HIMACHAL PRADESH
Pages 108–133

UTTAR PRADESH & UTTARANCHAL
Pages 166–211

BIHAR & JHARKHAND
Pages 212–225

ASSAM & THE NORTHEAST
Pages 322–339

• Lucknow

EASTERN INDIA
Guwahati

• Patna

WEST BENGAL & SIKKIM
Pages 284–303

CENTRAL INDIA

KOLKATA
Pages 266–83

Bhubaneswar •

MADHYA PRADESH & CHHATTISGARH
Pages 226–255

ORISSA
Pages 304–321

ANDHRA PRADESH
Pages 658–683

0 km   250
0 miles   250

KERALA
Pages 624–657

TAMIL NADU
Pages 576–615

ANDAMAN & NICOBAR ISLANDS (INDIA)
Port Blair

ANDAMAN ISLANDS
Pages 616–623

EYEWITNESS *TRAVEL GUIDES*

INDIA

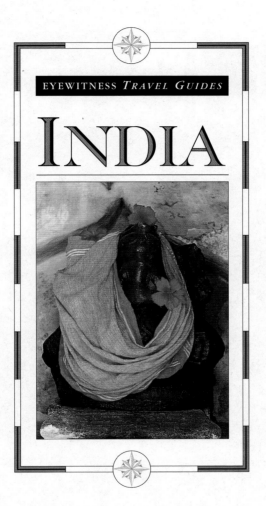

DK EYEWITNESS *TRAVEL GUIDES*

INDIA

DK

DK PUBLISHING, INC.
LONDON • NEW YORK • DELHI
MUNICH • MELBOURNE

DK PUBLISHING, INC.

Managing Editor Aruna Ghose
Managing Art Editor Bindia Thapar
Project Editor Nandini Mehta
Editors Madhulita Mohapatra, Vandana Mohindra,
Ranjana Saklani, Alissa Sheth
Designers Benu Joshi, Mugdha Sethi, Priyanka Thakur
Cartographers Uma Bhattacharya, Kishorchand Naorem
Photo Editor Radhika Singh
Picture Researcher Kiran K Mohan
DTP Coordinator Shailesh Sharma
DTP Designer Jessica Subramanian

Main Contributors
Roshen Dalal, Partho Datta, Divya Gandhi, Premola Ghose,
Ashok Koshy, Abha Narain Lambah, Annabel Lopez, Sumita Mehta,
George Michell, Rudrangshu Mukherji, Meenu Nageshwaran,
Rushad R Nanavatty, Ira Pande, Usha Raman, Janet Rizvi,
Ranee Sahaney, Deepak Sanan, Darsana Selvakumar,
Sankarshan Thakur, Shikha Trivedi, Lakshmi Vishwanathan

Consultant George Michell

Photographers
Clare Arni, Fredrik & Laurence Arvidsson, M Balan, Dinesh Khanna,
Amit Pasricha, Bharath Ramamrutham, Toby Sinclair, BPS Walia

Illustrators
Avinash, Dipankar Bhattacharya, Danny Cherian, R Kamalahasan,
Surat Kumar Mantoo, Arun P, Suman Saha, Ajay Sethi,
Ashok Sukumaran, Gautam Trivedi, Mark Warner

Reproduced by Colourscan, Singapore
Printed and bound by L. Rex Printing Company Limited, China

First American Edition, 2002

02 03 04 05 10 9 8 7 6 5 4 3 2 1

Published in the United States by DK Publishing, Inc.,

375 Hudson Street, New York, NY 10014

Copyright © 2002 Dorling Kindersley Limited, London

A Cataloging in Publication record is available from the Library of Congress.
ISBN 0-7894-8395-5

Throughout this book, floors are numbered
according to local usage, ie "first floor" is one flight up.

See our complete product line at
www.dk.com

**The information in this
Dorling Kindersley Travel Guide is checked regularly.**
Every effort has been made to ensure that this book is as up-to-date
as possible at the time of going to press. Some details, however, such
as telephone numbers, opening hours, prices, gallery hanging
arrangements and travel information are liable to change. The
publishers cannot accept responsibility for any consequences arising
from the use of this book, nor for any material on third party
websites, and cannot guarantee that any website address in this book
will be a suitable source of travel information. We value the views
and suggestions of our readers very highly. Please write to:
The Publisher, DK Eyewitness Travel Guides,
Dorling Kindersley, 80 Strand, London WC2R 0RL, Great Britain.
**The external boundaries of India as shown in this book are
neither correct nor authentic.**

Ashokan Capital, Sarnath

CONTENTS

INTRODUCING INDIA

◁ **Pilgrims taking an early morning ritual bath in the waters of the Ganges, Varanasi** *(See pp202–203)*

Mehrangarh Fort, towering over the city of Jodhpur

Fruit vendors on the pavements of
George Town, Chennai

Kandariya
Mahadev Temple
at Khajuraho,
Madhya Pradesh

INTRODUCING
INDIA

Putting Northern India on the Map

Encompassing an area stretching from the Greater Himalayan Range in the north to the upper part of the Deccan Plateau, northern India covers 2,331,318 sq km (900,127 sq miles). It is watered by three rivers – the Indus, the Ganges and the Brahmaputra – all of which originate in the Himalayas. The vast, densely-populated Indo-Gangetic Plains form its heartland. Some 705 million people, who speak 10 major languages, live here. The two largest cities are Delhi, the capital, and Kolkata (formerly Calcutta), both well-connected internationally by air.

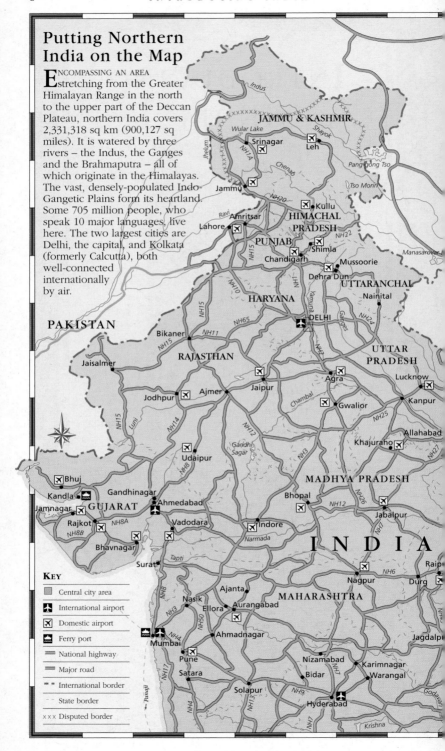

KEY

- Central city area
- ✈ International airport
- ✕ Domestic airport
- ⛴ Ferry port
- National highway
- Major road
- International border
- State border
- ××× Disputed border

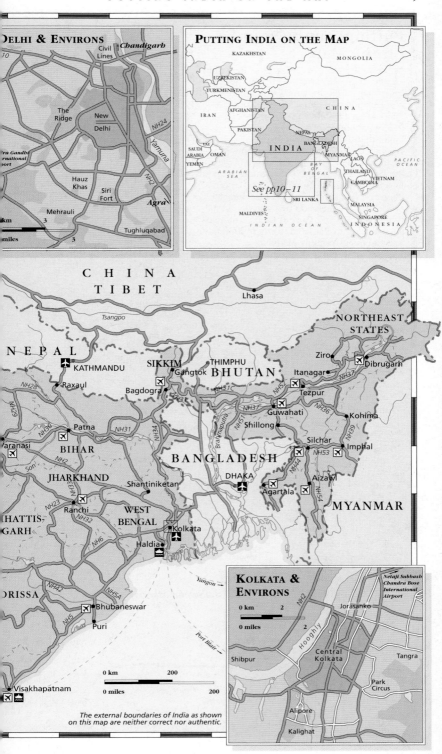

DELHI & ENVIRONS

Chandigarh

Civil Lines

The Ridge

New Delhi

NH24

Yamuna

ra Gandhi rnational ort

Hauz Khas

Siri Fort

NH2

Agra

Mehrauli

Tughluqabad

0 km 3

0 miles 3

PUTTING INDIA ON THE MAP

KAZAKHSTAN

MONGOLIA

UZBEKISTAN

TURKMENISTAN

CHINA

IRAN

AFGHANISTAN

PAKISTAN

NEPAL

BANGLADESH

INDIA

MYANMAR

LAOS

SAUDI ARABIA

UAE

OMAN

YEMEN

See pp10–11

ARABIAN SEA

BAY OF BENGAL

SRI LANKA

THAILAND

CAMBODIA

VIETNAM

PACIFIC OCEAN

SINGAPORE

MALAYSIA

MALDIVES

INDONESIA

INDIAN OCEAN

CHINA

TIBET

Lhasa

Tsangpo

NORTHEAST STATES

NEPAL

✈ KATHMANDU

SIKKIM

Gangtok

THIMPHU

BHUTAN

Ziro

☒ Dibrugarh

Itanagar

NH37

NH28

• Raxaul

Bagdogra ☒

NH31C

Tezpur

NH52

NH29

NH36

Patna ☒

NH31

NH34

NH37

NH51

Guwahati ☒

NH36

• Kohima

Brahmaputra

Shillong

Silchar ☒

NH39

aranasi ☒

NH2

BIHAR

Son

Imphal ☒

NH53

JHARKHAND

Shantiniketan

BANGLADESH

DHAKA ✈

NH44

Aizawl

HATTIS-GARH

NH23

Ranchi ☒

NH33

NH32

WEST BENGAL

Agartala ☒

NH54

MYANMAR

NH6

Kolkata ✈

ORISSA

NH42

Haldia ⚓

Yangon →

NH5A

Bhubaneswar ☒

NH5

Puri •

Port Blair →

KOLKATA & ENVIRONS

Netaji Subhash Chandra Bose International Airport

NH2

0 km 2

0 miles 2

Jorasanko

Hooghly

Shibpur

Central Kolkata

Tangra

Park Circus

0 km 200

0 miles 200

Alipore

• Visakhapatnam

☒ ⚓

Kalighat

The external boundaries of India as shown on this map are neither correct nor authentic.

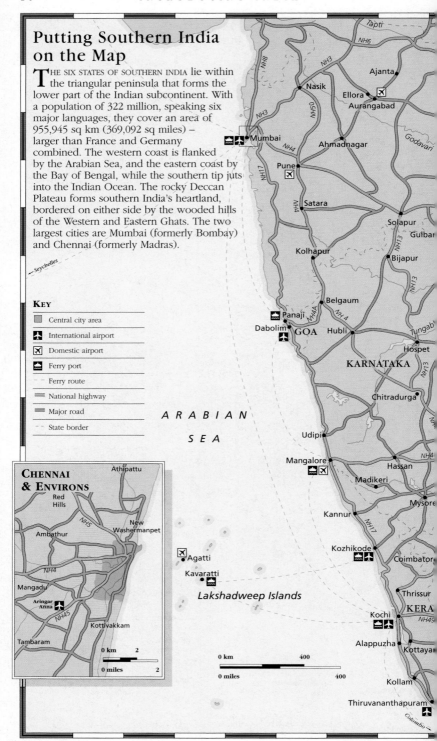

Putting Southern India on the Map

THE SIX STATES OF SOUTHERN INDIA lie within the triangular peninsula that forms the lower part of the Indian subcontinent. With a population of 322 million, speaking six major languages, they cover an area of 955,945 sq km (369,092 sq miles) – larger than France and Germany combined. The western coast is flanked by the Arabian Sea, and the eastern coast by the Bay of Bengal, while the southern tip juts into the Indian Ocean. The rocky Deccan Plateau forms southern India's heartland, bordered on either side by the wooded hills of the Western and Eastern Ghats. The two largest cities are Mumbai (formerly Bombay) and Chennai (formerly Madras).

KEY

- Central city area
- International airport
- Domestic airport
- Ferry port
- Ferry route
- National highway
- Major road
- State border

ARABIAN

SEA

CHENNAI & ENVIRONS

Athipattu
Red Hills
NH5
Ambathur
New Washermanpet
NH4
Mangadu
Aringar Anna
NH45
Kottivakkam
Tambaram

0 km   2
0 miles   2

Tapti
NH6
NH8
NH3
Ajanta
Nasik
Ellora
NSW
Aurangabad
NH3
Mumbai
Godavari
NH4
Ahmadnagar
Pune
NH17
Satara
NH4
Solapur
NH13
Gulbar
Kolhapur
Bijapur
NH13
Belgaum
Panaji
NH4A
NH 4
Dabolim
GOA
Hubli
Tungab
Hospet
KARNATAKA
NH13
Chitradurga
Udipi
Mangalore
NH4
Hassan
Madikeri
Mysore
Kannur
NH7
Kozhikode
Coimbator
Thrissur
KERA
NH49
Kochi
Alappuzha
Kottaya
Kollam
Thiruvananthapuram
Colombo

Agatti
Kavaratti
Lakshadweep Islands

Seychelles

0 km   400
0 miles   400

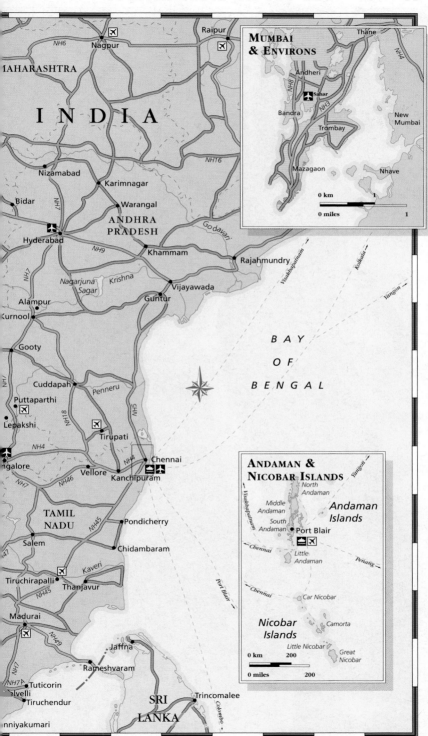

A PORTRAIT OF INDIA

NDIA IS POSSIBLY *the most diverse nation in the world. In area, it is the seventh largest country, and in population second only to China. Within its geographical confines, stretching from the Great Himalayas in the north to the tropical peninsular south, there is a dizzying variety of languages, cultures, ethnic groups, beliefs, and lifestyles that few continents, leave alone countries, possess.*

India, for first-time visitors and long-term residents alike, can be a powerful assault on the senses – noisy, frenetic, vibrant, and chaotic; a land of incredible contrasts and paradoxes. And yet, underlying the contrasts, there are patterns of continuity, an indefinable essence that is quintessentially Indian. Overwhelming at first, this country of a billion people and "a million mutinies" can gradually unfold rare delights. You may find it in the centuries-old temples, tombs and forts; in the exquisite crafts still made in the traditional way; in the bustle and aromas of its bazaars; or in the sudden glimpses of serene beauty that filter through the chaos.

Rose-ringed parakeet

LEGACY OF THE PAST

Much of India's fascination lies in the fact that it is both a young nation and an ancient country rolled into one, where the past and the present constantly collide. Its recorded history goes back 5,000 years to the Indus Valley Civilization, where excavations reveal a sophisticated urban culture *(see p41)*. This was followed, in around 1500 BC, by the arrival of the Aryans from Central Asia, who settled along the Gangetic Plains of northern India. The Indo-Aryans evolved a very distinctive culture that continues to be part of India's living tradition. The hymns of the *Rig Veda*, composed by them, are still recited in temples as well as in

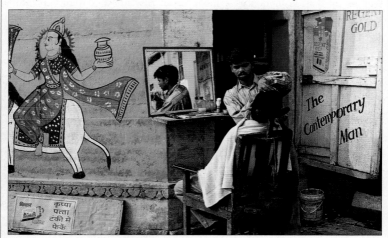

A roadside barber's stall – a common sight in India

◁ Village girls enjoying a monsoon shower, Tarnetar Fair, Gujarat

A typical scene from Kolkata's crowded streets

North Indians are usually light-skinned (or "wheat-complexioned", to use the language of matrimonial ads), southerners are darker, and people in the east have Mongoloid features. In addition, over 70 million Indians belong to a variety of tribes, ranging from Proto-Australoid groups in Orissa, to Mon-Khmer peoples in the northeast.

households in the 21st century. A less happy legacy of the Indo-Aryans was their division of society into four *varnas* (castes). This may have been a rational ordering of society in its time *(see p41)* but it has now degenerated into a system of inherited discrimination, which continues to have a hold on society and politics, even though such discrimination is banned by law.

A painted truck

Equally diverse are India's languages, with 17 major regional languages, and hundreds of dialects. Hindi is spoken by the largest number of people. But it is nowhere near displacing the powerful regional languages such as Tamil, considered India's oldest living language, or Bengali that boasts a rich literature and a Nobel laureate, poet Rabindranath Tagore *(see p292)* to boot. Though most Indian languages are derived from Sanskrit, they have developed their own distinct script and literature. The four main languages of the south, for instance, are more different from one another than, say, Italian is from Spanish. The Hindustani that is spoken in the streets of North and Central India is itself a blend of Sanskrit-derived Hindi and

PEOPLE AND LANGUAGE

One of India's great paradoxes is that the orthodoxy and rigidities of its society have been continually tempered by revolts and reforms, as well as by outside influences – India has an amazing ability to absorb and assimilate varied ways of being. Long before the New World created "melting pot" cultures, India played host (not always willingly) to invaders and conquerors, adventurers and traders, all of whom shaped, and were shaped by, the land they made their own. This is why there is no racial stereotype, no monolithic culture to define India. Broadly speaking (though there are many exceptions),

Chillies drying on the roof of a village house in Maharashtra

the Persian-inspired Urdu, a vibrant evidence of the cross-fertilization of cultures. The English language is among the lasting legacies of British rule in India. It is spoken by a pan-Indian elite, widely used as a link language, and is the surest passport to upward mobility and also, thanks to the Internet, to virtual reality.

CULTURE

India's culture, like its people, is a rich mosaic whose myriad elements have been born of its ancient roots, its foreign influences and its regional variety. Its richness also stems from the manner in which the "Great" and "Little" traditions intertwine. India's classical music and dance are highly developed forms, based on texts that are 2,000 years old. At the same time, there are earthier folk traditions, as well as the song-and-dance routine of Bollywood films, that form the staple of popular culture. It is the same story in the visual arts and architecture. On one hand is the breathtaking grandeur of Mughal monuments or South Indian temples. On the other, is the simple elegance of village homes, made with local materials to suit the climate, such

Children riding a haycart in Tamil Nadu

as the mud and thatch huts of the Rabaris of Kutch (see pp430–31).

Like elsewhere in the world, pre-modern Indian art is largely inspired by religious themes and nature. The Buddhist murals of Ajanta; the inlaid carvings of flowers and animals in Mughal and Rajput palaces; the exquisitely sculpted deities in Hindu and Jain temples; the miniatures and folk paintings illustrating scenes from the two great epics, the *Mahabharata* and the *Ramayana* (see pp26–7), are just a few examples.

Indian handicrafts, which have grown out of ancient traditions, continue to thrive despite rapid industrialization and a fast growing market economy. Objects of utility as well as beauty, such as quilts, shawls, copper pots, clay water jars, lamps and agricultural tools are in daily use in millions of homes, hand-made by artisans who keep alive the skills and traditions of their ancestors.

Odissi dancer

A woman drying saris at the river front in Varanasi

RELIGION AND SOCIETY

Religion and ritual pervade almost every aspect of life in India. Four major world religions – Hinduism, Buddhism, Jainism and Sikhism – were founded here. India has the third largest number of Muslims in the world, and Christianity has ancient roots here, introduced into the country by the apostle, St Thomas, around 2,000 years ago. The Zoroastrians, who fled persecution in Persia in the 9th century, also made India their primary home.

Indian Muslims, saying *namaaz* (prayers) in a mosque

On paper, 85 per cent of India's population are Hindus. But this figure does not quite convey the enormous fluidity of beliefs and practices that thrive under the broad rubric of Hinduism, which has evolved by interacting with all the other religions of India. It has become something of a cliché to say that Hinduism is not a religion *per se* but a way of life, but like most clichés it contains an essential truth. The Hindu religion has no single Book or God or prophet, and every community has its own favourite deity, chosen from an ever-expanding pantheon of gods.

The "Great" and "Little" traditions that underline so much of Indian life are intrinsic to Hinduism as well. At one level, it is a religion of abstruse philosophy and metaphysical quests. It is this philosophical strain which has given India the reputation of being a "spiritual" land. For most Indians, however, religion is more a matter of rituals and ceremonies that mark each day, season and passage in life. Gods are not remote figures, but part of every household and street corner, and worship can range from silent meditation to boisterous festivities. Though each sect has its own rules, rituals and taboos, ordinary Indians largely follow a "live and let live" philosophy. It is this underlying spirit of tolerance that has enabled India to remain a unique tapestry of varied cultures and faiths, notwithstanding periodic spells of strife.

While attitudes towards religion tend to be relaxed, social hierarchies are far more rigid. Though beginning to crumble in recent decades, the patriarchal joint family structure, with its deep-rooted belief in arranged marriages, obedience to elders, and emphasis on duty over individual liberties, remains the norm in much of India. Poverty, illiteracy, and caste-based divisions remain evident, particularly in the countryside. Women continue to face inequality and the girl child is still regarded as an unwanted burden in many communities.

A flower-seller outside the Minakshi Temple in Madurai

Cricket, a national passion in India

MODERN INDIA

But things are changing, and changing quite rapidly. Across the country, the old certainties are giving way to new equations, creating both conflict and hope. A great deal of this change has been fuelled by India's vibrant, secular democracy, the largest in the world and, in recent years, also by new economic opportunities.

Cinema, cricket and politics are arguably the three great national passions of India, enjoyed and dissected endlessly by all strata of Indian society. Of the three, politics offers  the greatest sense of participation. Though many of the country's millions are unlettered and poor, they unfailingly exercise their right to vote in election after election. The very fact that ordinary people can vote politicians in and out of office has given them a sense of power and pride that is gradually eroding their age-old subservience.

More visible evidence of a rapidly changing India is the emergence of a large "new middle

Indian beauty queens

class". For several decades after Independence in 1947 (see p56), India had a quasi-socialist mixed economy, dominated by the public sector. But in the 1990s, the government changed track and encouraged private enterprise and the entry of multinational corporations into India.

The Information Technology (IT) revolution has also had an enormous impact on India. Computers and satellite television have, in a remarkably short time, dramatically changed people's mindsets. Not everyone has gained from the new technologies, and vast stretches of India remain under the seemingly eternal haze of heat and dust. But in town after small town, there are growing numbers of people who are better off than their parents could ever dream of being, wielding mobile phones, driving cars and chatting in cyber cafés. Whether this consumerist boom will fuel an economic miracle or increase inequality is a topic of much heated debate. One thing is certain, though. Winds of change never lead to radical ruptures in India. The new blends with the old, traditions adapt to technology, continuity goes hand in hand with change.

Skyscrapers dominating the skyline of Mumbai

Landscape and Wildlife

INDIA HAS AN extraordinary diversity of landscapes and vegetation, supporting a rich variety of wildlife. The country is bounded on the north by the majestic Himalayas. Along their foothills, sweeping the breadth of Central India, are the fertile, densely populated Indo-Gangetic Plains, while the arid Thar Desert covers much of Western India. South of the Gangetic Plains is the Deccan Plateau, flanked by the hills of the Eastern and Western Ghats. India's 7,516-km (4,670-mile) long coastline borders on the Arabian Sea, the Indian Ocean and the Bay of Bengal.

Plum-headed parakeet

The Himalayan landscape *features snowcapped peaks, glacial streams and pine-covered slopes (see pp64–5).*

THE ARID WEST
The Thar Desert and the semi-arid scrublands adjoining it support a surprising variety of flora and fauna. The sand dunes of Rajasthan give way further west to the barren salt-flats and marshes of the Rann of Kutch.

THE GANGETIC PLAINS
The rich alluvial soil of these vast plains, which stretch across India from the northwest to the east, has been cultivated for thousands of years. Today rice, as well as wheat, sugarcane and pulses are grown here.

Blackbucks *are among the swiftest animals, covering up to 80 km (50 miles) per hour.*

Asian elephants *number only 45,000 in comparison to a quarter of a million African elephants, making this smaller species the more endangered one.*

Asiatic lions, *once found all over northern India, are now seen only in the Gir Sanctuary in Gujarat (see p423).*

Painted storks *migrate to lakes and swamps during their breeding season, between July and October.*

Crested serpent eagles *are large raptors with a distinctive pattern of black and white bands on their underwings.*

Wild boars *are common in most deciduous forests in India. The males have tusks and can be very aggressive.*

Avocets *migrate to the coasts and marshes of Gujarat and Maharashtra in November.*

THE COASTS
The diverse landscapes of the coasts include sandy beaches in Goa and Kerala, fringed by coconut palms, coral reefs in the Andamans, and mangrove forests in West Bengal and Orissa. The east coast is often hit by cyclones.

Starfish, *which cling tenaciously to rocks, can be seen in tidal pools all along the Indian coastline.*

THE DECCAN PLATEAU
Separated from the Gangetic Plains by the scattered ranges of the Vindhyas, the Deccan Plateau is covered with black volcanic soil and ancient crystalline rocks. The plateau's mineral wealth includes gold and diamonds.

THE GHATS
The hills of the Western and Eastern Ghats are covered with forests of teak, rosewood, *sal (Shorea robusta)* and sandalwood *(Santalam album)*, prized for its fragrant wood. Many orchid species also grow here.

Tigers, *an endangered species and numbering only 3,500 in the country, are found across peninsular India.*

Nilgiri tahrs *live in the higher elevations of the Western Ghats (see p649).*

Daniel butterflies *are common in the region.*

Bullfrogs *display their large vocal sacs during their mating season in the monsoon.*

Langurs *or Hanuman monkeys (Semnopithecus entellus), live in large groups, led by an adult male.*

Spectacled cobras *have characteristic spectacle-shaped markings on their hoods. Another reptile is the king cobra, the world's largest venomous snake.*

Peacocks, *India's national bird, perform a spectacular dance when rain clouds appear.*

Sacred Architecture

Ceiling panel from a Jain temple

INDIA'S 2,000-year-old architectural heritage is intrinsically linked to the country's major religions. Indigenous forms include Buddhist stupas and monasteries and Hindu and Jain temples *(see pp396–7)* in diverse styles. Many Indian temples, however, share common structural characteristics, being mostly built of stone columns and horizontal blocks, often richly carved with sacred imagery and decorative motifs. The true arch and the dome, as well as the use of mortar, were introduced in the 12th century by the Muslim conquerors.

Sculpted column, Narayana Temple, Melkote

BUDDHIST ARCHITECTURE

India's earliest religious monuments are stupas, hemispherical funerary mounds, and rock-cut shrines *(chaityas)* and monasteries *(viharas)*. While *chaityas* were places of worship, *viharas* were dwelling places for Buddhist monks and consisted of small residential cells arranged around four sides of an open court.

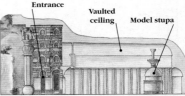

Entrance · Vaulted ceiling · Model stupa

Chaityas *served as halls* (grihas) *for congregational worship and enshrined a model stupa at one end.*

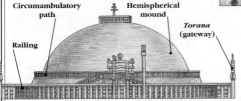

Circumambulatory path · Hemispherical mound · *Torana* (gateway) · Railing

Stupas *were monumental reliquaries in which the ashes of Buddhist teachers, including the Buddha, were interred. The Sanchi Stupa (see pp244–5) is faced in stone, and surrounded by a high railing with gateways (toranas).*

Rock-cut *chaityas have distinctive barrel-vaulted ceilings, expressed on the exterior as a horseshoe-shaped arch.*

HINDU TEMPLES

Vimana (pyramidal spire)

In North India, the soaring tower above the inner sanctum takes the form of a curving *shikhara* (spire) topped with a circular ribbed motif, the *amalaka*. South Indian temples, however, have multi-staged, pyramidal spires *(vimana)* crowned with a hemispherical or barrel-vaulted roof. Worship in both types takes place in a small dark sanctuary known as the *garbhagriha* (womb chamber).

Mandapa (hall or pillared pavilion) · Entrance

South Indian temples, *such as Thanjavur's Brihadishvara Temple (see pp598–9), have corridors and spacious halls* (mandapas), *with a profusion of decorated columns. These lead to the* garbhagriha, *above which rises the multi-staged spire.*

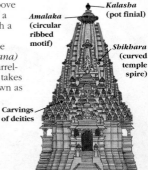

Kalasha (pot finial) · *Amalaka* (circular ribbed motif) · *Shikhara* (curved temple spire) · Carvings of deities

Khajuraho's *Kandariya Mahadev Temple's shikhara (see pp236–7) is considered the finest in North India.*

ISLAMIC ARCHITECTURE

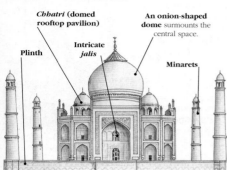

Mosques and tombs represent an imported tradition that was absorbed into Indian architecture. Mosques have domed prayer halls at one end of an open courtyard. The *mihrab* (arched niche) faces west, towards Mecca. The Mughals introduced the garden tomb, raised on a high plinth in the centre of a *charbagh*, an enclosed garden divided into four quarters. Decorative elements include Persian and Arabic calligraphy, geometric patterns and floral motifs, typical of Islamic art.

Chhatri (domed rooftop pavilion)

An onion-shaped dome surmounts the central space.

Plinth

Intricate *jalis*

Minarets

Mihrab, Bidar mosque (*see p545*)

Taj Mahal (*see pp172–3*), the zenith of Islamic architecture

GURDWARAS

The Sikh gurdwara, a prayer chamber where the *Granth Sahib*, or Holy Book, is housed, is often roofed with a dome flanked by arcades. Based on the late-Mughal style prevailing in North India in the 18th century, gurdwaras blend Islamic and Hindu architectural styles.

Gold plated dome

The prayer chamber houses the Holy Book.

The Golden Temple in Amritsar (*see pp106–107*)

CHURCHES

Though church architecture in Kerala predates the arrival of Europeans, most Christian places of worship, such as those in Goa (*see pp496–7*), are built in European styles. A common design has a Neo-Classical portico topped with a tapering steeple. Many Indian churches are also built in a Neo-Gothic style, such as the Afghan Memorial Church of St John the Evangelist (*see p447*).

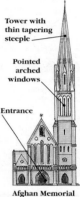

Tower with thin tapering steeple

Pointed arched windows

Entrance

Afghan Memorial Church, Mumbai

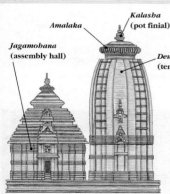

Jagamohana (assembly hall)

Amalaka

Kalasha (pot finial)

Deul (temple spire)

The Mukteshwar Temple (see p307) *typifies Orissa's temple architecture. The sanctuary has a curving spire* (deul) *and an adjoining assembly hall* (jagamohana).

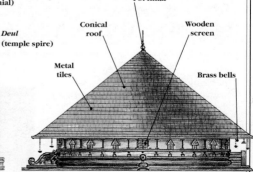

Pot finial

Conical roof

Wooden screen

Metal tiles

Brass bells

Kerala's temples, such as the one at Ettumanur (see p638), *have a distinctive form. The sanctums are often circular with roofs of sloping tiers of metal sheets or terracotta tiles. Carved woodwork and murals embellish the structure.*

Secular Architecture

Detail from a mirrored room

Mᴀɢɴɪꜰɪᴄᴇɴᴛ secular buildings, such as forts, palaces and mansions *(havelis)* were built by by powerful ruling and aristocratic families. Many of these, especially in Rajasthan and Gujarat *(see pp346–7)*, harmoniously combine monumental scale with superb decorative elements. The British imposed their own architectural stamp, a fusion of East and West. A variety of indigenous domestic forms that have remained unchanged through the ages can be seen throughout rural India.

Windows are inspired by Rajput palaces.

Mughal dome

Laxmi Vilas in Vadodara *(see p419)*, built in the late 19th century

CIVIC ARCHITECTURE

In the mid-19th century, the British began to incorporate elements from Indian Islamic architecture into European Neo-Classical or Gothic Revivalist styles. Known as Indo-Saracenic, this style reflected imperial and civic pride. Indo-Saracenic public buildings include Victoria Terminus *(see pp454–5)* and Mumbai University, and the High Court and Egmore station in Chennai. This culminated in the building of the new capital at New Delhi *(see pp72–3)*, where Sir Edwin Lutyens and his associates evolved a grand architectural style which was a more elegant synthesis of Indian and European traditions.

Sculpture, Churchgate Station, Mumbai

Gothic window, Mumbai University

End towers are surmounted by small bulbous cupolas.

Colonnaded verandahs run the length of the building.

A dome crowns the central chamber.

The entrance porch has a balcony above.

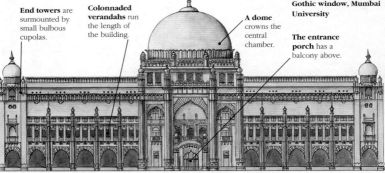

Prince of Wales Museum, Mumbai *(see pp450–51)*, inspired by Bijapur's Gol Gumbad *(see p543)*

THE COURTYARD

Domestic architecture in India is governed by public and private spaces. The front portion of the house was open to visitors and guests, but just beyond that was the courtyard, the heart of the house, restricted to the family. Larger mansions, such as those at Shekhawati *(see p372)*, Jaisalmer *(see p387)* and Chettinad *(see p612)*, had several courtyards surrounded by elaborate colonnades. The separation of private and public spaces within the home grew out of social conventions that secluded women from the public gaze.

Courtyard with wooden pillars and carved doors

VERNACULAR ARCHITECTURE

A painted niche

Rural houses in India reflect the country's varied climate and the range of available materials. In spite of the diversity, certain overall principles prevail. A typical dwelling is approached from the street through a formal doorway, often sheltered by a verandah, flanked by raised seating. The first room is usually used for both living and sleeping, and is thus larger. Cooking and eating take place to the rear, on the other side of an inner courtyard, near the well, or water supply. Hindu homes have a small masonry stand *(vrindavan)*, in the courtyard, where the sacred *tulsi* (basil) plant is grown for daily worship.

Walls are made with strips of bamboo.

Extended timber acts as supports.

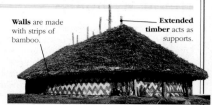

Tribal houses *in the forested northeast are quickly constructed from wood and bamboo. Rooms are added on as the family grows.*

Slate slabs are used to build strong, protective roofs.

Wooden pillars in the upper verandah.

Mountain homes *are built on high ground, and are double-storeyed, with the ground floor serving as a stable for livestock in winter.*

Central Indian villages *are tightly packed with houses that are either one-roomed tiled structures or larger ones. Some have flat-roofs where the family sleep at night in summer.*

Mud walls are reinforced with straw and cowdung.

Thatch roofs, made of local elephant grass, are replaced every year.

Coastal houses *have sloping tiled roofs as protection from sun and rain. The* tulsi *(basil) plant indicates that this is a Hindu home.*

Desert dwellings *are built with mud and consist of a single thatched room, enclosed by a wall. The circular* kothi *is used to store grain. Designs in white lime embellish the outer walls.*

MATERIALS FOR CONSTRUCTION

Circular thatch ceiling

Traditionally, most houses were built of locally available material. Bamboo and thatch were employed in house construction in Bengal, Orissa and the northeast, while stone and terracotta tiles were preferred in Madhya Pradesh, Maharashtra and South India. Sadly, such materials are now rapidly being replaced by steel and concrete. However, mud is still the most common material and is either applied directly or mixed with cowdung and straw.

Woven bamboo panel for walls

Coconut palm leaf roof

Thatched roof made of grass

Half-cylinder tiles

Terracotta sun-dried bricks

Stone slabs, ideal for walls

Hindu Mythology

Garuda, the great sun-eagle

T HE VAST PANTHEON of Hindu gods, goddesses and their divine exploits is best explored through sculpture. The principles of temple architecture were defined and established under the imperial Guptas (4th–6th centuries AD). Indian temples are adorned by a profusion of sculptures that are not merely decorative but also provide a visual interpretation of Hindu mythology. The numerous manifestations of deities, such as Shiva, Vishnu and Devi (the goddess also known as Parvati, Durga, Kali) are depicted in great detail. Semi-divine beings, such as devotees, nymphs and musicians complete the picture.

Dvarapala *is the armed guardian who stands outside the entrance of the temple or by the door of the inner sanctum. These forbidding figures carry weapons to protect the deity from intruders.*

Karttikeya is mounted on his peacock vehicle *(vahana)*.

Vedic gods, *such as Surya the Sun God, were manifestations of nature and the elements. They were absorbed into the Hindu pantheon of deities almost 2,000 years ago.*

Indra, the Vedic God of the Heavens, sits on Airavata, the four-trunked white elephant representing the rain-cloud.

Female attendant

Lakshmi, the consort of Vishnu

Garuda, the vehicle *(vahana)* of Vishnu, is half man and half eagle.

Lakshmi, *the Goddess of Wealth, appears as Gajalakshmi in this panel from Mamallapuram (see p579). She is seen with two elephants* (gaja) *who bathe her with their upturned trunks.*

Vishnu's *dwarf incarnation, Vamana (see p679) transforms himself into a giant to measure out the universe in three steps. This panel from Badami (see pp536–7) shows him with one leg raised skywards.*

Mohini, *the female form of Vishnu, is described as an enchantress, the most alluring maiden imaginable. Courtesans and nymphs are also carved as bracket figures.*

VISHNU ANANTASAYANA
This 5th-century panel from Deogarh *(see p233)* depicts Vishnu asleep on the serpent Ananta, whose hood shelters him. Brahma on a lotus rises from behind, while Shiva sits with Parvati on his *vahana*, the bull Nandi. Attendants and celestial beings surround the figure. The mace, discus, shield and sword, Vishnu's attributes, are personified below to ward off demons.

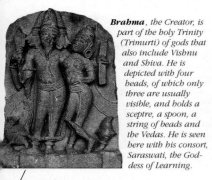

Brahma, the Creator, is part of the holy Trinity (Trimurti) of gods that also include Vishnu and Shiva. He is depicted with four heads, of which only three are usually visible, and holds a sceptre, a spoon, a string of beads and the Vedas. He is seen here with his consort, Saraswati, the Goddess of Learning.

Shiva, the God of Destruction, is seated with his wife, Parvati, who represents his peaceful and domestic aspect. Shiva holds an elephant goad and drum (dumroo), while Parvati has a lotus (kamal) in her hand.

Shiva and Parvati

Flying celestial figure

Ananta, the Many Headed Serpent, is also known as Adishesha.

Vishnu, the Preserver

Durga, the fierce form of gentle Parvati, slaying the buffalo-demon, Mahishasura. This panel from Mamallapuram, known as Mahishasuramardini, shows Durga riding a lion with a deadly weapon in each of her eight arms, given to her by the gods to annihilate the demon.

Karttikeya, Shiva's warrior son, has a peacock as his vahana. He is also known as Skanda, Subramanya and Murugan in South India. The other son of Shiva is Ganesha (see p467).

Attendants, the personifications of Vishnu's four attributes, protect the god from demons.

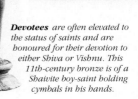

Dancers, musicians and other performers, usually carved on the lower plinths of temples

Devotees are often elevated to the status of saints and are honoured for their devotion to either Shiva or Vishnu. This 11th-century bronze is of a Shaivite boy-saint holding cymbals in his hands.

The Great Epics

Pandava hero on *ganjifa* card

THE TWO GREAT EPIC poems, the *Ramayana* and the *Mahabharata*, have had an abiding impact on Indian culture and philosophy. Over the centuries, their stories have inspired a great deal of art, music, dance, theatre and, more recently, popular TV serials. Containing a fund of wisdom about human behaviour, emotions and moral dilemmas, the epics continue to guide the daily lives of millions of Indians. Though known in their oral form since at least 500 BC, they were only put into writing around the 4th century AD.

Arjuna *shot the eye of a fish reflected in water, and won the hand of Draupadi, who then married all five brothers.*

In a game of dice *with the Kauravas, the Pandavas lost their kingdom and Draupadi. She was saved from the shame of being disrobed by the Kauravas when her sari kept growing magically to cover her.*

THE MAHABHARATA

This epic recounts the rivalry between the five heroic Pandava brothers – Yudishthira, Bhima, Arjuna, Nakul and Sahdeva – and 100 members of the Kaurava clan, headed by Duryodhana, and culminates in a great battle. Several other fables, legends and discourses are woven into the main story, making the *Mahabharata* eight times longer than the *Iliad* and the *Odyssey* put together.

Forced into exile *after the game of dice, the Pandavas wandered all over India for 13 years. In the final year, Arjuna lived in disguise as a eunuch, giving dance lessons.*

The **Bhagavad Gita** *is a sermon given to Arjuna by Lord Krishna, who acted as Arjuna's charioteer, on the battlefield of Kurukshetra. It is a famous discourse on ethics and morality, that contains the essence of Hindu religion and philosophy.*

In the final battle *the Kauravas created a cobweb-shaped defensive formation called the* chakravyuha, *inside which Arjuna's son was trapped and killed. However, on the 18th day of this fierce battle, the Pandavas, with Krishna's divine guidance, finally emerged victorious, and regained their kingdom, which they ruled with Draupadi as their queen.*

THE RAMAYANA

Rama, the ideal hero, was prevented from becoming king of Ayodhya by the intrigues of his stepmother, and sent into exile with his wife Sita and brother Lakshman. The demon-king, Ravana, abducted Sita, who was then rescued by the two brothers with the help of the monkey god, Hanuman. Rama is worshipped as an incarnation of Vishnu *(see p679)*.

The wedding of Rama and Sita took place after Rama succeeded in breaking the great bow of Shiva, which other suitors for her hand could not even manage to lift off the ground.

Exiled to the forest for 14 years, Rama, Sita and Lakshman lived simply and visited the hermitages of many holy sages.

Sita was abducted from her forest hut by Ravana, the demon-king of Lanka, who came disguised as a mendicant. The brave vulture Jatayu tried to save her, but his wings were slashed by Ravana. However, Jatayu was able to tell Rama what had happened before he died.

Ravana's ten heads and 20 arms signify his great intellectual and physical strength.

Hanuman, the Monkey God, is a much-loved figure in the pantheon of Hindu gods, worshipped for his miraculous powers, his courage and physical prowess.

Ravana's palace at Lanka was attacked by Rama and Lakshman who, with the help of Hanuman and his army of monkeys, rescued Sita and killed Ravana. Lakshman was gravely wounded in the battle, but saved by the magical mountain herb, Sanjivini, brought by Hanuman.

Rama's triumphant return to Ayodhya is celebrated in the festival of lights, Diwali (see p37), which symbolizes the victory of good over evil.

Classical Music and Dance

Sarangi and bow

INDIAN MUSIC AND DANCE are simultaneously modes of worship and a joyous celebration of life. Based on ancient codified texts, they originated as a form of worship in the temples, and gradually acquired a more secular character with royal patronage. Different regions of India have their own classical dance forms, while classical music is distinguished by two main styles – Hindustani and Carnatic *(see p595)*, the latter specific to South India.

Kuchipudi *is a highly dramatic dance form from Andhra Pradesh, which often enacts scenes from the great epics.*

The tiara is shaped like a temple spire.

Sensuous and spiritual at the same time, Odissi has sinuous movements and highly sculptural poses.

Frieze of a dancer from an 11th-century South Indian temple

Complex footwork and rhythms, and multiple pirouettes characterize this dance form.

Fan pleats decorate the front of the sari.

CLASSICAL DANCE

A wide range of hand gestures, facial expressions and body postures, codified in the *Natya Shastra*, a 4th-century treatise, constitute the "language" of Indian classical dance forms. Their themes are mostly based on religious mythology, and percussion and music play an important role.

A swirling skirt is worn over tight pyjamas.

Ghungroos (bells) help mark the rhythmic beat.

Kathak was a favourite dance at the royal courts of northern India.

Odissi developed in the temples of Orissa as an offering to the deities.

HINDUSTANI MUSIC

The origins of Hindustani classical music date to about 3000 BC. The raga (melodic line) and the *tala* (rhythmic cycle) are its foundation, and there is no formal written score. This gives artistes great latitude to improvise within the melodic framework of a raga. There are more than a 100 ragas, each assigned to a particular time of day or season, according to the mood or images its melody evokes. Royal patrons founded different *gharanas* or schools of music, which have preserved their individuality by passing knowledge down orally from guru (teacher) to *shishya* (disciple).

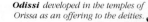

Ravi Shankar, *one of India's foremost sitar players, introduced Indian classical music to the West.*

Amjad Ali Khan *plays the sarod, an instrument developed by his grandfather from the* rabab, *a medieval Central Asian lute.*

Nine rasas (moods) are mentioned in the 4th-century treatise Natya Shastra. From the erotic, comic and pathetic to the odious, marvellous and quiescent, the rasas cover every mood and expression, whether in music, dance or painting. This 17th-century miniature painting depicts the serene mood of the morning Raga Todi.

Kerala's Kathakali dance featuring spectacular masks (see p657)

Fresh flowers adorn the hair.

Elaborate jewellery

Diaphanous veil

Red colour on the hands and feet draw attention to intricate movements.

Crinoline-like skirts and gentle swaying movements are typical of Manipuri dance.

Beautiful silk sari

Chiselled movements and symmetrical stances are typical of this dance form.

Bharat Natyam, from Tamil Nadu, has eloquent eye and hand movements (mudras).

Manipuri, from the northeast, enacts the legend of Radha and Krishna (see p179).

Bismillah Khan plays the shehnai, a ceremonial reed pipe of the oboe family, that is now also a concert instrument.

Zakir Hussain plays the tabla, a pair of drums that provide percussion at most music and dance performances.

Kishori Amonkar is a leading singer. A concert usually begins with a slow evocation of the raga, followed by an elaboration of the melodic line, and culminating in a fast-paced climax.

Costumes of India

ONE OF THE MOST REMARKABLE FEATURES of Indian apparel is the ingenious way in which a simple length of unstitched cloth is used. Gracefully draped as a sari, or wrapped around the head as a turban, the length of fabric is versatile, and is worn by both men and women. Stitched garments include the *kurta*, pyjama, sherwani, the voluminous skirt *(ghaghara* or *lehenga)*, and of course, the trouser, shirt and ubiquitous blue jeans. Today, despite the growing influence of contemporary Western fashion trends, most Indians continue to dress traditionally. The sari, particularly, is still worn all over India, even though the style of draping it differs from region to region.

The Veil (odhni *or* dupatta) *is an essential part of dress in conservative societies.*

The sari, *usually 5.5 m (6 yd) long, is tied around the waist, with the pleats tucked into an under-skirt. The pallav (end-piece) is either drawn over the left shoulder or draped over the head.*

Safa (turban)

Angavastram is the unstitched mantle draped over the shoulder.

Sari blouse

Sari

Salwar-kameez, *consisting of a baggy pyjama* (salwar), *a loose tunic* (kameez) *and* dupatta, *are worn by women in Punjab. This outfit is now worn all over India.*

THE INDIAN WEDDING
Festivals and weddings are glittering events that showcase the range and variety of clothes worn by both men and women in India. Such occasions are what keep traditional customs and attire alive today.

Bracelet-like folds of the *churidar.*

Maharashtrian *women wear 8-m (9-yd) saris in a style very similar to a dhoti. The extra fabric is pleated in front, drawn between the legs and tucked in at the back, to allow freedom of movement.*

In Kerala, *women wear a two-piece sari* (mundu-veshti), *of which the* mundu *forms the lower garment, while the* veshti *is tucked into the waist to form the pallav. Men just wear the lower garment, with an* angavastram.

HEADDRESSES

For Indian men, the most important accessory is the turban, (*pagri* or *safa*), an unstitched length of cloth that is deftly tied around the head. More than just a fashion statement, the turban's style and colour also indicates the wearer's social, religious, caste and regional status. Rajasthani turbans are intrinsic to the cultural ethos of the land, whereas in Punjab, the Sikh turban is characteristic of their identity as a martial community *(see p103)*. From the mid-19th century onwards, *topis* (caps) became popular, especially among courtiers in the Muslim courts. Even today, men wear plain or ornamental caps in mosques or during festivals.

A turbaned patriarch from Jodhpur, Rajasthan

Topi, worn by a young Muslim boy

Choli (tight-fitting blouse)

Odhni (veil)

Kurta

The bridegroom wears a formal sherwani-*churidar* in ivory silk.

The bride's *lehenga* is red silk, heavily encrusted with gold embroidery.

*The dhoti-**kurta*** *is the traditional male attire and comprises a dhoti (loincloth) or lungi, either tied around the waist or tucked between the legs. The upper garment is the stitched, long-sleeved* kurta.

***Sherwani**, a long coat with a high collar, is worn above the* churidar pyjama, *so-called because of the bracelet- (churi-) like folds near the ankles.*

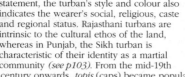

Ghaghara, *the ankle-length, gathered skirt worn in Rajasthan and Gujarat, is tied with a drawstring. A* choli *(tight-fitting blouse) is worn on top, while the* odhni *has one end tucked into the waist-band and the other taken over the right shoulder to cover the head.*

In Manipur, *women wear the sarong-like* phanek, *while men wear a garment known as the* khudei. *Each tribe, however, is indentified by its distinctive colours and stripes. This couple is from the Paite tribe.*

Bollywood's Magic Formula

HINDI FILMS from Bollywood (Bombay or Mumbai) are a fascinating mix of romance, violence, comedy, and tragedy, interspersed with song and dance sequences, and with a clear social or moral message. Ever since its inception in 1899, fashions in Bollywood have swung from mythological epics, to action thrillers to family dramas. But the basic *masala* (spicy mix) formula, which appeals to a large and diverse audience, remains unchanged.

Emotions are usually very melodramatic, as in this scene from Sarfarosh (1999), where a father laments over his wounded son.

Hero Hrithik Roshan is today Bollywood's most sought-after star. His electric good looks and powerful physique made him an instant hit with his first film.

Heroines add an essential touch of glamour. Slim, fashionable and gorgeously dressed film stars, such as Miss World 1997, Aishwarya Rai, set the standard for feminine beauty and grace.

The hero cult and Amitabh Bachchan are synonymous. Affectionately known as the "Big B", he has dominated Hindi cinema since the 1970s, with his portrayal of the Angry Young Man. He now hosts a TV game show and his wax statue is on display at Madame Tussaud's in London.

THE HINDI FILM INDUSTRY

It costs anywhere between US$1.75 million and $30 million to produce a Bollywood film. The budget is spent on massive fees for the stars, exotic locations, special effects, and on huge promotional campaigns. Of the more than 100 films produced every year, some are dubbed into regional Indian languages, or subtitled in English for international audiences.

Exotic locations are a must for romantic scenes. The musical courtship between the hero and heroine takes places against the backdrop of the Swiss Alps, the fountains of Rome, or while holidaying in Australia.

Family values form the core of most films. The home can be the scene of great happiness or discord, especially when there is a difference of opinion between generations.

Villains are portrayed as evil incarnate. In Jungle (2000), the villain is a dreaded bandit who terrorizes a wildlife sanctuary, and kidnaps a group of tourists, including the heroine.

Heroine Amisha Patel represents the fun-loving, urban, Westernized youth.

... Pyaar Hai

music RAJESH ROSHAN

Violence is generally of the comic-book variety. Dramatic fights are staged between the hero and villain at the climax, and invariably end with the triumph of good over evil.

Extras, the friends of the hero and heroine, are part of the chorus in the extravagant song and dance sequences.

NEW WAVE CINEMA

In the 1950s and 60s, parallel or "art" cinema was dominated by Satyajit Ray (*see p260*), whose thought-provoking films portrayed everyday life in Indian villages and small towns. By focusing on realism and social issues rather than fantasy and entertainment, he paved the way for internationally acclaimed directors such as Deepa Mehta and Mira Nair.

Deepa Mehta with actresses, Shabana Azmi and Nandita Das

Song and dance sequences range from duets between the hero and heroine to spectacular set pieces, with lots of male and female dancers. These are released before the film as music videos for TV, and often become hits, even if the film flops at the box office.

INDIA THROUGH THE YEAR

INDIANS LOVE celebrations and the year is filled with innumerable fairs and festivals. Almost every day marks a religious or social event celebrated by the diverse religious or local communities, where ritual fasting and feasting go hand in hand. Some festivals are linked to the pantheon of gods and goddesses, others follow the changing seasons and mark pastoral occasions. Some

Orchids in full bloom

commemorate anniversaries and events of national importance such as the Republic Day *(see p75)*. Hindu festivals usually follow the lunar calendar and both the full moon *(purnima)* and the new moon *(pradosh)* are considered auspicious. Muslim festivals, too, are determined by the new moon. This means that the dates of most religious festivals vary from year to year. See also special festival columns in each chapter.

Holi celebrations in the area around Mathura

SPRING (FEB–MAR)

FROM MID-FEBRUARY to the end of March, spring (Basant) is India's most glorious season with flowers in full bloom and pleasant, not-too-hot temperatures. It is also the main season for weddings, parades, cricket matches, horse racing, flower shows as well as a variety of other cultural events.
Basant Panchami *(Feb)*. Considered to be the first day of spring, Basant is celebrated all over North India. People dress in shades of yellow, echoing the yellow mustard blossoms that are in bloom. In Eastern India, the same day is celebrated as Saraswati *puja*, honouring the Goddess of Learning and Wisdom.
Vasantahabba *(Feb)*, Nrityagram. One of Bangalore's most awaited dance festivals. Acclaimed

artistes from all over India perform from dusk till dawn.
Delhi Horse Show *(Feb)*, Delhi. A two-day sporting event, where thoroughbred horses from all over the country take part in show-jumping, tent-pegging and dressage events.
Elephanta Festival *(Feb)*, Elephanta Island. An open air festival of classical dance and music, with performances by renowned artistes.
Kala Ghoda Festival *(Feb)*, Mumbai. A two-week extravaganza of the visual and performing arts is held in Mumbai's main cultural district of Kala Ghoda. The National Gallery of Modern Art and the Jehangir Art Gallery, as well as the area's sidewalks, become

venues for sitar and tabla performances, dance recitals and exhibitions of paintings, prints, photographs and installation art.
Nishagandhi Dance Festival *(Feb)*, Thiruvanan-thapuram. Artistes of almost all classical dance forms perform at the open air Nishagandhi Auditorium.
Id-ul-Zuha *(Feb)*. The Muslim feast of sacrifice popularly known as Bakr Id, commemorates Abraham's willingness to sacrifice his own son, Ismail. Since then, a goat is sacrificed to Allah on this day, prayers are offered in mosques and special delicacies are served.
Shivratri *(Feb/Mar)*. Devotees of Shiva observe the night of his celestial wedding to Parvati.
Delhi Dhrupad Samaroh *(Feb/Mar)*, Delhi. Leading exponents of Dhrupad, a classical musical tradition, present a series of recitals.
Four Square White-Water Rafting Challenge *(Feb/Mar)*, Rishikesh. The

Show jumping at the Delhi Horse Show

Namaaz (prayers) being offered during Id-ul-Zuha

premier white-water rafting event in India, this is also one of the richest competitions in the world with a cash prize of US$25,000. The week-long event is well attended by international as well as Indian teams.

Holi *(Mar)*. One of the most important Hindu festivals, Holi takes place on a full moon night and marks the end of winter. On the eve of Holi, bonfires are lit, and a effigy of the demon Holika is burnt to signify the triumph of good over evil. The next day, people swarm the streets, sprinkling coloured water and powder *(gulal)* on each other. This exuberant festival is especially dear to Lord Krishna, and around Mathura, his birthplace *(see p178)*, it is celebrated with great abandon.

Jamshed-e-Navroz *(Mar)*. Celebrated by the Parsi community as their New Year's Day, the festival is named after the Persian king Jamshed, who is believed to have first introduced the solar calendar. Devotees visit fire-temples and make offerings of sandalwood.

International Film Festival of Kerala *(Mar/Apr)*, Kerala. This event invites films from around the world, in categories such as world cinema, short films, documentary and Malayalam cinema.

Shankarlal Sangeet Sammelan *(Mar/Apr)*, Delhi. This is the capital's oldest classical vocal and instrumental music festival.

SUMMER (APR–JUN)

FROM EARLY April until June, the northern plains, and much of the south, undergo a hot and dry summer. By May and June, the heat in the north builds up to a scorching 40° C (104° F) and above – a signal for those who can afford it to move up to the hill stations in the Himalayas. Meanwhile, temperatures in the Deccan Plateau and the south rise to about 38° C (100° F). Most festivities come to a halt during this period.

Baisakhi *(13 Apr)*. This festival heralds the harvest season in the north.

Ramnavami *(Apr)*. Nine days of fasting *(navaratris)*, precede the birth of the hero-god Rama *(see p27)* on Ramnavami (the ninth day). During this period, many Hindu households maintain a strict vegetarian diet, and prepare special food cooked in ghee (clarified butter) without garlic or onions.

Mahavira Jayanti *(Apr/May)*. Jains celebrate the birth of the founder of Jainism, Mahavira *(see p396)*. Devotees visit shrines and offer prayers to the 24 *tirthankaras*. This festival is celebrated on a large scale in the states of Rajasthan and Gujarat.

Himachal Hang Gliding Rally *(May)*, Kangra. An international competition that draws professionals from around the world.

Symbol of National School of Drama

NATIONAL HOLIDAYS

Republic Day (26 Jan)
Independence Day (15 Aug)
Gandhi Jayanti (2 Oct)

PUBLIC HOLIDAYS

Id-ul-Zuha (Feb)
Shivratri (Feb/Mar)
Holi (Mar)
Good Friday (Mar/Apr)
Baisakhi (13 April)
Ramnavami (Apr)
Mahavira Jayanti (Apr/May)
Buddha Jayanti (May)
Milad-ul-Nabi (May)
Janmashtami (Jul/Aug)
Dussehra (Sep/Oct)
Diwali (Oct/Nov)
Guru Parab (Nov)
Christmas (25 Dec)

Buddha Jayanti *(May)*. The Buddha was born, attained enlightenment and died on the full moon of the fourth lunar month. Buddhists gather in *viharas* for prayers.

Milad-ul-Nabi *(May)*. Prophet Mohammed's birthday is observed with prayers and readings from the Koran.

International Flower Festival *(May)*, Gangtok. A rare show of exotic flowering plants found in Sikkim, including almost 500 varieties of orchids.

Summer Theatre Festival *(May/Jun)*, Delhi. This all-India festival is organized by the National School of Drama.

Procession of Buddhist lamas on Buddha Jayanti

Women teams participating in the Nehru Trophy Boat Race, Kerala

MONSOON (JUL–SEP)

JULY, AUGUST AND most of September make up the monsoon season, celebrated in India for the magical transformation of the earth. All newspapers eagerly report the progress of the monsoon. The south, especially the coastal areas, and the northeast, experience very heavy rains. Rainfall is fairly scanty in the northern plains, which remains hot and humid.

International Mango Festival *(Jul)*, Delhi. Held at the peak of the mango season, over 1,000 varieties of mangoes grown in North India are exhibited and sold at the Talkatora Stadium.

Kanwar Mela *(Jul/Aug)*, Haridwar. The largest religious congregation after the Kumbh *Mela (see p211)*, tens of thousands of Kanwarias (Shiva devotees), converge for a dip in the Ganges. During this time, devotees are seen travelling by cycle and on foot, carrying gaily decorated *kanwars* (vessels hung on bamboo poles).

Janmashtami *(Jul/Aug)*. The birth of Lord Krishna on a moonless night, is the season's most important festival. Celebrations reach their peak at midnight, while the day is given to fasting. The festivities in Mathura *(see p178)* and Brindavan *(see p179)* are especially grand.

Independence Day *(15 Aug)*. This is a national holiday, commemorating India's freedom from British rule in 1947. The Prime Minister addresses the nation from the ramparts of the historic Red Fort in Delhi.

Raksha Bandhan *(Aug)*. Young girls tie sacred threads *(rakhis)* on their brothers' wrists as a token of love, and receive in exchange gifts and a promise of everlasting protection.

Bangalore Flower Show *(Aug)*, Bangalore. A spectacular flower show is held in the Glass House of the sprawling Lalbagh Gardens. Hundreds of varieties of flowers, seeds and plants are on display and for sale.

A gaudy modern day rakhi

Nehru Trophy Boat Race *(Aug)*, Kerala. About 40 lavishly carved and decorated snake boats *(see p633)* take part in a thrilling race at Alappuzha.

WINTER (OCT–FEB)

THIS IS THE MOST perfect season. The monsoon is over, and the days now begin to grow cooler. It is also the most auspicious period in the Indian calendar and ushers in a number of festivals such as Dussehra and Diwali. Winter also marks the sowing of crops such as mustard and wheat. The chill is at its worst in the northern plains and hills between mid-December and mid-January, and though temperatures often fall below 3º C (37º F), the days are sunny. The southern region does not experience very low winter temperatures, the minimum being around 19º C (66º F).

Dussehra *(Sep/Oct)*. For nine days, episodes from the *Ramayana (see p27)* depicting Rama's adventures against Ravana are enacted all over India. The tenth day, Vijaya Dashami, celebrates Rama's defeat of Ravana, and huge effigies of the demon-king, his brother and son are burnt. In Delhi, the Shriram Bharatiya Kala Kendra's month-long dance-drama encapsulates the epic. Bengalis celebrate Durga Puja *(see p281)* at this time.

Gandhi Jayanti *(2 Oct)*. Mahatma Gandhi's birthday is widely celebrated as a national holiday.

Huge effigies of Ravana and his son during Dussehra, Delhi

Diwali *(Oct/Nov)*. Oil lamps illuminate each home to commemorate Rama's return to Ayodhya after 14 years of exile. Firecrackers are lit and sweets exchanged. During this period every locality holds Diwali *melas.*

Pushkar Fair *(Oct/Nov)*, Pushkar. Asia's largest camel, horse and cattle fair takes place in this pilgrim town.

Guru Parab *(Nov)*. On the first full moon night after Diwali, Sikhs celebrate the birthday of Guru Nanak, the founder of Sikhism.

Prithvi International Theatre Festival *(Nov)*, Mumbai. Prithvi Theatre is one of Mumbai's best known theatres. This week-long festival brings international theatre groups to the city, who perform plays in a variety of contemporary styles, along with a handful of Indian theatre groups.

International Trade Fair *(14–21 Nov)*, Delhi. In this major event for Indian industry, goods manufactured in India and abroad are exhibited at Pragati Maidan. Cultural events are also held in the fair grounds.

Id-ul-Fitr *(Nov/Dec)*. This festival marks the end of Ramzan or Ramadan, the 40-day long period of fasting for Muslims, that commemorates the period when the Prophet received the message of the Koran from Allah. The actual day varies according to the sightings of the new moon. A special *namaaz* is held at Delhi's Jami Masjid. It is also called Mithi (sweet) Id, as *sewian,* a delicacy made with sweetened vermicelli, is eaten and distributed at all homes.

International Seafood Festival *(Nov/Dec)*, Goa. A three-day festival of fresh seafood is held at Miramar Beach in Panaji, amid Goan music and revelry.

Madras Music Festival *(Dec)*, Chennai. The city celebrates its rich heritage of

Immaculate vintage cars at the Kolkata rally

Carnatic music and dance with recitals by numerous well-known artistes.

Mamallapuram Dance Festival *(Dec/Jan)*, Mamallapuram. Leading Indian classical dancers, perform Bharat Natyam, Kuchipudi, Kathakali and Odissi against a backdrop of the famous Pallava rock-cut sculptures.

Lohri *(13 Jan)*, Punjab. Bonfires and merriment mark what is believed to be the coldest day in winter.

Makar Sankranti *(14 Jan)*, Jaipur. Kites are flown to celebrate the return of the sun from the Equator to the Tropic of Capricorn. This day coincides with the Tamil festival of Pongal *(see p589)*.

Decorative paper kite

Republic Day *(26 Jan)*. A national holiday. Pomp and pageantry mark India's birth as an independent republic. In Delhi, a colourful military parade is held at Rajpath.

Beating of the Retreat *(29 Jan)*, Delhi. This beautiful

ceremony recalls the end of the day's battle when armies retreated to their camps. A grand display of regimental bands perform against the spectacular backdrop of North and South Blocks. As the sun sets, a bugle sounds the retreat, fireworks are lit and the buildings are framed with fairylights.

Vintage and Classic Car Rally *(Jan)*, Kolkata. *The Statesman* group of newspapers organizes this event when vintage cars, or the "grand old ladies", are flagged off on a short race. Their owners often dress up in period costumes. A similar rally is held in Delhi, in March each year.

Thyagaraja Aradhana Festival *(Jan)*, Thiruvaiyaru. An eight-day music festival is held in honour of the saint composer Thyagaraja, attracting eminent musicians from all over the country.

Island Tourism Festival *(Jan/Feb)*, Port Blair. A ten-day festival of dance, theatre and music reflects the multi-cultural population of the Andaman Islands. There are also exhibitions of local crafts, flora and marine life.

Desert Festival *(Jan/Feb)*, Jaisalmer. A cultural festival held on the sand dunes over three days, with camel races, camel polo, folk dances and music performances.

Bagpipers of an army regiment at the Beating of the Retreat ceremony

The Climate of India

SUMMER, MONSOON AND WINTER, with a brief but glorious spring and autumn, span the seasons in India. The climate changes with latitude and geographical location. In the north, temperatures soar in the vast Gangetic Plains, though the Himalayan belt remains pleasantly cool in summer. In winter, the high mountain passes remain snowbound. The central Deccan and deep south, however, have a tropical monsoon climate, with high temperatures and virtually no winter. India's coastal belts, on the other hand, remain humid and warm, with torrential rain. The semi-arid regions of Rajasthan and Kutch, as well as the rain shadow areas east of the Western Ghats, are among the country's worst drought hit areas, while the coasts and the northeast states, face the full onslaught of the monsoon, and are devastated by cyclones and floods each year.

Giant cacti growing in the arid Thar Desert, Jaisalmer

This arid region receives little rainfall.

India's highest temperatures, recorded in the Thar Desert in Rajasthan, rise above 48° C (118° F).

KEY

- Tropical rainy region: consistently high temperatures and heavy summer rainfall.
- Humid subtropical region: hot summer followed by heavy rainfall. Dry winter.
- Tropical savannah region: long, dry season with high summer temperatures. Mild winter.
- Tropical and subtropical steppe region: semi-arid. Low and erratic rainfall leading to drought.
- Tropical desert region: high summer and very low winter temperatures. Scanty rainfall.
- Mountain region: cold and dry climate. Short summer.
- Mountain region: cold, humid winter. Short summer.

JAIPUR

°C/°F				
	37/99	34/93	33/91	
	21/70	26/79	18/64	22/72
				8/46
☀ hrs	9.3 hrs	4.4 hrs	9.6 hrs	8.6 hrs
☂ mm	4.2 mm	193 mm	19.3 mm	14 mm
month	Apr	Jul	Oct	Jan

MUMBAI

°C/°F				
	32/90	30/86	32/90	29/84
	25/77	25/77	25/77	
				19/66
☀ hrs	9.6 hrs	2.5 hrs	8.3 hrs	9.1 hrs
☂ mm	2.8 mm	710 mm	88 mm	2 mm
month	Apr	Jul	Oct	Jan

Srina[...]

Jaisalmer

Jaip[u]

Mumbai

ARABIAN SEA

Torrential showers typify Kerala's monsoon

THE MONSOON

The word monsoon, from the Arabic *mawsim* (season), refers to South Asia's seasonal moisture-laden winds. In India, the Southwest Monsoon hits Kerala in end May. Simultaneously, one branch sweeps across the Bay of Bengal towards the Eastern Himalayas and the northeast, while the other, deflected westwards by the vast Himalayan barrier, moves towards the Gangetic Plains and gradually spreads across the mainland. At the end of September, the Southwest Monsoon begins to retreat southwards, and during October and November, southern Andhra Pradesh and the eastern coast of Tamil Nadu receive heavy rain. Nothing in India is awaited more eagerly than these annual rains; and songs and poems celebrate the months of Sawan and Bhadon (July and August), as a time of renewal and hope.

Lakshadweep Islands

Thiruvananthapur[am]

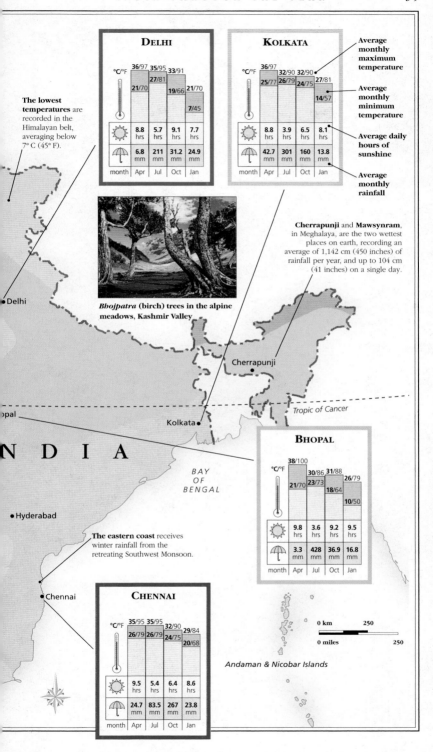

DELHI

°C/°F				
	36/97	**35**/95	**33**/91	
	21/70	**27**/81	**19**/66	**21**/70
				7/45

	8.8 hrs	5.7 hrs	9.1 hrs	7.7 hrs
	6.8 mm	211 mm	31.2 mm	24.9 mm
month	Apr	Jul	Oct	Jan

KOLKATA

°C/°F				
	36/97	**32**/90	**32**/90	**27**/81
	25/77	**26**/79	**24**/75	**14**/57

	8.8 hrs	3.9 hrs	6.5 hrs	8.1 hrs
	42.7 mm	301 mm	160 mm	13.8 mm
month	Apr	Jul	Oct	Jan

Average monthly maximum temperature

Average monthly minimum temperature

Average daily hours of sunshine

Average monthly rainfall

The lowest temperatures are recorded in the Himalayan belt, averaging below 7° C (45° F).

Cherrapunji and **Mawsynram**, in Meghalaya, are the two wettest places on earth, recording an average of 1,142 cm (450 inches) of rainfall per year, and up to 104 cm (41 inches) on a single day.

Bhojpatra (birch) trees in the alpine meadows, Kashmir Valley

Cherrapunji

Tropic of Cancer

opal

Kolkata

Delhi

N D I A

BAY OF BENGAL

BHOPAL

°C/°F				
	38/100	**30**/86	**31**/88	
	21/70	**23**/73	**18**/64	**26**/79
				10/50

	9.8 hrs	3.6 hrs	9.2 hrs	9.5 hrs
	3.3 mm	428 mm	36.9 mm	16.8 mm
month	Apr	Jul	Oct	Jan

• Hyderabad

The eastern coast receives winter rainfall from the retreating Southwest Monsoon.

• Chennai

CHENNAI

°C/°F				
	35/95	**35**/95	**32**/90	
	26/79	**26**/79	**24**/75	**29**/84
				20/68

	9.5 hrs	5.4 hrs	6.4 hrs	8.6 hrs
	24.7 mm	83.5 mm	267 mm	23.8 mm
month	Apr	Jul	Oct	Jan

0 km 250

0 miles 250

Andaman & Nicobar Islands

THE HISTORY OF INDIA

HE NAME INDIA *comes from "Indoi", a Greek word for the people who lived beyond the Indus river. The roots of Indian civilization lie in the country's precise and awesome natural boundaries, formed by the Himalayas in the north, and seas to the east, south and west. These have fostered a remarkable physical and cultural unity, despite the size and diversity of the area they enclose.*

INDUS VALLEY CIVILIZATION

Prehistoric sites in India date back to at least 250,000 BC, with agricultural settlements appearing around 7000 BC. By 2500 BC, a sophisticated urban civilization emerged, stretching across the Indus Valley and northwest India, all the way down to Gujarat. Its main cities were marked by solid brick structures, roads in a grid pattern, and elaborate drainage systems. Stone seals with an as yet undeciphered script, and standardized weights and measures were among the artifacts found in this culture (also known as Harappan Civilization), which had a thriving trade with Mesopotamia. Remains of two of these cities can be seen at Lothal and Dholavira in Gujarat. By 1800 BC, these cities declined, perhaps because of tectonic or ecological changes.

Dancing girl, 2500 BC

THE VEDIC AGE

Around 1500 BC, a people commonly known as Aryans, who were probably migrants from Central Asia, settled in the Indus region. Described in the *Rig Veda*, a Sanskrit text of that period, they had a mixed pastoral and agrarian economy. Three later Vedas, written between 1000–600 BC, and associated Sanskrit texts, record the extension of their settlements across the Gangetic Valley. This was also the time of the *Mahabharata* epic *(see p26)*, which describes a great war between two clans.

While the Rig Vedic religion worshipped nature gods, the deities of the later Vedic period were more complex. Later Vedic literature included a remarkable set of Sanskrit treatises called the *Upanishads*, which advocated a philosophical quest for truth, through enquiry. By this period, a social structure based on the caste system had developed. It was earlier occupational, but was now becoming hereditary and increasingly rigid. At the apex were the Brahmins or priests, followed by the *kshatriyas* (rulers and warriors). Below them were *vaishyas* (farmers and traders), and *shudras* (servants and labourers). Sacrifices and rituals to appease the gods were prescribed by the Vedas, and became a part of daily life.

TIMELINE

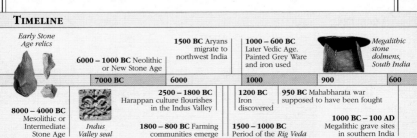

Early Stone Age relics		**1500 BC** Aryans migrate to northwest India	**1000 – 600 BC** Later Vedic Age. Painted Grey Ware and iron used		*Megalithic stone dolmens, South India*
	6000 – 1000 BC Neolithic or New Stone Age				
7000 BC	**6000**		**1000**	**900**	**600**
8000 – 4000 BC Mesolithic or Intermediate Stone Age	*Indus Valley seal*	**2500 – 1800 BC** Harappan culture flourishes in the Indus Valley	**1200 BC** Iron discovered	**950 BC** Mahabharata war supposed to have been fought	
		1800 – 800 BC Farming communities emerge	**1500 – 1000 BC** Period of the *Rig Veda*	**1000 BC – 100 AD** Megalithic grave sites in southern India	

◁ **Miniature painting of the Battle of Panipat, 1526, which established the Mughal dynasty in India**

THE AGE OF MAHAVIRA AND BUDDHA

The 6th century BC saw the rise of several urban centres in the north, accompanied by widespread trade. Urbanization led to changes in social stratification, and encouraged the emergence of new religious sects which challenged Brahmin dominance. Chief among these were Buddhism and Jainism, founded respectively by Gautama Siddhartha (566–486 BC) who became the Buddha, and Vardhamana Mahavira (540–467 BC). These religions gained popularity as they had neither caste nor sacrifice, and were open to everyone, including women. The Buddha's simple yet profound teachings *(see p221)* had particularly wide appeal. Mahavira believed in an ascetic life accompanied by truth and non-acquisitiveness *(see p396)*. Both religions disregarded god, discussed the laws of the universe, and advocated ahimsa – not harming any living being. Merchants, traders and others who adopted these religions gained new social status.

Ajanta painting of the Buddha with a monk

THE MAURYAN EMPIRE

The first empire in India was founded in 321 BC when Chandragupta Maurya, an unknown adventurer, defeated the ruling Nanda dynasty of Magadha (in Bihar) and established an empire extending down to the Narmada river in the Deccan. Chandragupta's grandson, Ashoka (269–232 BC) became one of India's greatest rulers, extending the Mauryan Empire to reach from Afghanistan to Karnataka. But after his bloody conquest of Kalinga *(see p309)*, Ashoka gave up violence and

Lion capital of Ashokan pillar

became a great patron of Buddhism. He recorded his ethical code on rocks and pillars all over his vast empire, enjoining his subjects to respect others' religions, give liberally to charity and avoid the killing of animals. These edicts were written in the Brahmi script, from which most Indian scripts have evolved. Ashoka also built many stupas enshrining Buddhist relics, including the one at Sanchi *(see pp244–5)*.

CENTRAL ASIAN INVADERS

After Ashoka, the Mauryan Empire soon declined. Local kingdoms arose across North India, while from the northwest a series of invaders, all from Central Asia, established successive dynasties. These included

TIMELINE

566 – 486 BC
Age of Buddha

327 – 325
Alexander the Great invades northwest India but soon retreats

321 BC
Accession of Chandragupta Maurya, founder of Mauryan dynasty

269 – 232 BC
Ashoka's reign

189 – 75 BC
Rule of Shunga dynasty

500 BC	400 BC	300 BC	200 BC	100 BC

540 – 467 BC
Age of Mahavira

Jain votive plaque from Mathura

315 BC
Megasthenes, the Greek writer, visits India

260 BC
Ashoka's conquest of Kalinga (now Orissa)

165 BC Menander, Indo-Greek king, rules in northwest India

100 BC– AD 220 Rule of Satavahanas in Deccan

the Indo-Greeks from Bactria (200–80 BC), the Scythians or Shakas with many branches (from 80 BC), the Parthians (1st century AD), and the Kushanas (AD 50–300). The territory of Kanishka, the greatest Kushana king, covered the northwest, Kashmir, and most of the Gangetic Valley. He too was a patron of Buddhism. Mahayana Buddhism developed at this time, reflected in two great schools of art, with Buddha sculptures in the Graeco-Roman Gandhara style in the northwest, and in a more indigenous style at Mathura.

As the Kushanas declined, the Gupta dynasty emerged in northern India, to establish another great empire (AD 320–500). The Gupta period saw a great cultural flowering, with fine sculptures, classical Sanskrit poetry and drama, and learned treatises on mathematics and astronomy produced at this time. In religion, the two Hindu sects of Vaishnavism and Shaivism (followers of Vishnu and Shiva) became prominent, and the Buddhist university of Nalanda was established (see pp218–19). But inroads by the Huns, marauding tribes from Central Asia, contributed to the decline of the Guptas after AD 450.

The next major empire was established by Harsha (AD 606–647) at Kanauj. His long and enlightened rule is described by the Chinese traveller Hiuen Tsang (see p219).

Buddha head, Gupta period

RULERS IN THE SOUTH
Meanwhile, in the Deccan region, numerous dynasties arose after the decline of the Mauryas. They included the Satavahanas (100 BC–AD 220), and the Ikshvakus (AD 225–310) in the eastern Deccan, under whom Buddhist stupas were constructed at Amravati (see p675) and Nagarjunakonda (see p676). Another Deccan dynasty were the Vakatakas (AD 250–550), during whose reign many of the superb sculptures and paintings at Ajanta (see pp479–81) were made. In the western Deccan, the Chalukyas came to power and built great temples at Badami (see pp536–7), Pattadakal (see pp538–9) and Aihole (see pp540–41). Their most powerful ruler, Pulakeshin II (AD 608–642), defeated Harsha, and stopped his southward advance.

In the far south, the three kingdoms of the Cheras (now Kerala), Cholas and Pandyas ruled between 400 BC and AD 400. The people of this region were of non-Aryan origin and were known as Dravids. Another major dynasty in the south were the early Pallavas, who ruled from AD 275–550, with their capital at Kanchipuram. During these centuries, cities, craft guilds, and inland and foreign trade flourished across India. The South Indian kingdoms grew rich on trade with Rome till AD 300, exporting luxury goods such as spices, fine silks, precious gems, and exotic creatures such as monkeys and peacocks.

The Drunken Courtesan, 2nd-century Kushana panel

4th-century Iron pillar, Delhi

AD 52 St Thomas in India	**250 – 300** Buddhist stupas of Nagarjunakonda and Amravati are built	**300 – 399** Ramayana and Mahabharata are compiled		**476** Birth of Aryabhata, great astronomer and mathematician **606 – 647** Harsha's reign **630 – 644** Hiuen Tsang in India
		320 – 500 Gupta dynasty		
AD 100	**200**	**300**	**400**	**500** **600**
AD 78 – 110 Reign of Kushana king Kanishka	*Statue of Kanishka*	**335 – 375** Reign of Samudra Gupta *Gold coin of Samudra Gupta*	**450** Hun invasions begin	**608 – 642** Reign of Pulakeshin II, Chalukyan king

Ceremonial procession of a Rajput prince

NORTHERN KINGDOMS (AD 750–1200)

Kanauj, once the capital of Harsha's empire, centrally located in the Gangetic Plains, had by 750 become the focus of conflict between three major dynasties – the Pratiharas, the Rashtrakutas and the Palas. The Pratiharas were a Rajput clan who ruled in Rajasthan and Malwa, while the Rashtrakutas (740–973) ruled in the northern Deccan. The Palas (750–1150), who were a Buddhist dynasty, ruled Bengal. Each captured Kanauj for a short while, but finally around 836, the Pratiharas gained control and held it for nearly two centuries. Soon other Rajput clans began to establish independent kingdoms.

The origins of the Rajputs are shrouded in mystery, but they are known from the 7th century AD in Western India. Some of them may have been descended from Central Asian tribes who settled in India in the wake of the Hun invasions *(see p43)*. They called themselves *rajaputra* or "sons of kings", and their 36 clans claimed descent from the sun and moon, from fire, or from mythical ancestors, in order to enhance their political

Woman writing a letter, Khajuraho

and social status. Early Rajput dynasties included the Paramaras in Malwa, the Solankis in Gujarat, the Tomars in Delhi, the Chandelas in Central India, and the Chauhans in Rajasthan, whose best known king, Prithviraj, is still extolled in Rajasthani ballads for his legendary valour and chivalry. During this period, independent kingdoms also existed in Kashmir, the northwest, the northeast, and in Orissa, where the Eastern Ganga dynasty, builders of the great temples at Konark and Puri *(see pp310–12)* ruled.

All these Rajput and non-Rajput dynasties fought frequent wars with each other to gain control of strategic areas, setting the stage for their downfall – they would be unable to form a united front to defend themselves against outside attack. In between wars, however, the rulers and princes lived in great luxury, in grand forts and richly ornamented palaces. Agriculture was well-developed, with over 100 types of cereals cultivated. Trade with the Arab lands flourished, bringing new prosperity to cities, merchants and craftsmen, and leading to the emergence of many new towns. This period also saw a flowering of literature, as well as sculpture and temple architecture. Outstanding examples, apart from those in Orissa, are the Khajuraho temples of the Chandelas *(see pp236–7)*, the Modhera Sun Temple *(see pp418–19)* and the Dilwara marble temples *(see p394)*, which were built under the Solankis of Gujarat.

TIMELINE

Rajput shield with sun emblem

700 Arab merchants arrive in Western India		**783 – 1036** Pratiharas rule Rajasthan and Kanauj	**871 – 1216** Rule of Imperial Cholas of Thanjavur

700	750	800	850	900

736 Dhillika (Delhi) founded by Tomars	**740 – 973** Rule of Rashtrakutas of the Deccan	**750 – 1150** Palas rule Bengal and Bihar	**800** Adi Shankaracharya preaches his philosophy	**900 – 1192** Rule of Western Gangas, builders of Shravana Belagola	**916 – 1203** Rule of Chandelas, builders of Khajuraho

SOUTHERN DYNASTIES (AD 600–1200)

In the Deccan and South India too several dynasties existed between 600 and 1200. A new Pallava dynasty had risen to power in the 6th century, at Kanchipuram. In 642, the Pallava ruler Narasimha Varman I defeated and killed the Chalukya king Pulakeshin II, after which the great Chalukya kingdom declined.

In the late 9th century, the Cholas *(see pp46–7)*, who had gone into decline in the 4th century, reasserted their power. They defeated the Pallavas, the Western Ganga dynasty which ruled near Mysore, and the Pandyas of Madurai, and established their supremacy in the south. They would later be challenged by the Hoysalas of Karnataka *(see p523)* who came to power in the 12th century.

As in northern India in this period, trade flourished in the south, despite constant wars. The Pallavas' maritime trade extended as far as Cambodia, Annam, Java, Sumatra, Malaysia and China.

In religion, this was a period of questioning and ferment. From the 7th century, itinerant Tamil poet-saints known as Alvaras and Nayannars, devotees of Vishnu and Shiva respectively, preached against caste divisions and orthodox Brahmanical practices, and emphasized a personal union with god through love and devotion *(bhakti)*. Their teachings had great popular appeal. Other influential sages were Adi Shankaracharya *(see p648)* who travelled across the country, elaborating on the ideas contained in the *Upanishads* *(see p41)* and challenging Buddhism, Jainism and the *bhakti* cult; and the 11th-century philosopher Ramanuja, who expanded on Shankaracharya's teachings. By the 12th century, with the reforms and revival that had taken place in Hinduism, Buddhism went into decline, except in Eastern India.

Bronze image of a Nayannar saint, 13th century

Great monuments were built in the Deccan and South India in this period, among them the magnificent temples of the Pallavas at Mamallapuram *(see pp578–81)* and Kanchipuram *(see p582)*, and the monolithic image of the Jain saint Bahubali at Shravana Belagola *(see p522)* erected by the Western Ganga kings. In the south-west, the superb rock-cut Kailasanatha Temple *(see pp476–7)* was built at Ellora by the Rashtrakutas.

The Shore Temple of the Pallavas, Mamallapuram

Image of Surya from Konark

	974–1233 Rule of Paramaras of Malwa	998–1030 Invasions of Mahmud of Ghazni	1032 Adinatha Temple, Mount Abu, built under Solankis		1110–1342 Hoysala rule		1192 Prithviraj Chauhan defeated by Muhammad of Ghur
950	**1000 AD**		**1050**	**1100**		**1150**	**1200**
973–1192 Rule of Chauhans of Ajmer	974–1238 Rule of Solankis of Gujarat	1050 Ramanuja preaches his Vaishnava philosophy		1076–1438 Eastern Gangas of Orissa build Konark and Puri	*Prithviraj Chauhan*		

The Chola Dynasty

BETWEEN THE 9th and 13th centuries, South India was dominated by the Chola dynasty, whose extensive empire covered much of peninsular India. Their two greatest kings were Rajaraja I (985–1014) and Rajendra I (1014–1044), under whom literature, architecture and sculpture reached new heights. They built magnificent temples, endowed with land and enormous wealth, and these became the focal point of their economy, as well as their social and cultural life. In 1216, the Cholas were defeated by the Pandyas, who then became the dominant power in South India.

Chola queen

King Rajaraja I
The first great Chola king, Rajaraja I (left) *subdued other southern kingdoms and conquered Sri Lanka.*

Infrastructure
The Cholas' irrig-ation dams on the Kaveri river (see p601) *ensured the fertility of their lands. Civil and military officials, provincial chieftains, and elected village committees formed part of their efficient administration.*

Wrestlers formed part of the Chola army.

CHOLA WARRIORS
This panel from the temple at Darasuram *(see p593)* celebrates the martial skills of the Cholas. Rajaraja I had a huge army of 31 regiments, which included elephant and horse cavalry, as well as foot soldiers.

Two faces of a copper coin of Rajaraja I

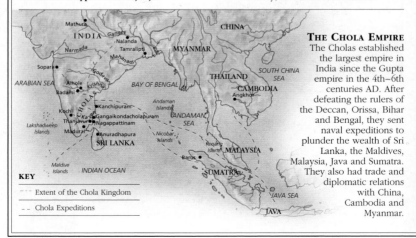

KEY

--- Extent of the Chola Kingdom

-- Chola Expeditions

THE CHOLA EMPIRE
The Cholas established the largest empire in India since the Gupta empire in the 4th–6th centuries AD. After defeating the rulers of the Deccan, Orissa, Bihar and Bengal, they sent naval expeditions to plunder the wealth of Sri Lanka, the Maldives, Malaysia, Java and Sumatra. They also had trade and diplomatic relations with China, Cambodia and Myanmar.

Architecture

The Brihadishvara Temple (see pp598–9) at Thanjavur, King Rajaraja I's capital, represents the zenith of Chola temple architecture, which is distinguished by its monumental scale and towering sculpted spires and gateways.

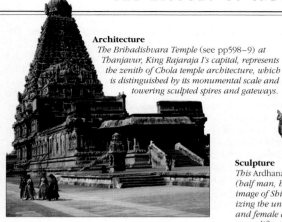

Sculpture

This Ardhanarishvara *(half man, half woman) image of Shiva, symbolizing the union of male and female aspects, exemplifies the superb grace of Chola bronze sculpture (see p566). Other famous sculptures portray queens, princely warriors, scenes from Shaivite texts, and Shiva as Nataraja, the God of Dance.*

Soldiers
used swords and shields with great skill.

Religion
The Chola kings, who spent lavishly on religion, worshipped Shiva, but Vishnu worship was also popular in South India. This stone sculpture of Harihara, a composite of Shiva and Vishnu, symbolizes a bridge between the two sects.

Seat of Power
Gangaikondacholapuram (see p592) was built in 1035 by King Rajendra I as his new capital, after his successful military expedition to the Gangetic Valley in northern India. The temple here, watched over by Shiva's bull Nandi, also served as a treasury, and a cultural and educational centre.

Dance and Music
Hundreds of musicians and dancers performed at the Chola temples every evening, under royal patronage.

THE COMING OF ISLAM (1206–1555)

Constant internal warfare between the different kingdoms, in the north as well as the south, had left them vulnerable to outside attack. From the 11th century, a volatile political situation in Central Asia, coupled with tales of India's fabulous wealth, fuelled a new wave of invasions by Muslim Turkic rulers from the northwest. Many of them stayed on in India to found dynasties, and with them came soldiers, scholars and merchants, artists and Sufi preachers, who brought new ideas in art, architecture, theology and warfare from the Islamic world. These were to have a lasting impact on religion, art, culture and history in the Indian sub-continent.

Ceramic tile detail, Lodi period

The first major invader was Mahmud of Ghazni who raided India repeatedly between 998–1030, and took back vast wealth from its temples. He was followed by Muhammad of Ghur, who conquered Punjab and Delhi, and established his control over areas earlier dominated by Rajputs, after defeating Prithviraj Chauhan in 1192. He was succeeded by his slave, Qutbuddin Aibak (1206–1210), who founded the first of many Muslim dynasties, collectively known as the Delhi Sultanate. Qutbuddin built

the towering Qutb Minar in Delhi. His successors included Iltutmish and Balban (see p93). Next came the Khiljis (1290–1320), whose ruler Alauddin conquered Gujarat, Rajasthan and Bengal, and made the kings of the Deccan and South India his tributaries. After the Khiljis came the Tughluqs (1320–1414), whose second ruler, Muhammad bin Tughluq, completed the conquest of the Deccan (see p475) and South India, and annexed them. But he was unable to maintain control over these distant areas, which soon began to reassert their independence. This process was accelerated by the devastating invasion of northern India by Timur of Samarkand in 1398, which further weakened the power of the Delhi Sultans. The last two Sultanate dynasties, the Sayyids (1413–1451) and the Lodis (1451–1526), were riven with infighting among their nobles, and had only a tenuous hold over their territories.

INDEPENDENT KINGDOMS

During the early years of the Delhi Sultans, a number of independent kingdoms, such as the Solankis in Gujarat, the Eastern Gangas in Orissa, and the Kakatiyas, Pandyas and Hoysalas of the Deccan and South India had been absorbed into the Sultanate. However, as the Tughluqs began to decline, many new independent states emerged. In 1336, the Hindu Vijayanagar Empire (see p530–31) in southern India established its independence,

The 13th-century Qutb Minar in Delhi

TIMELINE

Tughluq coin

1206 – 1290 Rule of first dynasty of Delhi Sultans	**1288 – 93** Venetian traveller Marco Polo visits South India	**1336 – 1565** Vijayanagar Empire
1228 Ahoms rule in Assam	**1320 – 1414** Rule of Tughluqs	**1347 – 1518** Bahmani kingdom

1250	1300	1350	1400	1450

1296 – 1316 Reign of Alauddin Khilji	**1327** Transfer of capital from Delhi to Daulatabad	**1398** Timur's invasion	**1440 – 1518** Kabir, saint-poet of the *bhakti* movement
1206 – 1210 Qutbuddin Aibak builds the Qutb Minar	*Sultanate weaponry*	**1345 – 1538** Rule of Ilyas Shahis of Bengal	**1394 – 1505** Rule of Sharqis of Jaunpur

The 14th-century Sufi saint Nizamuddin

while in 1347 the Muslim kingdom of the Bahmani sultans was founded in the Deccan, by a Tughluq noble. By the early 16th century, the Bahmani kingdom had broken up into the five smaller Muslim kingdoms of Bijapur, Ahmadnagar, Golconda, Berar and Bidar. In 1565, the combined forces of three of these kingdoms defeated the Vijayanagar forces, after which this powerful Hindu empire declined.

Meanwhile, as the Delhi Sultanate declined, its nobles and governors rebelled and founded their own kingdoms in Bengal (1388), Gujarat (1407), Mandu (1401) and Jaunpur (1408). In northeast India, the Ahoms who had migrated from Myanmar in 1228, established a kingdom in Assam (see p332). In Rajasthan too, several Rajput kingdoms, such as Mewar (see p398) and Marwar (see p380), reasserted their independence.

NEW CULTURAL INFLUENCES

Despite the turbulence throughout India between the 13th and 15th centuries, several new methods and technologies in agriculture, irrigation, administration, arts and crafts were introduced, many of them by the Muslim rulers. Trade flourished with Iran, the Arab countries, Southeast Asia, China and Europe, and a 14th-century historian records that Delhi was the largest city in the eastern Islamic world. The mosques, tombs and forts built by the Delhi Sultans ushered in new trends in architecture; and distinct regional styles, fusing Islamic and Hindu elements, developed at places such as Ahmedabad, Mandu, and the Muslim kingdoms of the Deccan.

In religion, mystical Sufi sects of Islam and saint-poets of the *bhakti* movement, such as Meerabai and Kabir, popularized the practice of religion as devotion to god, rejecting caste hierarchies. Guru Nanak (1494–1530) founded the Sikh religion (see p103), taking elements from the *bhakti* movement and Islam.

THE COMING OF THE MUGHALS

In 1526 Babur, a Central Asian prince descended from Timur, and a brilliant military campaigner, marched into India, overthrew the Lodis at the historic battle of Panipat, and laid the foundations of the Mughal Empire. Mughal rule was briefly interrupted when Babur's son Humayun was overthrown in 1540 by an Afghan chieftain, Sher Shah Sur. But Humayun regained his throne in 1555, and it was left to his son Akbar to consolidate and expand the Mughal Empire. The next two emperors, Jahangir and Shah Jahan, left a legacy of magnificent art and architecture. Aurangzeb, the last great Mughal, expanded the empire by adding new territories in the south.

Frieze of an elephant hunt from Hampi, Vijayanagar

Bara Gumbad, a 15th-century Lodi tomb

451 – 1526 Reign of Lodi sultans of Delhi		**1555** Reconquest of Delhi by Humayun		**1674** Shivaji crowned Chhatrapati
1469–1539 Guru Nanak, founder of Sikhism		**1571–85** Akbar builds Fatehpur Sikri	**1643** Shah Jahan begins Taj Mahal	**1690** Calcutta founded by Job Charnock
1500	**1550**	**1600**	**1650**	**1700**
1498 Portuguese Vasco da Gama reaches Calicut	**1540** Sher Shah Sur defeats Humayun and takes Delhi	**1600** Queen Elizabeth I grants charter to East India Company	**1661** Bombay transferred from the Portuguese to the English	
1526 Babur defeats Ibrahim Lodi at Panipat	**1530** Humayun succeeds Babur	**1556** Akbar becomes Mughal emperor		

The Great Mughals

THE MUGHALS, like their contemporaries the Ottomans of Turkey, the Safavids of Iran and the Tudors of England, were a powerful and influential dynasty. They ruled India for over 300 years, their empire extending at its height from Kandahar in the northwest to Bengal in the east, and from Kashmir in the north to the Deccan in the south. Great patrons of literature, architecture, and arts and crafts, which reached new heights under their patronage, the Mughals established a rich pluralistic culture, blending the best of Islamic and Hindu traditions.

Decorative Arts
Sumptuous objects, such as this blue glass and gold enamelled hookah base, were made in the royal Mughal workshops.

Emperor Akbar
The greatest Mughal, Akbar (r.1556–1605) was a brilliant administrator and enlightened ruler. He built the city of Fatehpur Sikri (see pp180–83).

A nobleman presents a gift to the emperor.

Weaponry
War elephants formed an important part of the Mughal army. They were controlled and commanded with sharp but beautifully crafted goads.

Court robes and turbans indicated status and religion.

Mughal Coins
Gold mohurs struck during the reigns of Akbar and his son Jahangir are renowned for their fine calligraphy.

Rajput princes were loyal allies.

Diwan-i-Khas was the special audience hall.

The Nine Jewels
Akbar gathered at his court brilliant men from different professions, whom he called his "nine jewels". They included the musician Tansen (centre) who, it is said, could light a lamp with the power of his voice.

Political Alliances
Raja Man Singh I of Amber gave his daughter in marriage to Akbar, beginning a tradition of Mughal-Rajput alliances that would bring peace and prosperity to the Mughal Empire.

Mughal helmet

Nur Jahan
A formidable combination of brains and beauty, Jahangir's Persian-born queen (b.1577) was the real power behind the throne.

Architecture
A monument of ethereal beauty, built by Shah Jahan for his wife, the Taj Mahal (see pp172–5) represents the zenith of Mughal architecture.

Jewellery
The legendary wealth of the Mughals included fabulous jewellery, such as this pendant encrusted with large, flawless diamonds.

Illuminated Manuscripts
Works of literature, history and biography were produced on gilded paper with beautiful calligraphy and illustrations.

Shah Jahan on his splendid throne.

SHAH JAHAN'S COURT
The splendour of the Mughal court is illustrated in this 17th-century painting of Emperor Shah Jahan, with his nobles grouped in strict hierarchical order around the throne. Mughal emperors, whose capitals were at Agra and later Delhi, used glittering court rituals and pageantry to display their supreme authority, as they took stock of the state of affairs in their empire.

Wars of Succession
Aurangzeb, the last great Mughal, came to power after imprisoning his father Shah Jahan, and killing his brothers. Ruthless and bigoted, he alienated many of his Hindu subjects, but expanded the Mughal Empire.

THE MUGHAL DYNASTY
The Mughal Empire flourished from 1526 until Aurangzeb's death in 1707. After that, the dynasty gradually declined under weak rulers, and finally ended in 1857. Its first six rulers were:
Babur (r.1526–30)
Humayun (r.1530–56)
Akbar (r.1556–1605)
Jahangir (r.1605–27)
Shah Jahan (r.1627–58)
Aurangzeb (r.1658–1707)

THE DECLINE OF THE MUGHALS

The death of Emperor Aurangzeb, the last great Mughal, in 1707, heralded the decline of the Mughal Empire. He left a ruined economy and weak successors, and independent states now began to be established by the Rajputs in Rajasthan, the nawabs of Avadh and Bengal, the nizams of Hyderabad, and the Wodeyars of Mysore. Two new powers were the Marathas in the Deccan and the Sikhs in the north. The Marathas under their leader Shivaji *(see p471)* expanded their territories after 1647. The Sikhs, originally a religious group, began to acquire territory in the hill states of the north, Jammu and Punjab. Under Ranjit Singh *(see p104)*, they became a powerful state in the early 19th century.

Sahib and mahout on elephant

THE EUROPEANS

But India would no longer remain a battleground for indigenous groups and dynasties – European traders, who had begun to arrive in the 16th century, were to change the course of its history. To set up trading factories in areas where their agents had settled, the Europeans began to acquire land, and fought numerous wars, both against one another and against Indian rulers. The trading groups were organized into companies, and included the Portuguese, French, Dutch and English. The Portuguese, who were the first to arrive, lost most of their territories to the Dutch and English by the end of the 17th century, retaining only Goa and a few adjacent enclaves. The Dutch, in turn, lost

out to the English. The 18th century saw major conflicts between the French and English, with three Carnatic Wars fought between 1740 and 1763, in South India and involving Indian powers on both sides. Ultimately, the English were the victors, the French retaining only Pondicherry and a few small settlements.

THE RISE OF THE BRITISH

Meanwhile, the English East India Company was acquiring territory in the north by gaining trade concessions from the Mughal emperors from the early 17th century onwards. They defeated the nawabs of Bengal in the Battles of Plassey (Palasi) in 1757 and Buxar in 1764. By this time, the invasions of Nadir Shah of Persia in 1739, and Ahmad Shah Abdali of Afghanistan in 1761, had further weakened the Mughals. In the battle with Abdali the Marathas, who had gained control of Delhi, suffered a crushing defeat. From these beginnings, the British began to expand their power. Robert Clive *(see p561)*, responsible for many of their successes, became Governor of Bengal in 1757. From 1773, the Parliament in England started to

Rachol Church in Portuguese Goa

Sepoys (Indian foot soldiers of the East India Company) rebelling at Fatehpur during the Mutiny of 1857

exercise some control over the Company. Warren Hastings, appointed Governor in 1772, was soon given the title of Governor General of Bengal (1774–1785), with supervisory powers over all the Company's territories. Under him and his successors (who from 1833 onwards were known as governors general of India), expansion continued, with major wars being fought against the Marathas, the Punjab, and Haider Ali and Tipu Sultan in Mysore. Other states too were conquered or brought under British control by various policies, such as the Subsidiary Alliance, under which Indian states had to maintain British troops and allow a British official to reside in the state and advise them. Another policy was the Doctrine of Lapse, under which states "lapsed" to the Company if a ruler died without a direct male heir. Thus by 1857, the Company's control extended over much of India, and obtained them vast profits. After the

Toy showing Tipu's tiger mauling a British soldier

Industrial Revolution, raw materials from India were exported to Britain, and machine-made British goods, particularly textiles, flooded the country. Artisans were impoverished, and crafts, towns and cities declined. Discontent with the alien rulers was growing. Unlike earlier conquerors of India, the British maintained their separateness, and their base in another country. In 1857, a combination of factors led to a major revolt, which began as a soldiers' mutiny, but soon had widespread civilian participation. Thousands of rebels marched towards Delhi in May and proclaimed the titular Mughal ruler, Bahadur Shah Zafar, emperor of India. By September the British had regained control over Delhi. Bahadur Shah was exiled to Rangoon (Yangon), and his young sons executed. Other rebel areas were also brutally taken over, ending the first major challenge to British rule.

1803 British capture Delhi from the Marathas

Queen Victoria's head on a Company coin

1799 – 1839 Reign of Ranjit Singh

1818 Rajasthani kingdoms accept British control

1825

1829 Governor General Bentinck bans *sati*, the Hindu practice of widow burning

1853 First railway from Bombay to Thana

1800

1850

1856 Annexation of Avadh

Nawab Wajid Ali Shah of Avadh

1857 The Indian Mutiny

1863 Simla becomes summer capital of the Raj

1858 Crown takes over the East India Company, Lord Canning becomes the first Viceroy

Pax Britannica

The Victoria Cross

THE FOUNDATIONS of British rule, or the Raj, were laid after the Indian Mutiny of 1857, which revealed the unpopularity of the East India Company's rule. By an Act of Parliament in 1858, the Company's rule ended, and its Indian territories became part of the British Empire, to be ruled through a viceroy. Though the *raison d'être* of the Raj was economic profit and political control, its abiding legacy was the political unification of the subcontinent, together with the introduction of Western education, a centralized administrative system, and a network of railways.

BRITISH INDIA

☐ *British territory, 1858*

Indian attendants in viceregal livery re-enact a Mughal procession.

Caparisoned elephants carry Raj officials.

Administration
Some 2,000 British officers, members of the prestigious Indian Civil Service, ruled over 300 million Indians. Dubbed the "Steel Frame of India", they brought British-style law and order to the remotest corners of the country.

A Sahib Travelling
A vast rail network was set up to facilitate commerce and travel. This 19th-century print shows first-class travel, a privilege of "whites only". The sahibs travelled in style, with several servants in attendance.

Lord Curzon
Viceroy from 1899 to 1905, Curzon believed British rule was necessary to civilize "backward" India. Paradoxically, the Western-style educational institutions set up by the Raj helped make Indians more aware of the injustices of colonial rule.

Raj Cuisine
The British soon developed a taste for Indian curries, toned down to make them a bit less spicy. Restaurants such as London's Chutney Mary *have been popular in Britain ever since.*

Memsahib and Tailor
Despite the climate, the British clung to their own dress and lifestyle. Children were sent "home" to study, and a large Indian staff enabled a leisurely lifestyle.

The Viceroy, Lord Curzon, and his wife lead the procession.

Crowds line the streets to see the grand spectacle.

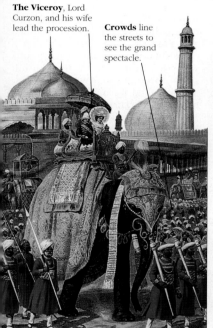

Cemeteries of the Raj
The harsh Indian climate took a heavy toll of British women and children, whose tombs fill the Raj's graveyards.

THE IMPERIAL DURBAR, 1903
This painting of Curzon's Delhi Durbar (1903), held to celebrate the coronation of Edward VII in London, shows a procession winding through the historic streets of Delhi. Held periodically, such assemblies announced the grandeur and the political might of British Rule in India.

The Company School
Paintings by Indian artists, such as this fanciful portrait of King Edward VII and Queen Alexandra in Indian royal attire, were specially commissioned for the British market.

Colonial Architecture
The most imposing edifice in New Delhi, built as the imperial capital between 1911 and 1931, was the viceroy's sprawling residence.

Crowds of supporters around Mahatma Gandhi

THE NATIONAL MOVEMENT

After 1857, nationalist aspirations began to grow, and the founding of the Indian National Congress in 1885 gave Indians a platform from which to demand self-goverment. A turning point came in 1919, when General Reginald Dyer's troops fired on an unarmed crowd in Jallianwala Bagh in Amritsar, which was protesting against the suppression of civil liberties. More than 300 people died, and Indians of every caste, class and religion united in their outrage at British brutality. By 1920, the leadership of the National Movement was taken over by Mohandas Karamchand Gandhi, a Gujarati lawyer who had recently returned from South Africa. Popularly known as Mahatma or "great soul", Gandhi's charismatic appeal and identification with the poor of India converted the freedom struggle into a mass movement. His strategy was to launch a moral crusade of non-violent resistance (*satyagraha*) to British laws and institutions, followed by

A popular poster of political heroes, past and present

periods of constructive village work. Working alongside Gandhi were several outstanding Indians, among whom was Pandit Jawaharlal Nehru.

At first, the movement for freedom was ruthlessly suppressed, but after World War II, Britain no longer had the strength or the will to enforce its rule. Meanwhile, from 1940 onwards, the Muslim League, led by Mohammad Ali Jinnah, had been demanding an independent state of Pakistan for Muslims.

Finally, at midnight on 14/15 August, 1947, the era of British rule ended, and the new nations of India and Pakistan were born. Casting a dark shadow over the celebrations was the Partition of the Indian subcontinent into two countries, accompanied by mass migrations of millions of Hindus and Muslims across the borders, and communal riots in which thousands were killed.

INDEPENDENT INDIA

After Independence, the new government integrated more than 550 princely states, which had been semi-independent in British days, into the Indian Union. In late 1947, a war between India and Pakistan took place over the accession to India of the princely state of Kashmir, and this continues to be a major point of dispute between the two countries. In 1948, Mahatma Gandhi was assassinated by a Hindu fanatic who felt he favoured Muslims. This so shocked and grieved both communities that peace was finally restored.

TIMELINE

1885 Indian National Congress founded

1905 Partition of Bengal

1911 Transfer of capital to Delhi announced at the Delhi Durbar

1910

1913 Rabindranath Tagore wins Nobel Prize

Gandhi's spinning wheel

1920 Non-cooperation Movement launched by Gandhi

1919 Jallianwala Bagh massacre

1920

1940 Muslim League adopts the Pakistan Resolution

1930–32 Civil Disobedience movement

1930

1942 Quit India Movement

1947 India attains Independence, Partition

1940

The Indian flag

1948 Mahatma Gandhi assassinated

1952 First General Election, with universal suffrage

1950

Nehru, with his daughter Indira and grandson Rajiv

As India's first prime minister, Jawaharlal Nehru laid the foundations of a modern nation state, with a democratic, secular polity, a strong industrial base and a planned economy, with Non-alignment as the keystone of its foreign policy. In 1962, China invaded north-east India and then withdrew after inflicting a humiliating defeat on the Indian army. This brought about much-needed modernization of India's military machine. Nehru died in May 1964, and in 1966 his daughter Indira Gandhi became prime minister. She continued his pro-poor and socialist policies, and in 1971, she stripped the Indian princes of their titles and abolished their privy purses. Later in the same year, she aided East Pakistan in its struggle against West Pakistan, leading to the formation of Bangladesh. But in 1975, perceiving a threat to her power and popularity, she declared a State of Emergency, under which the press was censored and dissidents imprisoned. When the general elections took place, in 1977, she was defeated, and the Congress party lost power for the first time

Rural women learning to read during a literacy campaign

since Independence. By 1980, Indira and the Congress were back in power, but a military action against Sikh terrorists holed up in their sacred Golden Temple led to her assassination by her Sikh guards in 1984. Her son, Rajiv Gandhi, took over in a sympathy wave, and began liberalizing the economy. He was assassinated by a Sri Lankan Tamil separatist during the 1991 election campaign, but economic reforms encouraging private enterprise and foreign investment continued. Since 1996, a series of coalition governments have been in power, with the Hindu nationalist Bharatiya Janata Party (BJP) emerging as a major force to challenge the Congress.

Significant progress has been made in the 55 years since Independence, though unemployment and poverty

A newly-built Info-tech park in Hyderabad

continue to exist. The literacy rate has risen from 18 per cent in 1951 to 66 per cent in 2001. In urban areas, women can be seen working in all professions. From frequent food shortages in the 1950s, India now has a food surplus, and its industrial base has expanded to produce a wide range of goods, from toys to aircraft. Economic reforms have flooded the market with consumer goods, and helped the rise of a prosperous middle class. In the field of information technology, there has been a veritable revolution, with India now established as a world leader in software development.

1961 Goa liberated from Portuguese rule	**1975** Indira Gandhi declares Emergency	**1992** Destruction of Babri Masjid leads to communal riots	**1998** Bharatiya Janata Party comes to power	**2001** Earthquake hits Gujarat
1962 India-China war		**1991** Rajiv Gandhi assassinated	**1998** Second Nuclear Test at Pokhran	**2001** India-Pakistan Summit meeting at Agra
1960	**1970**	**1980**	**1990**	**2000**
1965 War with Pakistan	**1971** Birth of Bangladesh	**1998** Amartya Sen wins the Nobel Prize for Economics	**2000** India's population reaches 1 billion	**2001** Terrorist attack on Indian Parliament
	1971 Princes lose titles and privy purses	**1982** India sends scientific team to Antarctica	**1998** AB Vajpayee becomes Prime Minister	**1999** India-Pakistan conflict in Kargil	

DELHI &
THE NORTH

Introducing Delhi & the North

AS RICH IN NATURAL BEAUTY as in historic
sites, North India is a much visited region.
A wide variety of landscapes can be enjoyed
here, from the snowcapped peaks, alpine
valleys and pine forests of Ladakh and Himachal
Pradesh, to the flat plains of Haryana and Punjab,
dappled with fields of golden mustard and wheat.
In sharp contrast is the urban sprawl of Delhi, a
bustling metropolis and the nation's capital. Ladakh's
dramatically sited cliff top monasteries and pristine
trekking trails are major attractions for visitors, as
are Shimla's Raj-era ambience and Dharamsala's
distinctive Tibetan flavour. Amritsar's great Sikh
shrine, the Golden Temple, and Delhi's magnificent
Mughal monuments are other popular destinations.

The lush green landscape of Srinagar, in the Kashmir Valley

Punjabi farmers enjoying a ride in a tractor-trailer

GETTING AROUND

Delhi has good air, rail and road links to the rest of the region. There are
daily flights to Leh, Srinagar, Amritsar and Chandigarh. Amritsar and
Chandigarh are also connected to Delhi by fast trains and a National Highway. From Chandigarh, there are air services to Shimla and Manali as well
as road links with frequent bus services. A particularly charming journey
is on the Toy Train, "Shivalik Queen" (see p777), which goes from Kalka,
near Chandigarh, to Shimla. Other great journeys, with spectacular
mountain scenery en route, include the trip by road from Manali to Leh,
and the journey along the old Hindustan-Tibet Road (National Highway
22), which runs from Shimla to the India-China border near Shipkila.

◁ A local woman crossing a barley field, nestled between the barren hills of Spiti (see p130), Himachal Pradesh

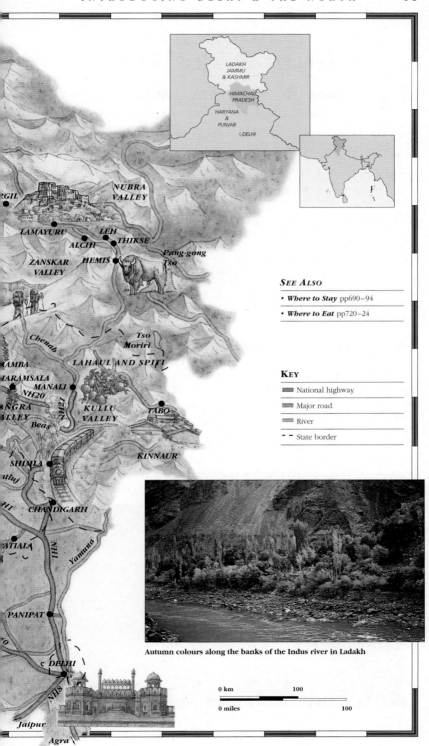

LADAKH
JAMMU
& KASHMIR

HIMACHAL
PRADESH

HARYANA
&
PUNJAB

DELHI

GIL

*NUBRA
VALLEY*

LAMAYURU   **LEH**
        ALCHI   **THIKSE**

*Pang-gong
Tso*

*ZANSKAR
VALLEY*   **HEMIS**

Chenab   *Tso
Moriri*

AMBA   *LAHAUL AND SPITI*
ARAMSALA   **MANALI**
        NH20
NGRA   *KULLU
LLEY   VALLEY*   **TABO**
        Beas

        KINNAUR

SHIMLA
utuj

CHANDIGARH

I

ATIALA   *Yamuna*

PANIPAT

DELHI

NH8

Jaipur

Agra

SEE ALSO

• *Where to Stay* pp690–94

• *Where to Eat* pp720–24

KEY

▬▬ National highway

▬▬ Major road

▬▬ River

– – State border

Autumn colours along the banks of the Indus river in Ladakh

0 km   100

0 miles   100

A PORTRAIT OF DELHI & THE NORTH

THE PEAKS OF THE HIMALAYAS, *the most spectacular natural barrier in the world, mark the boundaries of the area that extends northwards from Delhi. A variety of cultures and landscapes lies within this region. Delhi's bustling urban sprawl gradually gives way to the lush, flat farmlands of Punjab and Haryana, north of which are the serene mountainous lands of Himachal Pradesh and Ladakh.*

In geological terms, the Himalayas are very young *(see pp64–5)*, but for humans, they evoke a feeling of timeless eternity, and have been a source of spiritual inspiration for Indians for thousands of years. The monasteries and temples situated on their slopes perfectly complement the profound beauty of these mountains.

Saffron flowers

Most visitors to the region start out from Delhi, the country's capital, a city that is a blend of several historical eras. Its grand Mughal past is evident in its many superb monuments and tombs. The elegant tree-lined avenues and bungalows of New Delhi evoke the period of the British rule. Yet both coexist alongside the modern world of internet cafés, shopping arcades and posh multiplex cinemas.

Delhi's population swelled massively to accommodate the millions of people displaced by the Partition of India in 1947, when the western portion of Punjab became part of Pakistan. Homeless refugees from west Punjab have since prospered in Delhi, and now dominate the city's commercial life. As the nation's capital, Delhi continues to attract people from all over India, giving this vibrant city a resolutely cosmopolitan air.

The hardworking, resilient Punjabis have also transformed their home state with modern farming techniques, introduced in the 1960s. As a result of this "Green Revolution", Punjab and

A deep blue glacial lake near Thamsar Pass in Himachal Pradesh

Mustard fields in the fertile plains of Punjab

in their footsteps all year round. Himachal Pradesh has a number of delightful hill stations, such as Shimla, Kasauli and Dalhousie. The hillsides are covered with orchards, and apple farming is an important part of the state's economy. Himachal Pradesh also offers spectacular treks, some of which start from Dharamsala, a town with a distinct Tibetan flavour as the home of the Dalai Lama *(see p122)*

Haryana today produce much of India's wheat and rice, and one-third of its dairy products. Punjabis are also among the most successful immigrant communities in the world, and today, almost every family has at least one member living abroad, whether in London, New York, Vancouver or Hong Kong, as portrayed in Mira Nair's film, *Monsoon Wedding* (2001).

The name "Punjab" refers to the five *(panch)* rivers *(ab)* which traverse this green land. The sixth "river", if one can call it that, is the legendary Grand Trunk Road *(see p179)*. Travelling almost anywhere north of Delhi, one is bound to use this route. The kind of traffic may have changed since Rudyard Kipling's *(see p255)* day, and it is now rather prosaically rechristened National Highway 1, but it still lives up to the author's description: "Such a river of life exists nowhere in the world".

During the Raj-era, the British would escape from the summer heat of the plains and head for the hills. Today's visitors follow

A Delhi wedding procession

Jammu and Kashmir, which includes Ladakh, is India's northernmost state. Tragically, the militant separatist movement in the beautiful Kashmir Valley has effectively put an end to tourism there. But Ladakh remains an oasis of peace. Often perceived as having a purely Buddhist culture, its population is, in fact, almost equally divided between Buddhists and Muslims, who coexist here in harmony. Ladakh's uniquely syncretic culture, together with its astonishing natural beauty and the dramatic architecture of its monasteries, make it one of India's most fascinating areas.

A Kashmiri family gathered around their samovar

The Great Himalayas

Himalayan magpie

THE HIGHEST and youngest mountains in the world, the Himalayan Range stretches for 2,500 km (1,553 miles) along the Indian subcontinent's northern borders, separating it from Central Asia and the Tibetan Plateau. The Himalayas were formed about 30 million years ago, when the Indian plate broke away from Gondwanaland, drifted northwards and collided with the Eurasian landmass, driving the earth's crust up to form three parallel ranges, which include 30 of the world's highest peaks.

LOCATOR MAP

☐ *The Himalayas*

☐ *Area illustrated below*

High altitude desert, *where little grows except lichen, is found above the tree line. One such area is between Diskit and Hundar in Ladakh's Nubra Valley (see p143), which has sand dunes and camels.*

Glaciers *are especially abundant in the Western Himalayas. They are the source of three great Indian rivers – the Indus, the Ganges and the Brahmaputra.*

THE HIMALAYAS
Fourteen peaks in the Himalayas tower above 8,000 m (26,247 ft), including Mount Everest, the world's highest peak at 8,848 m (29,029 ft). The two highest peaks in India are Kanchendzonga *(see p302)* at 8,598 m (28,209 ft), and Nanda Devi (seen above) at 7,817 m (25,646 ft).

Bandar Punch ("Monkey Tail"), 6,316 m (20,722 ft), attracts many mountaineers. This peak is visible from Dodital *(see p188).*

Jaonali Peak, 6,633 m (21,762 ft)

Pithwar Peak, 6,904 m (22,651 ft)

Kedarnath, 6,940 m (22,769 ft), is regarded as Shiva's sacred mountain. Below it is the famous Kedarnath Temple.

A traditional Himalayan dwelling is generally built of stone and wood, or sun-dried mud bricks. Typically it has two or three storeys, the lowest level filled with stone to provide stability during earthquakes, the next level housing livestock, and the top floor where the family rooms are laid out.

FLORA AND FAUNA

Subtropical jungles, temperate coniferous forests and alpine meadows are among the varied vegetation zones in the Himalayas. They support a rich and abundant variety of plant and animal life.

Brahma Kamal (Saussurea obvallata) *is a popular offering at most hill temples.*

Deodar (Cedrus deodara) *is a towering conifer found in temperate forests in the Western Himalayas.*

Bar-headed geese (Anser indicus) *are attractive water birds that breed in high altitude lakes in Ladakh.*

Bharal (Pseudois nayaur) *are called blue sheep because of the blue sheen on their grey coats. They inhabit the harsh, stony slopes above the snow line.*

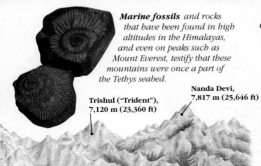

Marine fossils and rocks that have been found in high altitudes in the Himalayas, and even on peaks such as Mount Everest, testify that these mountains were once a part of the Tethys seabed.

Trishul ("Trident"), 7,120 m (23,360 ft)

Nanda Devi, 7,817 m (25,646 ft)

The snow leopard (Uncia uncia), *now endangered, lives above 4,000 m (13,123 ft). It preys on wild sheep and hares.*

Regional Food: North India

THE FOOD of the North Indian region is a hybrid cuisine which has grown out of several traditions and techniques. Among its chief influences are the classic Mughal cuisine born in the imperial kitchens, and the vegetarian food of Delhi's orthodox *bania* (merchant) community. Many of the area's most popular dishes are from Punjab, India's richest agricultural region. They include grilled *tandoori* food and robust farmhouse fare. Kashmiri cuisine, with distinct Central Asian influences, features local delicacies such as saffron, morel mushrooms and lotus roots.

Bharwa parathas *are pan-fried breads stuffed with vegetables or mince, eaten with yoghurt and pickles.*

Kadhai murgh (stir-fried chicken)

Dal (lentil purée)

Malai kofta (curried vegetable balls)

Milijuli sabzi (mixed vegetables)

Raita (whipped yoghurt)

Papad (lentil wafers)

Roti (unleavened bread)

Chawal (rice)

NORTH INDIAN THALI

Traditional North Indian meals are served on a *thali* (platter) with small *katoris* (bowls) of meat, vegetables and lentils. Pickles, chutneys, *raita* and *papad* are typical accompaniments that enhance the flavour of the main dishes. Many types of unleavened bread are served along with steamed rice.

Biryani *is a festive rice dish, slow-cooked with chicken or meat in a clay pot, and flavoured with cinnamon, saffron and cardamom.*

Pulao *is long-grained rice, enriched with ghee (clarified butter), and steamed with a variety of colourful vegetables, cottage cheese and spices.*

Pickled onions

Pickled garlic

Green chilli

Mint chutney

PUNJAB

Punjabi specialities include hearty dishes such as *murgh makhani* (butter chicken), *kaali dal* (black lentils), *sarson ka saag* (puréed mustard greens), and *baingan bharta* (smoked aubergine).

Kaali dal (black lentil stew)

Murgh makhani (butter chicken)

Sarson ka saag (mustard greens)

Makki roti (corn bread)

Baingan bharta (smoked aubergine purée)

Gucchi

Dhaniwal korma

Rishta

Walnut chutney

Nadru (lotus root)

Tabak maas

Haq ka saag

KASHMIR

Kashmiri feasts feature *rishta* (meat-balls in yoghurt sauce, flavoured with saffron and aniseed), *dhaniwal korma* (chicken simmered with milk and fresh coriander), *tabak maas* (sautéed lamb chops), lotus roots, *haq* (greens) and *guchhi* (morel mushrooms).

TANDOORI PLATTER

The *tandoor*, a clay oven from Central Asia, has generated a kind of barbecued cuisine now popular all over the world. Meats, fish, vegetables and cottage cheese are marinated in yoghurt and spices and grilled on skewers.

Gobhi (cauliflower)

Seekh kebab (minced lamb kebabs)

Paneer (cottage cheese)

Sabzi seekhs (skewered vegetables)

Murgh tikka (grilled boneless chicken)

Raan (leg of lamb)

Tandoori murgh (barbecued chicken)

Rotis *or breads, leavened or unleavened, made of flour, have different textures, flavours and names. They are served along with main dishes and help to scoop the food into the mouth.*

Sweets *are commonly made of milk, flavoured with rosewater and decorated with fine sheets of beaten silver. Kulfi, a pistachio and saffron ice cream, is especially delicious.*

Khasta roti (layered bread)

Pudina paratha (mint bread)

Naan (leavened white bread)

Kulfi kesari (saffron ice cream)

Gulab jamun (sweet dumplings)

Rasmalai (cottage cheese balls)

DELHI

DELHI, THE CAPITAL OF INDIA, *is also its third largest city, with a population of about 10 million. Its strategic location along the north-south, east-west route has given it a focal position in Indian history, and many great empires have been ruled from here. The monuments and ruins of these are scattered throughout the city, often cheek by jowl with modern structures and highrise towers.*

The vast urban sprawl of contemporary Delhi is, in fact, a conglomeration of several distinct enclaves, chief among which are Old Delhi, with its 16th- and 17th-century Mughal-built monuments and congested souk-like bazaars; and New Delhi with its wide avenues, grand vistas and colonial mansions, built by the British in the 1930s as their imperial capital. New Delhi has government buildings and also houses the Diplomatic Enclave where all the embassies are located. The picturesque 12th-century ruins of citadels built by the first Islamic rulers can be seen in the Qutb-Mehrauli area, and the affluent new middle class suburbs of South Delhi lie close by. Slums and shanty towns dot the outer fringes of the city.

All the contrasts and contra-dictions of India are particularly visible in the capital: denim-clad youngsters rubbing shoulders with robed sadhus (holy men), and bullock carts travelling alongside the latest luxury cars. Adding to Delhi's fascinating diversity is the fact that it is largely a city of migrants. After the violent Partition of India and Pakistan in 1947, millions of refugees, mainly from West Punjab, flocked here in search of a new life. Since then there has been a steady influx of people from all over India. Yet each regional community has retained its distinct cultural identity, making Delhi less a melting pot than a *thali* (platter) whose offerings may be savoured singly or in interesting combinations.

A view of the old city around Jami Masjid, with its bustling streets and crowded buildings

◁ India Gate and the elegant Statue Canopy designed by Sir Edwin Landseer Lutyens, completed in 1931

Exploring Delhi

Some of Delhi's most impressive buildings can be seen
in the area shown in this map. Vijay Chowk is the
vantage point for the grand sweep of Raj buildings
grouped on Raisina Hill. To the north, the magnificent
Jami Masjid with its busy hive of lanes, is the focus
of Old Delhi. To the southeast, the medieval quarter
around the tomb of the Sufi saint Nizamuddin Auliya
leads along Mathura Road to the ruined fort, Purana
Qila. And to the south, the Mehrauli area (shown on
the Greater Delhi map), has a fascinating cluster of
monuments built in the 12th and 13th centuries.

Vijay Chowk *(see pp72–3)*, at the base of
Raisina Hill, surrounded by government offices

SIGHTS AT A GLANCE

**Historic Buildings, Streets
& Neighbourhoods**

Around Kashmiri Gate **22**
Around Vijay Chowk pp72–3 **1**
Chandni Chowk pp84–5 **17**
Coronation Memorial **23**
Feroze Shah Kotla **21**
Hauz Khas **28**
Humayun's Tomb p83 **16**
Jahanpanah **30**
Jantar Mantar **9**
Khirkee **29**
*Mehrauli Archaeological
  Park pp92–4* **31**
Nizamuddin Complex **15**
Purana Qila **13**
Raisina Hill **3**
Rajghat **20**
Rajpath **4**
Rashtrapati Bhavan **2**
Red Fort **19**
Safdarjung's Tomb **26**
Tughluqabad **33**

Churches, Temples & Mosques

Baha'i House of Worship **34**
Jami Masjid **18**
Lakshmi Narayan Mandir **10**

Museums

Crafts Museum pp80–81 **14**
National Gallery of Modern Art **6**
National Museum pp76–7 **5**

Nehru Memorial Museum
  and Library **11**
Sanskriti Museum **32**
The National Rail Museum **25**

Shops & Markets

Connaught Place **8**
INA Market **27**

Parks & Gardens

Lodi Gardens **12**
The Ridge **24**

Theatres & Art Galleries

Mandi House Complex **7**

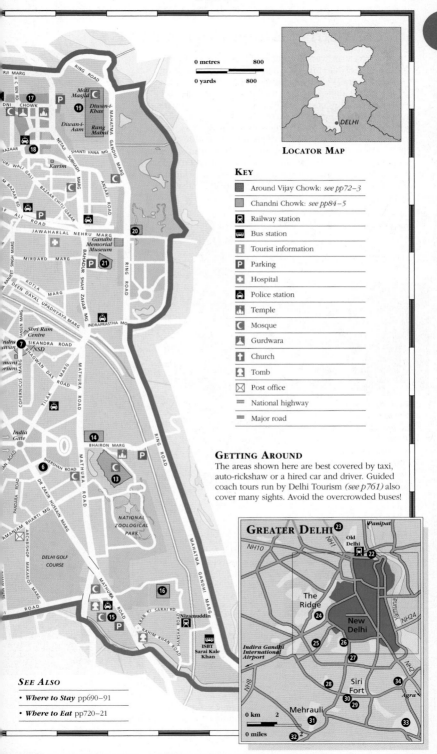

0 metres 800

0 yards 800

LOCATOR MAP

KEY

	Around Vijay Chowk: *see pp72–3*
	Chandni Chowk: *see pp84–5*
🚉	Railway station
🚌	Bus station
🛈	Tourist information
🅿	Parking
✚	Hospital
🚓	Police station
🛐	Temple
C	Mosque
⚕	Gurdwara
✝	Church
⚰	Tomb
⊠	Post office
═	National highway
═	Major road

GETTING AROUND

The areas shown here are best covered by taxi, auto-rickshaw or a hired car and driver. Guided coach tours run by Delhi Tourism *(see p761)* also cover many sights. Avoid the overcrowded buses!

GREATER DELHI

SEE ALSO

• *Where to Stay* pp690–91

• *Where to Eat* pp720–21

Street-by-Street: Around Vijay Chowk ❶

Vijay Chowk or "Victory Square", a large piazza at the base of Raisina Hill, was planned as a commanding approach to the Viceroy's House, now the Indian President's residence. This is where the "Beating of the Retreat" ceremony takes place each year on 29 January *(see p37)*. Vijay Chowk is flanked by two long, classical Secretariat buildings (the North and South Blocks), which house several ministries as well as the Prime Minister's Office. Ministers and government officials live in spacious bungalows on the tree-shaded avenues nearby. From Vijay Chowk, Lutyens's grand Central Vista lies ahead – large trees and fountains line the lawns of Rajpath up to India Gate, the Statue Canopy and the National Stadium at the far end.

★ Vijay Chowk
This piazza, flanked by red sandstone obelisk-shaped fountains, faces a grand vista.

North Block, designed by Herbert Baker, has an imposing Central Hall.

Sansad Bhavan is also known as Parliament House.

The Iron Gates
Copied from a pair Lutyens saw in Chiswick, England, these are set into ornamental sandstone gateposts. They lead to Rashtrapati Bhavan (see p74).

DALHOUSIE ROAD

THYAGARAJA MARG

KEY

– – – Suggested route

SIR EDWIN LANDSEER LUTYENS

The red sandstone National Archives, designed by Lutyens

Architect Sir Edwin Landseer Lutyens (1869–1944), President of the Royal Academy from 1938 to 1944, was commissioned to design India's new capital in 1911. With Herbert Baker, his colleague, it took him 20 years to build the city in a unique style that combined Western Classicism with Indian decorative motifs. The result is an impressive and harmonious synthesis, with Neo-Mughal gardens and grand vistas meeting at verdant roundabouts. Delayed by World War I and quarrels between Baker and Lutyens, spiralling costs met by Indian revenues led Mahatma Gandhi to term it a "white elephant". Ironically, the British lived here for only 16 years.

★ South Block
The Prime Minister's Office and the Defence Ministry are located within this section of the Secretariat.

Sunehri Bagh Mosque
This simple 18th-century mosque, built by a saint called Sayyid Sahib, makes for a picturesque roundabout. The adjoining Sunehri Bagh Road is lined with shady trees – a feature of all Lutyens's avenues.

LOCATOR MAP
See Delhi Map pp70–71

Roundabout
Beautifully landscaped road intersections are a haven for workers during lunch.

Udyog Bhavan
(Ministry of Commerce)

India Gate

Vayu Bhavan
(Air Headquarters)

TILAL NEHRU MARG

KAMARAJ ROAD

SUNEHRI BAGH ROAD

IX ROAD

KRISHNA MENON MARG

| 0 metres | 25 |
| 0 yards | 25 |

Statue of Kamaraj
K Kamaraj was Congress Party President (1963–6).

★ Bungalow-lined Avenues
Strict building bylaws preserve the original architecture of the colonial bungalows in the tree-lined avenues of this area.

STAR SIGHTS

★ **Vijay Chowk**

★ **South Block**

★ **Bungalow-lined Avenues**

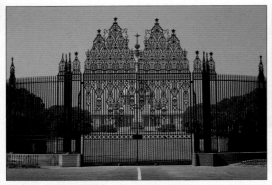

Ornate iron gates leading to Rashtrapati Bhavan, designed by Lutyens

Rashtrapati Bhavan ❷

C (011) 301 5321. ● to the public.
Mughal Gardens ○ Feb–Mar: daily.

DESIGNED BY Sir Edwin Lutyens *(see p72)* as the British Viceroy's Palace, Rashtrapati Bhavan, situated at the crest of Raisina Hill, is now the official residence of the President of India. A vast, copper-clad cupola soars over this elegant beige and red sandstone building which covers an area of 2 ha (5 acres). The *pièce de résistance* is the circular Durbar Hall, situated directly beneath the dome, where all important state ceremonies and functions are held.

To the west, the beautifully landscaped grounds include Rashtrapati Bhavan's famed **Mughal Gardens**. These terraced gardens with watercourses and fountains built on three levels, are open to visitors in the spring months.

Raisina Hill ❸

Cathedral Church of the Redemption **C** (011) 301 5396. ○ daily. ✝ 9am Mon–Sat; 8am Sun (summer); 8:30am Sun (winter).

THE BARREN, treeless grounds around Raisina Hill were selected by the British as the site of the new capital. Now a heavily-guarded, verdant area, it is dominated by stately buildings such as the twin North and South Blocks *(see*

p72) of the **Secretariat**. The two virtually identical buildings that rise impressively from the top of Raisina Hill, were designed by Sir Herbert Baker, who also designed the grand circular **Sansad Bhavan** (Parliament House) to the north of Vijay Chowk. Both the Rajya Sabha (Upper House) and the Lok Sabha (House of the People) convene here when Parliament is in session. The Lok Sabha's many heated debates take place in the Central Hall. After the December 2001 terrorist attack, Sansad Bhavan is now closed to visitors.

Behind Sansad Bhavan is the Anglican **Cathedral Church of the Redemption**, inspired by Palladio's Church of II Redentore in Venice. Originally built for senior British officials in 1931, it is now the diocese of the Bishop of the Church of North India.

Rajpath ❹

National Archives **C** (011) 338 5000. ○ Mon–Fri. ● public hols.
Indira Gandhi National Centre for the Arts **C** (011) 338 6345. ○ during exhibitions. ● Mon.

RUNNING EAST of Vijay Chowk is Rajpath, a two-mile-long avenue used for parades, with ornamental fountains, canals and lawns on either side. At the intersection of Rajpath and Janpath is the **National Archives** building, where important state records and documents are kept. Opposite this is the **Indira Gandhi National Centre for the Arts**. A major venue for large exhibitions and international symposia, it also houses a collection of rare manuscripts.

At Rajpath's eastern end is **India Gate**, a massive red sandstone arch, built to commemorate the Indian and British soldiers who died in World War I, and those who fell in battle in the North-West Frontier Province and the Third Afghan War. An eternal flame burns in memory of the soldiers who died in the 1971 India-Pakistan War. Facing India Gate is the sandstone canopy where a statue of King George V was installed in 1936. The statue is now at Coronation Park *(see p88)* and the canopy stands empty.

India Gate

National Museum ❺

See pp76–7.

Sansad Bhavan, where the Constitution of India was drafted

National Gallery of Modern Art ❻

Jaipur House, near India Gate.
📞 (011) 338 2835. ⏰ Tue–Sun.
⛔ public hols. 🏛 ♿

JAIPUR HOUSE, the former residence of the maharajas of Jaipur, is one of India's largest museums of modern art, covering the period from the mid-19th century to the present day. Its excellent collections include works by leading modern Indian painters such as Jamini Roy, Rabindranath Tagore, Raja Ravi Varma and Amrita Shergill, as well as contemporary artists such as Ram Kumar and Anjolie Ela Menon. Also on display are works by British artists such as Thomas Daniell and his nephew William Daniell, and an interesting group of "Company Paintings" – 18th-and 19th-century works by Indian artists commissioned specially for the British market.

Mandi House Complex ❼

Triveni Kala Sangam Tansen Marg.
📞 (011) 371 8833. ⏰ Mon–Sat.
⛔ public hols. 🏛 📷
Rabindra Bhavan Ferozeshah Rd.
📞 (011) 338 6626. 🏛
Kamani Auditorium Copernicus Marg. 📞 (011) 338 8084.
Shri Ram Centre Safdar Hashmi Marg. 📞 (011) 371 4307. 🏛 📷
National School of Drama Bhagwan Das Rd. 📞 (011) 338 9402.
For **Tickets** see **Entertainment** p96.

MANDI HOUSE, today the offices of the state-owned television centre, lends its name to this cultural complex encircling the roundabout. **Triveni Kala Sangam** has contemporary art galleries, an open air amphitheatre for concerts and plays, a popular café and a bookshop specializing in Indian arts publications. The state-sponsored **Rabindra Bhavan** arts complex houses the national academies of literature (Sahitya Akademi), fine arts and sculpture (Lalit Kala Akademi), and the

Connaught Place, the British-built shopping complex in New Delhi

performing arts (Sangeet Natak Akademi) in separate wings. All three have libraries and display galleries that sell reproductions and postcards. Regular exhibitions of photography, graphics and ceramics are also held here.
Kamani Auditorium, the **Shri Ram Centre** and the **National School of Drama** are vibrant centres for theatre, music and dance performances.

Mirrorwork skirts on sale at Janpath

Connaught Place ❽

Shops ⏰ Mon–Sat. ⛔ public hols.

OPENED IN 1931 and named after the Duke of Connaught, this shopping complex, with its Palladian archways and stuccoed colonnades, was designed by Robert Tor Russell as a deliberate contrast to the noise, smells and chaos of an Indian bazaar. The central circle of Connaught Place has now been renamed Rajiv Chowk, and the outer circle Indira Chowk. Its arcades and pavements spill over with *paan* kiosks, book stalls and shoe-shine boys, while the eclectic mix of shops is interspersed with eateries and cinema halls. Though no longer Delhi's premier shopping area, its shaded arcades are pleasant to stroll through. Other popular shopping centres around Connaught Place include the state emporia on **Baba Kharak Singh Marg**, **Shankar Market** in the outer circle, and the stalls along **Janpath**. **Cottage Industries** (see p97) is also located on Janpath.

REPUBLIC DAY PARADE

Ever since 1950, when India became a republic, this parade on 26 January has attracted large crowds despite the often chilly weather. Soldiers and sailors, war veterans and school children, and even elephants and camels, march

Republic Day Parade

smartly down Rajpath. Especially popular are the folk dancers and the inventive floats representing each state of the country. A ceremonial flypast by the Indian Air Force signals the end of the always colourful parade.

National Museum ❺

FIVE MILLENNIA OF INDIAN HISTORY can be explored at the National Museum, with its collection of nearly 200,000 pieces of Indian art. The nucleus collection of about 1,000 artifacts was sent to London in the winter of 1948–9 for an exhibition at the Royal Academy's Burlington House. After its return, it was housed in the Durbar Hall of Rashtrapati Bhavan *(see p74)* until the present building, built of the same beige and pink stone as the imposing new capital, was complete in 1960. The museum's collection of Harappan (Indus

Mother Goddess icon, Indus Valley

Valley) relics and Central Asian treasures from the Silk Route is considered among the finest in the world.

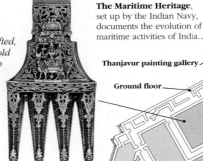

★ **Dara Shikoh's Marriage Procession**
An 18th-century Mughal miniature painting in gold and natural pigments.

Gold Tali Pendant
Delicately handcrafted, this 19th-century gold pendant from South India is part of the ceremonial jewellery displayed in this gallery.

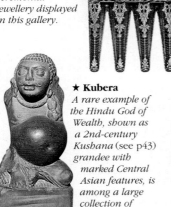

The Maritime Heritage, set up by the Indian Navy, documents the evolution of maritime activities of India.

Thanjavur painting gallery

Ground floor

★ **Kubera**
A rare example of the Hindu God of Wealth, shown as a 2nd-century Kushana (see p43) grandee with marked Central Asian features, is among a large collection of Mathura Art.

THE SERINDIAN COLLECTION

Almost 700 years after the Silk Route fell into disuse, Sir Aurel Stein, a British archaeologist, led a series of expeditions (1900–16) to uncover its treasures. Stein's collection of the artifacts he found in the Taklamakan Desert is on view at the museum's Central Asian Antiquities section. It includes silk paintings, Buddhist manuscripts and other valuable records.

Silk painting, 7th–8th century

Entrance

Auditorium

★ **Nataraja**
This 12th-century Chola statue of the cosmic dance of Lord Shiva is the centrepiece of the museum's South Indian bronzes.

Second floor

Aurangzeb's Sword
The personal sword of the Mughal emperor Aurangzeb, crafted in 1675 in the Indo-Persian style, has quotations from the Koran inscribed on it.

VISITORS' CHECKLIST

Janpath. 📞 (011) 301 9272.
🕐 Tue–Sun. 🔴 public hols. 📷
📷 extra charges. 📋 11:30am,
2:30pm, 4pm. 🚻 🍴 ♿ ⬆
Film shows, lectures,
presentations and special
exhibitions. Gallery talks on
Wednesdays on specific topics.

Gold Brocade
This 19th-century silk wedding sari woven in Varanasi (see p209) is embellished with motifs in gold thread.

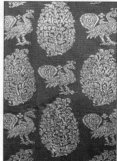

The Numismatics Gallery displays an impressive collection of coins and the evolution of the Indian script.

★ Illuminated Koran
A superb example of the elegant Islamic art of calligraphy, this gilded 18th-century Koran is one of a collection that also has an 8th-century Koran in the ancient Kufic script. The latter is among the oldest of its kind in the world.

First floor

Library

GALLERY GUIDE
The collection is displayed on three floors, grouped according to theme, epoch and style. The central foyer itself has a display of sculptures from various parts of the country. The museum also has a library and auditorium where film shows and lectures are regularly held. Information on these is published in the newspapers. The museum shop sells a range of handicrafts and other souvenirs, as well as replicas of select sculptures. The display is changed from time to time for variety, and special exhibitions are also mounted.

KEY TO FLOORPLAN

☐ Harappan Gallery
☐ Ancient and Medieval Sculpture
☐ Chola Bronzes
☐ Buddhist Art
☐ Tantra Art
☐ Decorative Arts and Jewellery
☐ Maritime Heritage
☐ Manuscripts and Miniatures
☐ Central Asian Antiquities
☐ Decorative Arts, Textiles, Arms and Armour, Musical Instruments

STAR EXHIBITS

★ **Dara Shikoh's Marriage Procession**

★ **Kubera**

★ **Nataraja**

★ **Illuminated Koran**

The brick and plaster astronomical instruments in Jantar Mantar

Jantar Mantar ❾

Sansad Marg. ◯ *daily.* 🖼

SAWAI JAI SINGH II of Jaipur, a keen astronomer, built this observatory in 1724 because he wanted to calculate planetary positions and alignments accurately, in order to perform sacred rituals and *pujas* at propitious moments. One of the five observatories he built *(see pp358–9)*, Jantar Mantar's instruments are large and fixed, making them resistant to vibration and therefore exact. The Samrat Yantra, a right-angled triangle whose hypotenuse is parallel to the earth's axis, is a gigantic sundial, with two brick quadrants on either side of it to measure the sun's shadow. The Ram Yantra, reads the altitude of the sun, and the Jai Prakash Yantra (invented by Jai Singh II himself) verifies the time of the spring equinox. Now obsolete, the observatory lies in the centre of a pleasant park surrounded by high-rises.

Lakshmi Narayan Mandir ❿

Mandir Marg. ◯ *daily.*

BUILT IN 1938 by the industrialist BD Birla, this was one of the earliest Indian temples without caste restrictions, and Mahatma Gandhi attended its first *puja*. A fairly typical example of modern Indian temple architecture, with its marble entrance and ochre and maroon *shikharas* (spires), the Birla Mandir, as it is popularly known, has images of Vishnu and his consort Lakshmi in its main shrine. Subsidiary shrines set around the courtyard, are inscribed with verses from sacred Hindu texts and are decorated with paintings depicting scenes from the *Mahabharata* and *Ramayana*.

Teen Murti Memorial

Nehru Memorial Museum and Library ⓫

Teen Murti Marg. ☎ *(011) 301 6350.* ◯ *Tue–Sun.* ● *public hols.* **Nehru Planetarium** ☎ *(011) 301 4504.* 🖼 *Shows 11:30am, 3pm.*

THE RESIDENCE OF Jawaharlal Nehru, India's first prime minister, Teen Murti Bhavan was converted into a museum and library for research scholars after Nehru's death in 1964. This house has a special place in modern Indian history because it was also the home of two future prime ministers – Nehru's daughter Indira Gandhi and his grandson Rajiv Gandhi, both of whom were assassinated *(see p57)*. Nehru's bedroom and study, still exactly as he left them, reflect his austere yet elegant personality and his eclectic taste in books.

The extensive grounds are home to the **Nehru Planetarium** and the square, three-arched **Kushak Mahal**, a 14th-century hunting lodge built by Sultan Feroze Shah Tughluq *(see p87)*. On the roundabout in front of the house stands the **Teen Murti** ("Three Statues") **Memorial**. This is dedicated to the Indian soldiers who died in World War I. The house derives its name from this landmark.

Teen Murti Bhavan, Nehru's official residence, now the Nehru Memorial Museum and Library

Athpula, the 17th-century bridge near the entrance to Lodi Gardens on South End Road

Lodi Gardens ⓬

Entrance on Lodi Rd & South End Rd.
◯ daily. ⓫

LODI GARDENS is one of Delhi's most picturesque parks, and a favourite haunt of joggers, yoga enthusiasts, political bigwigs accompanied by their bodyguards, and families who come to picnic on weekends. Landscaped at the behest of Lady Willingdon, the vicereine, in 1936, the park acts as a "green lung" for the people of Delhi. Its tree lined pathways and well-kept lawns and flowerbeds are laid out around the imposing 15th-century tombs of the Sayyid and Lodi dynasties, Delhi's last sultans. Many of them still have traces of the original turquoise tilework and calligraphy. The elegantly proportioned octagonal **Tomb of Muhammad Shah** (r.1434–44), the third ruler of the Sayyid dynasty, is said to be the oldest in the garden. The largest of the structures is the **Bara Gumbad** ("Big Dome") with an attached mosque built in 1494, and a guesthouse. At the South End Road entrance to the gardens is a lovely stone bridge called **Athpula** (literally "eight piers"), said to date from the 17th century. To its west are ramparts that enclose the **Tomb of Sikander Lodi** (r.1489–1517).

Purana Qila ⓭

Mathura Rd. ☎ (011) 462 9365.
◯ daily. **Son et Lumière** Sep–Oct & Feb–Apr: 8:30–9:30pm daily; Nov–Jan: 7:30–8:30pm daily; May–Aug: 9–10pm daily.
Tickets: from site and the Delhi Tourism office. ☎ (011) 331 4229.

PURANA QILA, literally "Old Fort", stands on an ancient site that has been continuously occupied since 1000 BC, as archaeological excavations have revealed. The brooding ramparts of the fort now enclose the remains of the sixth city of Delhi, Dinpanah (see p91), which was begun by the second Mughal emperor, Humayun. His reign, however, was short and in 1540 he was overthrown by the Afghan chieftain Sher Shah Sur (see p49). Sher Shah added several new structures and renamed the citadel Shergarh ("Lion's Fort"). After Sher Shah's death Humayun regained his throne. Of the many palaces, barracks and other edifices built by these two rulers, only Sher Shah's mosque and a building that was probably Humayun's library remain standing today.

The **Qila-i-Kuhna Mosque**, built in 1541, is a superbly proportioned structure with fine decorative inlay work in

Chhatri with decorative tilework

red and white marble and slate. To the south of the mosque is Humayun's library, known as **Sher Mandal**. A double-storeyed octagonal tower of red sandstone, it is crowned by an elaborate *chhatri* (open pavilion) supported by eight pillars. This was the tragic spot where the devout emperor, hurrying to kneel on the steps for the evening prayer, missed his footing and tumbled to his death in January 1556. The ramparts of the Purana Qila have three principal gateways, of which the imposing red sandstone **Bara Darwaza** on the western wall is the main entrance. Humayun's Tomb (see p83) can be seen from the southern gate.

Bara Darwaza, Purana Qila

Crafts Museum ⓮

Wooden doll on toy swing

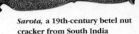

Sarota, a 19th-century betel nut cracker from South India

FOR CENTURIES, Indian craftsmen such as potters, weavers, masons and carvers, have created a range of objects for everyday use that are both beautiful and practical. A unique project was started in 1956 to promote indigenous artisans by giving them a place to display their work, and by the early 1980s, over 20,000 objects had been collected. This was the core around which India's first Crafts Museum developed.

★ **Bandhini Odhni**
This exquisite veil is the work of the Bhansali tribe in Kutch, Gujarat. Tie-and-dye (bandhini) is done by tying threads around grains to form a pattern, and dyeing the cloth in different colours.

Mukhalinga
This rare, late 19th-century phallic image (linga) with a human face (mukha) is made of brass and silver. The third eye and tiny snake-earrings are symbols of Shiva.

STAR EXHIBITS

★ **Bandhini Odhni**

★ **Charrake**

★ **Bhuta Figure**

Crafts Demonstration Area
Artisans from all over India set up workshops each month (barring the monsoon) to display their skills to visitors.

Amphitheatre

KEY

- ◻ Gallery of Aristocratic Arts
- ◻ Gallery of Ritual Arts
- ◻ Gallery of Folk and Tribal Cultur
- ◻ Gallery of Popular Culture
- ◻ Gallery of Textiles
- ◻ Non-exhibition space
- ◻ Temporary exhibitions gallery
- ◻ Visual store

Yashoda and Krishna
This mid-20th-century plaster cast statuette from South India is an interesting example of popular kitsch, inspired by gods and mythology. It is cheap and easy to reproduce for use in a domestic shrine.

VISITORS' CHECKLIST

Bhairon Marg. **▌** *(011) 337 1887.* ○ *Tue–Sun.* ● *public hols.* ▫ ▫ ▫ ♦ ♿
Crafts demonstration ○ *daily.*
● *Jul–Sep.*

★ Charrake
These enormous, circular vessels are cast of an alloy known as bell metal. They are still used in Kerala for wedding feasts or at temples for making payasam *(a type of rice pudding) for devotees during festivals.*

Madhubani Painting
This traditional wall painting in natural pigments, depicting a wedding scene, is by Ganga Devi, a famous 20th-century woman painter from Bihar (see p217).

★ Bhuta Figure
These life-sized wooden figures, artifacts from the Bhuta cult of spirit worship in the southern state of Karnataka (see p526), date back to the early 19th-century.

Library

Entrance

GALLERY GUIDE
The museum's exhibits are spread over two floors of the complex, divided into separate areas by courtyards that also double up as exhibition spaces. A large open area is used for live art displays by visiting artisans each month, except during the rainy season.

The Crafts Museum Shop
This shop sells a fine selection of items made by indigenous artisans, including house-hold objects, decorative pieces and textiles.

Nizamuddin Complex ⑮

W of Mathura Rd. **Dargah** ◯ *daily*.
Qawwali performance *7pm Thu.*
🎵 *Urs (Jul & Dec).*

THIS MEDIEVAL settlement, or *basti,* is named after Sheikh Hazrat Nizamuddin Auliya, whose grave and hospice are located here. Nizamuddin belonged to a fraternity of Sufi mystics, the Chishtis, respected for their austerity, piety and disdain for material desires, and was a spiritual descendant of Moinuddin Chishti *(see p376).* His daily assemblies drew both the rich and the poor, who believed that he was a "friend of God" who would intercede on their behalf on Judgement Day. He died in 1325 but his disciples call him a *zinda pir* (living spirit) who continues to heed their pleas. A three-day Urs is

Congregational area, Nizamuddin

observed, with qawwalis sung, on the anniversary of his death, and another on the death of his disciple Amir Khusrau.

A winding alley leads to the saint's grave. It is crowded with mendicants and lined with stalls selling flowers and *chadors* (ceremonial cloths), polychrome clocks and prints of Mecca. The main congregational area is a

**Colourful stalls in the alley
leading to Nizamuddin's tomb**

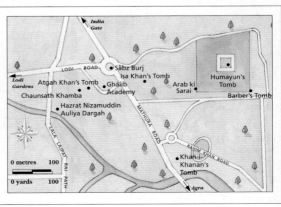

**Tomb of the famous
poet Mirza Ghalib**

marble pavilion (rebuilt in 1562) where, every Thursday evening, followers sing devotional songs composed by the celebrated Persian poet, Amir Khusrau (1253–1325). Women are denied entry beyond the outer verandah but may peer through *jalis* into the small, dark chamber where the saint's grave lies draped with a rose petal strewn cloth, surrounded by imams who continuously recite verses from the Koran. Amir Khusrau is buried in the complex, as

are other eminent disciples, such as Jahanara Begum.

Across the western side of the open courtyard is the red sandstone Jama't Khana Mosque, built in 1325. To its north is a *baoli* (stepwell), excavated in secret while Tughluqabad *(see p95)* was being built, because Ghiyasuddin Tughluq had banned all building activities elsewhere. Legend has it that labourers worked here at night with the help of lamps lit not with oil but with water blessed by Nasiruddin, Nizamuddin's successor. The early 16th-century **Tomb of Atgah Khan** is to the north. A powerful minister in Emperor Akbar's court, he was murdered by Adham Khan, a political rival *(see p93).* The open marble pavilion, **Chaunsath Khamba** ("64 pillars"), is close by and just outside is an enclosure containing the simple grave of Mirza Ghalib (1786–1869). One of the greatest poets of his time, Ghalib wrote in both Urdu and Persian, and his verses are still recited. Nearby is the **Ghalib Academy**, a repository of paintings and manuscripts.

Despite its crowds, the *basti* preserves with miraculous serenity the legend of Nizamuddin, described by Khusrau as "a king without throne or crown, with kings in need of the dust of his feet".

NIZAMUDDIN COMPLEX

One of Delhi's historic necropolises, many of the saint's disciples, such as Amir Khusrau and Jahanara Begum, Shah Jahan's favourite daughter, are buried close to their master. Jahanara's epitaph echoes her master's teachings: "Let naught cover my grave save the green grass, for grass well suffices as a covering for the grave of the lowly".

[Map: Nizamuddin Complex]
India Gate
LODI ROAD
Sabz Burj
Isa Khan's Tomb
Lodi Gardens
Atgah Khan's Tomb
Ghalib Academy
Arab ki Sarai
Humayun's Tomb
Chaunsath Khamba
Barber's Tomb
Hazrat Nizamuddin Auliya Dargah
MATHURA ROAD
LALA LAJPAT RAI PATH
0 metres   100
0 yards   100
Khan-i-Khanan's Tomb
BAHIM KHAN ROAD
Agra

Humayun's Tomb ⑯

Marble star inlaid on panel

Humayun, the second Mughal emperor *(see p79)*, is buried in this tomb, the first great example of a Mughal garden tomb, and inspiration for several later monuments, such as the incomparable Taj Mahal *(see pp172–3)*. Built in 1565 by Persian architect Mirak Mirza Ghiyas, it was commissioned by Humayun's senior widow, Haji Begum. Often called "a dormitory of the House of Timur", the graves in its chambers include Humayun's wives and Dara Shikoh, Shah Jahan's scholarly son. Also in the complex are the octagonal tomb and mosque of Isa Khan, a 16th-century nobleman, and the tomb of Humayun's favourite barber. The Arab ki Sarai was a rest house for the Persian masons who built the tomb.

VISITORS' CHECKLIST

Off Mathura Rd.
📞 *(011) 435 5275.*
🕐 *daily.* 🎫 🚻 ♿

The perfectly symmetrical Humayun's Tomb as seen from the entrance

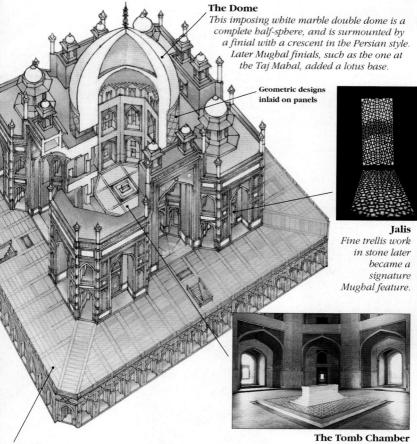

The Dome
This imposing white marble double dome is a complete half-sphere, and is surmounted by a finial with a crescent in the Persian style. Later Mughal finials, such as the one at the Taj Mahal, added a lotus base.

Geometric designs inlaid on panels

Jalis
Fine trellis work in stone later became a signature Mughal feature.

The imposing plinth is decorated with red sandstone arches and consists of multiple chambers, a departure from the single chamber of previous tombs.

The Tomb Chamber
The plain white marble sarcophagus stands on a simple black and white marble platform. The grave itself, no longer accessible, lies in the dark, bat-filled basement below.

Street-by-Street: Chandni Chowk ⓱

ONCE SHAHJAHANABAD'S *(see p91)* most elegant boulevard, Chandni Chowk ("Silvery, Moonlit Square"), laid out in 1648, had a canal running through it, and was lined with grand shops and mansions. Today, it is still the heart of Old Delhi, where religious and commercial activity mix easily. At the entrance to Chandni Chowk is the Digambar Jain Temple, the first of many shrines along its length. Built in 1656, it also houses a unique hospital for birds.

Charity box for donations at the Bird Hospital

Sisganj Gurdwara
Guru Tegh Bahadur, the ninth Sikh guru, was be-headed at this site in 1675.

Fatehpuri Masjid (built in 1650)

CHANDNI CHOWK

KINARI BAZAAR

DARIBA KALAN

Nai Sarak

Sunehri Masjid
The "Golden Mosque", with three gilt domes, was built in 1722. On 22 March 1739, Persian invader Nadir Shah stood on its roof to watch the massacre of Delhi's citizens.

CHEL PURI

BAZAAR GULIYAN

Shiv Temple

STAR SIGHTS
★ Kinari Bazaar
★ Lahore Gate
★ Dariba Kalan
★ Jami Masjid

★ Kinari Bazaar
Tightly packed stalls sell all manner of glittering gold and silver trimmings such as braids, tinsel garlands and turbans for weddings and festivals.

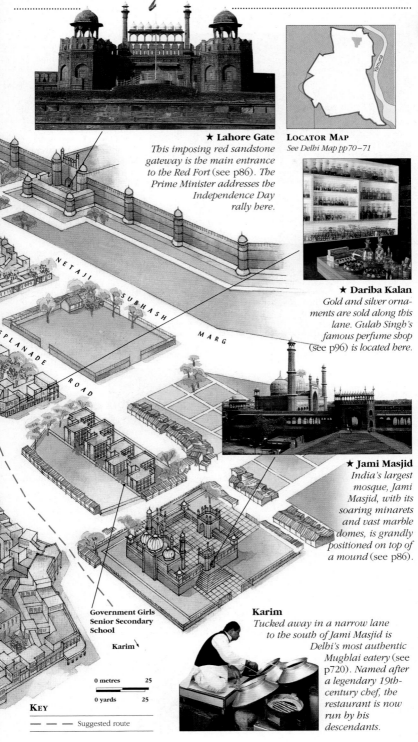

★ **Lahore Gate**
This imposing red sandstone gateway is the main entrance to the Red Fort (see p86). The Prime Minister addresses the Independence Day rally here.

LOCATOR MAP
See Delhi Map pp70–71

★ **Dariba Kalan**
Gold and silver ornaments are sold along this lane. Gulab Singh's famous perfume shop (see p96) is located here.

★ **Jami Masjid**
India's largest mosque, Jami Masjid, with its soaring minarets and vast marble domes, is grandly positioned on top of a mound (see p86).

Government Girls Senior Secondary School

Karim

Karim
Tucked away in a narrow lane to the south of Jami Masjid is Delhi's most authentic Mughlai eatery (see p720). Named after a legendary 19th-century chef, the restaurant is now run by his descendants.

| 0 metres | 25 |
| 0 yards | 25 |

KEY

– – – Suggested route

The sandstone and marble Jami Masjid, India's largest mosque

Jami Masjid ⑱

Off Netaji Subhash Marg. ⬜ *daily.* ⬛ *to non-Muslims during times of prayer and after 5pm.*

THIS GRAND MOSQUE, with three imposing black and white marble domes, and twin minarets framing its great central arch, was built in 1656 by the Emperor Shah Jahan, on a natural mound. It took six years and 5,000 workers to construct, at a cost of nearly a million rupees. A magnificent flight of sandstone steps leads to the great arched entrances. In Aurangzeb's time, the area attracted horse sellers and jugglers; today, shoe minders and beggars mill around. The huge 28-m (92-ft) square courtyard can accommodate up to 20,000 people at Friday prayer sessions and at Id, when it looks like a sea of worshippers. Next to the *dukka* (water tank) for the ritual ablutions, is the platform where, before loud-speakers took over, a second

prayer leader echoed the imam's words and actions for worshippers too far from the pulpit for a clear view.

Red Fort ⑲

Chandni Chowk. 📞 *(011) 327 3703.* ⬜ *Tue–Sun.* ⬛ *public hols.* 🖼 **Son et Lumière** *Sep–Oct & Feb–Apr: 8:30–9:30pm daily; Nov–Jan: 7:30–8:30pm daily; May–Aug: 9–10pm daily.* 🖼 **Museum** ⬜ *Tue–Sun.* 📷

RED SANDSTONE battlements give this imperial citadel its name, Lal ("Red") Qila ("Fort"). Commissioned by Shah Jahan in 1639, it took nine years to build and was the seat of Mughal power until 1857 when the last Mughal emperor, Bahadur Shah Zafar, was dethroned and exiled. Today, the Red Fort remains a powerful symbol of Indian nationhood.

The throne canopy at the Diwan-i-Aam

It was here that the national flag was hoisted for the first time when India became an independent nation on 15 August 1947.

Entry is through **Lahore Gate**. One of the fort's six gateways, this leads on to the covered bazaar of **Chatta Chowk**, where jewels and brocades were once sold. Beyond this lies the **Naqqar Khana**, a pavilion where ceremonial music was played three times a day.

A path from here leads to the **Diwan-i-Aam**, a 60-pillared, red sandstone hall where the emperor gave daily audience to the public. The emperor sat beneath the lavishly carved stone canopy, while the low bench in front of it was for his chief minister. Beyond this hall is the **Rang Mahal**. Inside its gilded chambers, once exclusively for women, is an inlaid marble fountain shaped like an open lotus.

Nearby, is the **Khas Mahal**, the emperor's royal apartments with special rooms for private worship and for sleeping. The Robe Room ("Tosh Khana") has a superb marble *jali* screen carved with the scales of justice, a motif seen in many miniature paintings. North of the Khas Mahal is the **Diwan-i-Khas**, built completely of white marble. The legendary Peacock Throne, embedded

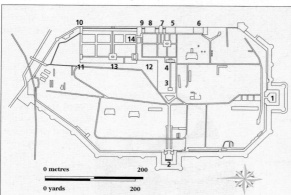

RED FORT

1 Delhi Gate
2 Lahore Gate
3 Naqqar Khana
4 Diwan-i-Aam
5 Rang Mahal
6 Moti Mahal
7 Khas Mahal
8 Diwan-i-Khas
9 Hamams
10 Shah Burj
11 Sawan
12 Bhadon
13 Zafar Mahal
14 Moti Masjid

0 metres   200

0 yards   200

with priceless jewels was kept here until it was taken away as war booty by the Persian chieftain Nadir Shah in 1739. The walls and pillars of this exclusive pavilion, where the emperor met his most trusted nobles, were once inlaid with gems. The ceiling was of silver inlaid with precious stones.

A little further away are the **Hamams** (Royal Baths) with inlaid marble floors and three enclosures. The first chamber provided hot vapour, the second scented rosewater through sculpted fountains, and the third cold water.

To the west of the baths is the elegant little **Moti Masjid** ("Pearl Mosque"), named after the pearly sheen of its marble. It was built by Emperor Aurangzeb in 1659.

Gandhi's *samadhi* at Rajghat

Rajghat ⑳

Mahatma Gandhi Rd. ⬤ *daily.*
Prayer meetings *5pm Fri.*
Gandhi National Museum
☏ *(011) 331 1793.* ⬤ *Tue–Sun.*
⬤ *public hols.* **Film shows** *4–5pm Sat & Sun.*

INDIA'S MOST POTENT symbol of nationhood, Rajghat is the site of Mahatma Gandhi's cremation. A sombre, black granite platform inscribed with his last words, *He Ram!* ("Oh God") now stands here. The only splash of colour comes from the garlands of orange marigolds that are draped over the platform. All visiting heads of state are taken to this *samadhi* (memorial) to lay wreaths in memory of the "Father of the Nation". On Gandhi's birthday (2 Oct) and death anniversary (30 Jan), the nation's leaders gather here for prayer meetings.

The Ashokan Pillar, rising above the ruins of Feroze Shah Kotla

Just across the road is the **Gandhi National Museum**, crammed with memorabilia, including Gandhi's letters and diaries. A framed plaque on the wall sets out his simple philosophy: "Non-violence is the pitting of one's whole soul against the will of the tyrant... it is then possible for a single individual to defy the might of an unjust empire".

Feroze Shah Kotla ㉑

Bahadur Shah Zafar Marg. ⬤ *daily.*

ONLY SOME RAMPARTS and ruined structures remain of Feroze Shah Kotla, the palace complex of Ferozabad, Delhi's fifth city *(see p91)*, erected by that indefatigable builder Feroze Shah Tughluq. Entry is from the gate next to the Indian Express Building. At one end of the walled enclosure stand the roofless ruins of the Jami Masjid, of which only the rear wall is

still extant. This was once Delhi's largest mosque and according to popular legend, Timur, the Mongol conqueror from Samarkand who sacked Delhi in 1398, came here to say his Friday prayers.

Next to the mosque are the remains of a pyramidal structure, topped by one of the Mauryan emperor Ashoka's polished stone pillars *(see p42)*. Brought from the Punjab, it was installed here in 1356 by Feroze Shah. It was from the inscriptions on this pillar that James Prinsep, the Oriental linguist, deciphered the Brahmi script, a forerunner of the modern Devanagari, in 1837.

Khuni Darwaza (the "Bloodstained Gate"), opposite the Express Building, was built by Sher Shah Sur as one of the gates to his city *(see p79)*. This was where the Emperor Bahadur Shah Zafar's sons were shot by Lieutenant Hodson after the Mutiny of 1857 was quashed *(see p53)*.

THE BAZAARS OF OLD DELHI

Old Delhi's bazaars are legendary. An English visitor over a 100 years ago, wrote in praise of the "Cashmere shawls, gold and silver embroidery, jewellery, enamels and carpets" found here. Today the great wholesale bazaars of Chandni Chowk still retain a souk-like quality. Their narrow streets are lined with shops, whose goods spill out onto the pavements. Each lane specializes in a commodity: Dariba Kalan, for instance, is the lane of jewellers and silversmiths, while Kinari Bazaar *(see p84)* sells a bewildering array of tinsel and sequins.

Indian spices on sale in Khari Baoli, Asia's largest spice market

Around Kashmiri Gate ㉒

Between Nicholson Rd, Ramlal Chandok Marg & Church Rd.
St James's Church Lothian Rd.
📞 *(011) 386 0873.* ☐ *daily.*
✝ *English: 9am Sun.*

THIS LANDMARK, from where the Mughals would set off to spend their summers in Kashmir, resonates with memories of the Mutiny of 1857 *(see p53)*. The short stretch between Kashmiri Gate and the Old Delhi General Post Office (GPO) witnessed bitter fighting, as the city of Delhi lay under siege by the British. A final assault led to the blasting of the Gate, and a plaque on its western side honours "the engineers and miners who died while clearing the gate for British forces on September 14, 1857". In the 1920s, this area was also a favourite haunt of the British residents living in nearby Civil Lines.

The historic **St James's Church**, Delhi's oldest, is the most striking sight in the vicinity. It was consecrated in 1836 by Colonel James Skinner. A flamboyant adventurer of mixed parentage who was rejected by the British Army, Skinner raised his own cavalry regiment which proceeded to fight with great distinction. The church was erected in fufillment of a vow Skinner made on the battlefield. An unusual structure, the church is in the shape of a Greek cross, surmounted by an imposing eight-leafed dome. Its two stained-glass windows were installed in the 1860s. A marble tablet in front of the altar marks Skinner's simple grave.

Statues of former viceroys around the Coronation Memorial

Coronation Memorial ㉓

S of NH1 Bypass. ☐ *daily.*

THE ROYAL DURBAR, held in 1911 to proclaim the accession of George V as King Emperor of India, was held at this site. A red sandstone obelisk commemorates the coronation. More than 100,000 people thronged to see the King Emperor and Queen Empress sit beneath a golden dome mounted on a crimson canopy. Today, it is a dusty and forlorn spot, surrounded by statues of former viceroys, including Lords Hardinge and Willingdon (distinguished for their role in the construction of New Delhi). Towering over them all is the 22-m (72-ft) high statue of the King Emperor himself, which was removed from the Statue Canopy at India Gate *(see p74)* and installed here in the 1960s. About 3 km (2 miles) southeast is a forested park area known as the **Northern Ridge**, cut through by Ridge

Coronation Memorial

Road and Rani Jhansi Road. At its southern end lies the **Mutiny Memorial** (known locally as Ajitgarh), a Victorian Gothic tower which commemorates the soldiers "both British and native … who were killed" in 1857. Panoramic views of Old Delhi can be enjoyed from here.

Running parallel to the Northern Ridge is the sprawling **Delhi University** area. St Stephen's College, the most distinguished of the colleges dotting the campus, was designed by Walter George in 1938. The office of the Vice Chancellor, once the guesthouse for British officials, is also the spot where the young Lord Louis Mountbatten proposed to Edwina Ashley in 1922. A plaque celebrates the event. They eventually became India's last viceroy and vicereine.

The Ridge ㉔

Upper Ridge Rd. ☐ *daily.* **Buddha Jayanti Park** ☐ *daily.*

DELHI'S RIDGE, the last outcrop of the Aravalli Hills extending northwards from Rajasthan, runs diagonally across the city from southwest to northeast. The area was originally developed by Feroze Shah Tughluq in the late 14th century as his hunting resort. The ruins of his many lodges can still be seen here. This green belt of

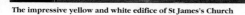
The impressive yellow and white edifice of St James's Church

undulating, rocky terrain is covered by dense scrub forest consisting mainly of laburnum *(Cassia fistula)*, kikar *(Acacia arabica)* and flame of the forest *(Butea monosperma)*, interspersed with bright splashes of bougainvillea.

A large area in the centre is now the **Buddha Jayanti Park**, a peaceful, well-manicured enclave, with paved paths. Pipal *(Ficus religiosa)* trees abound, and on a small ornamental island is a simple sandstone pavilion shading the large gilt-covered statue of the Buddha, installed by the 14th Dalai Lama in 1993. An inscription nearby quotes the Dalai Lama: "Human beings have the capacity to bequeathe to future generations a world that is truly human". Every year in May, Buddhist devotees celebrate Buddha Jayanti here *(see p35)*.

The National Rail Museum ㉕

Chanakyapuri. **C** *(011) 688 1816.* ◯ *Tue–Sun.* ◉ *public hols.* 🎞 *extra for train rides.* 🚻

INDIA'S RAILWAY NETWORK can boast of some astonishing statistics. It has a route length of 63,360 km (39,370 miles) and tracks that cover 108,513 km (67,427 miles). There are about 7,150 stations, 12,600 passenger trains, and 1,350 goods trains that run every day. The railways employ 1.6 million people, while 13 million passengers travel by train each day, consuming 6 million meals through the course of their journey.

This museum encapsulates the history of Indian railways. Steam locomotive enthusiasts

will appreciate the collection that traces the development of the Indian railways from 1853, when the first 34 km (21 miles) of railway between Bombay (now Mumbai) and Thane was laid. The wealth of memorabilia on display inside includes the skull of an elephant that collided with a mail train at Golkara in 1894, and a realistic model of an 1868 first-class passenger coach with separate compartments for accompanying servants. Outside, are several retired steam locomotives built in Manchester and Glasgow in the late 19th century, and the salon that carried the Prince of Wales (later King Edward VII) on his travels during the 1876 Royal Durbar. A "toy train" offers rides around the compound, and the shop sells a range of model locomotives.

Safdarjung's Tomb ㉖

Aurobindo Marg. **C** *(011) 301 7293.* ◯ *daily.* 🎞 📷 *extra charges for video photography.* 🚻

THIS IS THE LAST of Delhi's garden tombs and was built in 1754 for Safdarjung, the powerful prime minister of Muhammad Shah, the Mughal emperor between 1719 and 1748. Marble was allegedly stripped from the tomb of Abdur Rahim Khan-i-Khanan in Nizamuddin to construct this rather florid example of late Mughal architecture. Approached by an ornate gateway, the top storey of which houses the library of the

Archaeological Survey of India (ASI), the tomb has an exaggerated dome and stands in a *charbagh*, a garden cut by water channels into four parts. Its façade is extensively ornamented with well-preserved plaster carving and the central chamber has some fine stone inlay work on the floor.

A well-stocked shop selling imported foodstuffs at INA Market

INA Market ㉗

Aurobindo Marg. **Shops** ◯ *Tue–Sun.*

THIS LIVELY BAZAAR retains all the trappings of a traditional Indian market but also sells imported foodstuffs such as cheese, pasta and exotic varieties of seafood. The stalls are crammed together under a ramshackle roof, mostly corrugated iron and oilcloth, and sell every manner of stainless steel utensils, spices, Punjabi pickles, readymade garments and even live chickens. Tiny restaurants in between offer Indian fast food. Diplomats, out-of-town shoppers and locals all patronize this market for its reasonable prices and wide variety of products.

The name is derived from Indian National Airports, as the adjacent colony used to house employees of the nearby Safdarjung Aerodrome. Built in the 1930s, the aerodrome was the headquarters of the South Eastern Command Air Wing during World War II. It now contains the offices of the Ministry of Civil Aviation and the Delhi Gliding Club. Indian Airlines also has a 24-hour booking office here *(see p773)*.

A late 19th-century steam engine at the National Rail Museum

The double-storeyed *madrasa* (college) at Hauz Khas

Hauz Khas

W of Aurobindo Marg. **Monuments**
☐ *daily.*

BEYOND THE BOUTIQUES, art
galleries and restaurants
that have taken over the
village of Hauz Khas, are the
medieval monuments from
Feroze Shah Tughluq's reign.
In 1352, the sultan erected a
number of buildings on the
banks of Hauz Khas, the large
tank which was excavated by
Alauddin Khilji for his city of
Siri. The tank, which shares
its name with the surrounding
village, is now dry.

Contemporary accounts
claim that Feroze Shah was a
prolific builder, and during his
37-year reign he constructed
an astounding 40 mosques,
200 towns, 100 public baths
and about 30 reservoirs.

Among the buildings around
Hauz Khas are a *madrasa*,
Feroze Shah's tomb and the
ruins of a small mosque. The
madrasa is built close to the
edge of the tank. Plaster
carvings and niches for books
can be seen inside. The
chhatris (open pavilions) in
the entrance forecourt are
said to cover the teachers'
burial mounds. At one end of
the *madrasa* lies the austere
tomb of Feroze Shah. Wine-
red painted plaster calligraphy
decorates its interior.

The complex is best viewed
in the afternoon, when sunlight filters through the *jalis* to
cover the graves of the sultan,
his sons and grandson with
delicate star-shaped shadows.

East of Hauz Khas, off
Aurobindo Marg, is a small
tapering structure called **Chor
Minar** ("Tower of Thieves")
dating back to the 14th-
century Khilji period. Its walls,
pockmarked with holes, are
said to have held the severed
heads of thieves, intended to
deter others from crime.

Close by, to the northwest,
is the **Nili Masjid** ("Blue
Mosque"). Named after the
blue tiles above its eaves, it
was built in 1505 by a certain
Kasumbhil, nurse to the
governor of Delhi's son.

Khirkee

N of Press Enclave Marg.
Monuments ☐ *daily.*

THE UNUSUAL two-storeyed
Khirkee ("Windows")
Mosque, built by Feroze Shah
Tughluq's prime minister,
Khan-i-Jahan Junan Shah, in

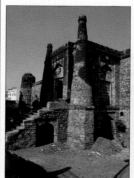
The fortress-like Khirkee Mosque

the mid-14th century lends its
name to this little village in
South Delhi. The mosque
has a fortress-like appearance,
broken by rows of arched
windows, which give the
mosque its name. Its innovative design was not repeated
again as its many pillared
divisions were found imprac-
tical for large congregations.

Further down is **Satpula**,
the seven-arched stone weir
built by Muhammad bin
Tughluq in 1326. It formed
part of a reservoir used for
irrigation, and also made up a
portion of the fortified wall
enclosing Jahanpanah.

An arched window with a carved
stone *jali*, Khirkee Mosque

Jahanpanah

S of Panchsheel Park. **Monuments**
☐ *daily.*

IN THE HEART of Jahanpanah,
Muhammad bin Tughluq's
capital, stands **Begumpuri
Mosque**, also built by Khan-i-
Jahan Junan Shah. (Ask specifically for the old mosque, as
a new one is located nearby.)
The mosque is remarkable for
its 44 domes which surmount
the cloisters surrounding the
central courtyard. It is said
that in times of need, this
mosque also functioned as a
treasury, a granary and a
general meeting place.

To the north is the palace of
Bijay Mandal, from where,
according to the 14th-century
Arab traveller Ibn Batuta,
Muhammad bin Tughluq
reviewed his troops. The
upper platform offers a grand
view of Delhi, extending from
the Qutb Minar to Humayun's
Tomb and beyond.

Early Capitals of Delhi

ᴅᴇʟʜɪ's ꜰᴀᴍᴏᴜs "seven cities" range from the 12th-century Qila Rai Pithora, built by Prithviraj Chauhan, to the imperial Shahjahanabad, constructed by the Mughals in the 17th century. Each of these cities comprised the settlements that grew around the forts erected by powerful sultans with territorial ambitions.

Purana Qila

As the Delhi Sultans consolidated their territories, they moved their defensively situated capitals in the rocky outcrops of the Aravallis, to the northeast, towards the open plains by the banks of the Yamuna. Today, Delhi is an amalgam of the ruins of medieval citadels, palaces, tombs and mosques, and an ever-expanding, modern concrete jungle.

Ferozabad (see p87), stretching north from Hauz Khas to the banks of the Yamuna, is Delhi's fifth city built by Feroze Shah Tughluq (r.1351–88).

Shabjabanabad was Delhi's seventh city, built between 1638 and 1649 by Shah Jahan who shifted the Mughal capital here from Agra (see pp168–77).

Shahjahanabad

Ferozabad

Purana Qila

Siri, Delhi's second city can still be seen near the Siri Fort Auditorium and the adjacent village of Shahpur Jat. The once prosperous city of Siri was built by Alauddin Khilji in 1303.

Purana Qila (see p79), the citadel of Delhi's sixth city, Dinpanah, was built by Humayun. It was captured and occupied by the Afghan chieftain, Sher Shah Sur (r.1540–45) who called it Shergarh.

Siri

Jahanpanah

Qila Rai Pithora

Tughluqabad

Jahanpanab was built by Muhammad bin Tughluq (r.1325–51) as a walled enclosure to link Qila Rai Pithora and Siri. The ruined battlements of Delhi's fourth city stand near Chiragh.

Qila Rai Pithora was the first of Delhi's seven cities, built by the Chauhans in about 1180. In 1192, it was captured by Qutbuddin Aibak who established his capital here (see pp92–3).

Tughluqabad (see p95), a dramatic fort on the foothills of the Aravallis, was Delhi's third city built during Ghiyasuddin Tughluq's four-year reign (1321–5).

Mehrauli Archaeological Park ㉛

Chhatri outside
Jamali-Kamali

BEST KNOWN FOR the Qutb Minar, a UNESCO World Heritage Monument, Mehrauli was built over Rajput territories called Lal Kot and Qila Rai Pithora. In 1193, Qutbuddin Aibak, then a slave-general of Muhammad of Ghur *(see p48)*, made it the centre of the Delhi Sultanate. By the 13th century the small village, Mehrauli, had grown around the shrine of the Sufi saint, Qutb Sahib. Later, Mughal princes came here to hunt and some 19th-century British officials built weekend houses, attracted by the area's orchards, ponds and game. Many of Delhi's rich and famous now own sprawling retreats in the area.

Dargah Qutb Sahib
The 13th-century dargah of Sufi saint Qutbuddin Bakhtiyar and the nearby Moti Masjid ("Pearl Mosque") attract many pilgrims.

Hauz-i-Shamsi reservoir was built in 1230 by Sultan Iltutmish *(see p48)*, who is supposed to have been guided to this site by the Prophet in a dream.

Zafar Mahal is a palace named after the last Mughal emperor, Bahadur Shah Zafar.

Mehrauli village

★ **Jahaz Mahal**
Venue of the Phoolwalon ki Sair (a colourful flower procession), this square pleasure pavilion, built during the Lodi era (1451–1526), seems to float on the Hauz-i-Shamsi tank.

Jharna (waterfall) was so-called because after the monsoon, water from the Hauz-i-Shamsi would flow over an embankment into a garden.

Bagichi Mosque

Madhi Masjid
Surrounded by bastions and a high wall, this fortress-like mosque, dating back to 1200, has a large open courtyard and a three-arched, heavily ornamented prayer hall.

STAR FEATURES

★ **Jahaz Mahal**

★ **Qutb Minar**

★ **Jamali-Kamali Mosque and Tomb**

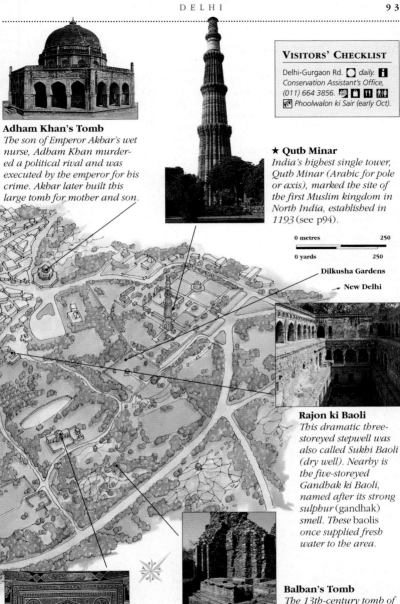

Adham Khan's Tomb
The son of Emperor Akbar's wet nurse, Adham Khan murdered a political rival and was executed by the emperor for his crime. Akbar later built this large tomb for mother and son.

★ Qutb Minar
India's highest single tower, Qutb Minar (Arabic for pole or axis), marked the site of the first Muslim kingdom in North India, established in 1193 (see p94).

0 metres   250

0 yards   250

Dilkusha Gardens

New Delhi

Rajon ki Baoli
This dramatic three-storeyed stepwell was also called Sukhi Baoli (dry well). Nearby is the five-storeyed Gandhak ki Baoli, named after its strong sulphur (gandhak) smell. These baolis once supplied fresh water to the area.

Balban's Tomb
The 13th-century tomb of Balban, Qutbuddin's successor, lies in a square rubble-built chamber.

★ Jamali-Kamali Mosque and Tomb
The tomb of Jamali (the court poet during the late Lodi and early Mughal age) is inscribed with some of his verses. Its well-preserved interior has coloured tiles and richly decorated painted plasterwork. The second grave is unidentified but is widely believed to be that of his brother, Kamali.

Mehrauli: The Qutb Complex

Floral motif

THE QUTB MINAR TOWERS over this historic area where Qutbuddin Aibak laid the foundation of the Delhi Sultanate *(see p48).* In 1193, he built the Quwwat-ul-Islam ("Might of Islam") Mosque and the Qutb Minar to announce the advent of the Muslim sultans. The mosque is a patchwork fusion of decorative Hindu panels, salvaged from razed temples around the site, and Islamic domes and arches. Later, Iltutmish, Alauddin Khilji and Feroze Shah Tughluq added more structures, heralding a new architectural style.

Iron Pillar
This 4th-century pillar, originally made as a flagstaff in Vishnu's honour, is a tribute to ancient Indian metallurgy.

Qutb Minar
The five-storeyed Victory Tower started by Qutbuddin Aibak was completed by his successor, Iltutmish.

Carved Panels
Panels carved with inscriptions from the Koran embellish the gateway.

Entrance

Alai Darwaza
This gateway to the complex, erected in 1311 by Alauddin Khilji, is one of the earliest buildings in India to employ the Islamic principles of arched construction.

Quwwat-ul-Islam Mosque
Hindu motifs, such as bells and garlands, are clearly visible on the pillars of this mosque.

Pots displayed at Sanskriti Museum

Sanskriti Museum 🈲

Anandgram, Mehrauli-Gurgaon Rd. ☎ (011) 650 1796. ☐ daily. ● public hols.

THIS UNUSUAL MUSEUM is set amidst beautifully land-scaped, spacious grounds. Exhibits are displayed both in the garden and in specially constructed rural huts. The collection itself is equally unusual in its devotion to objects of everyday use, that have been exquisitely crafted by unknown, rural artisans. OP Jain, whose personal collections gave birth to this museum, has donated combs, nutcrackers, lamps, toys, foot-scrubbers and kitchenware, to demonstrate how even the most utilitarian objects can possess an innate beauty. Terracotta objects from all over India, in every shape and size, are also on display. They include striking pots made in traditional techniques unchanged for centuries, and towering figures of South Indian village deities.

Tughluqabad 🈳

Off Mehrauli-Badarpur Rd.
Monuments ☐ daily.

THE THIRD OF DELHI'S early capitals (see p91), Tughluqabad is dominated by its spectacular fort, built by Ghiyasuddin Tughluq early in the 14th century. The fort was so sturdily constructed that its rubble-built walls, following the contours of the hill, survive intact all along the 7-km (4-mile) perimeter. Rising from the citadel to the right of the main entrance are the ruins of the Vijay Mandal ("Tower of Victory"). To the left is a rectangular area where arches are all that remain of a complex of palaces, houses and halls. Legend has it that when Ghiyasuddin tried to prevent the building of the *baoli* at Hazrat Nizamuddin Auliya's *dargah* (see p82), the saint cursed him, saying that one day only jackals and the Gujjar tribe would inhabit his capital.

A good view of the fort and of the smaller, adjoining Adilabad Fort, is possible from the walls. Adilabad was built by Muhammad bin Tughluq, who is believed to have killed his father Ghiyasuddin by

Ghiyasuddin Tughluq's Tomb

contriving to have a gateway collapse on him. Both are buried in **Ghiyasuddin's Tomb**, attached to the Tughluqabad Fort by a causeway that crossed the dammed waters of a lake. Constructed in red sandstone and inlaid with white marble, the tomb's sloping walls pioneered a style that was used in all subsequent Tughluq architecture.

Baha'i House of Worship 🈴

Bahapur, Kalkaji. ☎ (011) 644 4029. ☐ Tue–Sun. ● public hols. **Prayer services** 10am, noon, 3pm & 5pm.

DELHI'S most innovative modern structure, the Baha'i House of Worship is a world where silence and order prevail. Designed by Iranian architect Fariburz Sahba and completed in 1986, the arresting shape of its unfurling, 27-petalled, white marble lotus has given it its more popular name, the Lotus Temple. The edifice is circled by nine pools and 92 ha (227 acres) of green lawns.

The Baha'i sect originated in Persia and is based on a view of humanity as one single race. Followers of all faiths are invited to meditate and attend the daily 15-minute services in the lofty auditorium, which can seat up to 1,300 people.

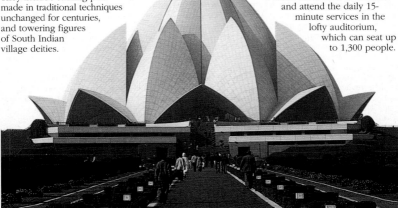

The lotus-domed Baha'i House of Worship, one of Delhi's most spectacular sights

Shopping & Entertainment in Delhi

THE HALLMARK OF SHOPPING in Delhi is the bewildering variety of merchandise, markets and styles. Besides Connaught Place, almost every residential colony boasts a market. Old, established shops, bazaars and markets co-exist happily with glitzy, high-end boutiques and department stores and one can buy anything from seasonal fruits and traditional handicrafts to designer clothes and the latest imported electronic items. Delhi also has a rich and varied cultural life. The city's cultural calendar livens up between October and March when the season is in full swing. The number of events multiply as all major festivals of music, dance, theatre and cinema are held at this time of the year.

SHOPS AND MARKETS

NEW DELHI'S main shopping centres are in and around **Connaught Place** and Janpath where the state emporiums and Cottage Industries offer an exciting and varied range of textiles, jewellery and souvenirs at fixed and reasonable prices. In the north is Chandni Chowk *(see pp84–5)*, the traditional market, while to the south are Khan Market, Sundar Nagar and Santushti, the old urban villages of Hauz Khas, Shahpur Jat and Mehrauli, and **Dilli Haat**, a crafts bazaar on Aurobindo Marg. The five-star hotels also have convenient shopping arcades selling carefully selected goods.

ANTIQUES, JEWELLERY AND SILVER

GENUINE ANTIQUES are rare to come by and, in any case, cannot be taken out of the country unless certified by the ASI *(see p759)*. However, the **Crafts Museum Shop**, hotel boutiques and Sundar Nagar market stock excellent reproductions of miniature paintings, woodcarvings and bronzes made by artisans today. Superb pieces of traditional jewellery, including *kundan* and *meenakari,* are available at Sundar Nagar market, especially at **Bharany's**. Silver jewellery, both traditional and modern, can be found in the gullies of Dariba Kalan, in Chandni Chowk and Sundar Nagar. **Ravissant** and **Cooke & Kelvy** are the best places for contemporary silverware.

TEXTILES, SHAWLS AND CARPETS

TRADITIONAL textiles are available in most of the better shops and emporiums, particularly **Cottage Industries. The Shop, Anokhi** and **FabIndia** are the best places for good quality readymade garments, linen and light cotton quilts. **Ogaan**, at Santushti, has a good range of eclectic Indian designer-wear, while its branch at Hauz Khas stocks bed linen, curtains and embroidered cushion covers from the "Shades of India" collection. **Shyam Ahuja** sells linen, textiles and *dhurries,* while **Khazana** is an excellent outlet for Afghan and Kashmiri carpets and pashmina shawls.

HANDICRAFTS AND GIFTS

THE Crafts Museum Shop, **Tulsi, Dastkar** and Dilli Haat have a wide selection of Indian handicrafts and other gift items, while **Tibet House** has woollen shawls, jackets, *thangkas* and carpets. For quality leather goods such as, handmade shoes and jackets, the many Chinese-owned outlets in Connaught Place, set the standards for comfort and durability. For trendier goods there are **Hidesign** and **Da Milano**.

In Chandni Chowk's Dariba Kalan is **Gulab Singh Johari Mal**, a marvellous old-fashioned shop where one can test Indian perfume *(attar)* from cut-glass bottles. Their soaps are also worth

buying. Herbal cosmetics, incense sticks, perfumed candles and aromatherapy oils and lotions are available in many of the larger stores, including **Good Earth**, which stocks the "Forest Essentials" range. Cosmetics by Biotique and Shahnaz Herbal are found at most chemists.

Spices and fresh seasonal fruit are found at INA Market *(see p89)* and Indian tea is sold in Kaka Nagar Market (near the Oberoi Hotel on Zakir Hussain Marg), Khan Market and at **Regalia**.

ENTERTAINMENT GUIDES, TICKETS AND VENUES

ALL NEWSPAPERS list the day's entertainment on their engagements page. Other useful sources of information on events, restaurants, sports and related activities are the weekly *Delhi Diary*, and the monthly magazines, *First City* and *Around Town*.

At several venues in the city, such as the **India International Centre**, entry is free. At others, such as the **Indian Council for Cultural Relations** (ICCR), it is by invitation only. Tickets for selected music and dance festivals and theatre, however, are advertised and sold at certain bookshops or at the box office.

Most of Delhi's cultural activities are clustered around Mandi House *(see p75)*. The largest auditorium, **Kamani** on Copernicus Marg, hosts concerts, plays and classical music and dance performances throughout the year. During the season, music and dance events are also held at FICCI Auditorium, on the roundabout, **Triveni Kala Sangam**, on Tansen Marg, and at Azad Bhavan, the main venue for performances organized by the state-run ICCR. Excellent plays, in both Hindi and English, are held at the open air auditorium of the **National School of Drama**, the main repertory company at Bhawalpur House, and at the **Shri Ram Centre** nearby. Colourful folk dances from all over India, organized by the **Trade Fair Authority of**

India, are held during the annual Trade India Fair in November, at Pragati Maidan, the huge exhibition grounds on Mathura Road.

Both the **India Habitat Centre** and the India International Centre, on Lodi Road, organize a variety of events that include films, plays, concerts, exhibitions, lectures and discussions. The mega **Siri Fort Complex**, in South Delhi, is the venue for most film festivals and other prestigious events.

Popular Indian and foreign films are screened at the many cinema halls dotted all over the city. Among the better equipped halls are **PVR Anupam** in Saket and **PVR Priya** in Vasant Vihar.

PERFORMING ARTS

DELHI IS THE BEST PLACE to experience the range and richness of classical dance and music. Performances by the best exponents of the major styles of Odissi, Kathak, Bharat Natyam and Kathakali take place during the high season, between October and March. The same is true of concerts of Hindustani and Carnatic classical music. India's vibrant folk dance and music traditions, such as the devotional music of the Sufis, dance-dramas from Kerala, puppet shows from Rajasthan and Karnataka, can also be seen at various venues. Check newspapers for details on location and tickets.

EXHIBITIONS

MAJOR EXHIBITIONS are held at the **National Museum**, **National Gallery of Modern Art**, **Indira Gandhi National Centre for the Arts** (IGNCA) and the Crafts Museum. These include special collections of rare sculpture and paintings from museums all over India, as well as from abroad. Recent years have seen exhibitions of Picasso's paintings, the Nizam of Hyderabad's fabulous jewels and Mughal paintings from Queen Elizabeth II's private collection.

Regular exhibitions of contemporary art are also held in the many art galleries around Mandi House.

DIRECTORY

ANTIQUES, JEWELLERY AND SILVER

Bharany's
Sundar Nagar Market.
((011) 435 8528.

Cooke & Kelvy
Janpath.
((011) 372 1081.

Crafts Museum Shop
Pragati Maidan.
((011) 337 1269.

Ravissant
Oberoi Hotel.
((011) 436 3030.

TEXTILES, SHAWLS AND CARPETS

Anokhi
Khan Market.
((011) 460 3423.

Cottage Industries
Janpath.
((011) 332 0439.

FabIndia
Greater Kailash I,
N-Block Market.
((011) 621 1032.

Khazana
Taj Mahal Hotel.
((011) 302 6162.

Ogaan
Hauz Khas Village.
((011) 685 3849.
Santushti.
((011) 467 2429.

Shyam Ahuja
Santushti.
((011) 467 0112.

The Shop
Connaught Place.
((011) 374 6050.

HANDICRAFTS AND GIFTS

Da Milano
Connaught Place.
((011) 335 2490.

Dastkar
45–B, Shahpur Jat.
((011) 649 5920.

Good Earth
M–1, Hauz Khas.
((011) 685 1757.

Gulab Singh Johri Mal
Dariba Kalan,
Chandni Chowk.
((011) 327 1345.

Hidesign
49G, Connaught Place.
((011) 332 7642.

Regalia
Sundar Nagar Market.
((011) 435 0115.

Tibet House
Lodi Rd.
((011) 461 1515.

Tulsi
Santushti.
((011) 687 0339.

ENTERTAINMENT VENUES

India Habitat Centre
Lodi Rd.
((011) 468 2222.

India International Centre
40, Lodi Estate,
Max Mueller Marg.
((011) 461.9431.

Indian Council for Cultural Relations
Azad Bhavan,
IP Estate.
((011) 331 2463.

Kamani Auditorium
Copernicus Marg.
((011) 338 8084.

National School of Drama
Bhawalpur House.
((011) 338 9402.

PVR Anupam
Community Centre,
Saket.
((011) 686 5999.

PVR Priya
Basant Lok,
Vasant Vihar.
((011) 614 0048.

Shri Ram Centre
Safdar Hashmi Marg.
((011) 371 4307.

Siri Fort Auditorium
Asian Village Complex.
((011) 649 3370.

Trade Fair Authority of India
Pragati Maidan.
((011) 337 1540.

Triveni Kala Sangam
205, Tansen Marg.
((011) 371 8833.

EXHIBITIONS

Indira Gandhi National Centre for the Arts
Central Vista Mess,
Janpath.
((011) 338 6345.

National Gallery of Modern Art
Jaipur House,
India Gate.
((011) 338 2835.

National Museum
Janpath.
((011) 301 9272.

HARYANA & PUNJAB

HARYANA AND PUNJAB cover the vast plains that stretch between the River Indus and the Gangetic belt. Fertile soil and the improved agricultural techniques of the 1960s Green Revolution (*see p62*), have made this region the granary of India, producing more than half the wheat, rice and millet grown in the country. Industrial development followed the success of the Green Revolution, and the two states now also have flourishing dairy and wool-based industries. Most visitors pass only briefly through Haryana and Punjab, usually on their way to

Himachal Pradesh, taking in en route the states' two best known attractions: Chandigarh, the planned city built by the famous architect Le Corbusier, which is the shared capital of Haryana and Punjab, and the Golden Temple at Amritsar, the holiest shrine of the Sikhs. For those who care to explore further, there are the former princely states of Patiala and Kapurthala, with their distinctive architecture, and the holy *dargahs* at Panipat and Sirhind. Above all, the warmth and hospitality of the people is this area's special attraction.

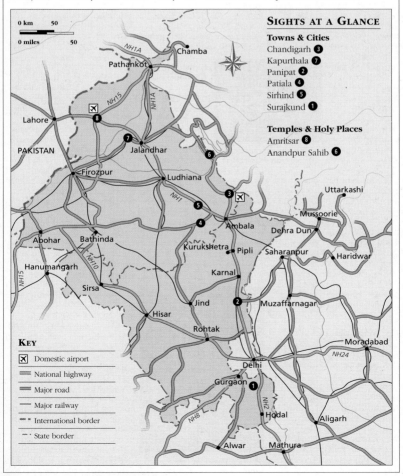

SIGHTS AT A GLANCE

Towns & Cities
Chandigarh **3**
Kapurthala **7**
Panipat **2**
Patiala **4**
Sirhind **5**
Surajkund **1**

Temples & Holy Places
Amritsar **8**
Anandpur Sahib **6**

KEY
☒ Domestic airport
══ National highway
━━ Major road
─── Major railway
▬▬ International border
--- State border

◁ **A view of the Hari Mandir or Golden Temple from across the sacred pool, Amrit Sarovar, at Amritsar**

Sufi saint Qalandar Shah's *dargah* at Panipat, built in the 14th century

Surajkund ❶

Faridabad district. 21 km (13 miles) S
of Delhi. ☒ ⓘ *Haryana Tourism,
Chanderlok Building, 36, Janpath,
New Delhi, (011) 332 4910.* ☒
Surajkund Crafts Mela (Feb).

T HIS HISTORIC RESERVOIR, built
between the 10th and 11th
centuries by King Surajpal of
the Rajput Tomar dynasty, is
today a popular picnic spot.
The original embankment of
stone terraces
surrounding the
tank, specially
built to trap rain-
water, still exists.
Nearby, an
artificial lake is
well-equipped
with boating
facilities. The
area comes alive
in the first two
weeks of February, when an
excellent crafts *mela* is held
here, with artisans from all
over India selling their wares
in a specially created village.
Puppets from Rajasthan, bell
metal beasts from Orissa, and
mirrorwork from Gujarat are
displayed alongside a variety
of food stalls, while musicians
and folk dancers weave
through the crowds, giving
the fair a joyous, carnival air.

**Folk singers performing at
the Surajkund Crafts Mela**

Panipat ❷

Panipat district. 85 km (53 miles) N of
Delhi. ☒ ☒ ☒ *Urs of Qalandar
Shah (Jan/Feb).*

T HE SITE of three decisive
battles that changed the
course of Indian history,
including one which led to
the founding of the Mughal
Empire *(see pp50–51)* in
1526, Panipat is situated on a
flat, dusty plain and traces its
history to the epic age. The
older part of the town has
some interesting *havelis*, and
a 14th-century tomb-shrine
dedicated to the Sufi saint
Qalandar Shah. The new
town is a busy, bustling
settlement, strung along
National Highway 1, which
follows the route of the
historic Grand Trunk Road
(see p179). Today, Panipat is
well-known for its furnishing
fabrics and carpets.

ENVIRONS:
Karnal, 34 km
(21 miles) north
of Panipat, lies
at the heart of a
rich pastoral
region and is an
important
agricultural and
cattle breeding
centre. The
National Dairy Research
Institute is situated here.
Some 90 km (56 miles) north
of Panipat, the pilgrim town
of **Kurukshetra** is dotted
with temples and marks the
mythical site of the epic battle
between the Pandavas and
Kauravas, the heroes of the
Mahabharata (see p26).

**Ritual prayers at the sacred
temple tank at Kurukshetra**

Chandigarh ❸

Chandigarh district. 238 km (148
miles) N of Delhi. ☒ *750,000.* ☒ *11
km (7 miles) S of city centre.* ☒ ☒
ⓘ *Punjab Tourism, Sector 22, (0172)
70 4570.* ☒ *Rose Festival (Feb).*

T HE STATE CAPITAL of both
Haryana and Punjab,
Chandigarh was built in the
early 1950s by the inter-
nationally renowned architect
Le Corbusier. It is considered
the first modern city of post-
Independent India and is laid
out on a grid, divided evenly
into 57 blocks or sectors.
Le Corbusier conceived the
city along the lines of a mod-
ular man, with the **Capitol
Complex**, which includes the
Secretariat, Assembly and
High Court buildings, as its
"head". The main shopping
area, **Sector 17**, is the
"heart" of Le Corbusier's plan,
and is set around a central
plaza and fountain, lined
with shops indicating that
Chandigarh's affluent citizens
are extremely fond of good
food and clothes. Adjoining
this sector is a gently
undulating stretch of green,
the city's "lungs", with an
enormous **Rose Garden**
that is at its best in February.
Over a 1,000 varieties of
colourful roses bloom amidst
winding paths, fountains
and sprawling, beautifully
tended lawns.
The city's extensive
residential sectors make up its
"torso", with neat houses and
gardens showing impressive
evidence of the residents'
green fingers. Each road is
lined with a different species
of flowering tree – laburnum,
jacaranda, *gulmohar* – adding
colour to the cityscape.
Chandigarh's **Museum and
Art Gallery** in Sector 10
houses one of the country's
finest collections of
Gandharan sculpture *(see
p43)* and miniature paintings.
Among the best exhibits are a
serene 6th-century Standing
Bodhisattva in the Gandharan
style, and a rare 11th-century
statue of Vishnu holding a
conch shell from Kashmir.
The miniatures section has a
comprehensive selection of
Pahari paintings *(see p121)*

Chandigarh's Capitol Complex, typical of Le Corbusier's functional style

from the Kangra, Basohli and Guler schools, while modern art includes mountainscapes by the Russian painter Nicholas Roerich (see p128).

Lying opposite the Capitol Complex, the **Rock Garden** is one of the city's most popular tourist spots. Spread over 1.6 ha (4 acres) in Sector 1, it was created in the 1970s by an ex-road inspector, Nek Chand, and is a refreshing contrast to Le Corbusier's severely symmetrical cityscape. The area encloses a unique "kingdom", a labyrinth with hills, waterfalls and caves, and serried ranks of sculptures crafted from such unlikely material as discarded neon lights, fuse switches, broken crockery and glass.

Ceramic figures at Nek Chand's Rock Garden

A short distance away is the man-made **Sukhna Lake**, where a pleasant promenade attracts joggers and walkers.

This is one of Chandigarh's prettiest areas, especially in the evenings, when visitors can enjoy dramatic sunsets and views of the twinkling lights of the nearby hill station, Kasauli (see p113).

🏛 **Museum and Art Gallery**
📞 (0172) 74 2501. ⬜ Tue–Sun. 📷

ENVIRONS: The **Pinjore Gardens**, lying 22 km (14 miles) north of Chandigarh, were designed in the 17th century by Fidai Khan, foster brother of the Mughal emperor Aurangzeb. They are terraced in the Mughal style and dotted with domed pavilions, fountains and water chutes. **Sanghol**, 40 km (25 miles) west of Chandigarh, has an excavated site of a 2nd-century Buddhist stupa with an interesting museum of Kushana sculpture.

FESTIVALS OF HARYANA & PUNJAB

Qalandar Shah's Urs (Jan/Feb), Panipat. This festival honours the Sufi saint Qalandar Shah with qawwali singing and a colourful fair at his shrine.
Surajkund Crafts Mela (1–15 Feb), Surajkund. Craftsmen from all over the country congregate with a fine selection of their wares, from hand-woven fabrics to folk toys.
Rose Festival (Feb), Chandigarh. The city's gigantic Rose Garden is at its best with flower shows and a weekend carnival of dance and music.

Skilled swordsmanship at the Hola Mohalla festivities

Hola Mohalla (Mar/Apr), Anandpur Sahib. The highlight of this fair, held the day after Holi, is a spectacular display of fencing and tent-pegging, as the Nihang Sikhs show off their legendary martial and equestrian skills.
Baisakhi (14 Apr). Gala processions, dancing and feasting take place all over Punjab to mark the spring equinox and the beginning of the harvest. Lively melas are held at all the major gurdwaras.
Guru Parab (Nov). Cele-brated across Punjab on the first full moon night after Diwali (see p37), the birthday of Guru Nanak, the founder of Sikhism, is particularly spectacular at the Golden Temple at Amritsar. Thousands of lamps illuminate the temple every night from Diwali onwards.

LE CORBUSIER'S CITY

The "open hand", Chandigarh's emblem

In 1950, India's first prime minister, Jawaharlal Nehru, commissioned the French-Swiss architect Charles Edouard Jeanneret ("Le Corbusier"), to create a new capital for Punjab, as the old capital, Lahore, had become a part of Pakistan after Independence in 1947. The result was a city of concrete blocks and straight arterial roads, projecting Le Corbusier's philosophy of functional efficiency, free of unnecessary ornamentation such as domes and arches. Without any crowded bazaars, Chandigarh lacks the typical bustle and vitality of older Indian towns, and some of Le Corbusier's buildings now look weather-beaten. Yet it remains the country's cleanest and most orderly city and this, perhaps, is Le Corbusier's lasting legacy.

The splendid Durbar Hall at the Qila Mubarak, Patiala

Patiala ❹

Patiala district. 63 km (39 miles) SW
of Chandigarh. 👥 *269,000.* 🚉 🚌
🎭 *Basant (Feb).* 🛍 *Mon–Sat.*

P ATIALA, SITUATED between
the Satluj and Ghaggar
rivers, was formerly a princely
state, ruled by a string of
flamboyant rulers in the 19th
century, who made its name a
byword for everything larger
than life. Thus, the
"Patiala Peg" is a
whopping measure
of whisky, the
Patiala *salwar* three
times the width of
an ordinary one,
and the gargantuan
palace, to quote an
overawed English
visitor, "makes
Versailles look like a
cottage". Its rulers were also
enthusiastic patrons of the
arts, architecture and sports,
and the city's gracious
ambience and its rich folk
crafts owe a great deal to
their generous encouragement.
  The present city has grown
around the **Qila Mubarak**, a
fort built in 1763. Its oldest
part, Qila Androon, though
derelict, has traces of fine
wall paintings. The **Durbar
Hall**, added later, stands to
the right of the entrance gates
and is now a museum with a
beautifully ornamented ceiling
and well-preserved murals.
Inside it, is a spectacular
display of cannons and arms,
including the sword of the
Persian ruler Nadir Shah *(see
p52)* who invaded India in
1739. The lively bazaar around
the fort offers the city's

A typical *phulkari*
motif

famous hand-crafted leather
shoes *(jutties)*, tasselled silken
braids *(pirandis)* and brightly
embroidered *phulkari* fabric.
  The enormous **Old Moti
Bagh Palace**, completed in
the early years of the 20th
century in the Indo-Saracenic
style, has as many as 15
dining halls. Counted as one
of the largest residences in
Asia, it is set amidst terraced
gardens and water channels,
inspired by Mughal
gardens. The
terraces lead to the
Sheesh Mahal,
where the **Art
Gallery** displays
miniature paintings,
rare manuscripts,
objets d'art, and
hunting trophies
from the former
royal collection.
Pride of place is given to a
collection of medals, some
awarded to, and some
collected by, the former
rulers. The Art Gallery
overlooks a large tank flanked
by two towers, with a rope
suspension bridge to connect
them. The main palace has

Hand-embroidered *jutties* on sale
in Patiala's bazaar

now been given over to the
National Institute of Sports
and the large pleasure pool
where the maharaja once
watched dancing girls
cavorting has been converted
into a wrestling pit.
  In the north of the city are
the **Baradari Gardens**, laid
out in the late 19th century by
Prince Rajinder Singh, an avid
horticulturist, who also
created a rock garden and
fern house here. The splendid
Kali Temple, which is located
within the walled city, has a
large marble image of Kali,
brought here all the way from
Makrana in Rajasthan.

🏛 **Durbar Hall Museum**
◑ *Tue–Sun.* 📷 *with permission.* 🚫
🏯 **Old Moti Bagh Palace**
◑ *Tue–Sun* 🚫

Sirhind ❺

Fatehgarh Sahib district. 55 km (34
miles) W of Chandigarh. 👥 *31,000.*
🚉 🚌 🚹 *Punjab Tourism, (01763)
22 170.* 🎭 *Urs at Rauza Sharif (Aug),
Shaheedi Jor Mela (Dec).*

T HE TOWN OF SIRHIND was
one of the most important
settlements in North India
between the 16th and 18th
centuries. Once the capital of
the Pathan Sur sultans, the
ruins of whose massive fort
can still be seen, Sirhind was
also a favourite halting place
for the Mughal emperors on
their annual journeys to
Kashmir. In the 11th century,
Mahmud of Ghazni *(see p48)*
expanded his empire up to
this area, thus giving the town
its name, which in Persian
means "Frontier of India".
  The Mughals constructed
several beautiful buildings
here, in the area now called
Aam Khas Bagh, which
today is a tourist complex run
by the government. Especially
interesting is the **Royal
Hamam**, a complex struc-
ture for hot and cold baths,
that uses water drawn from
wells nearby through an
intricate system of hand
pulleys. Close to the baths are
the ruins of Shah Jahan's
double-storeyed palace, the
Daulat Mahal, and the better
preserved **Sheesh Mahal**,

Rauza Sharif, Shaikh Ahmad Faruqi Sirhindi's *dargah* in Sirhind

whose walls still have traces of the original tilework and decorative plaster.

To the north of Aam Khas Bagh is the white **Fatehgarh Sahib Gurdwara**, standing in the midst of bright yellow mustard fields, which bloom in January. It was built to honour the memory of the martyred sons of the tenth Sikh guru, Gobind Singh, who were walled in alive at this spot by the Mughal emperor Aurangzeb in 1705, for refusing to convert to Islam.

Adjacent to the gurdwara is an important pilgrimage site for Muslims, the tomb-shrine of the Sufi saint and theologian, Shaikh Ahmad Faruqi Sirhindi, who is also known as Mujaddad-al-Saini ("The Reformer of the Millennium"). This magnificent octagonal structure, with its dome covered in glazed blue tiles, was built in the 16th century. Known as the **Rauza Sharif**, it is considered as holy as the

Dargah Sharif in Ajmer *(see p376)*. Standing close to it is a striking tomb from the same period, the **Mausoleum of Mir Miran**, son-in-law of one of the Lodi kings. Also of interest is the **Salavat Beg Haveli**, a fascinating and exceptionally well preserved example of a large Mughal-era house.

🏛 **Aam Khas Bagh**
🕐 *Tue–Sun.*

Anandpur Sahib ❻

Roopnagar district. 73 km (45 miles) N of Chandigarh. 🚶 *31,000.* 🚉 🚌
🎎 *Hola Mohalla (Mar/Apr).*

GUARDED BY the Shivalik Hills and a ring of imposing forts, Anandpur Sahib is a complex of historic Sikh gurdwaras. It was here that

the severed head of the ninth guru, Tegh Bahadur, was brought to be cremated, at a site now marked by the **Sisganj Sahib Gurdwara**. The gurdwara also marks the place where the tenth and last guru, Gobind Singh, founded the Khalsa or "Army of the Pure" in 1699, along with five volunteers to help him defend the faith. The **Kesgarh Sahib Gurdwara**, which was built to commemorate this event, is regarded as one of the four *takhts* or principal seats of the Sikh religion – the others are at Amritsar *(see p104)*, Nanded in Maharashtra, and Patna *(see p214)* in Bihar. A week-long celebration was held here in April 1999, to mark the 300th anniversary of the Khalsa.

A Nihang Sikh in full regalia

A series of forts surround Anandpur Sahib on all sides – **Lohagarh Fort** was used as the armoury of the Khalsa army, **Fatehgarh Fort** guarded the route between Delhi and Lahore, and **Taragarh Fort** protected it from attacks by the hill states lying to the north.

Anandpur Sahib comes to life every year during the Hola Mohalla festival *(see p101)* when thousands of devotees congregate here to watch the blue-robed Nihang Sikhs, descendants of the gurus' personal guards, display their formidable martial and equestrian skills.

SIKHISM

A mid-19th-century painting of Guru Nanak with his disciples

With their characteristic turbans and full beards, the Sikhs are easy to identify. The Sikh religion is a reformist faith, founded by Guru Nanak in the 15th century. Strongly opposed to idol worship, rituals and the caste system, it believes in a formless God. Sikhism is also called the Gurmat, meaning "the Guru's Doctrine" and Sikh temples are known as gurdwaras, literally "doors to the guru". Nanak, the first of a series of ten gurus, chose his successor from among his most devoted disciples. Gobind Singh (1666–1708), the tenth and last guru, reorganized the community in 1699 as a military order, the Khalsa, to combat religious persecution by the Mughals. He gave the Sikh community a distinctive religious identity, and from then onwards they were meant to wear the Khalsa's five symbols: *kesh* (long hair), *kachha* (underwear), *kirpan* (small sword), *kangha* (comb) and *kara* (bracelet). Their holy book, the *Guru Granth Sahib*, is kept in the Golden Temple *(see pp106–107)*.

Detail of a marble sculpture, Elysée Palace, Kapurthala

Kapurthala ❼

Kapurthala district. 165 km (103 miles) NW of Chandigarh. 🚉 🚌

THIS FORMER princely state owes its extraordinary architectural heritage to the eccentric Maharaja Jagatjit Singh, who created amidst the rich agricultural fields of Punjab, a corner that will be forever France. In 1906, this passionate Francophile, commissioned a French architect to build him a palace modelled on Versailles, with elements of Fontaineblue and the Louvre added on. This amazing structure, which he grandly named the Elysée Palace (now the **Jagatjit Palace**), sits amidst gardens embellished with stone statuary and fountains, and is surrounded by villas built for his officials, modelled on those that were in vogue in the suburbs of Paris in the late 19th century. The palace is now a school, but the building with its ornate interiors and Renaissance-style painted ceilings, is open to public.

After this palace was built, the maharaja went through a Spanish phase. This found expression in the **Buena Vista Hunting Lodge**. Located on the outskirts of the town, it is occupied by his descendants. Another impressive sight is the town's **Moorish Mosque**. Inspired by the grand Qutubiya Mosque in Marrakesh, this was designed by yet another French architect employed by Jagatjit Singh. Its inner dome has been beautifully painted by Punjabi artists.

🏛 **Jagatjit Palace**
⬭ *Tue–Sun.* 📷

The Jagatjit Palace at Kapurthala, modelled on Versailles in France

MAHARAJA RANJIT SINGH

Maharaja Ranjit Singh (r.1790–1839)

Maharaja Ranjit Singh was one of North India's most remarkable rulers. By persuading rival Sikh chieftains to unite, he established the first Sikh kingdom of the Punjab. A military genius, his strong army kept both the British and ambitious Afghan invaders at bay, making Punjab a prosperous centre of trade and industry. A devout Sikh who did much to embellish the Golden Temple, the one-eyed Ranjit Singh was an enlightened ruler who liked to say "God intended me to look at all religions with one eye". A decade after his death, the British annexed the Punjab and seized his fabulous treasures, including the famous Kohinoor diamond.

Amritsar ❽

Amritsar district. 217 km (135 miles) NW of Chandigarh. 🏠 *1,000,000.* ℹ️ *Palace Hotel opp railway station, (0183) 40 2452.* ✈️ *12 km (8 miles) NW of city centre.* 🚉 🚌 🎪 *Guru Parab (Nov).*

FOUNDED IN 1577 by the fourth Sikh guru, Ram Das, Amritsar was built on a site donated by the Mughal emperor Akbar. Located in the heart of the city is the **Golden Temple** (*see pp106–107*), the Sikh community's holiest shrine, surrounded by a maze of lanes and 18 fortified gateways. In 1984, parts of the Golden Temple were badly damaged during an army operation to flush out extremists holed up inside, who were demanding a separate Sikh homeland. It has now been repaired and carefully restored to its original glory.

The temple complex is actually a city within a city, and the main entrance is through its northern gateway, known as the **Darshani Darwaza**, which also houses the **Central Sikh Museum**. On display are collections of paintings, coins, manuscripts and arms, that combine to create a vivid picture of Sikh history. Steps lead down to the **Parikrama** (marble pathway) which encircles the **Amrit Sarovar** ("Pool of Nectar", after which the town is named), and the main shrine, the golden-domed **Hari Mandir** ("Temple of God"). Several holy and historic sites line the Parikrama, among them a tree shrine called the **Dukh Bhanjani Ber**, said to have miraculous powers for healing diseases, and the **Athsath Tirath** which represents 68 of the holiest Hindu pilgrim shrines.

The Parikrama continues on to the Akal Takht, the seat of the Sikh religious order. Its construction began in 1589 and was completed in 1601 by the sixth guru, Guru Hargobind, when he began organizing the Sikh community into a political entity. The upper floors were

View of the Golden Temple complex, with the central shrine and main entrance

built by Maharaja Ranjit Singh. As part of the daily ritual, the Holy Book of the Sikhs, the *Guru Granth Sahib*, is carried out of the Akal Takht to the Hari Mandir at daybreak. The head priest then opens it for the *vaq*, the message for the day. From dawn till late at night the temple echoes with the music of *ragis*, musicians employed by the temple trust to sing verses from the Holy Book. Every visitor entering the Hari Mandir (including non-Sikhs) is given a dollop of sweet *prasad* (holy offering), and no visit is considered truly complete without a meal at the **Guru ka Langar**, a free kitchen where all visitors are fed a simple meal of *dal-roti* (lentil curry and bread). Run by volunteers, this kitchen can feed 10,000 people a day. Its vast hall, which can seat 3,000 people at a time, serves as a symbol of the caste-free, egalitarian society that the Sikh gurus strove to create. The notion of *kar-seva* (voluntary manual labour for a cause) is an important part of the Sikh order. Tasks such as sweeping the temple precincts, cooking at the *langar* or looking after the pilgrims' shoes, are enthusiastically performed by volunteers either as penance or as acts of worship. The final evening prayers are over by 9:45pm,

Memorial, Jallianwala Bagh

when the Holy Book is reverently closed and carried in a silver palanquin back to the Akal Takht. The floors of the temple are then washed with milk and water before the doors of the Darshani Deorhi are closed.

A few other shrines are found just outside the Temple complex. These include a shrine dedicated to Guru Hargobind Singh, as well as the nine-storeyed **Baba Atal Tower** which marks the spot where Atal Rai, the son of Hargobind attained martyrdom. The 16th-century **Durgiana Temple**, dedicated to Durga, lies 2 km (1.3 miles) northeast of the Golden Temple.

Jallianwala Bagh, also a short distance from the Golden Temple, is the site of an infamous massacre that took place in 1919. Hundreds of unarmed demonstrators

were gunned down in this enclosed garden on the orders of General Reginald Dyer, who arrived heading a platoon of infantry from Jalandhar. It was an event which helped hasten the end of British rule in India. A memorial to those killed stands at the east end.

Environs: The last checkpost on the Indian border is at **Wagah**, just 9 km (6 miles) from Amritsar, separated from Attari in Pakistan by a thin ribbon of road. Each evening, as buglers sound the last post, two splendidly uniformed guards on either side of the border goose step across to the flagpoles to lower their respective national flags. Their steps are matched so perfectly that it is like watching a mirror image of the same exercise. The ceremony, which attracts crowds of spectators on both sides, is a poignant reminder of the Partition of 1947 (see p56), when Punjab was divided between two nations.

Ceremonial guards accompanying the Holy Book outside the Akal Takht

Amritsar: The Golden Temple

Pietra dura detail

THE SPIRITUAL CENTRE of the Sikh religion, the Golden Temple was built between 1589 and 1601, and is a superb synthesis of Islamic and Hindu styles of architecture. In keeping with the syncretic tradition of those times, its foundation stone was laid by a Muslim saint, Mian Mir. It was virtually destroyed in 1761 by an Afghan invader, Ahmed Shah Abdali, but was rebuilt some years later by Maharaja Ranjit Singh, ruler of Punjab, who covered the dome in gold and embellished its interiors with lavish decoration.

First Floor
The marble walls have pietra dura inlay and decorative plasterwork, bearing animal and flower motifs covered in gold leaf.

★ Sheesh Mahal
The Hall of Mirrors on the top floor has a curved bangaldar roof, and its floors are swept with a special broom made of peacock feathers.

Hari Mandir
The holiest site for Sikhs, the three-storeyed temple, decorated with superb pietra dura, is where the Holy Book is kept during the day.

The dome, shaped like an inverted lotus, is covered in 100 kg (220 lbs) of gold donated by Ranjit Singh in 1830.

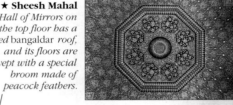

The lower wall of the temple is made of white marble.

STAR FEATURES
★ **Sheesh Mahal**
★ **Guru Granth Sahib**

★ Guru Granth Sahib
Covered by a jewelled canopy, the Holy Book lies in the Durbar Sahib ("Court of the Lord").

Darshani Deorhi
This gateway provides the first glimpse of the temple's inner sanctum. It has two splendid silver doors and sacred verses carved on its walls.

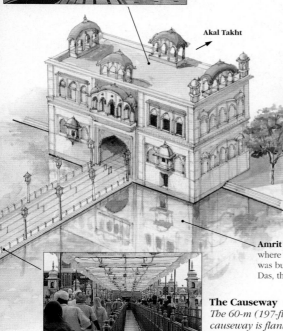

Akal Takht

Akal Takht
The seat of the supreme governing body of the Sikhs, it houses the gurus' swords and flagstaffs, as well as the Holy Book at night.

Amrit Sarovar, the pool where Sikhs are baptized, was built in 1577 by Ram Das, the fourth guru.

The Causeway
The 60-m (197-ft) long marble causeway is flanked by nine gilded lamps on each side, and leads to the temple across the Amrit Sarovar.

GOLDEN TEMPLE COMPLEX

1 Temple Office
2 Cloakrooms
3 Darshani Darwaza and Clocktower
4 Hari Mandir
5 Athsath Tirath (68 Shrines)
6 Guru ka Langar (Dining Hall)
7 Baba Karak Singh's Residence
8 Assembly Hall
9 Baba Deep Singh's Shrine
10 Darshani Deorhi
11 Arjun Dev's Tree
12 Akal Takht
13 Nishan Sahibs (Flagstaffs)
14 Gobind Singh's Shrine
15 Dukh Bhanjani Ber (Tree Shrine)

0 metres   50   **KEY**

0 yards   50   ⬜ Area illustrated above

HIMACHAL PRADESH

H IMACHAL, the "Abode of Snow", covers over 56,000 sq km (21,622 sq miles) of the Western Himalayas. The state's terrain rises from the foothills of the Shivaliks bordering the plains of Punjab, and extends to the trans-Himalayan heights of the Zanskar Range, bordering Ladakh and Tibet. Himachal's capital Shimla, famous as the summer capital of the British Raj, remains a popular destination for visitors. Manali, the state's other big hill station, is in the heart of the idyllic Kullu Valley. Watered by the Beas river, it is an excellent base for treks and excursions. West of Kullu, with the magnificent Dhauladhar Range as its backdrop, is the Kangra Valley, dotted with apple orchards. Its main town is Dharamsala, home to the Dalai Lama and a vibrant Tibetan community, and the seat of the Tibetan Government-in-Exile. In the eastern part of the state is Kinnaur with its green pastures and enchanting villages, while Lahaul and Spiti to the north are lands of rugged grandeur, with Buddhist monasteries clinging to steep, rocky cliffs.

SIGHTS AT A GLANCE

Towns & Cities
Mandi 10
Nahan 5
Rampur 6
Sarahan 7

Hill Stations & Areas of Natural Beauty
Bharmour 15
Chail 2
Chamba 14
Dalhousie 13
Dharamsala 12
Kasauli 4

Manali 19
Narkanda 3
Shimla 1

Monasteries
Tabo Monastery 21

Valleys & Districts
Kangra Valley 11
Kinnaur 9

Kullu Valley 16
Lahaul and Spiti 20
Parvati Valley 17

National Parks
Great Himalayan National Park 18

Tours
Sangla Valley Tour 8

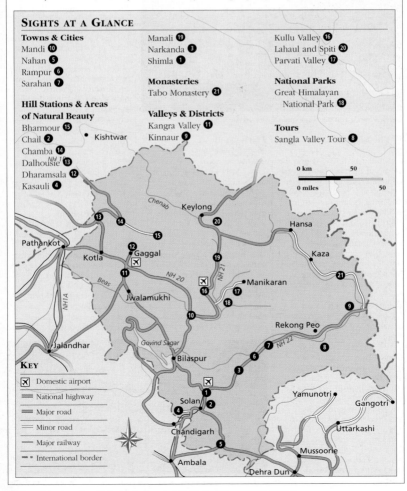

KEY

X	Domestic airport
=	National highway
=	Major road
=	Minor road
—	Major railway
- -	International border

◁ **Buddhist prayer flags fluttering in the wind, in the rugged mountains of Spiti**

Shimla **❶**

Stained glass, Christ Church

APOPULAR HILL STATION in North India, Shimla's spectacular location, thickly forested slopes and invigorating climate have attracted countless visitors since the small village was discovered by Captain Charles Kennedy in the early 19th century. In 1864, it became the summer headquarters of the British government in India. Today it is the fast-growing capital of Himachal Pradesh. Though many of the surrounding spurs and forests are now covered with concrete buildings, Shimla still retains much of its colonial charm.

fighter. The so-called "scandal" refers to the reputed abduction of an English lady in the late 19th century from this spot by Maharaja Bhupinder Singh of Patiala *(see p102)*. Nearby are the timber-framed Post Office, the Town Hall and the jewel-like Gaiety Theatre, opened in 1887, and still a popular venue for amateur dramatics. A favoured pastime for both local residents and visitors, is to stroll along The Mall, from Combermere Bridge to Scandal Point, passing the charming mock-Tudor Clarkes Hotel along the way.

Christ Church and the Municipal Library on the Ridge

🚋 The Ridge
N of The Mall.
A popular promenade and the centre of Shimla's busy social and cultural scene, the Ridge, situated at a height of 2,230 m (7,316 ft), is an open stretch of land on the western shoulder of Jakhu Hill. From here, the snowcapped peaks of the Himalayan Range stretch in an arc across the northern horizon. Ceremonial parades and official state functions are also held here.

🏛 Christ Church
☐ daily. 🕑 8am, 11am Sun. Contact caretaker if church is closed.
Dominating the eastern end of the Ridge is the Gothic Christ Church, a prominent landmark. Constructed in 1846, it was one of the first churches built in North India. Its fine stained-glass windows and impressive organ were acquired in the 19th century. The fresco around the chancel window was designed by Lockwood Kipling, Rudyard Kipling's father. Shimla's mock-Tudor **Municipal Library** is nearby.

🏛 The Mall
Shops ☐ *Mon–Sat. Restricted vehicular movement.*
This 7-km (4-mile) long thoroughfare, running from Boileauganj in the west to Chhota Shimla in the south-east, demarcates the original limits of the town. The central section of The Mall, flanked by rows of half-timbered buildings, has always been, and still remains, its most fashionable area with a profusion of restaurants, bars and up-market shops. The Mall's highest spot, Scandal Point, is marked by a statue of Lala Lajpat Rai, the famous freedom

🏛 Lower Bazaar
Shops ☐ *Mon–Sat.*
Below the central section of The Mall is the Lower Bazaar, which Kipling once referred to as "that crowded rabbit warren catering to the native popula-tion of Shimla". Offering the option of cheaper wares and less fashionable hostelries and eating places, it remains the poor man's Mall. Lower still is the **Ganj**, a congested bazaar where the town's wholesale trade in groceries takes place. This, more than any other part of town, retains a flavour of times gone by. Customers and coolies mingle in crowded lanes redolent with the aroma of the many spices on display.

🏛 State Museum
Chaura Maidan. **📞** *(0177) 20 5044.*
☐ *Tue–Sun.* ● *public hols.* 🚫 📷
The State Museum, housed in a reconstructed Raj building called Inverarm, was opened to the public in 1974. It has, since then, built up a fairly good collection of almost 10,000 artifacts from various parts of Himachal Pradesh. The exhibits, displayed in 15

The interior of the Gaiety Theatre, a focal point of Shimla's cultural life

galleries, include stone sculptures dating from the 6th to 11th centuries, belonging to the Gupta and Pratihara periods, and a collection of Kangra miniatures *(see p121)* representing various themes, based on the seasons *(Baramasa)*, musical modes *(Ragamala)* and episodes from the *Gita Govinda*, a devotional poem. Most impressive, however, is a spectacular series of mid-19th-century wall paintings from Chamba, housed in the ground floor galleries.

Jakhu Hill Temple

Jakhu Hill. ◯ *daily.*
The forested dome of Jakhu Hill, at 2,450 m (8,038 ft) is the highest point in Shimla. At its peak stands a temple dedicated to the monkey god, Hanuman. According to the epic *Ramayana (see p27)*, Hanuman rested here during his journey to fetch the Sanjivini herb from the Himalayas to save the wounded Lakshman's life. A steep 2 km (1.3 miles) climb from the Ridge to the summit through deodar and oak forests offers panoramic views of Shimla and its suburbs. Monkeys are a common sight all over Shimla but Jakhu is their kingdom. Visitors should watch out for simian hands rifling through their pockets and belongings.

Viceregal Lodge

The Mall. ◖ *(0177) 23 1375.*
◯ *daily.* 🎫 🚫
The most imposing British-built building in Shimla is the former Viceregal Lodge. Situated atop Observatory Hill, this grey stone structure in the English Renaissance style was built under the guidance of Lord Dufferin in 1888, as a suitable summer residence for the viceroys of India. Well-maintained gardens surround the stately mansion on three sides. The interior is as impressive, with two rows of

balconies overlooking the magnificent teak-panelled entrance hall. A bronze plaque behind the building lists the peaks visible at a distance. It is now called Rashtrapati Niwas and houses the Indian Institute of Advanced Studies. Only the entrance hall and the gardens are open to the public.

The stately Viceregal Lodge, set amid manicured lawns

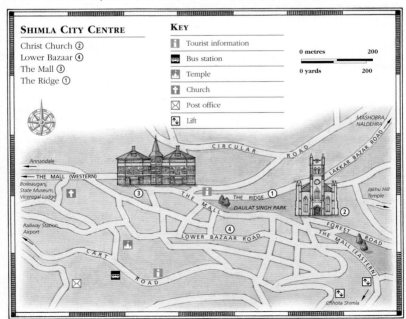

SHIMLA CITY CENTRE

Christ Church ②
Lower Bazaar ④
The Mall ③
The Ridge ①

KEY

ℹ Tourist information
🚌 Bus station
🏛 Temple
✝ Church
⊠ Post office
⇅ Lift

0 metres 200
0 yards 200

MASHOBRA / NALDEHRA

CIRCULAR ROAD

LAKKAR BAZAR ROAD

Annandale

← THE MALL (WESTERN)

Boileauganj, State Museum, Vicereagal Lodge

Railway Station, Airport

CART ROAD

THE MALL

THE RIDGE ①

DAULAT SINGH PARK

LOWER BAZAAR ROAD

ROAD

Jakhu Hill Temple

FOREST ROAD

THE MALL (EASTERN)

Chhota Shimla

Campsite at Kufri, under a heavy blanket of snow in winter

Exploring Shimla

The best way to explore Shimla is to walk along the many meandering roads and byways. Beyond the centre *(see pp110–11)*, the meadow of **Annandale** is 5 km (3 miles) north of the Ridge. During the Raj, all major social events, including races, cricket matches and fêtes, were held here. The **Glen**, another popular picnic spot, is further west and is reached by a path near the Oberoi Cecil *(see p693)*. This grand colonial structure, built on a precipice, is reminiscent of Raj-era luxury. Across the spur from here are the scenic **Chadwick Falls**. A 4-km (2.5-mile) long forest road, starting from Christ Church on the Ridge, continues along the wooded slopes of Jakhu Hill. This road winds southeast to end near one of Shimla's oldest educational institutions, St Bede's College for Women, en route overlooking the quaint bazaar of Chhota Shimla.

Musk deer in the Himalayan Nature Park

Deeper into the hills and along the same ridge system as Shimla, are a number of places to visit. At Charabra, 13 km (8 miles) north of Shimla, **Wildflower Hall**, the former retreat of the Commander-in-Chief, Lord Kitchner, is now a plush hotel *(see p694)*. About 10 km (6 miles) north along the old Hindustan-Tibet (HT) Road, just above the diversion to the left leading to the village of **Mashobra**, a gravel road barred by a gate to the right, indicates the entrance to the **Seog Wildlife Sanctuary** and the old Seog rest house. The sanctuary is home to local species of wildlife, including deer, hill fox and monal pheasants. At Mashobra, a steep forest pathway leads to a lovely little temple dedicated to a local goddess, set in a grove of deodars. The annual Sipi Fair is held here.

Continuing north from Mashobra, 3-km (2-mile) along a motor road, is the **Craignano Rest House**. Once the home of an Italian count, it commands superb views from its hilltop garden. Further north (10 km/6 miles) is **Naldehra** with a nine-hole golf course set amidst sloping meadows and fringed by deodar and blue pine. A British legacy dating from the 19th century, the golf course was

designed by the viceroy, Lord Curzon. About 16 km (10 miles) east of Shimla, is the picturesque little village of **Kufri**. At an altitude of 2,650 m (8,694 ft), it is now becoming a popular venue for winter sports. Kufri's small zoo, the **Himalayan Nature Park**, counts the Himalayan black bear and the musk deer among its residents.

⚔ Seog Wildlife Sanctuary
For permission contact: Divisional Forest Officer, Shimla Municipal Corporation. **(** *(0177) 25 2911.* 🚫
⚔ Himalayan Nature Park
Kufri. ⬭ *daily.* 🚫

Chail ❷

Solan district. 45 km (28 miles) SE of Shimla. 🚌🚆 **ℹ** *Hotel Chail Palace, (01792) 48 141*

THIS TINY HILL STATION is situated on a wooded ridge at a similar altitude to Shimla. Chail was developed as the summer capital of the Patiala maharajas *(see p102)* in the 1920s. **Chail Palace**, a stone mansion occupying a flattened hilltop, amid beautiful orchards and garden, is now a deluxe hotel *(see p692)*. The cricket pitch, near the top of a hill, is said to be the highest in the world. The Patiala rulers, enthusiastic cricketers themselves, invited the Marylebone Cricket Club (the MCC) to play here in 1933. Walks through the deodar forests of the Chail Wildlife Sanctuary, where Scottish red deer were introduced, are the best way to discover Chail's natural beauty.

Naldehra's scenic golf course

A temple on Hatu Peak, a day's hike from Narkanda

Narkanda ❸

Shimla district. 64 km (40 miles) N of Shimla. 🚌

NARKANDA, at a height of 2,750 m (9,022 ft), stands on the HT Road as it winds along the edges of the ridgeline dividing the Satluj and Yamuna catchments. From here, the Himalayan peaks are even closer, and the walks through dense temperate forests where spruce, fir and high-altitude oak take over from the deodar and blue pine, are quite spectacular. The best walk is the 6-km (4-mile) hike to Hatu Peak (3,300 m/10,827 ft), where the Gurkhas made one of their last stands against the British in 1815. The area around Narkanda is lush with apple orchards. In winter, the slopes are ideal for skiing.

Kasauli ❹

Solan district. 77 km (48 miles) S of Shimla. 🏠 *5,000*. 🚌

THE CLOSEST hill station to the plains, Kasauli offers the charm of quiet walks shaded by *chir* pine, oak and horse chestnut trees. It is at its best just after the monsoon, when colourful dahlias cover the hillsides. As an army cantonment, restrictions imposed by the authorities have prevented the old town from being taken over by concrete modern structures. As a result, old-fashioned buildings with gable roofs and wooden balconies remain intact on the **Upper** and **Lower Malls**, the two main streets that run right through the town. **Monkey Point**, the highest spot in the town, is 4 km (2.5 miles) from the bus station. From here there are clear views of Shimla, the meandering Satluj and Chandigarh. A particularly lovely trail across the hills is the 5-km (3-mile) walk to the **Lawrence School** at Sanawar, a public school founded by Sir Henry Lawrence (*see p197*) in 1847.

Postbox, Kasauli

ENVIRONS: About 60 km (37 miles) northeast of Kasauli is **Nalagarh**, the seat of the former princely state of Hindur. The palace is now a heritage hotel called the Nalagarh Resort (*see p693*).

(see p197)

FESTIVALS OF HIMACHAL PRADESH

Shivratri *(Feb/Mar)*, Mandi. Local deities are carried down from the surrounding hills on elaborately decorated palanquins, to pay homage to Lord Shiva at the Bhootnath Temple.
Summer Festival *(May/Jun)*, Shimla. This recently inaugurated festival, timed to coincide with the tourist season, attracts singers, musicians and dancers.
Minjar *(Jul/Aug)*, Chamba. Maize shoots or *minjars*, strung on silken threads, are cast into the Ravi river at the start of this week-long festival to seek blessings for a bountiful harvest.
Manimahesh Yatra *(Aug/Sep)*, Bharmour. The pilgrimage to the sacred Manimahesh Lake draws thousands of Hindu devotees. Its waters are believed to cleanse the sins of a lifetime.
Dussehra *(Sep/Oct)*, Kullu *(see p127)*.
Lavi Fair *(Nov)*, Rampur. Products from remote Tibet and Ladakh were once bartered with those from the plains and lower hills at this fair. Today, woollen goods and pashmina from Tibet, *chilgoza* nuts and shawls from Kinnaur and Changmurti horses from Spiti are briskly traded.
Renuka Fair *(Nov)*, Nahan. People from the surrounding villages gather at the shores of the Renuka Lake to celebrate the completion of the harvest, at this fair.

HILL STATIONS

By the late 19th century, when the British had consolidated their rule in India, families began to come over from Britain to join their menfolk. In the years that followed, more than 80 settlements were established in the lower hill ranges, as

summer retreats for the burgeoning expatriate population, keen to escape the intense heat of the plains. Hill stations endeavoured to recreate a way of life reminiscent of the home country, complete with half-timbered houses, clubs, churches, hospitals, parks with bandstands and a main street invariably known as The Mall. Boarding schools,

Kennedy's Cottage, by Captain J Luard, Shimla, 1822

with excellent teaching facilities, were also set up for children who were unable to go back to study in England.

Colourful Kinnauri shawls on sale at the Lavi Fair, Rampur

Trekking in Himachal Pradesh

A cone from a deodar tree

THIS MOUNTAINOUS STATE, with its vast variety of terrains, offers a wide range of treks from easy, one-day hikes to week-long routes. At lower altitudes, trails wind through forests of oak, deodar (*Cedrus deodara*) and pine, while steeper climbs lead to flower-strewn alpine meadows above the tree line. The towns of Manali and Dharamsala are starting points for several popular treks. The best season for trekking is during the month of June, and then later between mid-September and October, after the monsoon. During the rains (June–September), the trans-Himalayan cold deserts of Spiti *(see p130)* and Upper Kinnaur are ideal destinations, completely shielded from monsoon showers.

HIMACHAL PRADESH

LOCATOR MAP

◻ Area shown below

0 km   20

0 miles   20

Dharamsala to Macchetar

A challenging 75-km (47-mile) route crosses rocky terrain to the meadows at Triund. A steep ascent leads to the Indrahar Pass, with views of the Pir Panjal peaks, and ends at the small town of Macchetar, connected by road to Chamba.

Duration: *5 days*
Altitude: *4,350 m (14,272 ft)*
Level of difficulty: *moderate to tough*

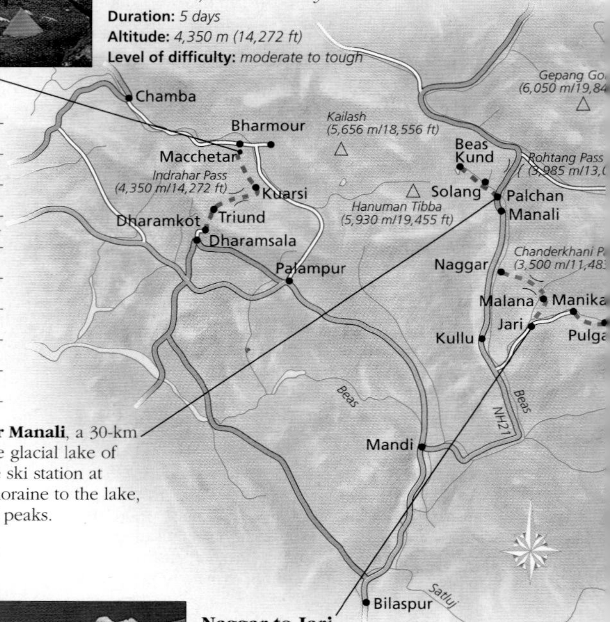

KEY

- ▪ ▪ The Pin Valley Trek
- ▪ ▪ Naggar to Jari
- ▪ ▪ Manali to Beas Kund
- ▪ ▪ Dharamsala to Macchetar
- ━━ National highway
- ━━ Major road
- ══ Minor road
- △ Peak
- ⌣ Pass

Starting at Palchan near Manali, a 30-km (19-mile) round trip to the glacial lake of Beas Kund, leads past the ski station at Solang and over glacial moraine to the lake, surrounded by snow-clad peaks.

Duration: *3 days*
Altitude: *3,980 m (13,058 ft)*
Level of difficulty: *easy*

Chamba

Bharmour

Kailash
(5,656 m/18,556 ft)
△

Gepang Go
(6,050 m/19,84...
△

Beas
Kund

Rohtang Pass
(13,985 m/13,0...

Macchetar
Indrahar Pass
(4,350 m/14,272 ft)

Kuarsi

△ Solang

Hanuman Tibba
(5,930 m/19,455 ft)

Palchan
Manali

Dharamkot

Triund

Dharamsala

Palampur

Naggar

Chanderkhani P.
(3,500 m/11,48...

Malana ● Manika

Kullu

Jari

Pulga

Beas

Mandi ●

NH21

Beas

Naggar to Jari

This 40-km (25-mile) trek crosses the Chandrakhani Pass, offering fine views of the peaks surrounding Solang Nala, and leads past the isolated Malana village (see p128) to end at Jari in Parvati Valley.

Duration: *4 days*
Altitude: *3,500 m (11,483 ft)*
Level of difficulty: *moderate*

Bilaspur

Satluj

The Pin Valley Trek
Starting at Manikaran, famous for its hot springs, the 130-km (81-mile) path goes over the Pin-Parvati Pass to the cold desert region of the beautiful Pin Valley. It ends at Mikkim, 40 km (25 miles) from the main roadhead at Kaza.

Duration: *7 days*
Altitude: *5,319 m (17,451 ft)*
Level of difficulty: *tough*

Kaza
Spiti
Dankar
Mikkim
irganga
Pin Valley
Sangam
Parvati
Pin
ndav Mantalai
idge
Mud
Pin Parvati Pass
(5,319 m/17,451 ft)

PRACTICAL TIPS

Be prepared: Acclimatization is essential for areas over 3,000 m (9,843 ft). See p767 for tips on altitude sickness. Guides are needed as maps are insufficient for safe passage across glaciers. For details on trekking see p751.
On the trek: Drink plenty of water. Carry a first aid kit and cooking fuel. Never burn wood, which is a scarce resource. Put out all fires properly, leaving no burning embers. Do not litter, and carry your rubbish back with you.
Permits: Foreign visitors require travel permits for parts of Spiti and Kinnaur, obtainable from the district or subdivisional magistrate's offices in Shimla (see p111), Rekong Peo (see p119), Kaza and Kullu (see p126). The offices at Kaza, (01906) 22 302 and Rekong Peo (01786) 22 253 are the most efficient. For general details see p758.
Equipment hire & operators: The Institute of Mountaineering and Allied Sports in Manali (01902) 52 342, and Yeti Trekking in McLeodganj (01892) 21 887, organize treks. The Regional Mountaineering Centre in McLeodganj, (01892) 21 787, offers mountaineering courses. In Manali, Himalayan Adventures, (01902) 52 365, is a reputable rafting agency, the Himalayan Institute of Adventure Sports, (01902) 53 050, offers para-gliding, and Himalayan Journeys, (01902) 52 365, offers mountain biking. For more details see p755.
Caution: Trekkers have gone missing in Parvati Valley. It is advisable to trek in groups and to take an experienced guide along.

OTHER ADVENTURE ACTIVITIES

Himachal Pradesh has several peaks over 3,000 m (9,843 ft), suitable for climbing. The Institute of Mountaineering and Allied Sports at Manali offers three-week courses. Skiing is possible at Narkanda, Kufri and at Solang Nala near Manali. Summer is the best season for rafting and kayaking on the Beas river at Manali, and for paragliding at Solang and Billing in Kangra. Himalayan Journeys *(see p752)* in Manali offers mountain biking near the Rohtang Pass.

Climbing a rock face, Tirthan Valley

Renuka Lake, venue of the Renuka Fair held in November

Nahan ❺

Sirmaur district. 100 km (62 miles) S of Shimla. 🚌 🚗 *Renuka Fair (Nov).*

LYING IN THE LOWER Shivalik Hills close to the plains, Nahan nestles sleepily on a low wooded ridge at 930 m (3,051 ft). The old town retains its network of narrow cobbled streets and has an interesting bazaar dating to the 17th century. The old palace (Raja Mahal) is closed to visitors. Other attractions include the Ranzore Palace facing the Chaugan (the royal polo ground), the lively Jagannath Temple in the bazaar, and the quiet walks through the *chir* pine forests on the Villa Round. Nahan serves as a convenient stopover for visiting the popular Renuka Lake nearby.

ENVIRONS: Lying 42 km (26 miles) east of Nahan, is the sacred **Renuka Lake**, whose shoreline traces the shape of a sleeping woman. According to Hindu mythology, Renuka was the wife of the sage Jamdagni and mother of Parasurama, an incarnation of Lord Vishnu *(see p679)*. She was killed by her son at his father's command, and miraculously came back to life, only to disappear again, leaving behind an imprint in the shape of her body. At the far end of the lake is a small wildlife park housing a pride of lions, Himalayan black bear and antelope. Nearby lies a smaller lake called Parasurama Tal, and below this, an open area where the Renuka Fair *(see p113)* is celebrated every year in November.

The pavilion in the spacious gardens of Rampur's palace

Rampur ⑥

Shimla district. 130 km (81 miles) NE of Shimla. 🚌 🚐 *daily.* 🎪 *Lavi Fair (Nov).*

ONCE ON the main trade route between India and Tibet, Rampur is today a big commercial town. It comes alive in November each year when the vibrant Lavi Fair *(see p113)* takes place.

The early 20th-century palace of the old kings is still their private residence, though visitors are allowed to walk around the sprawling gardens. A Hindu temple and a small pavilion are set in their midst.

Sarahan ⑦

Shimla district. 198 km (123 miles) NE of Shimla. 🚌 🚐 *daily.* 🎪 *Dussehra (Sep/Oct).*

PERCHED HIGH ABOVE the left bank of the Satluj, Sarahan was once the summer residence of the Rampur Bushahr kings. At 2,165 m (7,103 ft), it has a pleasant climate enhanced by the vista of the Srikhand Range across the valley, with the twin peaks of Gushu-Pishu and the holy mountain Srikhand Mahadev standing out prominently. Sarahan's most interesting sight is the spectacular tower temple, **Bhimakali**. It also has a short nature trail leading to a pheasantry. The many pheasants housed here include the monal and the near-extinct Western Himalayan tragopan.

Sarahan: Bhimakali Temple

Carved tiger

THE PALACE-CUM-TEMPLE COMPLEX of the Rampur Bushahr kings, Bhimakali owes its origin to the tradition of housing the family deity on the top floor of the feudal chief's home. Its elaborate layout consists of a series of courtyards connected by beautiful gateways. The presiding deity, Bhimakali, one of the myriad forms of the goddess Kali, is housed in the first floor of the pagoda-style temple.

Although the exact age of the temple is not known, it is associated with historical events dating to the 7th century, while parts of it are around 800 years old.

The Ram Mandir is located in the second courtyard.

View of the Bhimakali Temple Complex
The twin towers of the Bhimakali Temple, covered in snow and framed against the backdrop of the Srikhand Range, present an awesome sight.

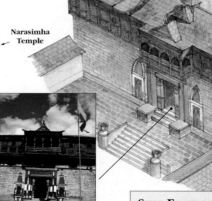

Slate roofs

Narasimha Temple

Main Entrance
An elaborately decorated metal door, at the entrance, opens into the first courtyard.

STAR FEATURES

★ **Carved Balconies**

★ **Tower Shrines**

★ **Silver Doors**

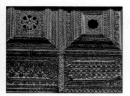

★ Carved Balconies

The uppermost storey of the renovated temple is fringed by overhanging balconies with exquisitely carved panels.

★ Tower Shrines

The Leaning Tower (on the right) was the main temple until it was damaged during an earthquake in 1905. The adjoining tower has since become the main shrine.

Golden Finials

The finials, a combination of symbols of the sun and the moon, represent the deity and the royal patrons.

Alternating bands of stone and timber

Wooden Skittles

Carved wooden skittles hang from the eaves of the temple roofs.

Carved tiger statue

★ Silver Doors

The silver doors that lead to the second courtyard are embellished with panels depicting various Hindu gods. They were added during the reign of Padam Singh (1914–47), a Rampur Bushahr king.

Dussehra Festival

Dussehra is the only time of the year when the original 200-year-old image of Bhimakali is actively worshipped.

Sangla Valley Tour  ➑

THE LARGEST VILLAGE in Kinnaur, Sangla, often lends its name to the whole Baspa Valley. A drive through this area takes two to three days and encapsulates a dramatic transition in landscape, from the spectacular river gorge at the entrance to Kinnaur to alpine valley pastures. It takes in awesome mountain scenery and mixed forests of oak and rhododendron, before reaching charming slate-roofed villages that nestle amidst orchards and fields.

Temple at Sungra Maheshwar ③
The temple's pagoda-like roof and the fine wooden carvings on its doorways and walls make this an interesting stopover.

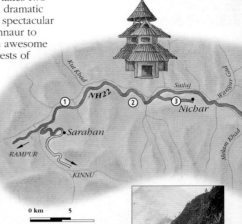

Kafour ①
Strung out along a little spur below the road, scenic Kafour is the first inhabited village in Kinnaur. The Hirma Temple, dedicated to a local mother goddess, stands out amid the slate rooftops.

0 km   5
0 miles   5

The Satluj Gorge at Tranda ②
From the road there are striking views of sheer rock walls falling 500 m (1,640 ft) to the river. On the other side, cliffs of equal magnitude enclose the Satluj in a narrow impenetrable gorge.

Kinnaur ➒

Kinnaur district. 244 km (152 miles) NE from Shimla to Rekong Peo. 🚶 19,250. 🚌 🚐 daily. 🎪 Sazi (Jan). **Travel permits** are required for parts of Kinnaur. Contact the Subdivisional Magistrate's office in Rekong Peo, (01786) 22 253. For details see p115.

KINNAUR, the remote north-eastern corner of Himachal Pradesh fringing the Tibetan Plateau, is a region of awesome grandeur. In the past, difficult terrain made Kinnaur inaccessible to all but the most intrepid of travellers, while in the 1950s, its proximity to the international border with Tibet resulted in restrictions on entry. However, these restrictions have been eased since 1992.

The variations in terrain, vegetation, climate and wildlife have broadly divided this region into Lower, Middle and Upper Kinnaur. Lower

View of the Kinner Kailash on a clear winter day

Kinnaur hugs both banks of a gorge-like Satluj river. The left bank's forested mountain slopes, contour-hugging terraced fields and tightly packed rows of houses clinging to the hillsides are picturesque in contrast to the right bank which is steeper, with higher peaks and a smaller population. Middle Kinnaur is much more rugged.

Dominating its heart are the majestic heights of the Kinner Kailash Range, while to its south is the gentler valley of the Baspa, one of the Satluj's largest tributaries. The arid sweep of the Zanskar peaks makes Upper Kinnaur a cold desert country of stark, barren mountains interspersed with occasional villages and irrigated fields.

Sapni ④
Sapni village has a tower temple that contains some of the finest examples of wooden sculpture in Kinnaur.

TIPS FOR DRIVERS

Length: 90 km (56 miles).
Getting around: The tour begins at Kafour village. The steep road is rough and winding, and is best negotiated with a 4-wheel drive. Sangla and Chitkul villages offer places to stay and eat, as well as a few shops with basic provisions.

Sangla ⑥
The largest among the villages that dot the Baspa Valley, Sangla has some beautiful walks to offer.

REKONG PEO

Chitkul ⑦
The tour ends at the village of Chitkul, just before the pastures of the Upper Baspa Valley. The valley's blue poppy was admired by the explorer Marco Pallis in 1933.

Kamroo ⑤
The tower of the Kamroo Narayan Temple commands a picturesque view of the valley. Fields and orchards slope down to the Baspa on one side of the river, while on the other side, thick forests rise up to pasturelands.

Rekong Peo, the new district headquarters, is a bustling little township on the right bank of Satluj river, with some shops and adequate transport connections. About 13 km (8 miles) higher up on the same mountain is **Kalpa**, the old headquarters. With its panoramic view of the Kinner Kailash Range, Kalpa is a must in any Kinnaur itinerary. The choice of walks include one to the upland pastures through deodar and *chilgoza* pine (*Pinus gerardiana*) forests. Some old temples can be seen in the nearby Chini village.

About 20 km (12 miles) from Rekong Peo, the Baspa river joins the Satluj at its left bank. The beauty of the **Sangla Valley** (or Baspa Valley) has been extolled both in local legend and by visitors over the years, and the region lends itself to a lovely trip by road. Apart from a furious rush in its last stretch of its course, the Baspa river ambles along a wooded valley past serene villages. Stupendous gneiss faces and forests of deodar, pine and birch reaching up to long swards of pasture and snow-covered peaks surround the valley. Every village in this valley, from Sangla to Chitkul, offers glorious walks and a choice of festivals to celebrate with the local people.

Buddhism holds complete sway throughout Upper Kinnaur. Fluttering prayer flags and mud-walled Buddhist temples with clay images and wall paintings dot the region, reflecting its proximity to Tibet. Many temples are credited to the 11th-century scholar Rinchen Zangpo, revered in Tibetan Buddhism as the Lotsawa (Translator), who initiated the mammoth task of translating Indian texts into Tibetan. He was also the main force behind a great temple-building movement and supposedly built 108 monasteries in one night. **Nako**, 100 km (62 miles) from Rekong Peo, has a small lake and is close to Reo Purgyal, the highest peak in Himachal Pradesh at 6,816 m (22,362 ft).

Young Buddhist monks in a monastery, Kinnaur

A cluster of village houses with sloping roofs in Mandi

Mandi ⑩

Mandi district. 156 km (97 miles) N of Shimla. 🏃 26,900. ☐ Joginder Nagar, 53 km (33 miles) NW of Mandi, then taxi or bus. ☐ 🎭 Shivratri (Feb/Mar).

Often referred to as the gateway to the Kullu Valley (see p126), Mandi is situated at the confluence of the Beas river with a small rain-fed tributary. The capital of the erstwhile princely state of Mandi, this small market town once functioned as a vital link between the hill communities on either side of it. The busy market located in a sunken garden in the centre of town, where all manner of merchandise is sold, is one of the more interesting sights here. Also situated in the town centre is the former residence of the Mandi kings, built in the colonial style, and now the heritage Rajmahal Palace Hotel. Several 16th- to 17th-century temples with beautiful stone carvings can be found all over the town. The most famous among these are the Madho Rai Temple, the Tarna Devi Temple and the Bhootnath Temple where the Shivratri festival is celebrated.

Environs: Rewalsar, a peaceful village at a height of 360 m (1,181 ft) is 24 km (15 miles) southeast of Mandi. On the shores of the Rewalsar Lake, resting in the hollow of a mountain spur, are a Buddhist monastery, three temples and a gurdwara commemorating the month-long stay of the tenth Sikh guru, Gobind Singh, in 1738. It is said that Padma-sambhava, the 8th century Indian apostle credited with bringing Buddhism to

Mandi district apple orchard

Tibet, used his legendary powers to fly from here to Tibet. His spirit is believed to reside in the tiny floating reed islands on the lake.

Mandi's hinterland contains many other places of scenic beauty. To the east, **Jhanjheli** and **Karsog**, both about 100 km (62 miles) away in apple orchard country, offer the possibility of some lovely treks to the hilltop temples of Shikari Devi and Mahunag.

Kangra Valley ⑪

Kangra district. 222 km (728 miles) NW of Shimla. 🏃 9,200. ☒ Gaggal, 55 km (34 miles) N of Kangra town. ☐ Joginder Nagar and Una. ☐

Located in the western part of Himachal Pradesh and spread between the Shivalik foothills and the Dhauladhar Range, the Kangra Valley is a land of gentle beauty. Undulating expanses of tea gardens and terraced paddy fields are crisscrossed by sparkling snow-fed rivulets. Kangra is the most populated district of Himachal Pradesh, and is well connected with the plains as it is situated along the border with Punjab.

The valley derives its name from the ancient town of Kangra, even though Dharamsala (see p122) is the present district headquarters. The history of the town goes back 3,500 years when it was called Nagarkot and was the capital of the kingdom of Trigartha. In 1620, Kangra and its fort were captured by Emperor Jahangir, after which it became a Mughal province. Dominating the town today are the ruins of the once formidable Kangra Fort, perched on top of a steep cliff overlooking the Banganga and Majhi rivulets. Within the fort's compound are two Hindu temples

The square-shaped Rewalsar Lake resting in the hollow of a mountain spur

The towering spire of Brajeshwari Devi Temple in Kangra town

dedicated to Ambika Devi (a local goddess) and Lakshmi Narayan, and a Jain temple with a stone image of Adinath. Behind the crowded bazaar is the Brajeshwari Devi Temple, whose fabled riches were plundered by Mahmud of Ghazni *(see p48)* in 1009. The present structure was built in 1920, after the terrible earthquake of 1905 destroyed the city and original temple.

Some 15 km (9 miles) southwest of Kangra town, are the 15 monolithic rock-cut temples of **Masroor**, dating to the 10th century and carved in a style similar to those at Ellora *(see pp476–8)*. The picturesque **Jwalamukhi**

Temple, 34 km (21 miles) southwest of Kangra, is one of North India's most important pilgrimage sites.

Further east of Kangra, the beauty of the tea garden country unfolds around **Palampur**, 45 km (28 miles) away. East of Palampur, are the 9th-century stone Baijnath Temple dedicated to Shiva, Bir with its Tibetan Buddhist monastery, and Billing, well-known as a take-off point for paragliding over the valley.

About 40 km (25 miles) southeast of Palampur, is the fortress of **Sujanpur-Tira**, located on the right bank of the Beas. Built by the Kangra kings in the early 18th century, it was the favoured

residence of Raja Sansar Chand, the renowned patron of Kangra miniature painting. The fortress also preserves some excellent wall paintings.

At the far end of the Kangra Valley is **Jogindernagar**, 55 km (34 miles) south of Palampur, the terminus of a narrow gauge railway line that winds up the valley from Pathankot in the west.

The **Maharana Pratap Sagar Lake**, created in 1979 by the construction of the Pong Dam across the Beas, lies to the southwest of Kangra district. This large wetland, spread over 45,000 ha (111,200 acres) when full, is a favoured stopover for migratory birds from Central Asia.

Terraced paddy fields in the Kangra Valley

PAHARI MINIATURE PAINTINGS

Pahari or "hill" painting refers to the various schools of miniature painting such as Kangra, Basohli, Mankot and Guler, that flourished between the mid-17th and the late 19th centuries in the Rajput kingdoms situated in the long, narrow region of the Himalayan foothills. Although there is evidence of painting in this region as early as 1552, the earliest group of distinctive Pahari style paintings appeared in about 1650 in the small state of Basohli. These miniatures, horizontal in format, use flat planes of bold colours, mainly reds and yellows.

Kangra miniature, 1788, depicting Krishna killing the serpent-demon, Kaliya

Stylized architecture and figures with large eyes and straight profiles wearing elaborate costumes and jewellery, are typical of these miniatures, which illustrate the *Rasamanjari*, a Sanskrit poem on the behaviour of lovers. In the 18th century, the neighbouring state, Mankot, developed an equally vibrant style, remarkable for a series of portraits of grandees of the court. By the late 18th century, the vitality of local tradition had mellowed under Mughal influence and a lyrical, more tranquil palette with a naturalistic rendering of forms characterized the miniatures from Guler and Kangra. Guler's painting tradition was dominated by one family of artists of whom the most talented was Nainsukh. Painting in Kangra flourished under the reign of Raja Sansar Chand (r.1775–1823). The highly refined style that emerged during this period concentrated on the lush, idyllic landscape as the backdrop for romantic scenes. Other centres of Pahari painting included Mandi, Jammu, Nurpur, Chamba and Kullu.

Dharamsala ⑫

Kangra district. 124 km (77 miles) NW of Shimla. 🏛 19,100. ✈ Gaggal, 11 km (7 miles) S of town centre. 🚊 Pathankot, 80 km (50 miles) NW of Dharamsala, then bus or taxi. 🚌 🛈 HP Tourism, McLeodganj (01892) 21 205. 🏪 daily. 🎭 Summer Festival (Jun), Bodh Festival (Oct/Nov).

Tibetan nuns in their red robes, a common sight in Dharamsala

Tʜɪs ʜɪʟʟ sᴛᴀᴛɪᴏɴ, established by the British in the mid-19th century, is today the home of the Dalai Lama and the Tibetan Government-in-Exile. Located on the lower spurs of the Dhauladhar Range, the town consists of two sections – the lower town with the main bus stand and bazaar, and the upper town, known as **McLeodganj**, 7 km (4 miles) to its north, which is the destination of most foreign visitors. There is little of interest in the lower town, apart from the lively **Kotwali Bazaar** and the **Museum of Kangra Art**. The museum has an excellent collection of Kangra miniatures (see p121), and also houses a school which teaches the art of miniature painting.

McLeodganj, the upper town, named after David McLeod, the lieutenant governor of Punjab in 1848, is primarily a Tibetan settlement. Its focal point is the **Tsuglagkhang Complex**, located at the southern edge of the town, which contains the residence of the Dalai Lama (not open to visitors), the **Namgyal Monastery** where monks can be seen debating in the afternoons, and the important **Tsuglagkhang Temple**. A

simple hall, painted in yellow, the temple has a raised dais from where the Dalai Lama holds discourses, and three beautiful images from the Buddhist pantheon – Sakyamuni (the Historical Buddha), Avalokitesvara (see p141), and Padmasambhava (see p120 & p139). The Dalai Lama is believed to be an incarnation of Avalokitesvara. Another temple in the complex has an intricate mural of the Kalachakra ("Wheel of Time") and beautiful sand mandalas, painstakingly created by the monks over a period of time and then ritually destroyed.

Situated at the northern edge of town are the **Tibetan Institute of Performing Arts**, and the beautiful **Norbulingka Institute**, where traditional arts and crafts are promoted and kept alive.

Gangchen Kyishong, the administrative centre of the

Stained glass, St-John-in-the-Wilderness

Tibetan Government-in-Exile, is midway between the upper and lower towns. This complex includes the excellent **Library of Tibetan Works and Archives**, a museum on the first floor with bronze images and *thangkas*, as well as the **Institute of Tibetan Medicine**. Nearby is the **Nechung Monastery**, the seat of the Tibetan State Oracle, whose predictions about major events in the coming year carry great weight in the Tibetan community. Also on the road to Kotwali Bazaar, just below McLeodganj, is the picturesque **Church of St-John-in-the-Wilderness**, a grey stone structure built in 1852. Brass plaques and superb Belgian stained-glass windows can be seen inside the church. The tomb of Lord Elgin, the British viceroy who died here in 1863 while on holiday, lies in the churchyard.

🏛 **Museum of Kangra Art**
Main Rd, Dharamsala. 🔾 Tue–Sun.
🏛 **Library of Tibetan Works and Archives**
Gangchen Kyishong, McLeodganj Rd.
🔾 Mon–Fri.
⛪ **St-John-in-the-Wilderness**
🔾 daily. ✝ 11am Sun.

Eɴᴠɪʀᴏɴs: The pretty village of **Dharamkot**, north of McLeodganj, is reached by a 3-km (2-mile) long road, lined with deodar and oak trees. There are superb views of the Kangra Valley from the village.

The brightly-painted façade of Namgyal Monastery, McLeodganj

Little Tibet

WHEN THE 14th Dalai Lama, Tenzin Gyatso, fled Tibet in 1959 after the Chinese occupation, Dharamsala became his new home, and the base of the Tibetan Government-in-Exile. The town is today often called Little Tibet, preserving Tibet's religious and

Butter lamp

cultural heritage, keeping the Tibetan cause alive internationally, and serving as the focal point for the 100,000 Tibetans scattered in refugee settlements all over India. Dharamsala also attracts Buddhists from across the world, such as the Hollywood actor Richard Gere.

The Tibetan flag is dominated by a snow-covered mountain representing Tibet. The six red bands symbolize the six Tibetan tribes.

RELIGION AND CULTURE

Dharamsala's many monasteries and crafts centres, and its performing arts school, ensure that Tibet's distinctive religion and culture continue to flourish.

Tibetan opera, known as lhamo, has traditional folk tales, legends and myths as its themes.

The Dalai Lama, who won the Nobel Peace Prize in 1990, is head of the Gelugpa or Yellow Hat sect (see p139) and is revered as Tibet's god-king.

Thunderbolt sceptre

Butter sculpture

Prayer bell

The altar in a Tibetan monastery includes, apart from images of the deities, seven ritual bowls of water, butter lamps, intricate butter sculptures, as well as a bell and a thunderbolt sceptre used during prayers and special rites.

Thangkas, or scroll paintings framed in silk depicting Buddhist divinities, are among the traditional arts kept alive by the refugees.

Sand mandalas symbolizing the universe are meticulously created and then ceremonially destroyed. They help monks to meditate.

See also features on Buddhist Iconography *(p141)* and In the Buddha's Footsteps *(p221)*.

Sylverton, one of the many colonial houses in Dalhousie

Dalhousie ⑬

Chamba district. 336 km (209 miles) NW of Shimla. 👥 7,400. 🚌 ℹ️ Geetanjali Hotel, near bus stand, (01899) 42 136. 🚤 daily. 🎭 Summer Festival (Jun).

SPRAWLING OVER five hills that range in height from 1,525 m to 2,378 m (5,003 ft to 7,802 ft), Dalhousie still retains its Raj-era ambience, with spacious, gable-roofed bungalows and churches flanking its leafy lanes. Originally conceived as a sanatorium for the expatriate population rather than as a fashionable summer retreat, it was founded in 1853 and named after Lord Dalhousie, the governor-general of British India between 1854 and 1856. The most popular walks are the twin rounds of **Garam Sarak** ("Warm Road") and **Thandi Sarak** ("Cold Road"), so called because one path is sunnier than the other. A shorter walk from the Circuit House to Gandhi Chowk – the central part of town where a school, church and the post office are situated – offers spectacular views of the Pir Panjal Range. From Gandhi Chowk, another pleasant ramble, about 3 km (2 miles) long, leads south to the pretty picnic spot of Panjpula or "Five Bridges".

For Raj aficionados, a track leading off to the right from the main bus stand moves past the old British cemetery in the woods, before reaching the cantonment. One of the two churches here boasts pretty stained-glass windows and sandstone arches.

ENVIRONS: A scenic road through dense forests of pine, deodar, oak, horse chestnut and rhododendron leads to the **Kalatope Wildlife Sanctuary**, about 8 km (5 miles) east of Dalhousie. With prior permission from the wildlife authorities at Chamba it is possible to take a diversion at Bakrota and drive to a rest house deep inside the sanctuary. About 26 km (16 miles) east of Dalhousie is **Khajjiar**, situated at a height of 2,000 m (6,562 ft). This saucer-shaped expanse of green meadow, bordered by towering deodars, has a picture postcard beauty, comparable with the finest views in Kashmir or Switzerland. In the centre is a small lake with a golden-domed Devi temple built on a floating island.

🦌 Kalatope Wildlife Sanctuary
For permission contact: Forest Department, Chamba. 📞 (01899) 22 639.

Chamba ⑭

Chamba district. 356 km (221 miles) NW of Shimla. 👥 20,300. 🚌 🚤 daily. 🎭 Sui (Apr), Minjar (Jul/Aug). **Travel permits** Contact the Deputy Commissioner, (01899) 25 371. For details see p758.

THIS TOWN WAS CHOSEN as the capital of the former princely state of Chamba in the 10th century, when Raja Sahil Varman moved here from Bharmour. He named it Chamba after his favourite daughter, Champavati, who legend says, sacrificed herself to provide water for the parched city. During the Sui festival, women and children sing her praises in the town's many temples.

A bridge over the Ravi river leads up to the town, situated on the ledge of a mountain, overlooking the right bank of the river. In the town's centre is the **Chaugan**, a huge expanse of meadow, that is the focal point of all cultural and social life. Clustered around it are a number of imposing buildings, including the old **Akhand Chandi Palace**, part

Silver mask of Parvati, Chamba

of which is now a college. The Chaugan is also the main marketplace with shops that sell a variety of merchandise, ranging from traditional silver jewellery with enamelled clasps to embroidered Chamba *chappals* (sandals) that may look flimsy but are excellent for walking up hillsides.

Chamba's towering stone temples are some of the finest in the region. The most

Images of deities on the walls of Lakshmi Narayan Temple, Chamba

Hillsides around Chamba ablaze with the colours of autumn

important are the six North Indian *shikhara*-style temples *(see p21)* that comprise the **Lakshmi Narayan Temple** complex, to the west of the Chaugan. Of these, three are dedicated to Vishnu and three to Shiva. The white marble image of Lakshmi Narayan, in the main temple, was brought from Central India in the 10th century. The carved panels on the temple walls illustrate mythological scenes as well as animal and floral motifs.

Other temples include the **Madho Rai Temple**, near the palace, with a bronze image of Krishna, and further up, the **Chamunda Temple**.

A glimpse of Chamba's rich heritage can be seen at the **Bhuri Singh Museum**, set up in 1908 by the king of Chamba at the time. His rare collection of miniature paintings formed the nucleus of the museum. Today, it has a fine collection of Pahari paintings *(see p121)*, murals, inscribed fountain slabs, carved stone panels and other artifacts, such as Chamba *rumals*, metal masks, copper plates and silver jewellery.

🏛 **Bhuri Singh Museum**
S of Chaughan. 🕐 *Tue–Sun.*

Bharmour ⑮

Chamba district. 64 km (40 miles) SE of Chamba. 🚌 📷 *Manimahesh Yatra (Aug/Sep).*

THE BHARMOUR region, homeland of the semi-nomadic, sheep-herding Gaddis and the first capital of the Chamba rulers, spreads across a steep mountainside, high above Budhil, a large tributary of the Ravi river. Bharmour's main attraction is the fascinating **Chaurasi** (literally, "Eighty-Four") **Temple** complex, built in the 10th century under Raja Sahil Varman, to honour the 84 saints who visited Bharmour. The major shrines are dedicated to Narasimha, Ganesha, and the local deities Larkana Devi and Manimahesh. The intricate wooden carvings on the temple lintels and the images of the main deities are outstanding, and it is said that the sculptor's hands were cut off to prevent him from replicating such remarkable work.

ENVIRONS: Situated at a height of 3,950 m (12,959 ft), **Manimahesh Lake**, 35 km (22 miles) from Bharmour, is the area's most sacred lake, as its holy waters are believed to cleanse all sins. In August/September, thousands of pilgrims converge here to participate in the annual Manimahesh Yatra *(see p113)*. The main motor road continues up to Hadsar, 16 km (10 miles) beyond Bharmour, and from there the *yatra* (procession) ascends in two stages via Dhanchho to the lake, nestling at the base of the Manimahesh Kailasa.

For the adventurous, Bharmour also offers a tough five-day trek over the Kugti Pass (5,040 m/16,535 ft) to Lahaul *(see p129)*. Holi, 26 km (16 miles) away in the main Ravi Valley, is the base for a number of trails over the Dhauladhar Range to the Kangra Valley. It offers the option of a longer walk to the Kullu Valley as well. Down the course of the Ravi, on the road to Chamba, the **Chatrari Temple** with its exquisite bronze image of Shakti Devi, is also worth a stop.

Well-preserved 10th-century temples at Bharmour

CHAMBA RUMALS

Chamba *rumals*, exquisitely embroidered handkerchiefs or coverlets, generally square in shape, were used primarily to wrap gifts, either for temple offerings or for ceremonial exchanges during wedding rituals. At times, they also formed the canopies draped above deities in temples. Pale colours, silk thread, a double-sided satin stitch and an unbleached muslin base were the framework within which intricate compositions, inspired by delicate Pahari miniatures, were created. Originally the work of the ladies of the court, the themes were religious, interspersed with animal and plant motifs, and enclosed within floral borders.

Hand-embroidered Chamba *rumal*

Brightly coloured tiger guarding the Jagannathi Devi Temple, Kullu

Kullu Valley 16

Kullu district. 240 km (149 miles) N of Shimla. 🏔 *18,300.* ✈ *Bhuntar, 10 km (6 miles) S of Kullu town.* 🚌
ℹ *HP Tourism, near Maidan, (01902) 22 349.* 🎭 *Dussehra (Sep/Oct).* **Travel permits** *Contact Deputy Commisioner, (01902) 22 727. For more details see p115.*

THE KULLU VALLEY in central Himachal Pradesh, watered by the Beas river, has long been a site of human habitation. In ancient Sanskrit texts it is referred to as Kulantapith, or "end of the habitable world" – an apt description when one compares the lush fields and apple orchards of this 80-km (50-mile) long valley with the desolate expanse of Lahaul (*see p129*), which is separated from it by the Pir Panjal Range. The local name for Kullu is the "Valley of the Gods" – its alpine setting is the gathering place for 360 gods from different temples in the region, who congregate here for the famous Dussehra festival.

Unlike British-built hill stations in the Himalayas, Kullu remained unknown to the outside world until it was "discovered" in the 1960s by the flower children, who were enchanted as much by its hillsides covered with marijuana plants (*Cannabis sativa*), as by its gentle beauty, superb mountain vistas and amiable people. The men of

Typical geometric pattern on the border of a Kullu shawl

Kullu Valley usually wear the distinctive Kullu *topi*, a snug woollen cap with a colourful upturned flap. The women weave thick shawls with striking geometric designs on their borders, and few visitors can resist acquiring these attractive products, now a flourishing local industry. Equally attractive are the village houses, their slate roofs rising above green meadows. **Kullu**, the district headquarters and the largest settlement in the valley, is located on the right bank of the Beas. The town's chief attraction is the 17th-century **Raghunath Temple**, dedicated to Rama and Sita, whose richly adorned images lead the processions at the Dussehra festival. Also worth exploring is the Akhara Bazaar, at the northern end of the town, famous for its handicrafts shops, selling shawls and traditional silver jewellery. At the southern end of town is the large green open space called **Dhalpur Maidan**, where the colourful Dussehra festivities take place.

A number of temples, all with superb stone carvings and impressive images, lie in the vicinity of Kullu town – the **Vaishno Devi Cave Shrine** is 4 km (2.5 miles) to the northeast;

the **Jagannathi Devi Temple** at Bekhli, 5 km (3 miles) to the north; and the **Vishnu Temple** at Dayar, 12 km (8 miles) to the west. The huge, pyramidal **Basheshwar Mahadev Temple** at Bajaura, 15 km (9 miles) to the south, has superb images of Vishnu, Ganesha and Durga. However, the most famous is the **Bijli Mahadev Temple**, dedicated to the "Lord of Lightning", 14 km (9 miles) to the southeast. Located on a high spur on the left bank of the river, opposite the town, this temple has an 18-m (59-ft) high staff, which periodically attracts lightning during thunderstorms especially in the monsoon. This is regarded as a divine blessing, even though it shatters the Shivalinga in the sanctum of the temple. The stone fragments are then painstakingly put together again with a mortar of clarified butter and grain, by the head priest.

ENVIRONS: Jalori Pass, about 70 km (44 miles) south of Kullu, on the ridgeline forming the divide between the Beas and Satluj rivers, offers two beautiful walks through dense, high-altitude oak forests and meadows. The first walk goes through a path with gentle gradients to the tarn of Saryolsar, 5 km (3 miles) away. The other walk, up a neighbouring hill, leads to the picturesque ruins of a fort occupied by the Gurkhas in the 19th century.

A waterfall in Kullu Valley

Hot springs in Manikaran, a popular pilgrim spot

Parvati Valley ⑰

Kullu district. 180 km (112 miles) NE of Shimla (via Jalori Pass). 🚌 ℹ️ HP Tourism, near Maidan, Kullu, (01902) 22 349.

THE SCENIC Parvati Valley, with its green, terraced rice fields and apple orchards, draws an increasing number of visitors. However, because of illegal marijuana cultivation in the surrounding country-side, the Parvati Valley has, in recent years, gained notoriety as a centre for the narcotics trade, and several foreign visitors have gone missing from the area. It is advisable to take guides and porters avail-able from Naggar *(see p128)* and **Manikaran**, for treks in this region.

The main settlement in the Parvati Valley is Manikaran, famous for its hot springs. It is also the starting point for a number of treks *(see pp114 –15)*. An interesting legend explains the origins of the hot springs. A serpent stole the earrings of Parvati, the consort of Lord Shiva, and disappeared with them into a deep burrow. On witnessing Shiva's terri-ble anger, the snake was too terrified to come out of its hole, but managed to snort the earrings out through the earth, thus creating vents from which the hot springs bubble out. A bath here is said to be good for the body and the soul, and local peo-ple sometimes boil rice in the geo-thermal steam. The Rama Temple and the Shiva Temple next to a Sikh gurdwara is always thronged with sadhus.

Great Himalayan National Park ⑱

Kullu district. 205 km (127 miles) N of Shimla, (via Jalori Pass). **Entry points:** Saing, Gushani. 🚌 Shamchi, 15 km (9 miles) S of Kullu, then jeep. 🛏 For bookings & permits contact Director, GHNP, Shamchi, (01902) 65 320. 📠

THE GREAT Himalayan National Park, covering an area of 754 sq km (291 sq miles), ranges in altitude from 1,300 m (4,265 ft) to 6,100 m (20,013 ft), and abuts the cold desert region of Pin Valley National Park *(see p130)*. The vari-ety of flora and fauna found here represents the entire Western Himalayas. A vast range of subtropical species along with alpine grasslands are covered with edelweiss and oak forests. Mammals include the Himalayan tahr, musk deer and the elusive snow leopard. Among the 300-odd species of birds, there are at least six kinds of pheasant.

Monal pheasant

A number of trekking trails and forest huts in the buffer zone offers an opportunity to explore the park.

GATHERING OF THE GODS

Kullu celebrates the festival of Dussehra with unique gusto. All over India, this festival commemorates the defeat of the demon-king, Ravana, by the god Rama, a story recounted in the Hindu epic, *Ramayana (see p27)*. In Kullu, local traditions add their own piquancy to this pan-Indian myth. These traditions originated in the 17th century, when the ruler, Jagat Singh, inadvertently caused the death of a Brahmin priest. To expiate his sin, he installed the deity Raghunath (an incarnation of Rama), on his throne and vowed that thereafter he and his descendants would rule Kullu only as regents. The image of this god was brought all the way from the holy town of Ayodhya *(see p199)*, the birthplace of Lord Rama. From then on, every September/October, Raghunath "invites" all the local gods of the valley, to celebrate Dussehra in Kullu. These gods, 360 of them, include Hadimba, the patron deity of the Kullu rajas from Manali *(see p128)*, and Jamlu, the reigning deity of Malana who administers justice via the village priest. The gods are carried on palanquins from their own temples and arrive at the Dhalpur Maidan in a cheerful procession accompanied by the frenzied beat of drums. Nine days of festivities follow when a tempo-rary market is set up, and sells everything from locally-made shawls and shoes, to brightly-hued plastic toys. The graceful *natti* dance, performed amidst a lot of friendly rivalry by several local groups, can also be watched.

Image of Vashishtha Devta, a local god

Preparing for the Dussehra festival celebrations

Manali ⑲

Kullu district. 281 km (175 miles) N of Shimla. 🚶 6,300. 🚉 ℹ️ *The Mall, (01902) 52 175.* 🏠 *daily.* 🎿 *Winter Carnival (Jan), Dhungri Mela (May).*

The 16th-century wooden Hadimba Temple in Manali

P ICTURESQUE MANALI, situated along the west bank of the Beas river, is a prime destination for visitors, offering a variety of scenic walks and treks through dense forests. Though a profusion of hotels and shops in recent years has overrun downtown Manali, its environs still retain much of the natural beauty that gives this hill station a unique flavour. Particularly charming is the original village, about 3 km (2 miles) north of the main bazaar, with its temple dedicated to Manu, the Hindu sage after whom Manali is named.

Located 1.5 km (1 mile) north of the main bazaar is the sacred **Hadimba Temple**, shaded by a grove of stately deodars. This four-tiered wooden temple with its pagoda-style roof was built in 1553 around a small natural cave enshrining the footprints of the demoness Hadimba, wife of Bhima, the mighty Pandava brother *(see p26)*.

On the left bank of the Beas, about 3 km (2 miles) north of the bazaar, the hot sulphur springs in the village of **Vashisht** are piped into Turkish-style baths. Further up, the lovely **Solang Valley**, 14 km (9 miles) from downtown Manali, is the scene of most of the area's outdoor activities. Treks lead up to the pastures of Dhumti and the small

snow-fed lake of Beas Kund *(see p114).* Paragliding, a popular activity, takes place on the nearby slopes, which also attract skiers in the winter.

ENVIRONS: Rohtang Pass, the perilous pass crossing into Lahaul, at an altitude of 3,980 m (13,058 ft), is 52 km (32 miles) north of Manali. It is a day's excursion, possible only in summer, with a brief halt at the spectacular Rahalla Falls along the way.

The first capital of the Kullu kings, **Jagatsukh** is 6 km (4 miles) south of

Woodcarving on a door in Malana

Manali, on the left bank of the Beas. The two *shikhara*-style *(see p21)* stone temples here possibly date back to the 6th century. **Naggar**, further south, on the same side of the river, succeeded Jagatsukh as the capital till it was moved to Kullu *(see p126)* in the 17th century. The Naggar Castle, built in the 15th century, is now a hotel. It is an excellent

example of traditional local architecture with walls composed of alternate layers of wooden beams and evenly hewn stone. It commands a fine view of the Beas Valley. Nearby is the **Roerich Museum** displaying the work of the Russian painter Nicholas Roerich. Lying across the river from Naggar, is scenic **Katrain**, surrounded by orchards. Trout fishing is a popular pastime here.

The remote village of **Malana**, beyond Chanderkhani Pass, is 25 km (16 miles) southeast of Naggar. Malana's isolated people live by their own code of conduct and shun contact with outsiders. Their unique culture, language and system of government set them apart from the rest of the valley. Visitors should enter the village only if invited.

🏛 **Roerich Museum**
Naggar. ⏱ *daily.* 🎫

NICHOLAS ROERICH (1874–1947)

This multi-faceted Russian who painted, wrote poetry and expounded a universalist philosophy distilled from many religions, travelled extensively through Tibet and the Himalayas. He is best remembered for the colourful celebration of nature in his trans-Himalayan landscapes. Roerich lived in Naggar where he died in 1947. His old home is now the Roerich Museum. His son Svyatoslav, also a painter, made India his home as well.

A mountainscape by Roerich

A tiny stream crisscrossing the lush landscape around Manali

Lahaul and Spiti 🔟

Lahaul and Spiti district. 350 km (217 miles) N from Shimla to Keylong. 🏔 *33,200.* 🚌 🎭 *Ladarcha Festival, Spiti (Aug).*

Aᴛ ᴀɴ ᴀʟᴛɪᴛᴜᴅᴇ of 2,750 m (9,022 ft), Lahaul and Spiti, bordering Tibet and Ladakh's Zanskar Valley, comprise the trans-Himalayan regions of western Himachal Pradesh. Unlike the lush meadows of the Kullu Valley, this is a barren land of rocky massifs and hanging glaciers, enclosed by the Himalayas to the north and the Pir Panjal to the south. Rainfall is scarce and the region is dependent upon glacial melt for the cultivation of its main crops, barley, millet and seed potato.

While the difficult terrain inhibits many travellers from going to Spiti *(see pp130–31),* Lahaul is more accessible. Upper Lahaul is a stark land of high mountains enveloping the deep valleys of the Chandra and Bhaga rivers, while Lower Lahaul lies below Tandi, where the two rivers meet and become the Chandrabhaga, or Chenab.

Today, Lahaul's social structure is an interesting mix of Buddhism and Hinduism, reflecting the close ties the region had with Tibet, Ladakh and neighbouring Kullu.

Keylong, the district head-quarters on the Bhaga river,

The meandering Chenab river, near Gondhla village

is the region's principal town. With many basic facilities, it is widely used as a stopover by travellers en route to Leh *(see pp136–7)* or as a base for treks. Across the river, opposite Keylong, a steep tree-shaded pathway leads to **Drugpa Kardang Gompa**, the largest monastery *(gompa)* in Lahaul. It has a fine collection of *thangkas (see p123),* musical instruments and old weapons. Nearby is the 16th-century **Shashur Gompa**. This monastery is renowned for its long 4.5 m (15 ft) *thangka.*

On the road to Manali, about 16 km (10 miles) south of Keylong, the eight-storeyed tower of the Gondhla chiefs

Detail of a prayer wheel at Keylong

dominates the landscape. The oldest monastery in Lahaul, the 800-year-old **Guru Ghantal Gompa** at Tandi, 11 km (7 miles) southwest of Keylong, is believed to have been established by Guru Padmasambhava, the founder of Tibetan Buddhism. Other places worth visiting are the carved wooden Mrikula Devi Temple at **Udaipur**, in the Pattan Valley, 44 km (27 miles) west of Tandi, and **Trilokinath**, with its marble image of Avalokitesvara *(see p141).*

Beyond Keylong, the road to Leh passes the last Lahaul village of **Darcha** with a trekking route to Zanskar *(see p152)* via the Shingo-la.

Suraj Tal, the glacial lake that is the source of Bhaga river, one of the main rivers in Lahaul

Spiti: The Sacred Valley

HIMACHAL PRADESH

THE HEART OF HIMACHAL'S cold desert, Spiti is a land of fascinating contrasts. Monasteries and prayer flags are dotted along the banks of glacial streams, while blue sheep and ibex graze amidst sparse pastures sprinkled with marine fossils. Once part of a West Tibetan kingdom, Spiti submitted to Ladakhi rule in the 17th century and became a part of British India in the 19th century. Through these changes in its political history, Spiti remained a locked land, enclosed between tall mountain ranges and international borders. Though now part of Himachal Pradesh, it has retained its Tibetan character and is an important preserve of ancient Buddhist heritage.

Bare multi-hued rock faces, a typical feature of the Spiti area

Chandra Tal, or the "Moon Lake", at a height of 4,270 m (14,009 ft), lies at the entrance to Spiti when approached from Lahaul. Oval in shape with deep blue waters, it is overlooked by craggy peaks and hanging glaciers.

Kaza is the administrative headquarters of Spiti.

Key Monastery, possibly founded in the 13th century, is the largest monastery in Spiti. Perched on an escarpment, it has a fine collection of thangkas *and is the seat of Lochen Tulku, a reincarnation of Rinchen Zangpo (see p119).*

Losar, the first Spiti village encountered en route from Lahaul, is beautifully situated below the wide confluence of the three rivulets that combine to form the Spiti river.

KEY

▨	Area illustrated
⛩	Monastery
▬	Major road
═	Minor road

0 km   25

0 miles   25

Kungri Monastery in Pin Valley belongs to the Nyingmapa sect *(see p139)*. The uppermost hall, in the main temple, contains some ancient wall paintings and wooden sculptures.

The land of the ibex and the snow leopard, the Pin Valley National Park is an untrammelled pastureland in the shadow of virgin snowcapped peaks. It surrounds the upper reaches of the Pin river and its tributary, the Paraiho. Among the carnivores, the fox and the snow wolf are common, while the beautiful snow leopard is more elusive.

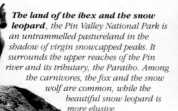

Chorten at a village in Pin Valley

Vibrant mural showing a scene from Buddhist mythology, Tabo Monastery

Dhankar, the old capital of Spiti, is wedged between the pinnacles of a razor sharp spur of crumbling rock and alkaline deposits. The old monastery here is richly endowed with beautiful frescoes, and a bronze statue of Avalokitesvara.

Children in Spiti

An impressive image of Guru Padmasambhava, covered in gold leaf, is the highlight of Lalung Monastery. This monastery is one of the 108 structures credited to Rinchen Zangpo.

Tabo Monastery ㉑

Lahaul and Spiti district. 442 km (275 miles) NE of Shimla. 🚌 ⬜ *Apr–Sep.* 🎏 *Monastery Festival (Oct/Nov).* **Travel permits** *required to travel between Tabo and Jangi (in Kinnaur). Contact Deputy Commisioner, Shimla (see p111), or SDM's office in Rekong Peo (see p118). For details see p115.*

TABO MONASTERY, Spiti's pride, is linked to an important era in the growth of Buddhism in Tibet. Tibetan Buddhism suffered a major setback during the reign of King Langdarma in the 9th century, and it took a whole century for the religion to recover. The resurgence, also known as the "second diffusion of Buddhism", was spearheaded by Ye-she-od, the Lama king of Guge in Western Tibet. Under his patronage, the legendary scholar Rinchen Zangpo spread the faith by translating Buddhist texts and promoting a tremendous temple-building movement.

The *gompa* at Tabo is one of the products of this movement, established in the 11th century by Rinchen Zangpo himself. Dating from a period when monastic temples were constructed close to villages, it is one of the largest of such centres. The squat, mud structures of Tabo are enclosed within a mud wall about 84 m by 75 m (276 ft by 246 ft) and appear quite unimpressive from the outside. The exquisite

wall paintings inside, however, make Tabo one of the most significant art treasures of the Tibetan Buddhist world. The earliest paintings in the *dukhang* (assembly hall) are from the 10th and 11th centuries and depict scenes from various incidents and tales associated with the life of the Buddha. The hall also contains imposing clay sculptures of the chief deities from the Buddhist pantheon. Seven other chapels in the complex contain paintings from the 15th and 16th centuries. One of the shrines houses a huge clay idol of a sitting Maitreya (the Future Buddha). Tabo is also a favourite retreat of the Dalai Lama.

Accessing parts of the Spiti Valley that lie below Tabo remains difficult. Travel is restricted due to the proximity of the border with Tibet.

Monks praying at Tabo Monastery

Fields of buckwheat in the Sangla Valley *(see pp118–19)* ▷

LADAKH, JAMMU & KASHMIR

LYING ACROSS six major mountain ranges, and covering an area of 222,000 sq km (85,715 sq miles), Jammu and Kashmir is India's northernmost state, bordering Pakistan and China's Tibetan Plateau. Its three distinct regions – Ladakh, Jammu and the Kashmir Valley – offer a rich diversity of landscapes, religions, and people. The predominantly Muslim Kashmir Valley is a mosaic of forests, ricefields, lakes and waterways, its gentle beauty now shattered by armed insurgency *(see p154).* Jammu, encompassing plains, mountains and foothills, boasts the famous hilltop shrine of Vaishno Devi, an important pilgrimage site for Hindus. Sparsely populated Ladakh, which accounts for two-thirds of the state's area, is a high altitude desert. Its harsh lines are softened by the emerald green of oasis villages, the crystal light of cloudless blue skies, and the dramatic silhouettes of ancient Buddhist monasteries which, for many visitors, are Ladakh's main attraction.

SIGHTS AT A GLANCE

Towns & Cities
Jammu ⑭
Kargil ⑩
Leh ①
Mulbekh ⑨
Srinagar ⑮

Monasteries & Palaces
Alchi Monastery ⑧
Hemis Monastery ⑤

Matho Monastery ④
Shey ③
Stok ②

Areas of Natural Beauty
Gulmarg ⑯
Pahalgam ⑰
Rangdum ⑫
Southeast Ladakh ⑥

Rivers & Valleys
Suru Valley ⑪
Zanskar ⑬

Tours
Nubra Valley Tour ⑦

KEY

☒	Domestic airport
▬	National highway
▭	Major road
—	Minor road
—	Major railway
▬	International border
×××	Disputed border

The abandoned Leh Palace, once the seat of the royal family

Leh ❶

Leh district. 1,077 km (669 miles) N of Delhi. 🚶 15,000. ✈ 11 km (7 miles) S of town centre on Srinagar Rd. 🚌 ℹ (01982) 52 297. 🎭 Muharram (Mar/Apr), Buddha Jayanti (May), Losar (Dec).

FROM THE 17th century right until 1949, Ladakh's principal town, Leh, was the hub of the bustling caravan trade *(see p142)* between Punjab and Central Asia, and between Kashmir and Tibet. The large **Main Bazaar**, with its broad kerbs, was clearly designed to facilitate the passage of horses, donkeys and camels, and to provide for the display and storage of merchandise.

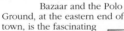

The Buddha, Leh Palace

The town is dominated by the nine-storeyed **Leh Palace**, built in the 1630s by Sengge Namgyal. A prolific builder of monasteries and forts, with many conquests to his name, he was Ladakh's most famous king. The palace's massive inward-leaning walls are in the same architectural tradition as the Potala Palace in Lhasa which, in fact, the Leh Palace antedates by about 50 years. Sadly, the solidity of its exterior belies the dilapidation inside, although some repair work is now being done. Visitors can go up to the open terrace on the level above the main entrance.

Much of Leh's charm lies in the opportunities it offers for pleasant strolls and walks. In the heart of town are the Main Bazaar and **Chang Gali**, with their eateries and curio shops selling precious stones and ritual religious objects such as prayer wheels. Along the Bazaar's wide kerb, women from nearby villages sit with large baskets of fresh vegetables, spinning wool on drop spindles and exchanging lively chatter in between intervals of brisk commerce.

The **Jokhang**, a modern ecumenical Buddhist establishment, and the town mosque, built in the late 17th century, are close to each other in the Main Bazaar. Between the Main Bazaar and the Polo Ground, at the eastern end of town, is the fascinating **Old Town**, with its maze of narrow alleys dotted with *chortens* and *mani* walls *(see p141)*, and its cluster of flat-roofed houses constructed of sun-baked bricks.

On the peak above the town are the small fort and monastery complex of **Namgyal Tsemo** (mid-16th century), believed to be the earliest royal residence in Leh. Next to its now ruined fort are a *gonkhang* (Temple of the Guardian Deities) and a temple to Maitreya (the Future Buddha), both of which have vibrant murals.

Those inside the *gonkhang* include a court scene with a portrait believed to be that of King Tashi Namgyal (mid-16th century), the founder of the complex.

At the western edge of Leh is the **Ecological Centre**, which runs development projects in agriculture, solar energy, health and environmental awareness in several of the surrounding villages. The centre also houses a library and a shop selling local handicrafts.

The gleaming white **Shanti Stupa** ("Peace Pagoda"), founded in the 1980s under the sponsorship of Japanese Buddhists, is situated on a hilltop west of the city.

Less than ten minutes' walk, in any direction away from the heart of town, will bring one to barley fields, green or

Barley fields around Leh

An archery contest near Leh

gold according to the season. Down the hill in the village of **Skara**, the massive mud walls of the 19th-century **Zorawar Fort** catch the eye. Another lovely walk is up past the **Moravian Church** to the serene village of **Changspa** with its ancient *chorten*. From here a road turns towards the beautifully-maintained 19th-century **Sankar Monastery**, with its impressive images of Avalokitesvara and of Vajra-Bhairav, Guardian of the Gelugpa order *(see p139)*.

ENVIRONS: Choglamsar, 7 km (4 miles) south of Leh, is the main Tibetan refugee settlement in Ladakh. It includes the Dalai Lama's prayer ground, known as Shanti Sthal, an SOS Children's Village, the Central Institute of Buddhist Studies, a solar-heated hospital and workshops that promote colourful Tibetan handicrafts.

Dramatically situated on a hilltop, so close to the airport that the wings of landing aircraft come perilously close to its walls, is the 15th-century **Spituk Monastery**, the oldest establishment of the Gelugpa sect in Ladakh. It houses the library of Tsongkapa, the sect's founder, and a shrine devoted to the goddess Tara *(see p141)*, with striking images of her myriad manifestations. Situated in one of Ladakh's most charming villages, **Phiyang Monastery**, is one of only two that represent the Drigungpa sect. It was founded by Ladakh's 16th-century ruler, Tashi Namgyal, supposedly as an act of atonement for the violence and treachery by which he came to the throne. Among its many treasures is a large and very interesting collection of Kashmiri bronzes of Buddhist deities, dating back to the 13th century, or possibly even earlier.

🛕 **Leh Palace**
⭕ daily. 📷 *Book in advance.* 🏞

🏔 **Namgyal Tsemo**
⭕ daily. 📷 *Book in advance.*

🏛 **Ecological Centre**
⭕ Mon–Fri. 📞 (01982) 53 221.

🏔 **Jokhang**
⭕ daily.

🏔 **Sankar Monastery**
⭕ daily. 🏞

🏔 **Spituk Monastery**
⭕ daily. 🏞 📷 *with permission of the lama-in-charge.*

🏔 **Phiyang Monastery**
⭕ daily. 🏞 📷 *with permission of the lama-in-charge.*

FESTIVALS OF LADAKH, JAMMU & KASHMIR

Hemis Festival *(Jun)*, Hemis. Of all Ladakh's monastery festivals *(see p140)* the one at Hemis is the most famous. This spectacular dance-drama, with colourful masks and costumes, offers a wonderfully authentic experience of Ladakhi culture.

Masked dancers performing at the Hemis Festival

Sindhu Darshan *(1–3 Jun)*, Leh. A recent introduction, this festival is a homage to the Indus. Held on the river banks, it includes exhibitions, polo matches and archery contests.

Ladakh Festival *(1–15 Sep)*, Leh and Kargil. Subsidized by the Tourism Department, this is held over two weeks in Leh's Polo Grounds, as well as in Kargil and some selected villages. Apart from the traditional masked dances, the events include polo matches and archery contests – both being popular traditional sports in the region. A handicrafts exhibition is also held.

Thikse Festival *(Oct/Nov)*, Thikse. The annual festival of the Gelugpa sect takes place in a beautiful setting. The precise dates of monastery festivals are fixed according to the Tibetan lunar calendar and vary every year.

Milad-ul-Nabi *(May)*, Srinagar. The Prophet's birthday is celebrated with special fervour at the Hazratbal Mosque, when its sacred relic, a lock of the Prophet's hair, is displayed to devotees.

Spituk Monastery's labyrinth of shrines linked by narrow passages

Monasteries Along the Indus

Maitreya in Thikse

SEVERAL OF LADAKH'S world-famous monasteries are situated along the Indus Valley, the region's historical and cultural heartland. Typically, a Ladakhi monastery *(gompa)* stands on a hill or ridge above the village that adjoins it. Its upper part consists of temples *(lhakhang)* and assembly halls *(dukhang)*, together with the *gonkhang*, the Temple of the Fearsome Guardian Deities. The monks' dwellings spill picturesquely down the hillside. The monasteries are still active centres of worship, so approach them respectfully.

Monks dancing in the courtyard of Lamayuru Monastery

Likir, *founded in the 12th century, houses a fine collection of thangkas and images, the latter enclosed in beautifully carved wooden frames.*

Basgo *has beautiful 16th-century murals in its fort and temple dedicated to Maitreya, the Future Buddha. It was the capital of Lower Ladakh in the 14th and 15th centuries.*

KARGIL

Indus

• Lamayuru

• Ri-dzong • Likir

• Basgo

• Alchi *(see pp144–6)*

NUBRA VALL

Leh *(see pp136–7)*

Indus

ZANSKAR VALLEY

• Shey

• Stok

Thi

Hemis *(see p140)* is Ladakh's largest and richest monastery. It has superb murals and *thangkas.*

Stakna •

0 km   15

0 miles   15

• Hemis

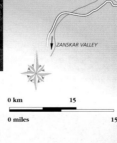

Ri-dzong *is built on top of a ridge of glacial debris which blocks a winding gorge. Founded in the 1840s by the Gelugpa sect, its monks follow a particularly austere regime.*

Lamayuru *is dramatically situated on a high spur overlooking an eerily eroded landscape. Believed to date to the 11th century, its oldest temple has a famous image of Vairocana, the Central Buddha of Meditation (see p146). Lamayuru also has a fine collection of thangkas.*

Stakna, *built in the early 17th century, has an exquisite silver chorten in its dukhang, surrounded by vividly-coloured murals.*

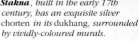

See also features on Little Tibet *(p123)*, Buddhist Iconography *(p141)*, and In the Buddha's Footsteps *(p221)*.

Thikse, *a 15th-century architectural gem crowning the crest of a hill, is a Gelugpa monastery which also has a modern Maitreya temple, consecrated by the Dalai Lama.*

Chemrey, *perched on a hilltop and dating from the 1640s, houses Buddhist scriptures with silver covers and gold lettering.*

Thak-thok Monastery belongs to the Nyingmapa sect. It is built around a cave which Guru Padmasambhava, the 8th-century saint, is believed to have used for meditation.

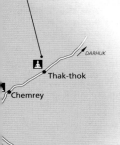

DARHUK

 Thak-thok

Chemrey

MANALI

KEY

 Monastery

= Road

Stok Palace, residence of Ladakh's erstwhile royal family

Stok ❷

Ladakh district. 17 km (11 miles) S of Leh. 🚌 🛈 *Leh Tourist Office,* *(01982) 52 297.* 🎭 *Stok Monastic Festival (Feb/Mar).*
Stok Palace ◯ *May–Oct.* 🎫 🚫

THE PALACE AT STOK has been the residence of the Namgyals, the former rulers of Ladakh, since its independence in 1843. Part of the palace has been converted into a fine museum of the dynasty and its history. Its collections include a set of 35 *thangkas (see p123)* representing the life of the Buddha, said to have been commissioned by the 16th-century king, Tashi Namgyal. Images and ritual religious objects, such as the bell and *dorje* (thunderbolt), are of unsurpassed workmanship. Secular objects include fine jade cups, the queens' jewellery, including a spectacular headdress, the kings' turban-shaped crown, and ceremonial robes. There is also a sword with its blade twisted into a knot, said to have been contorted by the enormous strength of Tashi Namgyal.

Shey ❸

Ladakh district. 15 km (9 miles) SE of Leh. 🚌 🛈 *Leh Tourist Office,* *(01982) 52 297.* 🎭 *Shey Strubla (1st week of Sep).*
Shey Palace ◯ *daily.* 🎫

SHEY was the ancient capital of Ladakh. Its abandoned palace contains a temple with a gigantic, late 17th-century Buddha image, surrounded by murals of deities, painted in rich colours and gold. Another beautiful Buddha image is housed in a nearby temple. Just below the palace, are huge 11th-century rock carvings of the Five Buddhas of Meditation *(see p146)*.

A Ladakhi couple bringing their baby to be blessed at Shey

BUDDHIST SECTS IN LADAKH

Five sects of Tibetan Buddhism are represented in Ladakh. Thak-thok monastery belongs to the Nyingmapa, which is based on the teachings of the 8th-century saint, Padma-sambhava *(see p120)*, while Matho *(see p140)* with its oracle monks belongs to the Sakyapa. The Drugpa and Drigungpa sects are based on the teachings of a line of Indian masters from the 11th century. The lamas of all these sects wear red hats on ceremonial occasions. The lamas who wear yellow hats belong to the reformist Gelugpa sect, headed by the Dalai Lama *(see p123)*, which exercised political control in Tibet until 1959. Apart from Thak-thok and Matho, and the two Drigungpa monasteries of Phiyang *(see p137)* and Lama-yuru, all Ladakh's monasteries belong to either the Drugpa or Gelugpa sects.

Monks of the Gelugpa sect chanting prayers

Dance of the Oracle at the 16th-century Matho Monastery

Matho Monastery ❹

Leh district. 30 km (19 miles) SE of Leh. 🚌 ◯ *daily.* 🎭 🖼 *Annual Matho Festival (Feb/Mar).*

THE ONLY MONASTERY in Ladakh of the Sakyapa sect *(see p139)*, Matho, built in the early 16th century, is also one of the few that continues to attract many new entrants. Its main importance, however, lies in its Oracles – two monks who, after months of purification by fasting and meditation, are possessed by a deity. This event takes place during Matho's annual festival, held between February and March. The drama of the occasion is tremendous as the Oracles traverse the topmost parapet of the monastery blindfolded, despite the 30-m

(98-ft) drop onto the rocks below. The Oracles answer questions put to them about public and private affairs, and great faith is reposed in their predictions. Matho also has a small museum with a rare collection of 16th-century *thangkas* and costumes.

Hemis Monastery ❺

Leh district. 43 km (27 miles) SE of Leh. 🚌 ◯ *daily.* 🎭 🖼 *Annual Hemis Festival (Jun).*

TUCKED AWAY up a winding glen in the mountains south of the Indus, Hemis is the largest as well as the richest of the central Ladakh monasteries. It was founded in the 1630s as a Drugpa establishment by King Sengge Namgyal, and continued to be

the most favoured monastery of the Namgyal dynasty. Of its several temples, the most rewarding is the *tshog-khang*, a secondary assembly hall which contains a fine image of the Buddha in front of a huge silver *chorten* set with flawless turquoises.

Hemis is also renowned for its spectacular annual festival, dedicated to Guru Padmasam-bhava, the 8th-century Indian apostle who took Buddhism to Tibet. A unique feature of this festival, which is held in the summer and attracts huge crowds, is the 12-yearly unveiling of the monastery's greatest treasure – an enormous, three-storey high *thangka* of Padmasambhava, embroidered and studded with pearls and semi-precious stones. The next unveiling of this *thangka* is due in 2004.

The giant *thangka* unfurled during the festival at Hemis Monastery

THE MONASTIC DANCE-DRAMAS OF LADAKH

The dance-dramas performed at Ladakh's annual monastery festivals are immensely popular events, constituting a link between popular and esoteric Buddhism. Attended by high lamas and novice monks in their ceremonial robes and hats, as well as by local families dressed in their splendid traditional costumes, these events are a vibrant expression of age-old cultural and religious values. The dancers, representing divine or mythological figures, wear colour-ful brocade robes and heavy masks as they perform ceremonial dances around the monastery courtyard. The solemnity of the occasion is lightened by comic interludes per-

formed by dancers in skeleton costumes, who bound into the arena performing agile gymnas-tics, and caricaturing the solemn rites just enacted, to the delight of the assembled specta-tors. In the climactic scene the masked figures ritually dismember a doll moulded from barley flour dough (perhaps symbolizing the human soul) and scatter its fragments in all directions. Besides attracting large numbers of outside visitors, these monastery festivals also provide people from far-flung Ladakhi villages an eagerly awaited opportunity to meet each other, and exchange news and views.

Masked dancers at a monastery festival

Buddhist Iconography

THE EXTERNAL manifestations of Buddhism are ubiquitous in Leh district and Zanskar – prayer flags fluttering in the breeze, prayer wheels turning in the hands of the elderly, *chortens* and *mani* walls inset with stone slabs carved with the sacred invocation *Om mani padme hum* ("Hail to the Jewel in the Lotus"). Inside the monasteries, the

Prayer wheel

iconography is more complex. Each divinity of the Mahayana Buddhist pantheon is depicted in several different manifestations, together with a host of saints, teachers and mythical figures, mandalas and allegorical compositions. Shown below are some images that are encountered most frequently.

THE BODHISATTVAS
Bodhisattvas are supremely compassionate almost-Buddhas who have attained enlightenment, but are willing to forgo nirvana so that they can help others obtain liberation from the endless cycle of rebirths.

Tara is the female form of Avalokitesvara and is depicted in 21 different forms.

Avalokitesvara, the Bodhisattva of Compassion, is often shown with 11 heads and multiple arms, symbolizing his benign omnipresence.

Manjushri, the Bodhisattva of Wisdom, bears a flaming sword in his hand, to cut through the fog of ignorance.

Guardian Deities are usually represented as fierce forms, with skull headdresses, wicked fangs and flames in place of hair. Most commonly seen is Mahakala, usually above the main door of a temple.

The Lords of the Four Quarters guard the four cardinal directions. The Lord of the North is recognized by the banner in his right hand, and a mongoose in his left hand.

The Wheel of Life, with animated human and animal figures on it, is mostly painted on temple verandahs. It shows the temptations and sins that make life on earth an endless misery.

See also features on Little Tibet *(p123)* and In the Buddha's Footsteps *(p221)*.

Glaciers and peaks encircling the blue-green waters of Pang-gong Tso

Southeast Ladakh ❻

Pang-gong Tso Leh district.150 km
(93 miles) E of Leh. **Tso Moriri** Leh
district. 220 km (1,137 miles) SE of Leh.
🅗 Leh Tourist Office, (01982) 52 297.
Travel permits Contact Deputy
Commissioner, Leh, (01982) 52 010.
The obligatory permits are granted on
condition that visitors travel in groups
of not less than four, with the tour
organized by a registered travel agent
and along specific tour routes.

SOUTHEAST LADAKH, on the
sensitive international
border with Tibet, is a region
with a series of spectacularly
beautiful lakes. The two major
lakes, **Pang-gong Tso** and
Tso Moriri, are accessible by
road, although there are no
scheduled bus services.

The biggest of the lakes is
the long and narrow Pang-
gong Tso. It is 130-km (81-
mile) in length and lies at an
altitude of 4,420 m (14,500 ft),
extending far into Western
Tibet. Visitors may go as far
as **Spangmik**, 7 km (4 miles)
along the lake's southern
shore, from where there are
spectacular views to the north
of the Chang-chenmo Range,
its reflection shimmering in
the ever-changing blues and

greens of the brackish water.
Above Spangmik rise the
glaciers and snowcapped
peaks of the Pang-gong Range.

Tso Moriri, 30 km (19 miles)
to the south of Pang-gong Tso
is a 140-sq km (54-sq mile)
expanse of intensely blue
water. At an altitude of 4,600
m (15,092 ft), it is set among
rolling hills behind which
lie snow-covered
mountains. The
region's only
permanent
settlement is on
the lake's
western shore,
Karzok – a
handful of houses and a
monastery, whose barley
fields must be among the
highest cultivated areas
anywhere in the world.

The lake and its freshwater
inlets are breeding areas for
many species of migratory
birds, such as the rare black-

necked crane and the great
crested grebe. Wild asses,
marmots and foxes can also
be seen in the region.

Among the human inhab-
itants of Southeast Ladakh are
the nomadic herders, known
as Chang-pa, who brave
extreme cold (-40° C/-40° F in
winter, and freezing nights
even in summer) throughout
the year, living in their black
yak-hair tents. They raise yak
and sheep, but their main
wealth is the pashmina goat.
The severe cold of winter
stimulates the goats to grow
an undercoat of soft warm
fibre, which they shed at the
beginning of summer. This
fibre, known as *pashm*, is the
raw material for Kashmir's
renowned shawl industry and
is, in fact, the unprocessed
form of the world-famous
cashmere wool. The lucrative
trade in *pashm* from Ladakh's
high-altitude
pastures as well
as from Western
Tibet was the motive
behind Ladakh's
annexation by the
Maharaja of
Kashmir in 1834.

Pashmina goat

ENVIRONS: The twin lakes of
Tso Kar and **Startsapuk Tso**,
are 80 km (50 miles) north of
Tso Moriri, on the road to
Leh. While Startsapuk Tso has
fresh water, Tso Kar is so briny
that the Chang-pa herders
regularly collect salt from the
deposits along its margins.

THE CARAVAN TRADE

For centuries, until 1949 Ladakh was the route for a busy
trade between Punjab and Central Asia. The caravans
invariably halted at Leh *(see pp136–7)*, where a lot of business was transacted, before proceeding to cross
the 5,578-m (18,301-ft) high Karakoram
Pass, one of the highest points on
any trade route in the world. In
summer the caravans traversed
Nubra, while in winter they crossed
the upper valley of the Shayok river.
Every year, over 10,000 pack
animals – horses, yaks, Bactrian
camels, and an especially sturdy
breed of local sheep – traversed
the Nubra region, carrying
Varanasi brocades, Chinese
silk, pearls, spices, Indian tea,
pashm wool, salt, indigo,
opium, carpets, and gold.

**A Ladakhi horseman taking a
break for prayers**

Tso Moriri, a breeding ground for
the great crested grebe

Nubra Valley Tour ❼

THE TOUR OF THE NUBRA REGION starts from Leh and follows the old caravan trade route to Central Asia, a "feeder" of the famous Silk Route. It takes in the world's highest motorable mountain pass – the Khardung-la, pretty villages with banks of wild flowers and stands of willow and poplar, valleys covered with seabuckthorn shrubs, stretches of sand dunes and double-humped Bactrian camels, remote monasteries, and medicinal hot springs.

The Karakoram Range, visible from the top of the Khardung-la

Panamik ⑥
A major halt on the caravan trade route, Panamik also has medicinal hot springs. This Panamik lady is seen in her local traditional dress.

Hundar ③
The fascinating vista of sand dunes between Diskit and Hundar can be explored on the back of a Bactrian camel.

LHAYUL GOMPA

Shayok-Nubra confluence ④
Flat sandy plains surround the confluence of these two rivers.

Samstangling ⑤
Overlooking the green fields of Sumur village, this 19th-century monastery has impressive images.

KARGIL

Leh

Diskit ②
Diskit, which has the region's only bazaar, also has a 17th-century monastery with exquisite murals.

SHEY

Khardung-la ①
From the top of this pass (5,578 m/18,301 ft) there are superb views, south over the Zanskar Range, and north to the towering Saser Spur of the Karakoram Range.

TIPS FOR DRIVERS

Length: 195 km (121 miles).
Getting around: This tour takes three days. Diskit, Hundar and Panamik have guesthouses and camps, for overnight stay.
Travel permits: Visitors must obtain an Inner Line Permit from the Deputy Commissioner, Leh, (01982) 52 010, to travel in the Nubra region. Permits are granted only to groups of four or more, and should be carried all the time.

0 km   8

0 miles   8

KEY

▬ Tour route

═ Other road

▬ River

Alchi Monastery ❽

Dancing deity in the Sumtsek

FOUNDED IN THE early 12th century AD, the religious enclave of Alchi is the jewel among Ladakh's monasteries. Because Alchi was abandoned as a site of active worship, for reasons unknown, as early as the 16th century, the 12th- and 13th-century paintings in its temples have remained remarkably well preserved, undimmed by the soot from butter lamps and incense sticks. Of the five temples in the enclave, the finest murals are in the two oldest, the Dukhang and the Sumtsek. These have been executed with great delicacy and skill by master painters who were probably from Kashmir.

Lhakhang Soma
This painting of a Guardian Deity and his female counterpart symbolizes the union of opposites.

Avalokitesvara
The legs of this gigantic statue in the Sumtsek are covered with exquisite miniature paintings of palaces and Buddhist pilgrimage sites.

★ Sumtsek
The carved wooden façade of this temple is in the style of Kashmiri temple architecture.

GREEN TARA

Green Tara or Prajnaparamita

There are several exquisite images of this goddess, variously identified as Green Tara, the Saviour, and Prajnaparamita (the Perfection of Wisdom) in the Sumtsek. Five of them are to the left of the gigantic Avalokitesvara statue, opposite his leg. The Green Tara seems to have held a special place in Alchi, since the goddess is not given such importance in other monasteries.

STAR FEATURES
★ Sumstek
★ Dukhang

View of Alchi
Idyllically located on a bend in the Indus river, Alchi's simple white-washed buildings with their band of deep red trim, stand out against an impressive backdrop of barren mountains.

VISITORS' CHECKLIST

Leh district. 70 km (44 miles) W of Leh on the Leh-Kargil Highway.
🚌 🛈 *Leh Tourist Office, (01982) 52 297.* 🗓 *daily.* 📷 🎥 *allowed without flash. Book ahead for a guide from Leh. Alchi village has accommodation as well as restaurants with toilet facilities.*

Chortens containing holy relics are dotted around the complex. They are often built in memory of a great lama.

★ Dukhang
The serene image of the Vairocana Buddha (see p146) is surrounded by elaborate wood-work, decorative friezes and superb mandalas.

Lotsawa Lhakhang

King and Queen
This mural in the Dukhang shows details of royal dress and hairstyles.

Rinchen Zangpo
This rare portrait of Rinchen Zangpo (see p119), an influential Tibetan saint known as the Great Translator, is in the 12th-century Lotsawa ("Translator") Lhakhang.

Manjushri Lhakhang,
one of the five temples, contains a large image of Manjushri *(see p141).*

Entrance

Exploring Alchi Monastery

UNKNOWN TO THE OUTSIDE WORLD UNTIL 1974, when Ladakh was opened up to tourists, Alchi is now one of Ladakh's major attractions, renowned as a great centre of Buddhist art. It was built as a monument to the Second Spreading – the revival of Buddhism that took place in Tibet in the 11th century, on the basis of religious texts brought from Kashmir. The entire Mahayana Buddhist pantheon of deities is represented within its five temples, together with superb paintings of court life, battles and pilgrimages, depicting the costumes, architecture and customs of the time.

The assembly hall, known as **Dukhang**, is the oldest of the five temples and holds some of Alchi's greatest treasures. The beautiful central image of Vairocana, the main Buddha of Meditation, is surrounded by a wooden frame exuberantly carved with dancers, musicians, elephants and mythical animals. It is flanked by four other Buddhas of Meditation. Even more impressive are the six elaborate mandalas painted on the walls, together with small scenes of contemporary life. The space between the mandalas is filled with fine decorative details that have an unexpectedly Rococo look about them.

In the three-storeyed **Sumtsek**, the second-oldest temple, are spectacular images and paintings. The temple's most unique features are the gigantic images of

One of the many prayer rooms in Alchi Monastery

Avalokitesvara, Manjushri (see p141) and Maitreya, that stand in alcoves in three of its walls. Only their legs and torsos are visible from the ground floor, while their heads protrude into the upper storey. From waist to knee they are draped in dhoti-like garments, covered with remarkably animated and sophisticated miniature paintings. It is advisable to take a torch to examine their incredible detail. The Avalokitesvara image is covered with shrines, palaces, and vignettes of contemporary life. The Maitreya image has scenes from the Buddha's life painted within roundels, and the Manjushri image depicts the 84 Masters of the Tantra.

The three other temples probably date from the late 12th to early 13th centuries, and though they would win acclaim in any other setting, they fade in comparison with the Dukhang and the Sumtsek. The **Manjushri Lhakhang** has murals of the Thousand Buddhas and an enormous, recently-repainted image of Manjushri. The **Lotsawa Lhakhang** has rather more austere paintings and images. It is dedicated to the saint Rinchen Zangpo, who was also closely associated with the Thikse (see p139) and Tabo (see p131) monasteries. The **Lhakhang Soma**, the last temple to be built at Alchi, has a profusion of fierce-looking deities on its walls, and scenes showing the Buddha preaching.

Riders, Central Asian in appearance, on the Avalokitesvara image

THE FIVE BUDDHAS OF MEDITATION

Buddhism in the 12th century laid emphasis on the Five Dhyani Buddhas, or Buddhas of Meditation, who feature in several mandalas in Alchi. Each of these Buddhas is associated with a direction and a colour. Vairocana (the Resplendent) is associated with the centre and the colour white; Amitabha (the Boundless Light) with the west and the colour red; Akshobhya (the Imperturbable) with the east and the colour blue; Amoghasiddhi (Infallible Success) with the north and the colour green; and Ratnasambhava (the Jewel-Born) with the south and the colour yellow. The Five Buddhas of Meditation symbolize the different aspects of the Buddha, and the mandalas help devotees to meditate on them.

Mandala with the Five Dhyani Buddhas

Mulbekh ⑨

Kargil district. 190 km (118 miles) NW of Leh. 🚌 ⓘ *Kargil Tourist Office, (01985) 32 721.*

APRETTY VILLAGE in the Kargil district, Mulbekh, spread over the broad green valley of the Wakha river, is the point at which the proselytizing tide of Islam, spreading towards central Ladakh, lost its impetus. As a consequence, Mulbekh has a mixed population of Buddhists and Muslims, and supports a mosque as well as a monastery, perched on a crag above the village. Its main attraction, however, is a giant engraving of Maitreya, the Future Buddha, on a huge free-standing rock by the roadside. It is believed to date back to the 8th century.

The 8-m (26-ft) high Maitreya Buddha at Mulbekh

Kargil ⑩

Kargil district. 230 km (143 miles) NW of Leh and NE of Srinagar. 🚌 ⓘ *Kargil Tourist Office, (01985) 32 721.* 🎭 *Muharram (Mar/Apr), Ladakh Festival (Sep).* **Travel permits** *are required for the Dha-Hanu region, available at Leh (see p142).*

FOR TRAVELLERS between Leh and Srinagar, Kargil town is a good place to stop for the night. The second largest urban centre in Ladakh, Kargil was an important trading centre before the Partition of India, when the road to Skardu in Baltistan (Pakistan) was still open. The majority of Kargil's population are Shia

View of the Nun-kun massif from Suru Valley

Muslims, an Islamic sect that regards Muhammad's cousin Ali and his successors as the true imams.

Kargil apricots are famous, and its hillside orchards are an enchanting sight in May when the trees are in bloom, and in July when the fruit is ripe. The town is also the base for expeditions to the Suru Valley, Zanskar and Nun-kun. Kargil suffered shelling during the conflict between India and Pakistan in 1999, so check the situation before a visit there.

Suru Valley ⑪

Kargil district. 19 km (12 miles) S of Kargil. 🚌 *to Sankhu.*

THE SURU VALLEY starts from Kargil and runs 100 km (62 miles) to the southeast. One of Ladakh's loveliest and most fertile regions, it boasts rolling alpine pastures, mud-walled villages and views of majestic snowcapped peaks. Abundant water from melting snows gives the Suru Valley rich harvests of barley and plantations of willow and poplar, especially around **Sankhu** village. Close to Sankhu are the ruins of ancient forts, together with rock engravings of Maitreya and Avalokitesvara from the valley's pre-Islamic past. The upper valley is dominated by the peaks, ridges and glaciers of the Nun-kun massif which is 7,135 m (23,409 ft) high. Expeditions to the mountain take off from the picturesque village of **Panikhar**, whose pastures are covered with alpine flowers in June and July.

Prehistoric rock paintings in the Suru Valley

THE DARDS

A conspicuous sight in the bazaars of Kargil and Leh are the Dards, in their colourful caps adorned with flowers. Their aquiline features and fair complexions set them apart from other Ladakhis, as do their customs and traditions. There are several theories about the origins of this small community – among others, that they are the descendants of Alexander the Great's soldiers. Anthropological research, however, indicates that their ancestors migrated from Gilgit in Pakistan before it came under the influence of Islam. There are Dard villages at Dha-Hanu, east of Kargil on the Indus, close to where the river leaves Ladakh for Baltistan (Pakistan).

A Dard in his distinctive cap

A view of the dramatically-situated Phugtal Monastery *(see p151)* in Zanskar ▷

Rangdum ⑫

Kargil district. 110 km (68 miles) SE of Kargil. 🚌 ⓘ *Kargil Tourist Office, (01985) 32 721.*

THE VILLAGE of Rangdum serves as a night halt between Kargil (*see p147*) and Zanskar. Though geographically part of the Suru Valley, its largely Buddhist population and its monastery orient it culturally towards Zanskar. Situated on a wide flat plateau at 3,800 m (12,467 ft), crisscrossed by water courses, and framed by snow peaks and hills of curiously striated rock, Rangdum has a wild, desolate beauty. The fortress-like 18th-century **Gelugpa Monastery** is built on a hillock, and a small temple in the complex has a fine wall painting of a battle-scene, with warriors sporting Mongolian-looking armour and battledress.

Zanskar ⑬

Kargil district. 230 km (143 miles) SE from Kargil to Padum. 🚌 *to Padum.* ⓘ *Padum Tourist Office, (01983) 54 017.* 🎭 *Karsha Monastery Festival (Jul/Aug).*

THERE IS A certain mystique about Zanskar. This is no doubt due to its remoteness and altitude, between 3,350 m (10,991 ft) and 4,400 m (14,436 ft), and the fact that the region is difficult to access – the only motorable road into the valley is usually open from around early June to mid-October. But Zanskar's reputation as a Shangri-la also derives from the grandeur of its landscapes, the simplicity of life in its villages, and the serene ambience in its *gompas*, often built around ancient cliff-top meditation caves.

Zanskar contains the valleys of two rivers, the Stod and the Lungnak which, flowing towards each other along the northern flank of the Greater Himalayas, join to become the Zanskar river. This continues north through a gorge in the Zanskar Range, to join the Indus.

The western arm of Zanskar, the Stod Valley, and its central plain are fertile and well-watered – villages form green pockets and the virtual absence of trees contributes to an extraordinary sense of light and space. The inhabitants of this region are mostly agricultural farmers, growing barley, wheat and peas in the lower villages, and raising livestock – yaks, sheep and *dzos* (a hybrid between cows and yaks) – in the higher villages. In winter, many of these farmers take the only route out of the area, trekking for six gruelling days across the frozen Zanskar river, to sell their highly prized yak butter in Leh. In contrast

The Zanskar river, running through a gorge

Perak, the traditional female headdress

to the fertile western arm and central plain, the eastern arm of Zanskar – the Lungnak Valley – is a forbidding and stony gorge, with few villages to be found in the vicinity.

The main gateway to Zanskar is the **Pensi-la** (4,400 m/14,436 ft), about 130 km (81 miles) southeast of Kargil. There are spectacular views from the top of this pass, especially of the impressive **Drang-drung Glacier**, which is the origin of the Stod river. The road then continues down to **Padum**, 230 km (143 miles) southeast of Kargil, at an altitude of 3,500 m (11,483 ft). Padum is Zanskar's main village and administrative headquarters. This is the only place in the region with basic facilities including accommodation, transport and a few rudimentary shops. It is also the starting point for a number of treks in the region (*see pp152–3*). Padum itself has few sites of interest, except for a rock engraving of the Five Dhyani Buddhas (*see p146*) in the centre of the village. A new mosque serves Padum's small community of Muslims. There are a number of interesting sites to explore in the vicinity. Within easy reach

Stucco decoration and images in bas-relief at Sani Gompa, Zanskar

on foot, is the village of **Pipiting**, which has a temple and *chorten* on top of a mound of glacial debris, and a pavilion which was specially constructed for the Dalai Lama's prayer assemblies.

A short distance away is **Sani**, 8 km (5 miles) northwest of Padum, one of the oldest religious sites in the Western Himalayas. Within the monastery walls stands the Kanika Chorten, its name possibly linking it to the Kushana ruler Kanishka *(see p43)*, whose empire stretched from Afghanistan to Varanasi in the 1st and 2nd centuries AD. The monastery itself is said to have been founded by Padmasambhava *(see p120)* in the 8th century, and its main temple has some fine murals. Even more interesting is another small temple in the complex, which has unique, beautifully painted stucco bas-relief decorations, and niches in the walls for images. Sani is surrounded by a stand of poplars, conspicuous in this otherwise treeless landscape.

Visible from Padum, the buildings of the Gelugpa monastery of **Karsha**, 10 km (6 miles) northeast of Padum, seem to spill down the mountainside west of the main valley, until they merge with the houses and fields of the village. This site includes ancient rock engravings, and the murals in its Avalokitesvara temple, just outside the main complex, seem to put it in the same period as Alchi *(see pp144–6)*. Tradition, however,

Fertile fields of barley and wheat in the Stod Valley in Zanskar

attributes the monastery's foundation to the ubiquitous Padmasambhava. Karsha has a large community of resident monks, and holds its colourful annual festival between July and August.

Stongde, on the opposite side of the valley, 12 km (7 miles) from Padum, is perched on a ridge, high above the mosaic of the village's fields. Believed to have been founded in the 11th century, it houses no fewer than seven well-maintained temples, some of them containing exquisite murals.

The villages of Sani, Karsha and Stongde are connected by motor transport, though the monasteries in the **Lungnak Valley** are less accessible. The narrow footpath leading up the valley winds along unstable scree slopes high above the river, and the walk is strenuous. It takes a sharp

Mandala, Bardhan
Monastery

climb on foot or on horseback to reach **Bardhan** and **Phugtal** monasteries.

Bardhan, 9 km (6 miles) southeast of Padum, is spectacularly located atop a crag jutting out from the mountain and rising some 100 m (328 ft) sheer out of the river. It has fine wall paintings dating back to the time of the monastery's foundation in the early 17th century. Of all Ladakh's many monasteries however, none, not even Bardhan or Lamayuru, can rival Phugtal, 60 km (37 miles) southeast of Padum, for the grandeur and drama of its location. Its main temples are constructed inside a huge cave on the mountainside above the Tsarap river, at a point where the drop to the water is almost sheer. Yet below the temples the monks' dwellings have somehow been built on or into the cliff-face, and the whole improbable complex is linked by a crazy system of ladders and walkways. There is no record of Phugtal monastery's foundation, but the style of its paintings, some of them quite striking, link it with the Tabo monastery in Spiti *(see p131)* and the traditions established by the Tibetan saint Rinchen Zangpo *(see p119)* in the 11th century. Its monks belong to the Gelugpa order.

🏛 **Sani, Karsha, Stongde, Bardhan and Phugtal Monasteries**
⭘ *daily.* 📷

Phugtal Monastery, built into a sheer cliff-face

Trekking in Ladakh and Zanskar

Black-necked crane

TREKKING IN THE ARID, extremely cold trans-Himalayan desert of Ladakh and Zanskar, very often at altitudes that exceed 5,000 m (16,404 ft), can be a uniquely exhilarating experience. The terrain, as starkly beautiful as any highland setting in the world, has a number of trails, many of which trace ancient trading routes to Central Asia. They lead past spectacularly located monasteries, remote passes, sometimes staggeringly high, deep river gorges and lush meadows scattered with *mani* walls and *chortens*. The best time to trek is between June and September, when the land is not snowbound and the terraced fields are being harvested.

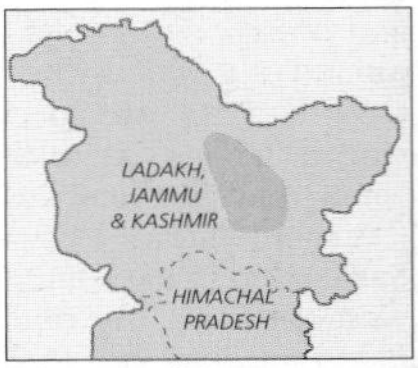

LOCATOR MAP

☐ Area shown below

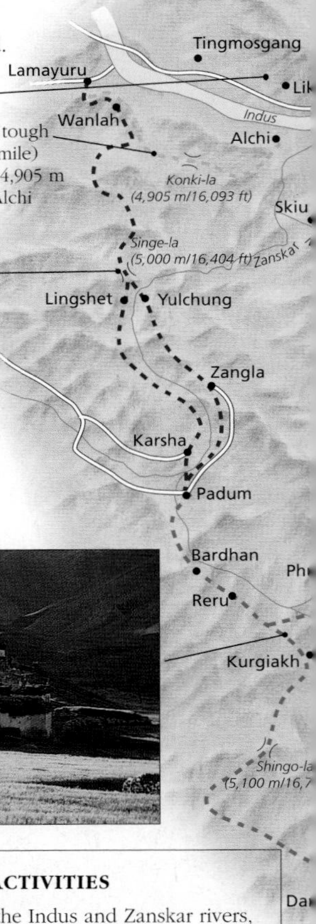

Likir to Tingmosgang is an easy, two-day, 22-km (14-mile) path, past a number of villages at 4,000 m (13,123 ft).

From Lamayuru, a tough five-day, 65-km (40-mile) trek, via Konki-la at 4,905 m (16,093 ft), ends at Alchi (*see pp144–5*).

Tingmosgang • Li
Lamayuru • Wanlah • Indus
Alchi •
Konki-la (4,905 m/16,093 ft)
Skiu
Singe-la (5,000 m/16,404 ft) Zanskar

Padum to Lamayuru

This 160-km (99-mile) path follows the Zanskar river via Karsha, past the impressive Lingshet Monastery and Singe-la ("Lion Pass"), ending at Lamayuru. A slightly easier route past Zangla, joins the main trail at Yelchang village.
Duration: 10 days
Altitude: 5,000 m (16,404 ft)
Level of difficulty: tough

Lingshet • Yulchung
Zangla
Karsha •
Padum

Padum to Darcha

The 115-km (71-mile) path goes from Zanskar into Himachal Pradesh, along the beautiful Tsarap river, past Phugtal Monastery and Kurgiakh, Zanskar's highest village at 4,100 m (13,451 ft).
Duration: 10 days
Altitude: 5,100 m (16,732 ft)
Level of difficulty: moderate

Bardhan •
Ph
Reru •
Kurgiakh •
Shingo-la (5,100 m/16,7

OTHER OUTDOOR ACTIVITIES

Rafting down the Indus river on rubber dinghies, a popular sport

White-water rafting on the Indus and Zanskar rivers, is a popular activity from July to mid-September. There are various options to consider on the Indus river, from calm "float trips" between Hemis and Choglamsar, to longer stints between Spituk and Alchi. **Jeep safaris** to the lakes of Tso Kar and Tso Moriri and back, take three days, with tents pitched near Karzok village. The region's rich wildlife include bar-headed geese, black-necked cranes and the *kiang* (Tibetan wild ass).

Spituk to Hemis

Ladakh's most popular trek, this 105-km (65-mile) path runs along the Indus river through Markha Valley, past Skiu village and the high pass of Kongmaru, and ends at Hemis Monastery (see p140).

Duration: *8 days*
Altitude: *5,274 m (17,303 ft)*
Level of difficulty: *easy*

Rafting trips on the Indus are organized by local agencies.

Leh
Choglamsar
Spituk
k Kangri
m/20,112 ft)
Hemis
Kongmaru-la
274 m/17,303 ft)
aling *Kang Yaze*
(6,400 m/20,997 ft) Upshi
Rumtse
Indus
Tanglang-la
(5,328 m/17,480 ft)
Debring
Tso-Kar
Puga
rap
Karzok *Tso Moriri*
Baralacha-la
(4,892 m/16,050 ft)

Leh to Tso Moriri is a 230-km (143-mile), ten-hour journey by jeep.

0 km		20
0 miles		20

Tso Kar or "White Lake", lying northwest of Tso Moriri

PRACTICAL TIPS

Be prepared: *Most of the walking is hard, and it is imperative to be well acclimatized to the altitude, as even the bottoms of river gorges are 3,000 m (9,843 ft) above sea level. For tips on altitude sickness, see p767. Guides and ponies are essential for all treks in the region. Maps are insufficient, so don't wander off on your own as it could prove fatal. For more details on trekking see p751.*
On the trek: *Drink plenty of water. Do not litter; carry all rubbish back with you. Plastics can be taken to the Ecology Centre (01982) 53 221 in Leh. Carry cooking fuel. Never burn wood, which is a scarce resource.*
Permits: *Permits are required for the Nubra Valley, Pang-gong Tso, Tso Moriri and the Dha-Hanu region (see p142). For general details on permits see p758.*
Equipment, jeep hire and operators: *The Traveller Shop in Leh, (01982) 52 248 hires out trekking gear. Rafting agencies include Indus Himalayan Explorers (01982) 52 735 and Rimo Expeditions (01982) 53 348. Jeeps are expensive and can be hired from Leh for trips to Nubra (see p143) and the lakes. Check the price list at the taxi stand. For more details see p755.*

KEY

- - Spituk to Hemis

- - Likir to Tingmosgang

- - Lamayuru to Alchi

▬ ▬ Padum to Lamayuru

- - Padum to Darcha

▬▬▬ Leh to Tso Moriri

══ Minor road

△ Peak

◡ Pass

Srinagar's 14th-century Shah Hamadan Mosque, made entirely of wood

Jammu ⑭

Jammu district. 500 km (311 miles) NW of Delhi. 🏘 378,400. ✈ 8 km (5 miles) SW of city centre. 🚐 🚍 ℹ J&K Tourism, Vir Marg, (0191) 54 8172. 📅 Lohri (13 Jan), Jammu Festival (Apr), Navratra (Sep/Oct).

THE WINTER CAPITAL of Jammu and Kashmir state, Jammu is located on a bluff of the Shivalik Range, overlooking the northern plains. The main site of interest is the **Amar Mahal**, once the residence of the maharajas, and today a museum with artifacts relating to the region's culture and history. Jammu is also the base for the pilgrimage to the cave shrine of the goddess **Vaishno Devi** in the Trikuta mountains, 50 km (31 miles) away. The shrine attracts four million Hindus every year.

🏛 **Amar Mahal Museum**
Off Srinagar Rd. ◯ Tue–Sun. 🎫

Srinagar ⑮

Srinagar district. 700 km (435 miles) NW of Delhi. 🏘 895,000. ✈ 8 km (5 miles) S of city centre. 🚍 ℹ J&K Tourism, (0194) 45 2690. 📅 Milad-ul-Nabi (May).

SRINAGAR, the summer capital of Jammu and Kashmir, is a city of lakes and waterways, gardens and picturesque wooden architecture. The old quarters of the city sprawl over both sides of the Jhelum river, crossed by seven bridges. Although the bridges have their own names (such as Amira Kadal and Zaina Kadal), they are also known by their numbers; an Eighth Bridge, built more recently (in the 20th century) above First Bridge, is known with typical Kashmiri wit as Zero Bridge. This serves the modern part of the city, built in the late 19th century. At the city's edge are the idyllic **Dal** and **Nagin Lakes**, linked by a network of backwaters. Srinagar's mosques and shrines are among the city's most attractive features. Typically, these are built of wood intricately carved in geometric patterns, and instead of a dome they are surmounted by a pagoda-like steeple. The most striking examples are the **Mosque of Shah Hamadan** in the old city, and the **Shah Makhdum Sahib Shrine** on the slopes of Hari Parbat hill. Two conventional stone mosques, the **Patthar Mosque** and the

Chinar leaves in autumn colours

Mosque of Akhund Mulla Shah, both beautifully proportioned structures, date from the 17th century. In an altogether different style is the **Hazratbal Mosque**, with its dazzling white dome and single slender minaret. Rebuilt in the Saracenic style after a fire in the 1960s, it contains Kashmir's most sacred relic, a hair from the beard of the Prophet Muhammad.

The Mughal emperors delighted in Kashmir's beauty and further enhanced it by introducing the stately *chinar* tree (*Platanous orientalis*) to the Kashmir Valley. They also created terraced hillside gardens designed around fountains and watercourses, which were formed by channeling water from natural springs or streams. Of the 777 Mughal gardens that reportedly once graced the Kashmir Valley, not many survive. There are three, however, within easy reach of Srinagar, on the eastern shore of the Dal Lake – **Chashmashahi**, **Nishat** and **Shalimar Gardens**. Above

The impressive ruins of the 8th-century Sun Temple at Martand

A house in Gulmarg, one of India's few ski resorts

the pretty Chashmashahi Garden, and rising tier upon tier on the mountainside, are the ruins of a 17th-century religious college. Built by a Mughal prince for his teacher, it is somewhat incongruously known as **Pari Mahal** or "Palace of the Fairies". From this vantage point, there are heart-stopping views of Dal Lake and the snowy ridge of the Pir Panjal Range.

ENVIRONS: Vestiges of Kashmir's pre-Islamic past can be seen in the ruins of magnificent Hindu temples at **Avantipora**, 28 km (17 miles) southeast of Srinagar, and **Martand**, 60 km (37 miles) southeast of Srinagar. The Sun Temple at Martand is believed to date from the 8th century AD, while the two Avantipora temples are probably from the 9th century AD. Built with great limestone blocks fitted together without mortar, these temples bear witness to the astonishing degree of technical expertise that prevailed in the early medieval period.

🌿 **Chashmashahi Garden**
⬜ daily. 🚫
🌿 **Nishat and Shalimar Gardens**
⬜ daily.

Gulmarg ⑯

Srinagar district. 58 km (36 miles) W of Srinagar. 🚌 ℹ️ *J&K Tourism, Gulmarg Tourist Office, (01953) 54 487.*

GULMARG, or the "Meadow of Flowers", at an altitude of 2,730 m (8,950 ft), was developed by the British around a meadow on the northern flank of the Pir Panjal Range. The central bowl has been laid out as a golf course, one of the highest in the world. Around it are fairy-tale cottages with pine forests behind them. Gulmarg, together with **Khilanmarg**, some 300 m (984 ft) higher up in the mountains, is among India's few ski resorts. Its facilities, catering to all levels of proficiency, also include beginner courses.

Pahalgam ⑰

Srinagar district. 96 km (60 miles) E of Srinagar. 🚌 ℹ️ *J&K Tourism, Pahalgam Tourist Office, (01936) 3224.*

IN THE VALLEY of the Lidder river, Pahalgam is on the southern slope of the Great Himalayas. It is the base for several treks to Kishtwar and the Suru Valley *(see p147)*, and for the pilgrimage to the holy cave of **Amarnath**, the destination of several thousand Hindu pilgrims, every August.

Pahalgam, dotted with mustard fields, also offers trout fishing, golf and short expeditions into the nearby mountains. The road from Srinagar to Pahalgam passes by **Pampore**, famous for its fields of saffron *(Crocus sativa)*, which has been cultivated in Kashmir since the 10th century. The saffron flower blooms in late autumn.

Mustard fields surrounding a farmhouse in Pahalgam

HOUSEBOATS AND SHIKARAS

In the 19th century, some of Srinagar's boat-dwelling community started building luxury versions of their own homes to cater to visitors. These houseboats, which remain moored in one place, have become the favoured accommodation for most visitors. Those in the deluxe

class are astonishingly elaborate, their plush living rooms and bedrooms a showcase for the celebrated Kashmiri handicrafts – exquisite woodcarving, embroidery, carpets and papier mâché. Mobility between houseboat and shore is ensured by a *shikara*, a skiff propelled by a boatman with a heart-shaped paddle. Whether luxuriating in the comfort of a houseboat, or accommodated more prosaically in a hotel on dry land, there can be no more idyllic way to spend a day in Srinagar than reclining on the cushions of a *shikara* in the shade of its awning, cruising the city's lakes and backwaters.

Houseboats and *shikaras* on Dal Lake

CENTRAL
INDIA

Introducing Central India

SOME OF INDIA'S most visited destinations are in this vast and varied region, which covers the flat Gangetic Plains, several Himalayan ranges and the verdant forests of the Central Indian heartland. These include the Taj Mahal at Agra, the holy city of Varanasi, the exquisitely sculpted temples of Khajuraho, and the great Buddhist sites of Sanchi and Bodh Gaya. Other attractions in Central India include the game sanctuaries of Kanha and Corbett, the medieval forts and palaces of Gwalior and Orchha, and the hill stations of Mussoorie, Nainital and Ranikhet, which are the base for many treks.

SEE ALSO

- *Where to Stay* pp695–8
- *Where to Eat* pp724–8

Luxuriant forested hills of *chir* pine and alpine meadows in Uttaranchal

0 km   80

0 miles   80

A view of the cenotaphs of the Orchha rulers, lying along the Betwa river

KEY

▬	National highway
▬	Major road
▬	River
- -	State border

◁ The glowing pastoral landscape of rural Kumaon near Mukteshwar (*see p190*), in the Western Himalayas

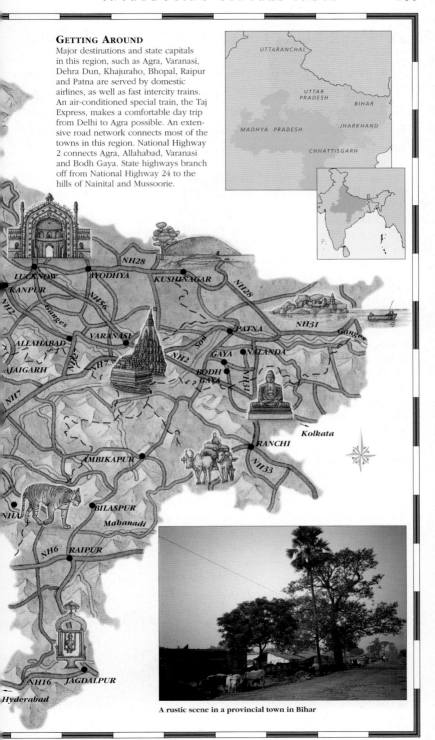

GETTING AROUND

Major destinations and state capitals in this region, such as Agra, Varanasi, Dehra Dun, Khajuraho, Bhopal, Raipur and Patna are served by domestic airlines, as well as fast intercity trains. An air-conditioned special train, the Taj Express, makes a comfortable day trip from Delhi to Agra possible. An extensive road network connects most of the towns in this region. National Highway 2 connects Agra, Allahabad, Varanasi and Bodh Gaya. State highways branch off from National Highway 24 to the hills of Nainital and Mussoorie.

A rustic scene in a provincial town in Bihar

A PORTRAIT OF CENTRAL INDIA

THREE OF INDIA'S LARGEST STATES – *Uttar Pradesh, Bihar and Madhya Pradesh – lie in Central India. This vast and densely populated region is the country's Hindi-speaking belt (often called the "cow belt"), an area remarkable as much for its rich historical past and religious and cultural diversity as for its mineral wealth.*

The River Ganges, which flows through Uttar Pradesh (UP) and Bihar, has shaped much of the history and culture of both states. On its fertile banks, civilizations, cities and empires have grown and flourished, from 1500 BC onwards *(see p41).*

Detail from the great stupa at Sanchi

Today, the river continues to play a crucial role in the economy, culture, religion as well as imagination of the millions of people who live in the surrounding Gangetic Plains.

UP is both the spiritual heartland of Hinduism and the cultural heartland of Indian Islam – the former symbolized by Varanasi, the holiest of Indian cities *(see pp202–208)*, and the latter by the Taj Mahal, the country's greatest Islamic monument *(see pp172–5)*. With a population of 148 million, UP elects more members to the Indian parliament than any other state, and therefore plays a dominant role in national politics. Six Indian prime ministers have been from here,

including Pandit Jawaharlal Nehru, his daughter Indira Gandhi and grandson Rajiv Gandhi and, more recently, Atal Behari Vajpayee. The tides of contemporary politics often hinge on the strength of caste and religious sentiments. One tragic result of this was the demolition of a 15th-century mosque in the town of Ayodhya in 1992, by Hindu religious extremists, because they claimed it stood at the spot where Lord Rama *(see p27)* was born. The incident led to widespread Hindu-Muslim riots and the issue continues to simmer.

In November 2000, several new states were created. In UP, the northernmost section, covering the Kumaon and Garhwal hills, became the new state of Uttaranchal. This is an area of great natural beauty, with picturesque hill stations, trekking trails, and ancient Hindu pilgrimage centres, in the shadow of towering Himalayan peaks.

The Chhota Imambara complex at Lucknow, capital of Uttar Pradesh

Pilgrims on the banks of the Ganges in Bihar

Bihar, like UP, is a densely populated state, and its political agenda too has in recent years been dominated by caste-based issues, at the expense of social and economic development. As a result, rural poverty is still widespread and the literacy rate remains abysmally low, at around 40 per cent. Ironically, this was a state that once had one of the ancient world's greatest universities, at Nalanda *(see pp218–9)*, and was the seat of two of India's greatest empires, the Maurya and Gupta empires *(see pp42–3)*. Bihar also occupies an important place in the history of Indian civilization, as the birthplace of Buddhism – for it was here, at Bodh Gaya *(see p222)*, that the Buddha gained enlightenment. This historic legacy can be seen in the state's famous Buddhist sites. Present-day Bihar has an earthy vitality, which can be experienced at the huge annual cattle fair at Sonepur *(see p216)*, where a prime attraction is the unique elephant bazaar.

The new state of Jharkhand, in what was southern Bihar, came into being in November 2000. An area of great natural beauty, Jharkhand comprises a forested plateau, home to a large population of tribal people with distinctive cultures, who now dominate the political and economic life of their nascent state. Jharkhand is blessed with great mineral wealth, and its rich deposits of coal and iron, in particular, ensure its future prosperity.

Madhya Pradesh (MP) provides a sharp contrast to the flat, crowded plains of UP and Bihar, with its varied terrain and relatively sparse population. The countryside here is an enchanting mosaic of cotton fields, craggy ravines, rolling hills, and vast tracts of forest and grassland, which are home to at least half of India's tiger population. A tragic industrial disaster in the state capital, Bhopal, in 1984 *(see p240)* has made the people of this state especially active in environmental issues, and many of them have been campaigning against a large dam on the Narmada river *(see p251)*. MP still gets relatively few visitors, yet few other states can rival its range of attractions, which include the World Heritage monuments at Sanchi *(see pp244–5)* and Khajuraho *(see pp236–8)*, and some of India's finest wildlife sanctuaries.

At the same time as Jharkhand and Uttaranchal, Chhatisgarh came into being. This southeastern part of Madhya Pradesh is a thickly forested area, populated by different tribal communities, engaged in agriculture and a variety of beautiful crafts *(see p253)*. Facilities are still being developed to welcome visitors to this fascinating part of the country.

A poster depicting Varanasi as the home of Shiva

The River Ganges

RISING IN an ice cave, 4,140 m (13,583 ft) high in the Himalayas, the Ganges flows for 2,525 km (1,569 miles) through the mountains of Uttaranchal, and the vast plains of Uttar Pradesh, Bihar and Bengal, before entering the sea in the Bay of Bengal. Through the ages, great civilizations have flourished on its banks, which are today lined with teeming cities, fertile paddy fields and innumerable temples and ghats. For, above all, the Ganges is India's main spiritual and religious artery, sacred to millions of Hindus who believe that to bathe in its waters is to be absolved of all sins, and to be cremated on its banks and have one's ashes immersed in its waters ensures salvation of the soul.

Goddess Ganga

Gaumukh *("Cow's Mouth") at the mouth of the Gangotri Glacier, is the source of the Ganges. Emerging as an icy torrent, the river is called the Bhagirathi here.*

Rishikesh *(see p184)* has famous ashrams offering yoga and meditation courses where studies in Hinduism are pursued.

Votive offering floated in the river

Devprayag (see p187), *set amidst dramatic mountain gorges, is an important pilgrimage town where the rivers Bhagirathi and Alaknanda meet to become the Ganges.*

UTTAR PRADESH

Kanpur

KEY

 International border

 State border

Allahabad

Haridwar*, the "Gateway to the Gods" (see p184), is where the Ganges finally descends from the Himalayas and begins its long journey through the plains that constitute India's heartland. Haridwar teems with temples, holy men and pilgrims, especially around its main ghat, Har-ki-Pauri, sanctified by the footprint of Lord Vishnu. It is one of the four sites where the mammoth Kumbh Mela is held every 12 years (see p211).*

Allahabad (see p210) *marks the confluence of three holy rivers, the Ganges, the Yamuna, and the mythical Saraswati. The Kumbh Mela held here in 2001 attracted some 30 million pilgrims.*

The Myth of the Ganges
holds that the celestial River Ganga was brought to earth by sage Bhagiratha so that he could sprinkle her holy water on the ashes of his ancestors, who were struck down by Lord Vishnu for their wickedness. The river water would ensure salvation for their souls. When the Ganga descended, Lord Shiva broke her enormous force by winding her through his hair, to save the earth from being destroyed in a deluge. This myth is often depicted in paintings and sculptures.

Varanasi (see pp202–208) *is regarded by Hindus as the holiest spot on this holiest of rivers. Around 90 ghats line the river front, where the living come to be purified by the waters of the Ganges, and the dead are brought to attain* moksha *(release from the endless cycle of death and rebirth).*

Fertile fields, *enriched by alluvial soil, can be seen all along the Indo-Gangetic Plains. These fields of wheat and mustard are in Bihar.*

Kanwarias *are devotees of Shiva who make an arduous annual journey every August, to the Ganges on foot, carrying back the river's sacred water in brightly decorated pots, to their temples at home.*

Ghaghara

Gandak

Gandak

Patna

Munger

Barges *laden with jute fibre are a common sight around the Gangetic Delta in Bengal.*

Varanasi

Son

BIHAR

Gaur

Patna *(see pp214–5) is always busy with river traffic as the Ganges is wide and easily navigable here.*

BANGLADESH

Nabadwip

The otter, *about 70-cm (28-in) long, has a brown waterproof coat, webbed paws and stiff whiskers. This playful creature can often be seen gambolling on the banks of the river.*

WEST BENGAL

Hooghly

Kolkata

Ganga Sagar Mela *is a colourful festival (see p295), held in January at Sagar Island, close to where the river enters the sea.*

Sagar Island

Ganges Delta

Bay of Bengal

Regional Food: Central India

THE VAST AND FERTILE Gangetic Plains cover much of Uttar Pradesh and Bihar, with Madhya Pradesh to their south forming India's geographic centre. The three states in this Hindi-speaking region grow much of India's three staple foods – rice, lentils and wheat – as well as superb mangoes, melons and litchis. There have been two major influences on the food of Central India – the sophisticated vegetarian cuisine of the holy city of Varanasi, and Lucknow's refined meat dishes and *biryanis*, developed in the royal kitchens of the hedonistic nawabs of Avadh.

Fresh fruit in this region includes melon, mango and litchi in summer, and papaya, guava and grapes in winter.

THE VEGETARIAN MEAL

The rich variety of vegetables eaten in Central India include the bitter gourd *(karela)*, believed to be a blood cleanser, tender okra *(bhindi)* which soothes the stomach, and crisp lotus roots *(kamal kakri)*. Lentil dumplings *(badi)* add a spicy flavour to vegetables.

Bhindi (okra)

Kamal kakri (lotus root)

Badi sabzi (vegetables with lentil dumplings)

Karela (bitter gourd)

Paneer bhurji (sautéed cottage cheese)

Kotoo roti

Sabudana kheer (sago pudding)

Aloo sabzi (curried potato)

The Navaratris, *a nine-day fasting period for Hindus, demands a special diet of milk-based foods, and* kotoo roti *(water chestnut flour bread).*

Mango pickle

Chilli pickle

Fruit *chaat*

Sprouted lentils

Chaat *is a spicy snack of vegetables, fruit, or sprouted lentils, seasoned with pepper, ginger and tamarind. It is a popular street food.*

Badam halwa

Shahi tukra

Savouries *made of wheat or gram flour, such as kachoris (stuffed fried bread), pakoras (vegetable fritters), and triangular samosas (turnovers filled with potato), are typical snacks offered to visitors.*

Malpua

Jalebi

Sweets *include rich* badam *(almond) halwa, a crunchy bread pudding called* shahi tukra *("emperor's morsel"),* jalebi *with its crisp golden spirals, and* malpua, *a syrup-soaked pancake.*

NAWABI CUISINE

The cuisine of the Muslim aristocracy of Patna, Lucknow and Bhopal is renowned for its tender meats and its aromatic blend of spices such as saffron, mace and nutmeg. Dishes slowly simmered overnight are often eaten to break the Ramzan fast at dawn.

Galauti kebab

Shami kebab

Kakori kebab

Nihari, *a breakfast stew of lamb shanks, is slow-cooked overnight and eaten with* rumali roti.

Rampur mutton *has tender pieces of meat in a rich yet mild gravy of cream and almonds.*

The Kebab Platter *can consist of* kakori *kebab, a melt-in-the-mouth lamb kebab, which was devised by cooks from Kakori near Lucknow for a toothless* nawab. Galauti *and* shami *kebabs are other Lucknow specialities.*

Roti, **poori**, **paratha** *are unleavened wheat breads, served with main dishes. They help scoop the food into the mouth.*

Chicken korma *is an elegant curry, with subtle flavours. It is simmered in yoghurt with saffron and cardamom.*

DUM PUKHT FOOD

The delectable *dum pukht* (dough-sealed) cuisine was invented in the kitchens of Lucknow's Nawab Asaf-ud-Daulah. During a famine, he directed his cooks to put rice, meat and spices into a gigantic cooking pot, seal it with dough and cook it slowly overnight. This *biryani* would then be fed to the poor every morning.

Dum pukht biryani

Raita (whipped yoghurt)

DALS

An extraordinary variety of *dals* (lentils) – black and white *urad*, red and brown *masur*, green and yellow *mung*, and deep yellow *arhar* – form part of the daily diet of this region. *Dals* are a rich source of protein.

SHERBETS

Made from thinned yoghurt *(lassi)*, fruits and herbs, these help combat the scorching summer, and ward off sunstroke and indigestion.

Kesar lassi (saffron-flavoured drink)

Khus sharbat (vetiver sherbet)

Nimbu pani (fresh lemonade)

Roob Afza (herbal syrup)

Betel leaves

Paan *or betel leaf with nut* (supari), *silver-coated cloves and cardamoms, are digestives and mouth fresheners, eaten after a heavy meal.*

UTTAR PRADESH & UTTARANCHAL

STRETCHING from the Himalayas to the Indo-Gangetic Plains, Uttar Pradesh (UP) and Uttaranchal cover a vast area of 294,000 sq km (113,514 sq miles), with a population of almost 175 million. Hindi is the main language. Both states offer a wide variety of landscapes and historic monuments. In UP's plains are the famous Taj Mahal and other great Islamic monuments, as well as the holy Hindu city of Varanasi and the Buddhist stupas of Sarnath. The mammoth Kumbh Mela takes place every 12 years at Allahabad as well as Haridwar. In November 2000, the hill areas of Uttar Pradesh became the separate state of Uttaranchal. Its numerous attractions include beautiful trekking trails, the picturesque hill stations of Mussoorie and Nainital, river rafting tours and yoga ashrams around Rishikesh, and Corbett National Park, famous for its tigers.

SIGHTS AT A GLANCE

Towns & Cities
Agra **1**
Aligarh **20**
Allahabad **28**
Dehra Dun **9**
Jaunpur **25**
Jhansi **21**
Kanpur **22**
Lucknow **23**
Rampur **19**

Hill Stations & Areas of Natural Beauty
Almora **13**
Kausani **16**
Lansdowne **15**
Mussoorie **10**
Nainital **12**

Ranikhet **14**
The Garhwal Hills **11**

Historic Sites
Ayodhya **24**
Fatehpur Sikri **5**
Kalinjar Fort **30**
Sarnath **27**
Sikandra **2**

Temple Towns & Holy Places
Brindavan **4**
Chitrakoot **29**

Haridwar **6**
Mathura **3**
Rishikesh **7**
Varanasi **26**

National Parks
Corbett National Park **17**
Dudhwa National Park **18**

Tours
River Tour along the Ganges **8**

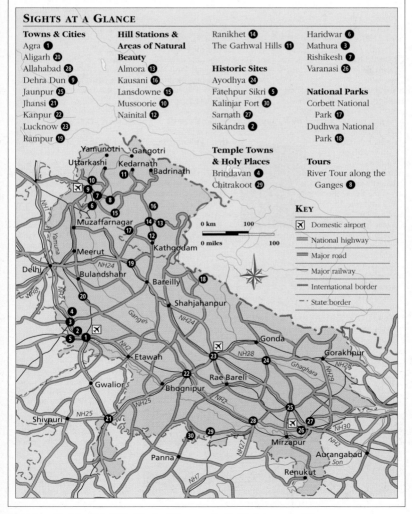

KEY

✈	Domestic airport
	National highway
	Major road
	Major railway
	International border
	State border

0 km   100
0 miles   100

◁ **Fatehpur Sikri's Jami Masjid, built in the 16th century by the Mughal emperor Akbar**

Agra **❶**

A *pietra dura* motif

AGRA WAS THE SEAT of the imperial Mughal court during the 16th and 17th centuries, before the capital was shifted to Delhi. The city, strategically located on the banks of the Yamuna and along the Grand Trunk Road, flourished under the patronage of the emperors Akbar, Jahangir and Shah Jahan, attracting artisans from Persia and Central Asia, and also from other parts of India, who built luxurious forts, palaces, gardens and mausoleums. Of these, the Taj Mahal, the Agra Fort and Akbar's abandoned capital of Fatehpur Sikri have been declared World Heritage Sites by UNESCO. With the decline of the Mughals, Agra was captured by the Jats, the Marathas, and finally by the British, early in the 19th century.

St John's College, designed by Sir Samuel Swinton Jacob

🏛 Agra Fort
See pp170–71.

🌙 Jami Masjid
◻ *daily.* ● *to non-Muslims during prayer times.*

A magnificently proportioned building in the heart of the historic town, the "Friday Mosque" was sponsored by Shah Jahan's favourite daughter, Jahanara Begum, who also commissioned a number of other buildings and gardens, including the canal that once ran down Chandni Chowk *(see pp84–5)* in Delhi. Built in 1648, the mosque's sandstone and marble domes with their distinctive zigzag chevron pattern dominate this section of the town. The eastern courtyard wing was demolished by the British in 1857 *(see p53).* Of interest are the tank with its

Detail of minaret, Jami Masjid

shahi chirag (royal stove) for heating water within the courtyard, and the separate prayer chamber for ladies.

The area around Jami Masjid was once a vibrant meeting place, famous for its kebab houses and lively bazaars. A stroll or rickshaw ride through the narrow alleys can be a rewarding experience, offering glimpses of an older and very different way of life, reminiscent of Mughal Agra. This is also the city's crafts and trade centre where a vast array of products such as jewellery, *zari* embroidery, inlaid marble objects, *dhurries,* dried fruit, sweets, shoes and kites are available. Some of the main bazaars are Johri Bazaar, Kinari Bazaar, Kaserat Bazaar and Kashmiri Bazaar. Quieter lanes such as Panni Gali have many fine buildings, with

imposing gateways leading into secluded courtyards where the thriving workshops of master craftsmen still exist.

🏛 St John's College
Mahatma Gandhi Rd. ☎ *(0562) 35 5147.* ◻ *Mon–Sat.* ● *public hols.*

The unusual architecture of St John's College has been described as "an astounding mixture of the antiquarian, the scholarly and the symbolic". It consists of a group of red sandstone buildings, including a hall and library, arranged around a quadrangle, all designed in a quasi-Fatehpur Sikri style by Sir Samuel Swinton Jacob *(see p353),* who perfected the Indo-Saracenic style of architecture. Started by the Church Missionary Society, the college was inaugurated in 1914 by the viceroy, Lord Hardinge, and it continues to be one of Agra's most prestigious institutions.

✝ Roman Catholic Cemetery
Opp Civil Courts. ◻ *daily.*

Towards the north of the town is the Roman Catholic Cemetery, the oldest European graveyard in North India, established in the 17th century by an Armenian merchant, Khoja Mortenepus.

A number of Islamic-style gravestones, with inscriptions in Armenian, survive today, and include those of the cannon expert, Shah Nazar Khan, and Khoja Mortenepus himself. The cemetery also contains tombs of European

Jami Masjid, built by Shah Jahan's favourite daughter, Jahanara

John Hessing's tomb in the Roman Catholic Cemetery

missionaries, traders and adventurers such as the 18th-century French freebooter, Walter Reinhardt. The largest tomb is that of John Hessing, a British commander in the army of the Scindias, the rulers of Gwalior *(see p228).* Hessing's red sandstone tomb, built after his death in 1803, is modelled on the lines of the Taj Mahal. One of the oldest tombs belongs to the English merchant, John Mildenhall (1614), envoy of Elizabeth I, who arrived at the Mughal court in 1603 seeking permission to trade. Other interesting graves include those of the Venetian doctor, Bernardino Maffi, and

Geronimo Veroneo (once wrongly regarded by some as the architect of the Taj). Near the chapel, an obelisk marks the grave of the four children of General Perron, French commander of the Scindia forces. Another Frenchman, Jean Philippe Bourbon, a kinsman of Henry IV of France, is also buried here.

🚂 Fort Railway Station
📞 *(0562) 36 9590.*

This memorable Raj building was constructed in 1891 as a stopping-off point for colonial tourists visiting Agra's monuments. The octagonal bazaar *chowk* that originally connected the Delhi Gate and Agra

Fort to the old city and the Jami Masjid was demolished and this station, with its French château-style slate-roofed platforms, was built in its place. It is still in use today. Agra's two other railway stations are located in the cantonment and at Raja ki Mandi.

Auto-rickshaws parked outside the Fort Railway Station

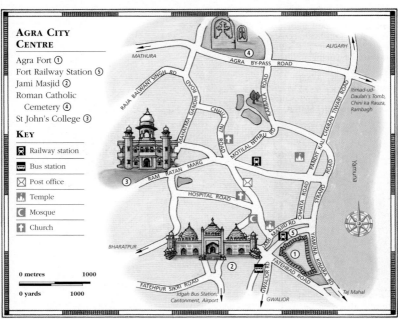

AGRA CITY CENTRE

Agra Fort ①
Fort Railway Station ⑤
Jami Masjid ②
Roman Catholic Cemetery ④
St John's College ③

KEY

🚉 Railway station

🚌 Bus station

⊠ Post office

🛕 Temple

🕌 Mosque

✝ Church

0 metres   1000

0 yards   1000

The colonnaded arches of the Diwan-i-Aam, the hall used for the emperor's public audiences

Agra Fort
daily. *free on Fri.*
Son et Lumière *7:30pm daily.*

Situated on the west bank of the Yamuna, Agra Fort was built by Emperor Akbar between 1565 and 1573. Its imposing red sandstone ramparts form a crescent along the river front, and encompass an enormous complex of courtly buildings, ranging in style from the early eclecticism of Akbar to the sublime elegance of Shah Jahan. The barracks to the north are 19th-century British additions. A deep moat, once filled with water from the Yamuna, surrounds the fort.

The impressive **Amar Singh Gate**, to the south, leads into the fort. To its right is the so-called **Jahangiri Mahal**,

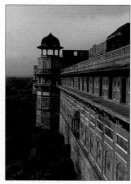

A riverside view of the Jahangiri Mahal, the emperor's main harem

the only major palace in the fort that dates back to Akbar's reign. This complex arrangement of halls, courtyards and galleries, with dungeons underneath, was the zenana or main harem. In front of the Jahangiri Mahal is a large marble pool which, according to legend, used to be filled in Nur Jahan's time with

thousands of rose petals so that the empress could bathe in its scented waters.

Along the river front are the **Khas Mahal**, an elegant marble hall with a vividly painted ceiling, characteristic of Shah Jahan's style of architecture, and two golden pavilions with *bangaldar* roofs (curved roofs derived from Bengali

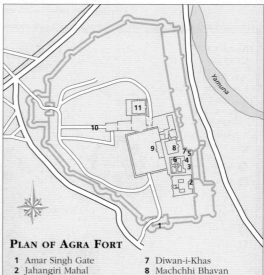

PLAN OF AGRA FORT

1 Amar Singh Gate
2 Jahangiri Mahal
3 Khas Mahal and Anguri Bagh
4 Sheesh Mahal
5 Musamman Burj
6 Mina Masjid
7 Diwan-i-Khas
8 Machchhi Bhavan
9 Courtyard of the Diwan-i-Aam
10 Nagina Masjid
11 Moti Masjid

St George's Church in Agra Cantonment, built in 1826

Firoz Khan Khwajasara's Tomb

S of Agra, on Gwalior Rd. ◯ *daily.*

A signpost on the Gwalior Road indicates the turning to this unusual 17th-century octagonal structure, standing on the edge of a lake. This marks the spot where Firoz Khan Khwajasara, a natural-born eunuch and the custodian of Shah Jahan's palace harem, is buried.

The red sandstone edifice stands on a high plinth and has a gateway attached to the main building. Steps lead to the upper storey where a central pavilion containing the grave is located. Highly stylized stone carvings embellish the surface. Interestingly, unlike other buildings of the period, there is an absence of calligraphic inscriptions. If the tomb is closed, the watchman from the village will open the gate.

huts). These pavilions were once associated with the princesses Jahanara and Roshanara, and have narrow niches which could have been used to conceal jewels. Facing them is **Anguri Bagh** ("Grape Garden") with its lily-pools and candle-niches. The **Sheesh Mahal** and royal baths are to the northeast, near the gloriously inlaid **Musamman Burj**, a double-storeyed octagonal tower with clear views of the Taj. This was where Shah Jahan, imprisoned by his son Aurangzeb, spent the last years of his life.

Mina Masjid ("Gem Mosque"), probably the smallest in the world and the emperor's private mosque, is nearby. Next to Musamman Burj is the **Diwan-i-Khas**, a lavishly decorated open hall with fine *pietra dura* work on its columns, where the emperor would meet his court. Two thrones, in white marble and black slate, were placed on the terrace so that the emper-or could watch the elephant fights below. Opposite is the **Machchhi Bhavan** ("Fish House"), once a magnificent water palace. To its west is the **Diwan-i-Aam**, an arcaded hall within a courtyard. Its throne-alcove of inlaid marble provided a sumptuous setting for the fabled Peacock Throne. To the northwest is the **Nagina Masjid** ("Jewel Mosque") built by Shah Jahan for his harem, and the **Moti Masjid** ("Pearl Mosque").

Musamman Burj

Cantonment

Enclosed by Mahatma Gandhi Rd, Grand Parade Rd & Mall Rd.

The pleasant, tree-shaded army cantonment area, with its own railway station and orderly avenues has many interesting public buildings, churches, cemeteries and bungalows in a medley of styles dating from colonial times. **St George's Church** (1826), a plastered, ochre-coloured building was designed by Colonel JT Boileau, architect of Shimla's Christ Church (*see p110*). **Havelock Memorial Church**, constructed in 1873 in a "trim Classical style", commemorates one of the British generals of the Indian Mutiny of 1857. Other buildings in this area include **Queen Mary's Library**, the **Central Post Office** and the **Circuit House**, which used to accommodate Raj officials.

A view of the 17th-century tomb of Firoz Khan Khwajasara

GOLD THREAD AND BEAD ZARDOZI

Agra's flourishing traditional craft of elaborate gold thread (*zari*) and bead embroidery is known as *zardozi*. This technique was Central Asian in origin and came to the region with the Mughal emperors. Local craftsmen in the old city developed further refinements and complex new patterns to create garments and accessories for the imperial court. However, with the decline of court patronage, the skill languished and almost vanished. It owes its recent revival to encouragement from contemporary fashion designers.

Detail of an embroidered textile

Agra: Taj Mahal

ONE OF THE WORLD'S most famous buildings, the Taj Mahal was built by the Mughal emperor Shah Jahan in memory of his favourite wife, Mumtaz Mahal, who died in 1631. Its perfect proportions and exquisite craftsmanship have been described as "a vision, a dream, a poem, a wonder".

Carved dado on outer niches

The Dome
The 44-m (144-ft) double dome is capped with a finial.

This sublime garden-tomb, an image of the Islamic garden of paradise, cost nearly 41 million rupees and 500 kilos (1,102 lbs) of gold. About 20,000 workers laboured for 12 years to complete it in 1643.

★ Marble Screen
The filigree screen, daintily carved from a single block of marble, was meant to veil the area around the royal tombs.

Four minarets, each 40 m (131 ft) high and crowned by an open octagonal pavilion or *chhatri*, frame the tomb, highlighting the perfect symmetry of the complex.

Plinth

★ Tomb Chamber
Mumtaz Mahal's cenotaph, raised on a platform, is placed next to Shah Jahan's. The actual graves, in a dark crypt below, are closed to the public.

Yamuna river

STAR FEATURES

★ Marble Screen

★ Tomb Chamber

★ Pietra Dura

The *charbagh*
was irrigated with
water from the
Yamuna river.

VISITORS' CHECKLIST

Tajganj. ☎ (0562) 33 0496.
○ Sat–Thu. 🚫 🔲
📷 Taj Mahotsava (Feb).
Museum ○ Tue–Thu.
● public hols. 🚫
Moonlight viewing 🚫

**Main
entrance**

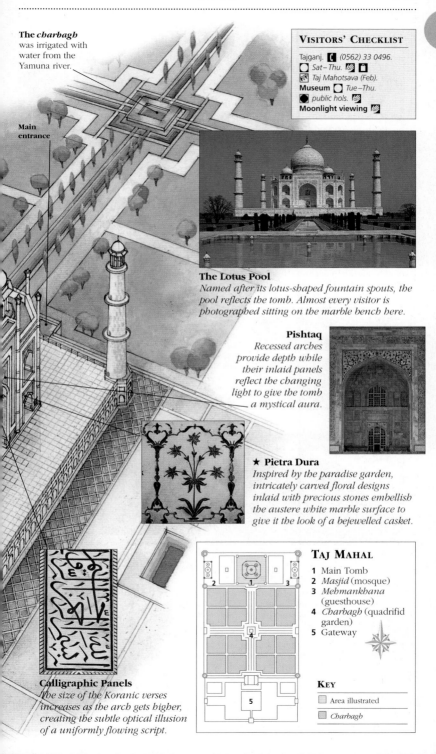

The Lotus Pool
*Named after its lotus-shaped fountain spouts, the
pool reflects the tomb. Almost every visitor is
photographed sitting on the marble bench here.*

Pishtaq
*Recessed arches
provide depth while
their inlaid panels
reflect the changing
light to give the tomb
a mystical aura.*

★ Pietra Dura
*Inspired by the paradise garden,
intricately carved floral designs
inlaid with precious stones embellish
the austere white marble surface to
give it the look of a bejewelled casket.*

TAJ MAHAL

1 Main Tomb
2 *Masjid* (mosque)
3 *Mehmankhana*
   (guesthouse)
4 *Charbagh* (quadrifid
   garden)
5 Gateway

Calligraphic Panels
*The size of the Koranic verses
increases as the arch gets higher,
creating the subtle optical illusion
of a uniformly flowing script.*

KEY

☐ Area illustrated

☐ *Charbagh*

Decorative Elements of the Taj

Stylized floral motif

IT IS WIDELY BELIEVED that the Taj Mahal was designed to represent an earthly replica of one of the houses of paradise. Its impeccable marble facing, embellished by a remarkable use of exquisite surface design, is a showcase for the refined aesthetic that reached its height during Shah Jahan's reign. Described as "one of the most elegant and harmonious buildings in the world", the Taj indeed manifests the wealth and luxury of Mughal art as seen in architecture and garden design, painting, jewellery, calligraphy, textiles, carpet-weaving and furniture.

Detail of the marble screen with an inlaid chrysanthemum

PIETRA DURA

The Mughals were great naturalists and believed that flowers were the "symbols of the divine realm". In the Taj, *pietra dura* has been extensively used to translate naturalistic forms into decorative patterns that complement the majesty of its architecture.

Flowers *such as the tulip, lily, iris, poppy and narcissus were depicted as sprays or in arabesque patterns. Stones of varying degrees of colour were used to create the shaded effects.*

Marble inlay above the mosque's central arch

White marble, black slate and yellow, red and grey sandstone used for decoration

THE ART OF PIETRA DURA

The Florentine technique of *pietra dura* is said to have been imported by Emperor Jahangir and developed in Agra as *pachikari*. Minute slivers of precious and semi-precious stones, such as carnelian, lapis lazuli, turquoise and malachite, were arranged in complex stylized floral designs set into a marble base. Even today, artisans in the old city maintain pattern books with the fine motifs on the Taj to recreate 17th-century designs in contemporary pieces.

A contemporary marble inlaid platter

A single flower, often with more than 35 variations of carnelian

CARVED RELIEF WORK

Decorative panels of flowering plants, foliage and vases are realistically carved on the lower portions of the walls. While the *pietra dura* adds colour to the pristine white marble, these highlight the texture of the polished marble and sandstone surface.

Floral sprays, carved in relief on the marble and sandstone dado levels, are framed with pietra dura and stone inlay borders. The profusion of floral motifs in the Taj symbolizes the central paradise theme.

Jali *patterns* on the octagonal perforated screen surrounding the tombs are a complex combination of the geometric and floral. The filtered light captures the intricate designs and casts mosaic-like shadows on the tombs.

CALLIGRAPHY

Inlaid calligraphy in black marble was used as a form of ornamentation on undecorated surfaces. The exquisitely detailed panels of inscribed Koranic passages, that line the recessed arches like banners, were designed by the Persian calligrapher, Amanat Khan.

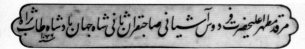

Exploring Agra: the East Bank

The picturesque east bank of the Yamuna is dotted with historic gardens, palaces, pavilions and the exquisite tomb of **Itimad-ud-Daulah**. North of Itimad-ud-Daulah is **Chini ka Rauza**, (literally "China Tomb", after its tiled exterior) built by Afzal Khan, a poet-scholar from Shiraz (Persia) who was Shah Jahan's finance minister. This large square structure is Persian in style, and at one time its surface was covered with glazed tiles from Lahore and Multan, interspersed with graceful calligraphic panels. The burial chamber within has painted stucco plaster designs that must have complemented the tiled exterior.

Lying further upriver is the quiet, tree-shaded **Rambagh** or Aram Bagh ("Garden of Rest"). This is believed to be the earliest Mughal garden, laid out by Babur, the first Mughal emperor, in 1526. The garden also served as his temporary burial place before his body was taken to Kabul to be interred. The spacious walled garden, divided by walkways that lead to a raised terrace with open pavilions overlooking the river, was further developed by the empress Nur Jahan.

♫ Chini ka Rauza
1 km (0.6 miles) N of Itimad-ud-Daulah's Tomb. ☐ daily. 🈲
♣ Rambagh
3 km (2 miles) N of Itimad-ud-Daulah's Tomb. ☐ daily. 🈲 free on Fri.

Riverside pavilion at Rambagh

Agra: Itimad-ud-Daulah's Tomb

A stylized floral motif

Lyrically described as a "jewel box in marble", the small yet elegant garden-tomb of Itimad-ud-Daulah, the "Lord Treasurer" of the Mughal empire, was built by his daughter Nur Jahan, Jahangir's favourite wife. Begun in 1622, it took six years to complete. The tomb is a combination of white marble, coloured mosaic, stone inlay and lattice work. Stylistically, this is the most innovative 17th-century Mughal building and marks the transition from the robust, red sandstone architecture of Akbar to the sensuous refinement of Shah Jahan's Taj Mahal.

Upper Pavilion
The replica tombs of Itimad-ud-Daulah and his wife are placed in the marble-screened upper pavilion.

Tapering pinnacles with lotus mouldings crown the minarets.

Mosaic Patterns
Panels of geometric designs, created by inlaid coloured stones, decorate the dado level of the tomb.

★ Marble Screens
Perforated marble screens with complex ornamental patterns are carved out of a single slab of marble.

STAR FEATURES

★ Marble Screens

★ Tomb Chamber

★ Pietra Dura

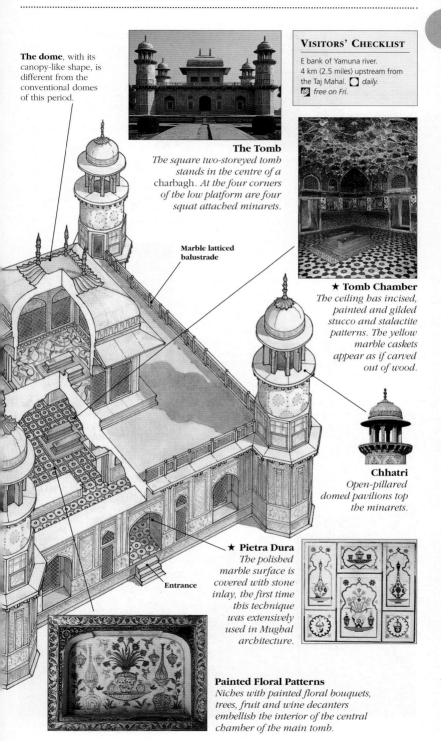

The dome, with its canopy-like shape, is different from the conventional domes of this period.

VISITORS' CHECKLIST

E bank of Yamuna river.
4 km (2.5 miles) upstream from the Taj Mahal. ◻ *daily.*
🎟 *free on Fri.*

The Tomb
The square two-storeyed tomb stands in the centre of a charbagh. At the four corners of the low platform are four squat attached minarets.

Marble latticed balustrade

★ Tomb Chamber
The ceiling has incised, painted and gilded stucco and stalactite patterns. The yellow marble caskets appear as if carved out of wood.

Chhatri
Open-pillared domed pavilions top the minarets.

★ Pietra Dura
The polished marble surface is covered with stone inlay, the first time this technique was extensively used in Mughal architecture.

Entrance

Painted Floral Patterns
Niches with painted floral bouquets, trees, fruit and wine decanters embellish the interior of the central chamber of the main tomb.

The entrance to Akbar's mausoleum at Sikandra

Sikandra ❷

Agra district. 8 km (5 miles) NW of Agra. 🚌 **Akbar's Mausoleum** 📞 (0562) 37 1230 (contact for permission to go to the tomb terrace). 🕒 daily. 🎫 free on Fri. 📷 ❌ ✅ 📹 Urs at Akbar's Tomb (mid-Oct).

THE MUGHAL EMPEROR Akbar is buried in this small village on the outskirts of Agra. It is believed that Akbar designed and started the construction of his own mausoleum, which was modified and completed by his son Jahangir. The result is this impressive, perfectly symmetrical complex, with the tomb located in the centre of a vast walled garden. The main gateway, to the south, is a magnificent red sandstone structure with a colossal central arch, finished with an exuberant polychrome mosaic of inlaid white marble, black slate and coloured stone. On each corner are four graceful marble minarets, considered

to be the forerunners of those that can be seen at the Taj Mahal in Agra *(see pp172–3)*.

The large garden, where monkeys frolic, is a typical *charbagh*, an enclosed garden divided into four quarters (representing the four quarters of life) by a system of raised walkways, sunken groves and water channels. Once impeccably maintained, much of the greenery is now an unkempt tangle.

The main tomb is a distinct departure from the conventional domed structure of the tomb of Akbar's father, Humayun, at Delhi *(see p83)*. The first three storeys of this majestic, four-tiered composition, consist of red sandstone pavilions. Above them is an exquisite marble-screened terrace enclosing the replica tomb, which is profusely carved with floral and arabesque designs, Chinese cloud patterns and the 99 names of Allah.

Mathura ❸

Mathura district. 62 km (39 miles) NW of Agra. 🚶 299,000. 🚪 🚌 ℹ️ Old Bus Stand, (0565) 40 5351. 🎎 Holi (Mar), Hariyali Teej (Jul), Janmashtami (Jul/Aug), Kansa Vadha (Sep), Annakut (Sep/Oct).

MATHURA, on the west bank of Yamuna river, is revered as the birthplace of one of India's most popular gods, Lord Krishna. A dark, cell-like room in the rather modern **Sri Krishna Janmabhoomi Temple**, on the periphery of the city, is reputed to be the actual site of his birth. Further away, along the river front, Mathura's 25 ghats form a splendid network of temples, pavilions, trees and stone steps leading down to the water. The **Jami Masjid**, with its striking tilework, lies behind the river front. A charming oddity is the Roman Catholic **Church of the Sacred Heart**, built in 1860, in the army cantonment. It combines Western elements with details taken from local temple architecture.

A religious image, Mathura

The **Government Museum** has a superb collection of sculpture in the distinctive local white-flecked red sandstone. These date from about the 5th century BC until the 4th century AD, when Mathura was part of the Kushana empire *(see p43)* and

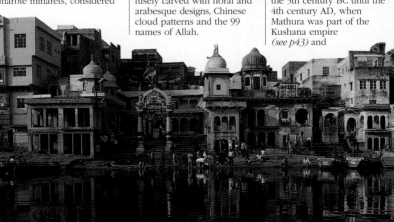

Vishram Ghat at Mathura, where every evening at sunset oil lamps are floated on the river

flourished as a major centre of Buddhism. Outstanding pieces include a Standing Buddha, and the famous headless statue of the great Kushana king, Kanishka.

🏛 **Government Museum**
Dampier Nagar. 📞 *(0565) 40 3191.* ⬜ *Tue–Sun.* ⬤ *public hols.* 🎟 📷 *extra charges.*

Brindavan ❹

Mathura district. 68 km (42 miles) N of Agra. 🚌 🚉 *daily.* 📅 *Holi (Mar), Rath ka Mela (Mar), Hariyali Teej (Jul), Janmashtami (Jul/Aug).*

Gopura of the South Indian-style Ranganathji Temple

SITUATED along the Yamuna, Brindavan ("Forest of Fragrant Basil") is an important pilgrim centre for devout Hindus who believe that the young Krishna once lived here as a humble cowherd and romanced the beautiful milkmaid Radha. Their love is widely celebrated in dance, art and literature. Brindavan's numerous temples, ashrams and ghats were mainly built by Hindu kings and rich merchants. Many Hindu widows, clad in white with their heads shaven, live in ashrams here, devoting their lives to the worship of Krishna. At the edge of the town is the historic **Govindeoji Temple** *(see p352),* built in 1590 by Raja Man Singh I of Amber. Across is the 19th-century **Sri**

Ranganathji Temple with a gold-plated ritual pillar and an interesting museum of temple treasures.

Amidst the narrow streets of the old town are the sacred walled groves of **Seva Kunj**, associated with the traditional Raslila dance which narrates the life of Krishna. Other notable temples in Brindavan include the red sandstone **Madan Mohan Temple**, built in 1580, which stands on a hill next to the river, the popular **Banke Bihari Temple**, near the main bazaar, and the 16th-century **Jugal Kishore Temple**. The **ISKCON Temple**, on the outskirts of the town, is a more recent addition to Brindavan.

FESTIVALS OF UTTAR PRADESH & UTTARANCHAL

International Yoga Week *(Feb),* Rishikesh. Yoga is taught on the banks of the Ganges during this rejuvenating week-long festival.
Taj Mahotsava *(Feb),* Agra. This ten-day cultural fiesta of music and dance is held in the vicinity of the Taj Mahal.
Jhansi Festival *(Feb),* Jhansi. A five-day arts and crafts extravaganza unfolds against the backdrop of Jhansi's historic fort.
Rang Gulal *(Feb/Mar).* The festival of colours, also known as Holi, is played with great abandon all over Uttar Pradesh.

Rang Gulal celebrations

Buddha Mahotsava *(May),* Sarnath and Kushinagar. Religious festivities mark the Buddha's birth, attainment of enlightenment and death. These are held at Sarnath, where he preached his first sermon, and at Kushinagar, where he attained nirvana.
Janmashtami *(Jul/Aug),* Brindavan and Mathura. To mark the birth of Krishna, pilgrims perform a circum-ambulation *(parikrama)* of sacred sites. Festivities reach a peak at midnight.
Ganga Festival *(Oct/Nov),* Varanasi. The ancient glory of the Ganges is celebrated by devotees, who pay homage to the sacred river.
Lucknow Mahotsava *(Nov/Dec),* Lucknow. Lucknow's historic past and continuing traditions are celebrated with food, crafts, music and dance.

THE GRAND TRUNK ROAD

A roadside *dhaba*

The Grand Trunk Road, Rudyard Kipling's "stately corridor" that linked Calcutta (now Kolkata) in the east with Kabul in the northwest, was laid out by Sher Shah Sur *(see p79)* in the 16th century. In those days, it resounded with the movement of armies on campaign, and in times of peace, with the pomp and pageantry that accompanied the Mughal emperors as their court moved from Agra to Delhi. This remains one of Asia's great roads and North India's premier highway. Some ancient shade-giving trees still stand, but the old caravanserais are now in ruins. Instead, at frequent intervals along the highway, there are *dhabas* where long-distance travellers, especially lorry-drivers, can stop for a cheap and filling meal of *dal* and *roti*, washed down with hot tea or cooling *lassi*. They can also snatch a quick nap on string cots *(charpoys)* thoughtfully provided by *dhaba* owners.

Fatehpur Sikri ❺

Fretwork *jali*

B UILT BY EMPEROR AKBAR between 1571 and 1585 in honour of Salim Chishti, a famous Sufi saint of the Chishti order *(see p376)*, Fatehpur Sikri was the Mughal capital for 14 years. A fine example of a Mughal walled city with defined private and public areas and imposing gateways, its architecture, a blend of Hindu and Islamic styles, reflects Akbar's secular vision as well as his style of governance. After the city was abandoned, some say for lack of water, many of its treasures were plundered. It owes its present state of preservation to the initial efforts of the viceroy, Lord Curzon, a legendary conservationist.

Pillar in the Diwan-i-Khas
The central axis of Akbar's court, supported by carved brackets, was inspired by Gujarati buildings.

Haram Sa
complex

Jami Masjid

Khwabgah
The emperor's private sleeping quarters, with an ingenious ventilating shaft near his bed, lie within this lavishly decorated "Chamber of Dreams".

Anoop Talao is a pool associated with Akbar's renowned court musician Tansen *(see p228)* who, as legend says, could light oil lamps with his magical singing.

Abdar
Khana

Entrance

★ Turkish Sultana's House
The fine dado panels and delicately sculpted walls of this ornate sandstone pavilion make the stone seem like wood. It is topped with an unusual stone roof of imitation clay tiles.

Diwan-i-Aam
This large courtyard with an elaborate pavilion was originally draped with rich tapestries and was used for public hearings and celebrations.

★ Panch Mahal
This five-storeyed open sandstone pavilion, overlooking the Pachisi Court, is where Akbar's queens and their attendants savoured the cool evening breezes. Its decorative screens were probably stolen after the city was abandoned.

Birbal's House

★ Diwan-i-Khas
This hall for private audience and debate is a unique fusion of different architectural styles and religious motifs.

Jodha Bai's Palace   **Sunehra Makan**

Ankh Michauli
Sometimes identified as the treasury, this building has mythical guardian beasts carved on its stone struts. Its name means "blind man's buff".

Pachisi Court is named after a ludo-like game played here by the ladies of the court.

PLAN OF FATEHPUR SIKRI

Fatehpur Sikri's royal complex contains the private and public spaces of Akbar's court, which included the harem and the treasury. The adjoining sacred complex with the Jami Masjid, Salim Chishti's Tomb and the Buland Darwaza *(see p183)*, are separated from the royal quarters by the Badshahi Darwaza, an exclusive royal gateway.

KEY

☐ Area illustrated

☐ Other buildings

☐ Sacred complex (Jami Masjid)

STAR SIGHTS

★ **Turkish Sultana's House**

★ **Panch Mahal**

★ **Diwan-i-Khas**

Exploring Fatehpur Sikri

Detail of a carved panel

THE PRINCIPAL BUILDINGS of the imperial palace complex, clustered on a series of terraces along the sandstone ridge, formed the core of Akbar's city. Stylistically, they marked the absorption of Gujarat into the Mughal Empire and reveal a successful synthesis of pre-Islamic, Hindu and Jain architecture (as in the carved brackets) with the elegant domes and arches of Islamic buildings. The concentric terraces clearly separate the public spaces from the private royal quarters. The buildings are mostly in Akbar's favourite red sandstone, which was quarried from the ridge on which they stand.

Stone "tusks" on the Hiran Minar

Aerial view of Fatehpur Sikri, Emperor Akbar's grand capital

Even today, access to the city that was Akbar's capital is provided by a straight road built by the emperor, once lined with exotic bazaars. It leads visitors through the Agra Gate to the triple-arched **Naubat Khana**, where the emperor's entry used to be announced by a roll of drums. Leading off from the Naubat Khana, is the western entrance to the imperial palace complex which opens into the spacious cloistered courtyard of the **Diwan-i-Aam**, where Akbar gave public audiences. A passage behind it leads into the "inner citadel". This contains the **Diwan-i-Khas**, **Khwabgah** and **Anoop Talao**, along with the treasuries and the **Abdar Khana** where water and fruit for the royal household were stored. It also contains the curiously named **Turkish Sultana's House**. Though probably built for one of Akbar's wives, the identity of the "Turkish

Sultana" remains unclear. The great courtyard in front of the Diwan-i-Khas has the **Pachisi Court**, named after the central space that resembles the board of *pachisi*, a traditional game.

The **Haram Sara**, or harem complex, was a maze of interconnected buildings beyond Maryam's House or **Sunehra Makan** ("Golden House"), named after its rich frescoes and gilding. The massive and austere exterior of the harem leads to **Jodha Bai's Palace**, a large inner courtyard, surrounded by pavilions decorated with azure glazed tiles on the roof. A screened viaduct, presumably for privacy, connected the palace to the **Hawa Mahal** facing a small formal garden. The **Nagina Masjid**, adjoining the garden, was the royal ladies' private mosque. The two-storeyed pavilion popularly said to be

Birbal's House, to the east of Jodha Bai's palace, has an unusual layout and fine carvings on its exterior and interior. Beyond this lie a large colonnaded enclosure surrounded by cells, probably meant for the servants of the harem, and the royal stables.

The **Hathi Pol** and **Sangin Burj**, the original gateways to the harem, lead to the outermost periphery of the palace complex. This was laid out in concentric circles around the inner citadel and is made up of ancillary structures, such as the caravanserais, the domed *hamams* (baths) and waterworks. The **Hiran Minar**, believed to be a memorial to Akbar's favourite elephant, was probably an *akash deep* ("heavenly light") with lamps suspended from stone "tusks" to guide visitors.

Entrance to Birbal's House

Jami Masjid

An inlaid panel

THIS GRAND OPEN mosque towers over the city of Fatehpur Sikri and was the model for several Mughal mosques. Flanked by arched cloisters, its vast congregational area has monumental gateways to the east and south. The spiritual focus of the complex is the tomb and hermitage of the Sufi mystic, Salim Chishti, as popular today as it was during the time of Akbar.

Tomb of Sheikh Salim Chishti
Exquisite marble serpentine brackets and almost transparent screens surround the inner tomb which has a sandalwood canopy inlaid with mother-of-pearl.

Hujra
Symmetrically flanking the main mosque, this pair of identical cloistered prayer rooms have flat-roofed pillared galleries that run round the complex.

Badshahi Darwaza
Akbar used the steep steps of this royal gateway to enter the complex. The view of the sacred mosque directly across, greeted his entry.

Corridors

Buland Darwaza
Erected by Akbar to mark his conquest over Gujarat in 1573, this huge 54-m (177-ft) gateway later inspired other lofty gateways.

MAKING A WISH IN SALIM CHISHTI'S TOMB

Ever since Akbar's childlessness was ended by the remarkable prediction of Salim Chishti in 1568, the saint's tomb has attracted crowds of supplicants, particularly childless women in search of a miracle. Visitors to the *dargah*, lavishly endowed by both Akbar and his son Jahangir, make a wish, tie a small cotton thread on the screen around the tomb, and go back confident that the saint will make it come true.

A thread tied to a screen in Chishti's tomb

Pilgrims taking a dip in the holy Ganges at Haridwar

A good way to experience Haridwar's ambience, which has changed little since ancient times, is to stroll along the riverside bazaar, lined with small eateries and stalls full of ritual paraphernalia – small mounds of vermilion powder, coconuts wrapped in red and gold cloth, and brass idols. The most popular items with the pilgrims are the jars and canisters sold here. These are used to carry back a vital ingredient of Hindu rituals: water from the Ganges (Gangajal) which, the faithful believe, remains ever fresh.

Haridwar ❻

Haridwar district. 214 km (133 miles) N of Delhi. 🚃 🚌 ℹ️ *GMVN, Lalta Bridge, (0133) 42 4240.* 🎉 *Kumbh Mela (every 12 years), Ardh Kumbha Mela (every 6 years), Haridwar Festival (Oct), Dussehra (Sep/Oct).*

THE GANGES, India's holiest river *(see pp162–3)*, descends from the Himalayas and begins its journey through the plains at Haridwar. This gives the town a unique status, making a pilgrimage to Haridwar every devout Hindu's dream.

Surprisingly bare of ancient monuments, Haridwar's most famous "sight", as well as a constant point of reference, is the Ganges itself with its numerous bathing ghats, tanks and temples. These bustling sites of ritual Hindu practices, performed by pilgrims for the salvation of their ancestors and for their own expiation, demonstrate their deep faith in the power of the river. The main ghat, **Har-ki-Pauri**, is named after a supposed imprint of Vishnu's feet at the site. Hundreds attend the daily evening *aarti* at this ghat, when leaf boats are filled with flowers, lit with lamps and set adrift on the Ganges. Further south, a ropeway connects the town to the **Mansa Devi Temple** on a hill across the river, which offers panoramic views of Haridwar. Also situated south of the town, is the famous **Gurukul Kangri University**. It is renowned as a centre of Vedic knowledge, and the students here are taught by their gurus in the traditional oral style. A section here displays archaeological finds.

Sign of Chotiwala, a popular restaurant

Rishikesh ❼

Haridwar district. 238 km (148 miles) N of Delhi. 🚌 ℹ️ *GMVN, Kailash Gate, Muni ki Reti, (0135) 43 1793.* 🎉 *International Yoga Week (Feb).*

THIS TWIN CITY of Haridwar, situated at the confluence of the Chandrabhaga and the Ganges, marks the starting point of the holy Char Dham pilgrim route *(see p187)*. Muni-ki-Reti (literally "Sand of the Sages"), lies upstream from the Triveni Ghat, and is said to be a blessed site since ancient sages meditated at this spot. It has several famous ashrams, including the Sivanand, Purnanand and Shanti Kunj ashrams, which offer courses in India's ancient knowledge systems *(see p754)*. North of Muni-ki Reti are two suspension bridges across the Ganges, Rama or Sivananda Jhula and Lakshman Jhula.

YOGA: THE ANCIENT PATH TO HOLISTIC HEALTH

Over 2,000 years ago, the sage Patanjali formulated a series of physical postures called *asanas* which, along with controlled breathing and meditation *(pranayama)*, were meant to set the individual on the path to self-realization. Ever since, yoga has been practised by ascetics and non-ascetics alike. Essentially, yoga calms and focuses the mind by stimulating blood circulation while relaxing nerves and muscles. This helps to combat the stress of daily life and is particularly suited to modern lifestyles as it does not require equipment or visits to the gym. Yoga entered the wider popular consciousness in the late 1960s when the Beatles paid a visit to the Maharishi Mahesh Yogi's ashram in Rishikesh, and today many schools of yoga have centres in India as well as in Europe and North America. Rishikesh, with its plethora of yoga ashrams, is touted as the yoga capital of the world. An International Yoga Week *(see p179)* is also held here in February.

A woman performing an *asana*

River Tour along the Ganges ❽

FROM SEPTEMBER TO APRIL, the Ganges, swollen by the monsoon rains of the upper catchment areas, becomes a torrent, gushing over rocky boulders as it hurtles out of the mountains to the plains. During this period a few stretches of rapids, where the flow is rough but safe, become a popular circuit for enthusiasts of white-water rafting. Only organized tours, run by certified experts, are allowed. For the less adventurous, a scenic driving tour meanders through this valley of the sages, whose ashrams nestle in the surrounding forests along the holy river.

The Ganges flowing serenely through a forested valley

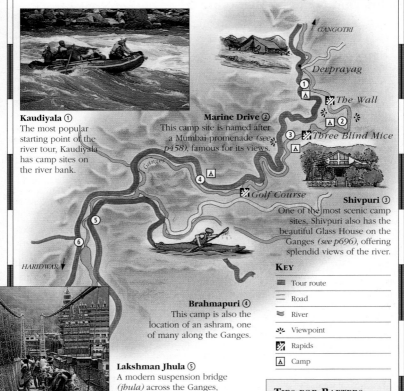

Kaudiyala ①
The most popular starting point of the river tour, Kaudiyala has camp sites on the river bank.

Marine Drive ②
This camp site is named after a Mumbai promenade *(see p458)*, famous for its views.

The Wall

Three Blind Mice

Golf Course

Shivpuri ③
One of the most scenic camp sites, Shivpuri also has the beautiful Glass House on the Ganges *(see p696)*, offering splendid views of the river.

Brahmapuri ④
This camp is also the location of an ashram, one of many along the Ganges.

Lakshman Jhula ⑤
A modern suspension bridge *(jhula)* across the Ganges, replaced the old rope bridge in 1929. This lies at the northern end of Rishikesh, and offers fine views of the river.

Rishikesh ⑥
An ancient spiritual centre, Rishikesh is serenely located on the banks of the Ganges amid lush, wooded hills.

GANGOTRI

Devprayag

HARIDWAR

KEY

▬	Tour route
═	Road
〰	River
☆	Viewpoint
🏴	Rapids
Ⓐ	Camp

TIPS FOR RAFTERS

Length: *36 km (22 miles).*
Getting around: *Rafting can be done over two or three days, with night halts at camps situated at Kaudiyala, Marine Drive, Shivpuri and Brahmapuri. A shorter tour of the same stretch can also be done in one day. For organized tours, tour operators and equipment hire (see p755).*

0 km ————————————— 10

0 miles ————— 5

The façade of the Forest Research Institute, Dehra Dun, established in 1914

Dehra Dun ❾

Dehra Dun district. 256 km (159 miles) NE of Delhi. 🏠 447,800. ✈ Jolly Grant, 24 km (15 miles) SE of town centre. 🚌 🚃 🛈 Directorate of Uttaranchal Tourism, Industrial Area, 3/3 Patel Nagar, (0135) 62 4147.

FRINGED BY the Shivalik Hills, Dehra Dun lies in the pretty Doon Valley, flanked by the Ganges to the west and the Yamuna to the east. The provisional capital of the newly-formed state of Uttaranchal, the town is also the gateway to the Garhwal Hills. A number of prestigious institutions have their head-quarters here, such as the Survey of India and the Forest Research Institute, with its botanical gardens. India's very own Eton, the Doon School, as well as the country's foremost training academy for army officers, the Indian Military Academy, are also situated here. Rajpur Road, the main link to the hills, is lined with bakeries and restaurants and has the old Clock Tower, the town's principal landmark, at one end. Dehra Dun's bracing climate and its proximity to Mussoorie, make it a popular retirement retreat. The Doon Valley is also famous for its fragrant basmati rice, and its mango and litchi orchards.

Little blue kingfisher

ENVIRONS: The **Rajaji National Park**, 5 km (3 miles) southeast of Dehra Dun, is a wildlife sanctuary covering over 800 sq km (309 sq miles). It is best known for its birdlife and herds of elephants.

Mussoorie ❿

Uttarkashi district. 35 km (22 miles) N of Dehra Dun. 🏠 26,000. 🚌 🛈 Uttaranchal Tourist Bureau, The Mall, (0135) 63 2863.

ONE OF THE RAJ'S most popular summer retreats, Mussoorie is perched on a horseshoe-shaped ridge above the Doon Valley at a height of 1,920 m (6,299 ft), and is inundated with Indian visitors in summer. Life in Mussoorie centres around The Mall, the main thoroughfare, which is lined with shops and eating places. The old library lies at the town's western end. About 7 km (4 miles) further west, is a house known as **Everest House**. This was the home of Sir George Everest, the legendary Surveyor-General who mapped Mount Everest,

and one of Mussoorie's earliest residents. The town's small Tibetan community is settled in **Happy Valley**, close to Convent Hill. The **Tibetan Market**, below The Mall, sells a range of woollens. A rope-way from The Mall leads up to **Gun Hill**, which, on a clear day, has fine views of many Greater Himalayan peaks, including Nanda Devi, Kedarnath and Badrinath (see pp64–5). **Camel's Back Road** named after a distinctively shaped rock, offers a pleasant walk along the upper ridge, and **Kempty Falls**, lying 12 km (8 miles) northwest of town, is a popular picnic spot.

Landour, a short distance east of Kulri bazaar, was originally a barracks and convalescence area for British soldiers. With its colonial bungalows and relative quiet, it has managed to preserve some of Mussoorie's old character and is the town's prettiest quarter.

THE PUNDITS

Up to the mid 19th-century, Tibet and Central Asia were vast blanks on the map of the world, yet strategically important to the British in their rivalry with Imperial Russia. As foreigners were forbidden from entering these lands, between 1865 and 1885, the Survey of India trained and sent an intrepid group of Indians to survey the region. Known as the Pundits, these men went disguised as

A portrait of Nain Singh (1830–95)

Buddhist pilgrims and traders, with compasses and survey notes con-cealed in their prayer wheels, and mercury thermometers hidden in their hollowed-out pilgrims staffs. The beads of a rosary helped them measure the distance they covered every day. The most remarkable of the Pundits was Nain Singh, who brought back invaluable and accu-rate topographical information on large tracts of Tibet.

The Garhwal Hills ⑪

Uttarkashi and Chamoli districts. 148 km (92 miles) N from Rishikesh to Uttarkashi. 🚌 ℹ *Uttaranchal Tourist Bureau, Uttarkashi, (01374) 22 290.*

THE NORTHERN stretches of Garhwal (Uttaranchal's western hills) are strewn with pilgrim towns, ancient shrines and forbidding snowbound peaks. **Uttarkashi**, the main town, lies 148 km (92 miles) north of Rishikesh *(see p184)*, and is an important starting point for treks to the upper reaches of Garhwal. A leading school for aspiring climbers, the **Nehru Institute of Mountaineering**, is situated in this town, and boasts of having trained Bachendri Pal, the first Indian woman to scale Mount Everest in 1984.

This region also encompass- es an area traditionally known as Dev Bhoomi ("Abode of the Gods"). The Char Dham or four major places of pilgrim- age, **Gangotri**, **Yamunotri**, **Kedarnath** and **Badrinath**, are all situated here at altitudes over 3,100 m (10,171 ft), in the shadow of some awe-inspiring Himalayan peaks. The pilgrimage season lasts from April to early November, after which the snows drive away all but the most devout. All four sites can be reached

Badrinath, Garhwal's foremost *dham* and source of the Alaknanda river

from Uttarkashi, Haridwar and Rishikesh.

Yamunotri, 209 km (130 miles) north of Rishikesh, is the source of the Yamuna, and a 13-km (8-mile) walk from Hanuman Chatti. Its temple was rebuilt in the 20th century after the earlier one was destroyed by floods. The small village of Gangotri, named after the Ganges which flows through it, lies 100 km (62 miles) northeast of Uttarkashi. Its 18th-century temple has images of Hindu deities. **Gaumukh**, the source of River Ganges, lies 18 km (11 miles) upstream, below the soaring Bhagirathi peaks, and can be reached via a path that follows the lovely river valley. At this point, the river is known as the Bhagirathi, and only becomes the Ganges proper after it joins the Alaknanda river at **Devprayag** *(see p162)*. The impressive Kedarnath peaks form the backdrop for the pilgrim town of Kedarnath, sacred to Shiva, and 223 km (139 miles) northeast of Rishikesh. A beautifully carved stone temple, said to be 800 years old, lies 4 km (9 miles) north of the road head at Gaurikund.

A mendicant in saffron robes

The most visited of all the Char Dham shrines, Badrinath is situated 298 km (185 miles) northeast of Rishikesh. Its colourfully painted temple, dedicated to Vishnu, is usually packed with pilgrims. The town has a spectacular setting, wedged between the Nar and Narayan ranges. The Neelkanth or "Blue Throat Peak", named after Lord Shiva, towers over Badrinath at a height of 6,957 m (22,825 ft).

Joshimath, lying 250 km (155 miles) northeast of Rishikesh at the confluence of the Dhauli Ganga and Alak- nanda rivers at Vishnuprayag, is one of the four *mathas* (seats of learning) established by the great 9th-century sage, Adi Shankaracharya *(see p648)*. It is also the junction of two ancient trans-Himalayan trading routes. The town was a gateway to the Nanda Devi Sanctuary *(see p189)*, until the sanctuary was closed to the public in 1983. Today, visitors head mostly for the ski slopes of **Auli**, reached via road or cable car from Joshimath. The popular trek to the Sikh shrine of **Hemkund Sahib** and the **Valley of Flowers National Park** *(see p189)* begins 20 km (12 miles) north of Joshimath, from Ghangaria. The Valley of Flowers, best visited between the months of June and September, is a carpet of anemones, roses, primulas and other alpine flora.

Gaumukh, the glacial source of the Ganges, backed by the Bhagirathi peaks

Trekking in Garhwal and Kumaon

Wild irises, Garhwal

NO HIMALAYAN RANGES are as rich in myth and legend as those of Garhwal and Kumaon (Uttaranchal's eastern hills). Known as Dev Bhoomi ("Abode of the Gods"), every peak, river and trail is either named after a Hindu god or goddess, or finds mention in holy scriptures. Relatively easy to access, Garhwal and Kumaon are a wonderful introduction to the Himalayas. A single walk can lead through forests, valleys bursting with wild flowers, and glacial moonscapes of rock and ice. The best seasons are between February and May and September and November.

LOCATOR MAP

Areas shown below

The Gaumukh Trail

This 26-km (16-mile) path traces the infant River Ganges along an ancient pilgrim trail, from Gangotri to its glacial source at Gaumukh (see p162). The route crosses the Gangotri Glacier and forks, leading to the meadows of Tapovan and Nandanvan, dominated by the imposing Bhagirathi and Shivling peaks.

Duration: 6 days
Altitude: 4,500 m (14,764 ft)
Level of Difficulty: moderate to tough

KEY

- - The Gaumukh Trail
- - Dodital
- - The Curzon Trail
- - Pindari Glacier
- - The Valley of Flowers
— Major road
= Minor road
△ Peak
⌣ Pass

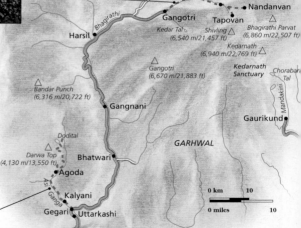

Dodital

One of Garhwal's popular treks, the 23-km (14-mile) path from Kalyani follows the Asi Ganga river valley, past Agoda to Dodital. This jewel-like lake, whose waters swarm with trout, is set in a densely wooded bowl. The pine and deodar forests are home to a variety of Himalayan birds.

Duration: 3 days
Altitude: 3,024 m (9,921 ft)
Level of Difficulty: easy

The Curzon Trail

The 70-km (44-mile) trail is named after the British viceroy who followed this route. From Ghat, it skirts the western edge of the Nanda Devi Sanctuary, crossing over the Kuari Pass, with clear views of Nanda Devi. It ends at Tapovan, 12 km (8 mile) northwest of Joshimath.

Duration: 6 days
Altitude: 4,268 m (14,003 ft)
Level of Difficulty: tough

The Valley of Flowers National Park, a 20-km (12-mile) climb from Govindghat, has a profusion of wild flowers *(see p187)*.

Duration: 3 days
Altitude: 3,352 m (10,997 ft)
Level of Difficulty: moderate

y of
vers
ngaria
◦ Hemkund
Bhiundhar

● Govindghat
● Joshimath
Auli   Tapovan
Kuan Pass
(4,268 m/
14,003 ft)   ● Pana
Pipalkoti   ● Jhinji
Gohna   Chechni Binayak
Tal   Pass
●Ramni
hamoli
● Nandprayag   ● Ghat
Bekhal
Tal

Rishi Ganga

*Nanda Devi East
(7,430 m/24,377 ft)* △

△ *Nanda Devi
(7,817 m/25,646 ft)*

**Nanda Devi
Sanctuary**

△ *Trishul
(7,120 m/23,360 ft)*

KUMAON

*Pindari
Glacier*

Phurkiya ●
Dwali ●

● Khati
Loharkhet ●
Dhakuri ●
Karmi
Song ●

Sundar-dhunga

Pindar

Pindari Glacier is a 50-km (31-mile) trek from Song, through dense forests with fine views of Trishul Peak.

Duration: 6 days
Altitude: 3,650 m (11,975 ft)
Level of Difficulty: tough

NANDA DEVI SANCTUARY

The 630-sq km (243-sq mile) Nanda Devi Sanctuary has three splendid peaks – Nanda Devi, Nanda Devi East and Nanda Kot, which form a snowy wall in the north. Nanda Devi *(see pp64–5)* is India's second highest peak at 7,817 m (25,646 ft). Believed to be the birthplace of Shiva's consort, Parvati, the mountain is revered as a goddess. The area was thought

Nanda Devi and Nanda Devi East

to be impenetrable till British mountaineers Eric Shipton and Bill Tilman discovered a route in 1936. A spate of expeditions followed, to the distress of the local people who believed this would incur the wrath of the goddess. In 1976, American mountaineer Willi Unsoeld, along with his 22-year-old daughter Nanda Devi (whom he had named after the peak), set off for the mountain, but Nanda Devi died tragically during the expedition. The core area of the sanctuary was closed in 1983 to protect its fragile ecosystem, which is the habitat of rare fauna such as the snow leopard and the monal pheasant.

Nainital ⑫

Nainital district. 322 km (200 miles)
NE of Delhi. 🚉 *Kathgodam, 35 km
(22 miles) S of Nainital, then taxi
or bus.* 🚌 ℹ *KMVN, Oṃ Park,
(05942) 35 700.*

The 11th-century complex of stone temples at Jageshwar, near Almora

THIS PRETTY hill station,
nestled in the Kumaon
Hills, is named after the
emerald green eyes *(naina)*
of Parvati, Shiva's consort. A
temple dedicated to the goddess stands on the northern
shore of the large freshwater
lake *(tal)*. The old summer
capital of the British Raj's
United Provinces, Nainital is
today part of the newly-formed
state of Uttaranchal. The lake
is encircled by the Mall Road,
and the "flats", a large field
which is a popular promenade
and recreation centre. The
Boat House Club, set up in
1890 on the water's edge, is
the hub of many activities and
has a number of sail boats and
rubber dinghies for hire. The
many attractive colonial buildings include the governor's
summer residence (built in
1899), St Joseph's School,
the old Secretariat (now
the Uttaranchal High Court)
and the Municipal Library. **St-
John-in-the-Wilderness** is an
evocatively named Gothic
church, with fine stained-glass
windows and dark wooden
pews. Nainital also has some
beautiful walking trails, one of
which leads up from the flats,
through the densely wooded
Ayarpata Hill, to **Tiffin Top**
and **Dorothy's Seat**, lookout
points offering panoramic
views of the lakeside. Close
by, and almost hidden by the
forest, is an old public school,
the appropriately named
Sherwood College. The
Upper Cheena Mall leads to
Naina Peak, with breathtaking
views of the mountain ranges.
Less energetic visitors can take
the cable car up to **Snow
View** for scenic views.

ENVIRONS: Described as
India's Lake District,
Nainital's environs have
a number of serene
lakes, surrounded by
thick forests. Excursions
are offered to **Bhim
Tal**, 22 km (14 miles)
east of Nainital;
Naukuchiya Tal, just
4 km (2.5 miles) from
Bhim Tal, is a lake with nine
corners, rich in birdlife; and
Sat Tal, a conglomeration of
seven lakes, located 21 km
(13 miles) northeast of
Nainital. **Mukteshwar**, 30 km
(19 miles) northeast of
Nainital, is one of the most
beautiful spots in the area,
along with the orchards at
Ramgarh, close by.

Sculpture,
Jageshwar

Almora ⑬

Almora district. 285 km (177 miles)
NE of Delhi. 🚉 *Kathgodam, 90 km
(56 miles) S of Almora, then taxi or
bus.* 🚌 ℹ *KMVN, Holiday Home,
(05962) 30 250.*

THE LARGE MARKET TOWN of
Almora is the headquarters
of the surrounding district.
Its curving ridge offers
expansive views of the
spectacular Greater
Himalayan Range, including
peaks such as Trishul and the
spectacular Nanda Devi *(see
p189)*. The cobbled street of
Almora's distinctive bazaar
lies above The Mall, where
locally crafted *tamta* products
(hand-beaten copper and
brass utensils plated with
silver) are on sale. The town's
trademark confectionery, the
bal mithai, is available
here as well. Also of
interest are the tall,
narrow houses with
their delicately carved
wooden façades, a
hallmark of local
architecture. The
historic **Almora Jail**,
probably one of the
few in the country
with such picturesque
surroundings, once
held important political
prisoners such as Mahatma
Gandhi and Jawaharlal Nehru.
A number of temples dot the
landscape; the most popular
of these are the **Chitai
Temple** and the **Udyot-
chandeshwar Temple**. On
the western edge of town,
Brighton End Corner has
fine mountain views.

ENVIRONS: Binsar, 34 km (21
miles) northeast of Almora, at
an altitude of 2,412 m (7,913
ft), is a wonderful spot from
which to view the mountains.
The steep drive up through
tangy forests of pine is very
pretty, and there is a 13th-
century Shiva Temple set in
the forest, just short of the
summit. **Jageshwar**, located
34 km (21 miles) east of
Almora, is of great religious
significance. This is an

The lake at Nainital, with facilities
for boating and water sports

Ranikhet's nine-hole golf course, offering fine mountain views

impressive complex of over 100 splendidly carved stone temples, dating back to the 11th century.

Ranikhet **⑭**

Almora district. 367 km (228 miles) NE of Delhi. *Tourist Reception Centre, Mall Rd, (05966) 20 227.*

PRIMARILY a cantonment town, Ranikhet is home to the Indian Army's renowned Kumaon Regiment. Not surprisingly, the army is the town's most visible presence, its many red-roofed bungalows spreading across the wide "Queen's Field", a literal translation of the town's name. **Sadar Bazaar** is the main market, while the **Upper Mall** leads away from the bazaar to the quieter part of town. **Chaubatia**, once a British sanatorium, lies further along The Mall and now houses the Government Fruit Garden, which grows 200 varieties of fruit. Ranikhet's true allure, however, lies in its untrammelled Himalayan views that offer a spectacular vista of nearly 350 km (217 miles) of the Greater Himalayan Range. The **Army Golf Course**, 6 km (4 miles) down the Almora Road at Uphat, is one of the country's highest golf courses, and was originally a racetrack. It welcomes visitors who are willing to pay green fees, so take no notice of the signboard that threatens trespassers.

Lansdowne **⑮**

Almora district. 216 km (134 miles) NE of Delhi. *Kotdwar, 37 km (23 miles) SW of town centre, then taxi or bus.*

THE CANTONMENT TOWN of Lansdowne, is one of the few hill stations that has managed to remain wonderfully unchanged over the last century. Away from the main tourist circuit, the town has been spared the frenzied building and modernization that has crept into other popular destinations. A loosely spread out jumble of bungalows and shops, it is set on gentle forested slopes of pine, deodar and silver oak. The Army's Garhwal Rifles have their regimental centre here, and a visit to

A green bee-eater with its catch

the beautifully maintained regimental mess is a must. A pleasant walk leads to **Tip-n-Top**, a lookout point 3 km (2 miles) from town, which offers excellent mountain views.

Kausani **⑯**

Almora district. 385 km (239 miles) NE of Delhi. *Tourist Reception Centre, (05962) 45 006.*

KAUSANI WAS Mahatma Gandhi's favourite abode in the hills. After a long stay here at the **Anashakti Yoga Ashram** in 1929, he remarked on how unnecessary it was for Indians to visit the European Alps for their health, when they had the beauty of Kausani at their doorsteps. A 400-km (249-mile) uninterrupted panorama of the Nanda Devi Range can be seen from the old **Circuit House**.

ENVIRONS: Baijnath, 20 km (12 miles) north of Kausani, is known for a cluster of temples, now in ruins, built in the 11th century. The main attraction is the **Parvati Temple**, with a 2-m (7-ft) high image of the goddess, dating from the 12th century. **Bageshwar**, 41 km (26 miles) east of Kausani, lies at the confluence of the Gomti and Saryu rivers, and was once a major trading post between Tibet and Kumaon. Although the link with Tibet no longer exists, local merchants still bring wool and animal hide to the town's annual Uttaryani Fair. With its stone temples dedicated to Shiva, Bageshwar is also an important pilgrimage centre in Kumaon. Nila Parvat (the "Blue Mountain"), stands proudly between the two rivers, and locals believe that it is home to all the 330 million deities of the Hindu pantheon. Many visitors to Bageshwar are en route to the Pindari Glacier (*see p189*).

Pumpkins drying on a slate roof below the peaks at Kausani

Corbett National Park ⑰

SITUATED ALONG THE VALLEY of the Ramganga river and
fringed by the Himalayan foothills in the north,
Corbett is considered one of India's finest wildlife
sanctuaries. The 1,318-sq km (509-sq mile) reserve was
originally a hunter's paradise during the British Raj. In
1936, it became India's first national park, largely due
to the efforts of the great British hunter-turned-
conservationist Jim Corbett, after whom the park is
named. The park encompasses varied terrain, from
savannah grasslands to hilly ridges of deciduous forests
with *chir* pine and *sal (Shorea robusta)*. Corbett is
renowned for its remarkable variety of wildlife,
notably tigers, elephants, *chausingha* (four-horned
antelopes) and an astonishing 600 species of birds.

Paradise Flycatcher
*The male has beautiful
plumage, and measures
50 cm (20 in) in length.*

**Coucal or
Crow Pheasant**
*This striking,
black and brown
bird is found
all over north-
ern India. Its
loud and
resonant call
echoes over the
valleys and forests in
and around Corbett.*

Sona Nadi
Wildlife Sanctuary

Kanda

Ramganga Reservoir

Dhikala   Khinnanauli

Paterpani

Chir Choti   Gaujpani

Dam
TAKESWAR   Kalagarh   Dhara   Jhirna

Grasslands
*Vast savannah grasslands (chaurs),
ideal for viewing deer and other wildlife, surround Dhikala, the park's hub,
located by the Ramganga Reservoir.*

Machaans or high
watchtowers, situated
around the park, are
ideal for viewing wildlife.

Gharial
*The gharial (Gavialis
gangeticus) is a species
that can be seen on the
banks of the Ramganga
Reservoir (formed by a
dam on the Ramganga
river). The reservoir also
attracts a variety of water
birds such as geese, ducks,
grebes and storks.*

VISITORS' CHECKLIST

Pauri Garhwal & Nainital districts. 436 km (271 miles) NW of Lucknow. **Entry points:** *Dhangarhi & Kalagarh.* 🚉 *Ramnagar, 20 km (12 miles) S of Dhangarhi.* 🚌 ℹ️ *For bookings and permits contact Ramnagar, (05945) 51 489.* 🕐 *Nov–Jun.* 🎥 💳 📷 *extra charges for video.* 🏠

Ramganga River
The lifeline of the park's wildlife, the Ramganga river is surrounded by tall elephant grass (nall) *and scrub.*

Elephant Safari
The highlights of a trip to Corbett are the sunrise and sunset elephant safaris, available from Dhikala and Bijrani. Apart from the herds of wild elephants and deer, it is sometimes possible to encounter a lone tiger or leopard.

Gairal Ⓐ   Ramganga
RANIKHET

Ⓐ Sarpduli   Sultan • Dhangarhi

Malani

Garjia•

Bijrani Ⓐ

dhang   Dhela   Amdanda

Ramnagar
HALDWANI

Indian Tiger
Corbett has about 140 tigers. It became India's first Tiger Reserve in 1973, under the aegis of Project Tiger (see p289).

0 km   5
0 miles   5

KEY

▪ ▪ Park boundary

▪ ▪ Trail

═══ Major road

═══ Minor road

ℹ️ Tourist information

☀️ Viewpoint

▣ Café

Ⓐ Accommodation

JIM CORBETT (1875–1955)

Jim Corbett was born in Nainital and developed a keen interest in the jungles of Kumaon. An avid hunter in his early years (he shot his first leopard when he was eight), the turning point came when, on a duck shoot, he was appalled by the mindless slaughter of 300 birds. Corbett then decided to use his rifle solely to kill the man-eating leopards and tigers that plagued the nearby villages. Riveting accounts in his first book, *Man-eaters of Kumaon*, describe how he tracked and shot the dreaded Champawat tigress who had killed 434 people. In 1956, after Corbett's death, the park was named after him as a tribute to his pioneering efforts at conservation.

Bust of Corbett, Dhikala

Dudhwa National Park ⑱

Lakhimpur-Kheri district. 220 km (137 miles) N of Lucknow. **Entry point:** *Palia.* 🚌 🚗 **ℹ** *For bookings contact Field Director, Dudhwa, (05872) 52 106.* 🕐 *15 Nov–15 June.* 📷 *extra charges. Jeeps available.* 🐘

LOCATED CLOSE to the border with Nepal, Dudhwa National Park covers 490 sq km (189 sq miles) of densely wooded plains. Its forests have some of the finest specimens of *sal* trees in India. In 1988, Dudhwa was recognized as a Tiger Reserve, mainly due to the efforts of Billy Arjan Singh, a legendary environmentalist. Arjan Singh is best-known for the tigress, Tara, he hand-reared and returned to the wild in 1978.

Today, the park has more than 30 tigers. The park is also well known for its herds of swamp deer *(Cervus duvauceli)*. Better known as *barasingha* (literally, 12-antlered), these deer find their ideal habitat in the grassy wetlands in the southern reaches of the park.

Other species include leopards, sloth bears and a small herd of rhinos, brought here from Assam and Nepal, in an attempt to re-introduce the species into Dudhwa. The park is also home to nearly 400 species of birds, among them swamp partidges, lesser floricans and hornbills. The park's lakes attract waterfowl such as fishing eagles and ibis.

Rampur ⑲

Rampur district. 310 km (193 miles) NW of Lucknow. 🚶 *281,500.* 🚗 🚌

EARLIER A STRONGHOLD of the Afghan Rohilla chieftains (highlanders from Peshawar), Rampur became a princely state under the British. It was ruled by a dynasty of Muslim nawabs who were great connoisseurs of the arts. They drew hundreds of scholars and artists to their court, whose books and paintings became part of the state collection. They also established a famous *gharana* (school) of classical music. The Hamid Manzil, built by Nawab Hamid Ali Khan Bahadur who came to the throne in 1896, now houses the renowned **Raza Library**, which has a collection of almost 1,000 Mughal miniatures, over 10,000 books, numerous rare manuscripts, and portraits dating from the 16th to 18th centuries. It is not officially open to the public, but permission to visit can be obtained from the curator. Hamid Ali Khan was also responsible for renovating many of Rampur's palaces, including the sprawling palace and fort complex to the northwest of the town. Rampur is a maze of bazaars and was once known for its fine cotton *khes* (damask). Traces of its Rohilla warrior ancestry are visible in the

Rampur knives and daggers, a local speciality

famous daggers, always on sale, and in the touches of Pashto (the native tongue of Peshawar) which pepper the Urdu that is spoken here.

 Raza Library
For permission to visit contact the curator. 📞 *(0592) 32 5045, 32 5346.*

ENVIRONS: The town of **Moradabad**, lying 26 km (16 miles) west of Rampur, is a small 17th-century settlement, best-known for its brass and metalware industries. The town's fort and mosque are now almost hidden by the many tenements and bazaars.

Nawab Hamid Ali of Rampur

Aligarh ⑳

Aligarh district. 371 km (231 miles) NW of Lucknow. 🚶 *667,700.* 🚗 🚌 🎪 *Numaish (Feb).*

HISTORICALLY important because of its location in an agriculturally rich region, Aligarh was a Rajput stronghold from the end of the 12th century onwards, until it was wrested by the Mughals. Its fort, which dates to 1524, fell to the British under Lord Lake in 1803. British presence influenced many of its foremost citizens, such as Sir Sayyid Ahmed Khan who founded the **Aligarh Muslim University** in 1875, for which the town is most famous today. The sprawling campus has many

Swamp deer, also known as *barasingha*, in Dudhwa's grasslands

imposing buildings, such as a mosque that is an exact replica of the Jami Masjid *(see p86)* in Delhi, only one-third its size.

Jhansi ㉑

Jhansi district. 301 km (187 miles) SW of Lucknow. 🚶 *383,200.* 🚗 🚌
ℹ️ *UP Tourism, Shivpuri Rd, (0517) 44 1267.* 🎭 *Jhansi Festival (Feb).*

Mᴏsᴛ ғᴀᴍᴏᴜs for the role that its queen, Rani Lakshmibai, played during the Indian Mutiny of 1857, Jhansi is a key transit point for visitors travelling from Delhi to the temples of Khajuraho *(see pp236–8)*. The main site of interest is **Shankar Fort**, built in 1613 by Raja Bir Singh Deo. It has 9-m (30-ft) high walls built in concentric rings around its centre, and offers fine views from its ramparts.

The **Archaeological Museum**, located outside the fort on the road back to town, has medieval Hindu sculpture, royal artifacts, and some prehistoric tools.

🏛 **Archaeological Museum**
⬜ *Tue–Sun.* ⬛ *2nd Sat.* 📷 📷
extra charges for video photography.

Kanpur ㉒

Kanpur district. 79 km (49 miles) SW of Lucknow. 🚶 *2,532,100.* 🚗 🚌

Oɴᴇ ᴏғ ʙʀɪᴛɪsʜ India's largest garrisons Kanpur, or Cawnpore as it was then known, witnessed some of

The ramparts of Shankar Fort at Jhansi, stormed by British forces in 1858

the bloodiest battles in 1857. More than 1,000 British soldiers and civilians were killed when Nana Sahib, the Maratha ruler, broke the British siege held by General Sir Hugh Wheeler in June 1857. When British reinforcements arrived, equally ferocious reprisals occurred.

Today, Kanpur is an industrial city with leather, cotton and oil as its main products. The old garrison, now an enclave of the armed forces, has some interesting relics of the Raj. Among them is the **All Souls' Memorial Church**, a grand Gothic style structure with an intricate stained-glass window over the west door. Built after 1857, it is a memorial to those killed during the siege. East of the church, the pretty **Memorial Garden** has a statue of an angel surrounded by a Gothic screen. This statue originally stood at the site of a terrible massacre, where British women and children were hacked and thrown down a well near Bibighar, in the

town's centre. Northeast of the church, **Sati Chaura Ghat** along the Ganges, is the spot where Indian forces killed 500 British soldiers and civilians. The **Military Cemetery** on the edge of the cantonment has many interesting graves, while in the town, the **King Edward VII Memorial Hall** and **Christ Church** (built in 1840) are also worth visiting.

Eɴᴠɪʀᴏɴs: Bithur, 25 km (16 miles) west of Kanpur, boasts a fort built by the Peshwas *(see p471)*. It is also the legendary birthplace of Lav and Kush, the twin sons of Rama and Sita *(see p27)*. About 60 km (37 miles) south of Kanpur, lies the beautiful 5th-century brick temple at **Bhitargaon**, built by the Gupta kings. The only one of its kind still surviving, most of the relief panels on the temple have vanished, but some terracotta sculptures inside remain.

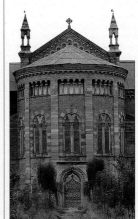

RANI LAKSHMIBAI OF JHANSI

India's Joan of Arc, Rani Lakshmibai single-handedly defied the British when her husband, Raja Gangadhar Rao, died in 1853 leaving no adult heir. She wished to rule as Regent but the British invoked the infamous Doctrine of Lapse

(see p53) and she was driven from her kingdom. While the Indian Mutiny of 1857 brewed in the north, the queen and her general, Tantia Tope, captured Gwalior Fort. She died defending it at Kotah-Sarai near Gwalior in 1858. According to the historian Christopher Hibbert, "she died dressed as a man, holding her sword two-handed and the reins of her horse in her teeth". She remains one of India's best-loved heroines.

Rani Lakshmibai astride her horse

Stained-glass window in the All Souls' Memorial Church, Kanpur

Lucknow ㉓

The fish emblem of the nawabs

As the Mughal Empire disintegrated, many independent kingdoms, such as Avadh, were established. Its capital, Lucknow, rose to prominence when Asaf-ud-Daula, the fourth nawab, shifted his court here from Faizabad *(see p199)* in 1775. The city was also North India's cultural capital, and its nawabs, best remembered for their refined and extravagant lifestyles, were patrons of the arts. Under them music and dance flourished, and many buildings were erected. In 1856 the British annexed Lucknow and deposed its last nawab, Wajid Ali Shah. This incident helped instigate the Indian Mutiny of 1857, when the city witnessed one of the bloodiest episodes in colonial history.

Sikander Bagh's stately gateway, adorned with the fish emblem

View of the Tomb of Khurshid Zadi, Qaiser Bagh

⌂ Qaiser Bagh Palace
Qaiser Bagh. ☐ *daily.*

Once the most magnificent palace in Lucknow, Qaiser Bagh, was built by Wajid Ali Shah (r.1847–56), the last nawab. When the British recaptured Lucknow in 1858, they demolished many of the complex's more fanciful structures, with their florid sculptures of mermaids and cherubs. However, the remaining buildings, although in ruins, hint at their former splendour. The **Lal Baradari** now houses a fine arts academy as well as the archaeological section of the State Museum; the **Pathar Wali Baradari** is a school for Hindustani music; and the **Safaid Baradari**, now an office building, was where the nawab, dressed as a fakir, used to hold court. Only two wings of the residential quarters that once housed the nawab's vast harem remain. Carvings of fish, the nawabs' royal emblem, adorn many of the structures. Nearby, lie two grand tombs, the **Tomb of Saadat Ali Khan** (the fifth nawab) and the **Tomb of Khurshid Zadi**, his wife.

Under Nawab Wajid Ali Shah, Lucknow witnessed an artistic flowering. An aesthete who was not interested in governance, he devoted himself to poetry and music and is believed to have introduced the *thumri* (a form of light classical music). Dance forms benefited as well, and the Lucknow *gharana* (school) of Kathak *(see p28)* reached new heights during his short reign, before he was deposed by the British in 1856 and exiled to Calcutta.

♣ Sikander Bagh
Sikander Bagh. ☐ *daily.*

Named after Wajid Ali Shah's favourite queen, Sikander Bagh was the royal pleasure garden of the nawabs. In 1857, British troops led by Sir Colin Campbell relieved the siege of the Residency at this site. The **National Botanical Gardens and Research Centre** are now located in its grounds. To the west, the **Shah Najaf Imambara** has the tomb of Ghazi-ud-din Haidar (the sixth nawab).

⌂ Chattar Manzil
NW of Qaiser Bagh. ☐ *daily.*

Built during Saadat Ali Khan's reign (1798–1814), the Chattar Manzil ("Umbrella Palace"), derives its name from the umbrella-shaped gilt dome *(chattar)* crowning the structure. A basement *(tehkhana)* was built below the level of the Gomti river, so that its waters could keep the area cool in the summer. The building now houses the Central Drug Research Institute.

⌂ The Residency
NW of Qaiser Bagh. ☐ *daily.* 🖼

Lucknow's most haunting monuments are the desolate ruins of the Residency. This complex of buildings which grew around the large brick home of the Resident, was an exclusive British enclave, protected by fortifications. In 1857, all the city's British

The British Residency before it was destroyed during the siege of 1857

citizens took refuge here during the five-month siege. Sir Henry Lawrence, the commander of the troops, expected relief to arrive within 15 days. But, it was 87 days before a force led by Sir Henry Havelock broke through the ranks of sepoys, only to find themselves trapped inside. For the next seven weeks they faced constant bombardment, until Sir Colin Campbell finally retook the Residency on 17 November. By then, almost 2,000 people had died either from bullet wounds or from cholera and typhoid.

Today, the Residency looks just as it did in 1857. In its small museum, the gaping holes made by cannon fire are still visible. The **Model Room** on the ground floor, has a model depicting British defences during the siege. Lying below, are the cellars where the women and children took shelter. The cemetery near the ruined church, has the forlorn graves of those who died, including that of Sir Henry Lawrence. An **Indian Martyrs' Memorial** stands opposite, on the banks of the Gomti river.

Bara Imambara

Hussainabad. ☐ daily. ● during Muharram (Mar/Apr).

Lucknow's most distinctive architectural structures are the *imambaras*, or ceremonial halls used during Muharram *(see p669)*. The Bara ("Great") Imambara, built by Asaf-ud-Daula in 1784, was essentially a famine relief project providing much-needed employment. It is said that while one group of workers were involved with its construction during the day, another group dismantled it at night. Elaborate gates lead to this sprawling, low edifice. Its most remarkable feature is a large hall, 50-m (164-ft) long and 15-m (49-ft) high, totally unsupported by pillars.

VISITORS' CHECKLIST

Lucknow district. 516 km (321 miles) E of Delhi. 1,917,000. Amausi, 15 km (9 miles) SW of Lucknow. UP Tourism, 3, Nawal Kishore Rd, Chitrahar Building, (0522) 24 8349. Muharram (Mar/Apr).

Above it is the *bhulbhulaiya*, a labyrinth of balconies and passages. The **Asafi Mosque** and a stepwell also lie in the compound.

Asaf-ud-Daula also erected the 18-m (59-ft) high **Rumi Darwaza**, just outside. This portal, embellished with lavish decorations, was the Imambara's west facing entrance.

The Bara Imambara complex, built in the late 18th century

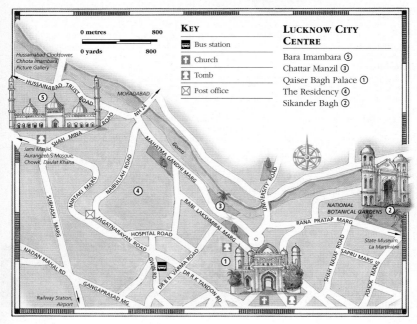

KEY

🚌 Bus station
✚ Church
🛕 Tomb
⊠ Post office

LUCKNOW CITY CENTRE

Bara Imambara ⑤
Chattar Manzil ③
Qaiser Bagh Palace ①
The Residency ④
Sikander Bagh ②

Lucknow: The Outer Sites

SOME OF LUCKNOW's best architectural sites lie beyond the city centre. The religious monuments, such as the *imambaras* and mosques, reveal a distinct Persian influence, while the secular buildings, which include the palaces of the nawabs as well as colonial structures, are more European in style. A particularly extravagant example among the latter is La Martinière. The home and mausoleum of a French adventurer, it later became a school, serving as the model for St Xavier's School which was immortalized in Rudyard Kipling's novel, *Kim*.

Portrait of Nawab Wajid Ali Shah in the Picture Gallery

Close to the Rumi Darwaza *(see p197)*, **Aurangzeb's Mosque** stands on high ground known as Lakshman Tila, the location of Lucknow's original township. To the east is the **Hussainabad Clocktower**, erected in 1887. The 67-m (220-ft) high Gothic tower was built to mark the arrival of Sir George Cooper, Avadh's first lieutenant governor. To its west lies the 19th-century Baradari, built by Muhammed Ali Shah (the eighth nawab), where the **Picture Gallery** is located. Splendid life-sized portraits of the ten nawabs, painted between 1882 and 1885 and recently renovated, are on display here.

To the west of the Picture Gallery is the Hussainabad Imambara, better known as the **Chhota Imambara**. This gem-like structure is surmounted by a delicate gold dome, and its outside walls are engraved with superb calligraphy. The interiors are adorned with gilt-edged mirrors, ornate chandeliers, silver pulpits and colourful stucco designs. The *tazias* (replica tombs) and *alams* (standards) used during the Muharram festival between March and April, are kept here. The **Jami Masjid**, to the southwest is another striking structure, built by Muhammed Ali Shah in the early 19th century. Its walls are heavily ornamented and its arches are covered with fine stucco work.

Northwest of the Jami Masjid, the **Daulat Khana** was the palace of Asaf-ud-Daula. Constructed in the late

Alam, **Chhota Imambara**

1780s, it includes numerous Indo-European buildings. The most prominent of these is the **Asafi Kothi**, its elegant façade marked by semi-circular bays.

Lucknow's main market is situated in the **Chowk**, the city's atmospheric old quarter. Stretching from Gol Darwaza to Akbari Darwaza, this maze of narrow *galis* (lanes) is lined with shops selling a range of goods from colourful kites to *paan* to Lucknow's famed *chikankari* – fine muslin delicately embroidered with threadwork. Wholesale flower markets overflow with roses and jasmine, and *attar* shops sell tiny bottles of fragrant perfume. The Chowk is also the best place to sample some authentic local cuisine (especially the many varieties of succulent kebabs), refined to an art form by chefs attached to nawabi households *(see p165)*.

At the southeastern corner of the city, situated in the Zoological Gardens, is Lucknow's **State Museum**. Its collection includes rare silver and gold coins, 16th-century paintings, and stone sculpture from the 2nd century BC.

The extraordinary **La Martinière** stands further south. It was

built by Major General Claude Martin, a French soldier of fortune and, in 1793, the richest European in Lucknow. A fanciful Gothic château, it has four enormous octagonal towers, containing numerous rooms. The exterior is lavishly decorated with a variety of animals and mythological figures, including lions, gargoyles and a female sphinx. One of the two cannons on the terrace was cast by Martin in his arsenal, as was the bronze bell. He died in 1800 and is buried in the basement. In 1840, the building, in accordance with Martin's will, became a school for boys. The school was evacuated during the siege of Lucknow, but re-opened a year later after extensive renovations.

🏛 **Picture Gallery**
⭘ *Mon–Sat.*
🏛 **State Museum**
📞 *(0522) 23 5542.* ⭘ *Tue–Sun.* 📷
🏫 **La Martinière College**
    Prior permission required
    from the principal.
    📞 *(0522) 22 3863.*

The elaborate façade of La Martinière College for boys

The colourful Hanuman Garhi Temple in Ayodhya

Ayodhya ㉔

Faizabad district. 134 km (83 miles)
E of Lucknow. 🚌 📷 *Kartik Purnima* (Oct/Nov).

LOCATED ON THE BANKS of the Sarayu river, Ayodhya is said to be the birthplace of Rama, the divine hero of the *Ramayana (see p27)*. Dozens of temples in this small pilgrim town commemorate his birth. Whether this is a historical fact or simply part of oral tradition, for devout Hindus Ayodhya remains inextricably linked with the legend of Rama. As a result, when the Mughal emperor Babur built a mosque near the supposed spot of Rama's birthplace in 1526, he left behind a bitterly contested site. Known as the **Babri Masjid** ("Mosque of Babur"), it was a long-simmering source of tension between Hindus and Muslims. In 1992, a mob of Hindus tore down the

mosque, leading to rioting all over the country. Security personnel now guard the site. A makeshift temple outside the security ring still attracts pilgrims, particularly during the full moon night of Kartik Purnima. One of the more renowned temples, among the hundreds of shrines on the river bank, is the **Hanuman Garhi**. Built within the walls of an old fort, it is dedicated to the monkey god, Hanuman.

ENVIRONS: Ayodhya's twin city, lying 6 km (4 miles) to its west, **Faizabad** has a sizeable Muslim population and was Avadh's first capital before it was shifted to Lucknow in 1775. In the town's centre is the Jami Masjid, built by the later Mughals, while the 18th-century tomb of Bahu Begum, the wife of Shuja-ud-Daula (Avadh's third nawab), is an austere structure built in marble. Faizabad also has a pretty rose garden.

THE MANGO: KING OF FRUITS

Langra mangoes, available in summer

The mango *(aam)* is considered the king of tropical fruits and is the best-loved fruit of the country. The Mughal emperor Babur called it the "finest fruit of Hindostan". The popular paisley motif is derived from the shape of the mango fruit, and mango leaves, considered auspicious, are used as buntings at festive occasions. Of the hundreds of varieties grown all over the subcontinent, few are as aromatic and juicy as the mangoes of Jaunpur. The *langra* is arguably the best among the varieties grown here. It is fleshy, juicy and sweet, and possessed of a distinct tangy flavour. It sells at a premium countrywide and is widely exported to the Middle East and Europe. The *dussehri* from Lucknow, and the *chausa* from the Rampur region, are also popular varieties. The raw *chausa* is considered ideal for spicy chutneys and pickles, without which no meal is complete.

Jaunpur ㉕

Jaunpur district. 60 km (37 miles)
SE of Lucknow. 🚶 *160,000*. 🚗 🚌

THOUGH LARGELY bypassed by visitors, Jaunpur has a wealth of medieval Islamic architecture. Located along the Gomti river, Jaunpur was established by Feroze Shah Tughluq *(see p91)* in the late 14th century and soon grew into an important trading post. It was subsequently ruled by the independent Muslim rulers of the Sharqi dynasty who held sway for much of the 15th century, until Ibrahim Lodi conquered the city in 1479. It eventually fell to the Mughals in the early part of the 16th century.

Jaunpur's many rulers each left a distinct architectural stamp on the city. The Mughal emperor Akbar built the great **Akbari Bridge** across the river, which still stands. To its north is the **Old Shahi Fort** from the Tughluq era. It contains a mosque, built with yellow and blue enamelled bricks, and an exact replica of a traditional Turkish bath or *hamam*. The most striking mosque, the **Atala Masjid**, just outside the fort, dates to the Sharqi period. It is embellished with recessed arches and ornamental fringes, and square courts surround the central structure. Though built on a grander scale, the 15th-century **Jami Masjid** borrows its basic architectural inspiration from the Atala Masjid.

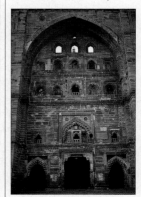

The grand façade of the Jami Masjid in Jaunpur

A view of the Taj Mahal *(see pp172–5)* from across the Yamuna river, Agra ▷

Varanasi 26

ALSO KNOWN AS KASHI ("the City of Light"), or as Benares, Varanasi is situated on the west bank of the Ganges and is India's holiest Hindu city, with a spiritual and religious legacy that goes back nearly 3,000 years. This is the city of Shiva, the foremost among the 12 places where the god burrowed and then burst into the sky in a fiery pillar of light (*jyotirlinga*). Sanctified by Shiva's all-pervading presence and the sacred Ganges, the 90 or so ghats along the river define the life and identity of Varanasi. Stretching from the southern Asi Ghat to the northern Adi Keshava Ghat, close to the Malviya Bridge, the ghats cover more than 6 km (4 miles). Lined with temples and shrines they reverberate with the endless cycle of Hindu religious practice – from daily rituals to profound rites of passage.

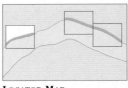

LOCATOR MAP
Asi Ghat to Shivala Ghat

Tulsi Ghat
One of Varanasi's oldest sites, this ghat (earlier known as Lolarka Ghat), was renamed after the poet-saint Tulsidas, who lived here in the 16th century. His house and temple still stand nearby.

Mural of goddess on the walls at Ganga Mahal Ghat

Asi Ghat
A linga stands beneath a pipal tree on Varanasi's southernmost ghat, which marks the confluence of the Asi and Ganges rivers.

Rewa Ghat

0 metres   50

0 yards   50

Bhadaini Ghat

Ganga Mahal Ghat

Janki Ghat
Brick-red steps distinguish Janki Ghat, in keeping with the Varanasi tradition of each ghat having its own distinctive colour.

Chet Singh Ghat
*The fort on this ghat marks the spot where Maharaja Chet
Singh was defeated by the British in the mid-18th century.*

Niranjani Ghat

Anandamayi Ghat
*The ashram founded by, the
Bengali female saint,
Anandamayi Ma, draws
thousands of devotees.*

**Panchkot
Ghat**

Jain Ghat

**Mahanirvani
Ghat**

Prabhu Ghat

Shivala Ghat
*This ghat, dating to 1770, was built by Chet
Singh, the maharaja of Varanasi.*

**Vatsaraj
Ghat**

RAMLILA

The Ramlila is a cycle of plays which tells the story of
the *Ramayana (see p27)*, in which Lord Rama is
exiled from his kingdom for 14 years. The Ramlila
tradition was started in Varanasi by Tulsidas, author
of the *Ramcharitmanas* (a popular version of the
epic). Street performances
take place in the evenings
at different venues, in
September/October, attracting thousands of spectators.
The performance at the
residence of the former
maharaja at Ramnagar Fort is
by far the most spectacular
of the Ramlilas in Varanasi.

**Young boys dressed as
the main characters**

Boat Building
*Planks lie waiting to be jointed
into boats, which are an essential
mode of transportation along the
busy river front.*

Varanasi: Digpatiya Ghat to Mir Ghat

THESE CENTRALLY LOCATED GHATS are the city's most sacred, and many of them were built under the patronage of India's erstwhile princely states, such as Darbhanga, Jaipur and Indore. One of Varanasi's two cremation ghats, Harishchandra Ghat, lies just to the south. Behind the holy Dasashvamedha Ghat meanders a winding lane known as Vishwanath Gali, lined with a multitude of shops that sell all manner of religious objects. It leads to the city's principal shrine, the Vishwanath Temple, said to be over 1,000 years old.

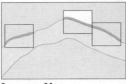

LOCATOR MAP
Digpatiya Ghat to Mir Ghat

Digpatiya Ghat

Chausatthi Ghat
Lessons in the scriptures take place at this ghat, named after the temple of the Chausath Yoginis or 64 female divinities.

Harishchandra Ghat

Rana Mahal Ghat

Munsi Ghat

Ahilyabai Ghat

Prayag Ghat

Darbhanga Ghat
The towers and turrets of old havelis, built in the early 1900s by two princes of Bihar, dominate this ghat. Some of the massive pillars in these havelis are reminiscent of the Greek style.

Dasashvamedha Ghat
This centrally located ghat, Varanasi's holiest spot, is named after the ten simultaneous horse sacrifices (dasashvamedh) performed by Brahma the Creator. Rows of priests sit under bamboo parasols, ready to perform ritual prayers for the pilgrims that swarm here.

Vishwanath Gali
*Lacquer jars, vermilion powder,
bottled Ganges water, bangles and
brocade, are all sold in the lane that
leads to the Vishwanath Temple, the
focal point of all worship in Varanasi.*

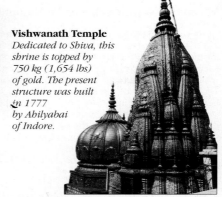

Vishwanath Temple
*Dedicated to Shiva, this
shrine is topped by
750 kg (1,654 lbs)
of gold. The present
structure was built
in 1777
by Ahilyabai
of Indore.*

Vishwanath
Temple

Man Mandir Ghat
*Jai Singh II of Jaipur built one
of his four Jantar Mantars* (see
pp358–9) *above Raja Man
Singh's palace in 1710. Its
sundial is visible from the ghat.*

The Palace of the Dom Raja, the king of the
Doms. The Doms are a caste who have
exclusive rights over the cremation ghats. They
sell wood and collect the ashes. The Dom
Raja's wealth derives from the cremation fees
his family have collected for centuries.

**Tripura
Bhairavi Ghat**

**Mir
Ghat**

0 metres   50

0 yards   50

BOAT RIDES

A sunrise boat ride is the highlight of a trip
to Varanasi, when the temples along the
river front are bathed in soft light. The
people of Varanasi trickle out of the labyrinthine lanes and head for the ghats at
dawn. Here, they wash clothes, perform
yoga *asanas,* offer flowers and incense to
the river, and take a ritual dip. The most
fascinating ride is from Dasashvamedha to Manikarnika Ghat *(see p206).*
Dozens of rowing boats ply up and down the river, and can be hired by
the hour. Rates are negotiable, so do fix the price before hiring one.

Dasashvamedha Ghat at sunrise

Varanasi: Nepali Ghat to Panchaganga Ghat

Along this stretch is the famed Manikarnika Ghat, one of the city's two cremation ghats. According to legend, Shiva's *mani* (crest jewel) and his consort Parvati's *karnika* (earring), fell into the nearby well while they were bathing, hence the name. Dying in Varanasi is a cause of celebration for Hindus, as it is believed to bestow instant salvation or *moksha* (liberation from the cycle of birth and death). It is said that Shiva whispers into the ears of the dying, and the old and infirm, sages and ordinary people, come here to breathe their last.

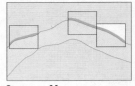

Locator Map
Nepali Ghat to Panchaganga Ghat.

| 0 metres | 50 |
| 0 yards | 50 |

Jalasen Ghat

Nepali Ghat
A lion stands outside a pagoda-style, woodwork temple, built by the royal family of Nepal.

Manikarnika Ghat
Funeral pyres burn day and night at this cremation ghat, while bodies wrapped in shrouds lie on biers besides piles of wooden logs. In the middle of the ghat is the well (kund) that Vishnu carved out with his discus before the Ganges flowed here.

Scindia Ghat
The elaborate structures on this ghat were so top heavy that they collapsed, and were rebuilt by Daulat Rao Scindia of Gwalior in 1937. A temple stands half submerged in the river, with its sanctum knee deep in the water.

RITUALS PERFORMED IN THE GANGES

A vessel for holy water

Although there are over 700 temples in Varanasi, none are more sacred than the river itself. The Ganges is worshipped as a living goddess, with the power to cleanse all earthly sins. Daily baths in her waters are advised by Hindu scriptures to prepare for the soul's final journey to liberation. Offerings of flowers and *diyas* floating down the river are a common and very pretty sight.

A Ritual Dip
Thousands come to Varanasi everyday, to bathe and pay obeisance to the Ganges.

Evening Aarti
The daily prayers (aarti) at dawn and dusk, serve as salutations to the river. Oil lamps are offered and bells rung while sacred mantras are chanted.

Wayside Shrine
A widow clad in white assembles flowers, incense and Ganges water in a small brass container, for paying homage at a wayside shrine.

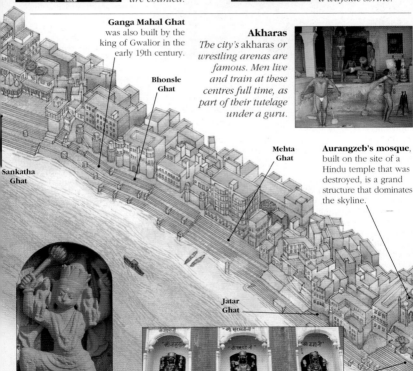

Ganga Mahal Ghat was also built by the king of Gwalior in the early 19th century.

Bhonsle Ghat

Akharas
The city's akharas or wrestling arenas are famous. Men live and train at these centres full time, as part of their tutelage under a guru.

Sankatha Ghat

Mehta Ghat

Aurangzeb's mosque, built on the site of a Hindu temple that was destroyed, is a grand structure that dominates the skyline.

Jatar Ghat

Panchaganga Ghat
This ghat marks the mythical meeting place of five sacred rivers, and has numerous images of the five river goddesses – Ganga, Yamuna, Saraswati, Dhupapapa and Kirana.

Adi Keshava Ghat

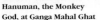

Hanuman, the Monkey God, at Ganga Mahal Ghat

Exploring Varanasi

VARANASI, ONE OF THE OLDEST CITIES in the world and a contemporary of Babylon and Nineveh, dates to the 7th century BC. This eternal city, where religion is an integral part of daily life, has drawn saints, poets and pilgrims through the ages. Behind the riverside ghats are narrow crowded lanes and bazaars, where people jostle with sacred cows, saffron-robed sadhus and devotees making offerings at roadside shrines. Varanasi is also renowned as a centre of Sanskrit learning and Hindu philosophy, attracting scholars and students from all over India. The Benares Hindu University, established in the early 1900s, perpetuates this tradition.

Dramatic ramparts of the Ramnagar Fort rising from the river bank

The narrow, winding Vishwanath Gali leads to the **Vishwanath Temple**, dedicated to Shiva, who is known here as Vishwanath, "Lord of the Universe". Painted floral carvings adorn its exterior and interior walls, and it is nearly always crowded. Adjacent to it lies the ancient **Jnana Vapi Well** ("Well of Wisdom"), whose waters are said to bring enlightenment. According to legend, this well is believed to contain the linga from the original Vishwanath Temple which was destroyed by the Mughal emperor Aurangzeb in the 17th century. The **Jnana Vapi Mosque** is built on the ruins of the temple.

Further south lies the sprawling **Benares Hindu University**, founded by the eminent Sanskrit scholar, Madan Mohan Malviya. Within the campus is the renowned **Bharat Kala Bhavan Museum**, known for having one of the country's best collections of Indian paintings. About 12,000 in number, they cover the period from the 11th century to the 20th century. Most impressive are the

Mughal miniatures, notably a depiction of the Emperor Shah Jahan. The Indian sculpture section is equally impressive, housing around 2,000 pieces, from 300 BC to AD 1400. Among them are a fine 10th-century sculpture of the marriage of Shiva and Parvati and an 11th-century statue of Vishnu as Varaha *(see p679)*. The display of Gandhara sculpture is also noteworthy.

The 17th-century **Ramnagar Fort**, lying across the river beyond Asi Ghat, has been home to the maharajas of Varanasi for 400 years. Although now in a state of disrepair, the palace still retains its charm. Ornamented swords, photographs of tiger shoots and visits by the King and Queen of Belgium line the walls. The Durbar Hall now houses the museum, where numerous objects are on display including palanquins and elephant howdahs.

🏛 Bharat Kala Bhavan
📞 *(0542) 31 6337.* ⭕ *Mon–Sat.* 📷
🚩 Ramnagar Fort and Museum
⭕ *daily.* 📷

Sarnath ㉗

Varanasi district. 10 km (6 miles) NE of Varanasi. 🚌 📷 *Buddha Mahotsava (May).*

TO BUDDHISTS, Sarnath is as sacred as Varanasi is to Hindus. The Buddha came to the Deer Park here in 528 BC, to preach the Dharmachakra, or the Wheel of Law, his first major sermon after gaining enlightenment *(see 221)*. Sarnath was then one of ancient India's greatest centres of learning, visited by Chinese travellers Fa-Hsien and Hiuen Tsang who wrote of its flourishing monasteries.

The central monument of the existing complex is the 5th-century AD **Dhamekh Stupa**, which is built at the site where the Buddha is believed to have delivered his sermon to five disciples. To its west, are the remains of the Dharmarajika Stupa, built by the Mauryan emperor Ashoka *(see p42)* to preserve the Buddha's relics. The complex also has several smaller monasteries and temples, as well as a Bodhi Tree, planted in 1931, and the statue of Anagarika Dharmapala, the founder of the society that maintained Sarnath and Bodh Gaya *(see pp222–3)*.

The **Archaeological Museum** exhibits a superb collection of Buddhist artifacts. The highlight is the Ashokan lion capital in polished sandstone *(see p4)*, India's national emblem.

🏛 Archaeological Museum
📞 *(0542) 58 5002.* ⭕ *Sat–Thu.* 📷

Dhamekh Stupa, Sarnath's principal monument

Brocades from Varanasi

VARANASI, India's most ancient pilgrimage centre, is also famous for its textiles. Renowned for its gossamer-fine cotton weaves for over 2000 years, its weaving traditions acquired new splendour from the 16th century onwards, with the patronage of the Mughal emperors. Varanasi's weavers soon became adept at weaving silk with gold and silver thread, to create sumptuous

Paisley pattern on silk

brocades for royal costumes and court furnishings, embellished with the exquisite floral, animal and geometric motifs favoured by the Mughals. They also produced brocades for Tibetan monasteries, decorated with Buddhist motifs such as clouds, lotus flowers and flames. Today, a wide range of brocade saris, scarves, and Tibetan-style fabrics are made and sold in the city.

The pallav, *the culminating end piece of a sari (see p30), is the most elaborately designed part of the sari. Its rich and complex weave requires very fine and deft craftsmanship.*

Gyaser *textiles* *were traditionally woven for trade with Tibet. This contemporary textile has taken a single element (the flame) from a ritual cloth to create a stunning pattern.*

A panel *of more than 600 geometric motifs has been specially created as a design directory for Varanasi's brocade weavers.*

The flower motif, *the classic* latifa buta, *combines gold and silver threads in a style known as Ganga-Yamuna, after the two rivers whose waters are pale and dark.*

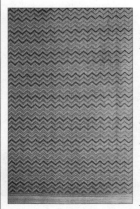

The Panch Ranga sari, *or the five-colour sari, creates a* leheriya *(wave) design in alternating colours of blue, orange, purple, pink and green, with a patterned edging in gold. The sheer richness of the design and colours are its distinguishing features.*

Contemporary brocades *recreate fish scale patterns in gold and silver threads, inspired by* Gyaser *textiles, as well as* jali *or trellis designs used in Mughal architecture.*

The creeper-covered ramparts of Allahabad Fort, built by the Mughal emperor Akbar

Allahabad ❷⑧

Allahabad district. 227 km (141 miles)
SE of Lucknow. 🚆 990,300. 🚉 🚌
🛈 Tourist Bungalow, 35 MG Marg,
Civil Lines, (0532) 60 1440. 📷
Kumbh Mela (every 12 years).

Aᴌʟᴀʜᴀʙᴀᴅ'ꜱ ꜱᴀᴄʀᴇᴅ location at the confluence (*sangam*) of three rivers – the Ganges, the Yamuna and the mythical Saraswati – has given it a cultural, political and religious importance for nearly 3,000 years. Hiuen Tsang, the Buddhist monk and scholar (*see p219*), visited the town, then known as Prayag, in AD 643, and wrote in great detail of its prosperity and fame.

In the 16th century it was captured by the Mughals who renamed it Allahabad. Later, the British maintained a large military presence in the city and established the law courts and the university. Jawaharlal Nehru (*see p57*), India's first prime minister, was born here in 1889, and the city later became a major centre of the Independence Movement. Today Allahabad is a quietly prosperous provincial centre, the broad, tree-lined avenues of the Civil Lines area contrasting with the congested bustle of the old city.

Allahabad Fort was built in 1583 by Akbar, who had a 3rd-century BC Ashokan pillar brought here from Kausambi. The pillar, unfortunately, is in a part of the fort that is not open to the public. On the fort's eastern side, is a temple complex with an undying banyan tree, the **Akshaivata**. Legend has it that anyone who leapt

from its branches would achieve salvation from the endless cycle of rebirths. After too many such attempts, the tree was fenced off, and a special permit is required from the local tourist office to view it.

Khusrau Bagh, a tranquil Mughal garden on the western edge of town, is named after Emperor Jahangir's eldest son who led an unsuccessful rebellion against his father and was later murdered during the battle over succession with his brother, Shah Jahan in 1615. His tomb lies next to those of his sister and his mother. The latter, a Rajput princess from Jaipur, distraught by the war between her husband and her son, took an overdose of opium. The *chhatris* on her tomb show Rajput influence.

Anand Bhavan, ancestral home of India's premier political dynasty, the Nehru-Gandhi family, now houses a museum of Nehru

Gothic façade of the All Saints Cathedral

memorabilia and chronicles the high points of the Independence Movement. Close by, in the Civil Lines area, is the fantastically arched and turreted **Muir College** built in 1870, and regarded a fine example of Indo-Saracenic architecture. Some glazed blue and white tiles still cling to the dome and a single tower soars to a height of 60 m (197 ft).

Across the road is the **Allahabad Museum** which has an interesting collection of terracottas from Kausambi and some 10th- to 13th-century sculpture from the Chandela era. Across Civil Lines to the west stands the **All Saints Cathedral**. Constructed in 1877 and designed by William Emmerson, architect of the Victoria Memorial in Kolkata (*see pp274–5*), it is lined with Jaipur marble inside.

🏛 **Allahabad Fort**
⬤ *closed to the public.*
🏤 **Anand Bhavan**
◻ *Tue–Sun.* 📷
🏛 **Allahabad Museum**
◻ *Tue–Sun.* 📷

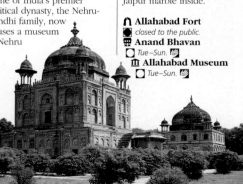

The tombs of Prince Khusrau and his sister, Khusrau Bagh

ENVIRONS: Kausambi, is 63 km (39 miles) and about an hour's drive from Allahabad on the eastern bank of the Yamuna. Excavated ruins of a stupa, a palace and extensive ramparts lie within a 2-km (1.3-mile) radius. While local legend holds that the city was built by the Pandavas, heroes of the *Mahabharata (see p26),* excavations reveal that a Buddhist community flourished here between 600 BC and AD 600. The Buddha himself came here to preach. The site contains the remains of a paved brick road, small houses, each with a ceramic drain, and the stump of an Ashokan pillar dating to the 3rd century BC (a second pillar was moved to the Allahabad Fort). Some terracotta artifacts and seals from 200 BC which were found here are now in the Allahabad Museum. Surrounded by fields and villages, with the river in the background, Kausambi has an aura of great serenity.

Chitrakoot's Ramghat, with temples on the banks of the Mandakini river

The remains of mud and brick ramparts at Kausambi

Chitrakoot ㉙

Banda district. 128 km (80 miles) SW of Allahabad. 🚉 *Karwi, 8 km (5 miles) NE of town centre, then taxi or bus.* 🚌 ℹ *MP Tourism Bungalow, (07672) 768 5326.* 🛏 *daily.*

THIS PILGRIM TOWN on the banks of the Mandakini river, though in neighbouring Madhya Pradesh, is easier to access from Allahabad. Chitrakoot, literally "the Hill of Many Wonders" refers to the forested **Kamadgiri Hill**, where according to the *Ramayana*, Rama, Sita and Lakshman spent a portion of their 14-year exile. Below the hill lies **Hanuman Dhara**, a natural spring that flows over a delightful image of the monkey god, Hanuman, placed in a recess. Dotted with numerous temples, and full of sadhus, the town has a unique charm. Boat rides from the attractive **Ramghat**, the town's main ghat, provide an impressive view of the temples along the river bank.

Kalinjar Fort ㉚

Banda district. 190 km (118 miles) W of Allahabad. 🚉 *Banda, 53 km (33 miles) N of Kalinjar Fort, then taxi or bus.* 🚌 🛏 *daily.*

ONE OF INDIA'S oldest forts, Kalinjar was called Kanagora by Ptolemy, the 2nd-century AD Egyptian geographer. Its strategic location on the route between North and South India made it a coveted target for many rulers. It has thus had a very turbulent history, and was successively occupied by many medieval rulers, until it fell to the Afghan ruler Sher Shah Sur *(see p79)* in 1545 .

Seven gateways, named after seven planets, and lined with sculptures and carvings lead to the fort. These include a giant Shiva with 18 arms and a dancing Ganesha. The **Neelkanth Temple** inside the fort, is dedicated to Shiva. Still in worship, the temple's inner sanctum contains an ancient linga.

THE KUMBH MELA

Hindu legend has it that during a war over the urn *(kumbh)* of immortal nectar *(amrit)* between the gods and demons, Vishnu gave the urn to Garuda, his winged mount. During his flight, four drops of the nectar fell on four places, Nasik *(see p474)*, Ujjain *(see p246)*, Haridwar *(see p184)* and Allahabad. A Kumbh Mela is thus held at each spot in turn,

Pilgrims at Allahabad's Kumbh Mela in 2001

every three years, when certain planetary configurations, transform the waters of the Ganges into nectar. Pilgrims from all over India, converge at the Kumbh Mela to wash away their sins, making it the world's largest religious gathering. Specially built tent-cities and stalls spring up to cater to the influx. At Allahabad's Kumbh Mela (Jan–Feb 2001) almost 30 million devotees took a bath on Mauni Amavasya (24 Jan), the most sacred of the six main bathing days. The next Kumbh Melas will be held in Ujjain in 2004, Nasik in 2007 and Haridwar in 2010.

BIHAR & JHARKHAND

THE NAME BIHAR derives from the Sanskrit word *vihara*, or monastery – an apt appellation for a state which was the birthplace of Buddhism. Major sites associated with the life and teachings of the Buddha, such as Bodh Gaya, Nalanda and Rajgir, lie in the dry plains of central Bihar and are the main attractions for visitors to the state. Northern Bihar is a fertile agricultural plain, watered by the River Ganges and its tributaries, where the famous Patna rice is grown. In November 2000, the southern part of Bihar became the new state of Jharkhand, which is dominated by a scenic and thickly forested highland called the Chhota Nagpur Plateau. The game sanctuaries of Palamau and Hazaribagh are located here. Jharkhand is rich in mineral resources, and is also the home of several indigenous tribes, believed to be among the earliest settlers of the Indian subcontinent.

SIGHTS AT A GLANCE

Towns & Cities
Jamshedpur 16
Munger 5
Patna 1
Ranchi 15

Hill Stations
Netarhat 14

Historic Sites
Nalanda 7
Rajgir 8
Sasaram 2
Vaishali 4

Temple Towns & Holy Places
Bodh Gaya 10
Deoghar 6

Gaya 9
Parasnath 11
Sonepur 3

National Parks
Hazaribagh Wildlife Sanctuary 12
Palamau National Park 13

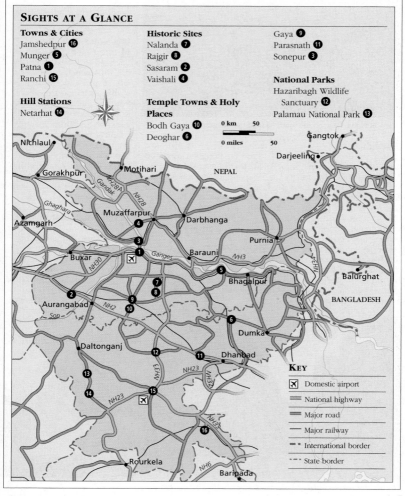

KEY

- ✕ Domestic airport
- National highway
- Major road
- Major railway
- ▪▪ International border
- ▪▪▪ State border

◁ **The Mahabodhi Temple at Bodh Gaya, the most important Buddhist pilgrimage site**

Patna ❶

T HE CAPITAL OF BIHAR is a modern city with ancient roots going back to 600 BC. During the reign of the Maurya and Gupta empires *(see p42)* Patna, then known as Pataliputra, was renowned as one of the great cities of Asia, but today it is a congested urban sprawl, stretching along the banks of the Ganges. West Patna, laid out by the British, has gracious mansions and administrative buildings, while the eastern end comprises the old city, a warren of crowded lanes surrounding medieval monuments and bustling bazaars.

Didarganj Yakshi

A view of Patna, lying on the south bank of the Ganges

⊞ Golghar
☐ *daily.*

Patna's signature landmark, the Golghar (literally "round house"), is an extraordinary dome that resembles a giant beehive. Built in 1786 by Captain John Garstin as a silo to store grain during the famines that occurred frequently in those days, the Golghar was never actually put to use. The structure is 125 m (410 ft) wide at the base and gradually tapers up to a height of 29 m (95 ft). Two external staircases spiral upwards

along its sides, with platforms to rest on along the way. The idea was to haul the grain up, and pour it down a hole at the top into the dome's pit, which had a capacity of 124,285 tonnes. A remarkable echo can be heard inside the structure. During the monsoon, the dome's summit offers impressive views of the Ganges which, in this season, can swell to a width of 8 km (5 miles).

⊞ State Museum
📞 *(0612) 23 0173.* ☐ *Tue–Sun.* 📷

Some remarkable treasures are displayed in the State Museum. Among them is the Mauryan-era (probably 3rd century BC) polished stone image of the Didarganj Yakshi (female attendant), considered a masterpiece of Indian sculpture. Other highlights include Gandharan style statues of Bodhisattvas; outstanding Buddha images in bronze and black stone, dating from the Pala period (8th–12th centuries); terracotta figurines, ancient Buddhist scriptures, and a collection of Tibetan *thangkas*. The museum also boasts a 15-m (49-ft) long fossilized tree trunk, believed to be 200 million years old.

⊞ Khudabaksh Library
📞 *(0612) 67 0109.* ☐ *Sat–Thu.*

Founded in 1900, this library has a renowned collection of rare Persian and Arabic manuscripts, including a group of beautiful illuminated medieval Korans, and superb Mughal miniature paintings. Its rarest exhibits are volumes salvaged from the sacking of the Moorish University in Cordoba, Spain, in the 11th century, though how they found their way to India still remains a mystery.

⊞ Harmandir Sahib
☐ *daily.*

This historic Sikh gurdwara marks the birthplace of the firebrand tenth guru, Gobind Singh *(see p103)*, who was born here in 1666. Regarded as one of the four holiest Sikh shrines, the marble temple was

The beehive-shaped Golghar, built as a granary in the 18th century

The eclectic private collection at the Jalan Museum

built in the 19th century by
Maharaja Ranjit Singh *(see
p104)*. On the floor above the
main sanctum is a museum
with the guru's relics.

🏛 Jalan Museum
By appointment. 📞 *(0612) 22 5070.*
Also known as Qila ("Fort")
House, this museum's eclectic
collection, gathered by a
19th-century ancestor of the
Jalan family, includes Chinese
paintings, Mughal jade and
silverware, Napoleon's bed
and Marie Antoinette's Sèvres
porcelain. Qila House itself is
an interesting structure, built
on the ruins of a 16th-century

fort constructed by the Afghan
ruler, Sher Shah Sur *(see p79)*.

🏛 Kumrahar
🕐 *Tue–Sun.* 📷
This site contains the ruins of
the ancient city of Pataliputra.
Excavations have unearthed
elaborately carved wooden
ramparts, polished sandstone
pillars and the remains of a
vast Mauryan assembly hall
that is said to have stood here
in the 2nd century BC. A
museum here displays some
of these finds, which date
from an era when Patna was
described by Megasthenes, the
Greek envoy to the Mauryan

VISITORS' CHECKLIST

Patna district. 1,015 km (631
miles) E of Delhi. 👥 *1,377,000.*
✈ *7 km (4 miles) W of the city
centre.* 🚉 🚌 ℹ️ *Bihar Tourism,
JP Loknayak Bhavan, Fraser Rd,
(0612) 22 5411.* 🛒 *Mon–Sat.*
🎭 *Patliputra Mahotsava (Mar).*

court, as "a city of light, where
even wooden walls shine
bright as glass".

🏛 Old Opium Warehouse
Gulzarbagh. 🕐 *Mon–Fri.*
Located in a walled compound
on the river bank, the opium
warehouse of the East India
Company is now the Government Printing Press. Visitors
can enter the three long,
porticoed buildings, where the
opium was packaged before
being sent by boat to Kolkata.

ENVIRONS: Maner, 30 km (19
miles) west of Patna, is a major
centre of Islamic learning. It
has the fine 16th-century sandstone mausoleum of the Sufi
saint Hazrat Makhdum Yahya
Maneri, set in a tranquil park.
Maner is also famous for its
laddoos, a round confection of
gramflour and molasses.

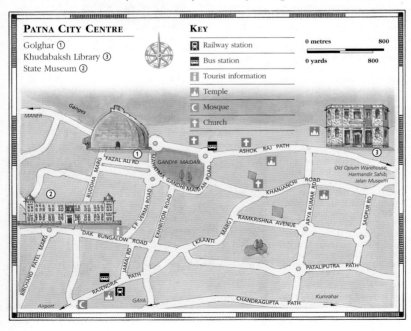

PATNA CITY CENTRE

Golghar ①
Khudabaksh Library ③
State Museum ②

KEY

🚉 Railway station

🚌 Bus station

ℹ️ Tourist information

🛕 Temple

☪ Mosque

✝ Church

0 metres   800

0 yards   800

The magnificent 16th-century tomb of the Afghan ruler Sher Shah Sur at Sasaram

Sasaram ❷

Rohtas district. 158 km (98 miles) SW of Patna. 🚉 🚌

THE DUSTY TOWN of Sasaram, a three-hour drive west of Patna on the historic Grand Trunk Road *(see p179)*, is famous for the **Mausoleum of Sher Shah Sur**, the great Afghan ruler *(see p79)*. This mid-16th-century architectural masterpiece is, to quote architectural historian Percy Brown, a testament to, "the aesthetic capacity of the Indian architect at its greatest, and his genius at its highest".

With a spectacular setting in the middle of an artificial lake, the pyramidal sandstone structure rises in five tiers to a height of 45 m (148 ft). The first two tiers comprise of a stepped basement and a high terrace that seems to emerge from the water, with a pavilion at each corner. The octagonal tomb is set on this plinth, and tapers towards the dome in three elegant layers of arches, crenellated parapets and small pillared kiosks. The broad dome is crowned by a large gilded lotus finial. All these elements combine to create a superbly proportioned structure that appears to float above the lake.

Curiously, the tomb is orientated eight degrees off its main axis – a mistake that the architect, Aliwal Khan, has skilfully disguised. The brilliant yellow and blue tiles are still seen in places. Nearby is the tomb of Sher Shah's father, Hasan Sur, built by the same architect.

Sonepur ❸

Saran district. 25 km (16 miles) N of Patna. 🚌 ℹ️ *Bihar Tourism, Patna, (0612) 22 5411.* 📷 *Sonepur Mela (Oct/Nov).*

NORTH OF PATNA, across the 7.5-km (5-mile) long Mahatma Gandhi Bridge over the Ganges, is the little town of Sonepur, known for its annual *mela*, reputedly the largest livestock fair in Asia. The month-long fair begins on the full moon of Kartik Purnima, which usually falls in October or November. The *mela* site is a sandy bank at the confluence of the

A mobile zoo at Sonepur's huge cattle fair

Ganges and Gandak rivers, and attracts millions of sadhus, pilgrims and local rural families, as well as livestock traders from all over India. On sale are elephants, camels, horses and cows, and an array of exotic birds. As a sideshow to the buying and selling of animals, grain and fodder, are several troupes of folk singers and magicians, *nautanki* (vaudeville) groups, dance bands, wrestlers and gymnasts, all exhibiting their skills on the sands. In between trading and entertainment, everyone takes a holy dip in the river during this most auspicious period in the Hindu calendar. The state tourism department sets up a tourist village a week in advance of the fair, and cottages and tents can be booked at their office in Patna. Even if buying an elephant (prices begin at about US$200) is not on a visitor's agenda, the Sonepur Mela, with its colourful combination of religion, entertainment and commerce, is an unforgettable experience.

Elephants being bathed during the Sonepur Mela

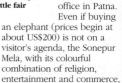

Vaishali ❹

Vaishali district. 55 km (34 miles) N of Patna. 🚍 ℹ️ *Tourist Information Centre, Vaishali (06225) 59 424.*

The renowned Bihar School of Yoga, inside Munger Fort

SET IN THE LUSH green landscape of north Bihar, dotted with groves of banana and litchi trees, Vaishali is an important religious site. Mahavira, founder of the Jain faith *(see p396)*, is said to have been born here in 599 BC. It is also the place where the Buddha preached his last sermon *(see p221)*. In the 6th century BC, Vaishali was a flourishing city under the Lichhavi rulers who established one of the world's first city republics here. A well-preserved **Mauryan Stone Pillar**, dating from the 3rd century BC, with a life-size lion sitting atop it, is located 4 km (2.5 miles) west of the Tourist Lodge.

Close to the pillar is the **Ramkund Tank**, also known as the Monkey Tank, which is now a stagnant pond. According to legend, it was dug by monkeys, who offered the

The lion atop the 3rd-century BC pillar, Vaishali

hungry Buddha a bowl of honey here – a scene often depicted in Buddhist sculpture and painting. Also near the pillar, are the ruins of a 5th-century BC brick stupa. It is believed to have been built by the Lichhavi rulers soon after the Buddha's death to enshrine his ashes. Ongoing excavations have revealed the brick foundations of various other stupas. In 1996, Japanese Buddhists built a temple and a huge white **Vishwa Shanti Stupa** ("World Peace Stupa"), re-establishing Vaishali on the Buddhist pilgrimage circuit.

MADHUBANI PAINTING

The vibrant Madhubani folk paintings *(see p81)* of north Bihar have now gained international acclaim and popularity. Painted on the walls of village homes by women, Madhubani art features motifs and themes inspired by Hindu mythology, nature and festivals, as well as by everyday life. Especially intricate compositions are created for the *kobbar*, or bridal room, for the wedding night, usually featuring a god and goddess surrounded by a host of small birds and animals, and watched over by the sun, moon and stars. In recent years, with Madhubani women having participated in international exhibitions in foreign countries, new motifs have crept into their work, such as skyscrapers, aeroplanes and women in stiletto heels. The vibrant colours used are made of vegetable and mineral dyes, and the paintings are drawn with thin bamboo sticks. Madhubani paintings are now also being done on paper and fabric, and are widely available for sale in many Indian cities.

A Madhubani painting, with its strong lines and colours

Munger ❺

Munger district. 180 km (112 miles) E of Patna. 🚆 ℹ️ *Tourist Information Centre, Fort Area, Munger (06344) 22 392.*

PICTURESQUELY located on the banks of the Ganges, Munger is home to the famous **Bihar School of Yoga**, established by Swami Satyanand, and now run by his disciple Swami Niranjananand. The school lies within the 15th-century Munger Fort, and welcomes visitors. The fort was successively occupied by the Mughals, various regional rulers and the British. Near the north gate of the fort is an 18th-century British cemetery with ornate pyramid-shaped tombs.

🏛️ **Bihar School of Yoga**
📞 *(06344) 22 430.* ⬜ *daily.*

Deoghar ❻

Deoghar district. 180 km (112 miles) E of Patna. ✈️ 🚍 ℹ️ *Tourist Information Centre, (06432) 22 422.* 🎪 *Mela (Jul/Aug).*

DEOGHAR'S **Baidyanath Dham** is an important Shiva temple in India. It is said to mark the spot where the heart of Shiva's consort Parvati fell, as the grief-stricken Shiva carried her corpse across the earth *(see p279)*. An object of special worship is the linga inside the temple, one of Shiva's 12 *jyotirlingas (see p202)*, believed to have miraculously materialized out of light. The month-long annual *mela* here attracts over 100,000 pilgrims every day.

Nalanda ⑦

Bodhisattva in
Temple 3

ONCE THE MOST PRESTIGIOUS centre of learning in Asia, the Buddhist University of Nalanda, founded in the 5th century AD, had over 5,000 international students and teachers, and a library of nine million manuscripts. Built on a hallowed site where the Buddha had often stayed, Nalanda flourished until AD 1199, when it was looted and destroyed by the Turkish raider, Bakhtiar Khalji. The evocative ruins of its monasteries and temples still convey a vivid impression of the serene and ordered life of contemplation and learning that prevailed here.

Temple 12
The remains of a torana stand in front of this 7th-century temple, which faces the row of monasteries.

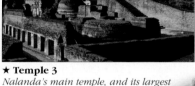

★ Temple 3
Nalanda's main temple, and its largest structure (31 m/102 ft high), dates to the 6th century. It has a shrine chamber at the top and small stupas at its corners.

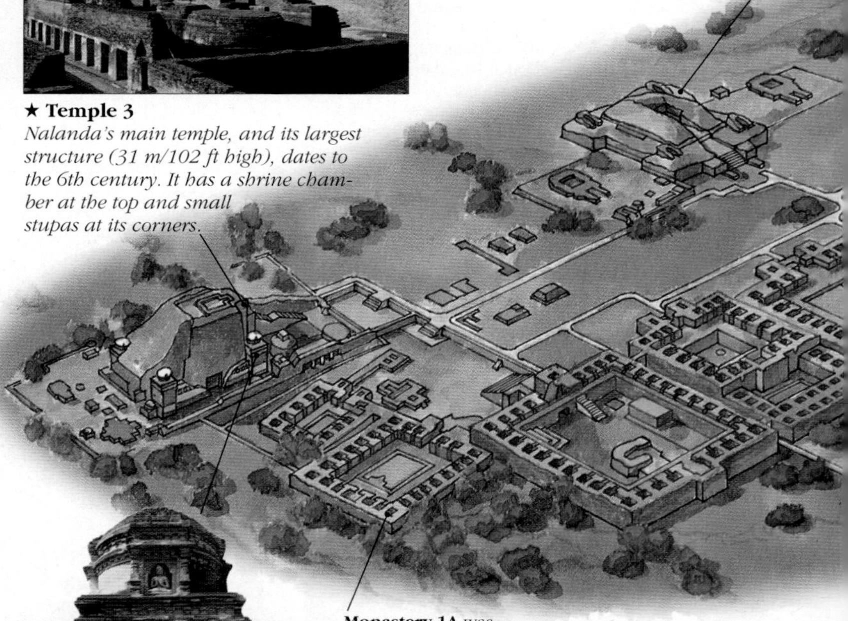

Monastery 1A was probably built by a king of Sumatra in the 9th century.

0 metres   50
0 yards   50

★ Votive Stupas
Located in the courtyard surrounding Temple 3, these have plaster images of standing Bodhisattvas and seated Buddhas.

STAR FEATURES

★ Temple 3

★ Votive Stupas

★ Dado Panels from Temple 2

A View of the Monasteries
Monks' cells surround a courtyard in each of the 11 monasteries. The ruins display skilful brickwork.

Temple 13 has a brick-making furnace to its north.

Temple 14
Traces of painting can be seen here in a niche with a pedestal, where a large image of the Buddha once stood.

Monastery 8 has an imposing shrine in its courtyard. All the monasteries stand on terraces.

Museum

★ Dado Panels from Temple 2
This 7th-century temple's basement, which is all that remains, has an elaborately sculpted dado with over 200 panels carved with deities, animals and floral motifs.

Brickwork
Layers of much earlier construction, some of it dating back to the 3rd century BC, are visible in the brickwork at Nalanda.

HIUEN TSANG IN NALANDA

The great Chinese scholar-monk, Hiuen Tsang, travelled across forbidding deserts and mountains to come to Nalanda in the early 7th century AD. He spent 12 years both studying and teaching here, and was dazzled by Nalanda's "soaring domes and pinnacles, pearl-red pillars carved and ornamented, and richly adorned balustrades". On his return to China he settled down at the Big Goose Pagoda in Xian, where he translated into Chinese the Buddhist scriptures he had brought back with him from Nalanda.

Chinese print of Hiuen Tsang

Hot sulphur springs at Rajgir, surrounded by temples and rest houses

Rajgir ❽

Nalanda district. 115 kms (72 miles) SE of Patna. 🚶 33,700. 🚉 🚌
ℹ Bihar Tourism, Kund Market.

SURROUNDED by five holy hills, the picturesque little town of Rajgir is important for Buddhists as well as Jains. Both the Buddha and Mahavira, founder of Jainism, spent many months meditating and preaching here. The hills around are dotted with Jain temples, the ruins of monasteries and meditation caves. Dominating Rajgir is the large new Japanese-built marble and sandstone **Vishwa Shanti Stupa** on Ratnagiri Hill, with its four gilded statues of the Buddha. Visitors can go up to the stupa by chairlift. From here, a path leads to the adjoining **Griddhakuta Hill** ("Vulture's Peak"), a site much venerated by Buddhists. Two rock-cut caves here were a favourite retreat of the Buddha, and it was on this hill that he preached two of his most famous sermons. The incident of the Buddha subduing a wild elephant, a scene often depicted in Buddhist art, also took place in Rajgir.

To the west of Griddhakuta Hill is **Vaibhava Hill**, at the foot of which are hot sulphur springs, crowded with people seeking a medicinal dip. On top of the hill are the seven **Saptaparni Caves** where the First Buddhist Council met soon after the Buddha's death to record his teachings. Below them on the hill is the **Pippala Watchtower**, a curious rock and stone structure, with cells for guards that were later used by monks. It dates to the 5th century BC, when Rajgir was the capital of the Magadha Empire (see p42), ruled by King Bimbisara who became a devotee of the Buddha. The remains of the great drystone cyclopean wall he built can still be seen on Rajgir's hills.

ENVIRONS: Pawapuri, 38 km (24 miles) east of Rajgir, is sacred to Jains as the place where the founder of their faith, Mahavira, died in 500 BC. A lotus-filled tank, with the marble Jalmandir Temple in the middle of it, marks the site of his cremation.

Gaya ❾

Gaya district. 100 km (62 miles) S of Patna. 🚶 383,200. 🚉 🚌
ℹ Bihar State Tourist Office, Railway Station, (0631) 32 155.

STRETCHING ALONG the banks of the Phalgu river, Gaya along with Varanasi and Allahabad, is regarded as one of the three most sacred sites for performing Hindu funeral rites. It is believed that Vishnu himself sanctified Gaya, decreeing that prayers for departed souls, performed here, would absolve all their earthly sins. Dominating the religious life of the city is the **Vishnupad Temple**, which is not open to non-Hindus, but no such restrictions apply to the picturesque ghats and shrines along the river front.

ENVIRONS: The **Barabar Caves**, cut deep into a granite hill, are 45 km (28 miles) north of Gaya, along a bumpy jeep road. They were the inspiration for the Marabar Caves in EM Forster's famous novel, A Passage to India. Dating to the 3rd century BC, these are the earliest examples of rock-cut caves in India. Of the four caves, built for ascetics on the orders of the Mauryan emperor Ashoka, the two most impressive are the **Lomas Rishi** and **Sudama Caves**. They are remarkable for the highly lustrous polish on the stone, and for the way in which the caves have been shaped to imitate the rounded wood and bamboo dwellings which were common at that time. Even the interior walls have perpendicular grooves cut into the stone, in imitation of bamboo strips. The façade of the Lomas Rishi Cave has fine lattice-work carving, and a charming row of elephants paying homage to stupas.

It is unsafe to explore this wild and rugged area without reliable guides, recommended by the Bihar Tourism office at Gaya's railway station.

Rituals being performed at the Phalgu Ghat in Gaya

In the Buddha's Footsteps

THE BUDDHA was born in 566 BC as Siddhartha Gautama, prince of the kingdom of Kapilavastu. Though born in Lumbini, in Nepal, all the places associated with his life and his teachings are in Bihar and Uttar Pradesh. These are now part of a well-travelled circuit for

The Buddha's footprints

Buddhist pilgrims, who follow in the Buddha's footsteps from Bodh Gaya, where he attained enlightenment; to Sarnath where he preached his first sermon; through other places he visited regularly, and finally to Kushinagar, where he died in 486 BC.

Renouncing *his princely life, Prince Siddhartha (represented here by a riderless horse) left his palace and his family at the age of 30, to search for answers to the meaning of human existence and suffering.*

Emaciated *by fasts and penances while he spent six years living with ascetics and wandering as a beggar, Prince Siddhartha found that such self-mortification gave him no answers.*

Enlightenment *came at Bodh Gaya where, after meditating for 49 days under the Bodhi Tree, he discovered that the cause of suffering is desire; and that desire can be conquered by following the "Eightfold Path" of Righteousness.*

The First Sermon, *delivered at Sarnath (see p208), contained the essence of his teachings. Eschewing asceticism, rituals, caste and class distinctions, his Eightfold Path prescribed Right Thought, Understanding, Speech, Action, Livelihood, Effort, Concentration and Contemplation.*

The Buddha's Death *took place in 486 BC. He fell ill after eating wild mushrooms prepared by one of his followers, and died in a grove of sal trees at Kushinagar, where a stupa marks the site of his cremation.*

BUDDHIST PILGRIM SITES

The Buddhist Trail *attracts Buddhists from all over the world, including countries such as Japan and Thailand. Many stupas and temples along the pilgrimage circuit owe their existence to these devotees. This Buddha image was built by the Japanese.*

See also the features on Little Tibet (p123) and Buddhist Iconography (p141).

The Thai Monastery in Bodh Gaya, built like a traditional *wat* (temple)

Bodh Gaya ⑩

Gaya district. 115 km (71 miles) SE of Patna. ⓧ 30,900. ⯑ Gaya, 13 km (8 miles) N of town centre, then taxi or bus. ⯑ ⯑ Bihar Tourism, 34 Mahabodhi Market Complex, (0631) 40 0672. ⯑ Monlam Chenmo Prayers (Jan/Feb), Buddha Jayanti (May).

THE HOLIEST SITE for Buddhists from all over the world, Bodh Gaya is the place where the Buddha attained enlightenment. The focal point of the town is the **Mahabodhi Temple**, whose soaring pyramidal spire dominates the landscape. The temple is enclosed on three sides by a 1st-century BC stone railing, carved with lotus medallions and scenes from the Buddha's life, and includes the sacred **Bodhi Tree**, under which the Buddha meditated before he attained enlightenment.

The original temple at this spot was a circular stupa, built by the Mauryan king Ashoka in the 3rd century BC, but a major reconstruction in the 7th century AD gave the temple its present form. In the 12th century, it was severely damaged by Muslim invaders, but faithfully restored in the 14th century by Burmese kings, who also added the replicas of the main spire at each corner of the temple. Then, as Buddhism went into near eclipse in northern India, the temple site was flooded and silted over, and effectively "lost" for centuries. Some Burmese Buddhists rediscovered it in the late 19th century. The temple ruins were then excavated and restored.

Today, Bodh Gaya once again flourishes as an international centre for Buddhism. Temples and monasteries built by various countries, including China, Japan, Sri Lanka, Vietnam, Thailand, Taiwan, Korea, Bhutan and Nepal, dot the town. The **Thai Temple** is the most picturesque, while the modern **Japanese Temple** is remarkable for the 25-m (82-ft) high Buddha statue that towers in front of it. The **Bhutanese** and **Tibetan Monasteries** are filled with colourful murals and prayer wheels, and both are always thronged by red-robed monks.

In the courtyard around the Mahabodhi Temple, monks meditate at the stupas, novitiates have their heads shaved, and pilgrims pray before the Bodhi Tree. For three weeks during the winter, a tented city springs up around the temple, as thousands of monks and pilgrims congregate here for the Monlam Chenmo Prayers, often presided over by the Dalai Lama and other venerated figures from the Buddhist world.

Across the street, the **Archaeological Museum** has fragments of the beautiful original 3rd-century BC temple railing, and bronze and stone images from the 8th to 12th centuries, which were excavated during the restoration of the temple.

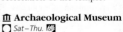
The 25-m (82-ft) Buddha statue, erected by the Japanese

🏛 **Archaeological Museum**
◻ Sat–Thu. 🞕

THE SACRED BODHI TREE

According to local lore, the original Bodhi Tree *(Ficus religiosa)* was cut down by Emperor Ashoka's wife because she was jealous of the time he spent at his Buddhist devotions. The emperor then revived the tree by nurturing its roots with gallons of milk, and built a protective stone railing around it. The tree that stands today is said to come from the same stock as the original tree. Ashoka's son Mahinda took a sapling from the original tree to Sri Lanka on one of his proselytizing missions. The tree flourished there, and its sapling was later brought back to be planted at Bodh Gaya after the original tree had died.

Pilgrims gathered around the Bodhi Tree

Beautifully carved stupas in the temple courtyard

Bodh Gaya: Mahabodhi Temple

Lotus carving on the Chakramana

T HE MAHABODHI TEMPLE complex marks the site where, more than 2,500 years ago, Prince Siddhartha meditated on the causes of human suffering, found the answers he was seeking under the Bodhi Tree, and became the Buddha – the Enlightened One. The best time to visit the complex is at dusk, when thousands of oil lamps bathe the temple in a golden light, and the sound of Buddhist prayers chanted in different languages fills the air.

The Buddha
This gilded stone image (late 10th century) in the main sanctum has an aura of great serenity. The pedestal is carved with alternating lions and elephants.

The Torana
The gateway to the temple is made of granite and covered with inscriptions from the Buddha's teachings. It dates from the 8th century.

The Spire, 54 m (177 ft) high, is carved in tiers and capped by an umbrella-like finial.

The Bodhi Tree under which the Buddha spent 49 days.

The entrance leads to the main sanctum with the Buddha image.

The Vajrashila
The red sandstone seat beneath the Bodhi Tree marks the spot where the Buddha sat. It probably dates to the 3rd century BC.

The Chakramana
Carved with lotuses, this sacred promenade was where the Buddha walked, meditating on whether to spread his message to the world.

Parasnath ⑪

Giridih district. 179 km (111 miles) NE of Ranchi. 🚉 🚌 *Madhuban.*

AN IMPORTANT destination for Jain pilgrims, Parasnath is named after Parsvanatha, the 23rd Jain *tirthankara (see p396)*, who is believed to have attained nirvana here. Clustered on top of Sikayi Hill, the highest peak in Jharkhand at 1,400 m (4,593 ft), are 24 Jain temples, each one dedicated to one of the Jain *tirthankaras.* The temple on the highest point is dedicated to Parsvanatha. Pilgrims begin their climb from Madhuban, a stopover at the foot of the hill, and it takes over three hours, through forested slopes. Palanquins are available to carry those who do not want to walk. The views from the top are magnificent.

Hazaribagh Wildlife Sanctuary ⑫

Hazaribagh district. 107 km (66 miles) N of Ranchi. 🚉 *Hazaribagh Rd Station, 67 km (42 miles) S of Pokharia, the main entry point, then bus.* 🚌 ℹ️ *Tourist Office, near bus stand, Hazaribagh town, (06546) 236, located 16 km (10 miles) S of Pokharia. For permission contact Divisional Forest Officer, Hazaribagh, (06546) 23 340.*

SET IN THE undulating Chhota Nagpur Plateau covered with tropical deciduous forests, this wildlife sanctuary is 16 km (10 miles) from Hazaribagh. Hazaribagh means "Thousand Tigers" and this quiet town's environs were once famous for their tiger population. However, as a result of deforestation, most

En route to Netarhat, through the picturesque Chhota Nagpur Plateau

of the tigers are gone, and spotting a tiger from one of the ten viewing platforms is now rare. The 190 sq-km (73 sq-mile) sanctuary, established in 1954, is bisected by the Ranchi-Kolkata Highway which, with its heavy traffic, has driven away many animals to other habitats. But there are plenty of wild boar, nilgai and leopard, and its thick forests are a haven for birdlife.

Leopard at Palamau Park

Palamau National Park ⑬

Palamau district. 170 km (106 miles) W of Ranchi. 🚉 *Daltonganj, 24 km (15 miles) NW of Betla, the main entry point.* 🚌 ℹ️ *Tourist Office, Betla, (06562) 56 513. For permits contact the Deputy Director, Palamau National Park, Daltonganj, (06562) 22 842. Jeeps are available at Betla.* 🏨

ALSO KNOWN AS Betla National Park, Palamau National Park, on the north-western edge of the Chhota Nagpur Plateau, is set in hilly tribal country, with the Koel and Burha rivers flowing

through it. The park is dotted with bamboo, *sal (Shorea robusta)* groves, towering *mahua (Madhuca indica)* trees from whose pale yellow flower the area's tribal people (Oraons and Mundas) make a potent liquor, and grassland. The sanctuary is inhabited by wild elephants, deer, leopards, tigers (44 at last count in 1997) and several bird species. There are numerous watchtowers and hides that have been strategically placed around the water holes. The picturesque ruins of two 16th-century forts, hot springs and a few tribal villages also lie within the park.

Netarhat ⑭

Palamau district. 156 km (97 miles) W of Ranchi. 🚌

THE ONLY hill station in Bihar and Jharkhand, Netarhat is situated at an altitude of 1,140 m (3,740 ft) and lies deep within the forested Chhota Nagpur hills, just off the Ranchi-Hazaribagh Highway. There are several pleasant rambles in the hills around this little town, and fine views of the surrounding countryside from **Magnolia Point**. The scenic **Burhaga Falls** make an enchanting picnic spot. A curious building here is a huge wooden Swiss-style chalet, formerly the country retreat of the British governors of Bihar, and now a boarding school for boys. The school authorities usually welcome visitors.

Watchtower in the Hazaribagh Wildlife Sanctuary

Fields on the outskirts of Ranchi

Ranchi ⑮

Ranchi district. 289 kms (180 miles)
E of Patna. 🚶 846,500. ✈ 5 km
(3 miles) S of town centre. 🚉 🚌
ℹ️ Birsa Vihar Tourist Complex, Main
Rd, (0651) 30 0646. 🛥 daily. 🎊
Rath Yatra (Jun/Jul).

THE CAPITAL OF the newly
formed state of Jharkhand,
Ranchi is a good base from
which to explore the natural
beauty of the Chhota Nagpur
Plateau. The summer capital
of Bihar in the days of the
British Raj, Ranchi still attracts
visitors keen to escape the
heat and dust of Bihar's
plains. The town's main
attraction is the 17th-century
Jagannath Temple, perched
on a hill in the south-
western outskirts.
Like the Jagannath
Temple at Puri (see
p313), this temple
also holds an annual
chariot festival.

The Chhota Nagpur
Plateau is the home
of the forest-dwelling
Munda and Oraon
tribes. The wide-
ranging exhibits and
collections of artifacts
in the **Ranchi
Museum** provide a
comprehensive picture of
their lifestyles and social
structures.

**Oraon tribal girls
dancing**

🏛 **Ranchi Museum**
◻ Mon–Sat. ● public hols.

**ENVIRONS: Hundru
Falls**, 45 km (28 miles)
east of Ranchi, is a
lovely picnic spot. This
is the point where the
Subarnarekha river
drops down dramati-
cally from the Chhota
Nagpur Plateau to form
a 100-m (328-ft) water-
fall, which splashes
into the pools below.
The sleepy town of
McCluskiegunj, 40 km
(25 miles) northwest of
Ranchi, is a quaint relic
of the Raj. It was estab-
lished as a settlement
for Eurasians who felt
they belonged neither
to British nor to Indian
society, and wanted a
haven of their own.
Today, only a handful
of the original settlers remain
(many have emigrated to
Australia), living out their old
age in cottages crammed with
their treasured collections of
English china ornaments, and
adorned with pictures of the
British royal family.

Jamshedpur ⑯

East Singbhum district. 130 kms (81
miles) SE of Ranchi. 🚶 570,300.
🚉 ℹ️ Tourist Information Centre,
Bistupur, (0657) 43 2892. 🚌 🛥
daily. 🎊 Founder's Day (Mar).

ONE OF INDIA'S major industrial centres, Jamshedpur
is a rare oasis of cleanliness
and efficiency in this region.
The planned township,
surrounded by lakes,
rivers and the pretty
Dolma Hills, was
established in 1908
by the Parsi tycoon,
Sir Jamshedji Tata (see
p446). He is regarded
as the father of
industrial develop-
ment in India. The
Tata Iron and Steel
Company (TISCO)
was set up by him
in this area because
of the rich deposits
of iron ore and coal found
here. The Tata empire continues to flourish, and several of
its research, educational and
cultural institutes here are
open to visitors.

FESTIVALS OF BIHAR & JHARKHAND

Maner Urs (Feb), Maner.
This festival honours the
Sufi saint Sheikh Yahya
Maneri with soulful
qawwali singing at his
mausoleum, and a lively
fair in the town.
Sarhool (Mar/Apr),
Jharkhand. The Munda
tribals perform tree-
worshipping ceremonies,
followed by much
dancing and feasting.
Jatra (Mar/Apr),
Jharkhand. The Oraon
tribals hold lively dances
during this festival, in
which the young people
choose their mates.
Buddha Jayanti (May),
Bodh Gaya. A fair and
special prayers are held to
celebrate the Buddha's
birth, attainment of enlightenment and nirvana.

**Pilgrims with offerings for
the Sun God at Chhat**

Batsavitri (May/Jun).
This festival commemo-
rates the legend of Savitri,
who brought her husband
Satyavan back from the
dead through the sheer
intensity of her prayer. It
is celebrated by married
women who fast and
pray, tie strings around
banyan trees and offer
sweets and fruits to
images of Savitri.
Sonepur Mela (Oct/Nov),
Sonepur (see p216).
Chhat (Oct/Nov). Flower-
shaped pastries called
thekua are made in every
home during this three-
day thanksgiving festival,
dedicated to the Sun God,
celebrated all over Bihar.

MADHYA PRADESH & CHHATTISGARH

COVERING A VAST AREA of 443, 406 sq km (171,200 sq miles), Madhya Pradesh and Chhattisgarh constitute the geographic heart of India. Between them, they border on to seven states, have one-third of India's forest cover, and are home to 40 per cent of the country's tribal population. Madhya Pradesh is crossed by the Vindhya and the Satpura mountains, and its main river is the Narmada. In the state's rugged north are the famous Khajuraho temples, while eastern Madhya Pradesh has two of India's finest game sanctuaries, Bandhavgarh and Kanha. The scenic Malwa Plateau in the southwest has the great Buddhist stupa of Sanchi and the romantic 15th–16th century citadel of Mandu.

In November 2000, the thickly forested and remote southeast, with its predominantly tribal population, became the new state of Chhattisgarh.

SIGHTS AT A GLANCE

Towns & Cities
Bhopal **9**
Chanderi **5**
Gwalior **1**
Gyaraspur **12**
Indore **13**
Jabalpur **19**
Mandla **20**
Shivpuri **4**

Historic Sites
Ajaigarh **7**
Bhojpur **10**

Khajuraho **6**
Mandu **15**
Orchha **3**
Sanchi **11**

National Parks
Bandhavgarh National Park **8**
Kanha National Park **21**

Hill Stations
Pachmarhi **18**

Temple Towns & Holy Places
Maheshwar **16**
Omkareshwar **17**
Ujjain **14**

Tours
A Tour of Bundelkhand **2**

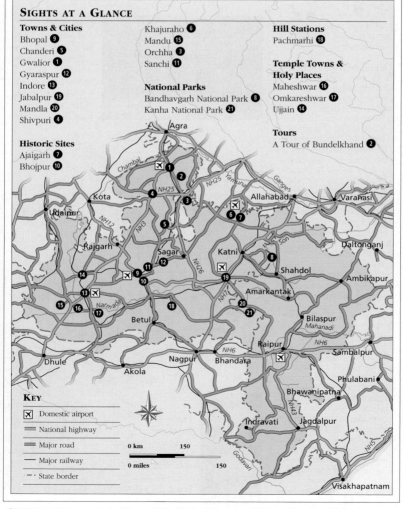

KEY

☒ Domestic airport
═══ National highway
━━━ Major road
──── Major railway
- · - · State border

0 km   150
0 miles   150

◁ Sculptures of *apsaras* (celestial nymphs) inside the 10th-century Lakshman Temple at Khajuraho

The Durbar Hall of Jai Vilas Palace
with its two gigantic chandeliers

Gwalior ❶

Gwalior district. 321 km (200 miles)
S of Delhi. 🏠 827,000. ✈ 14 km
(8 miles) N of city centre. 🚉 🚌
🛈 MP Tourism, 6 Gandhi Marg,
(0751) 34 2606. 🎭 Tansen Music
Festival (Nov/Dec).

APART FROM **Gwalior Fort**,
the main attraction for
visitors to Gwalior is the
opulent, Italianate **Jai Vilas
Palace**, south of the fort, built
for the maharaja of Gwalior
by his architect, Colonel Sir
Michael Filose, in the late
19th century. Still the residence
of the former Scindia rulers,
part of the palace has been
turned into a museum. The
most magnificent room is the
Durbar Hall. Hanging from its
ceiling are two of the world's
largest chandeliers, 13-m
(43-ft) high and weighing
3 tonnes each. Before
they were hung the
strength of the roof
was tested by having
several elephants
stand on it. Also on
view is an extra-
ordinary mechanical
silver toy train that
carried liqueurs around the
maharaja's dining table.

North of the fort is Gwalior's
old town, which has two
interesting Islamic monuments
– the 16th-century **Tomb of
Mohammed Ghaus**, a Mughal
nobleman, which has
outstanding stone latticework
screens; and the **Tomb of
Tansen**, the famous singer
who was one of the "nine
jewels" of the Mughal emper-
or Akbar's court *(see p180)*.

🏛 **Jai Vilas Palace Museum**
◯ Tue–Sun. 📞 (0751) 32 2390. 🈺

Gwalior Fort: Man Mandir Palace

Tile with
parrots

THE MASSIVE GWALIOR FORT stretches for
nearly 3 km (2 miles) atop a 100-m
(328-ft) high sandstone and basalt hill. Its
formidable bastioned walls, 10-m (33-ft)
high, enclose exquisite temples and palaces,
the most spectacular of which is the Man
Mandir Palace. Built between 1486 and
1516 by Raja Man Singh of the Tomar
dynasty, this double-storeyed palace is
regarded as one of the finest examples of
Rajput secular architecture, embellished with superb
stone carving and latticework. Brilliant blue, yellow and
green tiles depicting parrots and peacocks, rows of
ducks, elephants, banana trees and crocodiles holding
lotus buds, decorate the Man Mandir's façade.

Courtyard
*The interior court-
yard with its carved
pillars has rooms
around it. Two
subterranean floors,
with fountains and
baths, were later
used as dungeons.*

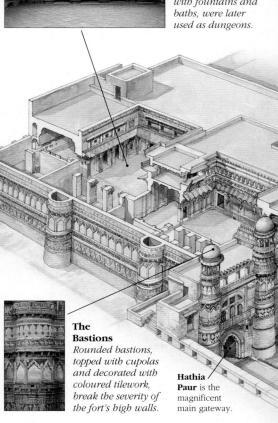

**The
Bastions**
*Rounded bastions,
topped with cupolas
and decorated with
coloured tilework,
break the severity of
the fort's high walls.*

**Hathia
Paur** is the
magnificent
main gateway.

The lavishly carved and decorated
south façade of Man Mandir

Stone Latticework
*The oriel window, in the
zenana quarters of the
palace, is framed against
intricately latticed stone
battlements. A pair of
caparisoned elephants
flank the window.*

Exploring Gwalior Fort

Described by a 16th-century
Persian chronicler as "the pearl
in the necklace of castles of
Hind", Gwalior Fort has had
a turbulent history. Founded
in the 8th century AD, it was
successively ruled by a series
of local Hindu dynasties,
followed by the Delhi Sultans,
the Mughals and finally the
Maratha Scindias (*see p471*),
who became the maharajas of
Gwalior in the 18th century.
It was also briefly in
British hands in the
19th century. The fort
is best entered from
the **Urwahi Gate** on
its western side, where
21 colossal **Jain
Sculptures** depicting
the *tirthankaras (see
p396)* and dating from
the 7th to the 15th
centuries, are carved
into the rock face.

Lying to their left is
the richly carved, 25-m
(82-ft) high temple, **Teli ka
Mandir**, the tallest temple in
the fort. Built in the 9th
century and dedicated to
Vishnu, it has an unusual
shikhara, rounded at the top.
After the Indian Mutiny of
1857 (*see p53*) British soldiers
occupied the temple and used
it as a soda factory. Situated
to its north are a pair of 11th-
century Vishnu temples, called
the **Saas-Bahu** ("Mother and
Daughter-in-Law") **Temples**.
They are covered with superb
sculptures of dancing girls and
deities, though their *shikharas*
were destroyed in an attack
by Sultan Qutbuddin Aibak
(*see p48*) in the 12th century.

North of them is the **Hathia
Paur**, entrance gateway to the

Rock-cut Jain
sculpture

VISITORS' CHECKLIST

N of city centre. ◻ *daily.* 🌐
Son et Lumière *daily, Apr–Sep:
8:30pm; Oct–Mar: 7:30pm.*
Archaeological Museum
◻ *Tue–Sun.* 🌐

Man Mandir Palace, its ornate
pillars supporting a dome
with a richly corbelled arch.
At the northeastern edge of
the fort is the 15th-century
Gujari Mahal, built
by Raja Man Singh for
his Gujar (tribal)
queen. Now the
**Archaeological
Museum**, its fine
collection of Jain and
Hindu sculpture
includes the cele-
brated statue of the
salabhanjika (wood
nymph), originally
from the temple at
Gyaraspur (*see p243*).

GWALIOR FORT

1 Urwahi Gate
2 Jain Sculptures
3 Teli ka Mandir
4 Saas-Bahu Temples
5 Hathia Paur Gate
6 Man Mandir Palace
7 Gujari Mahal

0 metres   700

0 yards   700

The 9th-century Teli ka Mandir,
the tallest temple in the fort

The strikingly ornamental façade of Gwalior Fort ▷

A Tour of Bundelkhand ❷

GWALIOR AND THE ADJOINING REGION of Bundelkhand, named after the Bundela Rajputs, make up a culturally distinctive area in Central India. Countless forts and monuments, situated in a boulder-strewn landscape of great beauty, still echo with stories of the pageantry of the Bundela Rajput courts, and the valour of warriors such as the Rani of Jhansi *(see p195)*. The area's glorious history and refined artistic traditions are reflected in the architectural treasures of Gwalior, the medieval city of Orchha, and the hilltop temples of Sonagiri.

Gwalior ①
The capital of many dynasties since the 8th century AD, Gwalior *(see p228)* is the most splendid of the "gateways" to the Bundelkhand region.

Pawaya ②
The remains of an ancient fort can be seen in this capital of the Nag kings (3rd century AD) from the highway at Dabra.

AGRA

Sonagiri ③
This impeccably maintained complex of 77 Jain temples is approached through a thriving pilgrim settlement.

Dabra

Sind

Jhansi ⑤
The town is known for its impressive fort and the heroic Rani Lakshmibai, who died leading her troops against the British in 1858.

Datia ④
This erstwhile Bundela capital surrounded by numerous small lakes, has scenically located palaces on hillocks.

BUNDELKHAND

Betwa

KEY

▰	Tour route
═	Other roads
≈	River

KHAJURAHO

Orchha ⑥
The temples, cenotaphs and tiered palaces of Orchha are perfect examples of Bundelkhand architecture.

0 km   20
0 miles   10

TIPS FOR DRIVERS

Length: *120 km (75 miles).*
Stopping-off points: *Gwalior, Sonagiri, Datia, Jhansi, Orchha and Taragram provide convenient stopovers. There is a petrol pump at Dabra, after Gwalior. State tourism hotels and guesthouses are available at Gwalior, Jhansi and Orchha. Local buses run between the major stops.*

Taragram ⑦
A fascinating handmade paper factory here is an interesting experimental centre aimed at upgrading local craftsmanship.

The marble cenotaph of Madhavrao Scindia at Shivpuri

Orchha ❸

See pp234–5.

Shivpuri ❹

Shivpuri district. 117 km (73 miles) SW of Gwalior. 🚶 *146,900.* 🚉 🚍 **ℹ** *MP Tourism, Railway Station, (0751) 54 0777.*

THE SUMMER CAPITAL of the Scindia rulers of Gwalior, Shivpuri was once a thickly forested region, and a favourite hunting ground of the Mughals. Most of the elephants in Emperor Akbar's army were taken from these forests. Today, the main attractions are the 19th-century white marble cenotaphs of Madhavrao Scindia and his mother, which stand facing each other in a formal Mughal-style garden. With their mix of *shikharas* (spires), domes and cupolas, they epitomize Indo-Islamic architecture. Madhavrao's cenotaph is decorated with *pietra dura* work in lapis lazuli and onyx. There are life-size statues of the ruler and his mother and, in accordance with family tradition, their favourite foods are brought and left here every day. The colonial-style **Madhav Vilas Palace** has airy terraces overlooking the town. The 156-sq km (60 sq-mile) **Madhav National Park** is a mixed deciduous forest with an artificial lake, surrounded by grasslands. **George Castle**, a hunting lodge, was built by Jiyajirao Scindia in honour of King George V, who stayed here in 1911.

Chanderi ❺

Guna district. 227 km (141 miles) S of Gwalior. 🚶 *28,300.* 🚍 **ℹ** *UP Tourism, Hotel Veerangana, Shivpuri Rd, Jhansi, (0517) 42 402.*

THE MEDIEVAL TOWN of Chanderi is dominated by the **Kirtidurga Fort**, perched 200 m (656 ft) above the Betwa river, and overlooking an artificial lake, Kirtisagar. Built by the Pratihara kings in the 10th century, Chanderi successively fell to the sultans of Delhi and Malwa, the Mughal emperor Babur and finally to the Marathas, becoming part of the Scindia kingdom of Gwalior. The entrance is through the Khuni Darwaza ("Bloody Gateway"), marking the point at which the Mughal emperor Babur broke through the 6-km (4-mile) long granite walls of the fort, when he conquered it in 1528. Cut into the

Minaret detail, Kirtidurga Fort

adjacent rock face are several imposing Jain statues. Most of the structures inside the fort are attributed to Sultan Mahmud of Malwa, and are executed in the graceful provincial Afghan style that distinguishes the buildings of Mandu *(see pp247–9)*. The most ambitious edifice here is the **Koshak Mahal**, built in 1445. The sultan originally planned it as a seven-storeyed palace, but only managed to complete two storeys, each with balconies, rows of windows and beautifully vaulted ceilings. Other notable buildings are the domed and arcaded **Jami Masjid** and the **Badal Mahal** with its elegant gateway. Chanderi was once a flourishing centre of trade, and an exploration of the town reveals large sandstone *havelis*, shops raised on plinths and ruined caravanserais lining the winding lanes. The town is also famous for its gossamer muslin saris and brocades.

ENVIRONS: Deogarh Fort, the "Fortress of the Gods", is 25 km (16 miles) southeast of Chanderi. Within it are a splendid display of sculptures from a group of 9th- to 10th-century Jain temples. Just below the fort is the 5th-century Vishnu Dasavatara Temple with its fine sculpture and carved pillars topped by celestial musicians. A statue of Vishnu asleep on Ananta, the cosmic serpent *(see pp24–5)*, on one of the outer walls, is among the early masterpieces of Indian art.

Chanderi's fort, the scene of many battles

One of the *chhatris* (cenotaphs)
of the Bundela kings at Orchha

Orchha ❸

Tikamgarh district. 120 km (75 miles)
SE of Gwalior. 🚪 *Jhansi, 19 km (12
miles) NW of Orchha, then taxi or bus.*
🚌 🛈 *MP Tourism, Sheesh Mahal,
(07680) 52 624.* 🎎 *Ramnavami
(Apr), Dussehra (Sep/Oct).*

ORCHHA is dramatically
positioned on a rocky
island, enclosed by a loop of
the Betwa river. Founded in
1531, it was the capital of the
Bundela kings until 1738,
when it was abandoned in
favour of Tikamgarh.

Crumbling palaces, pavil-
ions, *hamams*, walls and
gates, connected to the town
with an impressive 14-arched
causeway, are all that remain
today. The three main palaces
are massed symmetrically
together. These are the **Raj
Mahal** (1560), **Jahangiri
Mahal** (1626) and **Rai
Praveen Mahal** (mid-1670s),
named after a royal paramour.

The old town is dominated
by three beautiful temples –
the **Ram Raja**, the **Lakshmi
Narayan** and the **Chaturbhuj**.
A unique blend of fort and
temple styles, the Chaturbhuj
Temple is dedicated to Vishnu
and has huge arcaded halls
for massed singing, and a
soaring spire.

Lying along the Kanchana
Ghat of the Betwa are the 14
hauntingly beautiful cenotaphs of the Orchha rulers.
Along with the many *sati*
pillars in Jahangiri Mahal's
museum, these serve as
reminders of Orchha's feudal
past when queens sometimes
committed *sati* by jumping into
their husband's funeral pyres.

Orchha: Jahangiri Mahal

Flower motif
in turquoise
stone

AN EXCELLENT example of Rajput Bundela
architecture, this palace was built by
the Bundela king Bir Singh Deo and
named after the Mughal emperor Jahangir
who spent one night here. The many-
layered palace has 132 chambers off and
above the central courtyard and an almost
equal number of subterranean rooms. The
square sandstone palace is extravagantly
embellished with lapis lazuli tiles, graceful *chhatris* and
ornate *jali* screens. It also has a modest museum.

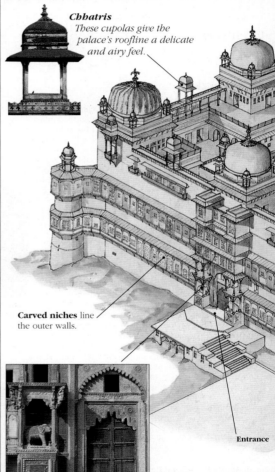

Chhatris
*These cupolas give the
palace's roofline a delicate
and airy feel.*

Carved niches line
the outer walls.

Entrance

★ **Entrance Gateway**
*The impressive entrance gate-
way, flanked by stone elephants,
leads up to the central courtyard.*

STAR FEATURES

★ **Entrance Gateway**

★ **Domed Pavilion**

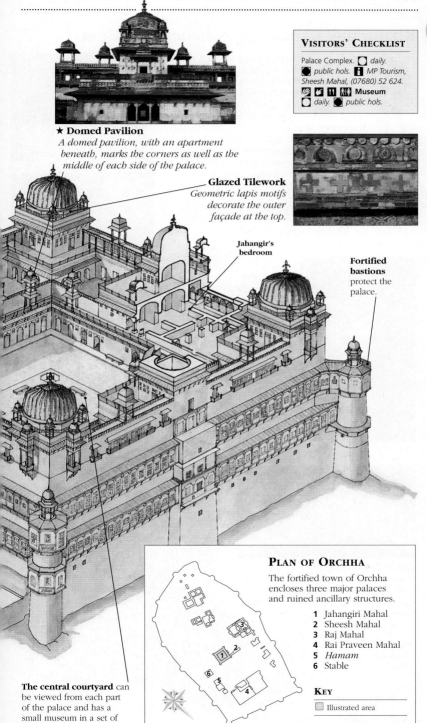

★ **Domed Pavilion**
*A domed pavilion, with an apartment
beneath, marks the corners as well as the
middle of each side of the palace.*

Glazed Tilework
*Geometric lapis motifs
decorate the outer
façade at the top.*

**Jahangir's
bedroom**

**Fortified
bastions**
protect the
palace.

VISITORS' CHECKLIST

Palace Complex. ◯ *daily.*
● *public hols.* ℹ *MP Tourism,
Sheesh Mahal, (07680) 52 624.*
▦ ♿ 🍴 🚻 **Museum**
◯ *daily.* ● *public hols.*

PLAN OF ORCHHA

The fortified town of Orchha
encloses three major palaces
and ruined ancillary structures.

  1 Jahangiri Mahal
  2 Sheesh Mahal
  3 Raj Mahal
  4 Rai Praveen Mahal
  5 *Hamam*
  6 Stable

KEY

☐ Illustrated area

The central courtyard can
be viewed from each part
of the palace and has a
small museum in a set of
rooms that run along it.

Khajuraho: Kandariya Mahadev Temple ❻

THE MAGNIFICENT GROUP of temples at Khajuraho, a UNESCO World Heritage Site, were built between the 9th and 10th centuries by the Chandela dynasty which dominated Central India at that time. The most impressive of the temples is the Kandariya Mahadev, which represents the pinnacle of North Indian temple art and architecture. It is remarkable for its grand dimensions, its complex yet perfectly harmonious composition, and its exquisite sculptural embellishment. Over 800 sculptures cover the temple, depicting gods and goddesses, beasts and warriors, sensuous maidens, dancers, musicians and, of course, the erotic scenes for which the Khajuraho temples are famous.

Amorous couple

View of the Kandariya Mahadev temple, built 1025-1050

★ Apsaras
Often carved as support-bracket figures, the celestial nymphs reveal the sculptors' mastery of the female form. Full of natural charm and sensuous grace, they are shown as dancers, attendants of the deities, or simply engaged in everyday activities.

The Maha Mandapa
Carved pillars, nymph-brackets, a corbelled ceiling and balconied windows add to the sumptuousness of the central hall's interior.

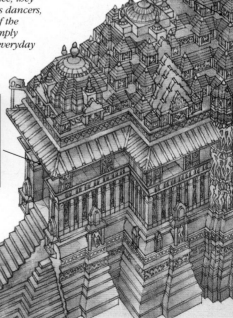

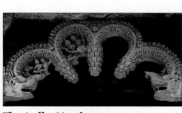

The Ardha Mandapa
The east-facing Ardha Mandapa (entrance porch) has an exquisite makara torana (ceremonial arch) flanked by two crocodile heads, and covered with floral tracery.

STAR FEATURES

★ **Apsaras**

★ **Main Shikhara**

★ **Erotic Panels**

★ Main Shikhara

The main spire soars to 30m (98ft), while 84 smaller spires rise in a crescendo towards it, to create the impression of a mountain range – more specifically, Mount Kailasa, the abode of Shiva.

★ Erotic Panels

The largest erotic panels are on the northern and southern facades, between the balconies. The erotic sculptures are variously believed to celebrate the marriage of Shiva and Parvati, serve as a love manual, or simply express an exuberant celebration of life and creation.

Garbhagriha

The dark and plain garbhagriha (inner sanctum), symbolizing a womb, houses a linga, the phallic symbol and principal object of worship in all Shiva temples. The sanctum is entered through a richly carved door frame.

The first tier above the terrace is carved with processional friezes and goddesses.

Exploring Khajuraho

THE 25 temples at Khajuraho represent the brilliant burst of artistic flowering that took place under the generous patronage of the powerful Chandela rulers, who made Khajuraho their peacetime capital. The remoteness of the temples' location saved them from the ravages of Islamic raiders, but also led to their being abandoned after the decline of the Chandelas in the 13th century. Hidden in a dense forest for 700 years, they were "rediscovered" in 1838 by Captain TS Burt of the Bengal Engineers. According to local tradition there were originally 85 temples, and ongoing excavations have unearthed extensive ruins in the area.

The polished stone image of Varaha, Vishnu's boar incarnation

The Khajuraho temples are divided into three groups. The most important are in the **Western Group** which, apart from the Kandariya Mahadev *(see pp236–7)*, includes the **Lakshman** and the **Vishwanath Temples**. Both are similar to the Kandariya Mahadev in composition, sculptural embellishments and themes, but they also have outstanding individual features.

The superb ceiling of the entrance porch and the female bracket figures inside the Lakshman Temple (built in AD 930) are worth special notice. The pair of street singers on the south façade are also remarkable, with their expressions of intense absorption. The master architect and his apprentices are exquisitely sculpted on the subsidiary shrine in the temple's eastern corner.

Opposite the Lakshman Temple is a pavilion with a magnificent statue of Varaha, the boar incarnation of Vishnu *(see p679)*, covered with carvings of several deities. In the Vishwanath Temple, dating to AD 1002, the *apsara* plucking a thorn from her foot (on the south façade) is outstanding, as is the *apsara* playing the flute, which can be seen in the interior chamber.

The **Matangeshwar Temple** (built AD 900), with its plain circular interior, is the only one still in everyday use *(see p243)*. The **Archaeological Museum**, near the entrance to the Western Group, has a

Apsara applying kohl

fine collection of sculptures found in the area, including a dancing Ganesha, and a fascinating frieze showing the construction of the Khajuraho temples, with scenes of stone being cut and transported.

A short distance away is the **Eastern Group** of temples. The Jain **Parsvanatha Temple**, built in AD 950, is the most remarkable, for the intricately carved ceiling pendants in its entrance porch. Three exquisite sculptures here show *apsaras* applying kohl around their eyes, painting their feet (both on the south façade), and fastening ankle bells (on the north façade). The last phase of temple-building in Khajuraho is seen in the **Southern Group**. The **Chaturbhuj Temple** (built AD 1090) has a superb, four-armed image of Shiva in the inner sanctum. It is the only

major temple in Khajuraho without any erotic sculptures.

🏛 **Archaeological Museum**
◯ *Sat–Thu.* 🔲 *(07686) 2028.*

ENVIRONS: Raneh Falls, 17 km (11 miles) south of the town of Khajuraho, provide a cool retreat. The 19th-century **Rajagarh Palace**, 25 km (16 miles) southeast of Khajuraho, is in the same Bundela style as the palaces at Datia and Orchha *(see pp234–5)*. Situated 32 km (20 miles) southeast of Khajuraho, along the Ken river, the **Panna National Park**, has herds of deer, leopards, crocodiles and the scenic Pandav Falls. A favourite spot for tourists in the park is Gille's Tree House restaurant, perched 20 m (66 ft) above the ground.

Ajaigarh ❼

Panna district. 75 km (45 miles) E of Khajuraho. 🚌 ◯ *daily.*

THIS GREAT Chandela citadel, built in the 9th century AD and perched 500 m (1,640 ft) above the plains, is now a spectacular ruin. The steep path up to the top goes past gigantic sculptures carved into the sheer cliff face, including a particularly enchanting one of a cow and calf. Within the fort lie the ruins of once-magnificent palaces, broken fragments of statues, and several poignant *sati* pillars, marking the self-immolation of countless Rajput widows.

Image of Vishnu in the Lakshman Temple

Bandhavgarh National Park ❽

VISITORS' CHECKLIST

Shahdol district. 237 km (147 miles) SE of Khajuraho. 🚉 Umaria, 33 km (21 miles) SW of Tala, the main entry point. 🚌 ℹ️ MP Tourism, White Tiger Lodge, Tala, (07653) 65 308. 🕐 Nov–Jun. 📷 🎟️ extra charges. 🎫 🚙 Jeep safaris available.

Indian tiger

ONE OF INDIA'S most important Tiger Reserves, the Bandhavgarh National Park sprawls across an area of 625 sq km (241 sq miles). Apart from some 50 tigers, the park's wildlife includes 250 species of birds, leopards, deer, jungle cats and packs of *dhole* (Indian wild dog). Great rocky hills, lush deciduous forests, marshes and meadows make Bandhavgarh one of India's most scenic areas. A picturesque hilltop fort with fine sculptures is part of the park's attractions.

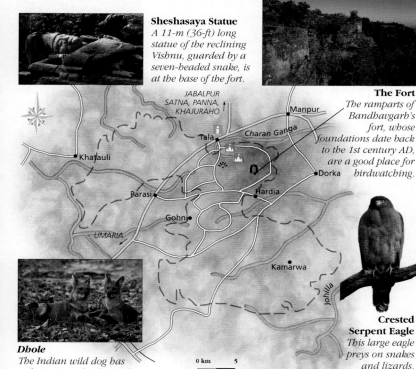

Sheshasaya Statue
A 11-m (36-ft) long statue of the reclining Vishnu, guarded by a seven-headed snake, is at the base of the fort.

The Fort
The ramparts of Bandhavgarh's fort, whose foundations date back to the 1st century AD, are a good place for birdwatching.

Crested Serpent Eagle
This large eagle preys on snakes and lizards.

Dhole
The Indian wild dog has a distinctive whistling call, to assemble the pack. It has a red coat, large upright ears and a bushy tail.

KEY

• ▬ Park boundary

═ Major road

═ Minor road

🛕 Temple

ℹ️ Tourist information

🔅 Viewpoint

⚲ Fort

THE WHITE TIGER OF REWA

In 1951, the maharaja of Rewa captured a white tiger in these forests. Named Mohan, he was mated in captivity with several tigresses, and all the white tigers in zoos across the world today are Mohan's descendants. A pair can be seen in the Bhopal zoo *(see p241)*. Since 1951, no other white tiger has been seen in the Bandhavgarh region. The white tiger is an "evolutionary colour aberration" and not an albino, nor a separate sub-species.

The white tiger, very rare in the wild

Bhopal

Arch detail, Moti Masjid

T HE CAPITAL OF MADHYA PRADESH, Bhopal was founded in the 11th century by Raja Bhoj of the Paramara dynasty. By the 18th century, it was held by a Muslim dynasty whose rulers included several remarkable women, the Begums of Bhopal. The city, ringed by hills, stretches along the shores of two artificial lakes, the Upper and Lower Lakes. The old quarter, north of the Lakes, is a maze of narrow lanes, bazaars and mosques. To the south is the new city, with its leafy suburbs and industrial enclaves. In December 1984, a toxic gas leak from the Union Carbide factory claimed the lives of 5,000 people, in one of the world's worst industrial disasters. With the wounds of this tragedy now healing, Bhopal is a good base for visiting some of the state's fascinating sites.

Fountain and tank inside the 19th-century Moti Masjid

◖ Taj-ul-Masjid

Hamidia Rd. ◗ *daily.* ● *to non-Muslims on Fri & on Muslim festivals.*

The most imposing monument in Bhopal, this large, pink-washed mosque was begun by Sultan Jehan Begum in 1878 but was left unfinished for almost a century before being completed in 1971. A progressive ruler, the begum established the city's postal system and hospitals, but virtually bankrupted the royal treasury as a result of her ambitious schemes. The enormous courtyard of the mosque has a *dukka* (water tank) for ritual ablutions, and the vast prayer hall is striking for its rows of pillars. This grandiose mosque is surmounted by three white domes and flanked by two 18-storeyed minarets. Its general ambience is majestic rather than beautiful.

Bhopali batua

♖ The Chowk

Bazaar ◗ *Tue–Sun.* Jami Masjid ◗ *daily.* ● *to non-Muslims on Fri & on Muslim festivals.*

Situated in the centre of the old quarter is the Chowk (literally, main square). Streets radiate out from it, each one specializing in a particular type of goods – the Bhopali *batuas* (elaborately beaded purses) for which Bhopal is famous, tussar silk, caps, drums and spices. *Havelis* line the streets, with wooden fronted shops on the ground floor, and elaborate wrought-iron balconies above. Dominating the area is the **Jami Masjid** with its gold finials, built in 1837 by Qudsia Begum, another of Bhopal's female rulers. It is surrounded by shops selling silver jewellery.

South of the Chowk is another mosque, the **Moti Masjid** ("Pearl Mosque") built in 1860 by Qudsia Begum's daughter and successor. With its striped dome and tapering sandstone minarets, it looks like a smaller version of the Jami Masjid in Delhi *(see p86)*.

Also worth visiting in this area is the **Shaukat Mahal**, a 19th-century Indo-Saracenic cum Rococo palace. Built by a French mercenary who claimed to be a descendant of the Bourbons, it now houses government offices, though visitors are usually allowed inside by the guards.

⛫ Bharat Bhavan

Shamla Hills. ◖ *(0755) 66 0353.* ◗ *Tue–Sun.* 🖼 🔢

A large cultural complex, Bharat Bhavan was established in 1982 to showcase and promote India's rich tribal and folk art heritage. To the right of the entrance is the Tribal Art Gallery, a superb collection that includes votive objects, terracotta figures, masks, wall paintings, wood-carvings, and the distinctive metal sculptures created by craftsmen from Bastar *(see p253)*. A gallery across the courtyard exhibits contemporary Indian art. Bharat Bhavan is also the venue for regular performances of theatre, music and dance in the evenings.

⛫ State Archaeological Museum

Banganga Rd. ◖ *(0755) 55 5099.* ◗ *Tue–Sun.* 🔢 🖼

A collection of 12th-century Jain bronzes, found in Dhar district in western Madhya Pradesh, form the highlight of

The Taj-ul-Masjid, Bhopal's most imposing monument

Replica of a tribal hut in the Rashtriya Manav Sangrahalaya

this museum's collection. It also has a series of stone sculptures, mostly from the 6th to 10th centuries. Older pieces include *yakshis* (female attendants) dating to 200 BC, and a Standing Buddha in black granite. The museum shop has good plaster replicas of some sculptures for sale.

🏛 Rashtriya Manav Sangrahalaya (Museum of Man)

S of Shamla Hills. 🏛 *Tue–Sun.* 🛈
Set in the hills overlooking the Upper Lake, this museum, which sprawls over a 40-ha (99-acre) site, has authentic replicas of Indian tribal dwell-

ings, built by the tribal people themselves. Tribal cultures from all over the country are represented in the museum, through comprehensive displays of utensils, ritual objects, musical instruments, tools, murals, carvings, jewellery and costumes. An Introductory Gallery, in a thatched hut, explains the museum's layout.

🐾 Van Vihar National Park

🏛 *Wed–Mon.* 🖼
The most famous inhabitants of this large park, near the Upper Lake, are the white tigers *(see p239).* A good time to see these rare creatures is at about 4pm, when they come

to the edge of their enclosure for their evening meal. The zoo is also home to lions, leopards and Himalayan bears.

🏛 Birla Museum

Near Lakshmi Narayan Temple. 🇨 *(0755) 55 1388.* 🏛 *Thu–Tue.* 🖼
This museum has a well-displayed collection of stone sculptures dating from the 7th to 12th centuries. Shiva, Vishnu and various goddesses are shown in their different incarnations. Particularly impressive are Vishnu in his boar (Varaha) incarnation, Goddess Durga in her ferocious Chamunda form, and Shiva and his consort Parvati in their celestial home on Mount Kailasa. Next to the museum is the large, recently-built and brightly painted Lakshmi Narayan Temple, overlooking the Lower Lake.

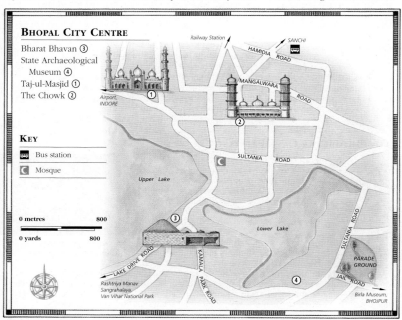

BHOPAL CITY CENTRE

Bharat Bhavan ③
State Archaeological Museum ④
Taj-ul-Masjid ①
The Chowk ②

KEY

🚌 Bus station

🇨 Mosque

0 metres   800
0 yards   800

Railway Station
SANCHI
HAMIDIA ROAD
MANGALWARA ROAD
Airport, INDORE
SULTANIA ROAD
Upper Lake
Lower Lake
SULTANIA ROAD
PARADE GROUND
LAKE DRIVE ROAD
KAMALA PARK ROAD
JAIL ROAD
Rashtriya Manav Sangrahalaya, Van Vihar National Park
Birla Museum, BHOJPUR

Sculpture from the incomplete Bhojeshwar Temple, Bhojpur

Bhojpur ⑩

Bhopal district. 28 km (17 miles) SE of Bhopal. 🚌 🛈 *MP Tourism, Bhopal, (0755) 77 4340.*

FOUNDED BY the 11th-century Paramara king, Raja Bhoj, who also established Bhopal *(see p240)*, Bhojpur is dominated by the monumental, though incomplete **Bhojeshwar Temple**. Impressive sculptures cover parts of its unfinished corbelled ceiling and its entrance doorway.

Inside, on a tiered platform, is an enormous stone Shivalinga, 2.3-m (8-ft) high and 5.3 m (17 ft) in circumference. Etched on the paving stones and rocks in the forecourt, are the architect's detailed plans for the finished temple, while on the northeast side are the remains of a massive earthen ramp used to haul stone up to the roof.

ENVIRONS: The **Bhimbetka Caves** with their prehistoric paintings, dating back some 12,000 years, are about 17 km (11 miles) south of Bhojpur.

Sanchi ⑪

Raisen district. 46 km (29 miles) NE of Bhopal. 🚇 🚌 🛈 *Traveller's Lodge, (07482) 62 723.* 🎭 *Chaityagiri Vihara Festival (Nov).*

THE TRANQUIL HILL of Sanchi contains one of India's best preserved and most extensive Buddhist sites. From the 3rd century BC to the 7th century AD, this was a thriving Buddhist establishment of stupas and monasteries. The complex of buildings at Sanchi therefore show the development of Buddhist art across different periods, stretching over more than a 1,000 years. Founded by Emperor Ashoka *(see p42)* whose wife came from nearby Vidisha, Sanchi grew and prospered under subsequent dynasties, largely through the generous patronage of the rich merchants of Vidisha. By the 14th century, Buddhism was on the wane in India and Sanchi was deserted and half forgotten, until it was "rediscovered" in 1818 by General Taylor of the Bengal Cavalry. Between 1912 and 1919 it was extensively restored by the Archaeological Survey of India (ASI) under Sir John Marshall. It was declared a World Heri-

Votive stupa with Buddha image

tage Site by UNESCO in 1989. Most of Sanchi's buildings are within an enclosure at the top of the 91-m (299-ft) hill, dominated by the **Great Stupa** and its four superb gateways *(see pp244–5)*. Nearby, to its north, is the smaller **Stupa 3** (built 2nd century BC), with its single gateway, which contained the relics of two of the Buddha's closest disciples, Sariputra and Maudgalayana.

Also within the enclosure are several monasteries, which are located on the eastern, western and southern sides. Of these the 10th-century **Monastery 51** is the most interesting, with its courtyard surrounded by a colonnade, behind which are 22 monks' cells. **Temple 17**, on the eastern side, dates to the 5th century AD. A flat-roofed structure with columns surmounted by double-headed lions, this is the earliest well-preserved example of an Indian stone temple, and its style and features considerably influenced the later development of temple architecture. Located below the Great Stupa, just outside the enclosure, is **Stupa 2** (2nd century BC), whose railings are carved with lotus medallions and mythical beasts. Also depicted is a horse with stirrups, the latter probably contemporary with their earliest use. Near the South Gateway of the Great Stupa lies the broken shaft of an Ashokan Pillar, made of

THE BHIMBETKA CAVE PAINTINGS

In 1957, the Indian archaeologist VS Wakanker discovered over 1,000 cave shelters in a rocky sandstone ridge near Bhimbetka village, surrounded by thick deciduous forest. More than 500 of these were covered with paintings done in bold, fluent lines, with the same power and energy as the cave paintings in Lascaux, France, or the Kalahari paintings in Africa. The earliest paintings, from the Upper Paleolithic period, are of large animals such as bison and rhino, done in red pigment, with humans drawn in green. The largest number of paintings are from the Mesolithic period (8000 to 5000 BC), and depict vivid vignettes of daily life, hunting scenes and a range of animals including, curiously, a giraffe. Later caves (1st century AD) show battle scenes and some Hindu deities.

Mesolithic period cave painting from Bhimbetka

Cave shelter at Bhimbetka

Stupa 3, which originally contained the relics of the Buddha's disciples

highly polished stone. It was used as a sugarcane press by a local landlord in the 19th century. Its four-headed lion capital, similar to the one at Sarnath *(see p208)* but not as fine, can now be seen in the Sanchi **Archaeological Museum**. Some other notable exhibits here include a pair of winged Mauryan lions, sculptural friezes from the gateways and statues of the Buddha and Bodhisattvas.

ENVIRONS: Besnagar, situated 10 km (6 miles) northeast of Sanchi, on the confluence of the Beas and Betwa rivers, was once a prosperous centre of trade. A unique relic of its past is the **Heliodorus Column**, with its fluted bell-shaped capital, dating to 113 BC. Dedicated to the god Vasudeva, it was erected by the envoy of the Greek king of Taxila (now in Pakistan), to commemorate his conversion to Hinduism.
Udayagiri, 20 km (12 miles) north of Sanchi, has fine examples of 5th-century AD rock-cut caves, carved

into the hillside. Most notable is **Cave 5**, with its impressive sculpture of Varaha, the incarnation of Vishnu as a boar, rescuing the earth goddess from the churning ocean.
    Raisen Fort straddles a hilltop 23 km (14 miles) southeast of Sanchi. Its 13th-century gates, palaces, temples and pavilions have lain in ruins ever since a devastating attack in the 16th century by the Sultan of Gujarat, but the site is still hauntingly atmospheric.
    Udayapur, 70 km (42 miles) northeast of Sanchi, has the exquisite 11th-century red sandstone **Nilkanteshwar Temple**, dedicated to Shiva. It is comparable in scale and sculptural beauty to the Khajuraho temples *(see pp236–8)*. The symmetry of its graceful *shikhara*, rising in a crescendo of delicately carved stone, is broken by a curious figure that seems to dangle in space. According to local legend, this figure represents the architect, trying to climb to the heavens.

Gyaraspur ⑫

Vidisha district. 64 km (40 miles) NE of Bhopal. 🚉 🏛 *MP Tourism, Bhopal, (0755) 77 4340.*

T HE ORNATELY CARVED 9th-century **Maladevi Temple** at Gyaraspur is built on a hillside. Partly carved out of a rock, it is now in ruins, and much of its superb sculpture has been pillaged. The exquisite statue of the *salabhanjika*, which is now the pride of the Archaeological Museum at Gwalior Fort *(see p229)*, was salvaged from here.

Sculpture of Varaha, Vishnu's boar incarnation, from Cave 5, Udayagiri

FESTIVALS OF MADHYA PRADESH & CHHATTISGARH

Shivratri *(Feb/Mar)*, Khajuraho. The celestial wedding of Shiva and Parvati is celebrated with colourful processions and an elaborate nightlong re-enactment of the wedding ritual in the Matangeshwar Temple.
Dance Festival *(Feb/Mar)*, Khajuraho. During this week-long festival, India's leading classical dancers perform in front of the Kandariya Mahadeva Temple. The postures and grace of the dancers are echoed in the exquisite stone sculptures of *apsaras* in the temple.

Classical dancer at Khajuraho Dance Festival

Dussehra *(Sep/Oct)* Chhattisgarh. This ten-day festival in honour of Rama is celebrated with great gaiety in the Bastar tribal heartland of Chhattisgarh. Along with lively dramatized episodes from the *Ramayana (see p27)* there are also colourful tribal fairs with dancing, cockfights and spirited bartering of goods.
Chaityagiri Vihara Festival *(Nov)*, Sanchi. Buddhists from all over the subcontinent gather at Sanchi to view the relics of two of the Buddha's closest disciples.
Tansen Music Festival *(Nov/Dec)*, Gwalior. Named after the great musician Tansen, one of the "nine jewels" at the court of Mughal emperor Akbar, this festival brings together the best classical musicians and singers from all over the country.

Sanchi:The Great Stupa

Animals on the torana

INDIA'S FINEST surviving Buddhist monument, the Great Stupa at Sanchi was built in the 2nd century. Its hemispherical shape is variously believed to symbolize the upturned alms bowl of a Buddhist monk, or an umbrella of protection for followers of the Buddhist dharma. The stupa's main glory lies in its four stone *toranas* (gateways), added in the 1st century BC. Their superb sculptures replicate the techniques of wood and ivory carving, and cover a rich variety of Buddhist themes.

West Gateway
This animated scene from the Jataka Tales shows monkeys scrambling across a bridge to escape from soldiers.

Circumambulatory Paths
The paths have balustrades carved with medallions of flowers, birds and animals, and the names of donors who funded them.

South Gateway
The Wheel of Law, being worshipped by devotees, symbolizes the Buddha.

The four gateways show scenes from the Buddha's life, and episodes from the Jataka Tales. The Buddha is not depicted in human form, but only through symbols such as a Bodhi Tree, footprints or a wheel.

Detail of Architrave
The intricate carving on the architraves is believed to be the work of ivory and wood carvers.

★ North Gateway
Sujata, the village chief's daughter, offers the Buddha (represented by the Bodhi Tree) kheer (rice pudding), as the demon Mara sends the temptress to seduce him.

The *vedika* (railings) are an impressive recreation in stone of a typical wooden railing design. They were the inspiration for the stone railings around Sansad Bhavan or the Parliament House *(see p74)* in New Delhi.

The Great Stupa and its West Gateway
Enclosing a smaller brick stupa built by Emperor Ashoka in the 3rd century BC, the Great Stupa is capped by a three-tiered stone umbrella, symbolizing the layers of heaven.

Statues of the Buddha meditating, added in the 5th century AD, face each of the gateways.

East Gateway
This scene shows a royal retinue at the palace of Kapilavastu, the Buddha's home before he renounced his princely life.

★ Salabhanjika
Supporting the lowest architrave of the East Gateway is this sensuous, voluptuous tree nymph, gracefully positioned under a mango tree.

STAR FEATURES

★ **North Gateway**

★ **Salabhanjika**

Indore ⓭

Indore district. 187 km (116 miles) W of Bhopal. 🏙 1,597,400. ✈ 10 km (6 miles) W of town. 🚊 🚌 🛈 MP Tourism, behind Ravindra Natyagriha, (0731) 52 8653. 🛒 Mon–Sat. 🎎 Ganesha Chaturthi (Aug/Sep).

THE BUSTLING commercial centre of Madhya Pradesh, Indore was a princely state until 1947, ruled by the Maratha Holkar dynasty.

At the heart of the city, surrounded by a lively bazaar, is the **Rajwada Palace**, now just an imposing façade following a fire in 1984. A short walk west of it stands the **Kanch Mandir** ("Glass Temple"), an opulent 19th-century Jain temple, extravagantly decorated with mirrors, glittering chandeliers, and murals on glass.

On the southwestern edge of Indore is the opulent Lalbagh Palace, built by the rulers of Indore in the early 20th century. Now a museum called the **Nehru Centre**, its gilded Rococo interiors house galleries of miniature paintings, medieval coins and tribal artifacts. In the garden is a statue of Queen Victoria, looking distinctly unamused.

🏛 **Nehru Centre**
Lalbagh Palace. [(0731) 47 3264. ◻ Tue–Sun. 📷

ENVIRONS: Dewas, 35 km (22 miles) northeast of Indore, was the setting for EM Forster's book, *The Hill of Devi* (1953).

The glittering interior of the Kanch Mandir in Indore

Sacred ghats on the Shipra river in Ujjain

Ujjain ⓮

Ujjain district. 56 km (35 miles) NW of Indore. 🏙 429,900. 🚊 🚌 🛈 MP Tourism, Railway Station, (0734) 55 9648. 🎎 Kumbh Mela (every 12 years), Shivratri (Feb/Mar).

ON THE BANKS of the Shipra river, Ujjain is one of India's seven sacred cities, and one of the four sites of the Kumbh Mela *(see p210)*. In the 4th–5th centuries AD it was the second capital of the Gupta Empire *(see p43)*, with the celebrated Sanskrit poet Kalidasa as one of its leading lights. Its glory was, however, eclipsed in the 13th century after it was sacked by the Delhi Sultans *(see p48)*.

The focal point of the town is the **Mahakaleshwar Temple** (an 18th-century reconstruction on the site of the original), with its much-venerated Shivalinga. In the main square is the **Gopal Temple**, whose silver doors are believed to be from the Somnath Temple in Gujarat, ransacked by Mahmud of Ghazni in the 11th century. A similar pair of doors are at the Golden Temple in Amritsar *(see pp106–107)*. **Ram Ghat**, the largest of sacred ghats on the banks of the river, is the site of the Kumbh Mela (the next one here is due in 2004). On the opposite bank is the **Chintaman Ganesha Temple** whose carved pillars, dating to the 11th century, are the only relics of the original temple. At the southwestern edge of the city is the **Vedh Shala Observatory**. Built in 1730 by Sawai Jai Singh II of Jaipur, the Mughal-appointed governor of Malwa, it is a smaller version of the one at Jaipur *(see pp358–9)*.

ENVIRONS: The charming 15th-century **Kaliadeh Palace**, 8 km (5 miles) north of Ujjain, on an island in the Shipra, was built by the sultans of Malwa. The basement has water channels cut in fantastic shapes.

THE HILL OF DEVI

The famous British writer Edward Morgan Forster (1879–1970) spent several months in the princely state of Dewas as private secretary to its eccentric and charming maharaja. *The Hill of Devi*, based on his letters home, provides a delightful inside view of life at a provincial court with its festivities, intrigues and complicated protocol. Dewas is dominated by a hill with the temple of the goddess Chamunda Devi, hence the title of the book. Curiously, tiny Dewas was divided and ruled by two brothers, each with his own palace, army and anthem. Forster was at the court of the elder maharaja. The experience also provided Forster with material for his best-known novel, *A Passage to India* (1924).

Devi image in the temple at Dewas

Mandu 🅖

Dhar district. 105 km (65 miles) W of Indore. 🚌 ℹ️ *Tourist Cottages, (07292) 63 235.*

A row of lofty arches in the Hindola Mahal or Swinging Palace, Mandu

PERCHED ON A CREST of the Vindhya Mountains is the deserted citadel of Mandu, one of India's most romantic and picturesque sites. Enclosed within its winding parapet walls, and surrounded by steep, wooded ravines, are palaces, mosques, lakes and pleasure pavilions, built between 1401 and 1529, by the sultans of Malwa *(see p49)*, who referred to it as Shadiabad, the "City of Joy". Mandu is spread over a 23-sq km (9-sq mile) area, but its major monuments are clustered in two groups – the Royal Enclave and the Village Group.

🅝 Royal Enclave
⬜ *daily.* 🖼️

Dominating the Royal Enclave are the **Jahaz Mahal** *(see pp248–9)* and the majestic T-shaped **Hindola Mahal** ("Swinging Palace"), whose massive inward-sloping walls give the impression that the building is swaying. Built in the late 15th century as the royal assembly hall, its austere façade is lightened by delicate tracery work on its arched windows. Next to it is a well, the **Champa Baoli**, connected to a series of subterranean rooms cooled by flowing water, where the ladies of the harem spent hot summer days. To its east are **Gada Shah's House and Shop**, which belonged to an ambitious Rajput chieftain at the court of Mandu. The so-called "Shop" was actually an audience hall, while the house, a luxurious double-storeyed structure with water channels and fountains, still has traces of two fine paintings of the chieftain and his wife. The earliest of the monuments in the Royal Enclave is Dilawar Khan's Mosque, built by the first Malwa sultan in 1405, using the stones and pillars of Hindu and Jain temples that had stood here earlier.

Detail from Hoshang Shah's tomb

🅝 Village Group
⬜ *daily.*

The first marble tomb to be built in India, **Hoshang Shah's Tomb** (1440) is a perfectly proportioned structure, where Malwa's most powerful sultan is buried. It has an inscription on the door recording the visit of four of Emperor Shah Jahan's architects in 1659. Opposite it is the magnificent **Jami Masjid** (built in 1454). It is said to have been inspired by the great Mosque at Damascus. Three large domes and 58 smaller ones surmount its colonnades, and the *mihrab* is decorated with beautiful calligraphy. Next to it is the **Ashrafi Mahal** *madrasa* with the ruins of a seven-storeyed Victory Tower, acclaimed in contemporary accounts as Mandu's finest structure. It was built by Sultan Mahmud in 1443, to mark his battle with the maharana of Mewar. Interestingly, the latter also built a Victory Tower at Chittorgarh *(see p402)* after the same battle.

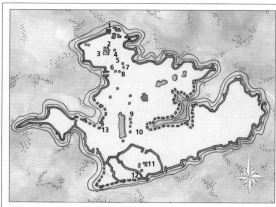

PLAN OF MANDU

1 Delhi Gate
2 Hindola Mahal
3 Champa Baoli
4 Gada Shah's House
5 Jahaz Mahal
6 Hoshang Shah's Tomb
7 Ashrafi Mahal
8 Jami Masjid
9 Malik Mugith's Mosque
10 Dai ka Mahal
11 Baz Bahadur's Palace
12 Rupmati's Pavilion
13 Neelkanth Mahal

| 0 metres | 800 |
| 0 yards | 800 |

Mandu: Jahaz Mahal

A pavilion window

THE JAHAZ MAHAL ("Ship Palace") was built by the fifth sultan of Malwa, Ghiyasuddin (r.1469–1500). Lying on a long, narrow strip of land between two of the many man-made lakes, Munja Talao and Kapur Talao, the palace gives the impression of an anchored ship, especially during the monsoon when the lakes are full. This pleasure palace was staffed entirely by the hedonistic sultan's harem of 15,000 women, who also served as his bodyguard.

The Pavilions
The juxtaposition of conical and domed roofs over the pavilions adds great charm to the Jahaz Mahal's silhouette.

Tilework
Blue and yellow tiles decorated the pavilions.

Entrance

The Terrace
The most spacious part of the palace, the terrace, with its pavilions and kiosks, overlooks the lakes.

STAR FEATURES

★ **Water Channels**

★ **Bathing Pool**

Exploring Mandu

Between the Village Group of monuments and Sagar Talao, Mandu's largest lake, are several monuments worth visiting. **Malik Mugith's Mosque**, built in 1432, has carved pillars taken from ruined Hindu temples. To its south are two impressive buildings in a pretty, wooded area – **Dai ki Chhoti Bahen ka Mahal** (the "Nurse's Younger Sister's Palace") and **Dai ka Mahal** (the "Nurse's Palace"). The two women were clearly royal favourites and the pretty, octagonal-domed houses show traces of blue and yellow tilework.

Shivalinga at Neelkanth Mahal

Southeast of Sagar Talao, down a winding road to the edge of a cliff, are the Rewa Kund Group of Monuments, associated with the legendary romance between Sultan Baz Bahadur and the beautiful singer Rupmati. Beside the Rewa Kund Stepwell, fed by an underground stream whose waters are said to be sacred, is **Baz Bahadur's Palace**, constructed between 1508 and 1509. Its most charming feature is an octagonal pavilion overlooking a garden, now covered with weeds.

Located just south of the palace is **Rupmati's Pavilion**, with its lovely fluted domes, from where there is a spectacular view of the surrounding countryside.

Baz Bahadur, the last sultan of Malwa, was defeated in battle by the Mughals in 1561. After this, Mandu fell into decline, as the Mughal emperors only used it as a halting place on their journeys to the Deccan. In 1616, Mandu briefly came to life again, when the Mughal emperor Jahangir spent seven months here, renovating the palaces and giving lavish parties at the Jahaz Mahal. Accompanying him was Sir Thomas Roe, the Elizabethan ambassador to the Mughal court. He has left a fascinating account of royal festivities and exciting lion and tiger hunts at Mandu.

★ **Water Channels**
The intricate spiral designs of the water channels are characteristic of the simple elegance of Mandu's architecture.

VISITORS' CHECKLIST

Royal Enclave. ☐ *daily.* 🖼 🎫
🛈 *Tourist cottages, Mandu, (07292) 63 235.*

The terrace pool, similar in design to the one on the ground floor, is fed by a water channel.

★ **Bathing Pool**
The beautiful pool at the northern end is surrounded on three sides by colonnades.

Narrow rooms lie at either end of the ground floor, with its three large halls.

A short distance west of Sagar Talao, a flight of steps leads down to a ravine to **Neelkanth Mahal**. This palace, with its many water channels and cascades, was built in 1574 on the site of an ancient Shiva shrine, for the Mughal emperor Akbar's Hindu wife. The main room, overlooking the valley, is once again in use as a Shiva temple, even though its walls are covered with fine Arabic calligraphy.

ENVIRONS: The **Bagh Caves**, lying 50 km (31 miles) west of Mandu, date from AD 400–700. Built by Buddhist monks, they have murals similar in style to those at Ajanta *(see pp480–81)*, but unfortunately these are in a very poor state of preservation.

BAZ BAHADUR AND RUPMATI

One day while out hunting, Sultan Baz Bahadur (r.1554–61) spotted a Hindu girl, Rupmati, singing as she bathed in the Narmada river. Bewitched by her beauty and her voice,

An 18th-century miniature of Rupmati and Baz Bahadur

Baz Bahadur persuaded her to live with him in Mandu. Thereafter, he spent his time in the pursuit of love and music, leaving his kingdom vulnerable to attack. When Emperor Akbar's general, Adham Khan, attacked Mandu in 1561, he won an easy victory. Baz Bahadur fled the battlefield, deserting Rupmati who was captured. But the courtesan proved more courageous than the king. Even as the Mughal general waited outside her room to claim her, she committed suicide by swallowing poison.

View of Maheshwar's fort, shrines and ghats, along the Narmada

Maheshwar 🔟

West Nimar district. 90 km (56 miles)
SW of Indore. 🚶 *19,600.* 🚉
*Barwaha, 39 km (24 miles) E of town
centre, then taxi or bus.* 🚌 **i** *MP
Tourism, Indore, (0731) 52 8653.* 📷
Panchkosi Yatra (Mar).

PICTURESQUELY sited on the
banks of the Narmada,
Maheshwar is an important
Hindu pilgrimage centre. It
was the site of the ancient
city of Mahishmati,
mentioned in classical
Sanskrit texts.
Maheshwar's beauti-
ful temples and ghats
were erected by
Queen Ahilyabai of
the Holkar dynasty
(see p246), in the
mid-18th century.

**Statue of Queen
Ahilyabai**

The 1.5-km (1-mile)
long river front is dotted with
shrines, ghats and the elegant
cenotaphs of the Holkar
rulers, and is usually thronged
with pilgrims taking a dip. A
magnificent fan-shaped
stairway leads from the river
front to Maheshwar Fort's
royal enclosure, and the
Ahilyeshwar Temple, built
in 1798. The richly carved
courtyard, leading on to the
palace, has an impressive
statue of Ahilyabai. This
benevolent queen, who also
built the Vishwanath Temple
(see p205) in Varanasi, was
described by a British colonial
official, Sir John Malcolm, as
"one of the purest and most
exemplary rulers that ever
lived". Also within the fort is
the Rehwa Weavers' Society,
where the famous gossamer-
fine Maheshwari cotton and
silk textiles are woven.

Omkareshwar 🔟

East Nimar district. 77 km (48 miles)
S of Indore. 🚉 🚌 🛥 **i** *MP
Tourism, Indore, (0731) 52 8653.*
📷 *Shivratri (Feb/Mar).*

THE ISLAND of Omkareshwar,
at the confluence of the
Narmada and Kaveri rivers, is
one of India's most enchanting
pilgrimage towns. Seen from
above, it is shaped like the
sacred *Om* symbol. The
island is 2-km (1.3-mile)
long and 1-km (0.6-
mile) wide, with
jagged cliffs on its
southern and east-
ern sides. It is
dotted with
temples, sadhus'
caves and bathing
ghats, and filled
with the sound of
chanting. A circumambulatory
path circles the island, marking
out the pilgrim trail.

Omkareshwar is linked to the
mainland by a concrete causeway, though visitors can also
come on the flat bottomed
barges that ply the river. The
island is dominated by the
towering white *shikhara* of the
Sri Omkar Mandhata
("Bestower of Desires")
Temple, within which is a
particularly sacred Shivalinga,
one of 12 *jyotirlingas* (natural
rock lingas said to have
miraculously emerged from
light) in the country.

At the eastern end of the
island is the 10th-century
Siddhnath Temple which has
beautiful sculptures of *apsaras.*
The northern end has a cluster
of Hindu and Jain temples.
Overlooking them is a ruined
palace, part of a fortified
township that stood here until
it was sacked by Muslim
invaders in the 11th century.

**A pilgrim praying on the banks of
the Narmada at Omkareshwar**

THE NARMADA DAM CONTROVERSY

Since the mid-1980s, an ambitious scheme to dam the
Narmada has been embroiled in controversy. The Narmada
Valley Authority claim that the Sardar Sarovar Dam will bring
electricity, irrigation and drinking water to millions of people.
Environmental activists opposing the dam, who include
Medha Patkar, leader of the "Save the Narmada" movement,
and Arundhati Roy, the 1997 Booker
Prize-winning author, say that the dam
will inundate some 37,000 ha (91,429
acres) of forest, and displace more
than 200,000 villagers, most of them
poor tribal people whose distinctive
culture and means of livelihood will
be wiped out along with their lands.
The Supreme Court of India has now
ruled that work on the dam can
continue. When completed, it will be
the second largest in the world, after
the Three Gorges Dam in China.

**Anti-dam activists at a
protest meeting**

The Narmada River

Image from Chausath Yogini Temple

RISING IN THE Amarkantak Plateau, where the Vindhya and Satpura ranges meet, the Narmada flows westward for 1,247 km (775 miles), across the states of Madhya Pradesh and Gujarat before entering the Arabian Sea. One of India's seven sacred rivers, the Narmada, according to Hindu mythology, was born of Lord Shiva's sweat when he performed his cosmic dance (*see p566*). The Narmada is also believed to be the embodiment of purity, and a legend holds that every year the polluted Ganges comes in the guise of a dark woman, and takes a purifying dip in the Narmada. Sugarcane, cotton and bananas grow along the river, whose banks are lined with temples.

Dhuandhar Falls *are a scenic spot, where the river drops 25 m (82 ft) down from the Amarkantak Plateau. The name Dhuandhar means "Stream of Smoke".*

Narmada Kund *at Amarkantak ("Neck of Shiva"), marks the source of the river. It is surrounded by 16th-century temples.*

Maheshwar has beautifully carved river front temples and 28 bathing ghats.

Omkareshwar is an *Om*-shaped island at the confluence of the Narmada and the Kaveri.

Chausath Yogini Temple which dates to the 10th century, is on a hilltop near the Marble Rocks.

Jabalpur

Bhedaghat • Chausath Yogini Temple

Dhuandhar Falls

Hoshangabad

Amarkantak

GUJARAT

Maheshwar

Omkareshwar

MADHYA PRADESH

Mandla

Sardar Sarovar Dam

Arabian Sea

MAHARASHTRA

At Mandla, the river takes a sharp turn.

Sethanighat Temple at Hoshangabad has an image of the Goddess Narmada.

The Narmada Parikrama, *undertaken by many sadhus, is a pilgrimage on foot along both banks of the river. It covers 2,600 km (1,616 miles) and takes about three years.*

The Marble Rocks *at Bhedaghat, where the fast-flowing river has cut a gorge, are especially spectacular on a moonlit night. Boat rides are the best way to experience their beauty.*

Pachmarhi's Christ Church, built in 1875, a relic of the Raj

Pachmarhi ⑱

Hoshangabad district. 210 km (130 miles) SE of Bhopal. 🚶 11,400. 🚉 Piparia, 47 km (29 miles) N of Pachmarhi, then taxi or bus. 🚌 🛈 MP Tourism, Amaltas Complex Station, (07578) 52 100. 🎭 Shivratri (Feb/Mar).

THIS DELIGHTFUL hill station, at an altitude of 1,067 m (3,501 ft), lies in the verdant hills of the Satpura Range. Its attractions include waterfalls and pools, and caves with prehistoric art. In 1857, Captain James Forsyth of the Bengal Lancers spotted this saucer-shaped plateau, and it was quickly developed into a sanatorium and army station by the British.

The town retains a genteel, Raj-era ambience, and among its colonial relics are the **Christ Church**, built in 1875, with beautiful stained-glass windows, and the **Army Music School** which still begins the day with rousing English martial tunes such as the Colonel Bogey March.

Pachmarhi means "Five Houses", and the town takes its name from the five ancient **Pandava Caves**, set in a garden south of the bus stop. From the caves, paths lead to the scenic **Apsara Vihar** ("Fairy Pool") and the **Rajat Prapat Waterfalls**.

The wooded hills around Pachmarhi, home of the Gond and Korku tribes, are dotted with cave shelters, some of them with paintings dating back 10,000 years. The most

accessible of them is the **Mahadeo Cave**, 6 km (4 miles) from the Jai Stambh ("Victory Pillar") in the centre of town. The **Jatashankar Cave Temple**, dedicated to Shiva, is a short excursion, 2 km (1.3 mile) from the main bus stop. At the Shivratri festival, a colourful gathering of pilgrims and sadhus takes place here. En route to it is the **Harper's Cave**, so called because it has a painting of a man playing an instrument that looks like a harp.

Jabalpur ⑲

Jabalpur district. 330 km (205 miles) E of Bhopal. 🚶 951,500. ✈ 14 km (8 miles) W of town centre. 🚉 🚌 🛈 MP Tourism, Railway Station, (0761) 32 2111.

THE GATEWAY to Bandhavgarh (see p239) and Kanha (see pp254–5), two of India's finest wildlife sanctuaries, Jabalpur was from the 12th to 16th centuries the capital of a powerful Gond tribal kingdom, whose most famous ruler was a brave and able woman, Rani Durgavati. In 1817 the British made it an army cantonment and administrative centre, to deal with the growing menace of gangs of highway bandits known as *thuggees*, who would rob travellers. In the 1830s, Colonel William Sleeman launched his famous campaign against the *thuggees*, and in a few years

Detail from a Gond tribal house

had wiped them out. The word thug (from *thuggee*), though, seems to have found a permanent place in the English language. In the bazaar is the **Rani Durgavati Museum** with stone sculptures and Gond tribal artifacts. The ruined **Madan Mahal Fort**, built by a Gond king in 1116, overlooks the town from a hill to the west.

🏛 **Rani Durgavati Museum**
◻ Mon–Sat.

ENVIRONS: The **Marble Rocks**, the **Chausath Yogini Temple** and the **Dhuandhar Falls** are 22 km (14 miles) southwest of Jabalpur.

Mandla ⑳

Mandla district. 95 km (59 miles) S of Jabalpur. 🚉 🚌 ⛴ daily.

THIS SLEEPY TOWN is situated on a loop in the Narmada river, which provides a natural moat for the 17th-century Gond Fort, now in ruins. Mandla is a sacred city for Gond tribals, whose warrior queen, Durgavati, committed suicide here in 1564 when she was defeated by the Mughal emperor Akbar's army. Temples and ghats line the banks of the river, where the Gonds perform their funeral rites. The main bazaar, near the bus stand, is interesting to explore with its shops selling tribal silver jewellery and bell metal.

The Narmada river at Mandla, lined by temples and ghats

The Folk Art of Bastar

BASTAR DISTRICT, in the newly-created state of Chhattisgarh, is a remote, thickly forested area, predominantly inhabited by tribal people and small communities of craftsmen. They live close to nature, and their arts and crafts have been inspired by the beauty, rhythm and vigour of forest creatures and plants. Animal, bird and plant motifs embellish many of the utilitarian, decorative and ritual objects that they fashion out of clay, wood, metal and cotton yarn. These can be seen at the weekly tribal markets held in Madhya Pradesh and Chhattisgarh, as well as in handicrafts shops in Delhi.

Clay toy on wheels

Wooden walking sticks, toys and ritual objects are carved out of the soft wood of roots and stems. The ingenious walking sticks make an eerie whistling sound, meant to scare away wild animals and evil spirits in the forest.

A newly-wed tribal couple in Bastar

Combs in wood and metal are exchanged between young tribal boys and girls of Bastar as tokens of love. The wooden combs are decorated with simple geometric motifs, while the brass ones are more ornately carved.

Iron lamps, embellished with leaf forms and lively animal and bird figures, are a speciality of Bastar's lohars (blacksmiths), who also make agricultural tools.

A brass comb, carved with the image of a deity

Tribal potters make fascinating clay ritual figures of mythical animals, horses and elephants. The materials used are the red and black clay from river banks, known for their strength and elasticity.

Bronze images, made by the Ghadva community of metalsmiths, using the lost wax technique, include this guardian deity of a Bastar village.

Textiles for festive occasions are woven from thick unbleached cotton by the Panka community of weavers. The motifs, always inspired by nature, are woven in red madder-dyed yarn.

Kanha National Park 🅪

O FTEN DESCRIBED as India's finest game sanctuary and a model for wildlife conservation, Kanha's magnificent landscape combines grassy meadows and flat-topped hills with meandering streams and lush deciduous forests. The setting for Rudyard Kipling's famous *Jungle Book,* Kanha is today an important Project Tiger *(see p289)* Reserve. Along with Bandhavgarh *(see p239),* it is one of the best places to spot these elusive creatures. The rich variety of wildlife found within this 1,954-sq km (754-sq mile) park, once the exclusive hunting ground of the British viceroys, includes deer, leopard, hyena, sloth bear, pythons and nearly 300 species of birds.

Common Mongoose
This ferret-like animal is a fierce fighter, particularly known for its masterly combats with snakes.

Dadars and Deer
Grassy meadows, known as dadars, characterize much of Kanha. They provide an ideal habitat for herbivores such as the spotted deer.

0 km   3
0 miles   3

Black Ibis
This elegant bird with glossy plumage is often found at the edges of Kanha's waterholes, looking for small fish, frogs and earthworms.

JABALPUR

Rondha

Sonph

Khatia

Kisli

Kanha

Khapa

Bisanpura

Sondh

Lapsi Kuba

Banjar River

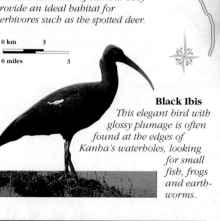

Kipling Camp
This British-run complex (see p698), close to the park entrance at Kisli, has pleasant chalets, surrounded by forest. The camp arranges guided safaris.

Interpretation centres, located at Khatia, Mukki and Kanha, have excellent films, models and books.

Shravantal
This tranquil waterhole attracts several water birds, such as the lesser whistling teal and the shoveller. There are viewing platforms located nearby.

VISITORS' CHECKLIST

Mandla district. 196 km (122 miles) SE of Jabalpur. 🚌 to Khatia and Kisli, the main entry points. 🛈 MP Tourism, Jabalpur, (0761) 32 2111; Bhopal, (0755) 77 8383. **Other entry points:** Mukki. 🌣 Nov–Jun. 📷 🎦 extra charges. 🎦 guides are compulsory. 🍴 🏠 from Kisli. Jeep safaris available. Visitors cannot walk in the park.

Tiger
Kanha's tigers now number about 100. Park guides expertly track them through pug marks and the alarm calls of deer and langurs.

BILASPUR

Central Indian Barasingha
Conservation has increased the numbers of this rare species, which was close to extinction 30 years ago.

● Bahmnidadar

🛈

▲ Mukki

KEY

- - Park boundary
= Major road
= Minor road
🛈 Tourist information
🌿 Viewpoint
▲ Accommodation

KIPLING'S JUNGLE BOOK

The English writer Rudyard Kipling (1865–1936) was born in Bombay (Mumbai), and though he spent little time in India, the country provided the setting for many of his books. Among his most enduring works is *The Jungle Books*, delightful stories of animal behaviour and the law of the jungle. Set in the Seonee Forests of Kanha, their endearing hero is the wolf-reared boy Mowgli; and the many enchanting animal characters include Rikki-tikki-tavi, the mongoose, Shere Khan, the tiger, Kaa, the python, and Baloo, the bear.

Jacket for Disney's version of *The Jungle Books*

EASTERN INDIA

Introducing Eastern India

KOLKATA, INDIA'S SECOND LARGEST CITY, is the best known destination for visitors to Eastern India. Apart from this endlessly fascinating metropolis, the region offers an astonishing diversity of landscapes, peoples and cultures. These include the steamy mangrove forests along the Bay of Bengal, habitat of the Royal Bengal tiger, the spectacular mountain vistas of Darjeeling (officially Darjiling) and Sikkim, and Orissa's magnificent temples and beaches. Further east are Assam and the northeastern states, home to many different tribal communities, whose distinct cultures flourish in areas of pristine natural beauty.

An agile Nishi tribesman of Arunachal Pradesh crossing the Siang, a tributary of the Brahmaputra river, on a tightrope

SEE ALSO

- **Where to Stay** pp699–702
- **Where to Eat** pp728–31

GANGTOK

DARJEELING • JALDAP

NH34

PANDUA

MURSHIDABAD

Varanasi

NH2

SHANTINIKETA

KOLK

Hooghly

SUNDERBA

Hirakud Reservoir

NH23

SIMLIPAL

Raipur

NH6

NH42

NH5

Bay of Bengal

Mahanadi

CUTTACK

BHUBANESWAR

NH5

PURI

Chilika Lake

GOPALPUR-ON-SEA

NH43

Visakhapatnam

0 km   80

0 miles   80

The 10th-century Mukteshwar Temple complex in Bhubaneswar

◁ **A woman fishing in Loktak Lake** *(see p338),* Manipur

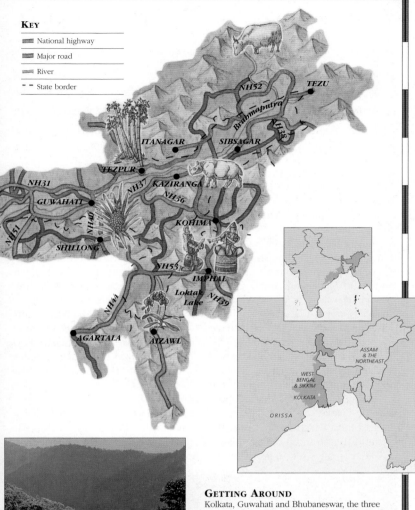

KEY

- National highway
- Major road
- River
- State border

TEZU

NH52

Brahmaputra

NH38

ITANAGAR

SIBSAGAR

TEZPUR

NH37

KAZIRANGA

NH31

NH36

GUWAHATI

NH51

NH40

KOHIMA

SHILLONG

NH53

NH44

IMPHAL

NH39

Loktak Lake

AGARTALA

AIZAWL

ASSAM & THE NORTHEAST

WEST BENGAL & SIKKIM

KOLKATA

ORISSA

Tea gardens in Darjeeling, nestling in the
foothills of the Eastern Himalayas

GETTING AROUND

Kolkata, Guwahati and Bhubaneswar, the three
major cities in this region, are well connected by
air and rail to most parts of India. From Kolkata
and Guwahati, there are regular flights to all the
northeastern states. The hill station of Darjeeling,
and Sikkim's capital, Gangtok, are accessible by air
or rail up to Bagdogra-Siliguri, from where buses
and taxis complete the journey up to the hills on
National Highway 31. The delightful Himalayan
Toy Train *(see p294)* also runs from Siliguri to
Darjeeling, providing panoramic views of the
Himalayas en route. From Kolkata, most destinations in West Bengal are reached on National
Highway 34. In Orissa, the major sights are
connected by National Highway 5. The gateway to
the northeast, Guwahati in Assam, has good road
links to the other six states on National Highways
37, 40 and 52. Visitors require travel permits for
some destinations in the northeast *(see p758)*.

A PORTRAIT OF EASTERN INDIA

THE PEOPLES AND CULTURES *to be found in India's eastern states are as varied as the landscape itself. Stretching from the crowded metropolis of Kolkata to the remote tribal settlements of Arunachal Pradesh, which border on China and Myanmar, the region includes mountainous Sikkim, tropical Orissa, and the lush valleys of Assam, watered by the mighty Brahmaputra river.*

West Bengal, the largest and most densely populated of the eastern states, offers the visitor a kaleidoscope of images. These range from the mangrove swamps of the Sunderbans, home of the Royal Bengal tiger, to the misty tea gardens of Darjeeling, and the unique vitality of the state capital Kolkata (formerly Calcutta).

Orchid from Meghalaya

Kolkata is a city that evokes extreme reactions: novelists exhaust metaphors trying to describe it, filmmakers are defeated by it, and even the average non-Bengali agrees that something about the city defines that abstract entity – "culture". As a headquarter of the East India Company, and later, the capital of British India, the city played an early host to crucial Western influences, especially English education. It witnessed the phenomenon popularly described as the Bengal Renaissance, a complex dynamic of socioreligious reform, and literary and artistic efflorescence, with a strong nationalistic undercurrent. Kolkata thus became the first Indian city to have an "intelligentsia". Rabindranath Tagore *(see p292)*, its most famous son, lives on through his stories, poems, plays and songs, loved to this day. Another cultural icon is the famous film director Satyajit Ray, whose work has had a profound impact on Asian art cinema. Since 1978, West Bengal has been under Communist rule. The culture of flag-waving processions, however, blends flawlessly with the

A village pond in Orissa, with a small Hindu temple on its banks

Statues being transported during Durga Puja, Kolkata's biggest festival

life still revolves around its serene and beautiful Buddhist monasteries.

In the extreme eastern corner of India are Assam and the six northeastern states of Arunachal Pradesh, Meghalaya, Manipur, Mizoram, Nagaland and Tripura, connected to the rest of the country only by a thin corridor of land. This region is home to dozens of tribal communities, each with its own language and culture *(see pp336–7)*.

typical Kolkata pastime of *adda* – a lively mix of heated political debate, highbrow analyses and lowbrow gossip. This is all played out against a backdrop of crumbling vestiges of some splendid colonial architecture.

From Kolkata, many visitors travel south to the beaches and exquisitely sculpted temples of Orissa. The highpoint of Orissa's cultural and religious year is the spectacular annual Rath Yatra, a festival held in the temple town of Puri *(see p312)*. The state pays a price for its scenic location on the Bay of Bengal – it is often hit by devastating cyclones during the monsoon. In recent years, however, Orissa's people, who include many forest-dwelling tribal groups, have enjoyed increasing prosperity, with schemes to develop the state's rich mineral resources and its growing tourism industry.

North of Kolkata lies Sikkim, its skyline dominated by the snow-capped peaks of India's highest mountain, Kanchendzonga *(see p302)*, which soars to a height of 8,598 m (28,209 ft). Sikkim's culture borrows much from neighbouring Tibet and Nepal, and many people practice the Tibetan form of Buddhism, introduced in the 15th century by its former rulers, the Chhogyals, who came from Tibet. Much of Sikkim's cultural and religious

Dancer at monastery festival, Sikkim

Tea dominates the economy of Assam, which produces more than half the tea grown in India, as well much of the country's oil. The other six states have rich agricultural and forest resources, and little industry. The isolation of the northeastern states, and their shared borders with Bangladesh, Bhutan, China and Myanmar, has led to violent separatist movements in some areas. Visitors need special permits *(see p759)* for this region whose main attraction is its pristine natural beauty and rare flora and fauna.

An Assamese woman pounding grain

The Story of Indian Tea

Tea leaves

INDIA IS THE WORLD's largest producer of tea, perhaps the world's most popular drink. The tea plant *(Camellia sinensis)* is indigenous to Northeast India, and though tea was cultivated and drunk for centuries by the Singpho tribe of Arunachal Pradesh as a stimulant and medicinal brew, tea plantations for commercial exploitation were only established in the mid-19th century. Today, the Indian tea industry employs over a million people, half of whom are women, and produces about 850 million kg (1,874 million lb) of tea every year, most of which is grown in Assam, northern Bengal and Darjeeling (Darjiling).

Darjeeling's tea gardens *are a picturesque sight, covering terraced hill slopes upto an altitude of 1,950 m (6,398 ft).*

Fresh tea leaves *are plucked from April to December. A skilled picker can harvest 37 kg (82 lbs) of leaves a day, enough to yield 20 kg (44 lbs) of processed tea.*

Shade trees

PICKERS IN A TEA GARDEN

The tea bush, with its bright green oval leaves, is regularly pruned to keep its height low, allowing for convenient picking. Left wild, the plant can grow into a tree up to 10 m (33 ft) tall.

The withering process blows warm air over the leaves, reducing their moisture content by half. The leaves are then rolled, pressed, fermented, and finally dried again.

Fresh tea leaves   Dried tea leaves

The CTC or crush, tear and curl method, is used to process a more robust, granular Assam tea. The leaves are crushed to release their enzymes, before they are fermented and dried.

Tea tasters *tell the quality of a tea by breathing on to leaves clutched in their fist, and inhaling the warmed aroma. To fix the base price at auctions, they also sample the brew, swilling the liquid round their tongues, in the manner of wine tasters.*

SPECIAL TEA

स्पेशल लज्जतदार चहा

A 1950s poster advertising a brand of Indian tea

GOLDEN ORANGE PEKOE

FINE DARJEELING TEA

Darjeeling tea logo

Assam tea logo

Darjeeling and Assam teas are the best known Indian varieties. Darjeeling teas are famous for their delicate muscatel flavour, and the best ones have been sold at auction for up to US$220 for 1 kg (2.2 lbs). Assam tea has a stronger taste and darker colour.

Women's supple fingers are preferred for the delicate task of plucking just the top two leaves.

Tea bush

Basket for carrying plucked tea leaves

Bronze tea kettles with dragon-shaped handles and elephant trunk spouts, are typical of the Darjeeling and Sikkim region.

Masala tea

Herbal tea

Assam Tender Buds

Green tea

Darjeeling Golden Tips

Assam Superior Buds

Different types of Indian tea include green (unfermented) tea which is drunk in Kashmir, and masala tea spiced with cardamom and ginger. Long leaves give a superior brew, while broken leaves and tea dust go into tea bags.

TEA ESTATES

In the early 19th century, the British began looking for a site in India, suitable for growing tea for the British market. They soon discovered wild tea plants growing in the northeast, and by 1850, vast tracts of tiger-populated jungle had been cleared in Assam, northern Bengal and Darjeeling to establish tea gardens. Today India has over 25,000 tea estates of varying size, each a self-contained world with its own school, shops and medical clinic. At its heart is the plantation manager's gracious bungalow, and a club where the planters meet for tennis and sundowners every evening.

A typical tea planter's bungalow in northern Bengal

Regional Food: Eastern India

T HE CUISINE OF West Bengal and Orissa has been
shaped by their landscape of lush riverine plains,
abundantly watered by the monsoon rains, and a
fertile coastline along the Bay of Bengal. Fish,
coconut, rice and an abundance of green vegetables
dominate their food, while mustard oil is the favoured
cooking medium, adding a distinct flavour and tang
to savoury dishes. Bengal is also famous for its wide
variety of sweet dishes. Sikkim and the landlocked,
forested northeastern states have a less spicy cuisine,
with many steamed dishes. Bamboo shoots and
other forest produce often feature on the menu.

Mustard oil, *leafy* poi *greens,*
patal *gourd, and a fragrant*
five-spice mix called panch
phoran *are typical ingredients*
of Bengali food.

**Shorshey maachh
(fish with
mustard)**

**Chholar dal
(split pea lentil
purée)**

**Moong dal
(moong lentil purée)**

**Ghonto
(mixed vegetables)**

**Ambal
(mango chutney)**

**Tamatar chatni
(tomato chutney)**

**Baingan
bhaja
(aubergine
fritters)**

**Shukto
(bitter vegetables)**

**Aloor dum
(braised potato)**

BENGAL

Fish is the centrepiece of a Bengali meal. Carp
with mustard, prawns in coconut gravy, and
steamed *bilsa* fish are special favourites. They are
accompanied by rice, *dal* (lentil purée), chutneys,
and vegetables such as crisp aubergine fritters
and *shukto*, a mixture of bitter leaves and
vegetables, believed to be good for digestion.

**Malai chingri
(prawns in coconut milk)**

**Ilish maachher jhal
(steamed bilsa fish)**

Bengali sweets *are*
mostly milk-based.
Mishti doi *is yoghurt*
sweetened with mo-
lasses, sandesh *is*
made of delicately
flavoured cottage
cheese, while
rosogullas are cottage
cheese balls in syrup.

Mishti doi

Sandesh

Rosogulla

THE NORTHEAST

Pork is a favourite meat with the largely tribal population of Arunachal Pradesh, Meghalaya and Nagaland. It is cooked with bamboo shoots or wild mushrooms, accompanied by *momos* (dumplings filled with meat, green vegetables or cottage cheese), and washed down with *chang* (rice or millet beer).

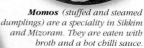

Momos *(stuffed and steamed dumplings) are a speciality in Sikkim and Mizoram. They are eaten with broth and a hot chilli sauce.*

Lentil purée

Chutney

Steamed rice

Steamed vegetables

Pork with bamboo shoot

Bamboo containers for *chang*

ORISSA

Orissa's cuisine is renowned for its inventive combination of ingredients, flavours and textures. A typical meal includes *besar maachh* (fish cooked with a long green vegetable called *Moringa oleifera* or drumsticks), *saag bhaja* (sauteed spinach garnished with coconut), and *aloo poshto* (potato with poppy seed).

Dalma (lentil stew)

Besar maachh (fish with *Moringa oleifera*)

Aloo poshto (potato with poppy seed)

Saag bhaja (sautéed spinach)

ANGLO-INDIAN CUISINE

Kolkata's Anglo-Indian (Eurasian) community has given a new twist to many English dishes by adding Indian flavours and spices. The bland English lentil soup is thus transformed into the delicious mulligatawny soup, with the addition of ingredients such as tamarind, used in *rasam (see p554)*. Caramel custard, a relic of the Raj, has now been enthusiastically adopted by the sweet-toothed Bengalis.

Mulligatawny soup

Caramel custard

KOLKATA

O NE OF THE WORLD'S GREAT CITIES, *Kolkata or Calcutta as it used to be known, has been through many incarnations. From an obscure village on the banks of the Hooghly river, it evolved into the capital of Great Britain's Indian empire. Today, this vibrant city with its distinct imperial flavour, is the capital of West Bengal, the only Indian state with a Communist-led government.*

In 1690, an English merchant, Job Charnock, established a trading post in the riverside village of Sutanuti which, together with neighbouring Govindapur and Kolikata, grew into the city of Calcutta. Over the next 200 years, the city became a flourishing commercial centre with imposing Victorian Gothic buildings, churches, and boulevards. Simultaneously, intellectual and cultural life bloomed, with a renaissance of Bengali art and literature, and the growth of a strong nationalist reform movement that led to the founding of the Brahmo Samaj, an enlightened off-shoot of Hinduism, and the establishment of Presidency College, then the foremost centre of English education. The decision to shift the capital to New Delhi in 1911 and the urban decay of the 1960s diminished some of the city's affluence, but never quenched its effervescence.

In 2001, Calcutta became Kolkata, the Bengali pronunciation of its name. The city is crowded and dirty in places, but is nevertheless full of character. The teeming life of the waterfront along the Strand, the noisy jumble of bazaars and pavement stalls, the residential streets with their once gracious mansions, all make for an electric, cosmopolitan atmosphere, rarely found in other Indian cities. Kolkata's charms straddle the decaying grandeur of the imperial capital and the smart restaurants and boutiques of Park Street. These coexist with the traditional Bengali world of Rabindranath Tagore's mansion at Jorasanko, the Kalighat temple and the potters' village of Kumartuli, and with the lively politics of the Coffee House and the Maidan, dominated by the Victoria Memorial, a spectacular symbol of imperial high noon.

View of the Hooghly river and the Howrah Bridge, the third longest cantilever bridge in the world

◁ Statue of the young Queen Victoria in the central hall, Victoria Memorial

Exploring Kolkata

THE CITY OF KOLKATA lies in a long strip, with the
river to its west and the wetlands to its east.
Along the river front, the Strand, is the city centre
with the Maidan, a large 400-ha (988-acre) park
where Kolkata's residents play football, hold political
rallies or enjoy the cool evenings. On the other side
of the park is the city's main thoroughfare, the
Chowringhee or Jawaharlal Nehru Road with shops,
hotels, offices and residential buildings. The southern part of the city has the middle-class residential
areas, while north Kolkata is the older part of the
city, its maze of narrow lanes crowded with houses,
cheek-by-jowl with shops and offices.

LOCATOR MAP

A street scene at New Market with Kolkata's distinctive taxis

SIGHTS AT A GLANCE

**Historic Buildings, Areas &
Neighbourhoods**
Alipore ⑬
Around BBD Bagh pp270–71 ①
Chowringhee ⑨
College Street ④
Jorasanko ⑱
Kumartuli ⑲
Marble Palace ⑰
Maidan ⑦
Mother House ⑪
Nilhat House ③
Nirmal Hridaya ⑮
Park Street Cemetery ⑫
Tangra ⑯

Museums
Indian Museum pp276–7 ⑩
Victoria Memorial pp274–5 ⑧

Churches, Temples & Mosques
Armenian Church of St Nazareth ⑥
Nakhoda Mosque ⑤
Kalighat ⑭
St John's Church ②

Parks & Gardens
Botanical Gardens ⑳

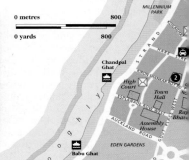

GETTING AROUND

Central Kolkata is compact and can easily be covered on foot. Alternatives include taxis, or the often crowded buses and mini-buses. Trams and the Metro, linking the southern and northern parts of the city from Tollygunge to Dum Dum, are other options. A local mode of transport are rickshaws that operate in the congested lanes and side streets.

A colourful stall in one of Kolkata's main flower markets

KEY

▢	Street-by-Street area: *see pp270–71*
🚉	Railway station
🚌	Bus station
⛴	Ferry port
Ⓜ	Metro station
ℹ	Tourist information
✚	Hospital
👮	Police station
🛕	Temple
☪	Mosque
⚔	Gurdwara
✝	Church
⊠	Post office
▬	National highway
▬	Major road
—	Minor road

SEE ALSO

• *Where to Stay* p699

• *Where to Eat* pp728–9

GREATER KOLKATA

Street-by-Street: Around BBD Bagh ❶

Signage of the Royal Insurance Building

THIS IS THE "HEART" OF KOLKATA and was the site of the original Kolikata, one of the villages from which the city grew. The small tank at its core was where three young Indian freedom fighters, Binay, Badal and Dinesh, shot the British inspector-general of police in 1930. The square, now named after them, is ringed by British colonial buildings, dating to the 18th and early 19th centuries. These were once the centres of British administrative and commercial control.

Job Charnock's Tomb
Job Charnock is believed to have laid the foundations of the English settlement in Kolkata.

★ St John's Church
The design of this church (see p272) was based on London's St Martin-in-the-Fields. The constructing engineers wanted the spire to be higher, but desisted fearing the soggy sub-soil.

High Court

STRAND ROAD

HARE STREET

Gates of Raj Bhavan
Magnificent Neo-Classical gateways lead to the old Government House, built in the mid-18th century. This is now the residence of the state governor, and can be viewed from across the road.

KS RAY ROAD

COUNCIL HOUSE

ESPLANADE ROW

TRAMS IN KOLKATA

Horse drawn trams first trundled their way from Sealdah station on 24 February 1873. Electric trams were introduced in March 1902 and have survived till today. Riding in them is a pleasant if rattly experience and the tram's slowly clanging bell is one of Kolkata's most characteristic sounds. Though an integral part of the city's transport network *(see p269)* and appreciated for being pollution free, they are under threat for being too slow.

An electric tram plying on the streets of Kolkata

STAR SIGHTS

★ St John's Church

★ GPO

★ Writers' Building

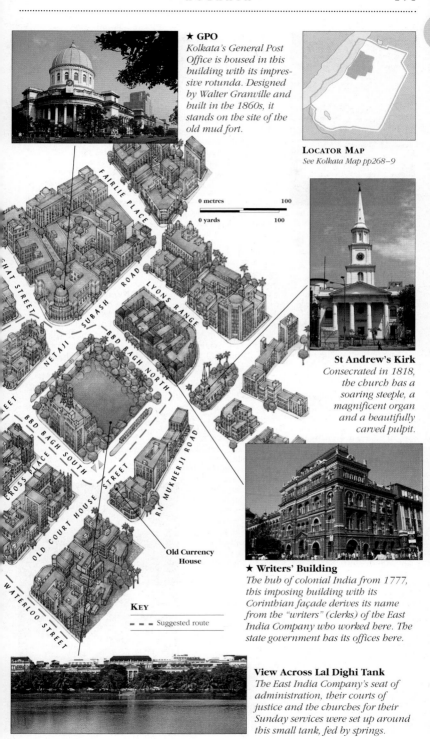

★ GPO
Kolkata's General Post Office is housed in this building with its impressive rotunda. Designed by Walter Granville and built in the 1860s, it stands on the site of the old mud fort.

LOCATOR MAP
See Kolkata Map pp268–9

FAIRLIE PLACE

0 metres 100
0 yards 100

SUBASH ROAD

LYONS RANGE

GHAT STREET

NETAJI

BBD BAGH NORTH

BBD BAGH SOUTH

CROSS PLACE

OLD COURT HOUSE STREET

RN MUKHERJI ROAD

WATERLOO STREET

St Andrew's Kirk
Consecrated in 1818, the church has a soaring steeple, a magnificent organ and a beautifully carved pulpit.

Old Currency House

KEY
- - - Suggested route

★ Writers' Building
The hub of colonial India from 1777, this imposing building with its Corinthian façade derives its name from the "writers" (clerks) of the East India Company who worked here. The state government has its offices here.

View Across Lal Dighi Tank
The East India Company's seat of administration, their courts of justice and the churches for their Sunday services were set up around this small tank, fed by springs.

View of St John's Church with its soaring spire

St John's Church ②

Council House St. ○ *daily.*
✝ *9am–Sat; 8am Sun.*

THE FIRST PARISH church in Kolkata, St John's Church was established in 1787. It boasts an impressive stained-glass panel of *The Last Supper*, in which the artist Johann Zoffany gave the 12 disciples the faces of British personalities famous in the city at the time.

St John's has many associations with the history of the English East India Company. Warren Hastings, Governor of Bengal, was married here. In the churchyard is a memorial to Lady Canning, the vicereine who died in 1861. Her name lives on in popular memory because she was much addicted to a fried, syrupy sweetmeat, which was named after her (it is pronounced "leddy-kenny" in Bengali). The mausoleum of Job Charnock (*see p270*) also stands here.

A short distance away is the memorial to the victims of the notorious "Black Hole Tragedy", an event which became one of the favourite horror stories of the Raj. When Siraj-ud-Daula, the Nawab of Bengal, captured the old British fort which stood on the site of the present General Post Office (*see p271*) in 1756, he imprisoned over 100 British inhabitants in a small, airless cell. Only 23 people were found alive the next morning – the rest had died of asphyxiation and thirst.

Nilhat House ③

Behind Old Mission Church. *Auctions held on Mon & Tue at 8:30am. Prior permission required from brokerage houses, J Thomas* 🔲 *(033) 248 6201 or Carritt Moran* 🔲 *(033) 220 2536.*

A TEA AUCTION CENTRE, Nilhat House stands on the site of an indigo trading house (*nil* means indigo, while *hat* is market). It dates to 1886; only the tea auction houses in London are older. Tea has always played an important role in the state's economy, especially in the colonial period. But even today, the bidding for teas from Darjeeling and the Dooars in northern Bengal and Assam (*see pp262–3*) is brisk. The auction prices are determined by the opinions of tea tasters, whose highly trained palates can immediately distinguish the type, plantation and year of each brew. Visitors can view and participate in these animated proceedings with prior permission.

College Street ④

Bidhan Sarani, North Kolkata.
Ashutosh Museum ○ *Mon–Fri.* 🈸

A S THE LOCATION of Kolkata's elite educational institutions, College Street is the heart of Bengali intellectual life. The pavements are crowded with stalls selling textbooks, exam guides, classics and second-hand books of all kinds – some people even claim to have discovered valuable first editions. Many of Kolkata's best bookshops are also found here.

The **Presidency College**, on this street, was established in 1817 and was then known as the Hindu College. Started as an institution for the city's rich citizens who wanted their sons to receive a Western-style education, it boasts great scholars, scientists and

writers such as the film director, Satyajit Ray (1922–92) and the economist Amartya Sen, who won the Nobel Prize for Economics in 1998.

Across the road is the dark, cavernous **Indian Coffee House**, the favourite haunt of the city's intelligentsia since it opened in 1944. Even today, waiters in shabby cummer-bunds serve endless cups of strong coffee to teachers, students, writers and poets.

Down a lane opposite Presidency College is the **Sanskrit College**, founded in 1824 to promote the study of ancient Indian languages, history and culture. Its ground floor has a small display of medieval Hindu sculpture and palm-leaf manuscripts.

Next to Presidency College are the buildings of **Calcutta University**, founded in 1857. Today, the gracious 19th-century main structure is dwarfed by modern high-rise additions, through which the old edifice, with its Ionic pillars and symmetrical proportions, is barely visible.

On the ground floor, the **Ashutosh Museum** specializes in the art of Eastern India. The exhibits include a fine collection of terracottas, bronzes, coins, old manuscripts and some exquisite examples of *kantha* (a quilting technique) and Kalighat paintings, or *pats* (*see p279*).

A second-hand bookstore on College Street

Detail of the ornamental entrance of Nakhoda Mosque

Nakhoda Mosque ❺

Zakaria St. ◯ daily. ⬤ to non–Muslims during times of prayer.

THE CITY'S LARGEST mosque, Nakhoda Mosque is based on the design of Akbar's tomb at Sikandra (see p178). Built in 1926, it is surmounted by a dome and faced with red sandstone, with minarets that rise to a height of 46 m (151 ft). It can accommodate over 10,000 people for prayer, but on major religious occasions, people spill out on to the street. Nearby is the **Hotel Royal**, famous for its rich *biryani* and *chaanp* (goat's ribs cooked in spiced gravy). This is a fascinating neighbourhood with 19th-century mansions, old bazaars and temples.

Armenian Church of St Nazareth ❻

Armenian St, near Brabourne Rd. ◯ daily. ⬤ 6pm Fri–Sat; 7am Sun.

BUILT BY Armenian traders in 1724, the Armenian Church of St Nazareth stands on the site of the original wooden church constructed in 1707, which had burnt down. Immigrants from Isfahan in Persia, the Armenians were among the earliest foreign traders to settle in Kolkata. Once a thriving community, today their numbers have dwindled. The church has a unique rounded spire, and its grounds house several graves with ornate tombstones.

Maidan ❼

Bounded by Strand Rd, AJC Bose Rd, Cathedral Rd & Eden Gardens Rd. **St Paul's Cathedral** ◯ daily. ✚ 7:30am, 8:30am & 6pm Sun.

IN THE HEART OF THE CITY, this 400-ha (988-acre) park stretches from the Hooghly river in the west to Chowringhee in the east, and contains several interesting areas and buildings. In the early 18th century, a dense jungle was cut down to build **Fort William**, after the earlier mud fort was destroyed in 1756. The present fort, a squat, irregular octagon, was completed in 1773. Today, it is the headquarters of the Indian Army's Eastern Command and not usually open to the public.

To the north of the fort are the pleasantly laid out **Eden Gardens**, where international cricket matches are held. They were conceived and designed in 1841 by Emily and Fanny Eden, the sisters of the governor general, Lord Auckland. At the northern corner of the Maidan is the **Burmese Pavilion** set in a small lake. This was brought here by Lord Dalhousie from Prome in Myanmar in 1854.

To its east is the **Shahid Minar**, literally "Martyrs' Memorial", originally called Ochterlony Monument. It was

Stained glass, St Paul's Cathedral

named after Sir David Ochterlony, one of the Raj's daredevil soldiers, who had led the British armies to victory in the Anglo-Nepal War in 1916. The monument is a fluted Doric column, 48 m (157 ft) high with a cupola for a roof. To its south is the Maidan's most impressive building, the **Victoria Memorial** (see pp274–5).

A short distance from the Memorial is **St Paul's Cathedral**. It was designed by Major WN Forbes in 1847 and its spire, modelled on Britain's Canterbury Cathedral, was added in 1938 to replace an earlier one. Its grounds are lined with trees and the interior is notable for a superb stained-glass window, designed by Edward Burne-Jones in memory of the viceroy, Lord Mayo. The **Race Course** is on the southwestern corner of the Maidan. Racing is popular in Kolkata and races are held throughout the year. Polo is played here for a few weeks in the winter season. The city's two famous football clubs, Mohun Bagan and East Bengal, are based in the Maidan, as are clubs for golf and bowling.

On Sunday afternoons, a lively fair with acrobats, magicians and jugglers takes place at the northern end of the Maidan. This is also the venue for large political rallies.

Eden Gardens, site of many cricket and football matches

Victoria Memorial 🔞

Imperial lion at the entrance

The City's most celebrated landmark, this monument to imperial self-confidence was the brainchild of Lord Curzon (1859–1925), one of British India's most flamboyant viceroys. The domed Classical structure, completed in 1921, was constructed with marble from Makrana, which also supplied marble for the Taj Mahal, and financed by "donations" from princes and ordinary citizens. Now a museum, its 25 galleries are spread over the ground and first floors. The collection, which covers a fascinating selection of Raj memorabilia, includes the Calcutta Gallery, with oil paintings and watercolours of the city's history.

★ Angel of Victory
Surmounting the dome is this 6-m (20-ft) high bronze revolving figure, with a trumpet, made in Italy.

Lord Cornwallis
This 18th-century governor general established the Raj's administration.

Durbar Hall

★ Statue of the Young Queen Victoria
The queen, sculpted in marble by Thomas Brock in 1921, holds an orb and a sceptre.

Entrance

General View
The impressive marble façade of the Victoria Memorial.

STAR SIGHTS

★ Angel of Victory

★ Statue of the Young Queen Victoria

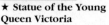

Bronze Panel
Two bronze panels depicting a vice-regal procession decorate the bridge at the northern entrance to the Memorial.

Dome
Skylights in the marble rotunda allow light to filter through to illuminate the lobby below.

VISITORS' CHECKLIST

Queen's Way. **C** (033)
223 5142. ◯ Tue–Sun. ●
public hols. 🏛 📷 ☑ **Son et
Lumière** (English) 7.15pm,
Oct–Nov; 7.45pm, Mar–Jun. 🏛

Exploring the Victoria Memorial

The foundation stone of this impressive structure was laid by the Prince of Wales, later King George V, during his visit to India in 1906. Designed by William Emerson, President of the British Institute of Architects, the building stands in spacious grounds, dotted with ornamental palms, ponds and statues. The museum contains over 3,500 artifacts that represent various facets of the Raj, such as a desk owned by Queen Victoria, embellished with paintings of Indian birds. Among the fine collection of paintings are works by the 18th-century landscape artists, Thomas Daniell and his nephew William Daniell, whose aquatints and lithographs of Indian scenes virtually determined the way India was perceived in 19th-century Britain. The collection also includes paintings by Johann Zoffany (1733–1810), portraits of imperial stalwarts, records of the East India Company, an exquisite set of Persian manuscripts, and paintings that depict Kolkata's history.

Calcutta Gallery
This gallery has an excellent collection of landscapes painted by 18th-century British artists.

Picture Gallery

A majestic bronze statue of Queen Victoria by Sir George Frampton

Chowringhee **9**

JL Nehru Rd. **The Asiatic Society**
Park St. **☎** *(033) 229 0779.* **Library**
◯ *Mon–Sat.* **Museum** ◯ *Mon–Fri.*

Now called Jawaharlal
Nehru Road, Chowringhee
was a fashionable promenade
during the Raj. This busy
thoroughfare derives its name
from a fakir (holy man),
Jungle Giri Chowringhee,
who once lived here. At its
northern end is the **Oberoi
Grand** *(see p699)*, one of
India's most elegant hotels.
Established in the 1870s, and
known as the Grand Hotel, it
was considered "the most
Popular, Fashionable and
Attractive Hotel in India".

Behind the Oberoi Grand is
New Market *(see p282)*, built
in 1874. This covered market,
surmounted by a clock tower,
has shops placed along many
interconnected corridors. One
of the oldest is the Jewish
confectionery and bakery,
Nahoum's, which has a
beguiling variety of cookies,
fudge and spiced cakes.

At its southern end, on Park
Street, is **The Asiatic Society**,
founded in 1784 by Sir
William Jones, a formidable
Oriental scholar. He was the
first to establish the common
origins of Latin and Sanskrit,
and called Sanskrit the
"mother of all languages".
The Society's **Museum** and
Library have a large collection of over 60,000 old and
rare manuscripts in Sanskrit,
Arabic and Persian, as well as
artifacts such as a 3rd-century
BC stone edict, and 17th-
century folios from the *Pad-
shahnama*, Abdul Hamid
Lahori's history of the Mughal
emperor Shah Jahan's rule.

**The well-preserved period façades
of buildings on Chowringhee**

Indian Museum **10**

**Gupta era
gold coin**

The oldest and largest museum in India,
the Indian Museum was founded in
1814. The imposing building, designed by
Walter Granville, also the architect of the
General Post Office *(see p271)*, dates to
1875. The museum's impressive collection
is noted for artifacts from the 2,500 BC
Indus Valley Civilization, sculpture from
Gandhara, the superbly sculpted
railings from the 2,000-year-old
Bharhut Stupa, and a fine collection
of 5th-century Gupta coins.

Kalighat Painting
*Painted in the folk style of the 19th-
century Kalighat school, this represents
the Vaishnava saint Chaitanya.*

**Arhat
Vanavasin
Thangka**
*This silk
painting of a
Buddhist sage is
from Tibet.*

Pala Bronze
*This 12th-century
Bodhisattva figure shows
the fluid grace of
Pala sculpture.*

STAR SIGHTS

★ **Gandhara Sculpture**

★ **Bharhut Railings**

Nautch Party
*This 19th-century
Company School
Painting of nautch
or dancing girls,
combines European
and Indian
techniques of art.*

VISITORS' CHECKLIST

JL Nehru Rd. [(033) 249
9902. ◯ Tue–Sun. ● public
hols. 🖾 📷 extra charges.
**Educational film shows daily,
and special exhibitions.**

KEY

◻ Art and Textile Gallery

◻ Geology Section

◻ Botany Section

◻ Zoological Section

◼ Anthropology Section

◻ Archaeology Gallery

◻ Egyptian Gallery

◼ Numismatics Gallery

◻ Library

Chandela Sculpture
*Dating to the 10th–11th
century, this sensuous
maiden from Khajuraho
holds a baby in her arms
while two small children
cling to her knees.*

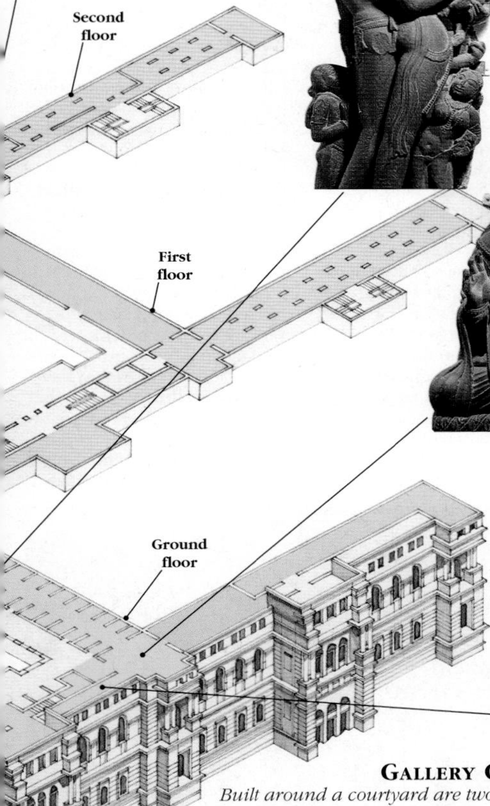

**Second
floor**

**First
floor**

★ **Gandhara
Sculpture**
*Dating to the 3rd
century, this image
of Maitreya, the
Future Buddha,
shows a strong
Greek influence
in the way the
folds of the robe
are sculpted.*

**Ground
floor**

GALLERY GUIDE
*Built around a courtyard are two storeys
of galleries. The Archaeology Gallery, to
the right of the main entrance, has railings
from the Bharhut Stupa as well as displays of ancient
and medieval sculpture. The Numismatics Gallery has
coins dating from 500 BC to the 17th century. The
Zoological Section, exhibits stuffed birds from British
zoological expeditions. The second floor has the Art
Gallery with paintings and miniatures.*

Entrance

★ **Bharhut Railings**
*Episodes from Buddhist
scriptures, events from the
Buddha's life and scenes
from daily life are carved
on these railings.*

A Sister of Charity outside the Mother House

Mother House ⑪

54A, AJC Bose Rd. 📞 *(033) 249 7115.* ⬜ *Fri–Wed. All donations are fully exempt from tax.*

THE CITY OF KOLKATA is inextricably linked to the name of Mother Teresa. At first a teaching nun at Loreto Convent, the death and devastation she witnessed in the city during the famine of 1943, and Partition of India in 1947 *(see p56),* made her leave this cloistered world and dedicate her life to the poor. The Missionaries of Charity was a new order she formed in 1950, with the Mother House as its headquarters. This simple building is today also her final resting place. Her grave is on the ground floor in a hall. It has no ornamentation, only a Bible placed on it. On a board on the wall are two words, "I thirst".

Park Street Cemetery ⑫

Bounded by Rawdon St & Park St. ⬜ *Mon–Fri.*

A ROMANTIC, overgrown haven of Raj nostalgia in the middle of the city, the Park Street Cemetery was opened in August 1767 to receive the body of John Wood, an official in the Custom House of the East India Company. From that date till the first half of the 19th century, it served as the resting place of many important Europeans who died in Kolkata. It was this graveyard which gave Park Street its original name, Burial Ground Road. Its name Park Street was derived from the park that Elijah Impey, the Chief Justice of the Supreme Court, established in the area. His grave is in this cemetery as well. William Jones, the great scholar and founder of The Asiatic Society, lies under a pyramid-shaped tomb. Henry Vansittart, one of the first governors of Bengal, is also buried here; so too is Henry Louis Vivian Derozio (1809-1831), a Eurasian teacher at Hindu College in the mid-19th century, who died at the young age of 23. Derozio inspired his students to question all established traditions and was one of the pioneers of what has come to be known as the Bengal

Renaissance *(see p260).* The best known tomb is that of Rose Aylmer, an early love of the poet, Walter Savage Landor. Her tomb, an unpretentious spiralled obelisk, is inscribed with lines by Landor. Also buried here is Colonel Kyd, founder of the Botanical Gardens *(see p281).*

Alipore ⑬

Bounded by AJC Bose Rd, Belvedere Rd & Alipore Rd. **Alipore Zoological Gardens** ⬜ *daily.* 📷 **National Library** 📞 *(033) 479 1384.* ⬜ *Fri–Wed.* ● *public hols.* 📷 **Agri Horticultural Society** 📞 *(033) 479 0834.* ⬜ *Tue–Sun.* 🌸 *Flower Show (Feb).*

B EST DESCRIBED AS the city's most fashionable address, the suburb of Alipore in south Kolkata is a sylvan world of tree-lined avenues, with palatial houses surrounded by well-kept lawns. Kolkata's zoo, the **Alipore Zoological Gardens**, was established here in 1875. It has a large collection of birds and mammals, and one of its main attractions is a tigeon, a crossbreed between a tiger and a lion. Nearby, the Belvedere Estate, in a broad expanse of lawn, today houses the **National Library**. This is the country's largest library with over two million manuscripts and books. Built in the Italian Renaissance style, the original

Weathered tombs in the tree-shaded Park Street Cemetery

The National Library in Alipore, with its colonnaded verandah

building, Belvedere, was the residence of the lieutenant governors of Bengal.

Further down are the lush gardens of the **Agri Horticultural Society**, founded in September 1820 by the missionary, William Carey *(see p287)*, to develop and promote agriculture and horticulture in India. In the first 40 years of its existence, seeds, bulbs and ornamental plants were imported from England, South Africa and Southeast Asia. Since then the Society has amassed a varied collection of rare flowering trees and shrubs, ferns and medicinal herbs. It is also an excellent place to buy winter annuals and other plants.

Kalighat ⓮

Ashutosh Mukherjee Rd. ◯ *daily.*

KOLKATA'S OLDEST pilgrimage site, Kalighat finds mention in medieval poems and ballads. Legend has it that the god Shiva, in a fury of grief at the death of his

wife, Sati (an incarnation of Parvati), slung her body on his shoulders and danced the terrible *tandava nritya* (dance of death), destroying everything in his path. To stop the carnage, Vishnu flung his magic *chakra* (discus) at Sati's body, and the dismembered pieces scattered across the land. The spot where the little toe fell became Kalighat, and some believe that the name Kolkata is derived from this.

The present Kali Temple dates to the early 19th century, but this has been a sacred spot for much longer. The image of the goddess in the dark inner sanctum is of a wild, untamed figure, with tangled tresses and wide, ferocious eyes. Her extended tongue has a gold covering which is changed every day. The temple is always crowded, especially on Tuesdays and Saturdays.

Kalighat has, over the years, become synonymous with Kalighat *pats*, a distinctive

The brick-and-mortar spire of the Kali Temple at Kalighat

painting style adopted by the scroll-painters of Bengal. They use paper and water-based paints, instead of tempera, to depict contemporary subjects. A good collection of Kalighat *pats* is on display at the Indian Museum *(see pp276–7).*

Nirmal Hridaya ⓯

251, Kalighat Rd. 📞 *(033) 464 4223.* ◯ *Fri–Wed.*

MOTHER TERESA'S home for the destitute, Nirmal Hridaya ("Pure Heart"), is near the Kali Temple. The site was probably chosen as this holy place teems with poor and old people, who come here to die and attain *moksha*. A large, scrupulously clean hall is full of beds for the sick and dying who are cared for by nuns, in their characteristic white and blue saris. Visitors who want to work as volunteers must first register at Mother House.

Kalighat painting of two wandering mendicants

MOTHER TERESA (1910–1997)

Mother Teresa, born Agnes Gonxa Bojaxhiu in Albania, came to Calcutta in 1929 to begin life as a teacher. The poverty and suffering she saw impelled her to leave the convent. She set up the order of the Missionaries of Charity and her indefatigable work among the lepers, the terminally ill, the unwanted and the poor earned her universal respect and love. To the people of Kolkata she was just "Mother" and their love for her transcended boundaries of religion, class and community. She was awarded the Nobel Peace Prize in 1979.

Mother Teresa on a postage stamp

Kim Li Loi, a family-run Chinese restaurant in Tangra

Tangra ⑯

Off the Eastern Metropolitan Bypass.
🎎 *Chinese New Year (Feb)*.

THIS EASTERN SUBURB is the city's new Chinatown. Chinese immigration to Kolkata began in the 18th century, and today large numbers of this still significant community have settled here. Tangra preserves the rich and varied culture of its immigrant population. A Chinese newspaper and journal are published from here, and there are many tiny restaurants, mostly extensions of family kitchens. "Tangra Chinese", with its discernibly Indian taste, is today as distinct a cuisine as Szechwan and Cantonese. All the city's leather tanneries are based at Tangra as, traditionally, the Chinese were involved with the very lucrative shoe trade.

Marble Palace ⑰

46, Muktaram Babu St. ◉ *Mon & Thu*. 📷 **Entry permit** *Contact Tourism Centre, 3/2 BBD Bagh, (033) 248 8271.*

THIS OPULENT mansion was built in 1835 by Raja Rajendra Mullick, a wealthy *zamindar* (landowner). His descendants still live here, but most of the house is open to visitors. Rajendra Mullick, who had travelled extensively in Europe, brought back an eclectic collection of Venetian chandeliers, Ming vases and Egyptian statuary that he housed in his Classical-fronted mansion, built around a colonnaded courtyard. Today, the Marble Palace provides a wonderful glimpse into the life of a rich 19th-century Bengali household. Nearly a 100 varieties of marble have been used on the floors and the dark halls are hung with paintings by European artists. In the courtyard is the family temple, while the grounds have a rock garden and aviary, home to mynahs and macaws.

Jorasanko ⑱

614, Dwarkanath Tagore Lane.
Rabindra Bharati Museum ◻
Tue–Sun. 📷 **Son et Lumière** *7pm daily.* ◉ *Mon & Thu.* 📷 🎎
Rabindranath Tagore's Birthday (May).

A MAJOR CENTRE of Bengali art and culture in the 19th century, Jorasanko is the ancestral home of Bengal's favourite son, Rabindranath Tagore *(see p292)*. Built in 1785, this simple three-storeyed, red brick structure housed the lively and cultivated Tagore family, many of whose members were prominent intellectuals and social reformers. The lane on which the house is located is named after Dwarkanath Tagore (1784–1846), the poet's father and a wealthy entrepreneur.

Today, the old house has been expanded and turned into **Rabindra Bharati University**, which specializes in the study of Bengali cultural forms. The house itself has been preserved as the **Rabindra Bharati Museum**. Beginning with the room in which Rabindranath Tagore died, it traces the history of the illustrious Tagore family with a large collection of art and memorabilia. There is an entire section devoted to paintings by Rabindranath.

The red brick Rabindra Bharati University, at Jorasanko

Final touches being given to a Durga image

Kumartuli ⑲

North Chitpur Rd.

LITERALLY, the "Area of the Potters", Kumartuli is a maze of alleys, where images of various Hindu gods and goddesses are made. The best time to visit is late August and early September as this is when potters create the idols for the ten-day-long Durga Puja. It is fascinating to watch them at work, moulding the clay, strengthened by straw and pith, to create images of the fish-eyed goddess Durga, her face often modelled on popular Hindi film actresses and her hair long and flowing.

Nearby is an ancient temple dedicated to Shiva, known as the **Buro Shiva** or "Old Shiva Temple". This is probably the only extant terracotta temple in the city, embellished with terracotta tablets in the frieze below the roof. Further away is Kolkata's celebrated landmark, the giant **Howrah Bridge** (now called Rabindra Setu), an airy, elegant mesh of steel that appears to float above the turgid Hooghly river *(see p267)*. The sunset behind the bridge is one of the loveliest sights in the city. Built in 1943 to replace the old pontoon bridge, this is the third longest cantilever bridge in the world, measuring 97 m (318 ft) in height and 705 m (2,313 ft) in length. The bridge links Kolkata with Howrah (Haora), the city's main railway station on the opposite bank, and is always clogged with traffic. To its south is the impressive Vidyasagar Setu. This massive cable-stayed suspension bridge was built in 1993 to connect South Kolkata with Shibpur and Howrah station.

Botanical Gardens ⑳

W bank of the Hooghly river, Shibpur. 🚢 from Babu Ghat. 📞 (033) 668 6226. ⬜ daily. **The Palm House** ⬜ Mon–Sat. **The National Herbarium** ⬜ Mon–Sat. ⬛ 2nd Sat.

THE BOTANICAL GARDENS, in the Shibpur suburb of Howrah, were established in 1786 by Colonel Kyd, an official of the East India Company. It has an astonishing array of flora including ferns, cacti and palms, and boasts of plants from every continent. The chief attraction is the magnificent banyan tree *(Ficus bengalensis)*. Claimed to be the largest banyan tree in the world, it is more than 200 years old and its branches, giving rise to nearly 300 aerial roots, spread over 60 m (197 ft). The central trunk was, however, struck by lightning in 1919 and was subsequently removed. The sight of this tree alone is worth the long journey.

The gigantic leaves of the *Victoria amazonica* lily, Botanical Gardens

THE DURGA PUJA

Image of the ten-armed Durga, slaying Mahisha

Durga Puja is West Bengal's favourite annual ritual in which simply everyone participates. Usually held between September and October, it heralds the advent of autumn and the new harvest. Each locality sets up its own *puja*, organized by local clubs and associations, financed through public subscriptions, though some of the old Bengali families perform their own *puja* in their ancestral houses. Brightly illuminated *pandals* (bamboo structures), often shaped like famous monuments such as the White House or the Taj Mahal, are erected on roads and in parks, and an image of the goddess Durga *(see p25)* is installed within. The goddess is elaborately decorated and in traditional Bengali homes, real jewellery is used. Presents are exchanged and great feasts are prepared. On the final day, the images are immersed in the Hooghly, to the frantic beating of drums and cries of "Jai Ma Durga!" ("Hail to Mother Durga!").

Shopping & Entertainment in Kolkata

KOLKATA IS A DELIGHTFUL PLACE to shop, even though it lacks the fashionable boutiques of Delhi or Mumbai. There are several old-style bazaars and street hawkers, and fewer glitzy shopping malls. Many shops stock a wide variety of goods, such as those in New Market; others cater to special niches. In certain places one needs to drive hard bargains – the shopkeepers both expect and enjoy this process. Kolkata was once famous for its auction houses, but sadly most of these have now shut down. This is also a culturally vibrant city, with regular performances of theatre, music and film shows. Exhibitions by well-known contemporary artists are also held throughout the year.

SHOPS AND MARKETS

KOLKATA'S **New Market** (see p276), on Lindsay Street, is the city's most famous shopping centre. Officially the Sir Stuart Hogg New Municipal Market, established in 1874, this is still a shopper's paradise, where one can find everything from Chinese sausages and fortune cookies to Tibetan curios and gold jewellery. **Sudder Street**, behind the Indian Museum, is another popular shopping centre. Each locality has its own bazaar; the best known of these are Gariahat, Bhowanipore (or Jadubabu's Bazaar), Bowbazaar and Maniktola. Wandering through bazaars offers a glimpse of street life, but be prepared for touts and beggars.

Shops usually open from 10am to 7pm and remain closed on Sundays and public holidays. New Market and some markets also close after 2pm on Saturday, so do check the timings in advance.

SARIS AND TEXTILES

THE BEST SHOPS for saris unique to West Bengal are **Ananda**, **Meera Bose** and **Kundahar**. Ananda also has an excellent selection of dhotis and *kurtas*. The upmarket boutique **Ritu's** has superb garments designed by Ritu Kumar, one of India's top designers. Exquisite hand-embroidered table linen and children's clothes are available at **Good Companions**. Carpets and *dhurries* are available at **Shyam Ahuja**.

HANDICRAFTS AND GIFTS

HANDICRAFTS special to West Bengal such as the terra-cotta Bankura horse (see p291), are on sale at **Bengal Home Industries**. The **Crafts Council of West Bengal** is another fascinating outlet that sells traditional saris as well as artifacts, while **Sasha** has a wide range of curios and bric-a-brac. Tea of the finest quality is available at **Dolly's Tea Shop** in the Dakshinapan shopping complex. This complex also has numerous other handicraft shops.

BOOKS AND MUSIC

THIS CITY of intellectuals and Nobel laureates, such as Rabindranath Tagore and Amartya Sen, is heaven for those willing to search for second-hand bargains in the shops that line the pavements of **College Street** (see p273) and **Free School Street**. Many of these shops have a good selection of rare and out of print books. **Dasgupta & Co** has a large choice, though there is no place to browse. The **Seagull Bookstore**, on the other hand, encourages browsing and is the best place for serious literature and academic books. **Landmark** too, has a large stock that ranges from thrillers to encyclopedias. The centrally located **Oxford Bookstore**, is also well-stocked and has a good café.

Music aficionados are advised to try **Music World** which has a good selection of

Indian and Western CDs and audio cassettes. On Chitpur Road towards Nakhoda Mosque (see p273), are music shops selling sitars, *sarods*, *veenas*, flutes and violins. Free School Street is about the only place in India where record albumns of 1950s Elvis Presley and Jerry Lee Lewis or 1960s Beatles and Rolling Stones are easily available.

SWEETS

WEST BENGAL'S sweets are famous. The variety is bewildering, but the two most popular are *sandesh* and *rosogulla* (see p264). The latter is on sale in every sweetshop, but those in **KC Das & Sons**, the family which invented this delicacy, are the best. *Sandesh*, made of cottage cheese and sugar (molasses or *gur* in the winter months), are of two kinds, those that are soft and those that have a harder outer crust. Both are widely available, but the best are found in **Nakur Nandy & Girish Chandra Dey**, **Makhan Lal Das & Sons** and **Balaram Mullick**.

ENTERTAINMENT GUIDES, TICKETS AND VENUES

THE *Sunday Telegraph* magazine and other English language dailies list the day's entertainment on their engagements page. Other useful sources of information are *Cal Calling* and *Kolkata: This Fortnight*, which is distributed by the West Bengal Tourist office. Information on tickets as well as reviews of plays and concerts also appear with the announcements.

Kolkata's cultural centre is just off the Maidan. The **Rabindra Sadan Complex**, named after Rabindranath Tagore, includes the **Academy of Fine Arts**. Next door is **Nandan**, where retrospectives of films by Satyajit Ray and other renowned directors, are regularly held. Other venues include **Madhusudhan Manch**, **Gorky Sadan**, **GD Birla Sabhaghar** and the **British Council**.

Exhibitions by well-known as well as up and coming artists are held at the city's many art galleries, especially the **Birla Academy of Art and Culture**, **CIMA Gallery** and **Chitrakoot Gallery**. CIMA Gallery also has a gift shop.

MUSIC AND THEATRE

PERFORMANCES of West Bengal's well-established classical and folk theatre (*jatra*) are staged throughout the year by semi-professional and amateur groups. Bengali theatre is perhaps the most vibrant in the country. Its rich repertoire includes plays with historical and socially relevant themes as well as translations of

Greek, European, Sanskrit and Hindi classics. *Jatra*, on the other hand, was introduced by the Vaishnava saint, Chaitanya Mahaprabhu, in the 16th century, and is based on musical plays that revolve around the Krishna legend (*see p179*). Characterized by dramatic acting interspersed with song and dance, the plays cater to both rural and urban audiences.

Another popular form of entertainment is Rabindra Sangeet. These melodious songs composed by Tagore include folk songs that are traditionally sung by boatmen who ply the Ganges. Regular concerts are held in the city, and attract audiences who continue to revere Tagore.

CLUBS AND NIGHTLIFE

KOLKATA IS A CITY of clubs which date to colonial times and are open only to members. Sometimes temporary membership can be arranged, particularly at the **Tollygunge Club** (*see p699*) which has huge grounds with rare trees and birds. Visitors can stay at the club, which has the comfort of a top hotel but at reasonable rates.

Kolkata's once glittering nightlife dwindled during the political upheavals of the 1960s. It is reviving now and affluent youth throng hotels where the city's nightclubs, such as **Anti-Clock**, **Someplace Else**, **Tantra** and **Big Ben**, are situated.

DIRECTORY

SARIS AND TEXTILES

Ananda
13, Russell St.
((033) 229 2275.

Good Companions
13 C, Russell St.
((033) 229 0473.

Kundahar
10, Dr Sarat Banerjee Rd.
((033) 466 7575.

Meera Bose
8, Dr Sarat Banerjee Rd.
((033) 466 4043.

Ritu's
111, Park St.
((033) 226 2792.

Shyam Ahuja
10, Azimganj House,
7, Camac St.
((033) 282 4041.

HANDICRAFTS AND GIFTS

Bengal Home Industries
11, Camac St.
((033) 282 1562.

Crafts Council of West Bengal
64, Lake Place.
((033) 473 9750.

Dolly's Tea Shop
G–62, Dakshinapan,
2, Gariahat (S).
((033) 483 4521.

Sasha
27, Mirza Ghalib St.
((033) 245 1586.

BOOKS AND MUSIC

Dasgupta & Sons
54/3, College St.
((033) 241 4609.

Landmark
3, Lord Sinha Rd.
((033) 282 2617.

Music World
18 G, Park St.
((033) 217 0751.

Oxford Bookstore
17, Park St.
((033) 229 7662.

Seagull Bookstore
31, SP Mukherjee Rd.
((033) 476 5869.

SWEETS

Balaram Mullick
2, Puddapukur Rd.
Bhowanipur.
((033) 475 9490.

KC Das & Sons
11, Esplanade East.
((033) 248 5920.

Makhan Lal Das & Sons
356, Upper Chitpur Rd.
((033) 555 8182.

Nakur Nandy & Girish Chandra Dey
56, Ramdulal Sarkar St.
((033) 241 0048.

ENTERTAINMENT VENUES

Academy of Fine Arts
2, Cathedral Rd.
((033) 223 4302.

Birla Academy of Art and Culture
108, Southern Ave.
((033) 466 2843.

British Council
5, Shakespeare Sarani.
((033) 282 5370.

CIMA Gallery
Sunny Towers, Ashutosh Chowdhury Ave.
((033) 474 8717.

Chitrakoot Gallery
55, Gariahat Rd.
((033) 475 2275.

GD Birla Sabhaghar
29, Ashutosh Chowdhury Ave.
((033) 476 8579.

Gorky Sadan
3, Gorky Terrace.
((033) 2475407.

Madhusudhan Manch
2, Gariahat Rd.
((033) 472 4148.

Nandan
1/1, AJC Bose Rd.
((033) 223 1210.

Rabindra Sadan
Cathedral Rd.
((033) 223 9917.

CLUBS AND NIGHTLIFE

Anti-Clock
Hotel Hindustan International,
AJC Bose Rd.
((033) 247 2394.

Big Ben
The Kenilworth,
Little Russell St.
((033) 282 8394.

Someplace Else
The Park Hotel, Park St.
((033) 249 7336.

Tantra
The Park Hotel, Park St.
((033) 249 7336.

Tollygunge Club
120, Deshpran Sasmal Rd.
((033) 473 4741.

WEST BENGAL & SIKKIM

WEST BENGAL HAS three distinct types of landscape. In the west, the red soil gives its rich colour to the terracotta temples of Bishnupur. The Ganges Delta in lower Bengal has dense, tangled mangrove swamps where Royal Bengal tigers roam, while the charming, Raj-era hill stations of Darjeeling and Kalimpong are located in the foothills of the Himalayas in the northern part of the

state. The neighbouring state of Sikkim, which also borders Bhutan, Nepal and China, is ringed by mountains. In its tranquil valleys, richly ornamented Buddhist monasteries stand amidst emerald-green terraced rice fields. The world's third highest mountain, Kanchendzonga (8,598 m/28,209 ft), dominates the skyline and the life of Sikkim's people. The two states have a combined population of 81 million.

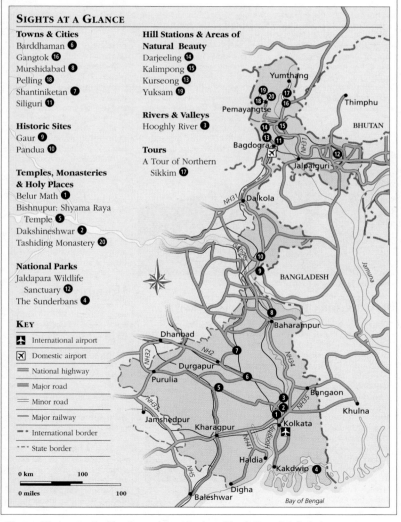

SIGHTS AT A GLANCE

Towns & Cities
Barddhaman ⑥
Gangtok ⑯
Murshidabad ⑧
Pelling ⑱
Shantiniketan ⑦
Siliguri ⑪

Historic Sites
Gaur ⑨
Pandua ⑩

Temples, Monasteries & Holy Places
Belur Math ①
Bishnupur: Shyama Raya
  Temple ⑤
Dakshineshwar ②
Tashiding Monastery ⑳

National Parks
Jaldapara Wildlife
  Sanctuary ⑫
The Sunderbans ④

Hill Stations & Areas of Natural Beauty
Darjeeling ⑭
Kalimpong ⑮
Kurseong ⑬
Yuksam ⑲

Rivers & Valleys
Hooghly River ③

Tours
A Tour of Northern
  Sikkim ⑰

KEY

✈ International airport
✕ Domestic airport
═ National highway
═ Major road
═ Minor road
— Major railway
- - - International border
- - - State border

0 km   100
0 miles   100

◁ **Image of the ten-armed goddess Durga, elaborately adorned for the Durga Puja festival**

Belur Math ❶

Howrah district. 10 km (6 miles) N of
Kolkata. 🚌 🚆 or taxi from Kolkata.
◯ daily. Conservative dress
appreciated.

JUST OUTSIDE KOLKATA, on the west bank of the Hooghly river, is Belur Math, the headquarters of the Rama-krishna Mission. The order was established in 1897 by the dynamic, reformist Hindu crusader, Swami Vivekananda (*see p615*), Ramakrishna Paramhansa's foremost disci-ple. The modern temple within the sprawling complex was built in 1938 and embod-ies Ramakrishna's philosophy, based on the unity of all faiths. The ground plan is in the shape of a cross, the windows have arches reminiscent of Mughal buildings, the gate shows Buddhist influence, and Hindu architectural motifs decorate the façade. Smaller temples and dormitories for the monks belonging to the order surround it. The place is spotlessly clean, and the atmosphere contemplative and calm. Today, the Mission has centres across the world.

Dakshineshwar ❷

24 Parganas district. 12 km (8 miles)
N of Kolkata. 🚌 🚆 or taxi from
Kolkata. ◯ daily. Conservative
dress appreciated.

NORTH OF Belur Math, on the east bank of the Hooghly river, stands the temple of Dakshineshwar, one of Bengal's most popular pilgrimage spots. The temple, built in 1855 by a rich and pious widow, Rani Rashmoni, was initially opposed by orthodox religious interests as she was not a Brahmin (the highest Indian caste). No Brahmin was therefore willing to be the temple priest. Only Ramakrishna Paramhansa, then still a boy, agreed, and he spent many years there, preaching and developing his

The curved *bangaldar* roof of the Kali temple, Dakshineshwar

philosophy of the essential oneness of all faiths. His room in the temple complex is still preserved in its original state.

The impressive whitewashed temple is set on a high plinth and topped by nine cupolas. The roof, with its line of rounded cornices, stands out impressively against the sky. Inside the sanctum is an image of Bhabatarini, an incarnation of the goddess Kali.

Within the large compound, strung along the river bank, are 12 smaller temples, each dedicated to the god Shiva. Crowds of pilgrims visit the Dakshineshwar temple daily, lending the sprawling temple complex a cheerful, bustling atmosphere.

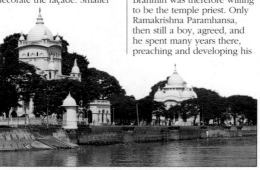

Belur Math, on the west bank of the Hooghly river

Hooghly River ❸

Hooghly district. 24 km (15 miles)
N from Kolkata to Shrirampur. 🚆
🚌 🚆 River cruises. ℹ Babu Ghat
(near Eden Gardens) or Tourist Office,
(033) 248 7302.

WHEN THE GANGES enters the Lower Gangetic Plains in West Bengal, the river breaks up into many channels. The main distributary, the Hooghly (now Hugli), flows 260 km (162 miles) from Nabadwip to the Bay of Bengal.

Between the 15th and 19th centuries, this easily navigable river attracted Dutch, French, Portuguese, Danish and British traders. The settlements they established transformed the

---

RAMAKRISHNA PARAMHANSA (1836–86)

Ramakrishna, one of modern India's greatest spiritual teachers, was born into a poor family of priests in 1836. He became a priest at Dakshineshwar, where he began a life of prayer and meditation. His philosophy was lucid – there is an inherent truth in all religions and a simple life is a pure life. A mystic who claimed to speak directly to God, he could explain complex and abstruse theological issues in the simplest language, which appealed to the poor and rich alike. His teachings were carried to the USA and to Britain by his main disciple Swami Vivekananda (1863–1902) who set up many Ramakrishna Mission centres abroad for education and religious studies.

Ramakrishna Paramhansa

**Visitors praying at the Church of
Our Lady of Bandel**

THE HOOGHLY RIVER

KEY

🚉 Railway station

🚌 Bus station

🛕 Temple

✝ Church

⛴ Jetty

0 km   5

0 miles   5

Bansberia

Bandel
Hooghly

Chinsurah

Chandannagar

Barakpur

Shrirampur

↓ KOLKATA

river banks into a mini Europe – the remnants of which can be best explored today by taking one of the river cruises.

Up river from Kolkata is **Shrirampur** (Serampore), a Danish colony until 1845. Dr William Carey, the first Baptist missionary in India *(see p279)*, set up the earliest printing press here in 1799 and translated the Bible into several Indian languages, including Bengali, marking the beginnings of modern Bengali prose. He also founded the first theological college, today Shrirampur College, in 1805. Its library houses a priceless collection of 18th- and 19th-century books.

On the east bank is **Barakpur** (Barrackpore), the site of the British viceroys' once gracious country house. The mansion, locally referred to as Lat Bagan ("Governor's or Lord's Garden"), was built by Lord Wellesley, the governor general in the early 19th century.

Chandannagar (Chandernagore), a French settlement from 1673 until 1952, still retains a Gallic ambience. The public benches on the waterfront (previously Quai Dupleix) are replicas of those found in Paris parks. The elegant Administrator's Residence, built in the 18th century, is now the Institut de Chandernagore, a library and

**Armenian
Church, Chinsurah**

museum, and contains an interesting collection of French-era documents and artifacts. The Église du Sacré Coeur has a statue of Joan of Arc and a Lourdes grotto.

North of Chandannagar is **Chinsurah** (Chunchura), an Armenian settlement, taken over by the Dutch in 1625, and later by the British. The Armenian Church was built in 1695, though the steeple was added a century later. The town of **Hooghly**, to the north, has an impressive *imambara* (mosque) built in 1836. Further upriver is **Bandel**, founded by the Portuguese in 1580. The Church of Our Lady of Bandel, consecrated

in 1599, is among the oldest in Eastern India. After being refaced in granite, it has, however, lost some of its charm. People of all faiths still pray at the statue of Our Lady of Happy Voyages, an icon with an interesting history. In 1632, while the city was being sacked by the Mughal emperor Shah Jahan, the icon was lost in the river, but later reappeared miraculously on the banks in front of the church.

Further north is **Bansberia**, site of several terracotta temples. The Ananta Vasudeva Temple, built in 1679, has a panel of warriors carved above the entrance, while the Hanseshwari Temple, built in 1814, has a fabulous array of Kremlin-like onion domes and an elaborately carved façade.

The French Administrator's Residence in Chandannagar

The Sunderbans ➍

White breasted kingfisher

THE VAST GANGES-BRAHMAPUTRA Delta stretching into Bangladesh, covers 18,000 sq km (6,950 sq miles) and has the world's largest tropical mangrove forest. The 2,585-sq km (998 sq-mile) Sunderbans Reserve, a UNESCO World Heritage Site created within the delta, was declared a Tiger Reserve in 1973 to protect the endangered Royal Bengal tiger. The intricate network of waterways, creeks and alluvial islands abounds in a variety of marine life, including crustaceans and dolphins, as well as reptiles such as Olive Ridley turtles and estuarine crocodiles. The swamps also attract an impressive array of birds, especially waterfowl. Guided boat tours take visitors for leisurely rides through the enchanting mangroves.

Fiddler Crabs
Male fiddler crabs have a large claw resembling a bow and fiddle, which they use to attract females and deter enemies.

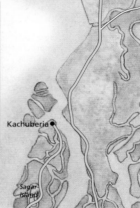

KOLKATA

Diamond Harbour

Jaynagar-Majilp

Raidighi

Kachuberia

Sagar Island

Lothian Island

Saptamukhi

Jamira

DIGHA

Ganga Sagar

Bakkhali

Mangrove Forests
Renowned for their variety of mangroves, the Sunderbans were once dominated by the sundari *tree (Heritiera fomes), now nearly extinct due to rampant timber poaching. Mangroves have ingeniously adapted to flooding and salinity, using breathing roots or pneumatophores.*

Country Boats
Small rowboats, available from Sajnakhali, take visitors along the reserve's many waterways. These craft are preferable to the noisier motorboats that tend to scare away wildlife, especially the rich variety of waterfowl.

MORE TO SEE

The western boundary of the Sundarbans boasts a number of popular beaches and reserves, all of which can be reached by road or boat. **Ganga Sagar** on Sagar Island, is the spot where millions of pilgrims gather for the annual Ganga Sagar Mela *(see p295)* during Makar Sankranti in January. **Diamond Harbour** is a popular picnic spot, while **Bakkhali** and **Digha** have beautiful beaches and are popular resorts. Bakkhali is also a haven for birdlife.

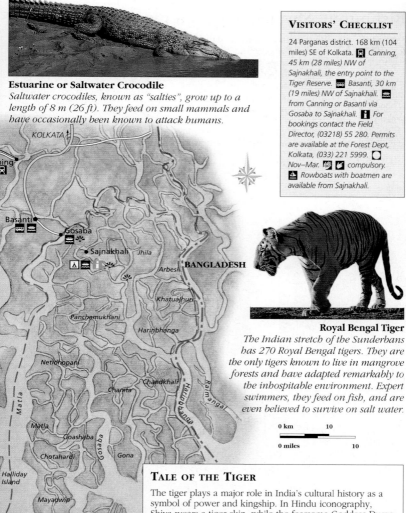

Estuarine or Saltwater Crocodile
Saltwater crocodiles, known as "salties", grow up to a length of 8 m (26 ft). They feed on small mammals and have occasionally been known to attack humans.

KOLKATA

Basanti

Gosaba

Sajnakhali

Jhila

Arbesi

BANGLADESH

Khatuajhuri

Panchemukhani

Harinbhanga

Netidhopani

Chandkhali

Chamta

Matla

Matla

Goashaba

Gosaba

Gona

Chotahardi

Halliday Island

Mayadwip

Bhangaduni

Royal Bengal Tiger
The Indian stretch of the Sunderbans has 270 Royal Bengal tigers. They are the only tigers known to live in mangrove forests and have adapted remarkably to the inhospitable environment. Expert swimmers, they feed on fish, and are even believed to survive on salt water.

```
0 km          10
0 miles       10
```

KEY

🚉 Railway station

🚌 Bus station

🛥 Jetty

ℹ Tourist information

Ⓐ Accommodation

☙ Viewpoint

═ Major road

═ Minor road

▪ ▪ Park boundary

▪▪▪ International border

TALE OF THE TIGER

The tiger plays a major role in India's cultural history as a symbol of power and kingship. In Hindu iconography, Shiva wears a tiger skin, while the fearsome Goddess Durga rides a tiger. Tiger images can also be seen in vibrant murals in Buddhist monasteries in Sikkim, Arunachal Pradesh and Ladakh. In the Sunderbans, ritual offerings are made to the forest deity, Banbibi, to seek protection from the tiger. Yet statistics belie the tiger's mythic status. In 1900, India's tiger population was about 40,000; by 1972 it had fallen to 1,800. Alarmed, the Indian government launched Project Tiger. Ever since, numbers have grown substantially and India now has between 2,750 and 3,500 tigers (about 60 per cent of the world's tiger population), protected in 27 Project Tiger Reserves across the country.

A play re-enacting Banbibi protecting a mother and child from the tiger

Bishnupur: Shyama Raya Temple ❺

Creeper
motif

Bishnupur, capital of the Mallabhumi kingdom between the 17th and the mid-18th centuries, is renowned for its elaborately adorned terracotta temples, made of the local red clay. The most imposing of these is the Shyama Raya Temple, built in 1643. It is richly decorated with scenes from Lord Krishna's life as well as episodes taken from the epic *Ramayana (see p27)*. Other motifs in the temple include scenes of hunting, boating and military processions.

Front façade of the Shyama Raya Temple

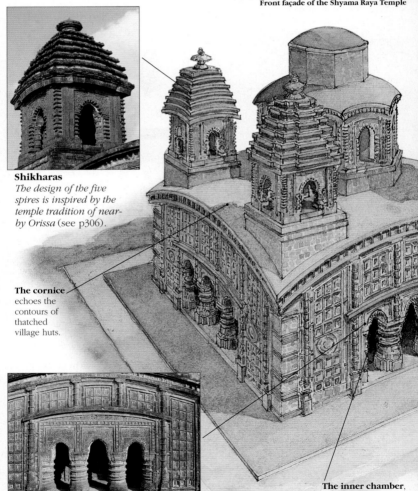

Shikharas
The design of the five spires is inspired by the temple tradition of nearby Orissa (see p306).

The cornice echoes the contours of thatched village huts.

The inner chamber, called *thakurbari* (god's house), has a finely decorated altar at one end.

Arched Façade
The arches, supported by squat, ornamented pillars, lead to a vaulted corridor.

VISITORS' CHECKLIST

Bankura district. 152 km
(94miles) NW of Kolkata.
🏛 62,000. 🚉 🚌 ☐ daily.
🎭 Rasa Festival (Aug).

Terracotta Friezes
*Scenes from the epics
alternate with scenes
from daily life.
Here, Krishna
plays his flute for
the* gopis
(milkmaids).

**The curved
cornice**
deflects rain
water.

Interior Arch
*This doorway has rich
carvings of creepers,
foliage and flowers.*

The twin hut-like roofs of the Keshta Raya Temple, Bishnupur

Exploring Bishnupur's Temples

The terracotta temples of Bishnupur are scattered over a 3-km (2-mile) radius, and stand out vividly against the vibrant green and ochre colours of the landscape.

The **Rasa Mancha Temple**, built by the ruler Bir Hambir in the early 17th century, has 108 pillars and a pyramidal roof. Images of Krishna and Radha were displayed here for the Rasa Festival, a tradition that still continues today.

North of the Rasa Mancha Temple is the large **Keshta Raya (Jor Bangla) Temple**, built in 1655. It has joined twin roofs, literally *jor bangla*. Floral motifs, scroll work and scenes from the *Ramayana* and *Mahabharata* embellish the friezes on the walls.

The **Madan Mohan Temple** further north, was built in 1694 and has friezes showing events from the life of Krishna.

To the northwest, the 19th-century **Shridhara Temple** has nine spires or *nav ratna*. The frieze at the entrance shows the god Shiva dancing.

Barddhaman ⑥

Barddhaman district. 125 km (78 miles) S of Kolkata. 🚌
🎭 Barddhaman Festival (Jan).

THE RAJAS of Barddhaman (Burdwan) were once powerful landlords and great patrons of the arts. Today, the small, nondescript town is a gateway to some interesting sites. The rajas built several temples at **Kalna**, 50 km (31 miles) to the east, in the 18th and 19th centuries today. The Shiva temple, with 108 minor shrines, is the most impressive. **Nabadwip**, 20 km (12 miles) to the north, was the birthplace of Sri Chaitanya (1486–1533), founder of the movement that revived the Krishna cult *(see p179)*. It is a charming town, with a few old houses built of the narrow red brick, unique to pre-British Bengal. Pilgrims singing *bhajans* throng the Gauranga Temple. Nearby, in **Mayapur**, is the large and modern Chandrodaya Temple built by ISKCON (International Society for Krishna Consciousness).

BANKURA HORSES

Bankura district's vibrant tradition of folk art includes a variety of clay handicrafts. The district's most famous product is the Bankura horse, a very stylized figure with a long neck and elongated ears, in warm terracotta colours. Artisans have used the same techniques of hollow clay moulding and firing for generations. Sizes vary from minute, palm-sized toys to gigantic creations over 1 m (3 ft) high. The horses are votive figures and are usually placed in front of local deities.

Bankura clay horse

Students attending open air classes at Visva Bharati University

Shantiniketan **❼**

Birbhum district. 213 km (132 miles) NW of Kolkata. 🚉 *Bolpur, 3 km (2 miles) S of Shantiniketan, then rickshaw.* 🚌 *Bolpur.* 🎪 *Kendulimela (Jan), Paush Mela (Dec).*

R ABINDRANATH Tagore founded the serene settlement of Shantiniketan in 1921. His aim was to establish an institution that followed the traditional Indian *gurukul* system of instruction where gurus would teach their disciples, while sitting on the grass under shady trees. The university also stressed the importance of community living, and specialized in all branches of the arts and humanities, with a special emphasis on Bengali culture.

Today known as the **Visva Bharati University**, its structure is more conventional, but certain traditions, such as open air lessons, remain sacrosanct. The place is still hallowed ground for admirers of Tagore.

In the campus is the Uttarayan Complex, where the poet lived and worked for many years. Other departments include **Kala** (Fine Arts) **Bhavan, Sangeet** (Music) **Bhavan** and **China Bhavan**, specializing in Chinese studies. Shantiniketan's association with contemporary Indian art is evident by the works on display by many of the country's leading artists, such as Binode Bihari Mukherjee (1904–80), Nandlal Bose (1882–1966) and Ram Kinkar

Baij (1910–80). The **Vichitra Museum** has memorabilia from the poet's life, including his paintings, developed from the sketches he made in the margins of his written work. Excellent performances of Rabindra Sangeet (songs written and set to music by Tagore) can be heard at the campus every evening.

The village of **Kenduli**, nearby, is the birthplace of the medieval poet, Jayadeva, who composed the *Gita Govinda*, a paean to Krishna. Every year in January the Bauls, wandering minstrels known for their soulful songs, gather here for Kendulimela a festival where they sing without pause for three days.

🏛 **Visva Bharati University** 📞 *(0346) 35 2751.* 🕐 *Thu–Tue.* 🎭 **Vichitra Museum** 🕐 *Thu–Tue.* 🚫 🎥

Murshidabad **❽**

Murshidabad district. 200 km (124 miles) N of Kolkata. 🚉 🚌

T HE FORMER CAPITAL of the nawabs of Bengal, Murshidabad lies in the green and gold Bengal countryside. This city, on the banks of the Bhagirathi river, was founded in 1704 by Nawab Murshid Quli Khan, governor of the Mughal emperor Aurangzeb. His grave lies beneath the stairs of the impressive **Katra Mosque**, built in 1724 along the lines of the Great Mosque at Mecca. The nawab chose this site because he wanted the footsteps of the faithful to pass over him.

Hazarduari ("A Thousand Doors"), the nawabs' palace, was built in the 1830s by General Duncan McLeod of the Bengal Engineers who,

The grand façade of Hazarduari Palace in Murshidabad

RABINDRANATH TAGORE (1861–1941)

Tagore was India's ultimate Renaissance man and his influence is still felt in all branches of the arts, particularly in Bengal. Born in 1861 into the rich and cultivated Tagore family *(see p280)*, he became a poet, lyricist, novelist, short story writer, essayist, painter, choreographer, actor and singer – as well as the author of India's national anthem. Following the translation of his poem *Gitanjali* into English by William Butler Yeats, he was awarded the Nobel Prize in 1913. He was knighted by the British government, but returned the honour in protest against the massacre at Jallianwala Bagh *(see p56)*. Mahatma Gandhi called him Gurudev ("Great Teacher"). Tagore died in August 1941, but his memory is still deeply revered by Bengalis and his portraits, if not his books, occupy pride of place in nearly all middle-class Bengali homes.

Nobel laureate Tagore, in 1930

inspired by Italian Baroque, gave it a banquet hall lined with mirrors and a striking circular Durbar Hall. The palace is now a museum with many fine exhibits, such as a gigantic chandelier, presented by Queen Victoria, which was hung directly over the nawabs' solid silver throne. The library has over 10,000 books, among them some beautiful illuminated Korans. Other items on display are a motley collection of arms and armour, including a cannon which was fired at the crucial Battle of Plassey in 1757 *(see p52)*, when Robert Clive defeated the nawab, Siraj-ud-Daulah – a battle which eventually paved the way for the establishment of the British Empire in India. The town declined after Kolkata grew in importance.

🏛 **Hazarduari Museum**
⬜ *Sat–Thu.* 📷 🚫

Gaur ⑨

Malda district. 325 km (202 miles) N of Kolkata. 🚉 *Malda, 16 km (10 miles) N of Gaur, then taxi or bus.* 🚌 **Monuments** ⬜ *daily.*

THE IMPRESSIVE RUINS of Gaur are an indication of its former glory, when the city caught the imagination of the second Mughal emperor Humayun who called it Jinnatabad ("Abode of Paradise"). This abandoned city, spread over 52 sq kms (20 sq miles), dates to the 15th and 16th centuries, though the area has a much older history. The Buddhist Pala kings ruled here from the 8th century onwards until they

The carved terracotta façade of the Eklakhi Mausoleum, Pandua

were ousted by the Senas, Bengal's last Hindu dynasty, in the 12th century. Thereafter, it was ruled by a series of Muslim sultans, including the Ilyas Shahi dynasty. Gaur was sacked by Sher Shah Sur *(see p79)* in 1537, and ravaged by plague in 1575, after which it became part of the Mughal Empire.

The oldest structure is the **Sagar Dighi**, a large tank built in the 12th century. On the eastern bank of the Bhagirathi river are the ramparts of a fort, within which is a brick wall that once enclosed a palace. The northern gate, the **Dakhil Darwaza**, built in 1425, has a soaring entrance archway and corners embellished with carving. To its north are the remains of **Sona Mosque**, built in 1526, and Gaur's largest mosque. Other interesting buildings include the many-arched **Qadam Rasul Mosque**, built in 1530 to enshrine an impression of the Prophet Mohammad's footprint, the brick

The Gumti Darwaza, Gaur

Tantipara Mosque and the **Lattan Mosque** with remnants of blue, green, yellow and white tiles. The **Gumti Darwaza**, the eastern entrance to the city of Gaur, still stands.

Pandua ⑩

Malda district. 360 km (224 miles) N of Kolkata. 🚉 *Malda, 18 km (11 miles) S of Pandua, then taxi or bus.* 🚌

THE creeper-covered ruins of Pandua lie on either side of a 10-km (6-mile) stretch of an old paved brick road. Between 1338 and 1500, Pandua replaced Gaur as the capital of Bengal's Muslim rulers. At the northern end, the 14th century **Adina Mosque**, built by Sultan Sikandar Shah, imitates the design of the great mosque at Damascus. Once the largest mosque in India, it contains Sikandar Shah's tomb. Further south, the early 15th-century **Eklakhi Mausoleum** has the grave of Sultan Jalal-ud-din. This stucture, built at great cost, was one of the earliest square brick tombs to be constructed in Bengal. The octagonal inner chamber, unusually, has an image of Ganesha, the Hindu elephant god, carved over the entrance archway. The **Qutb Shahi Mosque**, to the south, is sometimes called the "Golden Mosque" as its minarets were once topped with yellow tiles. It was built in 1585 by Sultan Makhdum Shah, whose grave lies adjacent to the mosque.

The Dakhil Darwaza in Gaur, built with small, red bricks

Tea plantations lining the road between Bagdogra and Siliguri

Siliguri ⓫

Darjeeling district. 79 km (49 miles) SE of Darjeeling. 🏠 470,300. ✈ Bagdogra, 12 km (7 miles) W of Siliguri, then taxi or bus. 🚊 New Jalpaiguri, 60 km (37 miles) SE of Siliguri, then taxi or bus. 🚌 ℹ Tourist Office, Siliguri, (0353) 51 1974.

Sᴵᴸᴵɢᴜʀᴵ, ꜱᴵᴛᴜᴀᴛᴇᴅ in the foothills of the Eastern Himalayas, was once a calm, provincial town, with quiet streets and well-equipped shops, where tea planters would come to stock up on provisions. Today, much of the town is a vast trucking depot, though it has some lively bazaars, such as the one on **Tenzing Norgay Road**. The

Tibetan woollens on sale here are good bargains, and cane furniture, a speciality of the area, is widely available. In the winter, Siliguri hosts international Buddhist conferences and also serves as the transit point for travellers to the Jaldapara Wildlife Sanctuary.

ENVIRONS: Clustered close to Siliguri are **New Jalpaiguri**, the railhead for the area, and **Bagdogra**, which has the airport. Along with Siliguri, these towns act as gateways to the hill stations of Darjeeling, Kurseong and Kalimpong, as well as to Bhutan and Sikkim. The drive between these towns goes past beautiful green acres of tea plantations.

Jaldapara Wildlife Sanctuary ⓬

Jalpaiguri district. 200 km (78 miles) E of Siliguri. 🚊 Madarihat, the entry point, then taxi. 🚌 Madarihat. ℹ For general enquiries and bookings for the Hollong Forest Lodge contact Tourist Office, Siliguri, (0353) 51 1974. ⏰ Oct–May. 🎦 📷 extra charges. ⓢ Hollong.

Tʜᴇ ʀᴇɢᴵᴏɴ around the Jaldapara Wildlife Sanctuary, in the richly forested Dooars Valley, was once the hunting ground of the kings of Bhutan. Today, it is one of the biggest reserve forests in West Bengal, covering an area of 115 sq km (44 sq miles). Established in

---

Tʜᴇ Dᴀʀᴊᴇᴇʟᴵɴɢ Hᴵᴍᴀʟᴀʏᴀɴ Rᴀᴵʟᴡᴀʏ (DHR)

The most attractive way to travel to Darjeeling from Siliguri is by the "toy train", officially known as the Darjeeling Himalayan Railway (DHR). The narrow gauge train gasps its way up from the railhead at New Jalpaiguri to Darjeeling, 2,134 m (7,001 ft) above sea level. The journey takes nine hours and the track rises a total of 2,088 m (6,850 ft) over its length of 80 km (50 miles). Constructed between 1879 and 1881, the train line was hailed as an engineering

The toy train pulled by steam engines

masterpiece and is now a UNESCO World Heritage Site. The line makes wide loops as it zigzags up the hill, requiring the train to backtrack for certain stretches. Each of the steam engines, one of which dates to 1892, hauls up three carriages. If nine hours sounds daunting, try journeying to Kurseong by train and taking a bus to Darjeeling, or travelling only the last stretch (from Ghoom to Darjeeling) by train. Tickets for the journey are available at New Jalpaiguri and Darjeeling stations. The train leaves both stations at 9am and 3pm during the peak season. For more details see p777.

1943, the reserve sprawls over lush, deciduous forests and dense scrubland, with the Torsa river flowing through it. This is one of the few places in India where the great Indian one-horned rhinoceros (*see p330*) can be easily spotted. About 50 of these magnificent animals live in the sanctuary, protected from poachers who hunt them for their horns, which are believed to be powerful aphrodisiacs. The sanctuary is home to various other rare and endangered species as well, including the leopard, tiger, hispid hare, hogbadger, and sloth bear.

Large numbers of hog deer, spotted deer, barking deer and gaur (Indian bison) can also be seen at Jaldapara. Bird species include the lesser pied hornbill, and the Bengal florican with its mottled and streaked plumage. In addition, there are eight species of freshwater turtles in Jaldapara's ponds.

The northern part of the sanctuary, known as Totopara, is located along the banks of the Torsa river. It is home to the Toto tribe, now only 950 strong, whose members have consistently refused to succumb to the comforts of civilization.

Jungle fowl, found in large numbers at Jaldapara

A delightful way to explore the Jaldapara Sanctuary is to take an early morning elephant safari through the park. The elephants belong to the forest department and spend their entire lives within the confines of the sanctuary. Quite often, the elephants taking visitors on safaris are accompanied by their calves, which gambol along closely beside them. The many waterholes in the sanctuary, where animals come to drink in the evenings, are excellent spots for wildlife sightings.

The elegant, colonial-style **Hollong Forest Lodge** within the sanctuary offers food and accommodation.

Kurseong ⑬

Darjeeling district. 31 km (19 miles) N of Siliguri. 🚉 🚌

Halfway between Siliguri and Darjeeling, on the Darjeeling Himalayan Railway line, secluded Kurseong has a quiet charm. It is smaller than Darjeeling, with a milder climate because of its lower altitude. Set amid tea gardens, with lush vegetation and a picturesque lake, Kurseong is known for its natural beauty. According to local legend, the place gets its name from *kurson-rip*, a beautiful wild orchid found in the area.

Kurseong is a walkers' paradise. The trek from **Mirik** to Kurseong (*see p303*), which takes about eight hours, runs through tea estates, orange orchards, cardamom plantations and small villages, and provides spectacular views of the valley. Similarly, the five-hour walk to **Ghoom** is also beautiful, winding along a ridge which runs through a thick, but well-shaded, forest.

FESTIVALS OF WEST BENGAL & SIKKIM

Saraswati Puja *pandal*

Ganga Sagar Mela (*mid-Jan*), Sagar Island. Thousands of pilgrims assemble for a fair, and a dip at dawn at the point where the Ganges enters the sea.
Saraswati Puja (*Jan/Feb*). Saraswati is the Goddess of Learning and her image is always dressed in pale yellow. School and college girls dress in yellow too, and place their books at the feet of the goddess during this festival, celebrated all over Bengal.
International Flower Festival (*Apr/May*), Gangtok. Held at the height of the flowering season, this festival showcases Sikkim's rare orchids, rhododendrons and other beautiful flowers.
Saga Dawa (*May*), Gangtok. Sacred scriptures are carried from monasteries through the streets by stately processions of lamas during this festival, which celebrates the Buddha's birth, his enlightenment and his attainment of nirvana.
Durga Puja (*Sep/Oct*) (*see p281*).
Burra Din (*25 Dec*), Kolkata. Otherwise known as Christmas, Burra Din is celebrated by Christians and non-Christians alike. Kolkata's main shopping streets are lit up and little plastic pine trees, decorations and thickly-iced fruit cakes are on sale at every local market.

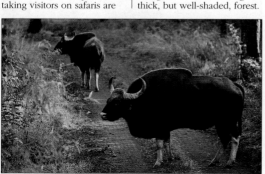

Gaur (Indian bison) roaming the scrubland at Jaldapara

A view of Darjeeling with Mount Kanchendzonga in the background

Darjeeling 🄬

Darjeeling district. 79 km (49 miles)
NW of Siliguri. 🄪 107,600. ✈
Bagdogra, 90 km (56 miles) S of city
centre, then bus or taxi. 🚉 🚌 🛈
Government Tourist Office, Chowrasta,
(0354) 54 050.

THE NAME DARJEELING derives
from the monastery of
Dorje Ling (meaning Place of
the Thunderbolt) that once
stood on Observatory Hill. The
British chose this sunny, west-
facing ledge of the Himalayan
foothills to build a sanatorium
in the mid-19th century.
Subsequently, it became
Bengal's summer capital and
the government would move
up here when the plains grew
too hot. Today, much of
Darjeeling's Raj splendour is
still in evidence and contrasts
with its Tibetan, Nepali and
Bengali character.

This picturesque town squats
rather precariously on the
hillside, and has three main
thoroughfares, **Hill Cart Road**,
Laden Road and **The Mall**.
The Mall is the hub of
Darjeeling, leading to the
crowded **Chowrasta** (crossroads), lined with bookshops
such as the **Oxford Book and
Stationery**, which has a wide
range of books on India. Other
shops sell teas, curios and
souvenirs. Vendors offer sets of
bright, out-of-focus postcards
and guided tours. A rather
jolting ten-minute pony ride
round the Chowrasta is also
available.

Nearby is the **Bhutia Busty
Monastery**, built in 1879.
The cult text, *The Tibetan Book
of the Dead*, was found in the
library attached to this shrine,
and was translated into English
in 1927. The murals in the
temple are beautiful – but
visitors should ask for
permission before entering.

The presence of **Kanchendzonga**, (8,598 m/28,209 ft),
India's highest peak *(see
p302)*, dominates the town.
Some of the best views of
the entire snow-clad range of
the Eastern Himalayan
peaks can be enjoyed from the
windy, prayer flag-lined
Observatory Hill.

At **North Point**, in the
northwest corner of Darjeeling,
is India's first passenger rope-
way, a cable car connecting
Darjeeling to **Singla Bazaar**
in the Little Rangeet Valley.
The hour-long journey provides a good view of the
mountains and the tea gardens
that cling to the sides and
bottom of the valley.

The **Himalayan Mountain-
eering Institute** is to the
south of North Point on Birch
Hill. Its Mountaineering
Museum has a fascinating
contour model of the
Himalayan peaks, while the
Everest Museum gives a
history of the various attempts
to climb Everest and other
Himalayan peaks. The
Himalayan Zoo is adjacent,
and is famous for its high
altitude fauna, including snow
leopards, Siberian tigers and
red pandas. To the south, the
Lloyds Botanical Gardens
are home to an interesting and
varied collection of Himalayan
flora – the hundreds of species
of orchids in its Orchid House

The carved and painted façade of the Yoga Choeling Monastery

are particularly lovely. The town also has some well-preserved colonial churches. **St Andrew's Church**, west of Observatory Hill, was built in 1873, though the clock tower was added later. **St Columba's Kirk**, near the train station, was built in 1894 and is worth a visit for its magnificent stained-glass windows.

Some of the best preserved examples of Raj-era grandeur in India are Darjeeling's hotels and clubs. Just above Observatory Hill is the rattan-and-chintz-decorated **Windamere Hotel** *(see p700)*. Open fires heat the sedate lounge where, to the accompaniment of a string quartet playing genteel tunes, maids in starched aprons serve sandwiches and Darjeeling tea to visitors and guests.

Ghosts of colonial planters can be sensed at the **Planters' Club**. Old hunting prints hang on the walls and visitors can sit in front of coal fires while bearers, who must have been robust young men in 1947, serve drinks in slow motion.

🏛 Bhutia Busty Monastery
Chowrasta. ⭘ daily.
🏛 Himalayan Mountaineering Institute
Birch Hill Park, entrance on Jawahar Rd West. 📞 (0354) 52 438. ⭘ daily.
⬤ Thu. 🎫 📷 extra charges.
🐾 Himalayan Zoo
⭘ Fri–Wed. 🎫

ENVIRONS: Those interested in Buddhism should visit the **Yoga Choeling Monastery**, 10 km (6 miles) south of Darjeeling, established in 1875 by the Gelugpa (Yellow Hat) sect. The monastery has murals of Buddhist deities and beautiful, if faded, frescoes in the prayer hall. Ask for permission before entering the shrine. **Tiger Hill**, 11 km (7 miles) south of Darjeeling, offers spectacular views of the mighty **Everest** (8,848 m/29,029 ft) and other peaks in the Eastern Himalayan Range, including **Makalu** (8,475 m/27,805ft) and **Janu** (7,710 m/25,295 ft), as they catch the first rays of the sun. Early risers can take a pre-dawn drive to Tiger Hill (about 45 minutes in a jeep).

Women tea pickers in northern Bengal's tea gardens, around Darjeeling

Senchal Lake, 5 km (3 miles) west of Tiger Hill, is a lovely mountain lake, but tends to be crowded with local tourists. For visitors who come to Darjeeling during the plucking season (April to November), the **Happy Valley Tea Estate**, just beyond the town, is a pleasant tea garden to visit.

Mural, Zangdopelri Fo-Brang Monastery

🏛 Yoga Choeling Monastery
⭘ daily. Donations welcome.

Kalimpong ⓯

Darjeeling district. 51 km (32 miles) E of Darjeeling. 🚶 43,000. 🚌

KALIMPONG WAS once part of Sikkimese and then Bhutanese territory, before it became part of British India in the 19th century. It was at the head of the ancient trade route to Tibet and still has the feel of a frontier town. Its market sells a mix of the exotic and the mundane, from fern shoots to plastic buckets. Memories of the Raj are recalled by the charming stone cottages and the quaint ambience of the **Himalayan Hotel** *(see p700)*, once a family home. The **Thongsa Monastery** is Kalimpong's oldest monastery. It was built in 1692, and is a brisk hour's walk above the town. To the south of the town, the **Zangdopelri Fo-Brang Monastery**, blessed by the Dalai Lama in 1976, has some interesting three-dimensional mandalas.

The town's many nurseries produce a large number of exotic orchids, gladioli, amaryllis lily and cactii. A good one to visit is the **Udai Mani Pradhan Nursery**.

TENZING NORGAY (1914–86)

Tenzing Norgay and Sir Edmund Hillary were the first two men to stand on top of Mount Everest. Tenzing Norgay was born in Tsa-chu, Nepal, into the Sherpa community, and later made his home in Darjeeling. He undertook his first climb as a porter with a British expedition in 1935 and climbed many mountain peaks, making at least six attempts on Everest before his successful one with Hillary in 1953, when he was the sherpa sirdar (head sherpa). Tenzing won the George Medal and later became the head of Darjeeling's Himalayan Mountaineering Institute. Tenzing's life highlighted the contributions, earlier seldom acknowledged, that sherpas make to Himalayan expeditions.

Statue of Tenzing, Himalayan Mountaineering Institute

Stupa at Gangtok's Namgyal Institute of Tibetology

Gangtok ⑯

East Sikkim district. 110 km (68 miles) N of Siliguri. 👥 29,200. ✈ Bagdogra, 117 km (73 miles) S of city centre, then taxi or bus. 🚉 Siliguri, 107 km (66 miles) S of city centre, then taxi or bus. 🚌 ℹ Sikkim Tourism, MG Marg, (03592) 21 634. 🎭 Losar Festival (Feb/Mar), Enchey Monastery Festival (Aug & Dec). **Travel permits** required to enter Sikkim (see p303).

T HE CAPITAL of Sikkim, Gangtok reflects this tiny state's extraordinary ethnic diversity. In the crowded city, which spills precariously down a ridge, Lepchas (the region's original inhabitants) live alongside Tibetans, Bhutias, Nepalis and Indians from the plains. Though now full of modern structures, Gangtok's "Shangrila" aspects can still be experienced in pockets of the city and in its alpine environs.

Until 1975, Sikkim was a kingdom, with the status of an Indian Protectorate. It was ruled by the Chogyals, Buddhists of Tibetan origin, whose dynasty began in the 17th century. However, the British Raj's policies of importing cheap labour from neighbouring Nepal for Sikkim's rice, cardamom and tea plantations drastically changed Sikkim's demography, soon Nepali Hindus constituted 75 per cent of the state's population. In 1975 the population of Sikkim voted overwhelmingly

to join the Indian Republic, ending the rule of Palden Thondup, the last Chogyal.

At the northern edge of the town is the early 20th-century **Enchey Monastery**, whose large prayer hall is full of vibrant murals and images, representing the entire pantheon of Mahayana Buddhist deities *(see p141)*. Enchey's festivals feature spectacular masked dances. At the southern end of the town is the **Namgyal Institute of Tibetology**. Established in 1958, it has a rare collection of medieval Buddhist scriptures, bronzes and embroidered *thangkas*.

⚑ Enchey Monastery
◻ daily 📷 only allowed outside the monastery.

🏛 Namgyal Institute of Tibetology
◻ Mon–Sat. ● 1st & 3rd Sat. 📷

Guardian of the East at Rumtek

ENVIRONS: Saramsa Orchidarium, situated 14 km (9 miles) south of Gangtok, displays many of the 450 orchid species found in Sikkim. They flower from April to May, and again in October.

Rumtek Monastery, 24 km (15 miles) southwest of Gangtok, is the headquarters of the Kagyupa (Black Hat) sect, one of the oldest Tibetan Buddhist sects, and the seat of its head, the Gyalwa Karmapa. The 16th Karmapa fled Tibet in 1959 after the Chinese invasion, and built a replica here of his monastery at Tsurphu in Tibet. Rumtek is an impressive

complex, its flat-roofed buildings topped with golden finials, and filled with treasures brought from the monastery in Tibet. Especially splendid is the reliquary *chorten* of the 16th Karmapa, behind the main prayer hall, made of silver and gold and studded with enormous corals, amber and turquoise. Since the 16th Karmapa's death in 1981, however, there have been two claimants to his title (and the monastery's legendary treasures), including one who dramatically escaped from Tibet into India in 2000. Until this dispute is resolved, the armed guards that surround the monastery will remain. Rumtek's main festivals are in February/March and in May/June.

Tsomgo Lake, 40 km (25 miles) northeast of Gangtok, lies at an altitude of 3,780 m (12,402 ft). Visitors to the lake require a special permit from the Sikkim Tourism office in Gangtok. The drive to Tsomgo Lake, close to the border with China, is spectacular, and the lake is an impressive sight both in spring and summer, when it is surrounded by alpine flowers in bloom, and in winter when it is frozen solid. Visitors can go for rides on the splendid shaggy black yaks that stand docilely on the lake's shores.

⚑ Rumtek Monastery
◻ daily. 📷 only allowed outside the monastery.

The richly decorated prayer hall of Rumtek Monastery

Flora and Fauna of the Eastern Himalayas

THE EASTERN HIMALAYAS and their foothills in northern Bengal, Sikkim and the north-eastern states are exceptionally rich in rare flora and fauna. This region receives the brunt of the Southwest Monsoon winds as they rise over the Bay of Bengal and hit the Eastern Himalayas with full force, gradually losing impetus as they travel westward. The resulting high moisture content in the air and soil has helped create a habitat

Primula calderina

of dense virgin forests, fertile hillsides and lush alpine pastures. Among the plants that can be seen in this region are over 50 species of rhodo-dendron, 500 species of orchid, and several varieties of primula and bamboo. Typical fauna of the region include yaks, blue sheep and red pandas. Local folklore adds another – the elusive Yeti or Abominable Snowman, glimpsed by many mountaineers.

The blue poppy (Meconopsis roylei), *which attracted famous 19th-century plant hunters such as Joseph Hooker to the Eastern Himalayas, grows above the tree-line, in alpine pastures where yaks graze.*

The cardiocrinum lily (Cardiocrinum giganteum) *is highly scented. It grows in temperate forests of oak, maple and rhododendron in Sikkim.*

Orchids, *such as this beautiful yellow* Dendrobium *species, festoon the forests of Arunachal Pradesh, Meghalaya, Manipur, Nagaland and Sikkim.*

The great pied hornbill, (Buceros bicornis) *with its huge yellow and black beak, is common in the forests of Arunachal Pradesh, where several tribes sport its black and white feathers in their headdress.*

Magnolia campbelli *with its lovely white blossom, blooms profusely in early spring in the temperate forests of the Darjeeling hills and Sikkim.*

The red panda (Ailurus fulgens), *also called the cat-bear, is a bright chestnut colour with white-rimmed ears and a bushy tail. One of its favourite foods is dwarf bamboo which grows in the temperate forests of Arunachal Pradesh and Sikkim.*

The yak *is greatly prized in Sikkim. It serves as a pack animal, and also provides milk, meat and wool from its shaggy coat.*

A Tour of Northern Sikkim ⑰

A N AREA OF unspoilt natural beauty, framed by snowcapped Himalayan peaks, northern Sikkim has only recently been opened to visitors. This tour, following the valley of the Teesta river, goes past tranquil monasteries and villages, through forests of rhododendron, to Yumthang where yaks graze in meadows filled with alpine flowers. Along the way there are charming rural markets, and superb views of the world's third highest peak, Mount Kanchendzonga.

TIPS FOR DRIVERS

Length: 149 km (93 miles).
Stopping-off points: The tour can be done in 2–3 days. Phodong, Mangan-Singhik and Lachung are stopping-off points.
Permits: Visitors require special permits for this region, issued by the Department of Tourism in Gangtok, (03592) 22 064. Travel is permitted in groups of two or more persons. For more details see p303.

Lachung ⑤
Just 15 km (9 miles) from Tibet, with which it used to trade before 1959, Lachung is a pretty village on both banks of the Lachung river.

Yumthang ⑥
The Lachung-Yumthang road crosses rhodo-dendron forests, which bloom between April and June. Yumthang, at 3,614 m (11,857 ft), also has hot sulphur springs.

0 km 5
0 miles 5

Mangan-Singhik ④
This market centre for northern Sikkim attracts local villagers selling oranges, apples and cardamom. There are breathtaking views of the Kanchendzonga Range from here.

Chungthang

KEY

━━ Tour route
━━ National highway
══ Minor road

Teesta

Kodyong

Phodong ②
This serene monastery, with 50 resident monks, has beautiful murals, woodcarving and Buddhist images. It was built in 1740.

Dik Chhu

Labrang ③
This monastery (built 1844), 4 km (2.5 miles) from Phodong, has an unusual octagonal shape. On the track below it are the ruins of Tumlong Palace, the seat of the Chogyals in the 19th century.

Gangtok ①
Built on a high ridge above the Ranipul river, Gangtok (see p298) is a bustling town, at an altitude of 1,675 m (5,495 ft).

NH31A

SILIGURI

Yumthang Chhu

Sebozung chhu

Pelling ⑱

West Sikkim district. 120 km (75 miles) W of Gangtok. 🚌 *Gezing, 9 km (6 miles) S of city centre, then local bus or taxi.* ℹ️ *Mount Pandim, Pemayangtse, (03595) 50 573.* 🎭 *Pemayangtse Festival (Feb/Mar).* **Travel permits** *required (see p303).*

SITUATED on a ridge, at an altitude of 2,040 m (6,693 ft), with excellent views of the peaks and glaciers of the Kanchendzonga Range, Pelling is a fast growing town. With plenty of accommodation, it is a convenient base from which to explore western Sikkim and embark on treks *(see pp302–303).* This is the state's most beautiful and unspoilt region, with expanses of forest, green river valleys, superb trekking trails, and Sikkim's oldest monasteries. Pelling is a day's drive from Gangtok, and is accessible from Darjeeling (72 km/45 miles south).

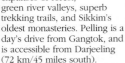

Detail of a door, Pemayangste

The main attraction here is the monastic complex of **Pemayangtse**, built in 1705, on a ridge a half-hour's walk from the town. Surrounded by picturesque monks' quarters and outhouses, the austere three-storeyed main monastery is a treasure house of beautiful *thangkas,* murals and images, with a breathtakingly intricate model of Zangdopelri, the seven-storeyed celestial home of Guru Padmasambhava *(see p139),* on the top floor. Pemayangtse has an annual festival, with spectacular masked dances. Sikkim's oldest monastery, **Sangachoeling**

(built in 1697), is a steep 40-minute hike through thick forests above Pemayangtse. It has exquisite murals. The ruins of Sikkim's 17th-century capital, built by the second Chogyal *(see p298),* are at **Rabdentse,** 3 km (2 miles) south of Pelling.

ENVIRONS: Khecheopalri Lake, 33 km (21 miles) north of Pelling, is an enchanting spot which is sacred to both Buddhists and Hindus, who come here to make a wish. Seen from above, the lake is shaped like the footprint of Buddha. Though surrounded by dense forest, it does not have a single leaf floating on its surface, and according to local belief, a holy bird swoops down and removes each leaf as it falls on the water.

Yuksam ⑲

West Sikkim district. 162 km (101 miles) W of Gangtok. 🚌 ℹ️ *Mount Pandim, Pemayangtse, (03595) 50 573.* **Travel permits** *required (see p303).*

YUKSAM WAS the first capital of Sikkim, where the first Chogyal of Sikkim was crowned in 1641 by three learned lamas. A stone throne and some *chortens* mark this historic spot. Below it is **Kathok Lake,** and **Dubdi Monastery,** built in 1700, with its exquisite Buddhist images and meditation cave, is a steep half-hour climb above. Yuksam is the starting point for the trek to Dzongri *(see p302).*

***Mani* stones being carved at Tashiding Monastery**

Tashiding Monastery ⑳

West Sikkim district. 145 km (90 miles) W of Gangtok. 🚌 ⭕ *daily.* 🎭 *Bumchu Festival (Feb/Mar).* **Travel permits** *required (see p303).*

BUILT in 1717, Tashiding Monastery stands on the summit of a heart-shaped hill, where Guru Padmasambhava is said to have shot an arrow and then meditated on the spot where it fell. Surrounded by *chortens, mani* stones, water-driven prayer wheels, and the Ratong and Rangeet rivers, with Mount Kanchendzonga looming behind the hill, this is a magical spot. During the annual Bumchu Festival it attracts large crowds from all over Sikkim.

During this festival, sacred water, said to have been put into a sealed jar by a 17th-century Buddhist saint, is mixed with river water and distributed as a powerful blessing to devotees. Miraculously, the supply of sacred water never runs dry, and each year when the jar is unsealed, oracle priests can predict the future of Sikkim from the water level in it – too much or too little water augurs ill for Sikkim's peace and prosperity. Tashiding also has the **Thongwa Rangdol Chorten,** a mere glimpse of which is supposed to wipe away all sins. The main temple, rebuilt in 1987, has large images of the Buddha and the Bodhisattvas.

Prayer flags fluttering near Yuksam, the first capital of Sikkim

Trekking in West Bengal & Sikkim

Rhododendron blossoms

THE EASTERN HIMALAYAS, spanning Tibet, Nepal, West Bengal and Sikkim, have some of the world's highest peaks such as Kanchendzonga, Everest, Lhotse and Makalu, and offer a variety of trekking options amidst lush hills bursting with orchids and rhododendron blossoms. The region is also alive with legends of the Abominable Snowman or Yeti, a huge, ape-like creature, who allegedly lives above the snowline. West Bengal's most popular trails are centred around the Singalila Ridge near Darjeeling, with views of Nepal's great massifs, while most of Sikkim's trails are dominated by the mighty Kanchendzonga. The best seasons are between October and November, and February and May.

LOCATOR MAP

☐ Area shown below

The Singalila Ridge

The Singalila Ridge, which begins near Darjeeling and extends to Kanchendzonga, has several trails. The Sandakphu-Phalut route beginning at Maneybhanjan has spectacular views of Everest, Lhotse, Makalu and Kanchendzonga, with plenty of lodges along the way. The 60-km (37-mile) path ends at the roadhead at Rimbik.

Duration: *6 days*
Altitude: *3,636 m (11,929 ft)*
Level of difficulty: *moderate*

MOUNT KANCHENDZONGA

Mount Kanchendzonga, the third highest peak in the world at 8,598 m (28,209 ft), dominates the skyline of Sikkim and West Bengal's Darjeeling district. Its name means "Five Treasures of the Snows", and the Sikkimese believe that the five summits of the Kanchendzonga Range conceal five treasures – salt, minerals and gems, grain, invincible armour and holy scriptures. This magnificent mountain is revered as the guardian deity of Sikkim and is worshipped all over the state during the Pang Lhabsol festival, which takes place in the seventh month of the Tibetan calendar (between August and September). Prayers, rituals and masked dances are performed at monasteries – with the massif represented by a red mask crowned with skulls – to ensure that the land is protected in the year to come. Such is the awe in which the Sikkimese hold the peak that in 1999, an Austrian expedition to scale it was cancelled after widespread public protest that this would dishonour the deity and bring catastrophe to Sikkim.

A panoramic view of Mount Kanchendzonga from Dzongri Peak

0 km   5

0 miles   5

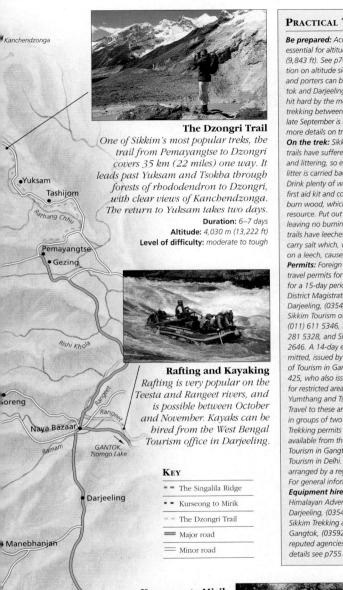

Kanchendzonga

Yuksam
Tashijom
Rathang Chhu
Pemayangtse
Gezing
Rishi Khola
oreng
Naya Bazaar
Rangeet
Rangeet
Ramam
GANTOK,
Tsomgo Lake
Darjeeling
Manebhanjan

The Dzongri Trail
One of Sikkim's most popular treks, the trail from Pemayangtse to Dzongri covers 35 km (22 miles) one way. It leads past Yuksam and Tsokha through forests of rhododendron to Dzongri, with clear views of Kanchendzonga. The return to Yuksam takes two days.
Duration: *6–7 days*
Altitude: *4,030 m (13,222 ft)*
Level of difficulty: *moderate to tough*

Rafting and Kayaking
Rafting is very popular on the Teesta and Rangeet rivers, and is possible between October and November. Kayaks can be hired from the West Bengal Tourism office in Darjeeling.

KEY
- - The Singalila Ridge
- - Kurseong to Mirik
- - The Dzongri Trail
== Major road
= Minor road

PRACTICAL TIPS
Be prepared: *Acclimatization is essential for altitudes over 3,000 m (9,843 ft). See p767 for information on altitude sickness. Guides and porters can be hired in Gangtok and Darjeeling. The region is hit hard by the monsoon and trekking between early June and late September is not advisable. For more details on trekking see p751.*
On the trek: *Sikkim's trekking trails have suffered deforestation and littering, so ensure that all litter is carried back with you. Drink plenty of water and carry a first aid kit and cooking fuel. Never burn wood, which is a scarce resource. Put out all fires properly, leaving no burning embers. Some trails have leeches (see p767), so carry salt which, when sprinkled on a leech, causes it to fall off.*
Permits: *Foreign visitors require travel permits for Sikkim, issued for a 15-day period from the District Magistrate's Office in Darjeeling, (0354) 54 233, or the Sikkim Tourism offices in Delhi, (011) 611 5346, Kolkata, (033) 281 5328, and Siliguri, (0353) 43 2646. A 14-day extension is permitted, issued by the Department of Tourism in Gangtok, (03592) 23 425, who also issue special permits for restricted areas such as Dzongri, Yumthang and Tsomgo Lake. Travel to these areas is permitted in groups of two or more persons. Trekking permits for Sikkim are available from the Department of Tourism in Gangtok, and Sikkim Tourism in Delhi. All treks must be arranged by a registered agency. For general information see p758.*
Equipment hire & operators: *Himalayan Adventures in Darjeeling, (0354) 54 004, and Sikkim Trekking and Tours in Gangtok, (03592) 23 638, are reputed agencies. For more details see p755.*

Kurseong
Mirik

Kurseong to Mirik
A great introduction to the West Bengal hills, this gentle 18-km (11-mile) hike goes past numerous villages and local tea estates.
Duration: *1 day*
Altitude: *1,767 m (5,797 ft)*
Level of difficulty: *easy*

ORISSA

BOUNDED ON THE WEST by the thickly forested hills of the Eastern Ghats, and on the east by nearly 500 km (311 miles) of coastline on the Bay of Bengal, Orissa covers an area of 156,000 sq km (60,232 sq miles). Its most famous sights are clustered together in a compact triangle on the eastern coast, in the fertile delta of its major river, the Mahanadi. These include the magnificent 13th-century Sun Temple at Konark, a UNESCO World Heritage Site, and other outstanding temples at Bhubaneswar and Puri. To recover from sightseeing fatigue, there are beaches within easy reach at Puri, Konark and Gopalpur-on-Sea, fringed by coconut groves and fishing villages. Just south of this triangle is Chilika Lake, Asia's largest lagoon and a paradise for birdwatchers. The hinterland of the coast is lush with green paddy fields, dotted with ancient Buddhist ruins and tranquil hamlets, where Orissa's beautiful traditional crafts flourish. The spectacular, unspoilt landscape of northern Orissa includes Simlipal National Park, with its wealth of wildlife, and settlements of tribal people who form nearly a quarter of Orissa's population of 35 million.

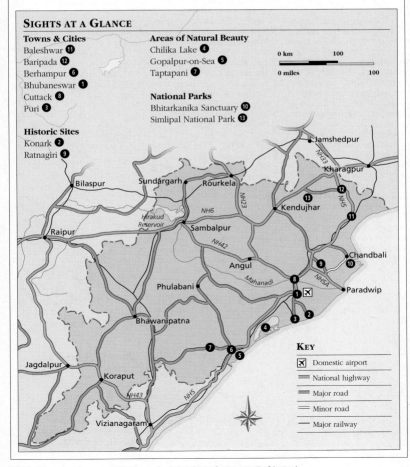

SIGHTS AT A GLANCE

Towns & Cities
Baleshwar ⑪
Baripada ⑫
Berhampur ⑥
Bhubaneswar ①
Cuttack ⑧
Puri ③

Historic Sites
Konark ②
Ratnagiri ⑨

Areas of Natural Beauty
Chilika Lake ④
Gopalpur-on-Sea ⑤
Taptapani ⑦

National Parks
Bhitarkanika Sanctuary ⑩
Simlipal National Park ⑬

0 km   100
0 miles   100

Jamshedpur
Kharagpur
Bilaspur
Sundargarh
Rourkela
NH33
Kendujhar ⑬
⑫
NH5
⑪
NH6
NH23
Hirakud Reservoir
Sambalpur
Raipur
NH42
Angul
Mahanadi
Chandbali
⑨
⑩
Phulabani
⑧
① ✖
③
②
Paradwip
NHSA
Bhawanipatna
④
⑦ ⑥
⑤
Jagdalpur
Koraput
NH43
NH5
Vizianagaram

KEY
✖ Domestic airport
National highway
Major road
Minor road
Major railway

◁ **Pilgrims swarming around the huge chariot at the Rath Yatra Festival in Puri**

Bhubaneswar ❶

Painted dowry box from Orissa

T HE CAPITAL OF ORISSA, Bhubaneswar is famous for its superb Hindu temples. Most of these are in the older, southern part of the city, while the new town, with its modern administrative buildings and wide tree-lined avenues, is in the north. The temples date from the 7th to the 13th centuries, a period which saw the waning of Buddhism and a revival of Hinduism under the successive dynasties that ruled Orissa: the Shailodbhavas and Bhauma Karas in the 7th–8th centuries; the Somavamshis in the 9th–11th centuries; and the Eastern Gangas in the 12th–13th centuries.

Exploring the temples

More than 400 temples remain of the 7,000 that are said to have once embellished Bhubaneswar, earning it the title, the "City of Temples". A distinctive version of the North Indian style of temple architecture evolved in Orissa over the centuries (see p21), under the patronage of the different dynasties. As the power and prosperity of these dynasties grew, the temples became bigger and more elaborate. Most of the temples have two main components – a convex curvilinear spire locally known as the *deul* (elsewhere called the *shikhara*), which towers over the inner sanctum where the deity's image is kept; and an entrance porch or assembly hall called the *jagamohan,* with a stepped pyramidal roof. Some of the bigger temples have two or three of these porches. Several smaller shrines and bathing tanks often surround the main temple, which is enclosed in a walled compound.

The magnificent 11th-century **Lingaraj Temple** represents the high point of the Orissan style, where both sculpture and architecture have evolved in perfect harmony. Its grandeur lies in its towering 55-m (180-ft) high *deul* (spire) with dramatic vertical ribs, and in the consummate artistry with which each sculpture and embellishment is executed. The female figures, animals, and friezes of ceremonial processions are full of grace and exuberance. The temple's large courtyard has more than 100 smaller shrines. The main deity here is Shiva as Tribhuvaneswar ("Lord of the Three Worlds"), from which the city takes its name. The intriguing image of a rampant lion springing on a crouching elephant is a powerful motif in this temple, as in many others in Orissa, and some scholars believe it is a royal emblem. Non-Hindus cannot enter the Lingaraj Temple, but can view it from a platform near its northern gateway. The other temples are open to visitors.

Devotees bathing in the sacred waters of Bindusagar

North of the temple is the large **Bindusagar Tank** with a pavilion in the middle. It is believed to contain water from every sacred river in India. The main deity of the Lingaraj Temple is brought here for a ritual bath (see p309) every year.

Udaigiri & Khandagiri Caves, Airport

BHUBANE

BARADANDA SAHI ROAD

VIVEKANANDA MARG

③

②

①

The impressive spire of the 11th-century Lingaraj Temple

BHUBANESWAR CITY CENTRE

Bindusagar Tank ②
Lingaraj Temple ①
Mukteshwar Temple ⑤
Orissa State Museum ⑦
Parasurameshwar Temple ④
Rajarani Temple ⑥
Vaital Deul Temple ③

The 8th-century **Vaital Deul Temple**, to the west of Bindusagar, is an unusual temple with eerie interior carvings. These indicate that it was probably used for macabre tantric rites, including human sacrifice. The main deity here is a terrifying, eight-armed Chamunda (a form of Durga), with a garland of skulls, seated on a corpse, flanked by a jackal and an owl.

Built in the 7th-century, the **Parasurameshwar Temple**, on the road to Puri, is the best preserved and most lavishly sculpted of the earliest group of temples. The square-towered shrine has a rectangular *jagamohan* adjoining it, decorated with wonderfully animated bands of dancers and musicians on its west window. The main entrance to the *jagamohan* also has a fine carving of domestic elephants capturing wild ones, to the left of the lintel. Set into the outer walls of the shrine are images of deities, among them a superb potbellied Ganesha, and his brother Karttikeya sitting on his vehicle, the peacock.

The nearby 10th-century **Mukteshwar Temple**, one of the jewels of Orissan temple architecture, is notable for its exquisite sculptures and elegant proportions. Its beautiful *torana* (gateway) is decorated with languorously reclining female figures. The *jagamohan* is illuminated by diamond-shaped latticed windows on the north and south walls, their outermost frames depicting enchanting scenes of frolicking monkeys. A unique feature of the *jagamohan* is the decorated ceiling, carved into a lotus with eight petals. The sculptures of female figures in this temple are remarkable for their expressive faces, with hairstyles and jewellery shown in exquisite detail. The octagonal wall surrounding

Guardian figures, Rajarani Temple

the temple has a number of niches, each containing a wheel, a lotus medallion or a delicate scroll.

Set amidst paddy fields, just off the main road, is the 11th-century **Rajarani Temple**. It has a particularly striking spire decorated with miniature replicas of itself, rising in continuous tiers around the tower. This temple is renowned for its fine sculptures of *dikpals* (the guardians of the eight cardinal directions) perched on lotus flowers. Of these, Agni, the God of Fire on a ram, and Varuna, God of the Oceans seated on a crocodile, are particularly impressive. Also remarkable are the tall and slender female figures, carved in high relief on the walls of the temple.

The highlight of this interesting museum is its rich collection of Buddhist and Jain sculptures, coins, and painted palm-leaf manuscripts. There are also collections of tribal art, traditional jewellery and musical instruments.

ENVIRONS: The **Nandan Kanan Zoo** and botanical gardens, 16 km (10 miles) north of Bhubaneswar, is famous for its white tigers (*see p239*). The zoo, surrounded by a thick forest, enables the animals to live in natural surroundings. Panthers and gharials (*Gavialis gangeticus*) have been successfully bred in captivity here.

🐾 **Nandan Kanan Zoo**
⬭ *Tue–Sun.* 📷 🖥 ⬛

Chausath Yogini Temple,
PIPLI, DHAULI,
PURI, KONARK

KEY

🚌 Bus station

🏯 Temple

ℹ Tourist information

0 metres   500

0 yards   500

The beautifully sculpted *torana* of Mukteshwar Temple

Exploring Bhubaneswar's Surroundings

Terracotta roof tile

MANY SITES OF HISTORICAL and architectural significance lie close to Bhubaneswar. They include Jain monastic caves, Hindu temples, Buddhist stupas and ancient rock inscriptions, dotting the lush green landscape around the city. Dating from the 3rd century BC (when the area was part of the great kingdom of Kalinga) to the 13th century AD, these sites bear witness to the region's political and religious importance for a continuous period of over 1,000 years.

Bagh Gumpha at Udaigiri, shaped like the open mouth of a tiger

🔼 Udaigiri and Khandagiri Caves

6 km (4 miles) NW of Bhubaneswar. ⬜ daily. 🖼 🎫 Sadhu Convention (Jan).

The twin hills of Udaigiri ("Sunrise Hill") and Khandagiri ("Broken Hill") were honeycombed to make retreats for Jain monks in the 1st century BC. Located just off the highway that runs from Bhubaneswar to Kolkata, the hills rise suddenly from the flat surrounding plains, and are separated from each other by the highway.

Carvings at Udaigiri Caves

As one approaches from Bhubaneswar, **Udaigiri** is the hill on the right, and is best explored first as it has the more interesting caves. The most impressive of its 18 caves is the double-storeyed **Rani Gumpha** or "Queen's Cave" (Cave 1), which has lavishly sculpted friezes of women dancing and playing music, kings and queens in courtly splendour, elephants, monkeys and foliage. The sculpture is remarkable for its expressive animation, and has

been compared with the famous sculpted gateways at Sanchi (see pp244–5).

Other notable caves are **Chhota Hathi Gumpha** or "Small Elephant Cave" (Cave 3), with six superb elephants flanking its entrance; **Ganesh Gumpha** (Cave 10) whose sculptures include an intriguing battle scene with a woman riding an elephant while soldiers in kilts chase her, and **Bagh Gumpha** or "Tiger Cave" (Cave 12), its front ingeniously shaped like a

tiger's head with the mouth open. The most significant cave historically is **Hathi Gumpha** or "Elephant Cave" (Cave 14). On the rock above its entrance is an inscription from the 1st century BC. It records that the caves were built by Kharavela, third king of the powerful Chedi dynasty, whose conquests included large parts of Bihar, the Deccan and South India. The inscription also states that King Kharavela rebuilt his capital, Kalinganagar, after it was destroyed by a cyclone. Even today, Orissa remains vulnerable to cyclones, the last one having devastated the state in October 1999. On the summit of Udaigiri stands a ruined apsidal structure, probably used as a place of worship by the monks.

Across the highway, on **Khandagiri**, are 15 caves with carvings of sacred Jain symbols. The **Ananta Cave** (Cave 3), with its figures of twin serpents on the arches above the doorways, is the most important and has superb ornamentation and lively friezes, including one of boys chasing lions, bulls and other animals. Another enchanting carving in this cave shows the goddess Lakshmi in a lotus pool, being bathed with water from pitchers held by two elephants (see p24). Three of the caves – numbers 5, 8 and 9 – have impressive carved figures of the Jain tirthankaras in high relief.

Unlike Buddhist caves such as those at Ajanta (see p479) and Ellora (see p478), most of the Udaigiri and Khandagiri caves are so low that it is impossible to stand upright in

Khandagiri, the site of a Jain monastery with rock-cut chambers

Hirapur's Chausath Yogini Temple, open to the sky

them. This was in keeping with the self-mortification and asceticism that Jain monks were expected to practise. The site still attracts sadhus, who gather here every year in January to meditate in the caves. A lively fair springs up below the hills to entertain the crowds that gather to seek the sadhus' blessings.

🏛 Dhauli
8 km (5 miles) S of Bhubaneswar.
A stark white Buddhist stupa in the middle of serene green paddy fields on the banks of the Daya river marks the site of the bloody battle of Kalinga, fought by one of India's greatest rulers, the Mauryan emperor Ashoka *(see p42)* in 260 BC. He won the war but the carnage and misery it inflicted on the people filled the emperor with remorse and brought about a dramatic change of heart. After this battle, he gave up *digvijaya* (military conquest) for *dharmavijaya* (spiritual conquest), embraced Buddhism, and publicized his new maxims in rock edicts, installed in different parts of his empire. One of these is here, at the base of Dhauli Hill, in which the emperor declares, "All men are my children", and enjoins his officials to ensure impartiality, non-violence, justice and compassion in administration. The top of the rock is sculpted into an imposing elephant's head, symbolizing the Buddhist dharma. This is one of the earliest sculptures found in the subcontinent. The huge white **Shanti Stupa** ("Peace Pagoda") at the top of the hill was built by Japanese Buddhists in the early 1970s.

🏛 Chausath Yogini Temple
15 km (9 miles) SE of Bhubaneswar.
This 9th-century, circular temple is dedicated to the *chausath yoginis* or 64 manifestations of the goddess Shakti, who symbolizes female creative energy. All the images, each about 0.6 m (2 ft) tall and carved out of black chlorite stone, are placed in niches in the inner enclosure. The presiding deity, a graceful 10-armed *yogini*, is in the 31st niche. The temple is located in the pretty village of Hirapur.

Garden umbrella from Pipli, with appliqué-work

ENVIRONS: Pipli, 15 km (9 miles) south of Bhubaneswar, on the highway to Puri, is a village of artisans famous for their colourful appliqué-work fabrics. The craft originated to serve temples, providing intricately stitched awnings and covers for deities, and hangings in vivid hues for festival days. Today, garden umbrellas, cushion covers, wall hangings and bags are made in Pipli using the same techniques, in which cloth is cut into bird, flower, animal and other decorative shapes, and stitched on to fabric of a contrasting colour. Shops selling these line both sides of the highway as it passes through Pipli, enveloping it in a blaze of colour.

FESTIVALS OF ORISSA

Tribal Mela *(Jan)*, Bhubaneswar. Orissa's large and varied tribal population exhibit their dances, music, arts and crafts at this colourful week-long festival

Makar Mela *(14 Jan)*, Chilika Lake. Pilgrims bring offerings to a cave and temple devoted to the goddess Kali on a rocky island called Kalijai in Chilika Lake.

Magha Saptami *(Jan/Feb)*, Konark. To honour Surya, the Sun God, pilgrims come for a purifying dip in the sea before they worship at the temple. A colourful fair is held, with stalls selling food and gifts.

Ashokashtami *(Mar/Apr)*, Bhubaneswar. The image of Shiva, the main deity of the Lingaraj Temple, is taken in procession in a chariot for a ritual bath in the sacred Bindusagar Tank.

Chaitra Parba *(Apr)*, Baripada. This spring festival is marked by displays of the spectacular martial dance known as Mayurbhanj Chhau.

Rath Yatra *(Jun/Jul)*, Puri *(see p313)*.

Konark Dance Festival *(1–5 Dec)*, Konark. Classical dancers perform on an open air stage near the Sun Temple during this five-day festival.

A dancer performing during Rath Yatra celebrations

Konark: The Sun Temple ❷

Colossal elephants in the temple complex

ONE OF INDIA'S GREAT architectural marvels, this temple to the Sun God, Surya, was conceived as a gigantic chariot, with 12 pairs of wheels to carry the Sun God on his daily journey across the sky. Built in the 13th century by King Narasimhadeva of the Eastern Ganga dynasty *(see p44)*, the temple is also remarkable for its superb sculptures. Gods and demons, kings and peasants, elephants and horses jostle for space on its walls with dozens of erotic couples. Konark is now a UNESCO World Heritage Site.

Maiden with Bird
Statues of graceful maidens in a variety of poses are carved on the temple's façades.

Court Scene
This enchanting relief of the king being presented with a giraffe indicates the existence of maritime trade between Orissa's Eastern Ganga kings and Africa.

Amalaka

★ Surya
The majestic image of the Sun God stands on a chariot, flanked by his wives, and other deities.

★ Wheels of the Chariot
The 12 pairs of exquisitely carved wheels represent the months in a year, while the eight large spokes mark the division of the day into three-hour sections. The seven horses pulling the chariot represent the days of the week.

VISITORS' CHECKLIST

Puri district. 65 km 40 miles) SE
of Bhubaneswar. 🚌 **ℹ** *Orissa
Tourism, Yatri Niwas, (06758) 358.*
⬜ *daily.* 🏛 🎫 📷 *Magha
Saptami (Jan/Feb), Konark Dance
Festival (Dec).* **Archaeological
Museum** ⬜ *Fri–Wed.* 🏛 📷

The Konark Sun Temple, on the shores of the Bay of Bengal

The three-tiered roof is
shaped like a stepped pyramid
and crowned with a round fluted stone called an *amalaka*.
The terraces between each tier
are covered with sculptures.

The Cymbal Player
*This sculpture is in a row
of wonderfully animated
dancers, musicians and
drummers on the terrace
of the pyramidal roof.*

Medallion
*Deities and dancers
decorate the medallions
on the hub and the
spokes of the wheels.*

Erotic Sculpture
*A demure snake
goddess provides
a contrast to the
amorous couple
beside her. The
erotic sculptures
at Konark are
a celebration of
the joys of life.*

→ *Bhogmandir*

Main entrance

STAR FEATURES

★ **Surya**

★ **Wheels of the
Chariot**

Bhogmandir
*The ruined "Hall of
Offerings" has gigantic
rampant lions on
cowering elephants.*

Exploring Konark

The Sun Temple at Konark originally had a towering *deul* (spire), 70 m (230 ft) high, over its main sanctuary. Visible far out at sea, the temple was an important navigational aid for European sailors headed for Calcutta (Kolkata), who called it the Black Pagoda. Over time, the temple's easily weathered khondalite stone was progressively corroded by seawinds and sand, and by the 19th century the great tower had completely collapsed. Only its base still remains. The temple's Bhogmandir or "Hall of Offerings", is now roofless, but its plinth and pillars remain, carved with figures of dancers, depicting the poses still used in classical Odissi dance *(see p28).*

The chariot-shaped *jagamohan* or assembly hall was buried for nearly two centuries under drifting sand. It was only unearthed and restored by the Archaeological Survey of India (ASI) in the early 20th century. Its many remarkable sculptures include no less than 1,700 elephants in animated motion, carved on the plinth; and several enchanting *alasa kanyas* (maidens at leisure), playing with a pet bird, holding a mirror, or leaning against a doorway.

Three life-size images of the Sun God, Surya, made of contrasting coloured chlorite stone, are positioned so that the sun's rays fall on their faces, turn by turn, at dawn, noon and sunset.

In the northeast corner of the compound is the **Shrine of the Nine Planets**, a large stone slab carved with the deities of the nine planets. Colossal sculptures of war horses and elephants stand at the north and south. Near the compound is the **Archaeological Museum** with fine sculptures recovered from the site. The beach is 3 km (2 miles) from the temple, but is unsafe for swimming because of treacherous undercurrents.

Puri's Jagannath Temple, topped with Vishnu's wheel and flag

Puri ❸

Puri district. 60 km (37 miles) S of Bhubaneswar. 🚩 157,650. 🚉 🚌 ℹ️ *Orissa Tourism, Station Rd, (06752) 22 664.* 🕐 *daily.* 🎏 *Rath Yatra (Jun/Jul).* **Jagannath Temple** 🕐 *daily.* ⬤ *to non-Hindus.*

Hand-painted *ganjifa* playing card from Puri

ONE OF India's most important pilgrimage centres, this seaside town is dominated by the towering Jagannath Temple. Early European sailors, for whom its 65-m (213-ft) high spire was an important landmark, called it the White Pagoda, to differentiate it from Konark's Sun Temple which they named Black Pagoda.

The **Jagannath Temple** was built in the 12th century by King Anantavarman of the Eastern Ganga dynasty *(see p44).* Surrounded by a 6-m (20-ft) high wall, its main gate is guarded by a pair of brightly painted stone lions. Non-Hindus are not allowed in, but can get a good view of the complex, with its multitude of small shrines and its courtyard thronged with pilgrims, from the roof of the Raghunandan Library across the street from the main gate.

The temple is similar in design to the Lingaraj Temple in Bhubaneswar *(see p306),* with three smaller shrines adjoining its tall sanctuary tower. The elegant stone column near the entrance, topped with the figure of Arun, charioteer of the Sun God, was brought here from the Sun Temple at Konark in the 18th century.

From the temple, Puri's main street, **Bada Danda**, runs through the town, crammed with pilgrims' rest houses and shops selling food, religious souvenirs and handicrafts. Local specialities are the colourful *pattachitra* paintings and round *ganjifa* playing cards painted with religious themes.

Puri's beach is its other attraction, though not always safe for swimming because of dangerous undercurrents. The long beach front is crowded with stalls and groups of pilgrims along Marine Parade. Sunbathers and swimmers should therefore head to the eastern end, which is cleaner and more secluded, or to the beaches attached to the better hotels. Local fishermen wearing conical hats serve as lifeguards on the beach, and take visitors out to sea in their boats to watch the sunsets.

A family picnic on Puri Beach

The Jagannath Cult

A UNIQUE CULT HAS grown around Jagannath (Lord of the Universe), an incarnation of Vishnu. At Puri's Jagannath Temple, 6,000 resident priests perform the elaborate daily rituals of bathing, dressing and worshipping the image of Jagannath, together with those of his brother Balbhadra and sister Subhadra. Sumptuous meals are offered to the three

Lord Jagannath

deities five times a day, prepared daily by 400 temple cooks. During the spectacular Rath Yatra (chariot festival) in June/July, the deities are taken out in a procession in mammoth wooden chariots, pulled by thousands of devotees. The word juggernaut (large truck) is derived from the size and unstoppable force of Lord Jagannath's chariot.

Temple offerings *are sold at numerous stalls at the gates of the temple.*

Devotees *try to spend at least three days paying obeisance to Jagannath.*

Balbhadra has a white face and rides in a chariot with 14 wheels and four horses.

Subhadra has a yellow face and rides in a red chariot.

Puri cityscape

Jagannath's chariot is 1,370 m (4,495 ft) tall and has 16 wheels.

Jagannath Temple

Policeman

Musicians and drummers

Temple priests

PATTACHITRA PAINTING OF THE RATH YATRA

The Rath Yatra marks Lord Jagannath's annual journey to his birthplace, the Gundicha Temple, just over 2 km (1.3 miles) away. Over 200,000 people, including priests pilgrims, musicians and drummers, join the procession.

Temple dancers*, young boys known as* gotipuas, *perform the classical Odissi dance (see p28) before the deities every night. They are accompanied by musicians singing verses from the* Gita Govinda*, a 12th-century epic poem (see p292).*

Balbhadra, Subhadra and Jagannath*, the three deities, are believed to be of tribal origin, but have been absorbed into the Hindu pantheon. They have huge, all-seeing eyes, and outstretched arms to protect and bless all mankind.*

A view of Chilika Lake, a haven for water birds and dolphins

Chilika Lake ❹

Puri, Ganjam & Khordha districts. 50 km (31 miles) SW of Puri. ▤ *Balugaon, then taxi or bus.* ▦ *Balugaon & Satpada.* ▯ *Orissa Tourism, Barkul, (06756) 20 855.* ▨ *Makar Mela (Jan).* **Satpada and Nalabana Islands** ▦ *hired from Barkul, Balugaon, Satpada & Rambha.*

A GREAT, SHALLOW lagoon covering 1,100 sq km (425 sq miles), Chilika is separated from the Bay of Bengal by a sandy ridge, with just a narrow channel connecting it to the sea. Believed to be the largest brackish lake in Asia, Chilika is recognized as one of the most important wetlands in the world because of the phenomenal variety of aquatic and birdlife it supports. From November to February, the lake and its reed islands teem with nesting birds, including several winter migrants, such as the golden plover, the flamingo, the purple moorhen and the osprey. A major attraction at Chilika are dolphins, which are often spotted off **Satpada Island**, located at the confluence of the lake and the sea. **Nalabana Island**, at the core of the lake, is the best place for birdwatching. Orissa Tourism arranges boat trips to both the islands. **Kalijai Temple**, built on a small rocky island which attracts festive crowds during the Makar Mela in January. The lake also supports the local people who earn their living from Chilika's prawns, crabs and fish.

Gopalpur-on-Sea ❺

Ganjam district. 172 km (107 miles) SW of Bhubaneswar. ▤ *Berhampur 18 km (11 miles) E of town centre, then taxi or bus.* ▦ ▯ *Orissa Tourism, Berhampur Railway Station, (0680) 20 3870.*

T HIS QUIET seaside town was, in ancient times, a great seaport for Orissa's maritime trade with Indonesia *(see p318).* The British later developed it as a beach resort and it now has a sleepy charm, except during the Durga Puja holidays *(see p281)* in October, when it swarms with tourists from Bengal. Swimming in the sea is not safe because of treacherous undercurrents. But the beach, lined with bungalows and dotted with casuarina groves, is a good place to spend the day, watching the fishing boats and the sunset.

Berhampur ❻

Ganjam district. 170 km (106 miles) SW of Bhubaneswar. ▤ ▦ ▯ *Orissa Tourism, Railway Station, (0680) 20 3870.*

T HE MAIN commercial centre in southern Orissa, Berhampur is famous for its beautiful handwoven ikat silk, available in its bustling bazaar where weavers sit at their looms. The railhead for the seaside town of Gopalpur-on-Sea, Berhampur is also a convenient base for visiting **Jaugarh**, 35 km (22 miles) north of the city. Jaugarh has a 3rd-century BC rock edict erected by the Emperor Ashoka following the Battle of Kalinga, after which he had a change of heart. The edict is similar to the one at Dhauli

Painted panel from the 17th-century temple at Buguda

Floral offering to a goddess of fertility at Taptapani's hot springs

(see p309), in which Ashoka declares "All men are my children" and spells out his ethical code. A short distance away, at **Buguda**, is the Biramchinarayan Temple, built in the 17th century, with beautiful murals depicting scenes from the *Ramayana*.

Taptapani ❼

Ganjam district. 51 km (32 miles) W of Berhampur. ▦ ▯ *Orissa Tourism, (06814) 47 531.*

P ICTURESQUELY located on a forested hill in the Eastern Ghats, this spa is renowned for its hot springs. The boiling, sulphurous water bubbles out of a crevice in the hillside and is piped to a pool in a clearing. Near the pool is a small shrine to a tribal goddess of fertility as, apart from being beneficial for various chronic ailments, the hot springs are also believed to cure infertility. A tree with seed pods overhangs the pool, and women seeking the infertility cure are supposed to pick up seeds from the tree that have fallen to the muddy bottom of the pool – a difficult feat, especially since the water is too hot for more than a quick dip. The Saora tribal women *(see p321),* whose villages are nearby, can often be seen taking the cure. The most comfortable way to enjoy the hot springs is by renting a room in the Orissa Tourism rest house just below the pool, which has hot water from the springs piped directly into its bathtubs.

The Orissa Weaver's Art

ORISSA HAS A LONG and rich tradition of handwoven textiles. Over 300,000 people work in the state's textile industry producing a range of materials, from the simple cotton weaves of tribal areas, to the elaborate painted textiles for use in temples. Orissa's forests yield a wealth of wild silk cocoons which, in recent years, have been supplemented by mulberry plantations. The state is famous for its silk ikat weaves, an intricate technique in which warp and weft threads are tie-dyed in such a way as to produce patterns when woven. Typical motifs include birds, animals, fish, seashells, holy *rudraksh* beads and temple spires.

Eagle motif in ikat fabric

Vriksba Pattachitra shows a contemporary minimalist version of the traditional painted textile, used as a temple hanging. The tree is painted on natural-colored wild silk (tussar).

The **bomkai** *cotton sari from Ganjam district was traditionally woven for the local aristocracy. Its distinguishing features are the temple spire pattern on the border, and the rich end piece with its elaborate ikat motifs.*

The **kotpad** *sari from the Koraput tribal region has a simple elegance, with unbleached cotton offset by a rich red madder-dyed border.*

The **ekphulia** *(one flower) sari achieves a striking effect by repeating the one-flower and fish motifs.*

The **conch-shell motif** *in this silk ikat panel with its delicate, curvilinear pattern, is an example of the fine sense of design and colour that Orissa's weavers have.*

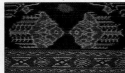

The **fish motif** *in this* tussar *silk textile symboilizes prosperity and luck. Below the fish are a row of* damroos *(hand-held drums).*

The **jotai** *ikat sari is inspired by the finger-painted patterns, called* jotai, *that adorn the walls of many village homes in Orissa. The rich red colour of the sari, and the rows of stylized trees and temple spires on the borders, add to the sumptuous effect.*

Cuttack ⓧ

Cuttack district. 35 km (22 miles) N of
Bhubaneswar. 535,150. Orissa Tourism, Arunodaya Market
Building, Link Rd, (0671) 61 2225.
Bali Yatra (Oct/Nov).

SITUATED ON the Mahanadi
Delta, Cuttack is Orissa's
most populous city, and was
its capital from the 10th
century onwards until 1956,
when the capital was moved
to Bhubaneswar (see p306).
There is little evidence today
of the city's historic past. The
gateway and moat of the
13th-century **Barabati Fort**,
in northwest Cuttack, are all
that remain of this great
citadel which once had a
nine-storeyed palace. The
eastern part of town is more
interesting, with silversmiths'
shops in **Balu Bazaar** and
Nayasarak, where Cuttack's
famous silver filigree jewellery is made. Nearby, in the
shops on **Jail Road**, the full
range of Orissa's beautiful
handicrafts are available,
including ikat silk, carved
hornware and paintings.

In this area, a cluster of
green domes marks the 18th-
century **Kadam Rasul
Mosque**, where the Prophet
Mohammed's footprints are
carved on a round stone.

The 18th-century Kadam Rasul Mosque in Cuttack

THE INDONESIAN CONNECTION

From the 4th century BC to the 14th century AD, the
power and wealth of successive kingdoms in Orissa
derived from their rich maritime trade, especially with Bali,
Java and Sumatra. Indeed, ever since the 10th century, the
word *kling*, derived from Kalinga which was the ancient
name of Orissa, has been used in Indonesia to refer to
India and Indians. With the trading links came cultural
influences, which are still visible in Orissa's crafts. The
state's weavers originally learned the intricate art of ikat
weaving (see p317) from Indonesia, and later were especially commissioned to weave all the silks for ceremonial
use in the royal courts and temples of Indonesia. Another
Orissa craft that originally came from Indonesia was the
silver filigree work that is still being done in Cuttack.
Today, Orissa's old maritime links with Bali, Java and

The colourful entrance gate to the
Bali Yatra fair at Cuttack

Sumatra are commem-
orated in a festival called
Bali Yatra (Bali Journey)
held in Cuttack during the
full moon of Kartik
(October/November).
A colourful fair is held on
the banks of the Mahanadi
river, and tiny boats made
of banana bark are lit
with clay lamps and
floated in the river.

Ratnagiri ⓧ

Cuttack district. 70 kms (44 miles) NE
of Cuttack. Orissa Tourism,
Link Rd, Cuttack, (0671) 61 2225.

THE THREE BUDDHIST sites of
Ratnagiri, Udaigiri and
Lalitgiri, situated close to each
other, are most conveniently
visited on a day trip from
Cuttack or Bhubaneswar,
driving through a beautiful
landscape of low hills and
lush paddy fields. The most
impressive of the three sites is
Ratnagiri ("Hill of Jewels")
which, between the 7th and
the 11th centuries, was a
major Buddhist university
and monastic establishment,
described by the 7th-century
Chinese traveller Hiuen Tsang
(see p219). Located on top of
a mound, crowned by a large
stupa, the best-preserved
structure here is a monastery
with a central courtyard and
an impressive colonnade
around the monks' cells. A
beautiful 4-m (13-foot) high
image of the seated Buddha
can be seen inside, together
with other Buddhist divinities,
and the entrance doorway
is superbly carved. A small
Archaeological Museum
displays other sculptures
found at the site.

Udaigiri ("Sunrise Hill"),
10 km (6 miles) south of
Ratnagiri, is still being
excavated and seems to have
better preserved sculptures.
The western spur of the hill
has a row of rock-cut

The serene 7th-century meditating
Buddha image at Ratnagiri

Flocks of waders amidst the mangroves at Bhitarkanika Sanctuary

sculptures, while the northern spur is covered with the ruins of brick stupas. A colossal sculpture of the Buddha here has an inscription dating it to the 8th century.

Lalitgiri ("Hill of Grace"), about 10 km (6 miles) south of Udaigiri (and directly connected by bus to Cuttack), is believed to be the oldest of the sites. The ruins, spread over two adjacent hills, include a terraced stone platform, a gallery of life-size Bodhisattva figures and an apsidal temple. Some of the better-preserved sculptures and a carved doorway have been incorporated into a modern Hindu temple. At the foot of a hill is a village of stone-carvers, who keep alive Orissa's fine tradition of stone sculpture.

🏛 **Ratnagiri Archaeological Museum**
◯ Sat–Thu. 🗺

Bhitarkanika Sanctuary ⑩

Kendrapara district. 106 km (66 miles) NE of Cuttack. **Entry points:** Chandbali, Rajnagar. 🚂 Bhadrakh, 50 km (31 miles) NW of Chandbali, then bus. 🚌 to Rajnagar. 🚌 from Rajnagar or Chandbali to Dangmal, Ekakula & Habalikhati. 🛈 For permits and bookings contact Bhubaneswar, (0674) 51 5840 or Rajnagar, (06729) 8460. ◯ mid-Oct–mid-Apr. 🗺

FAMOUS AS the nesting ground of the Olive Ridley turtle, this 170-sq km (66-sq mile) sanctuary is situated on

the delta of the Brahmani and Baitarani rivers on the Bay of Bengal. It also has the largest mangrove forests in the country after the Sunderbans in West Bengal (see pp288–9), with 63 of the 72 known mangrove species found here.

Encompassing 12 offshore islands, long sandy beaches and numerous rivulets and creeks, Bhitarkanika is home to an impressive range of fish, more than 170 species of birds such as storks, egrets, ibis and migratory ducks, and the largest number of estuarine crocodiles in the country.

Accommodation is available at a forest rest house at Chandbali, the entry point to the sanctuary, as well as deep within the sanctuary at Dangmal, Habalikhati and Ekakula (all three are accessible by boat). Orissa Tourism in Bhubaneswar and Cuttack organize tours and the necessary Forest Department permits for Bhitarkanika.

THE OLIVE RIDLEY TURTLE

Every year, in an awe-inspiring phenomenon, hundreds of thousands of Olive Ridley turtles arrive from as far away as South America, to nest at Gahirmatha, a 10-km (6-mile) stretch of beach near the mouth of the Brahmani river in Bhitarkanika Sanctuary. The world's largest arribada (Spanish for "the great arrival") occurs in February and March,

An Olive Ridley turtle nesting at Gahirmatha Beach

when some 200,000 nesting females congregate here, each laying between 50 and 200 eggs in deep hollows they excavate in the sand. After a two-month incubation with the sun's heat, the hatchlings emerge in millions and scamper out to the sea at night. Sadly, less than 0.1 per cent survive to adulthood, as dogs, seagulls, sharks as well as human poachers take an enormous toll on their numbers. The absence of arribadas in 1997 and 1998 caused much alarm among conservationists, until in March 2000 a record 700,000 Olive Ridleys arrived at Gahirmatha. Since the turtles return each year to nest at the spot where they were born, the cycle continues.

Olive Ridley hatchlings heading for the sea

Baleshwar ⑪

Baleshwar district. 214 km (133 miles)
NE of Bhubaneswar. 🚌 🚐
ℹ️ Orissa Tourism, SPA Complex,
Station Square, (06782) 62 048.

ONCE A BUSTLING seaport,
Baleshwar was established
by the British in 1642. It was
later in the possession of the
French and the Dutch, but
had lost its importance by the
18th century, with the silting
up of the port. Its colonial
past is visible in the ruins of
some Dutch tombs, and what
are said to be the remnants of
old canals which led to the
sea. Today Baleshwar is a
sleepy town, surrounded by
paddy fields and villages, and
renowned for the pretty
hand-crafted lacquer boxes
and brass fish made locally.

ENVIRONS: The tranquil
seaside village of **Chandipur**,
16 km (10 miles) east of
Baleshwar, is easily reached
by a short taxi or scooter ride
from the town. Here, the sea
recedes up to 5 km (3 miles)
at low tide, leaving an
expanse of clean white sand.
Orissa Tourism offers accommodation in a
picturesque old
bungalow a short
distance from the
beach, with the
day's fresh catch
served at dinner.
The only blot on this
peaceful landscape is
the Indian Army's test firing
range for rockets, just outside
Chandipur village, against
which environmentalists
and villagers have been
campaigning for many years.

Brass fish,
Baleshwar

Baripada ⑫

Mayurbhanj district. 295 km (183
miles) NE of Bhubaneswar. 🚌 🚐
ℹ️ Orissa Tourism (06792) 52 710.
📅 daily. 🎭 Chaitra Parba (Apr),
Rath Yatra (Jun/Jul).

THE MAIN MARKET TOWN of
northeastern Orissa,
Baripada is the headquarters
of Mayurbhanj district, which
is rich in forests and has a
large population of tribal
people. Baripada is also the
gateway to Simlipal National
Park. The town holds a Rath
Yatra (chariot festival) in
June/July, which takes place
around the **Jagannath
Temple**. This
festival is a small-
scale version of
the one that is held
in Puri (see p312),
but is equally lively
and vibrant, as the entire
town joins in the procession.
A unique feature in Baripada
is that the chariot of the
female deity, Subhadra, is
pulled only by women.

Another colourful festival
held here is Chaitra Parba
(in April), when tribal groups
perform the vigorous Chhau
dance wearing fabulous
costumes. It was originally
performed by warriors just
before they went on to the
battlefield. In the eastern part
of town, **Baripada Museum**
has fine sculptures, pottery,
and coins found in the area.

🏛 **Baripada Museum**
⏰ Tue–Sun. 🚫

ENVIRONS: Haripur, 16 km
(10 miles) southeast of Baripada, has the evocative ruins
of palaces and temples built
by the rulers of the Bhanja
dynasty who made this their
capital in the 15th century.
The most impressive ruins are
of the brick-built Rasikaraya
Temple, and the Durbar Hall
of the Bhanja kings.

Simlipal National Park ⑬

Mayurbhanj district. 320 km (199 miles)
N of Bhubaneswar. **Entry points:**
Lulung & Jashipur. 🚌 Baripada, 50 km
(30 miles) E of the park, then bus or
taxi. 🚐 to Lulung (via Baripada) &
Jashipur. ℹ️ For bookings and permits
contact Field Director, Simlipal Tiger
Reserve, Baripada, (06792) 52 593.
⏰ Nov–mid-June. 🚫 📷 extra
charges. 🚙 Jeeps available in the park.

THIS EXTRAORDINARILY beautiful park is located amidst
the pristine forests and hills of
northeast Orissa. Stretching
over an area of 2,750 sq km
(1,062 sq miles), Simlipal
comprises dense sal (Shorea
robusta) and rosewood
forests, broken by lush grasslands. Numerous rivers and
cascading rapids traverse the
forest, creating spectacular

Women tending their paddy fields near Baleshwar

A waterfall cascading down the hills at Barehipani, Simlipal National Park

(1,158 m/3,799 ft), one of the highest in the park. Basic food and accommodation are available in forest rest houses at Lulung, Barehipani, Chahala, Joranda and Nawana.

ENVIRONS: The capital of the Bhanja kings in the 10th and 11th centuries, **Khiching** has some of the finest examples of temple sculpture to be seen in Orissa. It is 20 km (12 miles) west of Jashipur, the western entry point to Simlipal National Park, and 114 km (71 miles) west of Baripada. The main sight here is the towering Khichakesh-wari temple, reconstructed in the early 20th century entirely from the ruins of the original temple that stood here. The temple is adorned with superb images of several deities, including a vibrant dancing Ganesha. A number of other temples, together with the ruins of two forts built by the Bhanja kings, dot this hamlet.

The small **Archaeological Museum** is well worth visiting. Among its highlights are outstanding life-size statues of Shiva and his consort Parvati, and exquisite sculptural panels from now-fallen temples.

🏛 **Archaeological Museum**
⭕ Tue–Sun. ⚫ public hols. 🈺

waterfalls, such as those at Joranda (150 m/492 ft) and Barehipani (400 m/1,312 ft).

Originally the maharaja of Mayurbhanj's private hunting ground, Simlipal was declared a wildlife sanctuary in 1957. One of the earliest tiger reserves in India, it is home to about 100 tigers, as well as an impressive range of other fauna including elephants, leopards, deer, gaur (Indian bison) and pangolins (or scaly anteaters). These curious-looking animals, covered with large overlapping scales, feed exclusively on termites and ants, tearing open anthills with their powerful claws and scooping up the insects with their long tongues. When threatened, the pangolin rolls up into an impenetrable armoured ball. Over 230

Pangolin at Simlipal

species of birds can also be seen at Simlipal.

The rare *muggers* (marsh crocodiles) can be spotted in rivers or basking on the banks where they dig tunnels to keep cool. At Jashipur, the western entry point to the park, there is a **Crocodile Sanctuary** where the reptiles can be observed at close quarters. One of the park's best spots for viewing wildlife is located in the grasslands at **Bacchuri Chara**, which are a favourite haunt of elephant herds. Another good area for sightings is at **Manghasani Peak**

An 11th-century sculpture of Shiva and Parvati, Khiching

TRIBES OF ORISSA

More than 60 different tribes, descended from the original, pre-Aryan inhabitants of the land, live in Orissa. Many still inhabit hills and forests in the remote interior of the state, relatively untouched by outside influences. The Saoras, who live in the vicinity of Taptapani *(see p316)*, are agriculturists whose mud houses are beautifully painted and decorated with carved doors and lintels. Further west live the Koyas, whose customs decree that their women must only marry considerably younger men. The dominant tribe in Orissa are the Kondhs, who used to perform human sacrifice to ensure the fertility of their land, until the British stamped out this practice in the mid-19th century. Today the Kondhs are renowned for their knowledge of medicinal herbs, and their beautiful metal jewellery. The Orissa government is now promoting tours of some tribal areas. Interested visitors should contact Orissa Tourism in Bhubaneswar, (0674) 43 2203, for information about the necessary permits, as well as accommodation in areas that have few facilities for travellers. For more details see pp754–55.

Kondh girl in her tribal jewellery

ASSAM & THE NORTHEAST

ASSAM and the six northeastern states, often called the Seven Sisters, make up the most geographically isolated and least visited part of India. This region, which has international borders with China, Myanmar (Burma), Bhutan and Bangladesh, has an unusually rich diversity of ethnic groups, languages, religions, climates and landscapes. The largest of the Seven Sisters is Assam, spread along the valley of the Brahmaputra river, and famous for its tea gardens and for the rare one-horned rhinoceros. The rolling green hills of Meghalaya boast the delightful hill station of Shillong, as well as one of the wettest places on earth, Cherrapunji. Arunachal Pradesh, Nagaland, Manipur, Mizoram and Tripura are home to more than 100 different tribes, with distinct and fascinating cultures. The Northeast is also a naturalist's paradise, with a wealth of rare flora and fauna.

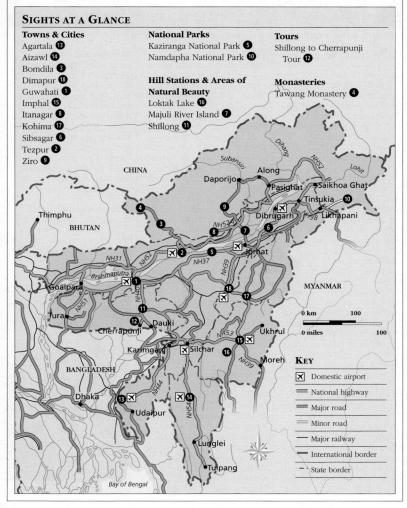

SIGHTS AT A GLANCE

Towns & Cities
Agartala ⑬
Aizawl ⑭
Bomdila ❸
Dimapur ⑱
Guwahati ❶
Imphal ⑮
Itanagar ❽
Kohima ⑰
Sibsagar ❻
Tezpur ❷
Ziro ❾

National Parks
Kaziranga National Park ❺
Namdapha National Park ⑩

Hill Stations & Areas of Natural Beauty
Loktak Lake ⑯
Majuli River Island ❼
Shillong ⑪

Tours
Shillong to Cherrapunji Tour ⑫

Monasteries
Tawang Monastery ❹

KEY
✕	Domestic airport
	National highway
	Major road
	Minor road
	Major railway
	International border
	State border

◁ **Lush ferns surrounding a small waterfall in the dense rainforests of Meghalaya, near Shillong**

Devotees at Guwahati's Kamakhya Temple, a major centre of pilgrimage for Hindus

Guwahati ●

Kamrup district. 1,081 km (672 miles) NE of Kolkata. 🏠 808,000. ✈ Borjhar, 25 km (16 miles) W of city centre, then bus or taxi. 🚉 🚌 ℹ Assam Tourism, Station Rd, (0361) 54 7102. 🎉 Rongali Bihu (Apr), Ambubachi (Jun), Assam Tea Festival (Dec).

THE CAPITAL of Assam, Guwahati is also the gateway to Northeast India. Ringed by the Neelachal Hills, the city stretches along both banks of the broad Brahmaputra river. An ancient seat of tantric Hinduism, with a number of interesting temples in its environs, Guwahati is now a busy commercial centre for Assam's tea and oil industries. Its outer fringes are dotted with the slender, graceful betelnut palm trees from which Guwahati (literally "Betel Nut Market") derives its name.

Brass utensil for serving betel leaf

🏛 Kamakhya Temple
Perched on Nilachal hill, 8 km (5 miles) northwest of the city, this temple is one of India's most important pilgrimage destinations. The present structure with its typically Assamese beehive-shaped *shikhara* dates to the 17th century, after the original temple was destroyed by Muslim invaders. According to legend, as a furious and grieving Shiva carried the corpse of his wife, Sati (also known as Parvati) around the skies, parts of her dismembered body fell to the earth *(see p279)*. All these sites have been sanctified by major temples. Kamakhya is believed to mark the place where her vagina fell, and is therefore said to have special powers associated with energy and creation. In accordance with tantric rituals, a goat is sacrificed here every day, and offered to the goddess. The giant turtles in the temple ponds look forward to being fed by visitors. The colourful annual Ambubachi festival, which marks the end of the earth's menstrual cycle, attracts pilgrims here from all over India, to be blessed by the goddess.

🏛 Navagraha Temple
On Chitranchal hill, in northeast Guwahati, is the Navagraha ("Nine Planets") Temple, believed to mark the site of the ancient city of Pragjyotishpur, Guwahati's old name, which was famous as a centre of astronomy. Beneath its red beehive-shaped dome is a dark chamber with nine lingas representing the nine planets.

🏛 Umananda Temple
Peacock Island. 🚤 Umananda Ghat, 1 km (0.6 miles) N of railway station. Enchantingly located on the lush green Peacock Island in the middle of the Brahmaputra, this 16th-century temple is also dedicated to Shiva's wife. The island, swarming with friendly langur monkeys, is an excellent place to stand and watch the river, deceptively slow on the surface but with swift undercurrents.

🏛 State Museum
GN Bordoloi Rd. ☎ (0361) 54 0651. ◐ Tue–Sun. 📷
This interesting museum, just east of the railway station, has fine reconstructions of tribal villages, a comprehensive

Umananda Temple, on a pretty island in the Brahmaputra

collection of local handicrafts and a gallery of medieval stone and bronze sculptures, which were excavated from Ambari, an archaeological site in the heart of the city.

🦏 Zoo & Botanical Gardens
RG Baruah Rd. ☐ Sat–Thu. 🎦 📷 extra charges.

The well-maintained zoo is in the eastern part of the city. A white tiger, clouded leopards, hornbills and, of course, the native one-horned rhinos, can be seen in spacious, moated enclosures. The Botanical Gardens adjoin the zoo.

Vashishtha Temple, on a wooded hill surrounded by streams

ENVIRONS: The **Vashishtha Temple**, 12 km (7 miles) southeast of Guwahati, stands in a pretty spot that marks the confluence of three streams, with a waterfall and groves of trees around it. This is said to be the site of the ashram of the sage Vashishtha, a character in the *Ramayana (see p27)*.
   Sualkuchi, 32 km (20 miles) south of Guwahati, is a major weaving centre for Assam's famous golden-hued *muga* silk. Several houses

here have women working at their looms, and they are happy to welcome visitors.
   Hajo, 32 km (20 miles) west of Guwahati, is a place of pilgrimage for Buddhists, Hindus and Muslims. The 16th-century Hayagriva Madhava Temple, on Manikuta Hill, is sacred to both Hindus and Buddhists, who believe that the Buddha died here. Fine bas-reliefs of scenes from the

Ramayana decorate its walls. Below the temple is a pond, home to Hajo's most famous resident – a giant turtle. On another hill in Hajo is the Pao Mecca ("Quarter of Mecca") Mosque, established by an Iraqi prince who came to Assam in the 12th century. A pilgrimage here is believed to be equivalent to a quarter of the piety attained by a Haj pilgrimage to Mecca.
   The spectacular temple ruins at **Madan Kamdev** are 50 km (31 miles) northwest of Guwahati. Exuberantly erotic carvings of deities and celestial nymphs lie strewn on a small hillock here. They date from the 10th to 12th centuries, when the area was ruled by the Pala dynasty *(see p44)*.

THE MIGHTY BRAHMAPUTRA

The Son of Brahma, Creator of the Universe, is the name of this majestic river which dominates life in Assam and much of Arunachal Pradesh. Curiously, it is the only Indian river to have a male name. The Brahmaputra begins its 2,900-km (1,802-mile) course from near the holy mountain of Kailasa in Tibet, where it is known as the Tsang Po. Plunging down from a height of 5,200 m (17,060 ft), it then carves a straight, deep 1,100-km (684-mile) long furrow through the Tibetan Plateau. As it continues, the river makes a great sweeping turn around the eastern end of the Himalayas, before plummeting through the deep gorges of upper

Arunachal Pradesh where it is called the Siang. Here, the river is crossed by a group of frighteningly fragile-looking bridges made of rope, including the 367-m (1,204-ft) long suspension bridge at Kamsing, one of the longest in the world.

The Brahmaputra river at dawn

The Brahmaputra enters the plains near the Assam-Arunachal border, and then flows eastward through Assam for 724 km (450 miles), broad and tranquil, except during the monsoon when it swells enormously, flooding flat land and forests, and sweeping away homes, crops and animals in an annual ritual of destruction. Just before the end of its course, the Brahmaputra merges with the Ganges to create the huge Bengal delta, before emptying into the Bay of Bengal in Bangladesh.

Sculpture of a goddess from the temple ruins at Madan Kamdev

The ruins of Tezpur's Da Parbatia Temple, dating to the 5th–6th centuries AD

Tezpur **❷**

Sonitpur district. 180 km (112 miles) NE of Guwahati. 👥 58,250. ✈ Saloni, 10 km (6 miles) N of town centre, then bus or taxi. 🚉 🚌 🛈 Tourist Office, Parvati Nagar, (03712) 20 241.

A PICTURESQUE TOWN on the north bank of the Brahmaputra river, Tezpur is surrounded by undulating green valleys covered with tea gardens. The hills of northern Arunachal provide a scenic backdrop to the town, and for visitors, Tezpur is a convenient stop and a take-off point for trips to Arunachal Pradesh.

Tezpur means "City of Blood", and this gory name is derived from its legendary past as the capital of the Hindu demon kings, the Asuras, said to have been vanquished here by Lord Krishna in a bloody battle. More recently, in 1962, Tezpur was close to another bloodbath when the invading Chinese army reached its outskirts before suddenly declaring a ceasefire *(see p57)*.

The ruins of the **Da Parbatia Temple**, 5 km (3 miles) west of the city, dating from the 5th to 6th centuries AD, bear testimony to Tezpur's ancient past, and represent the earliest example of sculptural art in Assam. All that is left of the temple are some sculptures and an exquisitely carved door

frame, with images of the river goddesses Ganga and Yamuna on either side. **Cole Park**, close to the Tourist Lodge, is Tezpur's prettiest spot, with a beautifully landscaped garden near a lake. It is embellished with 9th- and 10th-century sculptures unearthed in the city. A charming 19th-century colonial church stands behind the Tourist Lodge.

ENVIRONS: The scenic **Bhalukpong**, 58 km (36 miles) northwest of Tezpur, is set in green foothills that mark the border of Assam and Arunachal Pradesh. The Kameng river flows past it. Added attractions are medicinal hot springs, and an Orchid Centre, located 7 km (4 miles) away at **Tipi**, with some 500 varieties of orchids native to Arunachal. **Nameri Sanctuary**, 35 km (22 miles) north of Tezpur, covers 200 sq km (77 sq miles). The Jia Bhoroli river winds through its deciduous forests, which are home to clouded leopards, *mithuns* (Indian bison) and the rare white-winged wood duck. Nameri can be explored on elephant back. The Potasali Eco-Camp on the river, run by the Forest Department, organizes white-water rafting and *mahseer* fishing trips for visitors. **Orang Wildlife Sanctuary**, 65 km (40 miles) northwest of Tezpur,

Epiphytic orchid

is often described as a mini-Kaziranga *(see pp330–31)* since it has a similar landscape of marshes, streams and grassland, the favoured habitat of the one-horned rhinoceros. This little sanctuary is also home to the Asiatic wild buffalo and the Hoolock gibbon.

🦌 **Nameri Sanctuary**
Permits *Divisional Forest Officer, Koloabhomora, (03712) 20 854.* ◐
Sep–Apr. 📷 🎫 *extra charges.* 🎫 🏠
Potasali Eco-Camp (03712) 24 246.
🦌 **Orang Wildlife Sanctuary**
Permits *Divisional Forest Officer, Mangaldoi, (03713) 22 065.* ◐
Sep–Apr. 📷 📋

Bomdila **❸**

West Kameng district. 180 km (112 miles) NW of Tezpur. 🚌 🎉 *Losar (Feb/Mar).* **Travel permits** *required (see p758).*

T HE SCENIC ROAD from Tezpur winds steeply up through thick forests to this pleasant town, at an altitude of 2,530 m (8,301 ft). The headquarters of Arunachal's West Kameng district, Bomdila has Buddhist monasteries surrounded by apple orchards, with views of snowcapped peaks, terraced paddy fields and waterfalls. The **Crafts Centre** is famous for its carpet weaving. The town's inhabitants belong largely to the Monpa and Sherdukpen tribes, who combine Tibetan Buddhism with some of their original animist rituals and beliefs. They wear a curious black cap with five "tails" projecting from its rim, that serve to drain rainwater away from the face.

Monpas celebrating their New Year with a Yak Dance near Bomdila

Rows of prayer wheels at the 17th-century Tawang Monastery

Tawang Monastery ❹

Tawang district. 365 km (227 miles) NW of Tezpur. 🚌 🎭 *Losar (Feb/Mar)*. **Travel permits** *required (see p758)*.

T HE LARGEST Buddhist monastery in India, Tawang is situated in Arunachal Pradesh at an altitude of 3,050 m (10,007 ft). As the road ascends from Bomdila, the scenery becomes alpine, lush with pine, oak and rhododendron forests, and a short, high-altitude bamboo which is the favourite food of the red panda *(see p299)*. Past the Dirang Valley with its old *dzong* (fort), the road climbs sharply to the **Sela Pass**. At 4,249 m (13,940 ft), this is the second highest motorable pass in the world; the highest is in Ladakh *(see p143)*. This barren, desolate landscape is softened by a serene lake that lies below the Sela Pass.

Beyond a memorial to a valiant Indian soldier who held up the advancing Chinese army during the India-China conflict of 1962, the road descends to a beautiful, wide valley. The monastery, dramatically located on a spur surrounded by snowcapped peaks, dominates the valley. When the Dalai Lama fled Tibet in 1959, his route into India was through Tawang, and he still visits the area regularly to hold special prayers.

Founded in 1645 by a lama from Merak in neighbouring Bhutan, this Gelugpa (Yellow Hat) establishment *(see p139)*

has over 500 resident monks. It was also the birthplace of the sixth Dalai Lama. The three-storeyed *dukhang* (assembly hall) has a magnificent 8-m (26-ft) high statue of the Buddha. The ancient library, leading onto the main courtyard, has an excellent collection of *thangkas* and valuable Buddhist manuscripts.

The **Bramdungchung Nunnery**, associated with Tawang Monastery, is located 12 km (7 miles) northwest of Tawang. The road to the monastery, which can be reached by jeep, reveals a stunning alpine landscape of snowpeaks, Monpa hamlets with stone houses, and juniper and dwarf rhododendron bushes. Fluttering prayer flags and a long prayer wall mark the approach to the nunnery, guarded, as are most of the monasteries in this region, by fierce Tibetan mastiffs.

An intricately painted Wheel of Life mural at Tawang Monastery

The Brahmaputra river in full swell, flowing through Assam ▷

Kaziranga National Park ❺

Bar-headed goose in flight

Assam's magnificent Kaziranga National Park, declared a World Heritage Site by UNESCO, is the home of the Indian one-horned rhinoceros. Beautifully situated on the banks of the Brahmaputra, the 430-sq km (166-sq mile) park's landscape is characterized by vast grasslands and swamps, dotted with patches of semi-evergreen forest. The Mikir Hills, where several animals migrate during the monsoon, form its southern boundary. Kaziranga's rich variety of wildlife includes 80 tigers, large numbers of the Asiatic wild buffalo, herds of wild elephants, Hoolock gibbons, pythons and 300 species of birds, including the rare Bengal florican.

Exploring Kaziranga
Visitors on elephant-back are safe from charging rhinos and wild buffaloes.

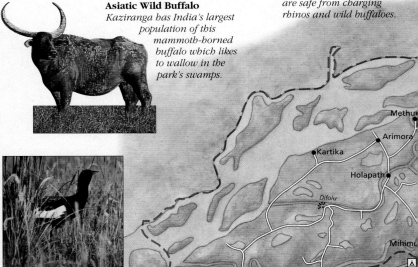

Asiatic Wild Buffalo
Kaziranga has India's largest population of this mammoth-horned buffalo which likes to wallow in the park's swamps.

Methu
Arimora
Kartika
Holapath
Difolu
Mihimu
GUWAHATI   NH37   Gotanga   Deopani   Kuthari   Baguri

Bengal Florican
This rare bird has beautifully streaked plumage.

THE INDIAN ONE-HORNED RHINOCEROS

Kaziranga is one of the last refuges of the Indian one-horned rhinoceros (*Rhinoceros unicornis*), an endangered species that was close to extinction at the beginning of the 20th century. Successful conservation measures have seen their numbers rise to 2,500 (across Assam and the foothills of Nepal), of which 1,500 are in Kaziranga. Once found extensively across the subcontinent, the rhino population dwindled dramatically because of widespread poaching for its horn, a prized ingredient in Chinese medicine. Actually a mass of closely matted hair, each rhino horn fetches an exorbitant price in Southeast Asia, where it is believed to have great medicinal and aphrodisiac properties.

A rhino mother and her baby in Kaziranga's vast grasslands

VISITORS' CHECKLIST

Golaghat district. 215 km (134 miles) NE of Guwahati. ✈ *Jorhat, 96 km (60 miles) NE of Kohora, the entry point, then taxi.* 🚆 *Furkating, 75 km (47 miles) E of Kohora, then taxi.* 🚌 ℹ️ *Bonani Tourist Lodge, Kohora, (03776) 62 423.* ⬜ *Apr–Oct.* 📷 🎥 *extra charges.* 🚙 *Jeeps available.* 🏠

Bheel (Shallow Lake)
Floods inundate the park every monsoon, leaving behind bheels *and marshes as they recede. These attract herds of wild elephants, and many other animals and water birds.*

Hog Deer
These animals, closely related to the spotted deer (chital), are found in large numbers in the park's riverine grasslands.

Wildgrass Resort
Located 5 km (3 miles) east of Kohora, just outside the park, this eco-friendly resort (see p702) arranges elephant rides and trips to nearby tea plantations (see pp262–3).

```
0 km                    8
───────────────────────
0 miles                 8
```

KEY

⚊	Park boundary
═	National highway
═	Minor road
ℹ️	Tourist information
🔆	Viewpoint
🅰	Accommodation

Hoolock Gibbon
This 1-m (3.3-ft) ape can be recognized by the distinctive silvery band above its eyebrows, and its loud whooping hoot, which resounds through the forest.

Sibsagar ⑥

Sibsagar district. 370 km (230 miles)
NE of Guwahati. 🚶 54,500. ✈
Jorhat, 60 km (37 miles) S of city
centre, then taxi or bus. 🚉 🚌 ℹ
Assam Tourism, near Shivadol Temple,
(03772) 22 394. 🎭 Shivratri (Feb/Mar).

AT THE HEART of Assam's tea
and oil-producing region,
Sibsagar is also the state's most
historic city, as the seat of the
Ahom dynasty *(see p49)* which
ruled Assam for 600 years.
Originally from Myanmar
(Burma), the Ahoms converted
to Hinduism and gradually
indigenized after conquering
Assam in 1228. The Ahoms
were defeated by the Burmese
in 1817, and their kingdom
became part of the British
Indian Empire in 1826.
    The Ahoms were great
builders, as is evident from
the ruins in and around
Sibsagar. Dominating
the town is the
enormous 103-ha
(255-acre) man-
made **Sibsagar
Lake**, with three
temples on its
banks. Especially
impressive is the
towering **Shivadol
Temple** with its 33-m (108-ft)
high gilded spire, built by an
Ahom queen in 1734. About
4 km (2 miles) south of the
town are the ruins of two

Vaishnavite mask, Majuli

18th-century brick palaces,
Karen Ghar and **Talatal
Ghar**. Both are seven storeys
high, and the latter also has
three underground floors and
a warren of secret tunnels.
To its northeast is the elegant
Rang Ghar, the oval, double-
storeyed royal sports pavilion,
constructed in 1746.

Majuli River Island ⑦

Jorhat district. 314 km (195 miles)
NE of Guwahati. 🚌 Neamati Ghat,
13 km (8 miles) N of Jorhat. 🚢 from
Neamati Ghat to Majuli, then bus to
Garamur. ℹ On arrival, foreigners
must register with the Sub-Divisional
Officer, Majuli, (03775) 74 424, who
also handles bookings.

PERHAPS THE LARGEST inhabited river island in the
world, Majuli covers an area
of 929 sq km (359 sq
miles). It is easy to
forget that
Majuli is an
island,
holding within
it hills, rivulets
and little islands
of its own. This
amorphous land-
mass is constantly being
sculpted into new dimensions
and shapes by the Brahma-
putra. Every year during the
monsoon, the river submerges

large tracts of land, forcing the
inhabitants to move to higher
ground. After the floods
recede, leaving behind fertile,
freshly silted land, the people
return to cultivate the area.
    As interesting as Majuli's
distinctive landscape are its
satras, unique monasteries
founded in the 15th century
by the Vaishnavite reformer-
philosopher, Shankardeva.
The *satras* are rich repositories of traditional Assamese
arts and crafts, and regularly
stage dance-dramas in praise
of Vishnu. Majuli's main
settlement is at **Garamur**
which has two *satras*. About
20 others are scattered across
the island. Visitors can stay in
the *satras*, and should offer to
make a donation towards
overnight stays or meals.

Itanagar ⑧

Papum Pare district. 420 km (261
miles) N of Guwahati. 🚶 35,000.
🚉 Lakhimpur, 60 km (37 miles) NE of
town centre, then taxi or bus. 🚌 ℹ
Sector C, Naharlagun, (0360) 4328.
Travel permits required (see p758).

UNTIL IT BECAME the capital
of Arunachal Pradesh in
1971, Itanagar was a settlement of the Nishi tribe, one
of the largest among the 26
major tribes that inhabit the
state. A few traditional Nishi

Bamboo forests in the vicinity of Itanagar, in Arunachal Pradesh

Apatani woman in the rice fields near Ziro

Namdapha National Park ⑩

Changlang district. 380 km (236 miles) NE of Itanagar. 🚉 *Margherita, 64 km (40 miles) SW of Miao, the entry point.* 🚌 ❱ *Director, Project Tiger, Miao, (03807) 79 2122.* 🕐 *Oct–Apr.* 🗺 **Travel permits** *required (see p758).*

THIS SUPERB PARK in remote eastern Arunachal Pradesh, bordering Myanmar, covers 1,985 sq km (766 sq miles). Rising from the plains to 4,500 m (14,764 ft) in the Himalayas, it covers a variety of habitats, and is the only reserve in India where all the four big cats of the Himalayas – tiger, leopard, clouded leopard and the rare snow leopard are found. It was declared a Tiger Reserve in 1983. Other wildlife includes the great Indian hornbill, the red panda *(see p299)*, and the Hoolock gibbon *(see p331)*.

ENVIRONS: The legendary Burma Road (or Stilwell Road) begins at **Ledo**, 60 km (37 miles) southwest of Miao. This 1,700-km (1,056-mile) road, of great strategic importance in World War II, connected Ledo, via the forbidding jungles and mountains of Arunachal Pradesh and Northern Myanmar, to Kunming in China's Yunnan province. Supervised by the American General Joseph Stilwell and built in two years at enormous human cost, it has now fallen into disrepair, but is still used by locals travelling on foot.

longhouses still remain, now all but swamped by Itanagar's newly-constructed government buildings. The Nishis are easily recognizable – they sport black and white hornbill feathers in their cane headgear, wear their hair in a bun on their foreheads and often carry bearskin bags.

The **Nehru Museum**, near the Secretariat, offers a comprehensive look at the arts and crafts of all the tribes of Arunachal Pradesh, with some lovely jewellery, textiles, cane and bamboo

Adi longhouse near Along

artifacts, and totem objects on display. A pretty but bumpy 6-km (4-mile) drive north from Itanagar leads to the lovely, emerald-green **Gyakar Sinyi Lake**, surrounded by dense forests. Many of the tall trees are festooned with orchids.

🏛 **Nehru Museum**
Siddharth Vihar. ☎ *(0360) 21 2276.* 🕐 *Tue–Sat.* 🗺 🚫

Ziro ⑨

Lower Subansiri district. 150 km (93 miles) NE of Itanagar. 👥 *12,300.* 🚌 ❱ *Deputy Commissioner's Office, (03788) 24 255.* **Travel permits** *required (see p758).*

THE PICTURESQUE town of Ziro in central Arunachal Pradesh, lies in a large, flat valley, surrounded by low pine-covered hills. This area, better known as the Apatani Plateau, is the home of the prosperous Apatani tribe who

practise a unique system of cultivation that combines rice-growing with pisciculture. The flooded paddy fields are stocked with fingerlings, the two staples of Apatani diet thus coming from the same plot of land. Like the Nishis, the Apatanis wear their hair in a bun on their foreheads, held with a brass skewer. Both the men and women are tattooed and the women sport huge bamboo noseplugs.

Northeast of Ziro, three other areas, **Daporijo**, **Along** and **Pasighat**, are now open to foreigners (with permits). The latter two are situated on the Brahmaputra river and are inhabited by the Adi tribe *(see p336)*. The drive from Ziro to Pasighat (300 km/186 miles) is wonderfully scenic, through dense virgin forest and tribal villages with thatched longhouses.

Tribal people of eastern Arunachal Pradesh on the Burma Road

Locally made bamboo baskets on sale in Shillong's Bara Bazaar

Shillong ⓫

East Khasi Hills district. 127 km (79 miles) S of Guwahati. 🚉 132,900.
🚌 🛈 Meghalaya Tourism, 3rd Secretariat, Lower Lachumiere, (0364) 22 6054. 🎭 Weiking Dance (Apr/May).

CAPITAL OF THE tiny state of Meghalaya, Shillong, with its mist-shrouded hills, pine forests, lakes and waterfalls, is sometimes described as the "Scotland of the East". Lying at an altitude of 1,496 m (4,908 ft), it was chosen as the headquarters of the British administration in Assam in 1874. It soon developed into a popular hill station, providing refuge from the searing heat of the plains.

The town still retains a distinctly colonial ambience, with its mock-Tudor bungalows, churches, polo ground and beautiful 18-hole golf course. It is also the home of the matrilineal Khasi tribe. The idyllic countryside around the town can be easily explored in short excursions.

🏠 Bara Bazaar

Bara Bazaar Rd. ⭘ Mon–Sat.
This sprawling market offers a vivid glimpse of Khasi tribal society. The stalls are piled high with produce from the surrounding villages – honey, pineapples, piglets, dried fish, wild mushrooms, raw betel nut and bamboo baskets. The market is dominated by Khasi women, who run most of the stalls. Dressed in their traditional tunic-like *jainsems* and tartan-checked shawls, these cheerful matriarchs can drive a hard bargain.

🏛 Museum of Entomology

Umsohsun Rd. 📞 (0364) 22 3411.
⭘ Mon–Sat. 🎟
This small private museum, situated north of Bara Bazaar, was established in the 1930s by the Wankhar family, and boasts a collection of rare butterflies and insects found in Meghalaya. Among them are huge stick insects, iridescent beetles, and the giant yellow and black birdwing butterfly which cloaks itself in a deadly poison to protect itself from predatory birds. The family also runs a breeding centre for rare species.

🌿 Ward Lake & Lady Hydari Park

Park ⭘ daily. 🎟 🎥 extra charges.
In the centre of town, the horseshoe-shaped Ward Lake has pleasant promenade paths around it, paddle boats for hire and a café. A short distance to its south is Lady Hydari Park, with a pretty Japanese garden and a mini

zoo which includes fauna native to Meghalaya's forests, such as hornbills, leopard cats, and the aptly named slow loris, a ferret-like creature that crawls around as though heavily drugged.

ENVIRONS: The beautiful **Bishop** and **Beadon Falls** are 3 km (2 miles) north of Shillong, just off the Guwahati-Shillong Highway. Along the same route, 17 km (11 miles) north of Shillong, is **Umiam Lake**, a large artificial reservoir set among forested hills. It offers facilities for angling, kayaking and water-skiing, and has an orchidarium in the adjacent park. The scenic **Elephant Falls** are 11 km (7 miles) south of Shillong. The road to **Mawphlang**, 24 km (15 miles) southwest of Shillong, is richly forested with pine and oak, and is a good place to see some of Meghalaya's rare species of orchids in their natural habitat.

The Elephant Falls, flowing over ferns and rocks

THE KHASIS

The Khasis are the predominant tribe in the Shillong area. Believed to have originated in Southeast Asia, their language belongs to the Mon-Khmer group. It is not known when they migrated to this region. Today, the majority of Khasis are Christians, their ancestors converted by British missionaries in the 19th century. Nevertheless, they retain many of their tribal customs. Chief among these is their matrilineal social structure, which dictates that landed property can only be inherited by females, with the youngest daughter given a special position as custodian of the family house and the clan's traditional rituals.

Khasi matriarch at her stall in Shillong's main market

Shillong to Cherrapunji Tour ⑫

T HE ROAD TO Cherrapunji through the East
Khasi Hills winds through dense pine and
oak forests, full of ferns and orchids. En route
are dramatic gorges and ravines, waterfalls
and limestone caves. Cherrapunji is one of
the wettest places on earth, and established a
world record of an incredible 2,621 cm (1,032
in) of rain in 1861. It continues to record an
average rainfall of 1,143 cm (450 in) in the
monsoon months of July to September.

Cherrapunji's famous oranges

Shillong Peak ②
The highest point in Meghalaya
at 1,965 m (6,447 ft), this
peak is named after the Khasi
deity, Ushyllong.

Shillong ①
Ward Lake
marks the
centre of
the town.

GUWAHATI

NH44

SILCHAR

Cherrapunji ④
Surrounded by groves of
orange and banana trees,
this little town has a lively
weekly market and is
famed for its delicious
orange-flower honey.

Mawphlang

Mylliem ③
A number of rare
species of orchids
grow around this
traditional Khasi
blacksmiths'
village, where
agricultural tools
are made.

NH40

Laitlyngkot

MAWSYNRAM

DAUKI

| 0 km | 5 |
| 0 miles | 5 |

Nohkalikai Falls ⑤
These are the second
highest falls in India. Tall
Khasi memorial stones dot
the area around them.

TIPS FOR DRIVERS

Length: 120 km (75 miles).
Stopping-off points: The tour
takes between 6–7 hours. Shillong
Peak, Cherrapunji (meals, toilets
available), Nohsngithiang Falls,
Nohkalikai Falls and Mawsmai
Caves are the best places to stop.
Getting around: Meghalaya
Tourism, (0364) 21 0358, and
several travel agencies run daily
tours from Shillong to Cherrapunji.
Take a torch to explore the caves.

Mawsmai Caves ⑥
Some of these
limestone caves
run more than
4 km (2 miles) deep.

KEY

▬ Tour route

═ Other roads

▬ National highway

Nohsngithiang Falls ⑦
On a clear day, there is a fine
view of the plains of
Bangladesh from these
impressive falls, also known
as the Seven Sisters Falls.

Tribal Peoples of the Northeast

Naga tribal basket

Northeast India is home to an extraordinary diversity of tribal peoples. Arunachal Pradesh alone has 26 major tribes, while Nagaland has 16. Dozens of others inhabit Assam, Manipur, Mizoram, Meghalaya and Tripura. Though living in the same region, they have been geographically isolated from each other by steep mountain ridges, rivers and gorges, and have therefore retained their distinct cultural identities and languages.

Gigantic stone megaliths *can be seen all over the state of Meghalaya. They were erected by the Khasi tribe as memorials to the dead.*

Pipes *of wood and metal are smoked by tribes in Arunachal Pradesh.*

Intricate beadwork, crafted by the Wanchos of Arunachal

The Adis of Arunachal Pradesh *are famous for their engineering skills and construct superb bridges, such as this tube of canework over the Brahmaputra river.*

The Konyaks of Nagaland, *who perform spirited martial dances, wear colourful costumes, with hornbill feathers, wild boar tusks and painted canework caps.*

The Thankuls of Manipur *are skilled at weaving, producing a distinctive red and white textile with a silken sheen.*

A chief's house in *Nagaland has crossed gables and is decorated with his tribe's symbols. The* mithun *(bison species) skull in the foreground symbolizes power and prosperity.*

This Naga chief *used to be a headhunter. The wooden heads on his basket indicate how many heads he took.*

The Cheraw dance *is performed at tribal festivals in Mizoram. The Mizos love music and dancing, and the Cheraw dance requires women to step agilely between rapidly moving bamboo poles.*

Ujjayanta Palace in Agartala, built in 1901

Agartala ⓑ

West Tripura district. 600 km (373 miles) S of Guwahati. 🏠 189,300. ✈ 12 km (7 miles) N of town centre, then bus or taxi. 🚌 ℹ Tripura Tourism, Ujjayanta Palace Complex, (0381) 22 3893.

T HE CAPITAL OF TRIPURA, a former princely state bordered by Bangladesh, Agartala is a pleasant little town, its lush tropical greenery dotted with red-brick civic buildings. Dominating the town is the sprawling white **Ujjayanta Palace**, built in 1901 in Indo-Saracenic style. Now the State Legislature, the palace's opulent interior includes a tiled Chinese Room with a magnificent ceiling crafted by Chinese artisans. It is open to visitors when the Assembly is not in session. Tripura is renowned for its exceptionally fine cane and bamboo work, freely available in the market.

Cane basket from Tripura

ENVIRONS: Neermahal Water Palace, 55 km (34 miles) south of Agartala, on an island in Rudrasagar Lake, was the summer home of the former maharajas of Tripura. Built in white marble and red sandstone, this fairy-tale palace has a profusion of pavilions, balconies, turrets and bridges, and part of it is open to the public. **Udaipur**, 58 km (36 miles) south of Agartala, is renowned for the **Tripurasundari Temple** with its distinctive Bengal-style curved roof. It was built in the 16th century.

Aizawl ⓒ

Aizawl district. 480 km (298 miles) SE of Guwahati. 🏠 229,700. ✈ 35 km (22 miles) W of town centre, then bus or taxi. 🚌 ℹ Mizoram Tourism, Chandmary, (0389) 34 1227. **Travel permits** required (see p758).

P ERCHED ALONG A RIDGE, its houses and churches standing out against the green hillside, Aizawl is Mizoram's capital, and home of the Mizo tribes, said to have migrated here from Myanmar's Chin Hills 300 years ago. In the centre of town is the lively **Main Market**, where local farmers congregate. Almost the entire population of Mizoram (as of Nagaland and Meghalaya) is now Christian, converted by missionaries who first came here in 1891. As a result of the schools they started, Mizoram has the second highest literacy rate in India. Blue jeans are more commonly seen today than tribal dress among the men, but the women still wear their elegant *puans* (long, narrow skirts). Visitors can see these being woven at the **Weaving Centre** in Luangmual, 7 km (4 miles) away.

Aizawl, stretching across a ridge

Fish sellers at Imphal's Ima Keithel

Imphal ⓯

Imphal district. 484 km (301) miles
SE of Guwahati. 🚂 217,300.
✈ 6 km (4 miles) S of city centre. 🚌
ⓘ Manipur Tourism, next to Hotel
Imphal, (0385) 32 0337. 🎭 Yaosang
(Feb/Mar), Lai Haraoba (Apr/May).
Travel permits required (see p758).

THE CAPITAL OF Manipur
(the "Jewelled
Land"), Imphal lies in a
broad oval valley
enclosed by forested
hills. Its inhabitants
mostly belong to the
Meitei tribe. The liveliest
part of the town is the
Ima Keithel ("Mothers'
Market") where more
than 3,000 women
congregate daily to
sell fresh produce, fish, grain,
canework and handicrafts,
including the elegant striped
textiles worn by the
Meitei women. These
formidable Imas, who
sport *tikas* of sandal-
wood paste on their
noses, have formed a
powerful union and
pride themselves on
charging fair prices.
Imphal's main temple,
the **Govindaji
Temple**, stands east
of the Bazaar, and on
festivals associated
with Lord Krishna
the graceful Manipuri
dance *(see p29)* is
performed here. Sagol
Kangjei, Manipuri
polo, is a favourite
sport in Imphal (they
claim to have invented
the game), and an opportunity
to see a match should not be
missed – the Polo Ground is in
the centre of the town. It is a
fast and furious game, with the
players dressed in dhotis and
often riding bareback on the
agile Manipuri horses. Two
well-tended **Commonwealth
War Graves Cemeteries** are
on the northern and east-
ern outskirts of town.
Buried here are the
men who died fight-
ing the Japanese during
the invasion of Manipur
in World War II. Also
worth visiting is an impressive **Orchidarium** displaying
various indigenous species. It
is 12 km (7 miles)
north of the town.

Manipuri dancer

ENVIRONS: Moirang, 45 km
(28 miles) south of Imphal,
with its ancient temple to the
pre-Hindu god, Thangjing, is
the spiritual home of the
Meiteis, who celebrate Lai
Haraoba here with great fanfare *(see p327)*. During World
War II, Moirang was the headquarters of the Indian
National Army (INA), led by
Subhash Chandra Bose, which
fought against the Allies.

Loktak Lake ⓰

Bishnupur district. 48 km (30 miles)
S of Imphal. 🚌 ⓘ For bookings on
Sendra Island contact Manipur
Tourism, (0385) 32 0337. 🚤 **Travel
permits** required (see p758).

LOKTAK LAKE is one of the
most enchanting places
in the northeast. Almost two-
thirds of this huge expanse
of freshwater is covered by
unique floating saucer-shaped
islands of reed and humus,
locally called *phumdi*, which
are home to a community of
fishermen. The southern part
of the lake forms the **Keibul
Lamjao National Park** where
contiguous masses of *phumdi*
form the very special habitat of
the endangered Manipur brow-
antlered deer called *sangai*.
These deer have divided
hooves, specially adapted to
their floating habitat, and
elegantly curved antlers. Only
a 100 or so of these graceful
animals are now left, found in
the wild only in an area of 6
sq km (2 sq miles) within the
park. **Sendra Island**, at the
heart of the park, provides a
magnificent view of the lake,
its islands and its rich birdlife.

Floating islands of reed and humus with fishermen's houses and moored boats, on Loktak Lake

The Baptist Church in Kohima, one of many churches in the area

Visitors can stay here, and the park also offers boat rides through the many labyrinthine waterways of the lake.

Kohima ⓱

Kohima district. 339 km (211 miles) E of Guwahati. ⓘ 78,600. ⓡ Dimapur, 74 km (46 miles) NW of Kohima, then taxi or bus. ⓿ ⓘ Nagaland Tourism, (0370) 22 2214. **Travel permits** required (see p758).

THE CAPITAL of Nagaland, Kohima, at an altitude of 1,500 m (4,921 ft), is a small, pleasant town surrounded by hills which are dotted with villages. Kohima is famous in World War II history for the decisive battle, fought on the tennis court of the British deputy commissioner's house, that finally stopped the Japanese advance into India in April 1944.

Those who fell in the battle are buried in the beautifully kept **War Cemetery** covering a terraced hillside. A poignant inscription at the base of one of the two large crosses here reads: "When you go home tell them of us and say, For your tomorrow we gave our today". The **Cathedral of Reconciliation**, which overlooks the cemetery, was built in 1995, partly funded by the Japanese government.

Kohima's main bazaar is a good place to encounter the handsome Naga people (see pp336–7) in their colourful woven shawls, who come from surrounding villages to sell their produce. The market also offers visitors a glimpse of the diet that supposedly made the Nagas such formidable warriors – bees' larvae and dog meat are favourites.

The **State Museum**, 2 km (1.2 miles) north of the bazaar, has an excellent anthropological collection of Naga masks, textiles, jewellery and totem pillars from all the 16 Naga tribes. Particularly intriguing is a large ceremonial drum that looks like a dugout canoe, kept in a shed outside the museum. The drum is engraved with stylized waves, and has gongs that look like paddles. This and other factors, such as the use of seashells in their costumes, has led some anthropologists to conjecture that the Nagas were originally a seafaring people, possibly from Sumatra. Today, a high percentage of Nagas are Christians and a church can be found in almost every corner of the state.

War Cemetery, Kohima

The original village of Kohima, **Bara Basti**, is a settlement of the Angami Naga tribe, located on a hill overlooking the town. Though now considerably modernized, it still has its ceremonial gateway, and a large traditional community house, the *morung*, with crossed horns surmounting its gable. A less modernized Angami Naga village is **Khonoma**, 20 km (12 miles) southwest of Kohima, with its wooden houses, carved gateway and surrounding stone wall. The villagers are renowned for their agricultural skills – terraced paddy fields cover the hillside, growing some 20 varieties of rice, and an intricate system of bamboo pipes irrigates the fields.

ⓜ State Museum
□ Mon–Sat. ● public hols.

Dimapur ⓲

Kohima district. 74 km (46 miles) NW of Kohima. ⓘ 107,400. ⓡ ⓿ ⓘ Tourist Office, near Nagaland State Transport Office,, (0386) 22 6355. **Travel permits** required (see p758).

THIS BUSTLING town in the plains functions as a gateway to the rest of Nagaland. It was founded by the Kachari rulers, a Tibeto-Burmese people who were displaced from their territories in Assam in the 13th century by the invading Ahoms (see p332). Some of the ruins of their old capital can be seen in the heart of the town. Most notable are 30 carved megaliths, believed to be fertility symbols. About 5 km (3 miles) from the city centre, on the road to Kohima, is the **Ruzaphema Bazaar** which displays a fascinating range of tribal handicrafts.

Carved monoliths in Dimapur erected by the Kachari kings

WESTERN INDIA

Introducing Western India

THIS REGION HAS SOME OF INDIA'S most popular destinations. In Rajasthan, the desert forts of Jaisalmer and Jodhpur, the palaces and lakes of Udaipur, and the Ranthambhore National Park evoke all the romance and splendour of the state's princely past. Gujarat's Jain temples and intricately designed stepwells are architectural marvels, while its natural wonders can be enjoyed on the beaches of Diu and at the lion sanctuary at Gir. The landscapes in this region range from the sand dunes of Rajasthan to the vast salt flats of Kutch, to the urban bustle of the two state capitals, Jaipur and Ahmedabad.

Rajasthani women in festive dress at the Pushkar Fair

Chillies drying in the desert sun near Osian, Rajasthan

0 km   50

0 miles   50

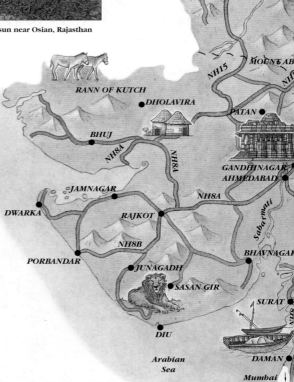

JAISALMER

BARMER

MOUNT AB

NH15

RANN OF KUTCH

DHOLAVIRA

PATAN

BHUJ

NH8A

NH8A

GANDHINAGAR
AHMEDABAD

JAMNAGAR

NH8A

DWARKA

RAJKOT

Sabarmati

NH8B

PORBANDAR

BHAVNAGAR

JUNAGADH

SASAN GIR

SURAT

DIU

Arabian
Sea

DAMAN

Mumbai

GETTING AROUND

Jaipur, Jodhpur, Udaipur and Ahmedabad are well-connected by air to Delhi and Mumbai as well as to each other. Trains travel between all the major cities, with fast trains connecting Delhi and Jaipur. Two luxury trains, the Palace on Wheels and the Royal Orient (see p777), offer a more romantic way to explore Rajasthan and Gujarat. Within Rajasthan, a network of national highways links most major destinations by road, while National Highways 8, 14 and 15 continue on to Gujarat.

◁ **Murals in glowing colours inside the Garh Palace in Bundi (see p404), Rajasthan**

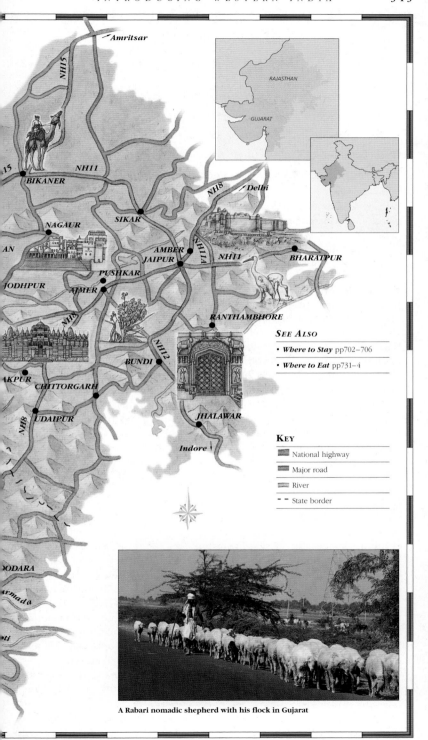

RAJASTHAN

GUJARAT

Amritsar

NH15

NH11

BIKANER

NAGAUR

SIKAR

NH8   Delhi

AMBER
JAIPUR

NH11   BHARATPUR

AN

JODHPUR

PUSHKAR

AJMER

NH8

RANTHAMBHORE

SEE ALSO

- *Where to Stay* pp702–706
- *Where to Eat* pp731–4

AKPUR   CHITTORGARH

NH8   UDAIPUR

BUNDI   NH12

JHALAWAR

Indore

KEY

	National highway
	Major road
	River
- -	State border

ODARA

rmada

ti

A Rabari nomadic shepherd with his flock in Gujarat

A PORTRAIT OF WESTERN INDIA

THE GREAT THAR DESERT *and the Arabian Sea have been two dominating influences in the history and culture of Rajasthan and Gujarat. Both these states have boundaries with Pakistan and, before 1947, contained a number of princely states. In most other respects, however, the two states are a study in contrasts.*

A many-splendoured land of fairy-tale palaces and vibrant fairs and festivals, Rajasthan fulfills everyone's favourite fantasies about India. Until Independence in 1947 Rajasthan, literally "the Land of Kings", was indeed just that. It was made up of more than 20 princely states, bastions of royal opulence and feudal pageantry. They were ruled by Rajput clans such as the Kachhawahas of Jaipur, the Rathores of Jodhpur and the Sisodias of Udaipur. Their legacy has helped make the state one of the country's most popular tourist destinations.

Today, Rajasthan's once-impregnable forts are open to visitors, and many of the old princely palaces and feudal castles have been converted into delightful hotels, often run by the erstwhile ruling families. Tourism has helped restore these historic buildings, and breathed new life into them. Apart from becoming successful hoteliers, many former princes have found new roles for themselves in politics, representing their constituencies in India's parliament. Rajasthan's traditional arts and crafts have also been revived, with tourists replacing maharajas as the new patrons.

A desert nomad's shelter in Rajasthan

Eighty per cent of Rajasthan's population still lives in rural areas, engaged in agriculture and livestock herding. The rhythm of life in the villages continues much as it has for hundreds of years, the drudgery of the daily grind broken every few weeks by religious festivals and cattle fairs, such as those at Pushkar *(see pp374–5)* and Nagaur *(see p376)*. These wonderfully colourful events provide Rajasthani villagers with an occasion for feasting, socializing, trading, and enjoying traditional entertainments such as camel races and puppet shows. The fairs have become a major attraction for visitors as well, offering a close and memorable encounter with the people and culture of rural Rajasthan.

Rajasthani society is still socially very conservative, with great value placed on

Camels for sale at the Pushkar Fair

ancient feudal codes of conduct and honour. As recently as 1987, an incident of *sati* took place here, when a young widow burnt herself on her husband's funeral pyre, while the whole village watched in admiration. But things are changing: female literacy in Rajasthan, which was just 20 per cent a decade ago, has doubled to 40 per

The Tarnetar Fair in Gujarat

cent in 2001, and women now head many village government councils. Rural development schemes have brought schools, hospitals and water to remote desert villages. What has still not changed, however, is the old-world courtesy and hospitality encountered everywhere in Rajasthan, be it in a princely palace or a mud hut in the desert.

In sharp contrast with Rajasthan, Gujarat is one of the most industrially advanced and urbanized states in the country – nearly 60 per cent of its population lives in cities. The Gujaratis' legendary business acumen has helped make the state one of the most prosperous in India.

While the forbidding expanses of the Thar Desert had for centuries effectively insulated Rajasthani society, Gujarat's 1,600 km (992 miles) of coastline on the Arabian Sea have helped foster contacts with other lands and cultures, and bred an adventurous spirit in the people. Since ancient times, Gujarat has traded with Arabs and Persians, East Africa, China, and Indonesia, through its ports at Surat *(see p420)* and Mandvi *(see p429)*, while from the 15th century onwards European

traders established their bases along the coastline. In the late 19th and early 20th centuries, many Gujaratis sailed to far off lands in search of new opportunities, and today their descendants (many of them with the surnames Patel and Shah) are flourishing – be it as hoteliers in America, retail traders in Britain, industrialists in Nigeria or lawyers in South Africa.

Gujaratis have been deeply influenced by Jainism *(see p396)*, which took hold in the region in the 11th century, during the reign of the Solanki kings. Jainism's emphasis on non-violence, community service, simple living and high thinking was an integral part of the philosophy of Gujarat's most famous son, Mahatma Gandhi, who led India's struggle for independence *(see p56)*. Ordinary mortals too try to follow this creed in their daily lives. Most Gujaratis, whether at home or abroad, are strict vegetarians, known for their toughness and self reliance, and for their thrift and philanthropy. These qualities were especially evident after the devastating earthquake that hit Gujarat in January 2001 *(see p428)*, from which the state is now slowly, but surely, recovering.

Rajasthani women preparing lunch

Forts and Palaces

Fort gate with spikes

THE SPECTACULAR FORTS of Rajasthan were originally forbidding, defensive citadels, but by the mid-16th century, when most Rajput states had made peace with the Mughals, luxurious palaces, pleasure pavilions and gardens were added to them, displaying many Mughal-inspired features. In the early 20th century there was another spate of palace-building in both Rajasthan and Gujarat. As a result of increasing contact between the British Raj and the princely states, a marked European influence in both architecture and decor is visible in these palaces.

Cannons *to defend the fort are mounted on the bastions, which tower high above the surrounding area.*

Sileh Khanas *(armouries) store a variety of weapons, from ceremonial jewelled swords to sharp knuckle-dusters, and even special armour for war elephants.*

Ramparts follow the contours of the hill.

Rana Kumbha's Palace

Entrance gates *are high enough for elephants to pass through. Their doors have huge spikes to prevent enemy elephants from storming them.*

Water reservoirs, *often fed by underground springs, are found in forts in the arid areas of Rajasthan and Gujarat.*

TYPES OF FORTS

Ancient Indian treatises list six types of forts for good defences. While *giri durgs* (hill forts) such as Chittor-garh are the most impregnable, other effective types are *dhanva durg*, protected by desert, such as Jaisalmer *(see pp388–9); vana durg*, protected by forest, such as Ranthambhore *(see p406); mahi durg*, protected by thick mud walls, such as Bharatpur's Lohagarh *(see p367); jala durg*, protected by water, such as Ghagron *(see p403);* and *nara durg*, a city fort such as Nagaur *(see p376)*, protected mainly by trusted men.

Ghagron Fort in Rajasthan, an example of a fort protected by water

PALACES

Palaces built by maharajas during the Raj, unlike those in the old forts, had modern plumbing, drawing rooms and dining halls suitable for entertaining British dignitaries.

Lalgarh Palace in Bikaner (see p379) was built in 1902. It beautifully combines Rajput decorative features with European elements, such as banquet halls and billiard rooms.

Wankaner Palace (see p427) was built in 1907. The ruler's travels in Europe gave him a taste for Italianate pillars and Gothic arches, crowned here with Mughal pavilions.

Corridors and staircases, that connect the private chambers in Rajput palaces, are often narrow and twisting to confuse enemy invaders.

The Victory Tower was built in 1458 after a successful battle. Each of its nine storeys is a temple.

Temples were built by rulers and merchants, who believed their deities protected the fort.

FORTS

Chittorgarh *(see p402)*, founded in AD 728 but added to at various times until the 16th century is, like many Rajput forts, built on a commanding height above the plains. Its massive ramparts encircle palaces, temples, stables and reservoirs.

Sheesh Mahals ("Halls of Mirrors") are ceremonial halls inlaid with mirror mosaic. One candle, reflected in the myriad mirrors, makes the whole room glitter.

Zenanas (women's quarters) have secluded courtyards and exquisite stone latticework (jali) screens. These let in light and air, yet maintain privacy. Most zenanas are large, because they also housed the rulers' many concubines.

Regional Food: Western India

VEGETARIAN FOOD dominates the cuisine of Gujarat and Rajasthan, both states having been strongly influenced by Jainism and Vaishnavism, which forbid animal slaughter. Two-thirds of Gujarat's population is vegetarian, and their food boasts a wide range of cereals, lentils and vegetables, distinguished by wonderfully subtle seasoning. Rajasthani cuisine is more robust, featuring many desert plants such as *kair (Capparis decidua)* berries and *sangri (Prosopis cineraria)* beans. It also includes the highly seasoned meat dishes of the martial Rajput community.

Rajasthani ingredients *include* sangri *beans, tangy* kair *berries and* amchur *(dried strips of sour mango).*

THE RAJASTHANI THALI

Though fresh vegetables are scarce in this desert land, a Rajasthani meal offers great variety. *Chilla* bread, *mirchi pakora* fritters and *gatta kadhi* curry show the many ways of cooking lentil flour. Vegetables include *makki* (corn) and *bhindi* (okra). *Laal maas* and *safed maas* are spicy mutton dishes, specialities of the Rajput community. *Ghewar* is a crunchy, syrup-soaked cake with a honeycomb texture, made of wheat or lentil flour.

Ghewar **(fried wheat cake)**

Khata (lentil and yoghurt soup)

Dahi pakora (lentil dumplings in yoghurt)

Sangri (desert bean)

Pudina chatni (mint chutney)

Mirchi pakora (chilli fritter)

Aam ka achaar (mango pickle)

Suji halwa (wheat germ pudding)

Dal (lentil purée)

Gatta kadhi (lentil rolls curry)

Poori (deep-fried bread)

Masala roti (flavoured bread)

Besan halwa (split pea flour pudding)

Lal maas **(mutton curry with red chillies)**

Safed maas **(mutton curry with almonds and yoghurt)**

Makki soyta **(corn kernels in gravy)**

Bhindi sabzi **(stir-fried okra and tomato)**

THE GUJARATI THALI

A variety of flavours, textures and tastes blend harmoniously in a vegetarian Gujarati *thali*. Protein-rich *dals* (lentils) are eaten with *undhiyo* (vegetables roasted in an earthen pot), savoury breads such as *thepla* and *rotli*, and crisp *khakra* wafers. Sweet *shrikhand* (saffron-flavoured yoghurt) and *aamras* (mango fool) are eaten with *poori* (fried puffed bread).

Rotli (baked bread)

Khakra (crisp wheat wafer)

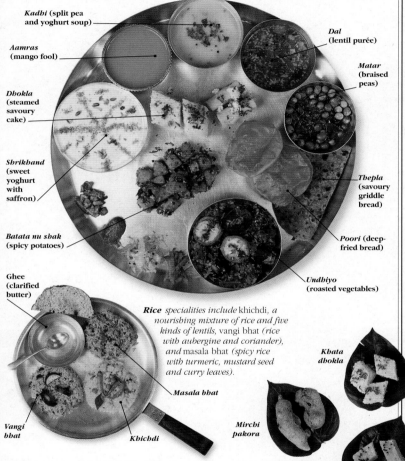

Kadhi (split pea and yoghurt soup)

Aamras (mango fool)

Dhokla (steamed savoury cake)

Shrikhand (sweet yoghurt with saffron)

Batata nu shak (spicy potatoes)

Ghee (clarified butter)

Dal (lentil purée)

Matar (braised peas)

Thepla (savoury griddle bread)

Poori (deep-fried bread)

Undhiyo (roasted vegetables)

Rice specialities include khichdi, *a nourishing mixture of rice and five kinds of lentils,* vangi bhat *(rice with aubergine and coriander), and* masala bhat *(spicy rice with turmeric, mustard seed and curry leaves).*

Masala bhat

Vangi bhat

Khichdi

Khata dhokla

Mirchi pakora

Khaman dhokla

Khandvi

Pickles are an essential part of the Gujarati meal. They are often made of keri *(sour green mango), seasoned with garlic, chillies and molasses, and spices such as aniseed, mustard and fenugreek.*

God keri (mango pickle with molasses)

Khati keri (sour mango pickle)

Chunda (sweet-sour mango chutney)

Farsaan, *delicious savoury snacks, include* dhokla *(steamed spongy cakes of split pea flour and yoghurt),* khandvi *(split pea flour rolls filled with coconut), and* mirchi pakora *(green chilli fritters).*

RAJASTHAN

N O STATE IN INDIA is as rich in magnificent palaces and forts, colourful festivals and bazaars, as Rajasthan. Stretching over 342,000 sq km (132,047 sq miles), the state is bisected by the Aravalli Range, which runs diagonally from the northeast to the southwest. Its main river is the Chambal. The Thar Desert, which covers western Rajasthan, was once ruled by three great kingdoms – Jaisalmer, Jodhpur and Bikaner. Shekhawati, with its painted *havelis,* is in the semi-arid north while the eastern plains have the bustling state capital, Jaipur, and the Ranthambhore National Park, famous for its tigers. In the hilly, wooded south are the fairy-tale palaces, lakes and forts of Udaipur, and the spectacular Jain temples at Ranakpur, and Dilwara in Mount Abu.

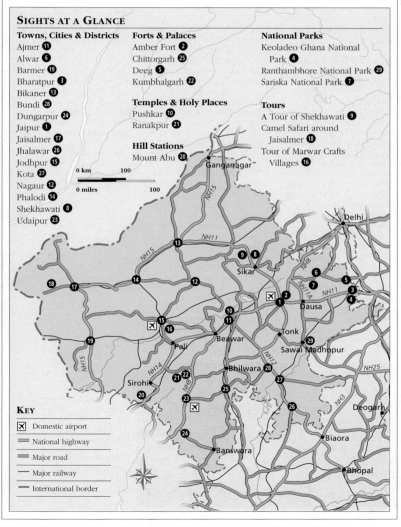

SIGHTS AT A GLANCE

Towns, Cities & Districts
Ajmer ⑪
Alwar ⑥
Barmer ⑲
Bharatpur ③
Bikaner ⑬
Bundi ㉘
Dungarpur ㉔
Jaipur ①
Jaisalmer ⑰
Jhalawar ㉖
Jodhpur ⑮
Kota ㉗
Nagaur ⑫
Phalodi ⑭
Shekhawati ⑧
Udaipur ㉓

Forts & Palaces
Amber Fort ②
Chittorgarh ㉕
Deeg ⑤
Kumbhalgarh ㉒

Temples & Holy Places
Pushkar ⑩
Ranakpur ㉑

Hill Stations
Mount Abu ⑳

National Parks
Keoladeo Ghana National Park ④
Ranthambhore National Park ㉙
Sariska National Park ⑦

Tours
A Tour of Shekhawati ⑨
Camel Safari around Jaisalmer ⑱
Tour of Marwar Crafts Villages ⑯

0 km   100

0 miles   100

KEY
☒ Domestic airport
▬ National highway
▬ Major road
— Major railway
⋯ International border

◁ **Detail of the exquisitely carved stone façade of the 19th-century Patwon ki Haveli, Jaisalmer**

Jaipur ❶

Stone guardian at Hawa Mahal

A LABYRINTH OF fascinating bazaars, opulent palaces and historic sights, Jaipur is often called the "Pink City" because its prominent buildings are washed in this colour. Tradition and modernity exist side by side here. On its colourful streets, motorbikes jostle for space with camels, and turbaned village elders rub shoulders with youngsters in jeans. Jaipur's old walled area has the City Palace, an astronomical observatory and bazaars that sell everything from shoes to jewellery. Recent additions include a multi-arts centre, but the focal point remains the Hawa Mahal.

Govind Dev Temple, dedicated to Krishna

🏛 City Palace Museum
See pp356–7.

🛕 Govind Dev Temple
Jaleb Chowk (behind City Palace). ◯ *daily.* 🎫 *Holi (Mar), Janmashtami (Jul/Aug), Annakut (Oct/Nov).*
The presiding deity of this unusual temple is the flute-playing Lord Krishna (also known as Govind Dev). The image of this god originally came from the Govindeoji Temple in Brindavan (*see p179*). It was brought to Amber (*see pp364–5*), then the capital of Jaipur's ruling family, in the late 17th century to save it from the iconoclastic zeal of the Mughal emperor Aurangzeb.

It is believed that this temple was once a garden pavilion called Suraj Mahal where Sawai Jai Singh II lived while his dream-city, Jaipur, was being built. Legend has it that one night the king awoke from his sleep to find himself in the presence of Krishna who demanded that his *devasthan* ("divine residence")

be returned to him. Jai Singh then moved to the Chandra Mahal, at the opposite end of the garden, and installed the image as the guardian deity of Jaipur's rulers.

Just behind the temple is the 18th-century **Jai Niwas Bagh**, a Mughal-style garden with fountains and water channels. Towards the north is the Badal Mahal, an enchanting hunting pavilion.

🛕 Chaugan Stadium
Brahmpuri. ◯ *daily.*
This large open area near the City Palace derives its name from *chaugan*, an ancient Persian form of polo played with a curved stick. The area was once used for festival processions and wrestling matches, as well as elephant and lion fights. Today the stadium, with its viewing pavilions, is the venue for the famous Elephant Festival (*see p371*) held at the same time as the Holi celebrations.

🛕 Hawa Mahal
Sireh Deori Bazaar. 📞 *(0141) 66 8862.* ◯ *daily.* ● *public hols.* 🎫 📷 *extra charges.* 🎫
A whimsical addition to Rajasthan's rich architectural vocabulary, the fanciful Hawa Mahal or "Palace of Winds" was erected in 1799 by the aesthete Sawai Pratap Singh (r.1778–1803). Its ornate pink façade has become an icon for the city. The tiered Baroque-like composition of projecting windows and balconies with perforated screens is

A view of the walled city of Jaipur

SIGHTS AT A GLANCE

five storeys high but just one room deep, its walls not more than 20 cm (8 inches) thick. Built of lime and mortar, the structure was designed in this way to enable the veiled ladies of the harem to observe unnoticed the lively street scenes below. Dedicated to Lord Krishna, the Hawa Mahal, seen from afar, looks like the *mukut* (crown) that

often adorns the god's head. Visitors can climb up the winding ramp to the top, and a gateway towards the west leads into the complex. Within are administrative offices and the **Archaeological Museum**, which houses a small collection of sculptures and local handicrafts, including some utensils dating back to the 2nd century BC.

VISITORS' CHECKLIST

Jaipur district. 261 km (162 miles) SW of Delhi. 🚇 2,324,500.
✈ 15 km (9 miles) S of city centre. 🚌 🚉 Paryatan Bhavan, Mirza Ismail Rd, (0141) 41 0595.
🕑 Mon–Sat. 🎏 Kite Flying Festival (14 Jan), Elephant Festival (Mar), Gangaur (Mar/Apr), Teej (Jul/Aug).

🏛 **Government Central Museum**

Ram Niwas Bagh. ☎ (0141) 56 5124. 🕑 Sat–Thu. ● public hols. 🎫 free on Mon.

Also known as Albert Hall, this grand, multi-layered museum was designed by Sir Samuel Swinton Jacob, a master of the Indo-Saracenic style *(see p22)*.

The museum's ground floor displays decorative shields, embossed salvers in Jaipur's famous metalware, and some good examples of local glazed pottery. A 9-m (30-ft) long *phad* (painted cloth scroll), depicts the life of Pabuji, a 14th-century folk hero *(see p381)*. The first floor has a fine collection of Mughal and Rajput miniature paintings. The museum's greatest treasure, one of the world's largest Persian garden carpets (dating from 1632), can be seen on request in the Durbar Hall.

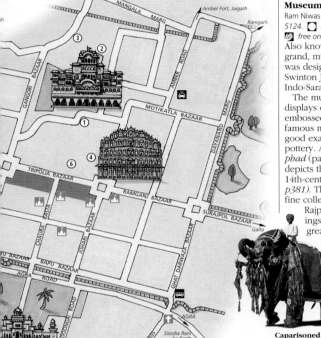

Caparisoned elephant at a festival

♫ **Jantar Mantar**
See pp358–9.

THE BUILDING OF JAIPUR

Sawai Jai Singh II was a keen scholar, statesman and patron of the arts. He was awarded the title of "Sawai" ("one-and-a-quarter"), a metaphor for one who is extraordinary, by the Mughal emperor Aurangzeb when he was just 11 years old. With the help of a gifted Bengali engineer, Vidyadhar Chakravarty, Jai Singh built a new capital south of Amber and named it Jaipur ("City of Victory"). Work began in 1727 and took six years to complete.

Sawai Jai Singh II (r.1700–43)

Surrounded by a crenellated wall pierced by seven gates, Jaipur is laid out in a geometric grid of streets and squares and is one of India's finest examples of a planned city.

KEY

■	Street-by-Street area: *see pp354–5*
🚌	Bus station
🛈	Tourist information
✉	Post office
🚓	Police station
🛕	Temple
✝	Church

Jal Mahal, Gaitor
MANGALA MARG
Amber Fort, Jaigarh
Ramgarh
GANGORI BAZAAR
AMBER ROAD
MOTIKATLA BAZAAR
DAYANAND MARG
TRIPOLIA BAZAAR
RAMGANJ BAZAAR
KASTA
CHAURA RASTA
JOHARI BAZAAR
GHAT DARWAZA BAZAAR
SURAJPOL BAZAAR
Galta
BAPU BAZAAR
U BAZAAR
AGRA ROAD
MOTI DOONGRI ROAD
NEB BYPASS
AGRA
Sisodia Rani ka Bagh
Moti Doongri Palace
awahar Kala Kendra, irport, ANGANER

Street-by-Street: Around Badi Chaupar

THE BADI CHAUPAR ("Large Square") is at one end of the colourful Tripolia Bazaar. Few changes have been made to the original 18th-century plan of streets and squares. Branching out of the main streets are narrow pedestrian lanes where artisans fashion puppets, silver jewellery, and other local handicrafts in tiny workshops. Behind are the *havelis* of eminent citizens, some used as schools, shops and offices. The area is a hub of activity, rich with pungent smells and vibrant colours, with temple bells adding to the cacophony of street sounds.

★ Jantar Mantar
Jai Singh II's observatory of astronomical instruments looks like a series of futuristic sculptures (see pp358–9).

Ishwar Lat
Ishwari Singh built this tower in 1749 to commemorate his victory over his stepbrother, Madho Singh I.

Tripolia Gate
Constructed in 1734, this impressive gate was once the main entrance to the palace.

City Palace

← Chandpol

Chhoti Chaupar
("Small Square") leads to Kishanpol Bazaar, famous for its shops selling rose-, saffron-, almond- and vetiver-flavoured sherbets.

TRIPOLIA

MANIHARON KA RASTA

NATANIYON KA RASTA

KISHANPOL BAZAAR

Maharaja Arts College

Flower Sellers
Marigolds and other flowers are made into garlands and used as offerings to beloved deities in temples and roadside shrines.

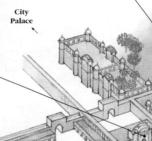

Lac Bangles
Maniharon ka Rasta is full of tiny workshops of lac bangle makers.

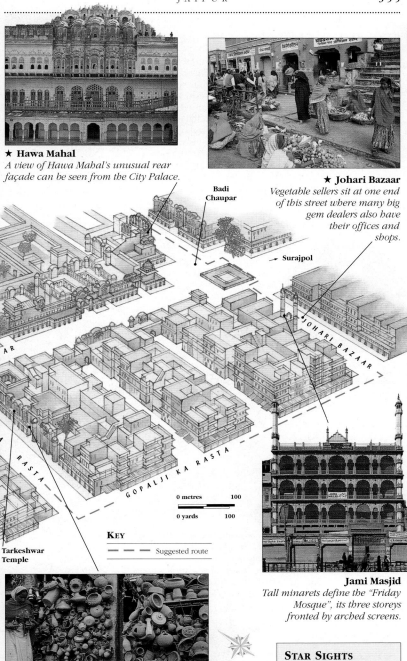

★ **Hawa Mahal**
A view of Hawa Mahal's unusual rear façade can be seen from the City Palace.

Badi Chaupar

★ **Johari Bazaar**
Vegetable sellers sit at one end of this street where many big gem dealers also have their offices and shops.

→ **Surajpol**

JOHARI BAZAAR

AAR

RASTA

KA RASTA

GOPALJI KA RASTA

0 metres	100
0 yards	100

KEY

– – – Suggested route

Tarkeshwar Temple

Jami Masjid
Tall minarets define the "Friday Mosque", its three storeys fronted by arched screens.

Pottery Shop
Large terracotta urns, pots of all sizes, bells, statues, foot-scrapers and oil lamps made by traditional craftsmen are sold here.

STAR SIGHTS

★ **Jantar Mantar**

★ **Hawa Mahal**

★ **Johari Bazaar**

City Palace Museum

Jaipur's coat of arms

OCCUPYING THE HEART of Jai Singh II's city, the City Palace has been home to the rulers of Jaipur since the first half of the 18th century. The sprawling complex is a superb blend of Rajput and Mughal architecture, with open, airy Mughal-style public buildings leading to private apartments. Today, part of the complex is open to the public as the Maharaja Sawai Man Singh II Museum, popularly known as the City Palace Museum. Its treasures, which include miniature paintings, manuscripts, Mughal carpets, musical instruments, royal costumes and weaponry, provide a splendid introduction to Jaipur's princely past, and its fascinating arts and crafts.

★ Pritam Chowk
The "Court of the Beloved" has four delicately painted doorways representing the seasons.

Sileh Khana
The erstwhile armoury houses the museum's collection of weapons, among the finest in India. Some pieces, such as this shield, are lavishly decorated.

Crafts demonstration area

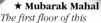

★ Mubarak Mahal
The first floor of this sandstone palace houses a dazzling collection of royal costumes and textiles, such as this gossamer-fine gold-embroidered skirt.

STAR FEATURES
★ Pritam Chowk
★ Mubarak Mahal
★ Rajendra Pol
★ Silver Urns

★ Rajendra Pol
Flanking this gateway are two large elephants, each carved from single blocks of marble.

Chandra Mahal

Each floor of this seven-storeyed palace is extravagantly decorated and has a specific name according to its function. The palace is closed to the public.

Riddhi-Siddhi Pol

★ Silver Urns

The two giant silver urns in the Diwan-i-Khas, listed in the Guinness Book of Records as the world's largest silver objects, carried sacred Ganges water for Madho Singh II's visit to London in 1901.

Shops

Transport gallery

Entrance   **Ticket counter**

Diwan-i-Aam

The former ceremonial hall now displays rare Mughal and Rajput miniature paintings, as well as carpets, manuscripts, a superbly crafted silver throne and an ivory elephant howdah.

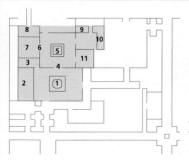

THE CITY PALACE

1 Mubarak Mahal
2 Crafts Demonstration Area
3 Sileh Khana
4 Rajendra Pol
5 Diwan-i-Khas
6 Riddhi-Siddhi Pol
7 Pritam Chowk
8 Chandra Mahal
9 Shops
10 Transport Gallery
11 Diwan-i-Aam

KEY

☐ Area illustrated

0 metres   200
0 yards   200

Jantar Mantar

Kantivrita Yantra

O F THE FIVE OBSERVATORIES built by Sawai Jai Singh II, the one in Jaipur is the largest and best preserved; the others are in Delhi *(see p78)*, Ujjain, Mathura and Varanasi. A keen astronomer himself, Jai Singh kept abreast of the latest astronomical studies in the world, and was most inspired by the work of Mirza Ulugh Beg, the astronomer-king of Samarkand. Built between 1728 and 1734, the observatory has been described as "the most realistic and logical landscape in stone", its 16 instruments resembling a giant sculptural composition. Some of the instruments are still used to forecast how hot the summer months will be, the expected date of arrival, duration and intensity of the monsoon, and the possibility of floods and famine.

Narivalaya Yantra
Inclined at 27°, these sundials represent the two hemispheres and calculate time by following the solar cycle.

Unnatansha Yantra
was used to determine the positions of stars and planets at any time of day or night.

Laghu Samrat Yantra
This "small sundial" is constructed on Latitude 27° North (Jaipur's latitude) and calculates Jaipur's local time up to an accuracy of 20 seconds.

City Palace Museum

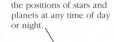

Chakra Yantra
A brass tube passes through the centre of these two circular metal instruments. They can be used to calculate the angles of stars and planets from the equator.

Entrance

★ Ram Yantra
Vertical columns support an equal number of horizontal slabs in the two identical stone structures that comprise this instrument. Its readings determine the celestial arc from horizon to zenith, as well as the altitude of the sun.

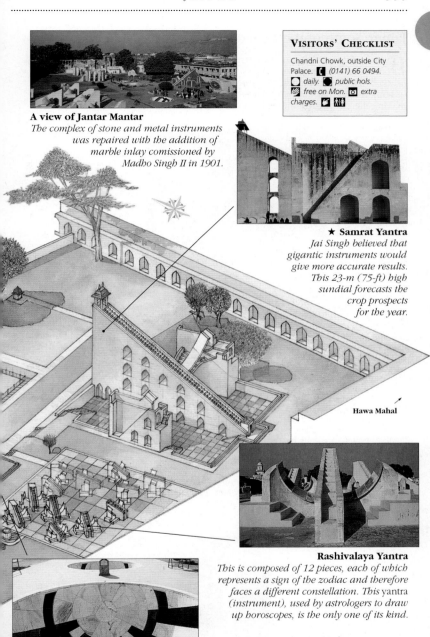

A view of Jantar Mantar
The complex of stone and metal instruments was repaired with the addition of marble inlay comissioned by Madho Singh II in 1901.

VISITORS' CHECKLIST

Chandni Chowk, outside City Palace. (0141) 66 0494. daily. public hols. free on Mon. extra charges.

★ Samrat Yantra
Jai Singh believed that gigantic instruments would give more accurate results. This 23-m (75-ft) high sundial forecasts the crop prospects for the year.

Hawa Mahal

Rashivalaya Yantra
This is composed of 12 pieces, each of which represents a sign of the zodiac and therefore faces a different constellation. This yantra (instrument), used by astrologers to draw up horoscopes, is the only one of its kind.

★ Jai Prakash Yantra
These two sunken hemispheres map out the heavens. Some historians believe that Jai Singh invented this instrument himself, to verify the accuracy of all the other instruments in the observatory.

STAR FEATURES

★ Ram Yantra

★ Samrat Yantra

★ Jai Prakash Yantra

Jaipur: South of the Walled City

BY THE END of the 19th century, Jaipur had expanded far beyond the boundaries of the walled city established by Sawai Jai Singh II. Many new pleasure palaces, hunting lodges and mansions came up on its outskirts, making the city a harmonious blend of old and new.

Lakshmi Narayan Temple, a white marble addition to the Pink City

🏯 Moti Doongri Palace

Jawaharlal Nehru Marg.
🔵 to the public.

Moti Doongri palace, perched on a low hillock, owes its florid exterior to Sawai Man Singh II, who converted the old fort of Shankargarh into a palace, and added turrets in the style of a Scottish castle. In 1940 he married the beautiful Princess Gayatri Devi of Cooch Behar, and this palace with its modernized interior became the venue for glittering parties hosted by the glamorous couple.

At the foot of Moti Doongri is the white marble **Lakshmi Narayan Temple**, a popular place of worship, admired for its elaborate carvings.

🏯 Rambagh Palace

Bhawani Singh Rd. 🗔 (0141) 38 1919. 🍽 open to non-residents.

The Rambagh Palace, now a splendid hotel (see p703), has a colourful past. Built in 1835, it was originally a small garden pavilion for Ram Singh II's wet nurse, but was used as a hunting lodge after she died in 1856. Later, on his return from England, Ram Singh II's son Madho Singh II transformed it into a royal playground with squash and tennis courts, a polo field and an indoor swimming pool. In 1933, it became the official residence of Madho Singh's adopted heir, Man Singh II,

who hired Hammonds of London to redo the interiors. New additions included an exotic red and gold Chinese room, black marble bathrooms, Lalique crystal chandeliers and an illuminated dining table. Surrounded by fairy-tale gardens, it became a hotel in 1957, when Man Singh II moved to the smaller Raj Mahal Palace.

Jawahar Kala Kendra

🏯 Raj Mahal Palace

Sardar Patel Marg. 🗔 (0141) 38 1757. 🍽 open to non-residents.

Now a grand heritage hotel (see p703), this pleasant 18th-

century palace, less opulent than the Rambagh Palace, occupies a special place in the history of Jaipur. Built in 1739 for Sawai Jai Singh II's favourite queen, Chandra Kumari Ranawatji, it was used as a summer resort by the ladies of the court. In 1821, it was declared the official home of the British Resident in Jaipur. However, the most glamorous and memorable phase of its history dates to the time when Man Singh II and Gayatri Devi moved here from Rambagh Palace in 1956. Among the celebrities they entertained were Prince Philip, a polo player like Man Singh II, and Jackie Kennedy.

🏛 Jawahar Kala Kendra

Jawaharlal Nehru Marg. 🗔 (0141) 51 0501. 🔵 daily. 📷 🎭

Designed by the Indian architect Charles Correa in 1993, this remarkable building pays vivid tribute to contemporary Indian design. Imaginatively patterned after the famous grid system of the city, each of its nine squares or courts houses a small *mahal,* or palace, named after a planet. Each one displays selected exhibits of textiles, handicrafts and weaponry, while in the centre there is a wonderfully conceived open-air plaza where performances of traditional Rajasthani music and dance are held.

The luxurious interior of Rambagh Palace, now a hotel

Jaipur Jewellery

BE IT THE FABULOUS rubies and emeralds sported by former maharajas and their queens or the splendid silver and bone ornaments worn by peasants, jewellery is an integral part of Rajasthani culture. Even camels, horses and elephants have specially designed anklets and necklaces. Jaipur is one of the largest ornament-making centres in India, and *meenakari* (enamel work) and *kundankari* (inlay work with gems) are the two traditional

A kundankari pendant

techniques for which it is most famous. In the 16th century, Man Singh I *(see p364)*, influenced by the prevailing fashions of the Mughal court, brought five Sikh enamel workers from Lahore to his state. Since then, generations of highly skilled jewellers have lived and worked here. Jaipur caters to every taste, from chunky silver ornaments to more sophisticated designs intricately set in gold with precious stones.

A jewelled trinket box *with a* kundankari *lid; the lower portion of this box is worked in fine* meenakari *and has traditional floral patterns in red, blue, green and white.*

Sarpech, *the cypress-shaped turban ornament, was a fashion statement introduced by the Mughal emperors in the early 17th century to display their finest gems. Rajput rulers, impressed by Mughal flamboyance, sported similar dazzling ornaments such as this piece of enamelled gold set with emeralds, rubies, diamonds and sapphires, finished with a pearl drop.*

The skill of stone-setting *can be seen in the crowded alleys of Haldiyon ka Rasta, Jadiyon ka Rasta and Gopalji ka Rasta. An inherited art, the jewellery trade is in the hands of artisans' guilds.*

Meenakari *embellishes the obverse side of* kundan *jewellery, for the Rajasthani love of adornment decrees that even the back of a piece of jewellery (left) must be as beautiful as the front (right).*

Kundankari *uses highly refined gold as a base, which is then inlaid with lac and set with precious and semi-precious stones to provide colour and design. Purified gold wire outlines the design and also conceals the lac background.*

Jaipur *is now a centre of lapidary, specializing in cutting emeralds and diamonds from Africa, South America and various regions of India. Gem-cutters learn their skill by cutting garnets.*

Exploring Jaipur: Outer Sites

A PARALLEL RANGE OF HILLS runs along Jaipur's eastern periphery, from Sanganer in the south up to Amber and beyond, enclosing a narrow valley. Consisting of thickly wooded slopes and rocky terrain, this was the area where the nobility built temples, gardens, pavilions and palaces. Perched high above the city are the dramatic fortresses of Nahargarh and Jaigarh that guarded the approach to both Amber and the new capital of Jaipur. The surrounding region also has the remains of fortified walls, temples, *havelis* and the marble cenotaphs of the Kachhawaha kings of Amber and Jaipur.

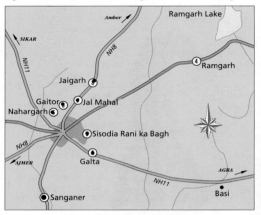

SIGHTS AT A GLANCE

Gaitor ⑥
Galta ②
Jaigarh ⑧
Jal Mahal ⑦
Nahargarh ⑤
Ramgarh ④
Sanganer ①
Sisodia Rani ka Bagh ③

KEY

■ Jaipur city centre
═ National highway
═ Major road

0 kms   25
0 miles   25

Marble statue of a Jain *tirthankara* at Sanganer's Sanghiji Temple

Sanganer

Jaipur district, 15 km (9 miles) SW of Jaipur.

This colourful town is famous for its blockprinted cotton. Today most of its printers and dyers belong to a guild, with retail outlets selling reasonably priced fabrics. Sanganer owes its success as a printing centre to a rivulet whose waters have a mineral content that fixes dyes. Sanganer is also a centre of handmade paper, and of Jaipur's renowned, hand-painted Blue Pottery, of which vases and tiles with delicate Persian, Turkish and Indian designs are made. Tucked away in the old walled town is the impressive 11th-century Jain **Sanghiji Temple**, lavishly decorated with carvings. Sanganer is now a busy suburb of Jaipur city and houses the city's airport.

A sacred tank in Galta

🏠 Galta

Jaipur district. 10 km (6 miles) E of Jaipur.

This picturesque gorge cradles Galta Kund, an 18th-century religious site with two main temples and a number of smaller shrines. Its seven sacred tanks, fed by natural spring water, are said to have curative powers. Two pavilions on either side of the complex have well-preserved frescoes. The Surya Temple, high on the ridge, provides spectacular views of Jaipur.

🍀 Sisodia Rani ka Bagh

Jaipur district. Purana Ghat. 6 km (4 miles) E of Jaipur. 📞 (0141) 64 0594. ◯ daily. 📷

This terraced garden was laid out in the 18th century for Sawai Jai Singh II's second

The picturesque Jal Mahal, seemingly afloat during the monsoon

wife, who married him on the condition that her son would succeed to the throne. To escape the inevitable palace intrigues, the queen moved to a more private home outside the walled city. Her little double-storeyed palace, decorated with lively murals, is surrounded by beautiful gardens. It is today a popular location for Indian films.

Ramgarh

Jaipur district. 40 km (25 miles) E of Jaipur.

Ramgarh is the site of one of the earliest Kachhawaha fortresses. The fort was built by the dynasty's founder, Duleh Rai (r.1093–1135), who also built a temple dedicated to the goddess Jamvai Mata, now visited by thousands of devotees. Ramgarh Lodge, on the northern bank of a man-made lake, is an elegant French villa-style hunting lodge built in 1931 for the Jaipur royal family. It is now a pleasant heritage hotel with one of the best polo grounds in the country.

Nahargarh

Jaipur district. 9 km (6 miles) NW of Jaipur. (0141) 32 0538. daily. public hols.

The forbidding hill-top fort of Nahargarh ("Tiger Fort") stands in what was once a densely forested area. The fierce Meena tribe ruled this region until they were defeated by the Kachhawahas. Its fortifications, strengthened by Sawai Jai Singh II, were subsequently expanded by successive rulers. Madho Singh II added a lavish palace called Madhavendra Bhavan for his nine queens. Laid out in a maze of terraces and

courtyards, it has a cool, airy upper chamber from which the ladies of the court could view the city. Its walls and pillars are an outstanding example of *arayish*, a form of plaster work that is hand-polished with a piece of agate to produce a marble finish.

Gaitor

Jaipur district. 8 km (5 miles) N of Jaipur. daily. public hols.

The marble cenotaphs of the Kachhawaha kings are enclosed in a walled garden just off the Amber road. This area was chosen by Sawai Jai Singh II as the new cremation site after Amber (*see pp364–5*) was abandoned. Ornate carved pillars support the marble *chhatris* erected over the platforms where the maharajas were cremated. One of the most impressive cenotaphs in the complex is that of Jai Singh II himself. It has 20 marble pillars carved with religious and mythological scenes and is topped by a white marble

dome. The most recent cenotaph was erected in 1997 in memory of Jagat Singh, the only son of Sawai Man Singh II and Gayatri Devi.

Jal Mahal

Jaipur district. 8 km (5 miles) N of Jaipur. daily.

During the monsoon, water fills the Man Sagar lake, and the Jal Mahal ("Water Palace") seems to rise from it like a mirage. Built in the mid-18th century by Madho Singh I, it is inspired by the Lake Palace at Udaipur, where the king spent his childhood. It was later used for royal duck-shooting parties, and a variety of water birds are still seen here. The terraced garden, enclosed by arched passages, has an elegant semi-octagonal tower capped by a cupola in each corner.

Jaigarh

Jaipur district. 12 km (8 miles) NW of Jaipur. (0141) 63 0848. daily. public hols.

Legendary Jaigarh, the "Victory Fort", watches over the old capital of Amber. One of the few surviving cannon foundries is located here. Its most prized possession is the monumental 50-tonne Jai Van, cast in 1726 and said to be the world's largest cannon on wheels. Ironically, despite its impressive size, the cannon has never been fired.

The famous Jai Van

Other interesting sights are the Diva Burj, a seven-storeyed tower where a huge oil lamp was lit on the king's birthday, two temples and a palace built over 200 years ago.

The ramparts of Jaigarh Fort, a feat of military engineering

Amber Fort ❷

Detail of door at Shila Devi

T̲HE FORT PALACE OF AMBER was the Kachhawaha citadel until 1727, when their capital moved to Jaipur. Successive rulers continued to come here on important occasions to seek the blessings of the family deity, Shila Devi. The citadel was established in 1592 by Man Singh I on the remains of an old 11th-century fort, but the various buildings added by Jai Singh I (r.1621– 67) are what constitute its magnificent centrepiece.

Elephant ride on the cobbled pathway to the fort

Aram Bagh, the pleasure garden.

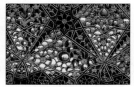

★ Sheesh Mahal
The flame of a single candle, reflected in the tiny mirrors embedded in this chamber, transforms it into a starlit sky.

Jas Mandir
This Hall of Private Audience has latticed windows, a floral ceiling of elegant alabaster relief work and glass inlay. A marble screen here overlooks the Maota Lake and allows in cool air.

Jai Mandir

A view of Amber Fort
Protected by Jaigarh Fort, the massive ramparts of Amber Fort follow the contours of a natural ridge.

STAR FEATURES

★ Sheesh Mahal

★ Ganesh Pol

★ Shila Devi Temple

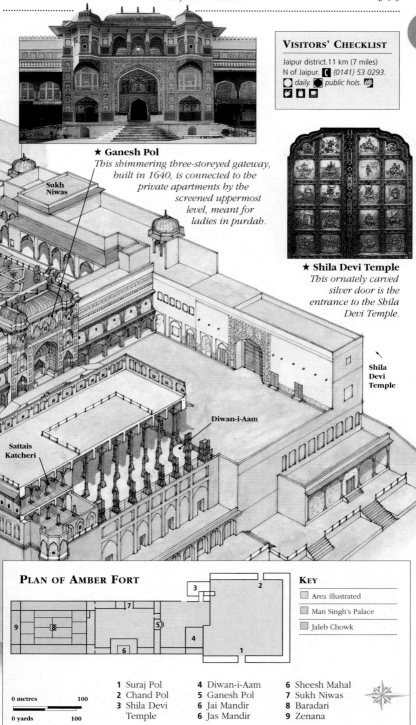

★ Ganesh Pol
This shimmering three-storeyed gateway, built in 1640, is connected to the private apartments by the screened uppermost level, meant for ladies in purdah.

Sukh Niwas

VISITORS' CHECKLIST

Jaipur district. 11 km (7 miles)
N of Jaipur. (0141) 53 0293.
daily. public hols.

★ Shila Devi Temple
This ornately carved silver door is the entrance to the Shila Devi Temple.

Shila Devi Temple

Diwan-i-Aam

Sattais Katcheri

PLAN OF AMBER FORT

KEY

Area illustrated
Man Singh's Palace
Jaleb Chowk

0 metres   100
0 yards   100

1 Suraj Pol	4 Diwan-i-Aam	6 Sheesh Mahal
2 Chand Pol	5 Ganesh Pol	7 Sukh Niwas
3 Shila Devi Temple	6 Jai Mandir	8 Baradari
	6 Jas Mandir	9 Zenana

Exploring Amber (the Old Capital)

Detail of painting on Ganesh Pol

CROWNING THE CREST of a hill, Amber Fort offers a panoramic view of Maota Lake and the historic old town at the base of the hill, which was the early seat of the Amber kings before they made the fort their capital. Several havelis, stepwells, and temples can be seen below the fort, pointing to the existence of a self-sufficient township, where the Mughal emperor Akbar used to stop on his annual pilgrimage to Ajmer *(see p376)*.

Sattais Katcheri, where the revenue records were written

The Fort Complex

The main entrance to the historic Amber Fort is through the imposing **Suraj Pol** ("Sun Gate"), so called because it faces the direction of the rising sun, the Kachhawaha family emblem. The gate leads into a huge courtyard, **Jaleb Chowk**, lined on three sides with souvenir and refreshment shops. A flight of steps leads to the **Shila Devi Temple**, which has silver doors, silver oil lamps, grand pillars carved to look like banana trees, and contains the Kachhawaha family deity, a stone *(shila)* image of the goddess Kali. The next courtyard is the

Diwan-i-Aam, the space for public audience. Near it is the **Sattais Katcheri**, a colonnade of 27 *(sattais)* pillars, where scribes once sat to record revenue petitions.

The magnificent **Ganesh Pol** is the gateway to three pleasure palaces, each with special features, built around a Mughal-style garden, **Aram Bagh**. Maota Lake, which provided water to the fort, is surrounded by two exquisite gardens. The **Kesar Kyari Bagh** has star-shaped flower beds once planted with

Marble carving of a Hindu deity

saffron *(kesar)* flowers, while **Dilaram Bagh**, built in 1568 as a resting place for Akbar on his way to Ajmer, is a clever pun on the name of its architect, Dilaram ("Heart's Ease"). A small Archaeological Museum is located nearby. The farthest and oldest end of the fort was converted into the zenana (women's quarters), with screens and covered balconies for the seclusion of the royal ladies in purdah. Faint traces of frescoes are still visible on the walls. In the centre of the courtyard is a pavilion with 12 pillars, the **Baradari**.

The Township

The **Chand Pol** ("Moon Gate"), directly opposite Suraj Pol, leads to the old town outside the fort. The beautiful **Jagat Shiromani Temple** with its remarkable *torana* (gateway) is one of the many temples that lies along this route. It also has a water tank, **Panna Mian ka Kund**. To the east lies **Sagar**, a popular picnic spot with two terraced lakes. The Jaipur-Delhi Highway cuts across the town, and Amber's main market and bus stand are located on this road. Further north stands the **Akbari Mosque**, built by Emperor Akbar in 1569, and towards the east is **Bharmal ki Chhatri**, a walled enclosure containing a group of memorials. This was the old cremation site for the rulers of Amber until a new spot was chosen at Gaitor *(see p363)*, near Jaipur.

Kesar Kyari Bagh, named after the rare saffron flowers once planted in its star-shaped flower beds

Bharatpur ❸

Bharatpur district. 181 km (112 miles)
E of Jaipur. 🚶 204,500. 🚌
ℹ️ RTDC Hotel Saras, (05644) 22 542.
🎭 Jaswant Mela (Oct).

MOST FAMOUS for its bird sanctuary, the kingdom of Bharatpur was founded by the fearless Jats, a community of landowners. Their

The moat and ramparts of Lohagarh

most remarkable leader, Raja Suraj Mal (r.1724–63), fortified the city of Bharatpur in 1733 and used the loot from Mughal buildings to embellish the forts and palaces of his kingdom.

In the centre of the town is **Lohagarh** ("Iron Fort"), a masterpiece of construction. Its massive double ramparts of packed mud and rubble surrounded by impressive moats withstood repeated attacks by the Marathas and the British until it was finally captured by Lord Lake in 1805. Three palaces built in the fort display a fine mix of Mughal and Rajput stylistic detail. One is now the site of a pharmaceutical

college, while the other two, around the Katcheri Bagh, house the **State Museum**. Its artifacts include a rare collection of 1st- and 2nd-century stone carvings. An interesting sunken *hamam* (bath) is close by. In 1818, Bharatpur became the region's first princely state to sign a treaty with the East India Company.

🏛 **State Museum**
📞 (05644) 28 185. ◯ Fri–Wed.
⬤ public hols. 🎫 free on Mon.
📷 extra charges.

Keoladeo Ghana National Park ❹

See pp368–9.

Deeg ❺

Bharatpur district. 36 km (22 miles)
N of Bharatpur. 🚌 ℹ️ RTDC Hotel
Saras, Bharatpur, (05644) 22 542. 🎭
Holi (Mar), Jawahar Mela (Aug).
Water Palace ◯ daily. ⬤ the day
after Holi (Mar). 🎫

ONCE THE CAPITAL of the Jat kings of Bharatpur, Deeg rose to prominence after the decline of the Mughal empire in the 18th century. Its square fort and fortified town, once filled with grand mansions and gardens, now lie unkempt

and forlorn. Deeg's Raja Suraj Mal and his son, Jawahar Singh, were keen builders of lavish pleasure palaces and the most remarkable of these is the **Deeg Water Palace**, a romantic summer retreat for the Jat kings. The magic of the monsoon inspired a lyrical composition of sandstone and marble pavilions replete with gardens and pools. A skilful cooling system drew water from a huge reservoir and used a number of innovative special effects to simulate monsoon showers and even

Sawan Pavilion, Deeg Water Palace

produce rainbows. The coloured fountains are now used only during the Jawahar Mela.

DEEG WATER PALACE

Sawan Pavilion is shaped like an upturned boat. Its ingenious water system created a semi-circle of falling water.

Nand Bhavan

Keshav Bhavan had heavy lithic balls placed on its roof, that rolled and produced "thunder" when water gushed up the hollow pillars and pipes inside the arches.

Entrance

Gopal Bhavan's numerous overhanging kiosks and balconies are reflected in Gopal Sagar from which it seems to rise. The interior still retains the original furnishings and objets d'art.

The roof-top reservoir had water drawn to it from four wells. Pipes leading from its sides supplied water to the chutes and fountains.

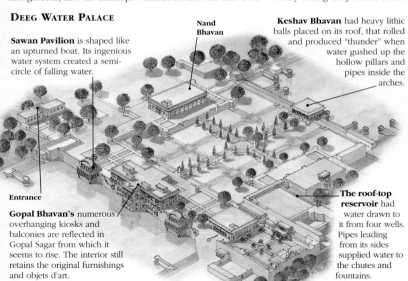

Keoladeo Ghana National Park ④

A UNESCO WORLD HERITAGE SITE regarded as one of the world's most important bird sanctuaries, Keoladeo Ghana derives its name from a Shiva temple (Keoladeo) within a dense forest *(ghana)*. This once-arid scrubland was first developed by Bharatpur's rulers in the mid-18th century by diverting the waters of a nearby irrigation canal to create a private duck reserve. Extravagant shooting parties for British viceroys and other royal guests were held here, and horrifying numbers of birds were shot in a single day. Today, the park spreads over 29 sq km (11 sq miles) of wetlands, and attracts a wide variety of migrant and water birds who fly in each winter from places as distant as Siberia. Keoladeo's dry area has mixed deciduous and scrub vegetation and is home to many animals, including the famed nilgai.

Shallow wetlands, one of the world's finest heronries

Getting Around the Park
Expert boatmen navigate the wetlands and point out bird colonies. Bicycles and cycle-rickshaws are also available for touring the forest paths.

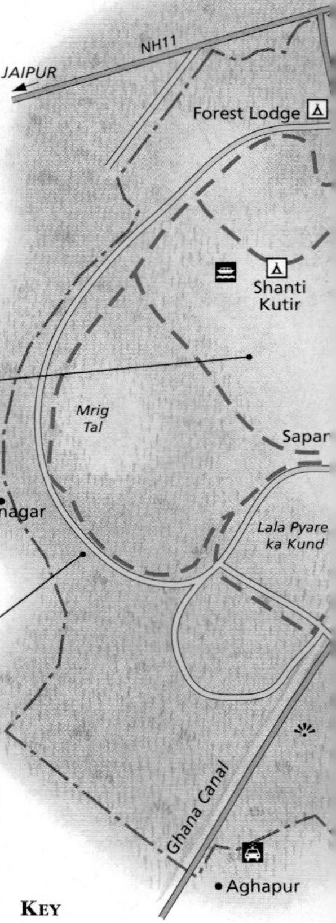

Dry scrubland provides good grazing for nilgai and other species of deer.

BIRDS, RESIDENT AND MIGRANT

The male Sarus crane dances to attract his mate

The park attracts over 375 bird species belonging to 56 families. Egrets, darters, cormorants, grey herons and storks hatch nearly 30,000 chicks every year. The park's most eagerly awaited visitor is the Siberian crane, now an endangered species. Other birds include the peregrine falcon, steppe eagle, garganey teal, snake bird and white ibis. Among the large variety of storks are the open-bill stork, the painted stork and the black-necked stork, considered to be the world's tallest stork. Standing on coral-coloured legs, the bird is 2 m (7 ft) tall, with a wingspan of 2.5 m (8 ft). The Sarus crane, a symbol of fidelity in Indian myth-ology, woos its partner for life with an elaborate mating dance.

Baby cormorants

KEY

═	Main road
=	Minor road
–	Park boundary
• •	Foot path/cycle trail
▨	Marshland
⚜	Viewpoint
▤	Jetty
⚓	Boating
▦	Police station
▨	Temple
Ⓐ	Accommodation

Map labels: JAIPUR — NH11 — Forest Lodge — Shanti Kutir — Mrig Tal — Sapar — Ramnagar — Lala Pyare ka Kund — Ghana Canal — Aghapur

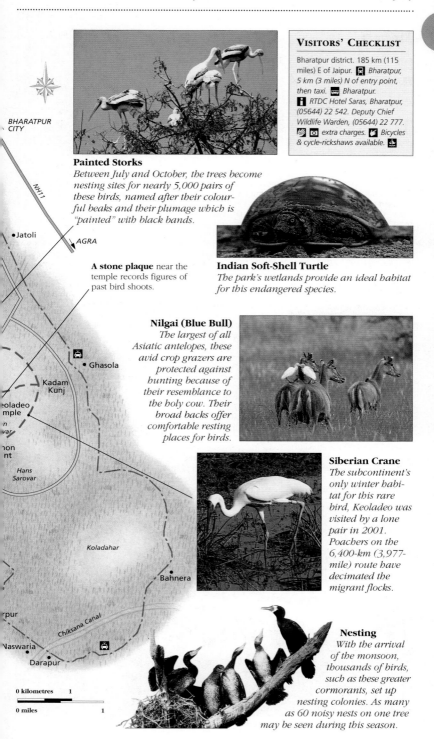

VISITORS' CHECKLIST

Bharatpur district. 185 km (115 miles) E of Jaipur. 🚉 Bharatpur, 5 km (3 miles) N of entry point, then taxi. 🚌 Bharatpur. ℹ️ RTDC Hotel Saras, Bharatpur, (05644) 22 542. Deputy Chief Wildlife Warden, (05644) 22 777. 📷 🎥 extra charges. 🚲 Bicycles & cycle-rickshaws available. ♿

Painted Storks
Between July and October, the trees become nesting sites for nearly 5,000 pairs of these birds, named after their colourful beaks and their plumage which is "painted" with black bands.

A stone plaque near the temple records figures of past bird shoots.

Indian Soft-Shell Turtle
The park's wetlands provide an ideal habitat for this endangered species.

Nilgai (Blue Bull)
The largest of all Asiatic antelopes, these avid crop grazers are protected against hunting because of their resemblance to the holy cow. Their broad backs offer comfortable resting places for birds.

Siberian Crane
The subcontinent's only winter habitat for this rare bird, Keoladeo was visited by a lone pair in 2001. Poachers on the 6,400-km (3,977-mile) route have decimated the migrant flocks.

Nesting
With the arrival of the monsoon, thousands of birds, such as these greater cormorants, set up nesting colonies. As many as 60 noisy nests on one tree may be seen during this season.

BHARATPUR CITY

NH11

AGRA

•Jatoli

• Ghasola

Kadam Kunj

eoladeo
mple

Hans Sarovar

Koladahar

Bahnera

Chiksana Canal

Naswaria

Darapur

0 kilometres 1

0 miles 1

Alwar ❻

Alwar district. 150 km (93 miles)
NE of Jaipur. 🚶 260,300. 🚉 🚌
🛈 RTDC, Nehru Marg, opp railway
station, (0144) 347 348.
📷 Jagannathji Fair (Mar/Apr).

T HE FORMER princely state
of Alwar is now a dusty,
provincial town, visited by
few tourists except those on
their way to the Sariska
National Park. Nevertheless it
has some remarkable monu-
ments, built by its wealthy
rulers in the 18th century, that
are well worth seeing. The
most significant of these is the
City Palace, whose extravagant architectural features
include a profusion of curved
bangaldar roofs and *chhatris*

Gate of the Tomb of Fateh Jang

(pavilions) as well as delicate
Mughal floral tracery and
jalis. The palace, built in
1793, now houses the District
Collectorate and Police Headquarters, and is best viewed
from the central courtyard
with its lovely marble
pavilions. The lavishly
decorated Durbar Hall and
the Sheesh Mahal, on the first
floor, can only be viewed
with special permission.

A door to the right of the
courtyard leads to the **City
Palace Museum**, spread over
three halls on the palace's

upper storey. Its treasures,
which bear witness to the
opulent lifestyles of Alwar's
maharajas, include rare and
exquisite copies of the Persian
poet Sa'adi's *Gulistan* (written
in 1258) and the *Babur Nama*
or "Memoirs of Babur" (1530),
superb Mughal and Rajput
miniatures and an awesome
armoury. Particularly
intriguing is a macabre coil
called *nagphas*, used for
strangling enemies. Another
unique exhibit is a silver
dining table with dividers,
through which shoals of metal
fish can be seen swimming.

The cenotaph of Maharaja
Bakhtawar Singh (r.1790–1815)
lies behind the palace, across a
magnificent *kund* (tank). It is
locally known as **Moosi
Maharani ki Chhatri**, after
his mistress who committed
sati here after he died. An
elegant monument that blends
brown sandstone with white
marble, its ceilings are adorned
with gold leaf paintings.

On a steep hill above the
city is the rugged **Bala Qila**, a
fort with extensive ramparts,
massive gateways and some
spectacular views from the
top. Originally a 10th-century
mud fort, it was added to by
the Mughals and Jats, and
captured by Pratap Singh of
Alwar in 1775. Within the fort
is a pretty frescoed palace, the
Nikumbh Mahal, in the
courtyard of which a police
wireless station is, rather
inappropriately, sited. Also

A page from the *Gulistan*

visible are the ruins of the
Salim Mahal, named after
Jahangir (Salim), Mughal
emperor Akbar's heir who was
exiled here after he plotted to
kill Abu'l Fazl, the emperor's
official historian. Near Alwar's
railway station is another fine
monument, the **Tomb of
Fateh Jang**, one of Emperor
Shah Jahan's ministers, built in
1647. Dominated by an enormous dome, the walls and
ceiling of this five-storeyed
structure have raised plaster
reliefs, with fine calligraphic
inscriptions on the first floor.

Alwar's green lung,
Company Bagh, is a lovely
garden with a greenhouse.

🏛 **City Palace**
Near Collectorate. ⬜ daily. 📷
🏛 **City Palace Museum**
⬜ Sat–Thu. ⬤ public hols. 📷 🚫
🕋 **Moosi Maharani ki
Chhatri**
⬜ Sat–Thu. ⬤ public hols. 📷
🕋 **Bala Qila**
⬜ daily. Written permission is
needed from the office of the
Superintendent of Police, City Palace.
🔲 **Tomb of Fateh Jang**
Near railway station. ⬜ daily.

The elegant marble pavilion at Moosi Maharani ki Chhatri

Sariska Palace, a luxury hotel just outside the Tiger Reserve

Sariska National Park ❼

Alwar district. 37 km (23 miles) NE of Alwar. 🚌 ℹ *Field Director, Project Tiger Sanctuary, Sariska (0144) 41 333.* ⬜ *Sep–Jun.* 📷 *extra for personal vehicles or jeeps.* 📷 🏨

DESIGNATED a Tiger Reserve under Project Tiger *(see p289)* in 1979, Sariska National Park, formerly the private hunting ground of the princely state of Alwar, sprawls over 800 sq km (309 sq miles), with a core area of 480 sq km (185 sq miles). The Aravalli Range branches out at Sariska, forming low plateaux and valleys that harbour a wide spectrum of wildlife in the dry jungles.

Silk cotton in bloom

The tiger population at Sariska is now believed to be between 20 and 30. Forest guides keep track of where a tiger was last seen and can sometimes lead visitors to spot this elusive predator.

There are a series of watering holes in Sariska, at Pandupol, Bandipol, Slopka, Kalighati and Talvriksha, that make good vantage points to view wildlife, especially at sunset when hoards of animals flock to them to quench their thirst. The gentle chital or spotted deer is commonly sighted at the park's watering holes, while the *chausingha* (four-horned antelope), unique to Sariska, can be spotted around Pandupol. Other species that can be seen here are panthers and black-faced langur monkeys, jackals and

hyenas, nilgai or blue bulls, wild boars and porcupines.

Among the birds that can be spotted, especially from the hides at Kalighati and Slopka, are the crested serpent eagle, the great Indian horned owl, woodpeckers, kingfishers and partridges.

The dry deciduous forests of Sariska come to life during the brief spring and early summer when the flowering *dhak (Butea monosperma)* and laburnum bloom. The date palm begins to bear fruit, while berries known locally as *kair (Capparis decidua)* appear on the bushes. The **Kankwari Fort**, dating to the 17th-century, and several ancient temple ruins, such as those of the **Pandupol Temple**, lie within the park.

The **Sariska Palace**, built at the end of the 19th century as a hunting lodge for Alwar's rulers, is now a luxury hotel *(see p705)*, with period furnishings and a collection of vintage *shikar* photographs.

Black-faced Hanuman langurs, a common sight at Sariska

Shekhawati ❽

Sikar & Jhunjhunu districts. 115 km (72 miles) NW from Jaipur to Sikar.
🚌 📷 *Gangaur Festival (Mar/Apr), Dussehra (Sept/Oct).*

A view of the impressive Char-Chowk Haveli, Lachhmangarh

THIS REGION, named after its 15th-century ruler Rao Shekha, has a number of fascinating small towns with well-preserved painted *havelis*, forts and temples. Among the most interesting are **Lachhmangarh** and **Fatehpur** with their grand *havelis*, and **Dundlod**, with its well-restored fort. Especially worth visiting is **Ramgarh**, 20 km (12 miles) north of Fatehpur. Famous for its Shani Temple which has an ornate interior of mirror-work and gilt, the town also has the Ram Gopal Poddar Chhatri, covered with more than 400 paintings. The main bazaar is crowded with "antique" dealers, who sell carved doors and windows from derelict *havelis*. Many of these are extremely skilful new copies of the originals.

Mahansar, 15 km (9 miles) northeast of Ramgarh, has the splendid Sone ki Dukan Haveli, abundantly worked in gold leaf. The paintings on its vaulted ceiling, depicting the incarnations of Vishnu, are perhaps the finest in the area.

Bissau, 10 km (6 miles) northwest of Mahansar, has the 18th-century Keshargarh Fort, which provides an excellent view of the sand dunes

Inside Dundlod Fort

to the north and west. It also has ten richly painted *havelis*. During Dussehra, Ramlila performances take place every evening, with the actors wearing masks and costumes made by local *sadhvis* (female ascetics) who started this tradition in the 19th century.

Churu, 12 km (8 miles) northwest of Bissau, is in the desert. Though not actually part of the Shekhawati region, it is included in the painted *haveli* circuit, as many merchants had homes here too. The Surana Double Haveli, with its imposing proportions and 1,111 windows, is the main attraction. The Banthia Haveli, east of the vegetable market, has interesting if bizarre frescoes, including one of Jesus smoking a cigar.

THE PAINTED HAVELIS OF SHEKHAWATI

The ancestral homes of some of India's leading industrialist families, such as the Birlas and Goenkas, can be seen in the many little towns of Shekhawati. These sprawling old *havelis* with their exuberantly frescoed walls were built between the late 18th and early 20th centuries by local Marwari merchants who had migrated to the port-cities of Bombay (Mumbai) and Calcutta (Kolkata) to seek their fortunes. Their interaction with the British and exposure to modern urban and industrial trends influenced their lifestyles. Consequently, their homes grew increasingly grand, reflecting the new ideas they brought back with them, as well as their new-found wealth and social status.

Fresco of a group of turbaned Rajput chieftains

The style and content of the Shekhawati frescoes are a telling comment on the urbanization of a traditional genre. The local artists still followed the one-dimensional realism of traditional Rajput painting *(see p405)*, but juxtaposed among the gods, goddesses and martial heroes are images from a changing world. In their celebration of contemporary "pop" themes, the frescoes of British ladies, top-hatted gentlemen, brass bands and soldiers, trains, motor cars, aeroplanes, gramophones and telephones, symbolize the industrial society emerging in the late 19th century.

The entrance to Biyani Haveli, Sikar

A Tour of Shekhawati ⑨

Sᴵᴛᴜᴀᴛᴇᴅ ᴀʟᴏɴɢ ᴛʜᴇ old camel caravan trade route, northwest of Jaipur, the Shekhawati ("Garden of Shekha") region resembles an open-air museum. A network of excellent roads through semi-arid scrubland connects numerous towns and villages, known for minor forts, *baolis* and the painted *havelis* of India's leading merchant families, still standing in all their evocative splendour.

A wall in the Poddar School, Nawalgarh, depicting gods and goddesses flying kites

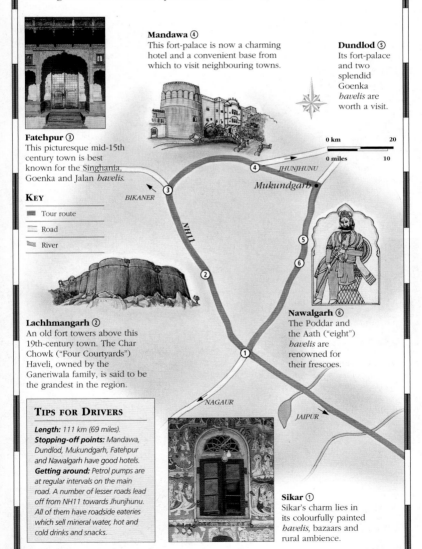

Mandawa ④
This fort-palace is now a charming hotel and a convenient base from which to visit neighbouring towns.

Dundlod ⑤
Its fort-palace and two splendid Goenka *havelis* are worth a visit.

Fatehpur ③
This picturesque mid-15th century town is best known for the Singhania, Goenka and Jalan *havelis*.

JHUNJHUNU

Mukundgarh •

BIKANER

KEY

▰	Tour route
═	Road
▱	River

NH11

Lachhmangarh ②
An old fort towers above this 19th-century town. The Char Chowk ("Four Courtyards") Haveli, owned by the Ganeriwala family, is said to be the grandest in the region.

Nawalgarh ⑥
The Poddar and the Aath ("eight") *havelis* are renowned for their frescoes.

0 km   20
0 miles   10

NAGAUR

JAIPUR

Sikar ①
Sikar's charm lies in its colourfully painted *havelis*, bazaars and rural ambience.

Tɪᴘs ғᴏʀ Dʀɪᴠᴇʀs

Length: 111 km (69 miles).
Stopping-off points: Mandawa, Dundlod, Mukundgarh, Fatehpur and Nawalgarh have good hotels.
Getting around: Petrol pumps are at regular intervals on the main road. A number of lesser roads lead off from NH11 towards Jhunjhunu. All of them have roadside eateries which sell mineral water, hot and cold drinks and snacks.

Street-by-Street: Pushkar ❿

A turtle shrine

APEACEFUL PILGRIM TOWN of lakes and 400 temples, Pushkar derives its name from *pushpa* (flower) and *kar* (hand) after a legend that claims its lakes were created from the petals that fell from the divine hands of Brahma the Creator. Today, life revolves around its lakeside ghats, temples and vibrant, colourful bazaars, and it is this harmonious mix of the spiritual and commercial that draws people to Pushkar.

Villagers at the Fair
Hundreds of thousands of people, camels and cattle attend the annual fair, said to be one of the largest in Asia.

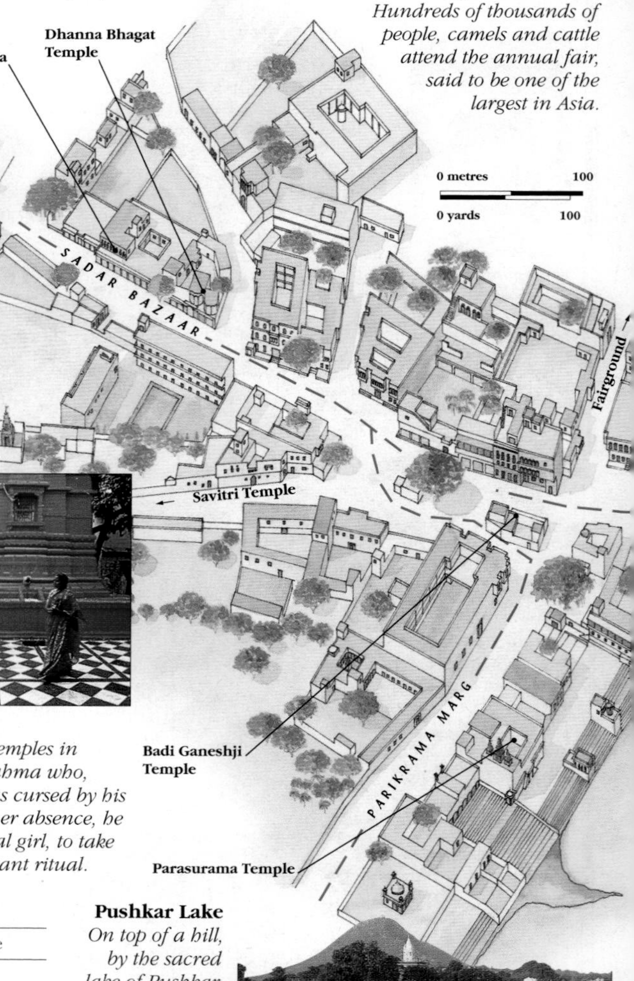

Dhanna Bhagat Temple

Residential area

SADAR BAZAAR

0 metres 100
0 yards 100

Fairground

Savitri Temple

PARIKRAMA MARG

★ Brahma Temple
This is one of the few temples in India dedicated to Brahma who, according to myth, was cursed by his wife Savitri when, in her absence, he invited Gayatri, a tribal girl, to take her place in an important ritual.

Badi Ganeshji Temple

Parasurama Temple

KEY

— — — Suggested route

STAR SIGHTS

★ Brahma Temple

★ Ghats

Pushkar Lake
On top of a hill, by the sacred lake of Pushkar, is the temple of Savitri. Across the lake, on another hill, is the Gayatri Temple.

Rangji Temple
This temple is conspicuous for its South Indian style of architecture (see p20). Its gopura (gateway), carved with over 360 images of deities, towers over the area.

Camel at the Pushkar Fair

VISITORS' CHECKLIST

Ajmer district. 144 km (90 miles) SW of Jaipur. 14,800. *RTDC Hotel Sarovar, (0145) 72 040.* daily. *Pushkar Fair (Nov). No eggs, meat or alcohol is available or allowed in Pushkar.*

Women at Sadar Bazaar

The Pushkar Fair
In the Hindu month of Kartik (October/November), ten days after Diwali, this peaceful town and its environs come alive as the much anticipated annual cattle fair begins. Tents and campsites suddenly spring up to accommodate the thousands of pilgrims, tourists and villagers with herds of cattle, horses and camels who come here to participate in this spectacular event.

Pushkar has always been the region's central cattle market for local herdsmen and farmers who buy and sell camels and indigenous breeds of cattle. Over the years, this trade in livestock has greatly increased in volume. The Pushkar Fair is now one of Asia's largest cattle fairs, and it transforms the quiet little village into a bustling market.

In the vast, specially-built amphitheatre on the outskirts of the town, numerous camel, horse and donkey races and contests take place amid lusty cheers from the spectators. A festive, carnival atmosphere prevails in Pushkar during the fair's two-week duration. Giant Ferris wheels and open air theatres offer amusement, while food stalls do a brisk trade, as do the shops that sell a fascinating variety of goods. In the evenings, people huddle round campfires, listening to the haunting strains of Rajasthani folk ballads. The fair reaches a crescendo on the night of the full moon *(purnima)*, when pilgrims take a dip in the holy lake. At dusk, during the beautiful *deepdan* ceremony, hundreds of clay lamps on leaf boats are lit and set afloat in a magical tableau.

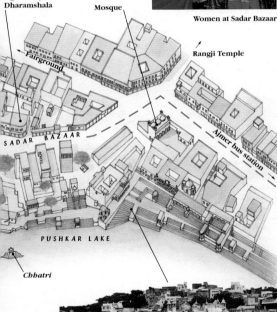

Digambar Jain Dharamshala · Mosque · Fairground · SADAR BAZAAR · Rangji Temple · Ajmer bus station · PUSHKAR LAKE · Chhatri

★ Ghats
Pushkar has 52 ghats. Devout Hindus make at least one pilgrimage to Pushkar and bathe at the holy ghats to wash away their sins, thereby earning themselves a place in heaven.

Ajmer **⑪**

Ajmer district. 135 km (84 miles)
SW of Jaipur. 485,200.
Rajasthan Tourism, near Khadim
Hotel, (0145) 62 7426. Urs (Oct).

AJMER IS FAMOUS throughout the subcontinent for the holy Muslim shrine, **Dargah Sharif**, the tomb of the great Sufi saint, Khwaja Moinuddin Chishti (1143–1235). Located in the southwest corner of the city, the saint's marble-domed tomb is at the heart of the Dargah complex, which is virtually a township in itself. It includes a bazaar and two marble mosques, built by the Mughal emperors Akbar and Shah Jahan in the 16th and 17th centuries. Akbar was Chishti's most famous devotee, and once walked barefoot all the way from Agra to Ajmer, a distance of 363 km (226 miles), as thanksgiving after the birth of his son Salim, the future Emperor Jahangir.

Millions of pilgrims come to Ajmer for the saint's annual Urs (death anniversary) in October, when spirited Sufi musicians sing the saint's praises in front of his tomb. A special rice pudding, cooked in giant iron cauldrons in the Dargah's courtyard, is offered to devotees.

West of the Dargah Sharif is Ajmer's architectural gem, the **Adhai-Din-ka-Jhonpra**, or "Hut of Two-and-a-Half Days". This strange name is said to derive from the duration of a religious fair that used to be held here. Though in ruins, the early 13th-century mosque complex, built into a hillside, is most impressive. Its main glory is its exquisite seven-arched screen in front of the colonnaded hall. Each

Pilgrims at Ajmer's Dargah Sharif, India's holiest Muslim shrine

Calligraphy, Adhai-Din-ka-Jhonpra

arch is different, and the numerous columns have elaborate carvings.

In the southeast corner of Ajmer is **Mayo College**, one of India's best public schools. An excellent example of Indo-Saracenic architecture, it was set up in 1875 by the viceroy, Lord Mayo, as an "Eton of the East" for Rajput princes. Its early students came accompanied by family retainers and private tutors, and some, like the prince of Alwar, even brought along their own elephants. Behind the 19th-century **Nasiyan Temple**, in the heart of the old city, is the Svarna Nagari Hall, vividly decorated with coloured-glass mosaics and large gilded wooden figures, recreating scenes from Jain mythology.

The **Rajputana Museum**, also in the old city, is located in Emperor Akbar's fort and palace. Its exhibits include impressive sculptures

dating from the 4th to the 12th centuries.

Around **Anasagar Lake**, to the northwest of the city, are elegant marble pavilions built by Emperor Shah Jahan in the 17th century. They are set on the lake's banks, in a pretty garden called Daulat Bagh. North of the city, on the summit of Beetli Hill, is the ruined 12th-century **Taragarh Fort**, which affords spectacular views of Ajmer and the surrounding countryside.

Nasiyan Temple
SM Soni Marg. daily.
Rajputana Museum
Near bus stand. daily.

Nagaur **⑫**

Nagaur district. 137 km (85 miles)
NE of Jodhpur. 83,400.
Cattle Fair (Jan/Feb).

THIS LITTLE desert town, midway between Jodhpur and Bikaner, is dominated by **Ahichhatragarh Fort**, dating to the 12th century. In the mid-18th century, the ruler of Jodhpur received the fort as a gift from the Mughals and embellished it with a charming pleasure palace. Several of its chambers have exquisite frescoes, now being carefully restored. The palace also has lovely water channels decorated with fish-scale patterns and ornamental spouts, as well as an ingenious system of airducts that used to supply the inner rooms with cool air.

The Nagaur Cattle Fair rivals the Pushkar Fair *(see p375)*, and is a dazzling kaleidoscope of animals, crafts and people, including Nagaur's famous puppeteers whose dramatic shows bring alive popular Rajasthani legends and folklore.

The exuberantly decorated seven-arched screen at the Adhai-Din-ka-Jhonpra, Ajmer

Ships of the Thar Desert

THE DESERT DWELLERS of Rajasthan could not survive without their camels. In the sandy, inhospitable expanse of the Thar Desert, it is their only means of transport, their beast of

Mural of camels

burden, as well as an important source of nourishment (camel's milk, slightly salty in taste, is drunk throughout Rajasthan's deserts). The hardy camel demands little in return. It can do without food and water for up to a month in winter, and a week in summer, tanking up on 70 litres (148 pints) of water at one go. The Rajasthani's affection for his camel is evident at all the desert fairs, where camels are given pride of place, resplendent in their colourful tassels and jewellery.

VARIETIES OF CAMEL

Three varieties of camel inhabit Rajasthan. All of them have two rows of eyelashes which help keep the sand out of their eyes. Their humps contain a thick layer of fat, which shields their bodies from the scorching desert sun.

Gujarati camels are darker-haired and adept at traversing marshy areas such as the Rann of Kutch.

Bikaneri camels have hairy ears, and great load-bearing capacity and stamina.

Jaisalmeri camels, with longer legs, can cover up to 22 km (14 miles) an hour.

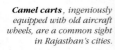

Camel carts, ingeniously equipped with old aircraft wheels, are a common sight in Rajasthan's cities.

Dhola and Maru, star-crossed lovers in Rajasthani folklore who eloped on their trusty camel, are a favourite theme in paintings.

Camelskin handicrafts include beautiful embossed water bottles. Bags, slippers, and lacquer-painted lampshades are other camelskin products.

Camel races at fairs test the evenness of a camel's gait by seeing how far it can carry a pot of milk without spilling any.

Camel cavalry regiments of the Indian Army have their origin in the camel regiments of the maharaja of Bikaner, which fought in Egypt in World War I. Today they patrol the desert borders.

Bikaner ⓭

Bikaner district. 361 km (224 miles)
NW of Jaipur. 🏛 529,000. 🚌 🚂
ℹ️ *Dhola Maru Hotel, Pooran Singh
Circle, (0151) 52 7445.* 🐪 *Camel
Festival (Jan), Jambeshwar Festival
(Feb/Mar), Kolayat Fair (Nov).*

The imposing ramparts of the 16th-century Junagarh Fort

ALONG WITH Jodhpur and
Jaisalmer, Bikaner was
one of the three great Desert
Kingdoms of Rajasthan and,
like them, prospered because
of its strategic location on the
overland caravan trade route
to Central Asia and China. It
was founded in 1486 by Rao
Bika, the disgruntled younger
son of Rao Jodha, the ruler of
Jodhpur *(see pp380–81)*, who
left home in search of new
territory to conquer.

Somewhat over-
shadowed by the
splendours of
Jodhpur and
Jaisalmer, Bikaner
nevertheless has a
great deal to offer
visitors, with its old
walled town where
camels saunter past
colourful stalls, its
many temples and
palaces, and the
magnificent
Junagarh Fort,
perhaps the best preserved
and most ornately decorated
of all the forts in Rajasthan.

**Maharaja's swing at
Junagarh Fort**

🏰 Junagarh Fort

▢ *Sat–Thu.* 📷 🎥 📷 *extra
charges.* **Museum** ▢ *daily.* 📷
Constructed between 1587
and 1593 by the third
ruler of Bikaner, Rai
Singh, Junagarh Fort is
protected by a 986-m
(3,235-ft) long sandstone
wall with 37 bastions, a
moat and, most effectively
of all, by the forbidding
expanse of the Thar
Desert. Not surprisingly,
the fort has never been
conquered, a fact which
explains its excellent state
of preservation. Within
the fort's austere stone
walls are no less than 37
profusely decorated
palaces, temples and
pavilions, built by its
successive rulers over the
centuries, though in a
harmonious continuity of
style. The most outstanding is
the **Anup Mahal**, built by
Maharaja Anup Singh in 1690
as his Hall of Private Audience.
It was sumptuously decorated
between 1787 and 1800 by
Maharaja Surat Singh.
In an ingenious
imitation of Mughal
pietra dura work
at a fraction of the
cost, the lime-plaster
walls of the Anup
Mahal have been
polished to a high
lustre. They are
covered with red
and gold lacquer
patterns, further
embellished with
mirrors and gold
leaf. The **Karan Mahal** (built
between 1631 and 1669) is the
Hall of Public Audience and is
ornamented in a similar if
somewhat less lavish style.

The luxurious interior of Anup Mahal with
ornamental lacquer work

Two other gorgeous, heavily
decorated palaces are the
17th-century **Chandra Mahal**
("Moon Palace") and **Phool
Mahal** ("Flower Palace"). The
latter contains Rao Bika's
small, low bed with curved
silver legs, on which he slept
with his feet touching the
ground. The bed was so
designed to enable Rao Bika
to jump quickly to his feet
and fight off murderous
intruders. The Chandra Mahal,
which was the queens' palace,
has carved marble panels
depicting the Radha-Krishna
legend, and both palaces
have superb stone carving
and *jalis*. The blue-and-gold
Badal Mahal ("Cloud
Palace") is covered with
paintings of clouds, yellow
streaks of lightning and rain
showers – a favourite fantasy
in this arid land. The **Hawa
Mahal** ("Palace of
Winds") has a huge mirror
positioned over the
maharaja's bed, which
apparently enabled him to
view the courtyard below,
thus alerting him to
approaching danger. The
oldest palace in the fort is
Lal Niwas, dating to
1595, and decorated with
floral motifs in red and
gold. The newest palace
is the huge **Durbar
Niwas** ("Coronation
Palace"), built in the early
20th century by Bikaner's
most progressive ruler
Sir Ganga Singh
(r.1887–1943), who gave
Bikaner its railway link
and built the Ganga Canal
which brought precious
irrigation water to his
kingdom. He was also

famous for hosting elaborate *shikars* (hunting expeditions) for visiting British dignitaries. The Durbar Niwas now houses the fort museum, whose armoury section includes such fascinating exhibits as a 56-kg (124-lb) suit of armour, a dagger with a pistol built into it, and swords with lion-shaped handles. Other exhibits include the fragrant sandalwood throne of the rulers, said to

Coat of arms of Bikaner's rulers

date back to their 5th-century ancestors who were the kings of Kannauj (Uttar Pradesh), and a curious half-spoon for soup, used by the maharaja to ensure that his luxuriant moustache remained pristine during mealtimes.

🏛 Walled City

West end of MG Rd. **Shops** ⬡ *daily.*
In the old walled city, entered through Kote Gate, is the bazaar, where excellent local handicrafts can be found, such as rugs and carpets, painted lampshades made of camel hide, and beautiful miniatures in the Bikaneri style. Savoury snacks (*bhujias*) are another local speciality, and Bikaneri *bhujias* are renowned throughout India, as are the sweets made of camel's milk. The grand 17th- and 18th-century *havelis* of Bikaner's wealthy merchants line the narrow lanes in the vicinity around Rampuria Street. Two of the most ornate are the **Rampuria** and

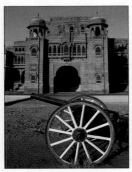

One of the two cannons flanking the entrance to Lalgarh Palace

Kothari Havelis. The former is now a delightful heritage hotel. In the southwestern corner of the walled town are two Jain temples, dating from the early 16th century, the **Bhandeshwar** and **Sandeshwar Temples**. Both are ornately carved and are embellished with frescoes, mirror-work and gold leaf scrollwork inside. They were built by two brothers who, having no children, constructed these masterpieces for posterity.

🏛 Lalgarh Palace

N of city centre. 📞 *(0151) 54 0201.*
Museum ⬡ *Thu–Tue.* 📷 🚫
Lalgarh Palace, outside the walled town, is a sprawling extravaganza of carved friezes, *jalis*, pillars and arches in the distinctive reddish-pink local sandstone (which resulted in Bikaner being dubbed the "Red City"). Constructed between 1902 and 1926, it was designed by Sir Samuel Swinton Jacob (*see p353*) in a style that combines traditional Rajput and Renaissance European features with Art Nouveau decor inside. Part of it has been converted into a hotel (*see p702*), and another section into a museum with vintage photographs and wildlife trophies. Lalgarh Palace's museum and beautiful gardens are open to visitors.

ENVIRONS: The **Camel Breeding Farm**, 9 km (6 miles) southeast of Bikaner, is best visited in the late after-noon when the camels return from grazing. Set up in 1975, the farm breeds nearly half the camels found in India, including those for the camel regiment of the Indian Army. **Gajner**, 30 km (19 miles) northwest of Bikaner, has the red sandstone Summer Palace of the maharajas, now a luxury hotel (*see p702*), and the Gajner National Park, home to blackbucks, wild boars, desert foxes and a large number of migratory birds. The 17th-century **Karni Mata Temple** at Deshnok,

30 km (19 miles) southeast of Bikaner, is also known as the Rat Temple, because of the hundreds of rats that swarm around the temple and its precincts. The rats are con-sidered sacred and are fed sweets and milk by the priests and visitors, who believe that they are reincarnated holy men. The temple is dedicated to Karni Mata, an incarnation of Durga, and is entered through intricately carved silver doors, presented by Sir Ganga Singh.

🐫 Camel Breeding Farm
⬡ *Mon–Sat.* 🚫 📷
🏛 Karni Mata Temple
⬡ *daily.* 📷 *Karni Mata Festival (Mar/Apr & Sep/Oct).*

Devotee feeding milk to rats at Karni Mata Temple, Deshnok

Phaiodi ❶

Jodhpur district. 150 km (93 miles) SW of Bikaner. 🚌

THIS LARGE TOWN attracts visitors because of the lovely hamlet of Khichan, 4 km (2.5 miles) to its east. Khichan is famous for the demoiselle cranes that gather around its lake between September and March. The birds migrate here from the Mongolian steppes for the winter. Every day, the villagers spread grain on the fields for the birds, and as a result the number of cranes that come here has increased substantially over the years. At last count, 7,000 cranes spent the winter at Khichan.

Jodhpur ⑮

Clock, Umaid Bhavan Palace

WITH THE MAJESTIC Mehrangarh Fort towering over opulent palaces, colourful bazaars and the sands of the Thar Desert, Jodhpur epitomizes all the romance and feudal splendour of Rajasthan. Now the second largest city in the state, Jodhpur was founded in 1459 by Rao Jodha, the Rathore ruler of the kingdom of Marwar. Strategically located on the overland trade route, it soon became a flourishing trade centre. Its merchant class, known as the Marwaris (see p372), have retained their entrepreneurial skills and continue to run many of India's leading business houses. The special riding breeches, known the world over as jodhpurs, were designed here.

Blue-washed houses around Jodhpur's Mehrangarh Fort

♕ Mehrangarh Fort
See pp382–3.

▣ Sardar Bazaar
◯ daily.
Jodhpur's bazaar lies in the heart of the old city, which is surrounded by a 10-km (6-mile) wall, pierced by eight gates. Clustered around a clock tower (built in 1912), the bazaar is a fascinating area to explore, with its little shops selling silver jewellery, lacquer bangles, tie-dyed fabrics, soft camel leather shoes, puppets, clay figurines and colourful heaps of sweets and spices. The pavements are lined with henna artists who decorate women's palms with intricate, lacy patterns.

An interesting building in this area is the early 17th-century **Taleti Mahal**, its carved balconies supported by temple pillars. Built for a favourite royal concubine, it now houses a school. There are several other beautiful houses in the bazaar area, mostly made of red sandstone and heavily carved.

♕ Jaswant Thada
◯ daily. 📷
This elegant pillared marble memorial with fine lattice carving is the *chhatri* (cenotaph) of Maharaja Jaswant Singh II (r.1878–95), whose innovative irrigation schemes brought water and prosperity to this parched land. Local people, who

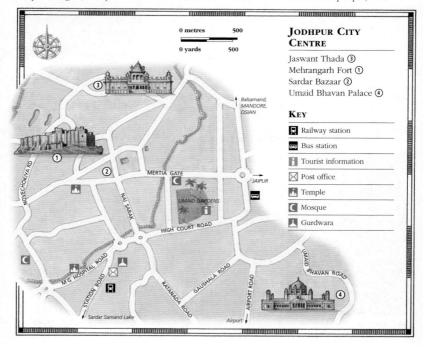

JODHPUR CITY CENTRE

Jaswant Thada ③
Mehrangarh Fort ①
Sardar Bazaar ②
Umaid Bhavan Palace ④

KEY

🚊 Railway station

🚌 Bus station

ℹ️ Tourist information

✉️ Post office

🛕 Temple

☪️ Mosque

🔱 Gurdwara

Map labels: Balsamand, MANDORE, OSIAN / JAIPUR / MERTIA GATE / UMAID GARDENS / HIGH COURT ROAD / NOVECHOKTA RD / NAI SARAK / M G HOSPITAL ROAD / STATION ROAD / RATANADA ROAD / GAUSHALA ROAD / AIRPORT ROAD / UMAID BHAVAN ROAD / Sardar Samand Lake / Airport

0 metres 500
0 yards 500

Umaid Bhavan Palace, a fusion of Rajput, Jain and Art Deco styles

VISITORS' CHECKLIST

Jodhpur district. 331 km (206 miles) W of Jaipur. 846,500. 5 km (3 miles) S of city centre. High Court Rd, (0291) 44 010. Mon–Sat. Marwar Festival (Oct).

believe the maharaja has retained his healing touch, come regularly to offer prayer and flowers at his shrine. Cenotaphs of subsequent rulers and members of the royal families are also located here, though earlier rulers have their memorials at Mandore.

🏛 **Umaid Bhavan Palace**

🔘 *daily.*

This immense palace, built of creamy-pink sandstone and marble, is a prime example of princely India's opulence. Its 347 rooms include eight dining halls, two theatres, a ballroom, several lavishly decorated reception halls and a vast underground swimming pool. A 60-m (197-ft) dome covers the cavernous central hall which, at its inauguration, seated 1,000 people for dinner.

The palace was commission-ed by Maharaja Umaid Singh, apparently to create jobs for his famine-stricken subjects. Begun in 1929, it took 3,000 men 15 years to complete; 19 km (12 miles) of railway tracks were also laid to bring the sandstone from the quarry. HV Lanchester, the architect of the Central Hall of Westminster in London, created a pleasing fusion of Rajput, Jain and European Art Deco styles for his royal patron.

Umaid Singh's grandson, Gaj Singh, still lives in a section of the palace, while the rest has been turned into a luxury hotel *(see p704)*. The palace museum is open to visitors and has an impressive collection of decorated weapons, watches and fantastically-shaped clocks, paintings, French furniture and porcelain.

The road in front of it, leading to the smaller Ajit Bhavan Palace, is lined with antique shops.

ENVIRONS: Mandore, 9 km (6 miles) north of Jodhpur, was the capital of the Rathore kings of Marwar until the 15th century, when Rao Jodha built a new capital at Jodhpur. Set around a beautiful terraced garden on a hillside are the red sandstone *chhatris* of Jodhpur's earlier rulers. The most imposing is that of Ajit Singh with its towering temple-like spire. When he died in 1724, his six wives and 58 concubines committed *sati* on his funeral pyre. Nearby, in the Hall of Heroes, are 15 life-size statues of religious deities and folk heroes, carved on a rock face. Further up the hill are the queens' cenotaphs (Raniyon ki Chhatri) and the tall and narrow 17th-century Ek Thamba Mahal Palace.

Balsamand, 6 km (4 miles) north of Jodhpur, has the 19th-century red sandstone water palace of the maharajas beside a large artificial lake. The **Sardar Samand Lake**, 55 km (34 miles) south of Jodhpur, attracts several water birds including egrets, ibis and pelicans. On its shores is the maharajas' Art Deco-style hunting lodge. The drive here passes through interesting Bishnoi villages *(see p384)*.

Jaswant Thada, the 19th-century cenotaph of Maharaja Jaswant Singh II

BHOPA BALLADEERS

Like the troubadours of medieval Europe, the nomadic Bhopa tribe of western Rajasthan enjoys a lively tradition of storytelling through song and dance. A long painted scroll (known as a *phad*) is, rather like a comic strip, crammed with paintings depicting dramatic events in the life of a Marwar hero, the brave warrior Pabuji. The Bhopa unrolls his scroll, and narrates the story through songs, highlighting relevant pictures on the scroll with a lantern, while his wife brings the tale to life with animated dance sequences. The Bhopas' performances draw enthusiastic crowds at fairs and festivals across the Marwar region.

Painted scroll used by Bhopas

Jodhpur: Mehrangarh Fort

Sati **handprints on Loha Pol**

RISING SHEER out of a 125-m (410-ft) high rock, Mehrangarh is perhaps the most majestic of Rajasthan's forts. Described by an awe-struck Rudyard Kipling as "the creation of angels, fairies and giants", Mehrangarh's forbidding ramparts are in sharp contrast to the flamboyantly decorated palaces within. Founded by Rao Jodha in 1459, the sandstone fort was added to by later rulers, mostly between the mid-17th and mid-19th centuries. The royal apartments within the fort now form part of an outstanding museum.

Chamundi Devi Mandir is dedicated to the goddess Durga in her wrathful aspect.

The Ramparts
The bastioned walls, parts of which are hewn out of the rock itself, are in places 24-m (79-ft) thick and 40-m (131-ft) high. Perched on them are old cannons.

Nagnechiaji Mandir has a 14th-century image of the goddess Kuldevi, the family deity of the rulers.

Zenana Chowk

★ **Phool Mahal**
Built between 1730 and 1750, this is the fort's most opulent chamber, richly gilded and painted. It was used for royal celebrations.

Suraj Pol is the entrance to the museum.

Palki Khana

Shringar Chowk

Carved balconies crown the towering bastions.

Shringar Chowk
This courtyard has the coronation throne of the Jodhpur rulers, made of white marble. Every ruler after Rao Jodha was crowned on it.

STAR SIGHTS

★ **Phool Mahal**

★ **Moti Mahal**

The blue-washed houses of Brahmapuri village, clustered below the ramparts of Mehrangarh Fort

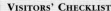

Chokelao Palace, now under restoration, was a pleasure palace built around a sunken garden.

★ **Moti Mahal**
Built between 1581 and 1595, this magnificent room was the Hall of Private Audience. Its ceiling is decorated with mirrors and gold leaf, and crushed seashells were mixed with plaster to give its walls a lustrous sheen.

Takhat Mahal
This exuberantly painted room with a wooden ceiling was the favourite retreat of Maharaja Takhat Singh (r.1843–73), who had 30 queens and numerous concubines.

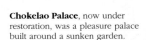

Jhanki Mahal is a long gallery with exquisite latticed stone screens.

Phool Mahal

Sileh Khana's exceptional collection of weapons includes damascened Mughal daggers, gem-studded shields, and special armour for war elephants.

Jai Pol
One of the seven fortified gates to the fort, it is now the main entrance. It was built in 1806 by Maharaja Man Singh to commemorate a victory in battle.

Exploring Mehrangarh Fort Museum

THE MEHRANGARH FORT MUSEUM is justly regarded as the best of the many palace museums in Rajasthan. Its rich and varied collection includes a golden throne, fine miniature paintings, traditional costumes and fascinating weapons. Particularly magnificent are the skilfully restored royal chambers, which present a vivid picture of princely life and culture in Rajasthan.

Maharaja's cradle with a mechanical rocking system, in Jhanki Mahal

The entrance to the museum is through the Suraj Pol on the fort's southeastern side. Inside, to the right, is the **Palki Khana** with a collection of richly gilded palanquins. Along with the impressive elephant howdahs on display in the **Howdah Gallery** next door, these reflect the importance of grand processions in courtly life. Particularly impressive is a 17th-century howdah made of solid silver, a gift from the Mughal emperor Shah Jahan. Another treasure is a spectacular palanquin covered in gold leaf, dating to 1730. This stands in the **Daulat Khana** (Treasury Hall), just before the **Sileh Khana** with its superb collection of weapons.

A gem-studded rhino-hide shield

From here, steps lead up to the **Umaid Mahal**, which exhibits miniature paintings of the Jodhpur School. Heavily influenced by the Mughal style, these paintings provide fascinating vignettes of life at court – the rulers riding camels with their courtesans, playing polo and leading ceremonial processions. Here too is a grand silk canopy, that was used by the rulers for outdoor camps.

The next chamber, on the floor above, is the splendidly gilded, 18th-century **Phool Mahal** ("Flower Palace"), the Hall of Public Audience. It also has superb miniatures, including a set of 36 *Raga-mala* paintings that depict the moods of various musical ragas.

The 19th-century **Takhat Mahal**, the chamber of a pleasure-loving ruler, is exuberantly painted with murals of Radha and Krishna and dancing maidens. The glass Christmas tree balls hanging from the ceiling were added in the 1930s. **Sardar Vilas**, just below Takhat Mahal, showcases Jodhpur's fine woodwork. Particularly striking is a door inlaid with ivory.

The next chamber is **Jhanki Mahal** or "Peeping Palace", so called because the women of the royal zenana could peep through its exquisite latticed stone screens to observe the ceremonies and festivities in the courtyards below. It now has a collection of royal cradles, including one with an ingenious mechanical rocking system, surmounted by guardian angels.

From here a courtyard leads to the 16th-century **Moti Mahal** or "Pearl Palace". A palmist sits in the courtyard to foretell the futures of visitors.

The museum also has a fine collection of Rajasthani turbans and folk music instruments. Rooms displaying costumes, royal tents and special treasures are under preparation.

ENVIRONS: Osian, 64 km (40 miles) northwest of Jodhpur, is the site of 16 outstanding Jain and Hindu temples. Built by wealthy traders between the 8th and 12th centuries, when Osian was an important stop on the caravan trade route to Central Asia, they represent the earliest phase of temple architecture in Rajasthan.

Famous for the rich variety and exuberance of their sculptural decoration are the 11 temples at the southern and western edge of Osian village. Of these, the most impressive is the 8th-century **Mahavira Temple** with a superb ceiling and 20 carved pillars holding up the main portico. Equally beautiful are the classically elegant 10th-century **Sun Temple** and the profusely sculpted **Vishnu** and **Harihara Temples**, from the 8th–9th centuries.

The other temples are on a hill east of the village, dominated by the 12th-century **Sachiya Mata Temple**, approached through a series of beautifully carved arches. This temple is particularly popular with infertile women who believe that Sachiya Mata, an incarnation of Durga, has special powers to help them bear children.

Sachiya Mata Temple, Osian

Tour of Marwar Crafts Villages 🔟

THE ARID COUNTRYSIDE south of Jodhpur is dotted with villages, their mud and thatch huts inhabited by the Bishnois and communities of potters and weavers. A daylong tour of this area provides a memorable opportunity to observe the rhythm of daily life in these hamlets, experience the warm hospitality of the villagers, and see beautiful traditional crafts being practised.

TIPS FOR DRIVERS

Length: 55 km (34 miles).
Getting around: Allow 6–7 hours for the trip. Refreshments are available at Gudda Bishnoi, Salawas and Kakuni. The heritage hotels at Rohet and Luni (Fort Chanwa) offer good food and are pleasant places for a break. Hotels and travel agencies in Jodhpur can arrange taxis. A four-wheel drive is recommended.

JAISALMER

Jodhpur ①
This historic and beautiful city is on the edge of the Thar Desert.

AJMER

Salawas ③
The villagers here are skilled weavers of *dhurries* (rugs) in traditional geometric patterns and vegetable colours. They are made of cotton or camel hair.

Gudda Bishnoi ②
The Bishnois in this hamlet tend camels and goats. The men wear only white, but the women wear vivid colours and silver jewellery.

KHEJARLI

Mogra

Kakuni ④
This village, 26 km (16 miles) south of Jodhpur, is famous for its pottery, made of the fine local clay.

Luni

Rohet ⑤
The 17th-century palace-fort here is now a heritage hotel *(see p704)*, surrounded by villages of leather craftsmen.

THE BISHNOIS

The Bishnois, passionate environmentalists, are followers of a 15th-century sage, Jambeshwar, whose creed is contained in 29 *(bis noi)* principles. Most of these focus on environmental protection, and the Bishnois' faith bids them to protect every living being, if necessary with their lives. Thus, the otherwise timid blackbuck can be seen roaming freely near Bishnoi villages, confident that it will be unharmed. Bishnois believe they will be reborn as deer.

Bishnoi woman

KEY

▬▬ Tour route
═══ Other roads
━━━ River

PALI, RANAKPUR, KUMBHALGARH

0 km   3

0 miles   3

Jaisalmer ⑰

TODAY A REMOTE OUTPOST in the Thar Desert, Jaisalmer was founded in the 12th century by Maharawal Jaisal of the Bhatti Rajput clan. It was once a flourishing trade centre, strategically located on the busy caravan trade route to Afghanistan and Central Asia. Its earlier rulers grew rich by looting gems, silk and opium from the caravans, but by the 16th century Jaisalmer had become a peaceful town, whose wealthy traders and rulers vied with each other to beautify their austere desert surroundings with splendid palaces and *havelis*. Made of the local golden-yellow sandstone, they are the most spectacular examples of the Rajasthani stonemason's art. In the 18th century, with the growth of sea ports at Surat and Bombay (Mumbai), Jaisalmer's importance dwindled. But the buildings from its golden age still stand, clustered around a magnificent fort *(see pp388–9)*.

VISITORS' CHECKLIST

Jaisalmer district. 285 kms (177 miles) W of Jodhpur. 🚉 58,300. 🚌 🚉 ℹ️ *Tourist Reception Centre, Station Rd, (02992) 52 406.* 🎭 *Desert Festival (Feb), Gangaur Festival (Mar/Apr).*

🏛 Manik Chowk
Located at the entrance to the fort, this is the main marketplace, where caravans used to halt in the past. The tiny shops sell camel hair blankets, silver jewellery and gorgeous embroidered textiles. Desert nomads and their camels add to the bazaar's colour.

🏛 Badal Vilas
Near Amar Sagar Gate. ⬜ *daily.*
This late 19th-century palace is distinguished by its multi-tiered tower in the shape of a *tazia* – the ornately decorated tower of wood, metal and coloured paper, carried by Shia Muslims at Muharram *(see p669)*. The Tazia Tower of Badal Vilas, built in the mid-20th century, was a parting gift to the maharawal from the town's Shia stone-carvers, many of whom moved to Pakistan after Independence.

🏛 Gadisagar Lake
SE of the city walls.
This rainwater reservoir, built in 1367, was once the city's sole source of water. Lined with ghats and temples, it comes alive during the Gangaur festival (March/April), when the maharawal leads a procession here. The beautiful gateway leading to the tank was built by a royal courtesan, Telia, whose audacity so enraged the queens that they demanded its instant demolition. The quick-witted Telia immediately had a statue of Krishna installed on top, thereby ensuring not only that the gateway would stand, but that everyone would bow before passing through it.

Jaisalmeri smoking a hookah

🏛 Salim Singh's Haveli
Near the Fort entrance.
Local guides can arrange visits for a fee.
This *haveli* was built in 1815 by a powerful prime minister of Jaisalmer. Narrow at the base, its six storeys grow wider at each level, and all its 38 balconies have different designs. Peacocks dance between the arches on the topmost balcony, and blue cupolas cap the roof. The rear portion of this *haveli* was, sadly, damaged during the Gujarat earthquake in January 2001, but visitors are still allowed in.

🏛 Nathmalji's Haveli
Near Gandhi Chowk. *Local guides can arrange visits for a fee.*
Built in 1855 by another prime minister of Jaisalmer, the particular charm of this five-storeyed mansion is that the two sides of its façade were carved by two craftsman-brothers, Hathu and Lallu. Though at first glance they seem identical, the details on each side are actually quite different. Besides the usual floral, geometric and animal patterns, this *haveli's* motifs also reflect new influences – a European-style horse and carriage, bicycles and steam engines.

🏛 Patwon ki Haveli
E of Nathmalji's Haveli. ⬜ *daily.*
This enormous and very elaborate *haveli* was built between 1805 and 1855 by Guman Chand Patwa, one of Jaisalmer's richest merchants and bankers, who dealt in silk, brocade and opium, and had a chain of trading stations stretching from Afghanistan to China. This six-storeyed mansion has five adjoining apartments for each of his sons, and 66 balconies. The curved eaves on the balconies suggest a fleet of sailing boats, and the numerous latticed windows are carved with breathtaking intricacy.

Gadisagar Lake, lined with ghats

The Jaisalmer Haveli

AFTER THE FORT, Jaisalmer's *havelis* are its greatest attraction. Built in the 19th century by the town's merchants and ministers, these mansions dominate its labyrinthine lanes. The *havelis* of Salim Singh, Nathmalji and Patwon are the finest examples of this type of architecture, their golden stone façades so finely carved that they could be made of lace.

Carved elephant

Several generations of an extended family lived together in these huge mansions, which usually contained secluded women's quarters that outsiders could not enter. Jaisalmer's stonemasons still practise their art, doing restoration work in the fort, and working abroad for wealthy new patrons in the Gulf and Saudi Arabia.

The entrance *of most* havelis *is on a plinth, raised high above street level, to prevent the desert sand from blowing into the rooms. The ground floor had no living rooms, and was usually used as a warehouse or storeroom.*

The inner courtyard, *found in all* havelis, *was a protected place for children to play in, and for women to attend to their daily chores in privacy.*

Jharokhas, *or projecting balconies, have curved* bangaldar *eaves. Their purpose was more decorative than functional, and they gave the stonemasons an opportunity to display the full range of their creativity and skill.*

Jalis, *or latticed stone screens, display a rich variety of patterns. They keep out the harsh desert sun but let in fresh air. They also enabled women to observe street life without being seen.*

Yellow sandstone *lends itself particularly well to fine carving. Soft when newly quarried, the stone gradually becomes harder with exposure.*

Narrow streets *in the neighbourhood of Patwon ki Haveli, lined with intricately carved façades, retain their traditional ambience.*

Jaisalmer Fort

Detail from Jaisalmer Fort

J AISALMER FORT rises like a fabulous mirage out of the sands of the Thar Desert, the awesome contours of its 99 bastions softened by the golden hue of the stone. Built in 1156 by Maharawal Jaisal, and added to by his successors, this citadel stands on the peak of the 80-m (263-ft) high Trikuta Hill. In medieval times, Jaisalmer's entire population lived within the fort and even now, thousands of people reside here, making it India's only living fort. Royal palaces, a cluster of Jain temples, mansions and shops are all contained within its walls.

The southern ramparts, built of stone without any mortar

Gyan Bhandar, in the basement of the Sambhavnatha Temple, is a library of illustrated Jain palm-leaf manuscripts, some of them dating to the 11th century.

Intricate sandstone carvings are found in these seven temples dedicated to the Jain *tirthankaras*, including Rishabdeo, Sambhavnatha Parsvanatha and others.

★ **Jain Temples**
Exquisitely carved Jain temples were built in the 15th and 16th centuries by the town's wealthy traders.

The ramparts, with an inner parallel wall, have huge cannonballs perched on top, ready to crush invaders.

JAISALMER IN JEOPARDY

The growth of tourism together with recent efforts to green the nearby desert have, ironically, posed a threat to the fort. Built for an arid climate that hardly ever experienced rainfall, the fort had no provision for water supply or drainage. Now, with rising ground water levels in the area, and the introduction of piped water in the fort, seepage has made the golden stone crumble in places. Conservation efforts by Indian and international organizations are now under way to save this unique fort and town.

The 12th-century Jaisalmer Fort, threatened by rising damp

STAR SIGHTS

★ **Jain Temples**

★ **Moti Mahal**

★ **Dussehra Chowk**

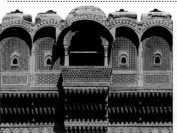

Royal Complex
The seven-storeyed palace complex consists of several interconnected palaces, built between the 16th and 19th centuries.

VISITORS' CHECKLIST

Jaisalmer Fort. Rajasthan Tourism, Station Rd, (02992) 52 406. ☐ daily. 🌐 📷 extra charges. ☑ 🚻 🍴 🎁 **Jain Temples** ☐ daily. 📷 extra charges. **Gyan Bhandar** ☐ daily.

Annapurna Bhandar was originally the fort's granary. Its ground floor has a temple.

Moti Mahal

Sarvottam Vilas
Brilliant blue tiles and glass mosaic work decorate this mid-18th century palace.

Naqqar Khana, or "Drummers' Gallery", has a richly carved octagonal balcony.

★ Moti Mahal
Floral paintings and carved doors embellish this 18th-century palace.

Rani Mahal

★ Dussehra Chowk
Festivals, royal performances and parades took place in this open plaza, framed by the palace complex. The rulers' marble throne overlooks the plaza.

Exploring Jaisalmer's Outer Sights

THE ENVIRONS OF JAISALMER are dotted with sites of both architectural and natural beauty. These include beautiful temples, the haunting ruins of the old capital, a fascinating desert village, rolling sand dunes, and the habitat of a rare desert bird, the great Indian bustard.

Manganiyar musicians, whose ballads recount Jaisalmer's history

⬛ Bhattiani Rani Temple
2 km (1.3 miles) S of fort. ⭘ *daily.*
This secluded Hindu shrine was built in honour of a 19th-century Jaisalmer princess who, surprisingly, committed *sati* on her brother-in-law's funeral pyre. A clan of Muslim musicians, the Manganiyars, are the caretakers of the temple, and recount this story, with its intriguing undertones, in their soulful ballads about Jaisalmer's history.

⬛ Bada Bagh
7 km (4 miles) N of fort. 🖼
The royal cenotaphs, with elaborately carved ceilings and fine equestrian statues of the rulers, are set in a green oasis. Next to them is the Bhaironji Temple, frequented by childless women who offer their silver girdles to the deity, in the hope that he will cure their infertility.

⬛ Lodurva
15 km (9 miles) NW of Jaisalmer.
The capital of the Bhatti Rajputs before they built the fort at Jaisalmer, Lodurva was abandoned after it was sacked by Muslim invaders in the 11th century. A group of Jain temples dominates this site, where the remains of many other fine buildings lie concealed beneath the desert sands. A beautiful *torana*

leads to the main temple, which houses a metal sculpture of the Kalpavriksha ("Celestial Tree"). It is believed to have wish-fulfilling powers.

⬛ Akal Fossil Park
17 km (11 miles) SE of Jaisalmer. ⭘ *daily.* 🖼 ☑
Extraordinary fossilized tree trunks, some of them 180 million years old, can be seen in this park. They bear witness to the fact that this arid area was once covered with dense forest.

Great Indian bustard

⬛ Khuri
40 km (25 miles) SW of Jaisalmer. Set among sand dunes, this little village is a superb example of desert architecture. Functional as well as beautiful, the village houses have thick mud walls that provide protection against the fierce desert heat and winds, while

the paintings that decorate their exteriors bring colour and beauty to the brown, parched environs.

⬛ Desert National Park
43 km (27 miles) W of Jaisalmer. *For permission, contact Collector's Office, Jaisalmer, (02992) 52 201.* 🖼 ☑ *Jeep & Camel safaris.*
This fascinating park is spread over 3,162 sq km (1,221 sq miles) of scrub and sandy wasteland, close to the border with Pakistan. Its star attraction is the great Indian bustard *(Choriotis nigriceps)*, a large bird with a height of 1.2 m (4 ft). The bustard had been hunted almost to extinction, and only about 1,000 remain now, but sightings are likely here. Other wildlife includes sand grouse, several species of falcon and vulture, desert fox, and *chinkara* (Indian gazelle).

Barmer ⓳

Barmer district. 160 km (99 miles) SE of Jaisalmer. 🚌 🚐 ⓘ *Rajasthan Tourism, Khartal, (02982) 22 956.* 🖼 *Tilwara Cattle Fair (Jan/Feb), Thar Desert Festival (Mar).*

THIS REMOTE DESERT town, whose arid soil cannot support agriculture, has become a major centre for desert handicrafts. Wood-carving, blockprinted textiles, embroidery and carpet weaving are the main source of livelihood for its people. They also lavish their skills on their mud huts, which are beautifully decorated with geometric and floral patterns. Barmer buzzes with activity during the annual Tilwara Fair (January/February), one of the many large cattle fairs in Rajasthan.

Visitors on a camel safari near Jaisalmer

Camel Safari around Jaisalmer ⑱

Window of a desert mud house

T HE FASCINATING desertscape around Jaisalmer is best explored on a camel safari. A two-day excursion takes in historic sights and villages of sheep and camel herders. Overnight stays in tents offer magical dawns and sunsets amid the dunes. Cushions are provided, but riders are advised to carry an extra one, to help soften the effects of the camel's lurching gait.

TIPS FOR RIDERS

Duration: Two days and two nights. Day 1: Jaisalmer to Lodurva via Bada Bagh and Ramkunda, 18 km (11 miles). Day 2: Lodurva to Sam via Kahala and Kanoi, 20 km (12 miles); Sam to Jaisalmer (by jeep), 45 km (28 miles). Overnight stays: Camps at Lodurva and Sam. For more details on safaris see p751; for tour operators see p755.

Jaisalmer ①
The camels set off from the First Gate of Jaisalmer's magnificent 12th-century fort.

Bada Bagh ②
The cenotaphs of the maharawals (rulers) of Jaisalmer are surrounded by green mango groves and thorny *khejri* (*Prosopsis cinerararia*) trees.

KISHANGARH

Baramsar

Ramkunda ③
A picnic lunch is served at this little village with a 15th-century Shiva temple.

Damodara

NH15

BIKANER

NH15

BARMER

Kuldhera

Kanoi ⑥
The older houses in this village are painted with flowers, animals and birds. The village craftsmen make elaborately carved camel saddles inlaid with brass.

Kahala ⑤
This hamlet of mud houses is inhabited by herders of goats and sheep. They also weave attractive blankets.

Lodurva ④
The night is spent at the old capital of the maharawals, which has lovely Jain temples. Dinner is served under a star-studded sky.

0 km   5

0 miles   5

KEY

━━ Tour route

═══ Other roads

▬▬ National highway

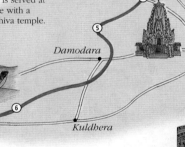

Sam ⑦
Rippling sand dunes stretch as far as the eye can see. The 45-km (28-mile) journey back to Jaisalmer the next morning is by jeep.

The City Palace, Udaipur *(see pp400–401)*, reflected in the waters of Lake Pichola ▷

The intricately carved Vimala Vasahi Temple

Mount Abu ⓴

Sirohi district. 185 km (115 miles) W of Udaipur. 🚶 22,100. 🚉 Abu Rd, 20 km (12 miles) SE of town centre, then bus. 🚌 ℹ️ opp main bus station, (02974) 3151. 🎉 Summer Festival (Jun).

RAJASTHAN'S ONLY hill station, Mount Abu has one of India's most spectacular sights – the **Dilwara Jain Temples**. This group of five marble temples is situated on a hill 3 km (2 miles) northeast of the town. The two most outstanding are the **Vimala Vasahi Temple** and the **Luna Vasahi Temple** which have incredibly intricate and delicate carvings. The sculptural details on the various doorways, archways, pillars, niches and ceilings of both these temples are simply breathtaking, the marble worked so finely that in places it is almost translucent.

The Vimala Vasahi Temple, dedicated to the first Jain *tirthankara*, Adinath, was built in 1031 by Vimala Shah, a wealthy prime minister of the Solanki kings of Gujarat. A statue of him seated on an elephant is in a pavilion to the right of the entrance. Inside, graceful nymphs and musicians, spirited horses and elephants adorn the arches and pillars, and the superb 11-tiered domed ceiling in the main hall. The inner sanctum has a statue of Adinath in tranquil meditation, while 52 carved niches contain images of the other *tirthankaras*.

The Luna Vasahi Temple, dedicated to Neminath, the 22nd Jain *tirthankara*, dates to 1231 and is even more ornately carved. Its most glorious feature, the main hall, has a magnificent lotus-shaped, tiered pendant carved from a single block of marble, descending from its domed ceiling. Behind the main shrine is the fascinating Hall of Donors, with a series of figures mounted on elephants, some in black marble. There are also life-size statues of the donors and their wives, with every detail of their dress and jewellery exquisitely and painstakingly carved.

The focal point of Mount Abu town is **Nakki Lake**, ringed by colonial mansions dating to the late 19th century, and the summer palaces of Rajput rulers. The curiously shaped **Toad's Rock** overlooks the lake, and **Sunset Point**, southwest of the lake, offers some spectacular views from a stone terrace.

About 4 km (2.5 miles) below Mount Abu, just off the main highway leading to the town, is the historic **Gaumukh** ("Cow's Mouth") **Temple** with a natural spring flowing from the mouth of a marble cow.

🏯 Dilwara Jain Temples
🔲 daily. ⬤ to menstruating women. Leather articles are not allowed inside.

ENVIRONS: Achalgarh, 8 km (5 miles) beyond Dilwara, has the ruins of a 15th-century fort, and a Shiva temple. The latter has a statue of Nandi made with over 4,000 kg (8,819 lbs) of gold, silver, brass and copper. A five-minute walk from the temple is **Guru Shikhar**, Rajasthan's highest point at 1,721 m (5,646 ft). It is marked by a small Vishnu temple.

Ranakpur ⓴

Rajsamand district. 90 km (56 miles) NW of Udaipur. 🚆 **Temple Complex** 🔲 daily. ⬤ to menstruating women. Leather articles are not allowed inside.

SET IN A SECLUDED, wooded valley of the Aravalli Hills, the 15th-century Ranakpur temple complex, dominated by the great **Adinath Temple**, is one of the five great holy places of the Jain faith. The grand scale and sheer architectural complexity of the white marble temple, along with its exquisite sculptural ornamentation, distinguish it as perhaps the single most impressive example of Western Indian temple architecture (*see pp396–7*).

Dancer, Luna Vasahi Temple

The temple has an unusual four-sided plan, with four separate entrances. Each entrance leads through a veritable forest of columns, and a number of beautifully ornamented halls and chapels, to the central sanctum containing a four-faced image of Adinath.

Each of the temple's 1,444 pillars is carved with different patterns of floral motifs, and the play of light and shadow

View of the Jain temple complex at Ranakpur

The winding ramparts of the indomitable Kumbhalgarh Fort

on the pillars, as the sun moves from east to west each day, is one of the glories of this monument. Equally stunning is the superb filigree carving on the concentric ceiling pendants, and the exuberant grace of the goddesses who form the support brackets. On one of the columns facing the sanctum, a carved panel with two figures on it depicts Dharna Shah, the builder of the temple, who was a minister of the maharana of Mewar, and his architect, Depa.

A wall topped with spires surrounds this serene temple complex, which also has a Hindu Sun Temple, and two other Jain temples. Of these, the 15th-century Parsvanatha Temple is distinguished by the exceptionally fine pierced stonework on its windows.

Kumbhalgarh ❷

Rajsamand district. 63 km (39 miles) N of Udaipur. 🚉 Kankroli, 35 km (21 miles) SE of Kumbhalgarh, then bus. 🏨 📷

LIKE A GIGANTIC brown snake, the great ramparts of Kumbhalgarh Fort wind along the rugged contours of the Aravalli Hills for 36 km (22 miles). This massive 15th-century fort, strategically located at a height of 1,050 m (3,445 ft) along the border between Marwar (Jodhpur) and Mewar (Udaipur), was

known as "The Eye of Mewar", because it offered a commanding view of the countryside for miles around. Built by Maharana Kumbha (r.1433–68), who also built the great fort of Chittorgarh (see p402), Kumbhalgarh was justly reputed to be the most impregnable fort in Rajasthan. Its ramparts are wide enough for six horsemen to ride a-breast, and seven fortified gates, studded with threatening spikes, lead to its entrance.

The crenellated walls of the fort enclose the smaller fortress of Kartargarh, several palaces and temples now in ruins, fields, water reservoirs and stables. Standing at the highest point of the fort is the **Badal Mahal**, a 19th-century addition with airy chambers painted in pink, green and turquoise, and fine wall paintings of hunting scenes.

A deity on the fort wall, believed to prevent evil happenings

The 15th-century **Neelkantha Temple**, which also lies within the fort, has a huge Shivalinga and is still in use.

Another interesting temple, the **Navachoki Mamdeva Temple**, is in a gorge to the east of Kartargarh. It contains several slabs of black granite inscribed with the history of Mewar, the earliest slab dating to 1491. Next to it is the cenotaph of Maharana Kumbha. Kumbhalgarh was also the birthplace of Maharana Pratap (1540–97), a great warrior king famous for his heroic stand against the armies of the Mughal emperor Akbar.

ENVIRONS: The **Kumbhalgarh Wildlife Sanctuary** covers 578 sq km (223 sq miles) of the Aravalli Hills, west of the fort, on the leeward side. Panther, flying squirrel, wolf and many bird species can be seen here.

Kankroli, 35 km (21 miles) southeast of Kumbhalgarh, has the 17th-century Dwarkadhish Temple on the southern shore of Rajsamand Lake. The western shore is lined with lovely marble pavilions and ghats.

The charming little town of **Deogarh**, 55 km (34 miles) north of Kumbhalgarh, set among lakes and hills, has the 17th-century Rajmahal Palace with exquisite wall murals, and the Anjaneshwar Mahadev Temple in a cave in the hillside. Deogarh is also a popular base for horse safaris (see p751) which explore this picturesque part of Mewar.

Marblework in Jain Temples

Detail from Ranakpur

RAJASTHAN's most outstanding Jain temples, at Ranakpur and at Dilwara in Mount Abu *(see p394)*, are breathtaking in the wealth and variety of their sculptural ornamentation. Made of white marble quarried at Makrana, which also provided the marble for the Taj Mahal, the Ranakpur and Dilwara temples are architectual marvels. Above all, they are testimony to the incredible artistry of the marble carvers who created these masterpieces. Visitors should use binoculars to fully appreciate the astounding work on the ceilings and pillars.

This four-faced image of Adinath, the first tirthankara, *stands in Ranakpur's main sanctum. It faces the four cardinal directions.*

THE JAIN RELIGION

Jain nuns with covered mouths

Jainism, founded in the 6th century BC, is based on a doctrine of non-violence towards all living beings. Jains are strict vegetarians, and the more orthodox ones cover their mouths to avoid inadvertently swallowing living organisms. Jains believe in 24 *tirthankaras* or crossing-makers, enlightened beings who guide others across the "river of transmigration" (the journey of the soul from one life to the next). The first of the *tirthankaras* was Adinath, also known as Rishabdeo, and the last was Mahavira (born in 540 BC). Regarded as the religion's founder, his 2,600th birth anniversary was celebrated in 2001. Jainism attracted many followers among the wealthy traders and merchants of Western India, who were also politically powerful as financiers and ministers in Rajput princely states. As acts of devotion and penance, they financed the building of several elaborately carved temples in Gujarat and Rajasthan.

HALL OF PILLARS

A forest of carved columns connected by wavy arches leads to the main sanctum at Dilwara's Vimala Vasahi Temple. It was built in the 11th century.

EXTERIOR

The uncarved exterior of Ranakpur's 15th-century Adinath Temple contrasts sharply with the profuse decoration inside. This symbolizes the Jain belief in the insignificance of outward forms, and the importance of a rich inner life.

CORBELLED CEILINGS

The ceilings are carved in concentric tiers to symbolize the Jain view of the universe as a series of cosmic cycles. Marble carvers were paid in gold according to the weight of the marble shavings they presented at the end of each day's work.

Dancers and deities, *gracefully sculpted, are the struts that support the ceiling.*

This Ranakpur ceiling *is a typical example of the Rajasthani marble carvers' art. It is so finely worked that the marble is translucent in places.*

Sculptured panels *at Ranakpur show dancers full of grace and movement.*

Pillars *in Dilwara are densely carved with floral motifs and figures in niches. No two pillars are identical in their ornamentation.*

Kalpavalli medallions, *with their exquisite patterns of foliage, tendrils and flowers, feature at both Dilwara and Ranakpur.*

The Parsvanatha plaque *shows the 23rd tirthankara protected by a multi-headed cobra. It is set into the southern wall of the Adinath Temple at Ranakpur.*

Udaipur ㉓

T HIS FAIRY-TALE CITY, with its marble palaces and lakes surrounded by a ring of hills, was founded by Maharana Udai Singh in 1559, and became the capital of Mewar after the fall of Chittorgarh in 1567 *(see p402)*. The rulers of Mewar, who belonged to the Sisodia clan of Rajputs, traced their dynasty back to AD 566. Fiercely independent, they refused matrimonial alliances with the Mughals, and took great pride in their reputation as the prime defenders of Rajput honour. The city is dominated by the massive City Palace, which overlooks Lake Pichola with its romantic island palaces. Picturesque *havelis*, ghats and temples line the lake front, with the lively bazaars of the old walled city stretching behind them.

A view of Lake Pichola, with the Jag Mandir Palace on an island

Jag Niwas, or the Lake Palace, in its magical setting on Lake Pichola

🏛 City Palace
See pp400–401.

🏛 Jag Mandir
Lake Pichola. ◯ *daily.* 🚢 *City Palace Jetty.* 📷 **Jag Niwas** ☎ *(0294) 52 8800.* 🍴 *open to non-residents.*

Jag Mandir, with its lush gardens and marble chambers exquisitely inlaid with coloured stone, was built in 1620. Eight stone elephants stand solemn guard at its entrance. Between 1623 and 1624, this island palace provided refuge for Prince Khurram (who would later become the Mughal emperor Shah Jahan) while he rebelled against his father. It is believed to have inspired many of his ideas for the Taj Mahal.

Jag Niwas, or the Lake Palace, built between 1734 and 1751, was once a royal summer retreat and is now one of the world's great hotels *(see p705)*. It is also a popular location for film shoots (including James Bond's *Octopussy*). Both palaces can be seen on a boat tour of Lake Pichola.

🏛 Jagdish Mandir
Moti Chhohta Rd. ◯ *daily.* **Bagore ki Haveli** Gangaur Ghat. ☎ *(0294) 52 3858* 📷

This 17th-century temple, just north of the City Palace's main gate, has an enormous black stone image of Vishnu in its profusely carved main shrine. The entrance is flanked by stone elephants, and a superb bronze image of Garuda (the mythical bird who is Vishnu's vehicle) stands in front of the temple. Nearby, at Gangaur Ghat, is the 18th-century **Bagore ki Haveli**, now a splendid museum exhibiting Udaipur's traditional arts and crafts, costumes, musical instruments and marblework. Folk music and dance performances are held here every evening at 7pm.

The old walled city, a jumble of shops and houses, many with beautifully painted façades, lies east of the Jagdish Mandir. In its narrow, lanes are the **Bapu** and **Bara Bazaars**, selling wooden toys, puppets, textiles, jewels and *pichhwais*.

Pichhwai painting

🦌 Fateh Sagar Lake
Fateh Sagar Rd.
North of Lake Pichola is Fateh Sagar Lake, with a garden café on its island. Overlooking it is Moti Magri Hill with a statue of Udaipur's great 16th-century warrior, Maharana Pratap, and his valiant steed, Chetak.

♣ Saheliyon ki Bari
Saheli Marg. ◯ *daily.* 📷
This delightful 18th-century retreat in the north of the city (its name means "Garden of the Maids of Honour") has ornamental fountains, a lotus pool and a rose garden. It was built for a queen of Udaipur, whose dowry included 48 maids.

🏛 Ahar
Ashok Nagar Rd. **Museum** ◯ *Sat–Thu.* ● *public hols.* 📷
Located 3 km (2 miles) east of Udaipur, Ahar has the impressive cenotaphs of 19 Mewar rulers, and a small archaeological museum.

ENVIRONS: Shilpgram, 8 km (5 miles) northwest of Udaipur, is a lively ethnographic crafts village, with artisans, folk performers, and replicas of traditional houses. Camel rides are also available.

Pavilion in the Saheliyon ki Bari, an 18th-century queen's garden

Nagda's Saas-Bahu Temples, seen through the finely-carved *torana*

VISITORS' CHECKLIST

Udaipur district. 269 km (167 miles) S of Jodhpur. 🚉 389,400. ✈ 25 km (16 miles) E of city centre. 🚌 🚍 ℹ Rajasthan Tourism, Suraj Pol, (00294) 41 1535. 🎭 Gangaur Festival (Mar/Apr), Mewar Festival (Apr).

Eklingji, 22 km (14 miles) northeast of Udaipur, is a complex of 108 temples and shrines, dedicated to Lord Shiva. It marks the site where the founder of the Mewar ruling dynasty, Bappa Rawal, received special blessings from a sage who lived here. The main temple dates to the 16th century. Built of marble and granite, it includes an impressive pillared hall and a four-faced image of Shiva crafted in black marble, with a silver Nandi facing it.

Nagda, a short distance away from Eklingji, is worth a visit for the Saas-Bahu Temples ("Mother and Daughter-in-law Temples"), twin structures dedicated to Vishnu. The 11th-century temples are entered through a finely carved *torana* and are renowned for their elaborate sculptures depicting amorous couples and scenes from the epic *Ramayana*.

One of Rajasthan's main pilgrimage sites is the 18th-century Shrinathji Temple at **Nathdwara**, 48 km (30 miles) northeast of Udaipur. The main deity is Lord Krishna, known locally as Shrinathji. His black stone image was brought here from Mathura *(see p178)* to save it from destruction by the Mughal emperor Aurangzeb in the 17th century. Beautiful painted cloth hangings known as *pichhwais* are hung behind it. Non-Hindus cannot enter the temple, but Nathdwara town's picturesque bazaar, with its *pichhwai* painters at work, is worth a visit. *Pichhwais*, one of the most vibrant forms of Indian painting, are done on stiff cloth in vegetable and mineral colours. They depict 24 scenes from the Krishna legend, each linked with a particular festival or holy day. At the centre of each painting is a stylised image of Lord Krishna, with dusky skin, slanting eyes and intricate jewellery, set against a background of verdant foliage, birds, animals and skyscapes. Around the deity are cows, milkmaids and devotees.

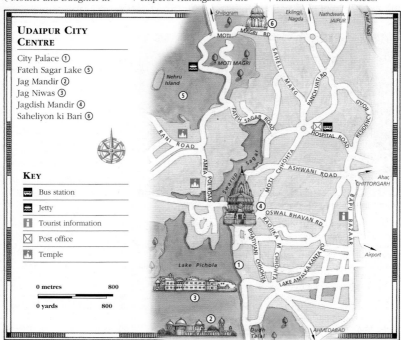

UDAIPUR CITY CENTRE

City Palace ①
Fateh Sagar Lake ⑤
Jag Mandir ②
Jag Niwas ③
Jagdish Mandir ④
Saheliyon ki Bari ⑥

KEY

🚌	Bus station
🚢	Jetty
ℹ	Tourist information
✉	Post office
🛕	Temple

0 metres   800

0 yards   800

Udaipur: City Palace

Royal sun symbol

Sᴛʀᴇᴛᴄʜɪɴɢ ᴀʟᴏɴɢ the eastern shore of Lake Pichola, Udaipur's City Palace is a fascinating combination of Rajput military architecture and Mughal-style decorative techniques. Its stern, fortress-like façade, topped by a profusion of graceful balconies, cupolas and turrets, has been aptly described by one writer as a massive plain cake topped with fabulous icing. The largest palace in Rajasthan, covering an area of **2 ha** (5 acres), the City Palace is actually a complex of several palaces, built or added to by 22 different maharanas between the 16th and 20th centuries. Much of it is now a museum, and parts of it are luxury hotels.

Fateh Prakash
This early 20th-century palace, now a hotel, has a magnificent Durbar Hall and a gallery of crystal furniture.

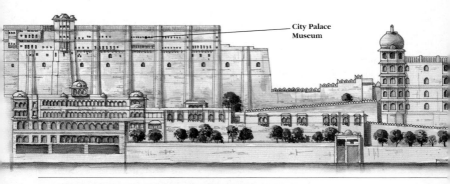

City Palace Museum

Rajya Angan Chowk, with a temple to the goddess Dhuni Mata

Exploring the City Palace

The older section of the City Palace complex dates from 1568. Behind its fortified walls is a maze of royal apartments, reception halls and court-yards. They are linked to each other by narrow passages and steep staircases – a feature typical of Rajput palaces of that period, designed to confuse invaders.

The superb **City Palace Museum** is spread out through several palaces in this section, and is entered through the imposing **Tripolia Gate** (built in 1713). Above the entrance is the Mewar crest – a large Sun face (reinforcing the Sisodia clan's claim to be descended from the Sun), flanked by Rajput and Bhil warriors (the tribal Bhils,

skilled archers, played a heroic role in Mewar's great battles). Beyond this is the **Ganesh Deorhi Gate** where entrance tickets for the museum are sold. It leads into a courtyard decorated with frescoes of horses and elephants, and a marble relief of the god Ganesha surrounded by dazzling mirror and glass inlay.

The next courtyard is the **Rajya Angan Chowk**, from where steps lead to the **Chandra Mahal** (built in 1620). One of the loveliest palaces in the complex, it has beautiful columns, fretwork windows and striking marble reliefs of Rajput women, one of whom carries a shield. There is a magical view of Lake Pichola and its island palaces from here.

Another flight of steps from here leads to the charming **Bari Mahal** (built in 1699). Perched 27 m (89 ft) above the ground, it is built on a terraced hillside that is com-

A view of the City Palace, on the eastern shore of Lake Pichola

VISITORS' CHECKLIST

City Palace Complex
📞 (00294) 528 016. ⬤ daily.
🚫 📷 restricted. 👥 **Museum**
📷 extra charges. ✗ 💻
Fateh Prakash 🍴 open to non-
residents. **Shiv Niwas** 🍴 open
to non-residents.

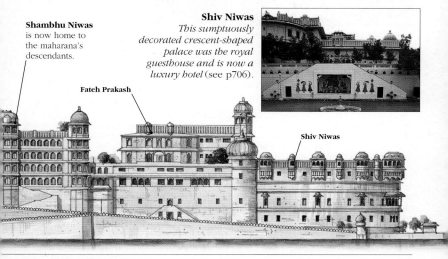

Shambhu Niwas
is now home to
the maharana's
descendants.

Shiv Niwas
*This sumptuously
decorated crescent-shaped
palace was the royal
guesthouse and is now a
luxury hotel (see p706).*

Fateh Prakash

Shiv Niwas

**Kanch Burj, with its dazzling
decoration of red and silver glass**

pletely enclosed within the
palace walls. Deep halls with
receding rows of carved
arches open into an enchanting courtyard with a marble
pool in the middle. Tall *neem*
trees stand around it, providing dappled shade.

The Bari Mahal leads to the
Dilkhushal Mahal (built in
1620) with two remarkable
chambers – the Kanch Burj
("Glass Turret") inlaid with
red and silver glass, and the
Krishna Niwas which exhibits
outstanding Mewar miniature
paintings *(see p405).* This was
the room of 16-
year-old Princess
Krishna Kumari,
who committed
suicide in 1807
when rival suitors
from Jodhpur and
Jaipur threatened
to go to war over
her hand.

To the left of this
palace is the
ornate **Moti
Mahal**, the cham-
ber of the
dissolute Maharana
Jawan Singh
(r.1828–38), who once
promised a dancing girl half
his kingdom if she could walk
a tightrope across Lake
Pichola. The girl had almost
reached when the maharana's
alarmed courtiers cut the
rope, and the dancer drowned.
Still further left is the **Mor
Chowk** ("Peacock Courtyard")
with its brilliantly coloured
19th-century mosaics of three
dancing peacocks.

**Mosaic of dancing pea-
cock in the Mor Chowk**

The southern end
of the City Palace
complex has three
other opulent
palaces built in the
late 19th and early
20th centuries –
Shambhu Niwas
where the descen-
dants of the rulers
now live; **Fateh
Prakash** with its
magnificent Durbar
Hall, fine portraits
and gallery of
crystal furniture;
and the semi-
circular **Shiv Niwas** built as
the royal guesthouse (Queen
Elizabeth II once stayed
here). Fateh Prakash and Shiv
Niwas are now luxury hotels,
but are open to non-residents
for tours and meals.

A colourfully painted chamber in Juna Mahal, Dungarpur

Dungarpur ㉔

Dungarpur district. 110 km (68 miles)
S of Udaipur. ☗ 42,550. ▤
🎦 Vagad Festival (Jan/Feb),
Baneshwar Festival (Feb).

THIS REMOTE, relatively unknown town boasts some
unexpected artistic treasures.
Dominating Dungarpur is the
seven-storeyed **Juna Mahal**,
built in the 13th century on a
large rock. The interior of this
palace-fort, in contrast to its
rather battered exterior, glows
with exuberant ornamentation,
and contains some of the
most beautiful frescoes to be
seen in Rajasthan. Remarkably
well-preserved, these include
a series of erotic paintings
from the *Kama Sutra* in the
erstwhile ruler's bedroom, on
the top floor of the palace.

The 19th-century **Udai Vilas
Palace** beside a lake, is built
of local grey-green granite in
a blend of Rajput and Mughal
styles. Rising from the centre
of its courtyard is a fantastic
four-storeyed pavilion with
cusped arches, densely carved
friezes, and a profusion of

canopies and balconies. The
large room on its top storey is
inlaid with a variety of semi-
precious stones.

Chittorgarh ㉕

Chittorgarh district. 115 km (72 miles)
NE of Udaipur. 🚉 ▤ 🛈 Janta Avas
Graha, Station Rd, (01472) 41 089.
🎦 Meera Utsav (Oct).

THE GREAT, battle-scarred
Chittorgarh Fort epitomizes
in its tragic history the valour,
romance, chivalry and strict
death-before-dishonour code
glorified in Rajput myths and
legends. Sprawling across 280
ha (692 acres), atop a steep
180-m (591-ft) high rocky hill,
Chittorgarh's ruined palaces,
temples and towers bear
witness to its illustrious and
turbulent past, when it was
the capital of the Sisodia
rulers of Mewar, between the
12th and 16th centuries.

As Rajasthan's mightiest fort,
it was the target of successive
invaders. The first siege, in
1303, was by Sultan Alauddin

Khilji *(see p48)*, whose goal
was to capture not only the
fort but also the queen, Rani
Padmini, whose legendary
beauty the sultan had glimpsed
reflected in a mirror. When
defeat seemed inevitable, Rani
Padmini along with 13,000
women committed *jauhar* – a
ritual form of mass suicide by
immolation, practised by
Rajput women to escape
dishonour at the hands of
their enemies. It is said that
50,000 Rajput warriors died in
the ensuing battle. Alauddin's
army then proceeded to sack
the fort and destroyed many
of its buildings. Within a few
years, however, the ruler's
grandson had regained it for
the Sisodia dynasty.

The next great battle, this
time against Sultan Bahadur
Shah of Gujarat in 1535, saw
the Queen Mother, Rani
Jawaharbai, lead a cavalry
charge and die on the battlefield along with the flower of
Rajput youth. Once again,
thousands of women inside
the fort committed *jauhar*.
The third and final assault on
Chittorgarh was led by the
Mughal emperor Akbar, who
was able to capture it in 1567.
Chittorgarh was abandoned
thereafter, and the Sisodias
moved their capital to
Udaipur *(see pp398–9)*.

Seven massive spiked gates
lead to the fort. The first
building to the right is **Rana
Kumbha's Palace** (built
between 1433 and 1468),
probably the earliest surviving
example of a Rajput palace.
Its northern side has a
profusion of richly
carved balconies,

A view of the impressive Chittorgarh Fort, spread over a rocky hill

and a unique stepped wall. Elephant stables and a council chamber comprise its public areas, while the private apartments are a maze of small rooms, including a zenana section. Near it are the 20th-century **Fateh Prakash Palace**, which now houses a museum of sculpture found on the site; the **Kumbha Shyam Temple**, dating to the 15th-century, with a fine sculpture of Vishnu in his Varaha (boar) incarnation; and the **Meerabai Temple**, built in 1440 by Meerabai, *(see p49)* another remarkable Mewar queen. A mystic and a poetess, she defied Rajput convention and devoted her life to the worship of Lord Krishna.

The main street runs south of this temple towards the nine-storeyed **Vijay Stambh** ("Victory Tower"), built by Maharana Kumbha between 1458 and 1468, to commemorate his victory over Sultan Mahmud of Malwa *(see p247)*. The view from the top of this extraordinary 36-m (118-ft) high sandstone structure, richly carved with gods and goddesses, is magnificent. The main street continues further south past noblemen's mansions to the **Gaumukh Reservoir**, fed by an underground spring, and the 16th-century **Kalika Mata Temple**, built over the original Sun Temple which was destroyed during the devastating siege of 1303.

Opposite this temple stands the 19th-century reconstruction of **Padmini's Palace** with a lake pavilion adjacent to it. The palace contains the mirror in which Alauddin Khilji supposedly saw her reflection. Standing further south, past some Jain temples, is the **Kirti Stambh**. This seven-storeyed tower is dedicated to the first Jain *tirthankara*, Adinath.

Vijay Stambh

🏛 **Fateh Prakash Museum**
◻ *Sat–Thu.* 🎟 *free on Mon.*

The 11th-century temple of the Sun God, in Jhalrapatan

Jhalawar ㉖

Jhalawar district. 323 km (201 miles) S of Jaipur. 🚶 48,100. 🚌 🛈 *Hotel Chandrawati, (07432) 30 081.* 📅 *Chandrabhaga Cattle Fair (Oct/Nov).*

THIS DELIGHTFUL little town, surrounded by orange groves and poppy fields, is dominated by a 19th-century fort, the seat of the erstwhile princes of Jhalawar. It now houses government offices. An incongruous yet charming part of the fort is the **Bhavani Natya Shala Theatre** (built in 1921), which was modelled on the grand opera houses the maharaja had seen on his European tours. The old walled town of **Jhalrapatan** ("City of Bells"), 6 km (4 miles) south of the fort, has a splendid cluster of 11th-century temples. Of these the most impressive is the **Surya Temple** with its stunning image of the Sun God. About 1.5 km (1 mile) south of this temple, on the banks of the Chandrabhaga river, stands the superbly carved 7th-century **Chandra Mauleshwar Temple**.

ENVIRONS: The 14th-century **Ghagron Fort**, 10 km (6 miles) west of Jhalawar, is spectacularly situated amid a picturesque landscape of hills, woods and fields, and surrounded on three sides by the Kali, Sindh and Ahu rivers.

The lush forests, cliffs and grasslands of **Darrah Wild-life Sanctuary**, 70 km (44 miles) west of Jhalawar, look just as they do in the famous Kota paintings *(see p405)* of hunting scenes – only the tigers and princes are now missing.

Kota ㉗

Kota district. 261 km (162 miles) S of Jaipur. 🚶 696,000. 🚉 🚌 🛈 *Hotel Chambal, (0744) 41 089.* 📅 *Dussehra Mela (Sep/Oct).*

THE IMPOSING façade of Kota's fortified **City Palace**, which dates back to 1625, stretches along the banks of the Chambal river, recalling the princely past of this now heavily industrialized city. Kota's rich artistic heritage is well-represented in the palace apartments – every available surface is covered with outstanding miniature paintings, mirrorwork, murals and mosaics. Particularly resplendent is the Durbar Hall, with its ebony-and-ivory doors, and paintings depicting Kota's history. Many of the royal apartments now form part of the excellent **Rao Madho Singh Museum**, which has a fine collection of weapons, paintings and royal regalia.

On Kishorsagar Lake, in the middle of the town, is the charming island palace known as **Jag Mandir** *(see front cover)*, built in the 18th century by a Kota queen who yearned for her childhood home in Udaipur *(see p398)*.

🏛 **Rao Madho Singh Museum**
◻ *Sat–Thu.* 🎟

ENVIRONS: Bardoli, 55 km (34 miles) southwest of Kota, has one of Rajasthan's most beautiful temple complexes. The 9th-century Ghateshwar Mahadev temple has an outstanding sculpture of Nataraja (the dancing Shiva) on the door of its sanctum.

Ebony-and-ivory door in the 17th-century City Palace, Kota

View of Bundi, nestled in a narrow valley of the Aravalli Hills

Bundi ㉘

Bundi district. 215 km (134 miles) S of
Jaipur. 🏛 88,350. 🚉 🚌
ℹ️ *Rajasthan Tourism, Circuit House,
(0747) 22 697.* 🏛 *daily.*
🎭 *Gangaur (Mar/Apr).*

BUNDI IS OFTEN described as
the undiscovered jewel of
Rajasthan. Surrounded on
three sides by the
rugged, thickly
forested Aravalli
Hills, this walled
town has retained
much of its
historic
character. The
Taragarh Fort
crowns the crest of a
steep hill overlook-
ing the town, while
the **Garh Palace**
spills picturesquely
down the hillside.
This palace is Bundi's
– and Rajasthan's –
jewel. Lieutenant
Colonel James Tod,
(1782–1835), the British
Political Agent and author of
the authoritative *Annals and
Antiquities of Rajasthan*,
wrote that "the *coup d'oeil* of
the castellated palace of
Boondi, from whichever side
you approach it, is the most
striking in India".

The state of Bundi was
founded in 1341 by Rao Deva
of the "fire-born" Hada
Chauhan Rajput clan, and the
massive, square Taragarh Fort
dates to his reign. Work on
the palace began in the 16th
century, and it was added to
by successive rulers over the
next 200 years, at different
levels on the hillside. Unlike
most other palaces in Rajasthan, there is very little Mughal
influence in its architecture.

**Painting from the
Chitrashala**

The Garh Palace represents a
rare example of the pure
Rajput style, with curved
roofs topping pavilions and
kiosks, a profusion of temple
columns and ornamental
brackets, and typically Rajput
motifs such as elephants and
lotus flowers. Unusually, the
palace is not built of the
sandstone favoured by most
other Rajput king-
doms, but of a hard,
green-tinged serpen-
tine stone, quarried
locally. This stone,
unlike sandstone,
does not lend itself
to fine carving.
Instead, Garh Palace
was embellished by
superb paintings.
The palace is
entered through the
imposing **Hathia
Pol** ("Elephant Gate-
way"), flanked by
two towers and
topped by a pair of
huge painted elephants. The
most spectacular parts of the
palace are the **Chattar Mahal**
(built in 1660), and the
Chitrashala, an arcaded
gallery (built between 1748
and 1770) overlooking a
hanging garden. The murals
in these are regarded as
among the finest examples of
Rajput painting. The
themes they cover
include scenes from
the Radha-Krishna
legend, religious
ceremonies, hunting
scenes and other
princely amuse-
ments. The colours
are predominantly
blue and green, with
touches of deep red
and yellow.

In the middle of the town is
the **Naval Sagar Lake**, with a
little temple on an island in
its centre. The fort and palace
reflected in the lake make an
enchanting sight.

Bundi has over 50 stepwells,
of which the most beautiful is
the 46-m (151-ft) deep **Rani-
ki-Baori**, also in the centre of
town. Built in the 17th century,
it is strikingly similar to Adalaj
Vav in Gujarat *(see pp414–15)*,
with richly decorated archways
and sculptures of Vishnu's ten
avatars *(see p679)*.

Situated at the northern
edge of the town is the 18th-
century **Sukh Niwas Mahal**,
a romantic summer palace
overlooking **Jait Sagar Lake**.
Standing at the opposite end
of the lake are the royal
cenotaphs, and at its western
edge is an elegant hunting
tower, the **Shikar Burj**.

ENVIRONS: Bijolia, 50 km (31
miles) southwest of Bundi, on
the road to Chittorgarh, has a
group of three beautiful 13th-
century temples, dedicated to
Shiva. **Menal**, lying 20 km (12
miles) further along the same
road is a delightful wooded
spot with 11th-century temples
standing near a gorge.

Tonk, 113 km (70 miles)
north of Bundi, was once the
capital of the only Muslim
princely state in Rajasthan.
Founded in the early 19th-
century, its main attraction is
the splendid Sunehri Kothi
("Golden Mansion") within the
palace complex, every inch of
its interior covered with gold
leaf, lacquerwork, moulded
stucco and striking mirrorwork.
Stained-glass windows bathe
this opulent hall in glowing
colours. Tonk's Arabic and
Persian Research Institute has
rare, illuminated medieval
Islamic manuscripts.

The gilded interior of Sunehri Kothi in Tonk

Rajasthani Miniature Painting

THE INTRICATE and vivid paintings of Rajasthan's princely states grew out of illustrated Jain and Hindu sacred texts. Originally, they depicted mainly religious themes, in bold lines and bright primary colours. After the 17th century, however, the influence of the more sophisticated Mughal-Persian art tradition brought greater delicacy of line, and a wider range of colours and themes into

Radha and Krishna, Bundi

Rajasthani art. By the 18th century, many princely states such as Kishangarh, Mewar, Bundi and Kota had developed their own distinctive styles. In most schools of Rajasthani painting, however, human figures are shown in profile, and different colours, seasons, flowers and animals are used symbolically to express a variety of moods. These various schools of miniature painting continue to flourish in Rajasthan today.

Jain religious text, early 17th century

MEWAR PAINTINGS
Large, detailed compositions, showing scenes from the lives of the maharanas of Udaipur, are characteristic of the Mewar School. The paintings depict festivals, grand processions, historic battles and religious ceremonies. The intricate detail was achieved by using just a single squirrel hair as a brush.

The Maharana Celebrating Gangaur **(1715)**

BUNDI AND KOTA PAINTINGS
The neighbouring princely states of Bundi and Kota produced outstanding miniatures. Bundi specialized in depicting palace life and scenes from Krishna's life, executed in soft blues and greens. Kota is renowned for its superb hunting scenes, set in dramatic forested landscapes, with wonderful depictions of animals and foliage. An 18th-century court painter named Sheikh Taju created many of them.

Bundi miniature depicting a palace scene

KISHANGARH PAINTINGS
Famous for his fine portraits, the 18th-century Kishangarh artist, Nihal Chand, found a favourite model in the royal courtesan, Bani Thani Radha, with her elegantly elongated features and enigmatic expression. He was also known for his lyrical depictions of skyscapes and seasons.

Bani Thani Radha, often called the Indian Mona Lisa

Maharao Durjan in the Kota Forest **(1730)**

Ranthambhore National Park ㉙

Park sign

THIS PARK LIES IN the shadow of the Aravalli and Vindhya mountain ranges and covers a core area of 275 sq km (106 sq miles). Its razor-sharp ridges, deep boulder-filled gorges, lakes and jungles are the habitat of carnivores such as the caracal, panther, jackal and hyena, numerous species of deer, and a rich variety of resident and migratory birds. The most famous resident, however, is the endangered tiger, which is spotted quite frequently at Ranthambhore. Like other parks in the region, this was originally the hunting ground of Jaipur's maharajas and it only became a Project Tiger Reserve in 1973.

Rajbagh Talao
Ruined pavilions stand on the banks of Rajbagh Talao, one of the three lakes in the park.

Ranthambhore Fort
The park derives its name from this great Rajput forest fort that is 1,000 years old and stands at a height of 215 m (705 ft).

Sambar
Large herds of sambar (Cervus unicolor) are seen around the lakes, wallowing in the water and feeding on aquatic plants, unperturbed by jeeps and visitors.

JAIPUR
TONK
Sawai Madhopur
MUMBAI

Padam Talao
Ranthambhore Fort
Rajbagh Talao
Jogi Mahal
Lahpur Valley
Nalghati Valley
Man Sarovar

Banyan Tree
This enormous banyan tree (Ficus bengalensis) lies in the grounds of Jogi Mahal. Its many spreading branches are all supported by roots.

0 km   5
0 miles   2

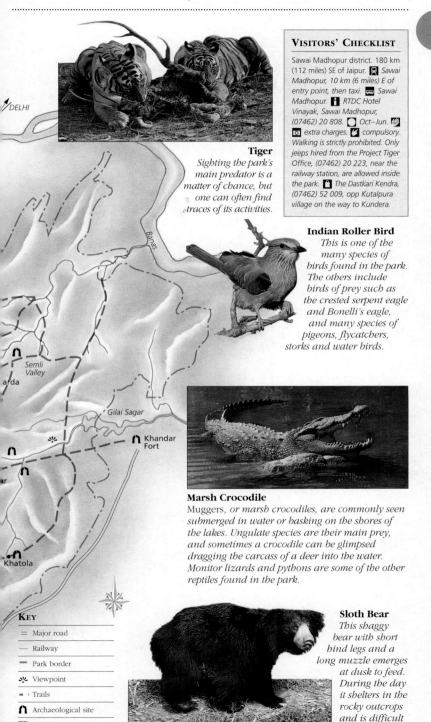

/DELHI

Banas

Semli
Valley

arda

Gilai Sagar

⋔ Khandar
Fort

r

⋔
Khatola

VISITORS' CHECKLIST

Sawai Madhopur district. 180 km
(112 miles) SE of Jaipur. 🚃 *Sawai
Madhopur, 10 km (6 miles) E of
entry point, then taxi.* 🚌 *Sawai
Madhopur.* 🛈 *RTDC Hotel
Vinayak, Sawai Madhopur,
(07462) 20 808.* ☐ *Oct–Jun.* 🎫
📷 *extra charges.* 📷 *compulsory.
Walking is strictly prohibited. Only
jeeps hired from the Project Tiger
Office, (07462) 20 223, near the
railway station, are allowed inside
the park.* 🛈 *The Dastkari Kendra,
(07462) 52 009, opp Kutalpura
village on the way to Kundera.*

Tiger
*Sighting the park's
main predator is a
matter of chance, but
one can often find
traces of its activities.*

Indian Roller Bird
*This is one of the
many species of
birds found in the park.
The others include
birds of prey such as
the crested serpent eagle
and Bonelli's eagle,
and many species of
pigeons, flycatchers,
storks and water birds.*

Marsh Crocodile
Muggers, or marsh crocodiles, are commonly seen
submerged in water or basking on the shores of
the lakes. Ungulate species are their main prey,
and sometimes a crocodile can be glimpsed
dragging the carcass of a deer into the water.
Monitor lizards and pythons are some of the other
reptiles found in the park.

KEY

═ Major road

─ Railway

━ Park border

☆ Viewpoint

∙ ∙ Trails

⋔ Archaeological site

🛈 Tourist information

Sloth Bear
*This shaggy
bear with short
hind legs and a
long muzzle emerges
at dusk to feed.
During the day
it shelters in the
rocky outcrops
and is difficult
to sight.*

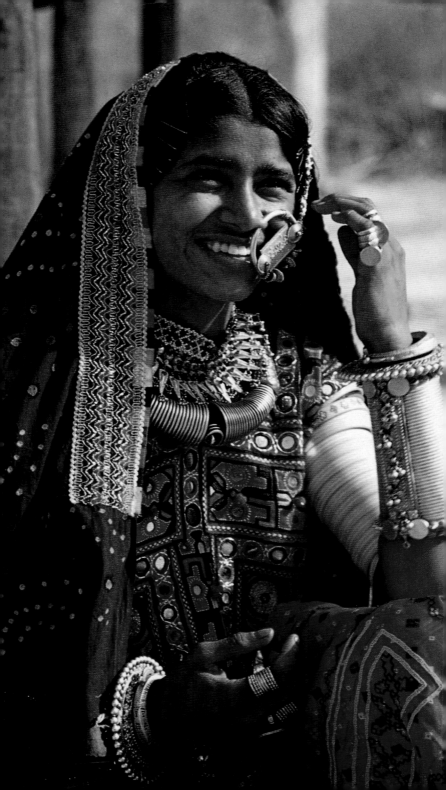

GUJARAT

THE STATE OF GUJARAT has three distinct regions – a corridor running north to south which is the industrial mainland, a peninsula known as Saurashtra, and Kutch, which is partly desert and partly marshland. The state's 1,600-km (994-mile) coastline has attracted seafarers through the ages, lured by the rich prospects of trade. The Arabs, Portuguese, Dutch, Mughals and British, as well as Parsis fleeing their native Iran, have all left their mark on Gujarat's culture. Fascinating archaeological sites, superb Jain, Hindu and Islamic architecture, exquisite crafts and rare wildlife, including the Asiatic lion, are among Gujarat's attractions, as are its hardworking, enterprising people. In January 2001, an earthquake hit Gujarat and devastated the region of Kutch. But with their legendary capacity to overcome hardship and disaster, the people lost no time in rebuilding their lives out of the debris around them.

SIGHTS AT A GLANCE

Towns & Cities
Ahmedabad ❶
Bhavnagar ⑫
Bhuj ㉒
Daman ⑪
Diu ⑭
Jamnagar ⑳
Junagadh ⑰
Mandvi ㉓
Patan ❻
Porbandar ⑱
Rajkot ㉑

Siddhpur ❼
Surat ⑩
Vadodara ❽

Historic Sites
Adalaj Vav ❷
Champaner ❾
Dholavira ㉔
Lothal ❸
Modhera Sun Temple ❺

Temples & Holy Places
Dwarka ⑲
Palitana ⑬
Somnath ⑮

National Parks & Areas of Natural Beauty
The Little Rann of Kutch Sanctuary ㉕
Nal Sarovar Sanctuary ❹
Sasan Gir National Park ⑯

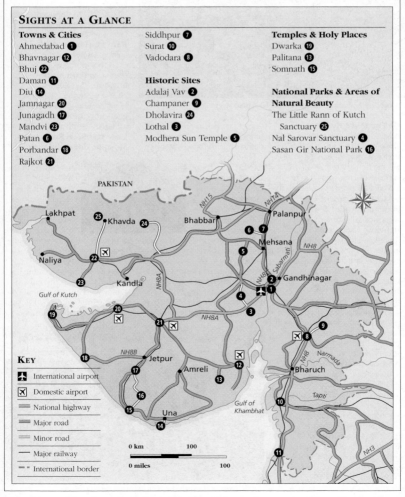

KEY

- ✈ International airport
- ✕ Domestic airport
- ═══ National highway
- ═══ Major road
- ═══ Minor road
- ─── Major railway
- ∙─∙ International border

◁ **Kutchi woman from the Meghwal tribe, in embroidered mirrorwork garments and heavy silver jewellery**

Ahmedabad ❶

G UJARAT'S LEADING CITY, Ahmedabad was the state capital until 1970. This bustling industrial and commercial centre also has a fascinating old quarter, redolent with Gujarat's traditional culture and history. Legend has it that the city owes its foundation to Sultan Ahmed Shah (r.1411–42), who, while out hunting, encountered a warren of rabbits on the banks of the Sabarmati river. Astonishingly, the rabbits turned fiercely on his hounds and defended their territory. Viewing this as an auspicious sign, the sultan built his new capital at this site and named it after himself – Ahmedabad.

A view of the crowded banks of the Sabarmati river

🏛 The Old City

Bounded by Lady Vidyagauri Rd, Sardar Patel Rd & Kasturba Gandhi Rd. **Heritage Walking Tours** 📞 *(079) 539 1811.*

A maze of crowded bazaars, *pols* (large gateways, leading to residential quarters), exquisitely carved façades, temples, mosques and subterranean stepwells *(vavs)* mark the 3-km (2-mile) square that makes up the Old City. This area is best explored on foot, and the Ahmedabad Municipal Corporation organizes a daily Heritage Walking Tour through the atmospheric bylanes.

Visitors can climb to the roof of the **Bhadra Fort**, the site of the original city, for panoramic views of the surrounding streets. Southwest of the fort is **Ahmed Shah's Mosque**, a simple place of worship, built in 1414 on the site of an early 13th-century Hindu temple.

Perhaps Ahmedabad's most photographed monument, **Siddi Saiyad's Mosque** in the northeast corner of Bhadra Fort, is renowned for its superb yellow stone latticework. Made by a slave of Ahmed Shah in 1572, the twin *jalis* on the western wall depict the intertwining branches of a tree, carved with extraordinary delicacy.

Southeast of the fort, the **Teen Darwaza** ("Triple Gateway") straddles the road, which is lined with shops selling blockprints, silverware and assorted bric-à-brac. Close by,

Tree of Life *jali* in Siddi Saiyad's Mosque

along Mahatma Gandhi Road, is the **Jami Masjid**, which Sultan Ahmed Shah built in 1423, to enable the faithful to congregate for Friday prayers.

The masons who constructed this yellow sandstone structure, ingeniously used pieces retrieved from demolished Hindu and Jain temples – the black slab close to the main arch is said to be the base of an inverted Jain idol. The mosque's 15 domes are supported by 260 pillars covered with intricate carvings. The interior is illuminated by natural light filtered through latticework screens.

Outside the east entrance of the Jami Masjid, close to the jewellery bazaar in Manek Chowk, is the **Tomb of Ahmed Shah**, with elegant pillared verandahs, where the sultan, his son and grandson are buried. In the heart of the market, echoing the plan and layout of the sultan's tomb, lies **Rani-ka-Hazira**, the mausoleum of his many queens.

To the southeast of Manek Chowk is **Rani Sipri's Mosque**, also known as Masjid-e-Nagina ("Jewel of a Mosque") because of its elegant proportions and slender minarets. Northwest of Manek Chowk is **Rani Rupmati's Mosque**, dedicated to the sultan's Hindu wife. Built in the mid-15th century, it has elements of Hindu and Islamic design, with perforated stone screens to provide privacy for women.

The city's famous Shaking Minarets, next to the railway station, were partly damaged in the earthquake of 2001, and are now closed to visitors.

Traffic moving through the Teen Darwaza thoroughfare

✿ Outside the Old City
N of the Old City.

Situated outside the Delhi Gate, the **Hatheesing Temple** was built in 1850 by Kesarsinh Hatheesing Shah, a Jain merchant. This intricately carved marble temple is dedicated to Dharmanath, the 15th Jain *tirthankara (see p396)*. A paved courtyard has 52 cubicles, housing shrines dedicated to different *tirthankaras*.

A fine example of Gujarat's stepwells is the **Dada Harir Vav** lying to the northeast of the old city. Built in 1500 for Bai Harir Sultani, a lady from the sultan's harem, its walls and pillars are beautifully decorated with elaborate carvings.

✿ New Ahmedabad
W of Sabarmati river.

Across the Sabarmati river, modern Ahmedabad has some fine examples of contemporary architecture designed by Le Corbusier *(see p101)* and the American architect, Louis Kahn. The **Sanskar Kendra**, designed by Le Corbusier, has a rare collection of miniature paintings. The Indian Institute of Management (IIM), India's top college for business studies, is in a campus designed by Louis Kahn. Close by, the **LD Institute of Indology** houses ancient manuscripts

and paintings, and the **Calico Museum** *(see pp412–13)* displays an outstanding collection of textiles. The prestigious National Institute of Design is on the south bank of the river.

✿ Sabarmati Ashram
⦿ daily. **Son et Lumière** *Mon, Tue, Wed & Fri: 6:30pm.*

A spartan colony of tiled houses, the **Sabarmati Ashram** was a second home to Mahatma Gandhi. It was from here that he orchestrated the final struggle for India's freedom. His cottage, Hriday Kunj, has been maintained much as he left it, and contains some personal items such as his round eyeglasses, wooden slippers, books and letters.

Gandhi's room in the Sabarmati Ashram, with his spinning wheel

VISITORS' CHECKLIST

Ahmedabad district. 545 km (338 miles) NW of Mumbai.
✈ 3,515,400. ✈ 10 km (6 miles) N of city centre. 🚉 🚌
🛈 HK House, Ashram Rd, (079) 658 9172. 🛍 Mon–Sat.
📅 Uttarayan (14 Jan), Navratri (Sep/Oct).

ENVIRONS: About 4 km (2.5 miles) south of the city is the **Vishala Complex** with a museum displaying traditional utensils and everyday objects. It also has an excellent outdoor restaurant for Gujarati cuisine, set in an attractive rural ambience *(see p733)*. A short distance to the southwest is the **Sarkhej Roja**, a beautiful complex of tombs and pavilions around an artificial lake, built as a retreat for Gujarat's rulers between 1445 and 1461. Its tombs include that of Ahmed Shah's spiritual advisor, Sheikh Ahmed Khattu. Finely carved brass latticework is a unique feature of this site. Built in the late 1960s, the state capital, **Gandhinagar**, is 25 km (16 miles) north of Ahmedabad. Spread over 60 sq km (23 sq miles), this planned township has the state's administrative complex at its centre.

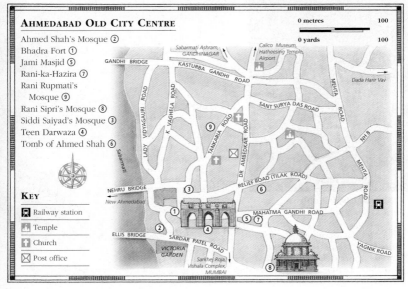

AHMEDABAD OLD CITY CENTRE

Ahmed Shah's Mosque ②
Bhadra Fort ①
Jami Masjid ⑤
Rani-ka-Hazira ⑦
Rani Rupmati's Mosque ⑨
Rani Sipri's Mosque ⑧
Siddi Saiyad's Mosque ③
Teen Darwaza ④
Tomb of Ahmed Shah ⑥

0 metres   100
0 yards   100

KEY
🚉 Railway station
🛕 Temple
✝ Church
✉ Post office

Ahmedabad: The Calico Museum

Detail from
kalamkari **fabric**

Aʜꜱ MAJOR centre of India's textile trade and industry since the 15th century, Ahmedabad is an appropriate location for this outstanding museum. Its collection of rare textiles includes royal tents, carpets and costumes; religious paintings on cloth; embroideries, brocades and silk weaves; and Kashmir shawls. The exhibits, most of which date to the 17th and 18th centuries, are displayed in a beautiful old *haveli*. The museum was established in 1949 by the Sarabhai family, textile mill owners and leading philanthropists of Gujarat.

Brocade Patka
This 18th-century gold brocade waist band, patterned with pink poppies, was part of a royal costume.

★ **Mughal Tent**
This sumptuous 17th-century tent is made up of intricately hand-painted cotton panels in the kalamkari *technique (see p680). Mughal kings used these tents during military campaigns, on hunting expeditions and while touring their kingdom.*

Ground floor

★ **Sharad Utsav Pichhwai**
Lord Krishna plays the flute in this exquisite 18th-century pichhwai from Nathdwara (see p399). It was hung in the temple on the autumn full moon, when nectar is believed to fall from heaven. Note the delightful cow licking Krishna's leg.

GALLERY GUIDE
The museum, set in the verdant Shahi Bagh gardens, is spread over 12 rooms on two floors of the haveli. *The exhibits are displayed with great imagination, and each gallery presents the craft of a region, a tribal group or a religious sect. Within the museum compound, housed in another fine* haveli, *are the Sarabhai Foundation Galleries, with a fine collection of bronze icons and paintings.*

A view of the Calico Museum, showing the richly carved wooden façade of the old *haveli* in which it is housed

VISITORS' CHECKLIST

Sarabhai Foundation, Shahi Bagh, N of Delhi Gate.
(079) 286 8172.
Thu–Tue. public hols.
Religious textiles: 10:30am; Secular textiles: 3pm; Garden tour by appointment only.
Sarabhai Foundation Galleries
Thu–Tue. public hols.

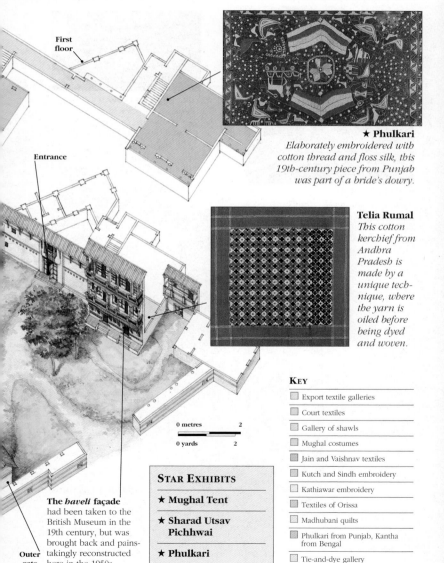

First floor

Entrance

★ **Phulkari**
Elaborately embroidered with cotton thread and floss silk, this 19th-century piece from Punjab was part of a bride's dowry.

Telia Rumal
This cotton kerchief from Andhra Pradesh is made by a unique technique, where the yarn is oiled before being dyed and woven.

0 metres 2
0 yards 2

The *haveli* façade had been taken to the British Museum in the 19th century, but was brought back and painstakingly reconstructed here in the 1950s.

Outer gate

KEY

- Export textile galleries
- Court textiles
- Gallery of shawls
- Mughal costumes
- Jain and Vaishnav textiles
- Kutch and Sindh embroidery
- Kathiawar embroidery
- Textiles of Orissa
- Madhubani quilts
- Phulkari from Punjab, Kantha from Bengal
- Tie-and-dye gallery

STAR EXHIBITS

★ **Mughal Tent**

★ **Sharad Utsav Pichhwai**

★ **Phulkari**

Adalaj Vav ❷

Detail of carving on a wall niche

T HE STEPWELLS *(vavs)* of Gujarat are an ingenious answer to the water scarcity in this arid region. Many of these elaborately ornamented, underground wells are dedicated to deities, acknowledging the hand of God in providing life-sustaining water. Adalaj Vav, perhaps Gujarat's finest stepwell, was built in 1499 by Rudabai, the wife of a local chieftain, to conserve water and provide a cool and pleasant ambience for social interaction. A series of beautiful platforms and galleries are built into the sides of the stepwell, all the way down to its subterranean depths.

Local women at the stepwell, which is still used for rest and recreation

The Stepped Corridor
The main corridor leads down five storeys to a depth of 30 m (98 ft), through pavilions whose walls, pillars and niches are covered with sculptures.

★ The First Well
Adalaj has an intermediate tank, 7 m (23 ft) in diameter, just before the main well. The octagonal well-shaft is entirely covered with fine carvings.

Ramp for drawing water

Stringed courses

The main well is no longer in use, but the ramp at the top, used for drawing water, still exists.

The steps surrounding the first well were used by people taking ritual baths.

STAR FEATURES

★ **The First Well**

★ **The First Landing**

★ **Wall Niches**

Ornamental Detail
*The well-shafts are pro-
fusely carved with intricate
floral and geometric motifs,
interspersed with figurines.*

VISITORS' CHECKLIST

Gandhinagar district. 17 km (11
miles) N of Ahmedabad. ▦ *Taxis
and autos are the best options
from Ahmedabad.* ◯ *daily.* ▣
flash photography is prohibited.

**One of the three
main entrances**

★ **The First Landing**
*Balconies, windows,
doors and shrines line
the first landing – a
large underground
platform. Adalaj is
best viewed at noon,
when sunlight filters
down to the bottom.*

Stringed courses,
or horizontal
detailing, break
the monotony of
plain walls.

The Pavilions
*The pavilions, supported by rows of carved
pillars, are flooded with diffused light and
provide ideal resting places.*

★ **Wall Niches**
*Niches feature in all the
pavilions, carved with
motifs of pots, horses,
flowers and leaves.*

OTHER STEPWELLS IN GUJARAT

The 11th-century **Rani ni Vav** in Patan *(see
p417)* is among the most elaborately carved
stepwells, with some 800 sculptures. Built in
1499, **Dada Harir Vav** *(see p411)* in Ahmedabad,
is one of the finest examples of a *vav* from the
Muslim period in Gujarat. The 15th-century
Ambarpur Vav, 18 km (11 miles) from
Ahmedabad, is one of the few *vavs* still in use.

Rani ni Vav in Patan, one of India's largest *vavs*

The dry dock at Lothal, dating to 2500 BC

Lothal ❸

Ahmedabad district. 75 km (47 miles) SW of Ahmedabad. 🚉 Lothal–Burkhi station, 6 km (4 miles) SW of Lothal, then local transport. 🚌 to Burkhi. ◻ Sat–Thu. 📷

EXCAVATIONS AT LOTHAL have unearthed the remains of a remarkable city of the Indus Valley Civilization (see p41) that existed 4,500 years ago. Located 6 km (4 miles) north-west of the confluence of the Sabarmati and Bhogavo rivers, Lothal (literally, "Mound of the Dead") had a navigable estuary to the sea through the Gulf of Cambay (now Gulf of Khambat), which made it a flourishing port that once traded with Egypt, Persia and Mesopotamia.

The site reveals the foundations of a well-planned city with blocks of houses, paved drains, channels and wells, and 12 public baths. Other finds include beautifully made beads and pottery decorated with bird and animal motifs. Seals with intriguing, pic-tographic writing (as yet undeciphered), and weights and measures were also found here. The city was surrounded by a mud brick embankment, to protect it from the peren-nial floods which, in all probability, caused the city's destruction around 1,900 BC.

Among the prize exhibits in the **Archaeological Museum** are a copper figurine and a gold-bead necklace.

In 2001, Indian oceanogra-phers carrying out water pollution tests in the Gulf of Cambay nearby, made an astonishing discovery. They found the foundations of two cities under the sea, complete with streets, houses, staircases and temples. Objects recov-ered from the seabed, such as a stone slab covered with mysterious markings (which could be the earliest form of writing yet dis-covered), and carved wooden logs, have been carbon-dated to 7500 BC. The discovery of this site, which has been dubbed "Asia's Atlantis", has excited historians and archaeologists all over the world, as it suggests that civiliza-tion may have started 5,000 years earlier than previously believed. They surmise that the city may have been submerged as sea levels rose at the end of the Ice Age in about 8000 BC.

🏛 **Archaeological Museum**
◻ Sat–Thu. 📷

Nal Sarovar Sanctuary ❹

Ahmedabad district. 60 km (37 miles) SW of Ahmedabad. 🚉 Viramgam, 35 km (22 miles) N of entry point, then taxi. 🚌 Viramgam.
🛈 Conservator of Forests (Wildlife), Gandhinagar, (07932) 54 133. 📷 🏊

NAL SAROVAR SANCTUARY is one of the largest bird sanctuaries in the country. The 115-sq km (44-sq mile) Nal Lake and the surrounding swamp forests are best visited between November and February, when they attract as many as 250 species of water-fowl, including flamingoes, geese, cranes, pelicans, storks, cormorants, ibis and spoon-bills. Winter migrants from as far as Siberia, such as the ele-gant bluish-grey demoiselle crane, also congregate here in

Reed beds on Nal Lake

hundreds, and can be observed at fairly close quarters from the boats that take visitors on the lake. A perennial resident is the Sarus crane, the largest species of crane in the world. Believed to pair for life, Sarus cranes enact a spectacular courtship ritual, performing a syn-chronized dance that involves bowing with out-stretched wings. Unfortuna-tely, pressures on the habitat from the resident fishing communities, and from growing numbers of tourists, are slowly depleting the Nal Lake's rich variety of birdlife.

Graceful flamingoes, a regular sight at the Nal Sarovar Sanctuary

Exquisitely carved images of Hindu deities at Rani ni Vav, Patan

Modhera Sun Temple ❺

See pp418–19.

Patan ❻

Mehsana district. 140 km (87 miles) from Ahmedabad. 🚶 112,050. 🚌 🚏 📷 *Jatar Fair (Sep/Oct).*

T HE TOWN OF PATAN was the capital of this region between the 8th and 15th centuries, before Sultan Ahmed Shah moved base to Ahmedabad *(see pp410–11)* in 1411. The ruins of the old capital, Anhilwada, lie 2 km (1.3 miles) northwest of Patan, and include an impressive stepwell, **Rani ni Vav**, and a water tank. The seven-storeyed stepwell ranks with Adalaj Vav *(see pp414–15)* as the finest in Gujarat. This splendid piece of architecture from the Solanki period (10th–14th centuries), now painstakingly restored, boasts some 800 individual, elaborately carved sculptures. Constructed in the 11th century by Queen Udaymati as a memorial to her husband, Bhimdeva, its unique feature is its direct as well as lateral series of steps leading to the water's edge. At the base are 37 niches, with the elephant god Ganesha carved into them. Nearby, the **Sahastralinga Talav**, a water tank with 1,000 shrines dedicated to the god Shiva, stands on the banks of the Saraswati river.

Patan also boasts more than 100 beautifully carved Jain temples, of which the **Panchasara Parsvanatha Temple** is the most striking. The town also has numerous traditional *havelis* with intricately carved façades.

Another attraction for many visitors is the beautiful *patola* sari. This lavish fabric is woven in Patan by a single family who have passed the craft down from one generation to the next. They are available locally and in major cities.

Siddhpur ❼

Mehsana district. 128 km (80 miles) N of Ahmedabad. 🚶 53,600. 🚌 🚏

L YING along the Anjuni river, Siddhpur was once famous for the Rudra Mala Complex of Shiva temples, dating from the 10th century. It was later destroyed by Muslim invaders in the 13th century. Historical accounts describe a three-storeyed complex, profusely carved in stone and supported by 1,600 pillars, with 11 smaller shrines and three 40-m (131-ft) tall gateways. Two porches and four columns from the main shrine are all that remain today, together with a well-preserved, carved gateway with two high columns. An exploration of the town reveals interesting wooden *havelis* and pillared mansions, built by Muslim traders in the 19th century.

ENVIRONS: This region has the popular temple towns of **Ambaji**, 88 km (55 miles) north of Siddhpur, and **Bahucharaji**, 55 km (34 miles) southwest of Siddhpur. Both temples are dedicated to the goddess Amba (a reincarnation of Shiva's consort, Parvati) and they attract large crowds of devotees during the four main full-moon festivals each year in March, June, September and November. The pilgrims have their heads shaved *en masse* at both temples.

Traditional houses in Siddhpur with finely carved façades

PATOLA WEAVING

Detail of a typical *patola* sari

Patola is an intricate silk weaving technique practised in Patan. The warp and weft threads are coloured in parts by tie-dyeing, and then woven to form clear designs in a method called double ikat *(see p666)*. Typical motifs include jewels, flowers, animals and dancing women, interspersed with geometric forms. The craft is laborious – a month's work goes into weaving one sari length (5.5 m/6 yards) – and its product is highly prized, especially in a bridal trousseau. This exquisite fabric was exported to Indonesia where it became the cloth of the royal court.

Modhera Sun Temple ❺

Surya, the Sun God

THE SUN TEMPLE at Modhera was built in 1026 by King Bhima I of the Solanki dynasty. It is so precisely laid out in an east-west direction that the sun's rays course through its chambers and strike the centre of the inner sanctum at high noon every day. The carvings, both inside and on the exterior, are extraordinarily detailed, depicting a pantheon of Hindu deities as well as scenes from everyday life. An impressive tank dominates the forecourt. The juxtaposition of a tank with a Sun Temple is inspired by Vedic scriptures, which say that the sun was born from the depths of a primordial ocean.

The Entrance Hall
This hall has 12 representations of Surya, that depict the phases of the sun in each month of the year.

Shrines
The tank is surrounded by miniature shrines, topped by curved shikharas.

The Kund
Flights of stairs create a ripple effect down to the base of the tank (kund), which is shaped like an inverted pyramid.

Vadodara ❽

Vadodara district. 113 km (70 miles) SE of Ahmedabad. 🏤 *1,306,100.* ✈ *8 km (5 miles) NE of town centre.* 🚉 🚌 ℹ *Gujarat Tourism, (0265) 42 7489.* 🏛 *Vadodara Municipal Corporation, (0265) 79 4456.*

SITUATED on the banks of the Vishwamitri river, Vadodara owes much of its splendour to Sayajirao Gaekwad (1875–1939), a former ruler who transformed his principality into a progressive centre of culture, education and industry. Today Vadodara, also known as Baroda, is a vibrant city with many interesting buildings, museums and parks. The **Laxmi Vilas Palace**, an Indo-Saracenic pile, was designed by the English architect, Major Charles Mant (*see p468*). It took 12 years to build and was finally completed in 1890. It is still the residence of the erstwhile ruling family, though there are plans to convert parts of it into a luxury hotel. The **Maharaja Fateh Singh Museum**, within the palace grounds, has a rare

The magnificent façade of the Laxmi Vilas Palace

The Torana
All that survives of the torana *or arched gateway are these two intricately carved columns leading into the temple.*

VISITORS' CHECKLIST

Mehsana district. 119 km (74 miles) NW of Ahmedabad. 🚆 *Mehsana, 25 km (16 miles) away, then taxi or bus.* 🚌 ℹ️ *(0273) 48 4334.* 🕐 *daily.* 🎫 📷 🚻 🎭 *Modhera Dance Festival (Jan).*

Garbhagriha
The walls and pillars of the inner sanctum are richly carved with images of deities, in strict order of their celestial hierarchy.

Sabha Mandapa, the assembly hall, was reserved for religious discourses and socio-cultural ceremonies.

Nritya Mandapa
This hall, which leads from the assembly hall towards the inner sanctum, was used for dance performances.

collection of paintings by one of India's leading painters, Raja Ravi Varma (1848–1906). **Sayaji Bagh**, a beautiful park in the heart of the city, houses a zoo as well as the **Vadodara Museum and Picture Gallery** which exhibits an eclectic collection of Mughal miniatures, European oil paintings, textiles, carved doors from old *havelis* and royal artifacts. Pride of place goes to its collection of 68 striking bronzes from Akota, a centre of Jain culture in the

Radha and Madhava by Raja Ravi Varma

5th century. Other notable sights are the **Kirti Mandir**, the *samadhi* (memorial) of Vadodara's royal family; the **Nyaya Mandir**, an Indo-Saracenic building which is now a law court; and a number of painted *havelis*. The city also has the Maharaja Sayajirao University's **College of Fine Art**, an institute of national eminence.

🏛 **Laxmi Vilas Palace**
📞 *(0265) 425 966.* 🕐 *Tue – Sun. Visits by prior appointment only.* 🎫

🏛 **Maharaja Fateh Singh Museum**
📞 *(0265) 42 6372.* 🕐 *Tue – Sun.* 🎫
🏛 **Vadodara Museum and Picture Gallery**
📞 *(0265) 79 3801.* 🕐 *daily.* 🎫

ENVIRONS: The famous Amul Dairy is located in **Anand**, 38 km (24 miles) northwest of Vadodara. Synonymous with the "White Revolution" that made India self-sufficient in milk, it helped pioneer India's dairy cooperative movement, and now procures one million litres of milk every day from 1,000 milk cooperative societies. It is open daily to visitors from 3 to 5pm.

Jain Temple in Pavagadh Fort, near Champaner

Champaner ❾

Vadodara district. 52 km (32 miles) NE of Vadodara. ▭ 🎭 *Mahakali Festival (Mar/Apr)*.

T HE DESERTED CITY of Champaner is situated at the foot of Pavagadh Hill. Originally the seat of a Rajput Chauhan dynasty, Champaner was conquered by the Muslim ruler Mahmud Begada in 1484. He spent 23 years rebuilding the citadel, adding mosques, palaces and tombs within its massive walls, guarded by huge gateways. Champaner remained the capital of Gujarat until 1535, when it was conquered by the Mughal emperor Humayun. Thereafter, it fell into gradual decline.

Much of Champaner lies in ruins today, with the remains of many old mosques and palaces reflecting a blend of Islamic and Jain traditions. The **Jami Masjid**, built in 1523, is a large, symmetrical structure with a perfectly pro-portioned dome. Its richly ornamented exterior with 172 pillars and 30-m (98-ft) high minarets, makes it one of the finest Islamic monuments in western India. Another ele-gant mosque here is the 16th-century **Nagina Masjid**.

The **Pavagadh Fort**, at the crest of the 820-m (2,690-ft) high Pavagadh Hill, is 4 km (2.5 miles) to the southwest of Champaner. It has a cluster of Muslim, Hindu and Jain shrines, and the ruins of an ancient fortification, reflecting its chequered past. On the

way up the hill are the ruins of the **Sat Mahal**, the seven-storeyed palace of the Chauhan kings. The kings were slain when they refused to embrace Islam after the Muslim conquest, and their women and children committed *jauhar*. There are also two domed granaries, the Makai Kothar and the Naulakha Kothar.

ENVIRONS: Dabhoi Fort, 75 km (47 miles) south of Champaner, was constructed in the 13th century by the Solanki Rajputs (10th–14th centuries). It is an interesting example of Rajput military architecture, with four gates, a water tank fed by an aque-duct and fields within the fort to provide food during a siege.

Detail from the Jami Masjid

Ruins of the 16th-century Jami Masjid in Champaner

Surat ❿

Surat district. 234 km (145 miles) S of Ahmedabad. 👥 *2,433,800*. ▭ 🚇 🛈 *1/847 Athugar St, Nanpura, (0261) 347 6586*. 🏛 *Mon–Sat*.

S TRATEGICALLY LOCATED on the coast, Surat was once a prosperous port and many powers battled to control it between the 16th and 18th centuries. At various times the Portuguese, Dutch, Mughals, Marathas and British held sway here, but its importance began to wane after 1837, when it was ravaged by flood and fire. Many of Surat's Hindu and Parsi merchants *(see p447)* left for Bombay (Mumbai), which then gradually overtook Surat as the premier port on the western coast. Though no longer a port of any consequence, Surat is today a major industrial centre.

The 16th-century **Surat Castle**, beside the Tapti Bridge, is the town's oldest structure. Built by Khudawan Khan, an Albanian Christian who embraced Islam, the castle has 12-m (39-ft) high battlements and 4-m (13-ft) thick walls. Iron strips were used to bind its various elements and all its joints were filled with molten lead, to make it as impenetrable as possible. Especially noteworthy is the imposing gateway in its eastern wing, with a menac-ingly spiked exterior, and a delicately carved interior. Sadly, sundry offices now housed within the castle have robbed it of its historic ambience.

Northeast of the castle, just beyond Kataragama Gate, are the English, Dutch and Armenian cemeteries, that bear witness to the city's cosmopolitan past. Though now overgrown, they are worth exploring for the intriguing personal histories recounted on the tombs' epitaphs. Particularly impres-sive is the mausoleum of Sir George Oxinden, a governor of the Surat Port, and his brother, in the British cemetery. The tomb of Baron Adriaan van Reede, built in the 17th century, in the Dutch cemetery has an enormous double cupola.

Modern Surat is known for its flourishing textile industry which produces the famous *tanchoi* (brocade) silk. It also specializes in jewellery and is a major diamond-cutting centre for suppliers from all over the world. During the 1980s, the city had, unfortunately, become a byword for urban squalor, and in 1994 suffered an outbreak of plague. This galvanized the city's admin-istration into a massive clean-up drive, which has resulted in the revival of Surat as a pros-perous commercial centre.

Daman ⑪

Daman Union Territory. 390 km (242 miles) S of Ahmedabad. 🛪 35,750. 🚉 Vapi, 10 km (6 miles) SE of Daman, then taxi or bus. 🚌 🛈 Nani Daman, (0260) 25 5104.

Tucked away in the southern tip of Gujarat, adjoining Maharashtra, is the tiny enclave of Daman which was a Portuguese colony until 1961. The Damanganga river, which flows into the Arabian Sea, divides the town into two distinct parts – Nani Daman (Little Daman) which is dotted with hotels and bars, and Moti Daman (Big Daman), the old Portuguese township.

Moti Daman is enclosed within the massive **Daman Fort**. Its ten bastions and two gateways date to 1559, and it is ringed by a moat linked to the river. Daman's well pre-served churches include the

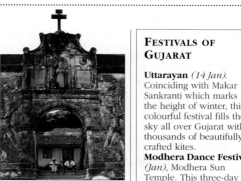

The gateway to St Jerome's Fort in Nani Daman

large **Bom Jesus Cathedral**, built in 1603, which has a richly carved portal and an ornamental altar. The smaller **Rosario Chapel**, outside the fort walls, has exquisite carved wooden panels, depicting scenes from the life of Jesus. The lighthouse, to the north of the fort, affords fine views of the Gulf of Cambay.

St Jerome's Fort, in Nani Daman, is less grand than Daman Fort but houses the lovely chapel of Our Lady of the Sea. The chapel has a del-icate, classical façade of 12 columns crowned with a cross.

Liquor flows freely in Nani Daman's dingy bars, attracting crowds of tipplers from the rest of Gujarat where alcohol is prohibited. Those who want to take in local colour would be well advised to avoid the bars and explore the farmers' market or the riverside fish market instead.

The Devka and Jampore beaches, 5 km (3 miles) north and south of Daman respec-tively, are not spectacular, but offer tranquil retreats among casuarina groves.

FESTIVALS OF GUJARAT

Uttarayan *(14 Jan).* Coinciding with Makar Sankranti which marks the height of winter, this colourful festival fills the sky all over Gujarat with thousands of beautifully crafted kites.

Modhera Dance Festival *(Jan),* Modhera Sun Temple. This three-day festival of Indian classical dance is a unique oppor-tuniy to enjoy these dance forms in the setting in which they were originally performed.

Bangles on sale at Tarnetar Fair

Tarnetar Fair *(Aug/Sep),* Tarnetar. This unique matchmaking *mela* sees prospective grooms prom-enading the fairgrounds, holding colourful umbrel-las, as young women wearing multi-pleated skirts swirl around in dance. A girl indicates her preference by approach-ing a youth for a chat, leaving it to the elders to settle matrimonial details.

Navratri *(Sep/Oct).* Navratri or "nine nights" is celebrated throughout Gujarat and is marked by nine nights of dancing in honour of the mother goddess. Women perform the *garba* dance, whirling around in a circle, clap-ping their hands. The exhilarating *dandia ras* is the highlight, when men and women strike small lacquered batons to a beat that gets faster and faster till it finally breaks in a frenzied crescendo.

View of the harbour below St Jerome's fort in Nani Daman, Daman

Bhavnagar ⑫

Bhavnagar district. 200 km (124 miles)
SW of Ahmedabad. 🏛 *511,000.* ✈
8 km (5 miles) SE of city centre. 🚉 🚌

F OR MOST VISITORS, Bhavnagar
is little more than a convenient base for exploring the
magnificent temple town of
Palitana. Yet Bhavnagar itself
is not without charm – its old
bazaar, dotted with merchants'
havelis, has shops specializing
in tie-dye textiles and gold
and silver jewellery. In the
southeast corner of the city,
on the road to the airport, is
the semi-circular **Barton
Museum** (built in 1895). It
houses the private collection
of coins, weapons and *objets
d'art* of a British officer,
Colonel Barton, who
served here in the
19th century.

The **Nilambagh
Palace**, once the for-
mer rulers' residence,
was built in 1859 and
is now a luxury hotel
(see p706) with a
great banquet hall   **Detail from the door**
and peacocks in   **of a temple in Palitana**
the garden.

🏛 **Barton Museum**
🅒 *(0278) 42 4516.* ⬜ *Mon–Sat.* 🖼
🏨 **Nilambagh Palace**
Ahmedabad Rd. 🅒 *(0278) 42 4241.*

ENVIRONS: The flat grasslands
of the 36 sq-km (14 sq-mile)
Velavadar National Park (65
km/40 miles north of Bhavnagar) are home to over 1,000
blackbucks. Blackbucks were
protected by the Bishnoi
community *(see p385)* until
the state took over this role.
A walk through the park at
dusk may provide a glimpse
of the wolves
that hunt

this Indian antelope, and of
the wild boars and nilgai that
congregate at the park's
watering holes.

🦌 **Velavadar National Park**
🛈 *Forestry Dept, Bhavnagar, (0278)
42 6425.* ⬜ *mid-Oct–May.* 🖼
🎦 *extra charges.* 🗹

Palitana ⑬

Bhavnagar district. 52 km (32 miles)
SW of Bhavnagar. 🚉 🚌
🎭 *Falgun Suth Tera (Feb/Mar).*

A N EXTRAORDINARY cluster of
863 Jain temples crowns
the twin summits of Palitana's
Shatrunjaya Hill and covers the
saddle linking them. The first
Jain *tirthankara*, Adinath
(see p396), is said to
have visited this hill,
while his chief disciple,
Pundarika, is believed
to have attained
enlightenment here.
Most of the temples
date to the 16th
century – earlier
temples on this site
were destroyed by
Muslim invaders in
the 14th and 15th centuries.
The temples are grouped into
nine fortified clusters called
tuks, and named after the
wealthy devotees who paid for
their construction. Each *tuk*
has a main shrine surrounded
by several smaller ones. The
most impressive of the main
shrines is the 17th-century
Adinath Temple, on the hill's
northern ridge. Its ceilings,
walls and supporting brackets
are covered with carvings of
saints, dancers, musicians and
lotus blossoms. Many images
of Adinath are enshrined

Sculptures of Jain *tirthankaras*
along a temple corridor, Palitana

inside. The southern ridge is
dominated by the 16th-century
Adishvara Temple, with its
richly ornamented spire. The
main image within portrays
Rishabhnath. It has eyes made
of crystal and is adorned with
necklaces and a magnificent
gold crown.

The 4-km (2.5-mile) ascent
to the summit of the hill takes
about two hours, a task made
lighter by the spectacular silhouette of hundreds of temple
spires and domes against the
sky. From the top, there is a
panoramic view of the Gulf of
Cambay and the countryside.

Diu ⑭

Diu Union Territory. 418 km (260
miles) S of Ahmedabad. 🏛 *21,600.*
🚉 *Delwada, 8 km (5 miles) N of
town centre.* 🚌 🛈 *Diu Jetty,
(02875) 52 212.*

T HE LITTLE ISLAND of Diu
covers an area of just 39
sq km (15 sq miles). Once
known as the "Gibraltar of the

The 19th-century Nilambagh Palace in Bhavnagar, set in a huge garden

The abandoned seaside fort at Diu, dating to the 16th century

East", it was a flourishing Portuguese colony from the 16th century onwards. It was ceded to India in 1961 and is today a Union Territory administered by the Central Government. The majestic **Diu Fort** on the eastern end of the island dominates the town. Built in 1535 when the Portuguese took control of Diu, it is worth a visit for its impressive double moat, its old cannons and for the superb views of the sunset it offers.

Diu town, sandwiched between the fort to the east and the city wall to the west, retains a distinctly Portuguese atmosphere in its churches and its many mansions. The **Nagar Seth Haveli** is particularly outstanding, with carved balconies and stone lions. The **Church of St Paul** (built in 1610) has a lovely, carved wooden altar, statues of the saints and a sonorous old organ. Its impressive Gothic façade was rebuilt in 1807. Nearby, the **St Thomas Church** (built in 1598) houses a museum of religious artifacts and stone inscriptions linked to the island's history.

The beach at **Nagoa**, 7 km (4 miles) from the town, has a long stretch of sand fringed with palm trees. Other beaches within easy reach of Diu are Jallandhar and Chakratirth which has a sunset viewpoint. As a Union Territory, Diu is not subject to Gujarat's prohibition laws. This explains the profusion of bars in the town, and the invasion, on weekends, by thirsty Gujaratis.

Somnath ⑮

Junagadh district. 406 km (252 miles) SW of Ahmedabad. 🚌

SITUATED ON THE COAST with a commanding view of the Arabian Sea, the **Somnath Temple** is revered as one of the 12 most sacred sites dedicated to Lord Shiva. The temple's legendary wealth made it the target of successive plundering armies, beginning with Mahmud of Ghazni in 1026, who is said to have made off with camel-loads of gold and precious gems, leaving the edifice in ruins. The cycle of pillage

and reconstruction at Somnath continued over the next seven centuries. The present temple, made of stone, was built in 1950.

East of the temple, at the confluence of three rivers, is **Triveni Tirth**. The ghats going down to the sea at this spot are said to mark the place where Lord Krishna's funeral rites were performed, after a hunter mistook him for a deer and killed him.

Sasan Gir National Park ⑯

Junagadh district. 368 km (229 miles) SW of Ahmedabad. **Entry point:** *Sasan Gir.* 🚃 🚌 ℹ️ *For permits contact Field Director, Sinh Sadan, Sasan Gir (02877) 85 541.* ⏰ *mid-Oct–mid-Jun.* 🎫 📷 *extra charges.* 🚙 *Jeeps available.*

UNTIL A CENTURY ago, the Asiatic lion roamed vast areas of India, from Gujarat all the way to Bihar in the east. Now, the Sasan Gir National Park is the only habitat left of the lion outside Africa. Asiatic lions are smaller than African lions, with a fold of skin along the belly. The males have shorter manes. About 320 lions live in Gir's 259 sq km (100 sq miles) of dry scrub forest. By the early 1900s, the Asiatic lion had been hunted and poached almost to the point of extinction. Their remarkable resurgence in Gir is attributed to the conservation efforts of the erstwhile nawab of Junagadh *(see p426)* and, subsequently, the Gujarat government.

A number of rivers wind through Gir, making it a haven for a range of wildlife, including the caracal, the *chausingha* (four-horned antelope), the blackbuck and a substantial leopard population.

THE MOON GOD AND SOMNATH

Legend weaves an interesting tale around the origins of the temple at Somnath. Som, the Moon God, was wedded to the 27 daughters of Daksha, a son of Brahma, but he loved only one of them, Rohini, causing great frustration to the other sisters. An infuriated Daksha cursed his son-in-law, causing him to lose his lustre. In despair, Som turned to Shiva and served him with such zealous devotion that Shiva gave him respite from the curse – he would wax for half the month and wane for the rest. In gratitude the Moon God built a Shiva temple at Somnath.

The Somnath Temple, visited by devotees of Shiva

An Asiatic lioness basking in the sun in Sasan Gir Sanctuary

A view of Palitana's 863 Jain temples, clustered on top of Shatrunjaya Hill ▷

The impressive Jain temple complex on Girnar Hill, just outside Junagadh

Junagadh ⑰

Junagadh district. 393 km (244 miles) SW of Ahmedabad. 🏛 168,700.
🚉 🚌 ℹ Majwadi Darwaza, (0285) 21 201. 🏛 Mon–Sat. 🔱 Bhavnath Fair (Feb/Mar), Kartik Mela (Oct/Nov).

JUNAGADH, WHICH MEANS "Old Fort", takes its name from the ancient fort of Uparkot, built in the 4th century on a plateau at the eastern edge of the town. The fort is surrounded by massive walls, over 20 m (66 ft) high in places, and a 90-m (295-ft) deep moat inside the walls. This once teemed with crocodiles that were fed on crimi- nals and political enemies. An ornate, triple-arched gateway marks the entrance to the fort. Inside, a cobbled path leads past Hindu temples to the now deserted **Jami Masjid** at the top of the plateau. Its carved stonework and pillars show that it was constructed on the remains of a destroyed Hindu temple. Nearby are a cluster of Buddhist caves dating to the 2nd century. The fort also has two fine 11th-century stepwells, the Navghan Kuan and the Adi Charan Vav.

In the mid-19th century, the nawabs of Junagadh moved down from the old fort into new colonial-style palaces in the city. The **Durbar Hall** of the City Palace, built in 1870, houses a museum with the typical trappings of royalty – palanquins, silver thrones and old armour. A complex of royal mausoleums can be seen

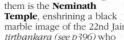

Intricate carving on Mahabat Maqbara

near the city's railway station, the most notable of which is the **Mahabat Maqbara** with splendid silver doors.

Junagadh's main attraction, however, is **Girnar Hill**, 6 km (4 miles) east of the city. An extinct volcano, this has been a holy site for Buddhists, Jains and Hindus since the 3rd century BC. Over 4,000 steps lead to the top of the 1,080-m (3,543-ft) high hill. En route is an **Ashokan Rock Edict**, dating to 250 BC (see p42), that conveys Emperor Ashoka's message of non-violence and peace. Halfway up the hill are a cluster of beautiful Jain temples. Most notable among them is the **Neminath Temple**, enshrining a black marble image of the 22nd Jain *tirthankara (see p396)* who

is believed to have died here. The 12th-century **Amba Mata Temple**, at the summit, is very popular with newlyweds, who come seeking blessings for conjugal bliss.

🏛 **Durbar Hall Museum**
📞 (0285) 62 1685. 🕐 Thu–Tue.
⚫ 2nd & 4th Sat. 🚫

Porbandar ⑱

Porbandar district. 404 km (251 miles) SW of Ahmedabad. 🏛 133,100.
🚉 🚌 🏛 Mon–Sat.

ONCE A MAJOR port on the Arabian Sea, Porbandar is today famous as Mahatma Gandhi's birthplace. The house where Gandhi was born in 1869 still stands in a small alley, in the western part of the city. Next door is the **Kirti Mandir Museum** with photographs from the Mahatma's life, and extracts from his speeches and

---

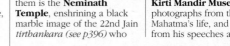

THE NAWAB OF JUNAGADH AND HIS DOGS

The 11th Nawab of Junagadh (1900–59), like his forebears, had a passion for breeding dogs, and these pedigreed pooches, 800 of them, were housed in luxury with separate rooms and personal attendants. The Nawab even held elaborate banquets to celebrate their "nuptials". On the eve of India's Independence, when the princely states were given the option of either remaining in India or becoming a part of Pakistan, the Nawab's decision to accede to Pakistan was thwarted by popular protest. The Nawab, however, decided to leave Junagadh. When the time for departure came, the Nawab, true to form, boarded the aircraft with his dogs, leaving behind his entire harem of concubines.

Portrait of the Nawab with his favourite dog

writings. The city has little else to attract visitors and in recent years it has gained the dubious distinction of housing local mafia dons. Interestingly, large sections of Gujarat's diaspora population, particularly the emigrants to Africa, originated from this district.

Entrance to the Kirti Mandir Museum, Porbandar

Dwarka 🔞

Jamnagar district. 453 km (282 miles) W of Ahmedabad. 🚆 🚌
🎪 *Janmashtami (Jul/Aug).*

LEGEND HAS IT that about 5,000 years ago, Lord Krishna *(see p679)* forsook his kingdom at Mathura *(see p178)* and came to live on the seafront at Dwarka, where he founded a glittering new city. It is believed that the city was subsequently submerged under the sea. Whether or not this is myth or fact, recent excavations of the seabed have indeed established the existence of a submerged city in the vicinity of Dwarka.

Hindu pilgrims flock to Dwarka throughout the year. The city's main temple is the towering **Dwarkadhish Temple**, dating to the 16th century. Built of granite and sandstone on a plinth area of 540 m (1,772 ft), it is supported by 60 pillars and rises seven storeys to an impressive height of 51 m (167 ft).

Situated a short distance to its east is the small, lavishly carved **Rukmini Temple**. Built in the 12th century, it is dedicated to Krishna's wife.

Jamnagar 🔞

Jamnagar district. 308 km (191 miles) SW of Ahmedabad. 🚶 *447,800.*
✈ *10 km (6 miles) W of city.* 🚆 🚌
🍴 *Mon–Sat.*

FOUNDED BY a local prince, Jam Rawal, in 1540, Jamnagar's old walled city is dominated by the **Lakhota Fort**, the original seat of its rulers, and the **Ranmal Lake** which surrounds it. The fort was badly damaged during the earthquake in January 2001, though visitors are still allowed inside. The museum in the fort has fine sculptures from nearby excavation sites, dating from the 9th to 18th centuries. Close by is the Kotha Bastion which once stored the rulers' arsenal.

In the heart of the old town is the circular **Darbar Gadh** where the Jamsahebs (as the rulers were called) held public audiences. This structure was also damaged heavily in the 2001 earthquake, but the ground floor is safe for visitors. The lanes leading off from here are worth exploring as the city is famous for its tie-dye fabric and silver jewellery. In this area are two Jain temples, the **Shantinath** and **Adinath Temples**, entirely covered with mirrorwork, gold leaf, murals and mosaics. Close to them is the 19th-century **Ratanbai Mosque**, its doors inlaid with mother-of-pearl. In the early 20th century, Jamnagar was ruled by the famous cricketer KS Ranjit Sinhji (r.1907–33). The city acquired several elegant public buildings and parks under his able administration.

🏛 **Lakhota Fort Museum**
⭘ *Thu–Tue.* ⬤ *2nd & 4th Sat.* 📷 🚫

ENVIRONS: The **Marine National Park**, in the Gulf of Kutch, is 30 km (19 miles) from Jamnagar. An archipelago of 42 islands, the park's rich and diverse marine life is best viewed from the tranquil island of Pirotan.

🦌 **Marine National Park**
🛥 *Jamnagar jetty. For permits contact the Park Director, Jamnagar, (0288) 55 2077.* ✓

Rajkot 🔞

Rajkot district. 216 km (134 miles) W of Ahmedabad. 🚶 *966,700.*
✈ *1 km (0.6 miles) NW of city centre.* 🚆 🚌 ℹ️ *Jubilee Gardens, (0281) 22 3264.* 🍴 *Mon–Sat.*

THE HEADQUARTERS of the Saurashtra region (southwest Gujarat) during the British Raj, modern Rajkot is a commercial and industrial town. The centre of the region's groundnut trade, it is also reputed for its handicrafts.

Rajkot's many 19th-century buildings give it a distinctly colonial flavour. The **Watson Museum** in Jubilee Bagh, named after a British Political Agent, has a fine collection of portraits of local rulers, tribal artifacts, archaeological finds from Harappan sites and a large statue of Queen Victoria. The impressive **Rajkumar College**, established by the British for the sons of the Gujarat nobility, remains a prestigious public school.

🏛 **Watson Museum**
📞 *(0281) 22 3065.* ⭘ *Thu–Tue.* ⬤ *2nd & 4th Sat.* 📷 📷 *extra charges.*

ENVIRONS: Wankaner Palace, 39 km (24 miles) northeast of Rajkot, is an eclectic mix of Mughal, Italian and Victorian-Gothic styles. Though still inhabited by the former royal family, a portion is now a luxury hotel *(see p706)*. **Halvad**, 125 km (78 miles) north of Rajkot, has a 17th-century lakeside palace with intricate wooden carvings.

Statue of the first principal, Rajkumar College, Rajkot

Rabari women near Bhuj, bringing water home

Bhuj ②

Kutch district. 217 km (135 miles) W of Ahmedabad. 121,100. ✕ 7 km (4 miles) N of city centre. 🚂 🚌 ℹ Gujarat Tourism, Toran Rann Resort, Madhapar Rd, (02832) 24 910. 🎭 Ashadhi Bij (Jul/Aug).

UNTIL THE EARTHQUAKE of January 2001 reduced much of Bhuj to rubble, this was a fascinating walled city, with beautiful palaces and *havelis*, and a bazaar famous for its rich handicrafts and jewellery. Bhuj was the capital of the prosperous princely state of Kutch, whose wealth derived from its sea trade with East Africa and the Persian Gulf ports. African slaves were an important part of Kutch's maritime trade, and their many descendants still live in the city. The town's main attraction was the **Darbargadh Palace** complex, which houses the fabulous **Aina Mahal** or "Palace of Mirrors". Built in 1752, it was badly damaged in the 2001 earthquake and is now closed. The palace and its contents are linked to the remarkable life of its Gujarati architect, Ramsinh Malam. Shipwrecked off the East African coast as a 12-year-old, he was rescued by a Dutch ship and taken to the Netherlands, where he spent the next 17 years. There, he blossomed as a craftsman, mastering Delft tile-making, glass-blowing, enamelling and clock-making. When he returned home, the ruler of Kutch, Rao Lakha, gave him an opportunity to display these skills. The Aina Mahal was thus decorated with Venetian-style chandeliers, Delft blue tiles, enamelled silver objects and chiming clocks – all made locally under Ramsinh's supervision. At the same time, local crafts of the highest quality were also displayed, such as a superb ivory-inlaid door, jewelled shields and swords, and a marvellously detailed 15-m (49-ft) long scroll painting of a royal procession, complete with African page-boys. All these formed part of the palace museum, which should reopen after repairs.

The royal cenotaphs, the Swaminarayan Temple and the bazaar are now unfortunately in ruins, but the excellent **Folk Arts Museum** still stands. It has a choice collection of Kutch textiles, embroidery, weaponry and other local crafts, and a reconstructed village of Rabari *bhoongas* (see p430).

🏛 **Folk Arts Museum**
Mandvi Rd. ◯ Mon–Sat. 🎫 🚫

EARTHQUAKE IN GUJARAT

On 26 January 2001, at 8.46am, as India celebrated its Republic Day, a devastating earthquake struck Gujarat. Its epicentre was in Kutch. Measuring 7.7 on the Richter Scale, it destroyed most of Bhuj, the headquarters of Kutch district, as well as Anjar, the second largest town in Kutch, and razed 450 villages in the district to the ground. Among the 20,000 people killed in the earthquake were 400 schoolchildren of Anjar, who were crushed under the rubble of falling buildings in a narrow street as they marched jauntily through town in the Republic Day Parade. In the state capital, Ahmedabad, most of those killed were trapped in recently-built highrise apartment buildings, which collapsed like houses of cards while, ironically, centuries-old historic monuments throughout the state suffered relatively little damage. An exception was the spectacular 18th-century Darbargadh Palace in Bhuj, with its richly decorated interiors showcasing the finest Gujarati craftsmanship – much of the damage it suffered is irreparable, and it is unlikely to open to visitors for some years. In contrast, the traditional, round mud *bhoongas* of the semi-nomadic Rabaris of Kutch withstood the earthquake remarkably well. Gujarat, and in particular Kutch, has always been an area of seismic activity, and some historians believe this is one reason that cities of the Indus Valley Civilization (see p41), such as Dholavira and Lothal, declined around 1900 BC. In more recent times, 1,100 people died in the 1819 earthquake and 7,000 in the 1956 earthquake. The disaster of 2001 made more than 250,000 people homeless. Although a massive rehabilitation effort began immediately, many Kutchi farmers, traders and skilled craftsmen, with characteristic grit and resilience, continued to work while living under plastic sheeting.

Bhuj after the earthquake that hit Gujarat in January 2001

The tranquil seafront at Mandvi, once a busy port

Mandvi ㉓

Bhuj district. 60 km (37 miles) SW of Bhuj. 👥 14,300. 🚌

THIS OLD PORT TOWN has fine beaches, good swimming, and camel and horse rides along the shore. Close to the beach is the **Vijay Vilas Palace**, an impressive Indo-Edwardian pile built in the 1940s as a royal summer retreat. Its lovely garden, drawing room and rooftop terrace are open to visitors and provide beautiful views of the sea. In the town is the curious 18th-century **Old Palace** of the Kutch rulers (now a girls' school). Architecturally a blend of local and European styles, its façade is decorated with cherubic Dutch boys holding wine goblets – architect Ramsinh Malam's touching salute to his adopted country.

🏯 **Vijay Vilas Palace**
⭕ Thu–Tue. 💰 📷 extra charges.

Dholavira ㉔

Bhuj district. 250 km (155 miles) NE of Bhuj. 🚌 ℹ️ For permission contact the Superintendent of Police, Bhuj, (02832) 50 444. ⭕ daily.

DHOLAVIRA IS a small village where archaeologists have unearthed extensive remains of a city that dates back to about 3000 BC. Lying on Khadir island in the Rann of Kutch it is, along with Lothal (see p416), the largest known Indus Valley settlement in India. The site reveals evidence of a remarkable, planned city with broad roads, containing a central citadel, a middle town with

spacious dwellings, a lower town with open spaces for markets and festivities, and two stadia. An intriguing ten-character inscription (which is still to be deciphered) is on the citadel's northern gate. The presence of large reservoirs and a dam reflect the existence of sophisticated systems for harvesting water.

The Little Rann of Kutch Sanctuary ㉕

Kutch district. **Entry points:** Dhrangadhra, 130 km (81 miles) W of Ahmedabad, & Dasada, 117 km (73 miles) NW of Ahmedabad. 🚊 Dhrangadhra, 20 km (12 miles) S of park. 🚌 Dhrangadhra & Dasada, then bus or jeep. ℹ️ Gujarat Tourism, Ashram Rd, Ahmedabad, (079) 658 9172. For permits & tours contact Forest Office, Dhrangadhra, (02754) 23 016. 🎫 💰 📷 extra charges.

AN EXPANSE OF SALT FLATS and grasslands in northwest Gujarat, the Little Rann of Kutch has a stark and unforgettable beauty – in sunlight, the salt crystals in the sand glitter like diamonds, while at night they bathe the landscape in an eerie blue haze. Every year, during the monsoon, when the sea and rivers flood the region, the salt flats are transformed into great marshy swamps, with patches of higher ground forming grassy islands known as *bets*. Some 4,841 sq km (1,869 sq miles) of this unique ecosystem, which supports a variety of rare fauna, form a wildlife sanctuary which is

one of the last refuges of the Asiatic wild ass (*Equus hemionus khur*), known locally as *ghorkhur*. Akin to the Tibetan *kiang*, the *ghorkhur* is distinguished by a dark stripe along its back. Only about 1,000 of them now remain. Known for its speed (up to 60 km or 37 miles per hour), the wild ass lives in herds led by a stallion, and survives by migrating between the grassy *bets* through the seasons, in search of food.

The sanctuary also has a large population of nilgai (blue bull), blackbuck, *chinkara* (Indian gazelle), wolves, and the rare caracal. Birdlife includes migratory demoiselle cranes, pelicans and flamingos who come to the salt marshes during the winter months.

The Asiatic wild ass, found in Kutch

Dhrangadhra and Dasada are both interesting bases from which to visit the Little Rann of Kutch Sanctuary. Dasada has a 15th-century fort and a village where potters and textile printers practise their craft. The family of Dasada's former feudal chiefs arrange accommodation and guided tours of the Rann. Dhrangadhra, capital of a former princely state, has a fine 18th-century palace, and a bazaar with interesting colonial buildings. Tours of the sanctuary can be arranged through the Forest office here. Accommodation is available in the government rest house.

Salt pans in the Rann, a major source of livelihood in Kutch

Rural Life and Art in Kutch

Clay storage niche

KUTCH IS HOME to several pastoral communities, many of them semi-nomadic herders of camels and sheep. Among them are the Rabaris, whose round houses *(bhoongas)* with conical roofs are a distinctive feature of the Kutch landscape. These communities are skilled in a variety of crafts, the vibrant hues and forms of their creations adding beauty to their stark surroundings. Anjar, which used to be the crafts centre of Kutch, was tragically destroyed in the January 2001 earthquake, as were many of the crafts villages near Bhuj. Despite this, the intrepid craftspeople continue to work and sell their creations at shops in Mumbai, Ahmedabad and Delhi.

A typical toadstool-shaped Rabari house in Kutch

THE RABARI BHOONGA

The *bhoongas* of the Rabaris, superbly designed for the hot, arid climate of Kutch, are also structurally solid. Most of them withstood the 2001 earthquake. A typical cluster of *bhoongas*, their beautifully decorated interiors displaying the artistic skills of the Rabaris, can be seen at Tunda Vandh, 15 km (9 miles) east of Mandvi.

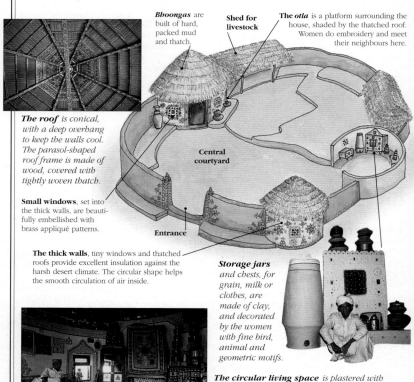

Bhoongas are built of hard, packed mud and thatch.

Shed for livestock

The otla is a platform surrounding the house, shaded by the thatched roof. Women do embroidery and meet their neighbours here.

The roof is conical, with a deep overhang to keep the walls cool. The parasol-shaped roof frame is made of wood, covered with tightly woven thatch.

Central courtyard

Small windows, set into the thick walls, are beautifully embellished with brass appliqué patterns.

Entrance

The thick walls, tiny windows and thatched roofs provide excellent insulation against the harsh desert climate. The circular shape helps the smooth circulation of air inside.

Storage jars and chests, for grain, milk or clothes, are made of clay, and decorated by the women with fine bird, animal and geometric motifs.

The circular living space is plastered with white clay, covered with relief patterns and studded with tiny mirrors to provide more light to its dark, cool interior. Niches and shelves built into the walls provide storage for items of everyday use.

PEOPLE

The pastoral communities of Kutch include Jaths, Ahirs, Meghwals, Bharwads and Sodhas, as well as Rabaris. While the men wander with their flocks, the women, children and elders stay at home, adding to the family income with their crafts skills.

Rabari women *dress in black wool, dramatically offset with silver jewellery. They also sport tattoos of peacocks and camels, as well as small crosses to keep away the evil eye.*

Rabari men*, in contrast to the women, wear only white, with fine embroidery at the back of their pleated* kediyans *(jackets). White and red woven shawls and voluminous turbans complete their attire.*

Rabari girls *wear the family's finest heirlooms. They begin embroidering their trousseau dresses as soon as they can hold a needle.*

CRAFT

Crafts are not just a means of earning and employment for the rural people of Kutch. They are also a proud and creative expression of each community's distinct culture and identity, through which utilitarian objects like cupboards, quilts, shoes, cowbells or clay dishes are transformed into art forms.

Embroidery *is done by most semi-nomadic communities. This section of a large wall hanging shows the work of a Rabari woman.*

Rogan, *a speciality of Niruna village near Bhuj, is a unique technique by which cloth is decorated with intricate, embossed lacquer-work patterns.*

Pottery *dishes such as this large platter are used at village feasts. They are made by the men of the Kumbhar (potter) community.*

Leather *objects are made by Meghwal men. They are embellished with bright tassels and embroidery.*

Patchwork *in vivid colours, using scraps and waste material, is done by Bharwad women to make items such as quilts, awnings and camel saddle covers.*

Silverwork *is crafted by the Sodha community, who also make jewellery to order in traditional designs, for the other pastoral communities.*

SOUTHWESTERN INDIA

Introducing Southwestern India

Encompassing the three states of Maharashtra, Goa and Karnataka, Southwestern India contains the central Deccan Plateau, the narrow Konkan coastline and the craggy Western Ghats that run parallel to the coast. Its major city is Mumbai (Bombay), India's vibrant commercial capital. The region's varied attractions include Goa's idyllic beaches and Portuguese churches, the ancient caves and temples of Ajanta and Ellora, and the magnificent ruins of Hampi. Further south are Bangalore, often described as Asia's Silicon Valley, the former princely state of Mysore, and the great Hoysala temples of Belur and Halebid.

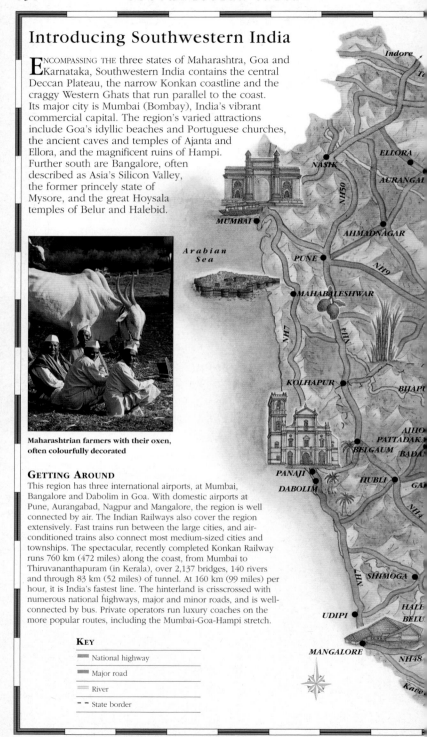

Maharashtrian farmers with their oxen, often colourfully decorated

Arabian Sea

GETTING AROUND

This region has three international airports, at Mumbai, Bangalore and Dabolim in Goa. With domestic airports at Pune, Aurangabad, Nagpur and Mangalore, the region is well connected by air. The Indian Railways also cover the region extensively. Fast trains run between the large cities, and air-conditioned trains also connect most medium-sized cities and townships. The spectacular, recently completed Konkan Railway runs 760 km (472 miles) along the coast, from Mumbai to Thiruvananthapuram (in Kerala), over 2,137 bridges, 140 rivers and through 83 km (52 miles) of tunnel. At 160 km (99 miles) per hour, it is India's fastest line. The hinterland is crisscrossed with numerous national highways, major and minor roads, and is well-connected by bus. Private operators run luxury coaches on the more popular routes, including the Mumbai-Goa-Hampi stretch.

KEY

▬ National highway

▬ Major road

▬ River

- - State border

(Map labels: Indore, Nasik, Ellora, Aurangabad, NH50, Mumbai, Ahmadnagar, Pune, NH9, Mahabaleshwar, NH7, Kolhapur, Bijapur, Aihole, Pattadakal, Belgaum, Badami, Panaji, Hubli, Gadag, Dabolim, NH4, Shimoga, Udipi, Halebid, Belur, Mangalore, NH48, Kaveri)

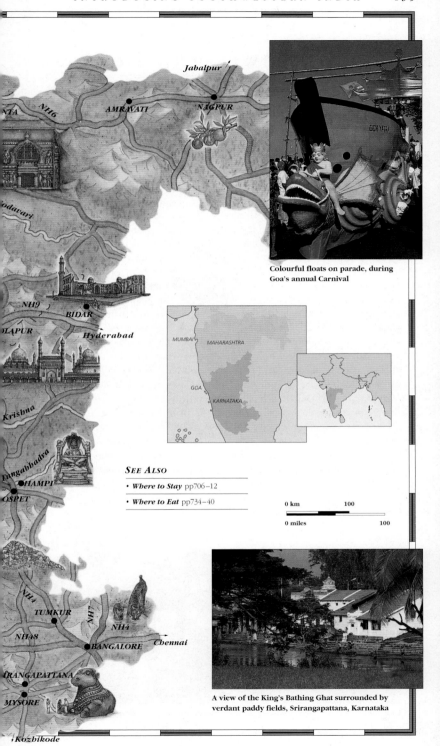

Jabalpur

AMRAVATI   NAGPUR

NTA   NH16

odavari

NH9

BIDAR

LAPUR   Hyderabad

Krishna

ungabbadra

HAMPI

OSPET

NH4

TUMKUR   NH7

NH48   NH4

BANGALORE   Chennai

RANGAPATTANA

MYSORE

Kozhikode

MUMBAI   MAHARASHTRA

GOA

KARNATAKA

Colourful floats on parade, during
Goa's annual Carnival

SEE ALSO

• *Where to Stay* pp706–12

• *Where to Eat* pp734–40

0 km   100

0 miles   100

A view of the King's Bathing Ghat surrounded by
verdant paddy fields, Srirangapattana, Karnataka

A PORTRAIT OF
SOUTHWESTERN INDIA

THE SOUTHWEST IS A REGION *of many and varied splendours. Its three states, Maharashtra, Goa and Karnataka, contain golden beaches, wooded hills, serene villages along the picturesque Arabian Sea coastline, and two of India's most cosmopolitan and dynamic cities – Mumbai (formerly Bombay) and Bangalore.*

Mumbai, capital of Maharashtra, is India's largest and most populous city, as well as its commercial and financial capital. It is also home to the world's largest cinema industry, popularly known as Bollywood. The city presents extraordinary and sometimes shocking contrasts – the glamorous world of film stars and business tycoons exists side by side with the squalor of slums and shantytowns, where over three million people (nearly one-third of Mumbai's population) live. The dominant image, however, is that of an upbeat, street-smart city full of dynamism and *joie de vivre.*

Mumbai's population includes Marathi-speaking Hindus, a sizeable

Green coconut

number of Muslims and Christians, as well as Jews, Parsis and other communities from different parts of India, drawn by its vibrant entrepreneurial culture, and often, by dreams of making it big in films. While this makes Mumbai remarkably cosmopolitan, it has on occasion led to sectarian strife, especially over the past decade, since the rise of the militant Hindu rightwing Shiv Sena Party.

Maharashtra is a vast state, its population of over 96 million making it politically important, and major industries based on cotton, sugar, engineering goods and processed foods lending it economic vitality. In recent years, strawberry fields and

Little fishing boats in Mumbai's harbour, against a backdrop of the city's skyscrapers

Goan women on their way to Sunday Mass

grape vineyards have made their appearance in its rich agricultural hinterland, but the most prized crop remains the Alfonso mango, a particularly sweet and luscious variety, which is exported across the world. Central Maharashtra has two World Heritage sites to its credit, at Ajanta and Ellora *(see pp476–81)*. The murals and sculptures found here testify to the common, ancient roots of Hinduism and Buddhism.

Many visitors travel by train from Mumbai to the tiny neighbouring state of Goa. The Konkan Railway which connects the two, and continues southwards to Karnataka, is a wonderful way to see the lush coastal scenery of coconut groves, spice plantations and fishing villages. Goa was a Portuguese colony from 1510 until 1961, when it was liberated by the Indian Army. The Portuguese departed peacefully, leaving behind a rich cultural legacy in cathedrals and mansions, music, dance, and in its distinctive cuisine. Another legacy of 450 years of Portuguese rule is in religion – almost one-third of Goa's population is Roman Catholic. Tourism and related industries are today a major source of livelihood here. Visitors from all over the world throng the beautiful beaches, which offer secluded palm-fringed retreats, as well as lively resorts buzzing with bars, cafés and discos.

A Hanuman statue in Nasik, Maharashtra

Karnataka is often described as the geographical and cultural meeting point between India's Dravidian south and its Indo-Aryan north. The state's varied landscape and architecture both reflect this unique melange. Karnataka's narrow strip of fertile coastland is backed by the green hills of the Western Ghats, covered with forests of fragrant sandalwood and teak. These slope down to a vast plateau, watered by the Kaveri and Krishna rivers. This is the state's historic and cultural heartland, dotted with architectural treasures in an extraordinary variety of styles. They were built by local Hindu and Muslim dynasties, as well as by ambitious rulers from the north, Maratha warriors and medieval Islamic chieftains, all of whom had once established kingdoms here.

Bangalore, the state capital, presents a sharp contrast to Karnataka's historic sites. As the ebullient centre of India's burgeoning computer software industry, this once laid-back town has been transformed into a globalized, high-tech showcase for contemporary India. Several multinational corporations have opened offices here, while pubs and shopping malls line its streets, catering to a young, cosmopolitan population.

The lush landscape along Karnataka's coastline

The Konkan Coast

A Konkani fisherwoman

Aʟʟ ALONG THE KONKAN COAST, from Mumbai to the south of Mangalore, are villages where, for over 2,000 years, fishing communities have harvested the fruits of the sea. A distinctive culture has developed in this area, protected by the forested hills of the Western Ghats. Beyond the coastline are fertile paddy fields, and plantations of coconut, cashew, betel nut, rubber, pepper and other spices. This is also India's monsoon land, where the Southwest Monsoon is at its heaviest, and where Arab merchants, drawn by the monsoon winds, came to trade long before the Europeans.

LOCATOR MAP

☐ *Extent of Area*

Harvesting ripe paddy is a full-time occupation for the entire village.

PADDY CULTIVATION
In wet paddy cultivation, seedlings are raised in a nursery and then transplanted in waterlogged fields when they are 30 cm (12 in) high.

Pepper, cashew and betel nut are some of the major cash crops that this region grows in abundance.

A rubber plantation bungalow is festooned with strips of cured rubber hanging out to dry.

FISHERFOLK OF THE COAST
Coastal people belong to different communities, speak their own dialects and celebrate local festivals. Strong and hard-working, their lives are ruled by natural forces.

Fishermen prepare their boats before they cast off just before dawn. The boats return by late morning.

A basket of freshly caught fish is carried to the shore to be sold directly to waiting customers.

**Small boats moored in the
Konkan backwaters**

Coastal dwellings have sloping
roofs made of tiles to deflect the
heavy rains during the monsoon.

These women *from Mumbai's
small Koli fishing community are
dressed in bright festival finery.*

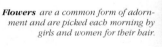

Flowers are a common form of adornment and are picked each morning by
girls and women for their hair.

KONKAN COAST

The narrow coastal
strip that runs along
the Arabian Sea is
sheltered by the
verdant slopes of the
Western Ghats. This
region can be explor-
ed either by road or
on the Konkan
Railway *(see p437).*

***Monsoon
clouds*** *herald
the onset of the
monsoon, when
the coast is
lashed by
torrential rain
from June to
early September.*

The Western Ghats, *or the Sahyadri Range,
run in an unbroken line along the coast.*

Dried fish is eaten during
the monsoon when heavy
rains prevent fishing.

Local fish markets
sell a large variety of
freshly caught produce.

Boat building is done by expert artisans
who repair old boats using traditional
methods, as well as build new ones from
locally procured wood.

Regional Food: Southwestern India

THOUGH SEAFOOD, coconut, red chillies and rice feature prominently in the cuisine of Maharashtra, Goa as well as Karnataka, the southwest is a region of great culinary variety. Persian influence is evident in the food of Mumbai's Parsis, while Goan cuisine has incorporated many Portuguese dishes and given them a local flavour. Karnataka is renowned for its out-standing vegetarian food, subtly seasoned with a range of spices, and its coffee grown in the hills of Coorg. Dishes such as *idli* and *dosa (see pp554–5)* are equally popular in neighbouring Tamil Nadu.

Sour ***kokum****, scarlet banana flower, jackfruit and drumsticks (Moringa oleifera) are favourite vegetables in this region.*

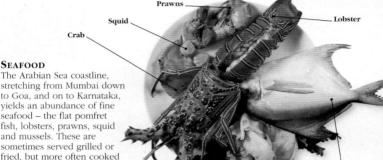

Prawns

Squid

Crab

Lobster

Pomfret

SEAFOOD

The Arabian Sea coastline, stretching from Mumbai down to Goa, and on to Karnataka, yields an abundance of fine seafood – the flat pomfret fish, lobsters, prawns, squid and mussels. These are sometimes served grilled or fried, but more often cooked as curries with fresh coconut and local spices, such as red chillies, pepper and tamarind.

GOAN SPECIALITIES

Goan cuisine is a delicious hybrid of Portuguese and local flavours and cooking methods. Among the most popular curries is *vindaloo*, whose name derives from the Portuguese words for its two main ingredients, *vinho* (wine vinegar) and *albos* (garlic). Coconut, red chillies and other spices are liberally used in other Goan curries, such as *xacuti* and *cafreal*. They are eaten with rice and *fugads* (stir-fried vegetables).

Camarão cafreal *is prawn with green herbs and coconut.*

Ambot-tik *is a tangy fish curry with tamarind.*

Galhina balchão *is a spicy chicken cooked with pickling spices.*

Vindaloo *is meat cooked in a marinade of vinegar and spices.*

Galhina indad *is spicy pot-roasted chicken.*

Xacuti *is braised meat with coconut and roasted spices.*

Fugads *of xango (beans) and* repolho *(cabbage) are garnished with coconut.*

Fugad de repolho

Fugad de xango

Bebinca *is a multi-layered cake made with eggs, molasses and coconut milk.*

MAHARASHTRA

Freshly-made relishes *(koshimbirs)* perk up a typical vegetarian meal in Maharashtra, which usually includes sautéed lentils and bean sprouts *(usal)*, steamed yam *(suran)* and sweet-sour lentils *(amti)*. *Bhelpuri* is a spicy street snack of puffed rice, sprouts and tamarind sauce.

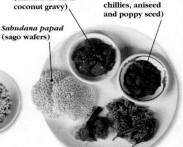

Malvani kombadi (chicken in thick coconut gravy)

Kolhapuri matan (mutton with chillies, aniseed and poppy seed)

Sabudana papad (sago wafers)

Gajar koshimbir (carrot relish)

Kheera koshimbir (cucumber relish)

Usal (sautéed sprouts)

Bhelpuri (street snack)

Amti (sweet-sour lentils)

Suran (steamed yam)

Non-vegetarian curries *include Kolhapuri mutton, robustly flavoured with red chillies, coconut, aniseed and poppy seed, and Malvani chicken in a thick gravy of coconut and roasted onion. They are served with spiced rice and crisp sago wafers.*

PARSI FOOD

The Parsis of Mumbai, whose ancestors came from Iran, serve dishes such as *patra ni machhi* (fish steamed in banana leaves), *dhansak* (a casserole of lentils, vegetables and meat), and *akuri* (spicy scrambled eggs).

Akuri (spicy scrambled eggs)

Dhansak (meat and lentil casserole)

Patra ni machhi (fish in banana leaf)

KARNATAKA

Karnataka is famous for its delicious vegetarian food. Specialities include *bisibele huliyana* (a nourishing lentil and rice mixture), *kolumbu* (vegetable curries with aromatic spices), *vaddhai* (black gram) and *holige* (chickpea stew).

Holige (chickpea stew)

Methi kolumbu (drumstick and aubergine curry flavoured with fenugreek)

Bisibele huliyana (lentils and rice)

Vaddhai (black gram curry)

Moru kolumbu (vegetables in yoghurt sauce)

Port wine **Beer** **Red wine**

DRINKS

In Goa, *feni*, a potent cashew-nut liqueur, and port are local favourites. In Karnataka, red and white wines are produced by Grover Vineyards. Beers are also brewed in the region.

MUMBAI

·······································

MUMBAI (FORMERLY BOMBAY), *capital of Maharashtra, is India's most dynamic, cosmopolitan and crowded city. The country's financial centre and its busiest port, Mumbai is also home to the world's biggest cinema industry, popularly known as Bollywood. Some 15 million people, from billionaire tycoons to homeless pavement dwellers, live in this teeming megalopolis.*

Consisting of seven swampy islands when the Portuguese acquired it in 1534, Bombay (from the Portuguese Bom Bahia or "Good Bay") came to the British Crown in 1661 as part of the dowry of Catherine of Braganza when she married Charles II. Finding little use for the islands, the British then leased them for a pittance to the East India Company, which quickly realized their potential as an excellent natural harbour in the Arabian Sea. By the 18th century, Bombay had become the major city and shipbuilding yard on the western coast, and by the 19th century land reclamations had joined the islands into the narrow promontory that it is today. The promise of commercial opportunities lured communities of Gujaratis, Parsis *(see p447)* and Baghdadi or Sephardic Jews to settle in Bombay, giving the city its vibrant multicultural identity. The city has now reverted to its local name, Mumbai, from Mumba Devi, the eight-armed goddess worshipped by the Koli fishermen who were the islands' original inhabitants.

Mumbai is a city of striking contrasts. Here skyscrapers stand next to stately Victorian buildings, noisy traditional bazaars adjoin glittering new shopping malls, and opulent neighbourhoods are surrounded by sprawling slums. Swelling Mumbai's population and stretching its sub-urban environs are migrants from all over the country who continue to flock to this "city of gold", in search of fame, fortune, or just a bit part in a Bollywood movie.

Swirling traffic around Flora Fountain in the heart of Mumbai

◁ **The Gateway of India, Mumbai's signature landmark, on the shores of the Arabian Sea**

Exploring Mumbai

MUMBAI IS A LONG, narrow promontory covering 430 sq km (166 sq miles), which juts into the Arabian Sea. Its downtown is the historic Fort area in South Mumbai, that derives its name from earlier colonial fortifications. This is the city's nerve centre, with the best known sights, hotels and restaurants. The posh residential area of Malabar Hill lies along the western coastline, just north of Marine Drive. Suburban Mumbai, with its sprawling new developments, stretches northwards from Bandra.

SEE ALSO
- **Where to Stay** pp706–708
- **Where to Eat** pp734–6

Fishing boats, decorated for Holi, at the seafront in South Mumbai

SIGHTS AT A GLANCE

Historic Buildings, Streets & Neighbourhoods
Ballard Estate **13**
Bandra **21**
Colaba Causeway **3**
Flora Fountain **9**
Gateway of India **1**
General Post Office **14**
Horniman Circle **7**
Kala Ghoda pp448–9 **4**
Khotachiwadi **18**
Malabar Hill **16**
Marine Drive **15**
Mumbai Stock Exchange **8**
Shahid Bhagat Singh Marg **12**
Town Hall **6**
Victoria Terminus pp454–5 **10**
Wellington Fountain **2**

Historic Sites
Elephanta Island **25**

Museums
The Prince of Wales Museum pp450–51 **5**

Temples & Mosques
Banganga **17**
Haji Ali Mosque **20**
Mahalaxmi Temple **19**

Beaches & Parks
Juhu Beach **22**
Sanjay Gandhi National Park **24**

Shops & Markets
Crawford Market **11**

Entertainment
Film City **23**

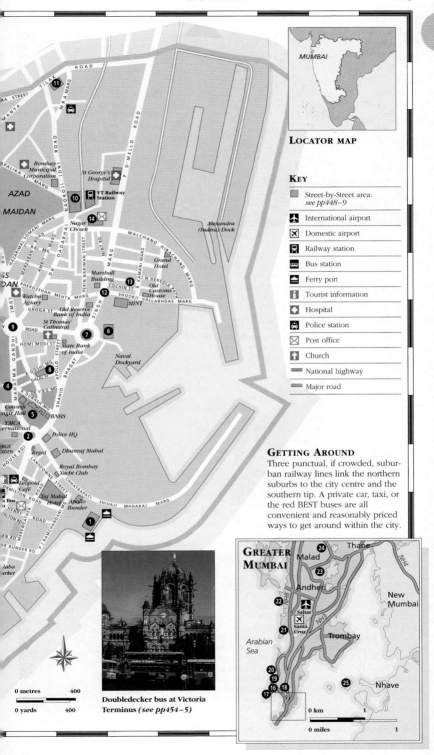

Doubledecker bus at Victoria Terminus (see pp454–5)

The Gateway of India with the red-domed Taj Mahal Hotel behind it

Gateway of India ①

Apollo Bunder, Chhatrapati Shivaji
Marg & PJ Ramchandani Marg.

MUMBAI'S most famous
landmark, the Gateway
of India, was the first sight
to greet travellers to Indian
shores during the heyday of
the British Raj. Ironically, it
also became the exit
point for British
troops after India
gained indepen-
dence in 1947. It
was built to com-
memorate the visit
of King George V
and Queen Mary
in 1911, en route
to the Delhi Durbar,
but in fact, the
King and Queen
were met with a
mock cardboard
and pastiche
structure – the
actual Triumphal Arch, built
in honey coloured basalt, was
only completed in 1924, years
after the royal visit. This monumental structure with two
large reception halls, arches
and minarets, and embellishments inspired by medieval
Gujarati architecture, was
designed by the Scottish
architect George Wittet, and
commands a spectacular view
of the sea. The Gateway
looks particularly impressive
at night when it is illuminated, with the inky black sea
stretching into the horizon
beyond it. This is the heart of
Mumbai's tourist district, the

Statue of Chhatrapati Shivaji
opposite the Gateway

city's most popular gathering
place, and always teems with
locals, visitors, vendors and
boatmen. Boats and barges
moored here provide regular
services across the bay and to
islands such as Elephanta (see
p461). They can also be hired
for leisurely trips down the
Mumbai coastline.

North of the Gateway of
India, towards Wellington
Fountain, is Chhatrapati
Shivaji Road. Formerly
Apollo Pier Road, it has now
been renamed after
Shivaji (see p471),
Maharashtra's great
warrior-hero.
Shivaji's eques-
trian statue is
placed here in a
pleasant garden,
in line with the
Gateway. Stand-
ing nearby is
another statue,
that of the great
19th-century Hindu philosopher and reformist, Swami
Vivekananda (see p615).

Around the Gateway are
some majestic buildings
dating from the colonial era.
These include the old **Yacht
Club** which now houses the
offices of the Atomic Energy
Commission (entry restricted),
the **Royal Bombay Yacht
Club**, originally built as a res-
idential annexe to the Old
Yacht Club, and the **Taj
Mahal Hotel** (see p707),
behind which lies the busy
Colaba Causeway.

The stately, red-domed Taj
Mahal Hotel was built in 1903
by a prominent Parsi industrialist, Jamshedji Tata (see p225)
who, it is said, decided to
construct this magnificent
hotel when he was barred
from entering the "Whites
Only" Watsons Hotel. The Taj,
with its splendid Moorish
arches and columns, majestic
stairways and galleries,
remains one of Asia's grandest
hotels, while Watsons is now a
dilapidated building, the hotel
having closed down long ago.

The eastern sea face stretching in front of the Gateway of
India is Mumbai's favourite
promenade. Called **Apollo
Bunder**, it was once the
traditional dockyard of the
local Koli fishermen, the
islands' original inhabitants.
Today, snake charmers and
performing monkeys, astrologers and ear-cleaners hustle
for business among the
strollers. Dozens of yachts,
fishing boats and ferries are
moored in the waters beyond.

The Royal Bombay Yacht Club, a
relic of the British Raj

The entrance to Cusrow Baug, a Parsi enclave along Colaba

Wellington Fountain ❷

Bounded by MG Rd, Shahid Bhagat Singh Marg, Chhatrapati Shivaji Marg & Madame Cama Rd.

BUILT TO commemorate the Duke of Wellington's visit to Bombay in 1801, Wellington Fountain (now renamed Shyama Prasad Mukherjee Chowk) is encircled by some magnificent colonial buildings. These include the old **Majestic Hotel** (now the government-owned Sahakari Bhandar) with its mock minarets and Gujarati balconies, and the elegant Art Deco **Regal Cinema**, designed by Charles Stevens and completed in 1934. His father, Frederick William Stevens, designed the imposing grey stone Indo-Gothic **Sailors' Home**, with a bas-relief of Neptune on its front gable, in 1876; it is now the Police Headquarters. Equally impressive are the Edwardian Cowasjee Jehangir Hall, now the **National Gallery of Modern Art** (see p449), and

the Indo-Saracenic **Prince of Wales Museum** (see pp450–51). Adjoining it is Hornbill House, the headquarters of the Bombay Natural History Society (BNHS), a prestigious institution established in 1883.

Colaba Causeway ❸

Shahid Bhagat Singh Marg. **Afghan Memorial Church** ◻ daily. ✝ 7am & 4:30pm, Sun.

CONSTRUCTED BY THE British in 1838, Colaba Causeway helped integrate the main city with Colaba, its southernmost spur. Today, the Causeway, also known as Shahid Bhagat Singh Road (see p456), is a lively mix of shops, restaurants and residential enclaves. Among them is the charming Parsi housing colony of **Cusrow Baug**, built in the 1930s, where the distinct culture and lifestyle of this dwindling community is preserved. Of the Causeway's many restaurants is one that has become an institution, the **Leopold Café and Bar** (see

p735), established in 1871, and a popular meeting place ever since. Further south are the **Sassoon Docks**, worth visiting early in the morning when they are buzzing with activity. This is when the fishermen bring in their catch and a wholesale fish market is set up by the lively, sharp-tongued Koli fishwives.

At the southern end of Colaba is the **Afghan Memorial Church of St John the Evangelist**, built between 1847 and 1858 (see p21). This grand Neo-Gothic structure with its tall spire and imposing front porch in buff basalt stone, was built in memory of the soldiers who died in the First Afghan War (1843), and the church is full of poignant memorial stones. It has superb stained glass, especially on its west windows, where an outstanding panel depicts the Crucifixion. A memorial to the martyrs stands in the garden.

Fishermen bringing in the day's catch at Sassoon Docks

THE PARSI COMMUNITY IN MUMBAI

Mumbai's cosmopolitan, progressive culture owes a great deal to the contribution of the Parsi community. Originally from Iran, where they followed the ancient Zoroastrian faith, they migrated to India in the 9th century AD when the advent of Islam brought with it the religious persecution of Zoroastrians. They settled along the west coast of Gujarat, absorbing many local traditions, and later moved to Mumbai where they made their name as brilliant financiers and traders. Often, they adopted the name of their trade, and so one finds Parsi surnames such as Mistry (mason) and Vakil (lawyer), or even Readymoney! A wealthy and talented community that has produced several leading industrial houses, such as the Tatas and the Godrejs, Parsis are also renowned for their philanthropy and have founded several cultural, educational and medical institutions in Mumbai.

Conductor Zubin Mehta, a Mumbai-born Parsi

Street-by-Street: Kala Ghoda ❹

Detail, Clock Tower

KALA GHODA, OR "BLACK HORSE", takes its name from an equestrian statue of King Edward VII that once stood at the intersection of Mahatma Gandhi Road and K Dubash Marg. The statue has long since been removed, but the name persists in public memory. Stretching from Wellington Fountain at the southern end of Mahatma Gandhi Road, to Bombay University at the north, and flanked by the Oval Maidan and the naval base at Lion Gate, this historic area is a hub of cultural activity. It also houses a number of art galleries, cafés, restaurants and fine shops and boutiques.

David Sassoon Library
The garden behind the library serves as a reading area.

Flora Fountain

Victoria Terminus

★ Rajabai Clock Tower
This 78-m (256-ft) high tower in Bombay University is adorned with figures representing different Indian communities.

Bombay University complex

MAHATMA GANDHI ROAD

ASH LANE

A DOSHI MARG

DALAL STREET

ELDON ROAD

UNIVERSITY ROAD

BHAURAO PATIL MARG

A S D'MELLO ROAD

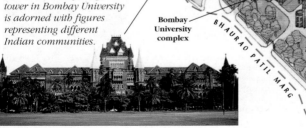

★ High Court
This fortress-like building, the second largest public building in the city, has a grand central staircase, well-appointed court rooms, and a large library.

Esplanade Mansion, formerly Watsons Hotel, witnessed the city's first motion picture in 1896.

Old Secretariat

<table>
<tr><td>

STAR SIGHTS

★ Rajabai Clock Tower

★ High Court

★ Prince of Wales Museum

</td></tr>
</table>

Army & Navy Building
The Neo-Classical Army & Navy Building, a departmental store in the early 1900s, is home to several offices of the Tata Group.

Kenneseth Eliyahoo Synagogue
This is the oldest Sephardic synagogue in the city, donated by the Sassoon family. It is used for prayer by Mumbai's Baghdadi and Bene Israeli Jewish community.

| 0 metres | 50 |
| 0 yards | 50 |

LOCATOR MAP
See Mumbai Map pp444–5

Elphinstone College
Part of this delightful Venetian Gothic building houses the State Archives.

KEY

– – – Suggested route

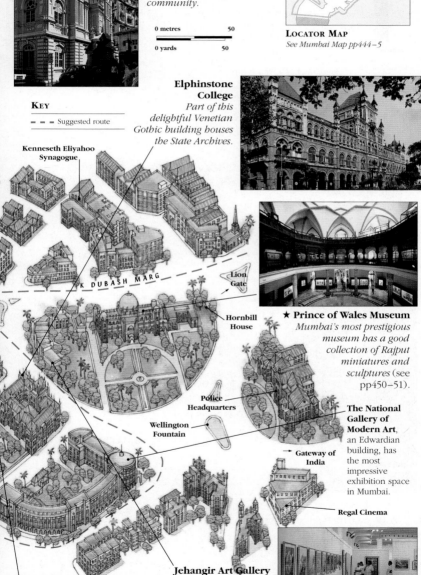

Kenneseth Eliyahoo Synagogue

K DUBASH MARG

Lion Gate

Hornbill House

Police Headquarters

Wellington Fountain

Gateway of India

Regal Cinema

David Sassoon Library

★ **Prince of Wales Museum**
Mumbai's most prestigious museum has a good collection of Rajput miniatures and sculptures (see pp450–51).

The National Gallery of Modern Art, an Edwardian building, has the most impressive exhibition space in Mumbai.

Jehangir Art Gallery
This gallery exhibits paintings by leading contemporary Indian artists, and also has a popular café.

The Prince of Wales Museum ❺

ESPECIALLY RENOWNED for its superb sculptures and miniature paintings, the Prince of Wales Museum's exhibits are housed in a grand Indo-Saracenic building, designed by George Wittet. Its foundation stone was laid by the Prince of Wales (the future George V) in 1905. During World War I, it served as a military hospital, and was formally inaugurated in 1923. Generous gifts from discerning private collectors have enabled the museum to build a collection of rare quality.

Damascened sword, Mysore, 1732

Japanese Cloisonné
This 19th-century vase forms part of an impressive collection of Far Eastern art.

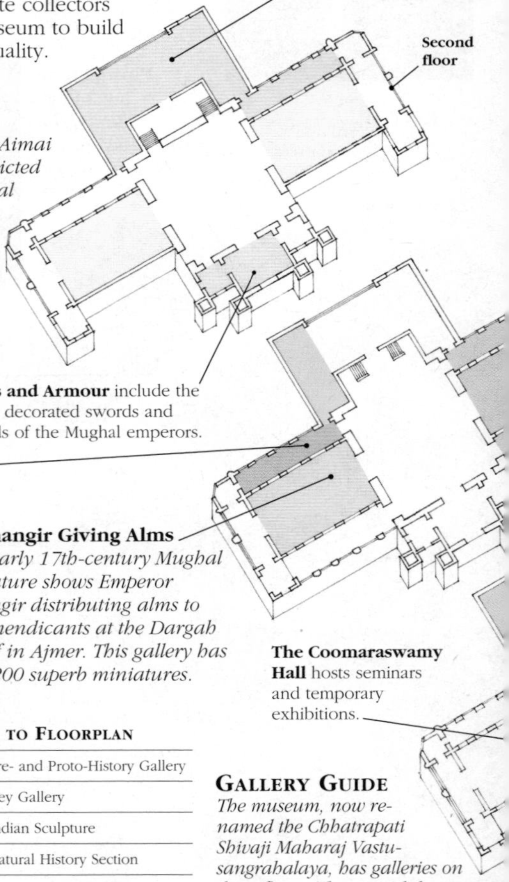

Second floor

Ivory Statuette
A Parsi girl, Bai Aimai Wadia, is depicted in traditional dress in this 19th-century piece from the Decorative Arts gallery.

Arms and Armour include the finely decorated swords and shields of the Mughal emperors.

★ Jahangir Giving Alms
This early 17th-century Mughal miniature shows Emperor Jahangir distributing alms to Sufi mendicants at the Dargah Sharif in Ajmer. This gallery has over 200 superb miniatures.

The Coomaraswamy Hall hosts seminars and temporary exhibitions.

KEY TO FLOORPLAN

- Pre- and Proto-History Gallery
- Key Gallery
- Indian Sculpture
- Natural History Section
- Decorative Arts
- Miniature Paintings
- Bronzes
- Nepalese and Tibetan Art
- Maritime History
- European Paintings
- Far Eastern Art
- Arms and Armour

STAR EXHIBITS

- ★ **Jahangir Giving Alms**
- ★ **Maitreya Buddha**
- ★ **Gandhara Sculpture**

GALLERY GUIDE

The museum, now re-named the Chhatrapati Shivaji Maharaj Vastu-sangrahalaya, has galleries on three floors. The central dome, the building's core, is encircled by galleries. The ground floor houses sculpture (including Gandhara masterpieces), the Pre- and Proto-History Gallery, and the Natural History Section. On the first floor are miniature paintings, decorative arts, arms and armour, and Nepalese and Tibetan Art. The second floor has European oil paintings.

VISITORS' CHECKLIST

Mahatma Gandhi Rd, Fort Area.
(022) 284 4519. Tue–Sun.
Students with an International
ID card get a discount.

Key Gallery
The central hall on the ground floor offers a sampling of the museum's treasures, with prize exhibits from different galleries.

First floor

★ Maitreya Buddha
An outstanding example of Nepalese art, this 12th-century gilt bronze statue of the Future Buddha was, like most of the museum's prized pieces, a gift from a private collector.

Ground floor

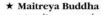

Entrance

★ Gandhara Sculpture
This 3rd-century AD sculpture of the Buddha meeting an ascetic shows strong Greek influence.

The Town Hall, Mumbai's most elegant public building

Town Hall **6**

Shahid Bhagat Singh Marg, Fort Area.
☎ (022) 266 0956. ◐ Mon–Sat.
● public hols. **The Asiatic Society**
☎ (022) 266 0956. ◐ Mon–Sat.

IN RECOGNITION OF Mumbai's importance as a burgeoning commercial centre in the 19th century, the city was bestowed with a Town Hall, facing the vast open space of Cotton Green (now Horniman Circle). Designed by Colonel Thomas Cowper and completed in 1833, the Town Hall is considered to be among the finest Neo-Classical buildings in India, and is one of the earliest surviving colonial buildings in Mumbai. Its impressive façade of pedimented porticoes surmounts a row of fluted Doric columns, which were shipped out from England. A grand flight of steps leads into a magnificent Assembly Hall, the venue for public meetings during the Raj.

The Town Hall's north wing houses **The Asiatic Society**, founded in 1804, with its imposing high ceiling, teak-panelled walls, and elegant cast iron balustrades. This institution's extensive library has a priceless collection of 800,000 volumes, including a first edition of Dante's *Divine Comedy*, ancient Sanskrit manuscripts and old Bombay gazetteers. On the first floor are marble statues of Mumbai's founding fathers, among them two governors, Mountstuart Elphinstone and Sir Bartle Frere, and the Parsi philanthropist, Sir Jamsetjee Jeejeebhoy.

Horniman Circle **7**

Veer Nariman Rd, Fort Area.
St Thomas' Cathedral ◐ daily.
✠ 8am & 4:30pm, Sun.

THE CENTRAL GREEN, the old Cotton Green where traders used to buy and sell bales of cotton, was laid out as a public garden in 1869. Later known as Elphinstone Circle, it was renamed after Independence in honour of Benjamin Guy Horniman, a former editor of the *Bombay Chronicle* who was an active supporter of India's Freedom Movement. Today, the garden remains a delightful spot, much frequented by students and office workers who relax here before the long commute back to their homes in the distant suburbs. The garden is also the venue for open-air theatrical

Stained glass, St Thomas' Cathedral

performances and cultural events in the winter.

The elegant circle of Neo-Classical buildings around the garden was built in the 1860s, and fashioned after acclaimed English examples such as Bath Crescent and Tunbridge Wells. Designed by James Scott, the buildings around the garden share a uniform façade with pedestrian arcades and decorative terracotta keystones from England, and represent the earliest planned urban compositions in Mumbai.

Anchoring the western edge of the flower-filled green patch of Horniman Circle is **St Thomas' Cathedral**, the city's oldest church, which was consecrated in 1718. Like many of Mumbai's great edifices, this too was funded by public donations, collected in large part by a young East India Company chaplain named Richard Cobbe. The church has an imposing bell tower and flying buttresses, and some fine 19th-century stained glass. The cathedral's spacious interior is especially remarkable for its splendid marble memorials to heroes of the Raj. An exceptionally fine one is the monument to Governor Duncan, which depicts him being blessed by Hindus for his efforts to stop infanticide. In front of the entrance porch is a charming Neo-Gothic fountain. Designed by Sir Gilbert Scott, it was donated by the Parsi financier, Sir Cowasjee Readymoney.

Opposite the Cathedral are some lovely older buildings – the Neo-Gothic **Elphinstone Building**, built in the late 19th century, and the Neo-Classical **British Bank of the Middle East**. Across the road is the **Readymoney Mansion** with its detailed timberwork, Mughal arches and carved balconies. Reminiscent of a Rajasthani *haveli*, it was also designed by George Wittet (*see p450*).

Greek-inspired keystone at Horniman Circle

The Mumbai Stock Exchange, India's financial epicentre

Mumbai Stock Exchange ⑧

Dalal Street, Fort Area. ◑ to public.

INDIA'S FINANCIAL epicentre, the Mumbai Stock Exchange towers above Dalal Street. This is Mumbai's Wall Street and derives its name from the many stockbrokers (*dalals*) in the area. The presence of close to 50 banks on a short stretch underlines the frenetic pace of its commercial activity. Just before lunchtime, the area swarms with *dabbawallahs (see p457)* who bring home-made lunch-boxes to the thousands of office workers in the area.

Flora Fountain ⑨

Junction of Veer Nariman Rd, MG Rd & Dr Dadabhai Naoroji Rd, Fort Area.

STANDING AT the intersection of three major streets is Flora Fountain, the quint-essential icon of Mumbai. Crafted out of Portland stone and shipped out from England, the fountain is sur-mounted by the Roman goddess Flora who stands above exuberantly carved seashells, dolphins and myth-ical beasts. Erected in 1869 in what was then a spacious open plaza, Flora Fountain is now swamped in a sea of traffic, and over-shadowed by a **Martyrs' Memorial** put up by the Maharashtra state government in 1960. The area has now been renamed

Hutatma Chowk ("Martyrs' Square"). This area marks the western ramparts of the now-vanished old Fort, built by the East India Company in 1716, which covered the southern part of the city. The Fort was demolished in the 1860s by the governor, Sir Bartle Frere, to allow the city to expand, and to accommodate the grandiose new civic and commercial buildings he had planned. All these buildings were designed with pedes-trian arcades, which today are crowded with hawkers selling a wide range of goods, from old books to clothes and electronic gadgets.

North of Flora Fountain, leading towards Victoria Ter-minus, is Dadabhai Naoroji (DN) Road, lined with some magnificent Victorian and later colonial structures such as the **Capitol Cinema** with its classical detailing, the **JN Petit Institute and Library** (1898) with its Venetian Neo-Gothic façade, and the Art Deco **Watcha Agiary** (Parsi Fire Temple) with its Assyrian-style carvings, built in 1881. Other interesting struc-tures include the Indo-Saracenic **Times of India Building** and the fanciful **Municipal Corporation Building**, with its Islamic minarets, Gothic towers and onion domes.

Flora Fountain, a favourite Mumbai landmark

Victoria Terminus ⑩

See pp454–5.

Crawford Market ⑪

Dr Dadabhai Naoroji Rd & Lokmanya Tilak Rd. **Shops** ☐ daily.

ONE OF MUMBAI'S most fascinating and lively areas, Crawford Market, now renamed Mahatma Jyotiba Phule Market, lies to the north of Victoria Terminus. Designed by William Emerson and completed in 1869, this architectural extravaganza of Moorish arches and half-timbered gables, topped by a clocktower, consists of a large central hall with two wings. Tiers of wooden stalls display nearly 3,000 tonnes of fresh produce daily, from fruit and flowers to fish and exotic birds. The floor is paved with stone from Caithness in Scotland, which remains cool through the day. The lamps are shaped like winged drag-ons. Above the entrance doors, the charming marble bas-reliefs depict scenes from market life. They were carved by Lockwood Kipling (*see p110*), father of the writer Rudyard Kipling, as was the fountain in the courtyard exuberantly decorated with Hindu river goddesses and animals.

Just west of Crawford Mar-ket is **Zaveri Bazaar**, where diamond, gold and silver merchants have their opulent stores. Northwest of Crawford Market, on Mutton Street, is **Chor Bazaar** ("Thieves' Market"), with its fascinating antique and bric-a-brac shops.

Vegetable stall at Crawford Market

Victoria Terminus ⑩

Central Railway emblem on the gate

The MOST IMPRESSIVE example of Victorian Gothic architecture in India, Victoria Terminus Railway Station (now renamed Chhatrapati Shivaji Terminus) is a richly ornamented extravaganza of domes, spires and arches. Designed by Frederick William Stevens and superbly decorated by local art students and craftsmen, it was completed in 1888 and named to commemorate Queen Victoria's Golden Jubilee. Now the busy headquarters of the Central Railway, over 1,000 trains and two million passengers, including crowds of suburban commuters, pass through the station daily.

Victoria Terminus, often mistaken for a grand palace or cathedral

The Gables
The gables are crowned by sculptures representing Engineering, Agriculture and Commerce.

★ Booking Hall
A Neo-Gothic vaulted roof with wooden ribs covers the hall. Stained glass, colourful tiles and decorative iron grilles add to its beauty.

Entrance
The entrance gate piers are topped by stone sculptures of a lion and a tiger, symbolizing Britain and India, respectively.

STAR SIGHTS

★ **Booking Hall**

★ **Stone Carvings and Sculptures**

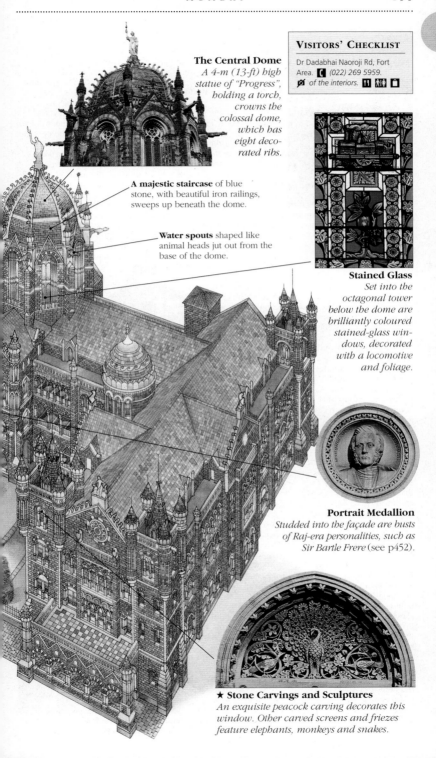

The Central Dome
A 4-m (13-ft) high statue of "Progress", holding a torch, crowns the colossal dome, which has eight decorated ribs.

VISITORS' CHECKLIST

Dr Dadabhai Naoroji Rd, Fort Area. ((022) 269 5959.
Ⓧ of the interiors. 🍴 ♿ 📷

A majestic staircase of blue stone, with beautiful iron railings, sweeps up beneath the dome.

Water spouts shaped like animal heads jut out from the base of the dome.

Stained Glass
Set into the octagonal tower below the dome are brilliantly coloured stained-glass windows, decorated with a locomotive and foliage.

Portrait Medallion
Studded into the façade are busts of Raj-era personalities, such as Sir Bartle Frere (see p452).

★ Stone Carvings and Sculptures
An exquisite peacock carving decorates this window. Other carved screens and friezes feature elephants, monkeys and snakes.

The Ruttonsee Mulji fountain, elaborately carved and embellished

Shahid Bhagat Singh Marg ⑫

Fort Area.

THIS BUSY STREET, also known as Colaba Causeway *(see p447)* towards its southern end, is the bustling commercial and administrative hub of the so-called Fort area *(see p453)*. Virtually no traces of this historic structure remain, but the area still offers a fascinating glimpse into the continuities between colonial and present-day Mumbai.

The **Reserve Bank of India**, which stands on the site of an old military barracks, is India's leading banking institution. Built in 1939 and designed by JA Ritchie, its grand Art Deco entrance, flanked by two impressive columns, enhances its air of respectable solidity. There are attractive cast iron grilles in the window panels. The new highrise offices of the Reserve Bank, across the road, stand in the grounds of the old **Mint**. This is a majestic Classical-fronted building, built in 1817 by Major John Hawkins, a member of the Bombay Engineers' Regiment. Entry into the Mint is restricted, but visible from its compound is a stone gateway erected by the Portuguese, now inside the naval establishment, INS Angre.

West of the Mint, occupying a corner site at the intersection of Pherozeshah Mehta and Shahid Bhagat Singh roads, is

the imposing **Gresham Assurance Building**. This Art Deco structure has an impressive basalt façade, with two grand pillars and a dome.

The **Marshall Building**, directly opposite, has a Florentine dome, and was constructed in 1898 to accommodate the warehouse and offices of a British engineering firm. Its façade, embellished with a medley of angels, portholes and pediments, is a wonderful example of how contemporary European architecture was successfully transplanted to eastern settings.

Drinking water fountains or *pyaus* were set up across the city by local philanthropists to provide respite from the hot Indian summer. At the point where Shahid Bhagat Singh Marg meets Mint Road is the **Ruttonsee Mulji Drinking Water Fountain** designed by FW Stevens, the leading architect of Victorian Bombay, who also designed the Municipal Corporation Building and the Victoria Terminus *(see pp454–5)*. This fountain was erected in 1894 by a local trader, in memory of his only son, whose statue stands beneath the dome. Made of limestone and red and blue granite, it is decorated with projecting elephant heads, whose trunks spout water. The dome, supported by columns made of blue granite, is crowned by the figure of a young boy. The fountain also has a special trough from which animals can drink.

Further down Mint Road, just before its junction with Walchand Hirachand Marg, is another *pyav* and the **Kothari Kabutarkhana**. Literally "Pigeon House", the Kabutarkhana is an ornate

Gresham Assurance Building

stone structure, constructed in the 18th century by a Jain merchant, Purushottamdas Kothari, and added to in the 19th and early 20th centuries. Jains, like Buddhists, believe that all living beings have souls, and that kind acts towards all life forms will earn the giver merit in the next life.

At the western end of Walchand Hirachand Marg is **Nagar Chowk**, an oasis of green in the midst of swirling traffic. It has an impressive statue of Sir Dinshaw Manekji Petit, a baronet, captain of industry and leading Parsi philanthropist of the early 20th century. The statue was sculpted by Sir Thomas Brock and the surrounding garden is a good place from which to view some of Mumbai's grand Victorian buildings – among them Victoria Terminus, the Bombay Municipal Corporation building and the General Post Office. Shahid Bhagat Singh Marg eventually runs into D'Mello Road, formerly known as Frere Road. This area lay under water until the 1860s, when it was reclaimed by the Port Trust. Today the road is lined with popular eateries.

Pigeons at the Kothari Kabutarkhana pecking at their daily supply of grain

Ballard Estate ⓭

Bounded by Shahid Bhagat Singh Marg, Walchand Hirachand Marg & Shoorji Vallabhdas Marg.

THIS ENTIRE AREA was once part of the sea until it was reclaimed by the Bombay Port Trust and converted into a business district. Planned between 1908 and 1914 by George Wittet, architect of the Gateway of India, the area was developed according to the strict guidelines he set, maintaining a restrained elegance in contrast to the over-ornamentation of the Victorian edifices in the Fort area. The district's broad pavements and neat tree-lined avenues are lined with stone buildings of uniform height and style, giving the Estate an atmosphere of calm tranquillity, unusual in a business quarter.

A convenient point of entry into Ballard Estate is from Shoorji Vallabhdas Marg, near the imposing Marshall Building. Among the most impressive buildings on this street is the **Customs House**. Designed by Wittet himself, it has a grand entrance portico in stately Renaissance style, framed by two columns rising to the height of the building. Next to it is the **Bombay Port Trust** also designed by George

The General Post Office, combining European and Indian styles

Wittet. Two striking ships in full sail are sculpted on its basalt façade. Further down the road, to the east, is the **Port Trust War Memorial**, honouring the memory of port officers who died in World War I. The memorial has a single, fluted column shaft in stone, surmounted by a lantern. The **Grand Hotel** dominates the corner of Walchand Hirachand Marg and Ram Gulam Marg. Another of George Wittet's designs, it has a striking central atrium. The grandiose **Mackinnon & Mackenzie Building** has an impressive portico, columns and statues. This, and other beautiful Edwardian buildings, such as **Darabshaw House** and **Neville House**, make Ballard Estate a uniquely elegant business district.

Port Trust Memorial

General Post Office ⓮

Walchand Hirachand Marg.
⬚ Mon–Sat.

COMPLETED IN 1911, this fantastic composition of minarets, domes and arches was designed by John Begg and supervised by George Wittet. A prime example of the Indo-Saracenic style, the General Post Office (GPO) building combines elements of Indian architecture, most notably an Islamic dome inspired by the Gol Gumbad in Bijapur *(see p543)*, with classical European traditions. Mumbai's main post office, the GPO has a lofty three-storeyed rotunda inside, which leads to its various departments. Business is transacted from behind delightful old-fashioned wooden counters.

THE DABBAWALLAHS OF MUMBAI

Among Mumbai's most characteristic sights are the *dabbawallahs*, men who pick up freshly cooked lunches from over 100,000 suburban homes and deliver them to offices all over the city. Most office workers spend an average of two hours travelling to work. Hot, home-cooked lunches therefore, would normally be an impossible luxury – if it weren't for the *dabbawallas*. They pick up the meals, usually *rotis*, vegetables and *dal*, packed in three or four round stainless steel containers, known as tiffin boxes or *dabbas* (hence the name

Dabbawallahs delivering home-cooked lunch to office workers

dabbawallah) from each house, colourcode the office addresses onto the lids, thread the *dabbas* onto long poles and cycle off to the nearest station. Here the *dabbas* are handed over to other *dabbawallas*, who deliver them to the right offices. Lunches rarely go astray, and empty *dabbas* are delivered back home by late afternoon. *Dabbawallahs*, traditionally migrants from the neighbouring city of Pune, are organized under the Mumbai Tiffin Box Suppliers Association. They provide one of Mumbai's most efficient services.

Marine Drive, sweeping in an arc along the sea, connecting the northern and southern ends of Mumbai

Marine Drive ⑮

Netaji Subhash Chandra Rd.

KNOWN as the "Queen's Necklace" after the glittering string of streetlights lining the road, Marine Drive (renamed Netaji Subhash Chandra Road) sweeps along a sea-facing promenade which runs from **Nariman Point** to Malabar Hill. Built on land reclaimed from the sea in the 1920s, it is also the main arterial link between the suburbs and the city's prime commercial and administrative centres, Nariman Point and the Fort area *(see p453)*. Situated at its eastern periphery is the **Oval Maidan**, nursery of such modern-day Indian cricketing heroes as Sachin Tendulkar (b.1973) and Sunil Gavaskar (b.1949).

The buildings of Marine Drive are characterized by a strong Art Deco flavour, popular in Mumbai during the 1930s and 1940s. With the advent of electric elevators, and with concrete replacing the earlier stone and brick, the apartment blocks on the seafront were built to a uniform height of five floors, making this the most fashionable residential area of the time.

The best way to enjoy Marine Drive during the day is from the upper floor of a red double-decker bus, which provides panoramic views of the sea and the city's skyline. In the evening, it swarms with people taking their daily walks, couples meeting after work and families gathering around the vendors selling coconut water and *bhelpuri*

(see p441). **Chowpatty Beach** is the city's most popular promenade and the southernmost of Mumbai's beaches. Earlier cluttered with food stalls and hawkers, the area has now been substantially cleaned up in a drive by the civic authorities. An inexpensive evening destination for the city's residents, it remains lively till late at night. It is also the venue for Mumbai's largest festival, Ganesha Chaturthi *(see p467)*, when huge crowds gather at Chowpatty Beach to immerse images of Ganesha, the elephant-headed god, in the Arabian Sea.

The **National Centre for Performing Arts (NCPA)**, at the southern tip of Marine Drive, is the city's most active venue for music, dance and theatre performances. Its Tata Theatre and Experimental Theatre stage works by international and Indian playwrights with the best of local talent, while India's finest musicians and dancers perform regularly in its other auditoriums *(see pp462–3)*.

Malabar Hill ⑯

Bounded by Napean Sea Rd, Ridge Rd & Walkeshwar Rd.

THIS LEAFY residential area, once dotted with bungalows set in large, forested compounds, is today crowded with highrise apartment blocks, home to Mumbai's rich and famous. The Parsi **Towers of Silence** are also located in this area. Parsis *(see p447)*, who believe that the elements of earth, water, air and fire are sacred and should not be defiled, place their dead in these tall, cylindrical stone towers to be picked clean by vultures. This, they believe, is one of the most environmentally friendly ways of disposing of the dead. A fall in Mumbai's vulture population, however, remains a cause of worry. A high wall and a thick belt of trees surround the Towers, which are closed to visitors.

The **Hanging Gardens** provide a pleasant open space in the vicinity, with good views of the city.

The Hanging Gardens, rising in tiers on Malabar Hill

Banganga ⑰

Walkeshwar, Malabar Hill.

HIDDEN AMIDST the soaring skyscrapers of Malabar Hill is the small settlement of Banganga, set around a sacred tank. According to legend, Rama, hero of the *Ramayana* *(see p27)*, pausing here while on his way to rescue his abducted wife Sita, shot an arrow into the ground and a spring gushed forth. This is the origin of the tank, and devotees take regular ritual dips in it. The site has several temples – the **Jabreshwar Mahadeo**, at the tank's corner, is the prettiest, while the **Walkeshwar Temple**, built in the 18th century, has a linga said to have been built by Rama himself. Around the tank and temples are rest houses (*dharamsalas*) for pilgrims.

The Mahalaxmi Temple, dedicated to Lakshmi, the Goddess of Wealth

point for most daytime activities. The inhabitants were converted to Christianity by Portuguese missionaries and adopted names such as Fernandes, D'Costa and D'Lima. Anant Ashram, a tiny eatery in Khotachiwadi's bylanes, serves excellent prawn curry and rice.

Mahalaxmi Temple ⑲

Mahalaxmi Temple Lane, off Bhulabhai Desai Rd.

DEVOTEES, both rich and poor, throng this temple dedicated to Lakshmi, the Goddess of Wealth and Prosperity, who is also known as Laxmi in Maharashtra and in parts of Gujarat *(see p419)*. The approach is lined with stalls selling religious offerings, such as coconuts, flowers and small plastic icons. The temple's history dates to the 18th century, when an embankment being constructed along the bay was repeatedly washed away. The contractor dreamt that if a temple was built to Laxmi, the wall would hold. And this

actually happened. Nearby is the **Mahalaxmi Race Course**, next to Mahalaxmi Station, which has horse races every weekend from November to April. In its crowded stands the city's fashionable set rub shoulders with the poor and hopeful.

Haji Ali Mosque ⑳

Off Lala Lajpat Rai Marg.

APPROACHED by a long causeway which gets submerged at high tide, is the *dargah* (tomb) of a rich merchant, Haji Ali Shah Bukhari, who gave up his wealth after a pilgrimage to Mecca. The *dargah* dates to the 15th century, but the dazzling white mosque was built in the 1940s and seems to float on its small island in the Arabian Sea. The causeway, usually lined with beggars, leads to a huge marble courtyard. The tomb lies at its centre and devotees touch their heads to the heavily embroidered *chador* (ceremonial cloth) covering it. Female devotees sit behind a a *jali* (stone screen).

Khotachiwadi's narrow lanes and balconied houses

Khotachiwadi ⑱

Bounded by Jagannath Shankarshet Rd & Raja Ram Mohan Roy Rd, Girgaum.

IN THE NARROW bylanes of Girgaum in central Mumbai is the old-fashioned neighbourhood of Khotachiwadi (literally, "Headman's Orchard"). Khotachiwadi grew as a suburban settlement, north of the Fort, in the 19th century, and retains the sleepy quality of a coastal village. The low, tile-roofed cottages have timber eaves and open verandahs with cast-iron balconies, the focal

Haji Ali Mosque, built on an island linked to the shore by a causeway

Bandra ㉑

N of Mahim Bay. **Mount St Mary Basilica** Mount Mary Rd. ◯ daily. 🎭 Bandra fête (Sep).

THE PROSPEROUS SUBURB of Bandra, in the north of Mumbai, is connected to the city by the Mahim Causeway. Amidst its new apartment blocks, swanky boutiques and restaurants, are vestiges of its past as a small Portuguese enclave. The quiet lanes with tile-roofed bungalows are inhabited by a community of local East Indian Christians, whose ancestors were converted by the Portuguese. A number of Roman Catholic churches, too, were built by the Portuguese, who retained Bandra until the late 18th century. The most important of these is the **Mount St Mary Basilica**, which attracts devotees of all faiths. Outside the church is a bizarre market selling wax models of various body parts. Devotees with ailing limbs buy the appropriate model and solemnly place it on the altar before the Virigin Mary in the belief that she will effect a miraculous cure. A deserted Portuguese fort, **Castella de Aguada**, on a hill, offers spectacular views of the sea and the hinterland.

Bandra's plush **Pali Hill** locality, which has the villas of several Bollywood stars, draws crowds of star-struck Indian tourists. Its other attractions are the seafront promenades at **Bandstand** and **Carter Road**, especially popular with local youth. Also situated on the seafront is a small Koli fishing village.

A green coconut vendor on Mumbai's crowded Juhu Beach

Juhu Beach ㉒

N of Bandra.

THE SANDY COASTLINE of Juhu Beach lies north of the city centre. This is not a beach for leisurely sunbathing, though, since it is always crowded. On weekends, especially, it is packed with families of pic-nickers playing cricket on the beach, paddling tentatively in the water and enjoying the sea breeze. Crowds of vendors offering snacks, toys and fairground rides add to the *mela* (fair) atmosphere. Juhu also has several luxury hotels that serve as weekend retreats for Mumbai's tycoons and Bollywood film stars.

The **Prithvi Theatre**, on Juhu Church Road, was founded in 1978 by one of Bollywood's leading families, the Kapoors. It stages plays in Hindi, Gujarati and English, and has a lively café, popular with Mumbai's arty crowd. A theatre festival is held in November (see p462).

Film City ㉓

Goregaon East. 🛈 Contact Film City's Public Relations Office (022) 840 1533.

BUILT IN 1978 to meet the needs of Mumbai's booming Hindi film industry, better known as Bollywood (see pp32–3), Film City sprawls over 140 ha (346 acres) in the city's northern outskirts. Bollywood produces some 120 feature films a year, making it the world's largest film industry, rivalled only by South India's Telugu and Tamil film industries. Film City is where many Bollywood blockbusters are shot, as are most TV soaps and serials. Song-and-dance routines, scenes of tear-jerking melodrama and action-packed fight sequences take place simultaneously on Film City's dozen shooting stages, against outsize backdrops of medieval forts, dense jungles and opulent cardboard palaces. In between takes, mythological heroes rub shoulders with rifle-toting bandits and skimpily clad vamps.

Sanjay Gandhi National Park ㉔

Borivili. 🛈 Conservation Education Centre, near elephant gate Goregaon, (022) 842 1174. ◯ Tue–Sun. 🎭 🎫 **Kanheri Caves** ◯ Tue–Sun. 🎭

AN HOUR'S TRAIN ride north of Mumbai, this national park is one of the few in India within the limits of a city. Surrounded by rolling hills, its deciduous forests harbour a wealth of birdlife and fauna, wild boar, cobras, as well as the occasional tiger. Tiger and Lion Safaris are offered in fenced-off sections of the park.

In a picturesque wooded area of the park is an extraordinary complex of 109 Buddhist caves, the **Kanheri Caves**, dating from the 2nd to the 9th centuries AD. The 6th-century **Cave 3** is the most impressive, with its colossal Buddhas, richly carved pillars and brackets and hemispherical stupa. The caves are best approached through the Park's northern entrance.

A film shoot in progress at Film City, Goregaon

Elephanta Island ㉕

Shiva and Parvati, carved in stone

LOCATED ON AN ISLAND off Mumbai's eastern shore, the 6th-century AD Elephanta cave temples, chiselled into a rocky cliff and dedicated to Shiva, contain some great masterpieces of Indian sculpture. Originally called Gharapuri or "Fort-City", the island was renamed Elephanta by the Portuguese after a huge stone elephant that once stood here. This is now in the garden of the Bhau Daji Lad Museum in Mumbai's Byculla area. A UNESCO World Heritage Site, the Elephanta cave temples can be visited on a day trip by boat from Mumbai.

VISITORS' CHECKLIST

9 km (6 miles) NE of Mumbai.
🚢 from Gateway of India. ℹ️
for ferries, (022) 202 6364. 🕐
Wed–Mon. 🎫 📷 🎵 Elephanta
Music & Dance Festival (Feb).

The Elephanta caves, cut into the cliff high above the water

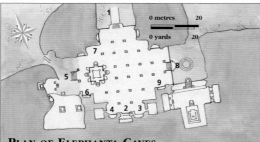

PLAN OF ELEPHANTA CAVES

1 Northern Entrance
2 Mahesamurti
3 Ardhanarishvara
4 Gangadhara
5 Western Entrance
6 Marriage of Shiva-Parvati
7 Shiva spearing Andhaka
8 Eastern Entrance
9 Shiva and Parvati Playing Dice

Exploring Elephanta

The origins of the cave temples at Elephanta are lost in obscurity, but in all probability they date to the 6th century AD and represent the period of Brahmanical revival after Buddhism began to decline. From the pier, where visitors disembark from the boats, a long flight of 125 steps leads to the temple's main **Northern Entrance**. This is a huge square hall with sides measuring 40 m (131 ft), supported by two dozen massive pillars. Here, in a deep recess against the rear (south) wall, is the huge triple-headed Shiva statue, the **Mahesamurti**. This is the glory of Elephanta, and few visitors can fail to be moved by this powerful, compelling image, hailed by art historian Percy Brown as "the creation of a genius". The three faces represent Shiva in his different manifestations. The central face with its towering, elaborate crown depicts Shiva the Preserver, sublimely serene and introspective. The one facing west represents Shiva the Creator, gentle, solicitous and graceful. The head facing east, with its cruel mouth, fiercely hooked nose and serpents adorning the hair, shows Shiva as the Destroyer. On either side of the statue are other superb sculptures.

The one on the east shows Shiva as **Ardhanarishvara** – the Lord who is Both Male and Female, and thus symbolizes the Divine Unity in which all opposites are resolved. The image on the west is of Shiva as **Gangadhara**, helping the river goddess Ganga descend to earth *(see p163)* while his consort Parvati and other deities look on.

Contrasting images of peace and violence, joy and fury, can be seen in exquisite sculptures throughout the temple. Thus, one sculpture near the **Western Entrance** lyrically depicts the marriage of Shiva and Parvati, while opposite it is a powerful panel showing Shiva brutally impaling the demon Andhaka. The **Eastern Entrance** has Shiva and Parvati contentedly playing dice in their mountain abode, as the demon-king Ravana tries to destroy their home by shaking the mountain.

The 5.5-m (18-ft) high Mahesamurti, dominating the cave temple

Shopping & Entertainment in Mumbai

MUMBAI IS ONE OF INDIA'S BEST shopping destinations. Large malls, department stores and exclusive boutiques stocking international brand names, coexist with traditional bazaars and pavement stalls selling everything from diamonds to dentures. Mumbai also has a vibrant nightlife, with more discotheques and pubs than any other Indian city. As the home of the Hindi film industry, Bollywood, Mumbai often holds gala premiere nights at its many cinema halls. The city's crowded cultural calendar also includes several concerts, exhibitions, theatre shows and festivals. But perhaps the best entertainment the city offers is the non-stop circus on its bustling streets and sidewalks.

SHOPS AND MARKETS

SOUTH MUMBAI'S main shopping areas include Colaba Causeway, Kemp's Corner, and the shopping arcade in the Oberoi Hotel at Nariman Point. The traditional market for fresh produce is Crawford Market *(see p453)*, while Bhuleshwar and Kalbadevi, north of the Fort area, are popular haunts for textiles and jewellery. Crossroads, a large new shopping mall, has come up in central Mumbai, close to the Haji Ali Mosque.

ANTIQUES AND JEWELLRY

A FASCINATING place for antiques is Chor Bazaar or "Thieves' Market" near Crawford Market. This warren of shops is crammed with colonial furniture, Victorian bric-a-brac and Chinese porcelain, along with a lot of junk and fakes. Very good bargains can still be found here. **Phillips Antiques**, on Shyama Prasad Mukherjee Chowk, stocks a fine collection of old postcards, prints and Raj-era lithographs. There are strict rules, however, regarding the export of antiques *(see p758)*.

Central Mumbai's Zaveri Bazaar is lined with jewellers' shops, **Tribhovandas Bhimji Zaveri** being the most famous. **Palazzo** at the Crossroads Mall has dozens of jewellery stores under one roof, offering elegant, exclusive designs. The shopping arcades at the **Oberoi** and **Taj Hotels** *(see p707 & p708)* are also good places to shop for jewellery.

TEXTILES AND FASHION

MUMBAI is a highly fashion-conscious city and most Indian designers have outlets here. Among the more exclusive boutiques are **Ensemble** and **Melange**, while casual ready-made garments are available at **Cotton World**. **Fantasia** and **Indian Textiles** specialize in a wide range of traditional Indian textiles and weaves, including silk saris, home furnishings and accessories. For good quality handwoven home furnishings and floor-coverings, the best shop is **Shyam Ahuja**.

HANDICRAFTS AND GIFTS

HANDICRAFTS from all over India are available in Mumbai. The widest range and best quality can be found at the **Cottage Industries Emporium**, **Contemporary Arts and Crafts** and **Bombay Store** in the Fort area. **Chimanlal's** has a good selection of handmade paper, while **Inshallah Maashallah** stocks pure perfume essence *(attar)* in tiny glass bottles capturing the fragrances of rose, vetiver and jasmine.

Mumbai is renowned for its high quality leather goods at reasonable prices. **Rasulbhai Adamji** at Colaba, **Csango** at Apollo Bunder, and many shops in the Oberoi Shopping Centre have a good range of jackets, handbags, wallets and luggage, some of it "inspired" by Gucci, Prada and Louis Vuitton. **Joy Shoes** at the Taj Hotel has high quality shoes

and leather accessories. Books, CDs and audio cassettes of both Indian and Western music, are available at various outlets throughout the city, including hotel book-shops. However, one of the best shops for music is **Rhythm House**.

ENTERTAINMENT GUIDES, TICKETS AND VENUES

DAILY NEWSPAPERS list the day's entertainment and events on their engagements page. Another good source of information is the magazine *Discover Mumbai*. A useful website which offers online information on cultural events and entertainment is *www.explocity.com* Tickets for most concerts and plays can be bought at **Rhythm House** or at the venue itself. The major venues for Mumbai's cultural events are the **NCPA** or the National Centre for the Performing Arts *(see p458)*, the **Nehru Centre** auditorium and **Shanmukhananda Hall**. **Prithvi Theatre** in Juhu *(see p460)* is a lively centre for stage productions. Other active exhibition venues include the **Jehangir Art Gallery**, the **NGMA** (National Gallery of Modern Art) and the Artists' Centre, located at Kala Ghoda *(see pp448–9)*.

PERFORMING ARTS

MUMBAI is a great centre of classical Indian music, and many well-known performers can be heard here. This cosmopolitan city also has many enthusiasts of jazz and Western classical music (conductor Zubin Mehta received his early training in Mumbai) and frequent concerts are held by both local and visiting international groups. Classical and folk dance performances from different parts of the country also feature regularly on the cultural calendar. Mumbai has a vibrant theatre tradition, with productions in English as well as Marathi, Gujarati and Hindi. These are often staged in the open at **Horniman Circle Gardens**

(see p452). The cultural high season is from November to April, though performances take place through the year.

CINEMA

AS THE CAPITAL of the Hindi film industry, Mumbai hosts a number of film-related events. Most of the film studios are located in the suburbs as are the private residences of screen celebrities. Great fanfare precedes the release of big-budget blockbusters, and glittering premieres are held at popular cinema halls such as **Sterling**, **Regal** and **Metro**. These draw star-struck fans who spend hours standing outside, waiting for a glimpse of their favourite stars. Film festivals, documentary film screenings, lectures, talks and exhibitions are also held throughout the year at various venues, such as the **British Council**.

HERITAGE TOURS

THE MAHARASHTRA Tourism Development Corporation (MTDC), offers guided tours of Mumbai on double-decker buses. **Bombay Heritage Walks**, organized by a group of young architects, take visitors through historical districts such as Banganga, Khotachi-wadi and the Fort area, on weekends, except during the monsoon (June to September). Prior booking is necessary.

NIGHTCLUBS AND BARS

MUMBAI'S NIGHTLIFE is more active than that of any other Indian city. While nightclubs and bars open and close at regular intervals, some have remained consistently popular. One of the liveliest is **Fire & Ice**, ingeniously housed in a mill compound in Parel. In south Mumbai, **Not Just Jazz by the Bay** has live music Wednesday through Saturday. Most hotels have their own bars and nightclubs such as **Infinity** in the Taj and Opium Den in the Oberoi, both of which attract Bollywood's A-list stars. Another favourite haunt of Mumbai's jetset is **Athena**, one of the city's trendiest new nightspots.

DIRECTORY

ANTIQUES AND JEWELLERY

Palazzo
Crossroads Mall.
(022) 494 5890.

Phillips Antiques
Shyama Prasad Mukherjee Chowk.
(022) 202 0564.

Tribhovandas Bhimji Zaveri
Zaveri Bazaar.
(022) 342 5001.

TEXTILES AND FASHION

Cotton World
Mandlik Rd, Colaba.
(022) 283 3294.

Ensemble
Great Western Bldg,
Shahid Bhagat Singh Marg.
(022) 287 2883.

Fantasia
Oberoi Shopping Centre.
(022) 284 6369.

Indian Textiles
Taj Hotel, Apollo Bunder.
(022) 202 8783.

Melange
Altamount Rd.
(022) 385 4492.

Shyam Ahuja
Crossroads Mall.
(022) 460 3078.

HANDICRAFTS AND GIFTS

Bombay Store
Western India House, PM Rd, Fort Area.
(022) 288 5048.

Chimanlal's
Fort Area.
(022) 207 7717.

Cottage Industries Emporium
Chhatrapati Shivaji M Rd.
(022) 202 6564.

Contemporary Arts and Crafts
Napean Sea Rd.
(022) 363 1979.

Csango
Apollo Bunder.
(022) 202 4309.

Inshallah Maashallah
Colaba.
(022) 204 9495.

Joy Shoes
Taj Hotel, Apollo Bunder.
(022) 202 3366.

Rasulbhai Adamji
Colaba.
(022) 202 1267.

Rhythm House
Kala Ghoda.
(022) 284 2835.

ENTERTAINMENT INFORMATION

w www.explocity.com

ENTERTAINMENT VENUES

British Council
Nariman Point.
(022) 282 3530.

Jehangir Art Gallery
Fort Area.
(022) 284 3989.

NGMA
Kala Ghoda.
(022) 285 2457.

NCPA
Nariman Point.
(022) 283 4500.

Nehru Centre
Worli.
(022) 496 4676.

Prithvi Theatre
Janaki Kutir,
Juhu.
(022) 614 9546.

Shanmukhananda Hall
King's Circle.
(022) 401 5164.

CINEMA

Metro
MG Rd,
Dhobi Talao.
(022) 203 0303.

Regal
Shyama Prasad Mukherjee Chowk.
(022) 202 1017.

Sterling
Hazarimal Somani Marg.
(022) 207 5187.

HERITAGE TOURS

Bombay Heritage Walks
(022) 834 4622.

NIGHTCLUBS AND BARS

Athena
Minoo Desai Marg,
Colaba.
(022) 202 3366.

Fire & Ice
Parel.
(022) 498 0444.

Infinity
Taj Hotel, Apollo Bunder.
(022) 202 3366.

Not Just Jazz by The Bay
Marine Drive.
(022) 285 1876.

Maharashtra

VERDANT HILLS, scenic coastal plains and busy industrial centres make up the varied landscape of Maharashtra, which covers an area of 300,000 sq km (115,831 sq miles). The hills of the Western Ghats, source of many rivers, run parallel to the narrow Konkan Coast, while cradled in the centre is the Deccan Plateau, formed from black volcanic lava 70 million years ago. This area saw a great flowering of art and architecture from the 2nd century BC onwards, and two famous UNESCO World Heritage sites are located here – the Buddhist caves at Ajanta and the rock-cut temples at Ellora. The rocky terrain around Pune is dotted with the massive forts built by the 17th-century Maratha leader, Shivaji, who launched successful guerrilla campaigns against the Mughals. His cult-like status is today perpetuated by the Shiv Sena, a nationalist political party.

Modern Maharashtra is a prosperous, highly industrialized region, with a strong agrarian base. Cotton and tobacco are widely cultivated, as are a variety of fruits including oranges, *chikoos* (sapodilla) and mangoes.

SIGHTS AT A GLANCE

Towns & Cities
Ahmadnagar ⑨
Aurangabad ⑪
Kolhapur ④
Nagpur ⑰
Pune ⑥
Wardha ⑱

Temple Towns & Holy Places
Nasik ⑩
Pandharpur ⑲

Historic Sites
Ajanta ⑭
Daulatabad ⑫
Ellora ⑬
Murud-Janjira ②

National Parks & Geographical Sites
Lonar ⑮
Melghat Tiger Reserve ⑯

Hill Stations
Lonavla ⑦
Mahabaleshwar ⑤
Matheran ⑧

Beaches
Alibag ①
Ganapatipule ③

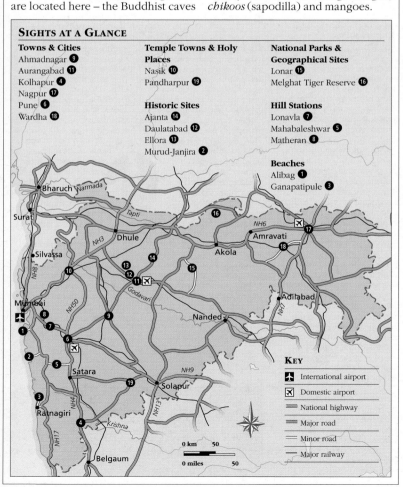

KEY

✈ International airport
☒ Domestic airport
━━ National highway
━━ Major road
━━ Minor road
━━ Major railway

0 km   50
0 miles   50

◁ **View of the votive stupa in the late 5th-century *chaitya* hall, Cave 19, at Ajanta**

View of the imposing Janjira Fort, built on an island

Alibag ❶

Raigarh district. 108 km (67 miles) S of Mumbai. 🚌🚕 *from Gateway of India, Mumbai, to Mandve, 18 km (11 miles) N of Alibag, then bus.*

THE PORT OF ALIBAG was developed by the Marathas in the 17th century to protect their kingdom from the Dutch, Portuguese and the increasingly powerful British. Alibag is today a quiet town, just across the bay from Mumbai. Its most impressive sight is its beach, a 5-km (3-mile) stretch of soft silver sand, lined by a stand of coconut and casuarina trees.

Kolaba Fort, constructed on an island in 1680 by the Maratha ruler Chhatrapati Shivaji (*see p471*), looms over the skyline. It is a forbidding grey mass of lead, steel and stone, built on a rock jutting from the sea, and can be reached on foot during low tide. Within its high ramparts are enclosed a temple dedicated to Lord Ganesha, and next to it a sweet-water well that must have been useful during sieges. There are two main entrances to the fort, one from the shore and another from the sea. The enormous shore-side doorway is decorated with sculptures of tigers, elephants and peacocks.

ENVIRONS: Kihim Beach, 9 km (6 miles) north of Alibag, is a tranquil getaway, with woods brimming with birds and wild flowers. It was the favourite haunt of the famous Indian ornithologist Salim Ali (1896–1987), author of the finest book on Indian birds.

Murud–Janjira ❷

Raigarh district. 185 km (115 miles) S of Mumbai. 🚌 *from Gateway of India, Mumbai to Mandve, 120 km (74 miles) N of Murud, then bus.* 🚤 *from Rajpuri to Janjira Fort.*

A SLEEPY COASTAL TOWN with Indo-Gothic houses and meandering pathways, Murud has a picture-perfect beach that promises lazy, sunny afternoons and cool dips in the clean sea. The little village of Rajpuri, 4 km (2.5 miles) south of the main Murud town, is the gateway to the Janjira Fort, the strongest island-fort in the Konkan, still enduring the surge and retreat of the Arabian Sea. Boats are available at Rajpuri to take visitors to the fort.

Also evocatively known as the Jazira-Mehruba or "Moon Fort", it was built in 1511 by the Siddis, who originally arrived in the Deccan from Abyssinia as slave-traders. The fortress, with its high ramparts, 22 bastions and granite walls jointed with lead to withstand the onslaught of the sea, proved invincible against attacks by the Portuguese and British, and even against the great

Maratha leader, Shivaji. Steps lead to a sturdy stone gate, where a stone engraving of a lion holding six diminutive elephants in captivity, represents six successive Siddi victories. Rusty cannons point outwards through niches in the ramparts. The palaces, gardens and mosques lie in silent ruin, and luxurious vegetation grows around the palace of the Siddi ruler, Sirul Khan.

Ganapatipule ❸

Ratnagiri district. 365 km (227 miles) S of Mumbai. 🚉 *Ratnagiri, 22 km (14 miles) S of Ganapatipule, then bus.* 🚌 🎪 *Gauri Ganapati (Sep/Oct).*

THE SMALL COASTAL village of Ganapatipule derives its name from the 400-year-old temple of Swayambhu Ganapati, where the naturally occurring idol of Ganapati (the local name of Lord Ganesha), is revered by Hindus as one of the eight sacred sites, or "Ashtha Ganapatis", in India. Despite attracting the usual smattering of holy men and mendicants, its beach has long stretches of pristine white sands and clear waters. Beyond the coast lie groves of fruit trees, including mango, banana, jackfruit, coconut and betel nut.

Alphonso mango

ENVIRONS: Ratnagiri, 19 km (12 miles) south of Ganapatipule, is famous for its groves of delicious Alphonso mangoes, locally known as *hapus*. Ratnagiri's fortress, Bala Qila, is situated along the coast, and is intact, with a notable Bhagavati temple within its walls.

The Swayambhu Ganapati Temple, at the base of a hill in Ganapatipule

Ganesha, the Remover of Obstacles

Lord Ganesha
imitating the
dance of Shiva

Lord GANESHA, the elephant-headed son of Shiva and Parvati, is the most auspicious and popular deity in India, and especially beloved in Maharashtra. Images of the endearing, potbellied god are found in every household, on temple doorways and shop entrances, on letterheads and wedding invitations. No task or enterprise is ever begun without invoking him, as he is the Lord of New Beginnings. Worshipped in many guises, he is Vighneshvara, the Remover of Obstacles, and Siddhidata, the God of Prosperity and Success. Ganesha is above all a friend, lovable and benign, and his festival, Ganesha Chaturthi, crosses all social boundaries uniting the people of Maharashtra in a frenzied ten-day celebration.

LORD GANESHA

Lord Ganesha's four arms hold his various attributes. Two of these, his broken tusk and a round sweetmeat called *modaka*, appear consistently. In the other two hands, he sometimes holds a lotus blossom, an elephant goad, an axe or prayer beads. According to legend, Ganesha gained his elephant head after Shiva, in a state of fury, cut his son's head off and then, in remorse, stuck on the head of a passing elephant.

Elephant goad

A half halo indicates his divinity.

Modaka

The broken tusk, used as a pen to write the *Mahabharata*, was the result of an encounter with Parasuram (*see p679*).

A rat is the vehicle of Ganesha

Intricate clay images *of Ganesha are made and consecrated on the first day of Ganesha Chaturthi (see p473). These are then enshrined in pandals or decorated stages, and worshipped continuously for ten days amidst Hindi and Marathi recitations and musical performances.*

Colourful floats, *accompanied by folk dancers, lead the serpentine processions that fill the streets, amidst chants and drumbeats. The processions end at the water's edge, where hundreds of idols are immersed in rivers, lakes or the sea. This final immersion on the tenth day marks the deity's return to his abode.*

See also features on Hindu Mythology (*see pp24–5*), Shiva (*see p566*) and Vishnu (*see p679*).

Colourful fishing boats docked off the Malvan coast

Kolhapur ❹

Kolhapur district. 225 km (140 miles)
S of Pune. 🏛 485,500. 🚉 🚌 🛈
Maharashtra Tourism, (0231) 65 2935.

SITUATED ON the banks of the
Panchganga river, the city
of Kolhapur is a thriving
commercial centre, noted
today for its flourishing dairy
industry. It is also one of
Maharashtra's most important
pilgrimage sites, associated
from early times with the
worship of Shakti (the Mother
Goddess). Ruled by the Hindu
Yadava dynasty between
the 10th and 13th centuries,
it was later occupied by the
Mughals. In 1675, Kolhapur
was finally seized by the
Maratha chief Shivaji *(see*

p471), and was later inherited
by his younger son. The state
remained with the Bhonsles
(one of the four Maratha
princely families) until
Independence.

Of the numerous
temples in Kolhapur,
the **Shri Mahalakshmi**
or Amba Bai Temple,
dedicated to the
Mother Goddess, is
the most venerated.
Built in the 7th century
by the Chalukya king
Karnadeva, the
temple's idol, said to
be a *swayambhu*, or
naturally occurring
monolith, is encrusted with
diamonds and other precious
stones. The *mandapa* has a
finely carved ceiling. Behind

**Kolhapuri
chappals**

the temple are the remains of
the **Old Palace** or Rajwada,
where members of the former
maharaja's family still live.

Its huge entrance hall was
once used for large public
wedding ceremonies.
Situated near the palace
gates are the town's
wrestling grounds,
where young men
practise traditional
Indian wrestling,
known as *kushti*.
The **New Palace**, 2 km
(1.3 miles) north of
the city centre, was
completed in 1881
and designed by Major
Charles Mant *(see p418)*,
who merged European, Jain,
Hindu and Islamic elements
to create a style which widely

THE MALVAN COAST

Fishing boat, Malvan coast

The southern Konkan coastline in the Sindhudurg district, known
as the Malvan Coast, is dotted with marine forts and pretty fishing
villages which, though off the beaten track, are worth visiting.
Vijaydurg Fort, 505 km (314 miles) south of Mumbai, stands on
the site of an 11th-century fort, rebuilt by the Bijapur sultans *(see
pp542–3)* in the 16th century. In 1654, it was further renovated by
Shivaji, who added three layers of fortifications, 27 bastions and
300 guns. It became the main naval base for the great Maratha
admiral, Kanhoji Angre, who used the fort to plunder European
ships in 1698. It fell to the British in 1756; a platform stands within the grounds, where British
astronomers set up their telescopes to study a solar eclipse. About 74 km (46 miles) south of
Vijaydurg, **Sindhudurg Fort**, built by Shivaji in 1664, lies deserted on an island known as
Kurte. With its 10-m (33-ft) high ramparts, it was a Maratha stronghold until power shifted to
Vijaydurg. It is the only place in Maharashtra where a statue of Shivaji depicts him without
a beard. His palm and feet impressions are preserved in mortar near the entrance. The small
port of **Malvan**, 4 km (2.5 miles) north of Sindhudurg, lends its name to this stretch of coast.
It is being developed into a beach resort, as is **Vengurla**, 52 km (32 miles) south of Malvan.
Savantwadi, 23 km (14 miles) east
of Vengurla, was the capital of the
Bhonsle kings. The art of making
ganjifa cards (painted, circular playing cards) was developed here. The
town is also known for its wooden
toys and lacquer work. **Amboli**,
25 km (16 miles) northeast of
Savantwadi, is a pretty hill station.

A view of Vijaydurg Fort, overlooking fishing boats in the bay

became known as the Indo-Saracenic style of architecture. The palace is today the Shahji Chhatrapati Museum and displays a collection of royal memorabilia, including garments, hunting photographs and one of Mughal emperor Aurangzeb's swords.

The **Town Hall**, another structure designed by Mant, has a small museum with a number of artifacts from nearby excavation sites. Kolhapur is also famous for its hand-crafted leather slippers, known as Kolhapuri *chappals*.

 Old Palace
○ *daily.*
 New Palace
○ *daily.*

ENVIRONS: One of the most important forts in the Deccan is at **Panhala**, a hill station 19 km (12 miles) northwest of Kolhapur. Situated on a steep hillside, the fortress is well protected by three impressive double walled gates, and 7-km (4-mile) long ramparts. Within its walls stand two temples, one dedicated to Amba Bai and the other to Maruti, the Wind God. The most interesting monuments are the huge stone granaries, the largest of which, Ganga Kothi, covers 948 sq m (10,204 sq ft). Established in the 12th century by Raja Bhoja II, the fortress fell successively to the Yadavas, the Adil Shahis of Bijapur, Shivaji, Emperor Aurangzeb and the British. There are

Panhala Fort in the picturesque Sahyadri Hills, after the monsoon

Panchgani, with spectacular views of the Krishna river

many private homes in Panhala as well, including that of the famous Indian singer Lata Mangeshkar *(see p503)*.

Mahabaleshwar ❺

Satara district. 115 km (72 miles) SW of Pune. 🚶 *12,800.* 🚲 *Cycles available.*

THE LARGEST hill station in Maharashtra, Mahabaleshwar is situated 1,372 m (4,501 ft) above sea level. In 1828, Sir John Malcolm, Governor of Bombay, chose this beautiful spot as the site for the official sanatorium. Soon after, the wooded slopes were covered with typical colonial structures, among them **Christ Church**, **Frere Hall**, **Government House** (which was the grand residence of the governor), the **Mahabaleshwar Club**, and the ever-popular polo grounds and race course.

Water spout, Krishna Temple

Due to its high altitude, the town has a cool climate and offers many pleasant walks. There are also several lookout points such as **Bombay Point**, from where the sea can be seen on a clear day, and **Arthur's Seat**, which affords panoramic views of the Konkan Coast. **Venna Lake** has facilities for boating.

In the old town is the sacred **Krishna Temple**, supposedly built on the legendary site of the Panchganga, or source of five rivers – the Koyna, Savitri, Venna, Gayatri and the mighty Krishna. The latter covers

1,400 km (870 miles), stretching from this spot to the Bay of Bengal on the east coast. The temple has a much venerated, naturally occurring Shivalinga, and a small tank. There are two other temples here, dedicated to Hanuman and Rama. There are also several berry farms close by, where visitors can help to pick strawberries, raspberries and mulberries.

ENVIRONS: The hill station of **Panchgani**, 18 km (11 miles) east of Mahabaleshwar, is surrounded by five hills. The town is the starting point for many scenic trekking trails *(see p473)*. It is also dotted with some charming old British and Parsi bungalows, some of which can be visited. The majestic hill-top forts of **Pratapgarh** and **Raigad**, 18 km (11 miles) west and 70 km (44 miles) northwest of Mahabaleshwar respectively, were both Maratha strongholds. They offer commanding views of the surrounding countryside.

About 111 km (69 miles) south of Mahabaleshwar is **Chiplun**, lying on the banks of the Vashishti river, whose waters supply Koyna Lake, a large man-made reservoir. The town is well-known for its irrigation scheme, developed in the 1980s, that provides water to the coastal fringe between the Sahyadri Hills and the sea. This quiet place offers splendid views of the Vashishti river as it winds through the hills.

The sprawling campus of Pune University

Pune ⑥

Pune district. 170 km (106 miles) SE of Mumbai. 🏙 2,540,500. ✈ 12 km (7 miles) NE of city centre, then taxi or auto. 🚉 🚌 🛈 Maharashtra Tourism, I Block, Central Bldg, (020) 612 6867. 🎎 Ganesha Chaturthi (Aug/Sep).

THE FAST-GROWING, industrial city of Pune is situated on the Deccan Plateau, at the confluence of the Mutha and Mula rivers, and is bounded by the Sahyadris in the west. Its pleasant climate and proximity to Mumbai made it the perfect monsoon capital for the British in the 19th century. Then called Poona, it became an important administrative centre and military cantonment. Even today, the Indian army's Southern Command is based here.

Pune was also the childhood home of the Maratha leader, Shivaji. From 1750 until 1817, it was the capital of the Maratha Confederacy and was ruled by the Peshwas. The remains of their **Shaniwar Wada Palace** is in the old city. Built in 1736, the palace was razed in a fire in 1828. Only its outer walls and the main entrance with large spikes, designed to deter the enemy's elephants, survive. Further south is **Vishram Bagh Wada**, a beautiful Peshwa palace with an elaborate wooden façade.

For many visitors, Pune is synonymous with the famous **Osho International Commune** founded by Bhagwan Rajneesh or Osho, and situated at Koregaon Park in the north of the city. The flamboyant pop mystic, or "sex guru" as he was called, had a meteoric rise in the West. Even after his demise in 1990, his well-appointed ashram continues to attract devotees from Europe and America.

Housed in a traditional Maratha house or *wada*, is the charming privately-owned **Raja Kelkar Museum**. On display are a collection of beautiful everyday objects such as pots, lamps, pens, ink stands, collection of nutcrackers, and other utilitarian items. An interesting piece is a Maharashtrian Chitrakathi scroll painting, used in folk theatre performances.

The **Tribal Museum**, east of the railway station, showcases the state's tribal cultures, especially from the Sahyadri and Gondwana regions.

The **Aga Khan Palace**, across the Mula river to the north of the city, was where Mahatma Gandhi was imprisoned by the British for two years; today, it is the Gandhi National Memorial. Gandhi's wife, Kasturba, died here and her ashes have been interred in a memorial in the gardens.

Other places of interest in the city include St Mary's Church, a fine garrison structure consecrated in 1825; the rock-cut Pataleshwar Temple, dating from the 8th century; the Parvati Temple perched on a hilltop; and many fine gardens, including the Empress Botanical Gardens and the Bund Gardens.

Pune is the centre of Maratha culture, with a lively tradition of theatre, classical music and dance. It is also an important university town and is home to the prestigious government-run Film and Television Institute and the National Film Archives.

A Warli painting from Raja Kelkar Museum

ENVIRONS: About 6 km (4 miles) southwest is the **National Defence Academy**, the training school for army, navy and air force cadets, at Khadakvasla. Further southwest are the spectacular forts of **Rajgad** and **Sinhgad** (the "Lion Fort"). The latter is associated with Shivaji's general, Tanaji Malasure. According to legend, he tied strong ropes to monitor lizards, made the creatures stick to the fort walls with their adhesive foot pads, and thus scaled the walls and captured the fort.

🏛 **Osho International Commune**
☎ (020) 613 6655. ⬤ daily. 📷 ▣
🏛 **Raja Kelkar Museum**
1378, Shukrawar Peth. ⬤ daily. ⬤ public hols. 📷
🏛 **Tribal Museum**
Off Koregaon Rd. ⬤ daily.
🏛 **Aga Khan Palace**
Ahmadnagar Rd. ⬤ Mon–Sat. ⬤ 2nd & 4th Sat, public hols. 📷

Vishram Bagh Wada, a Peshwa palace in the heart of the old city

Shivaji and the Marathas

MAHARASHTRA'S greatest hero, Shivaji, was born in 1627 to Shahji Bhonsle, a chieftain from Pune who served the sultans of Bijapur *(see pp542–5)*. Daring, ambitious and restless since his boyhood, by the age of 19 he had become the head of a band of intrepid fighters. Soon, Shivaji's brilliant guerrilla tactics against Emperor Aurangzeb and the powerful Mughal

Coronation Canopy at Raigad

army, and his swift conquests of mountain and sea forts, enabled him to establish a separate Maratha kingdom. In 1674, he was crowned Chhatrapati, the traditional title of a Hindu monarch, at his capital, Raigad. When he died in 1680, at the age of 53, he left behind a powerful Maratha state, which continued to play an important role in Indian history for the next 100 years.

Waghnakh ("tiger's claw"), a deadly hand weapon, was used by Shivaji to overcome and kill Afzal Khan, the Bijapur general, in a "friendly" meeting at Pratapgad.

Maratha horsemen were feared for their lightning raids which wrought havoc on enemy territory. The Deccan Plateau's hilly terrain aided their guerrilla tactics against the Mughals.

Shivaji is revered all over Maharashtra as a god-like hero. A fearless soldier and charismatic leader, he united the Marathas into a formidable force that defied the mighty Mughals. Today, he has become a symbol for the Hindu revivalist movement.

Fortresses, such as Rajgad and Raigad (see p469) and the sea forts (see p468) along the west coast, were the key to Maratha strategy and success. Shivaji's conquest of the crucial Purandhar Fort in 1649 compelled the sultan of Bijapur to condemn him as a rebel.

Shaniwar Wada was the former residence of the Peshwas, hereditary chiefs who came to power after Shivaji's death. The other main clans of the Maratha Confederacy – which was a significant power in the 18th century – were Holkars (see p246), Scindias (see pp228–9), Gaekwads (see p419) and Bhonsles (see p468).

The Buddhist *chaitya griha* at Karla Cave, near Lonavla

Lonavla ❼

Pune district. 62 km (39 miles) NW of Pune. 🛕 *55,700.* 🚉 🚌 **Karla Cave** ℹ️ *Maharashtra Tourism, Karla, (02114) 82 230.* ◯ *daily.* 📷 **Bhaja Caves** 📷

SITUATED ON the main train line from Mumbai to Pune, Lonavla was once a sleepy hill station famous for its *chikki,* a type of caramelized sweet. It has now become an extremely popular weekend getaway for city-dwellers from nearby Mumbai. Spread around the bustling main street, lined with souvenir shops, the town offers pleasant walks and is a convenient base for exploring the surrounding hills.

ENVIRONS: About 8 km (5 miles) northwest of Lonavla is **Khandala**, another pretty town with panoramic views of the scenic Western Ghats. The famous Buddhist rock-cut

Karla Cave, 11 km (7 miles) east of Lonavla, dates from the 2nd to 1st centuries BC. The splendid *chaitya griha (see p20),* the largest and best preserved of the early Buddhist caves in the Deccan, is the most significant sight here. It has a magnificently sculpted courtyard, a towering 14-m (46-ft) high façade with a horseshoe shaped window, and a large pillared hall with a monolithic stupa. The 20-odd **Bhaja Caves**, located 3 km (2 miles) off the Karla road, are the oldest in the region, dating from the 2nd century BC. Cave 12, a *chaitya griha,* still contains the remains of wooden beams on its ceiling. On either side of the façade are carvings

Statue of a divine couple, Karla Cave

of multistoreyed structures with windows and balconies. The **Bedsa Caves**, situated 9 km (6 miles) southeast of Bhaja, date to the 1st century AD. The roof of the main cave bears faint traces of paintings.

Matheran ❽

Raigarh district. 118 km (73 miles) NW of Pune. 🛕 *5,200.* 🚉 *From Neral Junction, take the toy train to Matheran (2 hrs).* 🚌 ℹ️ *Opp railway station.*

THE CLOSEST hill station to Mumbai, Matheran (which means "Mother Forest") lies at a height of 803 m (2,635 ft) above sea level. This picturesque town is situated in the forested Sahyadri Hills. In 1855, Lord Elphinstone, the governor of Bombay, visited Matheran, and the town soon became fashionable. The stately **Elphinstone Lodge** that he built became his weekend retreat. A railway line was laid in 1907, and a quaint toy train *(see p775)* still winds its way slowly through hills and forests from the junction at Neral. All motor vehicles are completely banned within the limits of the town, making it uniquely peaceful, despite the burgeoning crowds of visitors, particularly on weekends.

Matheran has as many as 33 lookout points. **Porcupine Point** or Sunset Point, a favourite with sightseers, is known for its spectacular sunsets. **Louisa Point** has views of the ruined Prabal Fort and a mountain trail called Shivaji's Ladder. By far the most impressive viewpoint is **Hart Point**, from where it is possible, on a clear day, to see Mumbai in the distance. St Paul's Anglican Church, the pretty Lord's Hotel and the Roman Catholic Church are among the many Raj-era buildings in Matheran.

Splendid views at Porcupine Point, also known as Sunset Point, Matheran

Carved stonework, Damri Mosque

Ahmadnagar ❾

Ahmadnagar district. 140 km (87 miles)
NE of Pune. 🚉 307,500. 🚏 🚌

THE SEAT OF a powerful Muslim kingdom in the 16th century, Ahmadnagar was founded in 1490 by Ahmad Nizam Shah Bahri, the son of a Hindu convert. In 1599, the Mughals, led by Akbar, invaded the city after his favourite commander Abu'l Fazl murdered the ruling sultan. However, the sultan's sister, Chand Bibi, ably defended the kingdom. The succeeding years saw the rise of Malik Ambar, a former African slave who fought successful battles against neighbouring Bidar (see p545) and Golconda (see pp666–7). In 1636, the kingdom finally submitted to Mughal rule.

The rulers of the Nizam Shahi dynasty were great builders, and their style of architecture shows an unmistakeable Persian influence. The **Ahmadnagar Fort**, 4 km (2.5 miles) northeast of the station, was built in 1490, though the impressive stone walls were added in 1563. Its palace, the only surviving structure, consists of a large hall with a series of domes. In 1942 it housed an important political prisoner, Jawaharlal Nehru, who wrote his famous book, *The Discovery of India*, here. The **Jami Masjid** dates to the same period. Nearby is the ornate **Damri Mosque**. Built in 1568, it has a cut-out trefoil parapet and finials topped by miniature pavilions.

Emperor Aurangzeb died in Ahmadnagar in 1707, and his body rested briefly at the small **Alamgir Dargah**, near the cantonment, before being interred at Khuldabad (see 475).

To the west of the town lies **Bagh Rauza**, a walled garden complex. It contains the mausoleum of Ahmad Nizam Shah Bahri, which has a lavishly decorated interior.

HIKING IN THE SAHYADRIS

The Western Ghats, also known in Maharashtra as the Sahyadris, run parallel to India's west coast and stretch across the states of Maharashtra, Karnataka, Tamil Nadu and Kerala. Formed from volcanic rock, the hills are a maze of ridges and valleys. In Maharashtra, the many popular hill stations serve as excellent starting points for a number of scenic walking trails. **Mahabaleshwar** and **Panchgani** are particularly well-marked with hiking routes that lead through lush forests and valleys. These hills also have a wealth of craggy rock-faces perfect for climbing and **Lonavla** is a favourite base for rock climbing enthusiasts. **Matheran** has a much-trodden path known as Shivaji's Ladder, which

leads from One Tree Hill down to the valley below. The Sahyadri Hills are particularly beautiful in September after the rains, when the hills are carpeted with wild flowers and cascading waterfalls seem to appear at every turn.

The rugged ranges of the Sahyadri Hills

FESTIVALS OF MAHARASHTRA

Janmashtami *(Jul/Aug)*. The birth of Lord Krishna is celebrated enthusiastically all over the state. Pots of butter are strung high in the streets and human pyramids attempt to reach them, imitating the god's childhood pranks.

Janmashtami in Mumbai

Naga Panchami *(Aug/Sep)*. Snakes, considered powerful creatures and revered across India, are worshipped during this festival. After being fed cupfuls of milk, they are taken out in colourful processions and later released into the fields.

Ganesha Chaturthi *(Aug/Sep)*. This is the most significant festival in Maharashtra, celebrated with particular fervour in Pune and Mumbai. Clay idols of Lord Ganesha *(see p467)* are made and then worshipped over 10 days, amidst lively festivities. After this they are led in colourful processions to the closest water body and immersed.

Kalidasa Festival *(Nov)*, Nagpur. Some of the most renowned exponents of classical music and dance gather at this festival, organized to honour the 4th-century Sanskrit dramatist and poet, Kalidasa.

Ellora Festival *(Dec)*, Ellora. This festival presents a variety of classical performing arts against the evocative setting of the Kailasanatha Temple.

The holy tank of Ramkund, Nasik

Nasik ❿

Nasik district. 187 km (116 miles) NE of Mumbai. 🏠 *1,077,000.* 🚌 🚂 ℹ️ *Maharashtra Tourism, (0253) 57 0059.* 📷 *Kumbh Mela (every 12 years).*

THE TOWN OF NASIK is one of India's most holy sites. A bustling temple town, built on both banks of the Godavari river, it has almost 200 shrines. The ghats that line the river front are the venue for the spectacular Kumbh Mela *(see p211).* Legend says that Rama, hero of the *Ramayana (see p27),* lived here during his 14-year exile. **Ramkund**, the centrally located tank and the town's focal point, is believed to mark the spot where Rama and his wife Sita bathed. The ashes of the dead are also immersed here.

Most of Nasik's temples date to the 18th century. The **Kala Rama Temple**, east of Ramkund, is built in black stone with a 25-m (82-ft) high *shikhara.* It supposedly marks the spot where Sita was abducted by Ravana. The **Rameshwar Temple** has splendid carvings on the roof of its hall, while the **Muktidham Temple**, close to the station, carries inscriptions from the *Bhagavad Gita* on its walls.

ENVIRONS: **Pandu Lena**, 8 km (5 miles) south of Nasik, has 24 Buddhist caves dating to the 1st and 2nd centuries BC. The oldest is Cave 10, a *vihara* (monastery) which has

splendid sculptures and inscriptions above its entrance. Cave 18, an early *chaitya griha,* has a beautifully carved exterior. Other fine caves include Caves 3 and 20. The sacred **Trimbakeshwar Temple**, 33 km (21 miles) west of Nasik, is built on the site of one of Shiva's 12 naturally-occurring *jyotirlingas* (lingas of light). It is surrounded by a large paved platform and has a carved *shikhara.* Though closed to non-Hindus, visitors can still get a good view of the courtyard and the shrine leading out of it. About 65 km (40 miles) south of Nasik is **Shirdi**, the temple complex of the first Sai Baba, Maharashtra's most popular saint, who died in 1918.

Aurangabad ⓫

Aurangabad district. 404 km (251 miles) NE of Mumbai. 🏠 *873,000.* ✈️ *10 km (6 miles) E of town centre, then taxi.* 🚌 🚂 ℹ️ *Maharashtra Tourism, Station Rd East, (0240) 33 1513.*

THE LARGEST CITY in northern Maharashtra, Aurangabad is the nearest air-link to the splendid caves at Ellora and Ajanta *(see pp476–81).* It was founded in 1610 by Malik Ambar, prime minister of the Nizam Shahi rulers of Ahmadnagar *(see p473).* In 1653 it became the headquarters of Aurangzeb, the last great

Detail of the entrance door, Bibi ka Maqbara

Mughal emperor. It was from this city – which he renamed after himself – that he conquered the Deccan states.

The city's most famous monument is the **Bibi ka Maqbara**. Located outside the walled city, this imitation of the Taj was built in 1678 by Aurangzeb's son, Azam Shah, in memory of his mother Rabia Durrani. Standing in the middle of a large Mughal garden, it has four disproportionately large minarets at the ends of its raised platform. Like the Taj, it uses white marble and stucco, but there is none of the fine *pietra dura* work that distinguishes Shah Jahan's creation *(see pp172–3).*

Aurangzeb's walled city makes up the central part of the town, although a few structures from Malik Ambar's older city remain, including the **Naukonda Palace** (largely in ruins) and the **Jami Masjid**. On the left bank of the Khan river is the **Dargah of Baba Shah Musafir**, a Sufi saint who was Aurangzeb's spiritual guide. The complex contains a small mosque, a *madrasa* (theological college), a law court, the zenana (women's quarters) and a water mill (Panchakki), fed by a rectangular tank. Also within the old city, close to Zafar Gate, is the **Himroo Factory**. Aurangabad is famed for its ancient art of weaving brocade, using silk and gold threads, known as *kamkhab.* When the city's prosperity declined, the weavers began

Bibi ka Maqbara in Aurangabad, an imitation of Agra's Taj Mahal

An ornately carved pillared hall in Cave 3, Aurangabad Caves

using less expensive cotton and silver threads, producing *himroo*, which literally means similar. A variety of such shawls and saris are available in showrooms across town. The factory also produces rich Paithani saris, intricately woven with gold thread.

ENVIRONS: About 3 km (2 miles) north are the **Aurangabad Caves**. Mainly excavated during the Vakataka and Kalachuri periods (6th and 7th centuries), these caves can be divided into two groups. Of the five caves in the western group, the oldest is Cave 4, dating to the 1st century AD. It is a fine *chaitya griha* with a monolithic stupa. Carved on the rock face outside is a superb image of the Buddha, seated on a lion throne. Cave 3 (5th century) has an ingeniously designed pillared hall that is acoustically sensitive and amplifies sound. Inside the inner sanctum, a Seated Buddha is flanked by devotees with floral offerings.

The eastern group, nearby, comprises four caves. Cave 6 has delicately sculpted Bodhisattvas, surrounded by flying figures. The most splendid of the caves is Cave 7, a sumptuous shrine with large sculptures of Tara and Avalokitesvara *(see p141)*. Its inner sanctum has a superb frieze of a female dancer accompanied by seven musicians.

Daulatabad ⑫

Aurangabad district. 13 km (8 miles) E of Aurangabad. 🚌 *Bus tours are offered by Maharashtra Tourism, Aurangabad, (0240) 33 1513. Taxis & jeeps also available from Aurangabad.* ⬜ *daily.* 📷

PERCHED ON a granite outcrop of the Deccan Plateau, this formidable fort has witnessed some of the greatest carnage in the region. Originally known as Deogiri, it was captured in 1296 by Alauddin Khilji, the Deccan's first Muslim invader from Delhi. He was followed by Muhammad bin Tughluq, who annexed the fort in 1328 and renamed the town Daulatabad ("City of Fortune"). In a fit of misguided reasoning, he decided to shift his capital here, and compelled Delhi's entire population to march across 1,127 km (700 miles). Thousands died of starvation or disease along the way, and when the move failed, the sultan and his court marched back to Delhi. Daulatabad was successively conquered by the Deccani Bahmani sultans, the Nizam Shahis, the Mughals, the Marathas and finally the Nizam

Himroo fabric, Aurangabad

of Hyderabad – each conquest proving more bloody and savage than the last.

The pyramid-shaped hill, on which the imposing fort is built, stands apart from the surrounding ranges, and towers to a height of 183 m (600 ft). This made Mughal emperor Shah Jahan's chronicler note that "neither ant nor snake could scale it". Four solid concentric walls protect the fort. The first of its three zones is **Ambarkot**, the outer fort. Within, stands the 60-m (197-ft) high victory tower, **Chand Minar**, built in 1435 by Alauddin Bahmani to celebrate his conquest of the fort. In the nearby **Jami Masjid**, 106 pillars from Jain and Hindu temples separate the main hall into 25 aisles. A triple gateway studded with iron spikes

provides access into **Kataka**, the inner fort. Gateways lead through fortified walls into the base of the citadel, known as **Balakot**, separated by a moat once infested with crocodiles.

Near the innermost gate lies the blue and white tiled **Chini Mahal**, where the last sultan of Golconda was imprisoned by Aurangzeb in 1687. On a nearby bastion is the enormous bronze cannon, the **Qila Shikhan** or "Fort Breaker". This 6-m (20-ft) long cannon has a splendid ram's head, and Persian inscriptions along its length refer to it as the "Creator of Storms". A series of dark tunnels lead to the heart of the citadel and end near a pillared pavilion, **Baradari**, a late Mughal building. The fort's ramparts offer sweeping views.

ENVIRONS: The walled village of **Khuldabad** ("Heavenly Abode") is 10 km (6 miles) north of Daulatabad. The Alamgir Dargah, dedicated to the Muslim saint, Sayeed Zain-ud-din, (d.1370), is its most famous monument. Also known as Rauza, this religious complex, established by Sufi saints in the 14th century, was considered so sacred that several Deccani sultans chose to be buried here. Emperor Aurangzeb, who died in the Deccan in 1707, is buried in a simple tomb in the courtyard. The beautiful tomb of Malik Ambar *(see p473)*, is a short distance to the north.

The Chand Minar, once covered in glazed Persian tiles, Daulatabad

Ellora: Kailasanatha Temple ⓭

Detail, roof of the entrance gateway

THE FINEST of the Ellora group of rock-cut caves is the magnificent Kailasanatha Temple (Cave 16), a UNESCO World Heritage Site. Commissioned by the Rashtrakuta king Krishna I in the 8th century, this mammoth complex, spanning 81 m (266 ft) by 47 m (154 ft), was carved out of a huge rocky cliff face. Sculptors chiselled through 85,000 cubic metres (approximately 3 million cubic ft) of rock, beginning at the top of the cliff and working their way down. The resulting marvel, embellished with huge sculptural panels, was meant to depict Mount Kailasa, the sacred abode of Lord Shiva.

★ **The Roof**
The mandapa *(assembly hall) roof is embellished by a lotus carved in concentric rings, topped by four stone lions.*

The Nandi Pavilion

Courtyard
On either side of the courtyard are two life-size elephants.

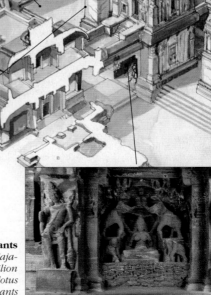

Obelisks
Flanking the Nandi Pavilion are two monolithic pillars, 17 m (56 ft) high, with carvings of lotus friezes and garlands.

★ **Lakshmi with Elephants**
Facing the entrance, the ornate Gaja-lakshmi panel in the Nandi Pavilion depicts Lakshmi seated in a lotus pond and being bathed by elephants bearing upturned pots in their trunks.

The tower rises 32.6 m (107 ft), and was once covered in white plaster, to replicate Mount Kailasa's snowy peaks.

Supporting Elephants
Elephants with lotuses in their trunks are carved all along the lower storey, and appear to support the structure.

| 0 metres | 10 |
| 0 yards | 10 |

Rock-cut monasteries

★ Ravana Shaking Mount Kailasa
A large panel depicts Ravana (the demon king in the Ramayana*) shaking Mount Kailasa in order to disturb Shiva and Parvati in their mountain home.*

Ramayana **panels** flank the south wall, while the north wall has *Mahabharata* and Krishna legends.

STAR FEATURES

★ The Roof

★ Lakshmi with Elephants

★ Ravana Shaking Mount Kailasa

Three Goddesses
The Hall of Sacrifice contains life-size images of Durga, Chamunda and Kali, as well as of Ganesha, Parvati and the seven mother goddesses.

Exploring Ellora

The 34 caves at Ellora, hewn from a 2-km (1.3-mile) long escarpment, are among the most splendid examples of rock-cut architecture in India.

The emergence and growing importance of Ellora coincided with the decline of Buddhism, and a Hindu renaissance under the Chalukya and Rashtrakuta dynasties (7th–9th centuries AD). Ellora was situated on an important trade route that ran between Ujjain in Madhya Pradesh and the west coast. It was the revenue from this very lucrative trade that sustained 500 years of excavation at Ellora, as the older Ajanta caves began to be abandoned.

The caves at Ellora fall into three distinct groups – Buddhist, Hindu and Jain – and they are numbered from the southern end. The **Buddhist Caves** (1 to 12) date from the Chalukya period, between the 7th and 8th centuries. The first nine are variations of *viharas* or monasteries, and are filled with fine Buddha figures, Bodhisattvas and scenes from Buddhist mythology. The most splendid is **Cave 10**, or Vishwakarma, named after the celestial carpenter. A striking *chaitya griha (see p20)*, it is dominated by a figure of the Teaching Buddha carved in front of a

View of the dramatic Ellora escarpment with its seasonal waterfall

votive stupa, placed under a vaulted roof. It is so intricately carved that it seems to be made of wood. Other important caves are **Cave 11**, or Do Thal (two-storeyed), and **Cave 12**, or Tin Thal (three-storeyed). The upper hall of Cave 12 has large Bodhisattvas carved on its walls, while rows of seven Buddha figures flank the entrance to the antechamber.

The **Hindu Caves** (13 to 29), were carved out between the 7th and 9th centuries, and represent the peak of Ellora's development. **Cave 14**, or Ravana ki Khai, contains impressive sculptures of deities from the Hindu pantheon, such as Durga slaying the buffalo demon, and Vishnu as the boar-headed Varaha. **Cave 15**, or Dashavatara, also has superb sculptural depictions.

Cave 21, or Rameshvara, and **Cave 29**, or Dhumar Lena, are other impressive caves.

The **Jain Caves** (30 to 34) date from Ellora's last stage, in the 9th century, and are simpler than the Hindu ones. **Cave 32**, or Indra Sabha, is the finest of the group. A monolithic shrine, it has carvings of elephants, lions and *tirthankaras (see p396)* on the courtyard walls. **Cave 30**, or Chhota Kailasa, is a small, incomplete replica of the Kailasanatha Temple *(see pp476–7)* and has sculptures of various *tirthankaras* and Mahavira on a lion-throne.

ENVIRONS: The 18th-century **Grishneshvara Temple**, nearby, is one of the 12 *jyotirlinga* shrines dedicated to Shiva, built by Rani Ahilyabai of Indore *(see p250)*.

The upper-storey hall, Vishwakarma (Cave 10)

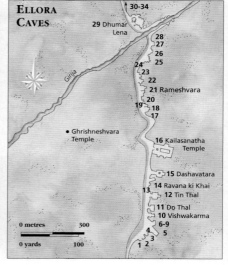

ELLORA CAVES

- 30–34
- 29 Dhumar Lena
- 28
- 27
- 26
- 25
- 24
- 23
- 22
- 21 Rameshvara
- 20
- 19
- 18
- 17
- 16 Kailasanatha Temple
- • Ghrishneshvara Temple
- Girija
- 15 Dashavatara
- 14 Ravana ki Khai
- 13
- 12 Tin Thal
- 11 Do Thal
- 10 Vishwakarma
- 6–9
- 5
- 4
- 3
- 1 2

0 metres   300

0 yards   100

Façade of Cave 19, Ajanta, with a
large horseshoe-shaped window

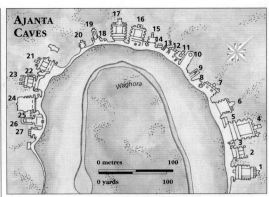

Ajanta ⑭

Aurangabad district. 110 km (68 miles)
NE of Aurangabad. from
Aurangabad. Tue–Sun.
flash photography is prohibited.
Organized tours & taxis are also
available from Aurangabad. Take a
packed lunch, bottled water, torch, and
wear comfortable shoes and a sun hat.

A UNESCO World Heritage Site,
the 30 extraordinary rock-
cut caves at Ajanta lie within a
horseshoe-shaped escarpment,
overlooking the narrow
Waghora river gorge. At its
head is a waterfall that drops
into the Saptakunda pool. The
caves were occupied for only a
short period and, over time,
the surrounding jungle con-
cealed their existence. They
were "rediscovered" quite acci-
dentally in 1819, when John
Smith, of the 28th Madras
Cavalry, suddenly saw the top
of the façade of Cave 10 while
on a tiger hunt.

Ajanta's caves fall into two
groups. The early group
belongs to the more austere
Hinayana phase of Buddhism
(2nd–1st century BC), during
which the Buddha was not
represented in human form
but only by symbols such as a
Wheel of Law or a Bodhi Tree.
The second group dates from
the Mahayana period (5th–6th
centuries AD), carved out during the rule of the Vakataka
dynasty, when artistic expression was more exuberant. The
caves were inhabited by
monks, artists and craftsmen,
who used them as varsh-
vatikas or monsoon shrines.
Stylistically they are of two

types – chaitya grihas (prayer
halls) and viharas (monasteries). The chaityas have
vaulted ceilings and octagonal
columns that divide the space
into a central hall with a votive
stupa, the object of veneration.
The side aisles that run around
the hall were used for ritual
circumambulation. The
Mahayana chaityas also have
Buddha images. Viharas
typically have a verandah, a
hall surrounded by cells, and
an inner shrine with enormous
Buddha figures.

Of the seven Mahayana
caves, dating from the 5th
century AD, Cave 1 is famous
for its splendid murals (see
pp480–81). Above its verandah are friezes of scenes from
the Buddha's life, while its ceiling is supported by 20 carved
and painted pillars. Cave 2 has
a superb façade carved with
images of Naga kings, and
their attendants (ganas), while
its main shrine has a magnificent painted ceiling.

Caves 8, 9, 10, 12, 13 and 15
are Hinayana caves. Cave 9,

a chaitya griha, has a façade
adorned with windows and
lattice-work. The large Buddha
figures along the sides were
a later addition (5th century)
and its murals are from both
periods. Cave 10 is thought to
be Ajanta's oldest cave and is
one of its finest chaitya grihas.

Caves 15 to 20 are late 5th-
century Mahayana caves.
Cave 16 has sculptures of
beautiful maidens flanking
the doorway, while in
Cave 17 the entrance to the
inner shrine is ornamented
with Buddha figures, god-
desses and lotuses.

Caves 21 to 27 (7th century),
make up the final group. Cave
26 displays the full magnificence of Ajanta's sculptural art.
Especially remarkable are two
splendid panels – one depicts
the Temptation of the Buddha
by the Demon Mara, while the
Parinirvana is a 7-m (23-ft)
image of the reclining Buddha,
with his eyes closed as if in
sleep. His disciples mourn his
passing, while above, celestial
beings rejoice in his salvation.

The moving Parinirvana, depicting the passing of the Buddha, Cave 26

The Ajanta Murals

THE EARLIEST AND FINEST examples of Buddhist painting in India can be seen at the Ajanta caves. Executed between the 2nd century BC and the 5th century AD, the murals show scenes from the Buddha's life, and from the Jataka Tales, which recount stories of the Buddha's previous incarnations as an enlightened being or Bodhisattva. Magnificent, detailed compositions, the murals include depictions of court scenes, princes and musicians, and offer fascinating glimpses of daily life in the 5th century. The colours, derived from plants and minerals, are in rich shades of ochre, lime, black, green and lapis lazuli.

Avalokitesvara, also identified as Vajrapani, is the most venerated Bodhisattva in the Mahayana pantheon, and can be seen to the right of the antechamber doorway.

CAVE 1
This late 5th-century *vihara* (monastery) contains some of Ajanta's most evocative murals.

Padmapani (Lotus-Holder), the Bodhisattva of Compassion, can be seen on the wall to the left of the antechamber doorway. He is surrounded by celestial beings and air-borne figures.

The Miracle of Sravasti, on the antechamber's right wall, depicts a famous miracle when the Buddha multiplied himself a thousand-fold.

The **Mahajanaka Jataka**, to the left of the antechamber, recounts the life of Prince Mahajanaka, who renounced the world to become an ascetic. Here, the prince is surrounded by female attendants.

A scene depicting a king, possibly the Vakataka ruler Harisena, greeting a Persian embassy

Scenes from the **Mahajanaka Jataka**, *from left to right, depict Prince Mahajanaka, Queen Shivali enticing the prince, palace maids, and a dancing girl.*

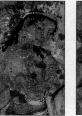

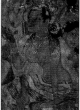

CAVE 2

Similar in design to Cave 1, this 5th-century *vihara* is profusely painted in lustrous colours. The walls, columns, capitals and ceiling are covered in scrollwork, geometric and floral patterns, and numerous Jataka panels, including stories connected with the Buddha's birth.

The large mandala (circular diagram) dominates the elaborately painted ceiling of this remarkable cave. A depiction of the cosmos, its outer ring is filled with lotus motifs.

CAVE 10

Considered to be Ajanta's oldest cave, this *chaitya griha* dates to the 2nd century BC. The left wall has its oldest mural, a frieze depicting a prince worshipping a Bodhi Tree.

CAVE 16

Outstanding paintings in this cave depict the conversion of Nanda, the Buddha's half-brother, and show his wife swooning when she hears the news of his becoming a monk.

Nanda's wife, Sundari, fainting upon hearing of his conversion

Numerous figures of the Buddha embellish some of the octagonal pillars (39 in all), that separate the aisles from the central nave in Cave 10.

CAVE 17

This cave has the largest number of paintings. Among the finest are a vast panel depicting Simhala's shipwreck and encounter with a man-eating ogress; and a lady at her toilet, gazing intently into a mirror.

Eight seated Buddha figures are depicted above the doorway in the verandah, with a row of amorous couples directly below them.

A panel from the Visvantara Jataka, to the left of the doorway, depicts Prince Visvantara and his wife drinking wine. They then move to the city gate and give alms to the needy.

This detail of an apsara (celestial maiden) adoring the Buddha, is part of a larger mural on the verandah to the right of the door. The Ajanta murals are renowned for their exquisite portrayal of women.

The enormous meteorite crater at Lonar, partially filled by a lake

Lonar ⓯

Buldana district. 130 km (81 miles)
E of Aurangabad. 🚉 Jalna, 83 km
(52 miles) W of Lonar, then bus. 🚌
from Aurangabad, taxis also available.

THE TINY VILLAGE of Lonar, is
famous for its remarkable
meteorite crater. Thought to be
the only hyper-velocity impact
crater in basaltic rock in the
world, the mammoth crater,
2 km (1.3 miles) in diameter
and 700 m (2,297 ft) deep, is
estimated to be about 50,000
years old. Scientists believe
that the meteorite is still buried
beneath the southeastern edge
of the crater. A lake fills the
bottom and the ruins of some
Hindu temples stand on its
shores. The crater is rich in
birdlife, and monkeys and
herds of deer can also be seen.
There are a few rest houses
that offer rooms and the village has some eateries as well.

Melghat Tiger Reserve ⓰

Amravati district. 400 km (249 miles)
NE of Aurangabad. 🚉 Amravati,
100 km (62 miles) SE of entry point.
Maharashtra Tourism, (0271) 67 4008,
organizes buses or jeeps from
Amravati to the park. ℹ️ For
bookings contact the Field Director,
(0721) 66 2792. ◐ Dec–May. 🎦

THE PROJECT TIGER RESERVE of
Melghat, which means
"Meeting Place of the Ghats",
spreads across the Gawilgarh
Hills in the southern part of
the Satpura Mountains. Its
highest altitudes are approximately 1,178 m (3,865 ft)
above sea level. These hills
have a dense canopy of the

country's finest deciduous
teak and bamboo forests,
which are now threatened by
rampant commercial exploitation for timber. Along with its
elusive 73 tigers, the reserve
is home to about 80 leopards,
chausingha (four-horned
antelope), *dhole* (Indian wild
dog), jungle cats, hyenas and
a rich variety of birds. The
sanctuary also supports the
state's largest concentration
of *gaur*, the endangered
Indian bison.

The best time to visit is
between January and April,
when the park is pleasantly
cool. Its five rivers, the
Khandu, Khapra, Sipna, Garga
and Dolar, dry out in summer,
and the few remaining pools
of rainwater are highly prized
as watering holes.

ENVIRONS: Chikhaldhara,
lying 25 km (16 miles)
northeast of Melghat, is a
quaint hill station established
by the British in 1839.

A tiger resting in a tree at the
Melghat Tiger Reserve

Nagpur ⓱

Nagpur district. 520 km (323 miles) NE
of Aurangabad. 👤 2,051,500. ✈️
10 km (6 miles) S of city centre, then
bus or taxi. 🚉 🚌 ℹ️ Maharashtra
Tourism, (0712) 53 3325. 🎭 Pola
(Jun/Jul), Kalidasa Festival (Nov).

SITUATED ON THE banks of
the Nag river, Nagpur was
the capital of the Central
Provinces until it became part
of Maharashtra state after
Independence. It is a fast
developing industrial city lying
on India's main north-south
railway line and is also the
country's orange-growing
capital. Historically, it was the
capital of the aboriginal Gond
tribals until it was captured by
the Maratha Bhonsles *(see
p468)* in 1740, and finally by
the British in 1861.

In October 1956, the city
witnessed an event of great
social importance, when
Dr BR Ambedkar, writer of
the Indian Constitution and a
freedom fighter born into a
lower caste Hindu family,
converted to Buddhism in a
stand against the rigid Hindu
caste system. Nearly 200,000
people followed him, and the
movement gathered great
momentum, resulting in about
three million conversions.

Nagpur town is built around
Sitabaldi Fort, which is
encircled by a deep moat. It
is open to the public only on
26 January and 15 August. In
the eastern part of the city are
the remains of the **Bhonsle
Palace**, which was destroyed
by fire in 1864. South of the
old city lie the **Chhatris**, or
memorials of the Bhonsle
kings, while a number of
colonial buildings are situated
in the western part of Nagpur.
Among the most noteworthy
are the High Court (1737–42)
and the Anglican Cathedral
of All Saints (1851).

ENVIRONS: Ramtek, 40 km
(25 miles) northeast of
Nagpur, is associated with the
14-year exile of Rama, Sita and
Lakshman, as told in the epic
Ramayana (see p27). It was
the capital of the Vakataka
dynasty between the 4th and
the 6th centuries, and the fort
on the Hill of Rama dates to

Baskets of juicy oranges on sale in Nagpur's thriving market

ENVIRONS: The ashram of Gandhi's disciple, Vinobha Bhave, is 10 km (6 miles) north of Sevagram at **Paunar**. Bhave started the successful Bhoodan Movement (which literally means "land donation") that sought to persuade wealthy landowners to give portions of their holdings to the poor.

Pandharpur ⑲

Sholapur district. 250 km (155 miles) SE of Pune. 🚶 *91,500.* 🚉 🚌
🎎 *Kartik Ekadashi Fair (Oct/Nov).*

THE SPIRITUAL capital of Maharashtra, Pandharpur is situated on the banks of the Chandrabhaga river and is the site of the sacred shrine of Vithoba, an incarnation of Lord Vishnu. The temple was built in 1228 and is the focal point of a sacred pilgrimage which draws thousands of Varakaris (members of one of the state's most popular religious sects) here every July to attend the Kartik Ekadashi fair. *Dindis* or group processions travel to Pandharpur from every village in the area, accompanied by devotional singing. The river front, lined with numerous bathing ghats, comes alive with crowds of people, who gather here for their ritual dip.

this period. Its walls, however, were built later, in 1740, by the founder of Nagpur's Bhonsle dynasty, Raghoji I. There are also several temples dedicated to Rama and Sita, dating to the 5th century.

Wardha ⑱

Wardha district. 493 km (306 miles) NW of Aurangabad. 🚉 🚌 *from Nagpur to Wardha, then bus or auto to Sevagram.* 🛈 *(07152) 84 753.*

MOST VISITORS to Wardha are en route to Mahatma Gandhi's historic **Sevagram Ashram**, now a national institution, 8 km (5 miles) northwest of Wardha town. Established by Gandhi in 1933, Sevagram ("Village of Service") was based on Gandhi's philosophy of rural economic development. It became the headquarters of India's

National Movement, where Gandhi lived and worked for over 15 years. Spread over 40 ha (99 acres) of farmland, the ashram has numerous *kutirs* or rural dwellings and several research centres. Gandhi's personal effects, such as his spinning wheel and spectacles, are on display, and khadi, the coarse home-spun cotton that Gandhi made famous as the symbol of India's freedom struggle, is also on sale. A photo exhibit opposite the main entrance depicts scenes from Gandhi's life, while a hospital catering to the needs of local villagers, is located on the main road. Prayers are held daily at 4.30am and 6pm under a pipal tree planted by Gandhi, which visitors can attend.

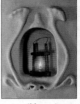

An oil lamp in a niche, Sevagram

The spartan interior of Mahatma Gandhi's ashram at Sevagram, near Wardha

GOA

THIS TINY STATE, along the Konkan Coast, covers 3,702 sq km (1,429 sq miles) and consists of just two districts, North and South Goa. Goa's distinct culture is a legacy of its colonial past. In 1510, Alfonso de Albuquerque established a small but powerful Portuguese enclave here. Though Goa became a part of the Indian Union in 1961, evidence of the 400-odd years of Portuguese rule is still apparent in the people's dress, language, religion and cuisine, and in their music, a fusion of the plaintive *fado* with the lilting rhythms of local Konkani folk songs. Today, Goa is one of India's most popular holiday destinations, with its idyllic beaches, lush paddy fields, coconut plantations and villages dotted with pretty white-washed churches and grand mansions. Its other attractions include the Hindu temples around Ponda, built between the 15th and 18th centuries, and the magnificent cathedrals of Old Goa. Goa's friendly, easy-going people go out of their way to make visitors feel at home.

SIGHTS AT A GLANCE

Towns & Cities
Mapusa ⑤
Margao ⑮
Panaji ①
Pernem ⑦

Churches, Seminaries & Temples
Pilar ⑪
Ponda ⑫
Rachol ⑭
Reis Magos ②
Tambdi Surla ⑬

Historic Sites
A Walk through Old Goa ⑩
Terekhol Fort ⑨
Braganza House ⑯

Beaches & Beach Towns
Anjuna ④
Arambol ⑧
Calangute ③
Cavelossim ⑱
Colva ⑰
Palolem ⑲
Vagator ⑥

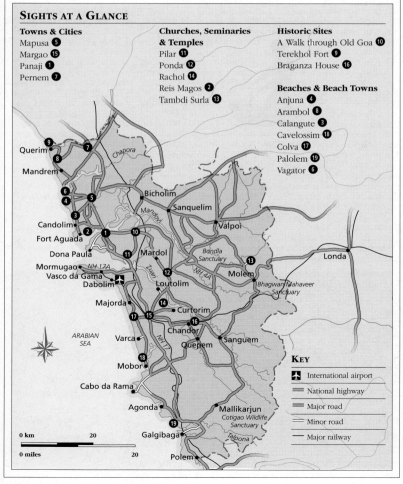

KEY
✈ International airport
National highway
Major road
Minor road
Major railway

◁ **Coconut groves and rice fields surrounding a village chapel in Goa**

Panaji ❶

G OA'S CAPITAL, Panaji, situated at the mouth of the
Mandovi river, is reminiscent of a provincial
Mediterranean town. Earlier a port of the Adil Shahi
kings of Bijapur *(see p542)*, it became a military landing
stage and warehouse after the arrival of the Portuguese
in 1510. In 1759, after a series of epidemics in Old Goa,
the viceroy was forced to move his residence to Panaji,
or Panjim as it was then called. However, it was only
in 1843 that the town became the official capital of
Portuguese territories in India. Today, Panaji has a
relaxed and friendly ambience, especially along the
leafy avenues of the old town *(see pp488–9)*. The newer
commercial hub, laid out on a grid, has concrete structures interspersed with colonial buildings and churches.

**The Church of Our Lady of the
Immaculate Conception**

🏛 Secretariat

Avenida Dom Joao Crasto. **(** *(0832)*
22 2701. ◯ *Mon–Sat.*
The river front Secretariat
housing the State Legislative
Assembly, is one of
Panaji's oldest buildings.
It was once the sum-
mer palace of Yusuf
Adil Shah, Goa's 16th-
century Muslim ruler,
and fell to the
Portuguese in
1510, despite a
formidable battery
of 55 cannons and
a salt-water moat
that protected it.

**The 19th-century
statue of Abbé de Faria**

Rebuilt in 1615, its strategic
location made it a point of
entry for ships and a stopover
for viceroys and governors en
route to Old Goa *(see p501)*.
In 1760, after Old Goa was
abandoned in favour of
Panaji, the Idalcaon's Palace
(a corruption of Adil Shah's or
Khan's Palace), as it was then

known, became the official
residence of the viceroys –
until 1918, when the residence moved to the Cabo
Palace, southwest of Panaji.
Extensive renovations have
transformed the original
Islamic structure into the
colonial building it is today,
with a sloping tiled roof,
wide wooden veran-
dahs and cast-iron
pillars. The Ashoka
Chakra and the
Buddhist Wheel of
Law, the emblems
of the Indian
government, have
replaced the Portuguese viceroys' coat of arms, above the
entrance to the building.

Standing west of the
Secretariat is the arresting
statue of Abbé de Faria. This
Goan priest, who was born in
Candolim in 1756, underwent
theological training in Rome.
After his ordination, he

moved to Paris, where he
won acclaim as the father of
modern hypnosis.

🔒 Church of Our Lady of
the Immaculate Conception

Church Square. **(** *(0832) 42 6939.*
◯ *daily.* **✝** *(English) 8am,
Mon–Sat; 8.30am, Sun.*
Overlooking Largo da Igreja
or "Church Square", Panaji's
main square, is the Church of
Our Lady of the Immaculate
Conception, the town's most
important landmark. Portuguese sailors used to come
to the original chapel, consecrated in 1541, to offer
thanksgiving prayers after
their long and treacherous
voyage from Lisbon.

The present church, with
its Baroque façade framed
by twin towers, was built in
1619. Its most striking feature,
the double flight of stairs
leading up to the church, was
added in 1871. The central
pediment was built at the

View of the the riverside Secretariat at Panaji, with its tiled roof and colonial façade

same time, as was the belfry to accommodate the huge bell brought from Old Goa's Augustinian monastery *(see p496)*. The chapel in the south transept has fine reredos (altar panels) retrieved from the viceroy's chapel in the Secretariat. The Baroque splendour of the main altar and the two transept altars is in sharp contrast to the otherwise simple interior.

🏛 Menezes Braganza Institute
Malaca Rd. 📞 *(0832) 22 4143.*
An excellent example of 19th-century Portuguese civic architecture, the Institute Vasco da Gama was built to impart knowledge in the arts and sciences. It was later renamed after the philanthropist Luis de Menezes Braganza (1878–1938), whose family home is in Chandor *(see p508).*

Today, this is Goa's Central Library, with a good collection of rare books. The superb mural in blue painted ceramic tiles *(azulezos)* was added to the entrance lobby in 1935, and depicts scenes from the epic *Os Lusiadas* (Lusiada, meaning the "people of Portugal", is derived from Lusitania, Portugal's old name). Written by the 16th-century Portuguese poet, Luis Vaz de Camões, this recounts the history of the Portuguese presence in Goa. The Institute used to have an art gallery with works by late 19th- and early 20th-century European

artists. These exhibits are now housed in the State Museum.

The grassy square in front of the Institute, **Azad Maidan**, is lined on one side by the Police Headquarters, built in 1832 with stones from Old Goa's abandoned buildings. The pavilion in the centre was made in 1847, using Corinthian pillars taken from a Dominican church, dating to the mid-16th century. Inside, a memorial to the freedom fighter, Dr Tristao de Braganza Cunha, has replaced an earlier statue of the first viceroy, Alfonso de Albuquerque, now in the Archaeological Museum in Old Goa *(see p500).*

The central pavilion, Azad Maidan

🏛 State Museum
Patto. 📞 *(0832) 22 6006.*
🔲 *Mon–Fri.* ⬤ *public hols.*
This museum houses a rather modest collection of pre-colonial artifacts, including statues, *sati* stones, antique furniture and carvings from

ravaged Hindu temples, as well as some Christian icons.

ENVIRONS: Panaji's nearest beach, **Miramar**, is 3 km (2 miles) west. **Dona Paula**, 7 km (4 miles) southwest of Panaji, is near the headland dividing the estuaries of the Zuari and Mandovi rivers. It is named after a viceroy's daughter who, the story goes, jumped into the sea when she wasn't allowed to marry a local fisherman. The jetty offers fine views of Fort Aguada across the bay. Jet skis are available for rent and visitors can also take an enjoyable ferry-ride to Vasco da Gama harbour.

A scene from *Os Lusiadas*, depicting Vasco da Gama's arrival in Goa

GOAN RIVER CRUISES
A delightful way to spend an evening in Goa is to take one of the many sunset cruises along the Mandovi river, organized by the Goa Tourism Development Corporation, (0832) 22 6728, and also by private operators. Most of the cruises begin from the jetty at the foot of Mandovi bridge, every day between 6 and 7pm (tickets are available at the jetty). Entertainment is provided by troupes of Goan dancers and musicians. On full moon nights, an excellent dinner is also provided on board. Full day cruises are on offer as well, and some operators, such as Classical Interlude, (0832) 22 2176, organize specialized tours focusing on culture, food or history. Hydro-Sports Goa, (0832) 22 1133, takes visitors out in traditional wooden canoes from Vainguinim Beach up the Cumbarjua Canal to Old Goa, passing mangroves populated with birds and crocodiles en route.

An evening cruise down the Mandovi river

Street-by-Street: Panaji Old Town

Terracotta medallion

Tucked away between Ourem Creek and Altinho Hill in Panaji are the old residential quarters of Fontainhas and São Tomé, built on reclaimed land in the 19th century. Fontainhas was named after the fountain of Phoenix, a spring that provided the quarter's only source of water, while São Tomé takes its name from the São Tomé Church. This old-world precinct, characterized by a jumble of painted, tile-roofed houses, has streets lined with taverns offering authentic Goan cuisine and *feni* (cashewnut liqueur), and bakeries serving *bebinca*, the delicious local cake. Many of the residents still speak Portuguese.

A priest in the doorway of St Sebastian's Chapel

Panjim Inn

FILIPE NERI XAVIER ROAD

CRUZADOR RAFAE

RUA DE NATALE

31ST JANUARY ROAD

RUA DE NATAL

CORTE DE OIT

RUA DE OUREN

Velha Goa Galeria, Dr Arminio Ribeiro de Santana Mansion

★ Fundação de Oriente
Originally a family home, it now houses a Portuguese foundation that promotes artistic, cultural and scientific work. Its library is open to the public.

★ St Sebastian's Chapel
The chapel, built in 1888, has a life-size crucifix that used to hang in the Palace of the Inquisition in Old Goa.

★ Rua de Natale
This road snakes up Altinho Hill and has steps laid out to help pedestrians negotiate the gentle climb.

STAR SIGHTS

★ **Fundação de Oriente**

★ **St Sebastian's Chapel**

★ **Rua de Natale**

Ourem Creek
The picturesque Rua de Ourem faces Ourem Creek. Behind it, colourful houses dot the slopes all the way up Altinho Hill.

Altinho Hill

KEY

- - - Suggested route

Venite Restaurant
This first-floor restaurant, overlooking the street below, has a wonderful ambience and serves excellent European and Goan food.

31ST JANUARY ROAD

GOMES PEREIRA ROAD

LUIS DE MENEZES ROAD

SÃO TOMÉ STREET

MAHATMA GANDHI ROAD

São Tomé, a tiny church built in 1849, was once the focus of a busy square. The nearby Mint marks the Inquisition's execution site.

0 metres 30
0 yards 30

Ourem Creek

Pato Bridge

Streetscape
Most houses are painted yellow, ochre, green or indigo with a white trim – in keeping with the old Portuguese building code.

Reredos behind the main altar, Reis Magos Church

Reis Magos ❷

North Goa district (Bardez taluka).
3 km (2 miles) NW of Panaji.
🎏 *Feast of Three Kings (Jan).*

THE FORT AT Reis Magos was built in 1551 by Don Alfonso de Noronha, the fifth viceroy, as a second line of defence after the forts at Aguada and Cabo (the tip of Dona Paula). It once housed a prison, which was moved to Mormugao in 1996. Adjacent to the fort is the Reis Magos Church. Constructed in 1555, this is one of Goa's earliest churches, and has the royal Portuguese coat of arms on its façade.

ENVIRONS: Fort Aguada, 4 km (2.5 miles) west of Reis Magos, was built in 1612 as a defence against the Marathas and the Dutch. Its church, dedicated to St Lawrence, the patron saint of sailors, was built in 1630, while the huge lighthouse dates to 1864. Some buildings within the fort now house the state prison. The local beach, Sinquerim, is known for its luxury resorts.

Calangute ❸

North Goa district (Bardez taluka). 16 km (10 miles) NW of Panaji. 🚌 ℹ️
GTDC Tourist Resort, (0832) 27 6024.

THE CENTRE OF the hippie scene in the 1960s and 1970s, Calangute is Goa's most popular beach. During the day, it is packed with sun-bathers, hawkers, masseurs, hair-braiders and ear-cleaners. The entire stretch of sand right up to the adjacent Baga Beach is lined with resorts, trinket stalls, bars and beach shacks such as Reggie's Bar and Souza Lobo (*see p738*), which serve excel-lent Goan food. **Goan Bananas**, another popular beach shack, offers facilities for water sports. Rides on fishing boats are also available at bargain prices. Calangute's church, **St Alex**, topped by a large dome, is on the road to Mapusa. Its Rococo-style white-and-gold interior has pretty, shell-shaped niches.

Soccer game in progress, Calangute

🍴 **Goan Bananas**
Cobravaddo, Calangute. 📞 *(0832) 27 6362.*

ENVIRONS: Extending north of Calangute, **Baga Beach** is far less crowded, although its expanse of soft, white sand has its share of guesthouses and bars. It hosts a leisurely Saturday flea market – a great alternative to the Wednesday market at nearby Anjuna. Tito's Bar, which has the only dance floor on the entire beach, is the hub of Baga's nightlife. **Candolim Beach**, 2.5 km (2 miles) south of Calangute, stretches all the way to Fort Aguada. Popular with large tour groups, the once peaceful waters now resound with the whir of speedboats and jet skis. **Saligao**, 2 km (1.3 miles) east of Calangute, has the pretty Church of Mae de Deus, in Neo-Gothic style, as well as a seminary which prepares boys for theological studies at Rachol Seminary (*see p504*).

Anjuna ❹

North Goa district (Bardez taluka).
18 km (11 miles) NW of Panaji. 🚌
🛍️ *Flea Market (Wed).*

ANJUNA HAS NOW replaced Calangute as a haven for backpackers. It is better known for its full-moon rave parties and sprawling flea market than for its beach. The popular market, held every Wednesday, is crowded with hawkers from all over India selling everything from Bali-nese batik, silver jewellery and papier-mâché boxes, to Tibetan prayer wheels, Rajas-thani mirrorwork and Kerala woodcarvings. Fluorescent rave gear and trendy beach-wear round off the selection, while added attractions are performing monkeys and fortune-telling Nandi bulls.

A woman selling sarongs at the Anjuna flea market

Beaches and Beach Life

Goa's splendid beaches stretch over 106 km (66 miles), from Querim in the north to Mobor in the south. Each beach has its distinct character, though in general, South Goa's beaches are far less developed than those in North Goa, and have only

Visitor under a beach umbrella

recently become popular as tourist destinations. To cater to the growing number of visitors, many beaches now have shacks serving beer, snacks and seafood, lively flea markets, and vendors offering a variety of services from head massages to dolphin-watching trips.

Querim, close to Terekhol, is a lovely, unspoilt stretch of sand.

Arambol, an idyllic, peaceful beach with fishing boats, has a picturesque freshwater lagoon that is fed by hot springs *(see p493)*.

Baga, an extension of Calangute, Goa's most developed beach, has lots of activity, with numerous bars, resorts and shacks, and some lively night spots.

Sinquerim, extending up to the ramparts of Fort Aguada, has three luxury hotels situated on its sands. A few reliable operators offer a range of water sports facilities as well as boat trips.

Vainguinim has facilities for sailing, wind-surfing, water-skiing, parasailing, canoeing and scuba diving, as well as motor boats and jet skis for hire.

Siridao, a small, secluded beach a short drive from Panaji, is strewn with pretty seashells.

Terekhol Fort *(see p493)*
Querim *(see p493)*
Arambol
Mandrem *(see p492)*
Morgim *(see p492)*
Vagator *(see p492)*
Anjuna
Baga
Calangute
Candolim
Sinquerim
Fort Aguada
Miramar *(see p487)*
Dona Paula *(see p487)*
Vainguinim
Siridao
Bogmalo
Majorda *(see p507)*
Colva
Benaulim *(see p507)*
Varca *(see p507)*
Cavelossim *(see p507)*
Mobor *(see p507)*
Cabo da Rama *(see p507)*
Agonda *(see p507)*
Palolem

Bogmalo, safe for swimming, is an ideal family beach with adequate facilities for water sports *(see p507)*.

Colva *has one of Goa's longest uninterrupted stretches of sand, backed by shady palms. It is the most popular of South Goa's beaches, and has a busy market square and a number of bars and seafood cafés* (see p507).

Palolem's crescent-shaped beach, the loveliest in South Goa, offers dolphin-watching trips and tree houses for rent. The sunset views here are spectacular *(see p507)*.

0 km 5
0 miles 5

The façade of St Jerome's Church (Our Lady of Miracles), Mapusa

Mapusa ⑤

North Goa district (Bardez taluka).
13 km (8 miles) N of Panaji.
🏛 40,150. 🚉 🚌 ℹ️ GTDC Hotel,
(0832) 26 2794. 🛒 Fri. 🎭 Feast of
Our Lady of Miracles (Apr).

THE LARGEST TOWN in north-ern Goa, Mapusa's main point of interest is the colourful Friday market, with its tan-talizing aromas of dried fish, spices, chillies, vinegar, local toddy and the spicy Goan sausages, chouriça. The region's famous cashewnuts are also much in demand. Hawkers peddle a range of beachwear, including cheap T-shirts and summer dresses, in the covered colonnades in front of the rows of shops. In the lanes leading off from the main market are stalls selling handicrafts and souvenirs from all over the country.

St Jerome's Church, also known as the Church of Our Lady of Miracles, was rebuilt twice, first in 1719 and again in 1838, after it was destroyed by fire. Its main altar, with the image of Nossa Senhora de Milagres, has some grand ornamental screens, salvaged from a church in Old Goa.

Interestingly, both Hindus and Catholics celebrate the Feast of Our Lady (held 16 days after Easter) with equal fervour. At the end of the festival Hindu devotees, accompanied by Catholics, take the holy oil from St Jerome's church back to the nearby Shanteri Temple.

ENVIRONS: Mayem Lake, 14 km (9 miles) southeast of Mapusa, is an ideal picnic spot, with boating facilities, a resort and a good restaurant.

Vagator ⑥

North Goa district (Bardez taluka).
17 km (11 miles) N of Panaji.
🚌 Chapora village.

A BEAUTIFUL BAY sheltered by rocky outcrops at both ends, Vagator consists of a number of small beaches fringed by shady coconut palms. Rarely crowded, it is the perfect place to discover Goa's unspoilt beauty.

The southernmost cove of **Ozran** lies below a steep cliff, where a freshwater stream empties into a clear pool, ideal for swimming. **Little Vagator**, to the north, is a secluded stretch of sand popular with more discerning visitors. **Big Vagator Beach** is dominated by the red laterite **Chapo-ra Fort** situated on top of a hill at its northern tip. Now in ruins, this fort

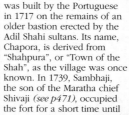

Brightly coloured fishing nets

was built by the Portuguese in 1717 on the remains of an older bastion erected by the Adil Shahi sultans. Its name, Chapora, is derived from "Shahpura", or "Town of the Shah", as the village was once known. In 1739, Sambhaji, the son of the Maratha chief Shivaji (see p471), occupied the fort for a short time until

it was returned to the Portuguese in exchange for Bassein, near Mumbai. Its ramparts, now desolate, offer sweeping views of the coast. Chapora village, below the fort, has many pleasant cafés.

ENVIRONS: The many fishing villages along the northern coastline can only be reached by taking a ferry across the Chapora river from Siolim, 10 km (6 miles) from Chapora village. The area around the village of **Morgim**, 5 km (3 miles) north of Chapora vil-lage, is ideal for birdwatching. **Mandrem** is another quiet village with a beautiful loca-tion, 12 km (7 miles) north of Chapora village.

Pernem ⑦

North Goa district (Pernem taluka).
29 km (18 miles) N of Panaji.
🚌 🚉 every half hour from Siolim.

THE HEADQUARTERS of Goa's northern most taluka, or sub-district, Pernem was occupied by the Portuguese in the mid-18th century. It was one of the last conquests they made between 1764 and 1788 – a period during which they expanded their territory to include Pernem, Bicholim and Satari in the north, and Ponda (see p502), Sanquem, Quepem and Canacona in the south. By this time, the fevour for conversions that existed during the period of the early conquests had waned, and these areas remained predom-inantly Hindu.

The brightly painted **Bhagavati Temple**, in the bazaar, stands on a 500-year-old site, although the present

Shack restaurant on Morgim Beach, a common sight in Goa

A fisherman casting his net at Querim Beach

structure dates to the 18th century. It is dedicated to the eight-armed Bhagavati, an incarnation of Shiva's consort Parvati. Its elaborate gateway is framed by two life-size elephants. A short distance from the bazaar is the palatial **Deshprabhu House**, the 19th-century mansion of the wealthy Hindu Deshprabhu family, who fought for Goa's liberation in 1961. This sprawling property, built around 16 courtyards, has a private temple and a museum displaying family portraits and antiques.

🏛 **Deshaprabhu House**
📞 (0832) 29 1275 to arrange a visit.

Arambol ⑧

North Goa district (Pernem taluka). 50 km (31 miles) N of Panaji.
🚌 🚕 every half hour from Siolim.

Also known as Harmal, Arambol is the only fishing village in North Goa that has some basic facilities for visitors. Situated along one of Goa's less commercial beaches, it still retains all the charm of a traditional fishing village, except for the occasional gypsy selling bright scarves

and skirts. Unlike in central Goa, the Hindu influence is apparent here; the numerous cafés and guesthouses are called Ganesha or Namaste instead of Pete's or Johnny's.

At the northern end, a rocky footpath leads to a second beach, entirely surrounded by cliffs. This sandy cove has a freshwater lagoon fed by hot springs and lined with sulphurous mud. A 5-km (3-mile) long path, heading north, leads to **Querim Beach** (pronounced "keri") – a pristine strip of white sand, backed by casuarina trees.

Terekhol Fort ⑨

North Goa district (Pernem taluka). 42 km (26 miles) N of Panaji. 🚌
🚕 every half hour from Querim.

Across the Terekhol river from Querim is the little hamlet of Terekhol, with Terekhol (Tiracol) Fort situated on a plateau above it. The early 18th-century fort was captured by the Portuguese in 1776 from the Bhonsles, a Maratha clan. It was the scene of an uprising in 1954, when a group of *satyagrahis* (freedom fighters) hoisted the Indian flag on its ramparts in an act of civil disobedience against colonial rule. The fort's high battlements face the sea, looking across the waters to Fort Aguada, Arambol and Chapora. The tiny chapel within the fort, with a statue of Christ in the courtyard, is usually closed but the atmospheric Terekhol Fort Heritage Hotel (*see p711*) offers some excellent views.

Carnival king on a float

FESTIVALS OF GOA

Jatra *(Jan)*, Quepem. A colourful festival *(jatra)* honouring local temple deities is celebrated at the Shantadurga Temple *(see p502)*. Other such festivals take place through the year at various temples in Ponda.
Carnival *(Feb)*, Panaji. Goa's grandest festival marks the beginning of Lent. "King Momo", who personifies fun and frolic, orders his subjects to forget their troubles, and leads a colourful parade through the streets. Three days and nights of nonstop revelry follow.

Masked dancers, Carnival

Shigmotsav (Shigmo) *(Mar)*. This joyous Hindu spring festival is celebrated acoss the state. Festivities continue for five days and include colourful street floats (in the larger towns), local folk theatre, sword dances and the lively spraying of coloured powder.
All Saints Procession *(Apr)*, Goa Velha, Pilar. Large crowds of devotees carry statues of 26 saints in procession from St Andrew's Church, in this small village near Pilar.
Feast of St Francis Xavier *(3 Dec)*, Old Goa. The feast of Goa's patron saint is held on the anniversary of his death (1552). Attended by Catholic pilgrims from all over the world, the feast is preceeded by novenas (nine days of prayer).

A holy cross on top of a knoll, Arambol Beach

Seagulls flocking around the day's catch at Arambol Beach ▷

A Walk through Old Goa ⑩

AMAGNIFICENT COMPLEX of cathedrals, churches and monasteries, spread along a 1.5-km (1-mile) stretch, marks the site of Old Goa, the Portuguese capital until the mid-18th century. The walk through this area, now a UNESCO World Heritage Site, takes in two of Goa's most important religious monuments, the Basilica de Bom Jesus and the grand Sé Cathedral, and ends on Holy Hill, where some of Goa's oldest churches are located.

Portrait of Vasco da Gama

Most of these buildings, designed by Italian or Portuguese architects, encompass a range of European styles, from sober Renaissance to exuberant Baroque and Portuguese Manueline *(see p501)*.

④ Sé Cathedral
This is thought to be Asia's largest church. The gilded high altar has six splendid panels depicting the life of St Catherine of Alexandria.

⑦ The Chapel of St Catherine, like Our Lady of the Rosary, was built to celebrate Albuquerque's victory in 1510, and served as Goa's only cathedral until the Sé Cathedral was built.

⑬ Our Lady of the Rosary was built on top of Holy Hill in 1526 by Alfonso de Albuquerque. He had watched Yusuf Adil Shah's defeat in 1510 from this very spot and vowed to build a church here.

⑫ Royal Chapel of St Anthony
St Anthony, Portugal's national saint, was also considered the Captain of the army.

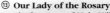
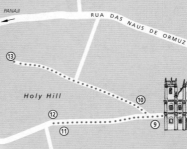

PANAJI

RUA DAS NAUS DE ORMUZ

Holy Hill

⑬ ⑫ ⑪ ⑩ ⑨ ⑦

⑩ Convent of St Monica, dating to the mid-17th century, will house Asia's first Museum of Christian Art, currently being relocated from Rachol *(see p504)*.

⑨ Church and Convent of St John of God
This convent was built in 1685 by the Order of the Hospitallers of St John of God, to tend to the sick. It was rebuilt in 1953.

⑪ Church and Monastery of St Augustine
The 46-m (151-ft) high laterite belfry dominates the remains of what was once India's largest church.

② Gateway of Adil Shah's Palace

The gate, comprising a lintel and basalt pillars, is all that survives of Adil Shah's palace, also used as the viceroys' residence from 1554 to 1695.

VISITORS' CHECKLIST

North Goa district (Tiswadi taluka). 9 km (6 miles) E of Panaji. Karmali, 9 km (6 miles) S of Old Goa. or taxi from Panaji. GTDC, Old Goa Tourist Hotel, behind Police Station, near MG Statue, (0832) 28 6127. Feast of St Francis Xavier (3 Dec). The Archaeological Survey of India's booklet on Old Goa is available at the Archaeological Museum.

① Viceroy's Arch

Over 1,000 ships a year brought new arrivals to Goa in the 17th century. They passed under this laterite archway, built by Francisco da Gama (viceroy 1597–1600).

③ Church of St Cajetan

Built by Italian friars in 1651, this church is renowned for the exuberant woodcarvings on its high altar and pulpit.

⑧ **Basilica de Bom Jesus** (see pp498–9).

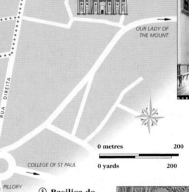

⑤ Church of St Francis of Assisi

Built by the Franciscan friars in 1521, this is one of Old Goa's most important churches. Its carved and gilded main altar depicts the crucified Jesus, four Evangelists, St Francis, and Our Lady with the baby Jesus.

⑥ Archaeological Museum

A bronze statue of the poet Luis Vaz de Camões, holding his epic Os Lusiadas (see p487), stands in the museum, now housed in the converted convent of St Francis of Assisi, adjoining the church.

Old Goa: Basilica de Bom Jesus

THE BASILICA DE BOM JESUS is revered by Roman Catholics all over the world since it houses the mortal remains of Goa's patron saint, Francis Xavier. It was the first church in South Asia to be granted the status of Minor Basilica, by Pope Pius XII in 1946. Built by the Jesuits in 1594, this grand Baroque structure blends Corinthian, Doric, Ionic and composite styles in its magnificent three-tiered façade. The Duke of Tuscany, Cosimo III, donated the elaborate tomb of St Francis in exchange for the pillow that lay under the saint's head. The tomb took the Florentine sculptor Giovanni Foggini ten years to build; it was finally assembled in 1698. The adjoining Professed House (1589) was used as the priests' quarters until it was damaged by a fire in 1633.

Doorway to Sacristy
An exquisitely carved wooden door leads to the sacristy.

★ Main Altar
The gilded reredos has a statue of St Ignatius of Loyola and another of the Infant Jesus. Local craftsmen, used to decorating temples, made plump, typically Hindu looking cherubs on the altar.

Altar of Our Lady of Hope

Chapel of the Blessed Sacrament

Altar of St Michael

ST FRANCIS XAVIER (1506–1552)

St Francis Xavier, Art Gallery

Francis Xavier was sent to Goa by the Portuguese king, Dom Joao III. He arrived in May 1542, aged 36, and worked tirelessly over the next few years, converting nearly 30,000 people. He died while on voyage off the coast of China in 1552, and was temporarily buried on an island. When his body was dug up three months later to transfer his bones, it showed no signs of decay. A year later, when his remains were enshrined in the Basilica in Goa, his body was still in pristine condition. This was declared a miracle, and in 1622 he was canonized. Expositions of his relics take place every ten years or so, the next one being due in 2004.

STAR FEATURES

★ Main Altar

★ Tomb of St Francis Xavier

★ Wooden Pulpit

★ Tomb of St Francis Xavier
*The marble and jasper tomb
has four bronze plaques
depicting scenes from the
saint's life. Built in a mixture
of Italian and Indian styles,
the silver reliquary containing
the sacred relics is surmounted
by a cross with two angels.*

Sacristy

★ Wooden Pulpit
*The figures of Jesus and
several Evangelists are
beautifully carved
on the pulpit.*

Basalt Stone Tablet
*The Jesuit motto, IHS
or Iaeus Hominum
Salvator, means "Jesus
the Saviour" in Greek.*

**Catholic nuns at the
entrance to the Basilica**

Façade
*This is the only Goan church not covered in
lime plaster. Its original coat was removed in
1956, exposing the soft red laterite beneath.
Each of the three doorways and six windows is
flanked by elegant pillars and basalt detailing.*

Exploring Old Goa

PORTUGAL'S GOA DOURADA ("Golden Goa") was once a vast city, inhabited by more than 30,000 people. In the 16th century, it attracted missionaries and soldiers, merchants and horse-traders, and its elegant palaces and mansions were much praised by contemporary visitors. However, by the mid-18th century, a series of epidemics and the silting up of the Mandovi river forced the viceroy to move his residence downstream to Panaji *(see p486)*. Thereafter, decline set in and, by the 19th century, the city was finally abandoned and its houses demolished. Today, Old Goa is a mere shadow of its former self, but the few churches and cathedrals that remain are considered to be among Goa's most significant monuments.

Rows of pillars on either side of the central nave, Sé Cathedral

⛪ Church of St Cajetan
E of Viceroy's Arch. ○ *daily.*

In the 17th century, Pope Urban III sent Italian priests from the Theatine Order to Golconda *(see pp666–7)*. When refused entry, they settled in Old Goa. Here, in 1651, they erected a church dedicated to their founder, St Cajetan, and designed along the lines of St Peter's in Rome. The distinctive dome and interior, laid out in the shape of a Greek cross, embody the majesty of Italian Baroque. The adjacent monastery is today a college of theology.

Detail of altar, Churh of St Cajetan

⛪ Sé Cathedral
Senate Square. 📞 *(0832) 28 6450.* ○ *daily.* ✝ *(Konkani) 7.30am & 6pm, Mon–Sat; 7.20am & 4pm, Sun.*

When ordered by the government in Portugal to build a church worthy of their mighty empire, Francis Coutinho (viceroy, 1561–4) envisaged a magnificent cathedral that would be the largest in Asia. The result is the Renaissance-style Sé Cathedral, designed in the 16th century by Julio Simao and Ambrosio Argueiro, and built over 80 years. Its 30-m (98-ft) high Tuscan-style façade was flanked by two square bell towers, only one of which survives. In it hangs the Golden Bell, known for its melodic tones, which rang out during the dreaded *auto da fé* trials, held in the cathedral's front square.

The interior, with intricate Corinthian detailing, has a 76-m (249-ft) long central nave. As many as 15 altars grace the interior, but the *pièce de résistance* is the gilded high altar, dedicated to St Catherine of Alexandria, with panel paintings depicting scenes from her life. Two of the eight chapels, the Blessed Sacrament and the Cross of Miracles, have delicate filigree work on their screens. The font, used by St Francis Xavier to baptize converts, is near the entrance. The sacred relics of his body, kept in the Basilica de Bom Jesus *(see pp498–9)*, are brought to the cathedral during the expositions held every ten years.

🏛 Archaeological Museum
Convent of St Francis of Assisi. 📞 *(0832) 28 6133.* ○ *Sat–Thu.* 📷

Once Goa's largest monastery, the Convent of St Francis of Assisi (built in 1517) now houses the Archaeological Museum, established in 1964. A huge bronze statue of Alfonso de Albuquerque, moved from Panaji, dominates the entrance hall. Among the objects of interest are a finely carved image of Vishnu and a Surya statue, dating to the Kadamba period (11th–12th centuries), and stone inscriptions in Marathi and Persian,

From right to left, Sé Cathedral, Church of St Francis of Assisi and Church of Our Lady of the Rosary in Old Goa

relics of earlier ruling dynasties. Other exhibits include Hindu *sati* stones, a model of *São Gabriel* (the ship in which Vasco da Gama sailed to India in 1498), and a bronze statue of St Catherine in the courtyard. The Portrait Gallery on the first floor has 60 paintings of Goa's viceroys and governors.

Detail of memorial, St Augustine's ruins

🔒 Church of St Francis of Assisi
W of Sé Cathedral. ☐ *daily.*
Built by the Franciscan friars in 1521, and rebuilt in 1661, this church has a beautifully carved doorway (taken from the original building). This is a rare example of the Portuguese Manueline style, which uses many nautical motifs, and was developed during

Façade with two octagonal towers, Church of St Francis of Assisi

the reign of King Dom Manuel (r.1469–1521). A pair of navigator's globes and a Greek cross (the emblem of all Portuguese ships) embellish the door. The superb Baroque interior has floral frescoes on the walls and ceiling, and the floor is paved with the sculpted tombstones of Portuguese nobility. The gilded altar has figures of St Francis and Christ. Other noteworthy features are the pulpit, which is carved in floral designs and the painted panels in the chancel, which depict various scenes from the saint's life.

🔒 Church and Monastery of St Augustine
Holy Hill.
Once the largest church in India, with a grand five-storeyed façade, St Augustine's now lies in ruins. Erected by the Augustinian order in 1512, the Gothic-style church was abandoned in 1835, and its roof caved in seven years later. Excavations begun in 1989 revealed eight chapels, four altars, wall sculptures and more than 100 splendid granite tombstones. According to contemporary descriptions, the church also had grand staircases and galleries, and a library that rivalled the one at Oxford (England), in the 17th century. Today, all that remains of St Augustine's is its soaring bell tower *(see p496).*

🔒 Church of Our Lady of the Rosary
Holy Hill. ☐ *daily.*
With its castle-like turrets and simple altar painted with baskets of flowers, this is one of Goa's earliest Manueline-style churches. The tomb of Dona Catarina, wife of Garcia de Sá (viceroy from 1548–9) and the first Portuguese woman to migrate to Goa, also lies here.

Further Afield
A few buildings of interest lie in Old Goa's southeastern corner. Marking the end of the Rua Direita, Old Goa's main street, is a desolate basalt pillar on a raised platform, the remains of the terrible **Pillory**. Criminals and heretics were strung up here as punishment, in the centre of the city square. Close by, on the road to Ponda, lies the **College of St Paul**. Founded by the Jesuits in 1541, it had 3,000 students, making it the largest Jesuit school in Asia. It also housed Asia's first printing press. St Francis Xavier stayed and preached here; the chapel further up the road was also used by him, and was later dedicated to his memory.
  The Church of Our Lady of the Mount, built in 1510, sits on top of a hill and is reached by a lane that leads off the Cumbarjua Road. Built by Alfonso de Albuquerque after his victory over Yusuf Adil Shah, the church has recently been restored. The views over Old Goa's towers and turrets are magnificent.

Altar in the Church of Our Lady of the Rosary, on Holy Hill

THE GOA INQUISITION
On the request of Francis Xavier *(see p498)*, a tribunal of Jesuits arrived in 1560 and took over Adil Shah's secondary palace (of which few traces now remain), to the south of Sé Cathedral. Their mission was to curb the libertine ways of the Portuguese settlers and convert "infidels". During the Inquisition in 1567, all Hindu ceremonies were banned,

Mural of a proselytizing priest

temples were destroyed and Hindus forcibly converted. Those who refused were locked away in the dungeons of the "Palace of the Inquisition" (as Adil Shah's palace was known) to await the *auto da fé* (acts of faith) trial. The condemned were burnt alive in front of a congregation of dignitaries. Over the next 200 years, 16,000 trials were held and thousands killed, and it was not until 1812 that the Inquisition was finally dissolved.

17th-century painting of St Cecilia, patroness of church choirs, Pilar

Pilar ⓫

North Goa district (Tiswadi taluka). 12 km (7 miles) SE of Panaji.

SET ON A HILLTOP, **Pilar Seminary** was originally built by the Capuchins (a Franciscan order) in 1613, on the site of an old Hindu temple. Abandoned in 1835, when all religious orders were disbanded, it was reopened by the Carmelites in 1858. In 1890, the Society of Pilar set up a mission college here, and classes are still held in the old seminary building.

The adjoining **Church of Our Lady of Pilar** has an elaborately carved stone doorway with a figure of St Francis of Assisi above it. Inside is a statue of Our Lady of Pilar, brought here from Spain. The tomb of Agnelo D'Souza (seminary director, 1918–27) lies adjacent to the church. The **New Seminary**, built in 1946, stands close by. Its museum displays fragments from the original temple, Christian art, Portuguese coins and a stone lion, the symbol of the Kadamba dynasty.

🏛 **Museum**
[(0832) 21 8529. ⃝ daily.

ENVIRONS: **Goa Velha**, 2 km (1.3 miles) southwest of Pilar, marks the site of Govapuri, the port-capital of the Kadamba rulers between the 11th and 13th centuries, of which few traces now remain.

Ponda ⓬

South Goa district (Ponda taluka). 28 km (17 miles) SE of Panaji. 🏛 17,700. 🚌 🚉 Urs of Shah Abdullah (Feb).

THE TOWN OF PONDA is a busy commercial centre, and its main sight is the **Safa Shahouri Mosque**, 2 km (1.3 miles) to the west. Built by Ibrahim Adil Shah (a successor of Yusuf Adil Shah) in 1560, it is a rectangular structure, with window arches, topped by a slanting tiled roof. A ritual tank to the south has the same designs as those on the *mihrabs* (arched niches).

Ponda also lends its name to the *taluka* (sub-district) of the same name, which is renowned for its numerous Hindu temples, tucked away in thick forests. As the Portuguese expanded their territory in central Goa, they destroyed over 550 temples. Hindu priests fled with their religious artifacts to regions that lay outside Portuguese control, especially the area around Ponda town, where they built new temples in the 17th and 18th centuries.

More than half of Goa's population is Hindu, and Goan temples, unlike those elsewhere in India, are a fascinating blend of European Baroque, Muslim and Hindu architectural styles. Their basic plan remains Hindu, but often Muslim domes replace the usual

Brass lamp tower, Shri Mahalsa Temple

shikharas (spires) over the main sanctum, and the prayer halls are decorated with ornate European chandeliers.

The **Shantadurga Temple**, 3 km (2 miles) southwest of Ponda at Quela, is Goa's most popular shrine. Built by Shahu, the grandson of the Maratha chief Shivaji *(see p471)*, the russet and cream coloured temple has an unusual pagoda-style roof, dominated by a five-storeyed octagonal lamp tower, unique to Goa. Grand chandeliers hang from the gilded roof in the huge central hall, and embossed silver screens shield the main sanctuary, which holds the silver deity of Shantadurga (a form of Shiva's consort Parvati), brought from Mormugao *taluka*. Also of interest are the huge *rathas* (chariots) that are used during the Jatra in January *(see p493)*.

The **Shri Ramnath Temple**, a short walk away, is noted for the grand silver screen embossed with animal and floral motifs, in front of its sanctum. Its linga, originally from Loutolim, is worshipped by devotees of both Shiva and Vishnu.

The **Shri Nagueshi Temple**, 4 km (2.5 miles) west of Ponda at Bandora, dates to 1780, though a temple may have stood here earlier. Built for the worship of Nagesh (Shiva as Lord of the Serpents), it is one of the oldest temples in this region. Its entrance hall

The large 18th-century water tank at the Shri Mangesh Temple

has carved wooden friezes depicting scenes from the epics *Ramayana* and *Mahabharata* (see pp26–7).

The 18th-century **Shri Lakshmi Narasimha Temple** is situated in Velinga village, 5 km (3 miles) northwest of Ponda. Its majestic image of Narasimha, Vishnu's man-lion incarnation (see p679), was brought here from Mormugao in the 1560s. Surrounded by forest, it is one of Goa's most attractive temples, with a sacred tank and an elaborate gateway. A tower standing close by houses the temple's musicians during the annual Jatra festival, held here in May.

Dedicated to Vishnu, the **Shri Mahalsa Temple** is 7 km (4 miles) northwest of Ponda, in Mardol village. The main deity (either a female form of Vishnu or his consort Lakshmi) was taken from Verna. The temple's distinguishing feature is an exceptionally tall brass pillar, 21 tiers in all, rising from a figure of Kurma (Vishnu's incarnation as a turtle), with Garuda (his vehicle) perched on top. The pillar symbolizes Mount Kailasa which, according to Hindu mythology, was placed on Kurma's back and was used to churn the primordial ocean. The original shrine is a wooden structure with a sloping roof, and the entrance porches have carvings of musicians and warriors. Its main hall has

A procession during the Shigmo Jatra, at the Shri Mahalsa Temple

The Kadamba-period Tambdi Surla Temple, set on the banks of a stream

intricately carved pillars, while the central part of the ceiling is raised, with painted images of gods set in niches.

A short distance to the northwest, at Priol, lies Goa's wealthiest temple, the 18th-century **Shri Mangesh Temple**, dedicated to Shiva. The courtyard has a sacred *tulsi* (basil) plant growing in a bright green urn, a characteristic Goan feature. There is a large sacred tank and a seven-storeyed lamp tower. Dance-dramas are performed here during the Jatra festivities in April and May. A vividly painted elephant on wheels stands at the entrance to the white and yellow temple. Inside, 19th-century Belgian chandeliers hang from the ceiling, while the main sanctum has a linga transferred from Mormugao. The childhood home of Lata Mangeshkar (b.1929), India's most famous singer of film songs, was near the temple.

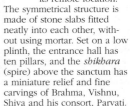

Detail, Tamdi Surla Temple

About 4 km (2.5 miles) northeast of Ponda town, near the village of Khandepar, is a cluster of **Hindu Rock-cut Caves** from the 10th–13th centuries, with carved lotus decorations on the ceiling, simple door frames and niches for oil lamps.

A few spice gardens that grow aromatic spices such as cardamom, nutmeg and cinnamon, make interesting day trips from Ponda. The Pascoal Plantation, 8 km (5 miles) east, and the Savoi Spice Garden at Savoi Verem, 12 km (7 miles) north, are easy to reach.

Tambdi Surla ⑬

South Goa district (Sanguem taluka). 73 km (45 miles) E of Panaji. *Taxis from Panaji or Ponda are the best option.*

HIDDEN AWAY IN the forests of Tambdi Surla, stands the oldest existing Hindu temple in Goa, dating from the Kadamba period (between the 11th and 13th centuries). Built in black basalt and dedicated to Shri Mahadeva (Shiva), the temple probably survived because of its remote location. The symmetrical structure is made of stone slabs fitted neatly into each other, without using mortar. Set on a low plinth, the entrance hall has ten pillars, and the *shikhara* (spire) above the sanctum has a miniature relief and fine carvings of Brahma, Vishnu, Shiva and his consort, Parvati.

ENVIRONS: The **Bhagwan Mahaveer Sanctuary**, 20 km (12 miles) southeast of Tamdi Surla, covers an area of 240 sq km (93 sq miles) and is home to leopards, deer and the Indian bison. The 600-m (1,969-ft) high **Dudhsagar Waterfalls** on the Goa-Karnataka border are its main attraction. The small **Bondla Sanctuary**, 30 km (19 miles) east of Tambdi Surla, is known for its variety of birds.

Bhagwan Mahaveer Sanctuary
☐ *daily.* 🎟
Bondla Sanctuary
☐ *Sep–Jun: Fri–Wed.* 🎟

Altar, Church of St Ignatius Loyola, Rachol

Rachol ⑭

South Goa district (Salcete taluka).
52 km (32 miles) SE of Panaji. 🚌

THE SMALL HAMLET of Rachol occupies the site of an old fortress built by the Bijapur sultans *(see p542)*, which was ceded to the Portuguese in 1520. A laterite archway and a dry moat are the only remnants of the bastion – once fortified with 100 cannons – that used to guard the southern borders of the Portuguese territories. The pretty **Church of Nossa Senhora das Neves** (Our Lady of the Snows), in the village, was built in 1576.

Silver reliquary, museum collection

Today, **Rachol Seminary**, built in 1606, is probably the most important of Goa's seminaries. First established in Margao in 1574, and known as the College of All Saints, the earlier seminary included a hospital, a school for the poor and a printing press. It was relocated here after the Margao institution was destroyed in a Muslim raid in 1579. For generations, this was Goa's most prestigious educational institution, both for secular and religious studies, offering a seven-year course in theology and philosophy, to prepare young seminarians for the priesthood.

Spectacularly located on the summit of a hill, the building has a grand fort-like façade, flanked by imposing watch-towers. The seminary's vast entrance hall is covered with impressive murals and opens on to a central courtyard, surrounded by cloistered rooms made of solid teak, each one with an adjoining wood-panelled study. The grand staircase is adorned with Hindu sculptures, excavated from the ancient Hindu temple on the site of which the seminary was constructed. This leads to the first floor and the library, which has a rare collection of Latin and Portuguese books, and portraits of Goa's archbishops.

Attached to the seminary is the **Church of St Ignatius Loyola**, dedicated to the eponymous saint. It has an ornately carved and gilded altar with a painting of St Constantine, the first Roman emperor to convert to Christianity. According to legend, a few bone fragments and a vial of his blood were brought to Rachol in 1782, and are supposedly enshrined near the entrance. The choir stall has delicate murals of the founding saints of various religious orders. On the first floor balcony is a beautiful 16th-century two-man pipe-organ from Lisbon.

Until mid-2001, Rachol Seminary also housed the renowned Museum of Christian Art, established in 1991 by the Indian National Trust for Art and Cultural Heritage (INTACH) and the Gulbenkian Foundation of Portugal. The entire collection is currently being shifted to the Convent of St Monica in Old Goa *(see p496)*, and will be set up in the Chapel of the Weeping Cross, adjacent to the convent. Its impressive collection of 17th- and 18th-century religious objects includes silver and ivory ornaments, ornate clerical robes, processional crosses and holy water sprinklers. Particularly charming is a portable altar for travelling missionaries, complete with candle stands and a mass kit.

Margao ⑮

South Goa district (Salcete taluka).
33 km (21 miles) S of Panaji.
🚶 78,500. 🚇 🚌 ℹ️ GTDC Tourist Hostel, (0832) 72 2513. 🎉 Feast of the Holy Spirit (Dec).

MARGAO (MADGAON), Goa's second most important city after Panaji, is the administrative and commercial capital of the South Goa district. This bustling town also serves as the area's main trading centre for local fish and farm produce.

The town square, **Praça Jorge Barreto**, has the large, colonial Municipal Building, which houses the library on its southern side, and a popular café called Longinhos

A view of the hilltop Seminary and Church at Rachol

nearby. Just behind the Municipal Building, to the south, are Margao's lively bazaars, selling the day's catch of fish and fresh fruit and vegetables. The **Covered Market**, close by, sells just about everything, including piles of soap flakes, pulses, dried fish, pickles, spicy pork sausages, tamarind, flower garlands, jaggery and crockery. A row of shops to the north sells locally brewed wines, and the lane just outside the market has a number of cloth merchants.

Abbé de Faria Street, winding north from the town square, is lined with some well-preserved colonial mansions, and leads to Margao's old Latin Quarter. Its central square, **Largo de Igreja**, is also surrounded by colourful 18th- and 19th-century town houses, with tiled roofs, wrought-iron balconies and balustrades. In the centre of the square is a monumental, 16th-century cross, overlooked by the towering Baroque **Church of the Holy Spirit**. Built in 1565 on the site of a ravaged Hindu temple, the church and the adjoining Jesuit College of All Saints, were ransacked numerous times by Muslim raiders. While the seminary was moved to Rachol, the church was rebuilt in 1675. Its whitewashed façade is flanked by two towers topped by domes and embellished with

The red and white Municipal Building, Praça Jorge Barreto, Margao

Monumental cross in Largo de Igreja

lanterns, though its side walls have been left unusually bare of lime-plaster. The grand interior has a stucco ceiling, a gilded pulpit decorated with carvings of the apostles, a Rococo altar, and elegant Baroque altarpieces in the transepts.

Just behind the church, Agostinho Lorenço Street leads east to the imposing mansion called **Sat Burnzam Gor**, or "Seven Gables" (see p506), named after the original seven gables and pyramidal crests on its roof. It is the only surviving example of a house with pyramidal roofs in Goa. Built in 1790 by Ignacio da Silva from his earnings as the viceroy's secretary, the huge, impressive salons are filled with richly carved rosewood furniture and priceless porcelain, and its private chapel was the first that was permitted in Goa. From the intersection lying

east of the church, a road winds up to **Monte Hill**. Although one cannot enter the tiny chapel at the top, the views across Margao's rooftops of the entire southern coast are spectacular.

⚏ Sat Burnzam Gor
☏ *(0832) 73 5728.* **◲** *Only by prior appointment; contact Mrs de Silva.*

ENVIRONS: The pretty villages around Margao have a number of colonial country mansions, dating to the prosperous period from the 18th to the 19th centuries, when local landlords began to profit from Portugal's control over the maritime trade routes from Africa to Malacca (in Malaysia). Many of these homes were also owned by Goans, who held high posts in the Portuguese government and were granted land in exchange for their services.

Loutolim, 10 km (6 miles) to the northeast, was once an important Portuguese administrative centre, and has a cluster of stately homes, all situated fairly close to the main church square. The Goa Tourism office, and Classical Interlude, (0834) 27 7022, which operates from the Casa dos Mirandos, can organize visits to these buildings. **Chandor**, 13 km (8 miles) east of Margao, has the palatial Braganza house, Goa's largest private dwelling (see pp508–9). **Chinchinim**, 10 km (6 miles) south of Margao, and **Benaulim**, 6 km (4 miles) southwest of Margao, also have fine mansions, with typical Goan *balcaos* (porches) and terracotta-tiled sloping roofs.

Fresh prawns, sardines, mackerel and salmon, Margao bazaar

Goa's Colonial Mansions

GOA'S COUNTRYSIDE is dotted with grand colonial mansions, built by the wealthy land-owning Goan gentry, who prospered in the 18th and 19th centuries. The homes of these local aristocrats were built in the traditional style of the region, with central courtyards, deep porches and window shutters

Chinese vase

made of oyster-shell. The furniture and interior decor, however, were largely European. Today, the Belgian chandeliers, Venetian cut-glass and gilded mirrors, Baroque-style rosewood furniture and Chinese porcelain, displayed inside, provide a fascinating picture of the tastes and lifestyles of a vanished era.

Oyster-shell window shutters *line the façade of Sat Burnzam Gor ("Seven Gables") in Margao. A unique feature of 16th- and 17th-century Goan architecture, oyster shells were used in place of glass panes and effectively kept out the heat and glare.*

A typical pyramidal **balcao**, *or porch, graces the entrance of the Figueredo House in Loutolim. Chairs were often placed under the* balcao, *as it was customary to socialize at the front door.*

This antique rosewood carving *from Goa's grandest mansion, Braganza House in Chandor (see pp508–509), is a typical example of Indo-Portuguese Baroque.*

European-style salons, *such as the regal ballroom in the Dr Alvaro Loyola Furtado Mansion in Chinchinim, built in 1833, have crystal chandeliers and elegant furniture.*

Carved antique furniture at the Casa dos Mirandos

WHERE TO SEE GOAN HOUSES

Loutolim has four houses of interest – Salvador da Costa House, Roque Caetan Miranda House, Figueredo House and Casa dos Mirandos, which is the finest. **Margao** has the Sat Burnzam Gor, **Chinchinim** has the Loyola Furtado Mansion, and **Chandor** has the Braganza House. For more details see page 505.

Colva ⑰

South Goa district (Salcete taluka).
6 km (4 miles) W of Margao.
ⓘ GTDC Tourist Cottage, (0832) 73
7753. 🎭 Fama de Menino Jesus (Oct).

COLVA'S PROXIMITY to Margao makes it an ideal summer retreat for Margao's residents. It is one of South Goa's oldest and most developed beach resorts, and its 25-km (16-mile) long sandy beach, from the Mormugao peninsula in the north to Mobor in the south, is the longest uninterrupted stretch in the state.

Today, Colva draws vast numbers of visitors, who spend the day enjoying the lively atmosphere of its many beach shacks, set high on stilts and backed by shady palms. These serve delicious grilled lobster and other seafood specialities. Numerous top-end and mid-range hotels stand on the main beach road, while the southern extremities have more pristine stretches of sand. Fisherfolk haul in their

A cheerful waiter, Mobor

catch on the beach front, which is also the venue for full-moon beach rave parties.

Standing a short distance from the sea, Colva's **Church of Our Lady of Mercy**, built in 1630, has an attractive Baroque interior and houses the famous statue of Menino (baby) Jesus, holding an orb and a flag, revered for its miraculous healing powers.

ENVIRONS: Majorda, 7 km (4 miles) north of Colva, has a wide beach dotted with luxury hotels. **Bogmalo Beach**, 20 km (12 miles) northwest of Colva, is a popular venue for wind-surfing.

Tourism has spilled over from Colva to the quiet village of **Benaulim**, 2 km (1.3 miles) south, whose roads are lined with small guesthouses, restaurants and bars. **Varca Beach**, 5 km (3 miles) further south, has many plush hotels, and a parish church with an imposing façade.

Cavelossim ⑱

South Goa district (Salcete taluka).
15 km (9 miles) S of Margao.

A FAVOURITE with Indian celebrities, Cavelossim has an enchanting 2-km (1.3-mile) stretch of sand. It also has a golf course, luxury resorts and excellent seafood restaurants, such as the Seaways Bar. The ornate **Church of the Holy Cross**, is situated in a pretty square.

ENVIRONS: Mobor, 5 km (3 miles) south of Colva, is an idyllic spot, with its backdrop of hills and the pretty fishing village of **Betul** nestling near the Sal river. The Leela Beach Resort is located here. **Cabo da Rama** ("Cape Rama"), the promontory just south of Betul, is named after Rama, hero of the *Ramayana*, who supposedly hid here during his 14-year exile *(see p27)*. It has the ruins of a Hindu fortress that fell to the Portuguese in 1763.

A thatch-roofed beach shack, Palolem Beach

Palolem ⑲

South Goa district (Salcete taluka).
37 km (23 miles) S of Margao.

FAMOUS FOR ITS spectacular sunsets, this bay is enclosed by a rocky outcrop at one end, and Canacona Island, a good camping site, at the other. Palolem's remote location, away from the crowded beaches of central Goa, makes it an ideal for a quiet holiday. A special attraction are the boat rides offered by fishermen, who take visitors out to sea for dolphin-watching trips.

ENVIRONS: Southern Goa is for the most part isolated and unspoilt by tourism. **Agonda**, 7 km (4 miles) north of Palolem, is even quieter than its neighbour. **Galgibaga**, 8 km (5 miles) south of Palolem, has a beautiful stretch of virgin sand, shaded by eucalyptus trees rather than palms. The remote **Cotigao Wildlife Sanctuary**, 18 km (11 miles) west of Palolem, is worth visiting for its tranquil beauty.

Visitors cycling on the sands at Colva, Goa's longest beach

Braganza House ⓰

Chinese blue porcelain dish

T̲HE AWESOME SCALE̲ of Braganza House, and the magnificence of its interior, make it Goa's grandest colonial mansion. This 17th-century building is still occupied by two branches of the Braganza family. The descendants of Antonio Elzario Sant'Anna Pereira occupy the east wing, while Francisco Xavier de Menezes Braganza's descendants live in the west wing. Both men received royal titles and a coat of arms from the king of Portugal in the late 19th century. The top floors of their private apartments have the splendid ballroom, library and chapel, and fine collections of 18th-century furniture and Chinese porcelain.

Dining Hall
A long table fills the first floor dining hall of this sprawling mansion.

★ The Chapel
The Baroque-style chapel has a diamond-encrusted fingernail of St Francis Xavier on its altar.

Guest Bedroom
A large rosewood four-poster bed dominates the bedroom. At its foot is a rosewood two-seater.

The East Wing
is owned by the Braganza Pereiras.

★ The Ballroom
A rosewood armchair with the Braganza coat of arms, and a gilded mirror are in the mansion's grandest room. The walls as well as the floors are of marble, and chandeliers hang from its floral-patterned zinc ceiling.

STAR FEATURES

★ The Chapel

★ The Ballroom

★ The Hallway

Menezes Braganza Salon
A collection of exquisite Chinese porcelain is displayed in one of the salons, where a large vase takes pride of place.

Portrait of Francisco Xavier de Menezes Braganza
A portrait of the grandfather of renowned journalist, Luis de Menezes Braganza (see p487), hangs in the ballroom of the west wing.

The West Wing is occupied by the Menezes Braganzas.

The Library
has Goa's finest private collection, with over 5,000 leather-bound books.

Entrance

0 metres   10
0 yards   10

★ The Hallway
A long and elegantly furnished hallway lies just behind the façade of the house. It is lined with 28 bay windows and overlooks a well-maintained garden.

Stairway
The monumental double staircase forms the core of the house, connecting the lower entrance level to the furnished top floors.

KARNATAKA

XTENDING from the Arabian Sea and the fertile forested ridges of the Western Ghats, with their thriving plantations of coffee, spices and fruit, to the drier, boulder-strewn region of the Deccan Plateau, Karnataka's scenic diversity is striking. Equally varied are its historical monuments. These range from the 6th–8th century Hindu temples at Badami, Pattadakal and Aihole, the earliest to be found in South India, to Tipu Sultan's 18th-century, European-style island fort at Srirangapattana, and the extravagantly turreted, early 20th-century palace in Mysore. Other sights include the superb temples at Halebid and Belur, the colossal Gommateshvara monolith at Sravana Belgola and the magnificent ruins of Hampi, the site of the great citadel of Vijayanagar. In northern Karnataka are the medieval citadels of the Deccan sultans at Bijapur, Gulbarga and Bidar, their walls enclosing mosques, audience halls and royal tombs.

SIGHTS AT A GLANCE

Towns, Cities & Districts

Bangalore ❶
Barkur ⓭
Belgaum ⓴
Bhatkal ⓮
Bidar ㉖
Bijapur ㉔
Gadag ⓳
Gokarna ⓯
Gulbarga ㉕
Kodagu ❻
Mangalore ⓫
Mysore ❺

Historic Sites

Aihole ㉓
Badami ㉑
Belur ❿
Chitradurga ⓱
Halebid ❾
Hampi ⓲
Pattadakal ㉒
Srirangapattana ❹
Talakad ❷

Mahbubnagar

Melkote ❼
Somnathpur ❸
Sravana Belgola ❽
Sringeri ⓰
Udipi ⓬

KEY

✈ International airport

☒ Domestic airport

━ National highway

━ Major road

═ Minor road

━ Major railway

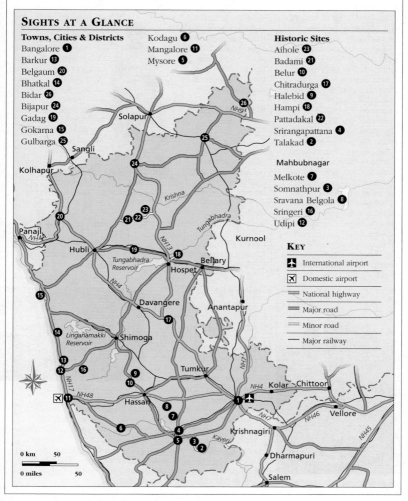

◁ **A mendicant at a shrine beside the Tungabhadra river, Hampi**

Bangalore ❶

Stone carving, Museum

OFTEN DESCRIBED AS Asia's Silicon Valley because of its thriving information technology industry, Bangalore is India's fifth-largest and fastest-growing city. Until its high-tech boom began in the late 1980s, it was known as the Garden City, with greenery flourishing in its pleasant, temperate climate. Today, with a growing population of young professionals, it has acquired a vibrant, cosmopolitan air. Bangalore was founded in the 16th century by a local chieftain, Kempe Gowda, but derives its name from the Kannada word *benda kaluru*, or "boiled beans", which an old woman gave a 10th-century Hoysala king when he turned up hungry at her doorstep.

🏛 Vidhana Soudha

W Vidhana Vidhi. ⬤ to the public.
Built of granite and porphyry, this imposing building houses the Secretariat and the State Legislature of Karnataka. Constructed in 1956 after the transfer of power from the ruling Wodeyar dynasty to the central government, it was designed by Kengal Hanumanthaiah, the then chief minister, who intended it to "reflect the power and dignity of the people". It is capped by a 20-m (66-ft) dome, which is surmounted by the four-headed Ashokan lion, symbol of the Indian state. With Rajasthani *jharokhas*, Indo-Saracenic pillars and other decorative elements, the Vidhana Soudha exemplifies the Neo-Dravidian style of post-Independence Bangalore. The woodwork inside is noteworthy, especially the sandalwood door to the Cabinet Room, and the Speaker's Chair made of rosewood from Mysore. The building looks spectacular on Sunday evenings when it is beautifully illuminated.

🏛 Attara Kacheri

E Vidhana Vidhi.
🕐 Mon–Fri.
This graceful, two-storeyed building with Corinthian columns, was completed in 1864 and housed the Public Offices from 1868 until 1956. These were later moved to the Vidhana Soudha, and this building became the High Court. On the ceiling of its Central Hall is a portrait of Sir Mark Cubbon, commissioner of Mysore from 1834 to 1861. Behind the building is an equestrian statue of him by Baron Marochetti.

♣ Cubbon Park

Cantonment. 🕐 daily. 🍴
Laid out in 1864 by Richard Sankey, the chief engineer of Mysore, and named in honour of the commissioner, Cubbon Park extends over 135 ha (334 acres). Its partly formal landscaping imaginatively integrates natural rock outcroppings with groves of trees and giant bamboos.

The park is liberally dotted with statues, such as that of the 19th-century ruler Chamarajendra Wodeyar (1868–94), overlooking the pond near an octagonal, cast-iron bandstand. There are also marble statues of Queen Victoria and Edward VII. In the middle of the park, a red-painted, Neo-Classical building known as the **Sheshadri Iyer Memorial**, houses a public library.

Chamarajendra Wodeyar

🏛 Government Museum

Kasturba Gandhi Rd.
📞 (080) 286 4483.
🕐 Tue–Sun. 🎟
Venkatappa Art Gallery
🕐 Thu–Tue. 🎟
Established in 1866, this is one of the oldest museums in the country. Housed in a

---

GARDEN CITY

The Cantonment in Bangalore was established in 1809, to house British troops quartered here during the 19th century. With its orderly streets, houses with characteristic "monkey top" eaves, and its lawns, trees, flowers and shrubbery, Bangalore was eventually christened the "Garden City of India". Two large parks, Cubbon Park and Lalbagh, along with numerous smaller ones such as the Kensington Gardens, act as the lungs of this verdant city. These gardens provide a welcome retreat from Bangalore's crowded streets and give a refreshing sense of space. The city is particularly charming in January and August when dahlias, marigolds and roses bloom in abundance.

A corner of Cubbon Park

The magnificent Vidhana Soudha, housing the Karnataka Secretariat

red stucco Neo-Classical building with Corinthian columns, it has 18 sections, with a fine collection of jewellery, miniature paintings, sculpture, artifacts from Mohenjodaro, and 5,000-year-old neolithic relics.

The **Venkatappa Art Gallery**, named after an early 20th-century artist patronized by the Wodeyar rulers of Mysore, forms one wing of this museum. It has watercolours and paintings made in the Mysore style.

Mysore painting from Venkatappa Art Gallery

These works still retain a greenish coating, imparted by a finishing rub with jade. The gallery also has a collection of leather puppets made of deer- and goat-skin (see p535), and fine sculptures from the Satvahana, Hoysala and Vijayanagar periods.

🏠 St Mark's Cathedral

Mahatma Gandhi Rd. ◯ Tue–Sun.
This simple, Neo-Classical cathedral was completed in 1812 and consecrated by the Bishop of Calcutta in 1816. An elegant, cream-coloured structure, it has an imposing portico in front and an apsidal recess at the rear. A shallow dome marks the internal crossing.

🏛 Bangalore Palace

N of Vidhana Soudha.
📞 (080) 336 0818 for permission to visit.
Built in 1880 at the exorbitant cost of one million rupees, the Bangalore Palace was modelled on Windsor Castle, complete with fortified towers and turreted parapets. It stands amid undulating lawns, partly converted into a formal garden with axial paths.

Spread over 13,700 sq m (147,466 sq ft), the palace fell into disrepair after 1949 when it was at the centre of an ownership dispute between the government and the ruling Wodeyars. It has since been restored to the Wodeyars and is now rented out as a popular venue for functions such as weddings and music concerts, and film shoots. No Kannada movie is considered complete if a scene is not shot here.

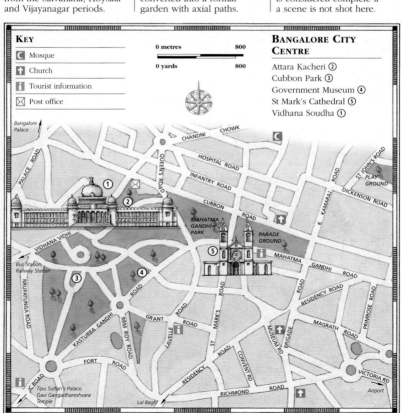

KEY

🄲 Mosque

🏠 Church

ℹ Tourist information

✉ Post office

0 metres   800
0 yards   800

BANGALORE CITY CENTRE

Attara Kacheri ②
Cubbon Park ③
Government Museum ④
St Mark's Cathedral ⑤
Vidhana Soudha ①

Exploring Old Bangalore

IN SPITE OF RAPID DEVELOPMENT, vestiges of the city's historic past are still found in the streets of Old Bangalore, south of the city centre. In contrast to the relentless modernization of the rest of Bangalore, this area contains monuments from the period of the Gowdas to that of Haider Ali and Tipu Sultan, and bears witness to the city's history from the 16th to the 19th centuries.

♛ Tipu Sultan's Palace
Albert Victor Rd.
◯ Sat–Thu. 📷
Within the original citadel, a mud-brick fort built by Kempe Gowda in 1537, lies Tipu Sultan's Palace, dating from about 1790. Made mostly out of wood with finely embellished balconies, pillars and arches, this two-storeyed structure, a replica of the Daria Daulat Bagh in Srirangapattana (see p516), served as a summer retreat of Tipu Sultan. He endearingly called it Rashk-e-Jannat, or the "Envy of Heaven". Although now dilapidated, it is still a hauntingly atmospheric place. While the palace retains the original elegant teak pillars, most of the painted decorations have been destroyed.

The palace housed the public administrative offices from 1831, until they were shifted to the Attara Kacheri in 1868 (see p512).

Dahlia bloom, Lalbagh

The Venkataramana-swamy Temple, nearby, dates from the early 18th century and was built by the Wodeyar kings.

♣ Lalbagh
Lalbagh Fort Rd.
◯ daily. 📷 🍴
📷 Flower Show (Jan & Aug).
Regarded as one of the most richly diverse botanical gardens in South Asia, Lalbagh, in the southern part of the city, was laid out by Haider Ali in 1740. Spread over 97 ha (240 acres) of parkland, many of its tropical and subtropical plants were brought here by Haider Ali's son, Tipu Sultan. Later, John Cameron, the Gardens' Superintendent in the 1870s, imported several more rare species from Kew Gardens in London. Cameron was also responsible for initiating work on Lalbagh's famous Glass House, modelled on London's Crystal Palace and conceived as a venue for horticultural shows.

Surrounded by *champaka* trees and pencil cedars, the Glass House has played host to several visiting dignitaries. An Annual Flower Show is still held here.

The entrance to the park is marked by an equestrian statue of Chamaraja Wodeyar of Mysore. Another popular attraction is the surreal Floral Clock, surrounded by Snow White and the seven dwarfs; this was a gift from Hindustan Machine Tools, leading Indian manufacturers of watches.

🛕 Gavi Gangadhareshvara Temple
W of Lalbagh. ◯ daily. 📷 Makar Sankranti (Jan).
One of Bangalore's oldest temples, the Gavi Gangadhareshvara Temple was built inside a natural cave in Gavipuram by Kempe Gowda in the 16th century. Legend has it that Kempe Gowda built this temple in gratitude after being released from his five-year imprisonment by Rama Raya.

The highlights here are the granite pillars, two of which support huge discs representing the sun and the moon, while the other two are topped by a Nandi and a trident. Devotees gather here during the Makar Sankranti festival to witness a unique phenomenon – the evening sun's rays passing between Nandi's horns and falling directly on the linga inside the cave.

The spacious, 19th-century Glass House at Lalbagh, with its intricate cast-iron frame

The Glitter of Gold

THE ANCIENT SEERS of India referred to gold by many names – synonyms for life, longevity, and beauty. Indians considered this metal auspicious and believed that wearing gold ornaments would ensure a long life. Craftsmen traditionally drew inspiration for their designs and motifs from nature, and also from the splendid temples with their ornately carved façades. The Kolar and Hatti mines in Karnataka were the repositories of the largest deposits of gold in ancient India. Due to the high price of gold, craftsmen mastered the technique of beating a minuscule quantity of gold into thin sheets and then transforming them into exquisite jewellery.

A gold *tali* pendant

Bangles

Earrings

Hair ornament

DECORATIVE ORNAMENTS

Gold ornaments were designed to be worn on practically every part of the body, from the crown of the head to the tips of the toes, to decorate and protect the wearer. Plants, animals and astral bodies inspired many of the shapes.

A Lady, late 19th-century painting by Raja Ravi Varma showing a woman in her finery

A large cobra head, set with rubies, emeralds and diamonds and edged with emerald beads, is tied to a plait to prevent it from unravelling. The snake form, as a symbol of fertility, occurs in many ornaments.

Temple deities are often adorned with ritual ornaments. These pieces display some of the forms and techniques used by ancient Indian jewellers, and show the evolution of their craft.

Pavan Sara, a necklace made of coins, is a piece of jewellery found all over the country. As an instrument of savings, the coins were redeemed for cash when the need arose.

Devotees congregating at the Vaidyeshvara Temple, Talakad

Talakad ❷

Mysore district. 45 km (28 miles) SE of Mysore. 🚌 🖼 *Panchalinga Darshana (at intervals of 4–12 years).*

THE HISTORIC CITY of Talakad, situated on the north bank of the Kaveri river, now lies partly buried under shifting sand dunes. From the 5th to the 10th centuries it was the capital of the Ganga dynasty *(see p522)*, but only two modest temples survive from that period. The largest edifice at this site is the 12th-century **Vaidyeshvara Temple**, dedicated to Shiva. Nearby is the more modest Kirti Narayana Temple, where the 3-m (10-ft) high image of Vishnu is still worshipped. A festival, the Panchalinga Darshana, is celebrated here at intervals ranging from four to 12 years.

Somnathpur ❸

Mysore district. 36 km (22 miles) E of Mysore. 🚌

ONE OF THE FINEST representations of Hoysala architecture *(see p524)*, the **Keshava Temple** is the highlight of this obscure little village. Built in 1268 by Somnatha, a general of King Narasimha III, its design is attributed to the celebrated sculptor and architect,

Janakacharya. The temple is accessed from the east, through a doorway with an open portico, where a slab records Somnatha's generous donations. Unlike the other Hoysala temples at Halebid and Belur *(see p523)*, this is well preserved and has complete towers. The temple has three star-shaped shrines that lead off a pillared hall; both the shrines and the hall stand on a high plinth. The basements of the inner sanctums and hall are profusely carved with animal and floral patterns, while images of deities under foliage canopies occupy the walls above. The interior of the hall is remarkable for its splendid columns and the elaborate ceilings which display lobed motifs, pendant buds and looped bands. The three shrines house fully-modelled, life-size images of Krishna playing the flute (south) and Janardana,

Insignia engraved on a horse-cart, Srirangapattana

a form of Vishnu (north). The Krishna image in the western shrine is a recent replacement of the original.

Also in Somnathpur is the ruined granite **Panchalinga Temple**, built in 1268 as a memorial in honour of Somnatha's family.

🖼 **Keshava Temple**
🕐 *daily.*

Srirangapattana ❹

Mandya district. 16 km (10 miles) N of Mysore. 🚉 *from Mysore.* 🚌 *from Mysore. Autos and cycles available.*

KNOWN TO the British as Seringapatam, this island fortress in the Kaveri river enjoys historical significance as the site of the battles between the British and Tipu Sultan, the "Tiger of Mysore". The British finally stormed the citadel in 1799, killing Tipu and consolidating their power in South India. Today, none of the structures within the fort survive, barring the bridges across the two arms of the Kaveri river, from which the bathing ghats and the ramparts can be seen.

To the east and the south, a broad moat surrounds the polygonal bastions and turreted parapets constructed by the French engineers employed by Tipu. The Mysore Gate and Elephant Gate, to the south, are flanked by guardrooms. Sultan Battery, the dungeons where Tipu used to keep British prisoners, is to the north; nearby is the Water Gate, where Tipu was killed.

The **Sri Ranganatha Temple**, after which the island is named, is a large complex that was substantially restored in the 19th century. The inner sanctum enshrines an image of the reclining Vishnu and is

Representations of Hindu deities at the Keshava Temple

Mural depicting a battle at the Daria Daulat Bagh, Srirangapattana

approached through pillared halls and an open courtyard with a gilded lamp column.

At the fort's eastern end is the **Jami Masjid**, erected by Tipu in 1787. It has an elevated prayer chamber with a tall minaret on either side.

The **Daria Daulat Bagh**, Tipu Sultan's summer palace, built in 1787, stands in the middle of a beautiful garden near the river, a short distance south of the fort. Each of its sides has three arched openings in the centre and the whole palace is surrounded by a pillared verandah. The east and west walls of the verandah are both covered with murals, restored in 1855. On the west wall are scenes of battle, one of which illustrates Haidar Ali's victory over the British at Pollilur (1780), while the east wall depicts courtly scenes. The carved woodwork and

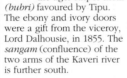

Snake shrine, Srirangapattana

the elegant painted floral designs on the wall reveal Mughal influence. The palace is now a museum, with paintings, maps and Tipu memorabilia on display. Further south, past the Church of the Abbé Dubois (where the learned French Jesuit priest and author lived between 1799 and 1823) and the British Cemetery, is the **Gumbaz** – the tombs of Haidar Ali and Tipu Sultan. The walls of the chambers are decorated with the tiger-stripes motif (*bubri*) favoured by Tipu. The ebony and ivory doors were a gift from the viceroy, Lord Dalhousie, in 1855. The *sangam* (confluence) of the two arms of the Kaveri river is further south.

🏛 **Daria Daulat Bagh Museum**
 (08326) 52 023. ⬜ *Sat–Thu.* 🈲

(see p531)

FESTIVALS IN KARNATAKA

Banashankari Temple Fair *(Jan/Feb)*, Badami. This 20-day festival combines religious rites with the excitement of a funfair. An annual cattle fair, specializing in white bulls, is held at the same time.

Hoysala Mahotsava *(Mar)*, Belur and Halebid. A festival of dance and music unfolds against the spectacular backdrop of these historic temples.

Royal Dasara *(Sep/Oct)*, Mysore. This grand, 10-day festival, known as Dussehra in North India, celebrates the victory of the goddess Chamundeshvari (Durga) over the buffalo demon, Mahishasura; it owes its origin to the Mahanavami festival (*see p531*). A royal elephant carrying an image of the goddess leads a splendid display of military bands, sports and parades, while religious ceremonies worship the elephant, the horse and weapons such as the State sword. Firework displays, concerts and wrestling matches liven up the evenings. A descendant of the former ruling Wodeyars plays a pivotal part and the famous golden throne, generally not on display, is used for the rituals.

Hampi Festival *(Nov)*, Hampi. Well-known dancers and musicians from around the country participate in this lively event.

TIPU SULTAN: "TIGER OF MYSORE"

Portrait of Tipu Sultan (1750–99)

Tipu Sultan, the ruler of Mysore, stands head and shoulders above the many Indian rulers who were his contemporaries. He was a shrewd diplomat, expert soldier, excellent scholar and accomplished poet, and his military and administrative skills were complemented by his dream of a modern industrial state. The latter found expression in his cultivation of European contacts and employment of French engineers. The Sultan's main adversaries were the British who had conquered part of his father Haider Ali's territory and wealth in the first two Mysore Wars (1767–9 and 1780–84). Tipu waged two further wars against them, culminating in the fall of Srirangapattana in May 1799, where he died fighting.

Caparisoned elephant at the Dasara celebrations, Mysore

Mysore: Amba Vilas Palace

THE MAGNIFICENT Amba Vilas Palace, a treasure house of exquisite carvings and works of art from all over the world, was built by the Wodeyar rulers. The main block of this Indo-Saracenic building, with domes, turrets, arches and colonnades, was designed by Henry Irving in 1897. It replaced an earlier structure that was destroyed by a fire. During weekends and festivals, thousands of light bulbs enliven the palace's stern grey exterior.

Public Durbar Hall
The richly decorated gold-and-turquoise Durbar Hall, on the second floor, exudes royal splendour. On its rear wall are a series of paintings by Raja Ravi Varma.

Amba Vilas Hall
The Private Durbar Hall is smaller than, but as sumptuous as, the Public Hall. It is roofed with stained glass imported from Glasgow. The central part of its ceiling is supported by cast-iron columns and arches.

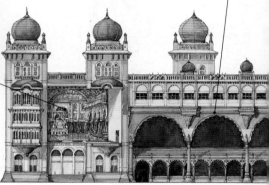

Mysore **❺**

Mysore district. 138 km (86 miles) SW of Bangalore. 🏃 742,500. 🚋 🚌 🛈 *Karnataka Tourism, Irwin Rd, (0821) 44 2096.* 🎭 *Vairamudi Festival (Mar/Apr), Feast of St Philomena (Aug), Royal Dasara (Sep/Oct).*

SITUATED AMONG fertile fields, and skirted by wooded hills, Mysore was the capital of the Wodeyar rulers, who were governors of southern Karnataka under the Vijaya-nagar kings. The Wodeyar dynasty ruled almost uninterrupted from 1399 until Independence, except for the 38-year rule of the Muslim warlord Haider Ali and his son, Tipu Sultan, in the 18th century *(see p517)*. Modern Mysore is the creation of Tipu Sultan who, in 1793, levelled the old city and built the present town. Today, Mysore is an important cultural centre, with the largest university in Karnataka. It is also renowned for its ivory work, silk-weaving, sandalwood incense and carvings.

Several elegant public buildings, erected under the Wodeyars, enhance the wide, tree-lined streets. In the heart of the city is the **Amba Vilas Palace**. To its west is **Jagan-mohan Palace**, built in 1902 to mark the coronation ceremony of Krishnaraja III. It partly obscures a Neo-Classical structure, now the **Chama-rajendra Art Gallery**, which houses an interesting collection of disparate objects including antique furniture, musical instruments, ceramics and ivory. On its top floor is a splendid collection of musical instruments, as well as magnificent paintings by the renowned 19th-century artist from Kerala, Raja Ravi Verma.

Near the northwestern corner of Amba Vilas Palace is **Krishnaraja Circle**, where

The crouching Nandi on Chamundi Hill

View of the Amba Vilas Palace, Mysore

VISITORS' CHECKLIST

Ramvilas Rd. (0821) 42
2620. daily.
Royal Dasara (Sep/Oct).

Golden Throne
*Originally made of fig-wood overlaid
with ivory, this jewelled throne was
later plated with gold and silver. It
is now brought out only during
the Dasara celebrations.*

Seating gallery for
viewing the annual
Mysore Dasara pro-
cession (see p517).

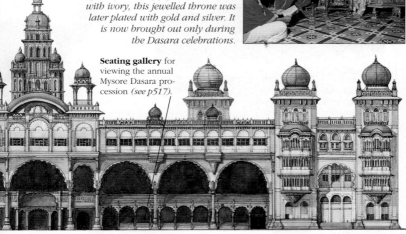

a statue of Krishnaraja Wodeyar stands beneath a pavilion.
The **Sayyaji Rao Road** that
leads out from this circle is
the principal shopping centre
of the town. A short distance
away is the Government
House, the seat of the British
Residents from 1805. Nearby,
the **Cathedral of St Philomena**, with a stained-glass
interior, is a new Neo-Gothic
structure, completed in 1959.

In the western part of the
city is the Neo-Classical **Man-
asa Gangotri**, the campus of
Mysore University. The
Oriental Research Institute
here houses a collection of
Sanskrit manuscripts, while
the **Folklore Museum** has
one of the most important
ethnographic collections of
South Indian toys, puppets
and household objects, as
well as two wooden chariots.

On the way to **Chamundi
Hill**, 3 km (2 miles) southeast
of Mysore, is **Lalitha Mahal
Palace**, built in 1930. Formerly a private royal guest house,
it is now a hotel (see p712).
About halfway up the hill is
the Nandi monolith, dating to
1659. Carved out of a single
boulder, it is 7.5 m (25 ft)
long and 5 m (16 ft) high.
The richly decorated bull is
depicted crouching. The
Chamundeshvari Temple,
at the summit of the hill, was
built in the 17th century by
the Wodeyars and was later
refurbished. It houses a
beautifully decorated idol of
Chamundeshvari, the family
deity of the Wodeyar kings.

ENVIRONS: The picturesque
Brindavan Gardens are 16
km (10 miles) to the north of
the city. This popular picnic

spot was laid out below the
Krishnarajasagar Dam by
Krishnaraja Wodeyar. Three
times a week the numerous
fountains are illuminated with
multi-coloured lights.

Cathedral of St Philomena

Wildlife Sanctuaries of Karnataka

THE NILGIRI Biosphere Reserve, encompassing six contiguous wildlife sanctuaries, spans the states of Karnataka, Kerala and Tamil Nadu. Created to protect the extraordinary biodiversity of the last surviving tracts of tropical evergreen and deciduous forests of the Western Ghats, it includes the area over which the

Heron

notorious sandalwood smuggler and bandit, Veerapan, holds sway.

This reserve, along with the adjacent Mudumalai Sanctuary *(see p604)*, forms one of the most important migratory corridors for animals such as the Asian elephant and the Indian bison. These parks are within convenient reach of Bangalore *(see pp512–3)* and Mysore *(see pp518–9)*.

The Ranganthittoo Bird Sanctuary *covers 540 sq km (209 sq miles) of riverine islands in the middle of the Kaveri river and attracts a large number of water birds during the nesting season, especially from June to November.*

Bandipur, *declared a wildlife sanctuary in 1931 by the then Maharaja of Mysore, has many* chausingha *(four horned antelope), and is also a Project Tiger Reserve* (see p289). *It spreads over 875 sq km (338 sq miles).*

The BRT Wildlife Sanctuary, *east of the Nilgiri Biosphere Reserve, is a corridor between the Western and Eastern Ghats. Covering an area of 540 sq km (209 sq miles), it supports a variety of birdlife, including storks.*

The Nagarhole Wildlife Sanctuary's *profusion of rivers and swampy grasslands keep it green all year. Established in 1983, the park has 645 sq km (249 sq miles) of deciduous vegetation. Its wildlife includes the bonnet macaque.*

The Kabini Reservoir, *separating Bandipur from Nagarhole, offers fine views. The Kabini River Lodge nearby is an excellent place for sighting wildlife, and a good place to stay* (see p712).

LOCATOR MAP

☐ *Wildlife Sanctuaries*

Coffee plantation in Madikeri

Kodagu ⑥

Kodagu district. 100 km (62 miles) S of
Mysore. 🚌 ℹ️ *Karnataka Tourism,
PWD Bldg, Mangalore Rd, (08272) 25
648.* 📷 *Keil Poldu (Sep), Huthri (Nov).*

PICTURESQUELY set amid the
forested mountains of the
Western Ghats, the district of
Kodagu (or Coorg) was an
independent state until it was
incorporated into the newly
formed state of Karnataka in
1956. **Madikeri**, the district
headquarters, situated 1,500
m (4,921 ft) above sea level
and surrounded by rolling
coffee and orange plantations,
is a charming hill town, and a
convenient base from which
to explore Kodagu.

Madikeri (or Mercara) was
once the capital of the Hindu
Lingayat kings, who ruled for
over 200 years from 1600,
except for a brief period
when Tipu Sultan seized
power. The **Fort**, at the centre
of the town, was built by the
third Lingayat king in 1812.
Within its stone ramparts,
it contains the simple,
unpretentious palace of the
Lingayat rulers, along with a
temple, an old church, a
museum and the local prison.

The famous **Omkareshvara
Shiva Temple**, situated in a
hollow east of the Fort, was
built by Linga Raja II in 1820
and dedicated to Vishnu and
Shiva. The temple complex
consists of brick buildings in
the Indo-Saracenic style set in

courtyards surrounded by
pillared verandahs. Other
notable monuments in
Madikeri are the **Royal
Tombs** of Raja Dodda Vira,
his wife and his son, Linga
Raja II. Curiously, these
display a distinct Islamic
influence, with onion-
shaped domes, minarets
and trellis work.

Kodagu remains pleasantly
cool all year round, and
the hills are at their most
lush after the heavy mon-
soon showers when they
make for delightful hikes.
The walk up to **Abbey
Falls**, 8 km (5 miles) from
Madikeri, is popular and
takes trekkers through
forests and coffee
plantations. Kodagu is
renowned for its sprawling
coffee plantations, first introduced in the mid-19th century
by the British. The Kodava
people bought back their land
after Independence, but
several estates still retain their
British names. Kodagu
produces some of the world's
finest varieties of mild coffee;
in fact, it is Karnataka's
richest district because it
accounts for the majority of
coffee exports from the state.
Coffee bushes are grown in
the benevolent shade of large
trees such as oak and rosewood, and in mixed plan-
tations with crops of oranges,
pepper vines and cardamom.

Nisargadhama, 27 km
(17 miles) from Madikeri, is a
beautiful forest retreat on a
riverine island on the Kaveri.
The bamboo cottages built
here by the forest department
are ideal for viewing wildlife.

Talakaveri, 45 km (28
miles) southwest of Madikeri,
at an altitude of 1,276 m (4,186
ft), is the source of the Kaveri,
one of India's seven sacred
rivers *(see p600)*; there is a
small shrine built around the
spring. At **Bhagamandala**,
36 km (22 miles) southwest of
Madikeri, the Kaveri meets its
two tributaries, Kanike and
Sujoythi. Several shrines dot
the area near the confluence –
also the site of the striking
Bhandeshvara temple, built in
the Kerala style *(see p21)*.

**The Talakaveri shrine, a place of
great religious significance**

THE KODAVAS

The people of Kodagu, known as Kodavas, are a distinct
ethnic group, and have their own language, Coorgi. The
Kodavas are proud of their martial origins and the country's armed forces have had a fair number of generals from
this community. They may no
longer live in the huge four-winged
homes called *ain mane*, but their
many traditional festivals, celebrated with great elan, still bring
them together. Coorgi weddings
are unique, in that there are no
priests and they are solemnized
by elders. The men dress in
traditional *kupyas*, or long black
coats tied at the waist by a gold-
and red-tasseled sash, while
women wear Coorgi-style saris
with pleats at the back. Their
distinctive cuisine includes
tangy pork curry served
with rice dumplings.

**A Kodava couple in
traditional dress**

Melkote ❼

Mandya district. 54 km (34 miles) N of Mysore. 🚌 🎦 *Vairamudi (Mar/Apr).*

A PICTURESQUE hill town of shrines and monasteries, Melkote is a major pilgrimage centre for devotees of Vishnu; it is also associated with Ramanuja, the renowned Hindu philosopher and social reformer who died in 1137. Ramanuja is worshipped along with Vishnu in the **Narayana Temple**, in the southern part of town. South of the temple stands a solitary gopura, while perched on the summit of a hill to the north-east of the town, is the small **Narasimha Shrine**, overlooking the large Kalyani Tank.

Daily life in Melkote still revolves around temple rituals, and the strong tradition of religious learning introduced by Ramanuja survives in its many institutions, of which the Academy of Sanskrit Research is the most famous.

Narasimha Shrine overlooking the Kalyani Tank at Melkote

Sravana Belgola ❽

Hassan district. 145 km (90 miles) W of Bangalore. 🚌 🅷 Tourist Office, (08176) 57 524. 🎦 *Mahamastakabhisheka (every 12 years; next one due in 2005).*

T HIS SMALL TOWN, situated between two granite hills, Indragiri and Chandragiri, is the most important Jain site in South India. It is dominated by the colossal 17.7-m (58-ft) high monolithic **Statue of Gommateshvara**, also known as Bahubali, son of the first Jain tirthankara *(see p396)*. On the summit of the 143-m (469-ft) high Indragiri

The head-anointing ceremony at Sravana Belgola

Hill, to the south, the statue of the naked saviour stands on an anthill, staring impassively ahead. Entwined around his legs and arms are creepers, indicating the length of time he stood immobile in meditation. An inscription at the base records its consecration in AD 981 by Chamundaraya, the powerful minister of Rajamalla IV, one of the Ganga kings.

The town, which lies at the base of the hill, has a large tank as well as a number of Jain temples *(bastis)*. Perhaps the most interesting of these is the *matha*, near the steps leading to Indragiri Hill. The walls of its courtyard have a series of vivid 18th-century murals illustrating the past and present births of Parsvanatha, the 23rd *tirthankara*, as well as scenes from the annual fair held here. Some fine Jain bronzes are displayed in the sanctuary that opens off the courtyard.

On Chandragiri Hill, to the north of the town, is another cluster of *bastis* established by the 10th–12th century Ganga kings and their powerful ministers. The **Neminatha Basti**, commissioned by Chamundaraya, enshrines an image of Neminatha, the 22nd *tirthankara*. The adjoining **Chandragupta Basti** has miniature panels carved on perforated stone screens depicting episodes from the life of Bahubali and his royal disciple, Chandragupta. A 5-m (16-ft) high sculpture of Parsvanatha, the 23rd *tirthankara*, is enshrined in another nearby *basti*.

Every 12 years, Jainism's most important festival, the spectacular Mahamastakabhisheka (head-anointing ceremony) is held here. The festival commemorates the consecration of the Bahubali monolith, and attracts thousands of monks, priests and pilgrims. A special scaffold is erected behind the statue so that priests can ritually bathe the god with milk, water from the holy rivers, ghee, saffron, sandalwood paste, vermilion and flower petals. At the last ceremony, held in 1993, a specially-hired helicopter flew overhead, showering the statue with 20 kg (44 pounds) of gold leaf, 200 litres (423 pints) of milk, marigolds and jewels, to the delight of the assembled crowds.

ENVIRONS: The village of **Kambadahalli**, 15 km (9 miles) east of Sravana Belgola, is another Jain settlement. The 10th-century Panchakuta Basti houses a trio of *tirthankaras* in three separate shrines.

A view of Chandragiri Hill above Sravana Belgola

A columned Nandi pavilion in the Hoysaleshvara Temple, Halebid

Halebid ❾

Hassan district. 220 km (137 miles) W
of Bangalore. 🚉 *Hassan, 31 km (19
miles) S of town centre, then bus or
taxi.* 🚲 *Cycles available on hire.*
ℹ️ *Tourist Office, (08172) 73 224.*

Set amid a lush agricultural
landscape ringed by distant
hills, this isolated site was the
Hoysala capital in
the 12th and 13th
centuries. While the
palace has yet to be
excavated, the
stone ramparts that
once surrounded
the city can still be
seen. Outside the
ramparts, to the
east, is the vast
tank known as
Dorasamudra,
which was also the
city's original name.
Today, the
principal attraction of Halebid
is the **Hoysaleshvara
Temple**, begun in 1121 by
King Vishnuvardhana, but
never finished. This structure
comprises a pair of identical
temples, each with its own
east-facing linga sanctuary
opening on to a hall and a
screened porch. Each temple
is also preceded by a pavilion
with a huge statue of Nandi,
the bull-vehicle of Shiva. As
the two halls are joined
together to create a spacious
columned interior, the temples
function as a single monument. The outer walls are
elevated on friezes of naturalistic and fanciful animals,
interspersed with animated
carvings of scenes from the
Ramayana and *Mahabharata*
(*see pp26–7*). Among the
finest wall panels here are
those of Shiva dancing on the

**A magnificent seated
Nandi at Halebid**

outstretched skin of the elephant demon he had slain,
Krishna playing the flute and
Krishna holding up Mount
Govardhan, on the south face
of the southern sanctuary. On
the north face of the northern
sanctuary is a a splendid
Nataraja (Shiva as the Lord of
Dance) and a panel depicting
a crouching multi-armed and -
headed Ravana
creeping up on
Shiva and Parvati
seated on Mount
Kailasa. Set on the
plinth on which
the temple is
raised is a three-
dimensional com-
position of a
warrior plunging
his sword into a
leonine beast with
a ferocious head,
interpreted as the
dynastic symbol of
the martial Hoysala rulers. The
landscaped garden in front of
the Hoysaleshvara Temple
serves as an **Archaeological
Museum**. Among the panels
exhibited here is one showing
a majestic seated Ganesha. A
short distance south of the
complex is a group of 12th-
century Jain *bastis*.

🏛 **Archaeological Museum**
⭕ *Sat–Thu.* 🚫

Belur ❿

Hassan district. 14 km (9 miles) SW of
Halebid. 🚉 *Hassan, 34 km (21 miles)
SE of town centre, then bus or taxi.*
🚌 ℹ️ *Tourist Office, (08177) 22 209.*

One of the jewels of South
Indian architecture, Belur's
Chennakeshava Temple was
built in 1117 by Vishnuvardhan
to commemorate the Hoysala
triumph over the Cholas (*see
pp46–7*). At the end of the
town's main street, a towered
gopura, erected by the kings
of Vijayanagar (*see p530*) in
the 16th century, marks the
entrance to the temple. Inside
is a spacious paved courtyard,
surrounded by subsidiary
shrines and colonnades. In
the centre is the main temple,
a single star-shaped sanctuary
opening onto a columned hall
fronted by a screened porch.
The entire surface of the
grey-green schist structure is
covered with richly textured
relief carvings. The lintels
have foliate frames running
between open-mouthed
aquatic monsters (*makaras*)
with exuberantly foliated tails.
The stone grilles that filter light
into the porch are raised on
friezes of elephants, lotus
stems, garlands and amorous
couples. Brackets fashioned as
female dancers, musicians and
huntresses, standing gracefully
under perforated trees, support
the sloping eaves above the
grilles. Many bear the artists'
signatures, a sign of their
elevated status under the
Hoysalas. Even finer bracket
figures can be seen inside the
temple. Though none of the
original votive figures are preserved within, ornate guardian
figures flank the doorway.

🎭 **Chennakeshava Temple**
⭕ *daily.* ⬤ *to non-Hindus.*

Belur's Chennakeshava Temple, in the centre of a large courtyard

Hoysala Art and Architecture

Frieze with mythological scene

THE TEMPLES of the Hoysala kings (12th–13th centuries) and their powerful ministers are among the wonders of South Indian art and architecture. They embody a fusion of the curving towers *(shikharas)* of North India with the columned *mandapas* of the south, and are characterized by their unique star-shaped plan and their rich surface decoration. The dense imagery of the basement friezes and wall panels, sculpted with religious and mythological scenes, as well as the exquisite bracket figures, are fashioned out of grey-green schist, a material that permits beautifully intricate carving.

Gods *seated with their consorts, such as this remarkable rendering of the Lakshmi-Narayana theme from Belur, are carved in full detail and set into the outer walls of Hoysala temples.*

Flowing foliate patterns, *derived from lotus stems and leaves, run continuously around the basements of Hoysala temples.*

Bracket figures, *fashioned as beautiful female dancers, are the highlights of Hoysala temples. This sculpture of a female drummer from Belur has an engraving of the artist's signature.*

Mandapa *interiors* *have spacious aisles lined with massive, highly polished lathe-turned columns, with undulating profiles and sharp ridges. A good example is this magnificent Nandi pavilion opposite the main shrine at Halebid.*

THE SOMNATHPUR TEMPLE

The perfectly proportioned triple-sanctuaried Keshava Temple at Somnathpur *(see p516)*, built in 1268, was the last of the great Hoysala temples.

The stepped outlines of the plinth echo the complex star-shaped plan of the sanctuary.

Towers over Hoysala sanctuaries have small spires arranged in tiers.

Miniature shrines flank the entrance steps.

Terracotta-tiled rooftops in Mangalore

Mangalore ⓫

South Kanara district. 357 km (222 miles) W of Bangalore. 🏠 399,000. ✈ 20 km (12 miles) N of city centre, then taxi or bus. 🚉 🚌 ℹ️ Karnataka Tourism, Hotel Indraprastha, (0824) 42 1692.

THIS THRIVING PORT on the estuary of the Netavati and Gurpur rivers is the largest city in Dakshina (South) Kanara, the coastal district famous for its coffee, cashewnut and pepper plantations. Rich harvests of these crops have attracted traders through the ages. Arab merchants first came here in the 13th and 14th centuries, and were later followed by the Portuguese and the British.

Mangalore today, presents a panorama of terracotta-roofed houses, whitewashed churches, temples and mosques, nestling amid groves of coconut palms. Among its historic monuments is the old watchtower, known as **Sultan's Battery**, built of laterite in 1763 by Haider Ali of Mysore (see p518).

Mangalore's 19th-century churches include the domed Church of the Most Holy Rosary and the Jesuit College of St Aloysius. Situated at the foot of Kadiri Hill, 3 km (2 miles) north of the city, is the 17th-century **Manjunath Temple**, with some superb bronze images of the Buddha, dating to the 10th–11th centuries, installed in the porch.

ENVIRONS: The pleasant beach resort at **Ullal** is just 12 km (7 miles) south of the city. Numerous Jain temples and monasteries dot the villages around Mangalore. The finest is the elaborate 15th-century Chandranatha Basti at **Mudabidri**, 35 km (22 miles) to the northwest. Dominating the summit of a hill at **Karkala**, 18 km (11 miles) further north, is the 13-m (43-ft) high Gommateshvara monolith (1432), an obvious imitation of the larger and earlier one at Sravana Belgola (see p522). The 16th-century Chaturmukha Basti, a perfectly symmetrical temple with a central chamber enshrining 12 tirthankaras, stands at the base of the hill. The pilgrimage town of **Dharmasthala**, 75 km (47 miles) to the east, is well-known for its Shiva temple. Its Gommateshvara statue was installed in 1973 by an influential local family.

Udipi ⓬

Udipi district. 58 km (36 miles) N of Mangalore. 🏠 113,100. 🚉 ℹ️ Tourist Office, Hotel Shri Krishna, (08252) 21 060. 🎉 Pargaya (Jan), Chariot Festival (Aug).

ALL ROADS in Udipi lead to the large open square in the city centre where the **Krishna Temple** is located. This is the focal point of all activity, spiritual and commercial, in this bustling pilgrim town. The famous 13th-century Vaishnava teacher, Madhava, is believed to have founded the temple by installing an image of Krishna he had rescued from a shipwreck. Parked outside the temple are the festival chariots with dome-like towers made of bamboo and covered with colourful textiles. After passing through the entrance gate, pilgrims bathe in the tank before entering the main sanctuary with its silver doors and viewing window. Surrounding the square are other temples and the eight mathas associated with the Krishna Temple, built in the typical Kanara style with wooden verandahs and sloping roofs.

Udipi also lends its name to the inexpensive eateries that originated here. Catering to a local clientele, the menu concentrated on traditional South Indian vegetarian food, such as the masala dosa and idli (see pp554–5). These restaurants, with their affordable rates, quick turnover and simple but good food, are now found all over India.

ENVIRONS: About 5 km (3 miles) west of Udipi is **Malpe Beach**, where fishing boats can be hired for excursions. **Manipal**, 4 km (2.5 miles) to the east, is an industrial and educational centre. The **House of Vijayanath Shennoy** in Manipal, now a museum, is an example of a traditional home, with a fine collection of everyday objects.

🏛 **House of Vijayanath Shennoy**
◻ Mon–Sat.

Priests performing rituals during the Chariot Festival at Udipi

Shop selling religious paraphernalia at Barkur

Barkur ⑬

Udipi district. 71 km (44 miles) N of Mangalore. 🏠 ⚑ *Navaratri (Sep/Oct).*

THE COASTAL TOWN of Barkur was a flourishing port in the 15th and 16th centuries until its river silted up. Today, the town's main attractions are its many temples with their typical sloping terracotta-tiled roofs. The largest is the **Panchalingeshvara Temple**, situated at the southern end of the town. Devotees gather at the stepped tank near the temple for a ritual bath before worshipping at the two east-facing linga shrines. The other temples include one dedicated to both Shiva and Ganesha, and the smaller Someshvara and Somanatheshvara temples.

ENVIRONS: The little hamlet of **Mekkekattu**, 8 km (5 miles) north of Barkur, is remarkable for its shrine of painted *bhuta* figures (local spirits). These are copies of the originals, which were removed to New Delhi's Crafts Museum *(see pp80–81)* and the Folklore Museum in Mysore *(see p519)*, after the shrine's renovation in the 1960s. The vividly painted deity Nandikeshvara, (the winged bull) stands in the lower shrine while his consort, who is flanked by attendants, occupies the upper one. Fierce guardian deities crowd a side chamber.

Bhatkal ⑭

North Kanara district. 120 km (75 miles) N of Mangalore. 🚌 *31,800.* 🏠 ⚑ *Navaratri (Sep/Oct).*

LOCATED ALONG a picturesque highway that follows the coastline, this town was an important port during the 16th and 17th centuries. The many beautiful Jain and Hindu stone temples found here date from those days of prosperity. Standing in the town's main street are the Chandranatheshvara and Parsvanatha *bastis.* Situated 2 km (1.3 miles) to the east, on the other side of the highway, is the **Khetapai Narayan Temple**, built in 1540. Its sanctuary and hall are enclosed within stone screens fashioned to imitate wood. As usual, finely sculpted guardian figures flank the doorway.

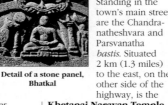

Detail of a stone panel, Bhatkal

ENVIRONS: Tucked away in the forested hills at **Kollur**, 35 km (22 miles) southeast of Bhatkal, is a shrine dedicated to the goddess Mukambika. This is the most popular pilgrimage site in the area.

India's highest waterfalls, the **Jog Falls**, lie 60 km (37 miles) northeast of Bhatkal. They can be seen at the head of the Sharavati river, framed by jagged pinnacles of rock.

Gokarna ⑮

SPECTACULARLY SITUATED by the Arabian Sea, Gokarna has now become a favourite destination of visitors in search of sun, sea and sand. A charming little town with two principal streets and clusters of traditional tile-roofed brick houses, Gokarna is also an important centre of Sanskrit learning.

The ancient **Mahabaleshvara Temple**, at the western end of the main street, was destroyed by the Portuguese in 1714 and then rebuilt later in the 18th century. In the sanctuary is a stone linga, encased in brass, placed on a coiled stone serpent. The floor of the hall in front has an intricate engraving of a giant tortoise. Shiva's birthday (Feb/Mar) is celebrated here with great fanfare. The two great temple chariots lead a procession through the town's narrow streets, while priests and pilgrims chant hymns in praise of Shiva.

BEACHES AROUND GOKARNA

Long stretches of beautiful, unspoilt beaches extend along the western coast from Gokarna to Karwar, a seaside town 60 km (37 miles) to the north. South of Gokarna are the Half Moon and Paradise beaches, while nearer Karwar are the lovely Binaga and Araga beaches. The gently curving bays, fringed by palms, are still occupied by small fishing villages where life revolves around the sea and the daily catch. Tourism remains unknown and only a few simple shacks offer basic food and shelter.

Waves breaking against rocks at a beach near Karwar

The two-storeyed Vidyashankara Temple at Sringeri

Sringeri 16

Chikmagalur district. 100 km (62 miles) NE of Mangalore. 🚆 🚌
🎭 *Navaratri (Sep/Oct).*

THE SMALL SETTLEMENT of Sringeri, tucked away in the forested ranges of the Western Ghats, is today an important pilgrimage centre and one of the most powerful seats of orthodox Hinduism in South India. This was where Shankaracharya, *(see p648)*, the great 9th-century philosopher and social reformer, established the first of his four *mathas*; the other three are at Joshimath in the Himalayas *(see p187)*, Puri *(see p312)* to the east and Dwarka *(see p427)* to the west. Today, his successors (also known as Shankaracharyas) wield tremendous influence in both

Floral offerings at Sringeri's temple

religious and temporal matters, while the *mathas* still function as centres of spiritual learning.

Standing on a paved terrace are two temples overlooking the Tunga river, crammed with sacred fish. The smaller temple, dedicated to Sharada, a popular form of the goddess Saraswati, is the principal destination for local pilgrims. Next to it is the 16th-century **Vidyashankara Temple**, where the Shankaracharya is worshipped in the form of a linga. This stone structure, which stands raised on a high platform, is laid out on an almost circular star-shaped plan. Friezes depicting the many forms of Shiva and Vishnu embellish the faceted walls. The hall that precedes the inner sanctum has massive piers carved as rearing *yalis* (mythical leonine beasts).

Chitradurga 17

Chitradurga district. 200 km (124 miles) N of Bangalore. 🚆 🚌

DRAMATICALLY positioned at the base of a rugged chain of hills, this town rose to prominence as an outpost of the Vijayanagar Empire *(see pp530–31)*. Later, in the 17th–18th centuries, it became the headquarters of a line of local chiefs known as Bedas, until it was occupied by Haider Ali *(see p517)* in 1799 and then by the British.

The **Fort**, defined by walls of huge granite blocks, rises above the town. A series of three gates leads into the irregular inner zone, strewn with striking granite boulders. There are several small temples here, as well as a number of ceremonial gateways erected by the Bedas. The platforms and pavilions within the compound of the Sampige Siddheshvara Temple mark the spot where the Bedas were crowned. The remains of rubble and mud-built granaries and residences, and a large circular well can be seen nearby.

In the town below, the local **Government Museum**, housed in a guardroom beside a gateway, displays artifacts from surrounding sites. The 17th-century Ucchalingamma Temple is on the main street.

🏛 **Fort**
⬜ *daily.* 🎫
🏛 **Government Museum**
☎ (08194) 24 202. ⬜ *Mon–Sat.*

The fort at Chitradurga, with gateways and shrines dotting the boulder-strewn landscape

A view of Hampi, with a ruined bridge over the Tungabhadra river in the foreground ▷

Hampi ⑱

Sculpted staircase, Mahanavami platform

AUNESCO WORLD HERITAGE SITE on the south bank of the Tungabhadra river, Hampi boasts the evocative ruins of Vijayanagar or the "City of Victory". The capital of three generations of Hindu rulers for more than 200 years, Hampi reached its zenith under Krishnadeva Raya (r.1510–29) and Achyuta Raya (r.1529–42). The site, which comprises the Sacred and Royal Centres, has a superb location, with rocky ridges and granite boulders acting as natural defences. The urban core of the city was fortified and separated from the Sacred Centre by an irrigated valley, through which ancient canals and waterways still run.

King's Balance
Ruling kings were weighed on this balance against gold or grain, for distribution to the poor.

Vitthala Temple
(see pp532–3)

Krishna Temple
Krishnadeva Raya erected this temple in 1516 to commemorate his victory over Orissa. It is no longer a place of worship.

Tiruvengalanatha Temple

Matanga Hill

★ Virupaksha Temple
The ancient temple of Virupaksha, dedicated to the goddess Pampa and her consort Shiva, is dominated by a 50-m (164-ft) high gopura. This is the principal place of worship in Hampi.

Tungabhadra

Hemakuta Hill

STAR SIGHTS

★ Virupaksha Temple

★ Narasimha Monolith

★ Lotus Mahal

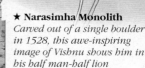

★ Narasimha Monolith
Carved out of a single boulder in 1528, this awe-inspiring image of Vishnu shows him in his half man-half lion incarnaton (see p679).

Chariot Festival
The bustling Bazaar Street is the main centre of activity and the venue for the colourful Chariot Festival. The temple chariot carries the main deity through the streets so it can be publicly honoured.

VISITORS' CHECKLIST

Bellary district. 460 km (286 miles) NW of Bangalore. 🚌 Hospet, 13 km (8 miles) W of site. 🚌 **ℹ** *Bazaar St, (08394) 51 339.* 📷 **Virupaksha Temple** ⭕ *daily.* **Lotus Mahal** 🎫 *also covers the Vitthala Temple.* 🎭 *Chariot Festival (Feb), Hampi Festival (Nov). Foreigners must register at Virupaksha Temple Police Station.*

0 metres 500

0 yards 500

Elephant Stables
An imposing structure of 11 chambers, this once housed the royal elephants. Especially noteworthy are the polygonal roofs, alternating with smooth or ribbed domes.

★ Lotus Mahal
A skilful blend of Hindu and Islamic architecture, this building may have served as a council chamber for the king.

Tiruvengalanatha Temple

Hospet

Hazara Ramachandra Temple

Ruined Palaces

Great Bath

The Queen's Bath, an open-air structure, seems to have been designed for royal recreation.

The Mahanavami Platform
was used by kings during the Mahanavami festival *(see p517)*, and for pre-war ceremonies.

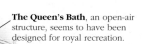

Archaeological Museum

Stepped Tank
This small, square tank with multiple steps was fed by a water chute, part of an extensive "hydraulic system" that brought water to the Royal Centre.

Hampi: Vitthala Temple

THE GRANDEST OF ALL THE religious monuments in the Sacred Centre, the Vitthala Temple represents the high point of Vijayanagar art and architecture. Though its founder remains unknown, it was enlarged in the 16th century by two of Vijaynagar's greatest rulers, Krishnadeva Raya and Achyuta Raya. Preceding the main shrine is the great open hall, or *mahamandapa*, built on a low platform and supported by intricately carved pillars. This was the gift of a military commander in 1554, just 11 years before the city was sacked and abandoned.

★ **Yalis**
Leaping yalis (*mythical leonine beasts), many with riders, adorn the outer piers of the temple.*

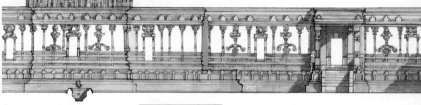

RECONSTRUCTION OF THE TOWER
This shows the pyramidal *vimana* (tower), over the main sanctuary of the Vitthala Temple, as it looked when it was built in the 16th century.

Relief
A niche in a stone pillar has a superb rendering of Garuda, the eagle mount of Vishnu.

STAR FEATURES

★ **Yalis**

★ **Chariot**

Exploring Hampi

The fabled city of the Vijaya-nagar kings (*see pp530–31*), covering an area of around 20 sq km (8 sq miles), sprawls across a spectacular barren and boulder-strewn landscape.

The **Sacred Centre**, on the southern bank of the Tungabhadra river, is dominated by the impressive **Virupaksha Temple**. It is dedicated to a form of Shiva (Virupaksha), known here as Pampapati (the "Lord of Pampa"), and commemorates his wedding to Pampa, the goddesss of the Tungabhadra. In front is the colonnaded **Bazaar Street** that dates mainly from the 16th to the mid-17th centuries, when it teemed with pilgrims and travellers in search of exotic wares. A path beside the river leads past the **Kodandarama Temple**, with its figures of

Rama, Sita and Lakshman carved on to a boulder inside the sanctuary. The bathing ghats here are considered to be the holiest at the site.

Beyond lies the **Temple of Achyuta Raya**, one of the major Hindu complexes at Hampi, dating from 1534 and dedicated to Tiruvengalanatha, the form of Vishnu that is venerated at Tirupati (*see p678*). Its perfect plan of two concentric enclosures, each entered by a towering *gopura* to the north, is clearly visible from the summit of **Matanga Hill**. The riverside path continues to the Vitthala Temple, from where a road proceeds to the village of

Kamalapuram, where the **Archaeological Museum** is located. En route is a gateway with a damaged façade with windows and battlements.

The road that runs south from Hampi village, through the Sacred Centre, leads up **Hemakuta Hill**, scattered with numerous pre- and early Vijayanagar shrines, many with small pyramidal towers. A large image of the elephant god, Ganesha, carved on a

A view of Matanga Hill

Vitthala Temple
*This striking temple with its elaborate
mandapas (columned halls) is dedicated to
Vitthala, an incarnation of Vishnu the Preserver, the second god in the Hindu Trinity.*

Musical Columns
*Small hollow columns
emit different tones
when lightly tapped.*

Chariot

Frieze Detail
*This panel depicts a trio of celestial
nymphs riding on parrots.*

★ Chariot
*This shrine in front
of the temple is
dedicated to
Garuda and is
fashioned as a
stone chariot.*

---

boulder, marks the top of the
ridge. Further south is the
Krishna Temple, erected in
the early 16th century during
the reign of Krishnadeva Raya.
It is entered through a
massive, though partly ruined
gopura. The colonnaded street
to the east now runs through
fields of sugarcane, while
the square tank nearby still
stores water. As it continues
south, the road travels past
the tremendous Narasimha
Stone Monolith, a representation of Vishnu's man-lion
incarnation *(see p679)*.

Fortified walls enclose the
Royal Centre. At the latter's
core is the superb **Hazara
Rama Temple**, built by Deva
Raya I, a Vijayanagar king of
the 15th century. Its outer
walls are covered with friezes
that depict the ceremonies
and parades of the Maha-
navami festival. Reliefs of
episodes from the *Ramayana*

**A coracle ferrying people across
the Tungabhadra river**

can be seen here. Around
the temple are excavated
remains of palaces, baths and
a hundred-columned audience
hall, while to its north are the
Elephant Stables and the
Lotus Mahal.

🏛 Archaeological Museum
Kamalapuram. ◻ *Sat –Thu.*

ENVIRONS: The historic village
of **Anegondi** lies on the
opposite bank of the Tungabhadra river. Until a bridge
under construction becomes
operational, it can be reached
only on the coracles that have
plied the river for centuries.

An important settlement
before the establishment of
Vijayanagar, Anegondi's now
dilapidated palaces, temples
and bathing ghats still preserve vestiges of their former
glory. The Kalyan Mahal, a
palace-like building reminiscent of Hampi's Lotus
Mahal *(see p531)*, stands in
the central square. Nearby are
a temple and a 14th-century
gateway. The massive walls
and rounded bastions of
Anegondi's citadel enclose
the rocky hills lying west of
the main town. Anegondi is
also of interest for its traditional mud-clad houses and
for the fine river views.

An outer wall of Gadag's Someshvara Temple, with temple towers in relief

Gadag ⑲

Gadag district. 450 km (280 miles) NW of Bangalore. 🚉 🚌 🛈 *Hotel Durga, Vihar Complex.* 🛗 *daily.*

A N IMPORTANT cotton collection centre, the sleepy little town of Gadag comes to life during the cotton season in May and June. During these months, the cotton market hums with activity and is well worth a visit.

A number of late Chalukyan monuments (11th–12th centuries) in the city indicate its historic past. Standing to the south is the **Trikuteshvara Temple**, remarkable for its three sanctuaries facing a common, partly open hall. Inclined slabs that serve as balcony seats are decorated with figurative panels, and are overhung by steeply angled eaves. Inside the hall, the columns have figures arranged in shallow niches. The east sanctuary accommodates three lingas, while the one to the south is dedicated to the goddess Saraswati.

In the middle of the city stands the **Someshvara Temple**. Though abandoned and now in a dilapidated state, its intricate carvings are fairly well preserved. The doorways to the hall have densely carved figures and foliation.

Sculpted figures

ENVIRONS: The small village of **Lakkundi**, 11 km (7 miles) east of Gadag, has temples dating from the 11th–12th centuries, built of grey-green chloritic schist. Surrounded by mud houses, a number of such temples are tucked away down narrow streets.

Jain Basti, the largest temple, has a five-storeyed tower. Its basement is adorned with friezes of elephants and lotus petals. Lathe-turned columns are seen in the entrance porch. The nearby Kashi Vishwanatha Temple has a pair of sanctuaries facing each other across a common porch. Relief carvings of a pair of *makaras* or aquatic monsters, sitting on the walls, are typical motifs of late Chalukyan art.

Belgaum ⑳

Belgaum district. 502 km (312 miles) NW of Bangalore. 🚉 🚌 🛈 *Tourist Office, Ashoka Nagar, (0831) 47 0879.*

T HIS BUSTLING CITY, on the border with Maharashtra, was an important garrison town under the British. Even today, the cantonment, with its bungalows and barracks, has a significant military presence. Earlier, in the 16th and 17th centuries, Belgaum was a provincial centre under the Adil Shahi rulers of Bijapur *(see p542),* the Marathas of Pune *(see p471),* as well as the Mughals when they occupied this part of Karnataka. The **Fort** to the east is unusually elliptical in layout and its stone walls incorporate many reused temple blocks. The **Safa Mosque** nearby was built in the first half of the 16th century by Asad Khan, the governor of Belgaum. The town also has three temples that date to the late Chalukyan period.

The elliptical fort at Belgaum

Performing Arts of Karnataka

KARNATAKA HAS A RICH and vibrant performing arts tradition. Story telling, with the help of media such as paintings and leather puppets, was among the most popular folk entertainments in the northern and northeastern part of the state, and in neighbouring Andhra Pradesh, before the advent of the cinema. Itinerant folk performers would delight rural audiences with

String puppet

stirring tales of good and evil, based on mythological episodes. A number of dance-dramas, such as the Yakshagana, developed in South Kanara, the region of Karnataka that borders Kerala. As in Kathakali *(see p657)*, Yakshagana actors dress in awe-inspiring costumes to perform a heavily mimetic dance, while the singer recites the story to the accompaniment of music.

KARNATAKA'S LEATHER PUPPETS

Huge figures made of goatskin are punched with holes of various shapes to allow light to filter through, thus creating the interplay of light and coloured shadow, so essential to shadow theatre. The chief puppeteer recites the story, while his assistants provide musical accompaniment.

Figures *are etched on the prepared skin with a sharp instrument, then cut along the outline and coloured.*

The chief puppeteer *manipulates the puppet with the help of an attached stick.*

Perforations on the figure allow light to pass through.

Bright colours and outlines are combined to create striking efects.

A stick is attached for manipulation.

Performances *take place at night. A light is placed behind a thin cotton screen, so that the audience, sitting in front, sees the moving shadows.*

Hanuman, the Monkey God, a major character in the *Ramayana*

YAKSHAGANA

This folk dance-drama originated in the early 16th century. An all-male cast consisting of about 20 actors and musicians

A man creating the elaborate headgear

act out a repertoire that is inspired mainly by episodes from the great epics *(see pp26–7)*, especially the *Mahabharata*. All-night performances, organized at the behest of a wealthy patron on special occasions, take place in the open, and no particular props are needed. Yakshagana's spectacular costumes are enhanced by tall headgear, a profusion of ornaments and elaborate make-up.

Actors performing a scene from the *Mahabharata*

Badami ㉑

Coiled Serpent, Ceiling, Cave 1

Columned verandah, Cave 3

DRAMATICALLY SITUATED within a horseshoe of red sandstone cliffs, overlooking the green waters of a large lake, this historic town was the capital of the powerful early Chalukya kings, who ruled the Deccan during the 6th–7th centuries AD. These rulers also held sway at Pattadakal *(see pp538–9)* and Aihole *(see pp540–41)*. Among the rock-cut and structural monuments, the most richly decorated are the cave temples, which are carved into the cliff on the southern side. Of these, Cave 1 is dedicated to Shiva, Caves 2 and 3 to Vishnu, and Cave 4 to the Jain saints.

A linga sanctuary is carved into the rear wall.

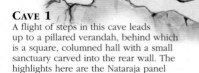

CAVE 1

A flight of steps in this cave leads up to a pillared verandah, behind which is a square, columned hall with a small sanctuary carved into the rear wall. The highlights here are the Nataraja panel and the carved panels on the ceiling.

Cave 2

This Vaishnava cave has a superb frieze of Varaha, the boar incarnation of Vishnu, on one end of the porch. A row of dwarfs is carved below it.

Cave 3

The verandah of this large and beautiful cave has an enormous four-armed figure of Vishnu seated on Adisesha, the serpent whose five hoods spread protectively over his crown. At his feet is the bird Garuda, his mount. This is the only cave with an inscription, dated AD 578.

Nataraja Panel
This 12-armed dancing Shiva is one of the earliest and finest depictions of the Nataraja in Karnataka.

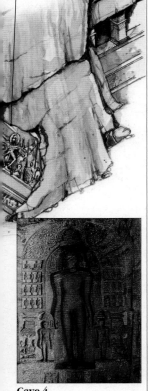

Cave 4
Standing and seated Jain tirthankaras cover the walls and columns in Cave 4, on top of a cliff. Some of these were added in the 11th and 12th centuries, when this part of Karnataka was governed by a later line of Chalukya rulers.

Exploring Badami

Most of Badami's temples are situated on the imposing cliff that lies north of the man-made Agastya Lake. The boulder-strewn landscape and the large lake acted as natural defences of the site. Standing on the embankment is the 11th-century **Yellamma Temple**, with its multi-storeyed tower. Further away, inside the village, is the **Jambulinga Temple**, dating to AD 699, with triple shrines dedicated to Brahma, Vishnu and Shiva opening off a common *mandapa*. The **Bhutanatha Temple** is scenically located at the end of the lake and was built in several phases. The core shrine, with a pyramidal tower, is from the 6th–7th centuries, while the porch, embellished with angled eaves and overlooking the water, dates to the 11th century. Several boulders lying around the temple have reliefs of a sleeping Vishnu, and a seated Jain figure. Lesser shrines nearby show the pyramidal layered towers that are typical of the late Chalukya style.

The **Archaeological Museum**, on the north side of the lake, displays a magnificent triangular panel depicting Brahma surrounded by elaborate foliage; this piece must have once surmounted a free-standing portal. Other items of interest include a squatting female divinity with a lotus head, and two panels showing Shiva – spearing a demon and shooting arrows as he rides in a chariot.

Steps ascend through a rugged gorge to the 7th-century **Upper Shivalaya Temple** that crowns the cliffs rising to the north of the town. Only the walls of the passageway and the multi-storeyed tower capped with a square-domed

The tower of the Upper Shivalaya Temple

roof still stand; the *mandapa* in front has been dismantled. Its simple basement mouldings and wall pilasters are typical of early structural architecture under the Chalukyas. Diminutive scenes of Krishna holding up Mount Govardhana, and Narasimha disembowelling his victim, are carved intricately on the walls. Perched on top of an isolated boulder near the main road north of the town, is the **Mallegitti Shivalaya Temple**, a well-preserved 7th-century structure. Perforated stone windows flank sculptured panels of Vishnu and Shiva, topped with garlands and various aquatic monsters.

ENVIRONS: A popular Devi shrine, facing a large tank dating from the 18th century, is situated at **Banashankari**, 5 km (3 miles) east of Badami. At **Mahakuta**, 10 km (6 miles) towards the east, a group of 7th-century temples built in contrasting North- and South-Indian styles *(see p20)*, are clustered around a small tank.

The Bhutanatha Temple overlooking the tank

Pattadakal ㉒

THE SACRED COMPLEX AT PATTADAKAL is picturesquely situated on the banks of the Malprabha river. A UNESCO World Heritage Site, its superb 8th-century temples are a fitting climax to the artistic achievements of the Chalukya kings, as seen in neighbouring Badami *(see pp536–7)* and Aihole *(see pp540–41)*. While these towns were important ancient settlements, Pattadakal, with only a small resident population, was mainly used for royal festivities and coronation ceremonies.

Shiva appearing out of the fiery linga, Virupaksha Temple

Exploring Pattadakal

The main temple complex is situated in landscaped gardens next to the small village. Built in a combination of the North Indian and South Indian temple styles *(see p20)*, these striking structures reveal a great deal about the evolution of temple architecture in South India.

The modest Galaganatha Temple, built of sandstone

cut tiers of horseshoe-shaped motifs and a ribbed finial. The **Kashi Vishvanatha Temple**, which lies to the west, dates from the mid-8th century and further illustrates the developments in the North Indian temple style. Its faceted tower is entirely covered with a mesh design of interlocking horseshoe-arched motifs. The columns inside the small vestibule preceding the sanctum are carved with a variety of mythological scenes.

North Indian-style Temples

Characterized by their curved towers *(shikharas)* over the inner sanctum, North Indian-style temples are exemplified in the **Kadasiddeshvara** and **Jambulinga Temples**, which are situated near the entrance. These are unassuming sandstone structures with damaged wall sculptures and curving tiered towers. The larger but incomplete **Galaganatha Temple** nearby has a well-preserved tower with sharply

South Indian-style Temples

South Indian temple towers *(vimanas)* rise in a stepped pyramidal formation, as in the **Sangameshvara Temple**, the earliest in the complex. It was erected by the Chalukya king, Vijayaditya, who died in AD 733 before the structure was completed. Its multistoreyed

tower is capped with a square domed roof. The incomplete hall in front has been restored.

The largest temples are the twin **Virupaksha** and **Mallikarjuna Temples** to the south. Both are dedicated to Shiva and were constructed in AD 745 by two sister queens of the powerful Chalukya king, Vikramaditya II, to commemorate his victory over the Pallava rulers of Tamil Nadu. These temples represent the climax of early Chalukya architecture and are said to be based on the Kailasanatha Temple in Kanchipuram *(see p582)*. They also served as the inspiration for the colossal Kailasanatha monolith at Ellora *(see pp476–8)*.

Today, the Virupaksha Temple is the only functioning shrine in this complex. In

View of the twin Virupaksha and Mallikarjuna Temples, Pattadakal

Nataraja, ceiling panel from the Papanatha Temple

front is a Nandi pavilion with a magnificently carved bull covered by a cloth. The temple itself consists of a spacious, columned hall with triple porches leading to the linga sanctum, surrounded by a passageway. The ornately carved pillars and ceilings portray mythological and religious stories. The finest reliefs are on either side of the east porch and include one of Shiva as *lingodbhavamurti*, appearing out of a fiery linga, and a depiction of Vishnu as Trivikrama, traversing the Universe in three steps.

The Mallikarjuna Temple, though identical, is smaller and more compact. The carvings on the columns of the interior hall show scenes from the *Panchatantra*, a collection of fables with bird and animal heroes. The walls surrounding the temple, and the Nandi pavilion in front of it, are incomplete.

A path from the Virupaksha Temple gateway along the river leads to the **Papanatha Temple**. This early 8th-century temple was extended several times, as can be seen in the unusual arrangement of double halls leading to the sanctuary, and in the later addition of passageway walls with porches on three sides. The interesting exterior combines South Indian-style pilastered wall niches with North Indian-style mesh patterns and curvilinear towers. Battle scenes from the *Ramayana* (*see p27*), carved on the east wall, conclude with Rama's coronation, shown on the column of the main porch. Both the halls have central aisles, with pot

Battle between Arjuna and Shiva, Virupaksha Temple

and foliage motifs carved on the capitals. Ornate brackets and beams support ceiling panels, the finest of which show a coiled *naga* (snake) deity and a Dancing Shiva (Nataraja), in the inner hall.

Jain Temple

To the west of the village, is a 9th-century Jain Temple built by the Rashtrakuta rulers, who succeeded the Chalukyas in the middle of the 8th century. A spacious open porch with peripheral lathe-turned columns is overhung with angled eaves. Some remarkable carvings of life-size elephant torsos are placed beside the doorway that leads into the inner hall.

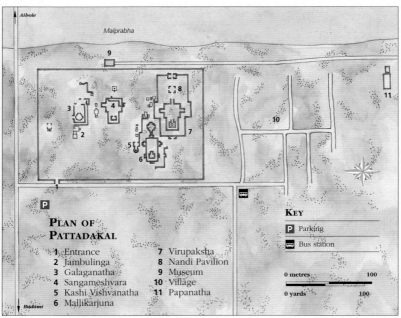

PLAN OF PATTADAKAL

1 Entrance
2 Jambulinga
3 Galaganatha
4 Sangameshvara
5 Kashi Vishvanatha
6 Mallikarjuna
7 Virupaksha
8 Nandi Pavilion
9 Museum
10 Village
11 Papanatha

KEY

🅿 Parking
🚌 Bus station

0 metres 100
0 yards 100

A view of the Gaudar Gudi with the Ladkhan Temple behind it, Aihole

Aihole ㉓

Bagalkote district. 27 km (17 miles) NE of Badami. 🚉 *Badami, 28 km (17 miles) SW of town, then bus or taxi.* 🚌 🎭 *Ramalinga Temple Chariot Festival (Feb/Mar).*

TIME SEEMS TO have stood still in this small, dusty town, situated on the Malprabha river, about 12 km (7 miles) downstream from Pattadakal *(see pp538–9)*. Fortifications encircle much of the town. Within are ancient sandstone temples of varying types, some of which were used as dwellings and are named after their former inhabitants. The temples are associated with both the early and later Chalukya rulers of Badami *(see pp536–7)*, and date from the 6th–11th centuries.

Most visitors begin their tour of Aihole at the **Durga Temple**. Nearby is a small complex with the **Ladkhan Temple**. This building is recognizable by the tiers of sloping slabs that roof the spacious hall as well as the adjoining entrance porch. River goddesses and amorous couples are carved on the columns of the porch, while images of deities can be seen on the side walls of a small chamber at the rooftop level. The adjacent **Gaudar Gudi** comprises a small sanctuary set within an open *mandapa*, with balcony seating on four sides. The ruined Chakra Gudi is near the stepped tank.

The **Kunti Group**, a quartet of temples conceived as open columned halls with interior sanctuaries, lies to the south. The temple to the southeast, probably the first to be built, has superbly carved ceiling panels portraying the Hindu Trinity of Brahma, Vishnu and Shiva. A similar trio of ceiling panels can be seen in the Hucchapayya Math, lying a short distance beyond.

A stepped path leads to the top of the hill southeast of the town, passing by a two-storeyed Buddhist temple. At the summit of the hill stands the serene **Meguti Temple** built in AD 634, the earliest dated structural monument in Karnataka. The temple's clearly articulated basement, plastered walls and eaves show the South Indian style of temple architecture *(see p20)* in its earliest phase. An impressive seated Jain figure is installed in the sanctuary. Prehistoric megalithic tombs are located to

the rear of the temple. The road, going downhill, follows the curving fortifications and passes the Jyotirlinga Group, until it ends at the Durga Temple. To the north of the Durga Temple is the **Chikki Gudi**, with exquisitely carved columns, beams and ceiling panels. A path to the right, leads to the small **Hucchimalli Gudi**, with a North Indian style tower, and an unusual icon of Karttikeya, Shiva's son, carved on the ceiling of the front porch.

Nearby lies the rock-cut **Ravala Phadi Cave**, dating to the late 6th century. Its interior is enhanced with splendid carvings of Hindu divinities. These include a Dancing Shiva in a subshrine; Ardhanarishvara, Harihara and Shiva with Ganga, on the walls of the main hall; and Varaha and Durga in the antechamber preceding the small linga sanctuary. Tiny shrines and a fluted column stand in front.

The exuberant Dancing Shiva relief in Ravala Phadi Cave

Aihole: Durga Temple

Medallion on porch pillar

THE LARGEST AND FINEST monument at Aihole, the Durga Temple is also the most unusual because of its apsidal sanctuary surrounded by an open colonnade. The temple is elevated on a lofty plinth, with steps at one end leading to a porch with elaborate carvings of sensuous couples and guardians on its columns. Other sculptural masterpieces, of Shiva with Nandi, Narasimha, Vishnu with Garuda, Durga and Harihara, are placed in the niches lining the colonnade. The interior of the hall is plain by contrast and the circular plinth within the sanctuary empty. The temple's name is a misnomer, as the identity of the image that was once worshipped here remains unknown.

A view of the semi-circular sanctuary of the Durga Temple

Naga Ceiling
A ceiling panel in the mandapa depicts a naga *with a coiled serpent body.*

The entrance porch has columns embellished with intricate carvings.

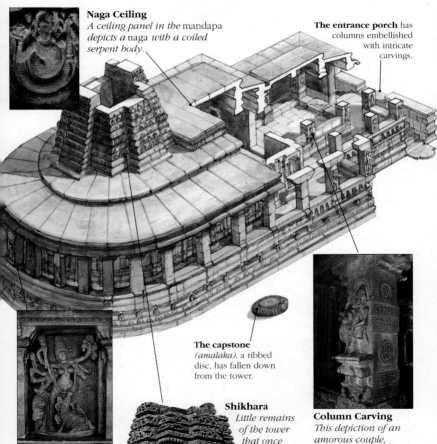

The capstone
(amalaka), a ribbed disc, has fallen down from the tower.

Shikhara
Little remains of the tower that once rose above the inner sanctum.

Durga
This niche shows a multi-armed Durga slaying the buffalo demon.

Column Carving
This depiction of an amorous couple, carved on one of the columns in the porch, is a masterpiece of Chalukyan art.

Bijapur ❷❹

Bijapur district. 550 km (342 miles) NW of Bangalore. 🚉 246,000. 🚌 ℹ️ Karnataka Tourism, Station Rd, (08352) 50 359. 🎵 Bijapur Music Festival (Jan), Asar Mahal Urs Festival (Sep).

A FTER THE FALL of the Bahmanis *(see p544)*, the Adil Shahi sultans emerged as the principal rulers of the Deccan in the 16th and 17th centuries. Their capital, the fortified city of Bijapur, was protected by ramparts with prominent bastions; many of the original cannons are still in place. The Malik-i-Maidan ("Lord of the Plain"), reputedly the largest cannon of the period in India, still guards the western entrance. Within the fort's walls are splendid mosques, palaces and tombs built by a succession of enlightened rulers.

🏛 The Citadel

The Citadel, in the heart of the city, is defined by its own fortified walls and surrounded by a wide moat. The south gate, the only one surviving, leads into what was once the palace complex. This ceremonial centre of Bijapur, surrounded by arcades, is known as the **Quadrangle**, and is today occupied by municipal offices. To its northwest stands the **Sat Manzil**, the seven-storeyed pleasure palace from the top of which the whole city could once be seen. Of this, only five storeys now remain. It overlooks an

Medallion at Jami Masjid

The arcaded prayer hall of the Jami Masjid

exquisitely ornamented miniature pavilion called the **Jal Mandir**. A short distance to the north are the **Gagan Mahal**, the audience hall of Ali Adil Shah I, with an arched façade facing an open space, and the **Anand Mahal**, or the "Palace of Joy", where the ladies of the seraglio lived. Other fine structures include the **Mecca Masjid**, a charming little mosque to the east of the Citadel, and **Karimuddin's Mosque** near the south gate, built with temple materials pillaged in 1310 by Alauddin Khilji *(see p48)*.

🏛 Outside the Citadel

The walled city, outside the Citadel, is scattered with monuments built by the Adil Shahi sultans. To the east of the Citadel is the double-storeyed **Asar Mahal**, built in 1646 as the hall of justice, and later converted into a sacred reliquary to house two hairs of the Prophet. Chambers on the upper level are decorated with murals depicting floral themes and courtly scenes with European-style figures. A short distance away is the elegant **Mihtar Mahal**, belonging to the period of Ibrahim II (1580– 1626) and entered through a triple-storeyed gateway. Balconies projecting over the street are supported on angled struts carved as if they were made of wood. The gateway leads to a small mosque.

The grandly conceived **Jami Masjid**, to the southeast, was begun by Ali Adil Shah I in 1576, but never finished. The marble floor of the capacious prayer hall has been divided into some 2,250 rectangular bays to resemble prayer mats. Even today, the mosque attracts more than 2,000 worshippers during Friday prayers. To the north and west are more tombs and mosques, including the Taj Baoli, a large square tank surrounded by steps.

🏛 Ibrahim Rauza

🕐 daily. 🎫 📷 extra charges. This exquisite mausoleum, often described as the finest Islamic building in the Deccan, was built by Ibrahim II for his wife. In fact, he predeceased her and is buried here too. The funerary complex consists of a tomb and a mosque, raised on a plinth in the middle of a formal garden. A huge tank nearby is named after his wife, Taj Sultana. The walls of the tomb, as seen within an arcaded verandah, are embellished with superb calligraphic and geometric designs. The tomb chamber is roofed by a flat vault with curving sides.

Ibrahim Rauza, the beautifully proportioned tomb of Ibrahim II

Bijapur: Gol Gumbad

BIJAPUR'S MOST CELEBRATED building, the monumental tomb of Muhammad Adil Shah (1627–56), second son and successor of Ibrahim II, is commonly known as the "Round Dome", or Gol Gumbad. The slightly bulbous dome, the largest in the world after St Peter's in Rome, rises on a base of petals to form a fitting climax to the whole composition. Completed in 1656, the tomb stands in the middle of a formal garden. On the west side is a small mosque with five arches flanked by slender minarets.

Detail of a medallion

VISITORS' CHECKLIST

Mahatma Gandhi Rd. ◯ daily. 📷
free on Fri. Autos & cycles available.

Circular gallery

The dome is nearly 44 m (133 ft) in diameter. It is carried on eight overlapping arches with intervening pendentives. The circular Whispering Gallery, over which the dome is raised, has remarkable acoustics.

A bulbous dome on a petalled base tops the minaret.

Minaret

The *mihrab* bay is within a part-octagonal projection, to the west. The walls are overhung by richly carved stone brackets with tiers of lotus buds.

Tomb of Muhammad Adil Shah.

Entrance Arch
The entrance façade has a wide, lofty arch in the centre, pierced with small windows on either side.

DECCANI PAINTING

The Muslim rulers of the Deccan, especially of Golconda *(see pp666–7)* and Bijapur, during the 14th and 15th centuries, encouraged art and established a Deccani School of Painting. This was influenced first by direct contact with Central Asia and Persia, and later by the Mughals. At the court of Bijapur, elements of European Renaissance and Persian art were assimilated into the classical Indian tradition, to create a distinctive Deccani style.

***Chand Bibi Playing Polo*, a Deccani painting**

The vaulted hall of the Jami Masjid at Gulbarga

Gulbarga 25

Gulbarga district. 616 km (383 miles)
NE of Bijapur. 🏛 428,000. 🚇 🚌
🛈 Hotel Mayura Bahumani, (08472)
40 947. 📷 Urs (Mar).

THIS SMALL provincial town contains some of the earliest examples of Islamic architecture in Karnataka. These date to the 14th and 15th centuries, when Gulbarga flourished as the capital of the Bahmani sultans (see p49), the first of the great Muslim kingdoms to dominate the Deccan.

The **Dargah of Gesu Daraz** (d.1422), to the northeast of the present town, is one of South India's holiest Muslim shrines. Khwaja Gesu Daraz, or Bande Nawaz as he was affectionately known, was a Sufi mystic from the Chishti sect (see p376). He fled from North India and sought refuge here at the court of Firuz Shah Bahmani, a pious and enlightened ruler. His simple tomb stands in the middle of a large, sprawling complex comprising a group of lesser tombs, mosques and madrasas, and is a major pilgrimage centre. The Dargah of Shah Kamal Mujarrad, another saint who lived in Gulbarga, lies further south.

A complex of seven royal tombs, known as the **Haft Gumbad**, lies to the west of the dargah. Firuz Shah Bahmani, who also died in 1422, is buried here in the largest and most elaborate of all the mausoleums. Immediately west of the city are the desolate ruins of the forbidding fort, almost circular and protected by a wide moat. Little of the royal centre remains intact today. Near the entrance gateway is the Bala Hisar, a solid keep dating from the 17th century, when the Adil Shahis (see pp542–3) occupied the city. The most interesting structure, however, is the large **Jami Masjid** nearby. Built in 1367, to commemorate Gulbarga's status as the capital, this is one of the earliest mosques in South India, and the only one without an open courtyard. To its rear is the 14th-century Bazaar Street, lined with small chambers now converted into dwellings. This leads to a series of gateways shielded by walls that protrude outwards from the fort walls. To the west of the fort are the derelict tombs of the early Bahmani sultans.

Another 14th-century monument is the **Shah Bazaar Mosque**, to the north of the fort. Its domed entrance chamber leads into a courtyard with a prayer hall beyond. A street from here proceeds westwards to an arcaded portal flanked by lofty minarets. Behind this portal lies the Dargah of Sheikh Sirajuddin Junaydi, a simple tomb with arcaded recesses and a flattish dome.

ENVIRONS: The picturesque ruins of **Firuzabad**, the palace city founded in 1400 by Firuz Shah Bahmani on the east bank of the Bhima river, are located 28 km (17 miles) south of Gulbarga. The massive stone walls with quadrangular bastions and arched gateways define an approximately square zone, almost 1,000 m (3,281 ft) wide. The best preserved structures are the Jami Masjid and a two-storeyed audience hall. Among the remains are the royal baths (hamams), with pyramidal vaults and fluted domes, said to be the oldest in the Deccan.

Bidar 26

Bidar district. 111 km (69 miles) NE of
Gulbarga. 🚌 Autos & cycles available.

BIDAR became the Bahmani capital in 1424, when Firuz Shah's brother and successor, Ahmad Shah, moved his court here. With the collapse of the Bahmani dynasty at the end of the 15th century, control of the region passed into the hands of the Baridis.

Bidar's **Fort**, built in 1428 by Ahmed Shah Bahmani, occupies a promontory that is defended by double rings of walls and a moat partly carved out of the bedrock. A trio of arched gates, one with polychrome tilework, another with a prominent dome, leads

Devotees at the gateway to the Dargah of
Gesu Daraz, Gulbarga

The walled road leading to the entrance gateway of Bidar's fort

into what was once the royal enclave. To the left is the Rangin Mahal, an exquisite palace built by Ali Shah Barid in the 16th century. The hall, with its original wooden columns displaying ornate brackets and beams, and the rear chamber adorned with magnificent tile mosaics and inlaid mother-of-pearl decoration, are especially striking. Nearby is the unusual Solah Khamba Mosque, with massive circular columns, built by the Tughluqs *(see p48)* in 1327. In front is the Lal Bagh, a walled garden with a central lobe-fringed pool. A short distance to the south is the ruined Diwan-i-Am, the Public Audience Hall, and the Takht Mahal, a monumental portal with traces of hexagonal tiles decorated with tiger and sun emblems in the spandrels.

The old walled town sprawls beneath the ramparts of the fort. On one side of the main north-south street is the **Takhti-i-Kirmani**, a 15th-century gateway embellished with bands of foliate and arabesque designs. Further south is the magnificent late 15th-century **Madrasa of Mahmud Gawan**, named after the erudite prime minister who was the virtual ruler of the Bahmani kingdom. This used to be a famous theological college, and at one time boasted a huge

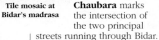
Tile mosaic at Bidar's madrasa

library, well-stocked with scholarly manuscripts. A superb example of Central Asian-style architecture, it has four arched portals that stand against a background of domes facing a central court. A pair of minarets flanks its façade. Tile mosaics on the exterior still survive, including a finely worked calligraphic band in rich blue and white. Still further south, the **Chaubara** marks the intersection of the two principal streets running through Bidar.

The **Mausolea of the Baridi rulers** lie west of Bidar. The largest is the Tomb of Ali Shah Barid (1577). This lofty, domed chamber, open on four sides, stands in the middle of a symmetrical four-square garden. Blank panels above the arches once contained tile mosaic, examples of which are preserved inside. The black polished basalt sarcophagus is still *in situ*.

Bidar is also known for a special type of encrusted metalware, often mistaken for damascening, known as *bidri (see p665)*. Introduced in the mid-17th century by artisans from Iran, the craft flourished under court patronage. The style, characterized by intricate floral and geometric designs, inlaid in gold, silver or brass onto a matt black surface, was used to embellish various objects, including platters, boxes, *huqqa* bases

and trays. Today, the finest pieces are housed in museums, and only a handful of artisan families still practise this craft in the town of its origin.

ENVIRONS: The Bahmani necropolis stands in the open countryside near **Ashtur**, a small village 3 km (2 miles) northeast of Bidar. The oldest and grandest of the tombs is the early 15th-century Tomb of Ahmad Shah. Splendid murals embellish the interior walls as well as the huge dome. The adjacent tomb of Alauddin Ahmad II, his successor, has coloured tile mosaics. Just outside is the Chaukhandi, the modest tomb of the saint Khalil Allah (d.1460), which has superb calligraphic panels over the doorways.

Façade of the Madrasa of Mahmud Gawan in Bidar

SOUTH INDIA

Introducing South India

SOUTH OF THE VINDHYA RANGE, India's Dravidian heartland has all that a visitor could look for. Dramatic coastlines, both on the Arabian Sea and the Bay of Bengal, meet at Kanniyakumari on the Indian Ocean. Isolated beaches, dense forests and game reserves are among its natural wonders. Tamil Nadu has some of India's most magnificent ancient temples, still active centres of religious practice. A different culture prevails in Pondicherry, which retains a strong French influence. Kerala is rich in beautiful scenery as well as in cultural heritage, while Andhra Pradesh has some of the region's most fascinating historic sites.

Fisherman at a sluice gate on the Kaveri river

A class in progress in a traditional Vedic school, Tamil Nadu

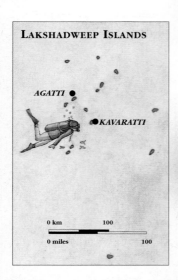

LAKSHADWEEP ISLANDS

AGATTI

KAVARATTI

Arabian Sea

0 km   100

0 miles   100

Mumb

NH7

PUTTAPARTH

LEPAKSHI

↑ *Panaji*

Bangalore

Hogenakkal Falls

KANNUR

NH17

Kaveri

SALEM

KOZHIKODE

NH47

COIMBATORE

THRISSUR

KODAIKANAL

KOCHI

NH49   MUNNAR

MADURAI

ALAPPUZHA

NH47

TIRUNELVELLI

NH7

THIRUVANANTHAPURAM

KANNIYAKUMARI
Indian Ocean

◁ **The spectacular Hogenakkal Falls on the Kaveri river** *(see p600)*

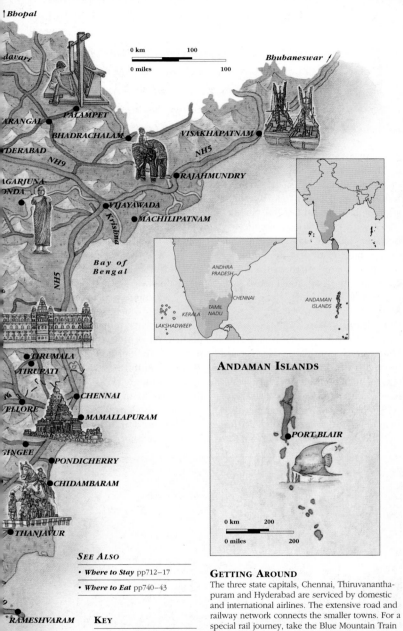

↑ *Bhopal*

0 km 100
0 miles 100

Bhubaneswar

davari

ARANGAL
PALAMPET
BHADRACHALAM
DERABAD NH9
AGARJUNA
ONDA
VIJAYAWADA
MACHILIPATNAM
Krishna

VISAKHAPATNAM
NH5
RAJAHMUNDRY

Bay of Bengal

NH5

ANDHRA PRADESH
CHENNAI
TAMIL NADU
KERALA
LAKSHADWEEP
ANDAMAN ISLANDS

TIRUMALA
TIRUPATI
ELLORE
CHENNAI
MAMALLAPURAM
GINGEE
PONDICHERRY
CHIDAMBARAM
THANJAVUR

RAMESHVARAM

ANDAMAN ISLANDS

PORT BLAIR

0 km 200
0 miles 200

SEE ALSO

- *Where to Stay* pp712–17
- *Where to Eat* pp740–43

KEY

Major road

River

- - State border

National highway

GETTING AROUND

The three state capitals, Chennai, Thiruvananthapuram and Hyderabad are serviced by domestic
and international airlines. The extensive road and
railway network connects the smaller towns. For a
special rail journey, take the Blue Mountain Train
from Coimbatore to Ooty *(see pp604–605)*. There
are regular flights from Kolkata and Chennai to
the Andaman Islands, and from Kochi (Kerala) to
Agatti (Lakshadweep). Cruises to Lakshadweep
are available from Kochi, and to the Andamans
from Chennai, Kolkata and Visakhapatnam.

A PORTRAIT OF SOUTH INDIA

T HE TERM "SOUTH INDIA", *though it conveys a sense of geographical unity, also encompasses a multitude of differences. While the three states – Tamil Nadu, Kerala and Andhra Pradesh – share, to some extent, an ancient heritage, they speak different languages, and each has its distinct artistic, cultural and political tradition.*

A popular view holds that while the history of North India is one of wars and invasions, the south remained cocooned in peaceful stagnation. In actual fact, the three states witnessed bloody conflicts between Jainism and Buddhism on the one hand, and Brahminical Hinduism on the other. They saw the rise and fall of powerful kingdoms, who fought many wars to establish their dominance. In the beginning of the colonial period, South India was also a battleground between the Europeans and the regional kingdoms. All these upheavals have left their mark on the region.

Wooden effigy, Thiruvananthapuram

Tamil Nadu, the heartland of Dravidian India has, for over three decades, been ruled by two regional parties. Though arch-rivals, they share a common platform, based on a strong advocacy of Tamil language and culture. Tamil is the oldest surviving Dravidian language, with a literature that goes back to AD 300. This period, known as the Sangam era, derives its name from the Tamil Sangams, gatherings of poets and writers, which produced countless poems, remarkably secular in nature, of which over 2,000 have survived. Another enduring expression of Tamil culture is visible in Tamil Nadu's Hindu temples – it has no less than 30,000 of them.

A more modern face of Tamil Nadu can be seen in the state capital, Chennai (earlier known as Madras).

A 16th-century Catholic church, overlooking a little fishing village at Kanniyakumari

A portrait of film star-turned-politician Jayalalitha

The city is a vibrant commercial and political centre, though it still values its traditional culture. Here, concerts of classical Carnatic music draw as large and enthusiastic crowds as the raucous political rallies held by its most popular politician, the former film star Jayalalitha.

In neighbouring Kerala, separated from Tamil Nadu by the magnificent forested hills of the Western Ghats, the main attraction is not temples (though it has those too), but natural beauty. It is easy to understand why this narrow strip of land between the Arabian Sea and the Western Ghats, with its verdant landscape of palm trees, paddy fields and coffee plantations, crisscrossed by enchanting waterways, has been dubbed "God's own country".

Modern-day Kerala, with a strong leftist political tradition, boasts of development indices that are exceptional among Indian states – the highest literacy rate in the country (the language spoken here is Malayalam), a low population growth rate, the lowest infant mortality rate, and a near-perfect record in communal harmony. Culturally, Kerala boasts spectacular dance forms such as Kathakali *(see p657)*, and the martial art form *kalaripayattu (see p626)*. It is also renowned for its superb Ayurvedic health resorts *(see p629)*, now a major draw for international travellers.

Telugu-speaking Andhra Pradesh is South India's largest state, with its capital, Hyderabad, located in the heart of the rocky Deccan Plateau. This city was once the seat of the powerful Nizams *(see p660)* whose wealth was legendary. Their legacy has given Hyderabad a unique flavour, rich in manifestations of an Islamic culture – in its architecture and cuisine, and in the widespread use of Urdu.

Andhra Pradesh shares with Tamil Nadu a penchant for film stars-turned-politicians. For many years it was ruled by Telugu cinema's most loved actor, NT Rama Rao, who specialized in playing mythological heroes. His son-in-law, Chandrababu Naidu, now the state's chief minister, has chosen a more down-to-earth way of winning popular support, with his ambitious schemes to modernize and develop the state. As a result of his efforts, Hyderabad is now vying with Bangalore for the title of India's information technology capital.

A truck overloaded with hay

Tamil Brahmin boys performing a religious ritual

Temple Towns

Religious symbol

SRIRANGAM *(see p601)* is typical of many towns in South India, especially in Tamil Nadu, that are dominated by sanctuaries dedicated to Hindu deities who protect the city and its population. Conceived as a vast religious complex, the town is enclosed by high fortress-like walls, and entered through towering gateways *(gopuras)*. The temple itself consists of multiple walled enclosures, often in concentric arrangements, surrounded by streets that echo the temple's layout. Though Srirangam is the largest and most perfect in layout, other such towns include Chidambaram *(see p590)* and Madurai *(see pp608–11)*.

Puja items being sold outside the temple enclosure

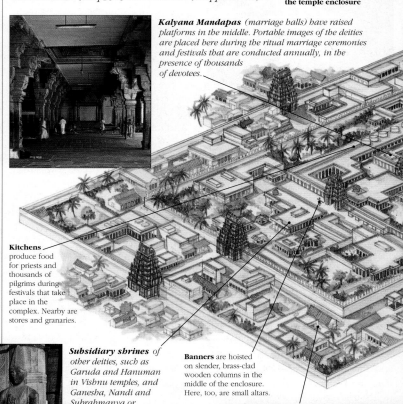

Kalyana Mandapas (marriage halls) have raised platforms in the middle. Portable images of the deities are placed here during the ritual marriage ceremonies and festivals that are conducted annually, in the presence of thousands of devotees.

Kitchens produce food for priests and thousands of pilgrims during festivals that take place in the complex. Nearby are stores and granaries.

Subsidiary shrines of other deities, such as Garuda and Hanuman in Vishnu temples, and Ganesha, Nandi and Subrahmanya or Murugan in Shiva temples, are also venerated within the complex.

Banners are hoisted on slender, brass-clad wooden columns in the middle of the enclosure. Here, too, are small altars.

The outer enclosures of temple complexes are packed with houses to accommodate the priestly community, which presides over the religious life of temple towns.

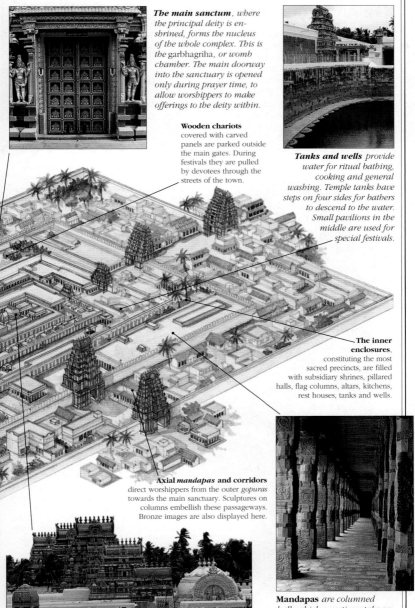

The main sanctum, where the principal deity is enshrined, forms the nucleus of the whole complex. This is the garbhagriha, or womb chamber. The main doorway into the sanctuary is opened only during prayer time, to allow worshippers to make offerings to the deity within.

Wooden chariots covered with carved panels are parked outside the main gates. During festivals they are pulled by devotees through the streets of the town.

Tanks and wells provide water for ritual bathing, cooking and general washing. Temple tanks have steps on four sides for bathers to descend to the water. Small pavilions in the middle are used for special festivals.

The inner enclosures, constituting the most sacred precincts, are filled with subsidiary shrines, pillared halls, flag columns, altars, kitchens, rest houses, tanks and wells.

Axial mandapas and corridors direct worshippers from the outer gopuras towards the main sanctuary. Sculptures on columns embellish these passageways. Bronze images are also displayed here.

Mandapas are columned halls which sometimes take on vast proportions, especially the so-called thousand-pillared halls. These can accommodate large numbers of visitors who come to listen to sermons or to enjoy performances of classical music and dance.

Gopuras, or ceremonial gateways, with soaring, pyramidal towers, are set into four sides of each of the concentric sets of walls that define the sacred complex. Their hollow brick towers are covered with brightly painted plaster sculptures. Barrel-vaulted roofs at the tops of the towers are crowned by gilded pot finials, visible from all over the town.

Regional Food: South India

Tamil Nadu, Kerala, Andhra Pradesh, as well as Karnataka *(see pp440–41)*, share a common culinary heritage that rests heavily on rice, lentils, coconut and spices. Similarities include a variety of snacks, such as *dosas*, *idlis* and *vadas* (deep-fried lentil doughnuts), and an amazing range of imaginatively cooked rice and vegetable specialities. Pungent lentil curries, pickles, chutneys and curd-based relishes are eaten throughout the south, yet each state's cuisine has its own distinct flavour, dictated by regional tastes and locally grown ingredients.

Pickles *and crisp sun-dried chillies accompany dishes cooked with green bananas or tapioca. Sambhar is made with curry powder and small onions.*

Uthapam (open rice pancakes)

Upma (savoury semolina snack)

Thengai saadham (coconut rice)

Thakkali saadham (tomato rice)

Vadas (fried lentil doughnuts)

Molaga-podi (chilli chutney)

Elimicham pazham saadham (lemon rice)

Sambhar (lentil purée)

Idli

Thayir saadham (curd rice)

Rasam (pepper water)

Puliyodharai (tamarind rice)

Poriyal

TAMIL NADU

Tamil vegetarian cuisine includes a choice of rice preparations, seasoned with curry leaves and chillies. Vegetables, either steamed or stir-fried *(poriyal)*, curries, such as *sambhar* (made with lentils) and *rasam* (pepper water), as well as curd, chutneys and poppadams, usually accompany the meal. Traditionally, fresh banana leaves were used instead of plates.

Dosa *and* idli, *crisp pancakes and steamed rice dumplings, are served with hot spicy* sambhar *and chutneys made with coconut, garlic and chillies.*

Meen varuval *(fried fish)* and pepper chicken *from Chettinad (see p613) are non-vegetarian dishes from Tamil Nadu. These were once served in "military hotels", so called to distinguish them from vegetarian eateries.*

KERALA

Rice and coconut form the base of Kerala's varied cuisine. The best-known dish is the *appam* (steamed rice pancake), served with stew. Other specialities are coconut-based curries, and fish *(meen)*, meat *(aadu)* and chicken *(kozhi)* preparations.

Avial *is a mixed vegetable curry cooked with coconut, turmeric and cumin.*

Kozhi varutha curry *is a chicken curry made with freshly ground spices and red chillies.*

Vegetable stew

Chicken stew

Appam

Meen moilee *is a delicately flavoured fish curry, simmered in fresh coconut milk.*

Aadu olathiayathu *is fried cubes of mutton, garnished with coconut and curry leaves.*

ANDHRA PRADESH

The liberal use of tamarind and red chilli give Andhra food its distinct flavour. A typical meal comprises a rice *pulao*, lentils, relishes and chutneys. Sautéed or curried vegetables, such as jackfruit *(Artocarpus heterophyllus)*, are also part of the menu. The coastal areas specialize in seafood.

Hyderabadi cuisine has a distinct Muslim influence (see p665). Savoury mutton or chicken pulaos are accompanied by dishes such as kebabs, mutton, chicken or vegetable curries (salans), sautéed vegetables and various breads.

Tahari (mince *pulao*)

Mirchi ka salan (green chilli curry)

Tamatar kutt (tomato purée)

Pachidi (curd relish)

Kodi pulao (chicken *pulao*)

Tamatar pappu (tomato-lentil curry)

Bagharey baingan (spicy aubergines)

Machli mahi khalya (tamarind fish curry)

Kurma pulusu (jackfruit curry)

COFFEE

Roasted and freshly ground coffee beans are filtered into a thick, aromatic "decoction" in a traditional brass container.

Royyalu pulusu (prawn curry)

Sabudana uthapam (sago pancakes)

CHENNAI

HENNAI, FORMERLY KNOWN AS MADRAS, *is the state capital of Tamil Nadu and the gateway to the rich and varied culture of the South Indian peninsula. Originally a cluster of fishing hamlets along the Coromandel Coast, the city developed its cohesive shape under the British. Today, it is South India's commercial and cultural capital, and the fourth largest metropolis in India.*

A modern capital, with the appearance of a gracious garden city, Chennai was once a group of villages set amidst palm-fringed paddy fields, until two English East India Company merchants, Francis Day and Andrew Cogan, established a factory-cum-trading post here. Completed on St George's Day, 23 April 1640, this fortified settlement came to be known as Fort St George. Outside its walls was George Town, the so-called "native town", whose crowded lanes, each devoted to a particular trade, serviced the British colonists. Colonial rule linked the various villages, including the settlement founded in the 16th century by the Portuguese at San Thomé, the sacred site associated with St Thomas the Apostle. Several centuries before the Europeans arrived, the great 7th-century Pallava port was at Mylapore; its Kapalesvara Temple, along with the Parthasarathi Temple at Triplicane, bear testimony to the city's antiquity.

Colonial rule marked the beginning of the city's growth as a major commercial centre. Today, most of the large business houses have their offices in George Town, while Fort St George is the power centre of the Tamil Nadu state government. Extending across 172 sq km (66 sq miles), Chennai today is a dynamic mix of the old and the new, its stately colonial structures juxtaposed with modern high-rises. Its rich cultural heritage of Tamil literature, music and dance is perpetuated in universities and performing arts centres. It is also a highly political city, as can be seen from the many grandiose memorials to politicians that line Marina Beach.

A huge hoarding depicting Jayalalitha, a Tamil Nadu political leader, looming above Marina promenade

◁ **Flower seller with fragrant garlands near the Kapalesvara Temple, Mylapore**

Exploring Chennai

A CONGLOMERATION OF SEVERAL overgrown villages, Chennai has no single centre, but can be divided into a numerous urban districts, connected by four main roads. George Town is to the northeast of Periyar EVR High Road (Poonamallee High Road), while Egmore, Triplicane and Mylapore are to the south. The city's main thoroughfare, Anna Salai (Mount Road), links Fort St George with Mount St Thomas, to the south. Chennai's other main roads, Rajaji Salai (North Beach Road) and Kamarajar Salai (South Beach Road), run along the seafront, along the popular Marina promenade towards Kalakshetra.

LOCATOR MAP

An early morning scene at a flower shop at Parry's Corner

SIGHTS AT A GLANCE

Historic Buildings, Areas & Neighbourhoods
Adyar ⑩

Anna Salai ⑥

Egmore ④

Fort St George ①

George Town ②

Triplicane ⑧

Churches & Holy Places
Little Mount & Mount of St Thomas ⑭

Mylapore & San Thomé ⑨

St Andrew's Kirk pp562–3 ③

Walk
A Walk along the Marina pp568–9 ⑦

Museums
The Pantheon Complex ⑤

Parks & Gardens
Guindy National Park ⑬

Entertainment
Kalakshetra ⑪

MGR Film City ⑫

GETTING AROUND

Public buses and private cars or taxis are the most convenient means of getting around within the city. The local (above-ground) trains of Chennai's Mass Rapid Transit System (MRTS) and the suburban railway together cover large sections of the city and its outskirts. Private tour operators have organized coach tours to most sites of interest.

SEE ALSO

- **Where to Stay** pp712–13
- **Where to Eat** pp740–41

Traffic on Anna Salai, Chennai's main thoroughfare

KEY

✈	International airport
✕	Domestic airport
🚉	Railway station
🚌	Bus station
M	MRTS train station
ℹ	Tourist information
✚	Hospital
🚓	Police station
🛕	Temple
C	Mosque
🏛	Gurdwara
✝	Church
⊠	Post office
══	National highway
══	Major road

0 km   1

0 miles   1

GREATER CHENNAI

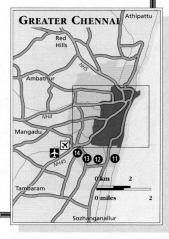

Athipattu

Red Hills

Ambathur

Mangadu

Tambaram

Sozhanganallur

0 km   2

0 miles   2

The Secretariat at Fort St George, the seat of Tamil Nadu's government

Fort St George ❶

Bounded by Sir Muthuswamy Iyer Rd, Flag Staff Rd & Kamarajar Salai (South Beach Rd). **Fort Museum**
○ Sat–Thu. ● public hols. 🎫

BRITAIN'S FIRST BASTION in India, the nucleus from which an empire grew, was established in a banana grove owned by a farmer called Madrasan. The official grant for the land, however, was given by Venkatadri Nayak, the deputy of the Raja of Chandragiri (see p680). The first factory within the fortified enclosure was completed on St George's Day, 23 April 1640, and named Fort St George. This was the East India Company's principal settlement until 1774, when Calcutta, now Kolkata, was declared the seat of the government.

The sloping ramparts, with battlements for gun emplacement that can still be seen today, were designed and constructed by Bartholomew Robins in 1750, after the

The altar in St Mary's Church with a painting of the Last Supper

original walls were destroyed by the French army in 1749. These ramparts form an irregular pentagon, further reinforced by a ring of earthen walls that slope down to a moat surrounding the entire complex. The drawbridges that once led to the Fort's five main gates have now been replaced by roads.

The first building to be seen on entering the Fort through the Sea Gate is the Neo-Classical **Secretariat**, which is today the seat of the government of Tamil Nadu. Behind it lie the **Legislative Council Chambers**. With their handsome classical lines and façades embellished with gleaming black pillars, these impressive buildings, built between 1694 and 1732, are said to be among the oldest surviving British constructions in India. The 45-m (148-ft) tall

flagstaff was erected by Governor Elihu Yale in 1687 to hoist the Union Jack for the first time in India. Today, the Indian tricolour flies in its stead. Yale began his career as a clerk with the East India Company and later founded Yale University in the USA, with his considerable fortune.

Standing to the south of the Legislature building is **St Mary's Church**, the oldest Anglican church in Asia. It was built between 1678 and 1680 by Streynsham Master, then the governor of Madras. Tombstones, memorials, registers and paintings, antique Bibles (including one printed in 1660) and silver are displayed in the church, and speak of its vibrant history. Both Elihu Yale and Robert Clive were married in this church, and the three daughters of Job Charnock (see p267) were baptized here before the family moved to Bengal. Arthur Wellesley, who later became the Duke of Wellington and triumphed at Waterloo, and Robert Clive, both lived in Fort St George. Their residences, Wellesley House and Clive House, still stand, albeit in a somewhat dilapidated condition, across from the church.

To the north is the **Parade Ground**, formerly Cornwallis Square, which was laid out in 1715. Magnificent parades and rallies were held here. To its east are ministerial offices, and barracks for regiments.

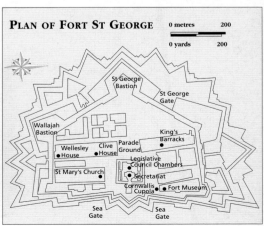

PLAN OF FORT ST GEORGE

0 metres 200
0 yards 200

St George Bastion
St George Gate
Wallajah Bastion
King's Barracks
Wellesley House
Clive House
Parade Ground
Legislative Council Chambers
St Mary's Church
Secretariat
Cornwallis Cupola
Fort Museum
Sea Gate
Sea Gate

Near the southeast corner of the Parade Ground is the **Fort Museum**, built in the 1780s. A treasure trove of colonial memorabilia, the museum is housed in what was built to be the Public Exchange. It has paintings of British royalty, 18th-century weaponry, emblems and other relics from the British era. Among its prized possessions are a scale model of the Fort and a painting of King George III and Queen Charlotte. There are lithographs on the second and third floors that provide fascinating perspectives of old Madras and other parts of South India.

Near the museum's southern end, and overlooking its cannon, is the **Cornwallis Cupola**, which originally stood in the Parade Ground. The statue of the governor-general, Lord Cornwallis, sculpted in 1800, shows him accepting the two young sons of Tipu Sultan *(see p517)* as hostages.

George Town ❷

Bounded by Rajaji Salai (North Beach Rd) & NSC Bose Rd.

IN THE 1640s, weavers and dyers from Andhra Pradesh were settled in this enclave to manufacture cloth for the East India Company's textile trade. The British referred to the settlement as "Black Town",

The General Post Office, George Town

while its inhabitants called it Chennapatnam, from where Chennai gets it name. After the entire area was rebuilt 100 years later, it was renamed George Town. During this period, most of the city's commercial activity was concentrated within this 5-sq km (2-sq mile) area. It still remains a busy hive of activity with public institutions in the south, trade and commercial premises in the centre, and residential quarters in the north.

The first feature of interest is the 38-m (125-ft) high

Fruit vendors on the pavements of George Town

Lighthouse on Rajaji Salai, whose beacon was visible 25 km (16 miles) out at sea. The adjacent red-brick **High Court**, designed by Chisholm in the Indo-Saracenic style, with stained glass and carved furniture, was opened in 1892, while the nearby **General Post Office** with its archways and square towers, is another fine Indo-Saracenic building. **Parry's Corner**, at the junction of NSC Bose Road and Rajaji Salai, is named after Parry and Company. Founded by Thomas Parry in 1790, it is the oldest British mercantile company still operating in Chennai. **Dare House**, the present headquarters of this 200-year-old company, now stands at the site.

The area's longest street, **Mint Street**, gets its name from the authorized mint that was set up here in 1841 to produce gold coins for the British as well as for various local rulers. The mint buildings are now part of the government printing press.

The 17th-century houses lining George Town were once the residences and business centres of Indian as well as Portuguese, Armenian and other foreign traders. **Armenian Street** is named after the many Armenians who lived here, while **Coral Merchant Street** housed a small Jewish community that traded in corals. Today, each street in George Town is dominated by a particular trade. Anderson Street specializes in paper, grain merchants operate from Audiappa Naicken Street, while textile salesalers have their warehouses on Govindappa Naicken Street and Godown Street. Some streets, such as Kasi Chetty Street and Narayanamudali Street, are lined with shops selling fancy goods and imported bric-a-brac.

ROBERT CLIVE (1725–74)

A portrait of Robert Clive by Nathaniel Dance (1773)

One of the most flamboyant personalities in the history of British India, Robert Clive was only 19 when he began his career as a clerk for the East India Company at Fort St George. Soon tiring of paperwork, he became a soldier and fought many successful battles *(see p52)*, including the Carnatic Wars, which established the Company's rule in South India. Clive was given the stewardship of Fort St George and later become Governor of Bengal. The wealth he amassed in India led to his trial, in England, on charges of corruption. Clive committed suicide in 1774.

St Andrew's Kirk ❸

A MAGNIFICENT EXAMPLE of Neo-Classical architecture, St Andrew's Kirk was consecrated in 1821. Inspired by St Martin-in-the-Fields in London, it was designed and executed by Major Thomas de Havilland and Colonel James Caldwell of the Madras Engineers, at a cost of £20,000. The body of the church is a circle, with rectangular compartments to the east and west. The circular part, 24.5 m (80 ft) in diameter, is crowned by a shallow masonry dome coloured a deep blue. This is painted with golden stars and supported by 16 fluted pillars with Corinthian capitals.

A memorial plaque

A view of St Andrew's Kirk with its towering steeple

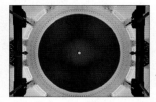

★ Dome
An architectural marvel, the dome has a framework of brick supported by an annular arch and is filled in by pottery cones. Its blue interior is formed by crushed sea shells mixed with lapis lazuli.

Stained glass
The stained-glass windows above the altar, in warm, rich colours, are among the glories of the church.

Pews
Superb mahogany pews and a pulpit furnish the interior. From 1839, the pews were let out to prominent citizens; the brass fittings that once held their name cards can still be seen.

Sixteen fluted Corinthian columns support the dome, lending beauty and balance to the design.

The steeple is 50 m (164 ft) high, 4 m (13 ft) taller than its inspiration, St Martin-in-the-Fields in London. On top of the slim pyramidal spire is a bronze weathercock.

VISITORS' CHECKLIST

Egmore. ☎ (044) 538 3508.
◯ daily. ✝ 9am & 6pm Sun.
✦ St Andrew's Day (Nov).

THE WELLS OF ST ANDREW'S KIRK

Because of sandy soil and a site prone to flooding during the monsoon, the church's foundations are actually a series of wells sunk to depths ranging from 4 m to 15 m (13 ft to 49 ft) below ground level. This example of engineering ingenuity is based on a structural practice followed by most indigenous buildings in the area. The wells are constructed either of specially made curved bricks, or pottery cylinders. These are placed so as to ensure maximum compaction of the soil, allowing the water to rise within them and thus protecting the main structure. The 150 wells were dug by a group of itinerant well-sinkers, the Mumvutties.

| 0 metres | 10 |
| 0 yards | 10 |

★ **Pipe Organ**
Dominating the altar is the handsome pipe organ in dull green and burnished gold. Installed in 1883, this instrument was built in Yorkshire, England.

STAR FEATURES

★ **Dome**

★ **Pipe Organ**

Entrance

A double colonnade of 12 polished Ionic columns is surmounted by a pediment.

A view of Egmore Railway Station, one of the city's major landmarks

Egmore ❹

Bounded by Periyar EVR High Rd & Pantheon Rd. 🚉 Egmore Railway Station, (044) 825 2165.

THE ENTIRE AREA south of Periyar EVR High Road (earlier known as Poonamallee High Road) and the curve of the Cooum river is known as Egmore. This was originally a small village that the East India Company acquired in the late 17th century, as it began to expand its territories. Egmore was also one of the earliest residential localities, where wealthy Company merchants built palatial homes surrounded by luxuriant gardens – the so-called "garden houses" that were extremely popular in colonial Chennai.

The **Government College of Arts and Crafts**, founded in 1850, stands on Periyar EVR High Road. This striking Gothic building and its art gallery were built by Robert Fellowes Chisholm (see p569), who was also appointed its superintendent (principal) in 1877. Its first Indian principal, Debi Prasad Roy Chowdhary, was a renowned painter and sculptor in the 1950s. The artists' village at Cholamandal (see p578) was established by bis successor, Dr KCS Panicker. Today the prestigious Government College is one of India's foremost art schools. Its gallery has regular exhibitions of contemporary painting and sculpture by artists and students.

To its west is the **Egmore Railway Station**, another of Chisholm's architectural gems. This is a handsome building, constructed in Indo-Saracenic style, with unconventional flattish domes and pointed arches. The station, operational since the early 20th century, connects Chennai with the rest of Tamil Nadu and the south.

Today Egmore is the up-market commercial heart of Chennai, a concrete jungle of offices, department stores, boutiques and hotels. On Pantheon Road are the largest showrooms of Co-Optex (see p574), a unit of the Tamil Nadu Handloom Textiles Cooperative, which sells handwoven silk and cotton saris and fabrics from the state.

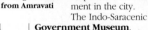

Standing Buddhas from Amravati

The Pantheon Complex ❺

Pantheon Rd. 📞 (044) 826 9638. ◐ Sat–Thu. ● public hols. 🅿 🚻
Connemara Public Library
📞 (044) 826 1151. ◐ daily.

THIS COMPLEX of cultural institutions derives its name from The Pantheon, where the Public Assembly Rooms were housed in the 18th century. At the time, its spacious tree-lined grounds were the venue for all public entertainment in the city.

The Indo-Saracenic **Government Museum**, with its faded red walls and labyrinth of staircases and

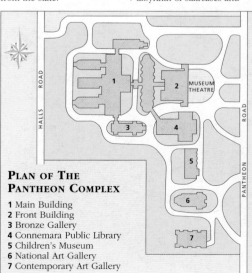

PLAN OF THE PANTHEON COMPLEX

1 Main Building
2 Front Building
3 Bronze Gallery
4 Connemara Public Library
5 Children's Museum
6 National Art Gallery
7 Contemporary Art Gallery

The façade of the National Art Gallery, built in Neo-Mughal style

interconnecting galleries, is spread over five sections of a large complex, each with a specific collection of objects. The 30,000-odd exhibits range from rocks and fossils to books and sculptures.

The Archaeological Section, in the main building, is noted for its exceptional collection of South Indian antiquities. The exhibits include stone and metal sculpture, woodcarvings and manuscripts. Its rare collection of Buddhist antiquities numbers over 1,500 pieces. A major section comprises artifacts from Amravati *(see p675)*, that were brought here in the early 1800s by an intrepid Englishman, Colonel Colin Mackenzie. On display are sculptural reliefs, panels and free-standing statues. Outstanding objects include a 2nd-century votive slab with a rendering of a stupa, and numerous stone panels with episodes from the Buddha's life depicted in low relief.

The Numismatics Section has a large collection of coins, particularly South Indian and Mughal coins. There are also some gold Gupta coins with Sanskrit inscriptions.

The Government Museum was one of the earliest institutions in India where ethnology and prehistoric archaeology were represented as museum subjects. The Anthropology Section, in the front building, has a good collection of prehistoric antiquities, including

cooking utensils and hunting tools, among them the first palaeolith in India, discovered in 1863 by Bruce Foote. The Zoological Section, in the main building, is one of the largest sections of the Museum. Although its scope is limited to South Indian fauna, a few non-indigenous animals and birds, such as the macaw, mandarin duck, and golden pheasant, have been added to enrich the collection. There is also an 18.5-m (60-ft) long whale skeleton on display. The adjoining 19th-century Museum Theatre, a semi-circular structure also built in Indo-Saracenic style, was initially used as a lecture hall. It is now a venue for public performances.

Some of the finest examples of South Indian bronze casting are on display in the **Bronze Gallery**. Its superb collection of almost 700 bronzes, specifically from the Pallava and Chola periods (between the 9th and 13th centuries) have been retrieved from temples and sites in the region. There are many impressive sculptures of the Nataraja – the depiction of Shiva performing his cosmic dance of creation *(see p566)*. Another outstanding piece is an 11th-century

Parvati, 9th century, Chola period

Chola Ardhanarisvara, a composite figure where Shiva and his consort Parvati are joined together to form a holistic entity. Bronzes of other gods and goddesses in the Hindu pantheon, including Rama, Sita and Ganesha, are on view as well. The panorama of images also includes Buddhist bronzes from Amravati, a Chola Tara and Maitreya Avalokitesvara, and 11th-century images of various Jain *tirthankaras*.

Opposite is the imposing **Connemara Public Library**, inaugurated in 1896. This structure, with its profuse stucco decoration, woodwork and stained-glass windows, was named after a dissolute brother of the viceroy, Lord Mayo. It is one of India's four national libraries and contains every book published in the country. Its oldest and most prized possession is a Bible, dated 1608.

The **National Art Gallery**, the former Victoria Memorial Hall and Technical Institute, is perhaps the finest building in the complex. Designed by Henry Irwin, one of the city's most celebrated architects, it was constructed in 1909 in Neo-Mughal style with a pink sandstone finish. Its immense door echoes the monumental gateways of Fatehpur Sikri *(see pp180–83)*. On display are more Chola bronzes, including two fine images of Rama and Sita, and a superb 11th-century Nataraja. Nearby, the **Contemporary Art Gallery** has a fine collection of contemporary Indian art, with a special focus on works by renowned South Indian artists, among them Raja Ravi Varma *(see p626)*.

A 2nd-century stupa panel from Amravati

Shiva, the Cosmic Dancer

Bronze sculptures depicting gods and goddesses, are the glory of South Indian art. Strict iconographic guidelines determine the proportions of each image and the symbolic meaning of every stance, hand gesture, weapon, and adornment. Master sculptors working within these rules were able, nevertheless, to create images of extraordinary individuality, power and grace.

Among the most remarkable bronze sculptures are those of Shiva as Nataraja, the Cosmic Dancer, and his wife Parvati. Richly symbolic in their iconography, they were made during the Chola period, from the 9th to the 13th centuries.

A slender bronze image of Parvati

NATARAJA

The Nataraja figure of Shiva as the Cosmic Dancer symbolizes nature's cycle of evolution and transmutation, and displays the Chola artists' mastery of form and expression.

A tiny crescent moon, a symbol of the passage of time, balances in his hair.

The fire in the left hand symbolizes destruction.

Goddess Ganga is shown among Shiva's flying locks since it was Shiva who eased her descent to earth (see p163).

The drum in his right hand symbolizes the rhythm of creation.

An open palm grants freedom from fear.

The left palm pointing to the foot symbolizes salvation from ignorance.

The left leg is lifted up in an animated dance movement.

The ring of flames symbolizes the cosmos.

The right leg tramples Apasmara, a dwarfish figure representing ignorance.

Bronze images representing the main temple deity are taken out in processions on festive occasions. These images are clad in silk and decked with sandalwood paste and floral garlands.

The marriage of Shiva and Parvati *is a beautiful example of Chola art. It shows Shiva, standing regal and tall, tenderly holding his bashful bride Parvati's hand. Vishnu, as the brother of Parvati, is shown as an onlooker.*

See also features on Hindu Mythology (see pp24–5), Ganesha (see p467) and Vishnu (see p679).

The multi-arched façade of the Thousand Lights Mosque

Anna Salai ❻

From Cooum Island to Little Mount.
Rajaji Hall ☐ daily.

A LONG ARTERIAL road leading from north Chennai to Little Mount at its southern end (see p573), Anna Salai (or Mount Road) is the city's main thoroughfare. The "garden houses" that belonged to Chennai's elite stood on either side of it until well into the early years of the 20th century. Today, it is a modern commercial road, lined with hoardings depicting film stars, and the expansive homes of the past have been replaced by multistoreyed buildings.

Anna Salai begins on an island in Cooum Creek, just south of Fort St George. The site is watched over by the statue of Sir Thomas Munro, the governor of the Madras Presidency from 1819 to 1826. Nearby, set in an expanse of greenery, is the prestigious **Gymkhana Club**. Sited close to the army headquarters, this was an exclusive facility for military officers. Until 1920, its membership was restricted to garrison officers only and, even today, the club grounds belong to the armed services.

The Old Government Estate, southwest of the Gymkhana Club, houses the mansion where the governors of Madras once lived in regal splendour. Though the main building is falling apart, the banqueting hall, built in 1802 by the second Lord Clive, the eldest son of Robert Clive, retains its grandeur. It was named **Rajaji Hall** after the first Indian governor-general, C Rajagopalachari, popularly known as Rajaji. Inside this elegant Neo-Classical building, an impressive broad staircase leads up to the vast banqueting hall, which has beautiful panelling and chandeliers.

Anna Salai then enters its commercial stretch. Along this length of the road are some of the city's oldest commercial landmarks, including one of India's largest bookshops, **Higginbotham's** (see p574), **Spencer's**, an international department store, and the **Taj Connemara**, one of the city's finest hotels (see p715).

Across the road from them is the **Old Madras Club**, now somewhat dilapidated. Established in 1832, it was known in its heyday as the "Ace of Clubs". Further down, the 19th-century **Thousand Lights Mosque** gets its name from the tradition of lighting 1,000 oil lamps to illuminate the Assembly Hall that once occupied the site. Standing further south is **St George's Cathedral**, planned by James Lillyman Caldwell and built by Thomas de Havilland in 1814. Its tall spire, measuring 42 m (138 ft), is one of Chennai's major landmarks.

Main altar in St George's Cathedral, built in the early 19th century

FILM STARS AND POLITICS

Hoardings depicting popular South Indian heroes

The South Indian film industry, particularly Tamil and Telugu cinema, is credited with having been the breeding ground of many politicians. The first chief minister from the Dravidian Party (then called DMK), the late Dr CN Annadurai, as well as his immediate successor, M Karunanidhi, were both scriptwriters with large followings. However, the most remarkable actor-turned-politican was Marudur Gopalamenon Ramachandran, whose portrayal of a swashbuckling hero made him the embodiment of righteousness. Popularly known as MGR, he acquired a cult status in the region and was chief minister of Tamil Nadu from 1977 to 1987. His co-star and protégée, Jayalalitha, was another charismatic chief minister until she was ousted on charges of corruption in 2001. Current heroes, such as Rajnikant and Chiranjeevi, have more macho images that depend heavily on daredevil stunts. They, too, have huge fan followings throughout South India.

A Walk along the Marina ❼

CHENNAI'S SEASHORE hosts one of India's largest urban beaches, stretching for 13 km (8 miles) along the city's eastern flank. The Marina, connecting Fort St George with San Thomé Basilica almost 5 km (3 miles) away, was built by Mounstuart Elphinstone Grant-Duff, the governor between 1881 and 1886. Described by architectural historian Philip Davies as "one of the most beautiful marine promenades in the world", it is a favourite place for Chennai's citizens to escape the humid heat of the city and enjoy the sea breezes. The walk along Kamarajar Salai (earlier known as South Beach Road) takes in parks, tree-lined cobbled streets and spectacular colonial and Indo-Saracenic buildings.

The Indo-Saracenic Presidency College, nucleus of Madras University

Anna Park

The walk starts from the Victory War Memorial ❶ which marks the north end of Kamarajar Salai. This memorial originally commemorated the victory of the Allied armies during World War I, and was later dedicated to the memory of those soldiers from the Madras Presidency who lost their lives in World War II. To its south, in Anna Park, is the Anna Samadhi ❷, a memorial erected in honour of CN Annadurai, the former chief minister of Tamil Nadu, who introduced significant political and social reforms in the state. Further south is the MGR Samadhi ❸, a commemorative garden with gateways and pathways, built in honour of the popular Tamil film icon and chief minister, MG Ramachandran (see p567). An array of souvenir shops and eateries can be found along this

Victory War Memorial, Kamarajar Salai

stretch of the beach, attracting tourists from the rest of the state. Particularly interesting is the Sunday market, with its curious jumble of goods.

North Marina

Across Kamarajar Salai is a series of imposing red brick buildings, built in a combination of architectural styles, which include Indian and Moorish features. The Indo-Saracenic Madras University ❹ was founded in 1857, making it one of the oldest universities in India. An architectural marvel, the Senate House ❺ was designed by Robert Chisholm in a mixture of Byzantine and Saracenic styles. This became the headquarters of Madras University in 1879. These buildings now stand in what was once the sprawling estate of the old Chepauk Palace ❻. This splendid Indo-

Saracenic structure, on Wallajah Road, was once the home of the Nawab of Arcot. Though the palace was built in 1768, Chisholm added the extensions, including the tower that once connected the two wings. It now houses government offices. Chepauk Stadium, Chennai's famous cricket ground, lies behind the palace. Further down the road is Presidency College ❼, the first institution in South India for higher education, founded in 1840. This rather austere structure has a ribbed dome with four clocks on its surface. Among the famous alumni of the college are the first Indian governor-general, C Rajagopalachari, and the Nobel Prize-winning physicists, CV Raman and his nephew, S Chandrasekhar.

South Marina

Further south, an impressive landmark on Kamarajar Salai is the statue *Triumph of Labour* ❽.

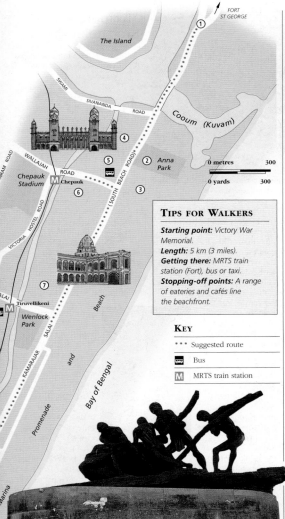

FORT
ST GEORGE

The Island

SWAMI

SIVANANDA ROAD

Cooum (Kuvam)

④

WALLAJAH ROAD

Chepauk Stadium

⑤

② Anna Park

Ⓜ Chepauk

⑥

③

VICTORIA HOSTEL ROAD

⑦

Ⓜ Tiruvellikeni

Wenlock Park

KAMARAJAR SALAI

Beach and Promenade

Bay of Bengal

Marina

0 metres   300

0 yards   300

TIPS FOR WALKERS

Starting point: Victory War Memorial.
Length: 5 km (3 miles).
Getting there: MRTS train station (Fort), bus or taxi.
Stopping-off points: A range of eateries and cafés line the beachfront.

KEY

••• Suggested route

🚌 Bus

Ⓜ MRTS train station

Triumph of Labour by Debi Prasad Roy Chowdhary, 1959

A busy evening scene on the Marina Beach

This sculpture was created by Debi Prasad Roy Chowdhary *(see p564)*, who became the first Indian principal of the Madras School of Arts and Crafts in 1929.

West of the main road, off Annie Besant Road, is the Ice House ⑨, till recently a women's hostel known as Vivekananda House. In the 1840s, this circular building, with a stone pineapple perched on its roof, was a storehouse for ice, which was imported all the way from New England (USA). It was also the site from which Swami Vivekananda *(see p615)* delivered his speeches when he visited the city. It has now been handed over to the Ramakrishna Mission which has plans to restore it. Further south is Queen Mary's College ⑩, today the Madras College for Women. Opened in July 1914, this was Chennai's first women's college. A bust of the queen still graces the entrance of the building. An imposing lighthouse ⑪ marks the southern end of the Marina.

ROBERT CHISHOLM'S LEGACY

Robert Fellowes Chisholm (1845–84) was among the most talented architects in India in the mid-19th century. In 1864, Chisholm's designs for the proposed Presidency College and Senate House won a competition, and he was appointed the consulting architect to the Madras government. The next 15 years saw considerable building activity along the Marina, where many innovative buildings were erected. Chisholm's designs blended Italian and Saracenic features so that the new structures would harmonize with the existing Chepauk Palace. For many years he was the head of the School of Industrial Art, founded in 1855 and now known as the Government College of Fine Arts.

Senate House, Robert Chisholm's signature building, completed in 1873

Watermelons and other fruit on sale at Triplicane Market

Triplicane ❽

Off Kamarajar Salai (South Beach Rd).
Parthasarathi Temple ☐ daily.
🎭 Neeratu Utsavam (Dec).

THE CROWDED SUBURB of Triplicane was among the first villages to be acquired by the East India Company in the 1670s. It derives its name from the sacred lily tank *(tiru-alli-keni)* that once stood here. One of the oldest temples in the city, the historic **Parthasarathi Temple**, is situated in Triplicane. Built in the 9th century, the temple is dedicated to Krishna (or Partha) in his role as Arjuna's divine charioteer *(sarathi)* in the epic, the *Mahabharata (see p26)*. The temple festival, in December, attracts thousands of devotees. At one time, the residences of the priestly Brahmin caste were clustered in the narrow lanes around the temple. Among them were the homes of the mathematical genius, Srinivasa Ramanujan (1887–1920), and the early 20th-century nationalist poet, Subramania Bharati.

Triplicane was once part of the kingdom of Golconda *(see pp666–7)*, and as a result this quarter has the largest concentration of Muslims in the city. The Nawab of Arcot, Muhammad Ali Wallajah (1749–95), an ally of the British in their struggle for power against the French, contributed generously to the construction of a large mosque here in 1795. Known as the **Wallajah (Big) Mosque**, this beautiful grey granite structure with slender minarets is situated on Triplicane High Road. The adjoining graveyard contains the tombs of various Muslim saints. The nawab's descendants still live in Triplicane, in a stately mansion known as **Amir Mahal**. Constructed in 1798, it became their residence after the Chepauk Palace *(see p568)* was taken over by the British.

The graceful façade of Wallajah Mosque, with its flanking minarets

Mylapore & San Thomé ❾

S of Triplicane. **Kapaleshvara Temple** ☐ daily. **Basilica of San Thomé** ☐ daily. **Luz Church** ☐ daily.

THE SITE OF a great Pallava port in the 7th and 8th centuries, Mylapore is today one of the busiest parts of the city. This traditional quarter, with its religious organizations, tiny houses and lively bazaars, is dominated by the **Kapaleshvara Temple**, the largest in Chennai. The main deity, Shiva, is symbolized as a peacock *(mayil)*, thus giving the area its original name, Mayilapura, the "Town of the Peacocks". According to legend, Shiva's consort, Parvati, assumed the form of a peahen to worship Shiva, represented here by his linga. A sculptural panel in a small

The Gothic-style Basilica of San Thomé

shrine in the courtyard depicts the legend. The present temple was built after the original was destroyed by the Portuguese in the 16th century. Mylapore's links with Christianity date to the 1st century AD, to the time of St Thomas *(see p573)*. In the 10th century, a group of Nestorian Christians from Persia (Iran) discovered the saint's burial site and built a church and tomb. The Portuguese, following the trail of the saint, established the settlement of San Thomé in the early 16th century. The present **Basilica of San Thomé**, over the tomb of the saint, is an impressive Gothic-style structure built in 1898. It has an ornate interior with magnificent stained-glass windows and a towering steeple. The crypt is said to contain a small bone from the saint's hand and the weapon that killed him.

Nearby is the **Luz Church**, which was built by a Franciscan monk in 1516, making it the oldest Catholic church in Chennai.

Adyar ⑩

S of San Thomé, across Adyar river.
Theosophical Society 🄲 *(044) 491 3528.* ⭘ *Mon–Fri & (Sat morn).*
Brodie Castle ⭘ *daily.*

Few places in Chennai offer greater serenity than the sprawling gardens of the **Theosophical Society**, situated in the city's Adyar neighbourhood, on the banks of the Adyar river. Founded in New York in 1875, the Society moved here seven years later when it acquired Huddlestone Gardens. Built in 1776 by John Huddlestone, a wealthy civilian, this large mansion is today the world headquarters of the Society. Its magnificent 108-ha (270-acre) estate comprises several 19th-century buildings, one of which is the former home of its founder Colonel Henry S Olcott.

The main building houses the Great Hall, almost spartan in its simplicity, where prayer meetings are held. Bas-reliefs, representing the different faiths, and engravings of verses taken from the holy books of all world religions can be seen here. There are also marble statues of the founders, Colonel Olcott and Helena Petrovna Blavatsky, as well as one of Annie Besant, who became president in 1907.

The Adyar Library and Research Centre, founded by Olcott in 1886, is one of the finest libraries in India. Its collection of 165,000 books and 20,000 palm-leaf and parchment manuscripts has made it a valuable repository for Indological research. The surrounding tranquil gardens have shrines dedicated to

The 400-year-old banyan tree in the gardens of the Theosophical Society

various faiths. The greatest attraction here, however, is the 400-year-old banyan tree, whose spreading branches cover an immense area of 4,180 sq m (44,993 sq ft). Over the decades, many of the Society's meetings and spiritual discourses were held under its canopy. Unfortunately, a terrible storm in 1989 destroyed its main trunk.

Brodie Castle, north of the Theosophical Society, is an imposing white structure on the banks of the Adyar. Now known as Thenral, it houses the prestigious College of Carnatic Music. Built in 1796 by James Brodie, an employee of the East India Company, it is said to be among the first "garden-houses" built in the city. These spacious, airy

houses with broad pillared verandahs, set in sprawling wooded gardens, were characteristic of colonial Chennai. This house later became the home of the first Chief Justice of the Madras Supreme Court.

Further north of Brodie Castle is the **Madras Club**, built by George Moubray, who came to India as an accountant in 1771. He acquired 42 ha (104 acres) of land on the banks of the Adyar, and built a house with a central cupola, surrounded by a beautiful garden. Known as Moubray's Cupola, this was once the exclusive preserve of the city's European population. Indians were only allowed membership in 1964, after it merged with the Adyar Club.

The pillared entrance of Brodie Castle in Adyar

THE THEOSOPHICAL SOCIETY

In the 1870s, Colonel Henry S Olcott, a veteran of the American Civil War, met the Russian aristocrat and clairvoyant, Madame Helena Petrovna Blavatsky in Vermont (USA) at the farm of the Christian Scientist, Mary Baker Eddy. Soon after, they launched a movement to foster the spirit of universal brotherhood, aiming to create a Utopian society in which people of all castes, creeds and colour could live in harmony. The movement attracted great thinkers and intellec-

Theosophical Society

tuals, among them Dr Annie Besant, president of the Indian National Congress in 1917. The idea of forming a national political party was, in fact, first voiced in the 1890s at the Society's headquarters in Adyar, under the banyan tree, by the British civil servant AO Hume. The famous philosopher Jiddu Krishnamurti was also associated with the Society.

A Bharat Natyam dance lesson in progress at Kalakshetra

Kalakshetra ⓫

Thiruvanmiyur, East Coast Rd. 🚌 or taxi. 📞 (044) 491 1844. ⭘ daily. 🎭 Kalakshetra Arts Festival (Dec/Jan).

THIS PIONEERING institution for classical dance, music and the fine arts, established in 1936, was the brainchild of Rukmini Devi. A protégée of Annie Besant, she was deeply influenced by the progressive views of the Theosophical Society (see p571). At 16, she scandalized conservative society by marrying George Sydney Arundale, the 40-year-old Australian principal of the Society's school. The couple's extensive travels around the world exposed Rukmini to the world of Western culture, specially dance, inspiring her to study ballet under the great Russian ballerina, Anna Pavlova. Back in Chennai, she again defied tradition by learning and performing the classical *dasi attam*, hitherto the domain of *devadasis* (temple dancers). The International Centre for the Arts, which she set up for the revival of this dance form, now called Bharat Natyam, (see p29), is today Kalakshetra, the "Temple of Art".

The school is set in a vast 40-ha (99-acre) campus, where classical music and dance are taught according to the traditional methods, by which a guru imparts knowledge to a small group of students. Some of India's best known dancers, such as Yamini Krishnamurti, Leela Samson and Alarmel Valli, were trained here. At the end

of each year, a festival is held and performances are staged in an auditorium designed like a *koottambulam*, the traditional theatre of Kerala temples (see p639).

MGR Film City ⓬

Near Indira Nagar. 🚌 📞 (044) 235 2212. ⭘ daily 🎥 📷 extra charges.

ONE OF CHENNAI'S newest attractions is a film city, dedicated to the memory of the hugely popular matinée idol, MG Rama-chandran (see p567). This is now the most popular location for Chennai's flourishing Tamil film industry, which is second only to Mumbai (see pp32–3) in film production. A fantasy world of extravagant sets and hi-tech equipment, Film City attracts starstruck fans from all over Tamil Nadu, who come here to catch a glimpse of their favourite film stars.

A film set in MGR Film City

Guindy National Park ⓭

S Chennai. Sardar Vallabhbhai Patel Rd. 🚉 Guindy station. 🚌 ⭘ Wed–Mon. 🏛 Raj Bhavan ⭘ to public.

ONCE A DISTANT suburb which was nearly twice its current size, Guindy has now been engulfed by the fast growing metropolis of Greater Chennai. Originally part of the private forest surrounding Guindy Lodge, a portion was officially declared the Guindy National Park in 1977. This predominantly dry deciduous scrub jungle of acacia is interspersed with larger trees such as sandalwood (Santalam album), banyan (Ficus bengalensis) and jamun (Syzygium cumini). Its most famous residents are the herds of endangered blackbuck (Antelope cervicapra), introduced in 1924. Among its 130 species of birds are raptors such as the honey buzzard and the white-bellied sea eagle. Winter is the best time for birdwatching, when migrant birds visit the forest. Also located within the park is the **Madras Snake Park**, established in the 1970s by Romulus Whitaker, the American zoologist, who also set up the Crocodile Bank outside Chennai (see p578). Today, the well-maintained Snake Park houses numerous species of snakes, among them king cobras, vipers and pythons. Other reptiles

A song-and-dance sequence being shot on location for a Tamil movie

include crocodiles, turtles and lizards. Large information boards, strategically placed, provide interesting details on the habitat and behaviour of the various species. For those who are interested, there are live demonstrations of venom extraction; the venom is used as an antidote for snake bites.

The historic 300-year-old Guindy Lodge, to the west of the Park, is now the **Raj Bhavan**, the residence of the governor of Tamil Nadu. Built as a weekend retreat for the city's British rulers, this handsome white building was renovated and expanded in the mid-1800s by the then governor, Grant-Duff.

Today, Guindy has some of the city's most prestigious institutions. The area also has many impressive memorials to modern India's leaders, Mahatma Gandhi, K Kamaraj and C Rajagopalachari.

Façade of the Church of Our Lady of Expectations, Mount of St Thomas

Little Mount & Mount of St Thomas ⑭

SW Chennai. Near Marmalog Bridge.
🚇 St Thomas Mount station. 🚌

A ROCK-HEWN CAVE on Little Mount is believed to be the place where, in AD 72, the mortally wounded St Thomas sought refuge. Near the modern **Church of Our Lady of Good Health** is the older **Blessed Sacrament Chapel** built by the Portuguese over the cave. Inside the cave is the opening through which the fleeing saint is said to have retreated, leaving behind a still visible imprint of his hand near the entrance. At the rear end of the cave is the Masonry Cross before which St Thomas is said to have prayed. By the **Church of the Resurrection** is a perennial

The Masonry Cross, engraved on a rock in the cave, Little Mount

spring with curative powers. Legend claims that the spring originated when St Thomas struck the rock with his staff to provide water for his thirsty congregation.

About 3 km (2 miles) southwest of Little Mount is the 95-m (312-ft) high Mount of St Thomas or Great Mount. A flight of 132 steps leads to the summit and the **Church of Our Lady of Expectations**, built by the Portuguese in the 16th century. The most important relic here is the ancient stone cross embedded into the wall of the altar. Said to have been engraved by the saint himself, this is the legendary "bleeding cross" that miraculously bled between 1558 and 1704.

Below the eastern flank of the Mount is the **Cantonment** area, with its shady streets lined with 18th-century Neo-Classical bungalows.

ST THOMAS IN INDIA

According to legend, St Thomas or Doubting Thomas, one of the 12 apostles, came to South India soon after Jesus Christ died. He is said to have arrived in Cranganore *(see p649)* in AD 52 and spent the next 12 years along the Malabar Coast, spreading the Gospel and converting the local population. He gradually moved eastwards and finally settled in Mylapore *(see p570)*. He spent the last years of his life in a cave on Little Mount, from where he would walk every day to the beach, resting for a while and preaching in the groves. It is said that one day in AD 72, while praying on the Mount of St Thomas, he was mortally wounded by a lance, and fled to Little Mount, where he died. His body was carried by his converts to San Thomé, where he was buried in the crypt of the small chapel he had built. This is today the Basilica of San Thomé, and the large stained-glass window depicts his story. The Portuguese colonized Mylapore in the early 16th century, lured by accounts left by the 13th-century Venetian traveller, Marco Polo, who had visited the early Nestorian chapel here. The saint holds a special place in the hearts of Indians, and was decreed the Apostle of India in 1972.

Portrait of St Thomas

Shopping & Entertainment in Chennai

As THE CAPITAL OF TAMIL NADU, Chennai has an excellent selection of handicrafts and handwoven textiles from the state. From shimmering silks in glowing colours and finely woven cottons to jewellery and replicas of Chola bronzes, the choice is enormous. The city's shopping centres include up-market department stores, malls and trendy boutiques, as well as the vibrant local bazaars which sell a wide range of merchandise. Chennai is also the cultural capital of South India, where performances of classical dance and music take place throughout the year. The height of the cultural season is from mid-December to mid-January, when the city hosts the prestigious Chennai Festival.

SHOPS AND MARKETS

THE BEST shopping in Chennai can be found in the more traditional areas, such as Panagal Park, Pondy and Burma bazaars, and the lanes around the temple at Mylapore. These were small street markets that have now grown into mini shopping malls, where everything is available at bargain prices. Chennai's oldest department store, Spencer's, partially burned down in the 1980s, and has now been rebuilt as a modern mall. It houses shops selling merchandise as varied as groceries and imported Swiss watches. Next door is the city's oldest landmark, **VTI** (Victoria Technical Institute), where handicrafts and a range of good quality linen are sold. This charitable organization supports South Indian Christian missions that specialize in exquisite hand-embroidery.

Most shops are open Monday to Friday, from 9:30am to 7pm. Bazaars, however, keep more flexible hours.

JEWELLERY AND ANTIQUES

THE BEST PLACE for high quality traditional South Indian gold jewellery is **Vummidi Bangaru Jewellers**. They also stock excellent reproductions of the gem-encrusted costume jewellery worn by classical dancers. **Prince Jewellery**, in Panagal Park, has jewellery from Kerala and also specializes in light weight gold

ornaments. Modern and traditional silverware and jewellery are available at **Sukha** and **Amethyst**.

Genuine antiques are hard to find. However, **Rani Arts & Crafts** stocks copies of old artifacts, including brass and metal images and objects, Tanjore (Thanjavur) paintings *(see p597)* and lacquerware.

TEXTILES AND SARIS

TAMIL NADU is renowned for the richness and variety of its silk and cotton textiles, a good selection of which is available in Chennai. **Radha Silks**, **Kumaran Silks** and **Sundari Silks** are famous all over India for their wonderful range of fabrics and silk saris from Kanchipuram *(see p583)*. **Nalli's**, a huge multistoreyed shop, has the widest range of Kanchipuram saris, and is always packed with local shoppers, particularly during the festival and wedding seasons. Other outlets are **Man Mandir** and **Shilpi**, a small boutique that sells saris and home furnishings. **Fabindia** too, stocks furnishings and ready-made garments. A good variety of textiles can be found at **Co-optex**, the large Tamil Nadu Cooperative of Textiles showroom. This pioneering society has encouraged the revival of handlooms.

HANDICRAFTS AND GIFTS

A FINE SELECTION of handicrafts can be found at **Poompuhar**, the Tamil Nadu State Emporium. VTI also sells

handicrafts, though hand-embroidered linen and nightwear are their main specialities. **Cane and Bamboo** is another interesting little shop with an assortment of gift items and souvenirs.

Apparao Galleries not only stocks paintings by contemporary Indian artists, but also has an accessory shop for gifts and home products. Their boutique sells trendy designer-wear.

Naturally Auroville specializes in natural products made in the Pondicherry Ashram and Auroville *(see pp586–8)*. The merchandise includes pottery, handmade paper, perfumed candles, incense sticks and aromatherapy oils and lotions.

Chennai is also a good place to shop for handcrafted musical instruments, such as the violin, *mridangam* and *veena*. While these are found at many outlets in the city, the best selections are available at **Musee Musicals** and **Saptaswara Music Store**. **Music World** stocks a wide range of CDs and audio cassettes by well-known Carnatic musicians. The city also has a number of excellent bookshops. Of these, the oldest and most well-stocked is **Higginbotham's**, established in 1844.

ENTERTAINMENT GUIDES, TICKETS AND VENUES

ANNOUNCEMENTS of performances of Carnatic music *(see p595)* and classical dance such as Bharat Natyam *(see p28)*, appear regularly in the entertainment columns of local newspapers. The city guides *Hallo! Madras* and *Chennai This Fortnight* list entertainment venues and information on tickets.

Performances of music and dance are held throughout the year. However, the peak season is from 15 December to 15 January, when the Chennai Festival, organized by the city's *sabhas* (cultural societies), takes place. During this period more than 500 concerts are held. The most prestigious cultural centre is the **Music Academy**. Other venues are **Narada Gana Sabha**, **Sri Krishna Gana Sabha** and **Karthik Fine Arts**. Classical dance and music performances are also held at the **Museum Theatre** in the Pantheon Complex *(see p564)* and the auditorium at **Kalakshetra** *(see p572)*.

MUSIC AND DANCE

SINCE the 1920s, Chennai has been the leading centre of Carnatic music and classical dance. The first music festival took place in December 1927 during the Madras session of the Indian National Congress. A year later, the Music Academy was established to promote Carnatic music, and in 1936, Rukmini Devi set up

Kalakshetra to popularize Bharat Natyam, the dance form once performed only in temples. Today, these two institutions along with the many *sabhas* are the major sponsors of music and dance events in the city.

During the season, music lovers gather in Chennai to hear India's top performers as well as promising new talent. Concerts of Carnatic music, both vocal and instrumental, begin in the morning and often last till midnight. Dance recitals are also held. Recently, some dancers have experimented with the traditional repertoire to create a contemporary form that is a fusion of Indian folk and classical forms with Western themes.

CINEMA

THE CHOICE OF FILMS that show at Chennai's many cinemas, such as **Devi**, **Ega**, **Gaiety** (founded in 1919), and the **Sathyam Cineplex**, ranges from Bollywood and Tamil blockbusters to the latest Hollywood releases. Tamil films are very similar to those produced in Mumbai's Bollywood, with song and dance sequences and a great deal of melodrama. But they play a role far beyond mere entertainment – their themes often have a social message and their charismatic actors, with their political links *(see p567)*, make them a potent medium of communication, especially among rural audiences.

DIRECTORY

JEWELLERY AND ANTIQUES

Amethyst
14 Padmavathi Rd,
Jeyapore Colony,
Gopalapuram.
(*(044) 820 3582.*

Prince Jewellery
13 Nagaeswara Rao Rd,
Panagal Park.
(*(044) 436 3137.*
769 Spencer Plaza,
Anna Salai.
(*(044) 855 5817.*

Rani Arts & Crafts
8 Nowrojee Rd, Chetpet.
(*(044) 643 0070.*
73 Gangadareswar Koil St.
(*(044) 643 0070.*

Sukhra
42 North Mada St,
Mylapore.
(*(044) 494 0699.*

Vummidi Bangaru Jewellers
Rani Seethai Hall,
603 Anna Salai.
(*(044) 852 3040.*

TEXTILES AND SARIS

Co-optex
Pantheon Rd, Egmore.
(*(044) 826 9231.*

Fabindia
Illford House, 3 Woods Rd,
off Anna Salai.
(*(044) 851 0395.*

Kumaran Silks
12 Nageswaran Rd,
T Nagar.
(*(044) 434 3544.*

Man Mandir
15 Khader Nawaz Khan Rd,
Nungamabakkam.
(*(044) 826 7648.*

Nalli's
9 Nageswaran Rd,
T Nagar.
(*(044) 434 4115.*

Radha Silks
Sannathi St, Mylapore.
(*(044) 494 1906.*

Shilpi
1 GG Minar, 23 College Rd,
Nungambakkam.
(*(044) 828 2603.*
29, CP Ramaswamy Rd.
(*(044) 499 7526.*

Sundari Silks
54–55 North Usman Rd,
T Nagar.
(*(044) 824 2064*

HANDICRAFTS AND GIFTS

Apparao Galleries
7 Wallace Garden, 3rd St.
(*(044) 855 5817.*

Cane and Bamboo
20 C-in-C Rd, Ethiraj Lane.
(*(044) 827 5180.*

Higginbotham's
116 Anna Salai.
(*(044) 852 2420.*

Musee Musicals
67 Anna Salai.
(*(044) 852 2780.*

Music World
Spencer's Plaza.
(*(044) 852 2717.*

Naturally Auroville
30 Khader Nawaz Khan Rd,
Nungambakkam.
(*(044) 821 7517.*

Poompuhar
818 Anna Salai.
(*(044) 852 0624.*

Sapthaswara Music Store
165 Royapetta H Rd,
Mylapore.
(*(044) 499 3274.*

VTI
New 180, Anna Salai.
(*(044) 852 3153.*

ENTERTAINMENT VENUES

Kalakshetra
Kalakshetra Foundation,
Thiruvanmiyur.
(*(044) 491 4359.*

Karthik Fine Arts
New 39, Bhimanna
Garden St, Alwarpet.
(*(044) 499 7788.*

Museum Theatre
Pantheon Rd, Egmore.
(*(044) 826 9638.*

Music Academy
306 TTK Rd, Alwarpet.
(*(044) 811 5162.*

Narada Gana Sabha
314 TTK Rd, Alwarpet.
(*(044) 499 3201.*

Sri Krishna Gana Sabha
8 Maharajapuram
Santhanam Salai,
T Nagar.
(*(044) 828 0806.*

CINEMA

Devi
47 Anna Salai.
(*(044) 855 5660.*

Ega
435 Poonamallee High Rd.
(*(044) 852 3813.*

Gaiety
Anna Salai.
(*(044) 853 5154.*

Sathyam Cineplex
Sathyam Theatre Complex,
8, Thiru Vi Ka Rd.
(*(044) 852 3813.*

TAMIL NADU

THE CRADLE OF ancient Dravidian culture, Tamil Nadu extends from the Coromandel Coast in the east to the forested Western Ghats in the west. At its heart is the fertile Kaveri valley, a land of rice fields and spectacular temples. This is the site of ancient Cholamandalam, where the Chola kings built magnificent temples at Thanjavur and elsewhere. Great temples also stand at Madurai and Chidambaram, which wit-nessed an efflorescence of dance, music and literature under their enlightened rulers. The 7th-century port-city of Mamallapuram with its spectacular rock-cut temples is now a World Heritage Site, while the former French enclave of Pondicherry, and British forts and churches reflect the state's colonial history. Many towns in Tamil Nadu have the prefix "Tiru", which means sacred, and indicates the presence of a major religious site.

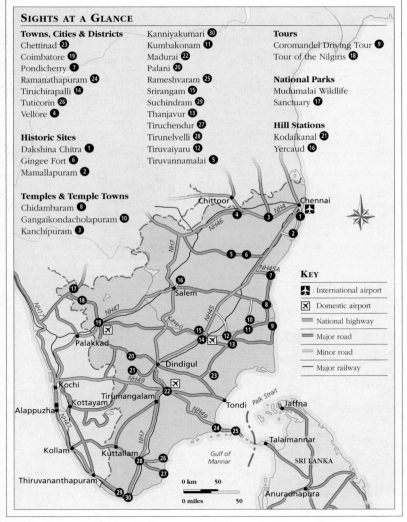

SIGHTS AT A GLANCE

Towns, Cities & Districts
Chettinad ㉓
Coimbatore ⑲
Pondicherry ⑦
Ramanathapuram ㉔
Tiruchirapalli ⑭
Tuticorin ㉖
Vellore ④

Kanniyakumari ㉚
Kumbakonam ⑪
Madurai ㉒
Palani ⑳
Rameshvaram ㉕
Srirangam ⑮
Suchindram ㉙
Thanjavur ⑬
Tiruchendur ㉗
Tirunelvelli ㉘
Tiruvaiyaru ⑫
Tiruvannamalai ⑤

Tours
Coromandel Driving Tour ⑨
Tour of the Nilgiris ⑱

National Parks
Mudumalai Wildlife Sanctuary ⑰

Hill Stations
Kodaikanal ㉑
Yercaud ⑯

Historic Sites
Dakshina Chitra ①
Gingee Fort ⑥
Mamallapuram ②

Temples & Temple Towns
Chidambaram ⑧
Gangaikondacholapuram ⑩
Kanchipuram ③

KEY
✈ International airport
✖ Domestic airport
National highway
Major road
Minor road
Major railway

Chittoor
Chennai
Salem
Palakkad
Dindigul
Kochi
Kottayam
Tirumangalam
Alappuzha
Kollam
Kuttallam
Thiruvananthapuram
Tondi
Jaffna
Talaimannar
SRI LANKA
Anuradhapura
Palk Strait
Gulf of Mannar

0 km 50
0 miles 50

◁ **Detail from a temple *gopura* with colourful stucco figures, Sarangapani Temple, Kumbakonam**

Dakshina Chitra ❶

Chingleput district. 26 km (16 miles)
S of Chennai. 🚌 📞 (04114) 45
303. ⭕ Wed–Mon. 🎫 📷 🍴 🏪

THIS HERITAGE VILLAGE, on
the Coromandel Coast,
provides a fascinating glimpse
into the homes and lifestyles
of the people of South India.
The village features reconstructions of traditional houses,
including, so far, six from
Tamil Nadu, three from Kerala
and one from Karnataka. The
handsome Chettiar mansion
(see p612) on view, with its
elaborately carved wooden
door, reflects the wealth of the
Chettiar merchant community,
while the homes of priests,
farmers, weavers and potters
are simple, utilitarian yet
elegant structures. Within the
complex is an Ayyanar shrine
(see p605) and an open courtyard, where folk and classical
dance performances and craft
demonstrations are held.

**ENVIRONS: Cholamandal
Village**, 12 km (7 miles) north
of Dakshina Chitra, is an
artists' village established in
1966 and the first of its kind
in India. For nature lovers,
the **Crocodile Bank**, founded
by an American zoologist,
Romulus Whitaker, is 15 km
(9 miles) south of the village.
It includes a snake farm and
a cooperative of Irulas, a
community of rat-catchers.

🏛 **Cholamandal Village**
📞 (044) 492 6092. ⭕ daily.
🏛 **Crocodile Bank**
⭕ Wed–Mon. 🎫 📷 extra charges.

**A colourful sign announcing the
entrance to the Crocodile Bank**

The sculpted relief at Mamallapuram, depicting Bhagiratha's Penance

Mamallapuram ❷

Kanchipuram district. 58 km (36
miles) S of Chennai. 🚌 🛈 Covelong
Rd, (04114) 42 232. ⭕ daily. 🎫 📷
🍴 🎭 Dance Festival (Dec/Jan).

THE UNESCO World Heritage
Site of Mamallapuram (or
Mahabalipuram) was once a
major port-city, built in the
7th century by the Pallava
king, Narasimha Varman I,
also known as
Mamalla, the "Great
Wrestler". This
spectacular site,
situated on the Bay
of Bengal, extends
across a boulder-
strewn landscape
and comprises rock-
cut caves and
monolithic shrines
(see pp580–81),
structural temples
and huge bas-reliefs
that are considered
the greatest examples of
Pallava art. The stone-carving
tradition that created these
wonders is still alive in the
many workshops scattered
around the village.

The spectacular **Shore
Temple**, perched dramatically
on a promontory by the sea,
has survived the ravages of
time and erosion. It was built
by Mamalla for Vishnu, while
the two Shiva shrines were
added by Mamalla's successor
Narasimha Varman II. The
temple has a low boundary
wall, with rows of seated
Nandis surrounding it. Placed
inside are a reclining Vishnu,
a 16-faceted polished linga
and reliefs of Somaskanda – a
composite form of Shiva with

**Krishna's Butter Ball,
a natural boulder**

his consort, Parvati and sons,
Skanda and Ganesha.

Inland from the Shore
Temple, in the village centre,
is the celebrated bas-relief
Bhagiratha's Penance, also
known as Arjuna's Penance or
the Descent of the Ganges.
Carved on an immense rock
with a natural vertical cleft,
symbolizing the Ganges, the
panel depicts in great detail
the story of the sacred river's
descent from the
sky (see p163). This
divine act, made
possible by the
penance of the sage
Bhagiratha, is wit-
nessed on the panel
by celestial and
semi-celestial
beings, ascetics,
and animals. The
symbolism is best
understood during
the monsoon, when
rainwater flows
down the cleft and collects
in the tank below. Nearby
are the unfinished **Panch
Pandava Cave Temple**, and
Krishna's Butter Ball, a
natural boulder perched
precariously on a slope.

South of Bhagiratha's
Penance is the **Krishna
Mandapa**, a huge bas-relief
showing the god lifting Mount
Govardhan to protect the
people from torrential rains,
as well as performing his
tasks as a cowherd. The
Olakkanatha Temple,
above the mandapa, was
once used as a lighthouse.

On the ridge southwest of
Bhagiratha's Penance are
three cave temples. The
Mahishasuramardini Cave

Temple has a graceful portrayal of Goddess Durga on her lion mount, subduing the buffalo-headed demon, Mahisha, on the northern wall. This panel seems to emanate life and motion, in contrast to the one on the southern wall, where Vishnu reclines in deep meditation before creating the earth.

Nearby, the **Adivaraha Cave Temple** has interesting panels of Pallava rulers with their consorts. The Lion Throne, on top of a hill further west, is a raised platform with a seated lion, discovered near the piles of brick rubble thought to be the remains of the palace of the Pallavas.

The **Trimurti Cave Temple**, northwest of Bhagiratha's Penance, is dedicated to three gods – Shiva, Vishnu and Somaskanda. The shrines are guarded by statues of graceful doorkeepers. A sculpture of Durga standing on Mahisha's head is on an outer wall. To its south, the **Varaha Cave Temple** has beautifully moulded lion pillars, while the relief sculptures of Lakshmi, Durga and Varaha, the boar incarnation of Vishnu, are among the masterpieces of Pallava art. The two-storeyed, rectangular **Ganesha Ratha**, further south, is attributed to Parameshvara Varman I (r.669–90). The temple, originally dedicated to Shiva, has beautifully carved inscriptions listing the royal titles of Parameshvara Varman.

A small **Archaeological Museum**, with sculptures and fragments excavated from the site, lies to its east.

🏛 **Archaeological Museum**
West Raja St. ◻ daily. 🈲 **Shore Temple** 🈲 also covers Panch Rathas.

ENVIRONS: The **Tiger's Cave**, 4 km (2.5 miles) north, is a shallow cave framed by a large boulder, with heads of *yalis* (mythical leonine beasts). It was probably a stage for outdoor performances.

The Vedagirisvara Temple, dedicated to Shiva, at the top of a hill in the village of **Thirukkazhukunran**, 17 km (11 miles) west, is famous for the two eagles that swoop down at noon to be fed by the temple priests. According to legend, these birds are saints who fly from Varanasi *(see pp202–208)* to Rameshvaram, stopping here to rest.

Fishermen with their boats on the beach at Mamallapuram

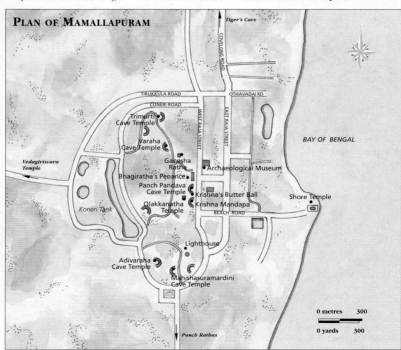

PLAN OF MAMALLAPURAM

- Tiger's Cave
- COVELONG ROAD
- TIRUKKULA ROAD
- CONERI ROAD
- OTHAVADAI RD
- Trimurti Cave Temple
- Varaha Cave Temple
- WEST RAJA STREET
- EAST RAJA STREET
- Vedagirisvara Temple
- Ganesha Ratha
- Bhagiratha's Penance
- Archaeological Museum
- BAY OF BENGAL
- Panch Pandava Cave Temple
- Krishna's Butter Ball
- Koneri Tank
- Olakkanatha Temple
- Krishna Mandapa
- BEACH ROAD
- Shore Temple
- Lighthouse
- Adivaraha Cave Temple
- Mahishasuramardini Cave Temple
- Panch Rathas
- 0 metres 300
- 0 yards 300

Mamallapuram: Panch Rathas

Sculpture of Subramanya

T HIS 7TH-CENTURY COMPLEX of mono-lithic rock-cut shrines called the Panch (five) Rathas (processional temple chariots) is named after the five Pandava brothers, heroes of the epic *Mahabharata (see p26)*, and their queen Draupadi. Although unfinished, these impressive temples are a tribute to the genius of the stone-cutters who carved these large boulders *in situ*. In an ambitious experiment, the styles and techniques of wooden architecture were imitated in stone, to create a variety of forms that later came to influence South Indian temple design.

Arjuna Ratha, Draupadi Ratha and Nandi

Arjuna Ratha
This two-storeyed temple has a graceful portrayal of Shiva leaning on his mount, the bull Nandi. Royal couples and other elegantly carved figures in the niches embellish the outer walls.

Nandi, carved out of a single rock, faces the Arjuna Ratha.

★ Durga Panel
A four-armed Durga is carved on the rear wall of the Draupadi Ratha's sanctum, with kneeling devotees in front. One of these is shown in the process of cutting his head off, as a supreme act of self-sacrifice.

STAR FEATURES

★ Durga Panel

★ Standing Lion

★ Harihara

Draupadi Ratha, a stone replica of a thatched tribal shrine, is the smallest *ratha* of the group, and is dedicated to the goddess Durga.

★ Standing Lion
The mount of Durga is placed in front of the Draupadi Ratha.

King Narasimha
The Pallava king Narasimha Varman I, the patron of this complex and after whose title, Mamalla, the site is named, is shown wearing a crown, a silk garment and jewellery.

Dharmaraja Ratha, an imposing three-storeyed *ratha,* is crowned by an octagonal domed roof. Sculpted panels are carved on the upper storeys.

Bhima Ratha, a gigantic, rectangular *ratha* with a barrel-vaulted roof and unfinished lower level, is named after the Pandava brother famed for his strength.

★ Harihara
Niche figures on the lower level include beautiful sculptures of Harihara, a composite form of Vishnu and Shiva (see p47). The right side of the body with matted locks of hair is Shiva, and the left is Vishnu, with a smooth, tapering cylindrical crown.

Nakul Sahdeva Ratha
Named jointly after the Pandava twins, this ratha is unique for its apsidal form, known in architectural terms as gajaprishta *(back of an elephant). As if to emphasize this, a perfectly sculpted elephant, carved from a single stone, stands next to it.*

Vaishnavite priests, Varadaraja Temple

Kanchipuram ❸

Kanchipuram district. 76 km (47 miles) SW of Chennai. ♔ 153,000. ☐ ☐ ☐ Hotel Tamil Nadu, 78, Kamakshi Amman Sannathi St, (04112) 22 461. ☐ Shivratri (Feb/Mar), Panguni Uthiram Festival (Mar/Apr), Brahmotsava (May/Jun).

THE SMALL TEMPLE TOWN of Kanchipuram, or Kanchi, as it is popularly known, is one of the seven sacred cities of the Hindus. From the 6th to the 8th centuries, it was the capital of the Pallavas (see p578), who built numerous temples here and founded universities for higher learning. Royal patronage from the succeeding Chola, Pandya and Vijayanagar dynasties further consolidated the city's reputation as a religious and commercial centre.

Kanchipuram is sacred to Shaivites (devotees of Shiva) as well as to Vaishnavites (worshippers of Vishnu). The town is thus divided into two distinct zones, with the Shaivite temples to the north and the Vaishnavite temples to the southeast.

It also has an important Devi (goddess) temple, the **Kamakshi Temple**, situated northeast of the bus stand. Dedicated to Kamakshi, or the "loving-eyed" Parvati, the temple was rebuilt in the 14th century, during the Vijayanagar period. It has four colourful gopuras and the main sanctum has a gold-plated roof.

The **Kailasanatha Temple**, to the west of the bus stand, is the oldest and grandest structure in the town. Built in the early 8th century by Rajasimha, the last great Pallava king, this Shiva temple is surrounded by 58 smaller shrines, each with splendid carvings of the various representations of Shiva. The recently discovered frescoes here are the earliest in South India. The sanctum has a circumambulatory passage with great symbolic meaning – seven steps (indicating seven births) lead to a dark passage (indicating the journey of life) and a narrow outlet (indicating death).

The great **Ekambareshvara Temple** on Car Street, constructed originally by the Pallavas, has a 16-pillared mandapa in front of it, that was added later by the Vijayanagar kings. This is one of the five panchalinga shrines (see p584) and houses a linga made of earth (prithvi). Legend says that the goddess Kamakshi, as part of her penance for disturbing Shiva's meditation, created this linga with earth taken from under a mango tree. Lingas abound in the corridors of the temple complex, while on the western side of the shrine stands the sacred mango tree, said to be 3,000 years old.

The **Vaikuntha Perumal Temple**, near the railway station, is one of the 18 temples dedicated to Vishnu. Erected by the Pallava king Nandi Varman II (r.731–96), this unique structure has three main sanctums, built one on top of the other. Each of them enshrines an image of Vishnu in a different form – standing, sitting and reclining. The hall in the lower shrine has panels depicting the genealogy, coronations and martial conquests of the Pallava kings.

The **Varadaraja Temple**, on Gandhi Road, is the town's main Vishnu temple. The chief deity is a form of Vishnu known as Varadaraja (the "King who Bestows Benediction"). It is believed that the temple stands on the site where Brahma performed a yagna (sacrifice) to invoke Vishnu's presence.

Among the temple's jewels is a valuable gold necklace, said to have been presented by Robert Clive (see p561). It adorns the deity during the Garuda festival.

Kanchipuram, famous for its silk, is also the seat of one of the four Shankaracharyas. They belong to the long line of head priests of the matha (religious centre) founded by the 9th-century philosopher-saint Adi Shankaracharya (see p648).

ENVIRONS: The bird sanctuary of **Vedanthangal**, 30 km (19 miles) southeast, attracts more than 30,000 migratory birds. Species such as cormorants, egrets, white ibis, and grey wagtails can be seen between October and February.

View of Kailasanatha, Kanchipuram's oldest temple

Kanchipuram Silk

INITIALLY, Kanchipuram was a weaving and trade centre for cotton textiles. But from the 19th century, with the increase in availability of mulberry silk from neighbouring Karnataka, the craftsmen turned entirely to silk weaving. Today, the silk fabric and saris created by the

Kanchipuram sari patterns

city's weavers and dyers are ritually offered to the gods before being sold. Kanchipuram silks, an essential part of every Indian bride's trousseau, are renowned for their lustre, and for their elegant combination of contrasting colours on the borders and end pieces *(pallavs)*.

Cocoons *of the silkworm* (Bombyx mori) *are reared on bamboo frames before being dropped into boiling water to preserve the length of the fibre.*

Yarn being sorted and graded before dyeing

Dyeing *is done by a special community which is skilled in this technique. The dyer first dips the yarn into a cauldron of colour and then dries the hanks in the sun.*

Warp and weft yarns *are prepared by family members. More than 5,000 families are involved in this very lucrative handloom industry.*

Classic Kanchipuram saris *are woven from twisted yarn, which makes them extremely durable. They are embellished with motifs such as temple spires, holy* rudraksha *beads, lotus flowers and peacocks, often woven in gold thread.*

Weavers' dwellings *are simple structures built around a courtyard, and serve as both a home and a work place. The loom is the main feature and occupies a large portion of the living area. Weaving skills are passed from generation to generation within families.*

Vellore ❹

Vellore district. 145 km (90 miles) W of Chennai. 🏯 *177,500.* 🚉 *Katpadi, 5 km (3 miles) N of town centre, then bus or auto.* 🚌 🛥 *daily.*

SURROUNDED by a deep artificial moat, the 16th-century **Vellore Fort** dominates the heart of this town. An impressive example of military architecture, the fort has a turbulent history. This formidable structure has withstood many battles, including an ill-fated mutiny led by the son of Tipu Sultan *(see p517)* in 1806 against the British East India Company. Today, part of the fort houses some government offices, including the Archaeological Survey of India (ASI), district courts and a prison. A museum within has a small but good collection of historical objects found in the area.

The only major structure to survive in the fort is the magnificent **Jalakanteshvara Temple**, constructed by the Nayakas, governors of the region under the Vijayanagar kings, in the mid-16th century. This Shiva temple is located near the fort's northern wall. It is surrounded by a low-lying boundary wall and contains a tank and subsidiary shrines. In the early 20th century, the temple was used as a garrison and its linga was removed from the sanctum. This was reinstated

The broad moat surrounding the quadrangular Vellore Fort

in 1981, after which worship recommenced. In the outer courtyard is the ornate Kalyana Mandapa. Its pillars are carved with magnificent horses and *yali* riders.

Vellore is renowned for its prestigious Christian Medical College, set up in 1900 by the American Dr Ida Scudder. This institution specializes in research on tropical diseases.

🏯 **Vellore Fort**
◻ *daily.* **Museum** ◻ *Sat–Thu.*
● *2nd Sat of every month.*
Jalakanteshvara Temple ◻ *daily.*
🚫 *inside the sanctum.*

ENVIRONS: Arcot, 27 km (17 miles) east of Vellore, is best known for its flamboyant nawabs *(see p570)* and their resistance to the British and French forces in the late 18th century. Some derelict tombs and a Jami Masjid are all that remain from that period.

Tiruvannamalai ❺

Tiruvannamalai district. 85 km (53 miles) S of Vellore. 🚉 🚌 🎊 *Karthigai Deepam (Nov/Dec).*

ONE OF THE MOST sacred cities of Tamil Nadu, this pilgrim town is the place where Shiva is believed to have appeared as a column of fire *(sthavara* linga *)* in order to assert his supremacy over Brahma and Vishnu. Arunachala Hill (the "Red Mountain"), which forms a backdrop to the town, is said to be the site where the fire manifested itself, and is thus perceived as the light of god himself. On the day of the Karthigai Deepam festival *(see p589)*, an enormous *deepa* (lamp), using 2,000 litres (528 gallons) of ghee and a 30-m (98-ft) wide wick, is lit on the hill, and burns for days. On a full moon night,

---

THE FIVE ELEMENTAL LINGAS

Hindu belief holds that five essential elements – air, water, fire, earth and ether – created man and the universe. Shiva, one of the three main gods of the Hindu Trinity, is represented as the embodiment of these five elements in five different places. At Sri Kalahasti in Andhra Pradesh *(see p680)*, he is represented as air; in Tiruvanaikka *(see p603)* he takes the form of water, so the linga (phallic symbol) in the main sanctum is partly

immersed in water. At Tiruvannamalai, Shiva represents fire, while in the Ekambareshvara Temple at Kanchipuram *(see p582)*, the linga is made of earth. Finally, at Chidambaram *(see p590)* Shiva represents ether, the most sacred of the five elements.

Nataraja Temple, Chidambaram, housing the ether linga

The 16th-century Arunachaleshvara Temple at Tiruvannamalai

pilgrims perform a 14-km (9-mile) long circumambulation on foot around the hill.

Arunachaleshvara Temple, the town's most important structure, is one of the five elemental shrines of Shiva, where the linga, encased in gold, represents fire. Covering a vast area of 10 ha (25 acres), this is also one of the largest temple complexes in India, parts of it dating to the 11th century. It has nine imposing towers, huge *prakaras* (walled and cloistered enclosures), the large Shivaganga Tank and a vast thousand-pillared hall.

Tiruvannamalai is also where Sri Ramana Maharishi, the famed 20th-century saint, spent 23 years in meditation. The **Sri Ramana Maharishi Ashram**, near Arunachala Hill, is an internationally renowned spiritual centre that attracts devotees from all walks of life.

Arunachaleshvara Temple

☐ *daily.* ● *to non-Hindus.*
Ø *inside the sanctum.*

Kalyana Mahal with Rajagiri Hill in the background, Gingee

Gingee Fort ❻

Viluppuram district. 37 km (23 miles) E of Tiruvannamalai. 🚌 ☐ *daily.* 📷

GINGEE (locally called Senji) Fort, is a remarkable example of military engineering. Its three citadels, dramatically perched atop three hills – Krishnagiri to the north, Rajagiri to the west and Chandrayandurg to the south-

The Krishna Temple and Durbar Hall on Krishnagiri Hill, Gingee Fort

east – are enclosed by solid stone walls to form a vast triangular-shaped area extending more than 1.5 km (1 mile) from north to south.

Built by the local Nayaka governors, feudatories of the Vijayanagar kings, in the 15th and 16th centuries, the fort was occupied by Bijapur's Adil Shahi Sultans *(see p542)*, the Marathas *(see p471)*, the French and finally the British.

This once-great fortress city is dotted with dilapidated arcaded chambers, mosques, *mandapas*, small shrines, tanks and granaries. Many temples, mostly dedicated to Vishnu, survive as well. These include the deserted temple in the main citadel on the 242-m (794-ft) high Rajagiri Hill. The most prominent, however, is the great **Venkataramana Temple**, in the foothills of the outer fort, near Pondicherry Gate. This was constructed by Muthialu Nayaka in the 17th century. Its original pillars were removed by the French and used in the Government Square at Pondicherry *(see p586)*. Near the gateway are

panels depicting scenes from the *Ramayana (see p27)* and the *Vishnu Purana.*

A Ranganatha Temple and a Krishna Temple, both smaller than the Venkataramana Temple, are located on Krishnagiri Hill, as is the **Durbar Hall**. The Durbar Hall has balconies extending to the edge of the hill which provide good views of the surrounding countryside.

The fort's finest monument is the **Kalyana Mahal**, a square hall built for the ladies of the court. The building has a central eight-storeyed pyramidal tower with a single large room on each floor.

There are also traces of a network of natural springs and tanks that provided an excellent supply of water to the citadel. One of the tanks, Chettikulam, has a platform where Raja Thej Singh, a courageous 18th-century Rajput chief and vassal of the Mughal emperor, was cremated. Tamil folk songs glorify Gingee and Raja Thej Singh, who was killed in a heroic battle against the Nawab of Arcot.

Gingee Fort sprawling across three hills

Street-by-Street: Pondicherry ❼

Government Square
A pavilion stands in the centre of this tree-lined square.

THE FORMER CAPITAL of French territories in India, Pondicherry was established in 1674 by François Martin, the first director of the French East India Company. The town is laid out in a grid pattern, with parallel streets cutting across each other at right angles. Its main promenade, the 3-km (2-mile) long Goubert Salai running along the Bay of Bengal, formed part of the French Quarter, with its elegant colonial mansions, tree-lined boulevards, parks, bars and cafés. Beyond this was a canal, now dry, that demarcated the Tamil Town, where the local populace once lived.

Statue of Jeanne d'Arc

VICTOR SIMONEL STREET

CASERNE STREET

MAHE DE LABOURDONNAIS STREET

GOUBERT SALAI (BEACH ROAD)

A Statue of Mahatma Gandhi, 4 m (13 ft) high, stands on a pedestal surrounded by eight stone pillars.

★ Church of Our Lady of the Angels
Built in 1865, this striking church boasts a rare oil painting of Our Lady of the Assumption, a gift from the French emperor, Napoleon III.

Le Café, a popular restaurant on Goubert Salai.

STAR SIGHTS

- ★ Church of Our Lady of the Angels
- ★ Aurobindo Ashram
- ★ View of the Seafront

JOSEPH FRANÇOIS DUPLEIX

Pondicherry's colonial past is intricately interwoven with the life of the redoubtable Marquis Joseph François Dupleix, governor between 1742 and 1754. This energetic statesman tried valiantly to prevent British supremacy by forming alliances with local princes. This power struggle was aggravated by the War of Austrian Succession in Europe between England and France. With the final defeat of the French in the Second Carnatic War, Dupleix relinquished his governorship and returned in disgrace to Paris. His memorial statue is on Goubert Salai.

Dupleix (1697–1764)

Raj Nivas

A harmonious fusion of French and Indian styles of architecture, Dupleix's palatial home is now the Lieutenant Governor's official residence.

VISITOR CHECKLIST

Union Territory of Pondicherry. 160 km (99 miles) S of Chennai. 🏃 220,800. 🚉 🚌 ℹ️ *Pondicherry Tourism, Goubert Salai, (0413) 33 9497.* 🛒 *Mon–Sat.* 🎭 *Masimagam (Feb/Mar), Ganesha Chaturthi (Aug/Sep).*

Manakula Vinayakar Temple

Dedicated to Ganesha, this temple has a golden spire, and walls portraying 40 different forms of Ganesha.

0 metres 80
0 yards 80

General Hospital

MANAKULA — VINAYAKAR

KOIL STREET

FRANCOIS MARTIN STREET

LAW DE LAURISTON STREET

CAMPAGNIE ST

TIN STREET

MARINE STREET

KEY

– – – – Suggested route

★ Aurobindo Ashram

Named after Sri Aurobindo (see p588), this serene ashram organizes regular meditation sessions to which all are welcome.

Pondicherry Museum's collection ranges from ancient Roman artifacts and Chola bronzes to beautiful snail shells.

★ View of the Seafront

Goubert Salai, the boulevard along the Bay of Bengal, is lined with grand colonial buildings.

Exploring Pondicherry

OFTEN DESCRIBED as a sleepy French provincial town, Pondicherry retains a distinct Gallic flavour. French is still spoken among the older residents, while stately colonial mansions stand in tree-lined streets that are still known by their colonial names. Even the policemen continue to wear the military-style caps, known as kepis. Today, Pondicherry, has been renamed Puduchcheri. Located on the east coast of Tamil Nadu, it is the administrative capital of a Union Territory that includes the former French enclaves of Mahe in Kerala *(see p655)*, Yanam in Andhra Pradesh and Karaikkal in Tamil Nadu.

A policeman wearing a kepi

🏛 Pondicherry Museum

49, Rue St Louis. ☑ *Director Art & Culture (0413) 33 6203.* ◯ *Tue–Sun.*
Located in the lovely old Law Building, near Government Park, the Pondicherry Museum has an out-standing collection of artifacts from the French colonial period. The rooms in one section are furnished in French style, and are decorated with marble statuary, paintings, mirrors and clocks. Prized exhibits include the bed that Dupleix slept in when he was the governor, and a *pousse-pousse*, an earlier version of the rickshaw.

The museum also displays rare bronzes and stone sculptures from the Pallava and Chola periods. Among the artifacts excavated from nearby Arikamedu, an ancient port that had trade links with Imperial Rome, are beads, am-phorae, coins, ornamented oil lamps, funerary urns and frag-ments of pottery and china.

Inside the same compound is the **Romain Rolland Library**. Established in 1872, the library now has a rich collection of more than 300,000 volumes, including many rare editions in both French and English. Its mobile library service takes more than 8,000 books in a bus to nearby villages. The reference

section, on the second floor, is open to the public.

🏛 Romain Rolland Library
◯ *Mon–Sat.*

🛡 Church of the Sacred Heart of Jesus
South Boulevard. ◯ *daily.*
A serene atmo-sphere cloaks this brown and white Neo-Gothic church, built in the 1700s. Its most interesting features are its large stained-glass panels depicting incidents from the life of Jesus Christ, and the handsome arches that span the nave. Further along the south-ern boulevard is the cemetery, which has some

Stained glass, Church of the Sacred Heart

interesting tombs with ornate marble decorations.

🌿 Botanical Gardens
S of City Bus Stand. 🅿
Lying at the far western end of the old Tamil Town, the Botanical Gardens, laid out in 1826, were designed in the formal French style with clipped trees, flower beds, gravel walks and fountains. The French introduced many unusual and exotic trees and shrubs from all over India and the world, many of which are still here. With its 1,500 species of plants, this is one of the best botanical gardens in South India. An interesting little aquarium displays some of the more spectacular marine species from the Coromandel Coast.

🏛 House of Ananda Rangapillai
Ananda Rangapillai St. ☑ *(0413) 33 9021 for permission to visit.*
This lavishly furnished house, once the home of an 18th-century Indian nobleman, offers fascinating glimpses into a vanished lifestyle. Now a museum, the house was owned by Ananda Rangapillai, Dupleix's favourite courtier and *dubash* (trade agent). A perceptive observer and com-mentator, he maintained a series of diaries between 1736 and 1760, recording his views of the fluctuating fortunes of the French in India. However, he displeased Madame Dupleix, who eventually ousted him from his post.

SRI AUROBINDO GHOSE

The firebrand Bengali poet-philosopher, Aurobindo Ghose, who joined the struggle for freedom in the early 1900s, was known for his extremist views. To escape from the British, he took refuge in the French territory of Pondicherry, where he was drawn into the spiritual realm. It was here that he studied, wrote about and popularized the principles of yoga. His disciple, Mirra Alfassa, known later as "The Mother", was a Parisian mystic, painter and musician, who first came to Pondicherry with her husband during World War I. Sri Aurobindo's philosophy so inspired her that she stayed on, and was later instrumental in the establishment of the Aurobindo Ashram.

Sri Aurobindo (1872–1950)

The verdant courtyard of the École Française de l'Extrême Orient

🏛 École Français de l'Extrême Orient

19, Rue Dumas. 📞 *(0413) 33 2504.*
An internationally renowned
research institution, the 19th-
century École Français de
l'Extrême Orient is noted for
its research in archaeology,
history and sociology.

🏛 French Institute of Indology

16, Rue Dumas. 📞 *(0413) 33 4539.*
The prestigious French
Institute of Indology was
established in the mid-1950s
by an eminent French Indo-
logist, Dr Jean Fillozet.
Originally set up for the study
of local language and culture,
this institute now has links
with many French universities
and research organizations.

🏛 Aurobindo Ashram

Rue de la Marine. 📞 *(0413) 33 4836.* ◯ daily.
Pondicherry's best-known
landmark, the Aurobindo

Ashram dominates life in
this town. Founded by Sri
Aurobindo in 1926, the
Ashram is a peaceful retreat
with tree-shaded courtyards.
The flower-festooned
samadhi (memorial) of Sri
Aurobindo and The Mother
lies under a frangipani tree
in the main courtyard. This
memorial, with two chambers,
one above the other, is the
focal point for all disciples
and followers.

ENVIRONS: Auroville, or the
"City of Dawn", 8 km (5 miles)
northwest of Pondicherry, was
designed by French architect
Roger Anger in 1968. Conceived as a utopian paradise by
The Mother, Mirra Alfassa,
it was planned as a futuristic
international city, where
people of goodwill would live
together in peace. The International Commune, with 40
settlements with names like
Grace, Serenity and Certitude,
and 550 permanent resi-
dents, are meant to
bring people from differ-
ent castes, religions and
nations under one roof,
where they could live in
harmony. Two important
settlements, Fraternité
and Harmonie, sell
handicrafts made by
local artisans. The Matri
Mandir, a meditation
centre set in an area of
25 ha (62 acres), reflects
The Mother's spiritual
beliefs. This spherical
marble chamber has a
crystal placed inside it,
reflecting the sun's rays.
The concentrated light
acts as a focal point
to aid meditation.

Matri Mandir, the spiritual and physical
centre of Auroville

FESTIVALS OF TAMIL NADU

Pongal *(mid-Jan).* A
thanksgiving festival in
praise of the sun, land
and cattle, Pongal is celebrated all over Tamil
Nadu. A sweet rice pud-
ding *(pongal)* is the main
offering. The southern districts organize a bull fight,
a popular martial event
known as *manju virattal.*
Chitirai *(mid-Apr).* The
Tamil New Year is cele-
brated all over the state
with offerings of food to
the gods. In Madurai, the
marriage of Minakshi
(Parvati) and Sundar-
eshvara (Shiva) is cele-
brated with much pomp.
Adi Perukku *(Jul/Aug).*
Sweets and different kinds
of rice preparations are
offered to the rivers of
Tamil Nadu to mark the
onset of the monsoon.
Navaratri Gollu
(Sep/Oct). Exclusively for
women, this nine-day fes-
tival marks the victory of
Goddess Durga over the
buffalo demon Mahisha.
Houses are decorated with
gollu dolls, which depict
gods and goddesses, as
well as with contemporary
secular icons.
Karthigai *(Nov/Dec),*
Tiruvannamalai. People
decorate their homes with
lights to celebrate the
birth of Murugan, son of
Shiva *(see p584).*

Tamil women making
preparations for Pongal

The gold-plated roof of the main sanctum, Nataraja Temple, Chidambaram

Chidambaram ❽

Thanjavur district. 60 km (37 miles) S of Pondicherry. 🚶 59,000. 🚉 🚌 ℹ Hotel Tamil Nadu, Railway Feeder Rd, (04144) 22 739. 🎭 Dance Festival (Feb/Mar), Arudhra (Dec/Jan).

Sacred chidambaram, where Shiva is believed to have performed his cosmic dance, the *tandava nritya*, is a traditional temple town where history merges with mythology to create a deeply religious ambience. All ancient Hindu beliefs and practices are zealously observed here, manifested in an endless cycle of rites and rituals.

The focal point of the town is the awe-inspiring **Nataraja Temple**, built by the Cholas (*see pp46–7*) in the 9th century to honour their patron deity, Shiva as Nataraja, the "Lord of Dance" (*see p566*). The temple has an unusual hut-like sanctum with a gold-plated roof, the huge, colonnaded Shivaganga Tank, and four colourful *gopuras*. The most interesting is the eastern *gopura* which features detailed sculptures of the 108 hand and feet movements of Bharat Natyam (*see p29*), and is considered a veritable encyclopaedia of this classical temple dance.

Within the temple's three enormous enclosures are five major halls (*sabhas*), each conceived for a special purpose. In the outer enclosure, next to the Shivaganga Tank, is the Raja Sabha ("Royal Hall"), a beautiful thousand-pillared hall, built as a venue for temple rituals and festivals. Many Chola kings were crowned here in the presence of the deity. In the central enclosure is the Deva Sabha ("Divine Hall"), where the temple bronzes are housed, and administrative functions performed. The adjacent Nritya Sabha ("Dance Hall") has a superb collection of sculptures, the finest being the **Urdhava Tandava**. The

Urdhava Tandava, Nataraja Temple

innermost enclosure, the holiest part of the complex, contains the Chit Sabha or Chitambalam ("Hall of Bliss"), from which the town derives its name. This is the main sanctum, housing one of the five elemental lingas of Shiva (*see p584*), the *akasha* linga, which represents ether, the all-pervading element central to human existence. The inner sanctum containing the linga is hidden behind a black curtain, symbolizing ignorance, which is removed only during prayer time. There is a certain aura of mystery to this veiled sanctum and it is often called the Sacred Secret of Chidambaram (Chidambara Rahasyam). Finally, the fifth hall, in front of the Chit Sabha, is the Kanaka Sabha ("Golden Hall"), where Shiva is supposed to have performed his cosmic dance.

Other areas of interest in the complex are the **Govindarajaswamy Shrine**, housing the reclining Vishnu, the **Shivakamasundari Shrine**, dedicated to Shiva's consort, Parvati, and the **Subramanyam Shrine**, in which Murugan is worshipped.

Religious traditions in the temple are preserved by a group of hereditary priests whose ancestors came to Chidambaram 3,000 years ago. Known as the *dikshitars*, they are easily recognized by their top-knots. Chidambaram's other claim to fame is the modern **Annamalai University**, which is located to the east. Founded by a philanthropist over 50 years ago, it is Tamil Nadu's first residential university, specializing in South Indian studies.

🏛 Nataraja Temple
Near bus stand. ◯ daily. 📷 ✂

Environs: Located 16 km (10 miles) east of Chidambaram, **Pichavaram's** maze of picturesque backwaters, with mangrove forests and 1,700 islands in 4,000 canals, can be explored in rowboats.

Coromandel Driving Tour 9

NAMED AFTER Cholamandalam ("the Realm of the Cholas"), the Coromandel Coast extends from the Godavari Delta in Andhra Pradesh in the north, to Point Calimere in the south. This spectacularly beautiful strip of land played a significant role in the maritime history of India. Its great ports have, through the ages, attracted traders and merchants in search of textiles and spices.

Dansborg Fort at Tarangambadi

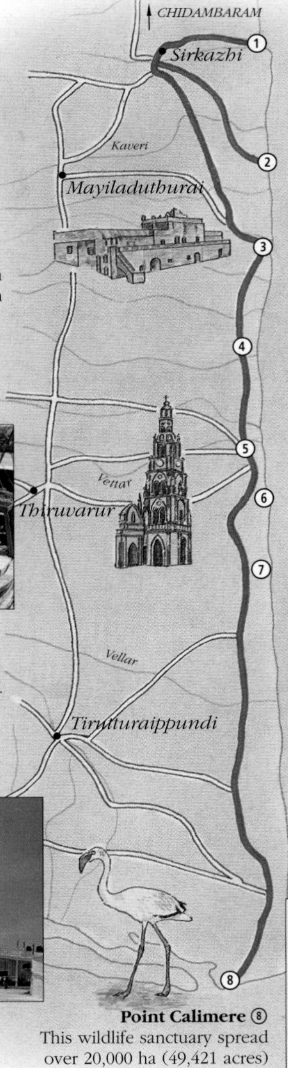

Tirumullaivasal ①
A magnificent shrine to Shiva dominates this small, coastal town.

0 km   10

0 miles   10

Tarangambadi ③
More popularly known as Tranquebar, this little town was a Danish settlement in the 17th century. It has an impressive fort, churches and a beautiful brick gateway, the Town Gate.

Nagapattinam ⑥
An old Chola port, this was also a major Buddhist centre till the 13th century. It was later occupied by the Portuguese, the Dutch and finally the British.

↑ CHIDAMBARAM

Sirkazhi ①

Kaveri

Mayiladuthurai ②

③

④

Bay of Bengal

⑤

⑥

Venar

Thiruvarur

⑦

Vellar

Tiruturaippundi

⑧

Poompuhar ②
This historic port city once had trade links with ancient Greece and Rome. An interesting museum here recreates stories of its past glory in bas-reliefs.

KEY

— Tour route

= Other roads

▬ National highway

Karaikal ④
This former French town has many 19th-century mansions and a Neo-Gothic church.

Nagore ⑤
The 16th-century tomb of Hazrat Sayyid Shahul, a Muslim saint who died in Nagore, attracts devotees of all religions, castes and creeds.

Velanganni ⑦
People of all religions seek cures at the Neo-Gothic Basilica of Our Lady of Good Health.

Point Calimere ⑧
This wildlife sanctuary spread over 20,000 ha (49,421 acres) of saline marshland is a haven for migratory birds.

TIPS FOR DRIVERS

Length: 90 km (56 miles).
Stopping-off points: Hotel Tamil Nadu at both Poompuhar and Nagapattinam are convenient stopping-off points. The route is well connected by government and private buses.

The superb Nataraja sculpture at Gangaikondacholapuram

Gangaikondachola-puram ⑩

Tiruchirapalli district. 40 km (25 miles) SW of Chidambaram. 🚌 *from Chidambaram or Kumbakonam.*

Grandly titled Gangai-kondacholapuram, "The City of the Chola who Took the Ganges", this now modest village was the capital of the powerful Chola dynasty *(see pp46–7)* during the reign of Rajendra I (r.1012–44). A great military commander like his father Rajaraja I, Rajendra I was the first Tamil ruler to venture northwards. He built this city to commemorate his successful campaign across the Ganges. According to an inscription, he then ordered the defeated rulers to carry back pots of sacred Ganges water on their heads to fill the Chola-Ganga tank, a victory memorial.

Except for the magnificent **Brihadishvara Temple**, little remains of his capital city. Built as a replica of Thanjavur's Brihadishvara Temple *(see pp598–9)*, the towered

sanctum of this granite Shiva temple is shorter than the one at Thanjavur. Adorning the lower walls, columns and niches are many remarkable sculptural friezes. One of the most outstanding is the panel depicting Shiva blessing Chandesha, a pious devotee sculpted to resemble Rajendra I himself. The sculptures of the *dikpalas* (guardians of the eight directions), *ekadasas* (the 11 forms of Shiva), Saraswati, Kalyanasundara and Nataraja *(see p566)* are also splendid examples of Chola art. Steps near the small Durga shrine in the courtyard

lead past a sculpture of a seated lion to a well, believed to have been filled with Ganges water for daily rituals.

The small **Archaeological Museum**, near the temple, exhibits Chola artifacts from neighbouring sites.

🏛 **Brihadishvara Temple**
⬜ *daily.* **Museum** ⬜ *Sat–Thu.*

Kumbakonam ⑪

Thanjavur district. 74 km (46 miles) SW of Chidambaram. 👥 140,100. 🚉 🚌 🚏 *Tamil Nadu Tourism, (0435) 30 422.* 🎭 *Nageshvara Temple Festival (Apr/May), Mahamaham Festival (every 12 years).*

Like Kanchipuram *(see p582)*, Kumbakonam is one of the most sacred cities in Tamil Nadu. Located on the southern bank of the Kaveri river, this is an ancient city where, as legend says, Shiva's arrow shattered the cosmic pot *(kumbh)* containing the divine nectar of creation *(amrit)*. This myth has given Kumbakonam both its name and sanctity. Today, the city represents the traditional cultural values of the Tamil heartland. It is also the region's main commercial and craft centre, famous for its textiles, jewellery, bronze casting and the superior quality of its locally grown betel leaves.

It is believed that when the divine nectar emerged from the pot, it filled the huge **Mahamaham Tank**. This is Kumbakonam's sacred centre and the site of the great Mahamaham Festival, held every 12 years (the next one will be held in 2004). At the

The 17th-century Adikumbheshvara Temple, Kumbakonam

auspicious time, thousands of devotees enter the tank for their holy dip. This is when the purifying power of the water is said to be at its height. The devout believe that all of India's nine sacred rivers (Ganges, Yamuna, Saraswati, Sarayu, Godavari, Narmada, Kaveri, Payokshini and Kanniyakumari) also bathe in the tank to cleanse themselves of the sins of humanity accumulated in their waters.

The tank, renovated by the Nayakas in the 17th century, has steps at the four cardinal points, and 16 ornate pavilions in honour of the 16 *mahadanas* (great gifts bestowed by a ruler on a spiritual centre). A fine example of Nayaka art is a relief depicting a king being weighed on a balance against gold (a ceremony known as *tulapurushadeva*), carved on the roof of a 16-pillared *mandapa* that stands at the northwest corner of the tank. To the north is the **Kashivishvanatha Temple**, which has a small shrine facing the water; this is dedicated to the nine sacred rivers, personified as goddesses. The shrine representing the Kaveri river occupies the central position.

To the east of the tank is the 17th-century **Adikumbheshvara Temple**, built on the legendary spot where Shiva shattered the pot. A unique feature is the depiction of 27 stars and the 12 zodiac signs carved on a large block of stone in the Navaratri Mandapa. It also has a superb collection of silver *vahanas* (vehicles) which are used during festivals to carry the temple deities. The grand, 12-storeyed **Sarangapani Temple**, to the east, is the most important Vaishnavite shrine in the city.

Nearby is the 9th-century **Nageshvara Temple**, a fine example of early Chola architecture. The town's oldest temple, this is the site of an annual festival that celebrates the worship of the linga by the sun. Niches on the sanctum walls contain exquisitely carved figures depicting the forms of Shiva, and scenes from the *Ramayana*.

Temple chariots at Kumbakonam's Adikumbheshvara Temple

ENVIRONS: The spectacular Airavateshvara Temple at **Darasuram**, 4 km (2.5 miles) west of Kumbakonam, was built by the Chola king, Rajaraja II (r.1146–73). This temple is dedicated to Shiva, who is known here as Airavateshvara, the "Lord of Airavata". Legend claims that after Airavata, the white elephant of Indra, the God of the Heavens, regained his lost colour, he worshipped Shiva at this spot.

Shiva's wedding procession, Darasuram

The four-tiered temple has a sanctum and three halls, of which the finest is the Rajagambira Mandapa, conceived as a stone chariot drawn by caparisoned horses, with Brahma as its driver. The outer walls have fine friezes and carvings of musicians, dancers and acrobats as well as depictions from the *Periya Puranam*, a Tamil treatise on the 63 Shaivite poet-saints, the Nayannars *(see p45)*.

The late Chola temple at **Tirubhuvanam**, 8 km (5 miles) northeast of Kumbakonam, is dedicated to Kumbheshvara, the "God who Removes Fear". This is also an old silk weaving centre. About 8 km (5 miles) west of Kumbakonam is **Swamimalai**, one of the six sacred shrines devoted to Lord Murugan *(see p25)*, who, legend says, propounded the meaning of "Om", the sacred mantra, to his father Shiva, and thus assumed the title Swaminatha ("Lord of Lords"). The temple, situated on a hill, has an impressive statue of Murugan in the sanctum; interestingly, he has an elephant as his vehicle instead of the typical peacock. This small village is also an important centre for bronze casting, where artisans still use traditional methods to create beautiful images for temples *(see p594)*.

Small votive shrines outside the Airavateshvara Temple, Darasuram

The College of Music at Tiruvaiyaru, on the Kaveri river

Tiruvaiyaru ⑫

Thanjavur district. 13 km (8 miles) N of Thanjavur. 🏘 14,500. 🚌 📷 Thyagaraja Music Festival (Jan).

THE FERTILE REGION watered by the Kaveri river and its four tributaries is known as Tiruvaiyaru, the sacred *(tiru)* land of five *(i)* rivers *(aru)*. For nearly 2,000 years the Tamil people have regarded the Kaveri as the sacred source of life, religion and culture. As a result, many scholars, artists, poets and musicians settled in this region, under the enlightened patronage of the rulers of Thanjavur *(see pp596–7)*. Among them was Thyagaraja (1767–1847), the greatest composer-saint of Carnatic music. The history of this small town is thus deeply linked with the growth and development of South Indian classical music.

The little **Thyagaraja Temple**, in the town, was built to commemorate the last resting place of the celebrated composer-saint. A musical festival is held here every year on the anniversary of his death, which falls, according to the Tamil calendar, in January. Hundreds of musicians and students of Carnatic music gather in the town and sing Thyagaraja's songs from morning till midnight for a whole week.

As dawn breaks over the river, a procession of musicians makes the short journey from Thyagaraja's house to the temple, singing continuously all the way. Music lovers wait eagerly at the shrine, seated on the mud floor of the thatch-roofed auditorium. To the sacred chants of priests, the stone image of Thyagaraja is ritually bathed with milk, rosewater, sandalwood and honey. The five songs known as the *pancha ratna* ("five gems") of Thyagaraja, which are considered unequalled masterpieces of Carnatic music, are sung in a grand chorus by all the assembled musicians. This ceremony is an annual reaffirmation of devotion to the composer and to a great tradition of music. For music lovers from all over India, it can be a magical experience.

Also in the town is the 9th-century **Panchanandishvara Temple** ("Lord of the Five Rivers"), built by the Cholas. Dedicated to Shiva, the shrines of Uttara (north) Kailasha and Dakshina (south) Kailasha, on either side of the main temple, were built by the wives of Rajaraja I and Rajendra I *(see pp46–7)*. The temple's huge *prakara* (boundary) walls, pillared *mandapas* and the Mukti Mandapa are immortalized in the songs of the Nayannars, a sect of 7th-century poet-saints *(see p45)*.

ENVIRONS: Pullamangai village, 12 kms (7 miles) northeast of Tiruvaiyaru, is noted for the **Brahmapurishvara Temple**, dating to the 10th century. The temple features elegant depictions of various gods and goddesses.

Children frolicking in the waters of the Kaveri, Tiruvaiyaru

THANJAVUR BRONZES

Artisan fashioning bronze idols

The Thanjavur region's wealth of artistic traditions includes the creation of exquisite bronze images through a process known as *cire perdue* or the "lost wax" technique. A model of the image is first made in wax and then coated with layers of clay to create a mould, which is heated to allow the melting wax to flow out through a hole at the base. A molten alloy of five metals *(panch loha)* is poured into the hollow. When it cools, the mould is broken and the image is finished and polished. Finally, the image's eyes are sealed with a mixture of honey and ghee and then ritually "opened" by a priest, using a golden needle. Even today, traditional artisans, known as *sthapathis*, create these images according to a fixed set of rules and guidelines laid down in the *Shilpa Shastra*, an ancient treatise on art. The main centre for bronze casting in Tamil Nadu is Swamimalai *(see p593)*.

Carnatic Music

T HE CLASSICAL MUSIC of South India is known as Carnatic music. Though based on the general concepts of raga (melody) and *tala* (rhythm) found in Hindustani music *(see pp28–9)*, Carnatic music differs in many respects. It is almost exclusively devotional in character, uses different percussion and musical instruments, and develops the melody in a more structured manner. It also lays more emphasis on rhythm. Some of the greatest Carnatic music was composed between 1750 and 1850, by the musical trinity of Thyagaraja, Syama Sastri, and Muthuswami Dikshitar who, between them, wrote over 2,500 songs in Sanskrit and Telegu, modifying and refining features that are now essential to the genre.

Thyagaraja, father of Carnatic music

ACCOMPANYING INSTRUMENTS
Traditional South Indian instruments such as the *veena*, the *nadasvaram*, the flute and the *thavil* are used for accompaniment, along with Western instruments such as the violin and saxophone.

MS Subbulakshmi is a leading vocalist.

The violin, a bow-string instrument of Western origin, is played in a seated position.

The ghatam, a mere clay pot, can produce fabulous rhythms in the hands of an accomplished performer.

Mridangam (two-headed drum)

Saraswati veena

Flute

Tanpura

Ghatam

Mridangam

Violin

Music festivals are often held in large cities, where concerts take place in small auditoriums, called sabhas. Most performers are accompanied by a violinist and two percussionists. A typical concert lasts for about three hours, during which a series of songs, usually in Telugu, are sung. The lyrics are as important as the melody, and many are devotional in nature.

The nadasvaram, which is a wind instrument, is a must at temple festivals, weddings and auspicious occasions. The thavil *(drum)* player performs complex rythmic improvisations to accompany the melody.

The veena, which resembles the more widely seen sitar, is a beautifully hand-crafted string instrument.

Thanjavur ⑬

THE CITY OF THANJAVUR, or Tanjore, lies in the fertile Kaveri Delta, a region often referred to as the "rice bowl of Tamil Nadu". For nearly a thousand years, this great town dominated the political history of the region as the capital of three powerful dynasties – the Cholas (9th–13th centuries), the Nayakas (1535–1676) and the Marathas (1676–1855). The magnificent Brihadishvara Temple *(see pp598–9)*, is the most important Chola monument, while the Royal Palace dates to the Nayaka and Maratha periods. Today, Thanjavur's culture extends beyond temples and palaces, to encompass classical music and dance. It is also a flourishing centre for bronze sculpture and painting.

Seven-storeyed observation tower of the Royal Palace, Thanjavur

🏰 Shivaganga Fort

Off Hospital Rd. ⃝ *daily.*

The quadrangular Shivaganga Fort, southwest of the old city, was built by the Nayaka ruler, Sevappa Nayaka, in the mid-16th century. Its battlemented stone walls, which enclose an area of 14 ha (35 acres), are surrounded by a partly rock-cut moat. The square **Shivaganga Tank** in the fort was excavated by Rajaraja I, and later renovated to provide drinking water for the city. The fort also contains the great Brihadishvara Temple, Schwartz Church, and a public amusement park.

Maratha ruler Serfoji II (r.1798–1832)

🏛 Brihadishvara Temple

See pp598–9.

⛪ Schwartz Church

Off West Main Rd. ⃝ *daily.*

The 18th-century Christ Church or Schwartz Church, a legacy of Thanjavur's colonial past, stands to the east of the Shivaganga Tank. This church was founded by the Danish missionary, Reverend Frederik Christian Schwartz, in 1779. When he died in 1798, the enlightened Maratha ruler, Serfoji II, donated a striking marble tablet to the church. This tablet, made by John Flaxman, has been placed at the western end of the church. It depicts the dying missionary blessing his royal patron, surrounded by ministers and pupils from the school that he established.

🏯 Royal Palace

East Main Rd. ⃝ *daily.* 🎥 📷 *extra charges.*

Resembling the shape of a flying eagle, this palace was built originally by the Nayaka rulers as their royal residence, and was subsequently remodelled by the Marathas. A large quadrangular courtyard leads into the palace complex, at one end of which is a pyramidal, temple-like tower. Outside the palace complex stands the seven-storeyed, arcaded observation tower, now without its capping pavilion.

The splendid Maratha Durbar Hall, built by Shahji II in 1684, has elaborately painted and decorated pillars, walls and ceiling. A wooden canopy embellished with glittering glass pieces and supported by four wooden pillars stands above a green granite slab on which the royal Maratha throne once stood. The other buildings include the Sadir Mahal, which is still the residence of the erstwhile royal family, and the Puja Mahal.

The **Rajaraja Museum and Art Gallery**, in the Nayaka Durbar Hall, was established in 1951 and has an impressive collection of bronze and stone idols dating from the 7th to the 20th centuries. Particularly noteworthy are the images of Shiva, such as the Kalyanasundaramurti, which depicts the wedding of Shiva and Parvati *(see p566)*, and the Bhikshatanamurti, which shows Shiva as a wandering mendicant, carrying a begging bowl and accompanied by a dog.

Next to the Rajaraja Museum is the **Saraswati Mahal Library**, constructed by the Maratha rulers. This is one of the most important reference libraries in India, with a fine collection of rare palm-leaf manuscripts and

Mural at the entrance of Saraswati Mahal, Royal Palace, Thanjavur

books collected by the versatile and scholarly Serfoji II. An adjoining **Museum** displays some of these valuable works.

The **Royal Museum** occupies part of the private quarters of the Maratha Palace, and exhibits the personal collection of Serfoji II.

Nearby is the Sangeeta Mahal (Music Hall), built by the Nayakas, and specially designed with acoustic features for musical gatherings.

Vithoba fresco in the Art Gallery, Royal Palace, Thanjavur

🏛 **Rajaraja Museum and Art Gallery**
◯ daily.
● public hols. 🎫
🏛 **Saraswati Mahal Library**
● to public. **Museum** ◯ Thu–Tue.
🏛 **Royal Museum**
◯ daily. 🎫

ENVIRONS: Lying 55 km (34 miles) east of Thanjavur, **Thiruvarur** is famous for its Thyagaraja Temple dedicated to the Somaskanda form of Shiva (see p578). The temple

has four *gopuras*, and a hall with a striking ceiling, covered with 17th-century paintings depicting scenes from the Shiva legend.

THANJAVUR PAINTINGS

A distinctive school of painting emerged during the rule of the Marathas, patronized by Serfoji II. This highly ornamental style was characterized by vibrant colours as well as decoration with gold leaf and precious and semi-precious stones. The themes are mostly religious, and the symbolic colour palette of red, black, blue and white depicts each deity in a specific colour. The subjects usually have rotund bodies and almond-shaped eyes. A favourite image is Krishna portrayed as a chubby infant.

Baby Krishna with his mother, Yashodhara

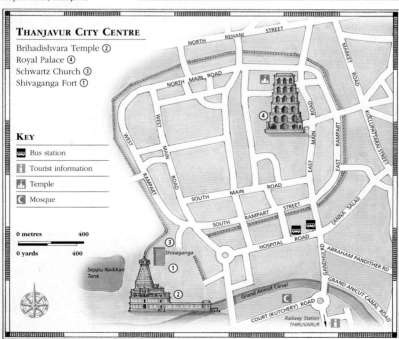

THANJAVUR CITY CENTRE

Brihadishvara Temple ②
Royal Palace ④
Schwartz Church ③
Shivaganga Fort ①

KEY

🚌 Bus station
🛈 Tourist information
🛕 Temple
☪ Mosque

0 metres   400
0 yards   400

Thanjavur: Brihadishvara Temple

A Shiva sculpture

THIS MONUMENTAL GRANITE temple, the finest example of Chola architecture, is now a UNESCO World Heritage Site. Completed in AD 1010 and dedicated to Shiva, it was built by Rajaraja Chola I (*see pp46–7*) as a symbol of the unrivalled power and might of the Cholas. The temple basement is covered with inscriptions that give details of the temple's administration and revenue, and provide valuable historical information on Chola society and government.

An octagonal cupola, beautifully carved out of a massive block of granite weighing 80 tonnes, crowns the *vimana*.

The passageway is circumambulatory and built on two levels, owing to the colossal height of the 4-m (13-ft) linga.

★ **Vimana**
The 66-m (217-ft) high pyramid-shaped vimana, *over the sanctum, is a 13-storeyed structure. Its gilded finial was presented by the king.*

★ **Dvarapala**
Two gigantic dvarapalas, *or doorkeepers, at the eastern entrance, direct devotees to the sanctum with their pointed fingers.*

Linga shrine

STAR FEATURES

★ Vimana

★ Dvarapala

★ Nandi Mandapa

Frescoes
Chola frescoes adorn the passage around the sanctum. They were discovered when the 17-century Maratha paintings covering them began to disintegrate.

VISITORS' CHECKLIST

Thanjavur. W of bus stand.
🔲 *daily. For permission to visit
inner chambers of the sanctum
and the top floors, contact the
temple, (04362) 43 139, or
Thanjavur tourist office.*
Archaeological Museum
🔲 *daily.* 🔲

General View of the Temple
*The Brihadishvara Temple stands
in the middle of a rectangular
court, surrounded by subsidiary
shrines. On the southern side of
the courtyard is an Archaeological Museum which displays,
among other things, photographs
of the temple before restoration.*

★ **Nandi Mandapa**
*Carved out of a single
block of granite weighing
25 tonnes, this huge
Nandi figure is 6 m
(20 ft) long, and faces
the inner sanctum.*

**Priests Outside the
Temple**
*Although under the
jurisdiction of the
Archaeological Survey
of India, the temple has
recently been opened
for worship.*

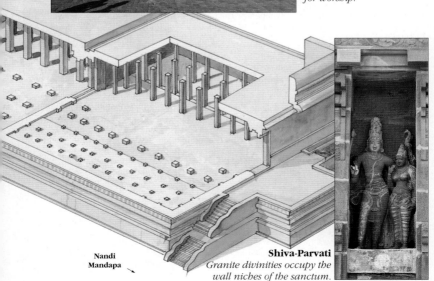

**Nandi
Mandapa**

Shiva-Parvati
*Granite divinities occupy the
wall niches of the sanctum.*

Tiruchirapalli's Rock Fort looming above the city

Tiruchirapalli ⑭

Tiruchirapalli district. 60 km (37 miles)
W of Thanjavur. 🏛 746,100. ✈ 7
km (4 miles) S of town centre, then
bus or taxi. 🚌 🚊 ℹ Hotel Tamil
Nadu, 1 Williams Rd, (0431) 46 0136.
🎏 Teppakulam Float Festival (Mar).

Situated at the head of the
fertile Kaveri Delta, this city
is named after the fierce three-
headed demon *(tirusira)* who
attained salvation after being
slain by Shiva. The town's
history is interwoven with
the political fortunes of the
Pallavas, Cholas, Nayakas
and finally the British, who
shortened its name to Trichy.
Today, Tiruchirapalli is Tamil
Nadu's second largest city.

Dominating the town is the
massive **Rock Fort**, perched
dramatically on a rocky outcrop that rises 83 m (272 ft)
above the flat plains. This
impregnable fortress was
constructed by the Nayakas of
neighbouring Madurai, who
made Tiruchirapalli their
second capital in the 16th and
17th centuries. They also
expanded the Shiva temple,
where the god is worshipped
as Thayumanavar (the "God
who Became a Mother").
Legend says that when a flash
flood prevented a mother
from coming to her pregnant
daughter's aid, Shiva assumed
her form and helped in the
childbirth. Further up, on the
summit, is a small Ganesha
Temple from where there are
spectacular views of verdant
rice fields and the sacred
island of Srirangam.

At the base of the southern
rock face is the first of the two
cave temples. The lower one
dates to the 8th century, and
the upper one to the reign
of the great Pallava ruler,
Mahendra Varman (r.600–630).
This contains one of the great
wonders of Pallava art, the
Gangadhara Panel, depicting
Shiva holding a lock of his
matted hair to receive the
River Ganga as she descends
from the heavens *(see p163)*.

Much of the present town
dates to the 18th and 19th
centuries, when the British
constructed the cantonment
and numerous civic buildings
and churches. Many of these
buildings are located around
the large Teppakulam Tank at
the base of the fort – a busy
area surrounded by fruit,
vegetable and flower markets.

Among the town's earliest
churches are Christ Church
(1766), founded by Reverend
Frederick Christian Schwartz
(see p596), to the north of
the tank; the Neo-Gothic
**Cathedral of Our Lady of
Lourdes** (1840), to the west
of the tank; and the Jesuit
St Joseph's College, also to
the west of the tank. In the
cantonment, which lies to the
southwest of the fort, is the
Church of St John (1816).

ⴖ **Rock Fort**
◻ daily. 🎞 📷 extra charges.

**The Cathedral of Our Lady of
Lourdes at Tiruchirapalli**

THE KAVERI RIVER

One of the nine sacred rivers of India, the Kaveri covers a length of
785 km (488 miles) from its source at Talakaveri in Karnataka *(see
p521)* to Poompuhar on the Bay of Bengal. Myths glorify the
Kaveri as the personification of a female deity (in some versions,
Brahma's daughter), who erupted from the sage Agasthya's
kamandala (water pot). From the early centuries of the Christian
era, the Kaveri has been central to Tamil culture, especially under
the Cholas, who ruled the region between the 9th and 13th centuries. The great temple cities that developed along its course became
centres of religion, dance, music and the arts. Farsighted water
management schemes in the delta, instigated by the Cholas, transformed the Thanjavur region into the "rice bowl" of Tamil Nadu,
and even today, devotees offer rice to the river goddess on the
18th day of the Tamil month Adi (July/August). Unfortunately, the
river has now become the subject of a bitter dispute over water
distribution between the Tamil Nadu and Karnataka governments.

**Shrine depicting the
legend of Goddess Kaveri**

ENVIRONS: At **Kallanai**, 24 km (15 miles) northeast of Tiruchirapalli, is a 300-m (984-ft) long earthen dam across the Kaveri river, the Grand Anicut. This formed part of the huge hydraulic system created by the Cholas *(see pp46–7)* to divert water from the river into a vast network of irrigation canals. The original no longer exists and the dam in operation today was rebuilt by British engineers in the 19th century.

Other places of interest are the 7th-century Shiva temple at **Narthamalai**, 17 km (11 miles) to the south, and the 9th-century Jain cave temples at **Sittanavasal**, 58 km (36 miles) to the southeast. Faded paintings here portray dancing girls, and a lotus tank with swans and fishes.

Srirangam ⑮

Tiruchirapalli district. 9 km (6 miles) N of Tiruchirapalli. 🚌 🚉 *Vaikuntha Ekadashi (Dec/Jan), Chariot Festival (Jan).*

THE SACRED 3-km (2-mile) long island of Srirangam, formed by the Kaveri and Kollidam rivers, is one of the most revered pilgrimage sites in South India. At its core is the majestic **Ranganatha Temple** *(see pp552–3)*. Dedicated to Vishnu, this is one of the largest temple complexes in Tamil Nadu and covers an enormous area of 60 ha (148 acres).

The complex as it exists today has evolved over a period of four centuries.

Extensive reconstruction first took place in 1371, after the original 10th-century temple was destroyed by the Delhi Sultan, Alauddin Khilji *(see p48)*. Its present form, however, includes extensions added in the 17th century by the Nayaka rulers, whose second capital was in neighbouring Tiruchirapalli. Interestingly, the last addition was as recent as 1987, when the unfinished southern gateway was finally completed.

Dominated by 21 impressive *gopuras* (gateways), the complex has seven *prakara* (boundary) walls defining its seven enclosures. The outer three comprise residences for priests, hostels for pilgrims, and small restaurants and shops selling religious books, pictures and sundry temple offerings. The sacred precinct begins from the fourth enclosure, beyond which non-Hindus are not allowed. This is where the temple's most important shrines are located. Among these are the spacious Thousand-Columned Mandapa, where images of Ranganatha and his consort are enthroned and worshipped during one of the temple's many festivals, and the magnificent **Seshagirirayar Mandapa**, with its rearing

A coracle ride on the Kaveri, Srirangam

stone horses with mounted warriors attacking fierce animals and *yalis* (mythical leonine beasts). A small museum close by has a good collection of stone and bronze sculptures.

The core of the complex is the sanctum, with its gold-plated *vimana*, where an image of Vishnu as Ranganatha, reclining on the cosmic serpent, Adisesha, is enshrined. This temple is also the place where the great 11th-century philosopher, Ramanuja *(see p522)*, developed the *bhakti* cult of personal devotion into a formalized mode of worship. Today, a constant cycle of festivals glorifying Vishnu are celebrated throughout the year.

Horse, Seshagirirayar Mandapa

East of the Ranganatha Temple is the mid-17th-century **Jambukeshvara Temple** in the village of Tiruvanaikka. The main sanctum contains one of the five elemental lingas *(see p584)*, representing Shiva as the manifestation of water. Legend says that the linga was created by Shiva's consort, Parvati, and in homage to her, the priest wears a sari when performing the *puja*. Non-Hindus can view the outer shrines in the complex, but not the main sanctum.

🏛 **Sri Ranganatha Temple**
🕐 daily. 📷 for viewpoint on top. 🎥 📷 extra charges. **Museum** 🕐 daily.
🏛 **Jambukeshvara Temple**
🕐 daily. 📷 🎥 extra charges.

One of the impressive gateways at the Ranganatha Temple, Srirangam

The verdant Marthanda Valley, with the misty Nilgiri Hills in the background ▷

Yerikadu Lake, from which Yercaud derives its name

Yercaud 🔟

Salem district. 32 km (20 miles) NE of Salem. 🚉 *Salem, then bus.* 🚌 ℹ️ *Hotel Tamil Nadu, Yercaud Ghat Rd, (04281) 22 273.* 🎭 *Shevaroyan Temple Festival (May).*

THIS ATTRACTIVE hill station, situated in the Shevaroy Hills, was established in the early 1800s by the British, who introduced the coffee plant here. Today, this is one of the state's most productive areas, and its surrounding slopes are entirely covered with plantations of coffee, tea, jackfruit and plantains.

The man-made **Yerikadu Lake** and the **Killiyur Falls** are two of the area's most scenic spots, while **Lady's Seat**, near the lake, offers delightful views of the surrounding countryside. The town and its environs have several apiaries that produce delicious honey. The **Horticultural Research Station** has an interesting collection of rare plants.

Mudumalai Wildlife Sanctuary 🔟

Nilgiris district. 64 km (40 miles) W of Udhagamandalam. 🚌 *Theppakadu, the main entry point.* ℹ️ *Tourist Office, Theppakadu, (0423) 56 235. For bookings contact Wildlife Warden's Office, Ooty, (0423) 44 4098.* 🔓 *daily (may be closed during Feb–Mar).* 🎟️ 📷 *Jeeps available.* 🏞️

MUDUMALAI OR "Ancient Hill Range", situated at the base of the Nilgiri Hills, is separated from Karnataka's Bandipur National Park *(see p520)* by the Moyar river.

This sanctuary is an important constituent of the 5,500-sq km (2,124-sq mile) Nilgiri Biosphere Reserve of the Western Ghats. Along with adjacent Bandipur and Nagarhole, it provides one of the most important refuges for the elephant and the bison in India. The park encompasses 322 sq km (124 sq miles) of undulating terrain, and rises to 1,250 m (4,101 ft) at Moyar

Tour of the Nilgiris 🔟

THE PICTURESQUE *nila giri* or "Blue Mountains", at the junction of the Eastern and Western Ghats, are so named because the shrub *kurunji (Strobilanthes kunthianus)* turns the hills blue with its blossoms every 12 years. Covered with high altitude grasslands and *sholas* (montane evergreen forests), they are of special interest to botanists and entomologists. This tour offers enchanting glimpses of lush green valleys, hill stations and hamlets inhabited by tribal people.

Jacaranda in full bloom in the Nilgiris

Pykara ⑥
Dams, fenced *sholas*, green meadows and conical-shaped Toda houses can be seen here.

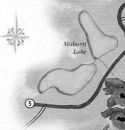

MUDUMALAI

Pykara Reservoir

Makurti Lake

TIPS FOR DRIVERS

Length: 90 km (56 miles).
Getting around: Avalanche and Pykara can only be reached from Ooty, as there are no road links from Coonoor. The route is well covered by public & private buses. An exciting alternative is the **Nilgiri Blue Mountain Train**, which runs from Mettupalayam to Ooty, via Coonoor (see p777).

Avalanche ⑤
This natural paradise has dense forests and a beautiful lake.

| 0 km | 3 |
| 0 miles | 3 |

KEY

—— Tour route

══ Other roads

Betta. The lowest point of the sanctuary is at the picturesque **Moyar Waterfalls**. Its topography is as varied as the vegetation, which ranges from dense deciduous forests of teak, laurel and rosewood in the west, to scrub jungle towards the east, interspersed with grassland, swamps and bamboo brakes.

The sanctuary provides a habitat for a rich diversity of wildlife, including the Nilgiri tahr *(see p19)*, sambar, tiger, leopard, spotted deer, flying squirrel, Malabar civet and Nilgiri langur. Over 120 species of birds, resident and migratory, can be seen here as well. These include the scops owl and the crested hawk eagle.

Coimbatore ⑲

Coimbatore district. 96 km (60 miles) NE of Chennai. 🏠 924,000. ✈ 10 km (6 miles) NE of city centre, then bus. 🚇 🚆 ℹ Tamil Nadu Tourism, Railway Station. 🏪 Mon–Sat. 🎪 Thaipoosam (Jan/Feb), Karthigai (Nov/Dec).

TAMIL NADU'S third largest city, Coimbatore is a major industrial centre and the state's commercial capital, with huge textile mills and engineering units. It is also a convenient base for visiting the Nilgiri hill stations. The city has a reputed Agricultural College, and two famous temples. The **Perur Temple** on the Noyyal river and the popular **Muruga Maruthamalai Temple**, on top of a hillock, are dedicated to Lord Shiva and his son, Murugan, respectively. They are visited by thousands of devotees during temple festivals.

The **Siruvani Waterfalls** are beautiful, and Siruvani water famed for its purity and taste.

GUARDIAN DEITIES

Huge figures made of burnt clay can be seen on the outskirts of villages in the southern districts of Tamil Nadu. They are worshipped as the guardians of the villages. The most prominent folk deity is Ayyanar, the son of Shiva and Vishnu. This mustachioed god, with prominent eyes, wears short trousers and carries a sword. His horse stands by his side so that he can ride through the night, keeping evil spirits at bay. Other deities are Munisami, who holds a trident and shield and rides a lion, and the black-hued Karuppusami, the nocturnal avenger who punishes thieves.

Guardian deities outside a village shrine

Ooty ①
Officially known as Udhagamandalam, this Queen of Hill Stations was originally inhabited by the Todas *(see p607)*. The century-old Blue Mountain Train terminates here.

Dodda Betta ②
The highest peak in the Nilgiris (2,623 m/8,606 ft) has fantastic views of the hills, valleys and plateaux.

Kotagiri ③
Known for its salubrious climate, this hill station is situated in the shadow of Dodda Betta Peak.

Nadubatti

METTUPALAYAM

Coonoor ④
A pretty town surrounded by hills and tea and coffee plantations, Coonoor hosts an annual fruit and vegetable show in May, at Sim's Park.

Tree-lined avenue in Kodaikanal

Palani ⑳

Madurai district. 100 km (62 miles) NW of Madurai. ✈ *Madurai, 119 km (74 miles) SE of town centre, then bus or taxi.* 🚃 🚌 ⛩ *Thaipoosam (Jan/Feb), Karthigai (Nov/Dec).*

A MAJOR PILGRIMAGE centre, Palani is situated on the edge of the great Vyapuri Tank. Its hilltop **Subrahmanyam Temple** is the most famous of the six abodes of Murugan, the son of Shiva, who is said to have come here disguised as a mendicant after quarreling over a fruit with his brother, Ganesha. Popularly known as Dandayutha Pani ("Bearer of the Staff"), Murugan is depicted with a clean shaven head, holding a stick. His image is made of medicinal herbs, mixed together to create a wax-like substance. During the Thaipoosam festival, the temple attracts thousands of pilgrims, many of whom shave their heads as an act of worship. An electric cable car takes devotees up the 600 steps to the hill shrine.

Palani is also a base for hikes in the surrounding hills.

Kodaikanal ㉑

Madurai district. 120 km (75 miles) NW of Madurai. 🚃 *Palani, 65 km (40 miles) N of town centre, then bus or taxi.* 🚌 🛈 *Tamil Nadu Tourism, (04542) 41 675.* 🕐 *Mon–Sat.* ⛩ *Summer Festival (May), Flower Show (May), Winter Festival (Dec).* 🛶

L USH GREEN VALLEYS, terraced plantations and a pleasant climate make Kodaikanal one of Tamil Nadu's most popular hill stations. Kodaikanal, or Kodai as it is commonly called, was first "discovered" by American missionaries in the 1840s. Drawn by its bracing climate and clean environs, they created a sanatorium-cum-retreat here. They also established Kodai's International School in 1901.

This picturesque town is today spread out around the man-made, star-shaped **Kodai Lake**, created by the dam built by Sir Vere Henry Levinge in 1863. The 3-km (2-mile) long trail around the lake makes for a pleasant walk. On the shore is a Boat House, built in 1910. East of the lake is **Bryant Park**, famous for its plant collection and its annual flower show, held in May.

Beyond the city centre are a number of scenic areas, such as Pillar Rocks, Silver Cascade and Green Valley View (originally known as Suicide Point), which offer enchanting picnic spots and views of the deep valley. Kodai also has many opportunities for cycling, riding and long, rambling walks. A trail following the hillside, called **Coaker's Walk**, provides a panoramic view of the hill station. The walk ends at the Church of St Peter, built in 1884, which has fine stained-glass windows. Nearby is a small **Telescope House**.

Some 3 km (2 miles) northeast of the lake is the **Kurunji Andavar Temple**, dedicated to Murugan. It is named after the amazing *kurunji* flowers *(see p649)*, associated with the god. The Chettiar Park nearby, laid out along the hillside, is where the *kurunji* blooms every 12 years.

Waterfall in the Nilgiris

HIKING IN THE NILGIRIS

Short excursions around Ooty offer many opportunities to explore the Nilgiris *(see pp604–605)* on foot. There are scenic trails in the grasslands around Mukurthi, an extinct volcano known to the Todas as the "Gateway to the Dead", and in the windswept Avalanche region, which consists of rolling, grassy downs, *shola* trees and rhododendrons. The western edge of this region falls away into the dense tropical jungles of Kerala. The eastern half of the range, largely deprived of the Southwest Monsoon, is dominated by dry scrub and volcanic rock.

Religious offerings for sale in Palani

The Todas

THE NILGIRIS ARE home to 18 tribal groups, among whom the Todas are the most remarkable. A pastoral community, the Todas are fair-skinned and curly haired, and are strict vegetarians. Their language, though of Dravidian origin, has no script. According to their creation myth, Goddess Teikirshy and her brother On first created the buffalo by waving a magic wand, and then created the Toda man. The first Toda woman was created from the right rib of the man. The Todas' first contact with civilization occurred when the East India Company annexed the Nilgiris in 1799. In 1823, John Sullivan, the then Collector of Coimbatore, built the first stone house in Ooty on land purchased from the Todas. Today, there are only about 1,100 Todas left.

Traditional silver jewellery

Toda buffaloes, pale brown with long horns, are deeply revered. A buffalo is often sacrificed after a funeral to accompany the deceased's soul in the afterlife.

Homespun cotton shawls called puthikuzhi have black-and-red embroidered motifs. Worn by both Toda men and women, they are tied around the waist, with one end thrown over the shoulder, almost like a Roman toga.

The dairy temple, conical in shape, is decorated with sun, moon, serpent and buffalo head motifs. Only men are allowed to go inside.

Elders are treated with great respect, and greeted by lifting their right foot and putting it on one's head for their blessings.

Dairy ceremonies are festive occasions, generally celebrated with dance and music. The lively songs consist of simple stanzas, describing important events from the Todas' past.

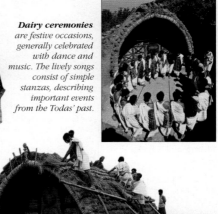

The barrel-shaped huts, made of bamboo, grass and cane, consist of a single room. Entry is through a carved wooden door, so small that one has to crawl through it to enter. Several of these windowless bamboo huts make up a Toda village, which is called a mund.

Madurai

ONE OF SOUTH INDIA'S great temple towns, Madurai is synonymous with the celebrated Minakshi Temple *(see pp610–11)*. This ancient city on the banks of the Vaigai river has, over the centuries, been a rich repository of Tamil culture. Some 2,000 years ago, it hosted the famous Sangams (gatherings of writers and poets), which were to provide Tamil literature with some of its most enduring works. From the 7th to 13th centuries, as the capital of the Pandyas, it saw art and trade with Rome and China flourish. It later became part of the Vijayanagar Empire, and was the Nayaka capital in the 16th–17th centuries. Today, religion and culture remain a vibrant part of the city's daily life.

Sculpted image

The grand pillared hall in the Thirumalai Nayaka Palace

Minakshi Sundareshvara Temple

See pp610–11.

Thirumalai Nayaka Palace

1.5 km (1 mile) SE of Minakshi Temple. ☐ *daily.* 🎞 **Son et Lumière** (English): 6.45pm, daily. 🎞
The power and wealth of the Nayakas is evident from the remains of this once grand palace, built by Thirumalai Nayaka in 1636. The building, with its interesting Islamic influences, was partially restored in the 19th century by Lord Napier, governor of Madras between 1866 and 1872. Today, only the spacious rectangular courtyard called

the Swarga Vilasam ("Heavenly Pavilion") and a few adjoining buildings survive, their awesome scale evoking the grandeur of a vanished era. The courtyard measures 3,900 sq m (41,979 sq ft), and is surrounded by massive circular pillars. To its west lies the Throne Chamber, a vast room with a raised, octagonal dome. This room leads to the Dance Hall, which now houses a display of archaeological objects.

Theppakulam

E of Minakshi Temple. ☐ *daily.* 🎞
Madurai's great tank is another marvel attributed to Thirumalai Nayaka. The square tank has steps, flanked

by animal- and bird-shaped balustrades, leading down to the rippling waters. This is the venue of the annual Theppam (Float) festival, celebrating the marriage of Shiva and Minakshi, when their images are taken in illuminated boats to the small pavilion in the centre of the tank.

Kadal Alagar Temple

1 km (0.6 miles) SW of Minakshi Temple. ☐ *daily.* ● to non-Hindus.
One of the 108 sacred Vaishnavite shrines, this glorious temple has three superimposed sanctuaries, of diminishing size, housing Lord Vishnu. From bottom to top, the images show Vishnu in the seated, standing and reclining position. The outer wall has beautiful sculptures and stone screens.

Anglican Cathedral

Off W Masi St. ☐ *daily.*
A fine example of Neo-Gothic architecture, this church was designed by Robert Fellowes Chisholm *(see p569)*, and consecrated in 1881.

Tombs of the Madurai Sultans

N of the Vaigai river. ☐ *daily.*
The sultans of Madurai ruled the city after the invasion in 1310 by Malik Kafur, a general of Alauddin Khilji *(see p48)*. They lie buried to the north of the city. The complex includes Alauddin's Mosque, with its flat-roofed prayer hall and tapering octagonal towers, and the tomb of a local Sufi saint, Bara Mastan Sada, built in the 16th century.

Entrance to the Anglican Cathedral at Madurai

A mural depicting a scene from the *Ramayana*, Alagarkoil Temple

VISITORS' CHECKLIST

Madurai district. 498 km (309 miles) SW of Chennai. 923,000. ✈ 12 km (7 miles) S of city centre. 🚉 🚌 ℹ 180, West Veli St, (0452) 73 4757. 🕐 Mon–Sat. 🎉 Theppam Festival (Jan/Feb), Navaratri (Sep/Oct), Avanimoolam (Aug/Sep).

The temple at **Alagarkoil**, 12 km (7 miles) north of Madurai, is dedicated to Kallalagar, a form of Vishnu who is regarded as Minakshi's brother. According to legend, when Kallalagar went to give his sister in marriage to Sundareshvara, he stayed on the banks of the Vaigai river during the ceremony. This event is celebrated every year, in April/May. On the summit of the hill is Palamudircholai, the last of the six abodes of Murugan, marked by a shrine, while further away is Nupura Ganga, a perennial spring, used for all rituals in the temple, and believed to have emerged from Vishnu's ankle.

ENVIRONS: Thiruparankunram, 6 km (4 miles) southwest of Madurai, is a small town known for its sacred granite hill. Regarded as one of the six sacred abodes of Murugan, the son of Shiva, the hill was the site of his marriage to Devayani, the daughter of Indra. There is a rock-cut temple here, built by the Pandyas in the 8th century. The temple is approached through a series of 17th- and 18th-century *mandapas*, at ascending levels, linked by stone steps. The entrance *mandapa* has typical Nayaka period pillars with horse and *yali* riders, while portraits of Nayaka rulers are carved on the columns. The temple's main sanctum contains five shrines.

The 14-day temple festival, in March/April, celebrates the victory of Murugan over the demon Suran, his coronation, and his subsequent marriage to Devayani.

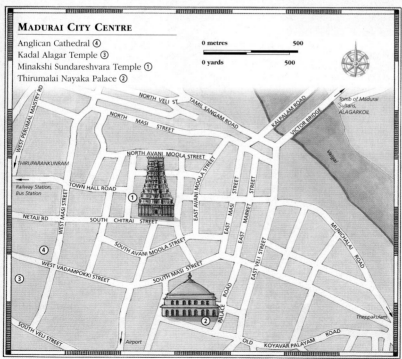

MADURAI CITY CENTRE

Anglican Cathedral ④
Kadal Alagar Temple ③
Minakshi Sundareshvara Temple ①
Thirumalai Nayaka Palace ②

0 metres   500
0 yards   500

Madurai: Minakshi Sundareshvara Temple

THIS ENORMOUS TEMPLE COMPLEX is dedicated to Shiva, known here as Sundareshvara (the "Handsome God"), and his consort Parvati or Minakshi (the "Fish-eyed Goddess"). Originally built by the early Pandyas (7th–10th centuries), it was extensively added to by succeeding dynasties, especially between the 14th and 18th centuries. The temple complex is within a high-walled enclosure, at the core of which are the two sanctums for Minakshi and Sundareshvara, surrounded by a number of smaller shrines and grand pillared halls. Especially impressive are the 12 *gopuras*. Their soaring towers rise from solid granite bases, and are covered with stucco figures of deities, mythical animals and monsters, painted in vivid colours.

Guardian Deities
Fierce monster images, with protruding eyes and horns, mark the arched ends of the vaulted roofs, and serve as guardian deities.

GOPURA
Pyramidal gates *(gopuras)* rise to a height of more than 50 m (164 ft). These towering gateways indicate the entrance to the temple complex at the four cardinal points, while lesser *gopuras* lead to the sanctums of the main deities.

Stucco Work
The figures of deities on the tower are repaired, repainted and ritually reconsecrated every 12 years.

Openings in the middle of the long sides allow light to enter the hollow chambers at each level.

The profusely carved pillars of the Thousand-Pillared Hall

Exploring the Minakshi Temple

The temple is entered from the eastern side through the **Ashta Shakti Mandapa** or the "Hall of Eight Goddesses", with sculpted pillars representing the various aspects of the Goddess Shakti. Next to this hall is the **Minakshi Nayaka Mandapa**, a spacious columned hall used for shops and stores. This hall has a votive lamp-holder with 1,008 lamps, which are lit on festive occasions and present a spectacular sight.

The adjacent seven-storeyed **Chitra Gopura**, is the tallest tower in the complex. Next to it is the **Potramarai Kulam**, or "Golden Lotus" Tank, with steps leading down to the water. It is surrounded by pillared corridors that once bore paintings from the Vijayanagar period. To the west of this tank is the **Minakshi Shrine**, one of the two main shrines, comprising two concentric corridors and many halls and galleries. Here lies the bed to which Minakshi's "husband", in the form of Sundareshvara's image, is brought every night from his own shrine, the **Sundareshvara Shrine**, which stands to the north. The god resides in this, the second

Kalyana Sundara, Vishnu giving Minakshi to Shiva

main shrine, amid columns that bear the fish motifs emblematic of his wife.

The 16th-century "Flagpole Hall" or **Kambattadi Mandapa**, in front of this shrine, has a pavilion with a seated Nandi, a gilded flagpole and ornately carved pillars depicting the 24 forms of Shiva. To its east is the **Thousand-Pillared Hall** with 985 beautifully decorated columns. Dating to the 16th century, this hall is now a museum, which displays bronze and stone images. A set of pillars, a marvel in stone, produce the seven notes of Carnatic music. The **Kalyana Mandapa**, to the south of the pillared hall, is where the marriage of Shiva and Parvati is celebrated every year during the Chitirai Festival in mid-April.

Pudumandapa, the 100-m (328-ft) long "New Hall" with portrait sculptures of the Nayaka rulers, is outside the main temple complex. Built by Tirumalai Nayaka in 1635, it now houses a market selling saris, jewellery and spices.

MINAKSHI SUNDARESHVARA TEMPLE COMPLEX

1 Ashta Shakti Mandapa
2 Minakshi Nayaka Mandapa
3 Chitra Gopura
4 Potramarai Kulam
5 Minakshi Shrine
6 Sundareshvara Shrine
7 Kambattadi Mandapa
8 Thousand-Pillared Hall
9 Kalyana Mandapa

0 metres   100
0 yards   100

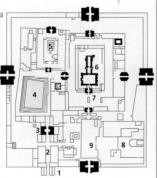

The Potramarai Kulam, surrounded by a colonnade

Chettiar Mansions

THE ARID REGION encompassing the towns of Karaikudi, Devakottai and their neighbouring villages, collectively known as Chettinad, is distinguished by large ornate mansions which are the ancestral homes of the Chettiars, Tamil Nadu's rich merchant community. Like the Marwaris of Shekhavati

An arched passageway

(see pp372–3), the Chettiars were astute businessmen who travelled far to make their fortunes. The wealth they acquired in Burma, Sri Lanka, Malaysia, and Vietnam was used to build these elaborate mansions. Today, the Chettiars are prominent bankers and industrialists based in Chennai and Bangalore.

CHETTIAR HOUSES

Built in the early 20th century, these houses reflect the social, ritual and kinship needs of the community, as well as its economic status. Though now unoccupied for most of the year, they are still used for family celebrations.

The splendid Chettinad Palace, Karaikudi

*A **long verandah** with wooden pillars leads to a series of open courtyards, surrounded by rooms to accommodate the growing family.*

*The **first pillared hall**, where each pillar is made from an entire tree trunk of Burma teak, is reserved for the men of the house to receive guests and conduct business.*

*The **formal reception room** has marble floors, stained-glass windows, painted cornices, teak and rosewood furniture and ornate chandeliers.*

*Elaborate **marble floors**, well-polished doorways, carved wooden beams, granite pillars, and other decorative elements in a Chettiar house display the skills of the Tamil craftsmen.*

Intricately carved wooden doorway

Chettinad ❷❸

Chettinad district. 82 km (51 miles)
NE of Madurai. 🚗 🚌 🚉 *daily.*
🎪 *Bullock Races (Jan/Feb).*

KARAIKUDI, THE HEART of the
Chettinad area, has several
temples, including the 7th-
century **Pillaiyarpati Temple**
dedicated to Lord Ganesha.
It also has fine Chettiar mansions, and antique shops
stocked with treasures from
these mansions. Chettinad is
famous for its hot, spicy, non-
vegetarian cuisine – pepper
chicken is one of the most
popular dishes. The food is
prepared in copper vessels
and served on plantain leaves.

Ramanathapuram ❷❹

Ramanathapuram district. 117 km
(73 miles) SE of Madurai. 🏠 62,000.
🚗 🚌 🚉 *daily.* 🎪 *Urs at Erwadi*
Dargah (Dec).

THIS ANCIENT TOWN is
associated with the
Setupatis, local rulers who
rose to prominence in the
late 17th century under the
Madurai Nayakas. They
derived prestige and income
by controlling the isthmus
that led to Rameshvaram
island. A century later, their
rule came to an end when
they surrendered to the East
India Company in 1792.
To the west of the present
town is the palace complex
of the Setupatis. Though little
remains, the 17th-century
Ramalinga Vilas, on the
north side of the palace complex, still has well-preserved
wall paintings. These depict
the epics as well as battle
scenes, business transactions
and royal ceremonies. The
upper chambers depict more
private royal scenes, such as
family gatherings, music and
dance recitals, and hunting
expeditions. A small shrine,
facing north, is dedicated to
the family goddess of the
Setupatis, Rajarajeshvari. It
stands immediately south of
the Ramalinga Vilas.
On the outskirts of the town
is the 800-year-old **Erwadi
Dargah**, housing the tomb of
Ibrahim Syed Aulia, a Muslim

The longest corridor at Ramanathaswamy Temple, with sculpted pillars

saint. It attracts devotees from
all over India, as well as from
Sri Lanka, Malaysia and
Singapore during its annual
festival in December.

Rameshvaram ❷❺

Ramanathapuram district. 163 km
(101 miles) SE of Madurai.
🏠 38,050. 🚗 🚌 ℹ️ *Tourist office,*
East Car Street, (04573) 21 371.
🎪 *Ramalinga (Jun/Jul).*

A MAJOR PILGRIMAGE SITE, the
sacred island of Ramesh-
varam juts out into the Gulf of
Mannar, the narrow body of
water separating Tamil Nadu
from Sri Lanka.
The **Ramanathaswamy
Temple**, in the middle of the
island, is dedicated to Shiva.
It houses the linga that Lord
Rama, the hero of the epic
Ramayana (see p27), is
said to have installed and
worshipped after his victory
against Ravana in Lanka.
Founded by the Chola rulers
but expanded extensively

Devotees taking a dip in the holy
waters of the Agni Tirtha

during the Nayaka period, in
the 16th to 18th centuries, this
massive temple is enclosed
within a high wall with five
gopuras. The most remarkable feature of this temple
is the **Sokkattan Mandapa**,
so called because it resembles
a *sokkattan* (dice) in shape.
It surrounds the core of the
temple on four sides in a
continuous corridor, and is
the largest and most elaborate
of its kind, with 1,212 pillars
extending 197 m (646 ft) from
east to west and 133 m (436
ft) from north to south. The
complex also has a staggering
22 *tirthas* (tanks) for ritual
ablutions; it is believed that a
dip in the Agni Tirtha, in front
of the temple, removes all
sins. The installation ceremony of the linga by Rama and
Sita is celebrated every year.
Standing on **Gandamadana
Hill**, the highest point of the
island, 3 km (2 miles) northwest of the Ramanathaswamy
Temple, is a two-storeyed
mandapa that is said to
shelter the footprint of Rama.
Dhanushkodi ("Rama's
Bow"), the southern-most tip
of Rameshvaram, about 18
km (11 miles) from the main
temple, has a spectacular
beach. From here, a series of
boulders, known as Adam's
Bridge, can be seen extending
far into the horizon. These
are believed to have been
used by Hanuman when he
crossed the ocean in search
of Sita. The Kodandarama
Temple, on the shore, is said
to be where Ravana's brother
surrendered to Rama. Miraculously, the temple survived a
devastating cyclone in 1964.

Tuticorin ㉖

Tuticorin district. 135 km (84 miles)
S of Madurai. 🏠 216,100. 🚉 🚌
🎪 Golden Chariot Festival (Aug).

THIS IS TAMIL NADU'S second
largest natural harbour,
and the main port of call for
ships from Southeast Asia,
Australia and New Zealand.
Tuticorin is also a major
industrial centre with thermal
power stations, spinning mills
and salt extraction units.

The city's other important
commercial activity is pearl
fishing. Since the early centuries of the Christian era, this
region's pearls have been in
demand throughout the
world. Ancient Tamil literature mentions a flourishing
trade with the Romans, who
bought Tuticorin pearls in
exchange for gold and wine.

Today the government,
which has set up a society of
divers, strictly regulates pearl
fishing, in order to protect the
oyster beds – sometimes pearl
fishing is allowed only once
in ten years. The pearl fishers
still use traditional methods,
diving to a depth of up to
70 m (230 ft) without oxygen
to extricate the pearls. Most
divers can remain underwater
for more than a minute; their
only safeguard against accidents or natural danger is
to dive in pairs.

Tuticorin was occupied by
the Portuguese in the 17th
century and later by the Dutch
and the British. Its colonial
past is visible in two elegant
churches, the Dutch **Sacred
Heart Cathedral**, built in the
mid-18th century, and the
beautiful 17th-century **Church
of the Lady of the Snows**,
built by the Portuguese.

Corridor of the Kanthimathi Nellaiyappar Temple, Tirunelvelli

Tiruchendur ㉗

Tuticorin district. 223 km (139 miles)
S of Madurai. 🚉 🚌 from Madurai,
Tirunelvelli, Tuticorin & Nagercoil.
🎪 Annual Temple Festival (Jun/Jul).

THIS BEAUTIFUL coastal town,
one of the six sacred
abodes of Shiva's son, Murugan (see p606), has the
impressive **Subramanyam
Temple**. Dating to the 9th
century, it was renovated in
the 20th century. The temple,
entered through the towering
Mela gopura, is built on a
rocky promontory overlooking the Gulf of Mannar, and
provides lovely views. On the
seashore are some caves and
rock-cut sculptures.

ENVIRONS: Manapad, 18 km
(11 miles) south, has one of
the oldest churches in India,
the Church of the Holy Cross.
Built in 1581, it preserves a
fragment of the "True Cross",
brought from Jerusalem. An
annual festival held every
September attracts pilgrims
from all over the region.
St Francis Xavier visited this
coastal village in 1542.

Tirunelvelli ㉘

Tirunelvelli district. 154 km (96 miles)
SW of Madurai. 🚉 🚌 ℹ Tamil
Nadu Tourism, Tirunelvelli Junction,
(0462) 50 0104. 🎪 Chariot Festival
(Jun/Jul).

SITUATED IN THE fertile tract
fed by the Tamaraparani
river, Tirunelvelli is dominated by the **Kanthimathi
Nellaiyappar Temple**, parts
of which date to the 13th
century. This complex of
twin temples, dedicated to
Shiva and Parvati, has two
huge rectangular enclosures
connected by a long corridor.
The Shiva temple is to the
north, while the Parvati
temple is to the south. The
elaborate mandapas here
include the Somavara Man-
dapa, which contains two
pillars carved like gopuras;
the Rishaba Mandapa, with
exquisitely carved sculptures
of Manmatha, the God of
Love, and his consort Rathi;
and the Mani Mandapa, with
a set of stone pillars that
produce the melodic notes
of Carnatic music (see p595)
when tapped.

Every summer, the temple's
wooden chariots are led in
procession through the town
during the annual Chariot
Festival, which attracts
thousands of devotees.

**ENVIRONS: Courtallam
(Kuttalam) Falls**, at an elevation of 170 m (558 ft), are
59 km (37 miles) northwest of
Tirunelvelli. This picturesque
spot is famed for its exotic
flora and the medicinal properties of its waters.

The Church of the Holy Cross in Manapad

Sthanumalaya Temple at Suchindram, overlooking the temple tank

Suchindram 29

Kanniyakumari district. 247 km (154 miles) S of Madurai. 🚉 Nagarcoil, 5 km (3 miles) NW of town centre, then bus. 🚌 📷 Arudhra Festival (Dec/Jan).

THIS SMALL temple town is closely linked with the legend of Kumari, the Virgin Goddess (an incarnation of Parvati). It is believed that Shiva rested at this quiet spot by the banks of the Pelayar river, while the goddess Kumari performed her penance at Kanniyakumari.

Suchindram's unique **Sthanumalaya Temple** is dedicated to the Hindu Trinity of Brahma, Vishnu and Shiva. The rectangular complex has enormous, brightly coloured *gopuras* dating from the 17th–18th centuries, which depict stories from the great epics *(see pp26–7)*. One of the two main shrines, built in the 13th century, contains the Sthanumalaya linga, which symbolizes Brahma, Vishnu and Shiva. The other is dedicated to Vishnu, whose image is made of a special kind of jaggery and mustard.

The temple also boasts a set of musical pillars made from single blocks of granite. When tapped, each pillar produces a different musical note. Other highlights are a 5-m (16-ft) high statue of Hanuman placed opposite the Rama shrine, and the exquisite sculptures in the Vasantha Mandapa. A special *puja* is held here every Friday evening, with music and a procession. In the complex is an ancient banyan tree, and a sculpture of Shiva's bull, Nandi, which locals believe actually continues to grow.

Kanniyakumari 30

Kanniyakumari district. 235 km (146 miles) S of Madurai. 👥 19,700. 🚉 🚌 ℹ️ Tamil Nadu Tourism, Beach Rd, (04652) 46 276. 📷 Chaitra Purnima (Apr), Navaratri (Sep/Oct).

THE SOUTHERNMOST TIP of the Indian subcontinent, where the Indian Ocean, the Arabian Sea and the Bay of Bengal meet, Kanniyakumari enchants visitors with its spectacular views, especially at sunrise and sunset. The most breathtaking of these occurs on Chaitra Purnima (the full moon night in April) when both sunset and moonrise occur at the same time.

Kanniyakumari is believed to be the abode of Kumari, the Virgin Goddess, who is supposed to have done penance here so that she could marry Shiva. The marriage, however, did not take place, since it was deemed that she remain a virgin in order to save the world. Her temple, the **Kumari Amman Temple**, a popular pilgrimage centre on the seashore, was built by the Pandya kings in the 8th century and was extensively renovated by the Chola, Vijayanagar and Nayaka rulers.

A magnificent structure, the temple has a Navaratri Mandapa with a beautifully painted panel of Mahishasuramardini (Durga killing the demon Mahisha). An 18th-century shrine within the temple contains the footprints *(sripadaparai)* of the goddess Kumari, who performed her penance at this spot.

The **Gandhi Memorial**, near the temple, is where Mahatma Gandhi's ashes were kept before immersion. The building is designed so that every year on October 2nd (Gandhi's birthday), at midday, the rays of the sun fall on the exact spot where his ashes were placed.

Just off the coast, on a rocky island, the **Vivekananda Memorial** marks the spot where the great Indian philosopher, Swami Vivekananda *(see p286)* meditated before attending the World Religious Conference in Chicago in 1893. Near the memorial is the imposing 40-m (131-ft) high statue of Tiruvalluvar, the 1st-century BC Tamil poet, who wrote the epic *Tirukural*, often referred to as one of the greatest classics of Tamil literature.

The **Church of Our Lady of Joy**, which was founded by St Francis Xavier in the 1540s, is located at the southern edge of the town. Other attractions include the sandy beaches and the multicoloured granite rocks.

🚩 **Kumari Amman Temple**
⭕ daily. ⬤ Sanctum closed to non-Hindus.

🏛 **Vivekananda Memorial**
⭕ Wed–Mon. 🎫 🚤 every 30 min.

A statue of the poet Tiruvalluvar, on the beach at Kanniyakumari

ANDAMAN ISLANDS

AN ARCHIPELAGO of 306 idyllic islands in the Bay of Bengal, about 1,000 km (620 miles) from the mainland, the Andamans and the neighbouring Nicobar Islands are actually the peaks of a submerged mountain range which extends from Myanmar to Indonesia. They encompass three distinct ecosystems – tropical forests, mangroves and coral reefs, which support a staggering variety of plant and animal life. Foreign visitors require a permit (see p758), and are not allowed on the Nicobar Islands. Many parts of the Andamans, too, are off-limits, to preserve their rare biodiversity and protect the six tribal groups, some of whom are fiercely independent. Their hostility was probably the reason why Marco Polo described the islands as being inhabited by cannibals. The Andamans acquired the sinister name Kala Pani ("Black Waters") in the 19th century, when the British established a penal colony here, and the terrible Cellular Jail in the capital, Port Blair. The islands' permanent population includes migrant Indians, Bangladeshis, Sri Lankans and Karens from Myanmar. The surrounding reefs are ideal for water sports.

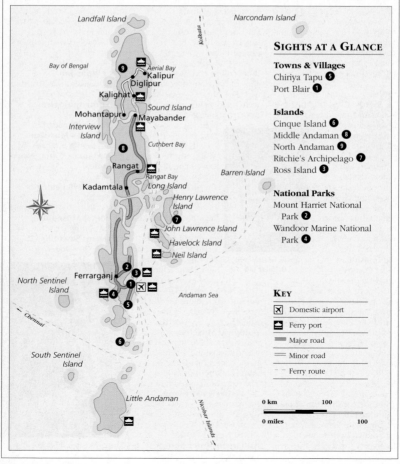

SIGHTS AT A GLANCE

Towns & Villages
Chiriya Tapu ❺
Port Blair ❶

Islands
Cinque Island ❻
Middle Andaman ❽
North Andaman ❾
Ritchie's Archipelago ❼
Ross Island ❸

National Parks
Mount Harriet National Park ❷
Wandoor Marine National Park ❹

KEY

☒	Domestic airport
⛴	Ferry port
▬	Major road
═	Minor road
- -	Ferry route

0 km — 100
0 miles — 100

◁ **An island in the Andamans covered by a dense, evergreen canopy of trees, surrounded by crystal waters**

An aerial view of the capital, Port Blair

Port Blair ❶

South Andaman Island. 1,190 km
(739 miles) E of Chennai. 🏯
100,200. ✈ 3 km (2 miles) S of town
centre, then bus or taxi. ⛴ 🛈 Govt
of India Tourist Office, 89 Junglighat
Rd, (03192) 33 006; Andaman &
Nicobar Tourism, (03192) 32 694.
Travel permits are required for the
Andaman Islands (see p758).
🎭 Island Tourism Festival (Dec/Jan).

THE CAPITAL, Port Blair, is
located to the southeast of
South Andaman Island. The
town is a base from
which to travel
around the archi-
pelago, and is well
equipped with
hotels, banks,
tour operators and
sports complexes.

The town's
tumultuous history
began in 1789,
when Lieutenant
Archibald Blair of
the British East
India Company
conducted a survey
to identify a safe harbour for
the Company's vessels. He
chose the site of what is now
Port Blair. Fifty years later
the islands became a penal
colony. Those incarcerated
were political activists
involved in the Indian Mutiny
of 1857 (see p53); by 1864,
the number of prisoners had
grown from 773 to 3,000. In
1896, the construction of the
Cellular Jail began; it soon
became an infamous symbol
of colonial oppression.
Designed specifically for
solitary confinement, it earned

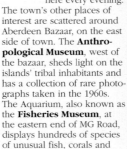

A row of tiny cells,
Cellular Jail

the Islands the dreaded name
of Kala Pani or "Black Waters",
reflecting the atrocities that
awaited the prisoners. It
remains Port Blair's most
prominent landmark.

Of the original seven wings
laid out around a central
watchtower, only three remain;
these are lined with cells, each
3 by 3.5 m (10 by 11 ft) in size.
Daily rations consisted of two
cups of drinking water and
two cups of rice. Executions
were frequent and many were
made to undergo hard labour.
Japanese troops,
who occupied the
Islands during
World War II, des-
troyed part of the
prison. In 1945, the
British moved back,
re-established their
headquarters at Port
Blair and closed the
jail. It is now a
memorial to the
political prisoners; a
moving sound and
light show is held
here every evening.
The town's other places of
interest are scattered around
Aberdeen Bazaar, on the east
side of town. The **Anthropological Museum**, west of
the bazaar, sheds light on the
islands' tribal inhabitants and
has a collection of rare photographs taken in the 1960s.
The Aquarium, also known as
the **Fisheries Museum**, at
the eastern end of MG Road,
displays hundreds of species
of unusual fish, corals and
shells. Next door, the
**Andaman Water Sports
Complex** offers a range of

activities, including wind-
surfing and parasailing, and
also hires out row boats and
rubber dinghies. The
**Samudrika Marine
Museum**, run by the Indian
Navy, has five galleries
devoted to the history,
geography and anthropology
of the Islands, and has a
superb display on marine life.
The tiny zoo at Haddo has
successfully bred saltwater
crocodiles and returned them
to the wild. At the **Forest
Museum** nearby, different
varieties of local wood are
on display.

Chatham Sawmills on
Chatham Island, 5 km (3
miles) north, is one of the
oldest and largest saw mills
in Asia. Established by the
British in 1836, this is where
many of the Islands' fast
disappearing species of trees,
including the towering
padauk (Andaman redwood),
are processed.

🏛 **Cellular Jail**
Son et Lumière (Hindi) 6pm, daily.
(English) 7.15pm, daily. 🎟
🏛 **Anthropological
Museum**
🕐 Tue–Sun. 🌑 public hols.
🏛 **Fisheries Museum**
🕐 Tue–Sun. 🌑 public hols. 🎟
🏊 **Andaman Water Sports
Complex**
🕐 daily.
🏛 **Samudrika Marine
Museum**
🕻 (03192) 32 719. 🕐 Tue–Sun. 🎟
🏛 **Forest Museum**
🕐 Tue–Sun. 🌑 public hols.
Chatham Sawmills
🕐 Mon–Sat, mornings are best. 🚫

The day's catch, a boatful of
fresh crayfish

ENVIRONS: The nearest beach from Port Blair is the crescent shaped **Corbyn's Cove**, 7 km (4 miles) south of the capital. **Viper Island**, named after a 19th-century British shipping vessel that was wrecked off its shore, can be reached via a cruise from Port Blair. Its sinister history involves the local prison, built in 1867, whose macabre gallows and torture posts can still be seen. Only daytime visits are allowed to Viper Island. About 15 km (9 miles) from Port Blair lies **Sippyghat Farm**, where many improved varieties of spices are grown along with a range of indigenous flowering plants and shrubs.

Orchid

Mount Harriet National Park ❷

South Andaman Island. 10 km (6 miles) N of Port Blair. 🚢 *From Chatham Wharf or Phoenix Bay Jetty (Fisheries Jetty) in Port Blair to Bamboo Flats Jetty, then taxi to park entry point. Tickets for day visits are available at entrance.* 🎫

SOME OF THE Andamans' highest peaks are in Mount Harriet National Park, lying across the inlet from Phoenix Jetty in Port Blair. Mount Harriet, at 365 m (1,198 ft), is surrounded by evergreen forests that support a remarkable biodiversity, predominantly birds such as the great black woodpecker and the green imperial pigeon. Well-marked hiking trails include the 2-km (1-mile) walk to Kalapathar, and the 16-km (10-mile) trail to Madhuban Beach, where elephants are trained for lumbering. Beware of leeches during the monsoon.

The **Forest Guest House**, on top of Mount Harriet, offers fine views of Port Blair and Ross Island. Overnight stays are possible with permission from the Wildlife Warden (*see p621*).

Ross Island ❸

Ross Island. 2 km (1 mile) E of Port Blair. 🚢 *from Phoenix Jetty.* **Travel permits** *required for the Andamans* (see p758). *Only day trips allowed.*

A SHORT FERRY ride from Port Blair leads to Ross Island, which served as the administrative capital for most of the Andaman Islands from 1858 until 1941. Ross Island's history, however, is much older, for it was the home of the indigenous Great Andamanese (*see p623*). Within 20 years of British occupation, diseases such as syphilis and measles virtually wiped out the tribe, whose numbers dropped from 5,000 to just 28. Ross Island was also the base for the British administrators of the penal colony in Port Blair, and was equipped with swimming pools and bungalows. In 1941, the Japanese converted the site into a POW camp, and built war installations, remnants of which can still be seen. It now lies deserted, and the few signs of its colonial glory, such as the chief commissioner's house and the Anglican church, are dilapidated and overgrown. The area is now under the control of the Indian Navy, whose museum, Smritika, records the lives of its political prisoners.

The rare Narcondam hornbill

SNORKELLING AND SCUBA DIVING

Snorkelling, a popular way to explore marine life

Snorkelling
Snorkels can be hired out for around Rs 70 per day, from numerous tour operators including the Andaman Water Sports Complex in Port Blair. Popular venues are Corbyn's Cove, Wandoor, Chiriya Tapu, Neil and Havelock Islands.

Scuba Diving
There are three registered dive centres in Port Blair. Samudra, (03192) 32 937, in Hotel Sinclair Bay View, is well established, and charges Rs 2,500 for a couple of dives near Port Blair, Rs 3,500 for areas further than Wandoor. It also runs diving courses. Port Blair Underwater, (03192) 85 389, at Peerless Resort in Corbyn's Cove, and Andaman Adventure Sports, (03192) 30 295 on MA Road, have similar rates. The recently opened Andaman Scuba Club on Havelock Island, is a pretty resort on the beach. @ info@andamanscubaclub.com

Eco-friendly Diving
Coral reefs are sensitive and even the gentlest touch can kill them. So avoid touching or treading on them, and be careful with your flippers. Practise descending into the sea before the actual dive, as descent is often too fast, leading to collision with reefs. Do not use anchors near reefs.

Wandoor Marine National Park ❹

CREATED IN 1983 to preserve the tropical ecosystems of 15 uninhabited islands in the Andamans, the Mahatma Gandhi Marine National Park at Wandoor stretches over 280 sq km (108 sq miles). It encompasses myriad bays, coral reefs, lagoons, rainforests and mangrove creeks, which teem with marine life. Ferries from Wandoor village skirt lagoons with kaleidoscopic sea beds, and are often chased by schools of playful dolphins. Most of the islands are protected and are therefore inaccessible; however, their coasts reveal a fascinating transition from towering tropical canopies to stilted mangroves that overhang the shores. The only two islands that allow visits are the popular Jolly Buoy Island, which is ideal for snorkelling, and Redskin Island, with a well-marked nature trail.

Types of Coral
Corals are of two broad types – either hard or soft. The colourful soft coral has no outer skeleton.

Angelfish
The angelfish is one of the reef's most vividly coloured fish. Its bright hues help to camouflage it as well as to advertise its territory.

Lion or Scorpion Fish
Measuring up to 40 cm (16 in), this ornate fish has deadly venom in its rays, which can be fatal for humans.

Giant Robber Crab
One of the largest and rarest crabs in the world, its powerful claws help it to climb trees such as the coconut palm, and break the hard shell of its fruit.

Grouper Fish
Among the most commonly found species, groupers can change their colour to match the rocks and surrounding reefs.

THE CORAL REEF

Referred to as rainforests of the sea, the multi-coloured reefs are delicate ecosystems that support an amazing variety of marine life *(see p647)*, and over 200 species of coral.

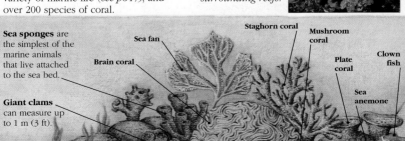

Sea sponges are the simplest of the marine animals that live attached to the sea bed.

Giant clams can measure up to 1 m (3 ft).

Brain coral

Sea fan

Staghorn coral

Mushroom coral

Plate coral

Clown fish

Sea anemone

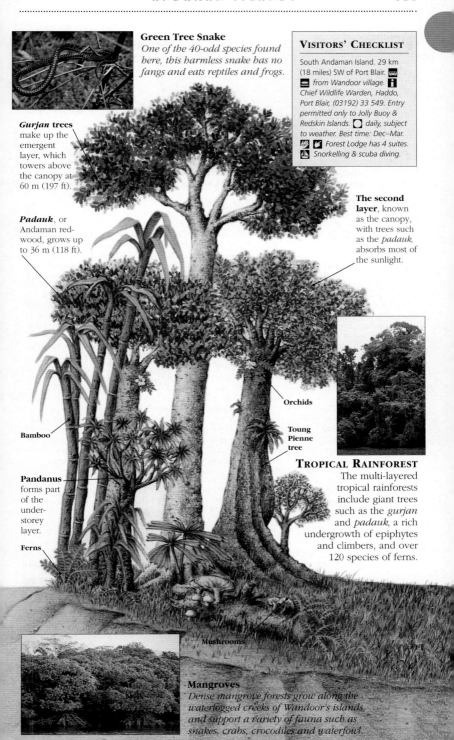

Green Tree Snake
One of the 40-odd species found here, this harmless snake has no fangs and eats reptiles and frogs.

Gurjan **trees** make up the emergent layer, which towers above the canopy at 60 m (197 ft).

The second layer, known as the canopy, with trees such as the *padauk*, absorbs most of the sunlight.

Padauk, or Andaman redwood, grows up to 36 m (118 ft).

Orchids

Bamboo

Toung Pienne tree

TROPICAL RAINFOREST
The multi-layered tropical rainforests include giant trees such as the *gurjan* and *padauk*, a rich undergrowth of epiphytes and climbers, and over 120 species of ferns.

Pandanus forms part of the understorey layer.

Ferns

Mushrooms

Mangroves
Dense mangrove forests grow along the waterlogged creeks of Wandoor's islands, and support a variety of fauna such as snakes, crabs, crocodiles and waterfowl.

A boat gliding across the glass-like surface of a lagoon, Andamans

Chiriya Tapu **❺**

South Andaman Island. 28 km (17 miles) S of Port Blair. 🚌 🛥 from Port Blair. Taxis available from Port Blair.

THE FISHING village of Chiriya Tapu ("Bird Island"), at the southernmost tip of South Andaman Island, is an hour's drive from Port Blair. Its white beaches, skirting a large bay, make it a popular day trip with visitors.

Forest trails through the surrounding tropical undergrowth are a birdwatcher's delight, as they teem with a vast variety of species, including rare sunbirds, kingfishers, woodpeckers and eagles. Its beaches, especially the picturesque **Munde Pahar Beach**, are excellent for snorkelling, and there are good camping facilities as well. The forest department is setting up a biological park, to house the animals from Port Blair's zoo (see p618).

Cinque Island **❻**

Cinque Island. 48 km (30 miles) S of Port Blair. 🛥 motor boats from Port Blair & Wandoor, fishing boats from Chiriya Tapu. **Travel permits** required for the Andamans (see p758). Only day visits are allowed.

THE VOLCANIC Cinque Island is perhaps the most beautiful of the entire Andamans group, as it has had little human interference over the years and is mostly uninhabited. Comprising two islands, North and South Cinque, connected by a sand bar, it was declared a sanctuary in 1987. The surrounding reefs of rare coral and varied marine life offer some of the best snorkelling and scuba diving in the Andamans. The sandy shores are also among the last refuges of the hawks-bill and green sea turtles, which nest here annually in their hundreds.

ENVIRONS: Tiny groups of islands known as the **Sisters** and the **Brothers**, lying 12 km (7 miles) and 32 km (20 miles) south of Cinque respectively, can be visited only with a professional diving group.

A hermit crab digging a temporary home

Large tracts of the remote southern island of **Little Andaman**, 70 km (44 miles) and eight hours by ferry from Port Blair, are a reserve for the 100-odd surviving members of the Onge tribe. It is not advisable to try and make contact with them. Part of northern Little Andaman is open to visitors.

Little Andaman
🛥 twice a week from Port Blair.

Ritchie's Archipelago **❼**

The group of islands lies between 20 km (12 miles) & 40 km (25 miles) E of South Andaman. 🛥 from Port Blair & Rangat Bay (Middle Andaman). **Travel permits** required for the Andamans (see p758).

THIS CLUSTER of tiny islands, collectively known as Ritchie's Archipelago, are for the most part protected as national parks to preserve their remarkable biodiversity. Only three islands are open to visitors and are connected to Port Blair by ferry on specific days of the week.

Neil Island, 36 km (22 miles) northeast, is the closest to the capital and is inhabited by settlers from Bengal. The interior is lush with paddy fields and plantations; the island is the region's main producer of fresh fruit and vegetables. The relatively untouched beaches offer superb snorkelling opportunities.

Havelock Island, 54 km (34 miles) northeast of Port Blair, is the most popular among visitors as it is well equipped, with government and private guesthouses, and also has a well-stocked main bazaar. It is worth trying out the tented accommodation on Radhanagar Beach, at the western tip of the island, where dolphins and turtles can be spotted from the long stretches of white sand. The elephants found on the island

A colourful sea fan and a grouper fish

Elephants, indispensable to the islands' lumber trade

were originally brought here to work the timber trade. Bikes and scooters are available and are the best way to explore.

The northernmost island in the archipelago, **Long Island**, 82 km (51 miles) north of Port Blair, attracts few visitors, perhaps because of the eight-hour journey to get there. It nevertheless has attractive beaches. There is just one rest house and virtually no public transport available, although bicycles can be hired. North Passage Island, 55 km (34 miles) S of Port Blair, has a beautiful white sandy beach at Merk Bay.

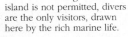

A vividly coloured local pineapple

ENVIRONS: Barren Island, 132 km (82 miles) northeast of Port Blair, has the only active volcano in India. It erupted twice in recent years, first in 1991 and then in 1994, after lying dormant for nearly two centuries. Rising sharply from the sea, its enormous crater continues to spew smoke. The island is now a wildlife sanctuary. There is no public ferry service and only chartered ferries make the long, 20-hour journey from Port Blair. Since landing on the island is not permitted, divers are the only visitors, drawn here by the rich marine life.

INDIGENOUS TRIBES

Until the 18th century, the Andaman and Nicobar Islands were inhabited by 12 distinct groups of aboriginal tribes. Now, overwhelmed by the immigrant population and threatened by disease and loss of land, their numbers have fallen from 5,000 to just 400. The Mongoloid Nicobarese and Shompen tribes of the Nicobars probably migrated from Myanmar, while the origins of the four Negrito tribes, the Jarawas, Great Andamanese, Onges and Sentinelese, continue to baffle anthropologists. Of these tribal groups, only the largest – the Nicobarese – have partially integrated into the mainstream, joining the public services. Meanwhile, the Onges and the Great Andamanese have become

A Jarawa tribesman

increasingly dependent on subsidies and live in tribal "reserves". The Sentinelese, from North Sentinel Island, are still hostile and continue to fend off strangers with showers of arrows. The Shompens of Great Nicobar are equally wary of outsiders. As the last representatives of truly independent indigenous peoples, perhaps their only chance of survival remains in self-imposed isolation.

Middle Andaman ❽

Middle Andaman Island. 170 km (106 miles) N from Port Blair to Rangat. from Port Blair. **Travel permits** required for the Andamans (see p758).

THIS IS LITERALLY the middle island among the Andamans trio. Large tracts of its interior are a part of the highly protected Jarawa Tribal Reserve. The Jarawas, traditional hunter-gatherers, are probably the last racially pure tribe left in India. The Andaman Trunk Road winds along the island's spine, running from Port Blair through Bharatrang Island to Middle Andaman. But with the welfare of the Jarawas in mind, only restricted public transport is encouraged. The area around **Rangat** is lush with tropical forests; the town itself has only a few provision stores. **Rangat Bay** is the point of departure for ferries to Port Blair and Havelock and Long Islands. Just 15 km (9 miles) away, **Cuthbert Bay** is a sanctuary for hundreds of marine turtles, which arrive here annually to nest. **Mayabander**, at the northern tip, 71 km (44 miles) from Rangat, is a beautiful spot. Some of its beaches, such as **Karmatang**, are famous for their spectacular sunrises, and are also nesting grounds for marine turtles.

North Andaman ❾

North Andaman Island. 290 km (180 miles) N from Port Blair to Diglipur. from Port Blair. **Travel permits** required for the Andamans (see p758).

NORTH ANDAMAN is the least populated of the three large islands. **Diglipur**, in the northeast, is one of the few places with accommodation. It is known for its beaches – in particular, Ram Nagar and Kalipur – and also has the islands' highest peak, **Saddle Peak** (737 m/2,418 ft), which was recently declared a national park. A scenic trail leads to the peak's summit.

From **Aerial Bay**, 9 km (6 miles) northeast of Diglipur, one can visit Smith and Ross Islands (see p619).

KERALA

ESTLING BETWEEN the Western Ghats and the Arabian Sea, Kerala is an enchanting mosaic of coconut groves and paddy fields, wide beaches and labyrinthine backwaters, verdant hills and rainforests. Its diverse culture is enriched by the three great religions that have ancient roots here. Hinduism is the religion of the majority, practised here with a rare rigour that prohibits non-Hindus from entering temples. Christianity, followed by a quarter of its population, was brought here by the Apostle St Thomas, while Islam was introduced by Arab traders in the 7th century. The architectural treasures of the state include the beautiful wooden palace at Padmanabhapuram, stately colonial buildings and a 16th-century synagogue in Kochi. This politically conscious state, where power alternates between Left and Centrist parties, boasts the highest literacy rate in India. Many of its people work in the Middle East, their remittances home adding greatly to Kerala's prosperity.

SIGHTS AT A GLANCE

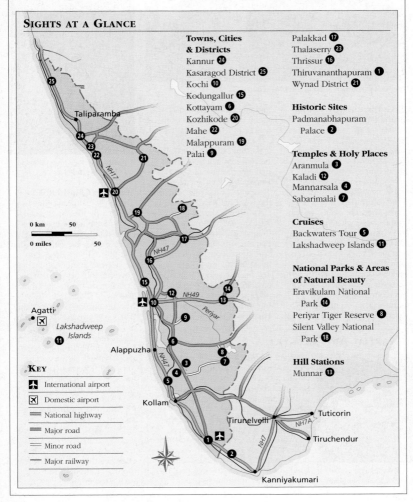

Towns, Cities & Districts
Kannur ㉔
Kasaragod District ㉕
Kochi ⑩
Kodungallur ⑮
Kottayam ⑥
Kozhikode ⑳
Mahe ㉒
Malappuram ⑲
Palai ⑨
Palakkad ⑰
Thalaserry ㉓
Thrissur ⑯
Thiruvananthapuram ①
Wynad District ㉑

Historic Sites
Padmanabhapuram Palace ②

Temples & Holy Places
Aranmula ③
Kaladi ⑫
Mannarsala ④
Sabarimalai ⑦

Cruises
Backwaters Tour ⑤
Lakshadweep Islands ⑪

National Parks & Areas of Natural Beauty
Eravikulam National Park ⑭
Periyar Tiger Reserve ⑧
Silent Valley National Park ⑱

Hill Stations
Munnar ⑬

KEY
✈ International airport
⊠ Domestic airport
═ National highway
═ Major road
═ Minor road
═ Major railway

◁ **Wooden canoes resting in the backwaters near Alleppey (Alappuzha)**

Thiruvananthapuram ●

Vishnu in wood

K ERALA'S CAPITAL, known until recently as Trivandrum, was the seat of the former royal family of Travancore from 1750 to 1956. The magnificent Anantha Padmanabhaswamy Temple has given the city its name, Thiruvananthapuram – literally the "Holy City of Anantha", the sacred thousand-headed serpent on whom Vishnu reclines. Built across seven hills, the city's old quarter clusters around the temple, while along busy Mahatma Gandhi Road are colonial mansions, churches and modern high-rises.

The Napier Museum, built in the 19th century

🏛 Government Arts and Crafts (Napier) Museum

Museum Rd. ● *Mon & (Wed morn) for all museums.* 📷 *covers all museums.* **Kanakakunnu Palace** 📞 *(0471) 31 4615 for permission.*
Located in a well-planned compound is a complex of museums and the city's zoo. The Government Arts and Crafts Museum, earlier known as the Napier Museum after John Napier, a former governor of Madras, is in a red and black brick Indo-Saracenic structure, designed by Robert Fellows Chisholm *(see p569)* in the 19th century. It exhibits a rare collection of bronzes, stone sculptures, exquisite gold ornaments, ivory carvings

and a temple chariot, all fashioned in the territories of the former kingdom of Travancore.

To the north of the Museum, is the **Shri Chitra Art Gallery**, housed in a beautiful building that incorporates the best elements of local architecture. The pride of its collection are the works of Raja Ravi Varma (1848–1906) and his uncle Raja Raja Varma, both pioneers of a unique academy style of painting in India. Raja Ravi Varma was considered the finest Indian artist of his time, and his mythological paintings have inspired the popular religious prints found in many Indian homes. The **Natural History Museum**, to the east,

has a fine replica of a typical Kerala Nair wooden house, *naluketu*, detailing the principles of its construction.

The **Kanakakunnu Palace**, where the Travancore royal family once entertained their guests, is adjacent to the complex, on top of a hill. Part of it is now rented out for official functions.

A short drive down the road from the complex leads to Kowdiar Junction, a roundabout of walls and ornate railings facing the Kowdiar Palace, the former maharaja's official residence.

A painting by Raja Ravi Varma in Sri Chitra Art Gallery

Mahatma Gandhi Road

The city's main road runs from the Victoria Jubilee Town Hall to the Anantha Padmanabhaswamy Temple. Among the many impressive buildings that line this road are the Secretariat, headquarters of the state government, the University College and the Public Library. The latter, founded in 1829, has a collection of more than 250,000 books and documents in Malayalam, Hindi, Tamil and Sanskrit. To the north, beyond the charming Connemara Market, are the Jami Masjid, St Joseph's Cathedral and the Neo-Gothic building of Christ Church.

🏯 Anantha Padmanabhaswamy Temple

Fort area. ● *to non-Hindus. Special rules for clothing apply (see p762).*
Located within the fort that encircles the old town, this is the only temple in the state with a towering seven-storeyed *gopura*, commonly

---

MARTIAL ARTS OF KERALA

Kalarippayat practice, CVN Kalari Sangham

Constant warfare in the 11th century gave rise to *kalaripayattu*, Kerala's martial arts. From it emerged two streams – the *chavverpada*, suicide squads, and the *chekavan*, warriors who fought duels to the death, in order to settle the nobility's disputes. Students learn to use weapons such as swords, spears, daggers, the *urumi*, (a flexible metal sword) and wooden poles. In the final stage, the student is taught how to defeat an opponent by applying pressure to nerve points.

The imposing *gopura* of the Anantha Padmanabhaswamy Temple

VISITORS' CHECKLIST

Thiruvananthapuram district. 708
km (440 miles) SW of Chennai.
744,800. 6 km (4 miles)
W of city centre, then bus or taxi.
Tourist Facilitation
Centre, Museum Rd, (0471) 32
1132; TRC, opp Chaitram Hotel,
(0471) 33 0031. Mon–Sat.
Chandanakuda (Mar/Apr),
Navaratri (Sep/Oct), Soorya
Dance Festival (Oct), Nishan-
gandhi Dance Festival (Nov).

seen in Tamil Nadu's temple architecture. The restrained ornamentation, however, is typical of Kerala. A flagstaff encased in gold stands in the huge courtyard. The main corridor, which runs around four sides of the courtyard, has 324 columns and two rows of granite pillars, each embellished with a woman bearing a lamp (*deepalaksh-mi*). The hall also has mythological animals, sculpted with rotating stone balls in their jaws. Rich murals adorn the outer walls of the inner shrine, where the 6-m (20-ft) long reclining Vishnu resides, with his head towards the south and feet towards the north.

🏛 Kuthiramalika Palace Museum

Fort area. ◻ Tue–Sun. 🎦 🎦 extra charges. 🎫 🎵 Carnatic Music Festival (Jan/Feb).

This interesting museum (also known as Puthen Malika) is housed in an 18th-century palace, built by Raja Swathi Thirunal Balarama Varma, a statesman, poet, musician and social reformer. A fine example of Kerala architecture, this wooden palace has polished floors and a sloping tiled roof. The wood carvings are particularly noteworthy, especially the 122 horses lining the eaves of the building. On display are various artifacts from the royal collection,

including a solid crystal throne given by the Dutch, and another carved out of the tusks of 50 elephants.

🏛 CVN Kalari Sangham

East Fort area. ◻ Mon–Sat. 🎦 🎫

This training centre for *kalaripayattu* was established in 1956 to revive Kerala's martial arts tradition. Each morning, students collect at the gymnasium (*kalari*) to perform a series of exercises that will help them develop the necessary combat skills. The centre also has a shrine to the deity of martial arts, Kalari Paradevata, and an Ayurvedic clinic where students are given oil massages.

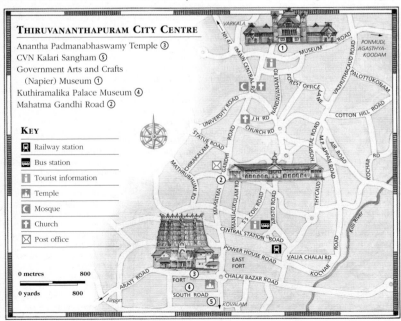

THIRUVANANTHAPURAM CITY CENTRE

Anantha Padmanabhaswamy Temple ③
CVN Kalari Sangham ⑤
Government Arts and Crafts
   (Napier) Museum ①
Kuthiramalika Palace Museum ④
Mahatma Gandhi Road ②

KEY

🚉 Railway station
🚌 Bus station
ℹ️ Tourist information
🛕 Temple
☪ Mosque
✝ Church
⊠ Post office

0 metres   800
0 yards   800

Exploring Thiruvananthapuram's Environs

THIRUVANANTHAPURAM IS THE GATEWAY to the southern tip of India. South of the city, along the Lakshadweep Sea, are many beach resorts, the most famous of which is Kovalam. The Padmanabhapuram Palace *(see pp630–31)*, the former residence of the Travancore kings, is to the southeast, while to its north and east are tranquil hill stations located picturesquely in the densely forested Cardamom (Ponmudi) Hills. Thiruvananthapuram also houses many important institutions, including the meteorological station, which performs the task of plotting the arrival of the Southwest Monsoon. The city is also one of Kerala's main centres of Ayurveda.

A fisherboy with his catch, Kovalam Beach

Lighthouse Beach, one of the many idyllic beaches in Kovalam

🚩 Kovalam

Thiruvananthapuram district.16 km (10 miles) S of Thiruvananthapuram. 🚌 ℹ️ *Ashok Hotel, (0471) 48 0101.*

Until the 1960s, Kovalam was just a sleepy fishing village with narrow lanes and thatched dwellings with wide courtyards for drying fish. However, once its spectacular beach and shallow, crystal-clear waters were discovered, it became a favourite with hippies and backpackers, and over the years acquired the reputation of being a shabby, downmarket resort. Today, however, it also attracts the rich and famous, who come here in private planes. As a result, the beaches are dotted with both luxury and budget resorts, as well as cafés and several government-approved Ayurveda centres that offer anything from a simple massage to three-week treatments. Hawkers, too, have set up stalls selling handicrafts and inexpensive beachwear. Despite

the onslaughts of mass tourism, Kovalam retains an inherent charm that makes it one of India's finest and most popular beach resorts.

Kovalam's sheltered natural bay is ringed by two rocky headlands. Its four beaches – Samudra Beach, Ashok Beach, Eve's Beach and Lighthouse Beach – all within short walking distance of each other, – provide visitors with their fill of sun, sea and sand. While the beaches to the south of the promontory are more crowded, the ones to the north offer ample secluded space for sunbathing, safe swimming in the placid blue waters, catamaran trips, and water sports.

Bananas and other fruit on sale, Varkala

🚩 Varkala

Thiruvananthapuram district. 40 km (25 miles) N of Thiruvananthapuram. 🚌 ℹ️ *Tourist Information Centre, near the helipad.*

This beautiful little beach town is better known among locals as a major pilgrimage centre. According to legend, the sage Narada flung a cloth made from the bark of a tree into the air, and it landed at the spot where the small town of Varkala now stands. Narada then directed his disciples to pray for salvation at the newly created beach, which came to be known as Papanasham Beach or the "Beach of Redemption". Since then, this beach has been associated with ancestor worship, as Hindus immerse the ashes of their dead here.

At the heart of the town is the sacred **Janardhana Swamy Temple**, believed to be more than 2,000 years old. This temple, dedicated to Krishna, attracts many pilgrims. One of the bells in the temple is said to have been given in gratitude by the captain of a 17th-century Dutch sailing ship, after his prayers were answered.

Varkala's other pilgrimage centre is the hilltop **Memorial of Sree Narayana Guru** (1855–1928) at Sivagiri, 3 km (2 miles) east of the temple. Every day, countless devotees flock to the memorial of this great saint and social reformer who advocated "one caste, one religion, one god for mankind".

With its backdrop of red laterite cliffs overlooking the beach, Varkala has now emerged as a popular resort

A view of the long sandy beach at Varkala

and spa. The town is famous for its natural springs with therapeutic qualities, and is also a centre for Ayurvedic treatment and yoga. To the south is the desolate Anjengo Fort, the main garrison of the Dutch East India Company in the 17th and 18th centuries.

Ponmudi
Thiruvananthapuram district. 61 km (38 miles) NE of Thiruvananthapuram. *Tourist Complex, (0471) 89 0230.*

Ponmudi, literally "Golden Crown", rises to a height of 915 m (3,002 ft) from the base of a thick tropical forest. Surrounded by tea estates and forested hills, this hill station is still unspoilt, refreshingly cool and mist-shrouded for most of the year. Its narrow winding paths and verdant environs offer pleasant walks. Wild flowers grow in abundance on the banks of gurgling brooks, adding to the charm of this peaceful place.

Agasthyakoodam
Thiruvananthapuram district. 60 km (37 miles) NE of Thiruvananthapuram. *Trekking permits Contact the Office of the Wildlife Warden, Thiruvananthapuram, (0471) 36 8607.*

At an elevation of 1,890 m (6,201 ft), Agasthyakoodam is the highest peak in southern Kerala. It forms part of the Western Ghats and the Agasthyavanam Forest, designated a sanctuary in 1992.

The mountain is revered by both Buddhists and Hindus, as it is believed to be the abode of the Bodhisattva Avalokitesvara *(see p141)*, as well as of the sage Agastya, a disciple of Shiva. The hills are rich in medicinal herbs and orchids, and harbour many species of birds and wildlife. Trekking to the top – a distance of 28 km (17 miles) – takes two days and is permitted only between December and April. The summit provides fine views of the large lake created by the Neyyar Dam.

AYURVEDA THERAPY

Ayurvedic treatment in progress

A classical text on medicine, the *Ashtangabridaya*, is the foundation of Ayurveda in Kerala. Its author, Vagbhata, was the disciple of a Buddhist physician, and received little recognition in the rest of India. It is believed that a few Nampoothiri (Brahmin) families were the original Ayurvedic physicians, and their descendants still carry the honorific title of *ashtavaidyan*. Today, this holistic science of healing is practised throughout India. However, the Kerala method is famous for its five-pronged treatment, *panchakarma*, in which medicated oils, herbs, milk, massage and a special diet are used to cure all types of ailments.

Caparisoned elephants and musicians, Thrissur Pooram

Padmanabhapuram Palace ➋

SET AMID LUSH HILLS, verdant paddy fields and perennial rivers, Padmanabhapuram Palace is the finest example of Kerala's distinctive wooden architecture. Laid out in a sequence of four adjoining walled compounds, comprising public and private zones, the palace has richly carved wooden ceilings, sculpted pillars, slatted windows, and pagoda-like tiled roofs. From 1590 to 1790, Padmanabhapuram was the home of the the former princely state of Travancore, which straddled parts of present-day Tamil Nadu as well as Kerala. By some quirk of fate, this beautifully kept palace now falls in Tamil Nadu but is maintained by the government of Kerala.

Detail from a carved rosewood door

The Lady's Chamber houses two large swings, a pair of enormous Belgian mirrors and a royal bed.

★ Prayer Hall
The prayer hall, on the third floor of the King's Palace, has exquisite murals on its walls. A medicinal bed here, carved from 64 different types of wood, was a gift from the Dutch.

The clock tower's chimes could be heard from a distance of 3 km (2 miles).

Entrance Hall
The entrance hall has a profusely carved wooden ceiling with 90 different inverted flowers, a polished granite bed and an ornate Chinese throne.

Main Gate
The main entrance to the palace complex is reached after crossing a large courtyard. This gate has a decorated gabled roof.

Entrance

| 0 metres | 20 |
| 0 yards | 20 |

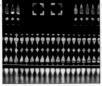

Carved bay window for watching processions

Guest house

The Bath House is a small airy room, where the male members of the royal family were given a massage before they descended, down covered steps, to a private tank to bathe.

★ Mother's Palace
Built in 1550, this is the oldest building in the complex. It contains intricately carved wooden pillars fashioned from the wood of the jackfruit tree. The floor was polished to a red gloss with hibiscus flowers.

Lamp
A horse lamp (the horse is a symbol of valour) in the entrance hall, hangs suspended from a special chain that keeps the lamp perfectly balanced.

The dining hall, laid out over two storeys, could seat 2,000 guests.

The palace museum houses artifacts including furniture, wooden and granite statues, coins, weapons and utensils.

STAR SIGHTS

★ Prayer Hall

★ Mother's Palace

★ Council Chamber

★ Council Chamber
The king's council chamber has wooden louvres to let in light and air. The gloss on the floor was achieved with a mixture of lime, sand, egg white, coconut water, charcoal and jaggery.

An elephant being led down the steps of Aranmula's Parthasarthy Temple

Aranmula ❸

Pathanamthitta district. 125 km (78 miles) NW of Thiruvananthapuram. 🚌 🚃 *from Alappuzha.* 🎭 *Onam Boat Regatta (Aug/Sep).*

THE PICTURESQUE VILLAGE of Aranmula, situated on the banks of the Pampa river, is famous as the venue for Kerala's magnificent snake boat races. The boat race festival has its origins in the legend of a devotee who once gave food to a Brahmin, believed to be Vishnu in disguise. However, the Brahmin, before disappearing, advised him to send his offering to Aranmula instead. Since then, during the festival, a ceremonial boat, carved out of a single block of wood, carries a consignment of food from a nearby village to the temple at Aranmula. On the last day of Onam *(see p629)*, this ceremonial boat leads a procession of about 30 snake boats to the temple. On this day, there is no racing and all the boats arrive together, as Krishna is said to be present on each boat at the same time.

The **Parthasarathy Temple**, one of the state's five most important temples, is dedicated to Krishna, and has an image of the god as Parthasarathy, the Divine Charioteer in the great epic, the *Mahabharata*. The image was brought here on a raft made of six bamboos, and this is what the town's name signifies – in Malayalam *aaru* means six and *mula*, bamboo.

Aranmula is also known for its unique metal mirrors made from an alloy of silver, bronze copper and lead. These mirrors were traditionally used as part of the arrangement of auspicious objects during Vishu, the Malayali New Year, in April *(see p629)*.

ENVIRONS: The 14th-century **Thiruvamundur Temple**, near Chengannur, 7 km (4 miles) west of Aranmula is dedicated to Krishna and attributed to Nakul, one of the five Pandava brothers *(see p26)*. Near Chenganacherry, 27 km (17 miles) northwest of Aranmula, is the **Tirukkotdittanam Temple**. This 11th-century temple is dedicated to Sahadev, Nakul's twin brother, and has lovely murals adorning its walls.

Metal mirror, Aranmula

Mannarsala ❹

Alappuzha district. 132 km (82 miles) NW of Thiruvananthapuram. 🚌 🎭 *Thulam (Oct/Nov).*

THE CUSTOM of worshipping snakes in Kerala reaches a climax at Mannarsala, the best known of the four main Naga temples in the state. According to legend, a woman from a family of great Naga devotees gave birth to two sons, one of whom was a serpent-child, who asked his family to worship him and vanished. The temples at Mannarsala, dedicated to the King of Snakes, Nagaraja, and his consort, Sarpayakshini, are situated in a thick grove of tall trees and dense bushes, surrounded by thousands of hooded stone serpents of various styles and sizes.

In Kerala, the ancestral home *(tharavad)* of every upper-class Namboothiri and Nair family is supposed to have a *sarpa-kavu* or snake-grove, housing a *nagakal* or snake stone. If a *tharavad* cannot afford to maintain its own shrine, the snake stones are offered to this temple.

The holy rites at Mannarsala are conducted by a priestess *(amma)*, a vestal virgin, who lives on the premises and is supported in her religious duties by her family.

Childless couples place a bell metal vessel *(uruli)* face down in front of the deities, to seek their blessings.

SACRED SERPENT SHRINES

In Kerala, the sacred serpent plays a significant role in belief and ritual. Malayali folklore speaks of a wooded, rural land inhabited mainly by Nagas (snakes) – the Lords of the Underworld – who were overthrown by the Brahmin settlers brought here by Parasurama *(see p679)*, the sixth incarnation of Vishnu. This mythological incident is the origin of snake worship in Kerala since, after their

defeat, Parasurama ordered that snakes be accorded divine status. Most temples thus have a niche for a snake god, amid dense sacred groves of ancient trees. The old ancestral homes *(tharavads)* also have private temples or groves for a snake deity.

Sacred grove with snake *(naga)* images, Mannarsala Temple

Boats of Kerala

KERALA'S ANCIENT boat-building industry is a specialized part of its rich wood-working tradition, that also includes architecture *(see p638)*. Boats built at Beypore *(see p653)* were highly prized and used by Arab merchants. The construction of a boat is always begun on an auspicious day in the Malayalam

Dugouts with carved sterns

calendar, and is marked by an invocation to the gods. The most sought-after wood is *anjili (Artocarpus hirsuta)*, though teak is also used. Racing boats of various sizes and shapes participate in the annual Onam regatta at Aranmula. Of these, the most magnificent is the long, narrow *chundanvallam*, or snake boat.

BOAT BUILDING
A master craftsman, assisted by a team traditionally drawn from different religions, builds the boat. No nails or metal pieces are used; only wooden pegs and joints hold the parts together.

SNAKE BOAT RACES
Snake boats *(chundan-vallam)*, once used to carry warriors, now participate in what is believed to be the world's largest team sport. The Nehru Trophy Boat Race *(see p36)*, introduced in 1952, is the most famous.

Rowing is perfectly synchronized to the pulsating rhythm of vanchipattu (boatmen's songs). Their themes are devotional, mythological, or related to rural life.

The prow of the boat is normally manned by four boatmen.

Oarsmen

Singers

Amaram, the stern, is decorated with brass studs and inlay work.

Kettuvallams *are now often converted into houseboats. Kettu means a bundle, while* vallam *is a big boat. Originally, these were used as ferries or to carry rice.*

Canoes*, usually made from a single log of wood, can carry no more than one or two people. They are commonly used to transport light cargo, such as coir fibre.*

Backwaters Tour ❺

A CRUISE ALONG THE BACKWATERS is one of the most enchanting experiences that Kerala offers. Exploring this labyrinthine network of waterways, which weave through villages set amidst lush vegetation, offers glimpses of Kerala's unique rural lifestyle, where land and water are inseparable. The most popular backwaters tour is from Kollam (Quilon), situated between Ashtamudi Lake and the Arabian Sea, to Alappuzha (Alleppey) on the edge of Vembanad Lake. The choice of transport ranges from local ferries and speedboats to *kettuvallams (see p633)*.

LOCATOR MAP

Water hyacinths *are the cause of a serious ecological problem since untamed growth has clogged the waterways of Kuttanad, the rice bowl of Kerala.*

Children going to school *by boat are a common sight. Various types of boats are used as transport along the backwaters, connecting the small villages with the mainland.*

Coconut palms fringe the waterways. In addition to coconuts, rice is cultivated extensively in Kuttanad, the area between Kottayam and Alappuzha.

Houses along a canal *have jetties with moored boats. The ground and water levels are often equal, which makes flooding a problem during the monsoon.*

Coconut Lagoon (see p715), *is a wonderful resort on Vembanad Lake, near the bird sanctuary in Kumarakom.*

Toddy tappers are expert at scaling coconut palms. The local brew, made from fermented coconut palm sap, is sold in shacks along the waterways. The first brew is light and delicious – however, potency levels rise with subsequent fermentation.

TIPS FOR PASSENGERS

Route 1: Kollam to Alappuzha
Dep: 10am. Maximum duration: 8 hrs. ℹ️ District Tourism Promotion Council (DTPC), Kollam, (0474) 74 5625.
Route 2: Alappuzha to Kollam
Dep: 10am. Maximum duration: 8 hrs. ℹ️ DTPC, Alappuzha, (0477) 25 3308.
For more details see p781.

Chinese fishing nets along the backwaters are used to trap fish. A popular fish in Kerala, karimeen (pearl spot), is found in these waters.

Children with banana trunks playing in the water

BACKWATERS

According to legend, Parasurama, the sixth incarnation of Vishnu, created Kerala by throwing his battle axe into the sea. The abundance of canals, lagoons and lakes in the state seem to reinforce this legend of a land born from the sea.

In this coir-producing village, women beat the husk and spin the fibre to make ropes or floor coverings. The fibre is often dyed to create brightly coloured mats with geometric designs.

Coconut husks soak in the shallow waters near the banks. This softens the husks before they are beaten to produce the fine fibre that is turned into coir. The flesh is converted into oil, or used in cooking.

Tea gardens surrounding the Mattupetty Reservoir, Munnar *(see p648)* ▷

Kottayam

Kottayam district. 160 km (99 miles)
N of Thiruvananthapuram.
60,750. District Tourist
Promotion Council, (0481) 56 2315.
Drama Festival (Jan).

ENCLOSED BY the blue waters of Vembanad Lake and the paddy fields of Kuttanad to its west, and by the lush hills of the Western Ghats to its east, Kottayam is one of Kerala's most beautiful districts. Its climate and landscape have combined to make the region prosperous. Kottayam town is surrounded by extensive plantations of rubber, and other valuable cash crops such as tea, coffee, cardamom and pepper. The first town in India to attain 100 per cent literacy, it is also the birth-place of Kerala's publishing industry and home to many Malayalam newspapers and magazines. A writers' co-operative society, the Sahitya Pravarthaka Sahakarana Sangham, which was set up here more than 50 years ago, has played a cardinal role in fostering the growth of Malayalam literature.

Kottayam also has an old Christian tradition that has been preserved by its large Syrian Christian population. It was one of the first towns to be patronized by St Thomas *(see p573)* in the 1st century AD. Of the many fine churches and seminaries that dot the landscape, the best known are the two Syrian Orthodox churches, **Valia Palli** and **Cheria Palli**, both dating to the mid-16th

Caption for top image:

Mural from the stately Shiva temple at Ettumanur

century. The churches stand on a hillock, about 2 km (1.2 miles) north of the city centre, and have colourful frescoes adorning their walls. The Nestorian cross at Valia Palli is said to have come from Ker-ala's first church, founded by St Thomas at Kodungallur *(see p649)*. Cheria Palli has painted panels behind its main altar, depicting scenes from the life of the Virgin Mary.

Nestorian cross at Valia Palli Church, Kottayam

ENVIRONS: Mannanam, 8 km (5 miles) north of Kottayam, is a pilgrimage centre for Syrian Christians, who gather in their thousands each January to attend a religious convention, one of the largest in Asia.

Kumarakom, a bird sanctuary on the banks of Vembanad Lake, is 12 km (7 miles) west of Kottayam. A variety of local and migratory birds can be observed from vantage points on the shore.

A large temple dedicated to Shiva at **Ettumanur**, 12 km (7 miles) north of Kottayam, has beautiful murals, similar to those found at Mattancherry Palace in Kochi *(see p642)*. The 11th-century Mahadeva Temple at **Vaikom**, 40 km (25 miles) northwest of Kottayam, is famous for its grand ele-phant pageants and traditional dance performances, which take place between November and December each year. It is also the site where Mahatma Gandhi led an important *satyagraha* (civil disobedience movement) to make temples accessible to untouchables.

WOODEN ARCHITECTURE IN KERALA

The importance of wooden architecture in Kerala is evident in legends that glorify the master carpenter, Perunthachhan. Palaces, temples, mosques and homes all have characteristic sloping tiled roofs to drain away the heavy rains during the monsoon. Roofs are generally hipped, often with decorated gables, topped by brass pot finials. To achieve height, they rise in two or more superimposed tiers to create steeply pyramidal profiles. Joints and wooden pegs, instead of nails, are used.

Brackets are often carved as *yalis* or figures of gods and goddesses.

Wooden pillars are ornate. These are decorative as well as functional, as they support the roof.

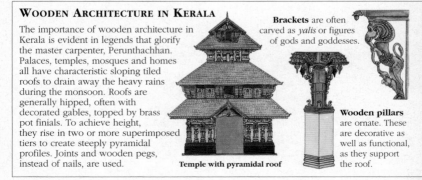

Temple with pyramidal roof

The Baroque façade of St Thomas Church, at Palai

Sabarimalai **7**

Pattanamthitta district. 191 km (119 miles) N of Thiruvananthapuram. 🚌 to Pamba, then by foot. 📅 Mandalam (Dec/Jan), Makaravilakku (mid-Jan).

ONE OF THE most famous pilgrimage centres in India, Sabarimalai lies in the Western Ghats at an altitude of 914 m (2,999 ft). The final 14-km (9-mile) approach from Pamba, through dense forest, is made on foot.

The focus of devotion here is the temple dedicated to the popular deity, Ayyappa. The temple stays open from November to mid-January, in April and during the first five days of each month of the Malayalam calendar. People of all religions can worship here, but women between the ages of 10 and 50 are restricted from entering. The final 18 sacred steps (each representing a sin that a devotee renounces on setting foot on it) are sheathed in *panchaloha*, an alloy of five metals, and lead to the

sanctum. Only those who have observed 41 days of penance (celibacy, wearing black and not shaving) are entitled to undertake the pilgrimage.

Periyar Tiger Reserve **8**

See pp640–41.

Palai **9**

Kottayam district. 175 km (109 miles) N of Thiruvananthapuram. 🚌 📅 Epiphany (6 Jan). **St Thomas Church** ✝ (Malayalam) 6am daily.

THE PROSPEROUS TOWN of Palai is surrounded by thick rubber plantations. The small but beautiful, 16th-century **St Thomas Church**, is its principal attraction. Constructed in the traditional style of early Christian churches in Kerala. It has a quaint wooden pulpit with a fish-like base, an elaborately carved main altar and two simpler side altars. A stone slab carries inscriptions in Syriac. Attractive glass candelabra are suspended from wall brackets, while a chandelier hangs from the ceiling. There is a wooden balcony at the rear. Services are still held in the church. Adjoining this building is a modern church, also dedicated to St Thomas.

THE AYYAPPA CULT

A Dravidian deity worshipped throughout Kerala, Ayyappa (or Sastha), was born out of the union between Shiva and Vishnu (who had transformed himself into a woman, Mohini). The baby, found on the banks of the Pamba river, was adopted by the childless king of Pandalam.

Ayyappa devotees, Sabarimalai

Ayyappa later revealed his divine status when he destroyed a demon. Before returning to his heavenly abode, however, the god shot an arrow into the air which landed near the ashram of the sage Sabari, where a temple was built. Ayyappa's warrior friend, Vavar, is a Muslim saint whose *dargah* nearby is visited by both Muslims and Hindus.

Ceilings are divided into panels carved with lotus designs or Hindu deities, such as Brahma, surrounded by *dikpalas* (guardian figures).

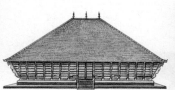

Koottambulams, traditional theatres, are usually situated in the precincts of large temples and palaces. They serve as the venue for staging Koodiyattam (dance-drama) performances.

Interiors of koottambulams have tall wooden pillars and *jalis* on three sides for ventilation. The roof is specially designed to provide excellent acoustic quality.

Periyar Tiger Reserve 8

THE CONSTRUCTION of the Mullaperiyar Dam across the Periyar river at Thekkady, in 1895, submerged large tracts of land and created a huge lake, covering an area of 26 sq km (10 sq miles). Years later, in 1935, the then Maharaja of Travancore declared 600 sq km (232 sq miles) of forest surrounding the lake a wildlife sanctuary. The Periyar Lake now forms the nucleus of the ecosystem of the sanctuary which, over the years, has been expanded to 777 sq km (300 sq miles). Declared a Tiger Reserve in 1978, the sanctuary is a rare example of human interference having enhanced rather than damaged an ecosystem.

Common kingfisher

Visitors viewing wildlife from a boat on Periyar Lake

Lake Palace
The former hunting lodge of the Maharaja of Travancore is now a delightful hotel inside the sanctuary (see p716).

Birdlife
The petrified tree trunks that jut out from the lake make convenient perches for birds looking out for fish.

0 km   1

0 miles   1

Wildlife
The deciduous forests, grasslands and tropical evergreen interiors of Periyar are the habitat of the endangered lion-tailed macaque (left), as well as Indian bison (gaur), sloth bears and the slender loris.

Herds of Elephants
The lake, a year-round source of water, and the abundant grassland make the sanctuary an ideal habitat for elephants, which now number approximately 800.

VISITORS' CHECKLIST

Idukki district. 190 km (118 miles) N of Kochi. 🚌 ℹ️
Wildlife Tourist Office, Kumily, (0486) 32 2028. 🐾 ✅ 🚤 🏠

Indian Giant Squirrel
This agile squirrel can make amazing leaps that cover about 6 m (20 ft). It is found in Periyar's deciduous and evergreen forests.

Mangaladevi
Temple

The Mangaladevi Temple, 15 km (9 miles) east of Thekkady, lies at a height of 1,337 m (4,387 ft), and offers excellent panoramic views of the forested hills of the ghats.

Mullakady

Periyar Lake
Two-hour boat cruises on the mist-shrouded lake offer excellent opportunities for spotting wildlife, especially herds of elephants.

Thannikudi

Periyar

KEY

🟰	National highway
═	Major road
─	Minor road
🚤	Jetty
ℹ️	Tourist information
🌿	Viewpoint
🏛️	Temple
⛺	Accommodation

Orchids
Periyar is known for its many species of flowering plants, including nearly 150 species of orchids. The rare orchid Habeneria periyarancis, *named after the region, is found only here.*

Kochi ❿

Antique mask

KOCHI, BETTER KNOWN AS COCHIN, is Kerala's most cosmopolitan city. It is also its main trading centre for spices and seafood. Built around a saltwater lagoon of the Arabian Sea, Kochi is in fact a collection of narrow islands and peninsulas. While mainland Ernakulam boasts of concrete shopping malls and glitzy apartment buildings, Mattancherry and Fort Kochi have an old world charm, with their blend of Dutch, Portuguese and English bungalows and quaint narrow streets *(see pp644–5)*. The scenic location of Kochi's natural harbour, surrounded by palm groves, green fields, inland lakes and backwaters, has enchanted visitors from across the globe for centuries.

Brahma emerging from Vishnu's navel, mural, Mattancherry Palace

🏛 Mattancherry Palace
Jew Town. 📞 *(0484) 22 6085.* ⏱ *Sat–Thu.*

The Mattancherry Palace, constructed by the Portuguese in the mid-1550s, was given to the ruler of Cochin as a token of goodwill in exchange for trading rights. It was later renovated by the Dutch, and so gained the misnomer, Dutch Palace. The two-storeyed structure, built around a courtyard with a small shrine to the goddess Bhagavati, is today a museum with a rare collection of murals and royal artifacts.

In the central Durbar Hall, where coronation ceremonies were once held, is the portrait gallery of the Kochi rulers; it also displays palanquins and textiles. The adjacent bedrooms and chambers are renowned for their fine 17th-century murals, representative of Kerala's temple art. Painted in rich, warm shades of red, yellow, black and white, they depict religious and mythological themes as well as episodes from the *Ramayana.*

✡ Paradesi Synagogue
Jew Town. ⏱ *Sun-Fri.* 📷

Nestling in a cul-de-sac at the end of a narrow lane, in the heart of Jew Town, is India's oldest synagogue. The first Jewish settlers are said to have reached Kodungallur *(see p649)* in the 1st century AD. Their settlement, then known as Shingly, prospered over the centuries.

However, persecution by the Portuguese in the early 16th century forced them to migrate to Cochin, where they settled on land given by the raja, and built a synagogue in 1568. Cochin's Jewish community was divided into two distinct groups – the so-called Black or Malabari Jews who claimed to be descendants of the original settlers, and the White or Paradesim Jews who came here from the Middle East, and after whom

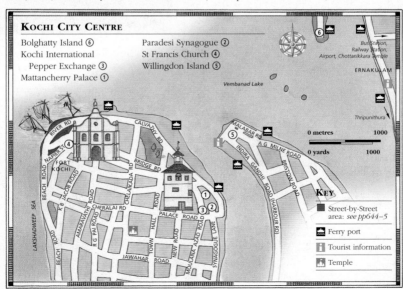

KOCHI CITY CENTRE

Bolghatty Island ⑥
Kochi International Pepper Exchange ③
Mattancherry Palace ①
Paradesi Synagogue ②
St Francis Church ④
Willingdon Island ⑤

KEY

▪ Street-by-Street area: *see pp644–5*
⚓ Ferry port
ℹ Tourist information
🛕 Temple

Main hall with brass pulpit and blue-tiled floor, Paradesi Synagogue

the synagogue is named. A third, smaller group was the Brown or Meshuhurarum Jews, descended from converted slaves, many of whom were in the spice trade. In 1940, there were 2,500 Jews in Kerala, but today only a dozen families remain, the rest having migrated to Israel.

The present synagogue, with its tiled roof and clock tower, was rebuilt in 1664 with Dutch help, after the Portuguese destroyed it in 1662. The synagogue's treasures include beautiful silver and gold Torah scrolls, a multitude of hanging oil lamps and crystal chandeliers, and a superbly crafted brass pulpit. The floor is covered with exquisite hand-painted blue willow-pattern tiles, which were brought from Canton in the mid-18th century by a powerful merchant, Ezekiel Rahabi.

The narrow lanes around the synagogue are crammed with Dutch-style residences. Today, most of these house antique shops.

♙ Kochi International Pepper Exchange

Jew Town. █ (0484) 22 4263. Passes required to enter hall. ☐ Mon–Sat.

This unique establishment reverberates with voices, seemingly raised in anger, as one ascends the stairs. However, nothing prepares the visitor for what lies within – the small hall is lined with tiny cubicles, each with a man talking animatedly on a telephone. Theatrical gestures accompanied by a loud cacophony of sounds mark the drama of each day's pepper auction.

♙ St Francis Church

Fort Kochi. ☐ Mon–Sat.
✝ (English) 8am, daily.

Established in the early 1500s by the Portuguese (who called it Santo Antonio) this is one of India's earliest European churches, with a simple façade that became the model for later churches. Taken over by the Dutch and then the British, it is today affiliated to the Church of South India.

Within are numerous gravestones with inscriptions, the earliest a Portuguese epitaph, dated 1562. Vasco da Gama (see p653) was buried here in 1524 until his body was taken to Portugal 14 years later.

Willingdon Island

This man-made island, named after the viceroy, Lord Willingdon, was created in the 1920s out of silt dredged to deepen Kochi port. Situated between Fort Kochi, Mattancherry and Ernakulam, it has some good hotels, as well as the main harbour, the Port Trust building, the customs house and the railway station. It is also an important naval base.

The gracious façade of Bolghatty Palace, now a hotel

Bolghatty Island

Bolghatty Palace Hotel █ (0484) 35 5003. 🍴 open to non-residents.

A narrow strip of land, this beautiful island with breathtaking views of the bay, is the location of Bolghatty Palace. Set in 6 ha (15 acres) of lush green lawns, this palatial structure was originally built by the Dutch in 1744 and later became the home of the British Resident. It has now been converted into a hotel run by the Kerala Tourism Development Corporation (see p714).

ENVIRONS: Kochi's bustling business centre, **Ernakulam**, is 10 km (6 miles) east of Fort Kochi. The Hill Palace at **Thripunithura**, 10 km (6 miles) southeast of Ernakulam, was built in 1895 and was the official residence of the former rulers of Cochin. The palace, set in spacious grounds, is now a museum with a fairly good collection of paintings, manuscripts and royal memorabilia. The exquisite floor tiles differ from room to room, and the sweeping wooden staircases have a grandeur all of their own. The 10th-century **Chottanikkara Temple**, dedicated to the mother goddess Bhagavati, one of Kerala's most popular deities, is 16 km (10 miles) northeast of Ernakulam.

🏛 Thripunithura Museum

█ (0484) 78 1113. ☐ Tue–Sun. ✍

Antique shops lining the narrow lanes in Jew Town

Street-by-Street: Fort Kochi

KOCHI'S NATURAL HARBOUR, created by a massive flood in 1341, attracted imperialists and merchants from all over the world. In the 16th century, the Portuguese built a fort here, which was later occupied by the Dutch and then the British. Today, this quarter, with its mixture of architectural styles, encapsulates Fort Kochi's tumultuous history. The most important building here is St Francis Church, erected by the Portuguese in 1502 and considered to be among the oldest churches built by Europeans in India. This area has now been declared a Heritage Zone to preserve its many historic buildings.

★ **Santa Cruz Cathedral**
Built in 1887, this cathedral has impressive murals on its ceiling.

Kashi Art Café
This charming restaurant, in an old Dutch building, houses an art gallery.

Mattancherry

Koder House
The residence of Satu Koder, patriarch of Kochi's Jews, was built by his ancestors in 1808.

★ **Chinese Fishing Nets**
First erected between 1350 and 1450, these cantilevered fishing nets indicate trade links with China.

Peter Celli Street
Many hotels and shops are located here.

Bishop's House
Once the Portuguese governor's house, this 16th-century structure is now home to Kochi's bishop.

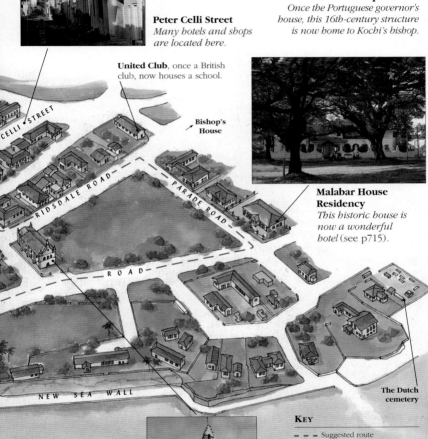

United Club, once a British club, now houses a school.

CELLI STREET

RIDSDALE ROAD

PARADE ROAD

Bishop's House

Malabar House Residency
This historic house is now a wonderful hotel (see p715).

ROAD

NEW SEA WALL

The Dutch cemetery

★ St Francis Church
Vasco da Gama was buried here in 1524, before his body was taken to Portugal.

KEY

– – – Suggested route

STAR SIGHTS

★ Santa Cruz Cathedral

★ Chinese Fishing Nets

★ St Francis Church

Lakshadweep Islands ⑪

Bird of paradise

FORMERLY THE Laccadives, the Lakshadweep Islands are an archipelago of 36 exquisite coral islands, with untouched beaches and verdant coconut groves, scattered off the Kerala coast in the Arabian Sea. With a total land area of only 32 sq km (12 sq miles), Lakshadweep (which means 100,000 islands) is the smallest Union Territory in India. The atolls enclose shallow lagoons harbouring India's richest diversity of coral varieties, and a multitude of colourful reef fish. Only two islands, Bangaram and Kadmat, are open to foreign visitors, while Indian visitors have a choice of six; all offer superb snorkelling and scuba-diving.

Cherbaniani Reef

Byramgore Reef

Bitra Island

Chetlat Island

Kiltan Island

Perumulappara

Kadmat Island

Bangaram Island

Amindivi Island

Agatti Island

Pitti Island   Androth Island

Kavaratti Island

Suheli Island

Kalpeni Island

0 km   50

0 miles   50

Minicoy Island

Wind-surfing in the Lakshadweep Islands

Kavaratti Island

450 km (280 miles) W of Kochi.
▦ ◯ *to Indian passport holders only.* ⬔

Lakshadweep's administrative headquarters, Kavaratti is the busiest island, and home to a large number of mainlanders, most of whom work for the government. It has beautiful white beaches and its crystal-clear lagoon is popular with water sports enthusiasts.

There are 52 mosques on the island that cater to the predominantly Muslim population. The **Ujra Mosque** has an ornate ceiling, carved from driftwood. The island also has a **Marine Aquarium**, which displays a variety of tropical fish and corals.

Huts at Bangaram Island Resort

Agatti Island

55 km (34 miles) NW of Kavaratti Island. ✈ ▦ ◯ *to Indian passport holders only.* ⬔

Lakshadweep's only airport is on Agatti Island. It has a fine lagoon and offers easy access for day visits to the uninhabited islands of Bangaram, Tinnakara and Parali I and II. Although all visitors arriving by plane must go through Agatti, the island itself is not open to foreign visitors.

Bangaram Island

58 km (36 miles) NW of Kavaratti.
▦ ⬔

The uninhabited Bangaram Island is covered with dense groves of coconut palms and has lovely sandy beaches.

The **Bangaram Island Resort** *(see p715)*, run by Casino Hotels of Kochi, has about 30 rooms as well as a restaurant and bar. Its lagoon, rich with corals and tropical fish, is excellent for scuba diving and snorkelling. Visitors can also choose from the variety of water sports

available, including sailing. A health certificate from a doctor is required for diving.

Kadmat Island

70 km (44 miles) N of Kavaratti Island. ▦ ⬔

Thickly covered with palm trees, Kadmat Island has two fine lagoons, to the east and west. The **Water Sports Institute** offers canoeing,

Snorkelling in Lakshadweep Islands' crystal-clear waters

Fisherfolk picking mussels among reefs in the shallows

VISITORS' CHECKLIST

Union Territory of Lakshadweep.
200–450 km (124–280 miles) W
of Kochi. 🏢 10,150 (Kavaratti).
✈ from Kochi to Agatti. 🚢
from Kochi (30 hours). 🚤 Boats
are available for trips between
the islands. ⓘ A trip to
Lakshadweep is only possible as
part of a package tour; individual
bookings are not permitted. For
bookings contact Lakshadweep
Tourism's Society for Nature
Tourism & Sports (SPORTS) office
in Kochi, (0484) 66 8387. For
enquiries contact the Delhi office,
(011) 338 6807. Travel permits
These are mandatory and take at
least two months to procure (see
p758), contact the Kochi SPORTS
office. Many agencies run tours
between October and March.

kayaking and glass-bottomed boat rides, and the **Lacadives Dive School**, on the same premises, offers snorkelling and scuba diving and has qualified instructors.

🤿 **Water Sports Institute**
SPORTS Office, Kochi.
📞 (0484) 66 8387.
🤿 **Lacadives Dive School**
📞 Mumbai, (022) 462 7381; Kochi, (0484) 36 7752.
🌐 www.lacadives.com

Kalpeni Island
125 km (78 miles) SE of Kavaratti Island. 🚢 🔲 to Indian passport holders only.
The clear, shallow lagoon of Kalpeni Island is the largest in Lakshadweep. With excellent reefs, Kalpeni is ideal for

diving and snorkelling. Coral debris, deposited by a storm in 1847, has formed raised banks on the eastern and southern shores. Kalpeni's inhabitants were among the earliest islanders to send girls to school, paving the way for other islanders who had traditionally kept their girls and women confined to the home.

A hermit crab coming out of a shell

Minicoy Island
250 km (155 miles) S of Kavaratti Island. 🚢 🔲 to Indian passport holders only.
Lakshadweep's southernmost island, Minicoy has a unique culture influenced by the neighbouring Maldives. Mahl, spoken here, is a dialect of the Maldivian Dhivehi, which is

related to the Indo-Persian languages with a script written from right to left. Minicoy is often referred to as "Minicoy's Island", as its ten villages are matrilineal. It is also rich in the performing arts; the traditional Lava dance is performed on festive occasions. Tuna fishing has become an important activity, with the establishment of a tuna canning factory.

Minicoy has a grand lagoon, and is the only island in the archipelago with a stretch of mangroves along its shores. A large lighthouse, built by the British in 1885, commands an impressive view of the sea.

MARINE LIFE IN THE CORAL REEFS

The Lakshadweep Islands are a conglomeration of atolls – ring-shaped coral reef formations – that are the richest coral reefs found in India. Formed over thousands of years, they are made up of billions of minute organisms called polyps. Related to sea anemones, polyps build their skeletons outside their body. As they grow, their limestone skeletons become elaborate coral formations, with new colonies spreading over dead ones, and eventually turn into formidable reefs. The complex and fragile reef ecosystem is alive with an extraordinary range of plants and marine life. Over 600 species of reef fish, such as clown fish and parrot fish in a dazzling array of colours, giant clams with purple lips, delicate sea fans and sea anemones, ink-blue starfish, dolphins, harmless sharks and marine turtles, make up the spectacular diversity of the underwater world. (For tips on eco-friendly diving, see p619.)

Parali Island, one of Lakshadweep's many atolls

Corals of a 100-odd varieties, including the boulder-like porites, the ridged brain (right), and the branched staghorn, can be seen here. The myriad colours are produced by the variety of algae that grow on them.

The nine-tiered tower dedicated to Shankaracharya, Kaladi

Kaladi ⑫

Ernakulam district. 35 km (22 miles) NE of Kochi. 🚌

THIS QUIET TOWN on the banks of the beautiful Periyar river is celebrated as the birthplace of the great philosopher, Shankaracharya. There are two shrines (built in 1910) to honour his memory, on the river bank. One is dedicated to him and the other to the goddess Sharada, and both are maintained by the Sringeri Matha (see p527).

Nearby is a spot locally known as Brindavan, where the Shankaracharya's mother, Aryamba, was cremated. The old Shri Krishna Temple, near the Sharada Temple, has an image of the deity, said to have been installed by Shankaracharya himself. On the road to the Krishna Temple is a 46-m (151-ft) tall, nine-tiered octagonal tower, the Shri Adi Shankaracharya Kirti Stambha Mandapa. Each of its floors commemorates the life and works of Shankaracharya.

ENVIRONS: The **Malayattor Church**, 8 km (5 miles) east of Kaladi, is said to be where St Thomas erected a cross.

The 1,000-year old rock-cut **Kalill Temple**, 22 km (14 miles) southeast of Kaladi, was originally a Jain temple. It is now dedicated to the mother goddess. Unlike at other temples, a female elephant is used in all ceremonial rituals.

Munnar ⑬

Idukki district. 130 km (81 miles) N of Kochi. 🚌 ℹ️ Tourist Information Centre, Old Munnar, (04865) 53 0679. 🔒 daily.

THE PICTURESQUE little town of Munnar lies at a height of about 1,800 m (5,906 ft), in a part of the Western Ghats known as the High Ranges. The name Munnar (which means "Three Rivers" in Tamil) is derived from its location at the confluence of three mountain streams – Kundala, Mudrapuzha and Nallathanni.

Located in 24,000 ha (59,305 acres) of sprawling tea estates, first established by the British in 1878, Munnar was once a summer resort for the British government in South India. The most important plantation in the High Ranges today belongs to Tata Tea, which oversees almost every public facility in the vicinity. The quaint High Range Club, made of wicker and teak, still serves as a social centre for Munnar's planters and, with its custom-ary "gentlemen's bar", retains an old-world atmosphere.

Munnar remains a popular destination for visitors from Tamil Nadu and Kerala. Because of this, the town and its environs have witnessed a proliferation of hotels, restaurants and shopping centres. However, areas further away from the city centre remain relatively un-spoilt, and the gentle hills of tea, coffee and cardamom plantations offer excellent cycle rides and walks.

ENVIRONS: Mattupetty Lake, 13 km (8 miles) north of Munnar, is surrounded by lovely semi-alpine scenery. A specialized cattle-breeding centre is located nearby.

A view of the tea plantations around Munnar

ADI SHANKARACHARYA (AD 788–820)

Adi Shankaracharya, only 32 when he died, travelled the length and breadth of India, wrote erudite commentaries on Hindu scriptures, and composed devotional poems and prayers. The core of his monist philosophy is that there is only one reality and that is Brahman, the all-pervading cosmic force of which the human soul is a part, while all material objects are mere illusions (maya). The Buddhist elements in his philosophy provoked, during his lifetime, the orthodox Brahminical charge that he was a "Buddha in disguise". His historical importance lies in the fact that he provided an intellectual basis to Hindusim.

The philosopher Adi Shankaracharya

The captivating landscape of Eravikulam National Park

Eravikulam National Park **⑭**

Idukki district. 16 km (10 miles) NE of Munnar. ▤ or auto-rickshaw from Munnar to Rajamalai, the entry point. ℹ For permits contact Divisional Forest Officer, Munnar, (04865) 53 0487. ◯ Aug–May. ▨

THE ROLLING high-altitude grasslands, a striking contrast to the dense *sholas* or tropical montane forests of the valleys, are unique to the mountain landscape of the Western Ghats. Easily the best pre-served stretch of this extraordinarily beautiful landscape is the Eravikulam National Park, spread across an area of 97 sq km (38 sq miles) at the base of the **Anaimudi Mountain**. With a height of 2,695 m (8,842 ft), this has the distinction of being the highest peak south of the Himalayas. Anaimudi, which means "Elephant Head", not surprisingly resembles one. The peak and its environs provide good hiking territory.

The park, on the border of Kerala and Tamil Nadu, was established in 1978 with the specific aim of conserving the endangered Nilgiri tahr, a rare breed of mountain goat *(see p19)*. Today, the park is home to about 3,000 tahr, the single largest population of this slate-grey goat in the world. Extremely agile, it inhabits the rocky slopes, and can be observed at surprisingly close quarters. The park is also home to macaques, leopards,

and packs of *dhole*, the rare Indian wild dog. Its streams contain trout, and there are also more than 90 species of birds, including song birds such as the laughing thrush.

Eravikulam is regarded as one of the best managed national parks in the country. The Muduvan tribals, who live at the periphery of the park, are employed to assist in its conservation. Their traditional method of selectively burning parts of the grassland prevents large forest fires, and also helps regenerate the tender grass on which young tahr feed. Eravikulam is also famous for the *kurunji (Strobilanthes kunthianus)*, the blue flowers that suddenly bloom en masse every 12 years and transform the rocky landscape into a sea of blue. The *kurunji* is next expected to bloom here in 2006.

Kurunji flower in full bloom

Kodungallur **⑮**

Thrissur district. 32 km (20 miles) N of Kochi. ▤ ◉ Id (Feb/Mar), Bharani Festival (Mar/Apr).

KNOWN AS MUZIRIS to the Greeks, and Cranganore to the Europeans, Kodungallur was the historic capital of the Cheraman Perumals, monarchs of the Chera empire *(see p43)*. Situated at the mouth of the Periyar river, this was the Malabar Coast's main port until a flood tide in 1341 silted up the harbour. After this catastrophe, Kochi *(see p642)* became the main port.

The town is today a major destination for Hindus, Christians and Muslims alike. The **Bhagavati Temple**, in the city centre, is the venue of a three-day festival of erotic song and dance. This temple was originally the shrine of a Dravidian goddess. It was then taken over by either the Buddhists or the Jains. The festival marks the reclaiming of the site for the goddess.

St Thomas *(see p573)* is said to have landed here in AD 52. The **Mar Thoma Pontifical Shrine** houses a sacred relic that was brought from the Vatican in 1953 to celebrate the anniversary of the saint's arrival 1,900 years earlier.

The **Cheraman Mosque**, 2 km (1.3 miles) from the city centre, was built in AD 629 by Malik Bin Dinar, who introduced Islam to Kerala. Perhaps the first mosque in India, it resembles a Hindu temple.

KERALA'S MATRILINEAL FAMILY SYSTEM

Called *marumakkathayam* in Kerala, the matrilineal family system, whereby inheritance is determined through the female line, is believed to have evolved in the late 10th century. This was a period of internecine warfare, and by placing women at the core of the inheritance, men could go to battle, knowing that their children's material well-being was protected. Children thus bear their mother's family name, and are identified as members of her family, with her brothers performing the role of the father figure. The Nairs are best known for this system, since warriors traditionally came from this community. Anthropologists, however, have traced its origin to the cult of the mother goddess widely prevalent in Kerala.

A Nair matriarch from Kerala

The Asian Elephant

LITERATURE, ART AND culture in India celebrate the elephant. Ganesha, the elephant-headed son of Shiva and Parvati, is the Remover of Obstacles, and his name is invoked before any important task is undertaken *(see p467)*. Unlike in the rest of India, Ganesha is a minor deity in Kerala. Yet, elephants play a major role in the daily life and festivals of the people

Ganesha, the elephant god

of Kerala, who have a uniquely close and affectionate relationship with elephants. Though mainly used as draught animals, elephants also participate in temple rituals, where they carry the deity in sacred processions. For such occasions, elephants are splendidly caparisoned with ornaments of gold. The wealthier temples have their own elephants.

The tusker *(a male with large tusks) faces great danger from poaching, despite the ban on ivory.*

ASIAN ELEPHANT
Denizen of the forests and floodplains of the Himalayan foothills, Central India and the southern highlands, the Asian elephant *(Elephas maximus)* is not as tall as the African elephant, and has smaller ears.

This 19th-century print *shows how trained elephants were used to capture wild ones by driving them into* khedas *(corrals).*

Temple elephants *are usually bought at the Sonepur Mela in Bihar* (see p216). *The mahout devotes hours every day to grooming and training them for temple festivals. All commands are given in Malayalam.*

In Kerala, *elephants are often seen carrying their own feed. Most people allow mahouts to cut as many fronds of palm as the animal needs – up to 200 kg (441 lb) a day.*

Icons and motifs *depicting the elephant are common in Indian art, as they are an integral part of Hindu mythology and pageantry.*

View of the Catholic Lourdes Cathedral in Thrissur

Thrissur ⓰

Thrissur district. 80 km (50 miles) N of Kochi. *317,500.* *Tourist Office, Govt Guest House, (0487) 32 0800.* *Thrissur Pooram (Apr/May), Kamdassamkadavu Boat Races (Aug/Sep).*

THIS TOWN, built around an elevated area called The Round, was planned during the reign of Raja Rama Varma, the ruler of Cochin (Kochi) in the 18th century. In the heart of The Round is the multi-roofed **Vadakkunnathan Temple**. This great Shiva temple was built in the 9th century, and has superb wood-carvings and rich decorative murals. The splendid Pooram festival is held here each year, with the main activities taking place outside the temple walls (non-Hindus are not permitted inside the shrine).

Northeast of the temple is the State Museum, displaying a good collection of murals, wood-carvings, sculpture and antique ornaments. The Archaeological Museum is nearby.

Entrance, Shri Krishna Temple

Thrissur is often dubbed Kerala's cultural capital as the town is home to two prestigious state-run cultural institutions. These are the Kerala Sangeetha Nataka Academy (for music and theatre) and the Kerala Sahitya Academy (for literature).

The town suffered political upheavals for centuries, having been successively ruled by the Zamorins of Kozhikode *(see p653)*, Tipu Sultan of Mysore and the rulers of Kochi. The Dutch and the British have also made their presence felt in the history of this district, as is evident from the many impressive churches, such as the late 19th-century **Lourdes Cathedral**, around the town.

ENVIRONS: Guruvayur, 29 km (18 miles) north of Thrissur, has Kerala's most popular temple. Legend has it that the 16th-century Shri Krishna Temple was created by Guru ("Instructor of the Gods"), and Vayu ("God of the Winds"). A large number of Hindu weddings take place here. The temple's elephant sanctuary is within the compound of an old palace nearby. It houses more than 40 elephants that belong to the deity – it is customary to present an elephant as an offering.

The renowned performing arts and teaching centre, the **Kerala Kala Mandalam**, is 32 km (20 miles) northeast of Thrissur. Founded in 1930 by the famous Malayali poet, Vallathol Narayan Menon, at Cheruthuruthy, it offers intensive training in Kathakali, Mohiniattam and Koodiyattam dance forms. Instrumental and vocal music forms are taught here as well. The complex also has a large *natyagriha* (dance hall) for performances.

Kerala Kala Mandalam
(0492) 62 2418 for permission.
Mon–Fri. *public hols, Apr/May.*

Vadakkunnathan Temple in Thrissur

THE POORAM FESTIVAL

A *pooram* (meeting) is a temple festival marked by the ceremonious congregation, at a particular temple, of deities from various other temples. Though a number of *poorams* are held throughout Kerala, Thrissur's Pooram is the most spectacular. Held between April and May, it celebrates the processional arrival of two goddesses before Shiva, after whom the town is named. Through a sea of devotees and the hypnotic beat of percussion instruments, two rows of elephants, with the central ones carrying the deities, move majestically towards each other. A firework display ends the celebrations.

Elephants at the Pooram festival

Palakkad ⓱

Palakkad district. 99 km (62 miles) N
of Kochi. 🚶 130,750. 🚉 ℹ️ Tourist
Information Centre, near Children's
Park, (0491) 53 8998. 🎪 Chariot
Festival (Oct/Nov).

Sɪᴛᴜᴀᴛᴇᴅ ᴀᴛ ᴛʜᴇ base of the
Western Ghats, Palakkad
(Palghat) derives its name
from the dense forests (kadu)
of pala (Alsteria scholaris)
trees that once covered the
land. Today, however, paddy
fields and tobacco plantations
have taken their place.

Tipu's Fort, in the heart of
the town, was built by Haider
Ali of Mysore in 1766; it was
subsequently occupied by
the British after they defeated
his son and successor, Tipu
Sultan (see p517), some 30
years later. This sombre,
granite structure now houses
various government offices.

The large **Vishwanatha
Temple**, on the banks of the
Kalpathy river, is famous for
its chariot procession.

On the outskirts of town are
the extensive **Malampuzha
Gardens**, laid out above a
huge irrigation dam built
across the Malampuzha river.
Pleasant boat cruises are
possible on a large lake,
nestling in the foothills.

ENVIRONS: The town of
Kollengode is 19 km
(12 miles) south of
Palakkad and is set
in beautiful pastoral
surroundings. The
Vishnu Temple and
Kollengode Palace are worth
a visit. **Thirthala**, 75 km (47
miles) west of Palakkad, has a
Shiva temple and the ruins of
a mud fort. Its most important
sight, the Kattilmadam Temple, is a granite Buddhist
monument dating from
the 9th–10th
centuries.

Silent Valley, a haven of rare plants and herbs

Silent Valley National Park ⓲

Palakkad district. 88 km (55 miles)
NW of Kochi. 🚌 Mannarkkad, the
entry point. Jeeps available to
Mukkali. ℹ️ For permits contact
the Wildlife Warden, Mannarkkad,
(0492) 422 056.

Tʜᴇ ѕɪʟᴇɴᴛ ᴠᴀʟʟᴇʏ National
Park, spread over an area
of 90 sq km (35 sq miles), preserves what is perhaps the
country's last substantial stretch
of virgin tropical evergreen
forest. An important part of
the Nilgiri Biosphere
Reserve (see p520), it
represents some of
the spectacular
biodiversity of the
Western Ghats. The
park is renowned
for its rare plants
and herbs, which
include over 100 species of
orchids. Wildlife includes
tigers, elephants, the Nilgiri
langur, the sloth bear, the shy
nocturnal slender loris, and the
endangered lion-tailed
macaque. A variety of
birds, as well as a
remarkable 100

Slender
loris

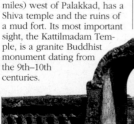

The desolate ruins of Tipu's Fort at Palakkad

species of butterflies and 400
species of moths, are also
found here. Visitors can trek to
the source of the Kunthipuzha
river which flows through this
valley. Accommodation is
available at the forest lodge in
Mukkali, just outside the park.

Malappuram ⓳

Malappuram district. 153 km (95
miles) N of Kochi. 🚌 ℹ️ (0493)
73 4311. 🏛️ daily. 🎪 Valiya Nercha
(Feb/Mar), Shivratri (Feb/Mar).

Tʜɪѕ "ʟᴀɴᴅ ᴀᴛᴏᴘ ʜɪʟʟѕ" stands
at the entrance to the
Malabar region, and is crossed
by three major rivers – the
Chaliyar, the Kadalundi and
the Bharatapuzha. A military
centre of the Zamorins of
Calicut, it was the scene of
fierce fighting between British
forces and the Mopplahs
(Muslim peasants), known as
the Mopplah Revolt. The most
serious uprising occurred in
1921, after which many rebels
were exiled to the Andamans
(see pp618-19). The old
British barracks, on a hilltop
overlooking the Kadalundi
river, now houses the district
administration. Malappuram is
also an important seat of both
Hindu and Islamic learning.

ENVIRONS: Kerala's pioneering Ayurvedic institution (see
p629), is at **Kottakkal**, 12 km
(7 miles) southwest of Malappuram. Started in 1902, the
Kottakkal Arya Vaidyasala is
based in a splendid building,
and has a research centre and

Arya Vaidyasala, at Kottakkal

hospital. **Tirur**, 32 km (20 miles) southwest of Malappuram, was the 16th-century birthplace of the father of Malayalam literature, Tunchat Ramanuja Ezhuthachan. He also taught the Malayalam alphabet to children, a practice that continues today at a shrine dedicated to him.

One of the earliest Portuguese settlements on the Malabar Coast was at **Tanur**, 34 km (21 miles) southwest of Malappuram. St Francis Xavier *(see p498)* is said to have come here in 1546.

Kozhikode ⑳

Kozhikode district. 254 km (158 miles) N of Kochi. 🏠 436,600. ✈ Karipur, 25 km (16 miles) S of city centre. 🚊 🚌 ℹ Kerala Tourism, SM Street, (0495) 72 2391. 🎭 Shivratri Utsavam (Feb/Mar).

THIS BUSY commercial town, better known throughout the world as Calicut, was the capital of the kingdom of the powerful Zamorins (a Portuguese corruption of their title, Samoothiri). Under them the town prospered as a major centre of the Malabar trade in spices and textiles, and it was from Calicut that the word calico originated as the term for white, unbleached cotton.

It was in Calicut, too, that Vasco da Gama, the intrepid Portuguese explorer who discovered the sea route to India, was first received by the Zamorin in his palace in May 1498. Dominating the city centre is the large Manamchira Tank, flanked by the Town Hall and the Public Library, both fine examples of traditional architecture. Nearby is the **Commonwealth Trust** (Com Trust) building, constructed over 100 years ago. Established by the Basel Mission in the 19th century, the Trust modernized the terracotta roofing-tile and textile industries. The Trust is also credited with developing the colour khaki, later used for the British Army field uniform on the recommendation of Lord Arthur Wellesley, the future Duke of Wellington. A shop on the premises sells textiles as well as terracotta products. A striking Roman Catholic cathedral also stands near the Manamchira Tank.

The town's Muslim heritage is indicated by its numerous mosques, remarkable for their massive size and elaborate wood carvings. Among these, the Mishqal Palli, near the port, is the most impressive, with a five-tiered tiled roof.

The **Pazhassirajah Museum** exhibits wood and metal sculptures, models of temples and reconstructions of megalithic monuments. The Art Gallery next door has paintings by Raja Ravi Varma, the 19th-century painter who belonged to a princely family from Travancore *(see p626)*.

Kozhikode's busy shopping area, the quaintly-named **Sweetmeats Street**, was once lined with shops selling the famous Calicut *halwa*, a brightly coloured sweet made of flour and sugar. Today, SM Street, as it is popularly known, has only a few shops that sell *halwa*. Court Road, leading off SM Street, houses the bustling Spice Market. Kozhikode is today the storage and trading centre for hill produce from Wynad *(see p654)*; spices such as cloves, cardamom, pepper, turmeric and coffee are sorted and packaged in the old warehouses along the waterfront.

🏛 Commonwealth Trust
South Manamchira St. 📞 (0495) 72 0704 for permission to visit.
🏛 Pazhassirajah Museum
East Hill. 📞 (0495) 38 1253.
🕐 Tue–Sun.

ENVIRONS: A short 16-km (10-mile) drive north of the city leads to the small village of **Kappad**, where a lonely stone plaque on the beach commemorates the spot where Vasco da Gama is supposed to have landed in 1498.

The historic village of **Beypore**, 10 km (6 miles) south of Kozhikode, is believed to be the fabled Ophir, referred to in ancient Greek and Roman texts. Artisans still follow the traditional methods of their forefathers at this ancient shipbuilding centre *(see p633)*. The type of dhows that were built here for Arab merchants more than 1,500 years ago are still in demand in West Asia. Old vessels are also brought here to be repaired.

The Commonwealth Trust, at the edge of the large Manamchira Tank, Kozhikode

The Tree House in Wynad, blending into the sylvan landscape

Wynad District ㉑

280 km (174 miles) NE from Kochi to Kalpetta. 🚌 🏧 *Tourist Information centre, Kalpetta, (0493) 60 2712.*

A REMOTE REGION of virgin rainforests and mist-clad mountain ranges, Wynad provides the ideal climatic conditions for Kerala's extensive plantations of cardamom, pepper, coffee and rubber. Relatively untouched by modernization, this is the homeland of large groups of indigenous tribal communities, such as the cave-dwelling Cholanaikens, and the downtrodden Paniyas, who until 50 years ago were sold as bonded labour to plantation owners. It is also the favoured habitat of animals such as the, Nilgiri langur, wild elephants and the giant Malabar squirrel.

The gateway to Wynad is **Lakkidi**, at its southern end. An ancient tree on the main highway, ominously draped with a heavy iron chain, presents a curious sight. Local legend claims that it binds the angry spirit of a Paniya tribal who showed a group of British surveyors the path through the dense forest. Instead of being rewarded, he was killed here and his spirit apparently haunted the highway until it was exorcised.

Kalpetta, the district headquarters, is 15 km (9 miles) to the north. Once a major Jain centre *(see p396)* this has two Jain temples situated nearby. The Anantanathaswami Temple is at Puliyarmala, 6 km (4 miles) away, while the Glass Temple of Koottamunda, dedicated to the third Jain *tirthankara*, Parsvanatha, is on the slope of Vallarimal Hill, 20 km (12 miles) to the south. The area's tallest peak, Chembara Peak

Coffee blossoms in a Wynad plantation

(2,100 m/6,890 ft) is 14 km (9 miles) southwest of Kalpetta, and is excellent for trekking and birdwatching.

Sulthan's Bathery (Sultan's Battery), 10 km (6 miles) east of Kalpetta, derives its name from Tipu Sultan of Mysore *(see p517)*, who built a fort here in the 18th century. The **Edakkal Caves** are 12 km (7 miles) away. Their inscriptions and carvings of human and animal figures are said to date to prehistoric times; some believe that these caves were the refuge of Jain monks. The caves' environs abound in megaliths. The **Wynad (Muthanga) Wildlife Sanctuary**, 16 km (10 miles) east of Sulthan's Battery, was established in 1973 and is part of the Nilgiri Biosphere Reserve *(see p520)*.

Mananthavady, 35 km (22 miles) north of Kalpetta, was the scene of a long guerrilla war between the local king, Pazhassi Raja, and British troops, led by Lord Arthur Wellesley, the future Duke of Wellington who defeated Napoleon at Waterloo. About 32 km (20 miles) to the north is the Vishnu Temple at Thirunelli, built beside the Paapanassini river. This is a major pilgrimage site, where Hindus perform funeral rites.

🗻 **Edakkal Caves**
⏰ *daily.* 📷 📹
🗻 **Wynad Sanctuary**
📷 📹 *extra charges. Permits from Wildlife Warden, Sulthan Bathery, (0493) 62 0454.*

The remains of Tipu's fort, Sulthan's Battery

Mahe ②

Union Territory of Pondicherry. Mahe
district. 48 km (30 miles) N of
Kozhikode. 🚌 🛈 *Govt Tourist
Home, (0497) 33 2222.*
🎭 *St Theresa's Feast (Oct).*

Sɪᴛᴜᴀᴛᴇᴅ ᴏɴ ᴛʜᴇ Mayyazhi
river, this former French
enclave is named after the
French admiral, Mahe de La
Bourdonnais, who landed here
in November 1741. A French
colony until 1954, it is today
part of the Union Territory of
Pondicherry (see p586). Only
some traces of Mahe's colonial
heritage remain, among them
the beautiful old residence of
the French administrator, at the
mouth of the river. It is now
the office-cum-residence of the
Indian government's administrator. Mahe's main church,
the whitewashed, Baroque St
Theresa's Church, is situated
on the highway. The town's
main "industry" seems to centre around the supply of cheap
alcohol, attracting truck drivers
and motorists who come here
from nearby areas to stock up.

Thalaserry ②

Kannur district. 255 km (158 miles)
N of Kochi. 🚉 🚌

Fɪꜱʜɪɴɢ ɪꜱ a major occupation in Thalaserry (once
known as Tellicherry), and
observing the bartering of the
day's catch can be an enjoyable experience. The British
East India Company estab-

Fishmongers awaiting the daily catch at Thalaserry

lished one of their first trading posts at Thalaserry at the
end of the 17th century. In
1708, they built the enormous
laterite fort on the coast. An
old lighthouse still stands on
its ramparts, and there are
also two secret tunnels, one
of which leads into the sea.

The Thalaserry Cricket
Club, founded in 1860, is one
of the oldest in
India, as cricket was
introduced here in
the late 18th century.

This region is one
of the main centres
of *kalaripayattu* (see
p626), a fact that has
made it a training
ground for circus
artistes as well. It is
a common sight to
see young men in
the *kalari* (gym-
nasium), exercising
to tone their muscles and
practising with wooden
weapons. Many images of
deities adorn the *kalari*,
giving it a sacred character.

**Façade of the fort,
Thalaserry**

Kannur ④

Kannur district. 66 km (41 miles) N of
Kochi. 🚉 🚌 🛈 *District Tourism
Promotion Council, Taluk Office
Campus, (0497) 70 6336.* 🏛 *daily.*

Tʜɪꜱ ꜱᴄᴇɴɪᴄ coastal town,
called Cannanore by Euro-
pean settlers, was an important
maritime centre in the 14th
and 15th centuries.
The Portuguese built
St Angelo Fort, 5
km (3 miles) south of
the city, in 1505. This
enormous laterite
structure overlooks
the fishing harbour
and is protected by
the sea on three
sides. It was later
occupied by the
British, who estab-
lished a large military
garrison here.

Muzhapilangad Beach, 15
km (9 miles) south of Kannur,
is a serene spot with a 4-km
(2.5-mile) long sandy beach,
safe for swimmers.

THEYYAM, KERALA'S SPECTACULAR DANCE-RITUAL

This dance-ritual, particular to the north Malabar region, was originally
aimed at appeasing ancient village deities, the mother goddess, folk
heroes, ancestors and spirits. With the advent of Brahminism, Hindu
divinities replaced many of the earlier ones, and the Theyyam
pantheon shrank from 300 to around 40. The Theyyam presentation begins with the singing of the *thottam* (song) in praise of the
deity relevant to that particular ritual. This is followed by the
dance, the steps and postures of which show the strong influence
of Kerala's martial arts tradition, *kalaripayattu*. Drums, pipes and
cymbals provide the accompaniment. The performers, all male, wear
masks, body paint, colourful costumes and imposing headgear
(*mudi*), which often rises to a staggering height of more than 2 m
(7 ft). The tender leaves of the coconut palm are cut to various
designs and shapes to form part of the elaborate costume of the
dancer. Theyyams, usually annual rituals, are held between December
and May. However, at the Parassinikadavu Temple, 20 km (12 miles)
north of Kannur, Theyyam is performed every day.

**A Theyyam dancer clad
in a colourful costume**

The laterite ramparts of Bekal Fort, outside Kasaragod town

Kasaragod District 25

400 km (249 miles) S from Kochi to Kasaragod. 🚉 🚌 🛈 *Tourist office, Bekal Fort, (0499) 77 2900.*

K ERALA'S northernmost district, flanked by the Western Ghats to the east and the Arabian Sea to the west, is a fertile region of thickly forested hills and meandering rivers. The district is named after its main town, Kasaragod, a bustling centre of the coir and handloom industries. About 8 km (5 miles) north of Kasaragod, is the **Madhur Temple**. This beautiful temple, with its copper-plate roofing, has a commanding location overlooking the Madhuvahini river.

Situated 16 km (10 miles) south of Kasaragod is **Bekal Fort**, the largest and best-preserved fort in Kerala. This enormous, circular structure is built with large blocks of laterite, and its outer wall rises majestically from the sea to a height of 39 m (128 feet). Inside is a cunningly concealed tunnel that leads directly to the sea. The fort's origins are shrouded in mystery, though it is generally thought to have been built in the mid-1600s by a local chieftain Shivappa Nayak, whose fiefdom was in neighbouring Karnataka. The scene of much conflict, the

fort was eventually occupied by the British after the defeat of Tipu Sultan *(see p517).*

Many beautiful beaches lie to the north and south of the fort. The closest, **Pallikere Beach**, provides a spectacular view of the fort. The Kerala government, along with the Bekal Resorts Development Corporation, have plans to develop this area as a major tourist complex. About 6 km (4 miles) north of Bekal, **Kappil Beach** is a secluded area, ideal for swimming. Kodi Cliff, at one end of the beach, is a scenic spot with wonderful views of the sunset on the Arabian Sea.

The **Chandragiri Fort**, on the banks of the Chandragiri river, is 10 km (6 miles) north of Bekal. This 17th-century fort is also attributed to Shivappa Nayak, who built it to defend his kingdom against the Vijayanagar rulers *(see pp530–31).* The imposing Malik Dinar Mosque, nearby, is said to have been

A typical temple lamp

founded by Malik Ibn Dinar, a disciple of the Prophet Muhammad, who introduced Islam to Kerala in about AD 664. The grave of Malik Ibn Muhammed, a descendant of Malik Ibn Dinar, lies here. The 9th-century **Ananthapura Temple**, 30 km (19 miles) north of Bekal, is the only temple in Kerala erected in the centre of a lake. It is said to be the original abode of Ananthapadmanabha, the presiding deity of the Anantha Padmanabhaswamy Temple in Thiruvananthapuram, the state capital *(see p627).*

The small hill station of **Ranipuram** is situated 85 km (53 miles) east of Kasaragod. Set amid acres of rubber and spice plantations, it offers good opportunities for trekking.

This region is also the centre for a number of performing arts, such as Theyyam *(see p655)* and Yakshagana, the elaborate folk art form from Karnataka *(see p535).*

Ananthapura Temple, built in the middle of a lake

Kathakali: Kerala's Classical Dance-Drama

LITERALLY MEANING "story-play", Kathakali is a highly evolved classical form of dance, drama and music (both vocal and instrumental), that is almost 400 years old. Male actor-dancers, in voluminous colourful skirts, elaborate headdresses and jewellery, enact stories from the Puranas and epics, mainly the *Mahabharata (see p26)*. The story unfolds simply at first, before building to a dramatic climax. The frenetic drumming, the emotive singing and the rhythmic movements of the dancers reach a crescendo, as the many scenes of love and valour culminate in the triumph of good over evil. These are traditionally all-night perform-ances, held in temple courtyards during religious festivals. Modern performances are shorter.

A noble *paccha* character

Make-up, a complex four-hour process, helps identify characters and define their roles. Mineral pigments and lamp black are the main ingredients. A paper frill defines the jaw line.

Facial movements are used to convey emotions, and to conduct dialogues.

Tadi characters wear red, white or black beards.

Mythical bird

Bejewelled crowns are worn by *kathi* characters.

Paccha character

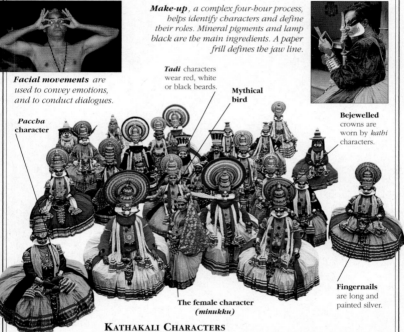

Fingernails are long and painted silver.

The female character *(minukku)*

Voluminous skirts

KATHAKALI CHARACTERS

Costumes and facial make-up use symbolic colours. Green *(paccha)* signifies divine and heroic characters, such as Krishna and Arjuna, while royal though arrogant personalities, such as Ravana, are distinguished by the red *(kathi)* patch applied over the bridge of the nose on a green background. Black *(kari)* is used for demons.

Actor-dancers, all male, do not speak but use symbolic mudras *(band gestures)* and facial expres-sions, with great elo-quence.

Percussion is provided by two drums, chenda and madalam. The lead singer marks the beat with a chengila (gong), and his assistant plays the cymbals.

ANDHRA PRADESH

FROM THE UNSPOILT beaches of Visakhapatnam along the Coromandel Coast, to the emerald green paddy fields of Nellore district, much of Andhra Pradesh is occupied by the rocky Deccan Plateau which rises 1,000 m (3,281 ft) above the fertile coastal plains. This is South India's largest state, covering an area of 275,000 sq km (106,178 sq miles). The main language spoken by its 78 million people is Telugu, though Urdu is also spoken in the state capital, Hyderabad. This vibrant city was until 1947, the seat of the fabulously wealthy royal family, the Asaf Jahi Nizams. Andhra Pradesh's varied cultural heritage is visible in its monuments. These include the ancient Buddhist site at Nagarjunakonda, the great Islamic fort of Golconda and the hilltop Hindu temple at Tirupati, which attracts more pilgrims than any other temple in India. The state's distinctive handicrafts include superb woven ikat textiles, pearl jewellery and inlaid metal *bidri* work.

SIGHTS AT A GLANCE

Towns, Cities & Districts
East Godavari District ❿
Hyderabad ❶
Kondapalli ⓭
Machilipatnam ⓫
Pochampalli ❸
Srikakulam District ❾
Vijayawada ⓬
Visakhapatnam ❻
Warangal ❹

Historic Sites
Amravati ⓮
Chandragiri ⓳
Golconda ❷
Nagarjunakonda ⓯
Penukonda ㉒
Ramatirtham ❽

Temples & Holy Places
Alampur ⓱
Lepakshi ㉓
Palampet ❺
Puttaparthi ㉑
Sri Kalahasti ⓴
Srisailam & Krishna Gorge ⓰
Tirupati ⓲

Areas of Natural Beauty
Borra Caves ❼

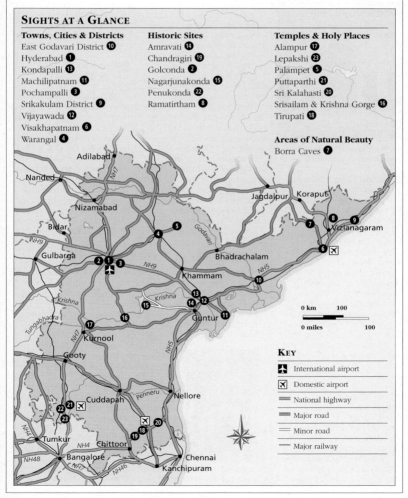

KEY

✈	International airport
⊠	Domestic airport
▬	National highway
▬	Major road
═	Minor road
▬	Major railway

◁ **Sunflowers, grown for their oil, in a field near Alampur in western Andhra Pradesh**

Hyderabad ❶

Enamel tiles, Badshahi Ashurkhana

THE SIXTH LARGEST CITY in India, Hyderabad was founded in 1591 and planned as a grid with the Charminar *(see pp662–3)* at its centre. It has now grown well beyond the confines of the original walled city, to include a new town north of the Musi river, the military cantonment at Secunderabad, and a burgeoning high-tech estate, nicknamed "Cyberabad". The city's sights include the grand palaces of its erstwhile rulers, the Nizams, and the colourful bazaars and mosques of the old city.

Portraits of Salarjung III and his son, painted on ivory

The Neo-Classical façade of the 19th-century Purani Haveli

🏛 Purani Haveli (Nizam's Museum)

Patthargatti Rd. 📞 *(040) 452 1029.* ⭘ *Sat–Thu.* 📷

This sprawling complex of mid-19th-century Neo-Classical buildings was the main residence of the sixth Nizam, Mahbub Ali Pasha. A glimpse of his lavish lifestyle can be seen in the eastern wing of the main building, in the Massarat Mahal. This has the Nizam's gigantic wooden wardrobe, a 73-sq m (786-sq ft) room with closets on two levels, and a mechanical elevator affording access to the upper tier. Its contents once included 75 identical tweed suits – the Nizam liked the pattern so much that he bought the Scottish factory's entire stock of it.

Purani Haveli also houses the Nizam's Museum, which displays china, silver objets d'art, and several fascinating photographs that capture the legendary opulence of the Nizam and his court.

🏛 Salarjung Museum

Near Naya Pul. 📞 *(040) 52 3211.* ⭘ *Sat–Thu.* ⬤ *public hols.* 📷

This eclectic collection of over 40,000 objects once belonged to Salarjung III, Prime Minister of Hyderabad between 1899 and 1949. Salarjung's highly individual taste ranged from objects of sublime beauty to some bordering on kitsch, which is what makes this museum so fascinating.

The pride of the museum is the outstanding Mughal jade collection, which includes an exquisite, translucent leaf-shaped cup. Miniature paintings are also well-represented, including those of the local Deccani School *(see p543)*, as are Indian stone and bronze sculpture, inlaid ivory objects and medieval Islamic manuscripts. A prized 13th-century Koran has the signatures of three Mughal emperors.

Salarjung's rather florid taste in European art is represented by some 19th-century statuary, while the collection of oil paintings include a Canaletto, a Guardi and a Landseer.

🏨 Osmania Hospital

Afzalganj. 📞 *(040) 461 9455.* ⭘ *daily.*

A spectacular stone building with soaring domes, Osmania Hospital was built in 1925 as part of the seventh Nizam's modernization plan after a catastrophic flood in 1908. Opposite it, across the river, are the **Boys' High School** and the **High Court**, built in pink granite and red sandstone. An imaginative blend of Islamic decorative detail and Western interior layouts, all three buildings, as well as

---

THE NIZAMS OF HYDERABAD

Hyderabad was India's biggest and richest princely state, as large as England and Scotland together. Its rulers, known as the Nizams, belonged to the Asaf Jahi dynasty, founded in 1724 by Nizam-ul-Mulk who first came to Hyderabad as the Mughal governor of the Deccan, and then established his independence as Mughal power in Delhi waned. The Nizams' fabulous wealth derived largely from their legendary hoard of emeralds and their diamond mines near Golconda, and many tales are told of their extravagance and eccentricities. The seventh and last Nizam, Osman Ali Khan, was the richest man in India but, unlike his ancestors, he was a notorious miser who smoked cigarette butts and wore the same set of shabby, patched clothes for weeks on end. After Independence in 1947, the Nizam resisted joining the Indian Union. However, riots broke out and Indian Army action to restore order finally led to the state's accession.

Portrait of the last Nizam (r.1911–48)

the city's Railway Station, were constructed between 1914 and 1936, and are the work of the British architect Vincent Esch.

🛕 Badshahi Ashurkhana

Afzal Ganj. ◯ *daily, with permission of the caretaker.*
This historic building, the Ashurkhana or "Royal House of Mourning", was built in 1595 by Muhammad Quli Qutb Shah, the fifth Qutb Shahi ruler *(see p667)*, as a congregation hall for Shias during the month of Muharram. It houses beautiful silver and gold *alams* (ceremonial standards) studded with precious stones, which are carried in procession during Muharram *(see p669)*, and are on display here through the year, on Thursdays.

Exquisite enamel-tiled mosaics adorn the central niche and the western wall, in glowing yellow, orange and turquoise. The outer hall with wooden colonnades was added later.

🛕 Charminar
See pp662–3.

🕌 Mecca Masjid
See pp662–3.

Splendid 17th-century tiled mosaics in the Badshahi Ashurkhana

VISITORS' CHECKLIST

Ranga Reddy district. 688 km (428 miles) N of Chennai. 🚶 3,449,900. ✈ 16 km (10 miles) N of city centre, then bus or taxi. 🚉 🚌 🛈 AP Tourism, (0930) 339 9247. ◯ daily. 🎉 Muharram (Mar/Apr), Mrigasira (Jun).

🛕 Falaknuma Palace
Near Naya Pul. 📞 (040) 444 0104.
The most opulent of the Nizams' many palaces, Falaknuma Palace was built in 1872. The front façade is in Palladian style, while the rear is a jumble of Indo-Saracenic domes and cupolas, added on to house the zenana. A huge amount of money was lavished on the interior, with tooled leather ceilings created by Florentine craftsmen, furniture and tapestries ordered from France, and marble imported from Italy.

The Nizams' most important guests, including King George V, stayed at Falaknuma, but after the death of the sixth Nizam here in 1911 (after a heavy bout of drinking), it was rarely used again. The palace is now being converted into a luxurious hotel.

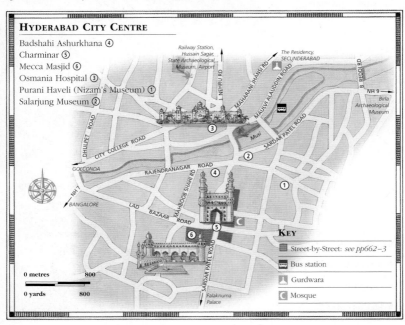

HYDERABAD CITY CENTRE

Badshahi Ashurkhana ④
Charminar ⑤
Mecca Masjid ⑥
Osmania Hospital ③
Purani Haveli (Nizam's Museum) ①
Salarjung Museum ②

Railway Station, Hussain Sagar, State Archaeological Museum, Airport

The Residency, SECUNDERABAD

Birla Archaeological Museum

NH 9

B. REDDI RD

MAULVI ALAUDDIN ROAD

MAHARANI JHANSI RD

SARDAR PATEL ROAD

Musi

DHULPET ROAD

CITY COLLEGE ROAD

GOLCONDA

RAJENDRANAGAR ROAD

NH 7

BANGALORE

LAD BAZAAR ROAD

MAHBOOB SHAHI RD

SARDAR PATEL ROAD

Falaknuma Palace

0 metres 800
0 yards 800

KEY

░ Street-by-Street: see pp662–3
🚌 Bus station
🛕 Gurdwara
🕌 Mosque

Hyderabad Street-by-Street: Charminar

Detail from arch, Charminar

I N THE HEART of the Old City, Charminar ("Four Towers") is Hyderabad's signature landmark. It was built in 1591 by King Muhammad Quli Qutb Shah of the Qutb Shahi dynasty *(see p666)* and, according to legend, marks the spot where he first saw his lover, the beautiful Hindu dancer Bhagmati. Another story says he built it as thanksgiving at the end of a deadly plague epidemic. Today, Charminar is the hub of a busy commercial area, where the grand mosques and palaces of the erstwhile rulers are surrounded by lively bazaars selling everything from pearls and perfumes to cabbages and computers.

Caps on sale on the pavement outside Mecca Masjid

Chowmahalla Palace

SHAH ALI DANDA ROAD

★ Mecca Masjid
Built between 1617 and 1694, this huge mosque has bricks from Mecca embedded in its central arch. Several Nizams are buried here.

Unani Hospital
was built by the last Nizam in the 1920s for the practice of traditional Graeco-Arab medicine.

```
0 metres        50
0 yards         50
```

KEY

– – – – – Suggested route

MAHAL ROAD

SARDAR

Silver-leaf is beaten into wafer-thin sheets in the shops in this street, and used to decorate sweets.

STAR SIGHTS
★ Mecca Masjid
★ Charminar
★ Lad Bazaar

★ Charminar
Grand arches frame Charminar's four sides. On the top floor is the city's oldest mosque. The minarets soar to 54 m (177 ft).

★ Lad Bazaar
Bangles, tinsel, embroidery, brocade turbans for bridegrooms, henna, herbal potions, and everything else needed for a bride's trousseau, are sold in this colourful bazaar.

Attar Shop
Perfume oils, sold in tiny bottles, include a local speciality called gil, *which captures the scent of wet earth after the first rainfall of a scorching summer.*

Charminar Kamaan served as the entrance to the royal mosque inside Charminar. Nearby are shops selling pearls.

Sher-e-dil Kamaan leads to shops selling gorgeous brocades and antique silk saris.

Machhli Kamaan
This is one of four ceremonial arches, built in 1594, around an open area where parades were held. It is carved with the auspicious fish symbol denoting prosperity.

GULZAR HAUZ ROAD

MITTI KA SHER ROAD

PANJERSHAH ROAD

PATTHERGATTI ROAD

Naya Pul

Jami Masjid
This simple whitewashed mosque, built in 1597, is the second oldest in Hyderabad.

Exploring Hyderabad & Secunderabad

BY THE 19TH CENTURY, Hyderabad had begun to
expand beyond the crowded confines of the old
quarter, clustered on both banks of the Musi river.
New palaces, and the British military cantonment of
Secunderabad, were now built on the city's outskirts.

🏛 Birla Archaeological Museum

Off Vijayawada Highway, Malakpet.
📞 *(040) 406 8204.* 🕐 *Mon–Sat.*
⬤ *public hols.* 🚫

Located in the 19th-century
hunting lodge of the sixth
Nizam, Asmangarh Palace is
the Birla Archaeological
Museum. Its exhibits include
sculptures and metal artifacts
found at excavation sites in
Andhra Pradesh, among them
some beautiful bronzes of
Shiva and Vishnu.

A short distance to the
south is an obelisk which
marks the Tomb of Michel
Raymond. A French mer-
cenary who fought in the
Nizam's army from 1785 till
his death in 1798, Raymond
became a local hero, revered
by both Muslims and Hindus.

🏛 The Residency

Koti. 🕐 *Mon–Sat.*
This elegant Palladian mansion, now the University
College for Women, was built
in 1805 by the third Nizam as a
gift for the British Resident at
his court, James Kirkpatrick. It
was decorated in style, with a
painted ceiling, and mirrors
and chandeliers from Brighton
Pavilion in England. The pediment above the portico still
bears the East India Company's
lion-and-unicorn coat of arms.

In the grounds is a small
replica of the main building,
which Kirkpatrick built for his
aristocratic Hyderabadi wife,
Khairunissa Begum – a liaison
that created a great scandal at
the time. There is a small
British cemetery in a corner
of the grounds.

🏛 State Archaeological Museum

Assembly Rd, N of Railway Station.
📞 *(040) 23 4260.* 🕐 *Tue–Sun.*
⬤ *2nd Sat, public hols.* 📷
Two large Norman-style gateways mark the entrance to
the Nampally Public Gardens,
which contain the State

Archaeological Museum. It
has a large collection of
Buddhist art, some fine Chola
bronzes, Roman coins, and
even an Egyptian mummy.
There are also replicas of
murals and sculptures from
the Ajanta and Ellora caves
(see pp476–81). Nearby is the
State Legislative Assembly
(built in 1913), a domed
complex modelled on a
Rajasthani palace.

**Hussain Sagar, with a gigantic
statue of the Buddha**

🛶 Hussain Sagar

This huge lake, created in the
17th century, lies off Mahatma
Gandhi Road, which bisects
Hyderabad and Secunderabad.
The 3-km (2-mile) stretch of
road along its southern
boundary is Hyderabad's most
popular promenade; it is lined
with statues of eminent figures
from Andhra Pradesh's

history. At the centre of the
lake is a rock, on which
stands a 17-m (56-ft) high
monolithic statue of the
Buddha, weighing 350 tonnes.
Completed in 1986, it sank to
the bottom of the lake when
the ferry carrying it capsized.
It was finally salvaged (intact)
seven years later and installed
on the rock in 1994.

🏛 Secunderabad

Northeast of Hussain Sagar
along the Tank Bund Road,
Secunderabad was established
in 1806 as a cantonment to
house British troops. It has
since grown into a teeming
city which is an extension of
Hyderabad. At its centre is the
Parade Ground, overlooked
by **St Andrew's Church** and
the imposing colonial-style
Secunderabad Club. The
Neo-Gothic **Holy Trinity
Church** (built in 1848) is 6 km
(4 miles) north of the Parade
Ground, and has beautiful
stained-glass windows, elegant
steeples on its square tower
and a British cemetery.

The walled compound of
the **Paigah Palaces**, where
the Hyderabadi aristocracy
lived, is 2 km (1.3 miles) west
of the Parade Ground, opposite Begumpet Airport. The
most imposing palace is Vicar
Manzil, built by the leading
nobleman at the sixth Nizam's
court, Sir Vicar-ul-Umra; he
had built the magnificent
Falaknuma Palace *(see p661)*
for himself but had to move
out when the Nizam decided
to acquire it. At its entrance is
the **Spanish Mosque** (built in
1906), with Moorish arches
and octagonal spires.

The Spanish Mosque at the entrance of Vicar Manzil, Secunderabad

Hyderabadi Culture

Golden lunch box

SULTAN MUHAMMAD Quli Qutb Shah, who founded Hyderabad in 1591, was an enlightened ruler, and a poet, scholar and patron of the arts. His kingdom was also a flourishing centre of trade, especially in pearls, diamonds and horses. At his court and in his bazaars, Hyderabadis rubbed shoulders with traders, scholars and artisans from different lands. This cosmopolitan tradition, and the culture of courtly elegance and etiquette, continued with the next dynasty – that of the Asaf Jahi Nizams, which ruled from 1724 until 1947. As a result, Hyderabad has a uniquely composite culture, a mélange of Hindu and Muslim customs, mingled with Arab, Persian and Turkish influences, evident in its language, food, manners and arts.

Bidriware *uses a technique introduced by Persians in the 16th century, by which black gunmetal is intricately inlaid with silver in floral and geometric patterns.*

Hyderabad's distinctive cuisine *includes dishes of Persian and Turkish origin such as* haleem *(minced meat cooked with wheat) and* lukmi *(puff pastry squares filled with meat).*

Falaknuma Palace, *photographed towards the end of the 19th century by the court photographer Lala Deen Dayal, captures the opulence of the Nizam of Hyderabad's lifestyle.*

The Nizams' jewels *were legendary, and included fabulous pieces such as this 19th-century turban ornament, set with rubies from Burma and diamonds from their mines at Golconda (see p666).*

Muharram *(see p669) is observed by processions of Shia Muslims carrying decorated* tazias *through the city. Hyderabad's Shia population is mostly descended from Persians who settled here several generations ago.*

Golconda miniatures *often depict the city's sophisticated, cosmopolitan culture. This 18th-century painting shows merchants from many lands calling on a lady.*

Golconda ❷

Sprawling across a boulder-strewn
plateau, Golconda ("Shepherd's Hill")
Fort was the citadel of the Qutb Shahi
dynasty, which ruled the Hyderabad
region from 1507 to 1687. The earlier
12th-century mud fort that stood here
was transformed between 1518 and
1580 into a splendid fortified city of

**Detail of a carving,
Bala Hisar gate wall**

grand palaces, mosques and gardens by successive
Qutb Shahi rulers. Golconda Fort was also famous for
its great hoard of diamonds, mined nearby, which
included the celebrated Kohinoor diamond, now part
of the British Crown jewels. The colossal ruins of
Golconda cover an area of 40 sq km (15 sq miles).

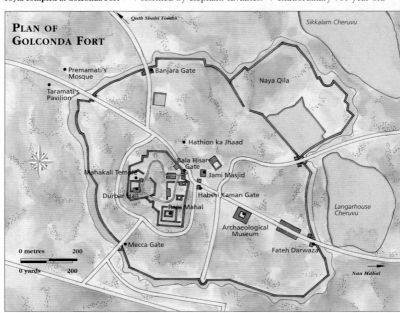

**Bala Hisar Gate, entrance to the
royal complex at Golconda Fort**

⋂ Golconda Fort

This great fortress is protected
by three formidable lines of
defence. The first, an outer
fortification made of enormous
blocks of granite, encircles the
citadel and its entire township.
The middle wall surrounds the
base of the hill, while the
innermost one follows the
contours of the highest ridge.
Visitors enter through the
Fateh Darwaza ("Victory
Gate"), on the east side, which
has a Hindu deity carved
above its arch. Huge iron
spikes are studded into the
gate to prevent it from being
stormed by elephant cavalries.

From the Fateh Darwaza, the
road curves past the **Archaeological Museum** (the old
Treasury), and through the
bazaar, once a famous centre
for cutting and polishing diamonds. Beyond are the two
massive arches of the **Habshi
Kaman Gate**, with rooms on
top. These used to house a
drummers' gallery and the
sultans' Abyssinian guards.
This gate leads to the middle
fortification wall.

To its north is the austere,
domed **Jami Masjid**, built in
1518 by Sultan Quli Qutb
Shah, the founder of the
dynasty; he was murdered
here while at prayer by his
son Jamshed in 1543. Beyond
is the ceremonial arch, the
Bala Hisar Gate, decorated
with various Hindu motifs,
including *yalis* (fantastic
leonine beasts). This is the
entrance to the inner citadel,
known as the **Bala Hisar
Complex**, where the royal
palaces, assembly halls, workshops and an armoury are
located. North of the Bala
Hisar is a walled enclosure,
begun in 1652, and planned
as an extension to the inner
fort. Within it is **Hathion ka
Jhaad** ("Elephant Tree"), an
extraordinary 700-year-old

PLAN OF GOLCONDA FORT

- Qutb Shahi Tombs
- Sikkalam Cheruvu
- Premamati's Mosque
- Banjara Gate
- Naya Qila
- Taramati's Pavilion
- Hathion ka Jhaad
- Mahakali Temple
- Bala Hisar Gate
- Jami Masjid
- Durbar Hall
- Habshi Kaman Gate
- Rani Mahal
- Langarhouse Cheruvu
- Archaeological Museum
- Mecca Gate
- Fateh Darwaza
- Nau Mahal

0 metres 200
0 yards 200

The royal bath near Rani Mahal, Golconda Fort

Baobab tree (*Adansonia digitata*), said to have been brought to Golconda by the sultans' Abyssinian guards.

The large-domed **Grand Portico** behind the Bala Hisar Gate is a good place to test the remarkable acoustics that were an important feature of the fort's defences. A soft handclap here can be heard in the king's chambers at the summit of the hill.

West of the Grand Portico are the ruins of the Qutb Shahi palaces. The most impressive of these is the **Rani Mahal**, a vaulted hall on a raised terrace, decorated with lovely floral arabesques. Hollows in these carvings were once inlaid with Golconda's famous diamonds and other precious stones. To the west of the Rani Mahal, a steep flight of 200 steps winds past royal baths, granaries, treasuries, water tanks and the remains of gardens, to the summit of the hill. Traces of the elaborate water supply system which carried water to the top of the citadel are visible along the route.

Just below the summit is a graceful mosque built by Sultan Ibrahim Qutb Shah, the third sultan, and the ancient Hindu **Mahakali Temple**, built into a cave.

At the summit of the hill is the three-storeyed **Durbar Hall** ("Throne Room"), with a rooftop pavilion. From here there are wonderful views of the entire fort and its surroundings, which include two pretty structures on hillocks – **Taramati's Pavilion** and **Premamati's Mosque**. These

Ceiling decoration, Bala Hisar Gate

are named after the two dancers who were royal favourites, and said to be so lightfooted that they could dance all the way from the pavilion to the Bala Hisar on a tightrope.

Standing outside the fort, east of the Fateh Darwaza, is the **Nau Mahal** ("Nine Palaces"), where the Nizams of Hyderabad held court whenever they came to Golconda.

Qutb Shahi Tombs

1 km (0.6 miles) NW of Golconda Fort.

This royal necropolis, where seven of the nine Qutb Shahi rulers are buried, is laid out in gardens with water channels, pools and tree-lined pathways. The tombs, built by each king in his lifetime, display a distinct and eclectic architectural style – they have large onion domes, Persian arches, Turkish columns and Hindu brackets and motifs.

Built of grey granite and plaster, each tomb's dome is set on a petalled base, with a richly ornamented gallery and small minarets surrounding it. The **Tomb of Muhammad Quli Qutb Shah**, the founder of the city of Hyderabad, is the most impressive. It is surrounded by a spacious terrace, where poetry and music festivals and Hyderabadi food festivals are occasionally held. Traces of brilliant turquoise and green enamelled tiles, which once

The elegant tomb of Muhammad Quli Qutb Shah, Golconda

covered the façades of all the tombs, still remain. Other remarkable monuments are the **Tomb of Queen Hayat Baksh Begum**, the wife of Mohammed Quli Qutb Shah, and the mosque behind it (both mid-17th century), decorated with exquisite floral designs and calligraphy.

At the centre of the complex is the simple but beautifully proportioned **Royal Mortuary Bath**. The bodies of the deceased kings were ritually bathed before burial on the inlaid, 12-sided platform; the surrounding 12 water tanks symbolize the 12 Shia Imams.

A panoramic view of Golconda Fort

Pochampalli ❸

Nalgonda district. 50 km (31 miles)
E of Hyderabad. 🚌 🚆 *daily.*

A NDHRA PRADESH'S ikat belt,
where intricate tie-and-dye
textiles *(see p317)* are woven,
borders Hyderabad.
Pochampalli, the name by
which most of the state's ikat
fabric is known, is the largest
centre for this craft. The technique in its present form was
first introduced in the 19th
century in Chirala, in Guntur
district, from where the fabric
was exported to Africa.

Pochampalli's main street is
lined with busy workshops
where the various stages of
production take place. Ikat
weavers first tie the yarn
according to the pattern and
then dye them in great vats. A
special oil-based technique is
used to restrict the dye to
those parts of the yarn that
need to be coloured. The
dyed yarn is then dried in the
sun and finally woven on
large hand-operated looms, to
produce a cloth called *telia
rumal (see p413).* The state
cooperative warehouses, as
well as several shops, sell a
wide range of beautiful silk
saris and fabrics.

ENVIRONS: The neighbouring
villages of **Koyalgudem** and
Choutuppal produce mainly
cotton ikat fabrics. **Narayan-
pur**, another major weaving
centre, is about 20 km (16
miles) further down the
Vijaywada Highway.

**Khush Mahal, the audience hall
at Warangal Fort**

Warangal ❹

West Godavari district. 140 km (87
miles) SW of Hyderabad. 🚆 🚌 🛈
Tourist Office, Kazipet, (08712) 76 201.

A MAJOR *dhurrie*-weaving
centre today, Warangal
was described by the 13th-
century Venetian traveller,
Marco Polo, as one of the
principal cities of South India.
It was the capital of the Hindu
Kakatiya kings, who domi-
nated this region until the
beginning of the 14th century.

An ancient fort at the edge
of the modern town is all that
remains of this once grand
city. Built during the reign of
the Kakatiya queen Rudrama-
devi (r.1262–89), its striking
circular plan, with three concentric rings of walls, is still
intact. The outer two rings,
both of mud, define a circle
1.2 km (1 mile) in diameter.
The innermost ring is made

of stone, with four massive
gateways at the cardinal
points. At its geometric
centre, four ornate *toranas*
(gateways), marking the sacred
precinct, are the only remains
of a great Shiva temple that
once stood here. The *toranas*
themselves are remarkable for
their size and beauty.

A short distance to the west
is the **Khush Mahal**, an
audience hall that was built
by Muslim invaders in the
14th century. Massive angled
walls with slit windows define
a lofty interior with vaulted
arches, though the roof is
quite damaged. It is remarkably similar to the Hindola
Mahal in Mandu *(see p247).*

ENVIRONS: Hanamkonda,
the site of the first Kakatiya
capital before it moved to
Warangal, is 3 km (2 miles)
northwest of Warangal. A
magnificent thousand-pillared
temple here, dedicated to
Shiva, was erected in 1163 by
Rudradeva (r.1158–95), the
first great Kakatiya king.

This grey-green basalt
temple, known as the *trikuta*
or triple shrine, consists of a
trio of shrines dedicated to
Shiva, Vishnu and Surya. They
are connected to a *mandapa,*
now roofless, by a platform
with a magnificently polished
Nandi bull. The columns have
sharply cut, lathe-turned
shafts. A ceiling panel carved
with an image of Nataraja *(see
p566)* covers the central bay.
The temple's tranquil gardens
contain several small linga
shrines, and an ancient well.

The magnificent thousand-pillared temple at Hanamkonda, near Warangal

The 13th-century Ramappa Temple at Palampet

Palampet ❺

Palampet district. 70 km (44 miles) SW of Hyderabad.

THIS VILLAGE is dominated by the **Ramappa Temple**, the best preserved example of Kakatiya architecture. Dedicated to Shiva, it was built in 1234 by Recherla Rudra, a general of the ruler Ganapatideva (r.1199–1262). Like the temple at Hanamkonda, it too has a spacious *mandapa* with beautifully sculpted black basalt columns. This *mandapa*, cruciform in plan, also has porches with balcony seats on three sides. The eaves sheltering the peripheral

Carving, Ghanpur

columns are supported by angled struts, many of which are fashioned as three-dimensional maidens with graceful bodies in dancing poses. Other similar but smaller relief figures, as well as scenes from the epics, are seen in the central ceiling panel within the *mandapa*.

The exterior of the sanctuary, in contrast, is devoid of any carvings. The restrained ornamentation and simple modelling are typical of the elegance of Kakatiya art. A stone pavilion sheltering a Nandi, smaller in size than the one at Hanamkonda, but as exquisitely carved, stands in front of the temple.

South of the Ramappa Temple is **Ramappa Cheruvu**, a vast artificial lake created by Recherla Rudra, and surrounded by picturesque hills.

ENVIRONS: More Kakatiya temples can be seen at **Ghanpur**, a little village 13 km (8 miles) northwest of Palampet. The largest consists of a pair of Shiva shrines, both with *mandapas* and balcony seats. The main shrine has delightful female *dvarapalas* (door-keepers), dancing maidens and finely carved brackets. Other minor shrines dot the walled compound.

TRADITIONAL ANDHRA DHURRIES

Although lustrous silk and wool carpets from Persia and Turkey embellished the palaces of the Nizams of Hyderabad, Andhra Pradesh has long had a local tradition of carpet weaving in Warangal and Eluru. Commonly known as *dhurries*, the rugs are made in both cotton and wool, in a variety of designs and colours. The cotton *dhurries* from Warangal are usually woven into geometric patterns, while the woollen carpets of Eluru (314 km/195 miles southeast of Warangal) sport floral designs that hint at a Western

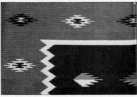

A *dhurrie* with geometric patterns

influence. The more expensive *shatranjis* (a chessboard-like pattern) are made with heavy cotton thread and produced on horizontal looms. The *kalamkari* craftsmen of Sri Kalahasti *(see p680)* make rugs in traditional designs on a jute base, using vegetable dyes.

FESTIVALS OF ANDHRA PRADESH

Ugadi *(Mar)*. Homes are spring-cleaned throughout the state and special food is prepared to celebrate the Telugu New Year.
Mrigasira *(Jun)*, Hyderabad. On this day a unique cure for asthma is administered to patients from all over India, who swallow live a small, freshwater fish called *maral*. Many sufferers claim miraculous cures.

Batkamma Festival, Warangal

Batkamma *(Sep/Oct)*, Warangal. This festival in honour of the goddess of wealth, Lakshmi, begins just before Dussehra and continues for nine days. Flowers are arranged over a turmeric representation of the goddess and carried on a bamboo tray to a lake or river, where the women dance in a circle around the floral offering before immersing it in the water.
Festival of Andhra Pradesh *(Nov)*, Hyderabad. This ten-day cultural festival marks the anniversary of Andhra Pradesh's statehood. The state's best musicians and dancers perform.
Muharram *(Mar/Apr)*, Hyderabad. The Shia Muslim community commemorates the martyrdom of the Prophet's grandson, Hussain, at the battle of Karbala, with 40 days of mourning. On the final day, gem-studded *alams* and colourful *tazias* (replicas of his tomb) are carried in procession through the Old City.

A view of the Visakhapatnam harbour on the Bay of Bengal

Visakhapatnam ❻

Visakhapatnam district. 350 km (218 miles) N of Vijayawada. ⚑ 969,600. ✈ 12 km (7 miles) W of town centre, then bus or taxi. 🚆 🚌 ℹ Vuda Complex, Siripuram, (0891) 54 6446. 🛑 daily.

THE SECOND BUSIEST port in India after Mumbai, Visakhapatnam, also known as Vizag, is rapidly becoming the largest shipyard in the country. It is an important industrial town and naval base as well. The town makes a convenient point from which to visit some of the beautiful beaches along the Bay of Bengal and the many picturesque temple towns of the northern coastal districts of Andhra Pradesh.

Named after Visakha, the Hindu God of Valour, Visakhapatnam was once part of the Mauryan emperor Ashoka's vast empire *(see p42)*. Later, it was ruled by the Andhra kings of Vengi, and other South Indian dynasties, including the Pallavas, Cholas and Gangas. In the 15th century, it became part of the Vijayanagar Empire *(see pp530–31)*. It finally came into British hands in the 17th century, after which it was developed into a major port.

Looming above the port is a hilly ridge with three crests, each with a religious shrine. On the southernmost one, **Venkateshvara Konda**, is a temple dedicated to Balaji (Krishna); in the middle is **Ross Hill**, with a mid-19th-century church; the third,

Dargah Konda, has a shrine dedicated to a Muslim saint, Ishaque Madina.

Along the southern coastline is **Dolphin's Nose**, a 358-m (1,175-ft) long rocky outcrop that rises 175 m (574 ft) above the sea. On it stands a lighthouse with a beam that can be seen 64 km (40 miles) out at sea. Vestiges of the city's colonial past are visible here in an old Protestant church, a fort, barracks and an arsenal, all dating to the 18th century.

Idyllic beaches, set on the fringes of the Eastern Ghats and bounded by forested hills and rocky cliffs, include the **Ramakrishna Mission Beach**, now being developed as a tourist resort by Andhra Pradesh Tourism, **Rishikonda Beach** and **Lawson's Bay**.

Towards the north of the town, beyond Lawson's Bay, is **Kailasagiri**, a forested hill which has several lookout

points for a panoramic view of the city and harbour. The twin town of **Waltair**, once a health resort for British officers, is north of the bay. Andhra University, one of the largest campuses in the state, is also situated here, along with a number of pretty 19th-century churches.

ENVIRONS: Simhachalam, the "Lion's Hill" Temple, dedicated to Lord Varaha Narasimha, an incarnation of Vishnu *(see p679)*, stands at the summit of the thickly forested Ratnagiri Hill, 16 km (10 miles) north-west of Visakhapatnam. A flight of steps leads to the northern gateway, an elaborately decorated *gopura* that is the main entrance to the temple. Inside the compound is a tall *dvajasthambha* (flagpole). Similar in style to Konark's Sun Temple *(see pp310–11)*, the temple was constructed in the 9th or 10th century, and was extensively rebuilt in the 13th century. It is believed that the presiding deity was originally Shiva, but he was replaced by this incarnation of Vishnu after the reformer-saint, Ramanuja *(see p522)*, visited the site in the 11th century.

Bheemunipatnam is a 24-km (15-mile) drive north from Visakhapatnam, along one of the longest stretches of beach road in the country. This quiet fishing village, situated at the mouth of the Gosthani river, was a Dutch settlement in the early 17th century.

Dutch heraldry, Bheemunipatnam

Obelisk-shaped Dutch tombs at Bheemunipatnam

Bimlipatam, as it was then known (locally referred to as Bhimli), was the site of Maratha attacks and Anglo-Dutch wars in the 17th and 18th centuries. Its Dutch legacy can be seen in some of the old colonnaded houses, the ruined fort, and the Dutch cemetery, which has unusual, obelisk-shaped tombstones.

A fascinating stalactite formation inside the Borra Caves

Borra Caves ❼

Visakhapatnam district. 100 km (62 miles) N of Visakhapatnam. 🚌
⭕ daily. 📷

CLOSE TO the northern border of Visakhapatnam district are these magnificent limestone caves, discovered in 1807 by William King of the the Geological Survey of India. The extensive underground chambers, lined by stalactites and stalagmites, are now being developed by the state tourism department as a major attraction for visitors. Some smaller stalagmites are worshipped as lingas, with Nandi bulls placed in front of them. The local people believe that the water trickling from the roof of the caves is from a mountain spring which is the source of the Gosthani river.

ENVIRONS: About 22 km (14 miles) northeast of Borra is the **Araku Valley**, home of several tribal communities, the state's original inhabitants. The road to Araku goes past forests and coffee plantations, and the valley, with its

Tribal women from Araku Valley

woods, waterfalls and bracing climate, offers pleasant walks.

Ramatirtham ❽

Visakhapatnam district. 72 km (45 miles) NE of Visakhapatnam. 🚌

RUINS FROM the Ikshvaku period (3rd to 4th centuries AD), when Buddhism flourished in this area, can be seen at Ramatirtham. Just outside the village is a group of structures on a hill known as Gurubhaktakonda ("Hill of the Devoted Disciple"). On a narrow rocky ledge about 165 m (541 ft) above the surrounding plains are the ruins of a stupa, monasteries, and prayer halls enclosing smaller stupas. Close by, on another hill called Durgakonda, is a similar set of ruins, along with carvings of Jain *tirthankaras* (*see p396*) that date from the 8th and 9th centuries.

Srikakulam District ❾

108 km (67 miles) N from Visakhapatnam to Srikakulam. 🚌

THE HEADQUARTERS of Andhra Pradesh's northernmost district, Srikakulam is located on the outskirts of the town, at **Arasavalli**, is a sun temple, ingeniously constructed at such an angle that the sun's rays fall directly on the deity's feet twice a year. The **Srikurma-natha Temple** at Srikurman, 13 km (8 miles) east of Srika-kulam, is dedicated to Kurma, the tortoise incarnation of Vishnu. It was built by the Chalukya kings in the 10th century but was substantially rebuilt by the Cholas in the 12th and 13th centuries. The colonnade around the main shrine has 19th century murals of Krishna and Vishnu.

Mukhalingam, 46 km (29 miles) north of Srikakulam, was the first capital of the Eastern Ganga kings, before they moved to Orissa (*see p44*). The temples here date to their reign, between the 9th and 13th centuries. The best preserved is the 9th-century Madhukeshvara Temple, with magnificent sculptures of Shiva and friezes of scenes from the Krishna legend. The 10th-century Someshvara Temple, at the entrance to the town, has beautiful statues of river goddesses and other deities, flanking the main doorway.

Mural showing Krishna surrounded by *gopis*, at Srikurmanatha Temple in Srikakulam district

Ripening fields of paddy with the Eastern Ghats in the background, near Rajahmundry

East Godavari District ❿

380 km (236 miles) E from Hyderabad to Rajahmundry. 🚃 Rajahmundry. 🚌

THE GODAVARI, one of South India's most sacred rivers, swells to a wide torrent (at places 6 km/4 miles across), just north of **Rajahmundry** town. Lush paddy fields and sugarcane plantations characterize the countryside.

Rajahmundry, the largest town in East Godavari district, is best known for the many Chalukya temples in its vicinity, and for the 2,743-m (8,999 -ft) long bridge that spans the river. The lookout points on **Dowleshvaram Dam** (built 1848–52), 10 km (6 miles) downstream, offer spectacular views of the river. Every 12 years, the Dakshina Pushkaram festival – the Kumbh Mela (see p211) of the South – takes place here.

Peddapuram, famous for its fine handwoven silk and cotton, is 30 km (19 miles) northeast of Rajahmundry, on the road to Visakhapatnam.

Annavaram, 70 km (44 miles) to the northeast of Rajahmundry, is the site of the Satyanarayana Temple, on Ratnagiri Hill, renowned for its 4-m (13 ft)-high statue of the Hindu Trinity, and its ancient sundial.

The **Godavari Gorge** begins 80 km (50 miles) north of Rajahmundry. A drive or boat ride along the Gorge, which cuts through the hilly Eastern Ghats, offers views of spectacular scenery, with a series of beautiful lakes that many visitors have found reminiscent of Italy and Scotland.

Ryali, 24 km (15 miles) south of Rajahmundry, has a Chalukya temple dedicated to Vishnu. It houses a stone image of the Goddess Ganga (see p163), from which flows a continuous trickle of water.

Draksharamam, 40 km (25 miles) southeast of Rajahmundry, is famed for its 10th-century Bhimesvara Temple, which combines the Chalukya and Chola styles of architecture, and houses a 5-m (16-ft) high linga. The Godavari is said to have been split into seven streams by the Saptarishis (seven great sages) of Hindu mythology and three of these streams are believed to have gone underground here. Close to the town is an old Dutch cemetery, locally known as Ollandu Dibba ("Holland Mound"), with gravestones dated between 1675 and 1728, some with very elaborate designs.

Antarvedi, on the banks of the Vashishta river, a branch of the Godavari, is 112 km (70 miles) south of Rajahmundry. It is best reached by boat from Narsapur on the south bank. The Lakshminarayana Temple (built in 1823), with its brightly painted tower stands on the river bank, and is usually thronged with pilgrims who come for a dip in the holy river.

Machilipatnam ⓫

Krishna district. 340 km (211 miles) E of Hyderabad. 🚃 🚌 🚆 daily.

ONE OF THE first European settlements on India's eastern coast, Machilipatnam ("City of Fish") was a thriving port and textile centre in the 17th and 18th centuries. It was also the headquarters of the English East India Company on the Coromandel Coast. The French and the Dutch briefly established themselves here as well. The Dutch cemetery, with its ornate tombstones, are all that remain from that period.

Machilipatnam was hit by a giant tidal wave in 1864, which drowned more than 30,000 people. It was caused by a volcanic eruption at Mount Krakatoa, 5,000 km (3,107 miles) away. After that it lost its importance as a port, but it remains famous for its *kalamkari* textiles (see p680).

A *kalamkari* blockprinter at work in Machilipatnam

Trade Textiles: Tree of Life

BETWEEN THE 17th and 18th centuries, the Coromandel Coast, with Machilipatnam as its trade centre and port, was one of the main producers and exporters of cotton textiles to Western Europe. At first just items of barter, they soon became fashionable in Europe, increasing the demand for the region's dye-painted cotton

Detail of flowers and foliage

kalamkari (see p680) fabric, known in Europe as chintz. Special designs were commissioned, among them the Tree of Life, which absorbed techniques and aesthetics from India, Persia, China and Europe. Valued for their richness of colour and design, they were widely used as hangings and spreads in European homes.

TREE OF LIFE

The Tree of Life was a very popular motif in textiles from the Coromandel Coast. Based on ancient nature myths that deified plants and trees, and inspired largely by Persian miniatures, its central flowering tree, rising from a rocky mound, linked earth to heaven and symbolized creation.

Birds, *real and mythical, inhabit the thickly foliated upper branches of the tree. Standing on the mound are two stylized peacocks holding snakes in their beaks.*

Aquatic creatures, *such as fish and tortoise, are depicted to show marine life in the holy waters below the Sacred Mound. Shades of painted indigo have been used to create the effect of rippling waves and flowing water.*

A bamboo thicket, *composed as a single Tree of Life, rises from the Sacred Mound. The painted and printed flowers and feathery leaves suggest nature's exuberance.*

A view of the Prakasam Barrage, built over the Krishna river at Vijayawada

Vijayawada **⑫**

Krishna district. 267 km (166 miles)
SE of Hyderabad. 🚂 825,400. ☐
🚌 ℹ AP Tourism, Hotel Krishnaveni,
(0866) 42 6382. 🚩 daily.

THE THIRD LARGEST CITY in the
state, Vijayawada is a busy
commercial town with one of
the largest railway junctions in
the country. In a picturesque
spot on the northern bank of
the Krishna river, it is bounded on three sides by the
Indrakiladri Hills. The area
around the river banks
is a pleasant contrast to the
noisy, crowded town.
   Within the city limits, on
a low hill to the east, is the
Kanakadurga Temple,
dedicated to the goddess
Lakshmi. The **Victoria
Jubilee Museum**, on Bunder
Road, houses a fine collection
of Buddhist and Hindu relics
from the 2nd and 3rd centuries. Especially impressive are
the white limestone Standing
Buddha from the nearby
Buddhist site of Alluru (3rd
or 4th century), and the
powerful depiction of Durga
slaying the buffalo demon
Mahisa (2nd century).
   On the outskirts of town is
the 1-km (0.6-mile) long
Prakasam Barrage, first built
in 1855 and extensively
reconstructed in 1955. It
irrigates nearly 1.2 million ha
(3 million acres) of land,
turning the Krishna Delta into
the richest granary in Andhra
Pradesh. **Bhavani Island**, a

scenic picnic spot, is just
upstream, reached by launch
from the river bank.

🏛 **Victoria Jubilee Museum**
◯ Sat–Thu. 📷 extra charges.

ENVIRONS: Mogalrajapuram,
3 km (2 miles) east of Vijayawada, and **Undavalli**, 4 km
(2.5 miles) to the south, on
the other side of the river, are
famous for their rock-cut
temples (5th–7th centuries).
   Mangalgiri, 12 km (7 miles)
south of Vijayawada, is a textile village, specializing in fine
cotton saris and striped and
checked fabrics. It also has
the impressive 14th-century
Lakshmi Narasimha Temple
complex, with a small Garuda
shrine in front of it.

Kondapalli **⑬**

Krishna district. 14 km (9 miles) W of
Vijayawada. 🚌

THIS PRETTY VILLAGE, famous
for its painted wooden
toys, is dominated by the 8th-
century Hill Fort built by the
Eastern Chalukya dynasty.
Encircled by ramparts and
towers, the fort was an important stronghold in the Krishna
Valley under the Qutb Shahis
of Hyderabad (see p666), in
the 16th century. At the crest
of the hill, a steep climb up,
is the ruined Tanisha Mahal
palace. The path descends
past a deep tank, the granary
and the armoury, to the
Golconda Gate, which faces
northwest towards Hyderabad.

KONDAPALLI TOYS

The craft of toy-making has been passed down for
many generations in Kondapalli. In the hands of
the deft artisans, the light yet strong and flexible
poniki wood is fashioned into
distinctive figures of gods and
goddesses, fruits and vegetables, which adorn many
Andhra homes during festivals.
Each part of the toy is
whittled into shape, and
then glued together
using a special tamarind-
seed glue. The piece
is then covered with
lime glue, which gives it a smooth
finish. It is allowed to dry before
being brightly painted in vivid
blues, greens, reds and yellows,
with touches of black.

**Lord
Krishna**

**A toy being painted in
bright colours**

The Maha Chaitya at Amravati, now only a low earthen mound

Amravati ⑭

Guntur district. 30 km (19 miles) W of Vijayawada. 🚌 from Guntur. 🚉 from Hotel Krishnaveni, Vijayawada. 🚗 run by AP Tourism, Vijayawada. ℹ️ Punnami Hotel, (08645) 55 332.

RENOWNED FOR ITS **Maha Chaitya**, or "Great Stupa", Amravati was once the most impressive of the many Buddhist religious settlements along the Krishna Valley. Today, nothing remains of this stupa except a low earthen mound, but in its day it was reputed to be the largest and most elaborate stupa in South India. It was built by the Satavahanas, the great Andhra dynasty, in the 3rd and 2nd centuries BC (see p43).

The Maha Chaitya was enlarged several times by the Ikshvaku kings, who succeeded the Satavahanas, reaching its final form between the 3rd and 4th centuries AD. Clad in the local white limestone, the Maha Chaitya was an earthen hemispherical mound about 45 m (148 ft) in diameter and more than 30 m (98 ft) in height, including its supporting drum and capping finial. It was surrounded by a 6-m (20-ft) high railing with posts and cross pieces, and lofty entrance gateways at the cardinal points, all exuberantly carved.

In the 5th century, when South India saw a revival of Hinduism, the stupa was

Amravati limestone carving with a scene from the Jataka Tales

abandoned, and remained so until a British official, Colonel Colin Mackenzie, began excavating the site in 1796. Unfortunately, by the time a thorough investigation of the ruins began in the mid-19th century, most of the limestone portions had been pillaged, many fine pieces having been shipped to Britain.

Nevertheless, a great deal of fine sculpture remains at the site, and is on display at the **Archaeological Museum**, next to the Maha Chaitya. Unlike the stupa at Sanchi (see pp244–5), where the Buddha is represented through symbols such as the Bodhi Tree or footprints, the Amravati sculptures show him in human form. The museum's display includes large Standing Buddha images, some more than 2 m (7 ft) high, whose natural poses and elegantly fluted robes suggest the influence of late Roman classical art. The second gallery has a remarkable life-sized ceremonial bull,

reconstructed from fragments discovered in 1980. A part of the stupa's railing, decorated with scenes from the Buddha's life, is reconstructed in the courtyard. Other exhibits include an instructive model of the original monument and superb sculptures of the Bodhi Tree, under which the Buddha is said to have meditated.

🏛 Archaeological Museum
🕐 Sat–Thu. 📷 extra charges.

ENVIRONS: Overlooking the Krishna river, just north of the museum, is the **Amareshvara Temple**. Built during the 10th and 11th centuries, it was renovated in the 18th century by a local chief whose statue stands in the outer hall. The sanctuary and the open-columned hall are in a walled compound. A basement, reached by a flight of stairs, is believed to conceal the remains of a stupa, suggested by the pillar-shaped linga in the sanctuary, which was probably part of the stupa dome.

Ceremonial bull, Amravati Museum

THE AMRAVATI SCULPTURES

The surviving limestone carvings from the Maha Chaitya are now divided between the Archaeological Museum at Amravati, the Government Museum in Chennai (see p565) and the British Museum in London. These reliefs testify to the vitality of early Buddhist art traditions in South India. Posts and railings show ornate lotus medallions, friezes of garlands carried by dwarfs, and Jataka Tales (see p480) illustrated with vivid scenes of crowds, horse riders and courtiers. Drum panels are adorned with pots filled with lotuses, model stupas with serpents wrapped around the drums, and flying celestials above the umbrella-like finials.

Limestone carving, Amravati Museum

Nagarjunakonda ⑮

Guntur district. 175 km (109 miles) W
of Vijayawada. 🚉 *Macherla, 22 km
(14 miles) SE of site, then bus to
Vijayapuri.* 🚌 🚉 *daily from
Vijayapuri, except Fri.* 🛈 *Project
House, Hill Colony, (08680) 76 333.*
🎫 *from Hyderabad.*

View of the hemispherical stupa, Bodhishri Chaitya, Nagarjunakonda

Nagarjunakonda or "Nagarjuna's Hill", on the banks of the Krishna river, was named after Nagarjuna Acharya, the 2nd-century Buddhist theologian and founder of an influential school of philosophy. Once a sophisticated Buddhist settlement, with large monasteries and stupas, wide roads and public baths, it was established in the 3rd and 4th centuries, when the area flourished under the rule of the powerful Ikshvaku kings.

Thereafter, Nagarjunakonda was ruled by a succession of dynasties, culminating with the Vijayanagar rulers, who built a fort around the Buddhist ruins. When the Vijayanagar Empire declined, the area was abandoned. It was rediscovered only between 1954 and 1961.

In the early 1960s, when the huge Nagarjuna Sagar Dam was being constructed across the Krishna, a number of these rediscovered ancient Buddhist settlements were threatened with submersion. However, the Archaeological Survey of India salvaged and reconstructed many of them, brick by brick, on top of the hill where the citadel once used to stand.

Today, most of the hill, and the secluded valley in which these settlements once stood, have been submerged by the waters of the Nagarjuna Sagar lake. Only the top of the hill, where the rescued remains have been reassembled, juts out like an island. The island is accessible by launches, which leave regularly from the small village of Vijayapuri, on the banks of the lake.

On the island, the path from the jetty leads first to the **Simha Vihara 4**. This comprises a stupa built on a high platform with a pair of *chaitya grihas* (prayer halls) adjoining it. While one of the *chaitya grihas* houses a second stupa, the other enshrines a monumental sculpture of the Standing Buddha. The **Bodhishri Chaitya**, opposite it, has a raised stupa contained within a semi-circular-ended brick structure. To its west is the **Maha Chaitya** stupa which, with a

**Detail of a carving,
Nagarjunakonda**

diameter of 27.5 m (90 ft), was one of the largest at Nagarjunakonda. Its internal rubble walls radiate outwards like the spokes of a wheel, and are filled with earth. Just ahead of it is the **Swastika Chaitya**, named after the Indian swastika emblem formed by its rubble walls.

Near the citadel walls is a stone megalith, some 2,000 years old. It conceals a simple burial chamber that once contained four skulls. To its east is the **Archaeological Museum**, which houses superb Buddhist sculptures from the ruins of Nagarjunakonda. They include limestone reliefs and panels carved with seated Buddhas, flying celestial beings and miniature replicas of stupas. Friezes from the railings which surrounded the stupas depict scenes from the Buddha's life. Among the free-standing sculptures are dignified Buddha figures dressed in elegant robes.

🏛 **Archaeological Museum**
🕐 *Sat–Thu.* 📷 🎫

ENVIRONS: More structures from the Ikshvaku period are reassembled at a site 15 km (9 miles) south of Vijayapuri. These include a Stadium, with tiered galleries around a central court, possibly used for musical and theatrical performances and sporting events. The adjacent Monastic Complex has shrines and *chaitya grihas* as well as a refectory, store and baths.

A giant-sized statue of the Standing Buddha in Nagarjunakonda

Srisailam & Krishna Gorge 16

Guntur district. 237 km (147 miles) W of Vijayawada. 🚉 *Macherla, 13 km (8 miles) NE of town centre, then jeep, book in advance.* 🚌 🚏 *from Nagarjuna Sagar.* 🏨 *Punnami Hotel, Srisailam, (08524) 88 311.* 📷 *Shivaratri (Feb/Mar).*

T HE PRETTY TEMPLE TOWN of Srisailam, situated in the thickly wooded Nallamalai Hills, overlooking the deep Krishna Gorge, is a popular pilgrimage spot. Dominating the town is the **Mallikarjuna-swamy Temple**, whose white tiered *gopuras*, standing atop fortress-like walls, are visible from a great distance. The temple, which houses one of the 12 *jyotirlingas* (naturally formed lingas said to contain the light of Shiva), is believed to date to pre-Vedic times, though the present structure was built in the 15th century. The carvings on the walls represent Shiva in his many forms. A pillared hallway leads to the inner shrine, guarded by a monolithic Nandi bull.

Further up the hill is the **Hatakesvaram Temple**, said to be the spot where the phil-osopher-saint Shankaracharya *(see p648)* wrote one of his celebrated treatises. A small Shiva temple at the summit, **Sikharam**, offers breathtaking views of the valley.

The dammed waters of the Krishna power a huge hydro-electric project at Srisailam. When the waters are high enough, a luxury launch, the *Zaria*, ferries visitors from the reservoir at Nagarjuna Sagar to Srisailam Dam. For almost half the distance between the reservoir and Srisailam Dam, the river passes through a thick forest reserve, habitat of the tiger, panther and hyena. The river, which runs very deep at Srisailam, is known here as the Patal Ganga ("Underground Ganges") – according to legend, it springs from an underground tribu-tary of the Ganges. On the ghats close to the dam, boatmen offer enchanting rides on their basin-shaped reed and bamboo boats.

The Sangameshvara Temple outside Alampur village

Alampur 17

Mahboobnagar district. 330 km (205 miles) E of Vijayawada. 🚉 🚌

T HIS VILLAGE, on the northern bank of the Tungabhadra river, is the site of the earliest Hindu temples in Andhra Pradesh. Constructed by the Chalukyas of Badami *(see pp536–7)* in the 7th and 8th centuries, the nine red sandstone shrines are collectively known as the **Nava Brahma Temples**, and are dedicated to Shiva. The layout conforms to a standard scheme – each temple faces east, has an inner sanctum, a pillared *mandapa*, and is surrounded by a passage. The tower over the inner sanc-tum, capped by an *amalaka* (circular ribbed stone), shows the dis-tinct influence of North Indian temple architecture *(see p20)*.

The later temples in the group have porches with per-forated stone screens on three sides of the passageways, as in the **Svarga Brahma Temple**,

Detail from the Padma Brahma Temple

built in AD 689. This beautiful temple has outstanding sculptures, including a comp-lete set of *dikpalas* (guardian figures) in the corner niches, and icons of Shiva in various forms. Some columns in the interior have been elaborately carved, such as those in the **Padma Brahma Temple**. The pillars here have seated lions at the base, fluted shafts and ribbed pot-shaped capitals.

The **Bala Brahma Temple** is the only one of the group, still in use. The **Archaeological Museum**, next to the complex, has a fine collection of early Chalukya sculptures. Just outside the village is the reconstructed **Sangameshvara Temple**, removed from a site that was submerged by the damming of the Krishna, 15 km (9 miles) to the north. Standing on a high terrace, it is similar to the Nava Brahma group, except that the sculp-tural details have eroded.

Just southwest of the Nava Brahma Temple complex are the **Papanashanam Temples** (9th–10th centuries). These temples have imposing multi-tiered pyramidal roofs but little external decoration, though the interior columns are ornately carved. One of the temples has a fine ceiling panel of Vishnu's incarnations *(see p679)*, and another has a powerful image of Durga.

🏛 **Archaeological Museum**
📅 *Sat–Thu.* 📷

Naga (Snake deity) from the Archaeological Museum, Alampur

View of Tirupati, with the gold-gilded *vimana* of the temple

Tirupati ⑱

Chittoor district. 585 km (364 miles) S of Hyderabad. 🏙 227,700. ✈ 12 km (7 miles) S of the city centre, then taxi. 🚌 🚍 ℹ *Andhra Pradesh Tourism, near Choultry No 3, (08574) 23 208.* 🎎 *Brahmotsavam (Sep/Oct).*

THE MOST popular destination for Hindu pilgrims in India, Tirupati is the site of the **Shri Venkateshvara Temple**, situated in the Tirumala Hills, 700 m (2,297 ft) above the town. The seven "sacred hills" of Tirumala are believed to symbolize the seven-headed serpent god Adisesha, on whose coils Vishnu sleeps. The temple dates to the 9th century, although it has often been expanded and renovated from the 15th century onwards.

The aura that surrounds Lord Venkateshvara (a form of Lord Vishnu, who is also known as Balaji) as the "Bestower of Boons" has made his shrine the most visited and the richest in India. It eclipses Jerusalem and Rome in the number of pilgrims it attracts – around 25,000 a day, and up to 100,000 on festival days. The gold *vimana* and flagpole, and the gold-plated doorway into the inner sanctum, proclaim the temple's wealth. The jet-black stone image, 2-m (7-ft) high, stands on a lotus and is adorned with rubies, diamonds and gold. The deity also wears a diamond crown, believed to

Lord Venkateshvara, the presiding deity at Tirupati

be the singlemost precious ornament in the world. He is flanked by his consorts, Sridevi and Bhudevi. The entrance portico has superb life-size images of the Vijayanagara king and queens *(see pp530–33)*, who worshipped Venkateshvara as their protective deity.

The entire complex is built to accommodate the huge influx of pilgrims, who come to seek favours from Lord Venkateshvara. This is one of the few temples in South India where non-Hindus are allowed into the inner sanctum. Devotees wait patiently in long queues for a special *darshan*, and make offerings of money, gold and jewellery that net the temple an annual income of nearly 1.5 billion rupees. The Tirumala Tirupati Devasthanam (TTD), which runs the temple, employs a staff of 6,000 to see to the pilgrims' needs and maintain the temple premises.

The temple complex includes a ritual bathing tank, and a small **Art Museum** with images of deities, musical instruments and votive objects. Surrounding it are green valleys and the Akash Ganga waterfall, which is the source of the holy water used for bathing the deity.

A unique feature at Tirupati is that many devotees offer their hair to the deity, and there are separate enclosures for this purpose. It is believed that since hair enhances a

person's appearance, shaving it off sheds vanity as well. This offering is usually made after the fulfilment of a wish. The hair-offerings are later exported to the United States and Japan where they are made into wigs.

Most pilgrims stop at the small Ganesha shrine in the foothills, and at the **Govindarajaswamy Temple** in Tirupati town, before driving up the hill to the Tirumala shrine. This temple, which dates to the 16th–17th century, is dedicated to both Krishna and Vishnu. Built by the Nayakas, the successors to the Vijayanagar rulers, it is approached through a massive, grey outer *gopura* that dominates Tirupati's skyline, and is carved with scenes from the *Ramayana (see p27)*. An exquisite pavilion in the inner courtyard has carved granite pillars, an ornate wooden roof, and impressive sculptures of crouching lions. The temple has a magnificent image of the reclining Vishnu, called Ranganatha, coated with bronze armour. A short distance north of the temple is the **Venkateshvara Museum of Temple Arts**, with temple models, photographs and ritual objects.

🛕 Shri Venkateshvara Temple
◯ *daily. Darshan: 6–11am. Extra charges to join the shorter queue for special darshan of the deity.*

The main gateway to Govindarajaswamy Temple

Avatars of Vishnu

VISHNU, THE SECOND GOD in the Hindu Trinity, personifies the preserving power of nature. Seen as the most "human" of the gods and the redeemer of humanity, he is said to have appeared on Earth in several avatars or incarnations, whenever the cosmic order was disturbed. From the 2nd

Krishna, the eighth avatar of Vishnu

century, a new devotional worship of Vishnu's incarnation as Krishna developed in South India, and, by AD 1000, Vaishnavism had become widespread. At his most famous temple, in Tirupati, Vishnu is worshipped as Venkateshvara, the God who Fulfills Desires. Lakshmi, the Goddess of Wealth, is his consort.

THE TEN INCARNATIONS

Vishnu descends to earth periodically, in order to redress the balance between good and evil. He is said to have ten main avatars, of which nine have already appeared; the tenth is yet to come.

Main image of Vishnu

Kavad *is a portable wooden shrine, which shows Vishnu in his Krishna avatar, protected by the serpent Adisesha, and with his brother Balrama.*

Krishna, who came to free the world from oppression.

Matsya, the fish and first avatar, rescued Manu (the first man) and the Vedas from a flood.

Rama, the seventh avatar, is the embodiment of goodness.

Buddha, is the ninth avatar *(see p221)*.

Kurma, the tortoise and second avatar, churned the ocean to produce *amrita*, the divine nectar.

Vamana, the dwarf priest and the fifth avatar, saved the world from a demon.

Parasurama, the sixth avatar, came to subdue the Kshatriyas who were overpowering the Brahmins.

Krishna

Varaha, *the boar and third avatar, saved the earth from drowning in the ocean by lifting it up on his tusks.*

Narasimha, *the half-man, half-lion fourth avatar, killed the demon Hiranyakshipu and delivered the earth from his evil deeds.*

Kalki, *the tenth avatar, is still to come. Vishnu will then appear for the final destruction and will recreate the world in perfect purity.*

See also features on Hindu Mythology *(see pp24–5)*, Ganesha *(see p467)* and Shiva *(see p566)*.

Rani Mahal, roofed by stepped pyramidal towers, at Chandragiri

Chandragiri ⑲

Tirupati district. 12 km (7 miles) W of Tirupati. 🚌 from Tirupati.

THIS SMALL VILLAGE was once an important outpost of the Vijayanagar kings. It later became the capital of the Aravidu ruler, Venkatapatideva (r.1586–1614), whose reign saw the decline of the Vijayanagar Empire.

Chandragiri's once glorious past is reflected in the massive walls of its late 16th-century fortress and some abandoned palaces. The most important of these is the **Raja Mahal**, which has an arcaded Durbar Hall and a domed pleasure pavilion. It was here that Sir Francis Day of the East India Company was granted land in 1639, in order to set up a factory in what later came to be known as Madras (see p557). Nearby is the **Rani Mahal**, with its striking pyramidal towers, and its façade decorated with foliate and geometric motifs.

A temple next to the ruined palaces at Chandragiri

Sri Kalahasti ⑳

Chittoor district. 36 km (22 miles) E of Tirupati. 🚌 from Tirupati. 🎭 Temple Festival (Sep/Oct).

LOCATED BETWEEN two steep hills, on the southern bank of the Svarnamukhi river, this town is one of the most important pilgrimage centres in Andhra Pradesh. Dominating one end of the crowded main street is a 36.5-m (120-ft) high free-standing *gopura*, erected in 1516 by Emperor Krishnadeva Raya of Vijayanagar (see pp530–33). The royal emblems of

Flower seller at Sri Kalahasti

the dynasty, depicting the boar and the sword together with the sun and the moon, are intricately carved on to the walls of this seven-storeyed towered gateway.

Nearby, similar but smaller *gopuras* provide access to the **Kalahastishvara Temple**, the town's main attraction, surrounded by a paved rectangular compound. A doorway to the south leads into a crowded enclosure of columned halls, pavilions, lamp columns and altars, connected by a maze of colonnades and corridors. Some of the columns are carved as rearing animal figures. In the north corridor are a set of bronzes of the 63 Shaivite saints called Nayannars (see p45). The inner sanctum, opening to the west, enshrines the *vayu* (air) linga, one of the five elemental lingas of Shiva (see p586) in South India. It is a curiously elongated linga protected by a cobra hood, made of brass. According to a local legend, a spider, a cobra and an elephant worshipped the linga in their own special way. The spider first spun a web around it to protect it from the sun's

KALAMKARI FABRICS

Deriving their name from the word *kalam* for pen and *kari* for work, these brightly coloured cotton fabrics are produced at Machilipatnam (see p672) and Sri Kalahasti. Using a mixture of painting and dyeing techniques, figures of gods, goddesses, trees and birds are first drawn on the fabric, and then painted with a "pen" made of a bamboo stick padded at one end with cotton cloth. The traditional natural colours of ochre, soft pink, indigo, madder red and iron black are characteristic of *kalamkari* textiles. *Kalamkaris* from Sri Kalahasti were part of temple ritual and, like temple murals, depict mythological themes, with gods, goddesses and other celestial beings. The ones from Machilipatnam display a distinct Persian influence (see p673) and once formed part of a lucrative trade with Europe, dating back to the 17th century.

Kalamkari depicting Shiva and Parvati

View of Sri Kalahasti town, with its towering *gopuras* and the Kannappa Temple on a hillock

rays. The cobra, when he reached the shrine, was so upset to see the linga covered with dirty cobwebs that he cleaned and covered it with little stones. The last to arrive was the elephant, who removed the stones and decorated the linga with flowers. This continued for some time until the three devotees, each sure that his way of worship was the purest and that the others had committed sacrilege, decided to confront each other. In the fight that ensued, they collapsed and Lord Shiva, pleased by their devotion, blessed them and named the shrine after them – Sri (spider), Kala (cobra) and Hasti (elephant).

Sri Kalahasti is also linked to the legend of Kannappa, the hunter, through its **Kannappa Temple**. One of the 63 Nayannars, Kannappa plucked out his eye in a frenzy of devotion and offered it to Shiva. A shrine commemorating him stands on the summit of the hillock that rises to the east.

Worshippers have thronged to this temple for generations to seek relief from the "evil effects" of Saturn. Some pilgrims also come here with their unmarried daughters in the hope that a special *puja* at the temple will help them find good husbands.

Puttaparthi ㉑

Ananthapur district. 437 km (272 miles) S of Hyderabad. ✈ 6 km (4 miles) S of ashram, then taxi. 🚂 Dharmavaram, 40 km (25 miles) N of Puttaparthi, then bus. 🚌 ℹ️ Sri Satya Sai Information Centre, Prasanthi Nilayam, (08555) 87 388. 🎉 Sai Baba's Birthday (23 Nov).

A**S THE BIRTHPLACE** of Sri Satya Sai Baba, the "godman" who preaches religious tolerance, universal love and service to others, Puttaparthi has special significance for his vast number of devotees from all over the world. Sai Baba's ability to produce *vibhuti* (sacred ash), seemingly miraculously out of thin air, is considered by his devotees to be an important symbol of his god-like status and powers.

Sri Satya Sai Baba, a popular godman

From a very young age, Sai Baba, born as Satyanarayana Raju in this village on 23 November 1926, claimed divine powers. When he was only 14, he declared that he was the reincarnation of a celebrated saint, Sai Baba from Shirdi in Maharashtra, who died in 1918. It is believed that he will return after his death as another saint called Prem Sai Baba. In 1950 Satya Sai Baba established an ashram for his followers, whose numbers had swollen to gigantic figures. Known as **Prasanthi Nilayam** or the "Abode of Highest Peace", it is today a large complex with guesthouses, dormitories, kitchens and dining halls. Over the years, several buildings have appeared around the ashram – schools, colleges, residential complexes, hospitals, a planetarium, a museum and recreation centres, transforming this tiny village into a cosmopolitan township. Outside the ashram, at the lower end of the village, rural life continues, seemingly unaffected by the ashram's activities. The countryside around is very fertile, with stretches of well-irrigated fields.

Women working in the fields, Puttaparthi

The ornate *mihrab* of the Sher
Shah Mosque, Penukonda

Penukonda ㉒

Anantapur district. 425 km (264
miles) S of Hyderabad. 🚌 📷
Babayya Fair (Dec).

A ROCKY HILL dominates
Penukonda, or the "Big
Hill", with walls rising up its
steep sides to form an almost
triangular fort. A strategic
Vijayanagar citadel from the
14th and to 16th centuries,
Penukonda was the capital of
the succeeding Aravidu rulers
until it was captured, first by
the Qutb Shahis, and then by,
the Mughals followed by the
Marathas. Today, gateways,
watchtowers, dilapidated
halls and shrines skirt the
path to the summit.

At the foot of the hill is the
walled city, with its main
gateways in the northern and
eastern sides. To the south is
a large tank. The main monuments are situated along the
city's north-south road. The
Parsvanatha Jain Temple
here contains a remarkable
sculpture, dating from the
Hoysala period (12th–13th
centuries), of the Jain saint
Parsvanatha *(see p396)* standing in front of an undulating
serpent. The 16th-century
Sher Shah Mosque, nearby,
has an arcaded façade and a
bulbous dome.

Further south, standing next
to each other, are two granite
temples dedicated to Rama
and Shiva. The pilastered
façade walls of the **Rama
Temple** are brought to life by

carvings depicting episodes
from the *Ramayana (see p27)*
and the Krishna legend, while
scenes from the Shiva mythology are sculpted on the walls
of the **Shiva Temple**.

The adjacent **Gagan Mahal**
is a palatial structure dating to
the Vijayanagar period. An
arcaded verandah leads to a
vaulted hall with rear chambers. The domed pavilion
above is topped by a pyramidal octagonal tower. A
similar, smaller tower tops the
adjoining staircase. To its east
is a square pavilion with
curving eaves, a
pierced parapet and
an octagonal pyra-
midal tower. The
interior has traces
of intricate plaster-
work. Nearby is a
well with an ornate
entrance shaped
like a lion.

A short distance
north of the walled
city is the **Dargah of
Babayya**, the shrine of a
16th-century Muslim saint. A
popular pilgrimage place
which was much patronized
by Tipu Sultan *(see p517)*, it
holds a big fair in December.

Lepakshi ㉓

Anantapur district. 460 km (286
miles) S of Hyderabad. 🚌 🏠 *daily.*
📷 *Shivratri (Feb/Mar).*

A N ENORMOUS monolith of
Nandi, Shiva's bull, stands
1 km (0.6 miles) east of
Lepakshi, welcoming
visitors to this impor-
tant pilgrimage town.

Lepakshi's top attrac-
tion is the **Virabhadra
Temple**, which stands
on a rocky outcrop. It
was built in the mid-
16th century, under the
patronage of two
brothers, Virupanna
and Viranna, governors
of Penukonda under
the Vijayanagar empire.

The temple is an
important repository of
the styles of sculpture
and painting that
evolved during this
period. Dedicated to
Virabhadra (Shiva in his

ferocious form), the temple
stands in the middle of two
concentric enclosures, built
on three levels. It is entered
through a *gopura* on the
north side. On either side of
the inner entrance are figures
of the river goddesses Ganga
and Yamuna, with a back-
ground of foliage. Among the
other notable sculptures here
are the carvings on the massive pillars that define the
central space in the open hall;
the deities, guardians and
sages carved on to the piers
of the unfinished Kalyana
Mandapa; and the
imposing monolithic
seven-headed *naga*
(serpent) sheltering
a granite linga, to
the southeast of
the main shrine.
Paintings in vibrant
vegetable and min-
eral colours cover
the ceilings of the
two adjoining

**Monolithic naga,
Virabhadra Temple**

mandapas (one open and the
other walled in), the walls of
the Ardha Mandapa and some
subsidiary shrines. Gods and
goddesses, groups of donors
and worshippers, and scenes
from myths and legends, bear
witness to the superb pictorial
art of the Vijayanagar empire.

A gory legend connected to
the Virabhadra Temple says
that Virupanna misused state
funds to build this shrine, and
then forestalled royal punishment by blinding himself. The
two dark reddish spots on the
western wall of the inner
enclosure are said to be the
marks left by his eyes.

Carved pillars at the Virabhadra Temple

Lepakshi Paintings

THE GLORY OF LEPAKSHI lies in the magnificent frescoed ceilings of the Virabhadra Temple, where a series of exquisite paintings illustrate in lively fashion episodes from the epics and the *Puranas*. The figures are shown in profile, with prominent eyes and sharply chiselled noses and chins. The frescoes are characterized by elegant black linework, set out against an orange-red background. Particularly

Lord Shiva as a mendicant

striking are the beautiful costumes and the detailed rendering of hairstyles, textile patterns, and jewellery. The palette of colours is limited to white, green, black and various shades of ochre and brown, applied to a stucco surface specially treated with lime. Some of the most beautiful paintings are on the ceiling of the open *mandapa*, arranged in long strips along the surrounding bays.

Ravana   Nandi   Shiva   Parvati   Brahma officiating as the priest   Garuda, Vishnu's bird-vehicle

THE MARRIAGE OF SHIVA AND PARVATI
This is Lepakshi's most spectacular fresco, and echoes the murals at Ajanta *(see pp480–81)* in its colours, detailed depiction of costumes and jewellery, and graceful female figures.

Dakshinamurti (Shiva as a Divine Teacher) is shown seated on a hillock, expounding on mysticism and philosophy to sages gathered at his feet.

Parvati, with her maids, is shown getting ready for the wedding. Flat figures in stylized poses, often arranged in rows, characterize these paintings.

The Boar Hunt *shows a wild boar charging at Arjuna and Shiva, who are preparing to shoot him.*

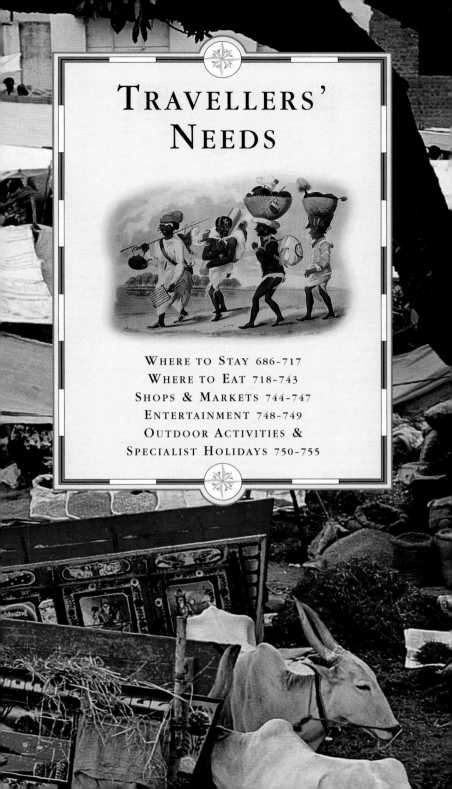

TRAVELLERS' NEEDS

WHERE TO STAY

A WIDE CHOICE OF accommodation is on offer for the rising number of visitors to India – from modern Western-style deluxe hotels and grand old palaces to budget hotels and tourist bungalows. Prices vary accordingly, depending on the quality of services offered, and the location. Star-rated luxury hotels, speciality hotels, health spas and heritage hotels are expensive, but the amenities they offer more than justify the high room rates. The moderately-priced budget hotels, often managed by state tourism departments, may lack the glamour of a five-star, but they are clean and excellent value for money. Cheaper accommodation is available at guesthouses, youth hostels and even spartan pilgrim abodes, such as *dharamshalas* and ashrams. Hotel rates fluctuate with the season and are usually cheaper during the off-season from April to September. The hotel listings on pages 690–717 provide a selection of some of the best hotels throughout India, to suit every taste and budget.

RAJVILĀS

Logo of an Oberoi luxury hotel

GRADING AND FACILITIES

AT THE TOP end of the scale are the five-star deluxe hotels. Most of these are part of international and Indian hotel chains, such as **Welcomgroup**, **Oberoi**, **Taj**, and the national India Tourism Development Corporation's (ITDC) **Ashok Group**. Many of the Ashok Group's properties, however, are now in the process of being sold to private operators. Next, are the four- and three-star hotels, many of them run by the state governments, followed by the cheaper guesthouses. The heritage hotels offer visitors a chance to stay in atmospheric, beautifully restored forts, palaces and stately homes.

PRICING AND BOOKING

THE MOST expensive establishments are the five-star and five-star deluxe hotels as well as the exclusive heritage hotels, although the smaller properties among the latter can be cheaper. Accommodation in the bigger cities is generally more expensive. Rates can differ among the state-run hotels, which have a good nationwide network. Prices vary at guesthouses, and seasonal discounts mean that prices can go down by almost 50 per cent.

Tariffs are based on the European system of room rent only, although in some places breakfast is included. Flexible prices dominate the market during the off-season and it is worth negotiating for a good discount. Often, hotels will also offer promotional discounts.

Foreigners have to pay the dollar room rate, plus any additional taxes on the listed price. This is payable in foreign currency or in Indian rupees. Hotel rates are usually revised every September, at the start of the tourist season.

Book well in advance during the peak tourist season (Oct–Mar). Since the classifications of hotels can be bewildering for first-time visitors, it's best to get a complete description of what to expect in terms of both room and service quality. Getting a reservation confirmed in writing is a sensible precaution.

While making reservations, especially for mid-range and budget hotels, do also check which credit cards are accepted. Another point to remember is that some hotels demand payment in advance and will refund only part of it if the booking is cancelled.

Check-out time is usually 12 noon, though some hotels are more flexible and allow a 24-hour departure, or accept a small fee for a few hours' extension. Sometimes, some of the smaller hotels allow a later check out, for free. When paying, scrutinize the bill thoroughly and retain all receipts on departure.

TAXES

THE HOTEL BILL includes taxes levied by the federal and state governments. The federal government charges a uniform 10 per cent hotel expenditure tax, which is imposed on all hotels. This is chargeable on all services. States levy a luxury tax on room rent as well, and this varies from 5 to 30 per cent. There may also be local taxes such as sales tax, service tax

The charming Raj-style Fernhill Palace Hotel in Ooty

◁ **Weekly market at Srirangapattana, Karnataka** *(see pp516–17)*

Udaipur's opulent Lake Palace Hotel in the middle of Lake Pichola

and special taxes on alcohol, which vary from state to state. Some hotels also levy a service charge.

HIDDEN COSTS

BE PREPARED TO PAY extra for breakfast, the mini bar, mineral water, telephone calls, laundry, room service (if this is not a regular sevice), extra bedding, business centre usage, e-mails and faxes, concierge services and even pay channels on television. Transfers to and from the hotel are complimentary only for up-market package tours.

For non-local and international telephone calls, check if there's an in-house ISD/STD facility, though it's cheaper to use an STD booth *(see p770)* outside the hotel. Small town hotels, with no running hot water, often charge extra for buckets of hot water.

LUXURY HOTELS

INDIA'S LUXURY HOTELS are comparable with the best anywhere in the world. They offer spacious suites and rooms, excellent service and a host of amenities. These usually include a travel desk, state-of-the-art conference facilities, shopping arcades, swimming pools, modern fitness centres, coffee shops and multi-cuisine restaurants. The staff are very polite and attentive and can help plan itineraries and make arrangements for activities such as tennis, golf or riding. Reservations should be made well in advance, especially during the peak season.

HERITAGE HOTELS

SEVERAL PALACES, FORTS and *havelis*, particularly in Rajasthan, Madhya Pradesh, Himachal Pradesh and Gujarat, have been restored, modernized and converted into plush, luxury hotels. These establishments have a gracious, old-world charm, and many are still run by former princely families, who treat visitors like honoured guests.

Classified as Grand, Classic and Ordinary under the umbrella of the **Heritage Hotels Association of India (HHAI)**, some can be booked through private agencies, such as **HRH Group of Hotels**, **Neemrana Hotels** and **WelcomHeritage**. Bookings can also be made through well-known travel agents.

MIDDLE-RANGE HOTELS

THE FOUR- AND THREE-star hotels offer a scaled-down version of five-star luxury and are less expensive. Levels of comfort, cleanliness and

professional services are, however, high. Rooms are air conditioned and have attached bathrooms. In addition, there are restaurants, gift shops, business centres and sometimes extensive gardens for dining outdoors.

BUDGET HOTELS AND TOURIST LODGES

BUDGET HOTELS are often found around bus stands and railway stations. They are inexpensive, with simple decor, Indian or Western-style toilets, ceiling fans and basic food options in a dining hall. Enterprising proprietors sometimes offer e-mail services for a fee. The tariff in major cities is higher than in smaller towns.

An excellent option, particularly in lesser known tourist destinations, is the country-wide network of tourist bungalows and lodges run by the state tourism departments or the Ashok Group. Moderately priced, they offer both independent rooms with attached baths as well as dormitory accommodation.

DAK BUNGALOWS

GOVERNMENT-RUN circuit houses, rest houses and dak bungalows (inns with very basic facilities) are conveniently located and are clean and cheap. Book in advance as priority usually goes to visiting government officials. Contact the local or district authorities for help in making reservations.

Cidade de Goa Beach Resort, designed by architect Charles Correa

GUESTHOUSES, PAYING GUESTS AND HOME STAYS

I N CERTAIN STATES, such as Goa, Tamil Nadu, Rajasthan and Madhya Pradesh, family cottages and old mansions have been converted (though sometimes only partially) into guesthouses. While these usualy fall into the mid-range or budget categories, the number of amenities, quality of service and price can be erratic. Look at rooms before checking in, as the difference between one room and another for the same price can be substantial. The better ones have air-conditioned rooms, with attached baths and Western-style toilets.

Home stays with local families are becoming a popular option, especially in Kerala. It is best to check with the state tourism offices (see p761) for a list of establishments under their Paying Guest Scheme. Rajasthan Tourism has a comprehensive list, as does Madhya Pradesh Tourism. In Kerala, **Sundale Vacations** specializes in home stays. The UK-based **Munjeeta Travels** also organizes home stay tours across India.

DHARAMSHALAS AND ASHRAMS

R ELIGIOUS CENTRES, among them *dharamshalas*, ashrams and monasteries, offer clean but basic accommodation all over the country. For most, prior booking is not essential and stay is often free, although donations are appreciated. It is wise to abide by the rules of the

Luxury campsite at Pushkar during the annual cattle fair

house and not offend any sentiments. Some ashrams in the older sections of town may provide only a mattress on the floor, which should suffice if the stay is just for a night. But be prepared to share rooms and bathrooms with others.

Popular ashrams such as the **Sri Aurobindo Ashram**, the **Ramakrishna Mission** and the **Sivananda Ashram**, have branches spread across the country, and bookings must be made in advance. Their head offices can be contacted for details.

In Ladakh, many monasteries run hotels fairly close to their premises. One of the best is the **Lamayuru Monastery Hotel** which has a great setting within the compound (see p138).

NATIONAL PARKS AND CAMPING SITES

M OST NATIONAL PARKS and wildlife sanctuaries have forest rest houses with basic facilities. Since most of these are often reserved for forest officials, many of the larger parks now have plush

private resorts located on their periphery. The most popular among these are in Ranthambhore (Sher Bagh), Corbett (Infinity Resorts), Kaziranga (Wildgrass) and Nagarhole (Kabini River Lodge). Reservations can be made through **Exotic Journeys**, or through travel agencies. Camping is not allowed inside wildlife sanctuaries, and as a rule, it is not even safe to venture out for unguided walks.

Tented camps are provided by operators who organize adventure tours, such as river rafting along the Ganges (see p185), or those that specialize in camping holidays (see p752). Check the arrangements in advance, as some may not provide mosquito nets or mineral water. In Rajasthan, some hotels offer guests the option of staying in luxury tents set in spacious gardens. During the Pushkar and Kumbh *melas* (fairs), the state governments provide tented accommodation.

SPECIAL HOTELS

T HE RISING INTEREST in holistic health and well-being has spawned a number of exclusive health spas and specialized resorts. The most popular are those that offer herbal treatments, such as Ayurveda, and yoga. Other services include massage therapies, such as aromatherapy and reflexology, and meditation. Usually, a strict diet is part of the spartan regime, although rules at the top-end resorts are flexible. Raj Vilas and Amar Vilas of the **Oberoi** Group and

Riceboat or *kettuvallam*, Kerala backwaters

Ananda are world class spas. Kerala's *kettuvallams* (converted rice boats) are luxurious and have good services. Trips can be organized by **Tourindia**.

YOUTH HOSTELS

INDIA HAS AN excellent network of youth hostels. Although these are available at very low rates, they also tend to be packed. Members of the **Youth Hostel Association of India** and Youth Hostel International get priority bookings, but non-members can get a room for a higher fee. Both room and dorm-style accommodation is available. The **YMCA** is better equipped, though more expensive and located in fewer towns.

TOUTS

VISITORS WITH NO prior bookings should contact tourist counters at the airport, railway station or bus stand to avoid being harassed by touts,

who also operate as taxi and auto-rickshaw drivers. Many are very persuasive and offer incredible discounts, all for a commission. Some, however, are genuinely helpful, and if there is no other option, keep the driver waiting until sure about the lodgings. Speak to a policeman if they become too persistent.

FACILITIES FOR THE DISABLED AND CHILDREN

THOUGH FACILITIES for the disabled are few, hotel staff are generally considerate. The government has recently initiated a move to add wheelchair ramps, special lifts and bathrooms wherever possible, although older properties, even the five-star hotels, may find it difficult to accommodate them.

Most hotels have no special amenities for children. However, Indian hotel staff are usually good with children and provisions can be made for extra beds. Only a few hotels offer baby-sitting services.

The impressive entrance foyer, Cecil Hotel, Shimla

TIPPING

DESPITE THE inclusion of service charges in the bill, tips are expected in most places. The amount is discretionary. A tip of Rs10 is fine for parking attendants, room service and porters, but waiters expect ten per cent of the bill. Taxi drivers don't need to be tipped. However, tipping is a great way to get things done quickly.

Choosing a Hotel

THE HOTELS in this guide, listed according to region, have been included because of their location, the excellence of their services and of the facilities available, and because they offer value for money. Colour-coded thumb tabs show the regions covered on each page. For restaurant listings see pp720–43.

	CREDIT CARDS	NUMBER OF ROOMS	AIR CONDITIONING	WESTERN BATHROOMS	COFFEE SHOP

DELHI

DELHI: *YMCA Tourist Hostel* ℞℞
1 Jai Singh Rd. 📞 *(011) 336 1915.* FAX *(011) 374 6032.* @ ymcath@ndf.vsnl.net.in
Reasonable rates, plain but comfortable rooms, and good access to the commercial heart of the city. 🔲 🔲 🔲 🔲 🔲 🔲 🔲

AE MC V	105	■	●	■

DELHI: *Jor Bagh "27" Guesthouse* ℞℞℞
27 Jor Bagh. 📞 *(011) 469 8647.* FAX *(011) 469 8475.* 🆆 www.budget-inns.com
This tranquil and comfortable guesthouse is located in Lutyens's Delhi, opposite the beautiful Lodi Gardens with its old trees and historic monuments. Meals are available on order. 🔲 🔲 🔲 🔲

AE MC V	18	■	◐	

DELHI: *Jukaso Inn Downtown* ℞℞℞
L–1 Connaught Circus. 📞 *(011) 332 4451.* FAX *(011) 332 4448.*
🆆 www.hoteljukasoinn.com
Very popular with business travellers, this friendly and efficient establishment, with a 24-hour business centre, is located close to the city's commercial and business centre. 🔲 🔲 🔲 🔲

AE DC MC V	36	■	◐	

DELHI: *La Sagrita Tourist Home* ℞℞℞
14 Sundar Nagar. 📞 *(011) 435 1249.* FAX *(011) 435 6956.*
Situated in a peaceful residential area near the Purana Qila and the zoo, this is a comfortable, up-market guesthouse with recently-refurbished rooms and a friendly atmosphere. 🔲 🔲 🔲

AE DC MC V	19	■	●	

DELHI: *Maharani Guest House* ℞℞℞
3 Sundar Nagar. 📞 *(011) 435 1129.* FAX *(011) 435 4562.*
Located in a converted residence, close to a market famous for its jewellery and antique shops, this clean and well-furnished guesthouse has extremely courteous and helpful staff. 🔲 🔲 🔲

AE DC MC V	24	■	●	

DELHI: *Nirulas* ℞℞℞
L–Block Connaught Circus. 📞 *(011) 332 2419.* FAX *(011) 335 3957.* 🆆 www.nirula.com
This hotel has spotlessly clean, comfortable rooms, excellent service, a central location and good wholesome food. 🔲 🔲 🔲 🔲

AE DC MC V	29	■	●	

DELHI: *The Ambassador* ℞℞℞℞
Sujan Singh Park. 📞 *(011) 463 2600.* FAX *(011) 463 2252.* 🆆 www.tajhotels.com
Built in the early 1900s as part of Lutyens's New Delhi, this hotel has spacious rooms with character, recently refurbished. There is also a good Chinese restaurant and a cosy coffee shop. 🔲 🔲 🔲 🔲 🔲 🔲 🔲

AE DC MC V	88	■	●	■

DELHI: *The Connaught* ℞℞℞℞
37 Shaheed Bhagat Singh Marg. 📞 *(011) 336 4225.* FAX *(011) 334 0757.*
🆆 www.hotelconnaught.com
This pleasant bed-and-breakfast hotel has clean and comfortable rooms, friendly staff and a 24-hour multi-cuisine restaurant. 🔲 🔲 🔲 🔲 🔲 🔲

AE DC MC V	79	■	●	■

DELHI: *Hans Plaza* ℞℞℞℞
15 Barakhamba Rd. 📞 *(011) 331 6861.* FAX *(011) 331 4830.* 🆆 www.hansgroup.com
Located in Delhi's main business district, this is a sleek boutique hotel, with elegant and comfortable rooms and efficient staff. 🔲 🔲 🔲 🔲 🔲 🔲

AE DC MC V	67	■	●	■

DELHI: *The Oberoi Maidens* ℞℞℞℞
7 Sham Nath Marg. 📞 *(011) 397 5464.* FAX *(011) 398 0771.* 🆆 www.oberoihotels.com
This gracious early 20th-century hotel in Old Delhi has an elegant ambience. The spacious rooms, where Ernest Hemingway once stayed, retain their period flavour. 🔲 🔲 🔲 🔲 🔲 🔲 🔲 🔲 🔲

AE DC MC V	54	■	●	■

DELHI: *The Park* ℞℞℞℞
15 Parliament St. 📞 *(011) 374 3000.* FAX *(011) 374 4000.* 🆆 www.theparkhotels.com
Located in Connaught Place, this hotel has luxurious rooms with views, a popular Spanish restaurant and a discotheque. 🔲 🔲 🔲 🔲 🔲 🔲 🔲 🔲 🔲

AE DC MC V	224	■	●	■

Price categories for a standard double room per night including tax and service charges but not including breakfast:
(Rs) under 550 rupees
(Rs)(Rs) 550–1,200 rupees
(Rs)(Rs)(Rs) 1,200–3,000 rupees
(Rs)(Rs)(Rs)(Rs) 3,000–6,000 rupees
(Rs)(Rs)(Rs)(Rs)(Rs) over 6,000 rupees

CREDIT CARDS
Indicates which major credit cards are accepted: AE American Express; DC Diners Club; MC Master Card/Access; V Visa.

WESTERN BATHROOMS
Indicates sit-down, flush toilets; showers and/or baths. Others have squat toilets and bucket-and-mug baths.

COFFEE SHOP
Hotels with 24-hour coffee shop, also serving hot meals.

AIR CONDITIONING
Hotels with air-conditioned rooms.

	CREDIT CARDS	NUMBER OF ROOMS	AIR CONDITIONING	WESTERN BATHROOMS	COFFEE SHOP
DELHI: *Claridges* (Rs)(Rs)(Rs)(Rs) 12 Aurangzeb Rd. (011) 301 0211. FAX (011) 301 0625. claridges.hotel@gems.vsnl.net.in A quiet elegant hotel situated in a tree-lined avenue in Lutyens's Delhi, the Claridges also has very good restaurants.	AE DC MC V	162	●	●	●
DELHI: *Grand Hyatt* (Rs)(Rs)(Rs)(Rs)(Rs) Vasant Kunj, Phase II. (011) 612 1234. FAX (011) 689 5891. W www.hyatt.com Set in ten acres of landscaped gardens, this impressive hotel combines high international standards with personalized services. The restaurants offer a range of cuisines.	AE DC MC V	390	●	●	●
DELHI: *Hyatt Regency* (Rs)(Rs)(Rs)(Rs)(Rs) Bhikaji Cama Place. (011) 679 1234. FAX (011) 679 1024. W www.delhi.hyatt.com A large hotel offering plush accommodation, the Hyatt is known for its superb restaurants and lively nightclub.	AE DC MC V	518	●	●	●
DELHI: *Imperial Hotel* (Rs)(Rs)(Rs)(Rs)(Rs) Janpath. (011) 334 1234. FAX (011) 334 2255. W www.theimperialindia.com This stately hotel has impeccable period décor in its rooms, fine restaurants, and a collection of paintings by the late 18th-century landscape artists Thomas and William Daniell.	AE DC MC V	263	●	●	●
DELHI: *The Manor* (Rs)(Rs)(Rs)(Rs)(Rs) 77 Friends Colony West. (011) 692 5151. FAX (011) 692 2299. W www.themanordelhi.com Perhaps the most elegantly designed boutique hotel in the city, The Manor is located in a quiet residential colony. It boasts of chic yet classic décor, and offers personalized service, privacy and gourmet food.	AE DC MC V	16	●	●	
DELHI: *The Oberoi* (Rs)(Rs)(Rs)(Rs)(Rs) Dr Zakir Hussain Marg. (011) 436 3030. FAX (011) 436 4758. W www.oberoihotels.com This exclusive establishment's plush executive centre, shopping arcade and beauty salon appeal to up-market visitors. Spectacular views of Humayun's Tomb from the hotel's top floor.	AE DC MC V	256	●	●	●
DELHI: *Park Royal* (Rs)(Rs)(Rs)(Rs)(Rs) Nehru Place. (011) 622 3344. FAX (011) 622 4288. W www.parkroyal.com.au A favourite with businessmen, this hotel is the venue for many conferences. It also has a lively bar.	AE DC MC V	217	●	●	●
DELHI: *Radisson Hotel* (Rs)(Rs)(Rs)(Rs)(Rs) NH 8, Mahipalpur. (011) 677 9191. FAX (011) 677 9090. W www.radisson.com Conveniently situated near the airport, this luxury hotel has excellent facilities for business travellers and good restaurants.	AE DC MC V	256	●	●	●
DELHI: *Taj Mahal Hotel* (Rs)(Rs)(Rs)(Rs)(Rs) 1 Mansingh Rd. (011) 302 6162. FAX (011) 302 6070. W www.tajhotels.com This beautiful hotel, located in Lutyens's Delhi, combines sumptuous traditional décor with modern facilities.	AE DC MC V	300	●	●	●
DELHI: *Taj Palace Hotel* (Rs)(Rs)(Rs)(Rs)(Rs) Sardar Patel Marg, Diplomatic Enclave. (011) 611 0202. FAX (011) 611 0808. W www.tajhotels.com Located between the airport and the city centre, this vast luxury hotel has efficient business facilities.	AE DC MC V	422	●	●	●
DELHI: *Welcomgroup Maurya Sheraton Hotel & Towers* (Rs)(Rs)(Rs)(Rs)(Rs) Sardar Patel Marg, Diplomatic Enclave. (011) 611 2233. FAX (011) 611 3333. W www.welcomgroup.com This hotel has superb decor and service, a solar-heated pool, and serves the finest tandoori fare in Delhi.	AE DC MC V	515	●	●	●

For key to symbols see back flap

Price categories for a standard double room per night including tax and service charges but not including breakfast:
Rs under 550 rupees
Rs Rs 550–1,200 rupees
Rs Rs Rs 1,200–3,000 rupees
Rs Rs Rs Rs 3,000–6,000 rupees
Rs Rs Rs Rs Rs over 6,000 rupees

CREDIT CARDS
Indicates which major credit cards are accepted: AE American Express; DC Diners Club; MC Master Card/Access; V Visa.

WESTERN BATHROOMS
Indicates sit-down, flush toilets; showers and/or baths. Others have squat toilets and bucket-and-mug baths.

COFFEE SHOP
Hotels with 24-hour coffee shop, also serving hot meals.

AIR CONDITIONING
Hotels with air-conditioned rooms.

	CREDIT CARDS	NUMBER OF ROOMS	AIR CONDITIONING	WESTERN BATHROOMS	COFFEE SHOP
HARYANA & PUNJAB					
AMRITSAR: *Mrs Bhandari's Guest House* Rs Rs 10 The Cantonment. (0172) 22 8509, 22 5714. FAX (0172) 22 2390. @ payal@mol.net.in Set in well-tended lawns, with a fireplace in each room, this comfortable guesthouse is run with warmth and efficiency. TV 🔌 ≈		14	■	●	
AMRITSAR: *Ritz Plaza Hotel* Rs Rs Rs 45 Mall Rd. (0183) 56 6818. FAX (0183) 22 6657. W www.sarovarparkplaza.com Recently refurbished, this hotel has attractively furnished rooms, a leafy garden and an excellent multi-cuisine restaurant. 🍴 Y 24 TV 🔌 ≈	AE MC V	50	■	●	
CHANDIGARH: *The Aroma Hotel* Rs Rs Rs Himalaya Marg, Sector 22–C. (0172) 70 0045. FAX (0172) 70 0051. W www.hotelaroma.com This hotel's main advantage is its proximity to the bus station and the city centre. The rooms have standard modern comforts. 🍴 Y 24 TV 🔌	AE DC MC V	30	●	●	■
CHANDIGARH: *Hotel Mountview* Rs Rs Rs Sector 10. (0172) 74 0544, 74 3268. FAX (0172) 74 2565. @ hmv10@glide.net.in Set in a pretty garden, this hotel has well-appointed rooms, a health club and a rooftop Chinese restaurant. 🍴 Y 24 TV 🔌 🛏 🔌 🎾 🍴 ≈ 🏊	AE DC MC V	156	■	●	■
GURGAON: *Bristol Hotel* Rs Rs Rs Rs DLF Qutab Enclave Phase I, Gurgaon. (0124) 635 6030. FAX (0124) 635 7834. W www.bristolhotel.com The only luxury hotel in Gurgaon, Delhi's fastest growing residential and commercial suburb, it has excellent business facilities and a rooftop swimming pool. 🍴 Y 24 TV 🔌 🛏 🔌 🎾 🍴 ≈	AE DC MC V	85	■	●	■
GURGAON: *Tikli Bottom* Rs Rs Rs Rs Manender Farm, Gairatpur BBS, Haryana. (0124) 666 6556. FAX (011) 335 1272. R (011) 335 1272; honiwala@vsnl.com Surrounded by the Aravalli Hills, this newly-built Lutyens-style country house, with lovely rooms, deep verandahs and friendly staff, is close to Delhi's airport. It is run by a charming English couple. 🍴 Y 🔌 🎾 ≈		3		●	
HIMACHAL PRADESH					
CHAIL: *Palace Hotel* Rs Rs Rs Palace Hotel, Chail. (01792) 48 141. FAX (01792) 48 142. Once the summer palace of the erstwhile royal family of Patiala, this beautiful property, set in 30 ha (75 acres) of gardens and deodar forests, offers a range of accommodation including nine cottages. There is also a pleasant outdoor café. 🍴 Y 24 TV 🔌 🛏 🔌 🎾	MC V	31		●	
DALHOUSIE: *Grand View Hotel* Rs Rs Rs Dalhousie. (01899) 40 760. FAX (01899) 40 609. @ grandview@rediffmail.com True to its name, this clean, comfortable hotel offers spectacular views of the Pir Panjal Range from its well-tended front lawn. 🍴 Y 24 TV 🔌 🔌 U	AE DC MC V	30	■	●	
DHARAMSALA: *Chonor House* Rs Rs Rs Thekchen Choeling Rd, McLeodganj. (01892) 21 006. FAX (01892) 21 468. @ chonorhs@sancharnet.in Traditional Tibetan wall paintings, teak and rosewood furniture and hand-knotted carpets adorn the elegant rooms, decorated by artists from the nearby Norbulingka Institute. 🍴 24 TV 🔌 🔌	MC	11	■	●	
DHARAMSALA: *Glenmoor Cottages* Rs Rs Rs McLeodganj. (01892) 21 010. FAX (01892) 21 021. W www.glenmoorcottages.com Five pleasant cottages, situated in quiet surroundings, provide comfortable and clean accommodation. 🍴		5	■	●	

KALPA: *Kinner Villa*   ⓇⓈⓇⓈ | 21 | ▨ | ● |
Village & PO Kalpa district, Kinnaur. 【 *(01786) 26 006.* ⓦ *www.himalayaindia.com*
This secluded hotel, built in stone and conifer wood, has comfortable
rooms with balconies offering fine views of the snows. 🍴 ⊗

KEYLONG: *Hotel Dekyid*   ⓇⓈ | 24 | ▨ | ● |
Town End Upper Keylong, Lahaul & Spiti district. 【 *(019100) 22 217.* ℻ *(01892) 22 217.*
@ *hoteldeykid@yahoo.com*
Spacious rooms are available at this budget hotel which has an amiable
staff and a decent restaurant. 🍴 24 📺 🛁 ⊗

KULLU: *Span Resorts*   ⓇⓈⓇⓈⓇⓈ | AE DC MC V | 25 | ▨ | ● |
Kullu-Manali Highway, Kullu district. 【 *(01902) 40 138.* ℻ *(01892) 40 140.*
ⓦ *www.spanresorts.com* ℝ *(011) 331 1434;* spanres@del3.vsnl.net.in
The Beas river runs right past this superbly located resort, with pretty cottages set in a sprawling garden. Each cottage has a patio, with splendid views
of the river and the mountains. 🍴 ☕ 📺 🛁 ⊗ ♨ 🏊 ⚡ 🚶 ⛷ 🎿 ♒ 🚣 ↻

MANALI: *John Banon's Hotel*   ⓇⓈⓇⓈⓇⓈ | AE DC MC V | 14 | ▨ | ● |
Near Circuit House. 【 *(01902) 52 335.* ℻ *(01892) 52 392.* ⓦ *www.fhrai.com*
This atmospheric Raj-era hotel is located in a pretty apple and cherry
orchard. It has large, clean rooms. 🍴 24 📺 ⊗ 🚶 ⛷

MANALI: *Snowcrest Manor*   ⓇⓈⓇⓈⓇⓈ | AE DC MC V | 32 | ▨ | ● |
Beyond Log Hut area. 【 *(01902) 53 351.* ℻ *(01892) 53 188.*
Large windows with splendid views across the valley to Rohtang Pass grace
every room in this plush modern hotel, built on a hillside. This is also a
good base for adventure sports. 🍴 📺 🛁 ⊗ 🍽 ☕ ⛷ ♒ 🚣

NALAGARH: *The Nalagarh Fort Resort*   ⓇⓈⓇⓈⓇⓈ | AE MC V | 22 | ▨ | ● |
The Fort, Nalagarh. 【 *(01795) 23 009.* ℻ *(01795) 23 021.* ⓦ *www.welcomheritage.com*
ℝ *(011) 656 1875;* welcom@ndf.vsnl.net.in
Housed in a fortress built by Raja Ajai Chand in AD 1100, this comfortably
refurbished hotel has a quaint medieval ambience. The extensive grounds
include orchards and forests. 🍴 ☕ 24 📺 🛁 ⊗ 🍽 ☕ ♒ ♨ 🚶

PRAGPUR: *Judge's Court*   ⓇⓈⓇⓈⓇⓈ | AE DC MC V | 10 | ▨ | ● |
Jai Bhavan, Tehsil Dehra, Kangra district. 【 *(01970) 45 035.* ℻ *(01970) 45 335.*
ⓦ *www.judgescourt.com* ℝ *(011) 467 4135;* info@judgescourt.com
Built in the early 20th century by an eminent judge, Justice Jai Lal, this
stately country manor in Indo-European style is surrounded by fruit
orchards and has been tastefully restored. 🍴 ☕ 📺 ⊗ 🍱

SARAHAN: *Srikhand*   ⓇⓈⓇⓈ | | 15 | | ● | ▨ |
Village & PO Sarahan, Rampur district. 【 *(01782) 74 234.*
This hilltop lodge run by Himachal Tourism commands great views and has
a range of rooms – dormitory style, standard and deluxe. 🍴 24 📺

SHIMLA: *Chapslee Hotel*   ⓇⓈⓇⓈⓇⓈⓇⓈ | MC | 5 | | ● |
Chapslee. 【 *(0177) 20 2542.* ℻ *(0177) 25 8663.* ⓦ *www.chapslee.com*
Formerly the summer residence of the erstwhile ruler of Kapurthala, this
charming hotel retains its old-fashioned atmosphere, and even offers a
game of croquet on its manicured lawns. The service and food are
impeccable, as is the decor. 🍴 ☕ 🛁 ⊗

SHIMLA: *Oberoi Cecil*   ⓇⓈⓇⓈⓇⓈⓇⓈ | AE DC MC V | 79 | ▨ | ● | ▨ |
Chaura Maidan. 【 *(0177) 20 4848.* ℻ *(0177) 21 1024.* ⓦ *www.oberoihotels.com*
ℝ *(011) 436 3030;* reservations@oberoihotels.com
Part of the Oberoi Group, this elegant hotel stands at the quiet end of
Shimla's Mall. A cozy atrium bar, log fires, parquet floors and a heated pool
add to the feeling of luxurious comfort. 🍴 ☕ 24 📺 🛁 ⊗ 🍽 ☕ ♒

SHIMLA: *Woodville Palace Hotel*   ⓇⓈⓇⓈⓇⓈⓇⓈ | AE MC V | 15 | | ● |
Raj Bhavan Rd. 【 *(0177) 22 3919.* ℻ *(0177) 22 3098.* ⓦ *www.welcomheritage.com*
ℝ *(011) 656 1875;* welcom@ndf.vsnl.net.in
This well-maintained palace-turned-hotel, built in 1938 by the Raja of
Jubbal, has a private forest perfect for woodland walks. 🍴 📺 ⊗

SHIMLA: *Wildflower Hall*   ⓇⓈⓇⓈⓇⓈⓇⓈⓇⓈ | AE DC MC V | 85 | ▨ | ● | ▨ |
Chharabra, Dhalli PO, Mashobra. 【 *(0177) 48 0808.* ℻ *(0177) 48 0909.*
ⓦ *www.oberoihotels.com* ℝ *(011) 436 3030;* reservations@oberoidel.com
Shimla's most luxurious hotel, this stately stone and slate building is set
amidst cedar and pine forests. It offers splendid mountain vistas and a host
of outdoor activities. 🍴 ☕ 24 📺 🛁 ⊗ 🍱 🍽 ♒ ♨ 🚶 ♒ 🚣 ↻ ✂

Price categories for a standard double room per night including tax and service charges but not including breakfast:
(Rs) under 550 rupees
(Rs)(Rs) 550–1,200 rupees
(Rs)(Rs)(Rs) 1,200–3,000 rupees
(Rs)(Rs)(Rs)(Rs) 3,000–6,000 rupees
(Rs)(Rs)(Rs)(Rs)(Rs) over 6,000 rupees

CREDIT CARDS
Indicates which major credit cards are accepted: AE American Express; DC Diners Club; MC Master Card/Access; V Visa.

WESTERN BATHROOMS
Indicates sit-down, flush toilets; showers and/or baths. Others have squat toilets and bucket-and-mug baths.

COFFEE SHOP
Hotels with 24-hour coffee shop, also serving hot meals.

AIR CONDITIONING
Hotels with air-conditioned rooms.

LADAKH, JAMMU & KASHMIR

	CREDIT CARDS	NUMBER OF ROOMS	AIR CONDITIONING	WESTERN BATHROOMS	COFFEE SHOP
ALCHI: *Alchi Resort* (Rs)(Rs)(Rs) Alchi. (01982) 52 520. Clean, comfortably furnished huts in a tranquil setting are located a stone's throw from the historic Alchi Monastery, with the Indus river flowing close by. The architecture and decor are traditional, and excursions to other monasteries in the vicinity can be organized.		15		●	
KARGIL: *Hotel D'zoji-La* (Rs)(Rs) Baru. (01985) 2227. FAX (01985) 2360. Situated 2 km (1.3 miles) out of town on the banks of the Suru river, this popular hotel has room service and STD and fax facilities.		41		●	
LEH: *Oriental Guest House* (Rs) Changspa. (01982) 53 153. FAX (01982) 53 345. www.hotelcaravancentre.com A favourite with budget travellers, this family-owned guesthouse on the road to Shanti Stupa exudes great warmth and hospitality.		25		●	
LEH: *Omasila* (Rs)(Rs) Changspa. (01982) 52 119. www.omasila.com Situated near barley fields on the outskirts of Leh, this quiet family hotel has clean food, with vegetables from its own garden.		35		●	
LEH: *Yak Tail* (Rs)(Rs) Fort Rd. (01982) 52 118. FAX (01982) 52 735. Centrally located in Leh, this hotel has balconies and a pleasant garden restaurant, and remains open through the winter.		23		●	
LEH: *Kang-lha Chen* (Rs)(Rs)(Rs) Zansti. (01982) 52 144. FAX (01982) 52 144. This quiet, old fashioned hotel has clean rooms, a good restaurant and a pleasant inner courtyard garden.	AE	25		●	
LEH: *Hotel Shambha-La* (Rs)(Rs)(Rs) Skara. (01982) 52 607, 53 500. FAX (01982) 51 100. @ ladakh_shambhala@vsnl.com (011) 686 7785. Located in a grove of poplars, surrounded by a large meadow, this hotel has clean, cheerful rooms and bright wall murals. The hotel arranges excursions and treks throughout Ladakh.	AE	24		●	
NUBRA: *Hotel Yarab Tso* (Rs)(Rs)(Rs) Tegar Village, PO Sumur. (01982) 20 008. FAX (01982) 52 607. This hotel offers a charming rural ambience, large, clean rooms and bathrooms, and room service. The tariff includes meals.		16		●	
PADUM: *Hotel Ibex* (Rs)(Rs) Padum. (01903) 45 012. Padum's best hotel has clean rooms with attached baths, laundry services, and a pleasant garden with outdoor seating and a sundeck.		15		●	
SASPUL: *Uley Tokpo Camp and Resort* (Rs)(Rs)(Rs) PO Box 268. (01982) 52 107, 53 640. FAX (01982) 52 107. @ phunchok@nda.vsnl.net.in Close to Alchi, this delightful resort set amidst apricot orchards on the banks of the Indus, offers clean thatched huts and tents.		43		●	
SRINAGAR: *Grand Palace Inter-Continental* (Rs)(Rs)(Rs)(Rs) Gupkar Rd. (0194) 47 0101. FAX (0194) 45 3794. www.inter-conti.com (011) 341 1001; newdelhi@inter-conti.com Built in 1910 as the Maharaja of Kashmir's palace, this hotel has sumptuous walnut wood interiors and a lovely garden shaded by *chinar* trees, overlooking Dal Lake.	AE MC V	125		●	■

UTTAR PRADESH & UTTARANCHAL

AGRA: *Hotel Agra Deluxe*   Rs Rs | MC V | 30
Fatehabad Rd. (0562) 33 0110. FAX (0562) 33 1330. @ hotelad@agr.dot.net.in
This clean and fairly basic budget hotel has simple rooms with attached
baths, and a multi-cuisine restaurant.

AGRA: *Taj View Hotel*   Rs Rs Rs | AE DC MC V | 100
Fatehabad Rd, Taj Ganj. (0562) 23 2400. FAX (0562) 23 2420. W www.tajhotels.com
(011) 332 2256; trn.delhi@tajhotels.com
Distant views of the Taj can be had from this multistoreyed hotel with landscaped gardens and Mughal-style interiors.

AGRA: *The Trident*   Rs Rs Rs | AE DC MC V | 140
Taj Nagari Scheme, Fatehabad Rd. (0562) 33 1818. FAX (0562) 33 1812.
reservations@tridentag.com
Surrounded by large, beautiful gardens, this low-rise hotel has a relaxed
ambience. The rooms are attractively furnished.

AGRA: *Amar Vilas*   Rs Rs Rs Rs | AE DC MC V | 106
Taj East Gate Rd, Taj Nagari Scheme. (0562) 23 1515. FAX (0562) 23 1516.
W www.oberoihotels.com (011) 389 0505; irsdesk@oberoidel.com
Set in elegant Mughal gardens with pavilions and pools, every room in this
luxurious spa-hotel run by the Oberoi Group offers views of the Taj Mahal,
which is just 600 m (1,969 ft) away.

AGRA: *Welcomgroup Mughal Sheraton*   Rs Rs Rs Rs | AE DC MC V | 285
Fatehabad Rd, Taj Ganj. (0562) 33 1701. FAX (0562) 33 1730.
W www.welcomgroup.com (011) 614 1821; rmonorth.welcomnet@welcomgroup.com
Recipient of the Agha Khan award for architecture, this imaginatively
designed hotel has a modern exterior, Mughal-style decor, immaculate
rooms and good Indian food.

ALMORA: *Kalmatia Sangam Himalaya Resort*   Rs Rs Rs | MC V | 9
Kalimat Estate, PO 002. (05962) 33 625. FAX (05962) 31 572.
@ kalmatia_sangam.vsnl.com
This resort offers nine cottages on a pretty hillside, and yoga and
meditation classes. The tariff includes meals.

ALLAHABAD: *Kanha Shyam*   Rs Rs Rs | AE DC MC V | 85
Civil Lines. (0532) 42 0281. FAX (0532) 62 2164. @ info@kanhashyam.com
Located in the Raj-era Civil Lines area with its broad avenues, this modern
well-run hotel is Allahabad's best.

CORBETT PARK: *Infinity Resorts*   Rs Rs Rs Rs | AE DC MC V | 24
PO Dhikuli via Ramnagar, Nainital district. (05947) 51 279. FAX (05947) 51 880.
W www.tigercorbettindia.com (011) 686 1189; kil@delhi.varunship.com
This comfortable, tile-roofed jungle lodge with a swimming pool also
organizes safaris and yoga classes.

DEHRA DUN: *Best Western Hotel Madhuban*   Rs Rs | AE DC MC V | 42
97 Rajpur Rd. (0135) 74 9990. FAX (0135) 74 6496. W www.madhuban.net
One of Dehra Dun's best, this centrally air-conditioned hotel has well-
appointed, spacious rooms, a mini golf course and a pretty garden. The
restaurant is very popular.

LUCKNOW: *Gomti*   Rs Rs | DC MC V | 65
6 Tej Bahadur Sapru Marg. (0522) 21 2291. FAX (0522) 21 2659.
@ upstdc@lw1.vsnl.net.in
A clean budget hotel run by the Uttar Pradesh Tourist Department, it has a
multi-cuisine restaurant and friendly service.

LUCKNOW: *Taj Residency*   Rs Rs Rs | AE DC MC V | 110
Vipin Khand, Gomti Nagar. (0522) 39 3939. FAX (0522) 39 2282.
W www.tajhotels.com (011) 332 2256; trn.delhi@tajhotels.com
Lucknow's top hotel is housed in a gracious colonial-style building topped
by a large dome. It has luxurious rooms, sprawling lawns and a restaurant
serving superb Avadhi cuisine.

MUSSOORIE: *Kasmanda Palace Hotel*   Rs | MC V | 14
The Mall Rd. (0135) 63 2424. FAX (0135) 63 0007.
This large white bungalow, built in 1836 as a summer retreat for the
erstwhile royal family of Kasmanda, has cosy interiors decorated with
family photographs and curios.

Price categories for a standard double room per night including tax and service charges but not including breakfast:
(Rs) under 550 rupees
(Rs)(Rs) 550–1,200 rupees
(Rs)(Rs)(Rs) 1,200–3,000 rupees
(Rs)(Rs)(Rs)(Rs) 3,000–6,000 rupees
(Rs)(Rs)(Rs)(Rs)(Rs) over 6,000 rupees

CREDIT CARDS
Indicates which major credit cards are accepted: AE American Express; DC Diners Club; MC Master Card/Access; V Visa.

WESTERN BATHROOMS
Indicates sit-down, flush toilets; showers and/or baths. Others have squat toilets and bucket-and-mug baths.

COFFEE SHOP
Hotels with 24-hour coffee shop, also serving hot meals.

AIR CONDITIONING
Hotels with air-conditioned rooms.

	CREDIT CARDS	NUMBER OF ROOMS	AIR CONDITIONING	WESTERN BATHROOMS	COFFEE SHOP
NAUKUCHIATAL: *The Lake Resort* (Rs)(Rs)(Rs) Naukuchiatal. ((05942) 47 183. FAX (05942) 47 061. W www.naukuchiatal.com lakeresort@naukuchiatal.com This secluded lakeside resort with large lawns has tasteful decor in its clean, comfortable rooms. Great for birdwatching. 🍴 📺 ⬛ 🏠 🏃 ♨ ⬆ ⏻	AE MC V	24		●	
NAINITAL: *The Palace Belvedere* (Rs)(Rs)(Rs) Awagarh Estate, Mallital. ((05942) 37 434. FAX (05942) 35 082. W www.welcomheritage.com The former palace of the Raja of Awagarh, this pleasant hotel boasts spacious rooms, many with lovely lake views, and great service. 🍴 24 📺 ⬛ ⬛	MC V	18		●	
RISHIKESH: *High Banks Peasant Cottage* (Rs) Tapovan. ((01364) 43 1167. FAX (01364) 43 1654. @ himalayas@vsnl.com A charming location above the Ganges in the Himalayan foothills, comfortable rooms, a pretty flower and vegetable garden, and fresh Indian food make this an attractive place to stay. 🍴 ⬛ ⬛ 🏃 ⬛		4		●	
RISHIKESH: *Hotel Ganga Kinare* (Rs)(Rs)(Rs) 16 Veerbhadra Rd. ((01364) 43 1658. FAX (0135) 43 5243. W www.uttarakhandtours.com (011) 572 7996; uttarakhandtours@hotmail.com Situated near the banks of the Ganges, this modern multistoreyed hotel has clean rooms, some with river views. 🍴 24 📺 ⬛ ⬛ ⬛	AE DC MC V	38	◼	●	
TEHRI GARHWAL: *The Glass House on the Ganges* (Rs)(Rs)(Rs) 23rd Milestone, Rishikesh-Badrinath Rd. ((01378) 69 218. W www.neemranahotels.com (011) 435 5214; sales@neemranahotels.com Located beside a secluded sandy beach on the banks of the Ganges, this delightful hotel offers spectacular views, log fires, riverside barbecues and a litchi orchard in its grounds. 🍴 ⬛ ⬛ ⬛	AE DC MC V	12	◼	●	
TEHRI GARHWAL: *Ananda–in the Himalayas* (Rs)(Rs)(Rs)(Rs)(Rs) Narendra Nagar. ((01378) 27 500. FAX (01378) 27 550. W www.anandaspa.com (011) 689 9999; anandaspa@vsnl.com This is among India's most luxurious spa-resorts, set in a tranquil 40-ha (100-acre) estate that once belonged to the Maharaja of Tehri Garhwal. It offers meditation, yogic and ayurvedic treatments, and other forms of holistic healing. 🍴 ⬛ 24 📺 ⬛ ⬛ ⬛ ⬛ ⬛ ⬛ ⬛ ⬛ ⬛ ⬛	AE DC MC V	75	◼	●	
VARANASI: *Scindia Guest House* (Rs) Scindia Ghat, Chowk. ((0542) 32 0319. FAX (0542) 32 7319. @ scindiaguesthouse@yahoo.com Located right on the river front, this guesthouse has small and simple but clean rooms, helpful, friendly staff and great views from its terrace and balconies. The food is home-cooked and excellent. 🍴 📺 ⬛		21	◼	●	
VARANASI: *Hotel Ganges View* (Rs)(Rs)(Rs) Asi Ghat. ((0542) 31 3218. FAX (0542) 36 9695. Housed in an atmospheric old *haveli* overlooking Asi Ghat, this hotel has attractively furnished rooms and a large terrace. The vegetarian food is excellent. The top-floor rooms are best. 🍴 ⬛		11	◼	●	
VARANASI: *Clarks Varanasi* (Rs)(Rs)(Rs)(Rs) The Mall, Cantonment. ((0542) 34 8501. FAX (0542) 34 8186. @ clarkvns@satyam.net.in Varanasi's oldest hotel has spacious rooms, inviting verandahs and a tree-shaded swimming pool. It also organizes cultural shows and yoga lessons at the Amrit Rao Haveli by the river. 🍴 ⬛ 24 📺 ⬛ ⬛ ⬛ ⬛ ⬛	AE DC MC V	113	◼	●	◼
VARANASI: *Taj Ganges* (Rs)(Rs)(Rs)(Rs) Nadesar Palace Ground. ((0542) 34 5100. FAX (0542) 34 8067. W www.tajhotels.com A luxury hotel with all modern facilities, including tennis courts, it also offers yoga and massage. Its Indian restaurant has classical music and dance performances in the evenings. 🍴 ⬛ 24 📺 ⬛ ⬛ ⬛ ⬛ ⬛ ⬛	AE DC MC V	130	◼	●	

BIHAR & JHARKHAND

BODH GAYA: *Mahayana Guest House* (Rs)(Rs) | 73
PO Box 04. **C** *(0631) 40 0756.* **FAX** *(0631) 40 0676.* **@** mahayanagt@yahoo.com
Run by a Tibetan monastery, this new hotel has pleasant rooms, airy
courtyards and a spacious lobby where monks often hold court. The Dalai
Lama stayed here during his 1998 visit. ▯ ▯ ▯ ▯

BODH GAYA: *Hotel Lotus Nikko* (Rs)(Rs)(Rs) | 32
Near Archaeological Museum. **C** *(0631) 40 0789.* **FAX** *(0631) 40 0788.*
@ *(011) 573 5073, 571 8125;* lotus@del3.vsnl.net.in
Walking distance from the Mahabodhi Temple, this pleasant hotel has
spacious, comfortable rooms. It also has an attractive garden. ▯ ▯ ▯ ▯

PATNA: *Republic* (Rs)(Rs) | MC V | 35
Lauriya Bagh, Exhibition Rd. **C** *(0612) 68 5021.* **FAX** *(0612) 68 5024.*
@ lovelysen@sancharnet.in
The attractions of this modest hotel include a multi-cuisine restaurant,
friendly service, conference facilities and a roof garden. The vegetarian
food is particularly good. ▯ ▯ ▯ ▯ ▯ ▯

PATNA: *Hotel Chanakya* (Rs)(Rs)(Rs) | AE DC MC V | 90
R–Block, Beerchand Patel Marg. **C** *(0612) 22 0590.* **FAX** *(0612) 22 0598.*
W www.chanakyapatna.com
This hotel has tastefully furnished rooms, a multi-cuisine restaurant and
conference facilities. ▯ ▯ ▯ ▯ ▯

PATNA: *Maurya Patna* (Rs)(Rs)(Rs)(Rs) | AE DC MC V | 75
South Gandhi Maidan. **C** *(0612) 20 3040.* **FAX** *(0612) 20 3060.*
R maurya2@dte.vsnl.net.in
The city's best hotel, this establishment offers all standard modern facilities,
and has a very helpful information desk. ▯ ▯ ▯ ▯ ▯ ▯ ▯ ▯ ▯

RAJGIR: *Centaur Hokke Hotel* (Rs)(Rs)(Rs)(Rs) | AE DC MC V | 26
Nalanda district. **C** *(06119) 55 245.* **FAX** *(06119) 55 231.* **@** centaur@sanchar.net.in
Built to attract well-heeled Buddhist pilgrim-tourists, this hotel's special
features include Japanese- and Western-style prayer rooms, a bath house, a
prayer hall, a restaurant that serves Japanese food, and an imposing tower
reminiscent of ancient Buddhist stupas. ▯ ▯ ▯

RANCHI: *Hotel Yuvraj Palace* (Rs)(Rs) | | 35
Doranda. **C** *(0651) 50 2842.* **FAX** *(0651) 50 0328.* **@** yuvrajpalace@ranchiexpress.com
This comfortable hotel with efficient, friendly service, is located in the leafy
Doranda quarter of this industrial town. It has a multi-cuisine restaurant
and conference facilities. ▯ ▯ ▯ ▯

MADHYA PRADESH & CHHATTISGARH

BANDHAVGARH: *Bandhavgarh Jungle Camp* (Rs)(Rs)(Rs)(Rs) | | 12
PO Tala, Umaria. **C** *(07627) 65 307.* **FAX** *(07627) 65 358.*
R *(011) 614 0091, 614 0116.*
Situated on the periphery of one of the country's finest wildlife sanctuaries,
the camp has attractive twin-bed safari tents with all mod-cons. There are
wildlife slide shows in the evening. ▯ ▯ ▯ ▯ ▯ ▯ ▯ ▯

BHOPAL: *Jehan Numa Palace* (Rs)(Rs)(Rs) | AE DC MC V | 60
157 Shamla Hills. **C** *(0755) 66 1100.* **FAX** *(0755) 66 1720.*
W www.hoteljehanumapalace.com **R** *(011) 542 3256;* solutions1@vsnl.com
Located on the slopes of the Shamla Hills, this hotel is a fusion of colonial
and classical European architecture. Attractions include a garden barbecue
and traditional massage. ▯ ▯ ▯ ▯ ▯ ▯ ▯ ▯ ▯ ▯ ▯ ▯ ▯ ▯

BHOPAL: *Noor-us-Sabah Palace* (Rs)(Rs)(Rs) | AE DC MC V | 39
VIP Rd, Kohe-Fiza. **C** *(0755) 74 9101.* **FAX** *(0755) 74 9110.*
W www.welcomheritage.com **R** *(011) 686 8992;* welcomheritage@bigfoot.com
Literally "The Light of the Day", this elegant palace is now a heritage hotel
with modern facilities. ▯ ▯ ▯ ▯ ▯ ▯ ▯

GWALIOR: *Usha Kiran Palace* (Rs)(Rs)(Rs)(Rs) | AE MC V | 28
Jayendraganj. **C** *(0751) 32 3993.* **FAX** *(0751) 32 1103.* **W** www.welcomgroup.com
R *(011) 614 1821;* rmonorth.welcomnet@welcomgroup.com
Once a palace of the Scindia family, this imposing heritage hotel is an
architectural jewel with a gracious ambience, featuring rich stone carvings
and sprawling lawns. ▯ ▯ ▯ ▯ ▯ ▯ ▯ ▯ ▯

Price categories for a standard double room per night including tax and service charges but not including breakfast:

- Rs under 550 rupees
- Rs Rs 550–1,200 rupees
- Rs Rs Rs 1,200–3,000 rupees
- Rs Rs Rs Rs 3,000–6,000 rupees
- Rs Rs Rs Rs Rs over 6,000 rupees

CREDIT CARDS
Indicates which major credit cards are accepted: AE American Express; DC Diners Club; MC Master Card/Access; V Visa.

WESTERN BATHROOMS
Indicates sit-down, flush toilets; showers and/or baths. Others have squat toilets and bucket-and-mug baths.

COFFEE SHOP
Hotels with 24-hour coffee shop, also serving hot meals.

AIR CONDITIONING
Hotels with air-conditioned rooms.

	CREDIT CARDS	NUMBER OF ROOMS	AIR CONDITIONING	WESTERN BATHROOMS	COFFEE SHOP
GWALIOR: *The Central Park* Rs Rs Rs 2–A City Centre, Side 1. ☎ (0751) 23 2440. ⓕ (0751) 34 6502. ⓦ www.centralpark.net This hotel offers personalized services for business executives, along with comfortable rooms and beautifully landscaped surroundings. Other facilities include a sauna and jacuzzi. ▮ ▮ 24 TV ▮ ▮ ▮ ≈ ▮	AE DC MC V	60	■	●	■
INDORE: *Taj Residency* Rs Rs Rs Rs Adjacent to Meghdoot Gardens. ☎ (0731) 55 7700. ⓕ (0731) 55 5355. @ residency.indore@tajhotels.com ⓡ (011) 332 2256; trn.delhi@tajhotels.com Located next to the city's Meghdoot Gardens, this excellent hotel offers elegant, spotless rooms, Indore's most exclusive multi-cuisine restaurant, and a poolside garden for parties. ▮ ▮ 24 TV ▮ ▮ ≈ ▮	AE DC MC V	78	■	●	
JABALPUR: *The Samadariya* Rs Rs 789 Russel Chowk. ☎ (0761) 31 6800. ⓕ (0761) 31 6354. The city's best hotel, it has well-equipped rooms, a jacuzzi and a very good vegetarian restaurant. ▮ ▮ 24 TV ▮ ▮	DC MC V	62	■	●	
KANHA NATIONAL PARK: *Kipling Camp* Rs Rs Rs Mocha Village, Mandla. ☎ (07649) 77 219. ⓕ (07649) 77 219. ⓡ (033) 473 3306. Blending in with the surrounding sanctuary, the cottages here have double-rooms with tiled roofs and whitewashed walls. Other attractions are excellent home food and guided tours of the park. ▮ ▮ A ▮ ▮		20		●	
KHAJURAHO: *Hotel Casa di William* Rs Rs Jhansi Rd. ☎ (07686) 44 244. ⓕ (07686) 42 252. Good views of the Western Group of temples can be had from this hotel which has simple, charming rooms and good food in its rooftop restaurant, including some Italian dishes. ▮ ▮		15	■	●	
KHAJURAHO: *Jass Trident* Rs Rs Rs Rs Bypass Rd. ☎ (07686) 72 344. ⓕ (07686) 72 345. ⓦ www.tridenthotels.com This hotel provides a relaxing retreat after the rigours of sightseeing in Khajuraho. The gardens are green and tranquil, with a large outdoor swimming pool, the rooms are attractively furnished, and there is a good restaurant and bar. ▮ ▮ 24 TV ▮ ▮ ▮ ▮ ≈	AE DC MC V	94	■	●	■
MAHESHWAR: *Ahilya Fort* Rs Rs Rs 3 RNT Marg. ☎ (0731) 52 0808, 24 4000. ⓕ (0731) 27 1000. ⓦ www.presidenthotels.com ⓡ (011) 462 5955; AhilyaFort@hotmail.com Built on the banks of the Narmada, this 18th-century fort with its simple yet stately ambience is a good example of Maratha architecture. The tariffs include meals, drinks, excursions and cultural programmes. ▮ ▮ ▮ ▮	AE DC MC V	15		●	
ORCHHA: *Betwa Cottages* Rs Rs Kanchanghat, Tikamgarh district. ☎ (07680) 52 618. ⓦ www.mptourism.com ⓡ (011) 334 1187; mpstdc@del6.vsnl.net.in These charming cottages on the banks of the Betwa river face some of Orchha's loveliest monuments. Each cottage has its own garden. ▮ ▮	AE DC MC V	18	■	●	
ORCHHA: *The Orchha Resort* Rs Rs Rs Kanchanghat, Tikamgarh district. ☎ (07680) 52 677. ⓕ (07680) 52 677. ⓦ www.orchharesort.com ⓡ (0562) 36 1820; oswalexp@nde.vsnl.net.in This low-rise hotel with the usual modern comforts is located opposite lovely monuments. The swimming pool has lovely views of the river. Only vegetarian food. ▮ ▮ 24 TV ▮ ▮ ▮ ≈	AE DC MC V	34	■	●	
UJJAIN: *Suvarna Palace* Rs Rs Rs 23 GDC Rd, Dashera Maidan. ☎ (0734) 51 3045. ⓕ (0734) 51 5045. @ hotelsuvarna@usa.net This well-managed hotel offers large, comfortable rooms as well as luxury suites. It is set in a well-tended garden. ▮ ▮ 24 TV ▮	MC V	22	■	●	

KOLKATA

KOLKATA: *Hotel Victerrace*   ⑧⑧   AE MC V   47
1–B Gorky Terrace. **▌** *(033) 240 8788.* **FAX** *(033) 240 4063.* **W** www.hotelvicterrace.com
Attractively furnished rooms, efficient and courteous staff, and an open-air
multi-cuisine restaurant. ▮▮ 24 TV ▮ ▮

KOLKATA: *The Astor Hotel*   ⑧⑧⑧   AE DC MC V   35
15 Shakespeare Sarani. **▌** *(033) 282 9957.* **FAX** *(033) 282 7430.*
W www.astorcalcutta.com
The name suggests a colonial ambience, a fact borne out by its red-and-
white brick façade and elegant rooms. ▮▮ ▮ 24 TV ▮

KOLKATA: *Fairlawn Hotel*   ⑧⑧⑧   AE DC MC V   20
13/A Sudder Street. **▌** *(033) 245 1510.* **FAX** *(033) 244 1835.* **W** www.fairlawnhotel.com
A relic of the Raj, this family-run hotel still retains its period flavour. Meals
are served at fixed times and feature a full English breakfast, and tea and
sandwiches on the lawns. ▮▮ 24 TV ▮ ▮ ▮

KOLKATA: *Lytton Hotel*   ⑧⑧⑧   AE DC MC V   80
14 Sudder Street. **▌** *(033) 249 1872.* **FAX** *(033) 249 1747.* **W** www.lyttonhotel.com
Located in the heart of the city, this tastefully decorated hotel has
comfortable rooms and also offers business facilities. ▮▮ ▮ 24 TV ▮

KOLKATA: *Tollygunge Club*   ⑧⑧⑧   MC V   70
120 Deshpran Sasmal Rd. **▌** *(033) 417 6022.* **FAX** *(033) 472 0480.*
@ tolly@cal3.vsnl.net.in
Spread over 40 ha (100 acres) in the heart of Kolkata, the club boasts an
18-hole golf course, spacious rooms and guest cottages with courteous, if
somewhat slow service. ▮▮ ▮ 24 TV ▮ ▮ ▮ ▮ ▮ ▮ ▮ ▮ ▮

KOLKATA: *The Kenilworth*   ⑧⑧⑧⑧   AE DC MC V   105
1 & 2 Little Russel Street. **▌** *(033) 282 8394.* **FAX** *(033) 282 5136.*
W www.kenilworthhotels.com **R** *(011) 332 1979, 332 3473.*
This quiet hotel has an elegant charm and comfortable rooms. It has
excellent breakfast and lunch buffets, and a cosy English-style pub,
complete with a red London phone booth. ▮▮ ▮ 24 TV ▮ ▮ ▮ ▮ ▮

KOLKATA: *Hotel Hindustan International*   ⑧⑧⑧⑧   AE DC MC V   186
235/1 AJC Bose Rd. **▌** *(033) 280 2323.* **FAX** *(033) 280 0111.* **W** www.hhihotels.com
Plush rooms with views of the city, a good Chinese restaurant and a
shopping arcade are the attractions of this hotel. ▮▮ ▮ 24 TV ▮ ▮ ▮ ▮

KOLKATA: *Oberoi Grand*   ⑧⑧⑧⑧⑧   AE DC MC V   213
15 Jawahar Lal Nehru Rd. **▌** *(033) 249 2323.* **FAX** *(033) 249 1217.*
W www.oberoihotels.com **R** *(011) 436 3030;* irsdesk@oberoidel.com
An institution in Kolkata, this grand Victorian building has sumptous
interiors, rooms with four-poster beds, an inviting tea lounge and
outstanding restaurants. ▮▮ ▮ 24 TV ▮ ▮ ▮ ▮ ▮ ▮ ▮

KOLKATA: *The Park*   ⑧⑧⑧⑧⑧   AE DC MC V   149
17 Park Street. **▌** *(033) 249 3121.* **FAX** *(033) 249 7343.* **W** www.theparkhotels.com
R *(011) 373 3737;* resv.del@park.sprintrpg.ems.vsnl.net.in
Comfortable rooms with jacuzzis, a swanky nightclub, and a well-stocked
library are this hotel's special features. ▮▮ ▮ 24 TV ▮ ▮ ▮ ▮ ▮ ▮

KOLKATA: *Taj Bengal*   ⑧⑧⑧⑧⑧   AE DC MC V   229
34–B Belvedere Rd, Alipore. **▌** *(033) 223 3939.* **FAX** *(033) 223 1766.*
W www.tajhotels.com **R** *(011) 332 2256;* trn.delhi@tajhotels.com
This luxurious hotel has beautiful interior decor, business facilities and
restaurants serving excellent Bengali food. ▮▮ ▮ 24 TV ▮ ▮ ▮ ▮ ▮ ▮

WEST BENGAL & SIKKIM

DARJEELING: *Cedar Inn*   ⑧⑧⑧⑧   MC V   22
Jalapahar Rd. **▌** *(0354) 54 446.* **FAX** *(0354) 53 764.* **W** www.cedarinnindia.com
There are great views of Kanchendzonga from this Victorian Gothic-style
hotel, with cosy wood-panelled interiors. ▮▮ ▮ TV ▮ ▮ ▮ ▮ ▮ ▮

DARJEELING: *New Elgin Hotel*   ⑧⑧⑧⑧   AE DC MC V   28
18 HD Lama Rd. **▌** *(0354) 54 114.* **FAX** *(0354) 54 267.* **W** www.elginhotels.com
R *(033) 226 9878;* newelgin@cal.vsnl.net.in
Landscaped gardens and views of Himalayan peaks are the special features
of this hotel, which also offers baby-sitting services. ▮▮ ▮ 24 TV ▮ ▮ ▮

Price categories for a standard double room per night including tax and service charges but not including breakfast:
Rs under 550 rupees
RsRs 550–1,200 rupees
RsRsRs 1,200–3,000 rupees
RsRsRsRs 3,000–6,000 rupees
RsRsRsRsRs over 6,000 rupees

CREDIT CARDS
Indicates which major credit cards are accepted: AE American Express; DC Diners Club; MC Master Card/Access; V Visa.

WESTERN BATHROOMS
Indicates sit-down, flush toilets; showers and/or baths. Others have squat toilets and bucket-and-mug baths.

COFFEE SHOP
Hotels with 24-hour coffee shop, also serving hot meals.

AIR CONDITIONING
Hotels with air-conditioned rooms.

	CREDIT CARDS	NUMBER OF ROOMS	AIR CONDITIONING	WESTERN BATHROOMS	COFFEE SHOP
DARJEELING: *Windamere Hotel* — RsRsRsRs Observatory Hills. (0354) 54 041, 54 042. FAX (0354) 54 043. www.windamerehotel.com A relic of the Raj, this delightful family-run hotel, established in the 19th century, is furnished in elegant colonial style, with coal fires and hot-water bottles in the rooms. It serves wholesome food and a string quartet serenades guests during dinner.	AE DC MC V	37		●	
GANGTOK: *The Chumbi Residency* — RsRsRs Tibet Rd. (03592) 26 618, 26 619. FAX (03592) 22 707. chumbi@dte.vsnl.net.in A four-storeyed modern hotel, with efficient and resourceful staff, and a coffee shop where good Chinese food is also available.	AE	25	●		■
GANGTOK: *Hotel Tibet* — RsRsRs Paljor Stadium Rd. (03592) 22 523. FAX (03592) 26 233. www.hoteltashidelek.com With its colourful Tibetan decor, excellent restaurant and bar, and friendly atmosphere, this hotel is deservedly popular.	AE DC MC V	33		●	
GANGTOK: *Nor-Khill Hotel* — RsRsRsRs Palijor Stadium Rd. (03592) 25 637, 20 064. FAX (03592) 25 639. www.elginhotels.com (033) 226 9878; newelgin@cal.vsnl.net.in Located in an old palace, this hotel set in a lovely garden, has spacious rooms with views of Kanchendzonga.	AE DC MC V	25		●	
GANGTOK: *Netuk House* — RsRsRsRs Tibet Rd. (03592) 22 374. FAX (03592) 24 802. www.netukhouse.com (0354) 54 041; windamere@vsnl.com The traditional hospitality of a Sikkimese family and excellent service adds warmth to this wonderful heritage hotel with gracious interiors. The tariff includes meals.		10		●	
KALIMPONG: *Himalayan Hotel* — RsRsRs Upper Cart Rd. (03552) 55 248. FAX (03552) 55 122. This heritage hotel is filled with fascinating photographs and Tibetan and Bhutanese art, and has a garden displaying Himalayan flora. It also offers excellent views of Kanchendzonga.	AE MC V	16		●	
SHANTINIKETAN: *Marks & Meadows* — RsRsRs Shantiniketan. www.deutech.com/markhotel (033) 244 8254; markhotel@indiamail.com Red-tiled cottages dot an expanse of manicured green lawns. The hotel also features a swimming pool, tribal dance performances in the evening and Bengali cuisine in its restaurant.	AE MC V		■	●	
SILIGURI: *Hotel Cindrella* — RsRsRs 3rd Mile, Sevoke Rd. (0353) 54 7136, 54 4130. FAX (0353) 53 1173. www.cindrellahotels.com Comfortable rooms, efficient service, and internet facilities make this Siliguri's best hotel. Only vegetarian food is served. The hotel also has a billiards room and a health club.	AE MC V	48	■	●	
SILIGURI: *Hotel Sinclairs* — RsRsRsRs PO Pradhan Nagar. (0353) 51 7674, 51 2675. FAX (0353) 51 7743. www.sinclairshotels.com (011) 335 4706; pressman@del2.vsnl.com Located near the Teesta river, this hotel has old-fashioned charm with spacious rooms and courteous and helpful staff. It offers conference facilities and an open-air garden café.	AE DC MC V	47	■	●	■
SUNDERBANS: *Sajnakhali Tourist Lodge* — Rs South 24, Parganas, PO Dayapur. (03219) 52 560. (011) 374 2840, (033) 221 5999. This lodge, which runs on solar energy, has basic accommodation, with meals served in a dining hall. It also has a watchtower and a crocodile pool.		30		●	

ORISSA

BHUBANESWAR: *Hotel Swosti* ⓇⓈ ⓇⓈ
103 Janpath. 【 *(0674) 53 5778.* FAX *(0674) 53 4794.* W *www.swosti.com*
Built in accordance with the ancient Indian architectural science of *Vaastu*,
this hotel also has a four-lane bowling alley for more modern tastes, and
good business facilities. 🟦🟦🟦🟦🟦🟦

	AE	57	■	●	
	DC				
	MC				
	V				

BHUBANESWAR: *Mayfair Lagoon* ⓇⓈ ⓇⓈ ⓇⓈ
8–B, Jayadev Vihar. 【 *(0674) 55 7701.* FAX *(0674) 55 7702.*
W *www.mayfair-resorts.com* 🔲 *(011) 332 0264;* conn@india.com
This elegant low-rise hotel has a lovely landscaped garden, a lake and
clean tile-roofed cottages for guests. It also has excellent restaurants, a pool
and a shopping arcade. 🟦🟦🟦🟦🟦🟦🟦🟦🟦🟦🟦🟦

	AE	64	■	●	■
	DC				
	MC				
	V				

BHUBANESWAR: *The Oberoi* ⓇⓈ ⓇⓈ ⓇⓈ ⓇⓈ
CBI, Nayapalli. 【 *(0674) 30 1010.* FAX *(0674) 30 1302.* W *www.oberoihotels.com*
🔲 *(011) 436 3030;* irsdesk@oberoidel.com
The classic ambience of Orissa's rich culture is recreated in this hotel. Everything here, from the temple-inspired architecture to its restaurants, has a
touch of class. It also has tennis courts. 🟦🟦🟦🟦🟦🟦🟦🟦🟦🟦🟦🟦

	AE	70	■	●	■
	DC				
	MC				
	V				

CHILIKA LAKE: *Barkul Panthnivas* ⓇⓈ ⓇⓈ
Barkul, Balugaon. 【 *(06756) 20 488.* W *www.orissa-tourism.com*
Situated on the banks of Chilika Lake, this modest hotel offers its guests
fresh seafood, yachting and speed boat excursions. 🟦🟦🟦

		25	■	●	

GOPALPUR-ON-SEA: *The Oberoi Palm Beach* ⓇⓈ ⓇⓈ ⓇⓈ ⓇⓈ
Gopalpur-on-Sea, Ganjam. 【 *(0680) 28 2021, 28 2023.* FAX *(0680) 28 2300.*
W *www.oberoihotels.com* 🔲 *(011) 436 3030;* irsdesk@oberoidel.com
This Oberoi-run hotel is situated near a tranquil, secluded beach. It has
beautifully kept gardens, with a mini zoo for children and stunning views
of the sea and the distant hills. 🟦🟦🟦🟦🟦🟦🟦🟦

	AE	18	■	●	
	DC				
	MC				
	V				

KONARK: *Yatri Nivas* ⓇⓈ ⓇⓈ
AT/PO Konark. 【 *(06758) 35 821.*
Run by the state's tourism department, this hotel is close to the Sun
Temple, and has clean, well-maintained rooms. Good value for money
makes it popular with visitors on a budget. 🟦🟦🟦🟦

		18	■	●	

PURI: *Toshali Sands* ⓇⓈ ⓇⓈ ⓇⓈ
Ethnic Village Resort, Konark Marine Drive. 【 *(06752) 23 571.* FAX *(06752) 23 899.*
W *www.toshaliresorts.com*
Overlooking the Balukhanda reserve forest, and sprawling across 12 ha (30
acres) of lush territory, the hotel offers cottages with modern amenities and
a soothing ambience. 🟦🟦🟦🟦🟦🟦🟦🟦🟦🟦🟦🟦

	AE	104	■	●	
	DC				
	MC				
	V				

PURI: *Mayfair Beach Resort* ⓇⓈ ⓇⓈ ⓇⓈ ⓇⓈ
Chakratirtha Rd. 【 *(06752) 27 800.* FAX *(06752) 24 242.* W *www.mayfair-resorts.com*
This imaginatively designed resort has comfortable rooms, each with its
own patio. Many of the rooms have sea views. Other attractions include a
good pool, and fresh seafood. 🟦🟦🟦🟦🟦🟦🟦🟦🟦

	AE	33	■	●	
	MC				
	V				

ASSAM & THE NORTHEAST

AGARTALA: *Royal Guest House* ⓇⓈ
Palace Compound, West Gate. 【 *(0381) 22 5652.* FAX *(0381) 23 899.*
Tucked away in one of the streets leading to the former maharaja's palace,
this guesthouse has large rooms, and good Indian and Chinese food. 🟦

		30	■	●	

AIZAWL: *Tourist Lodge* ⓇⓈ
Chaltlang. 【 *(0389) 21 083.*
A clean, reasonably-priced place run by the state tourism department, with
pleasing views and a good restaurant. 🟦

		14	■	●	

GUWAHATI: *Hotel Dynasty* ⓇⓈ ⓇⓈ ⓇⓈ
SS Rd, Lakhotia. 【 *(0361) 51 6021.* FAX *(0361) 52 2112.*
This hotel has clean and comfortable rooms, pleasant decor with lots of
greenery, and good fish dishes in its restaurant. 🟦🟦🟦🟦🟦🟦

	AE	86	■	●	■
	DC				
	MC				
	V				

IMPHAL: *Hotel Anand Continental* ⓇⓈ ⓇⓈ
Khoyathong Rd. 【 *(0385) 22 3422.* FAX *(0385) 24 0107.* @ dkbohra@37.com
Popular with the region's ministers and businessmen, this hotel has a well-
known kebab restaurant. 🟦🟦🟦🟦

	MC	30	■	●	
	V				

	CREDIT CARDS	NUMBER OF ROOMS	AIR CONDITIONING	WESTERN BATHROOMS	COFFEE SHOP

Price categories for a standard double room per night including tax and service charges but not including breakfast:
Rs under 550 rupees
Rs Rs 550–1,200 rupees
Rs Rs Rs 1,200–3,000 rupees
Rs Rs Rs Rs 3,000–6,000 rupees
Rs Rs Rs Rs Rs over 6,000 rupees

CREDIT CARDS
Indicates which major credit cards are accepted: AE American Express; DC Diners Club; MC Master Card/Access; V Visa.

WESTERN BATHROOMS
Indicates sit-down, flush toilets; showers and/or baths. Others have squat toilets and bucket-and-mug baths.

COFFEE SHOP
Hotels with 24-hour coffee shop, also serving hot meals.

AIR CONDITIONING
Hotels with air-conditioned rooms.

		CREDIT CARDS	NUMBER OF ROOMS	AIR CONDITIONING	WESTERN BATHROOMS	COFFEE SHOP
ITANAGAR: *Donyi-Polo Ashok* (Rs)(Rs)(Rs) C–Sector. ☎ *(0360) 21 2626.* FAX *(0360) 21 2641.* @ hoteldonyi@sancharnet.in ☎ *(011) 336 1607;* reservation@theashokgroup.com This hotel has some air-conditioned suites, offers guides for sightseeing, and also arranges for folk dances on request. 🍴 ▮ 24 TV ▮		AE DC MC V	18	■	●	■
JORHAT: *Hotel Paradise* (Rs)(Rs) Solicitor's Rd. ☎ *(0360) 32 1521.* FAX *(0376) 32 3512.* Located in the heart of the town, this hotel offers simple but decent accommodation and conference facilities. This is a good base from which to visit Majuli Island. 🍴 ▮ 24 TV ▮ ▮		MC V	31	■	●	
KAZIRANGA: *Wild Grass Resort* (Rs)(Rs)(Rs) Kaziranga National Park. ☎ *(03776) 62 011.* ☎ *(0361) 54 6827;* wildgrss1@sancharnet.in Near a pretty stream amidst paddy fields, this attractive resort organizes elephant safaris, forest walks and other interesting excursions. The lunch buffet is excellent. 🍴 ▮ ▮ ▮ ▮			18		●	■
KOHIMA: *Hotel Japfu* (Rs)(Rs) PR Hill. ☎ *(0370) 22 2721.* Situated on a hill, this simple, clean hotel has large, heated rooms, and a reasonable restaurant. 🍴 ▮ 24 TV ▮		MC V	27		●	
SHILLONG: *Hotel Pinewood* (Rs)(Rs)(Rs) Rita Rd, European Ward. ☎ *(0364) 22 3116.* FAX *(0364) 224 176.* @ pwhotel@neline.com This delightful Raj-era hotel, with mock-Tudor gables, is located close to the centre of town and to Ward Lake. The rooms and cottages are spacious and comfortable, and the gardens are lovely. 🍴 ▮ ▮ ▮ ▮ ▮			40		●	■
SHILLONG: *Hotel Polo Towers* (Rs)(Rs)(Rs) Polo Grounds. ☎ *(0364) 22 2341.* FAX *(0364) 22 0090.* @ hpt@vsnl.com A modern and efficient hotel located near the main shopping area, with comfortable rooms, a bar and a coffee shop. 🍴 ▮ TV ▮ ▮ ▮		AE MC V	50		●	■

RAJASTHAN

		CREDIT CARDS	NUMBER OF ROOMS	AIR CONDITIONING	WESTERN BATHROOMS	COFFEE SHOP
AJMER: *Mansingh Palace* (Rs)(Rs)(Rs)(Rs) Vaishali Nagar. ☎ *(0145) 42 5855.* FAX *(0145) 42 5858.* W www.mansinghhotels.com Originally an 18th-century fortress, this is now Ajmer's best hotel. Over-looking the scenic Anasagar Lake, it has atmospheric rooms, sprawling lawns and a bar. 🍴 ▮ 24 TV ▮ ▮ ⏾		AE DC MC V	54	■	●	■
BHARATPUR: *Laxmi Vilas Palace* (Rs)(Rs)(Rs) Kakaji Ki Kothi. ☎ *(05644) 23 523.* FAX *(05644) 25 259.* W www.laxmivilas.com One of Rajasthan's many heritage hotels, its unique features include a richly carved sandstone archway and spacious rooms furnished with antiques. Food comes from the home farm. 🍴 ▮ TV ▮ ▮ ▮ ▮ ▮		AE MC V	25	■	●	
BIKANER: *Lalgarh Palace* (Rs)(Rs)(Rs) Lalgarh Palace. ☎ *(0151) 54 0201.* FAX *(0151) 52 2253.* W www.welcomheritage.com ☎ *(011) 656 1869;* welcom@ndf.vsnl.net.in The deep red sandstone, opulent interiors and sprawling gardens of this converted palace, built in the early 20th century, is in striking contrast to the rugged sand dunes that surround it. 🍴 ▮ 24 TV ▮ ▮ ▮ ▮ ▮ ⏾		AE DC MC V	38	■	●	
BIKANER: *Gajner Palace Hotel* (Rs)(Rs)(Rs)(Rs) PO Gajner, Tehsil Kolayat. ☎ *(01534) 55 063.* FAX *(01534) 55 060.* This enchanting hotel with a fairy-tale setting beside a lake, used to be the Maharaja of Bikaner's hunting lodge. Surrounded by a forest, it offers comfortable rooms with period flavour, excellent birdwatching, jeep safaris and friendly service. 🍴 ▮ 24 ▮ ▮ ⏾		AE MC V	42		●	

BUNDI: *Royal Retreat* (Rs)(Rs) — 10
Garh Palace. [(0747) 44 4426. FAX (0747) 44 3278. W www.royalretreat.com
Located below the fort, this quiet, clean hotel is built around a courtyard.
Its rooftop restaurant has good vegetarian food.

CHITTORGARH: *Hotel Castle Bijaipur* (Rs)(Rs) — 24
Village Post Bijaipur. [No telephone
R (01472) 40 099; hpratapp@hotmail.com
This atmospheric feudal castle is picturesquely located in rural Mewar. It
organizes jeep safaris to nearby villages and forts, fishing trips and folk
entertainment in the evenings.

DEOGARH: *Deogarh Mahal* (Rs)(Rs)(Rs) — MC V — 42
PO Deogarh, Rajsamand district. [(02904) 52 777. FAX (02904) 52 555.
W www.deogarh.com
A beautiful, well-run heritage hotel, with traditional decor, a lotus-shaped
swimming pool, and views of the Aravalli Hills.

DUNGARPUR: *Udai Bilas Palace* (Rs)(Rs)(Rs)(Rs) — MC V — 20
Udai Bilas Palace. [(02964) 30 808. FAX (02964) 31 008. W www.udaibilaspalace.com
Run by the former ruling family who are attentive hosts, this hotel is near a
lake and a private forest. The Art Deco furniture blends harmoniously with
the traditional murals and decorative inlay work.

JAIPUR: *Rambagh Palace* (Rs)(Rs)(Rs)(Rs) — AE DC MC V — 95
Bhawani Singh Rd. [(0141) 38 1916. FAX (0141) 38 1098. @ rambagh.jaipur@taj.com
R (011) 332 2256; trn.delhi@tajhotels.com
Set amidst lush gardens, this hotel successfully combines princely Rajput
decor with modern amenities. Horse riding is on offer, and the grounds
include a polo field.

JAIPUR: *Samode Haveli* (Rs)(Rs)(Rs)(Rs) — AE MC V — 21
Ganga Pol. [(0141) 63 2370. FAX (0141) 63 1397. W www.samode.com
R reservations@samode.com
Built over 200 years, this gracious mansion has some stunning rooms with
original wall paintings and mirrorwork.

JAIPUR: *The Trident* (Rs)(Rs)(Rs) — AE DC MC V — 138
Opp Jal Mahal, Amer Rd. [(0141) 67 0101. FAX (0141) 67 0303.
W www.tridenthotels.com R reservations@tridentjp.com
This attractive, well-run hotel, located opposite the Jal Mahal, offers scenic
views of Man Sagar lake and the Aravalli Hills.

JAIPUR: *Raj Vilas* (Rs)(Rs)(Rs)(Rs)(Rs) — AE DC MC V — 71
Goner Rd. [(0141) 68 0101. FAX (0141) 68 0202. W www.oberoihotels.com
R (011) 436 3030; reservations@oberoidel.com
A luxury spa-resort run by the Oberoi Group, Raj Vilas has lovely gardens
with pools and pavilions, tasteful interior decor, excellent cuisine and
faultless service.

JAISALMER: *Killa Bhawan* (Rs)(Rs)(Rs) — MC V — 6
Jaisalmer Fort. [(02992) 51 204. FAX (02992) 54 518. @ kbhawan@yahoo.com
Expect the epitome of Rajasthani hospitality in this small, well-run
hotel. Other attractions include camel and jeep safaris to explore the
surrounding countryside.

JAISALMER: *Hotel Narayan Niwas Palace* (Rs)(Rs)(Rs) — AE MC V — 43
Malka Prol. [(02992) 52 408. FAX (02992) 52 101. W www.narayanniwas.com
R (0124) 56 2047.
Beautiful views of Jaisalmer Fort and the desert from the rooftop, and
friendly owners are the main attractions of this hotel, housed in a lovely
carved stone mansion.

JAISALMER: *Gorbandh Palace* (Rs)(Rs)(Rs)(Rs) — AE MC V — 67
1 Tourist Complex. [(02992) 53 801. FAX (02992) 53 811. W www.hrhindia.com
A new hotel with all modern conveniences, it is built in traditional style in
the carved golden Jaisalmer stone. It has an inviting central courtyard and a
good craft and book shop as well.

JODHPUR: *Devi Bhawan* (Rs)(Rs) — MC V — 10
1 Defence Lab Rd, Ratanada. [(0291) 51 1067. FAX (0291) 51 2215.
W www.devibhawan.com
This delightful, clean hotel has excellent food, lush gardens, and friendly
owners and staff. Jeep safaris are available.

Price categories for a standard double room per night including tax and service charges but not including breakfast:

Rs under 550 rupees
Rs Rs 550–1,200 rupees
Rs Rs Rs 1,200–3,000 rupees
Rs Rs Rs Rs 3,000–6,000 rupees
Rs Rs Rs Rs Rs over 6,000 rupees

CREDIT CARDS
Indicates which major credit cards are accepted: AE American Express; DC Diners Club; MC Master Card/Access; V Visa.

WESTERN BATHROOMS
Indicates sit-down, flush toilets; showers and/or baths. Others have squat toilets and bucket-and-mug baths.

COFFEE SHOP
Hotels with 24-hour coffee shop, also serving hot meals.

AIR CONDITIONING
Hotels with air-conditioned rooms.

Hotel	Price	CREDIT CARDS	NUMBER OF ROOMS	AIR CONDITIONING	WESTERN BATHROOMS	COFFEE SHOP
JODHPUR: *Ajit Bhawan Palace*	Rs Rs Rs	AE MC V	55	■	●	■
JODHPUR: *Welcomheritage Umaid Bhawan Palace*	Rs Rs Rs	AE DC MC V	98	■	●	■
KOTA: *Brijraj Bhawan Palace Hotel*	Rs Rs Rs	MC V	7	■	●	
KUMBHALGARH: *Aodhi Hotel*	Rs Rs Rs	AE MC V	26	■	●	
MOUNT ABU: *Palace Hotel*	Rs Rs Rs	AE DC MC V	35	■	●	
NEEMRANA: *Neemrana Fort Palace*	Rs Rs Rs	AE DC MC V	40	■	●	
PUSHKAR: *Hotel Pushkar Palace*	Rs Rs Rs	AE MC V	35	■	●	
PUSHKAR: *Pushkar Resorts*	Rs Rs Rs	AE DC MC V	40	■	●	■
ROHET: *Rohet Garh*	Rs Rs Rs	AE MC V	30	■	●	
SAMODE: *Samode Palace*	Rs Rs Rs Rs	AE MC V	44	■	●	■

JODHPUR: *Ajit Bhawan Palace*
Near Circuit House. ((0291) 51 0410. FAX (0291) 51 0674. W www.ajitbhawan.com
R (011) 622 1420; ajitbhawan@rediffmail.com
This home of a member of the former ruling family displays vintage cars, sepia photographs and antiques. Rustic cottages in the grounds recreate a village atmosphere for guests.

JODHPUR: *Welcomheritage Umaid Bhawan Palace*
Umaid Bhawan Palace. ((0291) 51 0101. FAX (0291) 51 0100.
W www.welcomheritage.com R (011) 656 1869; welcom@ndf.vsnl.net.in
With its monumental architecture and ambience of princely splendour, this is one of the finest heritage hotels.

KOTA: *Brijraj Bhawan Palace Hotel*
Civil Lines. ((0744) 45 0529. FAX (0744) 45 0057. @ brijraj@datainfosys.net
The erudite former ruler of Kota still lives in a part of this mansion which was once the British Residency. The food is excellent and the ambience regal yet friendly, with royal memorabilia, family souvenirs and wildlife trophies decorating the rooms.

KUMBHALGARH: *Aodhi Hotel*
PO Kelwara, Rajsamand district. ((02954) 42 341. FAX (02954) 42 349.
Located just below the great fort, this comfortable hotel with superb views of the hilly countryside, organizes fascinating horse safaris to view wildlife in the region, and to tribal villages.

MOUNT ABU: *Palace Hotel*
Bikaner House, Dilwara Rd. ((02974) 38 673. FAX (02974) 38 674. R (022) 492 6579.
Built as the summer palace of the ruler of Bikaner in 1894, this comfortably refurbished stately pile has a large garden, grand banquet hall and great period flavour.

NEEMRANA: *Neemrana Fort Palace*
Delhi-Jaipur Highway. ((01494) 46 007. FAX (01494) 46 005.
W www.neemranahotels.com R (011) 435 8962; sales@neemrana.com
This superbly renovated 15th-century Rajput fort has a series of charming courtyards and a swimming pool on the top floor, as well as a lovely shop. The village below has an impressive stepwell.

PUSHKAR: *Hotel Pushkar Palace*
Chhoti Basti. ((0145) 77 2001. FAX (0145) 77 2226. W www.hotelpushkarpalace.com
Stylishly furnished with family antiques, this heritage property's main attraction is its superb location by the lake.

PUSHKAR: *Pushkar Resorts*
Village Ganhera, Motisar Rd. ((0145) 77 2017. FAX (0145) 77 2946.
W www.pushkarresorts.com R (011) 464 7379.
With luxurious cottages set amidst orchards, this resort offers a golf putting range, and camel and jeep safaris.

ROHET: *Rohet Garh*
PO Rohet, Pali district. ((02936) 68 231. W www.rohetgarh.com
R (0291) 43 1161.
This tranquil fort-hotel, a favourite with authors Bruce Chatwin and William Dalrymple, has delightful owners who help guests explore the nearby villages and their crafts.

SAMODE: *Samode Palace*
Village Samode. ((01423) 40 013. FAX (01423) 44 815. W www.samode.com
R (0141) 63 2407; reservations@samode.com
This glittering palace, where scenes from the James Bond film *Octopussy* were shot, boasts a spectacular setting and interiors. It also runs a tented camp a short distance from the palace.

SARISKA: *Hotel Sariska Palace* Rs Rs Rs Rs | AE DC MC V | 125
Sariska. ((0144) 84 1322. FAX (0144) 84 1323. W www.sariska.com
R (011) 618 8861.
A former royal hunting lodge, this comfortable hotel also has an ayurvedic
and yoga centre. 🍴 🍷 📺 🛏 🏊 🎾 ⛳ 🚗 ⏱ 🏥

SAWAI MADHOPUR: *Sher Bagh* Rs Rs Rs Rs | | 12
Sherpur Khiljipur. W www.sherbagh.com
R (011) 331 6534; sherbagh@vsnl.com
This enchanting tented camp also organizes interesting forest excursions.
Great food, atmosphere and service. 🍴 🍷 24 🛏 🏊 🏥

SAWAI MADHOPUR: *Vanya Vilas* Rs Rs Rs Rs | AE MC V | 25
Ranthambore Rd. ((07462) 23 999. FAX (07462) 23 988. W www.oberoihotels.com
R (011) 389 0505.
The tents in this forest resort have teak floors and marble bathrooms. There
is also a heated pool and an amphitheatre. 🍴 🍷 24 📺 🛏 🏊 🎾

SHEKHAVATI: *Hotel Castle Mandawa* Rs Rs Rs | AE MC V | 70
Jhunjhunu district, Mandawa. ((015972) 23 124. FAX (015972) 23 171.
W www.castlemandawa.com
No two rooms are alike in this pleasant 18th-century fort-hotel. Dinners are
candle-lit, with folk dances and music. 🍴 🍷 24 🛏 🏊 ⛳ 🚗

UDAIPUR: *Jagat Niwas Palace* Rs Rs Rs | | 29
24–25, Lal Ghat. ((0294) 42 2860. FAX (0294) 41 8512. W www.jagatniwaspalace.com
Famous for its superb views of Lake Pichola, this delightful 17th-century
haveli has comfortable, palatial rooms and an inviting ambience. Horse
riding can be arranged. 🍴 🍷 24 📺 🛏 🏊 ⛳ 🎾 ⏱ 🏥

UDAIPUR: *Lake Palace Hotel* Rs Rs Rs Rs | AE DC MC V | 84
PO Box 5, Lake Pichola. ((0294) 52 8800. FAX (0294) 52 8700. W www.tajhotels.com
This fairy-tale island palace is among India's most romantic hotels. An expe-
rience not to be missed, if you can afford it. 🍴 🍷 24 📺 🛏 🏊 ⛳ 🏊 🏄

UDAIPUR: *Shiv Niwas Palace Hotel* Rs Rs Rs Rs | AE DC MC V | 34
City Palace. ((0294) 52 8016. FAX (0294) 52 8006. W www.hrhindia.com
Located next to the City Palace, this elegant crescent-shaped former royal
guesthouse is decorated with superb antique art and furniture. It also offers
a holistic health centre. 🍴 🍷 24 📺 🛏 🏊 ⛳ 🏊 🏄

UDAIPUR: *Udai Vilas* Rs Rs Rs Rs | AE DC MC V | 90
Haridas Ji Ki Nagri. ((0294) 43 3300. FAX (0294) 43 3200. W www.oberoihotels.com
R (011) 436 3030; reservations@oberoidel.com
This new luxury hotel is scenically located near Lake Pichola. The
landscaped gardens, fountains, pavilions and decor are inspired by
traditional Udaipuri decorative arts. 🍴 🍷 24 📺 🛏 🏊 ⛳ 🎾 ⏱ 🏊 🏄

UDAIPUR: *Devi Garh* Rs Rs Rs Rs Rs | AE DC MC V | 29
PO No 144. ((02953) 89 211. FAX (02953) 89 357. W www.deviresorts.com
R (011) 372 2200; reservations@deviresorts.com
Minimalist chic interiors harmonize with magnificent architecture in this pains-
takingly restored hill fort. The food and service are excellent, and a range of
Ayurvedic therapies is also on offer. 🍴 🍷 24 📺 🛏 🏊 ⛳ 🎾 ⏱ 🏊 🏥

GUJARAT

AHMEDABAD: *Cama Park Plaza* Rs Rs Rs | AE DC MC V | 50
Khanpur. ((079) 550 5281. FAX (079) 550 5285. @ camahotel@vsnl.com
Recently renovated, this elegant and comfortable hotel has pretty gardens,
a swimming pool, a coffee shop, and a good handicrafts boutique. It
overlooks the Sabarmati river. 🍴 🍷 24 📺 🛏 🏊 ⛳ 🎾 🏊

AHMEDABAD: *Hotel Holiday Inn* Rs Rs Rs Rs | AE DC MC V | 63
Near Nehru Bridge, Khanpur. ((079) 550 5505. FAX (079) 550 5501.
W www.sixcontinentshotels.com R (011) 331 0644; dso@bhrindia.com
Part of a well-known chain, this hotel has elegant rooms, a well-lit atrium,
a discotheque, a pool and efficient service. 🍴 24 📺 🛏 🏊 🎾 🏊 🏊

AHMEDABAD: *Taj Residency Ummed* Rs Rs Rs Rs | AE DC MC V | 91
International Airport Circle, Hansol. ((079) 286 4444. FAX (079) 286 4454.
W www.tajhotels.com R (011) 332 2256; trn.delhi@tajhotels.com
Imaginatively built round a central courtyard, the decor showcases Gujarati
crafts and antiques. Authentic Gujarati cuisine. 🍴 24 📺 🛏 ⛳ 🎾 🏊

Price categories for a standard double room per night including tax and service charges but not including breakfast:
Ⓡ under 550 rupees
ⓇⓇ 550–1,200 rupees
ⓇⓇⓇ 1,200–3,000 rupees
ⓇⓇⓇⓇ 3,000–6,000 rupees
ⓇⓇⓇⓇⓇ over 6,000 rupees

CREDIT CARDS
Indicates which major credit cards are accepted: AE American Express; DC Diners Club; MC Master Card/Access; V Visa.

WESTERN BATHROOMS
Indicates sit-down, flush toilets; showers and/or baths. Others have squat toilets and bucket-and-mug baths.

COFFEE SHOP
Hotels with 24-hour coffee shop, also serving hot meals.

AIR CONDITIONING
Hotels with air-conditioned rooms.

	CREDIT CARDS	NUMBER OF ROOMS	AIR CONDITIONING	WESTERN BATHROOMS	COFFEE SHOP
BHAVNAGAR: *Nilambagh Palace Hotel* ⓇⓇⓇ Nilambagh. ☎ (0278) 42 4241. FAX (0278) 42 8072. @ nilambag@ad1.vsnl.net.in This grand, 19th-century palace has richly carved pillars, glittering halls, antique teak furniture, and an enormous garden. Excursions to neighbouring tourist spots are also organized.	AE DC MC V	28		●	
DIU: *Hotel Radhika Beach Resort* ⓇⓇⓇ Nagoa. ☎ (02875) 52 553. FAX (02875) 52 552. Located near the beach, this clean and well-maintained resort has comfortable rooms in villas, and excellent service and food.	MC V	24	▨	●	
JAMNAGAR: *Orbit Park Inn International* ⓇⓇⓇ PO Baid. ☎ (0288) 44 484. FAX (0288) 44 486. Ⓦ www.sarovarparkplaza.com Ⓡ (011) 691 0544; reservations@sarovarparkplaza.com Well-appointed rooms and excellent service characterize this tranquil hotel. Enjoy lagoon views from its tea lounge.	AE MC V	60	▨	●	
SASANGIR: *The Gir Lodge* ⓇⓇⓇⓇ Sasangir, Junagarh district. ☎ (02877) 85 521. FAX (02877) 85 528. Ⓡ (011) 332 2256; trn.delhi@tajhotels.com Overlooking the river and hills, this lodge has comfortable rooms and friendly staff. Books and videos of wildlife films are available, as are jeeps for hire.	AE DC MC V	29	▨	●	
VADODARA: *Welcomgroup Vadodara* ⓇⓇⓇⓇ RC Dutt Rd. ☎ (0265) 33 0033. FAX (0265) 33 0050. Ⓦ www.welcomgroup.com Ⓡ (011) 614 1821; rmonorth.welcomnet@welcomgroup.com A blend of traditional hospitality with modern amenities, this hotel also boasts a fine art gallery. Special facilities include golf.	AE DC MC V	134	▨	●	▨
WANKANER: *Royal Oasis & Residency* ⓇⓇⓇ The Wankaner Palace. ☎ (02825) 20 000. FAX (02825) 20 002. This renovated guesthouse of the Wankaner Palace is on the banks of the Machhu river, amidst fruit orchards. An outstanding feature is its exquisite stepwell, three storeys deep.	AE DC MC V	12	▨	●	

MUMBAI

	CREDIT CARDS	NUMBER OF ROOMS	AIR CONDITIONING	WESTERN BATHROOMS	COFFEE SHOP
MUMBAI: *Chateau Windsor Guest House* ⓇⓇ 86 Vir Nariman Rd. ☎ (022) 204 4455. FAX (022) 202 6459. Ⓦ www.chateauwindsor.com The rooms are clean and comfortable, with arrangements for self-catering. The service is friendly, and the food is good.	AE MC V	45	▨	●	
MUMBAI: *Garden Hotel* ⓇⓇⓇ 42 Garden Rd, Colaba. ☎ (022) 283 4823. FAX (022) 284 1476. @ gardenht@bom5.vsnl.net.in This hotel has clean, well-furnished rooms, polite and efficient service and a tranquil terrace.	AE MC V	34	▨	●	▨
MUMBAI: *Hotel Harbour View* ⓇⓇⓇ 25 PJ Ramchandani Marg. ☎ (022) 282 1089. FAX (022) 284 3020. Ⓦ www.viewhotelsinc.com Spotless, tastefully furnished rooms are the main attraction of this hotel which offers panoramic views from its rooftop restaurant, cooled by refreshing sea breezes from the harbour.	AE MC V	21	▨	●	
MUMBAI: *Sea Green Hotel* ⓇⓇⓇ 145–A Marine Drive. ☎ (022) 282 2294. FAX (022) 283 6158. Ⓦ www. seagreenhotel.com Convenient location, spacious and clean rooms, friendly and attentive staff, and reasonable prices have made this hotel a Mumbai favourite for over 50 years. Many of the rooms look out on sea views across Marine Drive, while others overlook a stadium.	AE DC MC V	34	▨	●	

MUMBAI: *Hotel Suba Palace* (Rs)(Rs)(Rs) | MC V | 50
Near Gateway of India, Apollo Bunder. [C] *(022) 202 0636.* [FAX] *(022) 202 0812.*
[W] www.mrlgroup.com
Located near the Gateway of India, this hotel has tastefully decorated, comfortable rooms, and a large well-equipped conference room. [11] [24] [TV] [fridge] [AC]

MUMBAI: *West End Hotel* (Rs)(Rs)(Rs) | AE DC MC V | 79
45 New Marine Lines. [C] *(022) 203 9121.* [FAX] *(022) 205 7506.*
[W] www.westendhotelmumbai.com
Prime location, good food and excellent service have made this hotel popular. The clean, spacious rooms have an old-fashioned charm. [11] [Y] [24] [TV] [fridge]

MUMBAI: *YMCA International House* (Rs)(Rs)(Rs) | V | 292
18 YMCA Rd, Near Mumbai Central. [C] *(022) 309 1191.*
Offering security, reliable services and a relaxed atmosphere, rooms here are much in demand. Book at least a month ahead and pay an advance.

MUMBAI: *The Fariyas Hotel* (Rs)(Rs)(Rs)(Rs) | AE DC MC V | 87
Off Arthur Bunder Rd, Colaba. [C] *(022) 204 2911.* [FAX] *(022) 283 4992.*
[W] www.fariyas.com
Near the Gateway of India, with comfortable rooms, and a roof garden. Its restaurant, "Tavern", has a popular live band. [11] [Y] [24] [TV] [fridge] [AC] [RS] [W] [pool]

MUMBAI: *Gordon House* (Rs)(Rs)(Rs) | AE DC MC V | 29
5 Battery St, Apollo Bunder, Colaba. [C] *(022) 287 1122.* [FAX] *(022) 287 2026.*
[W] www.ghhotel.com.
The eclectic and tasteful interior decor of this charming hotel includes floors with Mediterranean, Scandinavian, country-cottage, and Louis Quatorze-style decor. The service is warm and efficient. [11] [Y] [24] [TV] [fridge] [AC]

MUMBAI: *Hotel Grand Maratha Sheraton* (Rs)(Rs)(Rs)(Rs)(Rs) | AE DC MC V | 386
Sahar. [C] *(022) 830 3030.* [FAX] *(022) 830 3131.* [@] itcgrandmaratha@welcomgroup.com
[R] *(011) 614 1821;* rmnorth.welcomnet@welcomgroup.com
A grand ballroom, English-style gardens, luxuriously appointed rooms, and a range of amenities are the attractions of this hotel. [11] [Y] [24] [TV] [fridge] [health] [W] [pool]

MUMBAI: *Hotel Marine Plaza* (Rs)(Rs)(Rs)(Rs)(Rs) | AE DC MC V | 68
29 Marine Drive. [C] *(022) 285 1212.* [FAX] *(022) 282 8585.* [@] hotelmarineplaza@vsnl.com
This new hotel has stunning views of the Arabian Sea and the glittering lights of Marine Drive. It also offers comfortable rooms, modern business facilities, and excellent service. [11] [Y] [24] [TV] [fridge] [AC] [W] [pool]

MUMBAI: *The Oberoi* (Rs)(Rs)(Rs)(Rs)(Rs) | AE DC MC V | 332
Nariman Point. [C] *(022) 232 5757.* [FAX] *(022) 204 3282.* [W] www.oberoihotels.com
[R] *(011) 291 4841;* irsdesk@oberoidel.com
Michael Jackson stayed at this plush hotel overlooking the Arabian Sea. There are separate floors for non-smokers and women travellers, an excellent shopping arcade, and a fleet of limousines. [11] [Y] [24] [TV] [fridge] [W] [pool]

MUMBAI: *The Oberoi Towers* (Rs)(Rs)(Rs)(Rs)(Rs) | AE DC MC V | 575
Nariman Point. [C] *(022) 232 4343.* [FAX] *(022) 204 3282.* [W] www.oberoihotels.com
[R] *(011) 291 4841;* irsdesk@oberoidel.com
Dominating Mumbai's shoreline, this enormous luxury hotel has non-smoking floors, rooms specially designed for the handicapped, and granite bathrooms well-stocked with herbal toiletries. [11] [Y] [24] [TV] [fridge] [health] [W] [AC] [pool]

MUMBAI: *The Orchid* (Rs)(Rs)(Rs)(Rs)(Rs) | AE DC MC V | 245
79–C Nehru Rd, near Domestic Airport. [C] *(022) 616 4040.* [FAX] *(022) 616 4141.*
[W] www.orchidhotel.com
Close to the airport, this hotel is famous for its eco-friendly policies, excellent restaurants and elegant rooms. [11] [Y] [24] [TV] [fridge] [AC] [W] [pool]

MUMBAI: *Ramada Hotel Palm Grove* (Rs)(Rs)(Rs)(Rs)(Rs) | AE DC MC V | 114
Juhu Beach. [C] *(022) 611 2323.* [FAX] *(022) 611 3682.* [W] www.krahejahospitality.com
[R] *(011) 373 5227;* delhi@krahejahospitality.com
Close to Juhu Beach, this hotel's special features include a poolside garden, large rooms, and attentive service. [11] [Y] [24] [TV] [fridge] [W] [pool] [pool]

MUMBAI: *Regent Mumbai* (Rs)(Rs)(Rs)(Rs)(Rs) | AE DC MC V | 508
Land's End, Bandstand, Bandra (W). [C] *(022) 655 1234.* [FAX] *(022) 644 1229.*
[W] www.regenthotels.com
This attractive hotel in the lively suburb of Bandra has an impressive three-storeyed marble lobby, tropical landscaping, and a separate swimming pool for women. All the rooms have sea views. [11] [Y] [24] [TV] [fridge] [health] [W] [AC] [RS] [pool]

Price categories for a standard double room per night including tax and service charges but not including breakfast:

- ⒭ under 550 rupees
- ⒭⒭ 550–1,200 rupees
- ⒭⒭⒭ 1,200–3,000 rupees
- ⒭⒭⒭⒭ 3,000–6,000 rupees
- ⒭⒭⒭⒭⒭ over 6,000 rupees

CREDIT CARDS
Indicates which major credit cards are accepted: AE American Express; DC Diners Club; MC Master Card/Access; V Visa.

WESTERN BATHROOMS
Indicates sit-down, flush toilets; showers and/or baths. Others have squat toilets and bucket-and-mug baths.

COFFEE SHOP
Hotels with 24-hour coffee shop, also serving hot meals.

AIR CONDITIONING
Hotels with air-conditioned rooms.

		CREDIT CARDS	NUMBER OF ROOMS	AIR CONDITIONING	WESTERN BATHROOMS	COFFEE SHOP
MUMBAI: *Taj Mahal Hotel* ⒭⒭⒭⒭⒭ Apollo Bunder, Colaba. 📞 *(022) 202 3366.* FAX *(022) 287 2711.* W *www.tajhotels.com* 📠 *(011) 332 2333;* trn.delhi@tajhotels.com One of Asia's great hotels, the Taj is an establishment of outstanding character and elegance. It has splendid views of the harbour and the Gateway of India, some of Mumbai's finest restaurants, and sumptuously decorated rooms. 🍴 🍸 24 📺 🛏 🚪 📻 🎿 ♨ 🏊 ♿ 🔌		AE DC MC V	582	●	●	●
MUMBAI: *The Taj President* ⒭⒭⒭⒭⒭ 90 Cuffe Parade, Colaba. 📞 *(022) 215 0808.* FAX *(022) 215 1201.* W *www.tajhotels.com* 📠 *(011) 332 2333;* trn.delhi@tajhotels.com Convenient for business travellers, this recently renovated hotel has panoramic views of the harbour and the city. The Konkan Café serves delicious regional food. 🍴 🍸 24 📺 🛏 🚪 📻 🎿 ◐ 🔌		AE DC MC V	292	●	●	●

MAHARASTHRA

		CREDIT CARDS	NUMBER OF ROOMS	AIR CONDITIONING	WESTERN BATHROOMS	COFFEE SHOP
AURANGABAD: *Taj Residency* ⒭⒭⒭⒭ 8–N–12 CIDCO. 📞 *(0240) 38 1106.* FAX *(0240) 38 1053.* W *www.tajhotels.com* Set amidst lovely gardens, this elegant hotel has spacious rooms leading onto private verandahs. Excellent service. 🍴 🍸 24 📺 🛏 🚪 ◐ 📻 🎿		AE DC MC V	40	●	●	●
AURANGABAD: *Welcomgroup Rama International* ⒭⒭⒭⒭ R–3 Chikalthana. 📞 *(0240) 48 5441.* FAX *(0240) 48 4768.* W *www.welcomgroup.com* Verdant gardens covering 5 ha (13 acres) surround this luxurious hotel. Special features include yoga and massage therapy, mini-golf and a poolside barbecue. 🍴 🍸 24 📺 🛏 🚪 ◐ 📻 🎿 🔌 ♿		AE DC MC V	90	●	●	●
CHIPLUN: *Gateway River View Lodge* ⒭⒭⒭ Village Dhamandivi, Tal-Chiplun. 📞 *(02356) 72 233.* FAX *(02356) 72 059.* 📠 *(011) 332 2256;* trn.delhi@tajhotels.com Perched on a hill with great views of the Vashishti river and green fields, this retreat has clean, comfortable rooms. 🍴 🍸 24 📺 🛏 ◐ 📻 🎿 🔌		AE DC MC V	37	●	●	
GANAPATIPULE: *MTDC Holiday Resort* ⒭⒭ Beach. 📞 *(02357) 35 248.* FAX *(02357) 35 328.* Located on the beach, this resort offers a range of accommodation, from large suites to tents. Some rooms have sea views, and there are facilities for a variety of water sports. 🍴 📺 📻 ◭		XX		●	●	
LONAVLA: *Fariyas Holidays Resort* ⒭⒭⒭⒭⒭ PO 8, Frichley Hill, Tungarli. 📞 *(02114) 73 852.* FAX *(02114) 72 080.* W *www.fariyas.com* Situated in the Western Ghats, this luxurious resort has a solar-heated pool, a health club, and a discotheque. 🍴 🍸 24 📺 🛏 🚪 ◐ 📻 📻 🎿 🏊 ⚲		AE DC MC V	90	●	●	●
MAHABALESHWAR: *Brightland Holiday Village* ⒭⒭⒭ Kates Point Rd, Nakhind Village. 📞 *(02168) 60 700.* FAX *(02168) 60 700.* W *www.brightlandholiday.com* This clifftop resort, with fine views of the Krishna river, has clean cottages and apartments. An Ayurvedic health centre, a children's park, and a discotheque are among its facilities. 🍴 🍸 24 📺 🛏 ◐ 📻 ◐ 🎿		MC V	60	●	●	●
MATHERAN: *The Rugby* ⒭⒭⒭⒭ Vithal Rao, Katwal Rd. 📞 *(02148) 30 291.* FAX *(02148) 30 259.* The hotel has a serene ambience and a pretty rock garden. The spotless rooms have private balconies with good views. Other attractions include an open air theatre and a discotheque. 🍴 24 📺 🛏 ◐ 📻 📻 🎿 🔌 ◉		AE DC MC V	60	●	●	●
NAGPUR: *The Pride Hotel* ⒭⒭⒭ Wardha Rd, opp. Airport. 📞 *(0712) 26 1102.* FAX *(0712) 26 0440.* W *www.pridegroup.com* Conveniently located, this hotel has well-furnished rooms, modern comforts and courteous staff. 🍴 🍸 24 📺 🛏 ◐ 📻 📻 🎿 ♿		AE DC MC V	99	●	●	●

NASIK: *Taj Residency* (Rs)(Rs)(Rs)(Rs) | AE MC V | 91
P–17 MIDC. **☎** *(0253) 38 4499.* **FAX** *(0253) 38 2638.* **@** *tajnsk@bom2.vsnl.net.in*
Located on a small hillock amid an expanse of greenery, its decor is
inspired by Maratha palaces. There are views of the Satpura Hills from
some rooms. Efficient staff. ⬛ ⬛ ⬛ ⬛ ⬛ ⬛ ⬛ ⬛ ⬛ ⬛

PUNE: *The Blue Diamond* (Rs)(Rs)(Rs)(Rs) | AE DC MC V | 108
11 Koregaon Rd. **☎** *(020) 612 5555.* **FAX** *(020) 612 7755.* **W** *www.tajhotels.com*
Located close to the Osho Commune, the rooms here are plush and the
service efficient. A well-designed golf course and a poolside restaurant are
added attractions. ⬛ ⬛ ⬛ ⬛ ⬛ ⬛ ⬛ ⬛ ⬛ ⬛

PUNE: *Holiday Inn Pune* (Rs)(Rs)(Rs)(Rs) | MC V | 115
Bund Garden Rd. **☎** *(020) 613 7777.* **FAX** *(020) 613 4747.* **@** *dine@holidayinnpune.com*
A luxurious hotel, its special attractions are a full American breakfast, a
pool with a sun deck, and a shopping arcade. Golf and tennis can be
arranged on request. ⬛ ⬛ ⬛ ⬛ ⬛ ⬛ ⬛ ⬛ ⬛ ⬛ ⬛

SEVAGRAM: *Ashram Yatri Niwas* (Rs)
Sevagram Ashram. **☎** *(07152) 84 266.*
This spartan but clean establishment, which can accomodate up to 70
persons, has a bookshop stocked with Mahatma Gandhi's works. Smoking
and consumption of alcohol and non-vegetarian food are not allowed. ⬛ ⬛

GOA

ANJUNA: *Laguna Anjuna* (Rs)(Rs)(Rs) | AE MC V | 12
Soranto Vaddo. **☎** *(0832) 27 3248.* **FAX** *(0832) 27 4310.* **W** *www.lagunaanjuna.com*
Simple yet tastefully designed beach cottages, excellent service and a
pleasant garden and swimming pool, have made this resort deservedly
popular with foreign visitors. ⬛ ⬛ ⬛ ⬛ ⬛

BAGA: *Captain Lobo's Beach Hideaway* (Rs)(Rs)(Rs) | MC | 21
Cobrowaddo, Baga. **☎** *(0832) 27 6103.* **FAX** *(0832) 27 6917.*
W *www.captloboshideawaygoa.com*
This friendly, family-run resort has comfortable suites in whitewashed
villas, with attached verandah and kitchenette. The location, on Baga
Beach, is ideal and the staff are friendly and helpful. ⬛ ⬛ ⬛ ⬛ ⬛ ⬛

BAGA: *Hotel Baia Do Sol* (Rs)(Rs)(Rs) | AE MC V | 23
Baga Beach. **☎** *(0832) 27 6084.* **FAX** *(0832) 27 6085.* **W** *www.ndnaik.com*
An idyllic location with spellbinding views of the sea, and a lively bar with
large bay windows, are the main attractions here. Music and barbecues
create a special ambience in the evenings. ⬛ ⬛ ⬛ ⬛ ⬛ ⬛ ⬛ ⬛

BAGA: *Ronil Beach Resort* (Rs)(Rs)(Rs) | AE MC V | 88
Baga. **☎** *(0832) 27 6101.* **FAX** *(0832) 27 6068.* **@** *ronil@goatelecom.com*
Offering guests a slice of traditional Goan life, this resort boasts excellent
Goan cuisine, rooms with fine views, attractively decorated with local
artifacts, and Ayurvedic massage therapy. ⬛ ⬛ ⬛ ⬛ ⬛ ⬛ ⬛ ⬛ ⬛

BARDEZ: *Nilaya Hermitage* (Rs)(Rs)(Rs)(Rs)(Rs) | MC V | 12
Apora Bhatti. **☎** *(0832) 27 6793.* **FAX** *(0832) 27 6792.* **W** *www.nilayahermitage.com*
Discreet luxury and delicious food are special features here. The resource-
ful and obliging staff can rustle up moonlight beach picnics or classical
dance performances. ⬛ ⬛ ⬛ ⬛ ⬛ ⬛ ⬛ ⬛ ⬛ ⬛ ⬛

BENAULIM: *Taj Exotica, Goa* (Rs)(Rs)(Rs)(Rs)(Rs) | AE DC MC V | 140
Calwaddo, Salcete. **☎** *(0832) 77 1234.* **FAX** *(0832) 77 1515.* **W** *www.tajhotels.com*
R *(022) 202 2626;* trn@tajhotels.com
Every room has a view of the sea; some even have a private plunge pool.
Excellent restaurants, water sports and a recreated fishing village are other
attractions here. ⬛ ⬛ ⬛ ⬛ ⬛ ⬛ ⬛ ⬛ ⬛ ⬛ ⬛ ⬛ ⬛ ⬛ ⬛ ⬛

CALANGUTE: *Paradise Village Beach Resort* (Rs)(Rs) | MC V | 83
Tivaiwaddo. **☎** *(0832) 62 6351.* **FAX** *(0832) 27 6155.* **W** *www.paradisevillage.org*
Comfortable suites and apartments are set in landscaped gardens, near the
beach. Excellent service and Goan cuisine. ⬛ ⬛ ⬛ ⬛ ⬛ ⬛

CALANGUTE: *Vila Goesa Beach Resort* (Rs)(Rs)(Rs) | MC V | 57
Cobrowaddo. **☎** *(0832) 27 7535.* **FAX** *(0832) 27 6182.* **@** *alobo@goatelecom.com*
A stone's throw from Calangute Beach, this attractively designed, well-
maintained resort has clean and comfortable rooms surrounded by
extensive gardens, and an excellent restaurant. ⬛ ⬛ ⬛ ⬛ ⬛

Price categories for a standard double room per night including tax and service charges but not including breakfast:
(Rs) under 550 rupees
(Rs)(Rs) 550–1,200 rupees
(Rs)(Rs)(Rs) 1,200–3,000 rupees
(Rs)(Rs)(Rs)(Rs) 3,000–6,000 rupees
(Rs)(Rs)(Rs)(Rs)(Rs) over 6,000 rupees

CREDIT CARDS
Indicates which major credit cards are accepted: AE American Express; DC Diners Club; MC Master Card/Access; V Visa.

WESTERN BATHROOMS
Indicates sit-down, flush toilets; showers and/or baths. Others have squat toilets and bucket-and-mug baths.

COFFEE SHOP
Hotels with 24-hour coffee shop, also serving hot meals.

AIR CONDITIONING
Hotels with air-conditioned rooms.

	Credit Cards	Number of Rooms	Air Conditioning	Western Bathrooms	Coffee Shop
CALANGUTE: *Pousada Tauma* (Rs)(Rs)(Rs)(Rs)(Rs) Porba Vaddo, Bardez. (0832) 27 9061. FAX (0832) 27 9064. W www.pousada-tauma.com Beautiful rooms built around a pool, and a well-run Ayurveda centre are the special attractions here.	MC V	12	■	●	
CAVELOSSIM: *Dona Sylvia Beach Resort* (Rs)(Rs)(Rs) Cavelossim Beach, Salcete. (0832) 87 1321. FAX (0832) 87 1320. W www.donasylvia.com This charming, Mediterranean-style resort, built around a pool, has excellent service, tennis courts, a good restaurant and bar, and a children's pool. It is popular with travellers on package tours.	AE DC MC V	176	■	●	
CAVELOSSIM: *The Leela Palace* (Rs)(Rs)(Rs)(Rs)(Rs) Mobor. (0832) 87 1234. FAX (0832) 87 1352. W www.theleela.com Situated on the tip of Mobor Beach, this imaginatively designed resort has a secluded private beach, and rooms with private gardens opening onto a lovely blue lagoon.	AE DC MC V	137	■	●	■
COLVA: *Silver Sands Beach Resort* (Rs)(Rs)(Rs) Colva Beach. (0832) 78 8099. FAX (0832) 78 8102. W www.silversandsresortgoa.com Located close to the beautiful beach, this resort has rooms with modern conveniences, a good swimming pool and health club, and live music in its excellent restaurant and bar.	AE DC MC V	66	■	●	■
MAJORDA: *Majorda Beach Resort* (Rs)(Rs)(Rs)(Rs) Salcete. (0832) 754 8710. FAX (0832) 88 1121. W www.majordabeachresort.com This large, plush resort has spacious and well-furnished rooms and suites, an enormous swimming pool and a covered street inspired by a Mediterranean village.	AE DC MC V	120	■	●	■
PANAJI: *Panjim Inn* (Rs)(Rs)(Rs) 212 Mala, Fontainhas. (0832) 22 6523. FAX (0832) 22 8136. W www.panjiminn.com Beautifully restored rooms, deep verandahs, a verdant garden and friendly staff make this stately 18th-century Fontainhas mansion a favourite with many visitors to Goa's capital.	MC V	22	■	●	
PANAJI: *Hotel Mandovi* (Rs)(Rs)(Rs) PO Box 164, DB Marg. (0832) 22 4405. FAX (0832) 22 5451. @ mandovi@goatelecom.com This staid but comfortable riverside hotel boasts a restaurant famous for its authentic Goan cuisine and pastry shop.	AE DC MC V	65	■	●	■
SINQUERIM: *Whispering Palms Beach Resort* (Rs)(Rs)(Rs) Candolim. (0832) 27 6140. FAX (0832) 27 6142. W www.whisperingpalms.com Popular with package tour groups, this resort has clean rooms, each with a private balcony overlooking either the sea or open fields. The food and service are excellent.	AE DC MC V	66	■	●	■
SINQUERIM: *The Taj Holiday Village* (Rs)(Rs)(Rs)(Rs) Bardez. (0832) 27 6201. FAX (0832) 27 6045. W www.tajhotels.com R (022) 202 2626; trn@tajhotels.com Charming cottages among palm trees, friendly and efficient service, water sports facilities, and excellent restaurants are the attractions of this popular resort.	AE DC MC V	144	■	●	■
SINQUERIM: *The Aguada Hermitage* (Rs)(Rs)(Rs)(Rs)(Rs) Bardez. (0832) 27 6201. FAX (0832) 27 6045. W www.tajhotels.com R (022) 202 2626; trn@tajhotels.com Built on a verdant hillock, each of these secluded, luxurious villas, run by the renowned Taj Group, has its own lovely garden. For food and facilities such as the pool, guests must use the Fort Aguada Beach Resort, situated at the foot of the hillock.	AE DC MC V	15	■	●	■

TEREKHOL: *Hotel Tiracol Fort Heritage* (Rs)(Rs)(Rs)
Querim, Pernem. 📞 (02366) 68 248. FAX (02366) 68 248. @ info@tiracolfort.com
The rooms in this romantic, atmospheric old fort have been restored and
furnished with charm, and have glorious views of the estuary and the
surrounding countryside. 🔒 📺 📺 🔲

	MC	10			
	V				

VAINGUINIM BEACH: *Cidade De Goa Beach Resort* (Rs)(Rs)(Rs)(Rs)
Vainguinim Beach. 📞 (0832) 22 1133. FAX (0832) 22 3303. W www.cidadedegoa.com
Imaginatively designed by one of India's leading architects, Charles Correa,
this luxury resort has a secluded beach, water sports facilities and some
outstanding restaurants. 🔒 📺 📅 📺 🔲 🔲 🔲 🔲 🔲 🔲 🔲 🔲

	AE	202	▦	●	▦
	DC				
	MC				
	V				

VARCA: *Renaissance Goa Resort* (Rs)(Rs)(Rs)(Rs)(Rs)
Salcete. 📞 (0832) 74 5200. FAX (0832) 74 5225. W www.renaissancegoa.com
Sea-facing rooms with private balconies, attractive architecture, a pristine
beach, water sports facilities and impeccable service make this a truly
luxurious resort. 🔒 📺 📅 📺 🔲 🔲 🔲 🔲 🔲 🔲 🔲 🔲

	AE	202	▦	●	▦
	DC				
	MC				
	V				

KARNATAKA

BADAMI: *Hotel Badami Court* (Rs)(Rs)(Rs)
17/3 Station Rd. 📞 (08357) 20 230. FAX (08357) 20 207.
📧 (080) 529 5451; rafiqmht@blr.vsnl.net.in.
Close to the monuments, this hotel has clean rooms, a swimming pool and
gym, and friendly service. 🔒 📺 📅 📺 🔲 🔲 🔲 🔲

		26	▦	●	▦

BANGALORE: *Windsor Manor Sheraton & Towers* (Rs)(Rs)(Rs)(Rs)
25 Sankey Rd, Windsor Square, opp Golf Course. 📞 (080) 226 9898. FAX (080) 226 4941.
W www.welcomegroup.com
This grand colonnaded hotel, with sumptuously elegant rooms, combines
old-fashioned colonial atmosphere with modern efficiency. It has superb
restaurants and an English-style pub. 🔒 📺 📅 📺 🔲 🔲 🔲 🔲 🔲 🔲 🔲

	AE	240	▦	●	▦
	DC				
	MC				
	V				

BANGALORE: *The Oberoi* (Rs)(Rs)(Rs)(Rs)(Rs)
37–39 MG Rd. 📞 (080) 558 5858. FAX (080) 558 5960. W www.oberoihotels.com
📧 (011) 436 3030; reservations@oberoidel.com
Near the city centre, this hotel has well-appointed rooms with private
balconies that look out on landscaped gardens. A business centre and
limousine service are also offered. 🔒 📺 📅 📺 🔲 🔲 🔲 🔲 🔲 🔲

	AE	158	▦	●	▦
	DC				
	MC				
	V				

BANGALORE: *The Taj West End* (Rs)(Rs)(Rs)(Rs)(Rs)
Race Course Rd. 📞 (080) 255 5055. FAX (080) 220 0010. W www.tajhotels.com
📧 (011) 332 2256; trn.delhi@tajhotels.com
Surrounded by pretty gardens, this superb hotel occupies a 19th-century
colonial mansion. The "Old World Rooms" near the lobby are enchanting,
with real period flavour. Other attractions include excellent restaurants and
a swimming pool. 🔒 📺 📅 📺 🔲 🔲 🔲 🔲 🔲 🔲 🔲

	AE	129	▦	●	▦
	DC				
	MC				
	V				

BIJAPUR: *Hotel Madhuvan International* (Rs)(Rs)(Rs)
Station Rd. 📞 (08352) 55 571. FAX (08352) 56 201. @ madhuvan_hotel@yahoo.com
Views of the monumental Gol Gumbad are the special feature of this
comfortable hotel. There is a pleasant garden restaurant serving regional
specialities, and the hotel also organizes excursions. 🔒 📺 📅 📺 🔲 🔲 🔲

		34	▦	●	

CHIKMAGALUR: *Taj Garden Retreat* (Rs)(Rs)(Rs)
KM Rd, PO Jyothinagar. 📞 (08262) 20 202. FAX (08262) 20 222. W www.tajhotels.com
📧 (011) 332 2256; trn.delhi@tajhotels.com
On the slopes of the Sahyadri Hills, this well-run hotel has small cottages
and a restaurant serving regional cuisine. It is a convenient base from
which to visit the Hoysala Temples. 🔒 📺 📺 🔲 🔲 🔲 🔲 🔲 🔲

	AE	29	▦	●	
	DC				
	MC				
	V				

COORG: *Orange County Resort* (Rs)(Rs)(Rs)
Karadigodu Post, Siddapur. 📞 (08274) 58 481. FAX (08274) 58 485.
W www.trailsindia.com 📧 (080) 558 2380; rhrl@vsnl.com
Set amidst coffee and spice plantations, this resort has attractive cottages.
Excursions to the surrounding forest, fishing in the Kaveri, and herbal
massages are also offered. 🔒 📺 📺 🔲 🔲 🔲 🔲 🔲 🔲 🔲

	AE	46		●	
	DC				
	MC				
	V				

HOSPET: *Malligi Tourist Home* (Rs)(Rs)(Rs)
6/143 Jambunath Rd. 📞 (08394) 28 101. FAX (08394) 27 038.
@ malligihome@hotmail.com
Close to Hampi, this well-managed hotel also runs an efficient travel
agency. Its most attractive feature is its swimming pool, inspired by the
royal Pushkarni pool at Hampi. 🔒 📺 📺 🔲 🔲 🔲 🔲 🔲 🔲 🔲

	AE	140	▦	●	▦
	MC				
	V				

<table>
<tr><td colspan="2"></td><td>CREDIT CARDS</td><td>NUMBER OF ROOMS</td><td>AIR CONDITIONING</td><td>WESTERN BATHROOMS</td><td>COFFEE SHOP</td></tr>
</table>

Price categories for a standard double room per night including tax and service charges but not including breakfast:

Rs under 550 rupees
Rs Rs 550–1,200 rupees
Rs Rs Rs 1,200–3,000 rupees
Rs Rs Rs Rs 3,000–6,000 rupees
Rs Rs Rs Rs Rs over 6,000 rupees

CREDIT CARDS
Indicates which major credit cards are accepted: AE American Express; DC Diners Club; MC Master Card/Access; V Visa.

WESTERN BATHROOMS
Indicates sit-down, flush toilets; showers and/or baths. Others have squat toilets and bucket-and-mug baths.

COFFEE SHOP
Hotels with 24-hour coffee shop, also serving hot meals.

AIR CONDITIONING
Hotels with air-conditioned rooms.

Listing	Credit Cards	Number of Rooms	Air Conditioning	Western Bathrooms	Coffee Shop
KARAPUR: *Kabini River Lodge* (Rs)(Rs)(Rs) Nagarhole National Park. ((08228) 32 181. FAX (08228) 44 405. (080) 559 7021; jungle@giasbg01.vsnl.net.in A former royal hunting lodge on the Kabini river, in the midst of wilderness, this excellently run establishment offers elephant safaris and coracle rides on the river.	AE MC V	25	●	●	
MANGALORE: *Manjarun Hotel* (Rs)(Rs)(Rs)(Rs) Old Port Rd. ((0824) 42 0420. FAX (0824) 42 0585. @ manjarun.mangalore@tajhotels.com (011) 332 2256; trn.delhi@tajhotels.com This multi-storeyed hotel has elegant and comfortable rooms, facilities for business travellers and a good restaurant.	AE DC MC V	97	●	●	●
MYSORE: *The Green Hotel* (Rs)(Rs)(Rs) Chittranjan Palace, 2270 VA Rd. ((0821) 51 2536. FAX (0821) 51 6139. @ grenhotl@sancharnet.in Originally built for the princesses of Mysore, this delightful palace-hotel has lovely gardens and elegant decor. Set up as a model of sustainable tourism by a UK charity, all profits go to worthy local projects.	MC V	31		●	
MYSORE: *Lalitha Mahal Palace Hotel* (Rs)(Rs)(Rs) Siddhartha Nagar. ((0821) 47 4266. FAX (0821) 57 1770. @ lmph@bgl.vsnl.net.in Overlooking the Chamundi Hills, this Italian palazzo-style structure was built by the Maharaja of Mysore for the then British viceroy. Today, it is an atmospheric hotel with lovely terraced gardens.	AE DC MC V	54	●	●	●

CHENNAI

Listing	Credit Cards	Number of Rooms	Air Conditioning	Western Bathrooms	Coffee Shop
CHENNAI: *Pandian* (Rs)(Rs) 15 Kennet Lane, opp. Egmore Railway Station. ((044) 825 2901. FAX (044) 825 8459. @ hotelpandian@vsnl.com One of Chennai's most popular budget hotels, the Pandian has clean rooms, a good restaurant and bar, and friendly staff.	AE DC MC V	90	●	●	
CHENNAI: *Grand Orient* (Rs)(Rs)(Rs) 693 Anna Salai. ((044) 852 4111. FAX (044) 852 3412. @ empeegrandorient@vsnl.com Conveniently located in the heart of the city, close to shopping centres, consulates and business centres, this hotel has very comfortable rooms and all modern amenities.	AE DC MC V	62	●	●	●
CHENNAI: *Hotel Residency* (Rs)(Rs)(Rs) 49 GN Chetty Rd. ((044) 825 3434. FAX (044) 825 0085. W www.theresidency.com The comfortable rooms on the upper floors offer good views of the city. Facilities include a bar with a Mexican theme.	AE DC MC V	112	●	●	●
CHENNAI: *Windsor Park* (Rs)(Rs)(Rs) 349 Poonamallee High Rd. ((044) 374 1999. FAX 374 3369. @ ampa@md3.vsnl.net.in An well managed establishment with business facilities, this hotel has clean rooms and a pool in the garden. It is conveniently located near the airport and the railway station.	AE DC MC V	50	●	●	
CHENNAI: *Ambassador Pallava* (Rs)(Rs)(Rs)(Rs) 30 Montieth Rd. ((044) 855 4476. FAX (044) 855 4068. @ pallava@vsnl.com This modern and efficiently run hotel has facilities for business travellers. The restaurant serves excellent seafood.	AE DC MC V	100	●	●	●
CHENNAI: *GRT Grand Days* (Rs)(Rs)(Rs)(Rs) 120 Sir Thyagaraya Rd, T Nagar. ((044) 822 0500. FAX (044) 823 0778. W www.grtgranddays.com An impressive atrium lobby sets the tone for this smart hotel with its elegant rooms and friendly, efficient service.	AE DC MC V	135	●	●	●

CHENNAI: *Quality Inn Aruna* ⒭⒭⒭ | AE DC MC V | 91
144–145 Sterling Rd, Nungambakkam. 【 *(044) 825 9090.* ⒻⒶⓍ *(044) 825 8282.*
@ qiaruna@satyam.net.in
Interiors with a clean, contemporary look, spacious rooms with a view, and
a convenient location near major shopping areas and consulates, are the
main attractions of this efficiently run hotel. 🍽 24 📺 ❖

CHENNAI: *ITC Park Sheraton & Towers* ⒭⒭⒭⒭ | AE DC MC V | 283
TTK Rd. 【 *(044) 499 4101.* ⒻⒶⓍ *(044) 499 7101.* ⓦ www.welcomgroup.com
Elegant rooms, fountains in the lobby, a shopping plaza and health club add
to the luxurious air of this hotel, located in an exclusive quarter. Suites in the
attached tower block have fine views. 🍴 🍽 24 📺 ❖

CHENNAI: *Taj Connemara* ⒭⒭⒭⒭ | AE DC MC V | 150
1 Binny Rd. 【 *(044) 852 0123.* ⒻⒶⓍ *(044) 852 3361.* ⓦ www.tajhotels.com
A charming heritage hotel with Art Deco interiors, a serene courtyard and a
beautiful pool. Authentic Chettinad cuisine is served at dinner in the open-air
restaurant, accompanied by a cultural show. 🍴 🍽 24 📺 ❖

CHENNAI: *The Trident* ⒭⒭⒭⒭ | AE DC MC V | 167
1/24 G S T Rd. 【 *(044) 234 4747.* ⒻⒶⓍ *(044) 234 6699.* ⓦ www.tridenthotels.com
This elegant low-rise hotel, located close to the airport, is surrounded by
gardens with luxuriant tropical foliage. There is a well-equipped gym, a conference hall and an excellent restaurant. 🍴 🍽 24 📺 ❖

TAMIL NADU

COVELONG: *Fisherman's Cove* ⒭⒭⒭ | AE DC MC V | 88
Covelong Beach, Kanchipuram District. 【 *(04114) 72 304.* ⒻⒶⓍ *(04114) 74 303.*
ⓦ www.tajhotels.com
This beach resort on the site of an old Dutch fort has charming rooms and
cottages (many of them facing the sea), and excellent seafood. Water sports
arranged on request. 🍽 24 📺 ❖

KARAIKUDI: *The Bangala* ⒭⒭⒭ | | 8
Devakottai Rd, Senjai. 【 *(04565) 42 0221.* ⒻⒶⓍ *(04565) 493 4543.*
ⓦ www.thebangala.com Ⓡ *(044) 493 4851;* vvisalam@vsnl.com
This heritage hotel is a delightful complex of old bungalows, renovated to
showcase Chettinad's distinctive and beautiful architecture and decor, with
teakwood fittings, colonnaded verandahs and airy rooms. 🍴 24 ❖

KODAIKANAL: *The Carlton* ⒭⒭⒭⒭ | AE DC MC V | 91
Lake Rd. 【 *(04542) 40 056.* ⒻⒶⓍ *(04542) 41 170.* @ carlton@md3.vsnl.net.in.
Ⓡ *(044) 852 3432;* chennai@krahejahospitality.com
A blend of vintage Raj and modern comforts, this superb hotel is set in
sprawling, landscaped grounds overlooking Kodai Lake. Scores high on
ambience, food and service. 🍴 🍽 24 📺 ❖

PONDICHERRY: *Anandha Inn* ⒭⒭⒭ | AE DC MC V | 70
154 SV Patel Rd. 【 *(0413) 33 0711.* ⒻⒶⓍ *(0413) 33 1241.* ⓦ www.anandhainn.com
Within easy reach of the city's picturesque beach boulevard, temples and
churches, this establishment has clean, well-equipped rooms, a business
centre, a bar, and a boutique. Service is efficient. 🍴 🍽 24 📺 ❖

PONDICHERRY: *Hotel De L' Orient* ⒭⒭⒭ | AE DC MC V | 10
17 Rue Romain Rolland. 【 *(0413) 34 3067.* ⒻⒶⓍ *(0413) 22 7829.* ⓦ www.neemrana.com
Ⓡ *(011) 435 6145;* sales@neemrana.com
This is an enchanting hotel, filled with fine colonial furniture, old maps and
prints, and furnishings made to 18th-century French colonial designs. The
restaurant serves excellent Franco-Indian fusion cuisine. 🍴 🍽 ❖

MADURAI: *Taj Garden Retreat* ⒭⒭⒭⒭ | AE DC MC V | 50
40 TPK Rd, Pasumalai Hill. 【 *(0452) 77 1601.* ⒻⒶⓍ *(0452) 77 1636.*
ⓦ www.tajhotels.com Ⓡ *(011) 332 2256;* trn.delhi@tajhotels.com
Built on a hillock overlooking the Minakshi Temple, this has beautiful
terraced gardens. Some rooms are in a 19th-century colonial house, while
others are in cottages with private terraces. 🍴 🍽 24 📺 ❖

MUDUMALAI WILDLIFE SANCTUARY: *Jungle Hut* ⒭⒭ | | 12
Near Bokkapuram. 【 *(0423) 52 6463.* ⒻⒶⓍ *(0423) 52 6240.* @ jungleht@yahoo.co.uk
The rooms in this attractive resort are in three stone cottages, set in a large
estate. A special attraction here are the 30 resident elephants who take part
in an enchanting ritual every evening, when they perform a *puja* (prayer)
to the elephant god, Ganesha. 🍴 🍽 ❖

<table>
<tr><td colspan="2">

Price categories for a standard
double room per night including
tax and service charges but not
including breakfast:
Rs under 550 rupees
Rs Rs 550–1,200 rupees
Rs Rs Rs 1,200–3,000 rupees
Rs Rs Rs Rs 3,000–6,000 rupees
Rs Rs Rs Rs Rs over 6,000 rupees
</td></tr>
</table>

CREDIT CARDS
Indicates which major credit cards are accepted: AE
American Express; DC Diners Club; MC Master
Card/Access; V Visa.

WESTERN BATHROOMS
Indicates sit-down, flush toilets; showers and/or baths.
Others have squat toilets and bucket-and-mug baths.

COFFEE SHOP
Hotels with 24-hour coffee shop, also serving hot meals.

AIR CONDITIONING
Hotels with air-conditioned rooms.

	CREDIT CARDS	NUMBER OF ROOMS	AIR CONDITIONING	WESTERN BATHROOMS	COFFEE SHOP
OOTACAMUND: *Savoy Hotel* Rs Rs Rs 77 Sylks Rd. (0423) 44 4142. FAX (0423) 44 3318. W www.tajhotels.com (011) 332 2333; trn.delhi@tajhotels.com Nestled in the Nilgiri Hills, amidst lovely gardens full of foxgloves and dahlias, this charming hotel has rooms with fireplaces, a cosy bar, good restaurants, and tennis courts.	MC V	40		●	■
THANJAVUR: *Hotel Parisutham* Rs Rs Rs Rs 55 GA Canal Rd. (04362) 331 801. FAX (04362) 330 318. @ hotel.parisutham@vsnl.com Friendly and helpful staff, a beautiful pool, comfortable rooms, and wholesome and tasty food, make this small, modern hotel a good choice. Cultural programmes by the poolside in the evenings, and excursions to nearby coconut plantations can be organized.	AE DC MC V	50	■	●	■
TIRUCHIRAPALLI: *Jenneys Residency* Rs Rs Rs Rs 3/14 Macdonalds Rd. (0431) 41 4414. FAX (0431) 46 1451. @ jenneys@satyam.net.in (011) 614 1821; rmonorth.welcomnet@welcomgroup.com Recently renovated, this spacious hotel has rooms with character, shops, a health club and efficient services.	AE DC MC V	93	■	●	■

ANDAMAN ISLANDS

	CREDIT CARDS	NUMBER OF ROOMS	AIR CONDITIONING	WESTERN BATHROOMS	COFFEE SHOP
PORT BLAIR: *Hotel Sinclairs Bay View* Rs Rs Rs South Point. (03192) 33 159. FAX (03192) 31 824. W www.sinclairshotels.com (011) 331 5292; pressman@del2.vsnl.net Located on the Bay of Bengal, overlooking Ross Island, the rooms offer spectacular sea views. The hotel runs a diving centre that arranges scuba diving, snorkelling and water sports.	AE DC MC V	30	■	●	■
PORT BLAIR: *Fortune Resort Bay Island* Rs Rs Rs Rs Marine Hill. (03192) 34 101, 32 065. FAX (03192) 31 555. W www.welcomgroup.com (011) 614 1821; rmonorth.welcomnet@welcomgroup.com Built almost entirely of the fabulous local *padauk* wood, this resort has lovely, imaginatively furnished rooms built into a hillside. The swimming pool here is filled with sea water.	AE DC MC V	45	■	●	■

KERALA

	CREDIT CARDS	NUMBER OF ROOMS	AIR CONDITIONING	WESTERN BATHROOMS	COFFEE SHOP
ALAPPUZHA: *Kayaloram Lake Resort* Rs Rs Rs Punnamada. (0477) 23 2040. FAX (0477) 25 2918. W www.kayaloram.com Built in the style of a traditional *tharavad* (ancestral home), the rooms have tranquil courtyards with bathrooms open to the sky. Kerala cuisine, Ayurvedic treatments, and backwaters cruises are on offer.	AE DC MC V	12	■	●	
KOCHI: *Bolgatty Palace Hotel* Rs Rs Rs Bolgatty Island. (0484) 38 4448. FAX (0484) 38 4457. @ bolgatty@md3.vsnl.net.in Its spectacular location on the tip of Bolgatty Island adds to the ambience of this hotel, in a lovingly restored 18th-century Dutch palace, which was later the British Residency.	AE DC MC V	26	■	●	
KOCHI: *The Trident* Rs Rs Rs Bristow Rd, Willingdon Island. (0484) 66 9595. FAX (0484) 66 9393. W www.tridenthotels.com (011) 436 3030; reservations@oberoidel.com Located on Willingdon Island, this hotel combines modern facilities with a relaxed ambience. Elegant rooms, a cheerful bar overlooking the pool and traditional Kerala cuisine.	AE DC MC V	96	■	●	■
KOCHI: *The Brunton Boatyard* Rs Rs Rs Rs Rs 1/498 Fort Kochi. (0484) 21 5461. FAX (0484) 21 5562. W www.casinogroup.com An architectural blend of Kochi's colonial Portuguese and Dutch styles and local building traditions, this resort (part of the Casino Group) has sloping tiled roofs, terracotta floors and lovely rooms with large four-poster beds and beautiful views of the harbour.	AE DC MC V	26	■	●	■

KOCHI: *The Malabar House Residency* ⓇⓈⓇⓈⓇⓈⓇⓈ
1/268 Parade Rd, Fort Kochi. 📞 (0484) 21 6666. 📠 (0484) 21 7777.
🌐 www.malabarhouse.com
Full of character, this is a well-restored 18th-century Dutch mansion in the heart of historic Fort Kochi. The rooms are elegant, the food excellent, and there is a pool and a stage for cultural events. 🍴 🍸 24 📺 🛏 🅿 🏫 🏊

	AE	17				
	DC					
	MC					
	V					

KOCHI: *Taj Malabar* ⓇⓈⓇⓈⓇⓈⓇⓈ
Malabar Rd, Willingdon Island. 📞 (0484) 66 6811. 📠 (0484) 66 8297.
🌐 www.tajhotels.com 📱 (011) 332 2256; trn.delhi@tajhotels.com
This charming hotel offers panoramic views and imaginative decor, with a hotel bar that is a replica of a traditional Malabar timber house. There is an Ayurvedic massage centre as well. 🍴 🍸 24 📺 🛏 🅿 🏫 🏊 🚗

	AE	96				
	DC					
	MC					
	V					

KOLLAM: *Aquaserene* ⓇⓈⓇⓈⓇⓈⓇⓈ
V/88 Kurumandai. 📞 (0474) 51 2410. 📠 (0474) 51 2104.
🌐 www.aquasereneindia.com
Comfortable cottages with red-tiled roofs nestle round the main building in this plush resort. An Ayurvedic massage centre, and luxurious houseboats are other attractions. 🍴 🍸 24 📺 🛏 🅿 🏫 🏊 ⛰ 🚗

	AE	28				
	DC					
	MC					
	V					

KOTTAYAM: *Coconut Lagoon Heritage Resort* ⓇⓈⓇⓈⓇⓈⓇⓈ
Kumarakom. 📞 (0481) 52 4491. 📠 (0481) 52 4495. 🌐 www.casinogroup.com
📱 (0484) 66 8221; casino@vsnl.com
Spectacularly located on an abandoned coconut plantation, this resort is only accessible by boat. Built in the style of traditional Kerala houses, the rooms are surrounded by a network of canals. 🍴 🍸 📺 🛏 🅿 🏫 🏊 ⬆ 🚗

	AE	50				
	DC					
	MC					
	V					

KOTTAYAM: *The Lake Village Heritage Resort* ⓇⓈⓇⓈⓇⓈⓇⓈ
Kodimatha. 📞 (0481) 36 3637. 📠 (0481) 36 3738. 🌐 www.thewindsorcastle.net
Built like a traditional Kerala village, this hotel offers guests fishing in the lake, directly from the patios adjoining their rooms. Other facilities include an Ayurvedic spa and a herb garden. 🍴 🍸 24 📺 🛏 🅿 🏫 🏊 ⬆

	AE	17				
	MC					
	V					

KOTTAYAM: *Taj Garden Retreat* ⓇⓈⓇⓈⓇⓈⓇⓈ
1/104 Kumarakom. 📞 (0481) 52 4377. 📠 (0481) 52 4371. 🌐 www.tajhotels.com
📱 (011) 332 2256; trn.delhi@tajhotels.com
On the banks of Vembanad Lake, this hotel has rooms in an atmospheric colonial bungalow and in cottages. Martial arts demonstrations, bird-watching and backwaters cruises are arranged. 🍸 24 📺 🅿 🏫 🏊 ⛰

	AE	22				
	DC					
	MC					
	V					

KOVALAM: *Surya Samudra* ⓇⓈⓇⓈⓇⓈ
Surya Samudra Beach Garden, Pulinkudi. 📞 (0471) 48 0413. 📠 (0471) 48 1124.
🌐 www.suryasamudra.com
Traditional wooden architecture, coconut groves, bathrooms open to the sky and a superb beach are the highlights of this well-run resort. The food too is excellent. 🍴 🍸 24 🅿 🏫 ⬆ 🏊

	MC	21				
	V					

KOVALAM: *Somatheeram Ayurvedic Beach Resort* ⓇⓈⓇⓈⓇⓈⓇⓈ
PO Chowara, south of Kovalam. 📞 (0471) 48 1601. 📠 (0471) 48 0600.
🌐 www.somatheeram.org
Renowned for its private beach, Ayurvedic spa, and yoga and meditation courses. The spacious rooms here are in attractive wooden houses or in stone bungalows and cottages. 🍴 🍸 📺 🛏 🅿 🏫 🏊

	AE	59				
	DC					
	MC					
	V					

KOVALAM: *Kovalam Ashok Beach Resort* ⓇⓈⓇⓈⓇⓈⓇⓈ
Kovalam. 📞 (0471) 48 0101. 📠 (0471) 48 1522. 🌐 www.kovalamashok.com
This luxurious modern hotel has an older wing in the atmospheric summer palace of the former maharaja. The sumptuous royal suites here attract the likes of former Beatle Paul McCartney. 🍴 🍸 24 📺 🛏 🅿 🏫 🏊 ⛰ 🏌

	AE	193				
	DC					
	MC					
	V					

KOZHIKODE: *Taj Residency* ⓇⓈⓇⓈⓇⓈ
PT Usha Rd. 📞 (0495) 76 5354. 📠 (0495) 76 6448. 🌐 www.tajhotels.com
📱 (011) 332 2333; trn.delhi@tajhotels.com
This hotel has elegant rooms, many of them facing the sea, and offers excellent service. Ayurvedic treatment for arthritis and other chronic ailments is also available. 🍴 🍸 24 📺 🛏 🅿 🏫 🏊 🏌

	AE	74				
	DC					
	MC					
	V					

LAKSHADWEEP: *Bangaram Island Resort* ⓇⓈⓇⓈⓇⓈⓇⓈ
Lakshadweep. 📞 (0484) 66 8221. 📠 (0484) 66 8001. 🌐 www.casinogroup.com
📱 (0484) 66 8221; casino@vsnl.com
A pristine island paradise, this imaginatively-designed resort consists of clean, attractively furnished beach huts and bungalows. Snorkelling, scuba diving and fishing are arranged. 🍴 🍸 🅿 🏫 ⬆ ⛰ 🚗

	AE	29				
	DC					
	MC					
	V					

Price categories for a standard double room per night including tax and service charges but not including breakfast:
Rs under 550 rupees
RsRs 550–1,200 rupees
RsRsRs 1,200–3,000 rupees
RsRsRsRs 3,000–6,000 rupees
RsRsRsRsRs over 6,000 rupees

CREDIT CARDS
Indicates which major credit cards are accepted: AE American Express; DC Diners Club; MC Master Card/Access; V Visa.

WESTERN BATHROOMS
Indicates sit-down, flush toilets; showers and/or baths. Others have squat toilets and bucket-and-mug baths.

COFFEE SHOP
Hotels with 24-hour coffee shop, also serving hot meals.

AIR CONDITIONING
Hotels with air-conditioned rooms.

	CREDIT CARDS	NUMBER OF ROOMS	AIR CONDITIONING	WESTERN BATHROOMS	COFFEE SHOP
MUNNAR: *Tea County Hill Resort* (Rs)(Rs) Munnar. (0486) 53 0460. FAX (0486) 53 0970. W www.ktdc.com (0471) 31 8976; ktdc@vsnl.com Idyllic surroundings, good service and clean rooms are the attractions of this pleasant resort.	AE DC MC V	43		●	
MUNNAR: *Windermere Estate* (Rs)(Rs)(Rs) Windermere House, Thrikakara Post. (0486) 53 0512. W www.windermeremunnar.com R (0484) 42 5237; son@windmeremunnar.com Set amidst tea and cardamom plantations, this establishment offers comfort, friendly service and enchanting surroundings and views.		7		●	
THEKKADY: *Spice Village Nature Habitat* (Rs)(Rs)(Rs)(Rs) Thekkady Kumily Rd. (0486) 32 2314. FAX (0486) 32 2317. W www.casinogroup.com Guests can avail of boat safaris to spot wildlife near the lake, and visit tribal hamlets at this resort in the Cardamom Hills. Accommodation is simple yet elegant huts, thatched with elephant grass.	AE DC MC V	52		●	
THEKKADY: *Taj Garden Retreat* (Rs)(Rs)(Rs)(Rs) Amalambika Rd, via Kumily. (0486) 32 2401. FAX (0486) 32 2106. W www.tajhotels.com R (011) 332 2256; trn.delhi@tajhotels.com This lovely resort is set among lush coffee and spice plantations, on the periphery of the Periyar Tiger Reserve. Rooms are in cottages built on stilts, and Ayurvedic therapy is also available.	AE DC MC V	32	●	■	
THEKKADY: *Lake Palace* (Rs)(Rs)(Rs)(Rs)(Rs) Periyar WIldlife Sanctuary. (0486) 32 2023. FAX (0486) 32 2282. W www.ktdc.com (0471) 31 8976; ktdc@vsnl.com Built on a peninsula jutting into Periyar Lake, this former royal summer palace still has a regal ambience. The surrounding forests offer plenty of opportunity for spotting wildlife.	AE MC V	6		●	
THIRUVANANTHAPURAM: *Muthoot Plaza* (Rs)(Rs)(Rs) Muthoot Centre, Punnen Rd. (0471) 33 7733. FAX (0471) 33 7734. @ muthoot@eth.com R (011) 691 0544; reservations@sarovarparkplaza.com Located in the city's commercial hub, this hotel has comfortable rooms, good business facilities and efficient service.	AE DC MC V	57	■	●	■
THIRUVANANTHAPURAM: *The South Park* (Rs)(Rs)(Rs) MG Rd, Palayam. (0471) 33 3333. FAX (0471) 33 1861. W www.thesouthpark.com In the heart of Thiruvananthapuram, this comfortable, recently-renovated hotel boasts a live band, a leafy garden where barbecue dinners are held, and Ayurvedic massage therapy.	AE DC MC V	83	■	●	■
VARKALA: *Taj Garden Retreat* (Rs)(Rs)(Rs)(Rs) Janardana Puram. (0472) 60 3000. FAX (0472) 60 2296. W www.tajhotels.com (011) 332 2256; trn.delhi@tajhotels.com Surrounded by green paddy fields, this hotel offers spectacular views of the coastline. A library, tennis courts, a freshwater pool, and a long, pristine beach are other attractions.	AE DC MC V	30	■	●	■
WYNAD: *Green Magic Nature Resorts* (Rs)(Rs)(Rs)(Rs)(Rs) Post Lakkidi, Vythiri. (0471) 33 1507. FAX (0471) 33 1407. @ tourindia@vsnl Set in the rainforests of northern Kerala, this magical resort offers accommodation in extremely comfortable tree houses atop tall ficus trees. There are ground level rooms as well, but no electricity.	AE DC MC V	12		●	
WYNAD: *Tranquil – The Plantation Hideaway* (Rs)(Rs)(Rs)(Rs)(Rs) Kuppamudi Estate, Kolagapara PO. (0493) 62 0244. FAX (0493) 62 2358. W www.plantationhideaway.com R (080) 558 9333; ivorytower@vsnl.com Located in the heart of a coffee plantation, this hotel has warm, attentive owners. Guests can avail of Ayurvedic massage therapy, and explore the verdant pepper, cardamom, coconut and banana plantations.	AE MC V	6		●	

ANDHRA PRADESH

HYDERABAD: *Green Park* (Rs)(Rs)(Rs) AE DC MC V 148
Greenlands, Begumpet. (040) 375 7575. FAX (040) 375 7677.
W www.hotelgreenpark.com
Close to the airport, this clean, modern and functional hotel also organizes tours and excursions for guests.

HYDERABAD: *Hotel Golconda* (Rs)(Rs)(Rs) AE DC MC V 150
1–1/124 Masab Tank. (040) 332 0202. FAX (040) 332 0404.
W www.hotelgolconda.com
This modern hotel, with comfortable rooms and efficient service, is located close to Banjara Hills. There is a multi-cuisine restaurant and a midnight buffet dinner for nightbirds.

HYDERABAD: *ITC Kakatiya Hotels & Towers* (Rs)(Rs)(Rs)(Rs) AE DC MC V 188
6–3–1187 Begumpet. (040) 340 0132. FAX (040) 340 1144. W www.welcomgroup.com
R (011) 614 1821; rmonorth.welcomnet@welcomgroup.com
This elegant hotel's special feature is a unique pool built around a natural rock. It is reputed for its excellent service and its cuisine, offered in three speciality restaurants.

HYDERABAD: *Taj Banjara* (Rs)(Rs)(Rs)(Rs) AE DC MC V 118
Rd 12, Banjara Hills. (040) 666 9999. FAX (040) 339 2218. W www.tajhotels.com
R (011) 332 2333; trn.delhi@tajhotels.com
Situated in the picturesque Banjara Hills, this hotel has elegant rooms, many of them overlooking a private lake. Other features include extensive business facilities, a tennis court, a swimming pool, and a charming lakeside café with a multi-cuisine menu.

HYDERABAD: *Taj Residency* (Rs)(Rs)(Rs)(Rs) AE DC MC V 140
Rd 1, Banjara Hills. (040) 339 3939. FAX (040) 339 2864. W www.tajhotels.com
R (011) 332 2333; trn.delhi@tajhotels.com
Lovely landscaping, an atrium that boasts natural rocks amidst lush greenery, elegantly furnished rooms, a private lake and outstanding regional Andhra Pradesh cuisine make this Hyderabad's most successful luxury hotel.

TIRUPATI: *Hotel Guestline Days* (Rs)(Rs)(Rs) AE DC MC V 140
14–37 Karakambadi Rd, PO Box 9. (08574) 80 800, 81 868. FAX (08574) 81 774.
@ guestlinetirupati@rediffmail.com
Overlooking the picturesque Tirumala Hills, this comfortable hotel has good food. Pilgrims hard-pressed for time can avail of the hotel's special service (for a fee) and bypass the long queues to enter the main sanctum of the Sri Venkateshvara Temple.

VIJAYAWADA: *Quality Inn D V Manor* (Rs)(Rs)(Rs) AE DC MC V 94
40–47 MG Rd. (0866) 47 4455. FAX (0866) 48 3170. W www.dvmanor.com
Centrally located, this modern, comfortable hotel has an central atrium with capsule lifts, a multi-cuisine restaurant and a bar.

VISAKHAPATNAM: *The Park* (Rs)(Rs)(Rs) AE DC MC V 61
Beach Rd. (0891) 75 4488. FAX (0891) 71 3603. W www.theparkhotels.com.
Conveniently located near the beach, this modern hotel's facilities include a crafts court where local artisans can be seen at work, and a bookshop. The air-conditioned rooms have sea views.

VISAKHAPATNAM: *Taj Residency* (Rs)(Rs)(Rs) AE DC MC V 93
Beach Rd. (0891) 56 7756, 56 4873. FAX (0891) 56 4370. W www.tajhotels.com
R (011) 332 2333; trn.delhi@tajhotels.com
With the usual standards of comfort and service associated with the Taj Group, this hotel also boasts panoramic views of the Bay of Bengal, and modern business facilities.

VISAKHAPATNAM: *Welcomgroup Grand Bay* (Rs)(Rs)(Rs) AE DC MC V 100
Beach Rd. (0891) 56 0101. FAX (0891) 55 0691. @ gm_grandbay@yahoo.com
Within walking distance from the sea, this well-run hotel offers elegantly appointed rooms, efficient staff and an excellent restaurant. The hotel has eco-friendly solar water-heating systems.

WARANGAL: *Ashoka Hotel* (Rs)(Rs) MC V 57
6–1–242 Main Rd, Hanamkonda. (08712) 57 8491. FAX (08712) 57 9260.
This large hotel has spacious and clean rooms, an efficient and friendly staff, good food, and a well-stocked bar.

WHERE TO EAT

INDIAN CUISINE is as rich in variety as the country itself. The delicate flavours of the classical cuisine that developed in the imperial courts of Delhi, Kashmir, Hyderabad and Lucknow are complemented by a vast range of regional specialities, made with a variety of exotic ingredients. From the arid deserts of Rajasthan come chilli-hot robust curries, whereas fish dominates in the cuisine of the lush, coastal areas of West Bengal, Goa and, to some extent, Kerala. Gujarat and Tamil Nadu are mostly vegetarian.

Red chilli

Eating habits in urban India have undergone considerable change in recent years, triggered off by rapidly changing lifestyles and the introduction of Western fast food chains. Though most Indians relish food cooked at home, eating out is becoming increasingly popular in the larger cities. Restaurants now offer anything from pizzas to sophisticated multi-course meals accompanied by local and imported wines. The restaurants on pages 720–43 have been selected for their quality, variety, service and price range.

ETIQUETTE

INDIANS ARE overwhelmingly hospitable and treat a guest as they would a favourite deity. In keeping with this tradition, many hotels and restaurants strive to follow a similar ethos. While it is customary for Indians to eat with their fingers, eateries do provide cutlery. There is usually a wash basin on the premises for washing hands before and after a meal, and restaurants often provide finger bowls with warm water and lemon for this purpose. Eating beef is taboo among Hindus, as is pork for Muslims.

RESTAURANTS

CHANGING LIFESTYLES have been widely responsible for the proliferation of eating places, not just in large cities, but in smaller towns as well.

Visitors savour a meal at one of Mumbai's many restaurants

A cook deftly prepares a paper-thin, plate-sized *rumali roti*

These range from luxurious gourmet restaurants to small cafés and roadside stalls, offering an eclectic choice of food, from Indian to Italian and Japanese. Most urban restaurants are air conditioned and the more expensive ones offer decor and service that is comparable with international standards. Traditional eating places, especially those that cater to a local clientele, are large, noisy halls, with special "family rooms", where parents can eat with their children. Simple and wholesome, mainly vegetarian, meals, are served here.

International chains, such as Pizza Hut and McDonalds, now have outlets in most big towns. They are becoming increasingly popular, particularly among the young. Special menus have been introduced to suit local tastes.

Most restaurants open by about 11am and close by midnight. In larger cities, it is best to book a table in

advance for weekends and holidays, especially at the more popular restaurants.

SPECIALITY RESTAURANTS

THE GROWING appreciation for international cuisine has led to a rise in up-market speciality restaurants in most major cities. Authentic Thai, Chinese, Mexican, Japanese and Italian dishes, prepared by expert chefs using choice imported ingredients, are enthusiastically patronized by discerning gourmands.

Regional Indian specialities, too, are equally in demand. Restaurants specializing in barbecued *tandoori* kebabs and breads, as well as cuisine from Goa, Kerala, Tamil Nadu, Kashmir, Lucknow, Hyderabad, West Bengal, Gujarat and Rajasthan, now offer a wide range of dishes derived from traditional family recipes. Certain select restaurants offering fusion food have begun to attract

Hotel Green, an improvised eatery in Rajasthan's Thar Desert

diners in search of unusual tastes and flavours. Here, inspired chefs experiment with recipes and ingredients from India and abroad, to create exciting new menus.

COFFEE SHOPS

L UXURY HOTELS have 24-hour coffee shops, which allow diners to grab a late dinner or early breakfast. Many local cafés and restaurants serving beverages and light snacks, however, also keep flexible hours. A recent addition is the small, bistro-type establishment in many shopping malls and at tourist sites. These are convenient places to relax and people-watch over sandwiches and a cup of tea.

ROADSIDE AND MARKET FOOD STALLS

F OR A GLIMPSE of the original Indian fast food industry, there is nothing better than a journey through the country's roadside and market food stalls. Improvised stalls, vans or carts, equipped with stoves and other cooking appliances, dish out tasty meals with speed and efficiency. The choice ranges from vegetarian snacks, such as spicy, deep-fried samosas, *dosas* and *idlis*, to *tandoori* chicken, kebabs, "fish fry" and Indian-style Chinese chow mein and spring rolls. If tempted to sample some of the fare, ask for a minimum of chillies. Indian sweets, fruit, ice cream and a variety of drinks, including mineral water, colas and juices, are also available. Unpretentious eateries also serve good food fast. These include the North Indian

*dhaba*s (which serve both non-vegetarian and vegetarian food), the Goan beach shacks (which specialize in fish curries with rice) and the South Indian Udipi restaurants (which serve only vegetarian meals). For health precautions, see pages 764–67.

VEGETARIAN FOOD

I NDIA'S EXCELLENT vegetarian food emanates from the country's largely vegetarian population. A simple but delicious meal of fresh seasonal vegetables, *dal* (lentil curry) and a wide choice of *rotis* and rice preparations can be had anywhere. Often these are served all together on a *thali* (platter) and are great value for money. The food's quality is endorsed by the displayed signs "Cooked in pure ghee" or "Cooked in ghee made from cow's milk".

ALCOHOL

T HE SERVING of alcohol is restricted, and some states, such as Gujarat, are officially "dry". Liquor is sold through government-

approved shops and licensed restaurants and prices vary across the country, because of the fluctuations in taxes from state to state. Luxury hotels are permitted to import wines and liquor, though they also serve Indian Made Foreign Liquor (IMFL), such as rum, beer, whisky and vodka. The quality of Indian wines and champagne is fast improving and some brands are even exported. Carrying alcohol for consumption in a restaurant is not permitted, nor is drinking in public places. National holidays and notified election days are "dry days" when no alcohol is served in hotels, bars and restaurants.

PRICES AND TIPPING

P RICES ARE fixed everywhere, be it in a luxury hotel or at a market stall. Luxury hotels also levy a Food and Beverage Tax (though the amount varies) which can escalate costs considerably.

Check your bill before paying. Even though a service charge is usually included, waiters do expect to be tipped – ten per cent of the bill is acceptable. Roadside eateries and street vendors are extremely cheap.

PAYING

C REDIT CARDS are usually accepted in up-market restaurants and bars, particularly if these are in luxury hotels. However, always keep cash (Indian rupees) on hand to pay for meals at eateries in small towns or roadside stalls and cafés.

Afternoon tea in a resort in the backwaters of Kerala

Choosing a Restaurant

THE RESTAURANTS in this guide have been selected to suit a wide price range and many are in recommended hotels (for hotel listings see pp690–717). Chosen for their good food, good value, and convenient or interesting location, they are listed region-wise. Entries are alphabetical within price category. Colour-coded thumb tabs show the areas covered on each page.

	Credit Cards	Regional Specialities	Pure Vegetarian	Western Dishes	Outdoor Tables
DELHI					
DELHI: *Berco's* ⓇⓈⓇⓈ E–8 Connaught Place. 【 (011) 331 8134. Best known for its spicy Chinese food, this restaurant also serves Thai and other Asian dishes. Generous helpings, good value for money. ▤ ○ *L, D.*	AE DC MC V				
DELHI: *Farsaan* ⓇⓈⓇⓈ M–27 Greater Kailash I. 【 (011) 646 4318. This speciality restaurant serves authentic Gujarati and Rajasthani food on traditional *thalis*. Though it now serves meat dishes as well it is best known for its vegetarian dishes and snacks (*farsaan* in Gujarati). ▤ ○ *L, D.*	AE	●			
DELHI: *Karim* ⓇⓈⓇⓈ 16 Jami Masjid. 【 (011) 326 9880. An institution among food lovers, this restaurant traces its ancestry to a legendary cook who served Mughal kings. Outstanding, but rich and spicy Mughal dishes include tender *burra* kebabs. ▤ ○ *B, L, D.* ● *Mon, Id Festivals.*	AE DC MC V	●			
DELHI: *Kwality* ⓇⓈⓇⓈ 67 Regal Building, Connaught Place. 【 (011) 374 2310. This restaurant's hearty Punjabi fare is perennially popular. Located in the heart of Delhi's central business district. ▤ ○ *L, D.*	AE DC MC V	●			
DELHI: *Sagar* ⓇⓈⓇⓈ Defence Colony Market. 【 (011) 462 1451. Clients line up to eat the wholesome South Indian food served at this excellent, value-for-money restaurant. ▤ ✍ ○ *B, L, D.*		●	▣		
DELHI: *Basil and Thyme* ⓇⓈⓇⓈⓇⓈ Santushti Shopping Complex. 【 (011) 467 3322. The innovative menu here changes everyday but old favourites such as chicken liver pâté, quiche Lorraine and date and walnut cake are always available. ▤ ○ *L.* ● *Sun.*	AE DC MC V			●	
DELHI: *DV8* ⓇⓈⓇⓈⓇⓈ 13 Regal Building, Connaught Place. 【 (011) 336 3358. Multi-cuisine food along with a lively bar. Happy hours are between 4 and 8pm daily and there is a "drinks only night" on Wednesdays when you can drink all you want for a fixed price. ▤ Ⓨ ♫ ℙ ○ *L, D.*	AE DC MC V			●	
DELHI: *Fabcafé* ⓇⓈⓇⓈⓇⓈ 1 N–Block Market, Greater Kailash I. 【 (011) 647 8559. Next to the popular Fabindia shops (*see p96*), this café is aimed at hungry, busy shoppers. The choice is wide, with snacks to go with coffee, and light lunch salads and platters. ▤ ℙ ○ *L, D.* ● *Holi.*	AE DC MC V			●	
DELHI: *Flavors of Italy* ⓇⓈⓇⓈⓇⓈ 52–C Moolchand Flyover Bank Complex, Defence Colony. 【 (011) 464 5644. The Italian owner dishes up delicious antipasti, pastas and salads. The *tiramisu* and espresso coffee are also good. ▤ ✍ ○ *L, D.*	AE DC MC V			●	▣
DELHI: *Lemon Grass* ⓇⓈⓇⓈⓇⓈ D–15 South Extension II. 【 (011) 625 0757. Fresh ingredients are flown in from Bangkok for the excellent Thai food here. Their curries are aromatic delights. ▤ ○ *L, D.*	AE DC MC V				
DELHI: *Park Baluchi* ⓇⓈⓇⓈⓇⓈ Inside Deer Park, Hauz Khas Village. 【 (011) 685 9369. Enjoy an alfresco lunch at this atmospheric restaurant located in a lovely, tree-shaded park, where deer and peacocks roam. All the *tandoori* dishes and Indian breads are outstanding. Try their *dal makhni* and vegetarian green kebabs as well. ▤ Ⓨ ○ *L, D.*	AE DC MC V	●			▣

Price categories for a meal for one, including tax and service charges but not alcohol:

Ⓡ under 100 rupees
ⓇⓇ 100–200 rupees
ⓇⓇⓇ 200–400 rupees
ⓇⓇⓇⓇ 400–700 rupees
ⓇⓇⓇⓇⓇ over 700 rupees

CREDIT CARDS
Indicates which major credit cards are accepted.

REGIONAL SPECIALITIES
Specialized cuisine is served from regions of India, such as Rajasthan, Gujarat or South India.

PURE VEGETARIAN
Restaurants serving only vegetarian food.

WESTERN DISHES
French, Italian or other Western fare is on the menu.

OUTDOOR TABLES
Tables for eating outdoors, often with a good view.

	CREDIT CARDS	REGIONAL SPECIALITIES	PURE VEGETARIAN	WESTERN DISHES	OUTDOOR TABLES
DELHI: *The Rampur Kitchen* ⓇⓇⓇ Khan Market. 🎧 *(011) 463 1222.* This little eatery serves specialities from Rampur *(see p194)*. Try the mutton stew and *sheermal* bread. 🍴 🔵 *L, D.* ⚫ *National hols.*	DC MC V	●			
DELHI: *Swagath* ⓇⓇⓇ Defence Colony Market. 🎧 *(011) 465 4537.* This new speciality restaurant serves excellent non-vegetarian South Indian food. The fish curries are delicious. 🍴 ⚡ 🔵 *L, D.*	AE DC MC V				
DELHI: *Dakshin* ⓇⓇⓇⓇ Marriott Welcome Hotel, District Centre, Saket. 🎧 *(011) 652 1122.* Specializing in spicy South Indian food, this restaurant offers aromatic dishes in an elegant ambience. 🍴 🎵 🅿 🔵 *L, D.*	AE DC MC V	●			
DELHI: *The Imperial Garden* ⓇⓇⓇⓇ E–3 Masjith Moth, Greater Kailash II. 🎧 *(011) 647 7798, 643 7288.* One of Delhi's finest Chinese restaurants, it is run by the "smiling Buddha" Baba Ling. Excellent food and friendly staff. 🍴 🔵 *L, D.*	AE DC MC V				
DELHI: *Bukhara* ⓇⓇⓇⓇⓇ Maurya Sheraton, Diplomatic Enclave. 🎧 *(011) 611 2233.* Undoubtedly one of the finest restaurants in the city, its celebrity guest list is impressive. Superb *tandoori* dishes, such as *sikandari raan* and the famous *naan* breads are not to be missed. 🍴 📺 🎵 🅿 🔵 *L, D.*	AE DC MC V	●			
DELHI: *Chor Bizzare* ⓇⓇⓇⓇⓇ Broadway Hotel, 4/15–A Asaf Ali Rd. 🎧 *(011) 327 3821.* Delicious Kashmiri food, such as the *yakhni*, *roghan josh* and lightly cooked green *haq* leaves, is served here. 🍴 📺 🎵 🅿 🔵 *L, D.*	AE DC MC V	●			
DELHI: *Dum Pukht* ⓇⓇⓇⓇⓇ Maurya Sheraton, Diplomatic Enclave. 🎧 *(011) 611 2233.* This restaurant specializes in Avadhi dishes, cooked slowly in their own steam. The *biryani* and *kakori* kebab are outstanding. 🍴 📺 🅿 🔵 *L, D.*	AE DC MC V	●			
DELHI: *House of Ming* ⓇⓇⓇⓇⓇ Taj Mahal Hotel, 1 Mansingh Rd. 🎧 *(011) 302 6162.* This restaurant offers great Cantonese and Szechwan fare. Specialities include Peking duck and date pancakes. 🍴 📺 🎵 🔵 *L, D.*	AE DC MC V				
DELHI: *La Piazza* ⓇⓇⓇⓇⓇ Hyatt Regency, Bhikaji Cama Place. 🎧 *(011) 679 1234.* The city's best Italian food is available here. There is an excellent lunch buffet daily, but the Sunday brunch, which offers as much pasta and pizza as you can eat, is even better. 🍴 📺 🎵 🔵 *L, D.*	AE DC MC V			●	
DELHI: *La Rochelle* ⓇⓇⓇⓇⓇ The Oberoi, Dr Zakir Hussain Marg. 🎧 *(011) 436 3030.* This elegant establishment prides itself on its authentic French cuisine, fine wines, and excellent service. 🍴 📺 🎵 🔵 *B, L, D.*	AE DC MC V			●	
DELHI: *Sakura* ⓇⓇⓇⓇⓇ The Metropolitan Hotel Nikko, Bangla Sahib Rd. 🎧 *(011) 334 2000.* Popular with visiting Japanese business travellers yearning for familiar food, and slowly catching on with local gourmets, this pricey restaurant serves authentic Japanese specialities. 🍴 📺 🔵 *B, L, D.*	AE DC MC V				
DELHI: *Spice Route* ⓇⓇⓇⓇⓇ Imperial Hotel, Janpath. 🎧 *(011) 334 1234.* The stunning interiors are a suitable background for the outstanding food, which features dishes from India as well as Southeast Asia. The service is discreet yet attentive. 🍴 📺 🎵 🔵 *L, D.*	AE DC MC V	●			

For key to symbols see back flap

Price categories for a meal for one, including tax and service charges but not alcohol:

Ⓡ under 100 rupees
ⓇⓇ 100–200 rupees
ⓇⓇⓇ 200–400 rupees
ⓇⓇⓇⓇ 400–700 rupees
ⓇⓇⓇⓇⓇ over 700 rupees

CREDIT CARDS
Indicates which major credit cards are accepted.
REGIONAL SPECIALITIES
Specialized cuisine is served from regions of India, such as Rajasthan, Gujarat or South India.
PURE VEGETARIAN
Restaurants serving only vegetarian food.
WESTERN DISHES
French, Italian or other Western fare is on the menu.
OUTDOOR TABLES
Tables for eating outdoors, often with a good view.

	CREDIT CARDS	REGIONAL SPECIALITIES	PURE VEGETARIAN	WESTERN DISHES	OUTDOOR TABLES

HARYANA & PUNJAB

		CREDIT CARDS	REGIONAL SPECIALITIES	PURE VEGETARIAN	WESTERN DISHES	OUTDOOR TABLES
AMRITSAR: *Kwality Restaurant* ⓇⓇ Novelty Building, Novelty Chowk, Lawrence Rd. 📞 *(0183) 22 4829.* Part of a well-known North Indian chain, this restaurant features authentic Punjabi food, served with efficiency. 🍴 🍷 ⚡ ◯ *B, L, D.*		DC MC V	●		●	
AMRITSAR: *Napoli* ⓇⓇ Hotel Blue Moon, The Mall, Queen's Rd. 📞 *(0183) 22 0416.* This popular restaurant, in business for over 30 years, serves international cuisine in generous portions. 🍴 🍷 ◯ *L, D.* ● *Diwali.*		AE MC V			●	■
AMRITSAR: *Crystal Restaurant* ⓇⓇⓇ Crystal Chowk. 📞 *(0183) 22 5555.* Good Punjabi food here, so stick with the standard *tandoori* fare most popular with clients. 🍴 🍷 ◯ *L, D.* ● *Diwali.*		AE MC V	●		●	
CHANDIGARH: *Ghazal Restaurant* ⓇⓇ SCO 189–91, Sector 17-C. 📞 *(0172) 70 4448.* This is well known for its Mughlai fare. Try the *murg lababdar, paneer dilruba* along with *naan* and *raita.* 🍴 🍷 🅿 ◯ *B, L, D.*		AE DC MC V				
CHANDIGARH: *Mehfil Restaurant.* ⓇⓇ SCO 181–3 Sector 17-C. 📞 *(0172) 70 4224.* Authentic Punjabi cuisine, served here with traditional warmth. The decor is a little overpowering. 🍴 🍷 🅿 ◯ *B, L, D.*		AE DC MC V	●			
CHANDIGARH: *Sagar Ratna* ⓇⓇ SCO 47 Sector 17-E. 📞 *(0172) 70 7710.* Specializing in South Indian food, this also serves fresh fruit drinks – the *chikoo* shake is a particular favourite with customers. 🍴 ⚡ 🅿 ◯ *B, L, D.*		MC V	●	■		
CHANDIGARH: *Salad Bar* ⓇⓇ SCO 76–9 Sector 17-C. 📞 *(0172) 72 3222.* Popular with the young and with shoppers in Sector 17, this establishment offers good salads and snacks. 🍴 🅿 ◯ *L, D.*		MC V				
CHANDIGARH: *Cinnamon Roof* ⓇⓇⓇ SCO 10–12, Sector 17-A. 📞 *(0172) 89 8822.* Vegetable sizzlers and Mexican food are offered here. In winter, little coal braziers are set up to ward off the chill. 🍴 🍷 🎵 🅿 ◯ *L, D.*		MC V			●	■

HIMACHAL PRADESH

		CREDIT CARDS	REGIONAL SPECIALITIES	PURE VEGETARIAN	WESTERN DISHES	OUTDOOR TABLES
CHAIL: *Palace Hotel's Restaurant* ⓇⓇ Palace Hotel. 📞 *(01792) 48 141.* Try the regional specialties offered in this delightful restaurant, such as *sepubadi* and Himachali *kadi.* 🍷 ◯ *B, L, D.*		AE MC V	●		●	
CHAMBA: *Ravi View Restaurant* ⓇⓇ Near Main Sehgal. 📞 *(01899) 22 671.* Great mountain views add to the ambience of this restaurant which serves good South Indian food and light snacks. ◯ *B, L, D.*			●			■
DHARAMSALA: *Ashoka Restaurant* ⓇⓇ McLeodganj, Jogiwara Rd. 📞 *(01892) 21 589.* *Tandoori* fare, curries and buttery *naans* are good choices in this pleasant, friendly restaurant. ◯ *B, L, D.* ● *Jan.*			●			■
DHARAMSALA: *Chonor Guest House Restaurant* ⓇⓇ Temple Rd, McLeodganj. 📞 *(01892) 21 006.* Spotlessly clean and attractively decorated, this restaurant serves wholesome Continental and Tibetan fare. Try the *momos.* ◯ *B, L, D.*		MC V			●	■

DHARAMSALA: *Nick's Italian Kitchen* ⓇⓇ
Kunga Guesthouse. **[** (01892) 21 180.
The pastas, pizzas and pies served here are recommended, as are the Tibetan
noodle soup and *momos*. ◻ B, L, D. ● *Tibetan New Year, Dalai Lama's Birthday.*

KALPA: *Kinner Villa Restaurant* Ⓡ
Hotel Kinner Villa. **[** (01786) 26 006.
Basic, simple Indian fare served here. There is some Chinese and Western
food as well, but it is best to stick to the *dal-roti*. ◻ B, L, D. ● *Nov–Apr.*

KULLU: *Silhouette – Hotel Le Grand* ⓇⓇ
National Highway 21, Kullu-Manali Rd. **[** (01902) 52 443.
Pure vegetarian food is served here on request. Chinese, Western and the
standard Indian *tandoori* food is also available. ▤ Ⲙ ◻ L, D.

MANALI: *Chopsticks* ⓇⓇ
The Mall. **[** (09102) 52 639.
Generous helpings of Japanese, Chinese and Tibetan food are served in
this friendly restaurant. Try their curd, pancakes, and the *gyakok*, a
delicious Tibetan hotpot. ◻ B, L, D.

MANALI: *Johnson's Cafe* ⓇⓇ
The Mall. **[** (09102) 53 023.
Fresh trout, homemade pasta, excellent ice cream and coffee, served in a
pleasant garden, make this restaurant a perennial favourite. Only organic
ingredients are used. ◻ B, L, D.

MANALI: *Mayur Restaurant* ⓇⓇ
Old Mission Rd. **[** (01902) 52 316.
For vegetarians, the restaurant will cook a special meal on request. The rest
of the menu is the usual *tandoori* and Indianized Chinese fare, but the
ambience is pleasant and the service efficient. ◻ B, L, D.

MANALI: *Rendezvous* ⓇⓇ
Hotel Snowcrest Manor, Log Hut Area. **[** (09102) 53 351.
There are spectacular views of the mountains from this restaurant, which
serves Indian and some Western dishes. Ⲙ ◻ B, L, D.

AE
DC
MC
V

MANDI: *Cabofrio Restaurant & Copacabana Bar* ⓇⓇ
Hotel Rajmahal, Near District Court. **[** (09105) 22 401.
Despite the Brazilian name, the usual mix of Western, Chinese and Indian
food is offered here. The snacks are good. Ⲙ ◻ B, L, D.

SHIMLA: *Davicos Bar & Restaurant* ⓇⓇ
5 The Mall. **[** (0177) 206 335.
An institution in Shimla, this restaurant serves good kebabs, snacks as well
as South Indian vegetarian food. Ⲙ ◻ B, L, D.

MC
V

SHIMLA: *Baljees* ⓇⓇⓇ
26 The Mall. **[** (0177) 252 313.
Among the town's oldest eateries, this offers delicious Indian and Western
food, and is conveniently located in the heart of The Mall. ◻ B, L, D.

SHIMLA: *Cecil Restaurant* ⓇⓇⓇ
Oberoi Cecil, Chaura Maidan. **[** (0177) 204 848.
This elegant restaurant serves Asian and European cuisine, and provides
the perfect setting for a quiet apéritif or a special occasion. ▤ ◻ B, L, D.

LADAKH, JAMMU & KASHMIR

JAMMU: *Falak* ⓇⓇⓇ
KC Residency Hotel, Vir Marg. **[** (01982) 52 0770.
Mainly Mughlai and Kashmiri cuisine here, though some Chinese food is
also served. ▤ Ⲙ ◻ L, D. ● *Nov–Mar.*

AE
DC
MC
V

LEH: *Budshah Inn Restaurant* ⓇⓇ
Main Bazaar, Leh. **[** (01982) 52 813.
Try this restaurant's Kashmiri *waazwan* (a traditional array of festive meat
dishes featuring lamb, lotus roots and other delicacies). The prices are
reasonable and the portions generous. ◻ B, L, D. ● *Nov–Mar.*

LEH: *Ibex Hotel Restaurant* ⓇⓇ
Leh. **[** (01982) 52 281.
This small eatery serves Indian and Chinese food, though Western food is
also available on request. Ⲙ ◻ B, L, D. ● *Nov–Mar.*

Price categories for a meal for one, including tax and service charges but not alcohol:

(Rs) under 100 rupees
(Rs)(Rs) 100–200 rupees
(Rs)(Rs)(Rs) 200–400 rupees
(Rs)(Rs)(Rs)(Rs) 400–700 rupees
(Rs)(Rs)(Rs)(Rs)(Rs) over 700 rupees

CREDIT CARDS
Indicates which major credit cards are accepted.

REGIONAL SPECIALITIES
Specialized cuisine is served from regions of India, such as Rajasthan, Gujarat or South India.

PURE VEGETARIAN
Restaurants serving only vegetarian food.

WESTERN DISHES
French, Italian or other Western fare is on the menu.

OUTDOOR TABLES
Tables for eating outdoors, often with a good view.

	CREDIT CARDS	REGIONAL SPECIALITIES	PURE VEGETARIAN	WESTERN DISHES	OUTDOOR TABLES
LEH: *Mentokling Garden Restaurant* (Rs)(Rs) Zangsti. (01982) 52 992. This pretty garden restaurant has tables under apple trees, and serves local and Western dishes. B, L, D. Nov–Feb.		●		●	▦
LEH: *Penguin Bar and Restaurant* (Rs)(Rs) Fort Rd. (01982) 52 107. Tables in the garden and a good German bakery are the highlights here. Pure vegetarian food is also available. B, L, D. Oct–May.		●		●	▦
LEH: *Summer Harvest Restaurant* (Rs)(Rs) Fort Rd. (01982) 53 226. A modest eatery with a selection of Tibetan, Ladakhi and Kashmiri dishes. Western food is also served here. B, L, D. Nov–Feb.		●		●	▦
LEH: *Zen Garden Restaurant* (Rs)(Rs) Shanti Stupa Rd. No telephone. A lovely riverside location is offered along with Chinese, Western and Indian food. B, L, D. Sep–May.		●		●	▦
LEH: *Amoo Cafeteria* (Rs)(Rs)(Rs) Main Market. (01982) 53 114. Good Tibetan and Kashmiri food is served at this rooftop restaurant, which offers great views of Leh Palace and the old fort. B, L, D.		●		●	▦
LEH: *Café World Peace* (Rs)(Rs)(Rs) Near New Gas Service. (01982) 52 988. The menu includes Indian, Chinese and Western food, as well as some delectable cinnamon rolls, pies and other baked goods. L, D. 15–20 Sep.		●		●	▦
LEH: *Omasila Restaurant* (Rs)(Rs)(Rs) Hotel Omasila, Changspa. (01982) 52 119. This pleasant garden restaurant prides itself on its organically grown fresh garden vegetables, and its quiet, scenic location. B, L, D.		●		●	▦
LEH: *Ostal Restaurant* (Rs)(Rs)(Rs) Ostal Guesthouse. (01982) 52 816. Pleasant and airy, with a Swiss bakery on the premises, this restaurant is situated in a picturesque village. L, D. end Sep.		●		●	▦
SRINAGAR: *The Chinar* (Rs)(Rs)(Rs) Gupkar Rd. (0194) 47 0101. This multi-cuisine restaurant's Kashmiri food is recommended, as is the outdoor barbecue against the majestic *chinar* trees. In more peaceful times, this was a favourite haunt of Bollywood filmstars. B, L, D.	AE MC V	●		●	▦

UTTAR PRADESH & UTTARANCHAL

	CREDIT CARDS	REGIONAL SPECIALITIES	PURE VEGETARIAN	WESTERN DISHES	OUTDOOR TABLES
AGRA: *Joney's Palace* (Rs) Kutta Park, Near Thana, Taj Ganj. No telephone. Good breakfasts and Israeli and Indian dishes are served here. Also well-known for its banana *lassi*. B, L, D.		●		●	
AGRA: *Dasaprakash* (Rs)(Rs) 1 Gwalior Rd, Meher Theatre Complex, Agra Cantonment. (0562) 36 3368. Reasonable prices for a good meal make this restaurant popular with clients seeking authentic South Indian cuisine. Try the *rawa dosa* and the *uthapam*. L, D.	MC V	●	▦		▦
AGRA: *Only Restaurant* (Rs)(Rs) 45 Taj Rd. (0562) 22 6834. Rather bland, staple fare is offered here. Performances of Indian music in the evening liven the atmosphere. B, L, D. Holi.	AE MC V	●		●	▦

AGRA: *Petals* 　　 Rs Rs 　 V ● ●
19–A Taj Rd. (0562) 22 5293.
A comfortable restaurant serving Indian, Chinese and Continental food. It offers good Mughlai cuisine. ▤ ◐ *L, D.* ● *Holi, Diwali.*

AGRA: *Zorba The Buddha Osho Restaurant* 　　 Rs Rs 　 MC ● ▣ ●
E–13 Shopping Arcade, Sadar Bazaar. (0562) 22 5055.
Run by the Osho order, this scrupulously clean restaurant serves highly recommended, reasonably priced vegetarian food. ▤ ⚡ ◐ *L, D.* ● *May, Jun.*

ALLAHABAD: *Elchico* 　　 Rs Rs 　 AE DC MC V
24 MG Road, Civil Lines. (0532) 42 0753.
One of the oldest in the city, this cosy restaurant serves Indian and Western dishes, and good pastry and coffee. ▤ ◐ *B, L, D.*

DEHRADUN: *Kwality Restaurant* 　　 Rs Rs 　 ● ●
19 Rajpur Rd. (0135) 65 7001.
This serves the wholesome and tasty Punjabi dishes which have been a feature of this chain for a long time. ▤ ◐ *B, L, D.*

FATEHPUR SIKRI: *Navratan Restaurant* 　　 Rs Rs 　 ● ● ▣
Gulistan Tourist Complex. (05619) 88 2490.
Popular as a stopover point, the restaurant here offers snacks and meals in a cheerful garden setting. ▤ Y ◐ *L, D.*

HARIDWAR: *Bestee* 　　 Rs 　 ● ▣ ●
18 Niranjani Akhara. (0133) 42 0082.
Good breakfasts are available here, although this eatery is most famous for its savoury snacks, fresh fruit milk shakes and *lassis.* ◐ *B, L, D.*

HARIDWAR: *Chinkara Hills* 　　 Rs 　 ●
Haridwar-Rishikesh Rd, Raiwala, Dehradun district. (0133) 48 4361.
This offers snacks to tourists en route to Haridwar. Non-vegetarian food and liquor, banned in Haridwar, are available here. Y ◐ *B, L, D.*

KANPUR: *Kwality Restaurant* 　　 Rs Rs 　 ● ●
16/97, The Mall. (0512) 31 2290.
As in the other restaurants of this chain, good, wholesome and reasonably priced Punjabi food is available here. ▤ Y ◐ *L, D.*

LUCKNOW: *Tunde ke Kebab* 　　 Rs 　 ●
Amina Chowk. No Telephone.
People travel long distances to eat the melt-in-the-mouth kebabs perfected by the legendary one-armed cook, Tunda. ◐ *L, D.*

LUCKNOW: *Vyanjan Restaurant* 　　 Rs Rs 　 MC V ●
Vinay Palace, 10 Ashok Marg. (0522) 28 0537.
The vegetarian food is excellent, and an effective cooling system adds to the pleasure of eating here. ▤ ◐ *L, D.*

LUCKNOW: *Zaika* 　　 Rs Rs 　 AE DC MC V ● ●
10 Rani Laxmi Bai Marg. (0522) 21 2155.
Avadhi dishes such as *biryani* and mutton *korma* are the specialities of this restaurant, which also serves other cuisines. ▤ ◐ *B, L, D.*

LUCKNOW: *Falaknuma* 　　 Rs Rs Rs Rs 　 AE MC V ●
Hotel Clark's Avadh, 8 MG Marg. (0522) 22 0131.
This rooftop restaurant, with great views of the city and the river, serves delicious traditional Dum Pukht cuisine *(see p165).* The service is efficient and the ambience pleasing. ▤ Y ◐ *L, D.*

LUCKNOW: *Oudhyana Restaurant* 　　 Rs Rs Rs Rs 　 AE DC MC V ●
Taj Residency, Vipin Khand, Gomti Nagar. (0522) 39 3939.
The luxurious ambience perfectly complements the regal Avadhi cuisine served here. Try the kebabs and *pulaos.* ▤ Y ◐ *L, D.*

MATHURA: *Best Western Radha Ashok* 　　 Rs Rs Rs 　 AE MC V ●
Masani Bypass Rd, Post. Chhatikara. (0565) 73 0395.
Conveniently located off the Delhi-Agra highway, this restaurant serves good multi-cuisine food, at reasonable prices. ▤ ◐ *B, L, D.*

MUSSOORIE: *Whispering Windows* 　　 Rs Rs 　 ● ●
The Mall. (0135) 63 2020.
This popular eatery, with views of The Mall, serves delicious Punjabi-style butter chicken as well as some Western dishes. ◐ *B, L, D.*

Price categories for a meal for one, including tax and service charges but not alcohol:

(Rs) under 100 rupees
(Rs)(Rs) 100–200 rupees
(Rs)(Rs)(Rs) 200–400 rupees
(Rs)(Rs)(Rs)(Rs) 400–700 rupees
(Rs)(Rs)(Rs)(Rs)(Rs) over 700 rupees

CREDIT CARDS
Indicates which major credit cards are accepted.

REGIONAL SPECIALITIES
Specialized cuisine is served from regions of India, such as Rajasthan, Gujarat or South India.

PURE VEGETARIAN
Restaurants serving only vegetarian food.

WESTERN DISHES
French, Italian or other Western fare is on the menu.

OUTDOOR TABLES
Tables for eating outdoors, often with a good view.

	Price	Credit Cards	Regional Specialities	Pure Vegetarian	Western Dishes	Outdoor Tables
NAINITAL: *Kumaon Retreat* Grasmere Estate, Mallital. (05942) 37 341. Views of the surrounding town, and wholesome food, make eating in this multi-cuisine restaurant a pleasant experience. B, L, D.	(Rs)(Rs)	AE DC MC V			●	
RISHIKESH: *Chotiwala* Swarg Ashram, across Shivanand Jhula. (0135) 43 0070. Great pure vegetarian pilgrim food (try the *aloo poori*) is served at lightning speed by cheerful waiters. Crowded at most times. B, L, D.	(Rs)	AE MC V	●	■		
VARANASI: *Keshari Restaurant* D14/90 Dasashvamedha Rd. (0542) 32 1475. This restaurant has a deserved reputation for its delicious pure vegetarian dishes which are specialities of Varanasi. B, L, D.	(Rs)(Rs)	MC V	●	■		■
VARANASI: *Achar Chutney* Best Western Kashika, The Mall. (0542) 34 8250. This offers a choice of good vegetarian, Mughlai and *tandoori* cuisine, with emphasis on fresh pickles and chutneys. B, L, D.	(Rs)(Rs)(Rs)	AE MC V	●			
VARANASI: *Café Sizzler's* Clarks Tower, The Mall. (0542) 34 8091. This clean, cheerful restaurant offers a wide range of multi-cuisine dishes. The lunch buffet is recommended. B, L, D.	(Rs)(Rs)(Rs)	AE MC V	●		●	
VARANASI: *Eden Restaurant* Hotel Pradeep, C–27/153 Jagatganj. (0542) 20 4963. This rooftop restaurant which even has a lawn, offers great views of Varanasi. Tasty Indian and Western dishes, good service. B, L, D.	(Rs)(Rs)(Rs)		●		●	■
VARANASI: *Mandap* Hotel Taj Ganges, Nadesar Palace Ground. (0542) 345 100. Delicately spiced vegetarian food, good multi-cuisine dishes, and pleasing views of the lush garden are on offer here. B, L, D.	(Rs)(Rs)(Rs)	AE DC MC V	●		●	

BIHAR & JHARKHAND

	Price	Credit Cards	Regional Specialities	Pure Vegetarian	Western Dishes	Outdoor Tables
BODHGAYA: *Café Om* Near Bank of India. No telephone. This popular eatery serves excellent breakfast, Tibetan and Japanese food as well as delicious cakes. It is open only during the pilgrimage season, from November to April. B, L, D. May–Oct.	(Rs)(Rs)		●		●	■
BODHGAYA: *Uruvelya Garden Restaurant* Hotel Niranjana. (0631) 40 0475. Pure vegetarian and regional food is served on request, along with standard multi-cuisine fare, in this pleasant outdoor restaurant. B, L, D.	(Rs)(Rs)	MC V	●		●	■
PATNA: *Darpan Restaurant cum Coffee Shop* Beer Chand Patel Marg. (0612) 22 6270. A choice of Indian, Chinese and Western cuisines as well as tasty snacks are available here. B, L, D.	(Rs)(Rs)	DC MC V	●		●	■
PATNA: *Samrat* Hotel Chanakya. (0612) 22 3141. Quiet and efficient service accompanies the wide choice of Indian, Chinese and Western food served here. B, L, D.	(Rs)(Rs)(Rs)	AE DC MC V	●		●	
RAJGIR: *Centaur Hokke Restaurant* Centaur Hokke Hotel. (06112) 25 245. This establishment prides itself on its authentic Japanese food, cooked by chefs trained in Japan. Try their fresh shrimps and *tempura*. Indian food is also available. B, L, D.	(Rs)(Rs)(Rs)(Rs)(Rs)	AE DC MC V	●			■

RANCHI: *Kaveri Restaurant* ⓇⓈ
11 GEL Church Complex, Main Rd. ☎ *(0651) 22 1464.*
The best-known vegetarian restaurant in town, this serves generous
portions of simple, wholesome food at reasonable prices. 🍽 ⭘ *B, L, D.*

DC
V

RANCHI: *Yuvraj Palace Restaurant* ⓇⓈⓇⓈ
Hotel Yuvraj Palace, Doranda. ☎ *(0651) 50 2842.*
Regional food, along with many other kinds of cuisine, is available here.
An attraction is the provision for alfresco meals. 🍽 🍷 ⭘ *B, L, D.*

MADHYA PRADESH & CHHATTISGARH

BANDHAVGARH: *Bandhavgarh Jungle Camp Restaurant* ⓇⓈⓇⓈⓇⓈ
Bandhavgarh National Park. ☎ *No telephone.*
English breakfast, Indian lunch and Continental dinner are served in a
delightful thatched roundhouse. 🍷 ⭘ *B, L, D.*

BHOPAL: *Jharokha Restaurant* ⓇⓈⓇⓈⓇⓈ
Hotel Amer Palace, 209 Zone I, Maharana Pratap Nagar. ☎ *(0755) 27 2110.*
A well-stocked bar, excellent pastry, and decent multi-cuisine fare makes
this one of Bhopal's most popular restaurants. 🍽 🍷 ⭘ *B, L, D.*

AE
MC
V

BHOPAL: *Shahnama Restaurant* ⓇⓈⓇⓈⓇⓈ
Jehanuma Palace Hotel, 157 Shamla Hills. ☎ *(0755) 66 1100.*
The lunch-time buffets in this elegant restaurant, decorated with Persian
miniature paintings, are very popular. Specially recommended is the
delicious Bhopali fare, such as mutton *razala* curry. 🍽 🍷 🎵 ⭘ *B, L, D.*

AE
DC
MC
V

GWALIOR: *Swad Restaurant* ⓇⓈⓇⓈ
Hotel Landmark, 47 Manik Vilas Colony. ☎ *(0751) 51 1271.*
Courteous staff, a cheerful ambience and appetizing multi-cuisine food
have made this restaurant very successful. 🍽 🍷 ⭘ *B, L, D.*

AE
DC
MC
V

GWALIOR: *Daawat Restaurant* ⓇⓈⓇⓈⓇⓈ
Hotel Gwalior Regency, Link Rd. ☎ *(0751) 34 0670.*
A popular venue for business lunches and family outings, this restaurant
serves very good Mughlai and Punjabi fare. 🍽 🍷 ⭘ *B, L, D.*

AE
DC
MC
V

GWALIOR: *Usha Kiran Palace Restaurant* ⓇⓈⓇⓈⓇⓈ
Usha Kiran Palace Hotel, Jayendraganj, Lashkar. ☎ *(0751) 32 3993.*
The Mughlai food served here is excellent and the royal
ambience complements it perfectly. Outdoor tables on request for those who wish to
enjoy an alfresco meal. 🍽 🍷 ⭘ *B, L, D.*

AE
MC
V

INDORE: *Santushti Restaurant* ⓇⓈⓇⓈ
R–3 City Centre, 570 Mahatma Gandhi Rd. ☎ *(0731) 24 2058.*
Pure vegetarian food, stylishly served on a traditional *thali*, is this
restaurant's speciality. There is also a mini-*thali* for children. 🍽 ⭘ *B, L, D.*

AE
DC
MC
V

JABALPUR: *Vatika Restaurant* ⓇⓈⓇⓈ
Hotel Samdariya, Russel Chowk. ☎ *(0761) 31 6800.*
A multi-cuisine restaurant with the usual mix of Indian, Chinese and Western
food. The South Indian dishes are specially recommended. 🍽 🍷 ⭘ *B, L, D.*

KHAJURAHO: *Raja Café* ⓇⓈⓇⓈ
Opposite entrance to Western Group of temples. ☎ *(07686) 42 307.*
Located near the temples, this popular rendezvous point in Khajuraho, run
by a formidable Indo-Swiss lady, is great on atmosphere, with tables set
out in a large tree-shaded courtyard. The juices, pasta dishes and chocolate
cake are recommended. 🍽 🍷 ⭘ *B, L, D.*

KHAJURAHO: *Gautama Restaurant* ⓇⓈⓇⓈⓇⓈ
Holiday Inn, Airport Rd. ☎ *(07686) 72 301.*
Overlooking the swimming pool, this airy restaurant with tinkling indoor
fountains serves wholesome multi-cuisine fare. 🍽 🍷 ⭘ *B, L, D.*

AE
DC
MC
V

KHAJURAHO: *The Jass Oberoi Hotel Restaurant* ⓇⓈⓇⓈⓇⓈ
Hotel Jass Oberoi, Bypass Rd. ☎ *(07686) 42 344.*
This good multi-cuisine restaurant offers Indian classical and folk dance
and music performances in the evenings. 🍽 🍷 ⭘ *B, L, D.*

AE
DC
MC
V

ORCHHA: *Hotel Sheesh Mahal Restaurant* ⓇⓈⓇⓈ
Hotel Sheesh Mahal. ☎ *(07680) 52 624.*
This atmospheric restaurant inside the 17th-century palace offers fresh
multi-cuisine meals. The lunch and dinner buffets are lavish. 🍽 ⭘ *B, L, D.*

Price categories for a meal for one, including tax and service charges but not alcohol:

Rs under 100 rupees
Rs Rs 100–200 rupees
Rs Rs Rs 200–400 rupees
Rs Rs Rs Rs 400–700 rupees
Rs Rs Rs Rs Rs over 700 rupees

CREDIT CARDS
Indicates which major credit cards are accepted.

REGIONAL SPECIALITIES
Specialized cuisine is served from regions of India, such as Rajasthan, Gujarat or South India.

PURE VEGETARIAN
Restaurants serving only vegetarian food.

WESTERN DISHES
French, Italian or other Western fare is on the menu.

OUTDOOR TABLES
Tables for eating outdoors, often with a good view.

	CREDIT CARDS	REGIONAL SPECIALITIES	PURE VEGETARIAN	WESTERN DISHES	OUTDOOR TABLES
PANNA: *Machaan Restaurant* (Rs)(Rs)(Rs) Ken River Lodge, Village Mandla. (07732) 75 235. This imaginatively designed tree house *(machaan)* built on stilts has an enchanting ambience, and offers good views of the scenic countryside. The food is simple but wholesome. ○ *B, L, D.*		●		●	■
UJJAIN: *White House Restaurant* (Rs)(Rs)(Rs) Hotel Suvarna Palace, 23 GDC Rd, Dashera Maidan. (0734) 51 3045. Reasonably-priced, this outdoor restaurant which serves Indian and Chinese food, is considered by many to be the best the town has to offer. ○ *B, L, D.*	MC V	●			■

KOLKATA

	CREDIT CARDS	REGIONAL SPECIALITIES	PURE VEGETARIAN	WESTERN DISHES	OUTDOOR TABLES
KOLKATA: *Charnok's* (Rs)(Rs) Charnok's City, KB–26 Salt Lake City, Sector III. (033) 335 1349. This offers a wide variety of options, from fast food to multi-cuisine main meals to fresh fruit juice and ice cream. ⚡ ○ *B, L, D.*	MC V	●		●	
KOLKATA: *Chung Wah* (Rs)(Rs) 13A–B Chittaranjan Avenue. (033) 27 7003. Established in 1920, this offers excellent Indian-style Chinese food. Try the chilli chicken, special fried rice and *chopsuey.* Prices are reasonable and portions generous. ▤ ▥ ○ *L, D.*	MC V				
KOLKATA: *Flury's Swiss Confectionery* (Rs)(Rs) 18 Park Street. (033) 229 7664. One of the first tearooms in Kolkata, Flury's attracts customers from breakfast onwards. It is particularly renowned for its pastries and confectionery. ▤ ○ *B, L.*	MC V			●	
KOLKATA: *Jimmy's Kitchen* (Rs)(Rs) 14 Lindsay Street, Esplanade. (033) 244 2584. Old fashioned, yet very popular, this Chinese restaurant serves good steamed dumplings and spicy Szechwan dishes. ▤ P ○ *L, D.*	MC V				
KOLKATA: *Kewpie's Kitchen* (Rs)(Rs) 2 Elgin Lane, Behind Netaji Bhawan. (033) 475 9880. The finger-licking fare served at this "food boutique" is so popular that it is crowded through the day. This is the best Bengali food in town. They sell their own well-regarded recipe book and pickles. ▤ ○ *L, D.*	MC V	●			
KOLKATA: *Kwality* (Rs)(Rs) 17 Park Street. (033) 229 7681. This well-established eatery is famous for its North Indian food, although their Western dishes are popular too. Also recommended are their ice cream sundaes and iced coffee. ▤ ▥ ○ *B, L, D.*	MC V	●		●	
KOLKATA: *Mocambo* (Rs)(Rs) 25B Park Street. (033) 229 0095. This renowned restaurant with its high ceilings and quiet elegance has a colonial ambience. It is justly famous for its grilled *hilsa* fish served appetizingly on a banana leaf. ▤ ▥ ○ *L, D.*	MC V	●		●	
KOLKATA: *Silver Grill* (Rs)(Rs) 18E Park Street. (033) 229 9086. This popular restaurant serves reasonably priced Indian-Chinese food. Their fried chicken *wonton* is recommended. Other good dishes are crispy chicken and Singapore-Thai fish. ▤ ▥ ○ *L, D.*	MC V				
KOLKATA: *The Starlit Café* (Rs)(Rs) Atrium, 3 Lord Sinha Rd. (033) 282 4446. This "new age" café serves healthy, light and well-balanced vegetarian food based on Ayurvedic principles. Try the Mexican dishes. ▤ ○ *B, L, D.*	MC V	●	■	●	

KOLKATA: *Suruchi* ® ®   MC V •
Park Circus, Elliot Rd. [(033) 229 1763.
Run exclusively by women, this little restaurant's tasty home-style Bengali
food is good value for money. 🅿 ◯ *L.*

KOLKATA: *Aheli* ® ® ®   AE DC MC V •
The Peerless Inn, 12 Jawahar Lal Nehru Rd. [(033) 228 0301.
The traditional Bengali meal here is served by courteous staff. The steamed
hilsa, malai prawns, *bhetki* fish steamed in banana leaves and the *bhapa doi*
(a yoghurt-based sweet) are recommended. ▤ 🍷 ⚡ 🅿 ◯ *L, D.*

KOLKATA: *Blue Fox* ® ® ®   MC V •
55 Park Street. [(033) 229 7948.
An old-fashioned British-style bar, once famous for its crooners, it is now
frequented for its excellent lobster and crab sizzlers. ▤ 🍷 🅿 ◯ *L, D.*

KOLKATA: *Zarauj & Tones* ® ® ®   AE DC MC V •
26 Jawahar Lal Nehru Rd. [(033) 249 0369.
Along with Indian and Chinese food, Thai and Japanese dishes are also
on offer here. ▤ 🍷 ⚡ ◯ *L, D.* ● *Tue.*

KOLKATA: *The Baan Thai* ® ® ® ®   AE DC MC V
The Oberoi Grand Hotel, 15 Jawahar Lal Nehru Rd. [(033) 249 2323.
For those in a hurry, lunches here are guaranteed not to take longer than
45 minutes. Others are welcome to linger over the wide variety of excellent
Thai dishes on offer. ▤ 🅿 ◯ *L, D.*

KOLKATA: *Main Land China* ® ® ® ®   AE DC MC V
3A Gurusaday Rd, Uniworth House. [(033) 280 2006.
Another of Kolkata's famous Chinese restaurants that attracts discerning
eaters, especially those with a taste for seafood. ▤ 🍷 🅿 ◯ *L, D.*

WEST BENGAL & SIKKIM

DARJEELING: *Glenary's* ® ®   MC V • • ▪
Nehru Rd. [(0354) 54 315.
This multi-cuisine restaurant is a popular meeting place for travellers. It has
an attached bakery that serves great breads and pastry, fine Darjeeling tea,
and dishes made with Kalimpong cheese. ▤ 🅿 ◯ *B, L, D.*

DARJEELING: *The Park Restaurant* ® ®   •
41 Laden La Rd. [(0354) 54 989.
Probably the best Indian cuisine in town, with tempting buffet lunches.
Packed lunches are also provided for travellers. ◯ *B, L, D.* ● *15 Jan–15 Feb.*

DARJEELING: *Windamere Hotel Restaurant* ® ® ®   AE DC MC • ▪
Windamere Hotel, Observatory Hills. [(0354) 54 041.
Great Darjeeling tea and cakes at this Raj-era establishment, where the views
and ambience make up for the rather stodgy meals. 🍷 🎵 🅿 ◯ *B, L, D.*

GANGTOK: *The Tea House Bar & Restaurant* ® ®   AE •
The Chumbi Residency, Tibet Rd. [(03592) 26 618.
Watch the twinkling lights of Rumtek Hill as you eat here. Good Tibetan,
Chinese and Indian fare. 🍷 ◯ *B, L, D.*

GANGTOK: *Wild Orchid Restaurant* ® ®   DC MC V •
Central Hotel, 31–A National Highway. [(03592) 22 553.
With traditional Sikkimese-style decor, this restaurant offers good Chinese
food as well as South Indian fare. ▤ 🍷 🅿 ◯ *B, L, D.*

GANGTOK: *Dragon Hall* ® ® ®   AE DC MC V • •
Hotel Tashi Delek, Mahatma Gandhi Rd. [(03592) 22 991.
The delicious buffets here offer a choice of Sikkimese, Tibetan, Indian and
Chinese food. Western fare is also available. 🍷 ◯ *L, D.*

GANGTOK: *Oyster Restaurant* ® ® ®   AE DC MC V •
Hotel Sonam Delek, Sonam Gyatso Marg. [(03592) 22 566.
The French toast and banana pancake here are justly popular. The view of
Kanchendzonga from the restaurant is an added attraction. ◯ *B, L, D.*

GANGTOK: *Snow Lion Restaurant* ® ® ®   AE DC MC V • •
Hotel Tibet, Paljor Stadium Rd. [(03592) 23 468.
This is an excellent place to sample Sikkimese and Tibetan food. The
momos and mandarin fish are specially recommended. 🍷 ◯ *B, L, D.*

Price categories for a meal for one, including tax and service charges but not alcohol:

Rs under 100 rupees
RsRs 100–200 rupees
RsRsRs 200–400 rupees
RsRsRsRs 400–700 rupees
RsRsRsRsRs over 700 rupees

CREDIT CARDS
Indicates which major credit cards are accepted.

REGIONAL SPECIALITIES
Specialized cuisine is served from regions of India, such as Rajasthan, Gujarat or South India.

PURE VEGETARIAN
Restaurants serving only vegetarian food.

WESTERN DISHES
French, Italian or other Western fare is on the menu.

OUTDOOR TABLES
Tables for eating outdoors, often with a good view.

	Price	CREDIT CARDS	REGIONAL SPECIALITIES	PURE VEGETARIAN	WESTERN DISHES	OUTDOOR TABLES
KALIMPONG: *Kalimpong Park Hotel* Kalimpong Park Hotel, Rinkingpong Rd. ((03552) 55 304. Along with the usual Sikkimese and Chinese food, some Nepali and Tibetan dishes are also available on request. ▮ ◯ *B, L, D.*	RsRs	DC MC V	●		●	
SILIGURI: *Amrapali* Hotel Cindrella, 3rd Mile, Sevoke Rd. ((0353) 54 7136. The hearty breakfasts and excellent lunches served at this vegetarian restaurant are recommended. Packed food is available for travellers who are in a hurry to hit the road. ▮ ▮ ◯ *B, L, D.*	RsRsRs	MC V	●	■	●	

ORISSA

	Price	CREDIT CARDS	REGIONAL SPECIALITIES	PURE VEGETARIAN	WESTERN DISHES	OUTDOOR TABLES
BHUBANESWAR: *Fish & Prawn Restaurant* P–1 Jaydev Vihar. ((0674) 30 1936. As the name suggests, this restaurant is famous for its fresh seafood delicacies, cooked in a variety of styles. The portions are generous and local specialities can be ordered in advance. ▮ ▮ ◯ *L, D.*	RsRsRs	AE DC MC V	●		●	
BHUBANESWAR: *Nakli Dhaba* Mayfair Lagoon Hotel, 8–B Jaydev Vihar. ((0674) 55 9533. Decorated to look like a *dhaba* (roadside eatery), this restaurant serves good *tandoori* and vegetarian food. The Western fast food and confectionery are also popular. ▮ ▮ ◯ *L, D.*	RsRsRs	AE DC MC V	●		●	
BHUBANESWAR: *Pushpanjali* CB–1 Nayapali. ((0674) 30 1010. This multi-cuisine restaurant offers an appetising buffet and a special dish of the day. The decor and ambience have been inspired by temple interiors in Orissa. ▮ ▮ ◯ *B, L, D.*	RsRsRs	AE DC MC V	●		●	
CHILIKA LAKE: *Panthanivas* Barkul, PO Balgaun. ((06756) 20 488. The best thing to sample in this restaurant, which has lovely views of the lake, is the very fresh seafood prepared in the local style. The menu also features some Western and Chinese dishes. ◯ *B, L, D.*	RsRs		●		●	■
CUTTACK: *Sagun* Hotel Akbari Continental, Haripur Rd. ((0671) 62 3251. Regional and vegetarian food may be had here on request, but the restaurant is best known for its rich Mughlai food. ▮ ▮ ▮ ◯ *B, L, D.*	RsRs	AE DC MC V	●		●	
GOPALPUR-ON-SEA: *Blue Wave* Oberoi Palm Beach Hotel, Beach Rd. ((0680) 24 2021. Situated right on the beach with great views, this luxury hotel has excellent buffet-style, fixed-priced dining for non-residents. ▮ ▮ ▮ ◯ *B, L, D.*	RsRsRs	AE DC MC V	●		●	
KONARK: *Gitanjali Restaurant* Panthanivas, OTDC Ltd. ((06758) 36 831. Located close to the Sun Temple, this restaurant offers Chinese, Indian and Western food. The seafood dishes are recommended. ◯ *B, L, D.*	RsRsRs		●		●	■
PURI: *Aquarium* Mayfair Beach Resort, CT Rd. ((06752) 27 800. The interior decor here is soothing. Indian, Chinese and Western food is always on the menu, and barbecue dishes and vegetarian food may be specially ordered. ▮ ▮ ◯ *B, L, D.*	RsRs	AE MC V	●		●	
PURI: *The Legend* SE Railways Hotel, CT Rd. ((06752) 22 063. The food here is a good example of Raj cuisine and traces its ancestry to the railway catering of colonial times. Multi-course meals, which are served at fixed times, offer fantastic value for money. ◯ *B, L, D.*	RsRs				●	

ASSAM & THE NORTHEAST

AGARTALA: *Hotel Radha International Restaurant* ℞℞
Central Rd. 【 (06381) 22 2615.
Pure vegetarian meals are cooked on request, otherwise guests can choose
from Indian, Chinese and Western dishes. 🍽 ◯ *B, L, D.*

DIMAPUR: *Hotel Tragopan Restaurant* ℞℞
Circular Rd. 【 (03862) 30 2911.
The menu here offers the usual multi-cuisine medley, but regional dishes,
such as bamboo shoot curry, can be prepared on request. 🍽 ◯ *B, L, D.*

GUWAHATI: *Ushaban Restaurant cum Coffee Shop* ℞℞ — DC MC V
MG Road. 【 (0361) 54 1064.
Good multi-cuisine snacks and meals are offered in this restaurant, where
outdoor seating is also available. 🍽 🍷 ◯ *B, L, D.*

GUWAHATI: *The Tandoor* ℞℞℞
Dynasty Hotel, SS Rd, Lakhtokia. 【 (0361) 51 0499.
Potted greenery and a fountain create a soothing ambience here. The
tandoori prawns and pomfret are recommended. 🍽 🍷 🎵 ◯ *L, D.*

IMPHAL: *Chamu Restaurant* ℞℞
Hotel Nirmala, Mahatma Gandhi Avenue, Thangal Bazaar. 【 (0385) 22 8904.
Ask for regional specialities such as *iromba* (fish with bamboo shoots).
Pure vegetarian food is available on request. 🍽 ◯ *B, L, D.*

ITANAGAR: *Bhismak Restaurant cum Coffee Shop* ℞℞ — DC MC V
Ashok Hotel, Sector–C. 【 (0360) 21 2626.
Good snacks and regular meals can be had here. The menu offers the
usual Chinese, Indian and Western dishes. 🍽 🍷 ◯ *B, L, D.*

KOHIMA: *Shilloi* ℞℞
Japhu Hotel, PO 140, PR Hills. 【 (06381) 22 2721.
A varied menu of standard but well-made multi-cuisine dishes, and a charm-
ing outdoor garden make this restaurant popular with travellers. ◯ *B, L, D.*

SHILLONG: *Pinecone* ℞℞ — AE DC MC V
Hotel Pinewood, Rita Rd, European Ward. 【 (0364) 22 3116.
Set in tranquil surroundings close to Ward Lake, this restaurant offers
popular Indian and Western buffet meals. 🍷 ◯ *B, L, D.*

TEZPUR: *Gabharu* ℞℞
Hotel Luit, RS Rd. 【 (03712) 22 084.
Friendly staff, attractive surroundings and reasonably priced Indian, Western
and Chinese food make eating here a pleasant experience. 🍽 ◯ *B, L, D.*

RAJASTHAN

AJMER: *Sheesh Mahal* ℞℞℞ — AE MC V
Hotel Mansingh Palace, Vaishali Nagar. 【 (0145) 42 5855.
The lake views are more attractive than the food here (standard multi-
cuisine fare). Puppet-shows and folk songs in the evenings. 🍽 🍷 ◯ *B, L, D.*

BHARATPUR: *Laxmi Vilas Palace* ℞℞℞ — AE MC V
Civil Lines. 【 (05644) 31 199.
Farm-fresh vegetables from the palace gardens are served here and the
cottage cheese is made in the palace dairy. The authentic Rajasthani dishes
include the famous *churma*, a sweet dish. 🍽 🍷 ◯ *B, L, D.*

BIKANER: *Hotel Bhanwar Niwas Restaurant* ℞℞℞ — AE MC V
Rampuria Street. 【 (0151) 20 1043.
Located in a splendid *haveli (see p379)*, this restaurant serves tasty vege-
tarian food. There is a concert in the courtyard every evening. 🍽 ◯ *B, L, D.*

BIKANER: *Manwar* ℞℞℞ — AE MC V
Hotel Karni Bhawan, Gandhinagar. 【 (0151) 52 4701.
Authentic Marwari cuisine and simple Continental dishes are served in this
heritage hotel restaurant with Art Deco interiors. 🍽 🍷 ◯ *B, L, D.*

JAIPUR: *Laxmi Mishthan Bhandar (LMB)* ℞℞ — AE DC MC V
Johari Bazaar. 【 (0141) 56 4844.
This pure vegetarian restaurant, in the centre of the old city, is an
institution in Jaipur. Try the *paneer tikka* and creamy *kulfi*. 🍽 ◯ *B, L, D.*

						REGIONAL SPECIALITIES	PURE VEGETARIAN	WESTERN DISHES	OUTDOOR TABLES

Price categories for a meal for one, including tax and service charges but not alcohol:

Rs under 100 rupees
RsRs 100–200 rupees
RsRsRs 200–400 rupees
RsRsRsRs 400–700 rupees
RsRsRsRsRs over 700 rupees

CREDIT CARDS
Indicates which major credit cards are accepted.

REGIONAL SPECIALITIES
Specialized cuisine is served from regions of India, such as Rajasthan, Gujarat or South India.

PURE VEGETARIAN
Restaurants serving only vegetarian food.

WESTERN DISHES
French, Italian or other Western fare is on the menu.

OUTDOOR TABLES
Tables for eating outdoors, often with a good view.

Restaurant	Price	Credit Cards	Regional Specialities	Pure Vegetarian	Western Dishes	Outdoor Tables
JAIPUR: *Niro's* MI Rd. (0141) 37 4493. Reservations are needed to eat at this popular restaurant, which serves excellent Chinese food, *reshmi* kebabs and *paneer tikka*. The iced coffee with a scoop of ice cream is another favourite. ▤ P ◯ L, D.	RsRs	AE DC MC V	●		●	
JAIPUR: *Surabhi* Old Amer Rd. (0141) 63 5954. Authentic Rajasthani cuisine is served in this atmospheric restaurant housed in an old *haveli*. Take a look at the fascinating collection of turbans here (200 styles are displayed). You can even try your hand at tying one while you wait for your meal. ▤ Y ◯ L, D.	RsRs	AE MC V	●		●	■
JAIPUR: *Swaad* B–Block, Ganapati Plaza. (0141) 38 8700. A wide variety of multi-cuisine dishes, from chicken *tikka* to baked Alaska, are available at this excellent eatery. ▤ ◯ L, D.	RsRs	AE DC MC V	●		●	
JAIPUR: *Four Seasons* D–43/A Subash Marg, C–Scheme. (0141) 37 5450. A favourite with locals for family outings, this multi-cuisine restaurant is particularly known for its vegetarian dishes. ▤ Y P ◯ L, D.	RsRsRs	MC V	●		●	
JAIPUR: *Mehfil Restaurant* Anukampa Mansion II, MI Rd. (0141) 36 7272. The multi-cuisine items here range from pizza and vegetable Manchurian to *hara bhara* kebabs and *kasturi tikka lajawab*. ▤ ♫ P ◯ L, D.	RsRsRs	MC V	●		●	
JAISALMER: *Cinera* Above Grand View, Central Market. (02992) 22 3116. An imaginative menu of Indian and Western dishes, and great views of the fort at sunset are the attractions of this restaurant. ◯ B, L, D.	RsRs		●		●	
JAISALMER: *Natraj* Next to Salim Singh ki Haveli. No telephone. This rooftop restaurant has good, reasonably priced Chinese and Indian food. It also has a beer bar. ▤ Y ◯ B, L, D.	RsRs		●			
JAISALMER: *Top Deck* Natraj, Gandhi Chowk. (02992) 52 229. A varied menu and reasonably priced food are offered by this rooftop restaurant. Their fruit *lassis* are specially recommended. ◯ B, L, D.	RsRs		●		●	■
JAISALMER: *Trio* Gandhi Chowk, Near Amar Sagar Gate. (02992) 52 538. Located near the Amar Singh Gate, this restaurant, which serves local desert cuisine, has great ambience and courteous service. ▤ Y ♫ ◯ B, L, D.	RsRs	AE MC V	●		●	
JODHPUR: *Kalinga Restaurant* Station Rd. (0291) 24 066. The traditional Rajasthani and Gujarati food served here is recommended. There is also a special menu for children. ▤ Y ◯ B, L, D.	RsRs	MC V	●			
JODHPUR: *On the Rocks* Hotel Ajit Bhavan, Opposite Circuit House. (0291) 51 0410. This garden restaurant, with lovely landscaping, has an enchanting ambience. It serves tasty Indian and Continental dishes. Y ◯ L, D.	RsRs	MC V	●		●	■
JODHPUR: *Reggie's Restaurant* Near Safari Club, High Court Colony. (0291) 37 023. This cheerful rooftop restaurant serves delicious *tandoori* as well as Western-style barbecued food. Their grilled chicken and baked fish are specially recommended. Y ◯ D.	RsRs	AE MC V	●		●	■

JODHPUR: *The Pillars* Rs Rs Rs
Welcomgroup Umaid Bhavan Palace. (0291) 51 0101.
This verandah restaurant overlooking the lush palace lawns, with a view of
the magnificent Mehrangarh Fort, has a magical ambience. Even the
standard multi-cuisine fare tastes special here. Y O B, L, D.
AE DC MC V

MOUNT ABU: *Palace Hotel Restaurant* Rs Rs Rs
Palace Hotel, Bikaner House, Dilwara Rd. (02974) 38 673.
The spacious, stately dining room of the Palace Hotel offers excellent
multi-cuisine food. They also prepare picnic hampers. ▤ O B, L, D.
AE DC MC V

PUSHKAR: *Sun and Moon* Rs Rs
Bramha Temple Rd. (0145) 72 883.
Relax in hammocks strung in the gardens of this charming open-air restau-
rant. The multi-cuisine food is very good and the staff friendly. O B, L, D.
AE DC MC V

PUSHKAR: *Sunset Café* Rs Rs
Next to Pushkar Palace. (0145) 72 725.
Try breakfast or tea here to watch sunrise and sunset over the tranquil
waters of the lake. The *dosas*, sizzlers and cakes are good. O B, L, D.
AE DC MC V

UDAIPUR: *Jagat Niwas Palace Restaurant* Rs Rs
Lal Ghat, Jagdish Mandir. (0294) 52 9728.
This open-air restaurant offers spectacular views of the Lake Palace. The
Indian food is good, and the ambience is spellbinding. O B, L, D.
MC V

UDAIPUR: *Ambrai* Rs Rs Rs
Amet ki Haveli, Outside Chand Pol. (0294) 43 1085.
A superb lakeside location, good multi-cuisine food and a lovely garden.
There is live Indian music in the evenings. ♫ O B, L, D. ● Holi.

UDAIPUR: *Gallery Restaurant* Rs Rs Rs
Fateh Prakash Palace, City Palace. (0294) 52 8016.
Superb lake views, splendid decor and elegantly presented food make
many visitors linger here for a leisurely meal. ▤ Y O B, L, D.
AE DC MC V

UDAIPUR: *Jharokha* Rs Rs Rs Rs Rs
Lake Palace Hotel, Lake Pichola. (0294) 52 7961.
Fabulously romantic interiors and lake views add enchantment to the buffet
meals served here. Reservations are essential. ▤ Y O B, L, D.
AE DC MC V

GUJARAT

AHMEDABAD: *Agashiye* Rs Rs
Opposite Siddi Saiyad Mosque, Lal Darwaza. (079) 550 6946.
Located on the roof of an old *haveli*, this restaurant's ambience and
outstanding Gujarati food make for a great dining experience. Don't miss
the delicious home-made ice cream. O L, D.
MC V

AHMEDABAD: *Bavarchi* Rs Rs
Astron Building, Sarkhej-Gandhinagar Highway. (079) 656 5370.
For those hungering for *tandoori* and Punjabi food in this mainly
vegetarian town, this is the place to eat. ▤ O L, D.

AHMEDABAD: *Khyber* Rs Rs
Fortune Landmark Hotel, Usmanpura Crossroads, Ashram Rd. (079) 755 2929.
This rooftop restaurant specializes in a variety of kebabs, including
vegetarian ones. The *tandoori* pomfret and *tandoori* cauliflower are
recommended, as is the excellent *kulfi*. O D.
AE DC MC V

AHMEDABAD: *Colours of Spice* Rs Rs Rs
Piyuj Chambers, Swastik Crossroads, Navrangpura. (079) 644 2324.
This plush restaurant's multi-cuisine menu includes Indonesian and Thai
food. The ambience and service are pleasant. ▤ ⚡ O L, D.
AE MC V

AHMEDABAD: *Rajvadu Restaurant* Rs Rs Rs
Behind Ambaji Temple, Jivraj Park. (079) 664 3845.
An enchanting, rustic ambience and excellent Gujarati cuisine in this open-air
eatery. Try the *bajri rotlas* (millet bread) and the sweet *malpuas*. ⚡ P O D.

AHMEDABAD: *Vishala* Rs Rs Rs
Opposite Vasna Tolnaka. (079) 643 0357.
This unique open air restaurant recreates the atmosphere of rural Gujarat,
with authentic Gujarati food served in traditional village huts. It also has a
superb museum of antique kitchen utensils. ♫ O D.

		CREDIT CARDS	REGIONAL SPECIALITIES	PURE VEGETARIAN	WESTERN DISHES	OUTDOOR TABLES

Price categories for a meal for one, including tax and service charges but not alcohol:

(Rs) under 100 rupees
(Rs)(Rs) 100–200 rupees
(Rs)(Rs)(Rs) 200–400 rupees
(Rs)(Rs)(Rs)(Rs) 400–700 rupees
(Rs)(Rs)(Rs)(Rs)(Rs) over 700 rupees

CREDIT CARDS
Indicates which major credit cards are accepted.
REGIONAL SPECIALITIES
Specialized cuisine is served from regions of India, such as Rajasthan, Gujarat or South India.
PURE VEGETARIAN
Restaurants serving only vegetarian food.
WESTERN DISHES
French, Italian or other Western fare is on the menu.
OUTDOOR TABLES
Tables for eating outdoors, often with a good view.

Restaurant		Credit Cards	Regional Specialities	Pure Vegetarian	Western Dishes	Outdoor Tables
BHAVNAGAR: *Nilambagh Dining Hall* (Rs)(Rs) Nilambagh Palace Hotel. (0278) 42 4241. Part of a heritage hotel, the ambience here is regal, with chandeliers and gleaming silver. Try the regional dishes and *tandoori* food. ○ B, L, D.		AE DC MC V	●		●	
DIU: *Apana Restaurant* (Rs)(Rs) Apana Guesthouse, Old Fort Rd. (02875) 52 112. The delicious food at this terrace restaurant with sea views includes a generous seafood platter with lobster and crab. ▤ ○ B, L, D.			●		●	■
DIU: *Rivera Restaurant & Bar* (Rs)(Rs) Radhika Beach Resort, Nagoa Beach. (02875) 51 553. This excellent restaurant offers a wide choice of cuisines, served by attentive staff in idyllic surroundings. ▤ ▾ ○ B, L, D.			●		●	
JAMNAGAR: *The Orion Restaurant* (Rs)(Rs) Hotel Orbit Park Inn, Khambalia Highway. (0288) 44 484. Modestly-priced multi-cuisine food is offered here in pleasant surroundings. Lavish buffets are also laid out on request, for groups. ▤ ○ B, L, D.		AE MC V	●		●	
VADODARA: *Mandap* (Rs)(Rs) Express Hotel, RC Dutt Rd. (0265) 337 001. The traditional décor goes well with the traditional Gujarati meals for which this restaurant is known. ▤ ○ L, D.		AE MC V	●	■		

MUMBAI

Restaurant		Credit Cards	Regional Specialities	Pure Vegetarian	Western Dishes	Outdoor Tables
MUMBAI: *Ankur* (Rs)(Rs) Meadows House, Tamarind Lane, Behind Kendeel Bar, Fort Area. (022) 265 4194. An old eatery that has re-invented itself, this now serves non-vegetarian food along with vegetarian delicacies. Their prawn *gassi* and chicken *aadajina* are highly recommended. ▤ ▨ P ○ L, D.		AE DC MC V	●			
MUMBAI: *The Bharat Bar & Restaurant* (Rs)(Rs) 317 Bharat House, SBS Rd, Fort Area. (022) 267 2677. Customers can take their pick from the live seafood in this excellent restaurant. The crab is particularly good. ▤ ▾ P ○ L, D.		AE DC MC V	●		●	
MUMBAI: *Fountain Restaurant* (Rs)(Rs) 57 Mahatma Gandhi Rd. (022) 267 5315. Despite its slightly faded air, you can be assured of a good meal here. The sizzlers are recommended. ▤ ▨ P ○ L, D.		AE DC MC V			●	
MUMBAI: *Palkhi* (Rs)(Rs) 15 Walton Rd, Near Electric House, Colaba. (022) 284 0053. Hidden among the fussy arches are the discerning eaters of the city who come here for the delicious kebabs. ▤ ▾ P ○ L, D.		AE DC MC V	●			
MUMBAI: *Rajdhani Restaurant* (Rs)(Rs) Abdul Rehman St, Crawford Market. (022) 342 6919. Specializing in regional Indian cuisines, this restaurant offers *thalis* from Gujarat, Rajasthan, Maharashtra and Kathiawar. ▤ ○ L, D.		MC V	●			
MUMBAI: *Apoorva* (Rs)(Rs)(Rs) Noble Chambers, SA Brelvi Marg, Near Horniman Circle, Fort Area. (022) 287 0335. This excellent restaurant specializes in Konkan coastal seafood. Try the fried *surmai* fish, crab and prawns with feather-light *neer dosas*. Kerala-style seafood is also delicious here. ▤ ▾ ▨ P ○ L, D.		MC V	●			
MUMBAI: *Café Royal* (Rs)(Rs)(Rs) 166 Mahatma Gandhi Rd, opp Regal Cinema. (022) 288 3982. Catering mainly to non-vegetarians, this restaurant's sizzlers, grilled sandwiches and burgers are especially popular. ▤ ▾ P ○ L, D.		AE MC V			●	

MUMBAI: *Gaylord Restaurant* (Rs)(Rs) — AE DC MC V
Mayfair, VN Rd, Churchgate. ((022) 282 1259.
The generous helpings in this multi-cuisine restaurant are served by friendly
staff. The pastry counter offers some tempting items. 🍽 Ⓨ Ⓟ ⚪ *B, L, D.*

MUMBAI: *Leopold Café* (Rs)(Rs)(Rs) — AE MC V
Colaba Causeway. ((022) 287 3362.
A longtime favourite with travellers, this restaurant, established in 1871, has
a large selection of well-made multi-cuisine dishes. The fruit bar and milk
shakes are legendary. 🍽 Ⓨ Ⓟ ⚪ *B, L, D.*

MUMBAI: *Little Italy* (Rs)(Rs)(Rs) — MC V
18–B Hotel Atlantic, Juhu Tara Rd, Juhu. ((022) 617 3885.
Run by an Italian, this offers pure vegetarian Italian food. The *fettucine
primavera* with capsicum, capers, and olives and the *risotto alla milanese*
are so good that you don't miss the absence of meat. 🍽 Ⓨ Ⓟ ⚪ *L, D.*

MUMBAI: *Only Fish* (Rs)(Rs)(Rs) — MC V
Hotel Rosewood, Tulsiwadi Lane, Tardeo. ((022) 496 3114.
This small, stylish restaurant offers a choice of regional Indian fish dishes.
Try their Bengali-style *machher jhol* and the banana flower with *luchis*
(fried bread). Their *rasmalai* makes a great dessert. 🍽 Ⓨ Ⓟ ⚪ *L, D.*

MUMBAI: *The Pearl of The Orient* (Rs)(Rs)(Rs) — AE DC MC V
The Ambassador, Churchgate. ((022) 204 1131.
This revolving restaurant, which offers superb views of Mumbai, serves
good Thai, Chinese and Japanese food. Try the lobster in garlic butter
sauce and the Peking pomfret. 🍽 Ⓨ Ⓟ ⚪ *L, D.*

MUMBAI: *Sanuk Thai* (Rs)(Rs)(Rs) — AE DC MC V
30 K Dubhash Marg, Kala Ghoda, Fort Area. ((022) 204 4233.
Spicy and aromatic Thai food is served here. Try the pepper and garlic
prawns and the crunchy bean sprouts. Ⓨ Ⓟ ⚪ *L, D.*

MUMBAI: *Bayview* (Rs)(Rs)(Rs)(Rs) — AE DC MC V
Hotel Marine Plaza, Marine Drive. ((022) 285 1212.
A palm-fringed view of the sea adds to the great multi-cuisine lunch and
dinner buffets served here. 🍽 Ⓨ 🍴 Ⓟ ⚪ *B, L, D.*

MUMBAI: *Indigo* (Rs)(Rs)(Rs)(Rs) — AE DC MC V
Behind Taj Hotel. ((022) 285 6316.
Situated in a pleasant old mansion, this restaurant's elegant surroundings
are in tune with the nouvelle Indo-English cuisine. Try the *rawas* (Indian
salmon), *filet mignon* and the tempting desserts. 🍽 Ⓨ Ⓟ ⚪ *L, D.*

MUMBAI: *Khyber* (Rs)(Rs)(Rs)(Rs) — AE DC MC V
145 Mahatma Gandhi Rd, Fort Area. ((022) 267 3227.
Waiters dressed as Pathans serve delicious grilled meats such as kebabs and
Khyber *raan* (leg of lamb), in this atmospheric restaurant which has murals
by renowned Indian artist, Anjolie Ela Menon. 🍽 Ⓨ ⚪ *L, D.*

MUMBAI: *Ling's Pavilion* (Rs)(Rs)(Rs)(Rs) — AE DC MC V
19/21 Mahakavi Bhushan Marg, Behind Regal Cinema. ((022) 285 0023.
A rather overpowering interior but the food here, including the
recommended baby lobsters, is excellent. Reservations are essential in this
family-run restaurant. 🍽 Ⓨ Ⓟ ⚪ *L, D.*

MUMBAI: *Mahesh Lunch Home* (Rs)(Rs)(Rs)(Rs) — AE DC MC V
8–B Cawasji Patel Street. ((022) 287 0938.
Credited with having popularised the seafood cuisine of the Konkan Coast,
this restaurant serves delicious and fresh seafood. Giant portions of crab
and *rawas* (salmon) are some specialities. 🍽 Ⓨ 🍴 Ⓟ ⚪ *L, D.*

MUMBAI: *Not Just Jazz By The Bay* (Rs)(Rs)(Rs)(Rs) — AE DC MC V
Marine Drive. ((022) 496 3114.
Great lunch buffets with a variety of salads and pastas are offered here, but
it is in the evenings that this restaurant comes into its own, with live jazz
from Wednesday to Saturday. 🍽 Ⓨ 🎵 Ⓟ ⚪ *L, D.*

MUMBAI: *Side Wok* (Rs)(Rs)(Rs)(Rs) — AE DC MC V
Nariman Centre of Performing Arts, Nariman Point. ((022) 281 8132.
Pan-Asian food with cheerful music makes a great combination. Try the
lemon grass pomfret, *tandoori* salmon, and the orange marmalade *crème
brulee* for dessert. 🍽 Ⓨ 🎵 Ⓟ ⚪ *L, D.*

	CREDIT CARDS	REGIONAL SPECIALITIES	PURE VEGETARIAN	WESTERN DISHES	OUTDOOR TABLES

Price categories for a meal for one, including tax and service charges but not alcohol:

Rs under 100 rupees
RsRs 100–200 rupees
RsRsRs 200–400 rupees
RsRsRsRs 400–700 rupees
RsRsRsRsRs over 700 rupees

CREDIT CARDS
Indicates which major credit cards are accepted.

REGIONAL SPECIALITIES
Specialized cuisine is served from regions of India, such as Rajasthan, Gujarat or South India.

PURE VEGETARIAN
Restaurants serving only vegetarian food.

WESTERN DISHES
French, Italian or other Western fare is on the menu.

OUTDOOR TABLES
Tables for eating outdoors, often with a good view.

MUMBAI: *Trishna Bar & Restaurant* RsRsRs 7 Rope Walk Lane, Sai Baba Marg. ☎ (022) 270 3213. Another of the city's great seafood restaurants, this attracts many celebrities. The Konkan-style lobster, king crab and *tandoori* pomfret are outstanding. Reservations are recommended. ▤ 🍸 🅿 ◯ *L, D.*	AE DC MC V	●			
MUMBAI: *Athena* RsRsRsRsRs 41/44 Minoo Desai Marg, Colaba. ☎ (022) 202 8699. This stylish restaurant, done in soft white and beige, serves innovative Continental food. It also has a lively bar and dance floor, the hottest new hangout for Mumbai's glitterati. ▤ 🍸 🅿 ◯ *L, D.*	AE DC MC V			●	
MUMBAI: *Olive Bar & Kitchen* RsRsRsRsRs Pali Hill Tourist Hotel, 14 Union Park, Khar West. ☎ (022) 605 8228. Mumbai's beautiful people dine at this trendy new restaurant, on pricey gourmet delicacies such as oysters, caviar and salmon. More down-to-earth treats include a velvety cocoa fudge. ▤ 🍸 🅿 ◯ *L, D.*	AE DC MC V			●	■
MUMBAI: *Zodiac Grill* RsRsRsRsRs The Taj Mahal Hotel, Apollo Bunder. ☎ (022) 202 3366. This restaurant serves fine Western food in an elegant atmosphere. Try their New Zealand steak, and grilled lobsters with herb butter. Other specialities are *camembert dariole* and kahlua mousse. ▤ 🍸 🅿 ◯ *L, D.*	AE DC MC V			●	

MAHARASHTRA

AURANGABAD: *Foodwalas Tandoor* Rs Shyam Chambers, Bansidal Nagar. ☎ (0240) 32 8481. The succulent and tender chicken dishes are recommended. The restaurant also has a bar and the service is good. ▤ 🍸 ◯ *L, D.*	MC V	●		●	
AURANGABAD: *Mingling Chinese Restaurant* RsRsRs Jaina Rd. ☎ (02991) 24 307. As the name suggests, this specializes in Chinese food, with just a hint of the Punjabi. There is a separate area for non-smokers here. ▤ ◯ *L, D.*	AE MC V				
AURANGABAD: *Residency Restaurant* RsRsRs Taj Residency, 8–N–12 CIDCO. ☎ (0240) 38 1106. A wide variety of Indian, Chinese and Western food is offered here, and a theme dinner or food festival is organized once a month. Good for regional food specialities. ▤ 🍸 ◯ *B, L, D.*	AE DC MC V	●		●	
CHIPLUN: *Riverview Restaurant* RsRsRs Gateway Riverview Lodge, Village Dhamandivi, Tal-Chiplun. ☎ (02356) 72 233. Though a wide selection of cuisines is offered here, Marwari and Konkani dishes are this restaurant's specialities. ▤ 🍸 ◯ *B, L, D.*	AE DC MC V	●			
LONAVLA: *Kailash Parbat Restaurant* RsRsRs Kailash Parbat, Pune-Mumbai Rd, Valvan. ☎ (02114) 73 086. A 24-hour coffee shop as well, this restaurant serves a wide variety of vegetarian food, with emphasis on regional specialities. ▤ 🍸 ◯ *B, L, D.*	AE DC V		■	●	
MAHABALESHWAR: *Brightland Holiday Village* RsRsRs Kates Point Rd, Nakhind Village. ☎ (02168) 60 700, 60 353. This has a cluster of eating places that cater to many palates. There is a choice of Indian, Mughlai, *tandoori* and barbecued food. The Village Pub offers a tempting array of cocktails and "mocktails", while the discotheque, "The Electric Mist", has a lively atmosphere. 🍸 🅿 ◯ *B, L, D.*	AE DC MC V	●		●	■
NAGPUR: *Ashoka Bar & Restaurant* RsRsRs Mount Rd, Sadar. ☎ (0712) 53 1141. This multi-cuisine restaurant overlooks a pool and green lawns. Their sizzlers are recommended. ▤ 🍸 ◯ *L, D.*	DC MC V	●		●	

NAGPUR: *Lahoree Deluxe Bar & Restaurant* ®®®
Lahoree Deluxe Building, Dharampeth. **(** *(0712) 53 3808.*
Hearty *tandoori* food is the speciality here, with some Chinese and Western
dishes also on offer. There is a lively bar as well. 目 🍸 🎵 🅿 🔾 *B, L, D.*
AE MC V

NASIK: *Nandinee Woodlands Restaurant* ®®
Nasiklub, Sarada Activity Centre, Nandinee Pune Rd. **(** *(0253) 55 7931.*
This restaurant set in a garden offers vegetarian food in a variety of styles.
The South Indian dishes are best. 🅿 🔾 *B, L, D.*
MC V

PUNE: *Arthur's Theme* ®®
Shop No 2, Vrindavan, North Main Rd, Koregaon Park. **(** *(020) 202 3366.*
This small and cosy restaurant prides itself on its French food. Both
vegetarian and non-vegetarian dishes are served here. 目 ⚡ 🔾 *L, D.*
MC V

PUNE: *Farshid's* ®®
Akshay Complex, Dhole Patil Rd. **(** *(020) 613 8941.*
This popular seafood restaurant serves excellent prawns and lobsters. Also
recommended are two Continental chicken dishes, *pollo arrosto* and *petti
di pollo*, specialities of the chef. 🍸 🅿 🔾 *L, D.*
MC V

PUNE: *Hotel Vaishali* ®®
1218/1 Shivajinagar, Fergusson College Rd. **(** *(020) 553 1244.*
This is a pleasant garden restaurant with good South Indian food.
Reasonable prices make it popular with local residents. 🔾 *B, L, D.*

PUNE: *Coffee House* ®®®
2–A Moledina Rd, Camp. **(** *(020) 63 0716.*
Part of an established chain, this has been refurbished in contemporary
style. Serves snacks and reasonably priced South Indian dishes. 目 🔾 *L, D.*
AE DC MC V

PUNE: *Jazz Garden* ®®®
ABC Farms Pvt Ltd, S No 35/36, Koregaon Park. **(** *(020) 681 7412.*
This open air multi-cuisine restaurant serves dishes from Kerala, Bengal and
Mexico. There is live jazz as well in the evening. 🍸 ⚡ 🎵 🅿 🔾 *L, D.*
AE DC MC V

PUNE: *The Place* ®®®
Clover Centre, 7 Moledina Rd. **(** *(020) 613 4632.*
Best known for its chicken and lamb sizzlers, this restaurant also offers
delicious homemade ice cream. 🍸 ⚡ 🅿 🔾 *L, D.*
AE DC MC V

GOA

ASSAGAO: *Axirwaad* ®®®
483 Rue De Boa Vista. **(** *(0832) 25 6949.*
This is an interesting mix of a restaurant and a private club with an art
gallery as well. The food is mainly Western with a few Middle Eastern
dishes prepared by the husband and wife team that runs it. 🍸 🔾 *L, D.*
AE DC MC V

BAGA: *Casa Portuguesa* ®®
Baga Beach. **(** *(0832) 27 7024.*
Located in a romantic old bungalow, this is a good place to sample the
special Goan-Portuguese cuisine of the region. 🍸 🎵 🔾 *D.* ● *May–Oct.*
AE DC MC V

BAGA: *Golden Nest* ®®
The Ronil Beach Resort, Saunta Vaddo. **(** *(0832) 27 6861.*
The food here is excellent. Try their pork *vindaloo*, fish and prawn curries,
pomfret *recheido* and the *soupa de camarão*. 🍸 🎵 🔾 *B, L, D.*
AE DC MC V

BAGA: *Fiesta Restaurant* ®®®
7/35 Saunta Vaddo, opp Tito's. **(** *(0832) 27 9894.*
Mediterranean dishes, such as *paella* and *moussaka*, are popular here.
Italian pasta and pizza are also available – the ten-inch *pizza margherita* is
specially recommended. 🍸 🔾 *D.* ● *Thur.*
MC V

BAGA: *J & A's Little Italy* ®®®
Between Arpora Hill and Baga Creek. **(** No Telephone.
Excellent pastas and wood-smoked beef are specially recommended here.
Salads are made from organically grown greens. 🍸 🎵 🔾 *D.* ● *May–Sep.*
DC MC V

BAGA: *Valerio's* ®®®
Hotel Baia do Sol, Baga Beach. **(** *(0832) 27 6084.*
This popular eatery has great sea views, and a brilliant Swedish chef.
Some of his specialities are superb seafood salad, and tomato soup with
lime and chilli. 🍸 🎵 *Wed, Sat.* 🔾 *B, L, D.*
AE DC MC V

	CREDIT CARDS	REGIONAL SPECIALITIES	PURE VEGETARIAN	WESTERN DISHES	OUTDOOR TABLES

Price categories for a meal for one, including tax and service charges but not alcohol:

Rs under 100 rupees
Rs Rs 100–200 rupees
Rs Rs Rs 200–400 rupees
Rs Rs Rs Rs 400–700 rupees
Rs Rs Rs Rs Rs over 700 rupees

CREDIT CARDS
Indicates which major credit cards are accepted.

REGIONAL SPECIALITIES
Specialized cuisine is served from regions of India, such as Rajasthan, Gujarat or South India.

PURE VEGETARIAN
Restaurants serving only vegetarian food.

WESTERN DISHES
French, Italian or other Western fare is on the menu.

OUTDOOR TABLES
Tables for eating outdoors, often with a good view.

BENAULIM: *Miguel Arcanjo* ⓇⓈⓇⓈⓇⓈ Taj Exotica, Colwaddo. 〖 *(0832) 70 5666.* Watch the chefs at work as they prepare delicious Mediterranean dishes such as tomato *tian*, *tabbouleh*, and Moroccan *tagine*. ▤ ▯ ♫ ◯ *L, D.*	AE DC MC V			●	■
BOGMALO: *Joet's* ⓇⓈ Bailli Chal, Bogmalo Beach. 〖 *(0832) 55 5036.* The mouth-watering Goan food here is cooked by the owners. Their prawn *balchão*, *vindaloo* and fresh fish dishes are great. ▯ ♫ *Tue.* ◯ *B, L, D.*	MC V	●			■
CALANGUTE: *Infanteria Restaurant* ⓇⓈⓇⓈ Vasco Da Gama, Calangute-Baga Rd. 〖 *(0832) 27 7421.* Essentially a pastry shop, their coffee, cakes and savoury snacks are recommended. Try their milkshakes and juices as well. ◯ *B, L, D.*				●	■
CALANGUTE: *Souza Lobo* ⓇⓈⓇⓈ Calangute Beach. 〖 *(0832) 27 6463.* A culinary institution since 1932, this is famed for its seafood and Goan cuisine. Top off the stuffed crabs, *vindaloo* and *sorpotel* with the memorable *crêpe Souza Lobo*. ▯ ◯ *L, D.* ● *Jun–Sep.*	MC V	●		●	■
CALANGUTE: *Cantorian* ⓇⓈⓇⓈⓇⓈ House No 1/281, Gauro Vaddo. 〖 *(0832) 28 1182.* The aromatic Thai, Vietnamese and Korean food here owes much to the organic herbs and vegetables that are used. ▯ ◯ *L, D.*					■
CALANGUTE: *Copper Bowl* ⓇⓈⓇⓈⓇⓈⓇⓈ Pousada Tauma, Porba Vaddo. 〖 *(0832) 27 9061.* Authentic Goan food, with levels of spice adjusted to suit different palates. A recent addition to the menu is Konkani food. ▯ ◯ *B, L, D.*	DC MC V	●			■
CALANGUTE: *Le Restaurant Français* ⓇⓈⓇⓈⓇⓈⓇⓈ Calangute-Baga Rd. 〖 *(0) 982 212 1712.* Famed for its authentic French food, including the exceptional *terrine de foies de volaille* and the *confiture d'oignons*. ▯ ◯ *D.* ● *May–Oct.*				●	■
CANDOLIM: *Palm & Sands* ⓇⓈⓇⓈⓇⓈ Dando. 〖 *(0832) 27 7161.* Simply outstanding seafood – the crabmeat *au gratin*, crab *xacuti*, lobster dishes and pork spareribs are highly recommended, as are the apple pie and date pancake. ▤ ▯ ◯ *B, L, D.*	DC MC V	●			■
DONA PAULA: *O' Pescador Restaurant & Pub* ⓇⓈⓇⓈ Near Dona Paula Jetty. 〖 *(0832) 27 9447.* This pleasant garden restaurant serves a variety of tasty pan-Indian, Goan, Chinese and Western dishes. ▯ ♫ ◯ *D.* ● *May–Sep.*	MC V	●		●	■
DONA PAULA: *Alfama Restaurant* ⓇⓈⓇⓈⓇⓈ Hotel Cidade de Goa, Vainguinim Beach. 〖 *(0832) 45 4545.* Good Goan, Western and Indian food here is accompanied by a delightful Goan band in the evenings. ▤ ▯ ♫ ◯ *L, D.* ● *May–Oct.*	MC V	●		●	
MARGAO: *Martin's Corner* ⓇⓈⓇⓈ Binvaddo, Betalbatim. 〖 *(0832) 88 0061.* Excellent seafood dishes in this homely restaurant include *masala* prawns. The *bebinca* makes a perfect end to the meal. ▯ ◯ *L, D.*	AE DC MC V	●		●	■
MOBOR: *Riverside* ⓇⓈⓇⓈⓇⓈⓇⓈ The Leela Palace, Cavelossim. 〖 *(0832) 87 1234.* Located on the banks of the Sal river, this restaurant serves authentic Italian cuisine. The homemade pasta, smoked mozarella with chargrilled tomatoes and seafood broth are recommended. The vanilla cream and berry compote are also delicious. ▯ ◯ *D.*	AE DC MC V			●	■

PANAJI: *Goenchin Restaurant* (Rs)(Rs)
Dada Vaidya Rd. 【 (0832) 22 7614.
AE DC MC V
Considered one of Goa's best Chinese restaurants. Try the roast lamb with mushroom and baby corn, and the honey noodles. 目 ￥ ○ *L, D.*

PANAJI: *Horse Shoe Restaurant* (Rs)(Rs)
E–245 Rua De Qurem. 【 (0832) 43 1788.
AE DC MC V
Tasty Goan dishes, cooked by a master chef, include fish curry, chicken in spicy sauce and a divine cashewnut cake. 目 ￥ ○ *L, D.*

PANAJI: *Rio Rico Restaurant* (Rs)(Rs)(Rs)
Hotel Mandovi, DB Rd. 【 (0832) 42 6270.
AE DC MC V
One of Goa's most respected establishments, its extensive menu offers a wide selection of Goan and Western dishes. 目 ￥ ♫ ○ *L, D.*

PANAJI: *Simply Fish* (Rs)(Rs)(Rs)(Rs)
Marriott Resort, Miramar Beach. 【 (0832) 43 7001.
AE DC MC V
The seafood here is displayed in a fisherman's basket, for clients to make their own selection. Try their lobster bisque and stews. ￥ ○ *D.* ● *May–Sep.*

SALIGAO: *Florentine* (Rs)(Rs)
Pequeno Morod. 【 (0832) 27 8249.
This restaurant, which serves only fish and chicken, is particularly famous for one dish – its Goan chicken *cafreal.* ￥ ○ *L, D.*

KARNATAKA

BADAMI: *Pulakeshi Restaurant* (Rs)(Rs)(Rs)
Hotel Badami Court, 17/3, Station Rd. 【 (08357) 20 230.
This multi-cuisine restaurant is named after the great Chalukyan king, Pulakesin. Try the regional Karnataka specialities. 目 ￥ P ○ *B, L, D.*

BANGALORE: *Mavalli Tiffin Room (MTR)* (Rs)(Rs)
11 Lalbag Rd. 【 (080) 222 0022.
MC V
Over 100 cooks labour to produce the *dosas*, *idlis* and fabulously frothy coffee at this noisy, crowded but perennially popular eatery, whose loyal clientele ranges from filmstars to hungry students. P ○ *L, D.* ● *Sun.*

BANGALORE: *Karavalli* (Rs)(Rs)(Rs)
Gateway Hotel, Residency Rd. 【 (080) 558 4545.
MC V
Famous for its coastal Karnataka seafood, this restaurant serves very fresh *bhetki* fish, scampi and squid. 目 ￥ P ○ *L, D.*

BANGALORE: *Koshy's Bar & Restaurant* (Rs)(Rs)(Rs)
39 St Mark's Rd. 【 (080) 221 1516.
AE DC MC V
A favourite haunt of Bangaloreans, this multi-cuisine restaurant's coconut soup and Kerala-style *appam* and stew are delicious. 目 ￥ P ○ *B, L, D.*

BANGALORE: *The Rice Bowl* (Rs)(Rs)(Rs)
Below Rama Hotel, 40/2 Lavelle Rd. 【 (080) 224 0216.
MC V
Generous portions of appetising Chinese and Tibetan food are served in this popular restaurant. ￥ P ○ *L, D.*

BANGALORE: *Sunny's Bistro* (Rs)(Rs)(Rs)
35/2, Kasturba Rd, Lavelle Rd. 【 (080) 224 3642.
MC V
Though it serves French and Italian cuisine, this restaurant is best known for its desserts, such as the sinful Devil's Food cake, the chocolate *ganache* in walnut crust, and the feather-light litchi soufflé. 目 ￥ P ○ *L, D.*

BANGALORE: *Cosmo Village* (Rs)(Rs)(Rs)(Rs)
29 Margrath Rd. 【 (080) 509 8237, 509 2709.
MC V
This is one of the trendiest of Bangalore's many pubs. Apart from a well-stocked bar and a swinging DJ, it has an eclectic menu that includes Mexican and Thai dishes. There is also a pleasant terrace. 目 ￥ P ○ *L, D.*

BANGALORE: *I-Talia* (Rs)(Rs)(Rs)(Rs)(Rs)
The Park Hotel, 14/7 Mahatma Gandhi Rd. 【 (080) 559 4666.
AE DC MC V
Run by a passionate gourmet, this restaurant offers excellent Italian food. Along with the pastas and salads, the special mango and Campari sorbet is highly recommended. 目 ￥ P ○ *L, D.*

BIJAPUR: *Hotel Madhuvan International Restaurant* (Rs)(Rs)
Hotel Madhuvan International, G–37 Brigade Garden, St Marks Rd. 【 (08352) 55 571.
Copious amounts of wholesome vegetarian food are served here on a traditional *thali*. The garden surroundings are very pleasant. P ○ *B, L, D.*

		CREDIT CARDS	REGIONAL SPECIALITIES	PURE VEGETARIAN	WESTERN DISHES	OUTDOOR TABLES

Price categories for a meal for one, including tax and service charges but not alcohol:

Rs under 100 rupees
RsRs 100–200 rupees
RsRsRs 200–400 rupees
RsRsRsRs 400–700 rupees
RsRsRsRsRs over 700 rupees

CREDIT CARDS
Indicates which major credit cards are accepted.

REGIONAL SPECIALITIES
Specialized cuisine is served from regions of India, such as Rajasthan, Gujarat or South India.

PURE VEGETARIAN
Restaurants serving only vegetarian food.

WESTERN DISHES
French, Italian or other Western fare is on the menu.

OUTDOOR TABLES
Tables for eating outdoors, often with a good view.

Restaurant	Price	Credit Cards	Regional Specialities	Pure Vegetarian	Western Dishes	Outdoor Tables
CHIKMAGALUR: *The Peaberry* Taj Garden Retreat, KM Rd, Jyothi Nagar. (08262) 20 202. This attractive multi-cuisine restaurant offers good coastal cuisine as well as standard North Indian favourites. *B, L, D.*	RsRsRs	AE DC MC V	●		●	
HAMPI: *Mango Tree Restaurant* 400m west of the ghats, on the south bank. No Telephone. Romantically situated on the banks of the river, under the shade of a mango tree, this restaurant serves its food on banana leaves. Delicious *dosas*, honey pancakes and *lassi*. *B, L, D.*	RsRs		●	■	●	■
HUBLI: *Hotel Naveen* Pune-Bangalore Rd, Unkal. (0836) 37 2939. The South Indian dishes here are recommended, though other cuisines also feature on the menu. *L, D.*	RsRsRs	AE DC MC V	●			
MANGALORE: *The Gallery* Manjarun Hotel, Old Port Rd. (0824) 42 0420. This restaurant specializes in the delicious coastal cuisine of the region. The spicy okra dish, *kane bezule*, is specially recommended. *B, L, D.*	RsRsRs	AE DC MC V	●		●	
MYSORE: *Dasaprakash Paradise* 105 Vivekananda Rd, Yadavgiri. (0821) 51 5565. Wholesome South Indian vegetarian food is served here. The breakfasts are particularly good, with *idlis* and filter coffee. *B, L, D.*	Rs	MC V	●	■		
MYSORE: *The Green Hotel Restaurant* 2270 Vinoba Rd, JL Puram. (0821) 51 2536. Delicious, subtly spiced food made from fresh ingredients, is served here in a charming verandah, or in the garden. *B, L, D.*	RsRsRs	MC V	●		●	■

CHENNAI

Restaurant	Price	Credit Cards	Regional Specialities	Pure Vegetarian	Western Dishes	Outdoor Tables
CHENNAI: *Copper Chimney* 74 Ground Floor, Cathedral Rd. (044) 827 5770. This spotlessly clean restaurant is best known for its North Indian and *tandoori* food. The kebabs and soups are recommended. *B, L, D.*	RsRs	MC V	●		●	
CHENNAI: *Dhabba Express* 9 Cenotaph Rd. (044) 432 8211. With *charpoys* (string cots) instead of chairs, this offers dishes typical of North Indian roadside eateries. Try the robust *dal makhni*. *L, D.*	RsRs	DC MC V	●			
CHENNAI: *Karaikudi Chettinad Restaurant* 84 Dr Radhakrishna Salat, Mylapore. (044) 811 1893. Recreating a traditional Chettinad ambience, down to the waiters' liveries, this restaurant's specialities include *pallathur* chicken, *chettiar* pepper chicken roast and pigeon *varuval*. *L, D.*	RsRs	AE DC MC V				
CHENNAI: *Ponnuswamy Hotel* 24–C IN Rd, Egmore. (044) 827 0784. Authentic Chettinad food with a variety of spicy dishes, featuring quail and crab. The *biryani* too is excellent. *L, D.*	RsRs	MC V	●			
CHENNAI: *Wang's Kitchen* 46 Pantheon Rd, Prince Plaza, Egmore. (044) 855 4928. The Chinese food here has distinctly Indian undertones. Try the spicy chicken Manchurian, and the hot-sour soup. *L, D.*	RsRs	MC V				
CHENNAI: *Amaravathi* 1 Cathedral Rd. (044) 811 6416. Reasonably priced authentic Andhra cuisine is the highlight here. The *biryani* is truly outstanding. *L, D.*	RsRsRs	AE DC MC V	●			

CHENNAI: *Annalakshmi*   Rs Rs Rs   AE DC MC V
804 Anna Salai. (044) 852 5109.
Run entirely by volunteers, this restaurant, named after the goddess of
food, serves sumptuous vegetarian fare, elegantly presented on silver and
gold *thalis*. Profits go to charity. ▤ ♫ ◐ *L, D.* ● *Mon.*

CHENNAI: *The Artz*   Rs Rs Rs   AE DC MC V
3 Kodambakkam High Rd, Nungambakkam. (044) 822 2211.
The décor here is pleasingly arty. A wide variety of cuisines is offered and
their *pudina parathas* are highly recommended. ▤ ◐ *L, D.*

CHENNAI: *Benjarong*   Rs Rs Rs   AE DC MC V
146 TTK Rd, Alwarpet. (044) 432 2640.
Orchids decorate the tables at this good Thai restaurant, which flies in fresh
ingredients daily from Bangkok. Try their unusual desserts. ▤ ✶ ◐ *L, D.*

CHENNAI: *The Rain Tree*   Rs Rs Rs Rs   AE DC MC V
Taj Connemara Hotel, 1 Binny Rd. (044) 852 0123.
This atmospheric outdoor restaurant serves mostly Chettinad food under a
huge rain tree. There are cultural shows in the evening. ▣ ◐ *L, D.*

TAMIL NADU

KANCHIPURAM: *Kanchi Kudil*   Rs Rs
53–A Sangeetha Vidwan, Nainar Pillai St. (04112) 27 680.
South Indian vegetarian snacks are served in this beautifully restored
traditional house. Fine handicrafts are also available here. ◐ *B, L.*

MADURAI: *Temple View Rooftop Restaurant*   Rs Rs   AE DC MC V
Hotel Park Plaza, 114–5 West Perumal Maistry St. (0452) 74 2112.
The superb views of the temple and the delicious chicken garlic fry make
this a popular eatery. ▤ Y ▣ ◐ *L, D.*

MADURAI: *The View*   Rs Rs Rs Rs   AE DC MC V
Taj Garden Retreat, 40 TPK Rd, Pasumalai Hill. (0452) 77 1601.
The tranquil ambience and multi-cuisine fare here make it an ideal place to
take a break from sightseeing in this temple town. ▤ ▣ ◐ *L, D.*

MAMALLAPURAM: *Moonrakers*   Rs Rs   AE DC MC V
Othavadai St. No Telephone.
This restaurant serves kebabs, *koftas*, pigeon and chicken, plus salads and
snacks, in a cheerful, friendly ambience. ◐ *B, L, D.*

OOTACAMUND: *Tandoori Mahal*   Rs
Commercial Rd.
Chilled beer with good *tandoori* vegetarian and non-vegetarian food can
be had in this well-run eatery. ▣ ◐ *L, D.*

OOTACAMUND: *The Nilgiri Woodlands Restaurant*   Rs Rs
Ettines Rd, opp Race Course. (0423) 42 551.
This value-for-money vegetarian restaurant serves a satisfying South
Indian *thali* meal. ▤ ✶ ▣ ◐ *L, D.*

PONDICHERRY: *Le Club*   Rs Rs Rs   AE DC MC V
Hotel de Pondicherry, 38 Rue Dumas St. (0413) 22 7409.
This classy French restaurant serves refreshing cocktails along with good
coq au vin, grilled prawns with basil, and *chateaubriand* steak. Their
fondant chocolate is also recommended. ▤ Y ▣ ◐ *L, D.* ● *Mon.*

PONDICHERRY: *Rendezvous Café*   Rs Rs Rs   AE DC MC V
30 Rue Suffren. (0413) 33 9132.
Along with French food, this also offers Italian, and Indian-style Chinese
dishes. Try their steak *de capitaine* and grilled prawns. The breakfasts here
are also good. ▤ ✶ ▣ ◐ *B, L, D.*

PONDICHERRY: *Carte Blanche*   Rs Rs Rs Rs   AE DC MC V
Hotel de L'Orient, 17 Rue Romain Rolland. (0413) 34 3067.
The atmospheric décor in this outstanding restaurant includes antique maps
of Pondicherry. The cuisine is superb, featuring an imaginative fusion of
Tamil and French flavours. ▤ Y ▣ ◐ *B, L, D* ● *Thu.*

THANJAVUR: *Geetham*   Rs   MC V
Hotel Parisutham, 55 Grand Anicut Rd. (04362) 31 801.
The vegetarian food here, presented on traditional *thalis*, features a
repertoire of no less than 72 curries. ▤ Y ▣ ◐ *L, D.*

Price categories for a meal for one, including tax and service charges but not alcohol:

(Rs) under 100 rupees
(Rs)(Rs) 100–200 rupees
(Rs)(Rs)(Rs) 200–400 rupees
(Rs)(Rs)(Rs)(Rs) 400–700 rupees
(Rs)(Rs)(Rs)(Rs)(Rs) over 700 rupees

CREDIT CARDS
Indicates which major credit cards are accepted.

REGIONAL SPECIALITIES
Specialized cuisine is served from regions of India, such as Rajasthan, Gujarat or South India.

PURE VEGETARIAN
Restaurants serving only vegetarian food.

WESTERN DISHES
French, Italian or other Western fare is on the menu.

OUTDOOR TABLES
Tables for eating outdoors, often with a good view.

ANDAMAN & NICOBAR ISLANDS

	CREDIT CARDS	REGIONAL SPECIALITIES	PURE VEGETARIAN	WESTERN DISHES	OUTDOOR TABLES
PORT BLAIR: *Waves* (Rs)(Rs) Carbyus Cove. **(** (0891) 45 110. This multi-cuisine restaurant, situated just across the Carbyus Cove beach, also has a pleasant garden. 📋 🍸 ⭕ *D.*		●		●	■
PORT BLAIR: *Mandalay Restaurant.* (Rs)(Rs)(Rs) Bay Island Hotel, Marine Hill. **(** (0891) 34 101. Located at the entry to Port Blair harbour, this multi-cuisine restaurant offers superb views of Ross and Havelock Islands. 📋 🍸 ⭕ *B, L, D.*	AE DC MC V	●		●	

KERALA

	CREDIT CARDS	REGIONAL SPECIALITIES	PURE VEGETARIAN	WESTERN DISHES	OUTDOOR TABLES
ALAPPUZHA: *Kayaloram Lake Resort Restaurant* (Rs)(Rs)(Rs) Kayaloram Lake Resort, Punnamada. **(** (0477) 23 2040. This open-air restaurant offers Continental food as well as delicious dishes from Kerala, such as *puttu* and *kadala, appams* and stew. ⭕ *B, L, D.*	AE DC MC	●		●	■
KOCHI: *Kashi Art Café* (Rs) Burgher St, Fort Kochi. **(** (0484) 22 1769. Perfect for coffee and light meals, this lovely old Dutch mansion has great ambience. Good breakfasts, cakes, and an art gallery as well. 🅿 ⭕ *B, L.*				●	■
KOCHI: *Fort House Hotel* (Rs)(Rs)(Rs) Calvathy Rd, Fort Kochi. **(** (0484) 22 6103. This charming family-run restaurant serves home-cooked Kerala food. Their fish and vegetable curries are recommended. 🅿 ⭕ *B, L, D.*		●			■
KOCHI: *The Old Courtyard* (Rs)(Rs)(Rs) Old Courtyard, 1/371 Princess St, Fort Kochi. **(** (0484) 21 6302. Shaded by an old mango tree, this lovely courtyard restaurant offers a range of cuisines. Great coffee is served through the day. ⭕ *B, L, D.*	DC MC V	●		●	■
KOCHI: *Fort Cochin* (Rs)(Rs)(Rs)(Rs) Casino Hotel, Willingdon Island. **(** (0484) 66 8421. Seafood, featuring the day's fresh catch, is the speciality in this outstanding restaurant, idyllically located on Willingdon Island. 📋 🍸 🎵 🅿 ⭕ *D.*	AE DC MC V	●		●	
KOCHI: *The Malabar Junction Restaurant* (Rs)(Rs)(Rs)(Rs) The Malabar House, Fort Kochi. **(** (0484) 21 6666. Excellent Western food is on offer in this small restaurant. Their seafood and Mediterranean dishes are recommended. 🍸 🅿 ⭕ *B, L, D.*	AE MC V	●		●	■
KOTTAYAM: *Vembanad Restaurant* (Rs)(Rs)(Rs) Vembanad Lake Resort, Kodimatha. **(** (0481) 56 4866. This multi-cuisine restaurant with splendid lake views offers authentic Kerala delicacies. The seafood is particularly good. 📋 ⭕ *B, L, D.*	AE MC V	●		●	
KOTTAYAM: *Coconut Lagoon Restaurant* (Rs)(Rs)(Rs)(Rs) Coconut Lagoon, PB No 2, Kumarakom. **(** (0481) 52 4491. As renowned for its superb Kerala cuisine as for its enchanting setting in a beautifully restored old *tharavad*. ⭕ *B, L, D.*	AE DC MC V	●		●	
KOVALAM: *Rockholm* (Rs)(Rs)(Rs) Hotel Rockholm, Lighthouse Rd. **(** (0471) 481 0306. There are breathtaking views from this terrace restaurant overlooking the sea. It serves excellent seafood and local dishes. ⭕ *B, L, D.*	AE DC MC V	●		●	■
KOVALAM: *Octopus* (Rs)(Rs)(Rs)(Rs)(Rs) Surya Samudra Beach Garden, Pulinkudi. **(** (0471) 48 0413. The ambience is magical in this multi-cuisine resort-restaurant located in reassembled old wooden Kerala houses. 📋 🍸 ⭕ *B, L, D.*	MC V	●		●	

KOZIKHODE: *Coral Reef Restaurant* ⓇⓈⓇⓈ
Hotel Taj Residency, PT Usha Rd. 📞 *(0495) 76 5354.*
A wide variety of cuisines is served in this pleasant restaurant, including healthy food based on Ayurvedic principles. 🍽 🍸 ◯ *L, D.*

AE
DC
MC
V

LAKSHADWEEP: *Restaurant Hut* ⓇⓈⓇⓈⓇⓈ
Bangaram Island Resort. 📞 *no telephone.*
Made of bamboo and palm fronds, this restaurant has a cheerful atmosphere. The evening barbecues are delightful. 🍸 ◯ *B, L, D.*

AE
DC
MC

THEKKADY: *Shalimar Spice Garden Resort Restaurant* ⓇⓈⓇⓈⓇⓈ
Shalimar Spice Garden Resort, Murikkady PO. 📞 *(0486) 32 2132.*
The food is as good as the traditional Kerala decor here. It includes Kerala delicacies served on banana leaves, and great pasta. 🍽 🍸 ◯ *B, L, D.*

MC
V

THIRUVANANTHAPURAM: *The Regency* ⓇⓈⓇⓈⓇⓈ
The South Park, Mahatma Gandhi Rd. 📞 *(0471) 33 3333.*
This newly renovated multi-cuisine restaurant offers a lavish buffet spread for lunch and dinner. 🍽 🍸 🎵 ◯ *L, D.*

AE
DC
MC
V

THIRUVANANTHAPURAM: *Tiffany's Restaurant* ⓇⓈⓇⓈⓇⓈ
The Muthoot Plaza, Punnen Rd. 📞 *(0471) 33 7733.*
Don't let the decor, a strange mélange of wall plates, stained glass and optical fibre lights, put you off your food. The multi-cuisine menu here is varied and well-made. 🍽 🍸 🅿 ◯ *B, L, D.*

AE
DC
MC
V

VARKALA: *Café Comorin* ⓇⓈⓇⓈⓇⓈ
Taj Garden Retreat, Janardana Puram. 📞 *(0472) 60 3000.*
Garden tables add to the atmosphere of this charming restaurant. Treat yourself to their Kerala cuisine. 🍽 🍸 🅿 ◯ *B, L, D.*

AE
DC
MC
V

ANDHRA PRADESH

HYDERABAD: *Ming's Court* ⓇⓈⓇⓈⓇⓈ
5–9–30/16/20 Basheerbagh, opp Gandhi Medical College. 📞 *(040) 323 6504.*
Shanghai lamb, fried rice and tiger prawns in a fiery Szechwan sauce are recommended in this popular Chinese restaurant. 🍽 🌿 🎵 ◯ *B, L, D.*

AE
DC
MC
V

HYDERABAD: *Dakhni* ⓇⓈⓇⓈⓇⓈⓇⓈ
Taj Banjara, Rd No 1, Banjara Hills. 📞 *(040) 339 9999.*
Try the Bijapuri *usli*, a dry lentil curry with *bajra* bread, and the *gosht gulbarga*, cooked in a delicious coconut sauce. 🍽 🍸 🌿 🎵 ◯ *L, D.*

AE
DC
MC
V

HYDERABAD: *Dum Pukht* ⓇⓈⓇⓈⓇⓈⓇⓈ
Grand Kakatiya Sheraton, 6–3–1187 Begumpet. 📞 *(040) 340 0132.*
To sample the city's rich Nizami cuisine, try *khwams*, which offers three different curries, *sheermal* bread, and skewered mutton kebabs and creamy curd on a silver platter. 🍽 🍸 🌿 🎵 ◯ *D.*

AE
DC
MC
V

TIRUPATI: *Bhima's Deluxe Restaurant* ⓇⓈⓇⓈ
Bhima's Deluxe Hotel, 38 Govind Raja Car St. 📞 *(08574) 25 521.*
In keeping with the aura of piety that envelopes this temple town, this restaurant serves wholesome, pure vegetarian Indian food. 🍽 ◯ *B, L, D.*

VIJAYWADA: *Aromas* ⓇⓈⓇⓈ
Quality Inn DV Manor, Mahatma Gandhi Rd. 📞 *(0866) 47 4455.*
This offers a choice of Indian, Mughlai and South Asian food, but is best known for its hearty Punjabi fare. 🍽 🍸 ◯ *L, D.*

AE
MC
V

VISAKHAPATNAM: *Dakshin Restaurant* ⓇⓈⓇⓈⓇⓈ
Hotel Daspalla, 28–2–48 Suryabagh. 📞 *(0891) 56 4825.*
This non-vegetarian speciality restaurant serves authentic hot and spicy Andhra cuisine. Try the *gongura* mutton. 🍽 🍸 🌿 ◯ *L, D.*

AE
DC
MC
V

VISAKHAPATNAM: *Bamboo Bay* ⓇⓈⓇⓈⓇⓈⓇⓈ
The Park, Beach Rd. 📞 *(0891) 75 4488.*
The only open-air, beach restaurant in the city, this serves mainly coastal cuisine – a combination of Andhra and Chettinad dishes, with some *tandoori* food thrown in. Try their *tandoori* pomfret, *gongura mamasam* and *yaar varuval*, all on one platter. 🍸 🎵 ◯ *D.*

AE
DC
MC
V

WARANGAL: *Kadambari Restaurant.* ⓇⓈⓇⓈ
Hotel Ashoka, 6–1–242 Main Rd, Hanamkonda. 📞 *(08712) 57 8491.*
This friendly restaurant specializes in Kerala cuisine, though it also offers Chinese and *tandoori* food. 🍽 ◯ *L, D.*

MC
V

SHOPS & MARKETS

I NDIA'S SUPERB TRADITION of textiles, arts and crafts makes shopping in this country tremendous fun. The range and quality is diverse – finely crafted bronzes and metal-ware, lustrous silks, jewellery, miniature paintings and handwoven carpets, as well as delightful, inexpensive tribal artifacts and souvenirs. The kaleidoscope of hues, textures and scents at local bazaars and markets, where flowers, fresh produce and spices are sold, is fascinating, as are the rows of pavement sellers hawking clothes and accessories. Though often a noisy and chaotic experience, browsing through the stalls can often lead to exciting bargains. Traditional bazaars co-exist with the multi-storeyed department stores and shopping malls of urban India, where all manner of goods, both local and imported, are sold under one roof. These are a favourite with local shoppers. For details on shopping in Delhi, see pages 96–7; for Kolkata, see pages 282–3; for Mumbai, see pages 462–3; and for Chennai, see pages 574–5.

Puppet

OPENING HOURS

M OST SHOPS in the principal shopping areas in urban India are open from about 10am to 7.30pm. Local stores keep longer hours, while markets selling fresh produce are open for business from dawn until late at night. Government emporia have fixed shopping hours, from 10am to 6pm with a lunch break between 1pm and 2pm. Shop timings vary from city to city, as do holidays. Republic Day (January 26th), Independence Day (August 15th) and Mahatma Gandhi's Birthday (October 2nd) are national holidays, and by law all shops and markets in the country remain closed.

HOW TO PAY

T HE RUPEE is accepted everywhere. All the larger stores now accept major international credit cards,

Interior of Camelot, an elegant boutique in Ribandar, Goa

such as MasterCard and Visa, but it is wise to carry some cash for purchases in bazaars and smaller shops. Some stores accept traveller's cheques as well, though a passport will be required for identification. International currency, too, can be used in certain places. If paying by credit card, ensure that the voucher is filled out in front of you, to avoid fraud. A sales tax, between seven to ten per cent, is charged on some items, unless the bill has been paid in foreign currency or with a foreign-based credit card.

RIGHTS AND REFUNDS

W HEN BUYING expensive items, such as carpets, jewellery or antiques, always insist on a receipt or cash memo. This is important in case damaged goods need to be returned or exchanged, though often in India this is less easy than it sounds. Refunds, too, are difficult.

Take particular care when purchases need to be shipped out. Check what costs are involved, including insurance, and ensure that all the paperwork is done correctly. International courier services (see p771) can also be approached to ship out large purchase.

BARGAINING

A GOOD WAY to get the best results when bargaining, is to check out costs and quality at a number of outlets. Usually, the big stores have fixed prices with no scope for bargaining, but haggling in bazaars and smaller shops can be quite rewarding. Try not to quote unrealistically low prices and miss out on a good deal in the process.

Flower-seller displaying garlands on a pavement, Kolkata

TOUTS

HANDLE TOUTS firmly and try not to succumb to offers of genuine antiques or fantastic bargains. They all operate on a commission basis, and taking visitors to shops of their choice is just a means of acquiring extra cash. Tourist coaches often stop at selected stores, but it is not obligatory to purchase anything. Don't be taken in by shops that say "government approved"; these are private enterprises not to be confused with government-run outlets.

DEPARTMENT STORES AND BOUTIQUES

PLUSH, air-conditioned department stores, malls and plazas, and up-market boutiques are now a regular feature in most large towns. They stock a variety of goods, ranging from clothes and leather items to kitchenware. International brands of cosmetics, perfume, fashion accessories, home appliances, glassware and more, are also available here. Boutiques specialize in popular Indian designer labels, including high-fashion Western-style and traditional Indian apparel.

GOVERNMENT EMPORIA

ALL STATE GOVERNMENTS have special outlets, with fixed prices, selling textiles and handicrafts from that particular region. These emporia have large premises in all state capitals, and although the range and quality of the items vary, they are good places to shop for gifts and souvenirs. Some of the well-stocked ones that also have branches in most larger cities are Poompuhar (Tamil Nadu), Rajasthali (Rajasthan) and Gurjari (Gujarat).

CRAFT CENTRES AND BAZAARS

THE DIVERSITY of traditional Indian crafts is one of the attractions of travelling in this country. Each region, town and village specializes in a particular skill, be it pottery,

Colourful paper kites on sale in a Rajasthan village

weaving, metalware or painting. In some smaller villages it is possible to observe artisans at work and buy directly from them. If a craft centre is not on your itinerary, many cities have arts and craft shops that sell handicrafts made in the region.

Shopping in local bazaars, with their noise and colour, is a unique experience. Located in the heart of old cities, bazaars are typically a maze of tiny shops and pavement stalls, selling a variety of merchandise, from flowers, vegetables and other fresh produce, to cooking utensils, textiles and jewellery.

SPECIALIST STORES

SPECIALIST STORES have built their reputation on the quality of merchandise they sell. The passion for antiques has led to a proliferation of shops selling bronzes, stone sculpture and metal artifacts.

If buying antiques, check with the Archaeological Survey of India *(see p759)* as objects over 100 years old cannot be taken out of the country. However, excellent reproductions can always be found. Exquisite gold and silver jewellery is readily available, though it is best to visit established jewellers. Jaipur is an excellent place to shop for precious stones, while Hyderabad is known for good-quality pearls.

Rajasthan, particularly Jaipur, Udaipur and Jodhpur, specializes in good quality miniatures, folk paintings and religious *pichhwais* on cloth. Other types of painting, such as Tibetan *thangkas* and the jewel-encrusted Tanjore paintings, are available in Ladakh, Himachal Pradesh and Tamil Nadu.

India's renowned textile tradition ranges from South India's glorious silk saris and Varanasi brocades to fine handwoven cottons, in a wide range of designs and colours. Inexpensive casual wear can be bought at pavement stalls. Boutiques are good places for designer clothes. Carpets and woollen goods, especially the pricey pashmina and *jamavar* shawls, should be bought only from reliable shops.

Tea, spices, herbal products and incense are also popular items. Kerala's spices are famous, while tea can be purchased all over the country. Herbal cosmetics and incense are usually sold in general stores, while *attar* (traditional perfume) can be found in most bazaars.

Mumbai's Chor Bazaar, a treasure trove of antiques

What to Buy in India

SHOPPING IN INDIA is a fascinating experience, since the bazaars and boutiques showcase a wide range of the country's decorative arts and crafts. The quality can vary, but the choice is enormous. Superb jewellery, colourful textiles, handicrafts and artifacts, as well as aromatic spices and herbal products, are all available. There are also elegant contemporary interpretations of traditional designs. In many places visitors can watch artisans at work and buy directly from them.

Wooden peacock head

Lacquerware
Bowls and platters in red and black lacquer were originally imported from Burma. Many of these can still be found in Chennai and on Kochi's Jew Street (see p643).

Brassware
A wide variety of perfectly proportioned ritual and utilitarian objects, such as boxes and lotas (water pots) were once an essential part of every household. They are now freely available in antique shops all over India.

Silverware
The choice of intricately carved and embossed silver artifacts includes salvers, candlesticks, nut bowls and decorative objects. Different parts of India usually specialize in a particular craft. Orissa is well known for its delicate filigree, while in Gujarat and Rajasthan, silversmiths carve elaborate designs on a solid base.

Stoneware
Stoneware is strongly influenced by the pietra dura motifs on the Taj Mahal (see pp174–5). Designers have now created a select range of tableware for the modern home that uses white marble as a base with delicate patterns printed in silver and gold foil.

Jewellery
Exquisite gem-encrusted kundan *and enamelled* meenakari *jewellery from North India (see p361), as well as gold ornaments from the south, are available in jewellery shops. Tribal or rural-style silver jewellery is also sold.*

Gold necklaces and bangle

Silver anklets, bracelet and armband

Navratna necklace and emerald earring

Textiles

A dazzling choice of blockprints, silk and cotton woven textiles and gold brocade can be bought by the metre or as ready-made garments, scarves, saris and home accessories. Good-quality paisley jamavar *and pashmina shawls are also available in select stores.*

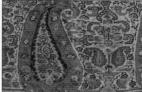

Printed and silk tissue cushion covers

Paisley *jamavar* shawl

Light-weight cotton quilts

Brocade textile and scarf

Bamboo and Cane Products

The northeastern states are famous for their fine bamboo and cane work. Besides objects of everyday use, such as large baskets for tea-pluckers, hats and utensils, artisans have now created a variety of trays, baskets, boxes and containers for the contemporary market. Good-quality furniture is also made for local and international buyers.

Bronze image

Tribal elephant

Paintings

Many places, especially Jaipur, Jodhpur and Udaipur in Rajasthan, have shops and ateliers where painters skilfully recreate old miniatures (see p405). Poster colours are now used instead of natural pigments, but the themes are still traditional. These range from court scenes to depictions of religious and mythological stories.

A miniature painting

Artifacts

Excellent reproductions of antique bronzes (see p594) are available in many shops. These include images of Hindu deities, such as Krishna and Ganesha, as well as objects made by tribal artisans.

Herbal and Beauty Products

Traditional herbal remedies have been re-invented to suit the modern-day need for eco-friendly soaps and cosmetics, soothing oils and lotions. Aromatherapy is highly popular, and Auroville (see p589) has developed a wide range of scented candles and joss sticks.

Aromatherapy candles from Auroville

Joss sticks *(agarbatti)*

Soaps

Bath salts

ENTERTAINMENT

ENTERTAINMENT IN INDIA offers fascinating insights into the religious, cultural and social diversity of the country. The vast and complex tradition of performing arts is an ancient one, inextricably linked to religion and mythology. Initially, classical music and dance were performed as part of temple ritual, while the rich repertoire of folk forms

Kathakali dancer

emerged as a response to local conditions, the land and community. Today, the choice of entertainment includes classical dance and music, religious dance-dramas, contemporary theatre and colourful temple festivals. There are popular alternatives as well, especially cinemas, where the latest Bollywood blockbusters are shown.

SOURCES OF INFORMATION

LOCAL NEWSPAPERS and magazines are good sources of information, as they carry regular listings and advertisements of events. Often, hotels have in-house publications highlighting the city's sights as well as its entertainment venues and programmes. If not, the travel desk can usually provide the necessary information. In addition, the India Tourism offices and website *(see p759)* publish an annual calendar of events. Good travel agents can also let visitors know what is happening where, and can help prepare an itinerary of cultural events. For details on entertainment in Delhi, see pages 96–7; for Kolkata, see pages 282–3; for Mumbai, see pages 462–3; and for Chennai, see pages 574–5.

BOOKING TICKETS

FOR CULTURAL programmes and the cinema, it is best to book tickets in advance at the venue itself. Tele-booking,

especially for the more popular shows, is not always reliable. Some stores in the larger cities also have ticket counters; event organizers will indicate where these are in the local newspapers. Hotels or tour operators can often arrange tickets as well.

CLASSICAL MUSIC AND DANCE

CLASSICAL MUSIC and dance are a dynamic reflection of India's rich cultural heritage *(see pp28–9)*. Regular performances of Odissi, Bharat Natyam, Kuchipudi and Kathakali, the dance-drama from Kerala, are organized by state tourism departments and private cultural organizations at auditoriums and hotels. In recent years, dance festivals against the backdrop of historic sites have become popular. Such events are now held at Ajanta and Ellora *(see pp476–81)*, Konark *(see pp310–12)*, Mamallapuram *(see pp578–81)*

Folk musicians from Rajasthan playing *sarangis* **(string instruments)**

as well as Khajuraho *(see pp236–8)*, and offer a unique way to enjoy India's many famed dance forms.

Concerts of Indian classical music, in the North Indian (Hindustani) and South Indian (Carnatic) styles, draw crowds of music lovers. Concerts by soloists as well as groups are held regularly in the larger cities. There is often a lively interaction between the artistes and the audience, who express their appreciation by exclaiming or clapping several times during a concert.

Devotional music, such as Sufi qawwalis and Hindu *bhajans*, also attracts large audiences. Other forms include *ghazals*, lyrical poems in Urdu, and Rabindra Sangeet, songs composed by the great Bengali poet, Rabindranath Tagore *(see p292)*.

FOLK THEATRE, MUSIC AND DANCE

THE TRADITIONS of folk and tribal theatre, music and dance are as vibrant as those of the classical forms.

A classical dancer performing at the dance festival at Mamallapuram

A movie theatre in Mumbai, with large posters of current Bollywood releases

At one time, these indigenous forms were restricted to the region of their birth. Today, promotion by various cultural organizations has given folk artistes greater exposure. As a result urban audiences can watch Chhau, a masked dance performed by men from Orissa, Bihar and West Bengal; balladeers *(bhopas)* and *manganiyars* from Rajasthan; the *garba* from Gujarat; the exuberant Punjabi *bhangra*; street theatre *(jatra)* from West Bengal; traditional martial arts from Kerala; and *tamasha*, a theatre troupe with dancers and musicians from Maharashtra. During the Dussehra festival, Ramlilas – exuberant dramatizations of the epic *Ramayana (see p27)* – are held all over North India. The most elaborate of these take place by the banks of the Ganges in Varanasi *(see p203)*.

CONTEMPORARY THEATRE

I N THE LARGER CITIES, good quality performances of Western shows are staged. However there is also a very strong tradition of Indian-language theatre in Marathi, Gujarati, Hindi and Bengali. The range covers adaptations of contemporary works by well-known Indian authors, musicals and political satires. Many of these productions, draw their inspiration from India's rich repertoire of classical and folk forms.

PUPPET SHOWS

P UPPETRY IN INDIA is an ancient tradition, especially in Orissa, Karnataka *(see p535)*, Rajasthan, Tamil Nadu, Andhra Pradesh and West Bengal, where itinerant folk performers use string, rod, glove and shadow puppets to tell mythological tales to a primarily rural audience. Today, many hotels organize cultural programmes for their foreign guests, which often include a traditional puppet show. A contemporary puppet theatre movement dealing with socially relevant themes related to education, health and gender and sexuality, is also becoming popular.

CINEMA

T HE MOST POPULAR form of entertainment is cinema, especially the extravagant blockbusters from Bollywood *(see pp32–3)*. Some excellent regional-language films, which touch on socially or politically relevant themes, are also made in Kerala, West Bengal, Tamil Nadu and Andhra Pradesh. Select theatres hold special screenings of avante-garde films, or New Wave Cinema, but these lack popular appeal. There are cinema halls in almost every town and large village, whereas the larger cities have multiplexes (with fast food eateries) that offer a mix of both Bollywood and Hollywood films. Tickets are more expensive here.

BARS AND DISCOS

N IGHTLIFE IN INDIA is definitely getting livelier. While Mumbai's night spots *(see p463)*, Bangalore's pub culture and Goa's night-long beach parties and moonlight raves have been much publicized, more conservative towns elsewhere in the country now have at least a few bars, pubs, pool lounges or discotheques.

INDIPOP

I NTERNATIONAL MUSIC channels such as MTV have given a tremendous boost to the Indian pop scene. Known as Indipop, the music of groups such as Indian Ocean and Euphoria, and singers such as Lucky Ali and Alisha Chenai has made pop stars as popular as film stars. The styles range from fusion music and folk-inspired *bhangra* pop to re-mixes of popular Hindi film hits. Some classical singers, such as Shubha Mudgal, have begun to experiment with popular music in order to reach a wider audience, particularly the MTV generation.

FAIRS AND FESTIVALS

T HE CONSTANT CYCLE of fairs and festivals is intrinsic to the Indian way of life, *(see pp34–7)*. From Holi, the festival of colour in spring, to Diwali, the festival of lights at the onset of winter, there are a series of colourful celebrations that mark the changing seasons or mythological events, as well as countless temple festivals. Visitors will usually have ample opportunity to witness these vignettes of the country's cultural and religious heritage, during their travels. Being invited to a home during a festival or a traditional celebration can also be an enjoyable experience.

Each chapter in this book has a column highlighting the main regional festivals.

A popular bar in the five-star Maurya Sheraton Hotel, Delhi

OUTDOOR ACTIVITIES & SPECIALIST HOLIDAYS

INDIA OFFERS a wide range of sporting and outdoor activities. The larger cities have facilities for golf, tennis, swimming and riding. Winter (Oct–Feb) is the main season for sports, such as polo and cricket. For the more adventurous, there are treks in the Himalayas, tiger tracking in India's many wildlife parks, and a choice of rivers for white-water rafting. Camel or horse

Batsman at the crease

safaris offer a memorable way to explore the Rajasthan desert. For the more spiritually inclined, there are yoga and meditation centres, and opportunities to spend time with renowned gurus at their ashrams. An increasing number of visitors are attracted by India's Ayurvedic health spas, and other holistic healing centres, which emphasize nature-based treatments.

SPECTATOR SPORTS

INDIANS ARE CRICKET-CRAZY and grab at any chance to watch or play the game. Winter is the main season, when world-class teams tour the country and test matches and one-day internationals are held in cities such as Delhi, Kolkata, Mumbai, Chennai, Bangalore and Kanpur. During these matches, fans of all age-groups crowd the stands, where a picnic atmosphere prevails. Announcements of match schedules and ticket details appear in the national and local newspapers.

Soccer does not have the high profile that cricket enjoys, but in certain places, such as Kolkata, Goa and Kerala, it is as popular. The game creates great hysteria in Kolkata, and professional clubs such as Mohun Bagan and its rival team East Bengal have mass followings. Check the local press for matches on in the city. Hockey, although a national passion, is not yet big enough to attract international events.

SWIMMING AND TENNIS

ALL FIVE-STAR HOTELS have excellent swimming pools with attached fitness centres. Non-residents are allowed to use hotel pools for a fee. In North India, outdoor pools close in winter. Beach resorts have pools as well as access to beaches. Before swimming in the sea, check with the lifeguard that it is safe. Swimming and sunbathing in the

nude are strictly prohibited.

Hotels offer grass or hard court tennis facilities and can also arrange games at certain local clubs, especially in the larger cities. India joined the Davis Cup fraternity in 1921, and has hosted the event numerous times. The **All India Tennis Association** also organizes tournaments. Currently among India's pride are the young Doubles team, Leander Paes and Mahesh Bhupathi, who won the French Open Men's Doubles title for the second time in June 2001.

GOLF

A VAST NETWORK OF clubs with well-maintained courses has made India a popular destination for golfers. The Royal Calcutta Golf Club was set up as early as 1829, and was followed by others in Raj-era hill stations, tea estates and cantonments. Exclusive golf resorts such as the ITC Classic Resort near Manesar,

designed by the international golfer Jack Nicklaus, are much frequented, especially by top executives who like to combine a round of golf with negotiating business deals.

The **Indian Golf Union** in Kolkata organizes a choice of activities, ranging from international events to leisurely games. It can also arrange temporary membership at the Royal Calcutta Golf Club and the Delhi Golf Club.

Many towns in India, such as Jaipur, Agra and Ranikhet, have well-maintained, army-run golf courses located in cantonment areas, which are open to foreigners for a fee. It is therefore worthwhile to enquire about facilities when in a new town.

POLO AND RIDING

STILL VERY MUCH an elitist sport, polo is enjoying a pleasant revival thanks to corporate sponsorships. The **Army Polo and Riding Club** in Delhi is the main centre,

A golfer beneath the ramparts of Jaipur's Moti Doongri Fort

and can be contacted for match schedules and other information. The season is in winter when regular matches are held in Delhi, Kolkata, Jaipur, Jodhpur and Mumbai.

Two of India's leading teams still play under the banners of the erstwhile princely houses of Jodhpur and Kashmir, while the Indian Army continues its long association with polo and fields its own team. Polo is extremely popular in Jaipur, and matches are held at the Rajasthan Polo Club near the Rambagh Palace Hotel. In some hotels in Rajasthan's Shekhawati district, visitors are taught how to play the game. Some variations are elephant and camel polo (both played in Jaipur), while in Ladakh, a rough and ready form of polo is played, with ponies instead of horses.

As for riding, thoroughbred horses can be hired at clubs in Delhi and Kolkata, as well as at the **Royal Equestrian Polo Centre** in Jaipur, after applying for a temporary membership. For joyrides there are always the hack ponies, found in most hill stations or on beaches.

HELI TOURISM

FOR SHORT but delightful package tours, **Deccan Aviation** organizes helicopter trips to many exotic destinations, such as the mountain ranges of the north and north-east, and around Bangalore and Mumbai. The cost includes food and lodging While expensive, these are perfect for tourists with plenty of cash but limited time. The government-run **Pawan Hans Helicopters Ltd** also offers heli-trips in collaboration with hotels or tour operators.

JEEP, CAMEL AND HORSE SAFARIS

OFTEN, THE BEST way to explore places that are off the beaten track is to take one of the many safaris on offer. Jeep safaris are popular in Ladakh, especially to the Nubra Valley (see p143) and to the lakes of Tso Moriri and

Horse safaris, a delightful way of exploring Rajasthan

Tso Kar. Jeep safaris are also popular in Lahaul, Spiti and Kinnaur in Himachal Pradesh. A good base is Manali which has a large number of adventure tour operators. Among them, **Himalayan Adventures** is a reputable agency that organizes jeep safaris as well as other adventure activities such as trekking and rafting. The two-day route from Manali to Leh is a very popular one.

Camel-owners in the Thar Desert in Rajasthan, around Jaisalmer, specialize in camel safaris between October and February. Most safaris last about four days, and the minimum charge is around Rs400 per day (inclusive of meals and blankets, with extra charges for tents). Among the many operators,is the **Desert Resort and Camp** at Manvar, which offers top-end safaris in luxury tents. A pleasant alternative is horse safaris around Jodhpur, Shekhawati, Kumbhalgarh and Udaipur.

These offer unique glimpses of rural life, taking in forts, palaces and remote villages. **Ghanerao Safari Tours** in Jaipur, specializes in horse safaris and offers both easy and challenging trips. Many hotels in Rajasthan organize horse safaris. Elephant safaris are also available (see p753).

TREKKING

INDIA HAS A fantastic range of trekking options. Besides the Himalayas, the Nilgiris (see p606) in South India, and in the Sahyadris (see p473) in Maharashtra, have many trails for short hikes.

The great Himalayas are a trekker's paradise. **Ibex Expeditions**, a reputable agency, organizes expeditions all over the Himalayas. For more detailed information on trekking and local adventure tour operators in Himachal Pradesh, see pages 114–15; in Ladakh and Zanskar, see pages 152–3; in Garhwal and Kumaon, see pages 188–9; and in West Bengal and Sikkim, see pages 302–303.

This guide divides trails into three types, based on levels of difficulty. "Easy" ones, which involve mildly strenuous walking at mid-high altitudes, are a good introduction. "Moderate" routes cover various terrains and should not be attempted by people with heart problems and serious ailments. Only experienced climbers should attempt "tough" treks, since these go to very high altitudes and require high levels of fitness. It is mandatory to carry a permit (see p758) near international border areas.

Trekking over the spectacular Shingo-la pass in Zanskar, Ladakh

Parasailing, popular in Himachal Pradesh and Uttaranchal

CAMPING AND ADVENTURE SPORTS

HOLIDAYS THAT combine camping and trekking can be particularly enjoyable. **Banjara Camps** specializes in tented holidays in the scenic Sangla Valley in Himachal Pradesh, while **Jungle Lodges and Resorts** organizes well-run luxury camps in Karnataka.

India also provides opportunities to pursue a range of adventure sports. However, it is advisable to take out extra cover on your insurance if you plan on trying any of these activities.

Hang-gliding and parasailing are offered in Himachal Pradesh, especially in Manali and Dharamsala, and near Billing in Kangra. Ooty in Tamil Nadu is another great hang-gliding site, while the Western Ghats in Maharashtra and Goa offer idyllic conditions for parasailing. Local tourism offices in each state organize these sports and can be contacted for bookings and equipment hire.

For mountaineering and rock climbing enthusiasts, the Himalayas offer a number of challenging peaks, many rising above 7,000 m (22,966 ft). Uttaranchal and Himachal Pradesh are India's main mountaineering regions, and Sikkim also offers climbing in the Himalayas. The **Indian Mountaineering Foundation** in Delhi is the central agency; it organizes expeditions and has an active rock climbing fraternity, too. It also provides information on the country's other institutes, such as the Himalayan Mountaineering Institute in Darjeeling (*see p296*), and the Nehru Intitute of Mountaineering in Uttarkashi *(see p187)*, both of which offer courses.

Auli in Uttaranchal is the best-equipped ski-centre in India, and is open between January and March. For bookings and skiing information, contact the **GMVN Office** in Dehra Dun, or the **GMVN Tourist Rest House** in Auli, which also hires out gear. Solang Nala, 13 km (8 miles) northwest of Manali, also has ski slopes that are open between February and March. The **Institute of Mountaineering and Allied Sports** in Manali rents out skiing equipment, offers mountaineering courses, and also organizes kayaking on the Beas river.

KAYAKING AND RIVER RAFTING

THE CHALLENGE of the fast-flowing rivers of the Himalayas makes India a popular destination for kayaking and white-water rafting. Rivers are graded from levels I to VI, and only professionals should attempt rapids that are graded IV and above. The main destinations are the Indus and Zanskar in Ladakh, the Beas and Satluj in Himachal Pradesh, the Ganges, Bhagirathi and Tons in Uttar Pradesh, and the Teesta in Sikkim. The best seasons are between September and December, and again between February and April.

Numerous agencies run organized trips and provide tents, rafts, life jackets and meals. The Ganges near Rishikesh is a popular site *(see p185)*, as it is just a few hours drive from Delhi. Many companies have set up rafting camps and provide equipment during the season. **Himalayan River Runners**, and **Aquaterra Adventures** are two of the reputable agencies that run various rafting camps in Uttaranchal and Ladakh.

WATER SPORTS

GOA IS A popular destination for water sports, where yachting competitions and wind-surfing regattas are attended by enthusiasts from all over the world. Sports such as water-skiing, sailing, wind-surfing and parasailing are offered by local agencies, on beaches such as Baga, Vainguinim, Sinquerim, Anjuna and Bogmalo. The **National Institute of Watersports**, located in Panaji, also offers training courses in wind-surfing, water-skiing, sailing and scuba diving, and hires out boats and equipment as well.

The **Royal Bombay Yacht Club** in Mumbai organizes sailing excursions for visitors every Saturday, while Kerala's popular Kovalam Beach has some facilities for surfing and snorkelling. In Tamil Nadu, a few water sports centres and hotels have recently opened, offering water sports facilities along the coast between Chennai and Mamallapuram.

The Lakshadweep Islands, off the Kerala coast, have excellent centres for wind-surfing, parasailing and water-skiing, as well as snorkelling and scuba diving. **Lacadives** on Kadmat Island has the best

White-water rafting on the Ganges

Colourful wind-surfing sails, Goa

equipped centre *(see p647)*. An equally exciting destination for snorkelling, scuba diving and other water sports is the tropical Andaman Islands in the Bay of Bengal. Quality equipment, including glass-bottomed boats and scuba gear, is available at the **Andaman Water Sports Complex** *(see p618)* in Port Blair, the best-known agency. Port Blair has many other agencies as well *(see p619)*.

FISHING

INDIA'S VAST NETWORK of rivers and lakes provides ample opportunity for fishing enthusiasts. All fishing in India requires a permit, which can be obtained from the Fisheries Officer at the various state Fisheries Departments. However, it is simpler to let an agency organize the permits for you. Himalayan River Runners organizes exciting *mahseer* fishing expeditions in the Ganges in February and March.

The best spots in North India are the Ramganga river, outside Corbett National Park; Gangalehri, off the Haridwar-Rishikesh road on the Ganges; and Pong Dam, on the Beas in Himachal Pradesh. This state also offers superb trout-fishing on the Beas river at Katrain, and in the scenic Sangla Valley on the Baspa river. In South India, **Jungle Lodges and Resorts** *(see p755)* run the Kali River Camp at Dandeli and the Cauvery Fishing and Nature Camp, in Karnataka. These are luxury camps for discerning visitors who wish to combine a fishing holiday with modern comforts.

WILDLIFE TOURISM

A RELATIVELY NEW concept in tourism, combining nature study with conservation activities, is becoming increasingly popular in India. The country has an extraordinary diversity of habitats that support a vast variety of plant and animal life, including many rare and endangered species.

Today, India has 70 protected national parks and over 400 wildlife sanctuaries that cover 4.15 per cent of its total area. Numerous societies are actively involved in environmental issues. The **World Wide Fund for Nature, India (WWF)**, with its headquarters in Delhi, has a regular programme of activities such as camping trips, film shows and seminars on wildlife. The **Bombay Natural History Society (BNHS)** is one of the foremost nature institutions in India. Its first Indian president was the renowned ornithologist, Dr Salim Ali *(see p466)*. The Society, dedicated to conservation, with special emphasis on bird studies, also organizes workshops. Another eminent institution is the **Madras Naturalists' Society**.

India's many wildlife reserves and game sanctuaries are the best places to see endangered species in the wild. **Ibex Expeditions** organizes eco-friendly trips to parks all over India; **Exotic Journeys** is another reputable agency *(see p689)*. Jungle Lodges and Resorts in Karnataka runs numerous luxury camps, spread across the Nagarhole and BRT Wildlife Sanctuaries *(see p520)*, with coracle boat rides, elephant safaris and film screenings on offer for visitors.

Corbett Park in Uttaranchal *(see pp192–3)*, Kanha in Madhya Pradesh *(see pp254–5)* and the Sunderbans in West Bengal *(see pp288–9)*, are among India's largest Tiger Reserves. Rajasthan's Keoladeo Ghana National Park *(see pp368–9)* attracts a large variety of migratory birds in winter and is a birdwatcher's paradise, while Kaziranga in Assam *(see pp330–31)* is one of the few places in the world where the Indian rhino can be found in the wild. The best park for observing Asian elephants is Periyar in Kerala *(see pp640– 41)*, which has the largest population of wild elephants in the country.

A few practical tips should be followed while visiting wildlife reserves. Do not litter, and be especially careful not to drop any plastic and synthetic materials. Carry a pair of binoculars, wear sturdy boots, and never wander off on your own, as this could be dangerous. Do not play loud music or blow horns within park limits since this disturbs the animals. Also, talk softly on safaris to improve the chances of spotting wildlife.

An elephant safari in Kaziranga National Park, habitat of the Indian rhino

A traditional head massage with Ayurvedic oils, Kovalam Beach

YOGA AND HEALING

YOGA, MEDITATION and Hindu philosophy are taught at ashrams and spiritual centres in most Indian cities. Some of the best are in Rishikesh, where courses are conducted by learned gurus, renowned in their fields. Of these, the **Sivananda Ashram** *(see p689)* is the most famous. Pune's **Osho International Commune** *(see p470)*, started in the 1960s by the charismatic guru Bhagwan Rajneesh, offers residential courses in meditation and philosophy. The **Ramamani Iyengar Memorial Yoga Institute**, run by the well-known Yogacharya BKS Iyengar is also in Pune, and offers a choice of *hatha* yoga courses. Among India's other reputed yoga and meditation centres are the **Sri Aurobindo Ashram** in Pondicherry *(see p689)*, the **Chinmaya Mission** at Mumbai and the **Ramakrishna Mission** at Belur Math *(see p689)*. Hotels and travel agencies can find out about local branches of many of these centres.

India also has numerous institutes that conduct courses in Buddhist meditation and *vipassana*. Dharamsala and McLeodganj, the home of the Dalai Lama, have some of the best centres. Residential courses are held at the **Tushita Meditation Centre**. Ayurveda and naturopathy

Logo of a yoga centre in Rishikesh

rely on the healing powers of herbs and natural foods, and are widely practised in India. Ayurvedic treatment using special herbal oils, is thought to have originated in Kerala *(see p629)*, and is widely practised there today. Almost all hotels in the state have Ayurvedic centres, especially around Kovalam and Thiru-vananthapuram. The **Kairali Ayurvedic Health Resort** at Palakkad (with branches in Delhi and Khajuraho), and the **Soma-theeram Ayurvedic Resort** *(see p715)* at Kovalam are among the best centres. For visitors in search of medical advice and treatment, the **Arya Vaidyasala** in Kottakal *(see p652)* is a pioneer institute.

India also has a handful of luxury spas, which emphasize holistic healing *(see p688)*. The **Institute of Naturo-pathy and Yogic Sciences** in Bangalore, also known as Jindal's Farm, admits patients for specialized treatments for respiratory and stomach disorders, ulcers, migraines and diabetes.

Other healing practices such as Reiki and Pranic healing (methods that channel positive forces through the body's *chakras* or energy centres), are practised in many larger cities, and it is best to check local city magazines for details. A magazine, published every month, called *Life Positive*, focuses on new-age healing techniques.

CULTURAL ACTIVITIES

INDIAN CLASSICAL dance and music are taught at renowned institutes all over the country. **Triveni Kala Sangam** *(see p75)* in Delhi holds courses in classical singing, dance and painting. Dharamsala's **Norbulingka Institute** teaches Tibetan arts and crafts, including *thangka* painting and embroidery. The dance village of **Nrityagram**, near Bangalore, offers long-term courses in classical dance, choreography, music and painting. **Kalakshetra** in Chennai *(see p572)* is a premier institute for teaching Carnatic music and classical dance, and the **Kerala Kala Mandalam** *(see p651)* near Thrissur, is another renowned centre for the performing arts.

A few travel agencies offer special interest tours on subjects such as architecture, rural and tribal culture, traditional arts and crafts, and cuisine. They make itineraries to suit individual tastes. **Incent Tours** focuses on textiles, architecture and food, while **Travel Link** specializes in tribal tours in Orissa.

Various institutions all over the country promote tradition-al crafts and artisans. The **Crafts Museum** *(see pp80–81)* in Delhi, and the **Dastkar Craft Centre**, which is near Ranthambhore in Rajasthan, are two places where visitors can observe artisans at work and learn more about their skills and way of life.

A classical Kuchipudi dance performance

DIRECTORY

SPORTS

All India Tennis Association
Tennis Stadium, Africa Avenue, Delhi.
((011) 617 6276.

Indian Golf Union
Room 1138–B, Jawaharlal Nehru Stadium, Gate 27, Lodi Rd, Delhi.
((011) 436 7161.

POLO & RIDING

Army Polo & Riding Club
C/o B Squadron, 61 Cavalry, Cariappa Marg, Delhi.
((011) 569 9777.
w indianpolo.com

Royal Equestrian Polo Centre
Dundlod House, Civil lines, Jaipur.
((0141) 21 1276.

HELI-TOURISM

Deccan Aviation
E–54 Anand Niketan, Delhi.
((011) 410 3520.
FAX (011) 410 3522.
w deccan-air.com

Pawan Hans Helicopters Ltd.
Safdarjung Airport, Delhi.
((011) 461 5711.
FAX (011) 461 1801.
w pawanhans.com

JEEP, CAMEL & HORSE SAFARIS

Desert Resort & Camp, Manvar
646, Hanuwant Nagar, 'A', BJS, Jodhpur.
((0291) 546 188.
FAX (0291) 546 188.
w manvaar.com

Ghanerao Safari Tours
B–II/302, Kamal Apts, Bani Park, Jaipur.
((0141) 20 1209.
FAX (0141) 20 1209
w horsesafari.com

Himalayan Adventures
The Mall, Manali.
((01902) 53 050.
FAX (01902) 52 182.
w shubhyatra.com

TREKKING

Ibex Expeditions
G-66 East of Kailash, Delhi.
((011) 691 2641.
w ibexexpeditions.com

CAMPING & ADVENTURE SPORTS

Banjara Camps
1 A, Haus Khas Village, Delhi.
((011) 686 1397.
FAX (011) 685 5152.
w banjaracamp.com

GMVN
74/1, Rajpur Rd, Dehradun.
((0135) 74 6817.
FAX (0135) 74 4408.

GMVN Tourist Rest House, Auli
((01389) 23 208.

Indian Mountaineering Foundation
6 Benito Juarez Marg, Delhi.
((011) 467 1211.
w indmount.com

Institute of Mountaineering & Allied Sports
Manali.
((01902) 52 342.

Jungle Lodges & Resorts
Shrungar Shopping Centre, MG Rd, Bangalore.
((080) 559 7021.
FAX (080) 558 6163.
w junglelodges.com

KAYAKING & RIVER RAFTING

Aquaterra Adventures
S–507 Greater Kailash II, New Delhi.
((011) 629 2760.
FAX (011) 623 2641.
w treknraft.com

Himalayan River Runners
F–5 Hauz Khas, Delhi.
((011) 685 2602.
FAX (011) 686 5604.
w hrrindia.com

WATER SPORTS

National Institute of Watersports
Sundial Apts, AS Rd, Altinho, Panaji, Goa.
((0832) 43 6550.
FAX (0832) 43 6400.

Royal Bombay Yatch Club
Apollo Bunder, Mumbai.
((022) 202 4607.

WILDLIFE TOURISM

Bombay Natural History Society
Hornbill House, Shaheed Bhagat Singh Marg, Mumbai.
((022) 282 1811.
w bnhs.org

Madras Naturalists' Society
8 Janaki Avenue, Abhiramapuram, Chennai.
((044) 499 7614.
w dmiactive.com

World Wide Fund for Nature, India
172–B, Lodi Estate, Delhi.
((011) 469 1227.
FAX (011) 469 1226.
w indev.nic.in

YOGA & HEALING

Arya Vaidyasala
Kottakkal.
((0493) 742216.
FAX (0493) 742210.
w aryavaidyasala.com

Chinmaya Mission
Central Chinmaya Mission Trust, Mumbai.
((022) 857 2367.
FAX (022) 857 3065.
w chinmayamission.com

Tushita Meditation Centre
McLeodganj.
((01892) 21866.

Institute of Naturopathy & Yogic Sciences
Jindal Nagar, Bangalore.
((080) 839 4926.
FAX (080) 839 4926.
w naturecure-inys.org

Kairali Ayurvedic Health Resort
Olassery, Post Kodumbu, Palakkad District.
((0492) 322 553.
FAX (0492) 322 732.
w kairali.com

Osho International Commune
17 Koregaon Park, Pune.
((020) 613 6655.
w osho.com

Ramamani Iyengar Memorial Yoga Institute
1107, B/1 Hare Krishna Mandir Rd, Model Colony, Shivaji Nagar, Pune.
((020) 565 3164.
w bksiyengar.com

CULTURAL ACTIVITIES

Dastkar Craft Centre
Kutalpura Village.
((07462) 52 049.

Incent Tours
113-A, Shahpurjat, Near Asiad Village, Delhi.
((011) 649 4075.
FAX (011) 649 5357.
w incenttours.com

Norbulingka Institute
Dharamsala.
((01892) 22 664.
FAX (01892) 24 982.

Nrityagram
The Dance Village, Hessaraghatta, Bangalore.
((080) 846 6312.
FAX (080) 846 6444.

Travel Link
10 Satya Nagar, Bhubaneswar.
((0674) 50 2310.
FAX (0674) 50 3778.

SURVIVAL
GUIDE

PRACTICAL INFORMATION

INDIA receives over 2.2 million visitors each year. The peak season is in winter (Oct–Mar), and it is wise to book ahead during this time. English is widely spoken in most parts of the country, so communication is rarely a problem. Tourist infrastructure (transportation, accommodation and restaurants) are of international standard in the larger cities; the remoter areas offer fairly basic accommodation

**Logo of the
Department of Tourism**

and some areas are still not equipped to cater to the international tourist, who may seek better banking services or prefer to pay by credit card. The Department of Tourism has offices across the country *(see p781)* as well as overseas, which provide brochures, itineraries and guided tours. There are many travel agencies in India, but it is wise to approach a reputable one for accommodation, tickets and tours.

WHEN TO GO

TRAVELLING IN INDIA is largely determined by the weather. The best time is between October and March, when conditions are pleasant across the country. Try to avoid the summer (Apr–Jun), which is unbearably hot in the north, and very sultry in the south. The rainy season (Jul–Sep) is also best avoided, as frequent heavy rainfall can make travel difficult, especially in the southwestern states of Goa, Maharashtra and Kerala. The Himalayan region can be very cold from November to January. The foothills, which provide a welcome escape from the heat of the plains, are at their best between March and June, and again in September (after the rains). Climate and rainfall charts can be found on pages 38–39.

WHAT TO TAKE

THE CLOTHES you need will depend on the time of year that you visit. In northern India, from November

until February, you will need a warm jacket, sweater and socks, especially after sundown, whereas in the south, the weather is balmy at that time. In February and March, and again in October, bring light woollens. During the summer and monsoon season (Apr–Sep) only loose-fitting cotton clothes are comfortable. Bring footwear that is easy to remove, as you will have to take off your shoes in places of worship. A first aid kit is a must *(see p766)*. A raincoat or umbrella, a hat to protect against the strong sun, and a torch are also useful.

ADVANCE BOOKING

IT IS ADVISABLE to have confirmed advance bookings for accommodation and travel, especially during the peak season (Oct–Mar). Airline tickets are available at short notice, but as trains are always crowded, bookings should be made ahead – ticket reservations can be made two months in advance. Insist on written confirmations.

VISAS AND PASSPORT

EVERYONE NEEDS a passport and visa to enter India. The Indian consular offices around the world issue a standard six-month multiple-entry visa for tourists, which is convenient for visiting neighbouring countries such as Nepal and Sri Lanka. Foreigners who arrive in India on this visa do not need to register themselves with a local authority and can travel freely in all areas except the so-called "Restricted Areas", which require special permits.

Visa extensions are sometimes granted for 15 days or, in exceptional cases, for a longer period. The application process is complicated. In Delhi, collect an extension form from the **Ministry of Home Affairs** office; then submit it to the **Foreigners Regional Regisration Office (FRRO)**; it will finally be issued by the Ministry of Home Affairs. In Mumbai, Chennai or Kolkata, contact the local FRRO.

Obtaining a visa extension, whether for 15 days or longer, is extremely difficult and extensions are only granted, if at all, in special circumstances.

PERMITS

IN ADDITION TO a visa, you may need special travel permits to visit what are known as "Restricted Areas". Obtaining a permit, can be complicated, so it is best to ask a reliable travel agent, at home or in India, to arrange it

A Goa café doing brisk business in winter, when the weather is balmy

◁ **The Blue Mountain Train on its scenic journey to Ooty** *(see p605)*

for you. This can take up to four weeks, so plan ahead. Permits are also issued by Indian embassies and consular offices abroad; from the FRRO in Delhi, Kolkata, Mumbai and Chennai; and from the Resident Commissioner's offices in Delhi. You will be asked to show these permits when travelling in restricted areas. You will also need trekking permits for the Himalayan regions bordering Pakistan, Tibet and China, and for treks in Uttaranchal (see pp188–9), Himachal Pradesh (see p115), Ladakh (see p143 & p153) and West Bengal and Sikkim (see p303). All visitors to Sikkim require 15-day travel permits, because of its proximity to a sensitive border with China.

Among the seven north-eastern states, no permits are required for Assam, Meghalaya and Tripura. However, permits are required for Arunachal Pradesh, Mizoram, Manipur and Nagaland, and can be acquired from any of the state tourist offices. In some areas, permits are issued only to groups of four or more – these are best organised by a travel agent.

Foreign nationals require a permit, valid for 30 days, for the Andaman Islands, but this excludes tribal areas and some islands, including Nicobar. Permits can be obtained on arrival at the immigration counter at Port Blair airport, or at Kolkata and Chennai airports. If travelling by ship, a permit can be obtained on arrival at Port Blair, as well as from the FRRO offices in the four main cities. For permits to travel to the Lakshadweep Islands, see page 647.

EMBASSIES AND CONSULATES

MOST COUNTRIES have embassies in Delhi, as well as consulates in Mumbai, Kolkata and Chennai. Consular offices can re-issue passports and assist in case of emergencies, such as theft,

imprisonment and hospitalization. All city telephone directories and information guides carry detailed listings of embassies and consulates, as does the Indian Ministry of Tourism's website. (www.tourindia.com)

CUSTOMS INFORMATION

WHEN ENTERING India, visitors have a duty-free allowance of 950 ml of alcohol and 200 cigarettes. For articles such as jewellery, video cameras, music systems or laptop computers, they must fill in the tourist baggage re-export form, undertaking to take these items back or else pay a fairly heavy duty on them on departure. They must also fill in the currency declaration form at the airport for more than US$2,500 in cash or traveller's cheques.

There is a duty of 60 per cent if the baggage value limit is exceeded. Antiques over 100 years old cannot be exported. Neither can wildlife products, such as animal pelts, *shahtoosh* shawls or ivory. Consult the **Archaeological Survey of India (ASI)** and the **Ministry of Environment and Forests** for details of these rules.

Visa Stamp

IMMUNIZATION

ONLY VISITORS travelling from certain countries in Africa, South America and Papua New Guinea require a valid vaccination certificate for yellow fever. However, vistors should get vaccinated against tetanus, typhoid and hepatitis A and B. It is also advisable to start a course of anti-malarial tablets before leaving for India, after consulting a doctor (see p767).

INSURANCE

IT IS ADVISABLE to take out an insurance policy for medical emergencies as well as theft before leaving home. Travel insurance is also essential to cover any adventure activity or sport that you may undertake on your trip.

TOURIST INFORMATION

Tourist information offices run by the **Government of India Department of Tourism** *(see p781)* can be found across the country and abroad. Each state also has its own tourism department, providing reliable and detailed advice and practical information on sightseeing, travel and stay. Tourist brochures and maps are readily available. A number of travel sites on the Internet, also provide up-to-date information. There are information counters in the arrival halls of international and domestic airports, as well as information booths at railway and bus stations.

Tourist brochures

ADMISSION CHARGES

Most museums, historical monuments and wildlife parks charge an entry fee. This is often a modest amount, though admission to UNESCO World Heritage Sites costs more – foreigners pay a fee of US$15 (payable in rupees) for the Taj Mahal, and US$5 for some of the other monuments, such as the Khajuraho temples.

There are often additional fees for cameras, video cameras, and for special shows such as the Son et Lumières. Most places of worship do not have any admission fee, but often have a donation box. If you are of a different religious denomination, it is advisable to ask if you may enter *(see p762)*.

HOLIDAYS AND OPENING HOURS

Each year, the government issues a new holiday list *(see p35)* that includes all major religious festivals, whose exact dates may change from year to year. Some are known as "restricted holidays", which means that though the office may be open, the staff may be on leave. Banks, offices and most markets remain closed on the three national holidays: Republic Day (26 January) Independence Day (15 August) and Mahatma Gandhi's birthday (2 October). Monuments and museums are normally open from 10am to 6pm with an hour's lunch break, and generally close on Mondays and government holidays. Markets and shops stay open until at least 7pm in most places. Temples tend to close between 1pm and 4pm when the deity is "at rest". Government offices work from Monday to Friday, from 9:30am to 6pm with, supposedly, a half-hour lunch break.

GUIDES

All tourist offices, travel agents and hotels can arrange a certified guide for fixed hourly rates. At popular monuments amateur guides can be a nuisance. Look instead for English-speaking guides who wear a metal badge certifying government tourist department approval.

French, Italian, Spanish, German, Russian and Japanese-speaking guides are also available at many popular destinations.

BACKPACKERS

For students and young travellers, most of the larger cities have branches of the **Youth Hostels Association of India** or **YHAI** *(see p689)*. Though it is not necessary to be a member of the International Association to stay, members do get priority and lower rates. **YMCA** hostels in larger cities also provide cheap lodgings for backpackers. Apart from these, plenty of cheap options are also available across the country, including the smaller towns. It is a good idea to buy a strong padlock as some of the budget hotels have flimsy locks. Many of these are not air conditioned, nor do they have mosquito nets – the latter are essential, and available locally. Do not leave money and important documents in your hotel; keep them with you at all times. Be wary of conmen enticing you with the promise of cheap accommodation and bargain shopping.

FACILITIES FOR THE DISABLED

Facilities for the disabled are still fairly basic and public buildings and places of interest seldom have ramps or rails. However, airports and all main railway stations do have wheelchairs and ramps, and porters are always available to carry luggage. Pavements are difficult to negotiate in a wheelchair as they are often uneven. Few hotels are equipped for the needs of the disabled visitor. The staff, however, will go out of their way to help.

FACILITIES FOR CHILDREN

Although some luxury hotels do have baby-sitting facilities, these services are rare. However, Indians are generally tolerant of children,

Visitors on a guided tour of the lake at Ranganthittoo Bird Sanctuary

who are warmly welcomed in most places. If travelling with very young infants, it is advisable to bring your own supplies of baby food and formula milk. Disposable nappies are now widely available in the larger towns.

LANGUAGE

THOUGH HINDI is the official language of India, there are several regional languages as well. Bengali is spoken in Kolkata and West Bengal, Marathi in Mumbai and Maharashtra, Tamil in Tamil Nadu, Telugu in Andhra Pradesh and Malayalam in Kerala. English has become the most convenient link language and is widely spoken in most Indian cities. Most people who deal with tourists, such as taxi drivers, guides, hotel staff, shop assistants and officials, speak English. Road signs and numbers are usually in English as well as in the regional language of the particular state. A few basic phrases in Hindi, Bengali, Marathi, Tamil and Malayalam are listed on pages 820–824.

ELECTRICITY

THE ELECTRICAL CURRENT in India is 220–240 volts, 50 Hz. The power supply is very erratic during summer months with low voltage, fluctuations and long power cuts. Triple round-pin sockets are the norm, but adaptors and transformers are available at the larger stores. It is advisable to carry a power surge cable to protect laptop computers against voltage fluctuations.

INDIAN STANDARD TIME AND CALENDAR

IN SPITE OF ITS SIZE, India has only one standard time. India is 5.5 hours ahead of Greenwich Mean Time (GMT) 4.5 hours behind Australian Eastern Standard Time, and 10.5 hours ahead of US Eastern Standard Time. The Western Gregorian calendar is used for all official work as this avoids the confusion of traditional calendars, which

vary between religions and regions. For example, in 2003, the official Indian calendar (Saka era) reads 1925, whereas the old Hindu calendar (Vikram era) reads 2060.

MEASUREMENTS AND CONVERSION CHART

THE METRIC SYSTEM IS most commonly used all over the country.

Imperial to Metric
1 inch = 2.5 centimetres
1 foot = 30 centimetres
1 mile = 1.6 kilometres
1 ounce = 28 grams
1 pound = 454 grams
1 pint = 0.6 litres
1 gallon = 4.5 litres

Metric to Imperial
1 centimetre = 0.4 inches
1 metre = 3 feet 3 inches
1 kilometre = 0.6 miles
1 gram = 0.04 ounces
1 kilogram = 2.2 pounds
1 litre = 1.8 pints

A range of plugs

PHOTOGRAPHY

SOPHISTICATED FILM and colour-processing facilities are readily available, even in smaller towns. Remember to check expiry dates when buying batteries and film. Larger photo shops also have excellent developing and printing facilities and offer quick services.

Taking pictures of women, tribal communities, and places of worship can be sensitive issues and it is best to ask before using your camera. Photographing security-sensitive areas, such as railway stations, dams, airports and military installations, is prohibited. Notice boards indicate where photography is not allowed.

Etiquette

INDIA IS STILL A TRADITIONAL society, governed by strong family values. Though in cities and larger towns you will find youngsters in Western dress with a modern, cosmopolitan outlook, they remain traditional in many ways. And though the diverse social, religious and caste groups have their own distinct customs, they share certain common values. Respect for elders is deeply ingrained, so it is important to treat older people with special courtesy. Indians are extremely hospitable and helpful to visitors – sometimes to an almost embarassing degree. It is a good idea to respond to this by bringing your hosts flowers, or a small gift, even though this is not an Indian custom. If you find yourself facing delays and inefficient services, or grappling with bureaucracy, it is far more effective to be firm and polite than to lose your temper.

Eating off banana leaves at a ceremonial temple feast

GREETING PEOPLE

THE TRADITIONAL greeting in India is the *namaskar* or *namaste* (pronounced "namastay") when meeting or parting. The palms are pressed together, raised towards the face, and the head is bent slightly forward. Greetings and gestures vary somewhat according to religion or regional group. Muslims raise their right hand towards the forehead with the words *adaab* or *salaam aleikum* (to which you reply *walekum salaam*). The Western handshake is also widely used, though more conservative women still prefer to greet visitors with a *namaskar*.

The suffix "*ji*" after someone's name is a mark of respect. Using first names only can be taken as overly familiar, so it's best to address new acquaintances as Mr, Miss or Mrs, or simply "*ji*".

Older people, particularly grandparents, are treated with great respect, and younger relatives often greet them by touching their feet. Your host will not expect you to do the same, but a courteous greeting in any form is important.

Indians will think nothing of asking you apparently very personal questions within minutes of first meeting you, so don't take offence if a relative stranger asks you how much you earn or whether you are married. Such questions are seen as nothing more than taking a normal friendly interest in a new acquaintance.

BODY LANGUAGE

THE FEET are considered to be the lowliest part of the body, and shoes are treated as unclean. People will usually take their shoes off before entering a house. Putting your feet up on the furniture is considered bad manners, as is touching someone inadvertently with your feet. If you are sitting on the floor, as is often the case, try to keep your feet tucked underneath rather than stretched out, and avoid stepping on people.

***Namaskar*, the traditional greeting**

The head, on the other hand, is thought to be a person's spiritual centre. An older person may bless someone younger by touching his or her head.

Living in close quarters with family and neighbours gives Indians a different sense of "personal space" than many Westerners are used to. If you find yourself crowded or jostled, particularly while travelling, be as tolerant as you can, since space is often at a premium.

You should also be aware that public displays of affection between couples is frowned on in Indian society.

SUITABLE DRESS

INDIANS TEND TO dress conservatively and keep the body well covered. In small towns, most women wear saris or *salwar-kameez (see p30)*. In cities, jeans, skirts, and t-shirts are common, particularly among the younger generation. However, men do tend to stare at skimpily-clad women, so try to avoid short skirts, halter-neck tops, or anything that might attract unwanted attention.

It is best to dress formally when visiting Indian homes. In fact, wearing an Indian outfit for the occasion will probably delight your hosts. Inexpensive, ready-made Indian clothes for men and women are widely available.

It is acceptable for men to go shirtless on the beach. Nude sunbathing is never allowed, and women are advised to wear full swimsuits, or sarongs over their bikinis. If you are going out for the evening, remember that most nightclubs have a dress code, and you may not get in if you are wearing shorts or sneakers.

PLACES OF WORSHIP

WHETHER you are visiting a Hindu temple, Buddhist monastery, Islamic mosque or Sikh gurdwara, make sure that you behave and dress appropriately. You should, for example, always ask permission to take photographs. Women should wear dresses that cover the upper arms, and are at least mid-calf length, and and take a scraf along to cover their head. It is acceptable for women to wear long trousers. Men should avoid shorts and may be asked to cover their heads with a hanky or scarf (rather than a hat).

Jain temples have strict rules, and will not allow leather items, even wallets or watch straps, inside. In some South Indian temples, men are expected to remove their shirts and wear a *dhoti* instead of trousers. These are often provided at the temple entrance. At most places of worship, shoes are taken off at the door, and you should sit with your feet facing away from the main shrine. In a temple or monastery, walk around in a clockwise direction. You may be offered *prasad* (sacred food) in most temples and gurdwaras, which must be taken only in the right hand. The segregation of men and women is common.

In Hindu temples, it is usual for devotees and visitors to offer flowers and incense. Do not sit on or lean against temple walls or shrines. Even those in ruins, as well as simple roadside graves are considered holy. Some Hindu temples, (especially in Kerala and a few in Orissa) are out of bounds for non-Hindus. If you are barred from entering,

Sign for removing footwear

do not take offence. Avoid entering a mosque during Friday prayers, and men should stay away from the women's enclosure.

BARGAINING

BARGAINING IS A way of life in India. Exchanges can be heated, but it is not necessary to be aggressive. Firmly state what you would like to pay and walk away if the shopkeeper does not agree. If you are buying in bulk, you may ask for an extra discount. The prices in larger shops and government emporia are usually fixed *(see p744).*

EATING INDIAN STYLE

EATING WITH your fingers can take a bit of getting used to, but it is the best way to enjoy traditional Indian food. If in doubt about how to eat a particular dish, don't be embarrassed to ask. It is considered impolite to use your left hand for eating. Sitting on the floor for meals is common and, in the south, banana leaves are often used instead of plates.

TIPPING

THERE ARE NO norms for tipping, or *baksheesh*, as it is called. Porters and doormen at hotels are usually happy with a 5 or 10 rupee tip. In restaurants, check the bill before you decide on the tip, since the larger ones usually include a service

charge. If not, ten per cent of the total amount is usually fine. Tipping taxi or autorickshaw drivers is optional, and not generally expected. If you hire a car with a driver, however, you are expected to give him a *baksheesh*. The same goes for hairdressers, masseurs or anyone offering you a personal service.

SMOKING AND ALCOHOL

ALTHOUGH SMOKING in public places is officially banned in some states (such as Delhi and Kerala), this rule is widely flouted. Smoking is banned on domestic flights, and in some hotels, restaurants and offices. Smoking or drinking within the precincts of a temple, gurdwara or mosque is strictly taboo, and in Amritsar, no smoking is permitted within the city limits.

Alcohol is available all over India, though the state of Gujarat is "dry", as are some religious sites and temple towns, such as Haridwar, Rishikesh and Pushkar. In addition, there are certain designated "dry days" all over the country, such as Mahatma Gandhi's birthday (2 October) and Independence Day (15 August). Only some restaurants are licensed to serve alchohol, and you are not allowed to drink alcohol in parks, buses or trains.

BEGGARS

AS A FOREIGN VISITOR in India, you will get more than your share of harassment from beggars at city traffic lights, markets and outside places of worship. Beggars can be extremely persistent. Although it's very difficult to refuse, visitors who give money to one, will soon find themselves surrounded by a throng. Be especially careful of being pickpocketed in the confusion. The best strategy is to ignore them, and walk on until they leave you alone. If necessary, complain to a nearby policeman. If you do wish to help monetarily, the staff at your hotel will be able to suggest deserving charities to whom donations can be made.

Hindu pilgrims outside a temple in Orissa

Personal Security and Health

Police officer's badge

Each state in india has its own police force, which is run from local police stations (*thanas*). If you need to report a crime, such as theft, to the police, try to do so within 24 hours of the incident. Although Indian police are generally helpful, the system itself is extremely bureaucratic and prone to corruption, so it is always best to contact your embassy or consular office for help and advice in the first instance. For a trouble-free visit, a few simple precautions are necessary. Protect your valuables and important documents at all times, stay and eat in places that look clean, and drink only mineral water. If you require medical attention, it is better to opt for a private clinic rather than one of the many government-run hospitals.

Policeman in summer uniform directing traffic in Kolkata

GENERAL PRECAUTIONS

Travelling in india is relatively safe for tourists. Take simple safety measures, such as wearing a money belt under your shirt for cash, traveller's cheques and important documents, such as passports and visas. Protect your camera and avoid wearing jewellery or carrying large amounts of cash in crowded areas. Valuables can be kept in a hotel safe, but do insist on a receipt. While shopping, ensure that shopkeepers make out a bill and process your credit card in front of you. There have been incidents of tourists being drugged and robbed, especially on trains, so it is not advisable to accept food or drink from strangers. Padlock your luggage to your seat during train journeys. It is a good idea to let your hotel know where you are going. Do not stray into deserted areas alone, especially at night, and avoid hitchhiking.

DANGER AREAS

The border areas are high-security zones, so when trekking or travelling in the Himalayan regions make sure you have an Inner Line Permit (*see p758*). The state of Jammu and Kashmir has had long-standing militant activity and much of the state is unsafe for visitors (*see p154*). Bihar too has a law and order problem and there have been incidents where buses and cars have been held up and robbed. Before travelling to such areas, it is a good idea to contact the state tourism department in Patna (*see p215*) for up-to-date information on the law and order situation. In restricted areas always travel in groups rather than on your own. Communal unrest and even riots are usually confined to the crowded older parts of cities. It is best to avoid these areas if the political situation is uneasy, or during important religious festivals which attract large crowds.

A police jeep

A hospital ambulance

SECURITY

Since the attack on New York's World Trade Center in 2001, security has been tightened throughout India, especially at airports and railway stations. Bag-and body-searches are usual when entering cinemas and public auditoria. Never pick up unattended baggage, and inform the police immediately if you notice anything suspicious.

NARCOTICS

Since the 1960s, India has been part of the "hippy trail" with marijuana easily available. With the arrival of Ecstasy and other harder drugs in the 1990s, particularly in places such as Goa, the law has tightened considerably. Possession, trafficking and use of narcotics (including marijuana) is now banned by law and punishable by tough jail sentences. Drug convictions lead to a minimum sentence of ten years without parole or remission. Never carry anything for strangers or check in their luggage for them at airports. A Narcotic Drugs and Psychotropic Substances Court has been established specifically to try drug-related offences.

WOMEN TRAVELLERS

Women, both indian and foreign, face a certain amount of unwanted male attention, even though "eve-teasing" is today a punishable offence. When travelling alone, the problems women encounter can range from being stared at to more active harassment such as suggestive comments and body contact in buses and crowded places.

Take your cue from Indian women who continue with their independent lifestyles despite such annoyances. Dress modestly, and avoid wearing clothes that can be thought of as provocative. Ignore men lounging at street corners and, if you find their attention offensive, approach the nearest policeman. Avoid walking about alone in quiet places and in the rougher parts of cities. When hiring a car or taxi, ask the hotel to book it for you and note the licence plate number. Hitch-hiking is not advisable under any circumstances.

When queuing for train or cinema tickets, use the "ladies' lines" which are usually much shorter. On many buses and on some trains there are "ladies only" seats or compartments to make the journey that much safer.

LEGAL ASSISTANCE

LEGAL PROBLEMS are rare for travellers, but if you do find yourself in a legal tangle, contact your embassy immediately. Always carry your passport and keep a photocopy handy. Do not hand over your travel papers to anyone until your embassy has been informed. Some insurance policies also cover legal costs for emergencies such as accidents.

PUBLIC TOILETS

WAYSIDE public toilets have poor hygiene and are best avoided. However, although few in number, those known as "Sulabh Shauchalayas" located on city roads are a great civic invention. Attractively designed, they are easy to spot, extremely clean and charge a nominal fee for use. They are, however, of the

Indian "squatting" variety and can be difficult to use if you are not used to them. Some hotels allow non-residents to use their toilets. It is always a good idea to carry your own toilet paper with you, just in case.

HOSPITALS AND MEDICAL FACILITIES

DO TAKE OUT comprehensive medical insurance before arriving in India. **MASTA** (Medical Advisory Service for Travellers Abroad) in the UK can give a health update for travellers to India. The larger cities have reasonably good government and private hospitals and nursing homes, with 24-hour services equipped to handle casualty and emergency cases. It is always best to contact your embassy for their list of approved hospitals, clinics, doctors and dentists. They may also be able to advise on sourcing safe, screened blood for transfusions. If in doubt, the local **Indian Red Cross Society** is one of the safest options for blood transfusion. Even in the best hospitals, it is imperative to ensure that staff use disposable syringes.

A local pharmacy or chemist shop

PHARMACIES

MOST BIG MARKETS in all cities and towns, have well-stocked pharmacies (or chemist shops, as they are known in India). They stock toiletries, sanitary napkins and tampons, baby food and disposable nappies. Pharmacists can also suggest simple remedies. For special medication, it is advisable to carry a prescription, or show the packaging with the generic name if the brand is unfamiliar, so that the pharmacist can suggest a suitable alternative. Antibiotics are sold only by prescription. Most pharmacies are open between 9am and 7:30pm. Many hospitals have 24-hour pharmacies.

HEAT AND HUMIDITY

NORTHERN, CENTRAL and western India are scorchingly hot *(see pp38–9)* during the summer (Apr–Jun). The east and the south are not as hot but can get oppressively humid during the monsoon.

Take things easy for a few days to get acclimatized. To prevent dehydration, drink plenty of fluids and add an extra pinch of salt to the food. It is wise to stay indoors during the hottest part of the day, and if outdoors wear a wide-brimmed hat and sunglasses, and use sun screen to protect your skin. Prolonged exposure to the sun can cause heat stroke, a serious condition with high body temperature, severe headaches and disorientation.

Polyester clothing and covered shoes and socks trap perspiration and can lead to prickly heat and fungal infections, especially in the scalp, between the toes, (athlete's foot), in the groin and other sensitive parts of the body. Prickly heat powder and anti-fungal ointments are available at most pharmacies. The best prevention is to wear light, loose-fitting cotton clothing and open sandals, and to always dry yourself well after washing.

In winter (Oct–Feb), cities have a lot of smog, as the pollution in the air tends to settle. This aggravates chest infections, and asthmatic travellers should always carry their own medication, although inhalers, such as Asthaline, are readily available on prescription.

FIRST AID KIT

A BASIC FIRST AID kit for travelling in India should include all personal medication, aspirin or painkillers for fevers and minor aches and pains, tablets for nausea, antiseptic and calamine lotion for cuts and bites, an anti-fungal ointment, plaster and crêpe bandages, a pair of scissors, insect repellent and tweezers. It should also have antihistamines for allergies, anti-diarrhoea tablets, water purification tablets, disposable syringes and a thermometer. Most of these items are also

Hand fan

available at Indian pharmacies. They stock effective herbal remedies as well; buy only brands that have been recommended by a reliable practitioner or pharmacist.

STOMACH UPSETS AND DIARRHOEA

D IARRHOEA, usually caused by a change of diet, water and climate, is common among visitors. Spicy Indian food often leads to digestive disorders, in which case it is best to eat plain boiled food until the attack subsides. Most importantly, drink plenty of liquids. Avoid raw salad, cut fruit, cold cuts, fresh juice and yogurt. Instead of tap water opt for bottles of sealed mineral water of well-known brands, such as Evian or Himalayan, if available. Most international brands of carbonated drinks are widely

Bottled mineral water

available, and fresh coconut water is also safe. Street food often looks tempting, but it is safer to avoid it unless it is hot and freshly cooked in front of you.

A good pharmacist can suggest standard diarrhoea medication, though if the attack is severe, it is best to consult a doctor. Also, take a course of oral rehydrating salts (ORS), commercially available under the popular Indian brand names of Electral or Electrobion. An effective home-made remedy is half a teaspoon of salt and three teaspoons of sugar mixed in boiled water.

FOOD AND WATER-BORNE DISEASES

V ISITORS MUST guard against dysentery. Bacillary dysentery lasts about a week and is accompanied by severe stomach pains, vomiting and fever, whereas amoebic dysentery has similar symptoms but takes longer to manifest. If left untreated, this can become chronic. The same is true of giardiasis, a type of diarrhoea caused by contaminated water. Vaccination against hepatitis A is advisable before travelling to India. The symptoms of this unpleasant disease include fever, fatigue, severe chills and jaundice. The only treatment is rest and a strictly controlled diet. Other waterborne diseases such as cholera (prevalent in flood-hit areas) and typhoid can also be prevented with vaccines.

Intestinal worms, common in most tropical areas, include tapeworms which are found in under-cooked meats and green leafy vegetables. Others, such as hookworms, can be contracted by walking barefoot on contaminated soil. Ensure that all food is well-cooked and always wear sturdy shoes in remote or waterlogged areas. A course of medication can be taken for worm infestation, which normally does not recur.

Green coconut-water, good for soothing an upset stomach

SEXUALLY TRANSMITTED AND OTHER INFECTIOUS DISEASES

AWARENESS OF sexually transmitted diseases such as HIV, which causes Acquired Immune Deficiency Syndrome (AIDS), is high in India. However, screening at blood banks is still unreliable, and for blood transfusions it is best to contact the **Indian Red Cross Society** *(see p765)*. Hepatitis B is also transmitted through infected blood, sexual contact, unsterilized needles, tattoos and shaves from roadside barbers. However, it can be prevented with a vaccine. Using a condom is essential for protection against all sexually transmitted diseases.

General precautions to follow are: before an inoculation, buy a disposable syringe, or insist that a new syringe and needle is unwrapped in front of you. Never have shaves from roadside barbers and stay away from seedy-looking beauty parlours, as you can pick up infections during manicures and pedicures. Any procedure using needles, such as tattooing and ear-piercing, is best avoided in places where hygiene is dubious.

Vaccination against tetanus is essential when travelling. Tuberculosis (TB), though common in India, is not a great risk for visitors. Meningitis, spread through droplet infection, is a more real threat – it needs immediate medical attention. Symptoms include fever, stiff neck and headache.

RABIES

ANIMAL BITES, especially from dogs and monkeys, can cause rabies. Clean the bite with an antiseptic solution and seek medical help at once, as treatment involves a course of injections, even if you have been bitten by a pet dog. There is a vaccination which partially protects against rabies, but this is only advised if you are going to high-risk areas. You should only take this vaccine if your doctor advises it.

INSECT-BORNE DISEASES

MALARIA IS prevalent in most parts of India during the summer and monsoon (Jul–Sep). The parasite is carried by mosquitoes, and symptoms include shivering followed by high fever and sweating. Seek medical help immediately. You should take a preventive course of anti-malarial drugs before, during and after your trip. For information on malaria medication, call a travel clinic or MASTA *(see p765)*.

Another serious mosquito-borne disease is dengue fever, with symptoms similar to malaria, including severe pain in the joints and muscles, and rashes. Seek medical treatment if you think you might be infected. Japanese B Encephalitis is a dangerous viral infection of the brain, and there have been outbreaks in rural areas. It is also mosquito-borne and its symptoms are similar to malaria, often with a loss of consciousness. Though there is a vaccine for this disease abroad, it is not always found in India.

To guard against mosquito bites, use mosquito repellent gadgets and a net over the bed while sleeping. If outdoors in the evenings, wear shoes and clothes that cover the arms and legs, and rub mosquito repellent cream on exposed skin. As a rule, carry mosquito repellent cream with you at all times.

Mosquito repellent coil and cream

CUTS AND BITES

INSECT BITES are common, especially in areas prone to heavy rainfall, such as the coasts, the Nilgiri Hills, parts of Kerala and the northeastern states. To avoid insect and ant bites, it is best not to sleep on the ground. Ticks, lice and mites are another problem, since they are carriers of typhus and Lyme's disease. Use insect repellents, avoid staying in places with poor hygiene and, if bitten, apply antiseptic cream. An antihistamine is the best antidote if you get stung by a wasp or bee. Rainforests are usually infested with bloodsucking leeches that attach themselves to the skin. Never try and pull them off since their heads remain embedded in the skin. A very effective way of getting them to drop off is to sprinkle them with salt, or touch them with a lighted cigarette. Clean the bite and apply an antiseptic.

Snake bites are rare, but if bitten, tie a tight crêpe bandage or tourniquet above the bite to prevent the blood flowing. Keep the limb immobile, note the time of the bite, and seek immediate medical help. Scorpion stings can also be serious, and the victim can sometimes go into shock. The treatment is similar to that of snake bite.

If you are stung by a jellyfish whilst swimming, vinegar or lemon juice, calamine lotion and antihistamines help reduce the pain and swelling. Clean the area with an antiseptic lotion.

ALTITUDE SICKNESS

A LACK of sufficient oxygen at altitudes higher than 2,500 m (8,202 ft), can cause attacks of Acute Mountain Sickness (AMS). This can lead to severe headaches, dizziness and loss of appetite. These often subside within a day or two, but if the symptoms persist beyond 48 hours, you should descend immediately to a lower altitude and seek medical attention. Though some doctors recommend Acetaolamide (Diamox) and dexamethasone, they are controversial drugs and should not be used.

A few tips to avoid AMS are: ascend slowly; once above 3,000 m (9,842 ft), do not increase camping altitude by more than 300 m (984 ft) a day; drink plenty of fluids; and avoid alcohol and sedatives.

Banking and Local Currency

**Logo, State
Bank of India**

INDIA PROVIDES A range of accessible banking facilities and money exchange services, with English speaking staff at the counters. These facilities are available in all the larger cities, at international airports, major banks and hotels, travel agencies and registered moneychangers. Touts might offer enticing exchange rates, but they are illegal operators and should be avoided. Traveller's cheques are the safest way to carry money, but always keep some cash for telephones, tips, transport and purchases, especially when travelling in smaller towns or off the beaten track, where credit cards and traveller's cheques are not always accepted.

BANKS AND BANKING HOURS

MOST INTERNATIONAL banks now have branches in all the larger cities across the country. The Indian bank with the largest distribution network is the **State Bank of India**, though there are other major banks with a national presence. The services they offer include international money transfers.

Banking hours are between 9.30/10am–2pm (Mon–Fri), and 9.30/10am–12 noon (Sat). Try to arrive early to avoid the long queues. Banks are always closed on regional and national holidays *(see p35)* and occasionally they shut down without any notice at all in response to public protests or strikes.

CHANGING MONEY

IN INDIA, banks offer the best exchange rates, though most good hotels also change money for resident guests. **LKP Merchant Financing Ltd** is a reliable foreign exchange broker, and there are numerous other brokers who also change money at the official rates for major international currencies. Rates of exchange are subject to

fluctuation, so check any national daily newspaper for the current rate. The "black-market" in India, operating through literally thousands of touts, offers much better rates than the official ones, but it is safer to go to authorized dealers.

TRAVELLER'S CHEQUES

TRAVELLER'S CHEQUES are convenient, safer to carry than large amounts of cash, and give better exchange rates than currency. All major brands of traveller's cheques are accepted in India, with **American Express** and **Thomas Cook** being the most widely used, and US dollars and pounds sterling the most widely exchanged currencies. Banks have the lowest surcharge and give the best value. They charge a small fee per cheque so using large denomination cheques is more economical. Traveller's cheques can be en-cashed easily in large cities and towns. Smaller towns, though not all of them, also have registered dealers. Keep a record of the serial numbers of cheques, as well as the proof of purchase slips, in case of loss or theft. Also, be

---

DIRECTORY

STATE BANK OF INDIA

Delhi
11 Sansad Marg.
((011) 374 7533.
Mumbai
State Bank Bhavan,
Madame Cama Rd.
((022) 202 2426.
Kolkata
Middleton Row.
((033) 29 8341.
Chennai
Circle Top House,
21 Rajaji Salai.
((044) 522 0141.

CITIBANK

Delhi
Jeevan Bharti Building,
124 Connaught Circus.
((011) 371 4211.

Mumbai
Bandra Karla Complex.
((022) 653 5757.
Kolkata
Kanak Building,
Chowringhee Rd.
((033) 288 2484.
Chennai
2 Clubhouse Rd.
((044) 846 1151.

HSBC

Delhi
15 Kasturba Gandhi Marg.
((011) 373 0001.
Mumbai
SK Ahire Marg,
Worli.
((022) 498 0000.
Kolkata
25-A Shakespeare Sarani.
((033) 280 5888.
Chennai
30 Rajaji Salai.
((044) 524 0205.

BUREAUX DE CHANGES

American Express
A Block, Wenger House,
Connaught Place,
Delhi.
((011) 332 5221.
Oriental Building,
364 Dr Dadabhai Naoroji
Rd, Mumbai.
((022) 204 3361.
21 Old Court House St,
Kolkata.
((033) 248 6282.
187 Anna Salai,
Chennai.
((044) 852 4320.

Thomas Cook
C–33, Connaught Place,
New Delhi.
((011) 335 6571.
Dr Dadabhai Naoroji Rd,
Fort, Mumbai.
((022) 204 8556.

Chitrakoot Building,
230–A Acharya Jagadish
Chandra Bose Rd,
Kolkata.
((033) 247 5378.
Ceebros Centre,
45 Monthieth Rd, Egmore,
Chennai.
((044) 855 4696.

LKP Merchant Financing Ltd
M-56, Connaught Place,
New Delhi.
((011) 373 9797.
22/B Cusrow Baug,
Colaba Causeway,
Mumbai.
((022) 288 5586.
Shop 41–A, Park
Mansions, 57A Park St,
Kolkata.
((033) 216 0055.
G14 & 15A Spencer Plaza,
769 Anna Salai, Chennai.
((044) 852 3393.

sure to keep records of encashment, as you will need these should you wish to reconvert rupees to other currencies when leaving the country.

CREDIT CARDS

CREDIT CARDS ARE now widely accepted in most big hotels, restaurants and department stores. The most common are VISA, Master-Card, Diner's Club and American Express. Air and rail tickets can also be paid for by credit card, and cash advances can be made at the parent bank. For example, Citibank account holders can directly access their account with their Citibank Card. However, many smaller establishments, even in the bigger cities, only accept cash.

Credit card-related fraud is on the increase, so keep your cards safe, and insist that receipt vouchers are made out in front of you.

ATM SERVICES

MOST FOREIGN, and many Indian, banks in large cities have 24-hour ATMs (automatic teller machines). Instructions are displayed in English, and cash is dispensed in rupees. Check with your bank at home which Indian banks will accept your ATM card, as not all machines are compatible. Some ATMs will dispense cash against credit cards. Cards with a PLUS or CIRRUS symbol are accepted at the following ATMs: Citibank, Standard Chartered, and Hong Kong and Shanghai Bank.

CURRENCY

THE INDIAN rupee (Rs) is divided into 100 paisas. The most commonly used coins are 50 paisa, 1, 2, and 5 rupee coins. Currency notes are available in denominations of Rs5, 10, 20, 50, 100, 500 and 1,000. Be careful not to mix up the 100 and 500 rupee notes as they look very similar. Beware of accepting torn or damaged notes, as shops and even banks are often reluctant to accept or exchange them. Banks often give notes stapled together in large packs. Ask them to remove the staples for you as you will find it difficult to do it yourself without tearing the notes.

Foreign nationals are not permitted to bring or take Indian currency into or out of the country.

Bank Notes
All currency is minted by the Reserve Bank of India. The notes have either Mahatma Gandhi or the Ashoka lion symbol on one side.

10-rupee note

20-rupee note

50-rupee note

100-rupee note

500-rupee note

Coins
Visitors should always keep some loose change handy. Some older variations of these silver coins are still in circulation.

50 paisa

1 rupee

2 rupees

5 rupees

Communications

Public telephone booth sign

THE INDIAN POSTAL SYSTEM is fairly efficient, with a wide variety of options from registered post to reliable courier services, offered by post offices countrywide. Telecommunications systems are sophisticated even in smaller towns: all main hotels have business centres and most markets have shops or booths from where international calls can be made, e-mails sent and the internet accessed. A range of English-language newspapers and magazines are available, and foreign newspapers and magazines are sold in bookshops, particularly in the main cities.

Postage stamps in 5-rupee denomination

INTERNATIONAL AND LOCAL TELEPHONE CALLS

ALL MAJOR HOTELS offer subscriber trunk dialling (STD) for calls within India, and international subscriber dialling (ISD) for international calls. Trunk calls can also be booked from private telephones. Calls made from STD/ ISD booths, identified by their yellow signage, are much cheaper than at hotels. Rates are fixed for international calls, but STD rates depend on the distance of the city called and the time of day when the call is made. Calls are cheapest between 11pm and 6am. Medium rate is between 8pm and 11pm. Local calls made from public booths take new 1 rupee coins for every three minutes.

The government-run Mahanagar Telephone Nigam Limited (MTNL) sells phone cards for both STD and ISD calls. For calling within India, you can buy cards for Rs200, Rs500 or Rs1,000. There is a 5 per cent service charge. For more information call 1600 11 1111 or contact the main telephone exchange offices. The service is currently available in Delhi and Mumbai.

MOBILE PHONE RENTALS

MOBILE PHONES can easily be rented from service counters at the international airports, as well as at registered offices located in most large cities. In Delhi, Airtel and Essar are the main

service networks, while in Mumbai, the networks are provided by BPL and Orange. Kolkata has Usha and Modi Telstra, and Chennai has RPG Cellular and Skycell. Hire charges range between Rs100 and Rs300 per day inclusive of a SIM card (rates are higher for roaming cards) and a handset. If hiring a handset, you will pay a fairly sizeable deposit, which is refundable.

FAX, E-MAIL AND INTERNET FACILITIES

FAX AND TELEGRAPH services are available at main post offices and also at local STD/ISD booths which, though often more accessible, have higher charges. The business centres of all large hotels also have centralized telecommunication services, which only residents can use.

The internet is widely used in India. Most large hotels offer net access to guests in their business centres, while privately operated internet cafés with the latest facilities can be found in markets and shopping areas in most large cities. Even smaller towns

usually have enterprising hole-in-the-wall internet outlets. Some main post offices and many STD/ISD phone booths also offer internet facilities. All outlets have fixed hourly or half-hourly rates.

POSTAL SERVICES

THERE ARE MANY different services offered by the Indian Postal Service – general or registered mail, parcel post, poste restante, and a special courier service known as EMS-Speed Post.

Letterboxes are colour coded: local letters, green; metropolitan and other cities, as well as international mail, red; and Quick Mail Service (QMS) yellow. Post offices are open Monday to Friday between 10am and 5pm, and on Saturdays until noon. Some services, such as registered mail, close earlier.

Letters sent poste restante are held at the **General Post Office** for up to one month, and you will need some form of identification – preferably your passport – to retrieve your mail. The same service is also provided by **Foreign Post Offices** in the four main cities, as well as American Express in most major cities. Envelopes should be addressed with the surname underlined and in capitals, c/o Poste Restante, followed by the name and address of the post office.

Internet café, Maurya Sheraton hotel, Delhi

Parcels sent overseas cannot exceed 20 kg (44 pounds). Check the details at the post office. Book Post is a cheaper option for documents, books and printed material. The maximum weight is 5 kg (11 pounds). Some hotels sell stamps and may offer to post letters and parcels. Always be sure to stick stamps and post postcards and letters yourself.

ADDRESSES

IN INDIA, addresses always begin with the house number, followed by the name of the street, and finally the city and its pin code. The newer residential localities are divided into blocks, and the block number usually appears with the house number. Therefore, B4/88 Safdarjung Enclave would be: house number 88 in the B4 block of Safdarjung Enclave Colony. Each state and city has its own variations, which can be confusing and hard to decipher, especially if trying to locate a house number. Often there may not even be a road sign. If you are lost, a passer-by will always help, but the best bet is to get directions from a taxi or rickshaw driver.

A typical post box

COURIER SERVICES

COURIER SERVICES are available across the country, but less so in rural and remote areas. While it is better to ship larger items such as furniture by regular land, sea or air cargo, letters, documents or smaller parcels are best sent through a courier agency, even though it may be more expensive. **United Parcel Service (UPS)**, **Federal Express** and **DHL Worldwide Express** are international courier agencies, with a widespread network all over India and the world. Many shops offer to send purchases by courier, but except for the government emporia and well-known establishments, you will be doing so at your own risk.

NEWSPAPERS AND MAGAZINES

INDIA'S LEADING national English language newspapers include *The Times of India*, *The Hindustan Times*, *The Indian Express*, *The Hindu* and *The Asian Age*. In the east, *The Statesman* and *The Telegraph* are widely read. There are other regional newspapers as well that provide local news. Many international newspapers, such as the *International Herald Tribune* and the *Financial Times*, are available alongside Indian weekly news magazines, such as *India Today* and *Outlook*. *Time* and *Newsweek* are available in large cities. For local news and cultural events, the city sections of the newspapers give reasonable coverage.

TELEVISION AND RADIO

THE STATE-RUN Doordarshan television network has programmes in English and the major regional languages.

With the arrival of satellite TV, the choice has become much wider. Cable TV is now also available everywhere, for international channels, such as the BBC World Service, CNN, Discovery, National Geographic and the Hong Kong-based Star network. Star Sports and ESPN are exclusive sports channels and Channel V and MTV are the main music channels. Most Indian TV channels show popular Hindi films or song and dance sequences; there are many regional Indian language channels as well.

India also has a wide radio network, with programmes in English and local languages. It is still the best form of communication, especially in the rural areas. Radio and television listings and reviews can be found in all major daily newspapers.

USEFUL DIALLING CODES AND NUMBERS

- To make an inter-city call, dial the STD code of that city and the local number. For Delhi, dial 011; Mumbai, 022; Kolkata, 033; Chennai, 044.
- To make an international call (ISD), dial 00, the country code, area code and the local number.
- Country codes: UK 44; France 33; USA & Canada 1; Australia 61; Ireland 353; New Zealand 64; South Africa 27; Japan 81.
- Dial 180 to book a trunk call in the country, and 186 to book an international call.
- Dial 197 to obtain a phone number in Delhi, Mumbai, Kolkata and Chennai.

TRAVEL INFORMATION

MOST INTERNATIONAL visitors to India arrive by air, though road and ferry links also connect India and her neighbours, such as Pakistan, Bangladesh, Nepal and Sri Lanka. Travelling within the country is possible by air, train, road and, in some places, either ferry or boat. Even remote regions are accessible. However, whatever your mode of transport, you should be prepared for delays and

The Maharaja, mascot of Air India

unexpected detours that may test your patience. The state-run Indian Airlines has the widest network of air routes. Private airlines, such as Sahara and Jet Airways, also cover a number of cities and offer excellent services. Indian Railways is one of the world's largest networks, and travelling first class is a good way to see the country. The long-distance air-conditioned luxury coach is another option.

ARRIVING BY AIR

ALL MAJOR international airlines fly to India, usually as stopovers on air routes between the East and West. Air India is India's international carrier. North American and European airlines such as British Airways, Lufthansa, KLM/Northwest, Air France and Swissair have regular flights to some or all of India's four main cities – Delhi, Mumbai, Chennai and Kolkata. There are also connections to the Far East and Australia, offered by Thai Airways, Singapore Airlines, Malaysian Airlines, Japan Airlines, Qantas and Cathay Pacific. Flights to destinations in the Gulf and Central Asia are offered by Emirates, Air Lanka and Gulf Air.

Austrian Airlines and Virgin Atlantic currently fly only to Delhi, though they plan to introduce flights to other Indian cities in the near future. Delta, South African Airways and Kenya Airlines fly only to Mumbai. Lufthansa flies to Bangalore, while Emirates flies

to Hyderabad; and Malaysian Airlines flies to both these cities. In addition, Air Lanka also flies to Thiruvanathapuram and Tiruchirapalli.

INTERNATIONAL FLIGHTS AND AIRPORTS

INDIA'S FOUR main international airports are at Delhi, Mumbai, Kolkata and Chennai. Other international airports offering flights to select destinations are at Hyderabad (Kuwait, Muscat, Sharjah and Kuala Lumpur), Bangalore (Muscat, Sharjah, Singapore, Kuala Lumpur, Frankfurt and a few flights via Mumbai to Paris, London, the Gulf and New York), Goa (UK and Germany), Ahmedabad (UK and the US), Kochi and Thiruvananthapuram (the Gulf, Singapore, Sri Lanka and the Maldives). A limited number of international flights also operate from Kozhikode, Amritsar, Varanasi, Lucknow, Guwahati, Tiruchirapalli, Jaipur and Agra. These are designated "customs airports" and permit landing of charter

planes as well as certain international flights.

AIR FARES

AIR FARES vary according to the airline and the season. It is best to book tickets well in advance of the peak season (October–March). At this time of year flights to India are overbooked, as apart from tourists, Indian families settled abroad and students at universities abroad, make their annual visit home.

ON ARRIVAL

BEFORE LANDING, visitors must fill in a disembarkation form that has to be submitted along with their passport at the immigration counter.

International airports offer a range of facilities that include currency exchange counters, left-luggage services, air-conditioned visitors' lounges, duty-free shops, restaurants, business centres and rest rooms with access for the disabled. In addition, there are counters for pre-paid taxis, car rentals and mobile phone rentals. Travel agencies located within the arrivals area can help with tour itineraries, hotel reservations and onward bookings. There is also a Tourism Department information counter.

CUSTOMS

THE GREEN CHANNEL is for those who do not have dutiable goods as listed in the Immigration Certificate. The

Indira Gandhi International Airport, Delhi

Red Channel is for passengers with any goods that are liable to customs duty, including money in excess of US$2,500.

GETTING FROM THE AIRPORT

COACHES CONNECT the airport with the city for a fee. Pre-paid taxis with fixed rates can be booked from counters outside the arrivals area. Metered auto-rickshaws are also available. Make sure you agree on the fare before taking one, and ask an airport policeman to note down its licence plate number. If you have booked accommodation, check if your hotel offers a free pick-up service.

AIRPORT TRANSFERS

VISITORS who are travelling onwards to other Indian cities will need to transfer to domestic terminals. Be sure to allow enough time to get between the two terminals. At all major airports there is a free transit service from one terminal to the other. Delhi's Indira Gandhi (IG) International Airport has two terminals: Terminal I (for domestic flights) is 7 km (4 miles) from Terminal II (the international terminal). In Mumbai, the international terminal at Sahar is 4 km (2.5 miles) from the domestic terminal. Kolkata's Netaji Subhash Chandra Bose International Airport, has both the international and domestic terminals in the same building. Chennai's Aringar Anna International Airport is next door to the Kamaraj Domestic Airport. In Thiruvananthapuram, both domestic and international flights operate from the same building.

Yellow licence plate of a taxi

DL·1Y 5732

CHECK-IN

FOR INTERNATIONAL flights, check-in is usually three hours ahead of departure. Tele-check-in is allowed by some airlines for business and first class passengers. Most airlines allow an economy-class passenger 20 kg (44 pounds) in the hold and one item of hand baggage. Make sure that your luggage is within the weight limit set by your airline, as excess baggage charges can be very high.

DEPARTURE TAX

A FOREIGN TRAVEL tax of Rs500–750 (US$10–15) has to be paid when leaving India, unless already included in your ticket. Only Rs150 (US$3) needs to be paid if travelling to neighbouring countries, such as Nepal, Pakistan or Sri Lanka.

DIRECTORY

AIRLINE OFFICES

Air India
- (011) 373 1225, Delhi.
- (022) 202 4142, Mumbai.
- (033) 282 6012, Kolkata.
- (044) 855 4477, Chennai.

British Airways
- (0124) 54 0543, Gurgaon.
- (022) 282 0888, Mumbai.
- (033) 288 3451, Kolkata.
- (044) 855 4680, Chennai.

Cathay Pacific
- (011) 332 3332, Delhi.
- (022) 202 9112, Mumbai.
- (044) 852 2418, Chennai.

KLM/Northwest Airline
- (011) 335 7747, Delhi.
- (022) 838 0838, Mumbai.
- (033) 240 3151, Kolkata.
- (044) 852 4427, Chennai.

Lufthansa
- (011) 332 3310, Delhi.
- (022) 230 1933, Mumbai.
- (044) 852 6331, Chennai.
- (080) 558 8791, Bangalore.

Virgin Atlantic
- (011) 334 3290, Delhi.

Qantas
- (0124) 35 9911, Gurgaon.
- (022) 282 8794, Mumbai.

Thai Airways
- (011) 623 9988, Delhi.
- (033) 280 1630, Kolkata.

AIRPORT	INFORMATION	DISTANCE TO CITY CENTRE	AVERAGE JOURNEY TIME
Delhi: IG International (Terminal II)	(011) 565 2011	20 km (12 miles)	Road: 45–60 minutes
Mumbai: Sahar International	(022) 611 6009	30 km (19 miles)	Road: 50 minutes
Kolkata: Netaji Subhash Chandra Bose International	(033) 511 9894	20 km (12 miles)	Road: 30–60 minutes
Chennai: Aringar Anna International	(044) 234 7500	12 km (8 miles)	Road: 30 minutes
Thiruvananthapuram: International Airport	(0471) 501 537	6 km (4 miles)	Road: 20 minutes
Bangalore: International Airport	(080) 526 6233	8 km (3 miles)	Road: 20 minutes
Goa: Dabolim International Airport	(0832) 51 2788	29 km (18 miles)	Road: 50 minutes
Kochi: Kochi International Airport	(0484) 6110 115	30 km (19 miles)	Road: 45–60 minutes

Domestic Air Travel

Logo of Indian Airlines

ALTHOUGH MORE EXPENSIVE than travelling by train, air travel in India is the most comfortable and convenient mode of travel. There are as many as 115 domestic airports in India, many of which have been greatly improved in terms of technology as well as customer services. The main cities of Delhi, Mumbai, Kolkata and Chennai are very well connected to all domestic airports within the country. The national carrier is the government-run Indian Airlines which, along with its subsidiary Alliance Air, offers the widest choice of routes and the most frequent services. If you have booked internal flights before leaving for India, do reconfirm on arrival. Erratic flight timetables, flight cancellations and delays due to bad weather conditions in winter (Dec–Jan) are common, so remember to reconfirm not just your ticket but the flight timing as well.

DOMESTIC AIRLINES

THE NATIONAL CARRIER **Indian Airlines** offers the largest number of routes and the most frequent connections across the country. Two major private airlines, **Jet Airways** and **Sahara Airlines**, also connect a number of cities. India's international carrier **Air India**, has domestic flights on the Delhi–Mumbai, Delhi–Kolkata, Mumbai–Kolkata and Mumbai–Chennai routes. A few regional airlines such as Archana Airways, Jagson Airlines and Gujarat Airways with limited operations within India, fly short feeder routes. Baggage allowance is 30 kg (66 pounds) for business class and 20 kg (44 pounds) for economy class.

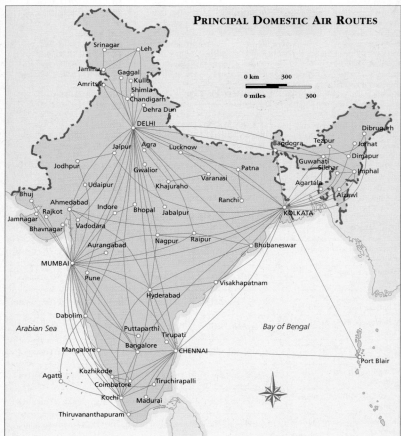

PRINCIPAL DOMESTIC AIR ROUTES

DOMESTIC AIRPORTS

AIRPORTS AT the four main cities of Delhi, Mumbai, Kolkata and Chennai, and cities such as Agra, Bhubaneswar, Hyderabad, Kochi and Bangalore have modern terminal buildings with up-to-date facilities. However, less-visited towns, such as Dehra Dun, have tiny airports with almost no facilities.

GETTING TO AND FROM THE AIRPORT

THE DISTANCE from airports to city centres varies, so it is useful to check the travel time beforehand. Also always allow time for unforeseen delays en route. Airport coaches run regularly for a fee. Pre-paid taxis with fixed rates can usually be booked from counters outside the arrivals area. Metered auto-rickshaws are also available. Make sure the meter is working, or agree on a fixed amount before taking one. If you are booking accommodation, check if your hotel offers a free pick-up service.

Indian Airlines air tickets

CHECK-IN

FOR MOST DOMESTIC flights, the check-in time is normally one hour before departure. If travelling to politically sensitive places such as Kashmir, Jammu, Leh and some of the northeastern states, security checks are more stringent and can require up to an extra half

hour. Make sure all bags are tagged, and do not carry batteries, lighters or any sharp objects, not even scissors, nail files or tweezers. As part of the security measures on some routes, you may be asked to identify your baggage on the tarmac, before boarding the flight.

RESERVATIONS

ALL DOMESTIC airlines have their own booking offices in the city, as well as a reservation counter at the airport (usually only in larger towns and cities). Tickets can also be booked through travel agents (see p759). Indian Airlines has computerized booking and flight information facilities all over the country, even in smaller towns. Tickets can be paid for in US dollars or sterling, as well as in rupees. Payment can also be made by credit card. All airlines require you to reconfirm your ticket 72 hours before flight departure. There are special fares for infants and children, and students carrying an international student ID card get a 25 per cent discount, Indian nationals aged 65 and above get a 50 per cent discount. All ticket cancellations must be done at least two hours before your flight. Some airlines will waive a cancellation charge if given sufficient notice. If you fail to do so, you may lose the full value of the ticket. If flights are cancelled or delayed you can claim a refund.

(see p759)

DIRECTORY

DOMESTIC AIRLINES

Indian Airlines
- (011) 462 0566, Delhi.
- (022) 202 3031, Mumbai.
- (033) 211 0810, Kolkata.
- (044) 855 3039, Chennai.

Air India
- (011) 373 1225, Delhi.
- (022) 202 4142, Mumbai.
- (033) 282 6012, Kolkata.
- (044) 855 4477, Chennai.

Jet Airways
- (011) 685 3700, Delhi.
- (022) 285 5788, Mumbai.
- (033) 229 2227, Kolkata.
- (044) 841 4141, Chennai.

Sahara Airlines
- (011) 335 9801, Delhi.
- (022) 283 5617, Mumbai.
- (033) 282 7686, Kolkata.
- (044) 826 3629, Chennai.

Airport Enquiries
- (011) 567 5433, Delhi.
- (022) 615 6367, Mumbai.
- (033) 211 6944, Kolkata.
- (044) 855 3397, Chennai.

TRAVEL PACKAGES

INDIAN AIRLINES offers two travel packages if the payment is in US dollars. The "Discover India Fare" for 15 or 21 days is about US$500–750, and allows unlimited travel with certain route restrictions. "India Wonder Fare" for about US$300 is for seven days of travel in one region. It does not include the Andaman Islands. The private airlines, Jet Airways and Sahara Airlines, also offer special packages for foreign nationals. The "Visit India" offer by Jet Airways ranges from US$550–800 for economy class travel over a period of 15–20 days. Sahara Airlines has a similar "Discover India" package, which costs US$475–725 for 15 or 21 days. Airlines have started offering discounts on tickets, and value add-ons such as free stays and gourmet dining to beat the competition, so it is worth doing a little research before purchasing your ticket.

Passengers waiting in the airport lounge at Delhi

Travelling by Train

Indian Railways logo

FOR MOST VISITORS, train journeys add a fascinating new dimension to their experience of India – there are few better ways of getting to know the people and see the countryside. The Indian Railways network is the fourth largest in the world, with tracks running over 108,513 km (67,427 miles) and connecting 7,150 stations. Over 10,000 trains run daily, transporting an average of 13 million people. Trains are always crowded, so try to book your tickets in advance. There are computerized ticket counters at railway stations, and most travel agents can also get tickets for you.

THE RAILWAY NETWORK

THE INDIAN RAIL network, established in 1853, runs the length and breadth of the country. The network is divided by region, and there are 16 zonal divisions. Delhi is served by Northern Railways, Mumbai by both Central and Western Railways, Kolkata by Eastern Railways and Chennai by Southern Railways. All four cities have either two or three main train stations, so it is important to confirm from which station your train is leaving. Indian Railways employ over 1.6 million people, making them the world's largest single employer.

TRAINS AND TIMETABLES

OF THE THREE kinds of trains (passenger, express and mail), it is best to take the air-conditioned express trains, as they have fewer stops and offer better facilities and services. They provide fast and punctual connections to some of India's most important cities. The Rajdhani Express links the capital,

Delhi, to most of the large cities such as Mumbai, Kolkata, Chennai, Thiruvananthapuram and others. The superfast inter-city train, the Shatabdi Express, connects main cities with many well-known tourist destinations, with connections such as Chennai–Bangalore, Delhi–Dehra Dun and Delhi–Agra. The recently opened Konkan Railway (see p437), on the western coast, offers speedy connections to Maharashtra, Goa, Karnataka and Kerala.

Each train is known by its name and number. When consulting the information board, do check both, since there may be more than one "Shatabdi" for example. Trains have first and second class chair-cars, and two- and three-tiered sleeper coaches. If these are air conditioned, the fares increase. Sleeper coaches have berths that fold back during the daytime to provide seating. Fares for express trains such as the Shatabdi or Rajdhani include meals and mineral water, and the Rajdhani also provides its overnight passengers with

bedding. Food items, such as biscuits, and reading material are sold by vendors en route. Try to get a window seat or the uppermost sleeper. Toilets are of the Indian and Western style. Carry your own toilet paper, soap and towel.

Train timings are subject to change. The printed timetable is available in most station bookshops, or check the very useful official website: www.indianrail.gov.in

TRAIN TICKETS, FARES AND RESERVATIONS

IT IS IMPORTANT TO make train bookings well in advance for a confirmed reservation. Railway stations now have computerized ticket counters, otherwise the hotel travel counter or a travel agent can arrange them for a fee. Never buy tickets from touts, as this is both illegal and unreliable.

Tickets can be booked up to six months in advance, and reservation fees are nominal. You will be asked for your age and gender and these details will appear on your ticket, along with the coach and seat number. Once at the station, find your coach and check for your name and seat number, which are usually posted on a list outside the coach. If wait listed, arrive at the station early to take advantage of any last-minute cancellations. The stationmaster will help.

If reserved tickets are unavailable, you can get an RAC (Reservation Against Cancellation) ticket. This allows you to board the train and get seating space. You may eventually be given a berth, but there is no guarantee. Reserved tickets can be cancelled, for a fee. If cancellation is more than a day in advance, a nominal fee is charged. Up to four hours before train departure, the charge is 25 per cent of the fare, and less than that, you forfeit 50 per cent of the fare.

Stations at Delhi, Mumbai, Kolkata and Chennai as well as other major cities have special booking counters for foreigners, called "Tourist Bureaus", within the main

Churchgate Station, Mumbai, during rush hour

booking offices. These provide information regarding reservations, itinerary and other inquiries. Payments may be made in US dollars or pounds sterling, or the rupee equivalent, and you must show your passport. You get priority reservation and are exempted from reservation fees. At New Delhi Railway Station, the International Tourist Bureau is located on the first floor of the main hall.

INDRAIL PASS

To TRAVEL extensively around India, the Indrail Pass is a convenient option. It offers unlimited travel across the country, and is available for second or first class and for different periods (half-day, 2 days, 4 days and anywhere between 7 and 90 days). It can be bought in India or abroad, but must be paid for in foreign currency. Indrail Passes are available from sales agents abroad, as well as overseas offices of Indian Airlines and Air India. They are also available at tourist counters and Tourist Bureaus at major railway stations, and from travel agents in Delhi, Mumbai, Kolkata and Chennai. Unless you do a lot of travelling, the pass may

Official porter in red jacket

work out more expensive than buying individual tickets. Even with a pass you will still need to reserve your seat.

SERVICES

At THE STATION, look for the licensed porters or coolies who wear a red shirt and an armband with a metal tag bearing a licence number on it. Porters are always well-informed about delays and platform changes which may not be announced on the board. Note your porter's number because you could lose sight of him in the crowds. His tariff varies according to weight, although Rs10–20 per item is acceptable. Indian stations are crowded and confusing. Keep your cool and keep an eye out for pickpockets who take advantage of the chaos. Railway waiting rooms (especially first class ones) are good places to spend the night if you are stranded. You need a valid ticket or Indrail Pass to use this facility. There are also waiting rooms only for women travellers. Left luggage facilities, called cloakrooms, are offered at most stations.

Station canteens are reasonably clean and provide mineral water and hygenically-packed meals.

DIRECTORY

RAILWAY ENQUIRIES

W www.indianrail.gov.in

Delhi
C *(011) 131.*
Mumbai
C *(022) 131, Western Railways.*
C *(022) 134, Central Railways.*
Kolkata
C *(033) 220 3545.*
Chennai
C *(044) 131, 132, 133.*

BOOKING CENTRES FOR SPECIAL TRAINS

Darjeeling Himalayan Railway
West Bengal Tourist Centre, Baba Kharak Singh Marg, Delhi.
C *(011) 374 2840.*
Matheran Hill Railway
Govt of India Tourist Office, 123 M Karve Rd, Mumbai.
C *(022) 203 3144.*
Palace On Wheels
Bikaner House, Delhi.
C *(011) 338 1884.*
The Shivalik Queen
Divisional Railway, Ambala.
C *(171) 261 0800.*
Blue Mountain Railway
Sangheetha Travel Agency, Ooty.
C *(0423) 44 266.*
Royal Orient
Tourism Corp of Gujarat Ltd, Baba Kharak Singh Marg, Delhi.
C *(011) 336 4724.*
Fairy Queen
Rail Museum, Delhi.
C *(011) 688 1816.*

SPECIAL TRAINS

You can travel in style on board some of India's luxury trains, particularly the **Palace on Wheels** and the **Royal Orient**. Both operate week-long tours from September to April. The former covers mainly Rajasthan, and includes Jaipur, Udaipur, Jaisalmer and Agra. The latter goes through Rajasthan to Ahmedabad in Gujarat. The **Fairy Queen**, a 150-year old restored steam engine, is the oldest in the world, featuring in the *Guinness Book of Records*. It runs from Delhi to Alwar between October and February. India's quaint "toy trains", connecting numerous hill stations with tracks laid across precariously steep slopes, include the World Heritage **Darjeeling Himalayan Railway** (see p294) which goes from New Jalpaiguri to Darjeeling. The **Shivalik Queen** runs between Kalka and Shimla (see p110–11), while the Kangra Valley Railway connects Pathankot and Jogindernagar (see p120). Another toy train, the **Matheran Hill Railway**, runs from Neral Junction to Matheran (see p472), while the luxurious **Blue Mountain Railway**, built in 1898, offers spectacular views of the Nilgiri Hills, up to Ooty (see p605).

Royal service in the Palace on Wheels

Travel by Road

**Logo of the Auto-
mobile Association**

INDIA HAS AN EXTENSIVE network of major and minor roads, as well as a number of well-maintained national highways, linking all the major cities. Driving is on the left, with right-hand drive cars. Indian traffic, particularly in the cities, is very chaotic, so visitors are strongly advised to hire a driver along with a car, rather than trying to negotiate the roads themselves. A number of international car rental companies, hotels and taxi stands provide excellent car rental services. In case of breakdowns, the remarkably ingenious roadside mechanics can solve most problems.

DRIVING LICENCES

IT IS NECESSARY to have an international driving licence to drive in India. If not, the **Automobile Association of India (AAI)** has several branches across the country that will issue a temporary licenses, provided you have a passport and an ordinary driving licence. This may take a day or two. You must be over 25 years old and there is a refundable insurance deposit of Rs10,000. You may be asked to take a driving test.

ROADS

INDIA HAS A NETWORK of over 3,000,000 km (1,860,000 miles) of roads. The primary arterial roads, the national highways, cover 52,000 km (32,240 miles) and carry 45 per cent of the country's total traffic. State highways run a total length of 128,600 km (79,732 miles). The National Highway Authority of India is in the process of improving links between the country's four major cities: Delhi, Mumbai, Chennai and Kolkata.

The countryside is criss-crossed with numerous major and minor roads of very variable quality. Some village roads are little more than dirt tracks riddled with potholes, so be prepared for a dusty, bumpy ride.

Most highways and major roads are well-equipped with tourist facilities such as motels, petrol pumps and STD/ISD telephone booths. Midway refreshment points and *dhabas (see p179)* are well-marked with hoardings, and provide clean food as well as toilets.

CAR RENTALS

SEVERAL REPUTED car rental companies, such as **Avis**, **Budget**, **Europcar** and **Autoriders Rent-a-Car** now operate in India. They offer both chauffeur-driven and self-driven cars, which can be hired at travel desks in larger hotels, tourist offices, travel agencies or directly from the companies themselves. Most of them operate through collaborations with local companies. Avis is in partnership with the Oberoi Group; Budget operates through Sapna Travel Agency while Europcar International has an arrangement with Travel House. Autoriders Rent-a-Car, a reliable Indian company, was earlier a partner of Hertz. Local hire services and private taxis are also available in cities from taxi stands and agencies. These can usually be arranged by your hotel or through a reliable local travel agent *(see p759)*.

HIRING A CHAUFFEUR-DRIVEN CAR

INDIAN ROAD AND traffic conditions can be a trial for anyone unused to these conditions. Hiring a driver is much the safest option, and not all that expensive. All taxis as well as agency-hired cars are distinguished by their yellow number plates with black lettering. Most taxi stands also have private cars for hire, which are usually white with yellow number plates. All car rental companies with "All India Tourist Permits" have licenses for interstate travel.

All drivers are familiar with Indian traffic rules, but insist on getting a driver who knows the area that you plan to visit. Also, do test both the driver and the car before embarking on a long journey.

Chauffeur-driven cars for long-distance travel usually charge per kilometre, with a minimum of 250 km (155 miles) per day plus additional charges per extra kilometre. If you are travelling only one way, additional charges will be levied for the return journey on the assumption that the car will return empty. Costs are also dependent on the car model and the region of hire, with air-conditioned cars being the most expensive. For travelling outside the state or city boundaries, extra charges as well as interstate

Traffic on Marine Drive in Mumbai

taxes are added. If the driver has to stay overnight, you will have to pay for his board and lodging, so it is best to negotiate a flat rate in advance. Car hire is more expensive in hill regions.

In certain areas, shared taxis are available for long journeys, which are cheaper. Certain companies require foreign nationals to pay in foreign currency, though most accept payment in rupees as well.

A typical Indian Oil pump at a filling station in Delhi

FUEL

Highways and main roads have well-maintained filling stations (or petrol pumps as they are called) at regular intervals, usually closer to towns. Many pumps in cities as well as on highways are open 24 hours, and carry both leaded and unleaded petrol, as well as diesel, which is cheaper. Most cars run on petrol, though some of the newer models also use diesel, as do most taxis. Unleaded petrol is not available everywhere, especially in remote areas, so ensure that your fuel tank is full when visiting these areas. Many petrol pumps in the main cities are now equipped with utility stores where mineral water, soft drinks, magazines and snacks are sold. Often they also have telephone booths and toilets.

Since 2001, most taxis, autorickshaws and buses in Delhi and Mumbai are being run on CNG (Compressed Natural Gas), in an effort to tackle the severe air pollution caused by vehicular emissions.

MAPS AND ROAD SIGNS

The Automobile Association of India, the Survey of India and the State Tourism offices provide good maps, brochures and information on all cities and regions in India. However, the placement of road signs is often erratic, and at times they are in the regional language rather than English. It is fine to stop and ask for directions, repeatedly if necessary – people are always happy to help.

RULES OF THE ROAD

If you plan to drive in India, you need to ensure that you are well accustomed to the chaotic traffic conditions. Though there are established traffic rules, such as lane driving and discreet use of high-beam lights, more often than not these are not followed. Vehicles drive on the left-hand side of the road, but often, you will find a stray car – or cow, for that matter – coming at you on the wrong side of the road.

On the highways, beware of trucks, who often use muscle power to force you off the road while overtaking. As a rule, stay clear of buses and trucks.

Few drivers adhere to the rules for overtaking, which is meant to be from the right. Many vehicles often overtake from the left, with no prior warning. Avoid night driving on highways unless absolutely necessary, as a lot of heavy traffic (especially trucks) use them then. Also, never offer lifts to strangers, as this could prove to be very dangerous. It is wise to make liberal use your horn. If you are unlucky enough to be caught speeding, or jumping a red light, a fine is payable on the spot.

In cities, ensure that your car is parked only in an authorized parking area, otherwise it may be towed away to the nearest police station, and released only on the payment of a heavy fine. Parking attendants should hand you a parking slip, with the parking charges printed on it. Charges are usually between Rs5 and Rs10.

Travelling by Bus, Coach and Ferry

Logo of the India Tourism Development Corporation (ITDC)

INDIA HAS AN EXTENSIVE bus and coach network, offering excellent connections to most cities as well as to the remotest parts of the country. Buses refer to the ordinary transport corporation-run vehicles, which are cheaper and ply interstate or within cities. Coaches are usually much more comfortable, with air conditioning. These are often hired out for guided tours and also ply between cities. The advantage of travelling by bus or coach rather than by train is that you have a wider choice of timings, stops and itineraries. A busy network of passenger ferries serve places along India's east and west coasts, and luxury cruises link the mainland to the Lakshadweep Islands as well as to the Andamans.

STATE TRANSPORT CORPORATION-RUN BUSES

THE VARIOUS STATE transport departments in India run extensive interstate bus services. The Interstate Bus Terminus (ISBT) in Delhi is the main point of departure for Punjab, Haryana, Himachal Pradesh, Uttar Pradesh and Rajasthan. Buses for Agra leave from Sarai Kale Khan, near Nizamuddin railway station. Mumbai's Central Bus Stand provides information on the Maharashtra Road Transport Corporation that runs services to all major cities within the state, as well as to Goa, Ahmedabad, Vadodara, Mangalore, Indore and Hyderabad. Kolkata too has an extensive network throughout West Bengal and the neighbouring states of Bihar, Orissa and Sikkim. Guwahati is the main entrance point for visitors to the northeastern states. The Assam State Transport Corporation runs buses within the city and to the neighbouring states. The Paltan Bazaar Bus Stand provides the best information on these services.

Computerized advance bookings can be made at the **Government of India Tourism Offices** in the four metropolitan cities.

Most interstate bus terminals are chaotic places, so do arrive early to book tickets. Then check at the enquiry counter to find the stand from where your bus will depart. Finally, be prepared for a lot of jostling as passengers tend to push to get the best seats.

STATE TOURISM-RUN COACHES AND PACKAGE TOURS

SOME OF THE best guided tours, both within cities and to neighbouring towns, are offered by the Government of India Tourism Department and the various state tourism departments (see p761). The Government of India Tourist Offices in most cities offer the latest information on schedules, routes and pick-up points. It is a good idea to buy tickets in advance though they can also be bought on the spot. Coach operators can also customize itineraries keeping in mind the size of the group and the destination.

Coaches run by the tourism departments are, by and large, clean, uncrowded and comfortable. Coach tours organized by them tend to include a guide, so you are also less likely to be surrounded by "freelance" guides or touts at your destination.

PRIVATE OPERATORS AND PACKAGE TOURS

PRIVATE TOUR operators and travel agencies also offer a wide variety of coach trips for visitors. These are good value for money, especially if you have a tight budget and limited time.

Agencies usually use either 18 seater or 35 seater super deluxe air-conditioned coaches with pushback seats. Tariffs depend on the quality of service and the itinerary. The ticket price will often include a guide as well as an overnight stay at a hotel as part of the package. Most travel agents have a partnership with luxury coach companies who pick up tourists from designated hotels. Reservations can be made either through the hotel's reception desk or from one of their recommended local agencies.

BUS AND COACH TICKETS AND FARES

BUS OR COACH fares are cheaper than train fares and depend on the kind of transport you opt for. Travel by "ordinary" bus is not advisable for tourists. Deluxe buses are somewhat better, but, if you are travelling in summer, the best option are the deluxe air-conditioned (a/c) coaches. Many deluxe coaches, known as "video coaches" blast loud music and Hindi movies through the

A luxury coach, run by Rajasthan Tourism

Passenger ferry near the Gateway of India, Mumbai

night. If you have an option, it is better to take a deluxe coach that is not a "video coach". If opting for a deluxe or a/c deluxe bus, you can book your ticket in advance and also reserve your seat.

The charges for bus and coach package tours often include airport transfers, road taxes, overnight stays, guides and any monument or museum entry fees en route.

FERRIES AND BOATS

Rajasthani coach ticket

FERRY CONNECTIONS link some of India's more exotic island destinations, as well as cities along the coasts. They are available from Kolkata to Chennai and Mumbai to Goa. There is also a catamaran service between Mumbai and Goa, although it is suspended during the monsoon season from July to September. Passenger liners also operate from both Chennai and Kolkata to the Andaman and Nicobar Islands, as well as from Kochi to Lakshadweep. Many luxury cruise fares include meals on board, ferrying charges between the ship and islands, sightseeing, lagoon cruising and land accommodation. These are very popular, so it is advisable to book at least two months in advance.

Two passenger liners, the *MV Nancowry* and *MV Akbar*, run by the **Shipping Corporation of India** (SCI), operate between Chennai and Port Blair in the Andaman Islands, once every ten days, and another SCI ship sails to Port Blair once a month from Visakhapatnam. Within the

Andamans, there are four passenger-cum-cargo ferries for transport from Port Blair to the other islands.

Ships also ply between Kochi and Lakshadweep.

S.P.O.R.T.S., the Society for Promotion of Nature Tourism and Sports, the official tourist agency of the Lakshadweep Islands, operates two ships, the *MV Bharatseema* and the *MV Tipu Sultan*, between Kochi and Lakshadweep. The Goa Tourism Development Corporation *(see p761)* operates river cruises within the state, whereas in Kerala, half- or full-day backwater cruises are organized by the Kollam (Quilon) District Tourism Promotion Council *(see p634–5)*. The Kerala Tourism Development Corporation in Kochi *(see p761)* also organizes cruises through the state's beautiful backwaters, on vessels ranging from luxury houseboats in traditional *kettuvallams* (rice boats) to modern 12-seater safari boats.

In Goa and Kerala, travelling by boat is often quicker than going by car. Ferries connect the mainland to nearby islands, such as Ernakulam to Willingdon Island. In Lakshadweep and the Andamans, they offer the only link for people travelling between the islands. In the northeastern states, ferry rides on the River Brahmaputra are available at Guwahati. In Varanasi, boats can be hired at the ghats on the River Ganges. Mumbai has taxi boats plying between the Gateway of India and Elephanta Island.

Local Transport in Cities

A regular taxi meter

Transport options vary from city to city. Most large cities have reliable bus, taxi and auto-rickshaw services. The main cities also have suburban trains that provide speedy connections to areas within city limits. There is also a wide variety of other transport available, especially in the smaller towns and in the old quarters of cities where it is better to opt for a small, light vehicle to cut through narrow congested lanes. Cycle-rickshaws, auto-rickshaws, vikrams (larger versions of auto-rickshaws), tempos and jeeps can be found in most cities, and in some areas horse-drawn carriages *(tongas)* and camel carts are still in use.

TAXIS AND AUTO-RICKSHAWS

Yellow-topped black taxis operate in most cities except Kolkata, where they are completely yellow, and Bangalore, where they are totally black. These metered taxis can be hailed in the street or hired from the local taxi stand.

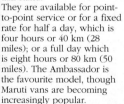

An auto-rickshaw, cheap, fast and sometimes hair-raising

They are available for point-to-point service or for a fixed rate for half a day, which is four hours or 40 km (28 miles); or a full day which is eight hours or 80 km (50 miles). The Ambassador is the favourite model, though Maruti vans are becoming increasingly popular.

Private cabs (some of which are air conditioned), are usually white in colour, and are also available at some of the regular taxi stands. In some cities, there are no yellow-topped taxis, but private taxis can be hired from agencies or hotels. Recently, Radio Cabs have been introduced in some cities such as Delhi and Mumbai. These are more expensive than the ordinary cabs, because they are air conditioned.

The ubiquitous auto-rickshaws (popularly called autos, scooters, or *phat-phats*) are the most common mode of transport in most places. Autos are more economical than taxis, but be prepared

for some hair-raising drives – they love squeezing between buses. In Delhi and Mumbai, the anti-pollution drive has seen the introduction of vehicles run on Compressed Natural Gas (CNG). Taxis and autos that have converted to CNG usage have a green band across the usual yellow and black body. All new autos run on CNG and are painted yellow and green, instead of yellow and black.

FARES AND METRES

All taxis and autos have meters, though fares fluctuate according to the prevailing price of fuel. Often, meters are not updated and drivers are required by law to carry a rate (tariff) chart listing both the old and current fare, based on the rate per kilometre. Night charges are higher than day fares and payment is extra for luggage. Drivers are notorious for overcharging passengers. The most common argument is that the meter is not working. It is best to firmly negotiate in advance, and insist on seeing the tariff chart. You can also negotiate a flat rate

before getting in. Carry some small change, as drivers often claim not to have return change. They are also prone to taking you via a long route so, if possible, try to find out the best route to take.

BUSES

Though city bus networks are very extensive, travelling by these buses is not a pleasant experience. Unable to cope with the large numbers of commuters, buses are overcrowded, and you will have to battle your way to even buy your ticket from the conductor. Buses that are full rarely stop at bus stops, which are usually seen full of waiting commuters. Drivers are known for their reckless driving. Even the so-called luxury buses drive at break-neck speed. Unless absolutely necessary, it is best to use some other form of transport.

SUBURBAN TRAINS AND METRO RAILS

Mumbai has the best suburban train network in India, providing efficient and affordable connections. However, it is extremely overcrowded and the rush hour is best avoided. Women should use the "ladies only" compartments. There are

The conductor standing at the door of a crowded city bus, Kolkata

Motorcycle taxis, a convenient way of getting around in Goa

three main lines, the most popular of which leaves from Churchgate and goes past Mumbai Central and Andheri. The others begin at Victoria Terminus (VT).

In Chennai, the surburban trains offer fast connections from Egmore to Central Station or George Town, and to Guindy or the airport.

India's first underground metro railway is in Kolkata. Limited routes in the northern and southern sectors are open, and the lines are still being extended. The service is clean and efficient and trains run between 7am and 10pm everyday. The main stations are situated opposite the Oberoi Grand and near Dr M Ishaque Road. Certain sections of Chennai's local above ground trains, the Mass Rapid Transit System (MRTS) are operational, while Delhi's metro, still under construction, is expected to be ready in 2004.

MOTORCYCLES AND BICYCLES

OFTEN THE BEST way to explore smaller towns and cities and their environs, is by motorcycle or bicycle. In Goa, motorcycle taxis are distinguished by their yellow mudguards and white number plates, and are available everywhere. If you prefer to travel independently, motorcycles are also available for

hire on a daily basis. Towns such as Pondicherry, Hampi, Belur and Halebid, can be explored by bicycle, available for rent at reasonable rates.

OTHER MODES OF TRANSPORT

OTHER TRANSPORT OPTIONS include minibuses, cycle-rickshaws and horse-drawn carriages. Cycle-rickshaws are a popular and practical means of transport to traverse the congested pockets of the old quarters of cities. They are more plentiful in smaller towns, where they can easily manoeuvre through narrow bylanes and *galis*. It is best to negotiate rates in advance, though some of them may have a flat rate for fixed routes. Tempos are battery-powered wagon-like vehicles, equipped with seats in the rear half. Uncomfortable and overcrowded, they charge flat rates for fixed routes. Horse-drawn carriages (*tongas* or *ikkas*) are also very common in small towns and around railway stations, and offer leisurely

rides. In Rajasthan, camel carts are also available – they offer a novel, if jerky, journey.

Jeeps and vans can be conveniently hired from cities (*see p779*), for short trips to explore the environs and neighbouring towns. They are also the main form of transport in Ladakh. Jeeps are also the best way of exploring the hills. Many areas have shared jeep taxis, which work out cheaper than private jeeps. A flat rate is usually charged, which includes any tolls en route. Private cars are often not allowed in hill towns, where the easiest options are to hire cycle-rickshaws or to explore the area on foot.

ROAD NAMES

IN MOST CITIES, especially in the four main cities, many roads which were named after Raj-era figures, have been renamed after well-known Indian and international figures. This might cause some confusion, as maps often carry the newer names, while locals usually refer to the road by the old name. When in doubt, it is best to ask two or three people, and cross-check the directions that you are given.

Hand-pulled rickshaws, found only in certain areas of central Kolkata

General Index

Acknowledgments

Dorling Kindersley would like to thank the following people whose contributions and assistance have made this book possible.

MAIN CONTRIBUTORS

ROSHEN DALAL has a PhD in Ancient Indian History from the Jawaharlal Nehru University, Delhi, and is the author of *A History of India for Children*.

PARTHO DATTA teaches Indian History at a college in Delhi University.

DIVYA GANDHI is an environmentalist and geographer, currently doing doctoral research at the University of Michigan.

PREMOLA GHOSE has travelled extensively, especially in Madhya Pradesh and Maharashtra. She is the Programme Officer at the India International Centre, Delhi.

ASHOK KOSHY is a senior civil servant who has spent many years in Gujarat and Kerala.

ABHA NARAIN LAMBAH is an architectural conservationist, who is the Director of Bombay Collaborative, a pioneering firm in the field of urban design and conservation in Mumbai.

ANNABEL LOPEZ is a practising architect as well as an architectural historian who has co-authored the book *Houses of Goa*.

SUMITA MEHTA is a journalist and travel writer based in Delhi, who has worked on conservation projects in Rajasthan.

RUDRANGSHU MUKHERJI is a leading columnist, journalist and author based in Kolkata

MEENU NAGESHWARAN runs a travel agency, Incent Tours, in Delhi.

RUSHAD R NANAVATTY is a keen mountaineer who has trekked extensively in northern, central and eastern India.

IRA PANDE is a Managing Editor with Dorling Kindersley in Delhi. She has also been a professor at Punjab University, Chandigarh.

USHA RAMAN is a freelance writer and editor based in Hyderabad.

JANET RIZVI, a PhD from Cambridge, is a leading authority on Ladakh and author of two books, *Ladakh, Crossroads of High Asia* and *Trans-Himalayan Caravans: Merchant Princes and Peasant Traders in Ladakh*.

RANEE SAHANEY is a well-known travel writer, and regular contributor to *outlooktraveller.com*.

DEEPAK SANAN is a senior civil servant who has spent many years working in Himachal Pradesh. He has written extensively on the region.

DARSANA SELVAKUMAR has a post-graduate degree in Ancient Indian History and archaeology.

SANKARSHAN THAKUR is a senior journalist and author of a book on Bihar.

SHIKHA TRIVEDI is an authority on traditional crafts. She is presently working with India's leading television news channel.

LAKSHMI VISWANATHAN is a Bharat Natyam dancer based in Chennai. She also sits on the governing body of the Music Academy Madras, one of South India's leading cultural organizations.

CONSULTANT

George Michell is an architectural and cultural historian specializing in India. Among his many publications are books on Hindu temples, royal palaces, the Vijayanagar Empire and Deccani art and architecture.

ADDITIONAL CONTRIBUTORS

John Abraham, Anvar Alikhan, Usha Balakrishnan, Manini Chatterjee, Anuradha Chaturvedi, Rta Kapur Chishti, Anna Dallapiccola, Dharmendar Kanwar, Ranjana Sengupta.

ADDITIONAL ILLUSTRATIONS

Naveed Ahmed Vali, Ampersand.

ADDITIONAL PHOTOGRAPHY

Akhil Bakshi, Benu Joshi, Aditya Patankar, Ram Rahman.

PROOF READER AND INDEXER

Anita Roy, Ranjana Saklani.

FACT CHECKING

Ranee Sahaney.

EDITORIAL, DTP AND CARTOGRAPHIC ASSISTANCE (DK LONDON)

Brigitte Arora, Jo Cowen, Emily Hatchwell, Jason Little, Casper Morris, Dave Pugh, Vivien Stone.

PUBLISHING MANAGER

Anna Streiffert.

ART DIRECTOR

Gillian Allan.

PUBLISHER

Douglas Amrine.

SPECIAL ASSISTANCE

Mahesh Buch; Tarun Chhabria; Manosh De; Sharada Dwivedi; Asit Gopal; GM Kakpori; Vijayan Kannampilly; Meenal Kshirsagar; Ritu Kumar; Anna Madhavan; Aditi Mehta; Milan Moudgill; Sheema Mukherjee; Sunil Philip; Nihar Rao; Anita Roy (Publisher, DK India); KJ Ravinder; Samit Roychoudhury; Shweta Sachdeva; Lalit Sharma; Parvati Sharma; Tara Sharma; Yuthika Sharma; Dr A Jaya Thilak; Maharao Brijraj Singh of Kotah; Maharaja Gaj Singh II of Jodhpur.

American Institute of Indian Studies.
Archaeological Survey of India, New Delhi.
Architecture Autonomous, Goa: Gerard da Cunha and Amit Modi.
Architectural Conservation Cell of the Associated Cement Companies Ltd.
Aurobindo Ashram.
Central Cottage Industries.
Department of Culture, Government of India: Kasturi Gupta Menon, Joint Secretary.
Department of Tourism, New Delhi: Rekha Khosla, Director; Ashwini Lohani, Director.
Indian Institute of Public Administration.
Indian Museum, Kolkata: Dr SK Chakravarty, Director; Chanda Mukherjee.
Indian National Trust for Art and Cultural Heritage: Martand Singh.
Maharana Mewar Historical Publications Trust, Mewar: Shriji Arvind Singhji, Chairman and Managing Trustee.
Mehrangarh Museum Trust, Jodhpur: Trustees; Mahendra Singh, CEO.
Sangath: BV Doshi.
Tibet House, New Delhi.
Tibetan Institute of Performing Arts, Dharamsala.
Wildlife Trust of India: Vivek Menon.
World Wide Fund: Krishna Kumar.

SPECIAL ASSISTANCE IN PHOTOGRAPHY
Archaeological Survey of India, New Delhi: Komal Anand, Director General;
    Dr KM Poonacha, Director (Monuments);
    Dr RC Aggarwal, Director (Museums);
    Mr Bakshi, Assistant Director (Monuments).
Crafts Museum, New Delhi: Dr Jyotindra Jain.
Government Museum, Chennai: R Kannan.
Khuda Baksh Oriental Library, Patna: HR Chigani.
Mathura Museum, Mathura: Jitendra Kumar.
Maharaja Fatehsingh Museum Trust, Baroda.
National Museum, New Delhi:
    RD Chowdhourie; U Dass; JC Grover;
    Dr Daljeet Kaur.
Prince of Wales Museum of Western India, Mumbai: Dr Kalpana Desai, Director.
Rampur Raza Library, Rampur: WH Siddiqi.
Sarabhai Foundation, Calico Museum of Textiles, Ahmedabad:
    DS Mehta, Secretary; A Sen Gupta.
Sanskriti Museum, New Delhi: OP Jain.
State Museum, Patna: Naseena Akhtar.

Dorling Kindersley would like to thank all regional and local tourist offices throughout India for their valuable help.
Particular thanks to Chandana Khan, Secretary, Tourism & Culture Department, Hyderabad; Victoria Memorial, Kolkata: CR Panda; Indian Museum, Kolkata: Shyamalkanti Chakravarti; The Asiatic Society, Kolkata: Ms Sarkar; Kunjo Tashi; Rajiv Mehrotra; Tenzin Geyche Tethong, Secretary to His Holiness, the Dalai Lama, Dharamsala; Chief PRO, Central Railways, Mumbai: Mukul Marwah; Quila House, Patna: BM Jalan; Secretary, Department of Cultural Affairs, Thiruvananthapuram.

FOOD PHOTOGRAPHY
Dorling Kindersley would like to thank Bhicoo Manekshaw; Farsaan, Uma Singh, New Delhi; Marriott WelcomHotel, New Delhi: Monisha Mukundan, PR Manager, Vijay Wanchoo, General Manager; Oberoi Hotel, New Delhi: Aruna Dhir, Manager Communication, Bruno Cerdan, Executive Chef and Chef Pankaj Mehra, Kandahar; for personally supervising the presentation of the food layouts for the book.

PHOTOGRAPHY PERMISSIONS
Dorling Kindersley would like to thank all those at temples, forts, palaces, museums, restaurants, shops and other sights, for their cooperation and contribution to this publication. The Publisher would also like to thank the following for their assistance and kind permission to photograph at their establishments: Brindavan, New Delhi; Crafts Museum, New Delhi; Good Earth, New Delhi; Annie Kumar, Regalia, India Tea House, New Delhi; Ramji Bharany, Bharany's, New Delhi. Particular thanks also to Urmila Dongre and Vivek Narang for their kind permission to photograph their products.

PICTURE CREDITS
t = top; tl = top left; tlc = top left centre; tc = top centre; tr = top right; cla = centre left above; ca = centre above; cra = centre right above; cl = centre left; c = centre; cr = centre right; clb = centre left below; cb = centre below; crb = centre right below; bl = bottom left; b = bottom; bc = bottom centre; bcl = bottom centre left; br = bottom right; bra = bottom right above; d = detail.

The publishers are grateful to the following individuals, picture libraries and companies, for permission to reproduce their photographs:

AMR Vastra Kosh Trust, New Delhi 317bra/bl/c.
Arya, Aditya 214c, 217c, 225cr, 233t/c/b, 239cr, 242bl/br, 246t, 252t, 261c, 338c, 457b, 459t, 748t, 777b.

Bagla, Pallava 17b, 19trb, 24-25d, 28tr, 65bl, 162cl, 193b, 221cl, 250b, 371c, 377cb, 641b.
Bahuguna, Manu 16t, 34b, 75b, 85c, 328 & 329, 408, 430tr, 445b, 454tr, 471bl, 521b, 543br, 556, 559c, 570t, 572t, 607t, 616, 618b, 619t, 622t, 646c, 750b, 752t, 753t.
Bakshi, Akhil 14c, 28b/br, 29bl, 186b, 219br, 391b, 436t, 770b, 778b.
Balan, M 18crb, 30br, 369b, 520b, 550t, 624, 626b, 627t, 628tl/tr, 629bl, 630tl/tr, 631tl, 633c/bl, 634-635c, 635tl/br, 640tl/cb, 641tl/cr, 646br, 647t/c/br, 648c, 649t/c, 650cl, 652b, 654t/c, 656t/c, 657t/cr/c, 688b, 719b.
Barkakoti, Kakoli 324c, 325br, 333t.
Bartholomew, Pablo/Mediaweb India 262cl, 262-263c.
Behl, Benoy 42t, 47tr, 136t/c, 137tr/b, 138tr/cl/cr/br, 139tl/cl/b, 140b, 141bl/b/br, 143cl/clb, 144tl/tr/cl/cr/b, 145tr/c/b, 146c/b, 147cl/b, 151c/b, 476tr/cb, 477t/c, 478t, 479t/b, 480t/cl/c/cr/clb/crb/bl/b/br, 481cr/bl/br, 565b, 566c.

Bhargava, Subhash 23clb, 56bl, 179c, 346br, 358c/bl, 364b, 367t/c, 373t, 377cl/bc/b, 378t, 379t, 380tl, 381b, 386t, 387t, 390b, 398tr, 401bl, 402t/b, 403t, 404t, 407t, 751t.
Bhojani, Namas 442.
Bihar School of Yoga Ganga Darshan, Munger, 217t.
Brown, Dean K 78b.
Chandola, Ashish 62t, 368b.
Chhabra, Tarun 607cl.
Chishti, Rta Kapur 209t/c/clb/crb/bl/br (a, b, c, d), 583t/c/cb/crb, 673cr (a, b, c, d, e, f).
Chopra, Tarun 14t.
Chundawat RS 13t, 18br, 19cl/bra, 64cla, 136b, 140t, 142c, 143t, 152t, 153b, 186t, 188t, 192c/cb, 194b, 255crb, 295b, 321c, 371b, 423br, 520crb.
Costumes & Textiles of Royal India, Ritu Kumar 30cl.
Crafts Museum 80tr/c/cb, 81tl/tc/crb, 252c.
Crampes, Gilles 123cl.

Das, Tanmoy 318bl.
Das, Vivek 262bl/br.
Dasgupta, Prosenjit 316tl.
Deen Dayal Trust 665clb.
Dilwali, Ashok 112t, 113c/br, 114b, 115tr, 116c, 117cr, 118c/b, 120t/c/b, 121t/c, 122t, 123tr, 124c, 125c/b, 126t/c, 127bl, 128c/bl, 129t/c/b, 130trb, 131br, 158t, 163c, 170t, 180tl, 182tl, 187t, 189b, 191b, 259b, 299crb, 300t, 301b, 302t/b, 618t/c, 619c, 620clb, 621b, 623t/c/b.
Dix, Thomas 226, 230 & 231, 236tr/c, 237b, 346-347c, 350, 371cr, 392 & 393, 394t, 397tr/bl, 414tr/cl/cr, 415tr/cl/b, 418tl/tr/c/cb, 419tr/c, 422t, 424 & 425, 464, 476tl/c/b, 477b, 478b, 481t/cl/crb, 679br.
DK Classic Cookbook 718t.
DK Picture Library Andy Crawford 27tr/bl, 141cr (Wimbledon Buddhist Temple, London); Geoff Dann (Ashmolean Museum, Oxford) 679ca; Gables 21c; Ellen Howdon (Glasgow Museum, Glasgow) 467c; Dave King 163b; Linda Whitwam 646tl.
Dongre, Urmila 3 (inset), 24tl/c, 25tl/b, 44t, 597tr, 746tl/cl (a, b, c, d).
Dube, DN 50cla, 172c, 173cr, 180tr, 181tl, 182tr/c.
Dubey, Suman 132 & 133.

Fotomedia Picture Library 32-33c, 55tr, 59(inset), 142t, 152b, 196b, 284, 286b, 433(inset), 471cl; Jyoti M Banerjee 193t, 334c; Francois Gautier 396cl, 441br, 754t/b, 783t; Nihal Mathur 406tr; Sanjiv Mishra 37b; Sundeep Nayak 368c; Christine Pemberton 22cl, 158b, 195t, 306tr, 308b, 443b, 444t, 454c, 473tr, 718b; Otto Pfister 130bl, 368t/cb, 369tl/c; Sanjay Saxena 185c, 303c, 355bl; Satish Sharma 467t; Mathew Titus 55tl; Henry Wilson 203br.
Gaur, RK 61b, 258t, 326b, 333b, 336cl,
Ghosh, Ashim 48bl, 183br.
Gruisen, Joanna van 18clb/bl/bla, 19tr, 34t, 64tl, 65tr, 127c, 138clb, 142cl/cr, 193cb, 224c, 254t, 288tr, 319t/c/b, 326c, 330tl, 388tl, 390c, 406cl, 520crc, 640tl/bl, 641tr.
Gupta, Nath 33br.
Tradition & Beyond: Handcrafted Indian Textiles, Roli Books India 2001 by Rta Kapur Chishti & Rahul Jain 317t/cl/cr (a) & (b)/br.

Husain, Fawzan 436b.
Image Bank/London 64-65c.
India Today Magazine 17c, 32tr/cl/clb/bl, 33tl/tr/cr/bl, 428b, 447b, 665cl.
Israni, Prakash 18tr, 36c, 63t, 101b, 183bl, 309c, 467b, 472c/b.
ITC Hotels/Maurya 749b.

Kaimal, Ravi 124t.
Kapoor, Prem 42c, 56br, 57br, 128t, 195bl, 632t, 639c, 748b.
Kapoor, Kanika 30-31c.
Kasliwal, Sudhir 360b, 361t/clb/bl/b, 746bl.
Khanna, Dinesh 12, 30bl, 31bl, 105b, 162tl, 163tl, 179b, 202cl/c/cr/b, 203cl/c/bl, 206cl, 207cr/bl, 313tr/br, 345t, 377c, 380tr, 421c, 437c, 438br, 439tl/tc/bc/br, 484, 494 & 495, 506b, 551t, 663tl, 665bl, 746cr.
Khazanchi, BN 15br, 34c, 36b, 37c, 327tr, 369cb.
Khokar, Ashish 28cl, 253br.
Khullar, Rupinder 30t,103b, 104b, 200 & 201, 221clb, 225b, 304, 312b, 318br, 321t/br, 458t, 459b.
Kohli, Bobby 263tl.
Kumar, Krishna 620t/cl/cr/crb, 622b.
Kumar, Poonam A 15bl.
Lewis, Karoki 204t, 207t/cl.
Mandhani, Pradeep 17t, 750t.
Mehrangarh Fort, Jodhpur 382b, 383b.
Mehta, Dalip 377bl, 299t/cr/c/clb.
Mehta Hemant/Picture India 31cr.
Mishra, Vishwanath 439bl.
Muthuraman, V 2 & 3, 6 & 7, 15t, 16b, 22b, 24cl, 25cr/br, 36t, 38b, 45bl, 47tl/bl/br, 54br, 204bl/br, 205tl/tr, 206bl, 207tr, 208t/b, 210t, 220t/b, 221b, 222c/br, 237c, 238c, 262tl, 267b, 269t, 271crb, 274trt/b, 275t, 281c, 324t, 334b, 335t/c, 516b, 517t/br, 518b, 519tl/tr, 524cr/crb/b, 535cla/cl/clb, 546 & 547, 548t/c, 551c/b, 554trb, 560t/b, 565t, 566bl/br, 569t/c/b, 571br, 576, 578t, 582t/b, 583cl/cr/clb/b, 584t/bl/br, 585t/c/b, 586tr, 587tl/tr/c, 588c, 589bl/br, 590b, 591br, 592t, 593t/c/b, 594t/c/b, 595t/bl/br, 596t/c/b, 597tl, 598b, 599t/c, 600t/c, 601t/c/b, 602 & 603, 604t/b, 605t/c/b, 606t/bl/br, 607c/cr/crb/bl/br, 608t/c/b, 609t, 610t/b, 611t/c/b, 612t/cl/cr/clb/crb/bl/br, 613t/b, 614t/b, 615t/b, 628b, 633cb, 636 & 637, 642t, 650t/clb, 652t, 653t/b, 654b, 655t/c/b, 656b, 657cl/bl/br, 753b, 762t.
Nath, Aman 45br, 50br.
Nath, Ashok 327tl, 332b, 336tc.
National Museum, New Delhi 24br, 26bla, 40, 41t/bl, 43t/br/bc, 48br, 49t, 50tl/c/clb, 51c/crb, 53bl, 76tl/tr/c/clb/bl/br, 77t, 141cl, 249b, 405cr/bl, 665br; JC Arora 52bl; RC Dutta Gupta 29tl, 42b, 44b, 52t;. P Roy 361crb (a) & (b)
National School of Drama, New Delhi 26crb.
Nehru Memorial Library, Teen Murti, New Delhi 57t.

Pasricha, Amit 18cr, 31br, 38t, 39t, 44c, 55bl, 60t, 98, 140c, 141t, 162br, 221crb, 256 & 257, 336bl/b, 337tl, 338t/b, 341(inset), 385t/cr/b, 400tr, 426b, 427t/b, 587b.
Pasricha, Avinash 28c/cr, 29cl/cr/bc/br, 102t, 313bl, 514t, 550b, 557b, 595cl/c/cr/crb/cra/bc, 772b, 775b.
Patankar, Aditya 28tl, 228tl/tr/c/b, 229t/cl/cr/b, 346tl/clb/bl, 347cr, 356tr, 372t/c, 390t, 403b, 748c.

Prabhakar, K 663tr/c/b, 665t, 666t, 667c, 669t/cr.
Prince of Wales Museum of Western India, Mumbai 450tl/tr/c/b, 451c/b.
Press Information Bureau 56t.
Rahman, Ram 72bl.
Rajamani, VK 25tr, 46tl/tr/bl/br, 46-47c, 552c/bl, 553tl/bl, 561b, 564c, 565c, 747cb.
Ramamrutham, Bharath 515 t/cl/c/ca/bl/b/br.
Rao, CR Anantha Padmanabha 652c.
Rao, E Hanumantha 19bl, 288tl, 407cb/b, 650cr.
Reshi Maryam 35t, 63b, 154t/c, 155t/c, 400tl, 430tl/c, 431c.
Rizvi, Janet 147t/cr.
Roli Books 27cl, 31tl, 236tl/b, 388b.

Sahai, Kamal 43bl.
Saith, Sanjeev 60b, 100b, 103t, 116b, 154b, 162tr, 163cb, 187b, 188c, 190t/c/b, 191t, 197c, 207crb, 209cl, 216c, 224t/b, 260t, 288c, 300b, 411c, 752b.
Sanan, Deepak 118t, 119t/c, 327b, 332t, 333c, 337cl.
Sanctuary Features & Photo Library 438cb, 439tr; Parvish Pandya 622c; Shailendra Yashwant 467cl.
Sanghvi, Hemen 23tr/cl/cr/crb/bl, 261b, 324b, 325t, 334tl, 336tl, 337tr/b, 339t/c/b.
Sankaran, R 619b.
Saran Shalini 13b, 35b, 48c, 50bl, 51tl/b, 52br, 54bl, 77c/b, 91b, 95t, 160t, 168tl, 170b, 171b, 183tl, 184b, 194t/c, 199br, 207br, 221t/tc, 240tr, 242c, 244tr/c/cb, 245t/bl/br, 248b, 251br, 374tl, 405crb, 429t, 431tl/tc/tr/bc, 685(inset), 757(inset).
Sarabhai Foundation, Calico Museum of Textiles, Ahmedabad 412tl/tr/c/b, 413t/c/b.
Satyan, TS 19br, 26tl, 27cr, 29tr, 165br (a, b), 517bl, 518tr/c, 535bl/br, 590t, 635tr, 762b.
Sekhsaria, Pankaj 369tr.
Seth, Pepita 216b, 649b.
Sethi, Ajay & Mugdha 101t, 164br, 165clb, 174c/bra, 175cl/bl, 203t, 205b, 206br, 281b, 291br, 631tr, 760t, 769bla.
Siddharth 263b.
Sinclair, Toby 7(inset), 18cl/bra, 19tl/clb/crb/b, 20tl, 25bl, 31tr, 113bl, 124b, 139tr, 155b, 157(inset), 159b, 161b, 163tr, 187c, 192t/b, 193c, 211t/b, 237t, 238t/b, 239t/cl/clb/crb/b, 254cl/clb/b, 255t, 257(inset), 261t, 288b, 289t/c/b, 291t, 292t, 298t/c, 299cl, 307t, 309t, 321bl, 322, 325bl, 326t, 330tr/c/b, 331t/cb, 335b, 336tr, 379c, 381t, 384b, 396b, 397cr, 401tr, 404b, 406tl/c/b, 407c, 416t, 423bl, 429c/b, 439bra, 461tl, 520t, 524t, 547(inset), 578b, 580tr, 621c, 631c, 634cl/br, 640c, 643tr, 644tl, 645c, 646bl, 647bl, 650crb, 670c/b, 679bc, 687t, 689t, 756 & 757, 760b, 781t.

Singh, NP 354bl.
Singh, Dhruv 394b, 396tl.
Singh, Hashmat 58 & 59, 62b, 64clb, 108, 114c, 115tl/b, 116tl/tr, 119b, 123clb/bl, 125t, 126b, 127br, 130tr/c/br, 131tl/cl/bl, 139cr, 143cr, 150t, 151t, 152c/cb, 153t, 189t, 262tr/clb, 294t, 296t, 297t/c/b, 298b, 301t, 302c, 303t/b, 345b, 377t, 381c, 395b, 397tl/crb, 688t.
Singh, Thakur Dalip 18tl, 19bc, 65cr/bra/br, 112c, 186c, 191c, 295c, 299bl, 331c, 482b, 520cl/clb.
Stock Transparency Services 460b, 466t/c, 471c, 482t, 483t.

Talwar, Amar 57bl, 65trb, 113t, 114t, 117br, 127t, 161t, 163cra, 182b, 188b, 225t, 248cr, 253cl, 428t, 430br, 431bl.
The Statesman/R De 37t.
V & A Museum, London (Courtesy of the Board of Trustees) 50tr, 53b.
Varuni, Ritu 336cr/br, 337cr.
Verma Bimla 23tl, 26tr, 27crb, 102c, 123crb/br, 162cr, 217b, 221cr, 253t/cr/cb/clb, 295t, 306tl, 308t, 309b, 312c, 320t, 398c, 431br, 470c, 679t/bl.
Wadhwa, Rajinder Kumar 313t.
Walia, BPS 101cl/cr, 103c, 104t/c, 105t/c, 106tl/tr/cl/cr/b, 107t/c/b, 121b, 123tl/t/cr (a) & (b), 141c, 199bl, 243c, 244tl/b, 245tr, 247t/c, 248tr/tl/cl, 249tl/tr, 255cr, 306b, 308cb, 310cl, 340 & 341, 396tr, 397br, 423t, 458b, 524cl.
Wedding Affair Magazine 31cl.
Whitaker, Rom 621t.
World Wildlife Fund 330cb, 331b.

Works of art have been reproduced with the permission of the following copyright holders © National Gallery of Modern Art, New Delhi 55br; Trustees of Rao Madho Singh Trust Museum, Kotah 405br; Courtesy Shriji Arvind Singhji Mewar, Chairman and Managing Trustee, Maharana Mewar Historical Publications Trust 405cl; Ramachandra Maharana, Puri, Orissa 313c; Mundrika Devi, Madhubani, Bihar 27tl;

Jacket
Anthony Cassidy/Stone/Getty Images front t, Benoy Behl front c, Dinesh Khanna front cr, Fredrik & Laurence Arvidsson front ba and spine b, Jitendra Singh spine t, National Museum spine c, RS Chundawat back, TS Satyan front clb, Urmila Dongre front cl, V Muthuraman front b.

All other images © Dorling Kindersley. For further information see: www.dkimages.com

Further Reading

HISTORY

A Discovery of India Jawaharlal Nehru, Oxford University Press, New Delhi, 1997.

A History of India (Vol 1) Romila Thapar, Penguin, New Delhi, 1990.

A History of India (Vol 2) Percival Spear, Penguin, New Delhi, 1990.

A History of South India KA Nilakanta Sastri, Oxford University Press, New Delhi, 1999.

A History of the Sikhs Khushwant Singh, Oxford University Press, New Delhi, 1991.

Alberuni's India Edward C Sachau, Routledge & Kegan Paul, London, 1988.

A New History of India Stanley Wolpert, Oxford University Press, New York, 1990.

Annals and Antiquities of Rajasthan Col James Tod, South Asia Books, Columbia, 1987.

Babur Nama: Memoirs of Babur (trans) Wheeler M Thackston, Oxford University Press, London, 1996.

Delhi Between Two Empires Narayani Gupta, Oxford University Press, New Delhi, 1981.

Freedom at Midnight Dominique Lapierre and Larry Collins, Avon Books, New York, 1955.

India: A History John Keay, HarperCollins, New Delhi, 2000.

India Britannica Geoffrey Moorhouse, Harvill, London, 1983.

India's Struggle for Independence Bipan Chandra et al, Penguin, New Delhi, 1989.

Ladakh: Crossroads of High Asia Janet Rizvi, Oxford University Press, New Delhi, 1996.

Liberty or Death Patrick French, HarperCollins, London, 1997.

Lives of the Indian Princes Charles Allen & Sharada Dwivedi, Century, London, 1985.

Plain Tales from the Raj Charles Allen, Andre Deutsch, London, 1975.

The Great Moghuls Bamber Gascoigne, Dorset Press, London, 1971.

The Great Mutiny: India 1857 Christopher Hibbert, Allen Lane, London, 1978.

The Idea of India Sunil Khilnani, Farrar Strauss Giroux, New York, 1997.

The Wonder that was India AL Basham, Rupa, New Delhi, 1967.

The Wonder that was India Part II, SAA Rizvi, Sidgwick & Jackson, London, 1987.

Tuzuk-i-Jahangiri: Memoirs of Jahangir (trans) Alexander Rogers and Henry Beveridge, London, 1909–14.

Xuanzang: A Buddhist Pilgrim on the Silk Road Sally H Wriggins, Boulder Press, Colorado, 1996.

RELIGION AND PHILOSOPHY

Buddhism Christmas Humphreys, Penguin, London, 1951.

Hinduism Kshiti Mohan Sen, Penguin, London, 1961.

Hindu Myths Wendy O'Flaherty, Penguin, London, 1974.

Manifestations of Shiva (exhibition catalogue), Stella Kramrisch, Philadelphia Museum of Art, Philadelphia, 1981.

The Bhagwadgita Robert Charles Zaehner, Oxford University Press, London, 1969.

The Ramayana and the Mahabharata Chakravarti Rajagopalachari, Bharati Vidya Bhavan, Mumbai, 1951.

CULTURE AND SOCIETY

A Taste of India Madhur Jaffrey, Atheneum Publishers, New York, 1986.

Banaras, City of Light Diana L Eck, Alfred A Knopf, New York, 1982.

Bombay: City of Gold Gillian Tindall, Penguin, London, 1992.

Bombay: The Cities Within Sharada Dwivedi & Rahul Mehrotra, India Book House, Bombay, 1995.

Butter Chicken in Ludhiana Pankaj Mishra, Penguin, New Delhi, 1995.

Calcutta, The City Revealed Geoffrey Moorhouse, Weidenfeld & Nicolson, 1971.

Dance of the Peacock: Jewellery Traditions of India Usha R Bala Krishnan & Meera S Kumar, India Book House, Mumbai, 1999.

Desert Places Robyn Davidson, Viking, London, 1996.

Eyewitness India, Manini Chatterjee & Anita Roy, Dorling Kindersley, London, 2002.

Garden of Life: An Introduction to the Healing Plants of India Naveen Patnaik, Doubleday, New York, 1993.

Hanklyn-Janklin Nigel B Hankin, Banyan Books, New Delhi, 1992.

Historical Dictionary of Indian Food KT Achaya, Oxford University Press, New Delhi, 1998.

India: A Million Mutinies Now VS Naipaul, Heinemann, Oxford, 1990.

India: A Wounded Civilization VS Naipaul, Vintage Books, New York, 1977.

Indian Cinema, Past and Present Feroze Rangoonwala, Clarion Books, New Delhi, 1983.

Madras Rediscovered S Muthiah, EastWest Books, Chennai, 1999.

May You Be the Mother of a Hundred Sons Elizabeth Bumiller, Random House Inc, New York, 1990.

No Fullstops in India Mark Tully, Viking, London, 1991.

The Great Indian Middle Class Pavan K Varma, Penguin, New Delhi, 1998.

The Muslim Community of the Indo-Pakistan Subcontinent Dr Ishtiaq Hussain Qureshi, Oxford University Press, New Delhi, 1977.

The Remembered Village MN Srinivas, Oxford University Press, New Delhi, 1996.

ARCHITECTURE

Forts Walks: Around Bombay's Fort Areas Sharda Dwivedi & Rahul Mehrotra, Eminence Designs, Bombay, 1999.

Indian Architecture Percy Brown, (2 vols), DB Taraporevala Sons and Co, Bombay, 1964

Mughal Architecture Ebba Koch, PRESTEL-Verlag, Munich, 1991.

Stones of Empire Jan Morris, Oxford University Press, Oxford, 1983.

The Moonlight Garden Elizabeth B Moynihan, Smithsonian Institution, Washington DC, 2000.

The Forts of India Virginia Fass, Collins, London, 1986.

The Hindu Temple George Michell, University of Chicago Press, Chicago, 1988.

The History of Architecture in India Christopher Tadgell, Phaidon, London, 1990.

The Palaces of India Virginia Fass and Maharaja of Baroda, Collins, London, 1980.

The Penguin Guide to the Monuments of India (2 vols) George Michell and Phillip Davies, Viking, London, 1989.

Rajput Palaces GHR Tillotson, Oxford University Press, New Delhi, 1987.

Traditional Buildings of India Ilay Cooper & Barry Dawson, Thames & Hudson, New York, 1998.

ARTS AND CRAFTS

Art of the Imperial Cholas Vidya Dehejia, Columbia University Press, New York, 1990.

A Second Paradise Naveen Patnaik, Sidgwick & Jackson, London, 1985.

Company Paintings: Indian Paintings of the British Period Mildred Archer, Victoria and Albert Museum, London in association with Mapin Publishing, Ahmedabad, 1992.

Costumes and Textiles of Royal India Ritu Kumar, Christie's Books, London, 1999.

Himalayan Art Madanjeet Singh, Macmillan, New York, 1963.

India: Art and Culture 1300–1900 (exhibition catalogue), Stuart Cary Welch, The Metropolitan Museum of Art, New York, 1985.

Indian Art Vidya Dehejia, Phaidon, London, 1997.

Indian Interiors Sunil Sethi, Taschen, Cologne, 2000.

Indian Painting MS Randhawa, and John Kenneth Galbraith, Vakils, Feffer and Simon, Mumbai, 1982.

Kalighat Paintings: Images from a Changing World Jyotindra Jain, Mapin Publishing, Ahmedabad, 1999.

Masterpieces from the National Museum Collection SP Gupta, New Delhi, 1985.

Paradise as a Garden Elizabeth B Moynihan, George Braziller Inc, New York, 1979.

Penguin Dictionary of Indian Classical Music Raghava Menon, Penguin, New Delhi, 1995.

South Indian Bronzes C Sivaramamurti, Lalit Kala Akademi, New Delhi, 1963.

The Art of India: Traditions of Indian Sculpture, Painting and Architecture Stella Kramrisch, Phaidon, New York, 1954.

The Essence of Indian Art (exhibition catalogue), Asian Art Museum of San Francisco, 1986.

The New Cambridge History of India: Architecture and Art of the Deccan Sultanates George Michell and Mark Zebrowski, Cambridge University Press, Cambridge, 1999.

The New Cambridge History of India: Mughal and Rajput Painting Milo C Beach, Cambridge University Press, Cambridge, 1992.

Tradition & Beyond: Handcrafted Indian Textiles Rta Kapur Chishti and Rahul Jain, Roli Books, New Delhi, 2000.

Traditions of Indian Classical Dance Mohan Khokar, Clarion Books, New Delhi, 1979.

NATURE AND WILDLIFE

Collins Handguide to Birds of the Indian Subcontinent Martin, Williams Woodcock, Collins Sons & Co, London, 1980.

Encyclopaedia of Indian Natural History RE Hawkins (ed), Oxford University Press, Bombay, 1986.

Flowers of the Himalaya Oleg Polunin and Adam Stainton, Oxford University Press, New Delhi, 1984.

Handbook of Birds of India and Pakistan, 2nd edition, Salim Ali and S Dillon Ripley, Oxford University Press, London, 1995.

In Danger Paola Manfredi (ed), Ranthambhore Foundation, New Delhi, 1997.

Indian Wildlife S Israel and T Sinclair (eds), APA Publications, Hong Kong, 1987.

India's Wildlife History: An Introduction Mahesh Rangarajan, Permanent Black, New Delhi, 2001.

Land of the Tiger Valmik Thapar, BBC Consumer Publishing, London, 1997.

Trees of India Pallava Bagla, Timeless, New Delhi, 2000.

LITERATURE

A Passage to India EM Forster, Harcourt, Brace & World, New York, 1924.

A Suitable Boy Vikram Seth, Viking-Penguin, New Delhi, 1993.

Gitanjali Rabindranath Tagore, Chiswick Press, London, 1912.

Heat and Dust Ruth P Jhabvala, John Murray, London, 1975.

In Custody Anita Desai, Heinemann, Oxford, 1984.

Kim Rudyard Kipling, Tuttle Publishing, Boston, 1994.

Malgudi Days RK Narayan, Viking, New York, 1982.

Midnight's Children Salman Rushdie, Penguin, London, 1991.

Such a Long Journey Rohinton Mistry, Faber & Faber, London, 1991.

Sunlight on a Broken Column Attiya Hussain, Virago Press, London, 1988.

The Far Pavilions MM Kaye, St Martin's Press, New York, 1978.

The Glass Palace Amitav Ghosh, Ravi Dayal, New Delhi, 2000.

The God of Small Things Arundhati Roy, IndiaInk, New Delhi, 1999.

The House of Blue Mangoes David Davidar, Viking in association with Weidenfeld & Nicolson, New Delhi, 2002.

The Jungle Books Rudyard Kipling, Lancer Books, New York, 1968.

The Raj Quartet Paul Scott, William Morrow and Company, New York, 1976.

The Shadow Lines Amitav Ghosh, Ravi Dayal, New Delhi, 1988.

Those Days Sunil Gangopadhyaya, Penguin, New Delhi, 1997.

Three Plays: Nagamandala, Hayavadana and Tughlaq, Girish Karnad, Oxford University Press, New Delhi, 1997.

Train to Pakistan Khushwant Singh, Ravi Dayal, New Delhi, 1988.

MEMOIRS/BIOGRAPHY

A Princess Remembers Gayatri Devi, Rupa, New Delhi, 1995.

India's Bandit Queen: The True Story of Phoolan Devi Mala Sen, Harvill, London, 1991.

Indira Gandhi Katherine Frank, HarperCollins, New Delhi, 2001.

My Experiments with Truth Mohandas Karamchand Gandhi, Navjivan, Ahmedabad, 1927.

The Hill of Devi EM Forster, Harcourt Brace, New York, 1953.

The Life of Mahatma Gandhi Louis Fischer, Harper & Row, New York, 1950.

The Tribal World of Verrier Elwin Ramachandra Guha, Oxford University Press, New Delhi, 1999.

TRAVELOGUES

Branch Line to Eternity Bill Aitken, Penguin India, New Delhi 2001.

Chasing the Monsoon Alexander Frater, Alfred Knopf Inc, New York, 1992.

City of Djinns William Dalrymple, Flamingo, London, 1994.

Elsewhere: Unusual Takes on India Kai Friese (ed), Penguin India, New Delhi, 2001.

India By Rail Royston Ellis, Bradt Publications, UK, 1997.

In the Court of the Fish-Eyed Goddess William Dalrymple, HarperCollins, New Delhi, 1998.

Sikkim: A Traveller's Guide Sujoy Das, Permanent Black, New Delhi, 2001.

Slowly Down the Ganges Eric Newby, Lonely Planet Publications, Hawthorn, 1998.

The Goddess in the Stones Norman Lewis, TransAtlantic Publications Inc, Philadelphia, 1995.

The Great Railway Bazaar Paul Theroux, Viking, London, 1995.

Travels on my Elephant Mark Shand, Penguin India, New Delhi, 1993.

Travels through Sacred India Roger Thorsons Housden, HarperCollins, London, 1996.

Travels with a Tangerine: A Journey in the Footnotes of Ibn Battuta Tim Mackintosh Smith, John Murray, London, 2001.

Glossary

ARCHITECTURE

amalaka circular ribbed stone atop a Hindu temple tower
apsara celestial maiden *(p236)*
bagh garden
bangaldar roof curved roof, like those on thatched huts in Bengal *(p290)*
baoli stone-clad stepwell, with galleries on its sides *(see vav)*
baradari 12-pillared pavilion
bhavan house or abode
bhulbhulaiya labyrinth
chaitya rock-cut Buddhist shrine
chaitya griha prayer hall in a rock-cut Buddhist shrine *(p20)*
charbagh formal Mughal garden, divided into four quarters *(p21)*
chhatri, cenotaph small ornamental pavilion or kiosk, topped by a cupola; also pavilion with a canopy, built at the site of a royal cremation
chorten Mahayana Buddhist reliquary shrine or memorial stupa
chowk courtyard in a palace or fort; also main square in a city
dargah shrine of a Muslim saint
darwaza door or gateway
Diwan-i-Aam Hall of Public Audience
Diwan-i-Khas Hall of Private Audience
dukhang assembly hall in a Mahayana Buddhist monastery
dvarapala guardian deities near Hindu temple doorways; literally, doorkeeper *(p24)*
garbhagriha womb chamber or inner sanctum in a Hindu temple
garh fort
ghat steps on river bank; also a hilly range
gompa Mahayana Buddhist monastery in Himachal Pradesh, Ladakh and Arunachal Pradesh
gonkhang temple of the guardian deities in a gompa
gopura towering pyramidal gateway in a South Indian Hindu temple complex *(p610)*
gurdwara Sikh temple *(p21)*
hamam traditional steam bath of the Turkish type
haveli large traditional town house or mansion, with inner courtyards *(p387)*
jali ornamental pierced or latticed stone screen *(p175)*
jharokha decorative projecting balcony *(p387)*
kalasha pot-like finial crowning a Hindu temple spire *(p21)*
khirkee window

kund tank or lake
lhakhang Mahayana Buddhist temple in Ladakh and Himachal Pradesh
mahal palace
mandapa pillared hall leading to a Hindu temple sanctuary
mandir Hindu temple
mani stones/mani walls stones carved with sacred Mahayana Buddhist chants
masjid mosque
mihrab arched niche in a mosque that faces west towards Mecca
pol fortified gateway
prakara wall enclosing South Indian Hindu temple compound
qila fort
salabhanjika tree nymph *(p245)*
shikhara spire of a North Indian Hindu temple *(p20)*
tharavad ancestral home in Kerala; also matrilineal clan
torana ceremonial gateway, usually leading to a religious site
tshog-khang/jokhang secondary assembly hall in a Buddhist monastery in Ladakh or Himachal Pradesh
vav stepwell in Gujarat *(p414)*
vihara Buddhist monastery
vimana multi-staged pyramidal spire above the inner sanctum of a South Indian Hindu temple
yakshi female attendant
yali fierce mythical leonine creature
yogini attendant, or manifestation, of Devi, a form of Parvati
zenana area of a palace or house where women live in seclusion

CRAFTS AND CULTURE

asanas physical postures in Yoga
Ayurveda ancient Indian system of medicine, largely based on plants *(p629)*
Baramasa series of paintings or verses depicting the seasons; literally 12 months
dhurrie woven cotton rug
ganjifa cards painted, circular playing cards *(p26)*
gharana school of classical music or dance *(p28)*
ikat textile pattern where the yarn is resist-dyed or tie-dyed before being woven *(p319)*
jauhar mass suicide by immolation practised by Rajput women, to escape dishonour at the hands of their captors
-ji honorific suffix added to a person's name
kundankari inlay work with gems *(p361)*

kushti Indian style of wrestling
meenakari enamel work *(p361)*
mela fair, fête
Natya Shastra ancient Sanskrit treatise on dance
nautanki vaudeville
pandit learned Sanskrit scholar, wise elder or priest
pattachitra religious paintings from Orissa *(p313)*
phad long painted cloth scroll from Rajasthan *(p381)*
pichhwai a vibrant form of painting on cloth from Rajasthan, depicting 27 scenes from the Krishna legend *(p399)*
qawwals Sufi musicians
raga melodic structure with a fixed sequence of musical notes
rasa mood or emotion; also essence
sati the custom of a widow immolating herself on her husband's funeral pyre
satyagraha a form of non-violent, moral protest started by Mahatma Gandhi
Shilpa Shastra ancient Sanskrit treatise on sculpture
shishya disciple
tala rhythm/rhythmic cycle in classical Indian music
thangka scroll painting framed in silk, depicting Mahayana Buddhist deities *(p123)*
thumri light classical music, sung in North India

DRESS

bindi circular dot on forehead
chappal handcrafted leather slippers; sandals
chikankari finely embroidered cotton textile from Lucknow
choli tight-fitting blouse
ghaghara/lehenga women's gathered skirt *(p31)*
juttis traditional leather shoes with pointed or upturned toes
kurta long stitched shirt *(p31)*
mukut crown
odhni/dupatta women's veil or long scarf *(p30)*
pallav end-piece of a sari *(p30)*
safa/pagri turban *(p30)*
salwar loose pantaloons, tapered at the ankle *(p30)*
sarpech jewelled turban ornament *(p665)*
sherwani long formal coat for men *(p31)*
topi cap *(p31)*
zardozi elaborate gold thread embroidery *(p171)*
zari gold thread

RELIGION

aarti Hindu prayer ritual with oil or butter lamps

ahimsa doctrine of non-violence

alams ceremonial standards used by Shia Muslims during Muharram *(p669)*

amrit divine nectar of immortality

ashram Hindu spiritual centre or religious retreat

avatar incarnation of a Hindu deity *(p679)*

bhajans Hindu devotional songs

bhakti cult of intense personal devotion to God, without going through priests

Bodhisattvas highly enlightened Mahayana Buddhist beings who refuse nirvana so that they can devote themselves to the service of others

chador ceremonial cloth to cover Muslim saint's grave; literally, a sheet

chakra discus or wheel; also Buddhist symbol of eight-spoked wheel, representing the Eightfold Path of Righteousness

darshan an auspicious sighting of a Hindu deity, religious person, temple or holy river; also formal audience given by a ruler or holy man

devadasi Hindu temple dancer

dharamshala rest house for pilgrims

dorje thunderbolt symbol in Mahayana Buddhism

dukka ablution tank in a mosque complex

Gangajal holy water from the Ganges river

gopis Lord Krishna's milkmaid companions

Hinayana "Small Vehicle" school of Buddhism practised in parts of India, Sri Lanka and Thailand, which emphasizes the impor-tance of an ascetic, monastic way of life

imam Muslim religious leader

imambara shrine of a Shia Muslim holy man; ceremonial halls used by Shia Muslims during Muharram *(p197)*

Jataka Tales stories based on legends of the Buddha's previous lives *(p480)*

jyotirlinga linga symbolizing Shiva's energy, believed to have miraculously materialized out of light; found in the 12 most sacred sites linked to Shiva

kumbh cosmic pot holding the nectar of immortality *(amrit)*

linga phallic emblem representing the Hindu god Shiva

madrasa Islamic theological school

Mahayana "Greater Vehicle" school of Buddhism which emphasizes the importance of Bodhisattvas

mandala circular diagram symbol-izing the universe, used as an aid to meditation by Buddhists

mantra meditational Hindu or Buddhist chant

matha Hindu or Jain religious centre

maya Hindu concept of illusion

moksha Hindu term for salvation

mudra symbolic hand gestures

namaaz Muslim daily prayers

navaratri nine-day fasting period preceding the Hindu festivals of Ramnavami and Dussehra

Om sacred Buddhist and Hindu syllable, invoking the divine

parikrama clockwise circumam-bulation of a Hindu or Buddhist holy site

prasad specially consecrated food from a Hindu or Sikh temple

puja Hindu prayer ritual

ratha temple chariot

samadhi memorial platform at Hindu cremation site

sangam holy confluence of rivers

Shaivite devotee of Lord Shiva

Shia a sect of Islam that reveres the Prophet Mohammed's cousin Ali and his successors as the true imams

Sufi mystical Islamic philosophy

Sunni a sect of Islam to which the majority of Indian Muslims belong; Sunnis follow traditional Islamic law, believed to be based on the words and acts of the Prophet Mohammed

takhts principal seats of Sikhism

tandava nritya Shiva's cosmic dance of destruction *(p590)*

tazia ornately decorated tower of wood, metal and paper carried by Shia Muslims at Muharram

thiru/tiru holy

tirtha Hindu holy place, usually near sacred river or tank

tirthankaras the 24 religious teachers worshipped by Jains

trishul trident carried by Hindu god, Lord Shiva

tuk fortified cluster of Jain temples

tulsi the sacred basil plant

Urs festival commemorating a Muslim saint

vahanas vehicles of Hindu gods

Vaishnavite devotee of Hindu god, Lord Vishnu

Vedas the oldest known Indian texts, written in Sanskrit, codifying Aryan beliefs and principles

vibhuti sacred ash

yagna Hindu ritual sacrifice

yatra Hindu pilgrimage

MISCELLANEOUS

adivasi tribal person

akash sky

attar/ittar perfume, usually distilled from flowers

badal cloud

bagh tiger

basti settlement or slum; also Jain temple complex

chaugan ancient Persian form of polo, played with a curved stick

diya oil or butter lamp

dhaba roadside eatery *(p179)*

durbar royal court or royal gathering; audience held by a ruler

dzo cross between yak and cow

gali lane or narrow alleyway

ghee clarified butter

gulal coloured powder used during the Holi festival *(p35)*

haat open-air market, usually held once a week

howdah ceremonial seat on an elephant's back

kettuvallam Kerala rice boat *(p633)*

kheda elephant corral

machaan raised observation platform in a forest

mahout elephant trainer

marg major road

mayil/mayur peacock

nava ratna nine principle jewels

nawab Muslim prince

paan betel leaf, a digestive *(p165)*

pandal marquee or decorated stage made of cloth and bamboo

padma lotus

prithvi earth

purnima full moon

pushpa flower

pyav drinking water fountain

rumal handkerchief or square cloth

sagar large lake or reservoir; also ocean or sea

shikar hunting expedition

shila stone

tal lake

taluka sub-district

thakur Hindu chieftain

thali platter

thuggees highway bandits

vayu air

zamindar landowner

Phrase Book

India has 18 major regional languages, many with their own scripts. While Hindi, spoken by 30 per cent of the people and widely understood throughout India, is the official national language, other languages enjoy predominance in their respective regions. Our phrase book covers five languages, four of them spoken in India's four largest cities and their surrounding regions: Hindi (spoken in Delhi); Bengali (spoken in Kolkata); Marathi (spoken in Mumbai); and Tamil (spoken in Chennai). The fifth language, Malayalam, is spoken in Kerala. While Hindi, Bengali and Marathi are Indo-European languages, descended from Sanskrit, Tamil and Malayalam are Dravidian languages, unrelated to the Indo-European group, though influenced by Sanskrit over the centuries. English is widely spoken and understood throughout the country and serves as a link language between the different regions. One can get by with English almost anywhere in India, but most Indians are delighted and warmly appreciative if a visitor makes an attempt to speak their language.

HINDI

IN AN EMERGENCY

Help!	Bachao!
Stop!	Roko!
Call a doctor!	Doctor ko bulao!
Where is the nearest telephone?	Yahan phone kahan hai?

COMMUNICATION ESSENTIALS

Yes	Haan
No	Na/Naheen
Thank you	Dhanyavad/Shukria
Please	Kripaya/Meharbani sé
Excuse me/Sorry	Kshama karen/ Maaf karen
Hello/Goodbye	Namasté
Stop	Rook jao
Let's go	Chalo
Straight ahead	Seedha
Big/Small	Bara/Chhota
This/That	Yeh/Voh
Near/Far	Paas/Door
Way	Raasta
Road	Sarak
Yesterday	Beeta hua kal
Today	Aaj
Tomorrow	Aane wala kal
Here	Yahaan
There	Wahaan
What?	Kya?
Where?	Kahaan?
When?	Kab?
Why?	Kyon?
How?	Kaisé?
Up	Upar
Down	Neeché
More	Aur zyada
A little	Thora
Before	Pehlé
Opposite/ Facing	Saamné
Very	Bahut
Less	Kam
Louder/Harder	Zor sé
Softly/Gently	Dheeré sé
Go	Jao
Come	Aao

USEFUL PHRASES

How are you?	Aap kaisé hain?
What is your name?	Aapka naam kya hai?
My name is ...	Mera naam ... hai
Do you speak English?	Angrezi ati hai?
I understand	Samajh gaya (male)/ gayi (female)
I don't understand	Nahin samjha (m)/ samjhi (f)
What is the time?	Kya baja hai?
Where is ...?	... Kahaan hai?

What is this?	Yeh kya hai?
Hurry up	Jaldi karo
How far is ...?	... Kitni door hai?
I don't know	Pata nahin
All right	Achha/Theek hai
Now/Instantly	Abhi/Isi waqt
Well done!	Shabash!
See you	Phir milengé
Go away!	Hat jao/Hato
I don't want it	Mujhe nahin chahiye
Not now	Abhi nahin

USEFUL WORDS

Which?	Kaun sa?
Who?	Kaun?
Hot	Garam
Cold	Thanda
Good	Achha
Bad	Kharaab
Enough	Bus/Kafi hai
Open	Khula
Closed	Bundh
Left	Baayan
Right	Daayan
Straight on	Seedha
Near	Paas/Nazdeek
Quickly	Jaldi
Late	Der sé
Later	Baad mein
Entrance	Pravesh
Exit	Nikas
Behind	Peechhé
Full	Bhara
Empty	Khali
Toilet	Shauchaalaya
Free/No charge	Nih shulka/Muft
Direction	Disha
Book	Kitaab
Newspaper	Akhbaar

SHOPPING

How much does this cost?	Iska kya daam hai?
I would like...	Mujhe ... chahiye
Do you have...?	Kya aap ké paas ... hai?
I am just looking	Abhi dekh rahen hain
Does it come in other colours?	Yeh dooserey rangon main bhi aata hai kya?
This one	Yeh wala
That one	Voh wala
Black	Kaala
Blue	Neela
White	Safed
Red	Lal
Yellow	Peela
Green	Hara
Brown	Bhura
Cheap	Sasta
Expensive	Mehanga
Tailor	Darzi

BARGAINING

How much is this?	Yeh kitne ka hai?

How much will you take?	Kya logé?
That's a little expensive	Yeh to mehanga hai
Could you lower the price a bit?	Daam thoda kam kariyé
How about xx rupees?	xx rupeye laingé?
I'll settle for xx rupees	xx rupeye mein dena hai to dijiyé

STAYING IN A HOTEL

Do you have any vacant rooms?	Aapke hotel mein khali kamre hain kya?
What is the charge per night?	Ek raat ka kiraya kya hai?
Can I see the room first?	Kya mein pehle kamra dekh sakta hoon?
Key	Chaabhi
Soap	Sabun
Towel	Tauliya
Hot/Cold water	Garam/Thanda pani

EATING OUT

Breakfast	Nashta
Food	Khaana
Water	Pani
Ice	Baraf
Tea	Chai
Coffee	Kaufi
Sugar	Cheeni
Salt	Namak
Milk	Doodh
Yoghurt	Dahi
Egg	Anda
Fruit	Phal
Vegetable	Sabzi
Rice	Chaawal
Pulses (lentil, split peas etc)	Dal
Fixed price menu	Ek daam menu
Is it spicy?	Mirch-masala tez hai kya?
Make it less spicy please	Mirch-masala kam, theek hai?
Knife	Chhuri
Fork	Kanta
Spoon	Chammach
Finished	Khatam

NUMBERS

1	Ek
2	Do
3	Teen
4	Char
5	Panch
6	Chhé
7	Saat
8	Aath
9	Nau
10	Dus

11	**Gyarah**	70	**Sattar**	Half past two	**Dhai**
12	**Barah**	80	**Assi**	A day	**Ek din**
13	**Terah**	90	**Nabbé**	A week	**Ek haftah**
14	**Chaudah**	100	**Sau**	Monday	**Somwar**
15	**Pandrah**	1,000	**Hazar**	Tuesday	**Mangalwar**
16	**Solah**	100,000	**Lakh**	Wednesday	**Budhwar**
17	**Satrah**	10,000,000	**Karod (crore)**	Thursday	**Veerwar**
18	**Atharah**			Friday	**Shukrawar**
19	**Unnees**	**TIME**		Saturday	**Shaniwar**
20	**Bees**	One minute	**Ek minit**	Sunday	**Raviwar**
30	**Tees**	One hour	**Ek ghanta**	Morning	**Subah**
40	**Chalees**	Half an hour	**Aadha ghanta**	Afternoon	**Dopahar**
50	**Pachaas**	Quarter hour	**Pauna ghanta**	Evening	**Shaam**
60	**Saath**	Half past one	**Derh**	Night	**Raat**

BENGALI

IN AN EMERGENCY

Help!	**Shahaajjo korun!**
Stop!	**Thamun!**
Call a doctor!	**Daktar dakun!**
Where is the nearest telephone?	**Ekhanay phone kothai?**

COMMUNICATION ESSENTIALS

Yes	**Haen**
No	**Na**
Thank you	**Dhonnobad**
Please	**Doya koray**
Excuse me/ Sorry	**Maap korben**
Hello/Goodbye	**Nomoshkar**
Stop	**Thamun**
Let's go	**Cholun**
Straight ahead	**Shoja**
Big/Small	**Boro/Chhoto**
This/That	**Eta/Ota**
Near/Far	**Kaachhé/Dooré**
Way	**Raasta**
Road	**Raasta**
Yesterday	**Goto kaal**
Today	**Aaj**
Tomorrow	**Kaal**
Here	**Ekhaané**
There	**Okhaané**
What?	**Ki?**
Where?	**Kothayé?**
When?	**Kokhon?**
Why?	**Kaeno?**
How?	**Ki koray?**
Up	**Opor**
Down	**Neeché**
More	**Aaro**
A little	**Ektu**
Before	**Aagey**
Opposite/ Facing	**Shaamney**
Very	**Khoob**
Less	**Kom**
Louder/Harder	**Jorey**
Softly/Gently	**Aastey**
Go	**Jao**
Come	**Esho**

USEFUL PHRASES

How are you?	**Kaemon aachhen?**
What is your name?	**Aapnaar naam ki?**
My name is ...	**Aamaar naam ...**
Do you speak English?	**Ingriji bolen?**
I understand	**Bujhi**
I don't understand	**Bujhi na**
What is the time?	**Kota bajé?**
Where is ...?	**... Kothhai?**
What is this?	**Eta ki?**
Hurry up	**Taarataari**
How far is ...?	**... Koto door?**

I don't know	**Jaani na**
All right	**Theek achhey**
Now/Instantly	**Ekkhuni**
Well done!	**Bah!**
See you	**Aashi**
Go away!	**Jao**
I don't want it	**Chai na**
Not now	**Ekhon na**

USEFUL WORDS

Which?	**Konta?**
Who?	**Kay?**
Hot	**Gorom**
Cold	**Thanda**
Good	**Bhalo**
Bad	**Khaaraap**
Enough	**Bus**
Open	**Khola**
Closed	**Bondho**
Left	**Baayen**
Right	**Daayiné**
Straight on	**Shojaa**
Near	**Kaachhey**
Quickly	**Taarataari**
Late	**Deri**
Later	**Porey**
Entrance	**Probesh**
Exit	**Prosthaan**
Behind	**Pechhoney**
Full	**Bhora**
Empty	**Khaali**
Toilet	**Shauchaalaya**
Free/No charge	**Bina poisha**
Direction	**Disha**
Book	**Boi**
Magazine	**Potrika**
Newspaper	**Khoborer kagoj**

SHOPPING

How much does this cost?	**Koto?**
I would like...	**Aami chaai**
Do you have...?	**Aapnaar kaachhe aachhe?**
I am just looking	**Shudhu dekchhi**
Does it come in other colours?	**Aaro rong aachhey?**
This one	**Eta**
That one	**Ota**
Black	**Kaalo**
Blue	**Neel**
White	**Shaadaa**
Red	**Laal**
Yellow	**Holud**
Green	**Shobuj**
Brown	**Khoiri**
Cheap	**Shostaa**
Expensive	**Daami**
Tailor	**Dorji**

BARGAINING

How much is this?	**Eta koto?**
How much will you take?	**Koto neben?**
That's a little expensive	**Beshi daam**

Could you lower the price a bit?	**Ektu komaan**
How about xx rupees?	**xx taka cholbé?**
I'll settle for xx rupees	**xx takar beshi debo na**

STAYING IN A HOTEL

Do you have any vacant rooms?	**Ghor khaali aachhey?**
What is the charge per night?	**Ek raater bhaara koto?**
Can I see the room first?	**Aagey ghor dekhte paari?**
Key	**Chaabi**
Soap	**Shaabaan**
Towel	**Towaaley**
Hot/Cold water	**Gorom/Thanda jol**

EATING OUT

Breakfast	**Jolkhaabaar**
Food	**Khaabaar**
Water	**Jol**
Ice	**Borof**
Tea	**Chaa**
Coffee	**Koffee**
Sugar	**Cheeni**
Salt	**Noon**
Milk	**Doodh**
Yoghurt	**Dohi**
Egg	**Deem**
Fruit	**Phol**
Vegetable	**Shobji**
Rice	**Bhaat**
Pulses (lentils, split peas etc)	**Daal**
Fixed price menu	**Ek daam menu**
Is it spicy?	**Jhaal ki?**
Make it less spicy	**Beshi jhaal chaai na**
Knife	**Chhuri**
Fork	**Kanta**
Spoon	**Chaamoch**
Finished	**Shesh**

NUMBERS

1	**Ek**
2	**Dooi**
3	**Teen**
4	**Chaar**
5	**Paanch**
6	**Chhoy**
7	**Shaat**
8	**Aath**
9	**Noy**
10	**Dosh**
11	**Egaro**
12	**Baaro**
13	**Tero**
14	**Chaudoh**
15	**Ponero**
16	**Sholo**
17	**Shotero**
18	**Aathero**
19	**Unneesh**
20	**Kuri/Beesh**

30	**Tirish**			Monday	**Shombar**
40	**Cholleesh**			Tuesday	**Mongolbar**
50	**Ponchaash**			Wednesday	**Budhbar**
60	**Shaat**			Thursday	**Bishuttbar**
70	**Shottor**			Friday	**Shukkurbar**
80	**Aashi**			Saturday	**Shonibar**
90	**Nobboi**			Sunday	**Robibar**
100	**Eksho**			Morning	**Shokaal**
1,000	**Haajaar**			Afternoon	**Duphur**
100,000	**Lakh**			Evening	**Bikel**
10,000,000	**Koti**			Night	**Raat**

TIME

One minute	**Ek minit**
One hour	**Ek ghonta**
Half an hour	**Aadh ghonta**
Quarter hour	**Pauney ghonta**
Half past one	**Derh**
Half past two	**Aadhai**
A day	**Ek din**
A week	**Ek shopta**

MARATHI

IN AN EMERGENCY

Help!	**Vachva!**
Stop!	**Thamba!**
Call a doctor!	**Doctorana bolwaa!**
Where is the nearest telephone?	**Ithé jawal phone kuthé aahé?**

COMMUNICATION ESSENTIALS

Yes	**Ho**
No	**Nahi**
Thank you	**Dhanyavad**
Please	**krupaya**
Excuse me/ Sorry	**Kshama pahijé**
Hello/ Goodbye	**Namaskar**
Stop	**Thamba**
Let's go	**Chala**
Straight ahead	**Saral**
Big/Small	**Mota/Lahan**
This/That	**Hé/Thé**
Near/Far	**Zawal/Laamb**
Way	**Marga**
Road	**Rastha**
Yesterday	**Kaal**
Today	**Aaj**
Tomorrow	**Udya**
Here	**Ithé**
There	**Tithé**
What?	**Kay?**
Where?	**Kuthé?**
When?	**Kenhvah?**
Why?	**Ka?**
How?	**Kasè?**
Up	**Varti**
Down	**Khali**
More	**Aankhi**
A little	**Thodé**
Before	**Aadhi**
Opposite/ Facing	**Samor**
Very	**Khoop**
Less	**Kami**
Louder/Harder	**Mothyané/Zorané**
Softly/Gently	**Haloo**
Go	**Za**
Come	**Ya**

USEFUL PHRASES

How are you?	**Kasa Kain?**
What is your name?	**Apla nao?**
My name is ...	**Maajhe nao ...**
Do you speak English?	**Inglish yeté ka?**
I understand	**Samazté**
I don't understand	**Kalale nahin**
What is the time?	**Kiti vajlé?**
Where is ...?	**Kuthé aahé?**
What is this?	**Hé kay aahé?**
Hurry up	**Aatpa lavkar**
How far is ...?	**Kiti laamb aahé?**
I don't know	**Mahiti nahin**
All right	**Theek aahé**
Now/Instantly	**Aathach**

Well done!	**Chhan!**
See you	**Bhétuya**
Go away!	**Chalta ho**
I don't want it	**Nakoy malaa**
Not now	**Aatha naahin**

USEFUL WORDS

Which?	**Konté?**
Who?	**Kon?**
Hot	**Garam**
Cold	**Thanda**
Good	**Changla**
Bad	**Vait**
Enough	**Puré**
Open	**Ughadé**
Closed	**Banda**
Left	**Davikadé**
Right	**Uzavikadé**
Straight on	**Saral**
Near	**Zawal**
Quickly	**Lavkar**
Late	**Ushira**
Later	**Nanthar**
Entrance	**Pravesh**
Exit	**Baaher**
Behind	**Maagé**
Full	**Bharalelé**
Empty	**Rikamé**
Toilet	**Shauchaalaya**
Free/No charge	**Mophat**
Direction	**Disha**
Book	**Pusthak**
Magazine	**Maasik**
Newspaper	**Vartaman patra**

SHOPPING

How much does this cost?	**Hé kevdyala?**
I would like…	**Mala... hava hotha**
Do you have…?	**Tumechyakadé ... aahé ka?**
I am just looking	**Ajun bagté/Aahé bagto**
Does it come in other colours?	**Aankhi ranga aahetka?**
This one	**Hé**
That one	**Té**
Black	**Kaala**
Blue	**Neelé**
White	**Pandhra**
Red	**Lal**
Yellow	**Piwala**
Green	**Hirvva**
Brown	**Chocoleti**
Cheap	**Svastha**
Expensive	**Mahaag**
Tailor	**Shimpi**

BARGAINING

How much is this?	**Hé kevdhyala?**
How much will you take?	**Kithi dyaché?**
That's a little expensive	**Zara mahaag aahe**
Could you lower the price a bit?	**Zara kami karana ka?**
How about xx rupees?	**Xx rupyé thik aahé?**
I'll settle for xx rupees	**Xx barobar aahé**

STAYING IN A HOTEL

Do you have any vacant rooms?	**Tumchya hotel madhé jagaa aahé ka?**
What is the charge per night?	**Eka ratri ché kiti**
Can I see the room first?	**Mee aadhi kholi baghoon ka?**
Key	**Killi**
Soap	**Saban**
Towel	**Towel**
Hot/Cold water	**Garam/Thanda pani**

EATING OUT

Breakfast	**Nasta**
Food	**Jewan**
Water	**Pani**
Ice	**Barpha**
Tea	**Chaha**
Coffee	**Kofi**
Sugar	**Saakhar**
Salt	**Mith**
Milk	**Doodh**
Yoghurt	**Dahi**
Egg	**Andé**
Fruit	**Phal**
Vegetable	**Bhaji**
Rice	**Bhath**
Pulses (lentils, split peas etc)	**Dal**
Fixed price menu	**Ekach bhav**
Is it spicy?	**Tikhat aahé ka?**
Make it less spicy please	**Har tikhat nakon bara ka?**
Knife	**Suri**
Fork	**Kata**
Spoon	**Chammcha**
Finished	**Samplé**

NUMBERS

1	**Ek**
2	**Don**
3	**Teen**
4	**Char**
5	**Pach**
6	**Saha**
7	**Sath**
8	**Aath**
9	**Nou**
10	**Daha**
11	**Akara**
12	**Barah**
13	**Terah**
14	**Chawda**
15	**Pandhra**
16	**Solah**
17	**Satara**
18	**Atharah**
19	**Ekonees**
20	**Vees**
30	**Tees**
40	**Chalees**
50	**Pannas**
60	**Saath**
70	**Sattar**
80	**Aishi**
90	**Nauwad**
100	**Shambhar**

1,000	Hazaar	Quarter hour	Pandhra minit	Thursday	Guruwar
100,000	Lakh	Half past one	Deed	Friday	Shukrawar
10,000,000	Koti	Half past two	Adhich	Saturday	Shaniwar
		A day	Ek divas	Sunday	Raviwar
		A week	Ek athavda	Morning	Sakali

TIME

One minute	Ek minit	Monday	Somwar	Afternoon	Dupari
One hour	Ek taas	Tuesday	Mangalwar	Evening	Sandhyakali
Half an hour	Ardha taas	Wednesday	Budhwar	Night	Ratri

TAMIL

IN AN EMERGENCY

Help!	Udhaivi véndum!
Stop!	Nillu!
Call a doctor!	Doctor koopiddunga!
Where is the nearest phone?	Pakkatatillé phone engu irrukku?

COMMUNICATION ESSENTIALS

Yes	Aama/Seri
No	Illai/Véndaam
Thank you	Nanri
Please	Daivusaidhu
Excuse me/Sorry	Mannikavum
Hello/Goodbye	Vannakkam/ Paankalaam
Stop	Nillu
Let's go	Pohalaam
Straight ahead	Néré
Big/Small	Perisu/Chinannadu
This/That	Idhu/Adhu
Near/Far	Pakkatilai/Dooram
Way	Vazhi
Road	Theruvu
Yesterday	Nétru/Néthiku
Today	Inru/Innikki
Tomorrow	Naallai/Naallaiku
Here	Ingé
There	Angé
What?	Ennai?
Where?	Engé?
When?	Eppo?
Why?	Ain?
How?	Eppiddi?
Up	Mélai
Down	Kizhai
More	Unnum konjam
A little	Konjam
Before	Minaalai
Opposite/Facing	Edhirai
Very	Romba
Less	Kammi
Louder/Harder	Perisa/Unnum ongi
Softly/Gently	Molla
Go	Pongo/Po
Come	Vaango/Vaa

USEFUL PHRASES

How are you?	Neenga eppudi irukénga?
What is your name?	Onge peyar enna?
My name is …	Enodia peyar …
Do you speak English?	English pése theriyuma?
I understand	Ennakku puriyum
I don't understand	Ennakku puriyadu
What is the time?	Ippo ena mani?
Where is …?	… Enga irrukku?
What is this?	Idhu ennadhu?
Hurry up	Seekrama vaango
How far is …?	… Evallavu dooram?
I don't know	Ennaku theriyadu
All right	Seri
Now/Instantly	Ippovai
Well done!	Shabash!
See you	Apram parkalaam
Go away!	Poividu!
I don't want it	Ennaku véndaam
Not now	Ippo illai

USEFUL WORDS

Which?	Edhu?
Who?	Yaaru?
Hot	Soodu
Cold	Kulluru
Good	Nalladhu
Bad	Kettadhu
Enough	Porum
Open	Thirandurikku
Closed	Moodirukku
Left	Edudhu
Right	Valadhu
Straight on	Nérai
Near	Pakkatillai
Quickly	Seekrama
Late	Nerama
Later	Apram
Entrance	Varuvu
Exit	Velivaasal
Behind	Pinalai
Full	Rombiruku
Empty	Kaali
Toilet	Kaizhupu arai
Free/No charge	Ilevasaasam
Direction	Disai/Pakkam
Book	Pustagam
Magazine	Patrigai
Newspaper	Samachara patrigai

SHOPPING

How much does this cost?	Idhodiya vilai ennai?
I would like…	Ennakku idhu venum …
Do you have…?	… onga kitta irrukka?
I am just looking	Naan summa paakaren
Does it come in other colours?	Idh vera colouril kidaikuma?
This one	Idhu
That one	Adhu
Black	Karuppu
Blue	Neelam
White	Vellai
Red	Seguppu
Yellow	Manjhal
Green	Pachchai
Brown	Kappi niram
Cheap	Maluvu
Expensive	Vilai jasti
Tailor	Theyalkaran

BARGAINING

How much is this?	Idhu enna vilai?
How much will you take?	Neengu evalave edithipél?
That's a little expensive	Adhu konjam vilai jasti
Could you lower the price a bit?	Vilai konjam kurrakkai mudduyuma?
How about xx rupees?	xx rubaai seria?
I'll settle for xx rupees	xx rubaai tharuven

STAYING IN A HOTEL

Do you have any vacant rooms?	Kaali arai irruka?
What is the charge per night?	Oru raatriku evaluvu caasu?
Can I see the room first?	Naan mudulai araiya parrakalama?
Key	Chaavi
Soap	Soapu
Towel	Thundu
Hot/Cold water	Soodu/Jillu thanni

EATING OUT

Breakfast	Kaalai chittrundi
Food	Saapadu
Water	Thanni/Jalam
Ice	Ice
Tea	Chai
Coffee	Coffee
Sugar	Shakarai
Salt	Uppu
Milk	Paal
Yoghurt	Thairu
Egg	Muttai
Fruit	Pazham
Vegetable	Kayagiri
Rice	Arusi
Pulses (lentils,etc)	Paruppu
Fixed price menu	Ore vilai menu
Is it spicy?	Naraya masala irukka?
Make it less spicy please	Masala seriya irukka?
Knife	Kaththi
Fork	Fork
Spoon	Spoon/ Theikarandi
Finished	Mudivu

NUMBERS

1	Onru/Onu
2	Erundu
3	Moonru
4	Naangu/Naalu
5	Anju/Aindhu
6	Aaru
7	Yezhu
8	Ettu
9	Ombodhu
10	Pathu
11	Pathinonru
12	Panandu
13	Pathimoonru
14	Pathinaalu
15	Pathinainthu
16	Pathnaaru
17	Pathinezhu
18	Pathinettu
19	Pathombadhu
20	Iravadhu
30	Mupaddu
40	Napadhu
50	Aimbadhu
60	Aravadhu
70	Yezhuvadu
80	Yenbadhu
90	Thonnuru
100	Nooru
1,000	Aayiram
100,000	Latcham
10,000,000	Kodi

TIME

One minute	Oru nimisham
One hour	Oru manéram
Half an hour	Ara manéram
Quarter hour	Kaal manéram
Half past one	Onre mani
Half past two	Erendarai mani
A day	Oru naal
A week	Oru vaaram
Monday	Thingakazhamai
Tuesday	Sevvaikazhami
Wednesday	Budhankazhami
Thursday	Viyaikazhami
Friday	Vellikazhami
Saturday	Nyayatrikazhami
Morning	Kaalai
Afternoon	Madhyanam
Evening	Sayankaalam
Night	Raatri

MALAYALAM

IN AN EMERGENCY

Help!	Sahayikoo!
Stop!	Nilku/Nirthu!
Call a doctor!	Doctore viliku!
Where is the nearest phone?	Evide annu aduth phone?

COMMUNICATION ESSENTIALS

Yes	Athe/Seri
No	Illa/Alla/Véndaa
Thank you	Nanni
Please	Dayavuchaidu
Excuse me/Sorry	Kshamikkanam
Hello/Goodbye	Namaskaram/ Veendum kanaam
Stop	Nilku
Let's go	Namuku pokaam
Straight ahead	Néré povuu
Big/Small	Valudu/Cherudu
This/That	Idhe/Adhe
Near/Far	Aduthu/Akalé
Way	Vazhi
Road	Patha/Road
Yesterday	Innalé
Today	Innu
Tomorrow	Naallé
Here	Evidé
There	Avidé
What?	Entha?
Where?	Evidé?
When?	Eppol?
Why?	Entha/Enthukonda?
How?	Enganế?
Up	Mukalil
Down	Kizhé/Thazhé
More	Eniyum kooduthal
A little	Kurachu/Alpam
Before	Munpé/Munnil
Opposite/Facing	Edhirvasam/Edhirai
Very	Valaré
Less	Kurachu/Kuravu
Louder/Harder	Uchchathil/Urakké
Softly/Gently	Pathiyé/Swaram thazhthi
Go	Pokoo/Po
Come	Varoo/Vaa

USEFUL PHRASES

How are you?	Sukhamano?
What is your name?	Ningaludé peru entha?
My name is ...	Ente peru ...
Do you speak English?	Ningal English samsarikumo?
I understand	Enikku manasilayi
I don't understand	Enikku manasilakilla
What is the time?	Samayam enthai?
Where is ...?	Evideyanu ...?
What is this?	Idhu enthanu?
Hurry up	Vegamakatté
How far is ...?	Ethra dooramundu...?
I don't know	Enikku ariyilla
All right	Seri
Now/Instantly	Ippol thanné
Well done!	Kémamai!/Nannai!
See you	Pinne kanaam
Go away!	Dooré po!
I don't want it	Enikku véndaa
Not now	Ippo illa/Véndaa

USEFUL WORDS

Which?	Edhu?
Who?	Aaré?
Hot	Choodé
Cold	Thanuppé/Kulluré
Good	Nalladhé
Bad	Cheetha/Mosam
Enough	Madhi
Open	Thurannu
Closed	Adachu
Left	Edadhu
Right	Valadhu
Straight on	Néré
Near	Aduthu
Quickly	Végum
Late	Vaiki
Later	Pinné/Pinneedu
Entrance	Munvasam/ Parvésana vathil
Exit	Purathékkulla vazhi
Behind	Pinnalé/Pinnil
Full	Nirayé
Empty	Kaali
Toilet	Moothrappura
Free/no charge	Saujanyam
Direction	Dikku
Book	Pustakam
Magazine	Masika/Varika
Newspaper	Newspaper

SHOPPING

How much does this cost?	Idhinu enthu vila?
I would like…	Enikku idhu venum ...
Do you have…?	... Ningaludé pakkal ondo?
I am just looking	Naan veruthé nokukayanu
Does it come in other colours?	Idhu vereyum colouril kittumo?
This one	Idhu
That one	Adhu
Black	Karuppé
Blue	Neela
White	Vella
Red	Chuvappé
Yellow	Manja
Green	Pachcha
Brown	Kappi niram
Cheap	Vilakuravu
Expensive	Vilakuduthal
Tailor	Thayalkaran

BARGAINING

How much is this?	Idhinu enthu vila?
How much will you take?	Idhu enthu vilaku tharum?
That's a little expensive	Vila kurachu kooduthalanu
Could you lower the price a bit?	Vila kurachu kuraikumo?
How about xx rupees?	xx rupaku tharumo?
I'll settle for xx rupees	Njyan xx rupaku edukkam

STAYING IN A HOTEL

Do you have any vacant rooms?	Muri (room) ozhivundo?
What is the charge per night?	Oru raatriku entha vaadaka?
Can I see the room first?	Eniku aadyam muri kaanan sadhikumo?
Key	Thakol
Soap	Soap
Towel	Thorthé/Towel
Hot/Cold water	Choodu/Thanutha véllam

EATING OUT

Breakfast	Prathal
Food	Aaharam/ Bhakshanam
Water	Véllam
Ice	Ice katta
Tea	Chaya
Coffee	Kaapi
Sugar	Panchasaara
Salt	Uppé
Milk	Paal
Yoghurt	Thairé
Egg	Mutta
Fruit	Pazham
Vegetable	Pachchakari
Rice	Ari/Choruế
Pulses (lentils, split peas etc)	Parippé
Fixed price menu	Otta vila menu/ Krithya vila menu
Is it spicy?	Ithu frivullathano?
Make it less spicy please	Erivu kooduthal vendaa?
Knife	Kaththi
Fork	Mullé/Fork
Spoon	Spoon
Finished	Kazhinju/Theernu

NUMBERS

1	Onné/Oru
2	Randé
3	Moonné
4	Naalé
5	Anché
6	Aaré
7	Yezhé
8	Etté
9	Onpadhé
10	Paththé
11	Pathinonné
12	Panthrandé
13	Pathimoonné
14	Pathinaalé
15	Pathinanché
16	Pathinaaré
17	Pathinezhé
18	Pathinetté
19	Pathompadhé
20	Irupadhé
30	Muppaddé
40	Nappadhé
50	Ambadhé
60	Arupadhé
70	Yezhupadé
80	Yenpadhé
90	Thonnuré
100	Nooré
1,000	Aayiram
100,000	Laksham
10,000,000	Kodi

TIME

One minute	Oru nimisham/ Minute
One hour	Oru manikoor
Half an hour	Ara manikoor
Quarter hour	Kaal manikoor
Half past one	Onnara mani
Half past two	Randara mani
A day	Oru divasam
A week	Oru aazhcha
Monday	Thingal
Tuesday	Chovva
Wednesday	Budhan
Thursday	Vyazham
Friday	Velli
Saturday	Sani
Morning	Raavilé
Afternoon	Uchcha
Evening	Vaikunneram
Night	Raatri

Railway Map of India

The external boundaries of India as shown on this map are neither correct nor authentic.